Seventh Workshop on Arabic Natural Language Processing (WANLP 2022)

Abu Dhabi, United Arab Emirates
8 December 2022

ISBN: 978-1-7138-9152-9

Printed from e-media with permission by:

Curran Associates, Inc.
57 Morehouse Lane
Red Hook, NY 12571

Some format issues inherent in the e-media version may also appear in this print version.

Printed with permission by Curran Associates, Inc. (2024)

For permission requests, please contact the Association for Computational Linguistics at the address below.

Association for Computational Linguistics
209 N. Eighth Street
Stroudsburg, Pennsylvania 18360

Phone: 1-570-476-8006
Fax: 1-570-476-0860

acl@aclweb.org

Additional copies of this publication are available from:

Curran Associates, Inc.
57 Morehouse Lane
Red Hook, NY 12571 USA
Phone: 845-758-0400
Fax: 845-758-2633
Email: curran@proceedings.com
Web: www.proceedings.com

WANLP 2022

The Seventh Arabic Natural Language Processing Workshop

Proceedings of the Workshop

December 8, 2022

The WANLP organizers gratefully acknowledge the support from the following sponsors.

Google Research

Preface

أهلاً وسهلاً ومرحباً بكم! حياكم في أبوظبي.

Ahlan wa-sahlan wa-marhaban bikum! Hayyaakum fi Abu Dhabi.
Hello and Welcome to Abu Dhabi!

Welcome to The Seventh Arabic Natural Language Processing Workshop (WANLP 2022) held with EMNLP 2022 in Abu Dhabi, UAE. Over the years, WANLP has developed a growing reputation as a high-quality venue for researchers and developers working on Arabic NLP, where they share and discuss their ongoing work. The first in the WANLP series was held in Doha, Qatar (EMNLP 2014), followed by Beijing, China (ACL 2015), Valencia, Spain (EACL 2017), Florence, Italy (ACL 2019), and in virtual mode in COLING 2020 and EACL 2021.

In this iteration of WANLP, we received 68 main workshop submissions (50 long, 14 short, and 4 demos). The total number of submissions is higher than all the earlier editions of the workshop. All papers submitted to the main workshop were reviewed by at least three reviewers each. Out of the 68 submissions, 36 were accepted: 31 long papers, two short papers, and three demo papers). We selected 13 papers for oral presentation and the rest as posters. We did not distinguish between long and short papers, or between oral and poster presentations in terms of quality.

WANLP 2022 included, for the first time, three shared tasks: The third edition of the Nuanced Arabic Dialect Identification (NADI) shared task, the Gender Rewriting Shared Task, and the Shared Task on Propaganda Detection in Arabic. NADI received submissions from 21 teams, 15 of which have system descriptions in the proceedings. The Gender Rewriting Shared Task received submissions from five teams, two of which have system descriptions in the proceedings. The Shared Task on Propaganda Detection in Arabic received submissions from 17 teams, 11 of which have system descriptions in the proceedings. The shared task system descriptions papers were reviewed by two reviewers each. Three additional shared task overview papers are included in the proceedings. The overview papers are presented in an oral session in the workshop.

For the second time, our workshop was able to secure sponsorship funding (Thanks to Google Research!) which we used to support student registrations.

In another success for the WANLP community, a new Special Interest Group on Arabic NLP (SIGARAB) was created in early 2022 by the advisory committee responsible for WANLP, building on its history of successful organization and collaboration.

Finally, we would like to thank everyone who submitted a paper to the workshop, as well as all the 83 members of the Program Committee, who worked hard to provide high-quality reviews on time. Organizing WANLP 2022 is a team effort.

Houda Bouamor, General Chair, on behalf of the workshop organizers.

Website of the workshop: `http://wanlp2022.arabic-nlp.net/`

Organizing Committee

General Chair

Houda Bouamor, Carnegie Mellon University in Qatar, Qatar

Program Chairs

Hend Al-Khalifa, King Saud University, KSA
Fethi Bougares, University of Le Mans, France
Kareem Darwish, aiXplain Inc.
Owen Rambow, Stony Brook University, USA

Publication Chairs

Ahmed Abdelali, Qatar Computing Research Institute, HBKU, Qatar
Nadi Tomeh, Université Sorbonne Paris Nord, France

Publicity Chairs

Salam Khalifa, Stony Brook University, USA
Wajdi Zaghouani, Hamad Bin Khalifa University, Qatar

Program Committee

Program Committee

Abdelmajid Ben-Hamadou, University of Sfax, Tunisia
AbdelRahim Elmadany, The University of British Columbia, Canada
Ahmed Abdelali, Qatar Computing Research Institute, HBKU, Qatar
Ahmed Ali, Qatar Computing Research Institute, HBKU, Qatar
Ahmed El Kholy, Columbia University, Microsoft, USA
Alexis Nasr, University of Marseille, France
Ali AlKhathlan, King Abdulaziz University, KSA
Almoataz B. Al-Said, Cairo University, Egypt
Aloulou Chafik, University of Sfax, Tunisia
Ann Bies, Linguistic Data Consortium, University of Pennsylvania, USA
Azzeddine Mazroui, University Mohamed I, Morocco
Bashar Alhafni, New York University in Abu Dhabi, UAE
Bashar Talafha, The University of British Columbia, Canada
Bassam Haddad, University of Petra, Jordan
Bayan AbuShawar, Al Ain University, UAE
Cal Peyser, Google Inc., USA
Chiyu Zhang, The University of British Columbia, Canada
Christian Khairallah, New York University in Abu Dhabi, UAE
Dana Abdulrahim, University of Bahrain, Bahrain
El Moatez Billah Nagoudi, The University of British Columbia, Canada
Fatemah Husain, Kuwait University, Kuwait
Fethi Bougares, Le Mans University, France
Firoj Alam, Qatar Computing Research Institute, HBKU, Qatar
Ganesh Jawahar, The University of British Columbia, Canada
Gilbert Badaro, American University of Beirut, Lebanon
Giovanni Da San Martino, University of Padova, Italy
Go Inoue, Mohamed Bin Zayed University of Artificial Intelligence, UAE
Hamada Nayel, Benha University, Egypt
Hamdy Mubarak, Qatar Computing Research Institute, HBKU, Qatar
Hend Al-Khalifa, King Saud University, KSA
Hossam Ahmed, Leiden Institute for Area Studies, Netherlands
Houda Bouamor, Carnegie Mellon University, Qatar
Ibrahim Abu Farha, University of Edinburgh, Scotland
Ife Adebara, The University of British Columbia, Canada
Imed Zitouni, Google Inc., USA
Imene Bensalem, Constantine 2 University, Algeria
Injy Hamed, New York University in Abu Dhabi, UAE
Jordan Kodner, Stony Brook University, USA
Kamel Smaili, LORIA, France
Kareem Darwish, aiXplain Inc., USA
Karim Bouzoubaa, Mohammad V University, Morocco
Khaled Shaalan, The British University in Dubai, UAE
Khaled Shaban, Qatar University, Qatar
Lamia Hadrich-Belguith, University of Sfax , Tunisia
Maram Hasanain, Qatar University, Qatar
Md Tawkat Islam Khondaker, The University of British Columbia, Canada

Mohamed Al-Badrashiny, aiXplain Inc., USA
Mohammad Abuoudeh, New York University in Abu Dhabi, UAE
Mourad Abbas, HCLA, Algeria
Muhammad Abdul-Mageed, The University of British Columbia, Canada
Mustafa Jarrar, Bir Zeit University, Palestine
Nada Ghneim, Higher Institute for Applied Sciences and Technology, Syria
Nada Almarwani, Taibah University, KSA
Nadi Tomeh, University Paris 13, France
Nizar Habash, New York University in Abu Dhabi, UAE
Nora Al-Twairesh, King Saud University, KSA
Omar Trigui, University of Sousse, Tunisia
Ossama Obeid, New York University in Abu Dhabi, UAE
Owen Rambow, Stony Brook University, USA
Peter Sullivan, The University of British Columbia, Canada
Preslav Nakov, Mohamed Bin Zayed University of Artificial Intelligence, UAE
Sahar Ghannay, LIMSI-CNRS, France
Sakhar Alkhereyf, King Abdulaziz City for Science and Technology, KSA
Salam Khalifa, Stony Brook University, USA
Salima Harrat, École Normale Supérieure (Bouzaréah), Algeria
Salima Mdhaffar, Le Mans University, France
Samah Aloufi, Taibah University, KSA
Samhaa R. El-Beltagy, Nile University, Egypt
Samia Touileb, University of Oslo, Norway
Seif Mechti, ISSEPS, Tunisia
Shady Elbassuoni, American University of Beirut, Lebanon
Shammur Absar Chowdhury, Qatar Computing Research Institute, HBKU, Qatar
Taha Zerrouki, Bouira University, Algeria
Tamer Elsayed, Qatar University, Qatar
Thamar Solorio, University of Houston, USA
Violetta Cavalli-Sforza, Al Akhawayn University, Morocco
Wajdi Zaghouani, Hamad Bin Khalifa University, Qatar
Wassim El-Hajj, American University of Beirut, Lebanon
Wei-Rui Chen, The University of British Columbia, Canada
Wissam Antoun, INRIA, France
Younes Samih, University of Düsseldorf, Germany
Yuval Marton, University of Washington, USA

Invited Speaker

Karim Bouzoubaa, Mohammadia School of Engineers at the Mohammed 5th University of Rabat

Keynote Talk: Digital Preservation of Arabic between Linguistics and AI

Karim Bouzoubaa
Mohammadia School of Engineers at the Mohammed 5th University of Rabat

Abstract: Languages are one of the oldest studied disciplines as they are intimately linked to the existence of human beings. The study of languages is a multidisciplinary field which has attracted the interest of several related fields such as linguistics and NLP, each providing additional knowledge for language understanding, learning, evolution, or preservation. From the technological point of view, computer science in general and artificial intelligence in particular study languages through natural language processing techniques, where the main goal is to discover linguistic patterns from corpora without resorting to linguists at all in many cases. Research in this field is diverse and currently benefits from advances in machine learning and deep learning techniques. One of the less studied aspects is the use and exploitation of these techniques for language preservation needs, for language comprehension needs or for the explanation of linguistic phenomena. The objective of this talk is to emphasize this perspective and to show through concrete cases how through the exploitation of several old and new computer and AI techniques, we can advance the digital preservation of Arabic and the explanation of some linguistic properties.

Bio: Karim Bouzoubaa is a Professor of computer science at the Mohammadia School of Engineers at the Mohammed 5th University of Rabat. Prof. Bouzoubaa holds a M.Sc. and a Ph.D. from Laval University in Canada in Artificial Intelligence and multi-agent systems fields. He is a research-driven professional with a distinctive combination of leadership, research and development, and education in the areas of Artificial Intelligence and Data Science. He contributed to the release of the Amine platform for the development of intelligent systems. He has published two books and over a hundred papers in top-ranked conferences and journals, taught at undergraduate and postgraduate levels, and worked on various R&D projects. He is the founding president of the Arabic Language Engineering Society in Morocco and the director of the Language Engineering lab. His research interests include Arabic NLP, NLP frameworks, Linguistic Resources and ontologies, IR and QA systems, Dialect processing, and Cognitive systems. He has led research teams, developed research programs, and has a long experience with most AI paradigms from the old to the newest ones. Prof Bouzoubaa is a Fulbright fellow and was a visiting professor at many institutions. He chaired and organized many international conferences, and was co-guest editor of the Special Issue on "Advances in Arabic Language Processing" for the International Journal on Information and Communication Technologies.

Table of Contents

Program

Thursday, December 8, 2022

09:00 - 09:05	*Opening Remarks*
09:10 - 10:00	*Invited Talk*
10:00 - 10:30	*Session 1 - Information Extraction (in-Person)*
	CAraNER: The COVID-19 Arabic Named Entity Corpus Abdulmohsen Al-Thubaity, Sakhar Alkhereyf, Wejdan Alzahrani and Alia Bahanshal
	Joint Coreference Resolution for Zeros and non-Zeros in Arabic Abdulrahman Aloraini, Sameer Pradhan and Massimo Poesio
10:30 - 11:00	*Coffee Break*
11:00 - 12:30	*Session 2 - NLU/NLG (in-Person)*
	SAIDS: A Novel Approach for Sentiment Analysis Informed of Dialect and Sarcasm Abdelrahman Kaseb and Mona Farouk
	AraBART: a Pretrained Arabic Sequence-to-Sequence Model for Abstractive Summarization Moussa Kamal Eddine, Nadi Tomeh, Nizar Habash, Joseph Le Roux and Michalis Vazirgiannis
	Towards Arabic Sentence Simplification via Classification and Generative Approaches Nouran Khallaf, Serge Sharoff and Rasha Soliman
	Generating Classical Arabic Poetry using Pre-trained Models Nehal Elkaref, Mervat Abu-Elkheir, Maryam ElOraby and Mohamed Abdelgaber
	A Benchmark Study of Contrastive Learning for Arabic Social Meaning Md Tawkat Islam Khondaker, El Moatez Billah Nagoudi, AbdelRahim Elmadany, Muhammad Abdul-Mageed and Laks Lakshmanan, V.S.
	Adversarial Text-to-Speech for low-resource languages Ashraf Elneima and Mikołaj Bińkowski

Thursday, December 8, 2022 (continued)

12:30 - 14:00 *Lunch Break*

14:00 - 14:45 *Panel discussion: Young Researchers in Arabic NLP*

14:45 - 15:00 *Best Paper Award Oral Presentation (in-Person)*

15:00 - 15:30 *Shared Task Papers (in-Person)*

NADI 2022: The Third Nuanced Arabic Dialect Identification Shared Task
Muhammad Abdul-Mageed, Chiyu Zhang, AbdelRahim Elmadany, Houda Bouamor and Nizar Habash

The Shared Task on Gender Rewriting
Bashar Alhafni, Nizar Habash, Houda Bouamor, Ossama Obeid, Sultan Alrowili, Daliyah AlZeer, Kawla Mohmad Shnqiti, Ahmed Elbakry, Muhammad El-Nokrashy, Mohamed Gabr, Abderrahmane Issam, Abdelrahim Qaddoumi, Vijay Shanker and Mahmoud Zyate

Overview of the WANLP 2022 Shared Task on Propaganda Detection in Arabic
Firoj Alam, Hamdy Mubarak, Wajdi Zaghouani, Giovanni Da San Martino and Preslav Nakov

15:30 - 16:00 *Coffee Break*

16:00 - 17:00 *Session 3 - Arabic Dialects (in-Person)*

ArzEn-ST: A Three-way Speech Translation Corpus for Code-Switched Egyptian Arabic-English
Injy Hamed, Nizar Habash, Slim Abdennadher and Ngoc Thang Vu

Maknuune: A Large Open Palestinian Arabic Lexicon
Shahd Salah Uddin Dibas, Christian Khairallah, Nizar Habash, Omar Fayez Sadi, Tariq Sairafy, Karmel Sarabta and Abrar Ardah

Developing a Tag-Set and Extracting the Morphological Lexicons to Build a Morphological Analyzer for Egyptian Arabic
Amany Fashwan and Sameh Alansary

A Weak Supervised Transfer Learning Approach for Sentiment Analysis to the Kuwaiti Dialect
Fatemah Husain, Hana Al-Ostad and Halima Omar

Thursday, December 8, 2022 (continued)

17:00 - 18:15 *Main Workshop Posters (in-Person & virtual)*

Mawqif: A Multi-label Arabic Dataset for Target-specific Stance Detection
Nora Saleh Alturayeif, Hamzah Abdullah Luqman and Moataz Aly Kamaleldin Ahmed

Assessing the Linguistic Knowledge in Arabic Pre-trained Language Models Using Minimal Pairs
Wafa Abdullah Alrajhi, Hend Al-Khalifa and Abdulmalik AlSalman

Identifying Code-switching in Arabizi
Safaa Shehadi and Shuly Wintner

Authorship Verification for Arabic Short Texts Using Arabic Knowledge-Base Model (AraKB)
Fatimah Alqahtani and Helen Yannakoudakis

A Semi-supervised Approach for a Better Translation of Sentiment in Dialectical Arabic UGT
Hadeel Saadany, Constantin Orăsan, Emad Mohamed and Ashraf Tantawy

Cross-lingual transfer for low-resource Arabic language understanding
Khadige Abboud, Olga Golovneva and Christopher DiPersio

Improving POS Tagging for Arabic Dialects on Out-of-Domain Texts
Noor Abo Mokh, Daniel Dakota and Sandra Kübler

Domain Adaptation for Arabic Crisis Response
Reem Alrashdi and Simon O'Keefe

Weakly and Semi-Supervised Learning for Arabic Text Classification using Monodialectal Language Models
Reem AlYami and Rabah Al-Zaidy

Event-Based Knowledge MLM for Arabic Event Detection
Asma Z Yamani, Amjad K Alsulami and Rabeah A Al-Zaidy

Establishing a Baseline for Arabic Patents Classification: A Comparison of Twelve Approaches
Taif Omar Al-Omar, Hend Al-Khalifa and Rawan Al-Matham

Towards Learning Arabic Morphophonology
Salam Khalifa, Jordan Kodner and Owen Rambow

AraDepSu: Detecting Depression and Suicidal Ideation in Arabic Tweets Using Transformers
Mariam Hassib, Nancy Hossam, Jolie Sameh and Marwan Torki

End-to-End Speech Translation of Arabic to English Broadcast News
Fethi Bougares and Salim Jouili

Arabic Keyphrase Extraction: Enhancing Deep Learning Models with Pre-trained Contextual Embedding and External Features
Randah Alharbi and Husni Al-Muhtasab

ArabIE: Joint Entity, Relation and Event Extraction for Arabic
Niama El Khbir, Nadi Tomeh and Thierry Charnois

Emoji Sentiment Roles for Sentiment Analysis: A Case Study in Arabic Texts
Shatha Ali A. Hakami, Robert Hendley and Phillip Smith

Gulf Arabic Diacritization: Guidelines, Initial Dataset, and Results
nouf alabbasi, Mohamed Al-Badrashiny, Maryam Aldahmani, Ahmed AlDhanhani, Abdullah Saleh Alhashmi, Fawaghy Ahmed Alhashmi, Khalid Al Hashemi, Rama Emad Alkhobbi, Shamma T Al Maazmi, Mohammed Ali Alyafeai, Mariam M Alzaabi, Mohamed Saqer Alzaabi, Fatma Khalid Badri, Kareem Darwish, Ehab Mansour Diab, Muhammad Morsy Elmallah, Amira Ayman Elnashar, Ashraf Hatim Elneima, MHD Tameem Kabbani, Nour Rabih, Ahmad Saad and Ammar Mamoun Sousou

Learning From Arabic Corpora But Not Always From Arabic Speakers: A Case Study of the Arabic Wikipedia Editions
Saied Alshahrani, Esma Wali and Jeanna Matthews

A Pilot Study on the Collection and Computational Analysis of Linguistic Differences Amongst Men and Women in a Kuwaiti Arabic WhatsApp Dataset
Hesah Aldihan, Robert Gaizauskas and Susan Fitzmaurice

17:00 - 18:15 *EMNLP Findings Posters (in-Person & virtual)*

Improving English-Arabic Transliteration with Phonemic Memories
Yan Song, Shengyi JIANG, Lianxi Wang, Xiangyu Pang, Renze Lou and Yuanhe Tian

Sarcasm Detection is Way Too Easy! An Empirical Comparison of Human and Machine Sarcasm Detection
Walid Magdy, Silviu Oprea, Steven Wilson and Ibrahim Abu Farha

17:00 - 18:15 *Demos (in-Person & virtual)*

Beyond Arabic: Software for Perso-Arabic Script Manipulation
Alexander Gutkin, Cibu Johny, Raiomond Doctor, Brian Roark and Richard Sproat

Coreference Annotation of an Arabic Corpus using a Virtual World Game
Wateen Abdullah Aliady, Abdulrahman Aloraini, Christopher Madge, Juntao Yu, Richard Bartle and Massimo Poesio

NatiQ: An End-to-end Text-to-Speech System for Arabic
Ahmed Abdelali, Nadir Durrani, Cenk Demiroglu, Fahim Dalvi, Hamdy Mubarak and Kareem Darwish

17:00 - 18:15 *NADI Shared Task (in-Person & virtual)*

Optimizing Naive Bayes for Arabic Dialect Identification
Tommi Jauhiainen, Heidi Jauhiainen and Krister Lindén

iCompass Working Notes for the Nuanced Arabic Dialect Identification Shared task
Abir Messaoudi, Chayma Fourati, Hatem Haddad and Moez BenHajhmida

TF-IDF or Transformers for Arabic Dialect Identification? ITFLOWS participation in the NADI 2022 Shared Task
Fouad Shammary, Yiyi Chen, Zsolt T Kardkovacs, Mehwish Alam and Haithem Afli

Domain-Adapted BERT-based Models for Nuanced Arabic Dialect Identification and Tweet Sentiment Analysis
Giyaseddin Bayrak and ABDUL MAJEED ISSIFU

Benchmarking transfer learning approaches for sentiment analysis of Arabic dialect
emna fsih, Sameh Kchaou, Rahma Boujelbane and Lamia Hadrich-Belguith

SQU-CS @ NADI 2022: Dialectal Arabic Identification using One-vs-One Classification with TF-IDF Weights Computed on Character n-grams
Abdulrahman Khalifa AAlAbdulsalam

Ahmed and Khalil at NADI 2022: Transfer Learning and Addressing Class Imbalance for Arabic Dialect Identification and Sentiment Analysis
Ahmed Oumar and Khalil Mrini

Arabic Sentiment Analysis by Pretrained Ensemble
Abdelrahim Qaddoumi

Dialect & Sentiment Identification in Nuanced Arabic Tweets Using an Ensemble of Prompt-based, Fine-tuned, and Multitask BERT-Based Models
Reem Abdel-Salam

On The Arabic Dialects' Identification: Overcoming Challenges of Geographical Similarities Between Arabic dialects and Imbalanced Datasets
Salma Jamal, Aly M .Kassem, Omar Mohamed and Ali Ashraf

Arabic dialect identification using machine learning and transformer-based models: Submission to the NADI 2022 Shared Task
Nouf AlShenaifi and Aqil Azmi

NLP DI at NADI Shared Task Subtask-1: Sub-word Level Convolutional Neural Models and Pre-trained Binary Classifiers for Dialect Identification
Vani Kanjirangat, Tanja Samardzic, Ljiljana Dolamic and Fabio Rinaldi

Word Representation Models for Arabic Dialect Identification
Mahmoud Sobhy, Ahmed H. Abu El-Atta, Ahmed A. El-Sawy and Hamada Nayel

Building an Ensemble of Transformer Models for Arabic Dialect Classification and Sentiment Analysis
Abdullah Salem Khered, Ingy Yasser Hassan Abdou Abdelhalim and Riza Batista-Navarro

Arabic Dialect Identification and Sentiment Classification using Transformer-based Models
Joseph Attieh and Fadi Hassan

17:00 - 18:15 *Gender Rewriting Shared Task Posters (in-Person & virtual)*

Generative Approach for Gender-Rewriting Task with ArabicT5
Sultan Alrowili and Vijay Shanker

17:00 - 18:15 *Propaganda Detection Shared Task Posters (in-Person & virtual)*

AraProp at WANLP 2022 Shared Task: Leveraging Pre-Trained Language Models for Arabic Propaganda Detection
Gaurav Singh

TUB at WANLP22 Shared Task: Using Semantic Similarity for Propaganda Detection in Arabic
Salar Mohtaj and Sebastian Möller

SI2M & AIOX Labs at WANLP 2022 Shared Task: Propaganda Detection in Arabic, A Data Augmentation and Name Entity Recognition Approach
Kamel Gaanoun and Imade Benelallam

iCompass at WANLP 2022 Shared Task: ARBERT and MARBERT for Multilabel Propaganda Classification of Arabic Tweets
Bilel - Taboubi, Bechir Brahem and Hatem Haddad

ChavanKane at WANLP 2022 Shared Task: Large Language Models for Multi-label Propaganda Detection
Tanmay Chavan and Aditya Manish Kane

AraBERT Model for Propaganda Detection
Mohamad Sharara, Wissam Mohamad, Ralph Tawil, Ralph Chobok, Wolf Assi and Antonio Tannoury

AraBEM at WANLP 2022 Shared Task: Propaganda Detection in Arabic Tweets
Eshrag Ali Refaee, Basem Ahmed and Motaz Saad

IITD at WANLP 2022 Shared Task: Multilingual Multi-Granularity Network for Propaganda Detection
Shubham Mittal and Preslav Nakov

Pythoneers at WANLP 2022 Shared Task: Monolingual AraBERT for Arabic Propaganda Detection and Span Extraction
Joseph Attieh and Fadi Hassan

CNLP-NITS-PP at WANLP 2022 Shared Task: Propaganda Detection in Arabic using Data Augmentation and AraBERT Pre-trained Model
Sahinur Rahman Laskar, Rahul Singh, Abdullah Faiz Ur Rahman Khilji, Riyanka Manna, Partha Pakray and Sivaji Bandyopadhyay

NGU CNLP atWANLP 2022 Shared Task: Propaganda Detection in Arabic
Ahmed Samir Hussein, Abu Bakr Soliman Mohammad, Mohamed Ibrahim, Laila Hesham Afify and Samhaa R. El-Beltagy

17:00 - 18:30 *Closing Ceremony*

CAraNER: The COVID-19 Arabic Named Entity Corpus

Abdulmohsen Al-Thubaity [1], **Sakhar Alkhereyf** [1], **Wejdan Alzahrani** [2], **Alia Bahanshal** [1]
[1] King Abdulaziz City for Science and Technology, Riyadh, Saudi Arabia
[2] King Saud University, Riyadh, Saudi Arabia
{aalthubaity,salkhereyf,abahanshal}@kacst.edu.sa
444203310@student.ksu.edu.sa

Abstract

Named Entity Recognition (NER) is a well-known problem for the natural language processing (NLP) community. It is a key component of different NLP applications, including information extraction, question answering, and information retrieval. In the literature, there are several Arabic NER datasets with different named entity tags; however, due to data and concept drift, we are always in need of new data for NER and other NLP applications. In this paper, first, we introduce Wassem, a web-based annotation platform for Arabic NLP applications. Wassem can be used to manually annotate textual data for a variety of NLP tasks: text classification, sequence classification, and word segmentation. Second, we introduce the COVID-19 Arabic Named Entities Recognition (CAraNER) dataset extracted from the Arabic Newspaper COVID-19 Corpus (AraNPCC). CAraNER has 55,389 tokens distributed over 1,278 sentences randomly extracted from Saudi Arabian newspaper articles published during 2019, 2020, and 2021. The dataset is labeled by five annotators with five named-entity tags, namely: Person, Title, Location, Organization, and Miscellaneous. The CAraNER corpus is available for download for free. We evaluate the corpus by finetuning four BERT-based Arabic language models on the CAraNER corpus. The best model was AraBERTv0.2-large with 0.86 for the F1 macro measure.

1 Introduction

Named entity recognition (NER) is a classical sequence classification problem where each word in a given sentence is assigned to one of a predefined list of tags such as person name (شاكر Shaker, بايدن Biden), location (القاهرة Cairo, واشنطن Washington), and organization (الأمم المتحدة United Nations, نادي الاتحاد Al-Ittihad Club).

NER is a key component and a fundamental task for many NLP applications, including information extraction (Liu et al., 2021; Nasar et al., 2021), question answering (Xu et al., 2021; Peng et al., 2021), content recommendations (Harrando and Troncy, 2021; Grewal and Lin, 2018), customer support (Brahma et al., 2021; Bozic et al., 2021), and information retrieval (Aliwy et al., 2021). It is one of the earliest tasks of NLP using classical statistical algorithms such as maximum entropy (Chieu and Ng, 2003) and has been developed for many years. However, it is still relevant in the current time where we are using transformer-based language models such as Bidirectional Encoder Representations from Transformers (BERT) (Liu et al., 2022).

Despite the recent advances in the NLP systems due to the usage of deep learning models, especially transformer-based language models, the need for new annotated datasets for developing NER systems is still crucial, where each domain and application requires its own dataset and tags. In general, NER systems, from our perspective, face three challenges:

First, the widespread use of NLP applications in different domains necessitates the usage of texts from these domains, which are probably different in their genre, style, and vocabularies, from the available annotated NER datasets. Out-of-vocabulary (OOV) will be the first challenge the NER system will face. For instance, if we need high-performance NER models, a NER dataset for the legal domain can not be used for the medical domain, and a NER dataset for Moroccan newspapers will not be the best choice for NER applications for UAE newspapers.

Second, unlike fixed tagset applications such as part-of-speech tagging or word segmentation, each NER application requires different tagsets. Most of the NER available datasets concentrate on person names, location, and organization tags with slight differences among them on other tags, such as the availability of geopolitical entities tags for government entities such as the Ontonotes 5 NER

Proceedings of the The Seventh Arabic Natural Language Processing Workshop (WANLP), pages 1 - 10
December 8, 2022 ©2022 Association for Computational Linguistics

dataset (Weischedel et al., 2013). Consider the need for a NER dataset for a food delivery chatbot; in this case, we may need a tagset containing tags for: a) the person's name to know who ordered the food, b) different tags for food items to direct the order to a relevant restaurant, and c) address to know the delivery location. Or suppose a system to analyze newspaper articles for military clashes; such a system, in addition to time, location, and the number of injuries, will need different tags to identify different kinds of weapons, for example.

Third, even if there is a dataset for particular domains or genres, there are always new topics, interests, and concepts introduced to those domains and genres that may degrade the models trained on older datasets. Such a challenge is well known in the machine learning community as data and concept drift (Celik and Vanschoren, 2021; Maheswari et al., 2022; Mei et al., 2022). Consider, for instance, a NER system trained on annotated texts from newspapers during the 2000s and then applied to newspaper texts during the COVID-19 pandemic; will this system perform well?

The contribution of this paper is in three folds. First, we introduce *Wassem* (وسم in Arabic, "annotate" in English), a platform for Arabic textual data annotation based on the Django framework. Second, we used Wassem to prepare COVID-19 Arabic Named Entity Recognition dataset (CAraNER): a NER dataset annotated with six tags (Person, Organization, Location, Title, Miscellaneous, and Other) covering 1,278 sentences, randomly extracted from Saudi Arabian newspapers part of Arabic Newspapers COVID-19 Corpus (AraNPCC) (Al-Thubaity et al., 2022). The COVID-19 part of the corpus name "CAraNER" is a temporal reference to the COVID-19 period as the AraNPCC corpus covers one year before the COVID-19 pandemic and two years after the emergence of the pandemic (i.e. 2019 - 2021).

Third, using CAraNER, we evaluate four BERT-based Arabic language models, namely bert-base-multilingual-cased (Devlin et al., 2019) (baseline), AraBERTv0.2-large (Antoun et al., 2020), CAMeLBERT-MSA (Inoue et al., 2021), and GigaBERT-v4 (Lan et al., 2020).

The rest of this paper is organized as follows: In section 2, we review the related work on Arabic NER. We briefly describe the main building blocks for Wassem in section 3. Section 4 describes the process of the CAraNER dataset construction and annotation and its basic statistics. Section 5 illustrates and discusses the result of fine-tuning four language models using CAraNER. We conclude the paper in section 6.

2 Related Work

Previous works on NER can be divided into two categories: building named-entity-tagged corpora and building NER models. In this section, we focus on previous work on building named-entity tagged Arabic corpora. Previous works on building named-entity corpora cover a variety of languages, genres, and domains. These studies focused on many tag sets that differ according to the application and domain requirements. Some corpora in the literature cover general-purpose tag sets from broad domains such as newswire and Wikipedia. In contrast, others focus on specific tag sets, such as the medical domain. Most previous studies include the four named-entity tags: Person, Location, Organization, and Miscellaneous.

The interest in building Arabic NER corpora dates back to the 2000s. One of the earliest studies for building an Arabic named-entity annotated corpus is the ACE 2004 Multilingual Training Corpus (Mitchell et al., 2005). The ACE 2004 corpus is developed by LDC and contains text in Arabic, Chinese, and English, covering a variety of genres. It was annotated for many NLP tasks, including named entity recognition and relation extraction. The ACE 2004 entity tags are Person (PER), Geo-Political Entity (GPE), Organization (ORG), and Facility (FAC). The size of the Arabic portion of ACE 2004 is around 10K tokens and collected from newswire texts.

Another LDC-licensed multilingual corpus is Ontonotes 5 (Weischedel et al., 2013), which is collected from various genres, including newswire and conversational telephone speech in three languages: Arabic, Chinese, and English. The Arabic portion of Ontonotes 5 contains around 300K tokens. Similar to our corpus, the Arabic Ontonotes 5 corpus was collected only from newswire sources in Modern Standard Arabic (MSA) and annotated with 18 entity types.

The ANERcorp corpus (Benajiba et al., 2007) is collected from Modern Standard Arabic media texts. It contains around 150K tokens tagged with four entity types: person, organization, location, and miscellaneous.

For genres other than newswire, Mohit et al.

(2012) developed the American and Qatari Modeling of Arabic (AQMAR) corpus for Wikipedia articles. It consists of 74K tokens tagged with domain-specific categories covering four topics: technology, science, history, and sports. Salah and Zakaria (2018) developed the Classical Arabic Named Entity Recognition Corpus (CANERCorpus) for text for the Islamic Hadith. It contains around 72K tokens tagged with categories relevant to the field, such as "Prophet".

Darwish and Gao (2014) have developed the first NER dataset for Arabic Tweets. Their dataset comprises 5,069 tweets tagged with three tags, namely: person, location, and organization. Recently, Jarrar et al. (2022) released the Nested Arabic Named Entity Corpus (Wojood). Wojood comprises 550K tokens from Modern Standard Arabic (MSA) and different Arabic dialects. Wojood annotated with 21 entity types, including person, organization, location, product, and unit. Wojood is the largest Arabic NER dataset and the first Arabic NER dataset using nested tagging.

The most important factor that may distinguish the CAraNER dataset is that it was sampled from the COVID-19 period. Regarding the CAraNER size (~50K tokens), we are working to increase its size to reach a level that can produce good results using state-of-the-art machine learning algorithms, specifically neural language models.

3 Annotation Platform

The motivation behind the development of *Wassem* is the shortage of open source annotation platforms suitable for Arabic NLP annotation tasks such as word segmentation and diacritization. We designed Wassem to help in the following tasks: a) Text and sentence annotation for applications such as text classification and sentiment analysis, b) Sequence annotation for applications like NER and POS tagging, c) Subword annotation for applications like Arabic words segmentation, and d) for Arabic word diacritization.

Wassem has four main functions, which are described as follows:

a. **Annotation task initialization:** The system administrator is responsible for this function. Four steps are needed to complete this process as follows: First, the administrator needs to define the list of tags used for the annotation task, with a brief description for each tag if they do not exist before in the database. Also, the administrator can attach a list of words with fixed tags such that the corresponding tag for each word in the list does not change when the context changes; this accelerates the annotation process. For example, for POS tagging, this list may include particles and prepositions such as "إلى" (to), "عن" (about), "لكن" (but) or part of the most frequent words in the data that have the same characteristic, i.e., they have fixed tags such as "الله" (Allah), "قال" (Said), "إلى" (To). The system will automatically annotate words with their corresponding tags in the list such that the user does not need to consider them during manual annotation. Such lists of words and their fixed tags can be used in the future for other annotation tasks. Second, the system currently provides manual annotation on the document level and word level. Based on the type of annotation task, the system administrator should determine the level of the task. The difference between the two levels is the text unit that will be annotated with the tag. Hence, in the case of the document level, a label will be assigned to the entire sentence/text, for example, sentiment analysis on the document level. In contrast, for the word-level annotation, each word/token in the text will be labeled with a tag, for example, POS tagging. Moreover, for the case of word-level annotation, the administrator should specify if the task is a segmentation, diacritization, or tagging the whole token (e.g., NER). Third, the administrator needs to provide a description of the annotation tasks and identify the minimum number of annotators who can participate in the task. The system can automatically assign a final label using the majority vote if there are three or more annotators. Fourth, the administrator should upload the raw data that will be tagged if it was not in the system before (i.e., used previously on other annotation tasks), and link this annotation task with the appropriate list of tags.

b. **Annotation task assignment:** After creating the annotation task, the administrator should assign it to the annotators. The administrator can add new annotators or select annotators already existing in the system. Wassem's website provides a link to a registration form for volunteer annotators where they need to pro-

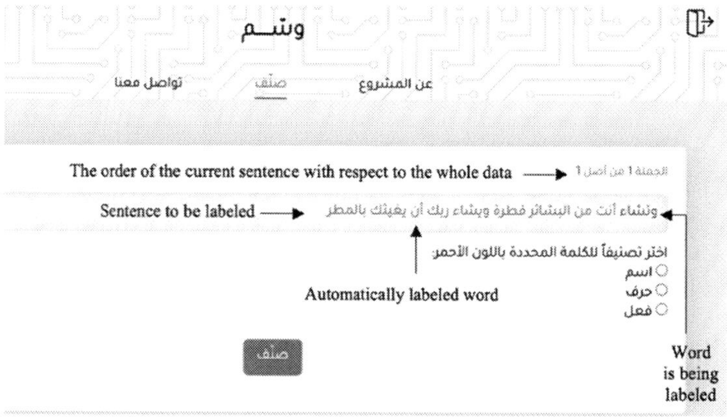

Figure 1: An example of a word-level annotation task (POS tagging) on Wassem.

vide their contact information, gender, age, and educational background. Such information will help the administrator to identify the best annotators for each annotation task.

c. Annotation process: When the annotator starts the annotation process for the first time, the system will welcome her/him and provide them with a description of the annotation task and a description for each tag. Then the system will display the data for the annotator to start annotating it. To keep the user concentrated on the annotation task, the system uses three colors for the words in the displayed sentence during annotation:

- Red: highlights the word that is being annotated.
- Gray: indicates the word that was labeled automatically by the system using a predefined list of words and their tags.
- Green: for the rest of the words.

Figure 1 shows an example of word-level annotation for a simple Arabic POS annotation task.

d. Exporting data: Finally, the annotated data can be exported in a CSV file format. The system applies the majority voting approach to determine the final tags for each example. If there is no agreement (i.e., tie), the final tag will be set as "*No_agr*". In the case of uncompleted tasks (i.e., some annotators have not completed their tasks yet), the system will set the tag as "*Not_Annot*" to the examples which are not annotated yet.

4 Data

In this section, we describe our work to prepare the raw data for the annotation process, the tagset used for annotation, the annotators' training and annotation process, and the final data after annotation. We made the dataset is available for free download on GitHub [1].

4.1 Data Preparation

The raw CAraNER data is randomly selected sentences from 826,323 Modern Standrad Arabic (MSA) texts that constitute Saudi Arabia newspapers in AraNPCC (Al-Thubaity et al., 2022). AraNPCC comprises more than 1.7 million texts automatically collected from the newspapers of 12 Arab countries for one year before the COVID-19 pandemic and two years during the pandemic (from 1 January 2019 until 31 December 2021). We focus on the Saudi part of the AraNPCC corpus as we had the chance to hire annotators only from Saudi Arabia, who are more familiar with the local named entities such as town names.

To prepare the data for annotation, we followed the following steps:

4.1.1 Texts Selection

There are 8 Saudi newspapers in AraNPCC. The texts from these eight newspapers are categorized into 19 classes: health, corona, culture, economy, international, local, opinion, society, sport, politics, technology, journal, last page, lifestyle, main, religion, story, women, and not classified. Each Saudi newspaper has its own classification system, so not all these classes are available in every Saudi newspaper. For each year (2019, 2020, and 2021) and

[1] https://github.com/kacst-ncdaai/caraner

from each of the eight newspapers, we randomly selected 6 texts from each class. Finally, we got 1,271 texts comprising 322,907 tokens. The number of tokens exceeds our need for this stage of the project; however, it will allow us to extend our work in the future.

4.1.2 Preprocessing

Instead of annotating the entire text, we preprocessed each text and divided it into sentences. Building a NER system based on sentences will allow all ML algorithms to handle the input data easily and will make the data more diverse. For each text, we carried out the following steps to achieve our goal:

a) Replace each new line marker "\n" with a space.

b) Replace each URL with a special marker "<link>".

c) Remove Arabic diacritics.

d) Replace repeated punctuation marks such as "!", "?", "." and "-" with a single punctuation mark of its kind.

e) Separate punctuation marks from words by a space and parentheses from words and numbers by a space.

f) The above step will affect the dots that come after the title abbreviations of Doctor "د." (Dr.), Engineer "م." (Eng.), Professor "أ." or "ا." (Prof.), which will negatively affect the process of sentence segmentation. So, we replace each dot after these abbreviations with a special marker "/".

g) We use the *sent_tokenize(text)* function in the NLTK python package to segment the text into sentences. This step will produce a list of sentences.

h) Select sentences with a length of more than 10 characters.

i) Replace "/" that comes after "د، م، ا، أ" with a dot "." on the selected sentences and save them in a list. This step allows us to preserve these abbreviations.

Applying the above steps for all texts produced 8,371 sentences comprising 370,138 words. We shuffled these sentences randomly and saved them in 75 text files, each file compromising approximately 5,000 words. Note that the preprocessing steps increase the number of words due to the application of step "e" mentioned above. Dividing the produced sentences into separate files (75) allows managing the annotation process as batches and handle any misconceptions or mistakes by the annotators during the revision of the annotation process for each batch before the beginning of the next batch.

4.2 Tagset

For CAraNER we choose the following tags:

- **PER:** person names such as "محمد" (Mohamad); nicknames such as "أخو نورة" (Nora's brother) and "الجاحظ" (Al-Jahiz).

- **TIT:** job title such as "رئيس مجلس الوزراء" (Prime Minister); military and civilian ranks "فريق أول بحري" (Admiral); academic or professional title such as "المهندس" (engineer); political or social title such as "صاحب السمو الملكي" (His Royal Highness).

- **LOC:** countries such as "مصر" (Egypt); regions, provinces, cities, and villages such as "بيروت" (Beirut); landmarks and sites such as "غار حراء" (Cave of Hira).

- **ORG:** government and commercial organizations and bodies such as "الهيئة السعودية للبيانات والذكاء الاصطناعي" (Saudi Data and Artificial Intelligence Authority); sports clubs such as "فريق نيوكاسل" (Newcastle United Football Club); international bodies such as "المنظمة العربية للتربية والثقافة والعلوم" (Arab League Educational, Cultural and Scientific Organization); countries and capitals as political entities such as "المغرب" (Morocco) in such a following context: "أعربت المغرب عن استنكارها ...." (Morocco has expressed its disapproval ....).

- **MIS:** For other named entities (miscellaneous). It includes but is not limited to diseases such as "كوفيد-١٩" (COVID-19), medicines and chemical compounds such as "كلوروكين" (Chloroquine); events such as "إكسبو ٢٠٢٠" (Expo 2020); Currencies such as "درهم إماراتي" (Arab Emirates Dirham); beliefs and ideologies such as

"الديمقراطية" (Democracy); products such as "إيباد برو" (iPad Pro); measurement units such as "كيلو جرام" (Kg); regulations and laws such "قانون كرة اليد الدولي" (international handball federation regulations); tribes such as "تغلب" (Taghlib).

Since the named entities can be in chunks with more than one word, we adopt the most used tagging format for NER: Inside–Outside–Beginning (IOB) format such that tags will be prefixed either with "I" or "B". The non-named entities will be tagged as "O".

In addition to these tags, we use the "N" tag to indicate when the annotator can not determine the right tag for a given word. This tag helps us track the annotators' learning curve and highlight the difficulties they may face during the annotation process. In total, the annotators will work on 12 tags, namely: *B_PER, I_PER, B_TIT, I_TIT, B_LOC, I_LOC, B_ORG, I_ORG, B_MIS, I_MIS, O,* and *N*. The N tag does not appear in the final revised tags for the dataset, as it is revised by other annotators.

4.3 Annotation Process

We have hired five annotators for the annotation process of CAraNER. All annotators are Saudi nationals, two males and three females, in the final semester of their university undergraduate study, and all were around 21 years old.

We followed the following steps to train the annotators:

- We introduced the problem of NER to the annotators.
- We introduced different examples of each tag and discussed them with annotators.
- We asked each annotator, based on their first impression, to annotate three short sentences and ask the other annotators if they agreed or disagreed and why. This discussion allowed us to clarify several issues regarding the annotation process to the annotators.
- We provided the annotators with 25 sentences and asked them to annotate them. Furthermore, we asked the annotators not to discuss the annotation process with each other to reduce cognition bias.
- We reviewed the annotation results with the annotators, gave them our feedback, and answered their questions and ambiguities regarding tags.
- We train the annotators on Wassem.

The training process for annotators took more than two weeks. After the annotators' training, we provide each annotator with one batch at the beginning of the week. Then, we ask them to annotate the batch during the week using Wassem unless they feel tired, bored, or sick. We do so to assure the quality of the annotation. In the following week, we annotate the same five batches as the previous week, but each annotator will annotate another batch. By the end of the second week, each batch will be annotated by two annotations. Within five weeks, the annotators were able to annotate 27 batches.

After annotating a batch, we asked all annotators to discuss the disagreement cases and to agree on a decision regarding a disagreement case.

The data shows that there are 2,949 disagreement cases (5.3%) during the annotation process, i.e., the annotators agreed on 94.7% of annotation examples. Furthermore, the annotated data shows that there were 506 cases (0.9%) where a single annotator could not determine the tag for a given word. 21 of these words were shared between two annotators. All these cases were resolved each week during the process of annotation revision.

4.4 Statistics

The statistics on the data show that the CAraNER corpus comprises 55,389 tokens distributed over 1,278 sentences containing 3,813 named entities. Table 1 illustrates the distribution of named entities and examples of each named entity type. Note that the percentage of words that have "O" tags in the dataset is 84.5%.

5 Evaluation

NER is usually treated as a sequence labeling problem. In the literature, early studies used CRF models (Konkol and Konopík, 2013). Later, deep learning sequence models such as LSTMs have been used in many studies for NER (Zhang and Yang, 2018). More recently, pre-trained language models have been used to model NER, and they outperform previous models (Yohannes and Amagasa, 2022).

Tag	%	Examples
PER	19.3%	ماكاريوس، خالد بن فهد، وليد الصمعاني، سلمان بن عبدالعزيز، كرستيانو رونالدو، نوف بنت خالد الجريوي، أبو فراس الحمداني، محمد بن سلمان بن عبدالعزيز، رجب طيب أردوغان، جو بايدن. Makarios, Khalid bin Fahd, Walid Al-Samaani, Salman bin Abdulaziz, Cristiano Ronaldo, Nouf bint Khalid Al-Jeriwi, Abu Firas Al-Hamdani, Mohammed bin Salman bin Abdulaziz, Recep Tayyip Erdogan, Joe Biden
TIT	21.4%	السفير السوفيتي، الرئيس القبرصي، الأمير، معالي وزير العدل، الدكتور، فضيلة الشيخ، الرئيس التنفيذي لنوفا، المهندسة، خادم الحرمين الشريفين Soviet Ambassador, Cypriot President, Emir, Honorable Minister of Justice, Dr., Sheikh, CEO of Nova, Engineer, Custodian of the Two Holy Mosques
LOC	12.9%	المسجد الحرام، معدن شمام، وادي الفرع، كولومبيا، لوسون، القاهرة، بحيرة مالاوي، ولاية كارولاينا الشمالية، مسرح نورد، مأرب Al-Masjid Al-Haram, Ma'aden Shemam, Wadi Al-Fara', Columbia, Lawson, Cairo, Lake Malawi, North Carolina, Nord Theater, Ma'rib
ORG	25.0%	فيسبوك، جماعة الإخوان، قوات الأمن البيئي، وزارة الداخلية، إدارة سقيا زمزم، الهيئة السعودية للبيانات والذكاء الاصطناعي، المركز الوطني للوقاية من الأمراض ومكافحتها، مليشيات الحوثي، ليفربول، الكونجرس الأمريكي Facebook, Brotherhood, Environmental Security Forces, Ministry of Interior, Zamzam Water Department, Saudi Authority for Data and Artificial Intelligence, National Center for Disease Prevention and Control, Houthi militias, Liverpool, US Congress
MIS	21.4%	ماء زمزم، فيروس كورونا المستجد، العلمانية، الفضة، قبيلة باهلة، دوري أبطال آسيا، توكلنا،السكري، مهرجان أفلام السعودية، نظام حماية الأجور للعمالة المنزلية Zamzam water, the emerging coronavirus, secularism, silver, the Bahla tribe, the Asian Champions League, Tawakkalna, diabetes, the Saudi Film Festival, the wage protection system for domestic workers.

Table 1: Named entities distribution with examples from the CAraNER corpus.

We evaluate the CAraNER dataset by fine-tuning four BERT-based language models: bert-base-multilingual-cased (baseline), AraBERTv0.2-large, CAMeLBERT-MSA, and GigaBERT-v4. All of these models are based on BERT-base except AraBERT, which is based on BERT-large.

We fine-tuned the language models on the Google Colab platform using Tesla GPUs. We considered the following for experimentation setup for all models:

- From Huggingface, we used *transformers* v4.21.1, *AutoTokenizer*, and *BertForTokenClassification* libraries.
- We use *AdamW* for optimization with learning rate = 3e-5.
- We split data into 80% for training and 20% for testing (randomly selected).
- We select the number of Epochs = 16.
- We set the value for Max_grad_norm = 1.0.
- We set sentence_max_length = 295 (length of the longest sentence in the corpus).
- We choose batch size = 4.

Model	Acc.	Prec.	Recall	F1
mBERT	0.95	0.78	0.77	0.77
AraBERT	**0.97**	**0.86**	**0.86**	**0.86**
CAMeLBERT	0.96	0.83	**0.86**	0.84
GigaBERT	0.96	0.81	0.8	0.8

Table 2: Performance measures (accuracy, macro averaged precision, recall, and F-1) for the fine-tuned language models. mBERT: *bert-base-multilingual-cased.*

Table 2 shows the performance measures (macro avg) for the four fine-tuned language models. We consider the macro F1 measure when comparing the models. The results suggest that the

Tag	mBERT	AraBERTv0.2-large	CAMeLBERT-MSA	GigaBERT-v4
B-LOC	0.63	**0.75**	0.71	0.71
B-MIS	0.61	**0.74**	0.69	0.64
B-ORG	0.69	0.83	**0.85**	0.8
B-PER	0.89	**0.97**	0.94	0.91
B-TIT	0.86	**0.92**	0.88	0.86
I-LOC	0.61	0.76	**0.78**	0.74
I-MIS	0.58	**0.64**	**0.64**	0.55
I-ORG	0.79	0.9	**0.91**	0.82
I-PER	0.94	**1**	0.98	0.97
I-TIT	0.9	0.91	**0.93**	0.85
O	0.98	**0.99**	0.98	0.98

Table 3: F1 measure for each named entity tag. mBERT: *bert-base-multilingual-cased.*

AraBERTv0.2-large language model outperforms the other models followed by CAMeLBERT-MSA.

The superiority of the AraBERT over other models can be explained by the fact that AraBERTv0.2-large is much larger than the other models. In particular, AraBERTv0.2-large has 371M parameters, whereas the other models are based on the smaller model BERT-base, which has less than half this number of parameters. However, we observe that CAMeLBERT-MSA achieved a comparable performance by only using less than half of the model size. This relatively good performance of CAMeLBERT-MSA can be attributed to the size of the data on which the model was trained compared to the other models.

From these results, we observe that all models achieved an accuracy score of more than 95%. This can be attributed to the fact that most of the words have an "O" tag, which makes it easy to achieve such a high accuracy score. In particular, only 3,813 (∼7%) out of 55,389 tokens are named entities, and 51,576 (∼93%) of the tokens are not.

Table 3 shows the F1 score of the four fine-tuned models on CAraNER for each tag. The results show that all models have the same relative performance order for named entity tags. We observe that the best performance was on the PER tag, followed by the TIT, ORG, LOC, and MIS tags, respectively. The relatively high performance on the PER and TIT tags is probably due to the repetition of public figures' person names and their titles in newspapers. For the ORG and LOC tags, the errors were due to wrong identification for the beginning of their named entities. The low performance of the MIS tag can be attributed to the diversity of named entities it contains.

6 Conclusion

In this paper, we introduced a web-based annotation platform for Arabic NLP (Wassem) and a new dataset for Arabic NER (CAraNER) annotated with five tags (PER, TIT, LOC, ORG and MIS) using Wassem. Experimentation on four BERT-based language models shows that fine-tuning AraBERTv0.2-large on CAraNER gives the best results among the other models, with a 0.86 macro F-1 score. Also, the relatively good performance of CAMeLBERT-MSA (0.84 macro F-1 score) may suggest that using large and diverse datasets for pre-training smaller language models (i.e., BERT-base) gives similar performance to larger models (i.e., BERT-large) pre-trained on smaller datasets. In the future, we plan to double the size of CAraNER to improve the performance and experiment with different Arabic language models.

Acknowledgment

The authors would like to thank the anonymous reviewers for their valuable comments and feedback. Also, they would like to thank the annotators for this corpus during their summer internships at KACST, namely, Abdulaziz Alghuwainem, Amjad Alshalhoub, Dalal Alqahtany, Dana AlDukhail, and Marwan Alobathani.

References

Abdulmohsen Al-Thubaity, Sakhar Alkhereyf, and Alia O. Bahanshal. 2022. AraNPCC: The Arabic newspaper covid-19 corpus. In *Proceedinsg of the 5th Workshop on Open-Source Arabic Corpora and Processing Tools with Shared Tasks on Qur'an QA and Fine-Grained Hate Speech Detection*, pages 32–

40, Marseille, France. European Language Resources Association.

Ahmed Aliwy, Ayad Abbas, and Ahmed Alkhayyat. 2021. NERWS: Towards improving information retrieval of digital library management system using named entity recognition and word sense. *Big Data and Cognitive Computing*, 5(4):59.

Wissam Antoun, Fady Baly, and Hazem Hajj. 2020. AraBERT: Transformer-based model for Arabic language understanding. In *LREC 2020 Workshop Language Resources and Evaluation Conference 11–16 May 2020*, page 9.

Yassine Benajiba, Paolo Rosso, and José Miguel Benedíruiz. 2007. Anersys: An Arabic named entity recognition system based on maximum entropy. In *International Conference on Intelligent Text Processing and Computational Linguistics*, pages 143–153. Springer.

Bojan Bozic, Jayadeep Kumar Sasikumar, and Tamara Matthews. 2021. KnowText: Auto-generated knowledge graphs for custom domain applications. In *The 23rd International Conference on Information Integration and Web Intelligence*, pages 350–358.

Aditya Kiran Brahma, Prathyush Potluri, Meghana Kanapaneni, Sumanth Prabhu, and Sundeep Teki. 2021. Identification of food quality descriptors in customer chat conversations using named entity recognition. In *8th ACM IKDD CODS and 26th COMAD*, pages 257–261.

Bilge Celik and Joaquin Vanschoren. 2021. Adaptation strategies for automated machine learning on evolving data. *IEEE Transactions on Pattern Analysis and Machine Intelligence*, 43(9):3067–3078.

Hai Leong Chieu and Hwee Tou Ng. 2003. Named entity recognition with a maximum entropy approach. In *Proceedings of the seventh conference on Natural language learning at HLT-NAACL 2003*, pages 160–163.

Kareem Darwish and Wei Gao. 2014. Simple effective microblog named entity recognition: Arabic as an example. In *Proceedings of the Ninth International Conference on Language Resources and Evaluation (LREC'14)*, pages 2513–2517.

Jacob Devlin, Ming-Wei Chang, Kenton Lee, and Kristina Toutanova. 2019. BERT: Pre-training of deep bidirectional transformers for language understanding. In *Proceedings of the 2019 Conference of the North American Chapter of the Association for Computational Linguistics: Human Language Technologies, Volume 1 (Long and Short Papers)*, pages 4171–4186, Minneapolis, Minnesota. Association for Computational Linguistics.

Ajeet Grewal and Jimmy Lin. 2018. The evolution of content analysis for personalized recommendations at Twitter. In *The 41st International ACM SIGIR Conference on Research & Development in Information Retrieval*, pages 1355–1356.

Ismail Harrando and Raphaël Troncy. 2021. Improving media content recommendation with automatic annotations. In *KaRS 2021, 3rd Edition of Knowledge-aware and Conversational Recommender Systems*.

Go Inoue, Bashar Alhafni, Nurpeiis Baimukan, Houda Bouamor, and Nizar Habash. 2021. The interplay of variant, size, and task type in Arabic pre-trained language models. In *Proceedings of the Sixth Arabic Natural Language Processing Workshop*, pages 92–104.

Mustafa Jarrar, Mohammed Khalilia, and Sana Ghanem. 2022. Wojood: Nested Arabic named entity corpus and recognition using BERT. In *Proceedings of the International Conference on Language Resources and Evaluation (LREC 2022), Marseille, France, June*.

Michal Konkol and Miloslav Konopík. 2013. Crf-based czech named entity recognizer and consolidation of czech ner research. In *International conference on text, speech and dialogue*, pages 153–160. Springer.

Wuwei Lan, Yang Chen, Wei Xu, and Alan Ritter. 2020. Gigabert: Zero-shot transfer learning from English to Arabic. In *Proceedings of The 2020 Conference on Empirical Methods on Natural Language Processing (EMNLP)*.

Chenguang Liu, Yongli Yu, Xingxin Li, and Peng Wang. 2021. Named entity recognition in equipment support field using tri-training algorithm and text information extraction technology. *IEEE Access*, 9:126728–126734.

Hao Liu, Qinjun Qiu, Liang Wu, Wenjia Li, Bin Wang, and Yuan Zhou. 2022. Few-shot learning for name entity recognition in geological text based on GeoBERT. *Earth Science Informatics*, pages 1–13.

A Uma Maheswari, N Revathy, T Guhan, B Praveen, and R Magesh Kumar. 2022. A systematic bpclstm algorithm for concept drift detection incorporated sentiment mining. In *2022 International Conference on Computer Communication and Informatics (ICCI)*, pages 1–8. IEEE.

Songzhu Mei, Cong Liu, Qinglin Wang, and Huayou Su. 2022. Model provenance management in mlops pipeline. In *2022 The 8th International Conference on Computing and Data Engineering*, pages 45–50.

Alexis Mitchell, Stephanie Strassel, Shudong Huang, and Ramez Zakhary. 2005. Ace 2004 multilingual training corpus. *Linguistic Data Consortium, Philadelphia*, 1:1–1.

Behrang Mohit, Nathan Schneider, Rishav Bhowmick, Kemal Oflazer, and Noah A Smith. 2012. Recall oriented learning of named entities in Arabic wikipedia. In *Proceedings of the 13th Conference of the European Chapter of the Association for Computational Linguistics*, pages 162–173.

Zara Nasar, Syed Waqar Jaffry, and Muhammad Kamran Malik. 2021. Named entity recognition and relation extraction: State-of-the-art. *ACM Computing Surveys (CSUR)*, 54(1):1–39.

Keqin Peng, Chuantao Yin, Wenge Rong, Chenghua Lin, Deyu Zhou, and Zhang Xiong. 2021. Named entity aware transfer learning for biomedical factoid question answering. *IEEE/ACM Transactions on Computational Biology and Bioinformatics*.

Ramzi Esmail Salah and Lailatul Qadri Binti Zakaria. 2018. Building the Classical Arabic named entity recognition corpus (canercorpus). In *2018 Fourth International Conference on Information Retrieval and Knowledge Management (CAMP)*, pages 1–8. IEEE.

Ralph Weischedel, Martha Palmer, Mitchell Marcus, Eduard Hovy, Sameer Pradhan, Lance Ramshaw, Nianwen Xue, Ann Taylor, Jeff Kaufman, Michelle Franchini, et al. 2013. Ontonotes release 5.0 ldc2013t19. *Linguistic Data Consortium, Philadelphia, PA*, 23.

Gezheng Xu, Wenge Rong, Yanmeng Wang, Yuanxin Ouyang, and Zhang Xiong. 2021. External features enriched model for biomedical question answering. *BMC bioinformatics*, 22(1):1–19.

Hailemariam Mehari Yohannes and Toshiyuki Amagasa. 2022. Named-entity recognition for a low-resource language using pre-trained language model. In *Proceedings of the 37th ACM/SIGAPP Symposium on Applied Computing*, pages 837–844.

Yue Zhang and Jie Yang. 2018. Chinese ner using lattice LSTM. In *Proceedings of the 56th Annual Meeting of the Association for Computational Linguistics (Volume 1: Long Papers)*, pages 1554–1564.

Joint Coreference Resolution for Zeros and non-Zeros in Arabic

Abdulrahman Aloraini[1,2] **Sameer Pradhan**[3,4] **Massimo Poesio**[1]
[1]School of Electronic Engineering and Computer Science, Queen Mary University of London
[2]Department of Information Technology, College of Computer, Qassim University
[3]cemantix.org
[4]Linguistic Data Consortium, University of Pennsylvania, Philadelphia, USA

a.aloraini@qmul.ac.uk spradhan@cemantix.org / upenn.edu m.poesio@qmul.ac.uk

Abstract

Most existing proposals about anaphoric zero pronoun (AZP) resolution regard full mention coreference and AZP resolution as two independent tasks, even though the two tasks are clearly related. The main issues that need tackling to develop a joint model for zero and non-zero mentions are the difference between the two types of arguments (zero pronouns, being null, provide no nominal information) and the lack of annotated datasets of a suitable size in which both types of arguments are annotated for languages other than Chinese and Japanese. In this paper, we introduce two architectures for jointly resolving AZPs and non-AZPs, and evaluate them on Arabic, a language for which, as far as we know, there has been no prior work on joint resolution. Doing this also required creating a new version of the Arabic subset of the standard coreference resolution dataset used for the CoNLL-2012 shared task (Pradhan et al., 2012) in which both zeros and non-zeros are included in a single dataset.

1 Introduction

In pronoun-dropping (pro-drop) languages such as Arabic (Eid, 1983), Chinese (Li and Thompson, 1979), Italian (Di Eugenio, 1990) and other romance languages (e.g., Portuguese, Spanish), Japanese (Kameyama, 1985), and others (Young-Joo, 2000), arguments in syntactic positions in which a pronoun is used in English can be omitted. Such arguments–sometimes called null arguments, empty arguments, or zeros, and called anaphoric zero pronouns (AZP) here when they are anaphoric, are illustrated by the following example:

... المفارقة الأخرى عن بوش هي عدم حماسته للمؤتمر الدولي
، لأن بوش من البداية ، يريد * اجتماعا مختلفا ...

Ironically, Bush did not show any enthusiasm for the international conference, because Bush since the beginning, (he) wanted to attend another conference ...

In the example, the '*' is an anaphoric zero pronoun–a gap replacing an omitted pronoun which refers to a previously mentioned noun, i.e. Bush.[1]

Although AZPs are common in pro-drop languages (Chen and Ng, 2016), they are typically not considered in standard coreference resolution architectures. Existing coreference resolution systems for Arabic would cluster the overt mentions of Bush, but not the AZP position; vice versa, AZP resolution systems would resolve the AZP, to one of the previous mentions, but not other mentions. The main reason for this is that AZPs are empty mentions, meaning that it is not possible to encode features commonly used in coreference systems–the head, syntactic and lexical features as in pre-neural systems. As a result, papers such as (Iida et al., 2015) have shown that treating the resolution of AZPs and realized mentions separately is beneficial. However, it has been shown that the more recent language models and end-to-end systems do not suffer from these issues to the same extent. BERT, for example, learns surface, semantic and syntactic features of the whole context (Jawahar et al., 2019) and it has been shown that BERT encodes sufficient information about AZPs within its layers to achieve reasonable performance (Aloraini and Poesio, 2020b,a). However, these findings have not yet led to many coreference resolution models attempting to resolve both types of mentions in a single learning framework (in fact, we are only aware of two, (Chen et al., 2021; Yang et al., 2022), the second of which was just proposed) and these have not been evaluated with Arabic.

In this paper, we discuss two methods for jointly clustering AZPs and non-AZPs, that we evaluate on Arabic: a *pipeline* and a *joint learning* architecture. In order to train and test these two architectures, however, it was also necessary to create a

[1]We use here the notation for AZPs used in the Arabic portion of OntoNotes 5.0, in which AZPs are denoted as * and we also use another notation which is ***pro***.

Proceedings of the The Seventh Arabic Natural Language Processing Workshop (WANLP), pages 11 - 21
December 8, 2022 ©2022 Association for Computational Linguistics

new version of the Arabic portion of the CoNLL-2012 shared task corpus in which both zeros and non-zeros are annotated in the same documents. To summarize, the contributions of this paper are as follows:

- We introduce two new architectures for resolving AZPs and non-AZPs together, the *pipeline* and the *joint learning* architecture. One of our architectures, the *joint learning*, outperforms the one existing joint end-to-end model (Chen et al., 2021) when resolving both types of mentions together.
- We create an extended version of the Arabic portion of CoNLL-2012 shared task in which the zero and non-zero mentions are represented in the same document. The extended dataset is suitable for training AZPs and non-AZPs jointly or each type separately.

2 Related Work

Most existing works regard coreference resolution and AZP resolution as two independent tasks. Many studies were dedicated to Arabic coreference resolution using CoNLL-2012 dataset (li, 2012; Zhekova and Kübler, 2010; Björkelund and Nugues, 2011; Stamborg et al., 2012; Uryupina et al., 2012; Fernandes et al., 2014; Björkelund and Kuhn, 2014; Aloraini et al., 2020; Min, 2021), but AZPs were excluded from the dataset so no work considered them. Aloraini and Poesio (2020b) proposed a BERT-base approach to resolve AZPs to their true antecedent, but they did not resolve other mentions.

There have been a few proposals on solving the two tasks jointly for other languages. Iida and Poesio (2011) integrated the AZP resolver with a coreference resolution system using an integer-linear-programming model. Kong and Ng (2013) employed AZPs to improve the coreference resolution of non-AZPs using a syntactic parser. Shibata and Kurohashi (2018) proposed an entity-based joint coreference resolution and predicate argument structure analysis for Japanese. However, these works relied on language-specific features and some assumed the presence of AZPs.

There are two end-to-end neural proposals about learning AZPs and non-AZPs together. The first proposal is by Chen et al. (2021) who combined tokens and AZP gaps representations using an encoder. The two representations interact in a two-stage mechanism to learn their coreference information, as shown in Figure 5. The second proposal, just published, is by (Yang et al., 2022), who proposed the CorefDPR architecture. CorefDPR consists of four components: the input representation layer, coreference resolution layer, pronoun recovery layer and general CRF layer. In our experiments, we only compared our results with the first proposal because the second system was only evaluated on the Chinese conversational speech of OntoNotes[2] and the model is not publicly available which makes it difficult to compare our results with theirs.

3 An Extended Version of the CoNLL Arabic dataset with AZPs

The goal of the CoNLL-2012 coreference shared task is to learn coreference resolution for three languages (English, Chinese and Arabic). However, AZPs were excluded from the task even though they are annotated in OntoNotes Arabic and Chinese. This was because considering AZPs decreased the overall performance on Arabic and Chinese(Pradhan et al., 2012), but not on English because it is not a pro-drop language (White, 1985). So in order to study joint coreference resolution for explicit mentions and zero anaphors, we had to create a novel version of the CoNLL-2012 dataset in which AZPs and all related information are included. The CoNLL-2012 annotation layers consists of 13 layers and they are in Appendix A.

Existing proposals evaluated their AZP systems using OntoNotes Normal Forms (ONF)[3]. They are annotated with AZPs and other mentions; however, they are not as well-prepared as CoNLL-2012. To create a CoNLL-like dataset with AZPs, we extract AZPs from ONF and add them to the already-existing CoNLL files. The goal of the new dataset is to be suitable for clustering AZPs and non-AZPs, and can be compared with previous proposals that did not consider AZPs and as well as with future works that consider them.

To include AZPs and their information (e.g., Part-of-Speech and parse tree) to CoNLL-2012, we can use ONF. However, while adding AZPs to the clusters, we realized that there is one difficulty:some

[2]The TC part of the Chinese portion in OntoNotes.

[3]The OntoNotes Normal Form (ONF) was originally meant to be an human-readable integrated representation of the multiple layers in OntoNotes. However, it has been used by many as a machine readable representation–as it is also more or less true–to extract annotations, primarily zeros that are typically excluded from the traditional CoNLL tabular representation.

```
Chain 71 (IDENT)
          6.2-13    الجَيْشِ الشَعْبِيَ لِ- -تَحْرِيرِ السُودانَ " سمسون خواجة
          7.2-2     *

Chain 92 (IDENT)
          8.1-11    وزارَةِ الخارِجِيَّةِ السُودانِيَّةِ مُطْرِف صِدِيق الَذِي يَرْأَسُ
                    الحُكُومِيَّ
          8.16-16   ه

Chain 95 (APPOS)
    ATTRIB 8.1-4    وَكِيلُ وِزارَةِ الخارِجِيَّةِ السُودانِيَّةِ
    HEAD   8.5-6    مُطْرِف صِدِيق
```

Figure 1: A screenshot of OntoNotes Normal Forms (onf). Chain 71 is not considered part of a CoNLL-2012 shared task because the cluster would become a singleton when we remove the AZP (denoted as *).

coreference chains only exist in ONF, but not in CoNLL-2012. These are clusters consisting of only one mention and one AZP, as in the example illustrated in Figure 1. Chain 71 has two mentions, an AZP (denoted with *) and a mention. Since CoNLL-2012 does not consider AZPs in coreference chains, this cluster would only have a single mention because CoNLL-2012 removed AZPs (these clusters are known as singletons, contains only one mention). Our new dataset includes AZPs; therefore, such clusters should be included. To add them to the existing CoNLL-2012, we have to assign them a new cluster. We did this by writing a script that automatically extracts AZPs from ONF and adds them in CoNLL-2012 following these steps:

1. Finds all clusters that have AZPs in ONF and extracts AZPs.

2. Each extracted AZP is either:

   (a) Clustered with two or more mentions: For this case, CoNLL has already assigned a coreference-chain number and we assign the AZP to the same number.

   (b) Clustered with only one mention: We create a new cluster that include the single mention and the AZP.

3. Adds the AZP and writes other relevant information, such as, Part-of-Speech, syntax, and all the annotation layers.

Adding AZPs to CoNL-2012 is beneficial to learn how to resolve them with other mentions or can be useful for future CoNLL-shared tasks and any other related NLP task. After preparing the new CoNLL dataset as discussed, we used it to train the joint coreference model. This new version

Category	Training	Development	Test
Documents	359	44	44
Sentences	7,422	950	1,003
Words	264,589	30,942	30,935
AZPs	3,495	474	412

Table 1: The documents, sentences, words and AZPs of the extended version of CoNLL-2012. We follow the same split as in the original CoNLL-2012 for training, development and test.

of Arabic OntoNotes will be made available with the next release of OntoNotes. The distribution of documents, sentences, words, and AZPs of this extended dataset are in Table 1.

4 The Models

Earlier proposals resolved AZPs based on the antecedents that are in the same sentence as the AZP or two sentences away (Chen and Ng, 2015, 2016; Yin et al., 2016, 2017; Liu et al., 2017; Yin et al., 2018; Aloraini and Poesio, 2020b). However, it has been shown that learning mention coreference in the whole document is beneficial for AZP resolution (Chen et al., 2021). Therefore, we apply two novel methods for resolving AZPs using clusters and coreference chains. The *pipeline* resolves AZPs based on the output clusters from the coreference resolution model while the *joint learning* learns how to resolve AZPs from the coreference chains, we show an example of these two in Figure 2. In the example, the *pipeline* resolves AZPs to clusters, instead of mentions and the *joint learning* finds the coreference chains for mentions, including AZPs. Earlier proposals suffered from two main problems. First, they consider a limited number of candidates (i.e mentions in two sentences away from the AZP) as possible true antecedents; however, the true antecedent might be far away from the AZP. Second, other mentions can share salient context as the true antecedent which can introduce more noise to the learning. Our methods mitigate these problems by considering all mentions in the document and employing more relevant information. The *pipeline* resolves AZPs based on clusters which decreases dramatically the number of AZP candidates. The *joint learning* resolves AZPs using coreference chains which incorporates broader context for AZPs, insufficient contexts results in many errors (Chen and Ng, 2016).

4.1 The Pipeline Model

In a *pipeline* setting, the inputs are the extended version of CoNLL, the one we described in Section 3. Each file consists of multiple sentences and we follow the same splits in CoNLL-2012 (Pradhan et al., 2012) for train, development and test. We initially fed the documents for training into two models: *coreference resolution* and *AZP identification.* We used the Arabic coreference resolution by (Aloraini et al., 2020) and the proposed AZP identification by (Aloraini and Poesio, 2020a). The outputs of coreference resolutions are clusters and each one has its own mentions. The outputs of the AZP identification are the predicted gap positions of AZPs. The *AZP resolution* model by (Aloraini and Poesio, 2020b) learns how to resolve the identified AZPs with their clusters. We show how we represent the input in the following:

The *input* is a document with sentences separated with periods, and has a total of *n* words. The *input* does not consider AZPs initially, they are masked.

$$input = (w_1, w_2, w_3, ..., w_n) \tag{1}$$

We first feed the *input* into the *coreference resolution* model which outputs the mention clusters, c_1, c_2, to the last cluster index, *k*.

$$output\_clusters = coref\_res(input) \tag{2}$$
$$output\_clusters = (c_1, c_2, ..., c_k) \tag{3}$$

After finding the coreference clusters, the *AZP Identification* model predicts the AZP positions in two steps. First, the *AZP identification* uses a Part-of-Speech tool to tag words and mark gaps after verbs as potential AZPs. Second, *AZP identification* classifies these marked gaps as AZPs or not. Therefore, not every gap between words has an AZP. For example, in (5) there is no AZP between the words w_2 and w_3, but there is one between w_1 and w_2 (i.e. a_i). We find AZP locations and extract their positions.

$$input\_with\_azp = AZP\_Id(input) \tag{4}$$
$$input\_with\_azp = (w_1, a_i, w_2, w_3, ..., w_n) \tag{5}$$
$$AZPs = (a_i, ..., a_k) \tag{6}$$
$$ss = same\_sentence(a_i, c_j) \tag{7}$$
$$cd = azp\_cluster\_distance(a_i, c_j) \tag{8}$$
$$AZP_i = (a_i\_pre, a_i\_next, ss, cd) \tag{9}$$

We follow the same representation for AZPs as (Aloraini and Poesio, 2020b):

- embeddings for previous word to AZP.
- embeddings for next word to AZP.
- Whether the AZP and the candidate entity (represented either as the last mention or first mention) are in the same sentence or not.
- The distance between the AZP and its cluster representation.

The four features are concatenated, as shown in (9).

Clusters can be represented in different ways, including, e.g, the representation of the first mention or the last mention. We found empirically that representing clusters with the nearest mention to the AZP (the last added mention to the cluster) produces better results.

$$c_i = \{m_1, m_2, ..., m_z\} \tag{10}$$
$$c_i = \begin{cases} m_1 & \text{the first mention to represent } c_i \\ m_z & \text{the last mention to represent } c_i \end{cases} \tag{11}$$

Next, the AZP and cluster representations are joined together through a concatenation layer. The variable *input* contains the concatenated representation of a mention pair - the AZP and its corresponding cluster. The binary variable *AZP res* receives *input* and is 1 if the AZP and the cluster corefer. The model also outputs the final clusters.

The following equations specify how the output of the network is computed:

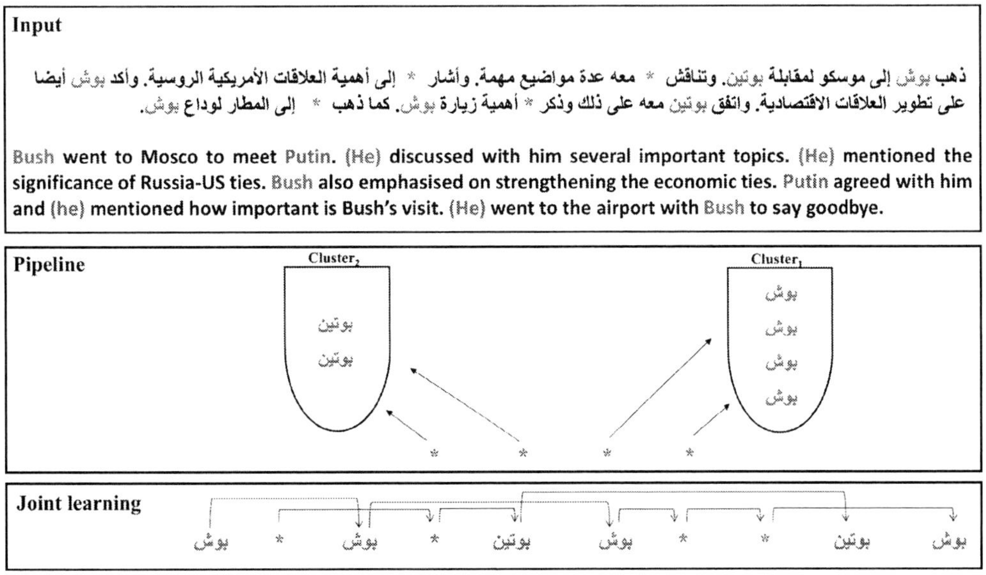

Figure 2: The input is a document and the asterisk * represents the AZPs in the text. For AZP resolution, The *pipeline* resolves AZPs with the output clusters and the *joint learning* resolves AZPs based on coreference chains.

$$input = concat(c_i, a_j) \tag{12}$$

$$input = [c_i, a_j] \tag{13}$$

$$results = AZP\_Res(input) \tag{14}$$

$$results = (r_1, r_2, ..., r_s) \tag{15}$$

The variable *results* consists of the final clusters of the resolved AZPs and non-AZPs. We show the model architecture in Figure 3.

4.2 The Joint Learning Model

Our *joint learning* architecture learns to resolve AZPs by using the explicitly represented AZP gaps. This way, AZPs would be learned as any other overt mention. In our extended CoNLL-2012 documents, AZPs have the special identified *pro*. Table 2 shows an example of a CoNLL-2012 original sentence and its extended version. However, we consider AZPs only in the training phase when we apply the coreference resolution model. At test time, AZPs are not considered, same as in a real life application. Instead, we use the *AZP identification* model by (Aloraini and Poesio, 2020b) to tag AZP gaps. After tagging, the input is ready for clustering using the trained coreference resolution model. This is how we represent the inputs for both training and testing:

The *input* is a CoNLL-2012 document with many sentences that has a set of *n* mentions. A mention can be a word or an AZP tag (*pro*).

$$input = (m_1, m_2, m_3, ..., m_n) \tag{16}$$

The variable *input* is fed into the *coreference resolution* (coref_res) model which outputs clusters. The clusters contain mentions and AZPs that refer to the same entity.

$$output\_clusters = coref\_res(input) \tag{17}$$

$$output\_clusters = (c_1, c_2, ..., c_k) \tag{18}$$

For the test phase, we assume a document is not labeled with AZP tags, which reflects real-life applications. Therefore, we first feed *input* into the *AZP identification* (AZP_Id) which outputs *input_with_azp*, that is *input* but with tagged AZPs. The *AZP identification* is pre-trained on the train set of CoNLL-2012 to detect AZP locations.

$$input\_with\_azp = AZP\_Id(input) \tag{19}$$

$$input\_with\_azp = (w_1, a_i, w_2, ..., m_n) \tag{20}$$

After preparing *input_with_azp*, we feed it into the trained *coreference resolution* model which outputs the clusters.

$$results = coref\_res(input\_with\_azp) \tag{21}$$

$$results = (r_1, r_2, ..., r_s) \tag{22}$$

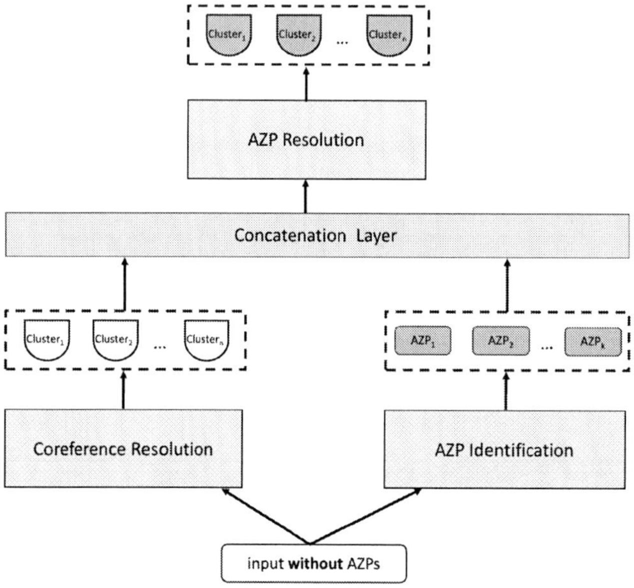

Figure 3: The input without AZPs is fed into the *Coreference Resolution* and *AZP identification* models. The outputs of the two models are clusters and AZPs respectively. Their representations are concatenated, and then their coreference information is learned through the *AZP Resolution* model.

Original CoNLL-2012 sentence	كانا في الوضع نفسه
Extended CoNLL-2012 sentence	كانا *pro* في الوضع نفسه

Table 2: An example of how we explicitly represent AZPs.

The variable *results* has the resolved AZPs and non-AZPs. We show the overall architecture in Figure 4.

5 Evaluation metrics

5.1 Coreference resolution

For our evaluation of the coreference system, we use the official CoNLL-2012 evaluation metrics to score the predicted clusters. We report recall, precision, and F_1 scores for MUC, B^3 and $CEAF_{\phi_4}$ and the average F_1 score of those three metrics.

5.2 AZP resolution

We evaluate AZP resolution in terms of recall and precision, as defined in (Zhao and Ng, 2007):

$$Recall = \frac{AZPhits}{Number\ of\ AZPs\ in\ Key}$$

$$Precision = \frac{AZPhits}{Number\ of\ AZPs\ in\ Response}$$

Key represents the gold set of AZP entities in the dataset, and *Response* represents the predicted resolved AZPs. *AZP hits* are the reported resolved AZP positions in *Response* which occur in the same position as in *Key*.

6 Training Objectives

6.1 Pipeline

The training objective of the AZP identification is binary cross-entropy loss, as introduced in (Aloraini and Poesio, 2020a):

$$L(\theta) = -\frac{1}{N}\sum_{i=1}^{N}[y_i \log \hat{y}_i + (1 - y_i)\log(1 - \hat{y}_i)] \tag{23}$$

θ is the set of learning parameters in the model. N is the number of training samples in the extended CoNLL-2012. y_i is the true label i and $\hat{y}_i$ is its predicted label.

For the AZP resolution, the goal is to minimize the cross entropy error between every AZP and its

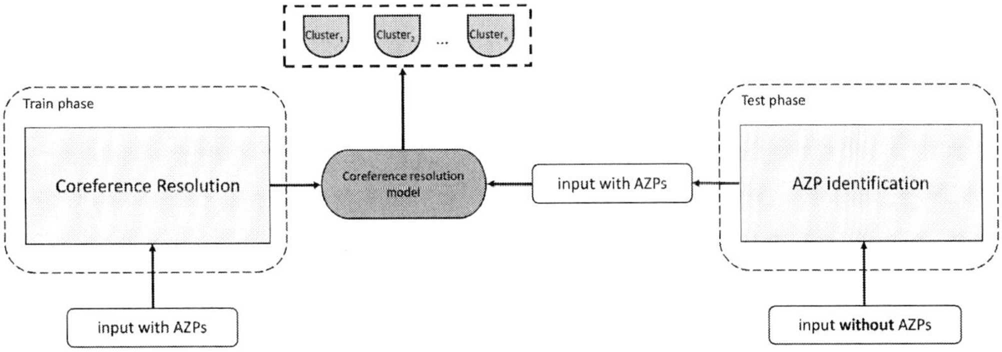

Figure 4: In the train phase, the model learns how to resolve mentions and AZPs. AZPs are represented with the *pro* tag and treated like any other mention. The test phase predicts and tags AZPs locations. We use the model proposed by (Aloraini and Poesio, 2020a) to find AZPs. The pretrained coreference resolution model is used in the test phase to cluster mentions and AZPs.

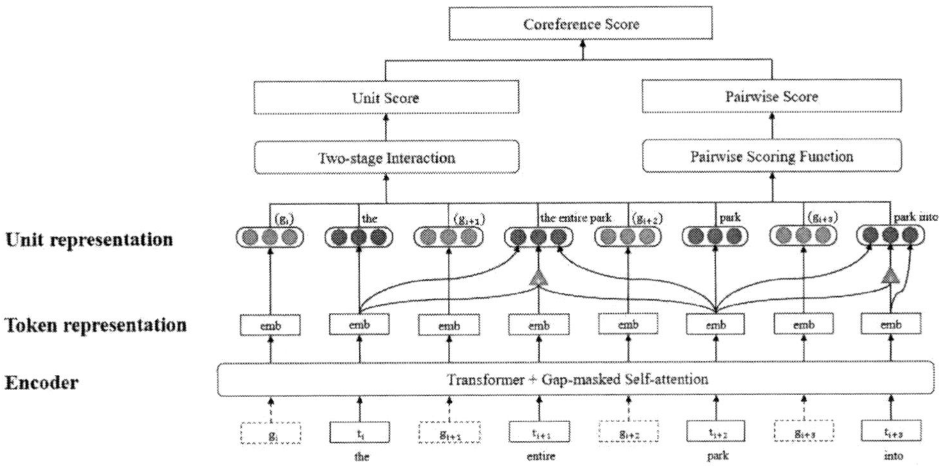

Figure 5: Resolving AZPs and non-AZPs in an end-to-end model (Chen et al., 2021).

antecedents, as defined in Aloraini and Poesio's (2020b) model; however, we resolve AZPs with clusters, instead of mentions:

$$L(\theta) = -\sum_{t \in T}^{n} \sum_{c \in C}^{k} \delta(azp, c) \log(P(azp, c)) \quad (24)$$

T consists of the n training instances of AZPs, and C represents the k candidate clusters from the coreference resolution. □*(azp, c)* returns whether a candidate cluster c is the correct one for the *azp*, or not. *log(P(azp, c)* is the predicted log probability of the *(azp, c)* pair.

The training objective of the coreference resolution is to optimize the log-likelihood of all correct mentions (Lee et al., 2017), as the following :

$$L(\theta) = \log \prod_{i=1}^{N} \sum_{\hat{y} \in \mathcal{Y}(i) \cap \mathrm{G}(i)} P(\hat{y}) \quad (25)$$

G represents the spans in the gold cluster that includes i.

6.2 Joint Learning

In the *joint learning*, we only use the (24) for training. AZPs are treated as any other mention; therefore, they become part of the coreference resolution learning objective. We also do not have to train the AZP identification model because we only use the AZP identification in the test phase and we use the pre-trained one on the original CoNLL-2012 from (Aloraini and Poesio, 2020a).

Models	MUC			B^3			$CEAF_{\phi_4}$			CoNLL Average
	R	P	F_1	R	P	F_1	R	P	F_1	F_1
Pipeline	62.9	70.7	66.5	57.3	65.6	61.2	61.1	64.5	62.7	63.5
Joint learning	65.2	75.5	70.0	62.6	68.3	65.3	64.8	67.7	66.2	67.1
Chen et al. (2021)	62.7	71.1	66.6	58.5	65.7	61.6	61.4	67.2	64.2	64.2

Table 3: Resolving AZPs and non-AZPs together.

7 Results

We compare the results of the *pipeline* and *joint learning* models with the results of Chen et al. (2021). We followed Chen et al. (2021)'s approach for hyperparameter tunning, but we changed the language model to AraBERT-base (Antoun et al., 2020). We evaluate two tasks. First, we assess the results at joint coreference resolution of both AZPs and non-AZPs. Second, we evaluate AZP resolution only. Unlike previous proposals that resolve AZPs with their antecedents, the AZPs of our methods and the Chen et al.'s (2021) model resolve AZPs differently. The *pipeline* uses the output clusters, the *joint learning* uses the coreference chains and Chen et al. (2021) uses two scoring components.

7.1 Resolving AZPs and non-AZPs

In Table 3, we see the results of resolving AZPs and non-AZPs. Chen et al.'s (2021) model achieves 64.2% F_1 score, which is 0.7% more than the *pipeline*, but less than the *joint learning* with 2.9%. Our *joint learning* approach outperforms our *pipeline* and Chen et al.'s (2021) system, achieving the best F_1 average score of 67.1%.

7.2 AZP resolution

Next, we compare the AZP resolution results. For the *pipeline*, we used two settings to represent clusters. First, we used the first mention in the cluster to be concatenated with the AZP representation. Second, we used the last-added mention. The *pipeline* approach achieves an F_1 score of 58.08% when using the first mention as the cluster representation and 58.59% when using the last mention. The *joint learning* provided better results with an F_1 score of 59.33%. Chen et al.'s (2021) model resolved more AZPs correctly than the *pipeline* and *joint learning* methods, achieving an F_1 score of 59.49% which is 0.19% more than the *joint learning* score. It seems the two components of Chen et al.'s (2021) model, the Unit Score and Pairwise Score, are able to distinguish AZPs and mentions effectively for the AZP resolution. However, for coreference resolution, they have showed the performance is better when they did not consider AZPs as part of the coreference resolution.

Training Settings	Test Evaluation		
	P	R	F_1
Pipeline (CR: FM)	60.34	55.98	58.08
Pipeline (CR: LM)	60.97	56.39	58.59
Joint Learning	61.41	57.40	59.33
Chen et al. (2021)	61.67	57.45	59.49

Table 4: AZP resolution results of *pipeline*, *joint learning* and Chen et al. (2021). FM refers to using the first mention as the cluster representation while LM refers to the last mention.

,

8 Discussion

The main difference between our *joint learning* approach and Chen et al. (2021) is how AZPs are detected and learned. In our approach, we detect AZPs initially before we cluster them with other mentions, while Chen et al.'s (2021) model learns clustering AZPs and mentions in an end-to-end system. Our results appear to confirm earlier results that considering AZP identification end-to-end in the coreference resolution task can negatively affect the performance on the task (Iida and Poesio, 2011; Chen et al., 2021) One possible explanation might be the overall performance of the mention detection on non-AZPs is better than AZPs (Chen et al., 2021). Chen et al. (2021) consider every gap as a candidate AZP, which increases the space of possible candidates and affects their detection recall. To mitigate this problem, we use a different neural component for AZP detection. The AZP identification that we used in the *joint learning* and *pipeline* settings only considers gaps that appear after verbs which limits the number of candidates. Moreover, the AZPs in the *joint learning* have explicit tags which might have resulted in their correct detection, which could be why the approach achieved better results. The main limitation of our proposed approaches is if the AZP identification fails to detect many AZPs in the test phase, it might have dropped the evaluation of the coreference resolution and AZP resolution. Pre-training BERT with AZPs can be beneficial. Existing language models (LMs) learn by masking words or perturbing their order (Qiu et al., 2020), but this is not applicable to AZPs. (Konno et al., 2021) have shown two approaches to improve LMs so they work for AZPs, first by introducing a new pre-training task and second by a new fine-tuning technique. They showed an increased performance for AZP resolution for Japanese. In future works, we intend to pre-train a large-scale LM using their methods and see if it can improve the performance of the AZP and coreference resolution tasks.

9 Conclusion

We proposed two architectures to resolve AZPs and non-AZPs jointly. The first approach is in a *pipeline* setting and the second in a *joint learning* representation. The *joint learning* outperformed the *pipeline* and another approach (Chen et al., 2021) in the joint coreference resolution. We also extended the Arabic portion of CoNLL-2012 to include AZPs which will be suitable for future works and shared-tasks that resolves AZPs and non-AZPs together.

Acknowledgements

We would like to thank the anonymous reviewers for their insightful feedback which helped to improve an early version of the paper.

References

Abdulrahman Aloraini and Massimo Poesio. 2020a. Anaphoric zero pronoun identification: A multilingual approach. In *Proceedings of the Third Workshop on Computational Models of Reference, Anaphora and Coreference*, pages 22–32.

Abdulrahman Aloraini and Massimo Poesio. 2020b. Cross-lingual zero pronoun resolution. In *Proceedings of The 12th Language Resources and Evaluation Conference*, pages 90–98.

Abdulrahman Aloraini, Juntao Yu, and Massimo Poesio. 2020. Neural coreference resolution for arabic. *arXiv preprint arXiv:2011.00286*.

Wissam Antoun, Fady Baly, and Hazem Hajj. 2020. Arabert: Transformer-based model for arabic language understanding. *arXiv preprint arXiv:2003.00104*.

Anders Björkelund and Pierre Nugues. 2011. Exploring lexicalized features for coreference resolution. In *Proceedings of the Fifteenth Conference on Computational Natural Language Learning: Shared Task*, pages 45–50.

Anders Björkelund and Jonas Kuhn. 2014. Learning structured perceptrons for coreference resolution with latent antecedents and non-local features. In *Proceedings of the 52nd Annual Meeting of the Association for Computational Linguistics (Volume 1: Long Papers)*, pages 47–57.

Chen Chen and Vincent Ng. 2015. Chinese zero pronoun resolution: A joint unsupervised discourse-aware model rivaling state-of-the-art resolvers. In *Proceedings of the 53rd Annual Meeting of the Association for Computational Linguistics and the 7th International Joint Conference on Natural Language Processing (Volume 2: Short Papers)*, pages 320–326.

Chen Chen and Vincent Ng. 2016. Chinese zero pronoun resolution with deep neural network. In *Proceedings of the 54th Annual Meeting of the Association for Computational Linguistics (Volume 1: Long Papers)*, pages 778–788.

Shisong Chen, Binbin Gu, Jianfeng Qu, Zhixu Li, An Liu, Lei Zhao, and Zhigang Chen. 2021. Tackling zero pronoun resolution and non-zero coreference resolution jointly. In *Proceedings of the 25th Conference on Computational Natural Language Learning*, pages 518–527.

Barbara Di Eugenio. 1990. Centering theory and the italian pronominal system. In *Proc. of the 13th COLING*, Helsinki, Finland.

Mushira Eid. 1983. On the communicative function of subject pronouns in arabic. In *Journal of Linguistics 19.2*, pages 287–303.

Eraldo Rezende Fernandes, Cícero Nogueira dos Santos, and Ruy Luiz Milidiú. 2014. Latent trees for coreference resolution. *Computational Linguistics*, 40(4):801–835.

Ryu Iida and Massimo Poesio. 2011. A cross-lingual ilp solution to zero anaphora resolution. In *Proceedings of the 49th Annual Meeting of the Association for Computational Linguistics: Human Language Technologies-Volume 1*, pages 804–813.

Ryu Iida, Kentaro Torisawa, Chikara Hashimoto, Jong-Hoon Oh, and Julien Kloetzer. 2015. Intra-sentential zero anaphora resolution using subject sharing recognition. In *Proceedings of the 2015 Conference on Empirical Methods in Natural Language Processing*, pages 2179–2189.

Ganesh Jawahar, Benoît Sagot, and Djamé Seddah. 2019. What does bert learn about the structure of language?

In *57th Annual Meeting of the Association for Computational Linguistics (ACL), Florence, Italy.*

Megumi Kameyama. 1985. *Zero Anaphora: The case of Japanese*. Ph.D. thesis, Stanford University, Stanford, CA.

Fang Kong and Hwee Tou Ng. 2013. Exploiting zero pronouns to improve chinese coreference resolution. In *Proceedings of the 2013 conference on empirical methods in natural language processing*, pages 278–288.

Ryuto Konno, Shun Kiyono, Yuichiroh Matsubayashi, Hiroki Ouchi, and Kentaro Inui. 2021. Pseudo zero pronoun resolution improves zero anaphora resolution. *arXiv preprint arXiv:2104.07425*.

Kenton Lee, Luheng He, Mike Lewis, and Luke Zettlemoyer. 2017. End-to-end neural coreference resolution. *arXiv preprint arXiv:1707.07045*.

Baoli li. 2012. Learning to model multilingual unrestricted coreference in ontonotes. In *Joint Conference on EMNLP and CoNLL2012-Shared Task*.

Charles N. Li and Sandra A. Thompson. 1979. Third person pronouns and zero anaphora in chinese discourse. In *Syntax and Semantics*, volume 12: Discourse and Syntax, pages 311–335. Academic Press.

Ting Liu, Yiming Cui, Qingyu Yin, Weinan Zhang, Shijin Wang, and Guoping Hu. 2017. Generating and exploiting large-scale pseudo training data for zero pronoun resolution. In *arXiv preprint arXiv:1606.01603*.

Bonan Min. 2021. Exploring pre-trained transformers and bilingual transfer learning for arabic coreference resolution. In *Proceedings of the Fourth Workshop on Computational Models of Reference, Anaphora and Coreference*, pages 94–99.

Sameer Pradhan, Alessandro Moschitti, Nianwen Xue, Olga Uryupina, and Yuchen Zhang. 2012. Conll-2012 shared task: Modeling multilingual unrestricted coreference in ontonotes. In *Joint Conference on EMNLP and CoNLL-Shared Task. Association for Computational Linguistics, Association for Computational Linguistics.*, pages 1–40.

Xipeng Qiu, Tianxiang Sun, Yige Xu, Yunfan Shao, Ning Dai, and Xuanjing Huang. 2020. Pre-trained models for natural language processing: A survey. *Science China Technological Sciences*, 63(10):1872–1897.

Tomohide Shibata and Sadao Kurohashi. 2018. Entity-centric joint modeling of japanese coreference resolution and predicate argument structure analysis. In *Proceedings of the 56th Annual Meeting of the Association for Computational Linguistics (Volume 1: Long Papers)*, pages 579–589.

Marcus Stamborg, Dennis Medved, Peter Exner, and Pierre Nugues. 2012. Using syntactic dependencies to solve coreferences. In *Joint Conference on EMNLP and CoNLL2012-Shared Task*.

Olga Uryupina, Alessandro Moschitti, and Massimo Poesio. 2012. Bart goes multilingual: the unitn/essex submission to the conll-2012 shared task. In *Joint Conference on EMNLP and CoNLL-Shared Task*, pages 122–128. Association for Computational Linguistics.

Lydia White. 1985. The "pro-drop" parameter in adult second language acquisition. *Language learning*, 35(1):47–61.

Jingxuan Yang, Si Li, Sheng Gao, and Jun Guo. 2022. Corefdpr: A joint model for coreference resolution and dropped pronoun recovery in chinese conversations. *IEEE/ACM Transactions on Audio, Speech, and Language Processing*, 30:571–581.

Qingyu Yin, Yu Zhang, Weinan Zhang, and Ting Liu. 2016. A deep neural network for chinese zero pronoun resolution. In *arXiv preprint arXiv:1604.05800*.

Qingyu Yin, Yu Zhang, Weinan Zhang, and Ting Liu. 2017. Chinese zero pronoun resolution with deep memory network. In *Proceedings of the 2017 Conference on Empirical Methods in Natural Language Processing*, pages 1309–1318.

Qingyu Yin, Yu Zhang, Weinan Zhang, Ting Liu, and William Yang Wang. 2018. Zero pronoun resolution with attention-based neural network. In *Proceedings of the 27th International Conference on Computational Linguistics*, pages 13–23.

Kim Young-Joo. 2000. Subject/object drop in the acquisition of korean: A cross-linguistic comparison. In *Journal of East Asian Linguistics 9.4*, pages 325–351.

Shanheng Zhao and Hwee Tou Ng. 2007. Identification and resolution of chinese zero pronouns: A machine learning approach. In *Proceedings of the 2007 Joint Conference on Empirical Methods in Natural Language Processing and Computational Natural Language Learning*, pages 541–550.

Desislava Zhekova and Sandra Kübler. 2010. Ubiu: A language-independent system for coreference resolution. In *Proceedings of the 5th International Workshop on Semantic Evaluation*, page 96–99.

A CoNLL-2012 Annotation Layers

The CoNLL-2012 annotation layers consists of the following (Pradhan et al., 2012):

1. Document ID: Contains the file name.
2. Part number: Some files are divided into several files and this number shows the sentence number.
3. Word number: Word position in the sentence.
4. Word itself: This represents the tokenized token.
5. Part-of-Speech: The Part-of-speech of the word.
6. Parse bit: This is the bracketed structure broken before the first open parenthesis in the parse, and the word/part-of-speech leaf is replaced with a *.
7. Lemma: Used to show the gold and predicate lemma.
8. Predicate Frameset ID: This is the PropBank frameset ID of the predicate in Column 7.
9. Word sense: The word sense.
10. Speaker/Author: The speaker or author name, where available. Mostly in broadcast conversation and web log data. However, this is not available for Arabic because all texts are extracted from newspapers.
11. Named Entities: Named entity for the word.
12. Arguments: Predicted and gold arguments.
13. Coreference: Coreference chain which can be single or multiple tokens.

SAIDS: A Novel Approach for Sentiment Analysis Informed of Dialect and Sarcasm

Abdelrahman Kaseb and **Mona Farouk**
Computer Engineering, Cairo University
Giza, Egypt
{abdelrahman.kaseb,mona_farouk}@eng.cu.edu.eg

Abstract

Sentiment analysis becomes an essential part of every social network, as it enables decision-makers to know more about users' opinions in almost all life aspects. Despite its importance, there are multiple issues it encounters like the sentiment of the sarcastic text which is one of the main challenges of sentiment analysis. This paper tackles this challenge by introducing a novel system (SAIDS) that predicts the sentiment, sarcasm and dialect of Arabic tweets. SAIDS uses its prediction of sarcasm and dialect as known information to predict the sentiment. It uses MARBERT as a language model to generate sentence embedding, then passes it to the sarcasm and dialect models, and then the outputs of the three models are concatenated and passed to the sentiment analysis model. Multiple system design setups were experimented with and reported. SAIDS was applied to the ArSarcasm-v2 dataset where it outperforms the state-of-the-art model for the sentiment analysis task. By training all tasks together, SAIDS achieves results of 75.98 FPN, 59.09 F1-score and 71.13 F1-score for sentiment analysis, sarcasm detection, and dialect identification respectively. The system design can be used to enhance the performance of any task which is dependent on other tasks.

1 Introduction

Sentiment analysis (SA) is one of the main tasks in the natural language processing (NLP) field. It is used for opinion mining which supports decision-makers. Working on sentiment analysis starts relatively early, for example, Pang et al. (2002) analysed the sentiment to positive and negative in movie reviews. Following this paper, sentiment analysis becomes one of the most important topics in NLP, especially with the increasing number of reviews on websites and social media platforms. Since then, a lot of work has been done in English sentiment analysis, while Arabic has relatively much less. Since Abbasi et al. (2008) started their work on Arabic SA, multiple researchers also began theirs. Now there are well-known Arabic SA models like (Alayba et al., 2018; Abdulla et al., 2013; Abu Farha and Magdy, 2021; Elshakankery and Farouk, 2019). Of course, working with Arabic has many challenges, one of the most challenging issues is the complex morphology of the Arabic language (Kaseb and Farouk, 2016; Abdul-Mageed, 2019). Another challenge is the variety of Arabic dialects (Abdul-Mageed, 2019). Moreover, one of the well-known challenges in SA for all languages is sarcasm, as the sarcastic person uses words and means the opposite of it. For example, "I'd really truly love going out in this weather!", does it reflect a positive or negative sentiment? because of the sarcasm, we cannot judge the sentiment correctly.

Several related works tackle English sarcasm detection with sentiment analysis (Oprea and Magdy, 2020; Abercrombie and Hovy, 2016; Barbieri et al., 2014). On the other hand, there are only a few works on both sentiment and sarcasm in Arabic. There are two shared tasks on sarcasm detection (Ghanem et al., 2019), but for both sarcasm and sentiment there was only one shared task Abu Farha et al. (2021) but each sub-task is independent, meaning that participating teams can submit a different model for each task. Some participants used the same model for both sentiment and sarcasm (El Mahdaouy et al., 2021).

Instead of training sentiment independently of sarcasm, this work introduces a new model architecture that works with multi-task training which trains both at the same time. There are other additions to the proposed architecture; firstly, it trains with dialect also. Secondly, the sarcasm and dialect that are initially predicted are used in the prediction of the sentiment. In other words, the sentiment model is informed by the sarcasm and dialect model output. The contributions offered by this work are:

- Design a novel model architecture that can be

Proceedings of the The Seventh Arabic Natural Language Processing Workshop (WANLP), pages 22 - 30
December 8, 2022 ©2022 Association for Computational Linguistics

used for a complicated task that is dependent on another task, e.g. sentiment analysis which is dependent on sarcasm detection.

- Investigate the design setups for the new architecture and find the best setup that could be used.
- Train the model on ArSarcam-v2 dataset and achieve the state-of-the-art results recorded as 75.98 FPN on sentiment analysis.

This paper is organized as follows Section 2 shows the related work on sentiment analysis, sarcasm detection, and dialect identification. Section 3 describes the dataset used in this work and shows data statistics. Section 4 describes SAIDS model and all the design setups. Section 5 shows the experimental results and finally section 6 concludes the work.

2 Related Work

SAIDS works on three tasks sentiment analysis, sarcasm detection, and dialect identification. In this section, the existing methods for each task are discussed.

2.1 Sentiment Analysis

Arabic sentiment analysis started with Abbasi et al. (2008) work. Since then, it is developed by multiple researchers. In the beginning, the main focus was on modern standard Arabic (MSA), but over time the researchers start to focus on dialectal Arabic (Mourad and Darwish, 2013; Kaseb and Farouk, 2021).

Regarding the datasets, based on Alyafeai et al. (2021), there are more than fifty datasets for sentiment analysis, including Elshakankery et al. (2021); Kaseb and Farouk (2019); Kiritchenko et al. (2016); Rosenthal et al. (2017); Elmadany et al. (2018) datasets. Because of the massive number of datasets, there are a massive number of system approaches for Arabic sentiments (Abu Farha and Magdy, 2019; Alayba et al., 2018; El-Beltagy et al., 2017). Based on Abu Farha and Magdy (2021) comparative study, using the word embedding with deep learning models outperform, the classical machine learning models and the transformer-based models outperform both of them. There is a reasonable number of Arabic transformer-based models like AraBERT (Antoun et al., 2020) and MARBERT (Abdul-Mageed et al., 2021) which are used by most Arabic sentiment analysis papers.

2.2 Sarcasm Detection

Unlike Arabic sentiment analysis, Arabic sarcasm detection has not gotten much attention yet. Only a few research works tackle the problem and still there is an obvious shortage of the Arabic sarcasm datasets, like Karoui et al. (2017); Abu Farha et al. (2022). Abbes et al. (2020) collected a dataset for sarcastic tweets, they used hashtags to collect the dataset for example #sarcasm. Then, they built multiple classical machine learning models SVM, Naive Bayes, and Logistic Regression, the best F1-score was 0.73.

After that, Ghanem et al. (2019) organized a shared task in a workshop on Arabic sarcasm detection. They built the dataset by collecting tweets on different topics and using hashtags to set the class. An additional step was added, by sampling some of the datasets and manually annotating them. In this shared task, eighteen teams were working on sarcasm detection. Khalifa and Hussein (2019) was the first team and achieved a 0.85 F1-score.

Then Abu Farha et al. (2021) made two tasks based on the ArSarcasm-v2 dataset; sentiment analysis and sarcasm detection. They have 27 teams participating in the workshop, the top teams achieved 62.25 F1-score and 74.80 FPN for sarcasm detection and sentiment analysis respectively.

2.3 Dialect Identification

Arabic dialect identification is an NLP task to identify the dialect of a written text. It can be on three levels, the first level is to identify MSA, classical Arabic (CA), and dialectical Arabic (McWhorter, 2004). The second level is to identify the dialect based on five main Arabic dialects EGY, LEV, NOR, Gulf, and MSA (El-Haj, 2020; Khalifa et al., 2016; Sadat et al., 2014; Al-Sabbagh and Girju, 2012; Egan, 2010). The third level is to identify the country-level dialect (Abdul-Mageed et al., 2020).

Regarding the datasets, there are datasets more than twenty Arabic datasets labeled with dialect. One of the most popular datasets is MADAR (Bouamor et al., 2018) where the data is labeled at the city-level for 25 Arab cities. Abdul-Mageed et al. (2020) built a shared task to detect the dialect, they published three different shared tasks. In the 2020 task, sixty teams participated, and the best results were 26.78 and 6.39 F1-score in the country-level and the city-level dialects respectively.

3 Dataset

ArSarcasm-v2 (Abu Farha et al., 2021) is the main dataset used in this work, it was released on WANLP 2021 shared task for two tasks sarcasm and sentiment analysis. It has about 15k tweets and is divided into 12k for training and 3k for testing, the same test set, as released on WANLP 2021, was used. Each tweet was labelled for the sentiment (positive (POS), neutral (NEU), and negative (NEG)), sarcasm (true, and false), and dialect (MSA, Egypt (EGY), Levantine (LEV), Maghreb (NOR), and Gulf). The authors of the dataset annotate it using a crowd-sourcing platform. This dataset originally consisted of a combination of two datasets, the first one is ArSarcasm (Abu Farha and Magdy, 2020) and the second one is DAICT (Abbes et al., 2020), Abu Farha et al. (2021) merged the two datasets.

3.1 Dataset Statistics

In this subsection, we introduce some dataset statistics that motivated us to work on SAIDS. The ArSarcasm-v2 dataset has 15,548 tweets, 3000 tweets are kept for testing and the rest of the tweets for training. Table 1 shows the number of examples for all task labels on the training set, as we can see, most of the data is labeled as MSA and non-sarcastic in dialect and sarcasm respectively.

Task	Label	Count
Sentiment	Positive	2,180
	Neutral	5,747
	Negative	4,621
Sarcasm	Sarcastic	2,168
	Non-sarcastic	10,380
Dialect	MSA	8,562
	EGY	2,675
	Gulf	644
	LEV	624
	NOR	43
Total		12,548

Table 1: Number of labels of sentiment, sarcasm and dialect on the training set

The relationship between sentiment labels and both sarcasm and dialect independently can be shown from Table 2. For the sentiment/sarcasm part, we can see that about 90 percent of sarcastic tweets are sentimentally labeled as negative, and about 50 percent of non-sarcastic tweets are sentimentally labeled as neutral. On the other hand, for the sentiment/dialect part, we can see that about 50 percent of MSA tweets are sentimentally labeled as neutral and about 50 percent of EGY tweets are sentimentally labeled as negative. From this table, we can conclude that the information we can get on sarcasm and dialect will benefit the sentiment analysis task.

	POS	NEU	NEG
Non-sarcastic	2,122	5,576	2,682
Sarcastic	58	171	1,939
MSA	1,405	4,486	2,671
EGY	506	793	1,376
Gulf	121	259	264
LEV	142	197	285
NOR	6	12	25

Table 2: Cross tabulation between sentiment labels and both sarcasm and dialect labels on the training set

Table 3 shows the percentage of sarcastic tweets on each dialect. As the number of NOR tweets is limited, its percentage is not reliable, so we can see that Egyptians' tweets are the most sarcastic. This supports the facts from table 2 that most EGY tweets are negative and most of the sarcastic tweets are negative tweets.

Dialect	Sarcasm percentage
MSA	10.83 %
EGY	34.77 %
Gulf	24.38 %
LEV	22.12 %
NOR	34.88 %

Table 3: Percentage of sarcastic tweets for each dialect on the training set

4 Proposed System

This section presents a detailed description of the proposed system. SAIDS learns sentiment analysis, sarcasm detection, and dialect identification at the same time (multi-task training), in addition, it uses the sarcasm detection and dialect outputs as an additional input to the sentiment analysis model which is called "informed decision". SAIDS decides the sentiment class using the information of sarcasm and dialect class which are both outputs itself. The main idea behind SAIDS is based on analyzing the dataset statistics, as shown in section

3, which says that most sarcastic tweets are classified as negative tweets and most MSA tweets are classified as neutral tweets.

4.1 System Architecture

Figure 1 shows the SAIDS architecture. The architecture consists of four main modules, the first module is MARBERTv2 (Abdul-Mageed et al., 2021), it is a transformer-based model, its input is the tweet, and its output is a sentence embedding which is a vector of length 768. The second module is the "Sarcasm Model", it is a binary classifier for sarcasm, its input is the sentence embedding, and its output is two values one for sarcastic tweets and another for non-sarcastic tweets. The third module is the "Dialect Model", which is identical to the "Sarcasm Model" except that it outputs five classes (EGY, LEV, NOR, Gulf, and MSA). The fourth module is the "Sentiment Model", it is a classifier for sentiment, its input is the concatenation of the sentence embedding, sarcasm model outputs and dialect model outputs.

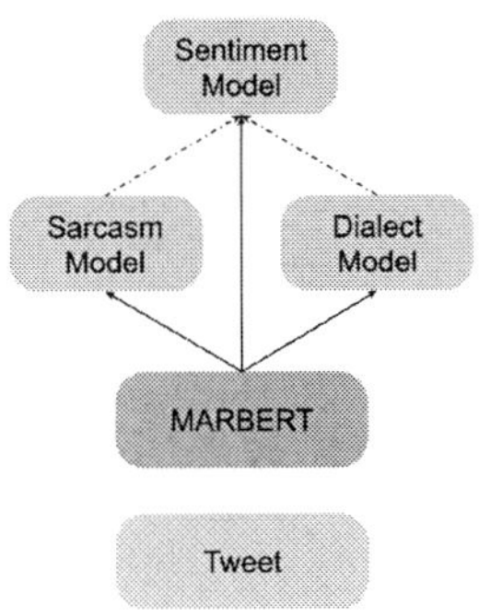

Figure 1: SAIDS architecture

The loss function used is Cross-Entropy for sentiment and dialect. Of course, since sarcasm is binary, we used binary Cross-Entropy for it.

4.2 Training Setups

This subsection describes the multiple setups that were used to arrive at the best model performance. The experiments carried out utilized multiple setups regarding the architecture and the training strategies.

Modules Architecture Multiple architectures were tested for the "Sentiment Model", "Sarcasm Model" and "Dialect Model". As a proof of concept for the idea, we first built a simple random forest model in each task model (random forest version). For the real scenario, we used multi-layer neural network (MNN) models. The first and the simplest is one output layer model and zero hidden layers. The second is one or two hidden layers, then the output layer. The third is one or two hidden layers the output of the module is the output of the hidden layer, which means that "Sentiment Model" inputs is not the output layer of the "Sarcasm Model" but the last hidden layer of it. The fourth setup is to concatenate the last hidden layer with the output layer and then pass it to "Sentiment Model".

What Should Be Informed The SAIDS architecture Figure 1 shows that the "Sentiment Model" inputs are "Sarcasm Model" and "Dialect Model" outputs but we experimented with multiple settings in this part; sentiment analysis informed of sarcasm only, dialect only, and both sarcasm and dialect.

Limited Backpropagation We limited the backpropagation over the dotted lines in Figure 1. It is used to ensure that the "Sarcasm Model" and the "Dialect Model" learn their main target correctly. When the model predicts sentiment incorrectly, its loss propagates directly to the MARBERTv2 model via the solid line and does not propagate via the dotted lines. Also, we evaluate SAIDS without limiting backpropagation which means the loss propagates everywhere, and with partial limiting. The partial limiting can be only set when the "Sarcasm Model" has hidden layers. We then limit the backpropagation through the sarcasm model's output layer but propagate it through the hidden layers.

Activation Function The experiments were carried out with Softmax as the activation function for the output of all modules. However, for the sake of comparison, we run the training without Softmax for the modules outputs, which means that the values are not from one to zero.

Task By Task Training As we train all the three tasks together with the same model, we experimented to train the first layer models, "Sarcasm Model" and "Dialect Model", for some epochs first, then train the full system together for multiple epochs. The motivation behind this idea is that as long as the first layer models work correctly, the sentiment analysis will correspondingly work correctly. We train in multiple orders like alternating between first layer models and full system and so on.

Other Training Parameters In our experiments, we built SAIDS and used the MARBERTv2 model provided by HuggingFace's transformers library (Wolf et al., 2020). Most of the experiments trained for five epochs except for a low learning rate where it was twenty epochs. For the learning rate, we used a range from $1e^{-4}$ to $1e^{-6}$. The sequence was truncated to a maximum length of 128 tokens. Adam (Kingma and Ba, 2015) was used as an optimizer for all models.

5 Results

In this section, the results achieved with SAIDS are discussed. For the sake of comparison, baselines were built for the system. To initially evaluate the idea itself, a random forest model baseline was built and compared with the random forest version of SAIDS. Baselines for real scenario are baseline one (B1) which is identical to BERTModelForSequenceClassification class in HuggingFace's (Wolf et al., 2020), which takes the MARBERTv2 sentence embedding and passes it to the output layer for classification, and baseline two (B2) which uses two hidden layers before the classification layer, the hidden layer size is equal to the "Sentiment Model" hidden layer size, and baseline three (B3) which uses a larger hidden layer size to match the total number of trained parameters of SAIDS model.

For evaluation, we used the original metrics described for the dataset (Abu Farha et al., 2021). For sentiment analysis, the metric is the average of the F1-score for the negative and positive classes (FPN). For sarcasm detection, the metric is F1-score for the sarcastic class only (FSar). For dialect identification, we used the weighted average of the F1-score for all dialects (WFS).

5.1 Results of Different Training Setups

This subsection presents the results of the training setups and describes the best setup that was chosen for the proposed model. For each part of this subsection, every other setup was not changed to make the comparison fair.

Modules Architecture As a proof of concept for our system, the random forest (RF) model baseline was compared with the informed random forest (IRF) which is the random forest version of SAIDS. Table 4 shows that IRF outperforms RF where the FPN is improved by 3 percent which is due to the proposed architecture. The information gained from the new inputs, "outputs of sarcasm model" and "outputs of dialect model", was 5 and 4 percent respectively. This means that about 10 percent of the sentiment analysis decision came from the newly added information.

Model	FPN
Random Forest	59.36
Informed Random Forest	62.34

Table 4: Performance comparison for the proof of concept on the validation set

For the MNN architecture of the modules, multiple numbers of hidden layers were trained. At each experiment, all the modules have the same number of hidden layers. Table 5 shows that using zero hidden layers gives the best results. So no hidden layer setup was used in SAIDS.

Model	FPN
0 Hidden Layer	75.23
1 Hidden Layer	74.90
2 Hidden Layer	74.89

Table 5: Performance comparison for the number of hidden layers in modules on the validation set

What Should Be Informed Experiments were also done to find the best features to use while analysing sentiment. Table 6 shows that using both dialect and sarcasm is better than using only one of them and of course better than not using any of them which is the baseline. With a quick observation, it was found out that the dialect benefits the sentiment more than the sarcasm, this can be obvious when speaking about MSA tweets because most of them are labeled as neutral on sentiment. Accordingly, sarcasm and dialect information was used in SAIDS.

Model	FPN
Not Informed (B1)	72.40
Informed of sarcasm	73.67
Informed of dialect	74.41
Informed of sarcasm and dialect	75.23

Table 6: Performance comparison for what should be informed on the validation set

Limited Backpropagation Experiments were also done to find the best path for backpropagation to work with. "Full limit" is when the loss does not propagate through the "Sarcasm model" and "Dialect Model", "Partial limit" is when it propagates through some layers, and "Unlimited" is when it propagates through all layers. The model was composed of two hidden layers while running these experiments. Table 7 shows that "Partial limit" gets better results than the others, but on SAIDS we did not use it as we used a no hidden layer setup, so we used the "Full limit" backpropagation.

Model	FPN
Full limit	74.23
Partial limit	74.89
Unlimited	72.31

Table 7: Performance comparison for limiting backpropagation on the validation set

Activation Function For the sake of comparison, the Softmax layer was removed from the output layer of the model in the experiments. Table 8 compares both setups, it shows that, as expected, using Softmax is better than not using it, as it quantify the probability of being sarcasm or being a certain dialect. So in SAIDS, Softmax was used on each module.

Model	FPN
With Softmax	75.23
Without Softmax	72.15

Table 8: Performance comparison for the activation function setting on the validation set

Task By Task Training Experiments were also done with training the three tasks together at the same time (All tasks), and multiple sets of the training sequence. The first is one epoch of training for sarcasm and dialect, and the rest for the full system (Seq 1). The second is odd epochs for sarcasm and dialect and even epochs for the full system (Seq 2). The third is two epochs of training for sarcasm and dialect and the rest for sentiment only (Seq 3). Table 9 shows that Seq 1 performs better than the other sequences, so we used it for the final model training.

Model	FPN
All tasks	74.35
Seq 1	75.23
Seq 2	73.49
Seq 3	73.01

Table 9: Performance comparison for different model training sequences on the validation set

Summary of Used Setups SAIDS used information from sarcasm and dialect models, which are both one classification layer with no hidden layers, the sentiment loss does not propagate through sarcasm and dialect models, and the Softmax activation function was used on each model output. The used training sequence was one epoch of training for sarcasm and dialect, and the rest epochs for the full system.

5.2 Results comparison with literature

SAIDS was trained and compared to the baselines we built and also the state-of-the-art models. Table 10 shows that SAIDS outperforms the existing state-of-the-art models on the sentiment analysis task. SAIDS's main task is sentiment analysis, the sarcasm detection and dialect identification are considered secondary outputs. Although the FSar score for SAIDS is considerably high, it is ranked third in the state-of-the-art models. On the other hand, most works that achieve state-of-the-art results are using different models for each task but in the proposed architecture, one model is used for both. The model also outputs the dialect, it achieves 71.13 percent on the weighted F1-score metric, but the literature has not reported the dialect performance so it is not included in the table.

Model	FPN	FSar
Baseline 1	71.60	58.41
Baseline 2	72.53	58.61
Baseline 3	73.11	58.62
El Mahdaouy et al. (2021)	74.80	60.00
Song et al. (2021)	73.92	**61.27**
Abdel-Salam (2021)	73.21	56.62
Wadhawan (2021)	72.55	58.72
SAIDS	**75.98**	59.09

Table 10: Performance comparison for the state-of-the-art models and SAIDS on the test set

6 Conclusion

Sentiment analysis is an important system that is being used extensively in decision-making, though it has different drawbacks like dealing with sarcastic sentences. In this work, we propose SAIDS which is a novel model architecture to tackle this problem. SAIDS essentially improves the sentiment analysis results while being informed of sarcasm and dialect of the sentence. This was achieved by training on the ArSarcasm-v2 dataset which is labeled for sentiment, sarcasm, and dialect. SAIDS's main target is to predict the sentiment of a tweet. It is trained to predict dialect and sarcasm, and then make use of them to predict the sentiment of the tweets. This means that while the model is predicting the sentiment, it is informed of its sarcasm and dialect prediction. SAIDS achieved state-of-the-art performance on the ArSarcasm-v2 dataset for predicting the sentiment; 75.98 percent average F1-score for negative and positive sentiment. For sarcasm detection, SAIDS achieved a 59.09 percent F1-score for the sarcastic class, whereas for dialect identification it achieved a 71.13 percent weighted F1-score for all the dialects. We believe that this model architecture could be used as a starting point to tackle every challenge in sentiment analysis. Not only sentiment analysis but also this is a general architecture that can be used in any context where the prediction of a task depends on other tasks. The idea behind the architecture is intuitive, train for both tasks and inform the model of the dependent task with the output of the independent task.

References

Ahmed Abbasi, Hsinchun Chen, and Arab Salem. 2008. Sentiment analysis in multiple languages: Feature selection for opinion classification in web forums. *ACM Trans. Inf. Syst.*, 26(3).

Ines Abbes, Wajdi Zaghouani, Omaima El-Hardlo, and Faten Ashour. 2020. DAICT: A dialectal Arabic irony corpus extracted from Twitter. In *Proceedings of the 12th Language Resources and Evaluation Conference*, pages 6265–6271, Marseille, France. European Language Resources Association.

Reem Abdel-Salam. 2021. WANLP 2021 shared-task: Towards irony and sentiment detection in Arabic tweets using multi-headed-LSTM-CNN-GRU and MaRBERT. In *Proceedings of the Sixth Arabic Natural Language Processing Workshop*, pages 306–311, Kyiv, Ukraine (Virtual). Association for Computational Linguistics.

Muhammad Abdul-Mageed. 2019. Modeling arabic subjectivity and sentiment in lexical space. *Information Processing & Management*, 56(2):291–307. Advance Arabic Natural Language Processing (ANLP) and its Applications.

Muhammad Abdul-Mageed, AbdelRahim Elmadany, and El Moatez Billah Nagoudi. 2021. ARBERT & MARBERT: Deep bidirectional transformers for Arabic. In *Proceedings of the 59th Annual Meeting of the Association for Computational Linguistics and the 11th International Joint Conference on Natural Language Processing (Volume 1: Long Papers)*, pages 7088–7105, Online. Association for Computational Linguistics.

Muhammad Abdul-Mageed, Chiyu Zhang, Houda Bouamor, and Nizar Habash. 2020. NADI 2020: The first nuanced Arabic dialect identification shared task. In *Proceedings of the Fifth Arabic Natural Language Processing Workshop*, pages 97–110, Barcelona, Spain (Online). Association for Computational Linguistics.

Nawaf A. Abdulla, Nizar A. Ahmed, Mohammed A. Shehab, and Mahmoud Al-Ayyoub. 2013. Arabic sentiment analysis: Lexicon-based and corpus-based. In *2013 IEEE Jordan Conference on Applied Electrical Engineering and Computing Technologies (AEECT)*, pages 1–6.

Gavin Abercrombie and Dirk Hovy. 2016. Putting sarcasm detection into context: The effects of class imbalance and manual labelling on supervised machine classification of Twitter conversations. In *Proceedings of the ACL 2016 Student Research Workshop*, pages 107–113, Berlin, Germany. Association for Computational Linguistics.

Ibrahim Abu Farha and Walid Magdy. 2019. Mazajak: An online Arabic sentiment analyser. In *Proceedings of the Fourth Arabic Natural Language Processing Workshop*, pages 192–198, Florence, Italy. Association for Computational Linguistics.

Ibrahim Abu Farha and Walid Magdy. 2020. From Arabic sentiment analysis to sarcasm detection: The ArSarcasm dataset. In *Proceedings of the 4th Workshop on Open-Source Arabic Corpora and Processing Tools, with a Shared Task on Offensive Language Detection*, pages 32–39, Marseille, France. European Language Resource Association.

Ibrahim Abu Farha and Walid Magdy. 2021. A comparative study of effective approaches for arabic sentiment analysis. *Information Processing & Management*, 58(2):102438.

Ibrahim Abu Farha, Silviu Vlad Oprea, Steven Wilson, and Walid Magdy. 2022. SemEval-2022 task 6: iSarcasmEval, intended sarcasm detection in English and Arabic. In *Proceedings of the 16th International Workshop on Semantic Evaluation (SemEval-2022)*, pages 802–814, Seattle, United States. Association for Computational Linguistics.

Ibrahim Abu Farha, Wajdi Zaghouani, and Walid Magdy. 2021. Overview of the WANLP 2021 shared task on sarcasm and sentiment detection in Arabic. In *Proceedings of the Sixth Arabic Natural Language Processing Workshop*, pages 296–305, Kyiv, Ukraine (Virtual). Association for Computational Linguistics.

Rania Al-Sabbagh and Roxana Girju. 2012. YADAC: Yet another dialectal Arabic corpus. In *Proceedings of the Eighth International Conference on Language Resources and Evaluation (LREC'12)*, pages 2882–2889, Istanbul, Turkey. European Language Resources Association (ELRA).

Abdulaziz M. Alayba, Vasile Palade, Matthew England, and Rahat Iqbal. 2018. A combined cnn and lstm model for arabic sentiment analysis. In *Machine Learning and Knowledge Extraction*, pages 179–191, Cham. Springer International Publishing.

Zaid Alyafeai, Maraim Masoud, Mustafa Ghaleb, and Maged Saeed AlShaibani. 2021. Masader: Metadata sourcing for arabic text and speech data resources. *CoRR*, abs/2110.06744.

Wissam Antoun, Fady Baly, and Hazem Hajj. 2020. AraBERT: Transformer-based model for Arabic language understanding. In *Proceedings of the 4th Workshop on Open-Source Arabic Corpora and Processing Tools, with a Shared Task on Offensive Language Detection*, pages 9–15, Marseille, France. European Language Resource Association.

Francesco Barbieri, Horacio Saggion, and Francesco Ronzano. 2014. Modelling sarcasm in Twitter, a novel approach. In *Proceedings of the 5th Workshop on Computational Approaches to Subjectivity, Sentiment and Social Media Analysis*, pages 50–58, Baltimore, Maryland. Association for Computational Linguistics.

Houda Bouamor, Nizar Habash, Mohammad Salameh, Wajdi Zaghouani, Owen Rambow, Dana Abdulrahim, Ossama Obeid, Salam Khalifa, Fadhl Eryani, Alexander Erdmann, and Kemal Oflazer. 2018. The MADAR Arabic dialect corpus and lexicon. In *Proceedings of the Eleventh International Conference on Language Resources and Evaluation (LREC 2018)*, Miyazaki, Japan. European Language Resources Association (ELRA).

Kathleen Egan. 2010. Cross lingual Arabic blog alerting (COLABA). In *Proceedings of the 9th Conference of the Association for Machine Translation in the Americas: Government MT User Program*, Denver, Colorado, USA. Association for Machine Translation in the Americas.

Samhaa R. El-Beltagy, Mona El Kalamawy, and Abu Bakr Soliman. 2017. NileTMRG at SemEval-2017 task 4: Arabic sentiment analysis. In *Proceedings of the 11th International Workshop on Semantic Evaluation (SemEval-2017)*, pages 790–795, Vancouver, Canada. Association for Computational Linguistics.

Mahmoud El-Haj. 2020. Habibi - a multi dialect multi national Arabic song lyrics corpus. In *Proceedings of the 12th Language Resources and Evaluation Conference*, pages 1318–1326, Marseille, France. European Language Resources Association.

Abdelkader El Mahdaouy, Abdellah El Mekki, Kabil Essefar, Nabil El Mamoun, Ismail Berrada, and Ahmed Khoumsi. 2021. Deep multi-task model for sarcasm detection and sentiment analysis in Arabic language. In *Proceedings of the Sixth Arabic Natural Language Processing Workshop*, pages 334–339, Kyiv, Ukraine (Virtual). Association for Computational Linguistics.

AbdelRahim A. Elmadany, Hamdy Mubarak, and Walid Magdy. 2018. An arabic speech-act and sentiment corpus of tweets. In *Proceedings of the Eleventh International Conference on Language Resources and Evaluation (LREC 2018)*. European Language Resources Association (ELRA). The 3rd Workshop on Open-Source Arabic Corpora and Processing Tools, OSACT3 ; Conference date: 08-05-2018.

Kariman Elshakankery and Mona Farouk. 2019. Hilatsa: A hybrid incremental learning approach for arabic tweets sentiment analysis. *Egyptian Informatics Journal*, 20(3):163–171.

Kariman Elshakankery, Magda Fayek, and Mona Farouk. 2021. Lastd: A manually annotated and tested large arabic sentiment tweets dataset. In *2021 the 5th International Conference on Information System and Data Mining*, ICISDM 2021, page 62–66, New York, NY, USA. Association for Computing Machinery.

Bilal Ghanem, Jihen Karoui, Farah Benamara, Véronique Moriceau, and Paolo Rosso. 2019. Idat at fire2019: Overview of the track on irony detection in arabic tweets. In *Proceedings of the 11th Forum for Information Retrieval Evaluation*, FIRE '19, page 10–13, New York, NY, USA. Association for Computing Machinery.

Jihen Karoui, Farah Banamara Zitoune, and Véronique Moriceau. 2017. Soukhria: Towards an irony detection system for arabic in social media. *Procedia Computer Science*, 117:161–168. Arabic Computational Linguistics.

Gehad S. Kaseb and Mona Farouk. 2016. Arabic sentiment analysis approaches: An analytical survey. *International Journal of Scientific & Engineering Research*, 7(10).

Gehad S. Kaseb and Mona Farouk. 2019. Extended-atsd: Arabic tweets sentiment dataset. *Journal of Engineering and Applied Sciences*, 14.

Gehad S. Kaseb and Mona Farouk. 2021. An enhanced svm based approach for sentiment classification of arabic tweets of different dialects. *International Journal of Advances in Electronics and Computer Science*, 8.

Muhammad Khalifa and Noura Hussein. 2019. Ensemble learning for irony detection in arabic tweets. In *Working Notes of FIRE 2019 - Forum for Information Retrieval Evaluation, Kolkata, India, December 12-15, 2019*, volume 2517 of *CEUR Workshop Proceedings*, pages 433–438. CEUR-WS.org.

Salam Khalifa, Nizar Habash, Dana Abdulrahim, and Sara Hassan. 2016. A large scale corpus of Gulf Arabic. In *Proceedings of the Tenth International Conference on Language Resources and Evaluation (LREC'16)*, pages 4282–4289, Portorož, Slovenia. European Language Resources Association (ELRA).

Diederik P. Kingma and Jimmy Ba. 2015. Adam: A method for stochastic optimization. In *3rd International Conference on Learning Representations, ICLR 2015, San Diego, CA, USA, May 7-9, 2015, Conference Track Proceedings*.

Svetlana Kiritchenko, Saif Mohammad, and Mohammad Salameh. 2016. SemEval-2016 task 7: Determining sentiment intensity of English and Arabic phrases. In *Proceedings of the 10th International Workshop on Semantic Evaluation (SemEval-2016)*, pages 42–51, San Diego, California. Association for Computational Linguistics.

John H. McWhorter. 2004. Review of the syntax of spoken arabic: A comparative study of moroccan, egyptian, syrian, and kuwaiti dialects. In *Language (Volume 80)*, pages 338–339. Association for Computational Linguistics.

Ahmed Mourad and Kareem Darwish. 2013. Subjectivity and sentiment analysis of Modern Standard Arabic and Arabic microblogs. In *Proceedings of the 4th Workshop on Computational Approaches to Subjectivity, Sentiment and Social Media Analysis*, pages 55–64, Atlanta, Georgia. Association for Computational Linguistics.

Silviu Oprea and Walid Magdy. 2020. iSarcasm: A dataset of intended sarcasm. In *Proceedings of the 58th Annual Meeting of the Association for Computational Linguistics*, pages 1279–1289, Online. Association for Computational Linguistics.

Bo Pang, Lillian Lee, and Shivakumar Vaithyanathan. 2002. Thumbs up? sentiment classification using machine learning techniques. In *Proceedings of the 2002 Conference on Empirical Methods in Natural Language Processing (EMNLP 2002)*, pages 79–86. Association for Computational Linguistics.

Sara Rosenthal, Noura Farra, and Preslav Nakov. 2017. SemEval-2017 task 4: Sentiment analysis in Twitter. In *Proceedings of the 11th International Workshop on Semantic Evaluation (SemEval-2017)*, pages 502–518, Vancouver, Canada. Association for Computational Linguistics.

Fatiha Sadat, Farnazeh Kazemi, and Atefeh Farzindar. 2014. Automatic identification of arabic dialects in social media. In *Proceedings of the First International Workshop on Social Media Retrieval and Analysis*, SoMeRA '14, page 35–40, New York, NY, USA. Association for Computing Machinery.

Bingyan Song, Chunguang Pan, Shengguang Wang, and Zhipeng Luo. 2021. DeepBlueAI at WANLP-EACL2021 task 2: A deep ensemble-based method for sarcasm and sentiment detection in Arabic. In *Proceedings of the Sixth Arabic Natural Language Processing Workshop*, pages 390–394, Kyiv, Ukraine (Virtual). Association for Computational Linguistics.

Anshul Wadhawan. 2021. AraBERT and farasa segmentation based approach for sarcasm and sentiment detection in Arabic tweets. In *Proceedings of the Sixth Arabic Natural Language Processing Workshop*, pages 395–400, Kyiv, Ukraine (Virtual). Association for Computational Linguistics.

Thomas Wolf, Lysandre Debut, Victor Sanh, Julien Chaumond, Clement Delangue, Anthony Moi, Pierric Cistac, Tim Rault, Remi Louf, Morgan Funtowicz, Joe Davison, Sam Shleifer, Patrick von Platen, Clara Ma, Yacine Jernite, Julien Plu, Canwen Xu, Teven Le Scao, Sylvain Gugger, Mariama Drame, Quentin Lhoest, and Alexander Rush. 2020. Transformers: State-of-the-art natural language processing. In *Proceedings of the 2020 Conference on Empirical Methods in Natural Language Processing: System Demonstrations*, pages 38–45, Online. Association for Computational Linguistics.

AraBART: a Pretrained Arabic Sequence-to-Sequence Model for Abstractive Summarization

Moussa Kamal Eddine,[1] **Nadi Tomeh,**[2] **Nizar Habash,**[3]
Joseph Le Roux,[2] **Michalis Vazirgiannis**[1,4]
[1]École Polytechnique, [2]Université Sorbonne Paris Nord - CNRS UMR 7030,
[3]New York University Abu Dhabi, [4]Athens University of Economics and Business
{moussa.kamal-eddine,michalis.vazirgiannis}@polytechnique.edu
{tomeh,leroux}@lipn.fr, nizar.habash@nyu.edu

Abstract

Like most natural language understanding and generation tasks, state-of-the-art models for summarization are transformer-based sequence-to-sequence architectures that are pretrained on large corpora. While most existing models focus on English, Arabic remains understudied. In this paper we propose AraBART, the first Arabic model in which the encoder and the decoder are pretrained end-to-end, based on BART (Lewis et al., 2020). We show that AraBART achieves the best performance on multiple abstractive summarization datasets, outperforming strong baselines including a pretrained Arabic BERT-based model, multilingual BART, Arabic T5, and a multilingual T5 model. AraBART is publicly available on github[1]and the Hugging Face model hub[2].

1 Introduction

Summarization is the task of transforming a text into a shorter representation of its essential meaning in natural language. *Extractive* approaches (Nallapati et al., 2017; Narayan et al., 2018b; Zhou et al., 2018; See et al., 2017) identify informative spans in the original text and stitch them together to generate the summary. *Abstractive* approaches on the other hand are not restricted to the input (Rush et al., 2015; Chopra et al., 2016; Dou et al., 2021).

While the vast majority of published models in both categories focus on English, some tackle other languages including Chinese (Hu et al., 2015) and French (Kamal Eddine et al., 2021b), while Arabic remains understudied. In fact, most Arabic summarization models are extractive (Qassem et al., 2019; Alshanqiti et al., 2021). They generate explainable and factual summaries but tend to be verbose and lack fluency. Addressing this problem, abstractive models are flexible in their word choices, resorting to paraphrasing and generalization to obtain more fluent and coherent summaries. Sequence-to-sequence (seq2seq) is the architecture of choice for abstractive models. Al-Maleh and Desouki (2020), for instance, apply the pointer-generator network (See et al., 2017) to Arabic, while Khalil et al. (2022) propose a more generic RNN-based model.

There are, however, two main issues with abstractive models as applied to Arabic. First, they are trained and evaluated either on extractive datasets such as KALIMAT (El-Haj and Koulali, 2013) and ANT Corpus (Chouigui et al., 2021), or on headline generation datasets such as AHS (Al-Maleh and Desouki, 2020), which only contains short and rather extractive headlines. Second, despite their state-of-the-art performance, abstractive models frequently generate content that is non-factual or unfaithful to the original text. Maynez et al. (2020) showed that English models that are based on the Transformer architecture such as BERT2BERT (Rothe et al., 2020) efficiently mitigate this phenomenon thanks to pretraining on large corpora. Therefore, Elmadani et al. (2020) finetuned a pretrained BERT using the encoder-decoder architecture of BERTSUM (Liu and Lapata, 2019). However, only the encoder is pretrained, the decoder and the connection weights between the encoder and the decoder are initialized randomly which is suboptimal.

To address these two problems, we propose AraBART, the first sequence-to-sequence Arabic model in which the encoder, the decoder and their connection weights are pretrained end-to-end using BART's denoising autoencoder objective (Lewis et al., 2020). While the encoder is bidirectional, the decoder is auto-regressive and thus more suitable for summarization than BERT-based models. We finetuned and evaluated our model on two abstractive datasets. The first is Arabic Gigaword (Parker et al., 2011), a newswire headline-generation dataset, not previously exploited in Ara-

[1]https://github.com/moussaKam/arabart
[2]https://huggingface.co/moussaKam/AraBART

Proceedings of the The Seventh Arabic Natural Language Processing Workshop (WANLP), pages 31 - 42
December 8, 2022 ©2022 Association for Computational Linguistics

bic abstractive summarization; the second is XL-Sum, a multilingual text summarization dataset for 44 languages including Arabic (Hasan et al., 2021). We evaluate our model and the other baselines using both automatic and manual evaluation. In the former we use ROUGE (Lin, 2004) and BERTScore (Zhang et al., 2020), while in the latter we collect human annotations assessing the quality and the faithfulness of the individual summaries generated by different systems. AraBART achieves state-of-the-art results outperforming pretrained BERT-based models, T5-based models (Xue et al., 2021; Al-Maleh and Desouki, 2020), as well as a much larger model, mBART25 (Liu et al., 2020), a multilingual denoising auto-encoder pretrained on 25 different languages using the BART objective. This improvement is observed in both automatic and manual evaluation.

In Section 2, we present the architecture and the pretraining settings of AraBART. In Section 3, we conduct an automatic evaluation of AraBART against four strong baselines on a wide range of abstractive summarization datasets. In Section 4, we present a detailed human evaluation using quality and faithfulness assessments. Finally, we discuss related work in Section 5.

2 AraBART

AraBART follows the architecture of BART Base (Lewis et al., 2020), which has 6 encoder and 6 decoder layers and 768 hidden dimensions. In total AraBART has 139M parameters. We add one additional layer-normalization layer on top of the encoder and the decoder to stabilize training at FP16 precision, following (Liu et al., 2020). We use sentencepiece (Kudo and Richardson, 2018) to create the vocabulary of AraBART. We train the sentencepiece model on a randomly sampled subset of the pretraining corpus (without any preprocessing) with size 20GB. We fix the vocabulary size to 50K tokens and the character coverage to 99.99% to avoid a high rate of unknown tokens.

2.1 Pretraining

We adopt the same corpus used to pretrain AraBERT (Antoun et al., 2020). While Antoun et al. (2020) use a preprocessed version of the corpus, we opted to reverse the preprocessing by using a script that removes added spaces around non-alphabetical characters, and also undo some words segmentation. The use of a corpus with no preprocessing, makes the text generation more natural. The size of the pretraining corpus before/after sentencepiece tokenization is 73/96 GB.

Pretraining Objective AraBART is a denoising autoencoder, i.e., it learns to reconstruct a corrupted text. The noise functions applied to the input text are the same as in Lewis et al. (2020). The first noise function is *text infilling*, where 30% of the text is masked by replacing a number of text spans with a [MASK] token. The length of the spans is sampled from a Poisson distribution with $\lambda = 3.5$. The second noise function is *sentence permutation*, where the sentences of the input text are shuffled based on the full stops.

Pretraining Settings AraBART pretraining took approximately 60h. The pretraining was carried out on 128 Nvidia V100 GPUs which allowed for 25 full passes over the pretraining corpus. We used the Adam optimizer with $\epsilon = 10^{-6}$, $\beta_1 = 0.9$, and $\beta_2 = 0.98$ following Liu et al. (2019). We use a warm up for 6% of the pretraining where the learning rate linearly increases from 0 to 0.0006, then decreases linearly to reach 0 at the end of the pretraining. We fixed the update frequency to 2 and we used a dropout 0.1 in the first 20 epochs and we changed it to 0 in the last 5 epochs. Finally we used FP16 to speed up the pretraining. The pretraining is done using Fairseq (Ott et al., 2019).

3 Experiments

Although AraBART can be adapted to be finetuned on different NLP tasks, our main focus in this work is abstractive summarization. Our motivation is that other tasks (e.g., text classification, named entity recognition, etc.) can be performed using other existing pretrained models with BERT-like architectures. However, when it comes to generative tasks, these models underperform and cannot be easily adapted.

3.1 Datasets

To evaluate our model, we use several datasets that consist mostly of news articles annotated with summaries with different level of abstractiveness. The first 7 datasets (*AAW*, *AFP*, *AHR*, *HYT*, *NHR*, *QDS* and *XIN*) are subsets of the Arabic Gigaword (Parker et al., 2011) corpus.[3] Each one is a differ-

[3]The datasets come from different Arabic newswire sources: AAW (Asharq Al-Awsat), AFP (Agence France Presse), AHR (Al-Ahram), HYT (Al Hayat), NHR (An Nahar), QDS (Al-Quds Al-Arabi), XIN (Xinhua News Agency).

		Datasets									
		AAW	*AHR*	*AFP*	*HYT*	*NHR*	*QDS*	*XIN*	*MIX*	*XL-S*	*XL-T*
Average	*document*	453.3	394.2	232.8	474.0	455.9	450.6	187.2	364.5	428.7	428.7
# of Tokens	*summary*	15.5	9.2	8.3	11.2	10.4	8.0	8.2	9.4	25.6	9.4
% Novel	*unigrams*	44.2	46.5	30.7	42.4	46.5	24.9	26.4	40.0	53.5	44.3
N-grams	*bigrams*	78.5	78.4	63.6	78.6	80.7	46.9	48.5	72.2	85.8	81.2
in Summary	*trigrams*	91.2	91.3	81.9	92.0	92.8	57.5	60.8	86.3	95.2	94.1

Table 1: Statistics of Gigaword subsets, as well as XL-Sum summaries (XL-S) and titles (XL-T). The first two lines show the average document and summary lengths. The last three lines show the percentage of n-grams in the summary that do not occur in the input article, used here as a measure of abstractiveness (Narayan et al., 2018a).

	Layers	Params	Vocab. size	Pretraining hours	Pretraining devices	Corpus size	Multilingual
AraBART	12	139	50	60	128 GPUs	73	No
mBART25	24	610	250	432	256 GPUs	1369	Yes
mT5$_{base}$	12	390	250	-	-	27,000	Yes
AraT5$_{base}$	12	282	30	80	TPUs v3-8	70	No
C2C	24	275	30	108	TPUs v3-8	167	No

Table 2: Sequence-to-sequence models used in the experiments. Parameters are given in millions, vocab sizes in thousands, and corpus sizes in GB. C2C stands for CAMeLBERT2CAMeLBERT. - refers to unspecified information.

ent news source, composed of document-headline pairs. In all these datasets we use a train set of 50K examples, a validation set of size 5K examples and a test set of size 5K examples, selected randomly. The *MIX* dataset consists of 60K examples uniformly sampled from the union of the 7 different sources.

In addition to the Arabic Gigaword corpus, we use XL-Sum (Hasan et al., 2021). The news articles in XL-sum are annotated with summaries and titles, thus creating two tasks: summary generation, and title generation.

Table 1 shows that the different datasets used in our experiments cover a wide range of article/summary lengths and levels of abstractiveness. This variation can be explained by the fact that the target sentences in each dataset follow a different headline writing style. For example, the summaries of the *QDS* dataset which are the shortest and the less abstractive on average, are more like titles extracted from the first paragraph with minimal reformulation. On the other hand, the summaries of XL-Sum, which are the longest and the most abstractive, contain information interspersed in various parts of the input text.

3.2 Baselines

We compare our model to four types of state-of-the-art sequence-to-sequence baselines. The first, called CAMeLBERT2CAMeLBERT (C2C), is a monolingual seq2seq model based on BERT2BERT (Rothe et al., 2020). The encoder and decoder are initialized using CAMELBERT (Inoue et al., 2021) weights while the cross-attention weights are randomly initialized.[4] C2C has 275M parameters in total.

The second baseline is mBART25 (Liu et al., 2020) which is a multilingual BART pretrained on 25 different languages including Arabic. Although mBART25 was initially pretrained for neural machine translation, it was shown that it can be used in monolingual generative tasks such as abstractive summarization (Kamal Eddine et al., 2021b). mBART25 has 610M parameters in total.

Another multilingual model that we include as a baseline in our experiments is mT5$_{base}$ (Hasan et al., 2021). mT5 is a multilingual variant of T5 (Raffel et al., 2020) pretrained on the mC4 dataset - a large corpus comprising 27T of natural text in 101 different languages including Arabic. mT5$_{base}$

[4] We experimented with ARABERT (Antoun et al., 2020) which was slower to converge and didn't achieve better performance.

has 390M parameters in total. Another recently released T5-based model is AraT5, pretraind on 70GB of natural text written in modern standard Arabic. For a fair comparison, we use the *base* version of mT5 and AraT5. Table 2 summarizes the specifications of the different models used in our experiments.

3.3 Training and Evaluation

We finetuned each model for three epochs, using the Adam optimizer and 5×10^{-5} maximum learning rate with linear decay scheduling. In the generation phase we use beam-search with beam size of 3. Ideally, an optimal hyperparameter search should be applied for each model. However, given the huge hyperparameter space on the one hand and the significant number of evaluation datasets, on the other hand, searching for optimal hyperparameter combinations would be considerably time-consuming and energetically inefficient. Given that, we opted for a fixed configuration for all models chosen based on the previous similar efforts (Lewis et al., 2020; Kamal Eddine et al., 2021b).

For evaluation, we first normalized the output summaries as is common practice in Arabic: we removed Tatweel and diacritization, normalized Alif/Ya, and separated punctuation marks. We report ROUGE-1, ROUGE-2 and ROUGE-L F1-scores (Lin, 2004). However, these metrics are solely based on surface-form matching and have a limited sense of semantic similarity (Kamal Eddine et al., 2021a). Thus we opted for using BERTScore (Zhang et al., 2020), a metric based on the similarity of the contextual embeddings of the reference and candidate summaries, produced by a BERT-like model.[5]

3.4 Results

We observe in Table 3 that AraBART outperforms C2C on all datasets with a clear margin. This is probably a direct consequence of pretraining the seq2seq architecture end-to-end.

AraBART also outperforms mBART25 on XL-Sum which is the most abstractive dataset. On Gigawords, AraBART is best everywhere except on AHR with mitigated results. On QDS, the set with the least abstractive summaries (see Table 1), however, it falls clearly behind mBART25 on all metrics. In fact, we notice that the gap between AraBART and the baselines is greater on the XL-Sum dataset than on Gigaword. For instance, our model's ROUGE-L score is 2.9 absolute points higher that mBART25 on XL-S while the maximum margin obtained on a Gigaword subset is 1.4 points on AAW and HYT. We observe a tendency for AraBART to outperform mBART on more abstractive datasets. In fact, the margin between their BERTScores is positively correlated with abstractiveness as measured by the percentage of novel trigrams.[6]

Figure 1 presents some examples of the output of the various systems we studied. The input news articles corresponding to the summaries in Figure 1 are shown in Appendix A.

4 Human Evaluation

To validate the automatic evaluation results, we conducted a detailed manual evaluation that covers two aspects: **quality** and **faithfulness**. We considered 100 documents randomly sampled from the test set along with their respective candidate summaries. The systems included in the manual evaluation are: AraBART, mBART25, mT_{base} and CAMeLBERT2CAMeLBERT (C2C).[7] In addition to the generated summaries, we include the reference summaries following Narayan et al. (2018a); Kamal Eddine et al. (2021b). The annotations were carried out by 14 Arabic native speaker volunteers. To guarantee a better quality assessments, each example was annotated by two volunteers separately. The guidelines provided to the annotators are presented in Figure 2.

4.1 Quality Evaluation

To assess the overall quality of system summaries we use the *Best-Worst Scaling* (BWS) method (Narayan et al., 2018a). For each document, the annotators were provided with the list of all possible combinations of summary pairs. They were asked to choose the best summary of each of the pairs. To help them in their decisions the annotators were asked to focus on three aspects: *factuality* (does the summary contain factual information?), *relevance* (does the summary capture the important information in the document?) and *fluency* (is the summary written in well-formed Arabic?).

[5]We use the official implementation (`https://github.com/Tiiiger/bert_score`) with the following options: `-m UBC-NLP/ARBERT -l 9` (Chiang et al., 2020)

[6]With a Pearson R score of 0.6625 and p-value<0.05.

[7]We separately evaluate the AraT5 model (Al-Maleh and Desouki, 2020), which was not yet published at the time of this human evaluation, in Section 4.3.

Source	Model	R1	R2	RL	BS
AAW	AraBART	**30.7**	**15.3**	**27.4**	**62.5**
	mBART25	29.5	14.4	26.0	61.5
	mT5$_{base}$	26.3	11.9	23.3	61.5
	AraT5$_{base}$	24.1	9.8	21.3	56.7
	C2C	24.6	9.9	21.7	58.3
AFP	AraBART	**55.0**	**37.9**	**53.4**	**77.5**
	mBART25	54.8	37.3	52.8	77.2
	mT5$_{base}$	52.8	35.8	51.0	61.5
	AraT5$_{base}$	47.8	29.6	46.3	73.6
	C2C	50.0	32.2	48.4	74.8
AHR	AraBART	**39.1**	25.4	**37.7**	**68.2**
	mBART25	**39.1**	**26.1**	37.5	68.1
	mT5$_{base}$	33.3	20.1	31.7	64.7
	AraT5$_{base}$	25.6	12.9	24.4	59.4
	C2C	33.0	19.7	31.8	63.5
HYT	AraBART	**33.1**	**17.5**	**30.7**	**63.8**
	mBART25	32.0	16.2	29.3	63.1
	mT5$_{base}$	29.9	14.5	27.5	62.0
	AraT5$_{base}$	26.3	10.7	24.2	58.0
	C2C	27.4	11.5	25.2	59.6
NHR	AraBART	**32.0**	**17.2**	**30.3**	**61.2**
	mBART25	31.0	16.2	29.2	60.3
	mT5$_{base}$	27.3	13.3	25.6	58.5
	AraT5$_{base}$	19.5	7.5	18.3	51.1
	C2C	24.1	10.0	22.9	53.0

Source	Model	R1	R2	RL	BS
QDS	AraBART	62.1	53.9	61.4	80.3
	mBART25	**62.4**	**54.1**	**61.7**	**80.4**
	mT5$_{base}$	59.3	50.5	58.5	78.7
	AraT5$_{base}$	56.3	47.1	55.6	76.4
	C2C	57.9	48.9	57.4	77.3
XIN	AraBART	**66.0**	**53.9**	**65.1**	**84.4**
	mBART25	65.1	53.4	64.2	84.0
	mT5$_{base}$	64.1	52.2	63.2	83.4
	AraT5$_{base}$	61.5	48.5	60.6	82.3
	C2C	62.4	50.1	61.6	82.5
MIX	AraBART	**39.2**	25.5	**37.6**	**67.6**
	mBART25	39.0	**25.6**	37.1	67.2
	mT5$_{base}$	33.1	20.0	31.5	64.0
	AraT5$_{base}$	32.2	18.8	30.8	62.2
	C2C	32.8	19.1	31.4	62.5
XL-S	AraBART	**34.5**	**14.6**	**30.5**	**67.0**
	mBART25	32.1	12.5	27.6	65.3
	mT5$_{base}$	32.8	12.7	28.7	65.8
	AraT5$_{base}$	25.2	7.6	21.6	58.1
	C2C	26.9	8.7	23.1	61.6
XL-T	AraBART	**32.0**	**13.7**	**29.4**	**65.8**
	mBART25	29.8	11.7	26.9	64.3
	mT5$_{base}$	25.7	9.3	23.5	61.6
	AraT5$_{base}$	24.0	7.1	21.8	57.3
	C2C	25.2	7.9	22.9	61.1

Source	Model	R1	R2	RL	BS
Macro Averages	AraBART	**42.4**	**28.8**	**40.3**	**69.8**
	mBART25	41.5	28.1	39.2	69.1
	mT5$_{base}$	38.5	24.0	36.5	66.2
	AraT5$_{base}$	34.2	20.0	32.5	63.5
	C2C	36.4	23.1	34.6	65.4

Table 3: The performance of AraBART, mBART25, mT5$_{base}$, AraT5$_{base}$, and C2C (CAMeLBERT2CAMeLBERT) on all datasets in terms of ROUGE-1 (R1), ROUGE-2 (R2), ROUGE-L (RL) and BERTScore (BS). Macro averages are computed over all datasets.

Table 4 shows a pairwise comparison between the models with regard to their overall quality. The scores represent the percentage of the times the *row* model was chosen as better than the *column* model. The last column in the table represents the BWS score, which is, for each model the percentage of time the model's summary was chosen as best minus the percentage of time it was chosen as worst (Narayan et al., 2018a).

The manual quality assessment showed the same ranking as the automatic evaluation presented in Table 3. However, in the current assessment, the differences between the models' performances vary. For example, AraBART, which is the top performing model, has a wider margin compared to mBART25. On the other hand, mBART25 lost its significant margin compared to the mT5 model. These findings highlight the importance of carrying out manual evaluation in the context of abstractive summarization generation. Finally, AraBART summaries were even judged as being of better quality than some references by the annotators. While this finding could seem problematic, it is in line with previous efforts (Narayan et al., 2018a; Ka-

	System	Arabic	English
(a)	**Reference**	تنظر محكمة عسكرية امريكية في وقت لاحق من اليوم في قضية الطبيب النفسي العسكري الامريكي ، نضال حسن ، الذي اعترف بقتل 13 شخصا واصابة اكثر من ثلاثين اخرين في اطلاق نار بقاعدة فورت هود منذ اربعة اعوام .	A US military court will hear, later in the day, the case of the US military psychiatrist, Nidal Hassan, who confessed to killing 13 people and wounding more than thirty others in a shooting at Fort Hood base four years ago.
	AraBART	مثل نضال حسن ، المتهم بقتل 13 جنديا امريكيا في قاعدة عسكرية في افغانستان ، امام محكمة عسكرية في مدينة فورت هود .	Nidal Hassan, accused of killing 13 US soldiers at a military base in Afghanistan, appeared before a military court in Fort Hood.
	mBART25	اعترف رجل افغاني بقتل 13 جنديا امريكيا وجرح اخرين في قاعدة عسكرية امريكية في ولاية فرجينيا في نوفمبر / تشرين الثاني الماضي .	An Afghan man confessed to killing 13 US soldiers and wounding others at a US military base in Virginia last November.
	C2C	قال رجل الدين الامريكي ، حسن حسن ، انه " لا يستطيع ان يقتل احد جنوده " ، بعد ان قتل جنديا امريكيا في قاعدة عسكرية	The American cleric, Hassan Hassan, said that he "could not kill one of his soldiers", after he killed an American soldier in a military base
	mT5	قضت محكمة عسكرية في ولاية كاليفورنيا الامريكية باعدام رجل قتل 13 جنديا امريكيا في قاعدة للجيش الامريكي عام 2009 .	A California military court has sentenced to death a man who killed 13 US soldiers at a US military base in 2009.
	AraT5	قال مسؤولون أمريكيون إن قائد قاعدة عسكرية أمريكية في أفغانستان، عبد الله حسن، قتل 11 جنديا في هجوم على قاعدة عسكرية أمريكية في أفغانستان.	US officials said that the commander of a US military base in Afghanistan, Abdullah Hassan, killed 11 soldiers in an attack on a US military base in Afghanistan.
(b)	**Reference**	توفي يوم الثلاثاء عن عمر ناهز 89 عاما النجم البريطاني السير روجر مور .	British star Sir Roger Moore died on Tuesday at the age of 89.
	AraBART	توفي الممثل البريطاني روجر مور عن عمر يناهز 91 عاما بعد صراع مع مرض السرطان .	British actor Roger Moore has died at the age of 91, after a battle with cancer.
	mBART25	قالت اسرة النجم السينمائي الشهير روجر مور ان والدهم توفي عن عمر يناهز 91 عاما بعد صراع طويل مع مرض السرطان .	The family of famous film star Roger Moore said that their father passed away at the age of 91 after a long battle with cancer.
	C2C	توفي الممثل البريطاني الشهير روجر مور ، الذي اشتهر بدور جيمس بوند في فيلم " غراند سلام " ، عن عمر يناهز 91 عاما	Renowned British actor Roger Moore, best known for his role as James Bond in the movie "Grand Slam", has died at the age of 91.
	mT5	توفي السير روجر مور ، بطل دور الجاسوس جيمس بوند ، عن عمر يناهز 67 عاما في سويسرا بعد صراع قصير مع مرض السرطان .	Sir Roger Moore, star of James Bond, has died at the age of 67 in Switzerland after a short battle with cancer.
	AraT5	قالت اسرة الجاسوس البريطاني جيمس بوند، الذي كان كان كان كان في عمر يناهز 65 عاما، إن والدها الراحل توفي في فرنسا بعد صراع طويل مع مرض السرطان.	The family of British spy James Bond, who was was was was at the age of 65, that their late father died in France after a long struggle with cancer.
(c)	**Reference**	كشفت دراسة حديثة - تناولت الخلايا الجذعية - عن تاثير السجائر علي الاجنة .	A recent study - dealing with stem cells - revealed the effect of cigarettes on fetuses.
	AraBART	توصلت دراسة علمية الي ان تدخين الامهات اثناء الحمل له اثار ضارة علي الاجنة .	A scientific study concluded that smoking by mothers during pregnancy has harmful effects on fetuses.
	mBART25	خلصت دراسة علمية حديثة الي ان تدخين الامهات السجائر له اثار ضارة علي اجنة الذكور واجنة الاناث .	A recent scientific study concluded that cigarette smoking by mothers has harmful effects on male fetuses and female fetuses.
	C2C	قال علماء ان تدخين السجائر في الامعاء قد يكون له تاثير علي صحة الانسان .	Scientists said that smoking cigarettes in the intestines may have an effect on human health.
	mT5	اظهرت دراسة حديثة ان السجائر قد يؤدي تدخين الامهات الي اضرار كبيرة علي الاجنة .	A recent study showed that smoking by mothers may cause significant harm to fetuses.
	AraT5	قال علماء إن التدخين في النساء في سن السن المبكر قد يسبب أضرارا خطيرة على خلايا الكبد.	Scientists said that smoking in women at the age of early age may cause serious damage to liver cells.

Figure 1: Three selected examples contrasting the output of the various systems we studied. All examples are from the XL-Sum summaries test set. We provide English translations to provide context for the general readers.

Quality Assessment	Faithfulness Assessment
In this task, pairs of generated summaries (headlines) are compared together. If we judge the first summary to be better than the second one you fill the scores column with 1, otherwise fill it with 2. To make a decision you can think of different aspects of quality: factuality (does the summary contain factual information?), relevance (does the summary capture the important information in the document?) and fluency (is the summary written in well-formed Arabic?).	In this task we have 5 summaries (headlines) generated by 5 different models. Some of them contain unfaithful information, that is information that is not covered by the source document (even if it is factual). The unfaithful information should be replaced by a # symbol. If we have multiple consecutive information judged as unfaithful, the text span should be replaced with multiple # symbols.

Figure 2: The guidelines we provided to the human evaluators to evaluate in terms of Quality and Faithfulness.

System	Reference	AraBART	C2C	mBART	mT5	BWS Score
Reference	-	44.7	79.0	53.0	56.5	16.65
AraBART	55.3	-	82.85	54.75	58.5	**25.6**
C2C	21.0	17.15	-	14.5	15.5	-65.9
mBART	47.0	45.25	85.5	-	50.5	14.2
mT5$_{base}$	43.5	41.5	84.5	49.5	-	9.55

Table 4: Human evaluation using Best-Worst Scaling (BWS). The numbers in the first five columns represent the percentage of the times the *row* model was chosen as better than the *column* model. The BWS score is the percentage of time the model's summary was chosen as best minus the percentage of time it was chosen as worst.

mal Eddine et al., 2021b). The lower scores of the reference summaries are related to the nature of the task itself. The news headline generation task considers headlines as summaries. However these headlines, while being relevant and fluent, may contain some information that is not presented by the input document such as names and dates. These bits of information are considered by the human annotators as inaccurate or non-factual. This assumption is confirmed in the next section.

System	Unfaithful Spans #	Faithful Words %
Reference	2.31	77.91
AraBART (ours)	**1.36**	**84.47**
C2C	3.18	61.80
mBART	1.68	81.31
mT$_{base}$	1.49	81.62

Table 5: Faithfulness results in terms of the average number of unfaithful spans of text in summaries (less is more faithful), and the percentage of faithful words in summaries (higher is more faithful).

4.2 Faithfulness Evaluation

Recent efforts have shown that automatic systems are highly prone to generate content that is unfaithful to the source document (Maynez et al., 2020; Chen et al., 2021). Thus, we opted for a manual evaluation that focuses on the summaries' faithfulness. In this evaluation task, we asked the annotators to detect *unfaithful spans*. A span is considered as unfaithful if it contains information that is not covered by the input document even if the information is factual (Maynez et al., 2020).

Automatic metrics based on surface token (e.g., Rouge) or distributional semantic (e.g., BERTScore) overlap between the reference and the generated summaries are not sufficient for abstractive summarization evaluation. This is mainly because they are not able to capture the faithfulness of the summary with respect to the input document. This is why, manually assessing the faithfulness of the summary could be very useful for evaluating the summarization systems. Table 5 shows the degree of faithfulness of each model to the input document.

Here again, AraBART outperforms all the other systems, obtaining a lower number of unfaithful spans and a higher percentage of faithful summary words. On the other hand, the reference summaries are outperformed by AraBART and two other baselines which confirms our assumption in Section 4.1 about the underperformance of the reference summaries compared to AraBART. The difference in the system rankings and the improvement margins between the automatic, the quality and the faithfulness evaluations, highlights the importance of conducting a detailed evaluation considering various aspects and dimensions.

4.3 AraBART vs AraT5

At the time we carried out the manual evaluation, the AraT5 model (Al-Maleh and Desouki, 2020) was not yet published. For this reason we performed a separate quality assessment evaluation comparing AraT5 to AraBART only. We used the same 100 documents as previously, and the annotators had to choose the better summary among those of AraT5 and AraBART following the same guidelines of the overall quality assessment. Three annotators participated in this evaluation task, and each document was annotated by only one participant. The final score shows that 91.5% of the time AraBART summaries were chosen as best, which again shows the superiority of AraBART in the abstractive summarization task.

5 Related Work

Arabic Summarization The overwhelming majority of past Arabic models are extractive (Douzidia and Lapalme, 2004; Azmi and Althanyyan, 2009; El-Haj et al., 2011; El-Shishtawy and El-Ghannam, 2012; Haboush et al., 2012; Belkebir and Guessoum, 2015; Qaroush et al., 2021; Ayed et al., 2021). Recently, seq2seq abstractive models for Arabic have been proposed in the literature (Al-Maleh and Desouki, 2020; Suleiman and Awajan, 2020; Khalil et al., 2022), but none of them used pretraining. Fine-tuning Transformer-based language models like BERT (Devlin et al., 2019) has been shown to help Arabic abstractive (Elmadani et al., 2020) and extractive (Helmy et al., 2018) summarization, but unlike AraBART, not all components of the model are pretrained. Readily-available multilingual pretrained seq2seq models have been applied to Arabic summarization. Kahla et al. (2021) uses mBART25 (Liu et al., 2020) in cross-lingual transfer setup on an unpublished dataset, while Hasan et al. (2021) experiment with mT5 (Xue et al., 2021) on XL-Sum. Our model, tailored specifically for Arabic, outperforms mBART25 and mT5 for almost all datasets despite having a smaller architecture with less parameters.

Arabic Datasets Most available datasets for Arabic are extractive (El-Haj et al., 2010; Chouigui et al., 2021), use short headlines that are designed to attract the reader (Webz.io, 2016; Al-Maleh and Desouki, 2020), or contain machine-generated (El-Haj and Koulali, 2013) or translated (El-Haj et al., 2011) summaries. Notable exceptions we choose for our experiments are Gigaword (Parker et al., 2011) and XL-Sum (Hasan et al., 2021) because they cover both headline and summary generation, contain multiple sources, and manifest variable levels of abstractiveness as shown in Table 1.

Pretrained seq2seq models BART-based models have been developed for multiple language including English (Lewis et al., 2020), French (Kamal Eddine et al., 2021b) and Chinese (Shao et al., 2021) in addition to multilingual models (Liu et al., 2020). While they can be finetuned to perform any language understanding or generation tasks, we focus on summarization in this work.

6 Conclusion and Future Work

We release AraBART, the first sequence-to-sequence pretrained Arabic model. We evaluated our model on a set of abstractive summarization tasks, with different level of abstractiveness. We compared AraBART to a number of state-of-the-art models and we showed that it outperforms them almost everywhere despite the fact that it is smaller in terms of parameters.

In future work, we are planning to extend the model to multitask setups to take advantage of availability of both titles and summaries in some datasets including XL-Sum, and use external knowledge sources to improve faithfulness. We will also explore new directions for automatic summarization evaluation on morphologically rich languages like Arabic. We would like to use AraBART in other text transformation and generation tasks, such as spelling and grammar correction.

Acknowledgments

This work was granted access to the HPC resources of IDRIS under the allocation 2021-AD011012694 made by GENCI.

Ethical Considerations

Limitations Our models are optimized for news text summarization; we do not expect comparable performance on other summarization tasks without additional training data.

Risks We acknowledge that our models sometimes produce incorrect non-factual and non-grammatical output, which can be misleading to general users.

Data All the data we used comes from reputable news agencies and does not contain unanonymized private information or malicious social media content.

Models We will make our pretrained and fine-tuned models available on the well known Hugging Face models hub[8], so they can be easily used and distributed for research or production purposes.

References

Molham Al-Maleh and Said Desouki. 2020. Arabic text summarization using deep learning approach. *Journal of Big Data*, 7:1–17.

Abdullah Alshanqiti, Abdallah Namoun, Aeshah Alsughayyir, Aisha Mousa Mashraqi, Abdul Rehman Gilal, and Sami Saad Albouq. 2021. Leveraging distilbert for summarizing Arabic text: An extractive dual-stage approach. *IEEE Access*, 9:135594–135607.

Wissam Antoun, Fady Baly, and Hazem Hajj. 2020. AraBERT: Transformer-based model for Arabic language understanding. In *Proceedings of the 4th Workshop on Open-Source Arabic Corpora and Processing Tools, with a Shared Task on Offensive Language Detection*, pages 9–15, Marseille, France. European Language Resource Association.

Alaidine Ben Ayed, Ismaïl Biskri, and Jean-Guy Meunier. 2021. Arabic text summarization via knapsack balancing of effective retention. *Procedia Computer Science*, 189:312–319. AI in Computational Linguistics.

Aqil Azmi and Suha Al-thanyyan. 2009. Ikhtasir — a user selected compression ratio Arabic text summarization system. In *2009 International Conference on Natural Language Processing and Knowledge Engineering*, pages 1–7.

Riadh Belkebir and Ahmed Guessoum. 2015. A supervised approach to Arabic text summarization using adaboost. In *New Contributions in Information Systems and Technologies*, pages 227–236, Cham. Springer International Publishing.

Sihao Chen, Fan Zhang, Kazoo Sone, and Dan Roth. 2021. Improving faithfulness in abstractive summarization with contrast candidate generation and selection. In *Proceedings of the 2021 Conference of the North American Chapter of the Association for Computational Linguistics: Human Language Technologies*, pages 5935–5941, Online. Association for Computational Linguistics.

Cheng-Han Chiang, Sung-Feng Huang, and Hung-yi Lee. 2020. Pretrained language model embryology: The birth of ALBERT. In *Proceedings of the 2020 Conference on Empirical Methods in Natural Language Processing (EMNLP)*, pages 6813–6828, Online. Association for Computational Linguistics.

Sumit Chopra, Michael Auli, and Alexander M. Rush. 2016. Abstractive sentence summarization with attentive recurrent neural networks. In *Proceedings of the 2016 Conference of the North American Chapter of the Association for Computational Linguistics: Human Language Technologies*, pages 93–98, San Diego, California. Association for Computational Linguistics.

Amina Chouigui, Oussama Ben Khiroun, and Bilel Elayeb. 2021. An Arabic multi-source news corpus: Experimenting on single-document extractive summarization. *Arabian Journal for Science and Engineering*, 46(4):3925–3938.

Jacob Devlin, Ming-Wei Chang, Kenton Lee, and Kristina Toutanova. 2019. BERT: Pre-training of deep bidirectional transformers for language understanding. In *Proceedings of the 2019 Conference of the North American Chapter of the Association for Computational Linguistics: Human Language Technologies, Volume 1 (Long and Short Papers)*, pages 4171–4186, Minneapolis, Minnesota. Association for Computational Linguistics.

Zi-Yi Dou, Pengfei Liu, Hiroaki Hayashi, Zhengbao Jiang, and Graham Neubig. 2021. GSum: A general framework for guided neural abstractive summarization. In *Proceedings of the 2021 Conference of the North American Chapter of the Association for Computational Linguistics: Human Language Technologies*, pages 4830–4842, Online. Association for Computational Linguistics.

Fouad Douzidia and Guy Lapalme. 2004. Lakhas, an Arabic summarization system. In *Proceedings of DUC'04*, pages 128–135, Boston. NIST, NIST.

M. El-Haj, Udo Kruschwitz, and C. Fox. 2010. Using mechanical turk to create a corpus of Arabic summaries. In *Proceedings of the 7th International Conference on Language Resources and Evaluation : Workshops & Tutorials May 17-18, May 22-23, Main Conference May 19-21, Valletta*. ELRA, Paris.

Mahmoud El-Haj and Rim Koulali. 2013. Kalimat a multipurpose Arabic corpus. In *Second Workshop on Arabic Corpus Linguistics (WACL-2)*, pages 22–25.

Mahmoud El-Haj, Udo Kruschwitz, and Chris Fox. 2011. Exploring clustering for multi-document Arabic summarisation. In *Information Retrieval Technology - 7th Asia Information Retrieval Societies Conference, AIRS 2011, Dubai, United Arab Emirates, December 18-20, 2011. Proceedings*, volume 7097 of *Lecture Notes in Computer Science*, pages 550–561. Springer.

[8]`https://huggingface.co/models`

Mahmoud El-Haj, Udo Kruschwitz, and Chris Fox. 2011. Multi-document Arabic text summarisation. *2011 3rd Computer Science and Electronic Engineering Conference (CEEC)*, pages 40–44.

Tarek El-Shishtawy and Fatma El-Ghannam. 2012. Keyphrase based Arabic summarizer (kpas). In *2012 8th International Conference on Informatics and Systems (INFOS)*, pages NLP-7–NLP-14.

Khalid N. Elmadani, Mukhtar Elgezouli, and Anas Showk. 2020. BERT fine-tuning for Arabic text summarization. *CoRR*, abs/2004.14135.

Ahmad Haboush, Ahmed Momani, Maryam Al-Zoubi, and Motassem Al-Tarazi. 2012. Arabic text summerization model using clustering techniques. *World Comput Sci Inf Technol J*, 2.

Tahmid Hasan, Abhik Bhattacharjee, Md. Saiful Islam, Kazi Mubasshir, Yuan-Fang Li, Yong-Bin Kang, M. Sohel Rahman, and Rifat Shahriyar. 2021. XL-sum: Large-scale multilingual abstractive summarization for 44 languages. In *Findings of the Association for Computational Linguistics: ACL-IJCNLP 2021*, pages 4693–4703, Online. Association for Computational Linguistics.

Muhammad Helmy, R. M. Vigneshram, Giuseppe Serra, and Carlo Tasso. 2018. Applying deep learning for Arabic keyphrase extraction. In *Fourth International Conference On Arabic Computational Linguistics, ACLING 2018, November 17-19, 2018, Dubai, United Arab Emirates*, volume 142 of *Procedia Computer Science*, pages 254–261. Elsevier.

Baotian Hu, Qingcai Chen, and Fangze Zhu. 2015. LCSTS: A large scale Chinese short text summarization dataset. In *Proceedings of the 2015 Conference on Empirical Methods in Natural Language Processing*, pages 1967–1972, Lisbon, Portugal. Association for Computational Linguistics.

Go Inoue, Bashar Alhafni, Nurpeiis Baimukan, Houda Bouamor, and Nizar Habash. 2021. The interplay of variant, size, and task type in Arabic pre-trained language models. In *Proceedings of the Sixth Arabic Natural Language Processing Workshop*, pages 92–104, Kyiv, Ukraine (Virtual). Association for Computational Linguistics.

Mram Kahla, Zijian Győző Yang, and Attila Novák. 2021. Cross-lingual fine-tuning for abstractive Arabic text summarization. In *Proceedings of the International Conference on Recent Advances in Natural Language Processing (RANLP 2021)*, pages 655–663, Held Online. INCOMA Ltd.

Moussa Kamal Eddine, Guokan Shang, Antoine J-P Tixier, and Michalis Vazirgiannis. 2021a. Frugalscore: Learning cheaper, lighter and faster evaluation metricsfor automatic text generation. *arXiv preprint arXiv:2110.08559*.

Moussa Kamal Eddine, Antoine Tixier, and Michalis Vazirgiannis. 2021b. BARThez: a skilled pretrained French sequence-to-sequence model. In *Proceedings of the 2021 Conference on Empirical Methods in Natural Language Processing*, pages 9369–9390, Online and Punta Cana, Dominican Republic. Association for Computational Linguistics.

Ahmed Mostafa Khalil, Y. M. Wazery, Marwa E. Saleh, Abdullah Alharbi, and Abdelmgeid A. Ali. 2022. Abstractive Arabic text summarization based on deep learning. *Computational Intelligence and Neuroscience*, 2022:1566890.

Taku Kudo and John Richardson. 2018. SentencePiece: A simple and language independent subword tokenizer and detokenizer for neural text processing. In *Proceedings of the 2018 Conference on Empirical Methods in Natural Language Processing: System Demonstrations*, pages 66–71, Brussels, Belgium. Association for Computational Linguistics.

Mike Lewis, Yinhan Liu, Naman Goyal, Marjan Ghazvininejad, Abdelrahman Mohamed, Omer Levy, Veselin Stoyanov, and Luke Zettlemoyer. 2020. BART: Denoising sequence-to-sequence pre-training for natural language generation, translation, and comprehension. In *Proceedings of the 58th Annual Meeting of the Association for Computational Linguistics*, pages 7871–7880, Online. Association for Computational Linguistics.

Chin-Yew Lin. 2004. ROUGE: A package for automatic evaluation of summaries. In *Text Summarization Branches Out*, pages 74–81, Barcelona, Spain. Association for Computational Linguistics.

Yang Liu and Mirella Lapata. 2019. Text summarization with pretrained encoders. In *Proceedings of the 2019 Conference on Empirical Methods in Natural Language Processing and the 9th International Joint Conference on Natural Language Processing (EMNLP-IJCNLP)*, pages 3730–3740, Hong Kong, China. Association for Computational Linguistics.

Yinhan Liu, Jiatao Gu, Naman Goyal, Xian Li, Sergey Edunov, Marjan Ghazvininejad, Mike Lewis, and Luke Zettlemoyer. 2020. Multilingual denoising pre-training for neural machine translation. *Transactions of the Association for Computational Linguistics*, 8:726–742.

Yinhan Liu, Myle Ott, Naman Goyal, Jingfei Du, Mandar Joshi, Danqi Chen, Omer Levy, Mike Lewis, Luke Zettlemoyer, and Veselin Stoyanov. 2019. Roberta: A robustly optimized bert pretraining approach. *arXiv preprint arXiv:1907.11692*.

Joshua Maynez, Shashi Narayan, Bernd Bohnet, and Ryan McDonald. 2020. On faithfulness and factuality in abstractive summarization. In *Proceedings of the 58th Annual Meeting of the Association for Computational Linguistics*, pages 1906–1919, Online. Association for Computational Linguistics.

Ramesh Nallapati, Feifei Zhai, and Bowen Zhou. 2017. Summarunner: A recurrent neural network based sequence model for extractive summarization of documents. In *Proceedings of the Thirty-First AAAI Conference on Artificial Intelligence*, AAAI'17, page 3075–3081. AAAI Press.

Shashi Narayan, Shay B. Cohen, and Mirella Lapata. 2018a. Don't give me the details, just the summary! topic-aware convolutional neural networks for extreme summarization. In *Proceedings of the 2018*

Conference on Empirical Methods in Natural Language Processing, pages 1797–1807, Brussels, Belgium. Association for Computational Linguistics.

Shashi Narayan, Shay B. Cohen, and Mirella Lapata. 2018b. Ranking sentences for extractive summarization with reinforcement learning. In *Proceedings of the 2018 Conference of the North American Chapter of the Association for Computational Linguistics: Human Language Technologies, Volume 1 (Long Papers)*, pages 1747–1759, New Orleans, Louisiana. Association for Computational Linguistics.

Myle Ott, Sergey Edunov, Alexei Baevski, Angela Fan, Sam Gross, Nathan Ng, David Grangier, and Michael Auli. 2019. fairseq: A fast, extensible toolkit for sequence modeling. In *Proceedings of the 2019 Conference of the North American Chapter of the Association for Computational Linguistics (Demonstrations)*, pages 48–53, Minneapolis, Minnesota. Association for Computational Linguistics.

Robert Parker, David Graff, Ke Chen, Junbo Kong, and Kazuaki Maeda. 2011. Arabic gigaword fifth edition. https://doi.org/10.35111/p02g-rw14.

Aziz Qaroush, Ibrahim Abu Farha, Wasel T. Ghanem, Mahdi Washaha, and Eman Maali. 2021. An efficient single document Arabic text summarization using a combination of statistical and semantic features. *J. King Saud Univ. Comput. Inf. Sci.*, 33:677–692.

Lamees Al Qassem, Di Wang, Hassan Barada, Ahmad Al-Rubaie, and Nawaf Almoosa. 2019. Automatic Arabic text summarization based on fuzzy logic. In *Proceedings of the 3rd International Conference on Natural Language and Speech Processing*, pages 42–48, Trento, Italy. Association for Computational Linguistics.

Colin Raffel, Noam Shazeer, Adam Roberts, Katherine Lee, Sharan Narang, Michael Matena, Yanqi Zhou, Wei Li, and Peter J. Liu. 2020. Exploring the limits of transfer learning with a unified text-to-text transformer. *Journal of Machine Learning Research*, 21(140):1–67.

Sascha Rothe, Shashi Narayan, and Aliaksei Severyn. 2020. Leveraging pre-trained checkpoints for sequence generation tasks. *Transactions of the Association for Computational Linguistics*, 8:264–280.

Alexander M. Rush, Sumit Chopra, and Jason Weston. 2015. A neural attention model for abstractive sentence summarization. In *Proceedings of the 2015 Conference on Empirical Methods in Natural Language Processing*, pages 379–389, Lisbon, Portugal. Association for Computational Linguistics.

Abigail See, Peter J. Liu, and Christopher D. Manning. 2017. Get to the point: Summarization with pointer-generator networks. In *Proceedings of the 55th Annual Meeting of the Association for Computational Linguistics (Volume 1: Long Papers)*, pages 1073–1083, Vancouver, Canada. Association for Computational Linguistics.

Yunfan Shao, Zhichao Geng, Yitao Liu, Junqi Dai, Fei Yang, Li Zhe, Hujun Bao, and Xipeng Qiu. 2021. Cpt: A pre-trained unbalanced transformer for both chinese language understanding and generation.

Dima Suleiman and Arafat Awajan. 2020. Deep learning based abstractive arabic text summarization using two layers encoder and one layer decoder. *Journal of Theoretical and Applied Information Technology*, 98:3233.

Webz.io. 2016. Webz.io's Arabic news articles. https://webz.io/free-datasets/arabic-news-articles/.

Linting Xue, Noah Constant, Adam Roberts, Mihir Kale, Rami Al-Rfou, Aditya Siddhant, Aditya Barua, and Colin Raffel. 2021. mT5: A massively multilingual pre-trained text-to-text transformer. In *Proceedings of the 2021 Conference of the North American Chapter of the Association for Computational Linguistics: Human Language Technologies*, pages 483–498, Online. Association for Computational Linguistics.

Tianyi Zhang, Varsha Kishore, Felix Wu, Kilian Q. Weinberger, and Yoav Artzi. 2020. Bertscore: Evaluating text generation with bert. In *International Conference on Learning Representations*.

Qingyu Zhou, Nan Yang, Furu Wei, Shaohan Huang, Ming Zhou, and Tiejun Zhao. 2018. Neural document summarization by jointly learning to score and select sentences. In *Proceedings of the 56th Annual Meeting of the Association for Computational Linguistics (Volume 1: Long Papers)*, pages 654–663, Melbourne, Australia. Association for Computational Linguistics.

A Example Input Documents

(a)	نضال حسن واعترف نضال حسن، الذي يدافع عن نفسه، بقتل الجنود، متحججا بحماية المسلمين وعناصر طالبان في أفغانستان، ولكن القاضي العسكري رفض حجته "بحماية الآخرين". وإذا أدين حسن، البالغ من العمر 42 عاما، بقتل 13 شخصا وجرح آخرين فإنه سيواجه عقوبة الإعدام. ويعتبر الحادث الأكثر دموية من بين الهجمات غير القتالية التي وقعت في قاعدة عسكرية أمريكية. وقال شهود عيان دخل في 5 نوفمبر/تشرين الثاني عام 2009 مصحة تعج بالجنود الذين كانوا ينتظرون أدوارهم إجراء فحوصات طبية أو التلقيح، ثم صعد على مكتب، وأطلق النار من سلاحين بيديه، دون توقف إلا لإعادة تعبئة السلاح. مواضيع قد تهمك نهاية وسيقدم ممثلو الادعاء أدلة تفيد بأن حسن مال إلى الأفكار المتطرفة، وكان يزور المواقع بحثا عن "الجهاديين" وطالبان، ساعات قبل الهجوم. وكان الرائد حسن سيلتحق بالقوات الأمريكية في أفغانستان قبل أن ينفذ هجومه. "عنف في مكان العمل" وصنفت وزارة الدفاع الأمريكية الحادث باعتباره "عنفا في مكان العمل" بدلا من تصنيفه "عملا إرهابيا"، وهو ما أغضب عئلات الضحايا، حسب ما أفاد به مراسل بي بي سي، نك براينت، في فروت هود. ويتوقع أن يدلي العديد من جرحى الحادث بشاهاداتهم أمام المحكمة. وسيواجه حسن عددا من ضحاياه في قاعة المحكمة لأنه سيتولى الدفاع عن نفسه. وهو يستخدم كرسيا متحركا لأنه أصيب بالشلل، عندما أطلق عليه شرطي في القاعدة العسكرية النار.
(b)	روجر مور ونال مور شهرة عالمية لادائه دور الجاسوس جيمس بوند. وأعلنت اسرته نبأ وفاته عن طريق تغريدة في تويتر نشرتها في حسابه الرسمي. وقال اولاده في التغريدة، "بقلب يعتصره الأسى، نعلن عن ان والدنا الحبيب السير روجر مور وافته المنية اليوم في سويسرا بعد صراع قصير ولكن بطولي مع مرض السرطان." وجاء في التغريدة، "نحن منكوبون. شكرا يا أبانا لأنك من أنت ولكونك عزيزا عند العديد من الناس." وأصبح مور، بفضل السنوات الـ 12 التي قضاها في اداء دور بوند، مليونيرا وشخصية محبوبة حول العالم. بدأ مور مساره الفني في ستينيات القرن الماضي، ولكن شهرته لم تنطلق بشكل حقيقي حتى عام 1973، عندما اختير لاداء دور بوند في فيلم " Live and Let Die". أدى مور دور البطولة في 6 من افلام جيمس بوند التالية، كان آخرها فيلم " A View to a Kill" في عام 1985 عندما كان يبلغ من العمر 57 عاما. وكان من آخر نجوم "المدرسة القديمة" من النجوم السينمائيين من امثال فرانك سيناترا وديفيد نيفين. وفي السنوات التالية، عرف مور بنشاطاته الانسانية، وعلى وجه الخصوص ما قام به كسفير لمنظمة يونيسيف لجمع التبرعات للاطفال الفقراء. وقال اولاد مور إن والدهم كان يعتبر عمله مع يونيسيف "اعظم انجازاته". وستجرى مراسم دفنه في موناكو.
(c)	وتوصل علماء إلى أن خليط المواد الكيماوية في السجائر ضار على نحو خاص بعملية تشكيل خلايا الكبد. وابتكر العلماء أسلوبا لدراسة أثر تدخين الأمهات على أنسجة الكبد، وذلك باستخدام تحليل خلايا جذعية جنينية. ووجد فريق العلماء، الذين قادتهم جامعة إدنبرة، أن تأثير المواد الكيماوية في السجائر يتفاوت بين أجنة الذكور وأجنة الإناث. وأثناء الدراسة، استخدم الباحثون خلايا جذعية محفزة - وهي خلايا قادرة على التحول إلى أشكال أخرى من الخلايا - في تخليق أنسجة كبد جنينية. وتم تعريض خلايا الكبد المخلقة للمواد الكيماوية الضارة الموجودة في السجائر، بما في ذلك مواد معينة من المعروف أنها منتشرة في الأجنة التي تكون أمهاتها من المدخنين. وأظهرت الدراسة أن خليطا كيماويا - يشبه ذلك الموجود في السجائر - ألحق أضرارا بحالة الكبد أكثر من التأثير السلبي الذي تخلفه كل مادة منها على حدة. أضرار دائمة وقال الطبيب دايفيد هاي، من مركز الطب التجديدي بجامعة إدنبرة، إن "دخان السجائر معروف بآثاره الضارة على الأجنة، لكننا نفتقر إلى الأدوات المناسبة لدراسة هذه الظاهرة بالتفصيل اللازم". وأضاف هاي "هذا المنهج الجديد يعني أن لدينا الآن مصادر لأنسجة متجددة، وهو ما يمكننا من فهم الأثر الخلوي للسجائر على الأجنة". ويلعب الكبد دورا هاما في مساعدة الجسم على التخلص من المواد السامة، بالإضافة إلى دوره الرئيسي في تنظيم عملية التمثيل الغذائي. وتحتوي السجائر على سبعة آلاف مادة كيماوية قد يؤدي تدخينها إلى تلف أعضاء الأجنة، وإلى أضرار دائمة. وسلطت الدراسة، التي جرت بالتعاون مع جامعتي أبردين وغلاسغو، الضوء على الفرق بين تأثير تدخين السجائر أجنة الذكور وأجنة الإناث. وظهرت ندوب في أنسجة أجنة الذكور، بينما لحق ضرر أكثر بالتمثيل الغذائي لخلايا أجنة الإناث. وقال بول فاولر، مدير معهد علوم الطب بجامعة أبردين، إن "هذا العمل جزء من مشروع يستهدف التعرف على الآثار الضارة لتدخين الأمهات أثناء الحمل على الأجنة في الأطوار المختلفة من النمو". وأضاف فاولر أن "هذه النتائج سلطت الضوء على الفروق الأساسية بين الأضرار التي تتعرض لها أجنة الذكور وأجنة الإناث". ونُشرت نتائج الدراسة في دورية أرشيف علم السموم.

Figure 3: The input news articles corresponding to the summaries in Figure 1

Towards Arabic Sentence Simplification via Classification and Generative Approaches

Nouran Khallaf
University of Leeds, UK
Alexandria University, Egypt
mlnak@leeds.ac.uk

Serge Sharoff , Rasha Soliman
University of Leeds, UK
s.sharoff,r.k.soliman@leeds.ac.uk

Abstract

This paper presents an attempt to build a Modern Standard Arabic (MSA) sentence-level simplification system. We experimented with sentence simplification using two approaches: (i) a classification approach leading to lexical simplification pipelines which use Arabic-BERT, a pre-trained contextualised model, as well as a model of fastText word embeddings; and (ii) a generative approach, a Seq2Seq technique by applying a multilingual Text-to-Text Transfer Transformer mT5. We developed our training corpus by aligning the original and simplified sentences from the internationally acclaimed Arabic novel "Saaq al-Bambuu". We evaluate effectiveness of these methods by comparing the generated simple sentences to the target simple sentences using the BERTScore evaluation metric. The simple sentences produced by the mT5 model achieve P 0.72, R 0.68 and F-1 0.70 via BERTScore, while, combining Arabic-BERT and fastText achieves P 0.97, R 0.97 and F-1 0.97. In addition, we report a manual error analysis for these experiments.

1 Introduction

Text Simplification (TS) is a Natural Language Processing (NLP) task that aims to reduce the linguistic complexity of the text while maintaining its meaning and original information (Saggion, 2017; Siddharthan, 2002; Collados, 2013). According to Shardlow (2014) definition, TS involves text transformation with new lexical items and/or rewriting sentences to ensure both its readability and understandability for the target audience (Bott and Saggion, 2011). TS could be classified as a type of Text Style Transfer (TST), where the target style of the generated text is "simple" (Jin et al., 2020). Evidence suggests the importance of TS involves : (i) its usage in designing and simplifying the language curriculum for both second language and first language learners, in making text easy-to-read for first language early learners; in assisting first-language users with cognitive impairments and low literacy language level; (ii) being a fundamental pre-process in NLP applications such as text retrieval, extraction, summarization, categorization and translation (Saggion, 2017); and (iii) acting as a post-process step in Automatic speech recognition. Hence, there are various types of simplification systems based on the purpose and who is the end-user of the system. There are three key aspects of simple text that: (i) it is made up of frequent simple words, grammatically simple sentences, and direct language; (ii) unnecessary information is omitted ; (iii) it can be shorter by the number of words, but also with shorter sentences, which might lead to their increased number (Bott and Saggion, 2011; Collados, 2013). Collados (2013) approached TS differently as he came up with different opinion, that is a slightly simplified text for one user is generally simpler for any other users. But a more extensive simplification for a specific user, may lead to a more complex text for another user. Most of TS techniques were borrowed from closely related NLP tasks such as Machine Translation (Sikka and Mago, 2020) . This has influenced our experiments to demonstrate the effectiveness of two different methods to address the sentence simplification (SS) task as follows:

(1) Classification Approach SS is considered as a classification task that requires a decision on which word to replace or syntactic structure to regenerate in each complex sentence. This approach allows the application of the Lexical Simplification (LS) task pipeline, i.e that aims to control the readability attribute of the text and make it more accessible to different readers with various intellectual abilities. LS particularly involves word change, thus we experiment the effect of different embedding representation on word classification decision. This approach highlights the impact of how the text is simplified either by applying word embedding, or

Proceedings of the The Seventh Arabic Natural Language Processing Workshop (WANLP), pages 43 - 52
December 8, 2022

contextualised embedding such as BERT (Devlin et al., 2018).

(2) Generative Approach SS is considered as a translation task, in which the translation is done within the same language from a complex sentence as the source to a simplified sentence as the target (Zhu et al., 2010). According to this perspective, SS generative model could be implemented using Machine Translation (MT) and monolingual text-to-text generation techniques. Thus, we combined all SS steps into one process which learns from the complex sentence how to generate the simple version. For this purpose, we applied a BERT-like pre-trained transformer to perform a sequence-to-sequence (Seq2Seq) algorithm.

The main contribution of this paper is to examine different approaches for Arabic sentence simplification task using automatic and manual evaluation. To our knowledge, this is the first available Arabic sentence-level simplification system.

2 Corpus and Tools

The corpus used for training is a set of complex/simple parallel sentences that have been compiled from the internationally acclaimed Arabic novel "Saaq al-Bambuu" which has an authorized simplified version for students of Arabic as a second language (Familiar and Assaf, 2016). We assume that a successful sentence simplifier should be able to detect word/sentences in the original text that require simplification and simplify them in such a way as the original simple counterpart. The dataset consists of 2980 parallel sentences as illustrated in Table 1 and classified according to The Common European Framework of language proficiency Reference (CEFR) .i.e is an international standard for describing language ability ranging from A1, A2 ... up to C2.

Levels	**Sentence**	**Tokens**
Simple A+B	2980	34447
Complex C	2980	46521
Total	**5690**	80968

Table 1: Number of Sentences and Tokens available per each CEFR Level in Saaq al-Bambuu parallel corpus

We aligned the words in the parallel "Saaq al-Bambuu" sentences using Eflomal word aligning tool that uses a Bayesian model with Markov Chain Monte Carlo (MCMC) inference (Östling and Tiedemann, 2016). After aligning the words, we automatically identified four basic simplification types on word-level and sentence-level (Alva-Manchego et al., 2017), then annotate these types with the following labels :

- Deletions, DELETE (D) in the complex sentence. [word-level]
- Additions, ADD (A) in the simplified sentence. [sentence-level]
- Substitutions, REPLACE (R), a word in the complex sentence is replaced by a new word in the simplified sentence. [word-level]
- Rewrites, REWRITE (RW) words shared in both complex and simple sentence pairs. [sentence-level]

The overall calculation of the simplification processes in the "Saaq al-Bambuu" corpus illustrated in figure 1. The $REWRITE$ operation has the highest proportion of the simplification processes [keeping the word as it is in both versions] in which 21899 words were copied in the simplified version. Whereas, 12561 words have been deleted to simplify the sentence that annotated with $DELETE$ label. In the third position comes $REPLACE$ operation in which 9082 words where subsisted with their simple counterparts. At last, only 362 words were added to simplify the sentences that annotated with ADD label.

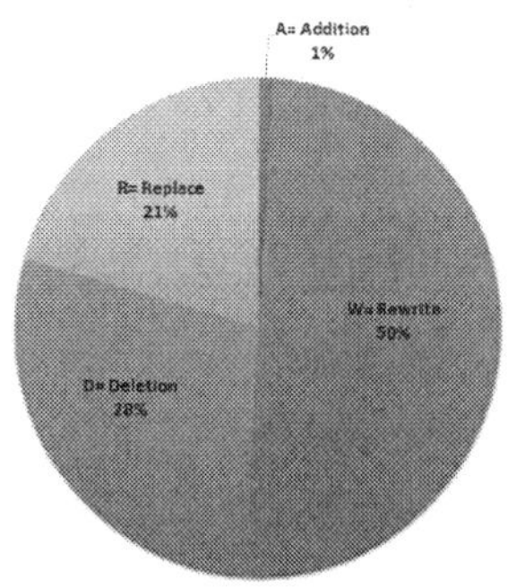

Figure 1: Represents the percentage of each simplification operation on Saaq al-bambuu corpus

Regarding Part-Of-Speech features (POS-features) extraction we used MADAMIRA a robust Arabic morphological analyser and part of speech tagger (Pasha et al., 2014).

3 Method One - Classification approach

The reference for this approach is the pipeline of the LS task, that focuses on LS by replacing complex vocabularies or phrasal-chunks with suitable substances (Paetzold and Specia, 2017b). To reach this goal, we decided to implement three classification models:

1. classification model which is based on *word embedding*, thus we applied ***fastText*** word embedding tool that represents words as vectors embedding.Those vectors embedding was trained on Common Crawl and Wikipedia. We used the Arabic ar.300.bin file in which each word in WE is represented by the 1D vector mapped of 300 attributes(Grave et al., 2018);
2. classification model which is based on *transformers*. Using ***Arabic-BERT*** a pre-trained transformer model on both filtered Arabic Common Crawl and a recent dump of Arabic Wikipedia contain approximately 8.2 Billion words (Safaya et al., 2020) ;
3. classification model combining both *fastText* and *Arabic-BERT* results with post-editing rules;

Considering the definition of the four main steps applied in the pipeline for LS as follows:

Complex word identification [CWI] is the main first step performed at the top of the pipeline that employed to distinguish complex words from simple words in the sentence. *Substitution Generation [SG]* involves generating all possible substitutions but without including ambiguous substances that would confuse the system in the Substitution Selection step. *Substitution Ranking [SR]* is to order the new generated substitution list to ease the selection step by giving high probability of the most appropriate highly ranked word. *Substitution Selection [SS]* is responsible for selecting from the ordered SG's generated list the most appropriate substitute according to the context while preserving the same meaning and grammatical structure.Taking into account the fact that, a word may have multiple meanings, and different meanings will have different relevant substitutions, then the SS task may generate a miss-substitution, which may lead to meaning corruption. The following part of this paper moves on to describe in greater detail the implementation of each step concentrating on employed methods and tools.

3.1 Complex word identification

CWI step could be viewed as a layered analysis opt for a better understanding of word complexity. Hence, we applied a lexicon-based approach. Taking into account one sentence per time, the first level relates to identifying POS-tags along with other features produced by MADAMIRA to be used in further steps. The second layer of analysis moved to assign each word a CEFR complexity level adopting a Lexical based approach using CEFR vocabulary Listas a reference to allocate each word in the target sentence to a readability level. At CWI, with identifying the complex words, these words become the targets to simplify. It is impractical to simplify all complex words in a sentence at once. So that ordering words according to their CEFR level and taking into account each of these words as the target per time to deploy the simplification process. For example, if a sentence has three complex words assigned with B2, C2, C1, firstly we order them to be C2, C1, and B2 and then start the simplification process with targeting C2 tagged word, followed by C1 and so on. In this example, this operation results in generating three sentences each with different masked word slot.

3.2 Substitution Generation and Ranking

These two steps were considered in one process using different methodologies to generate the substitution list and ranking them considering semantic similarity measures. For this purpose we obtained different sentence embedding to produce ten top ranked substitution list of the masked token.

3.2.1 Arabic-BERT prediction

Arabic-BERT model has different tasks to use in various NLP tasks. Here, for each *complex word* use applying BERT's task $MaskedLanguageModeling$ (MLM). This task predicts a substitution list of a masked [not shown, complex] token in a sequence given its left and right context. At this process, the MLM requires a concatenation between the original sequence and the same sentence sequence where the target word is replaced by [MASK] token as a sentence pair, and feed the sentence pair into the BERT to obtain the probability distribution of the possible replacements corresponding to the MASK word. **For example**, given this sentence from Arabic Wikipedia:

تَتطَلب مِن هَيئَة المَحكَمَة وُجوب تَحدِيد الحُقُوق

tatatalabu min hay'atu almaḥkamatu wujūba taḥdīda alḥuqūq

[require the judge or the court to necessarily determine the rights]

The ranking probability of Arabic-BERT's prediction list using fastText was shown on the right side of figure 2.

3.2.2 fastText prediction

Using *fastText* model in two folded processes, first ranking the previously produced substitutions obtained by MLM BERT. This is done by calculating the semantic cosine similarity between each word in the produced list to the target complex word. The second process is using fastText word embedding itself to generate a list of possible replacements [SG] and then ranking by the nearest neighbour [SR]. For example, the fastText generated list given the target complex word in the previous example is shown on the left side of the figure 2.

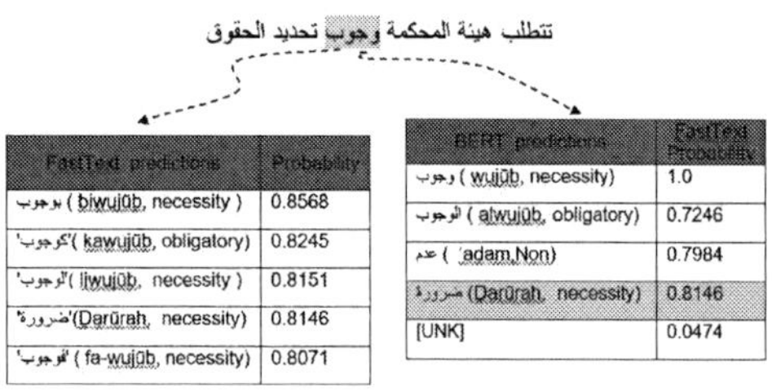

Figure 2: Arabic-BERT and fastText predication lists along with the probability obtained from fastText for the word "wujūba" ('وُجُوبَ', 'necessity')

3.3 Substitution Selection

At this stage, each complex word in the sentence has different ordered substituted lists based on Arabic-BERT and fastText. Taking into account each prediction list to analyse individually and select the more logical substitute based on the probabilities and some linguistics rules. This allowed the system to generate a set of simplified versions of the target sentence. In addition, keeping a record of the semantic similarity and the readability level of the new produced sentences. The system produces three different simple sentences based on Arabic-BERT substitute selection, fastText, and Combined decision from both generated lists. The combined decision is a very crucial stage and the system needs to be careful when selecting the best substitute based on different measures. Starting with the Arabic-BERT list, the greater the value the most common or familiar is the word for a person referring to simple words. If the word is tagged with replacement with [UNK] the decision is to ignore the results from Arabic-BERT and rely on fastText results. Then, applying the following four rules to limit incorrect selection:

1. `Rule1:` if [UNK] is a top-ranked substitute then go to fastText results.Check if the first substitute is [UNK] in this case the system completely ignores BERT results and keep the original then rely on FastText results immediately.

2. `Rule 2:` if any word's lemma in the generated list equal the lemma of the original word excludes these words from the list.Check if the lemmas in the predicted list matches the same lemma of the target word. In this case, we exclude these words from the potential replacement for the target word and keep only the words with a different lemma. These replacements should also share the same POS and Number with the target word.

3. `Rule 3:`CEFR list placement for difficulty. Check the word CEFR level of the new substitute word. The new word's CEFR level should be equal to or less than the CEFR level of the target word. Because sometimes the generated list may have a more frequent substitute which is more difficult than the original word but more frequent.

4. `Rule 4:` check if the new substitute shares the meaning. The system use this rule as it gives a level of confidence to the system selection. After the system makes the final decision either, keep the target word or select the suggested substitute based on previous rules. At this stage, comparing both target and substitute MADAMIRA English translation feature [appeared in Gloss feature]. If both words share part or all possible translation this gives the system confidence to replace the target with the substance.

4 Method Two: Generative Approach

Here, we employ a Seq2Seq approach adopting ***T5 "Text-to-Text Transfer Transformer"***. T5 is a BERT-like transformer that takes input a text and training it on the model to generate target text of a different variety of NLP text-based tasks such as (summarization, translation, question answering and more) (Raffel et al., 2019). The main difference between BERT and T5 is that BERT uses a Masked Language Model (MLM) and an encoder-decoder, although T5 employs a unified Seq2Seq framework (Farahani et al., 2021). T5 model initially targeted English-Language NLP tasks. Recent research extended the model to include more than 101 languages including the Arabic Language. A "multilingual Text-to-Text Transfer Transformer", Multilingual T5, mT5 (Xue et al., 2020), a new variant of T5 and pre-trained on Common Crawl-based dataset. The pre-trained language model was very successful for the Natural Language Understanding (NLU) task.

Considering the multilingual capabilities of mT5 and the suitability of the Seq2Seq format for language generation. This gives it the flexibility to perform any NLP task without having to modify the model architecture in any way. This experiment employs the 'MT5-For-Conditional-Generation' class that is used for language generation. Training a TS model using "Saaq al-Bambuu" parallel sentences, over the mT5-base model. The system was developed in $Python3.8$ environment with using other toolkits such as Natural Language Processing Toolkit $NLTK$ and $Scikit-learn$. Our sentence corpus was randomly split into 80% for training and 20% for testing.

5 Evaluation

Likewise, most TS evaluation approaches have been driven from other similar NLP research areas. Various evaluation methods have been applied across researches to measure the three main aspects of the newly generated text. These aspects are, i) fluency, referring to the grammatically well-formedness and structure simplicity; ii) adequacy, meaning preservation; iii) simplicity, more readable. All methods were evaluated on the same test dataset that consisted of 299 randomly chosen sentences excluded from training. We employed both automatic and manual evaluation comparing both systems.

5.1 Automatic Evaluation

BERTScore is an evaluation metric that computes cosine similarity scores using BERT-style embedding from a pre-trained transformer model. As such models provide a better representation of the linguistic structure, BERTScore evaluation correlates better with human judgments regarding the measurements of sentence similarity. BERTScore evaluation metric overcome the limitations of the previous Machine translation evaluation metrics such as BLEU(Papineni et al., 2002) and SARI(Xu et al., 2016), n-gram based evaluation metrics. These methods were not able to capture two main simplification features: 1) changing word order as paraphrasing simplification method, 2) maintaining the deep structure meaning, despite changes in the surface form structure. Moreover, the BERTScore evaluation method gives the option to use different pre-trained transformer models by applying *baseline rescaling* to adjust the output scores. This allowed determining the performance of different Arabic-language trained BERT models;(i) the default in multilingual BERT (mBERT)(Devlin et al., 2018) that is based on the selected language which is Arabic in this case; (ii) ARBERT, that trained on a collection of six Arabic datasets comprising 61GB of text (6.2B tokens) (Abdul-Mageed et al., 2021); (iii)AraBERTv0.2-base model consist of 77GB of sentences (8.6B tokens) (Antoun et al., 2020). However, AraBERT has been trained on a larger corpus than ARBERT, the latter uses WordPeice tokeniser as illustrated before. Whereas, AraBERT relies on SentencePiece tokeniser that uses spaces as word boundaries. Considering these two parameters reflected in BERTScore metrics.

Classification approach - Automatic Evaluation The classification system produced three simple versions of the target sentence using BERT-alone, fastText-alone, and combined version. This automatic evaluation was applied to compare different BERT models resolutions of these sentences as represented in Table 2. Figure 3 represents the number of changes performed by each classification model. These primarily results suggests that using fastText-alone perform unneeded simplification resulting in lower F-1. Whereas, a higher F-1 measure in Arabic-BERT-alone generated sentence suggest that using BERT eliminate necessary changes. While the combination of both tools suggestions enhances the substitution ranking and choice process. That eliminates unnecessary changes and enhance performance. In this case, combined produced sentences achieved P 0.97, R 0.97 and F-1 0.97 using ARBERT.

Generative Approach-Automatic Evaluation Testing the 299 sentences for evaluating the generated simplified sequences compared to the original sentences and the target simple sentences. Using three measures as presented in Table 2.

Classification	P	R	F1
	Default mBert		
Target/fastText	0.962	0.966	0.964
Target /BERT	0.991	0.990	**0.990**
Target / Combined	0.974	0.975	0.975
	ARBERT		
Target/fastText	0.958	0.960	0.959
Target /BERT	0.990	0.991	**0.990**
Target / Combined	0.976	0.976	0.978
	AraBERT		
Target/fastText	0.962	0.963	0.963
Target /BERT	0.989	0.989	0.989
Target / Combined	0.975	0.976	0.976

Generation	P	R	F1
	Default mBert		
Original/Target	0.889	0.838	0.862
Generated/Original	0.806	0.725	0.762
Generated/ Target	0.754	0.723	0.736
	ARBERT		
Original/Target	0.840	0.754	0.790
Generated/Original	0.647	0.529	0.573
Generated/ Target	0.570	0.524	0.538
	AraBERT		
Original/Target	0.879	0.823	0.848
Generated/Original	0.787	0.693	0.734
Generated/ Target	0.723	0.686	0.701

Table 2: Precision, recall and F1 measures using BERTScore with different transformer models

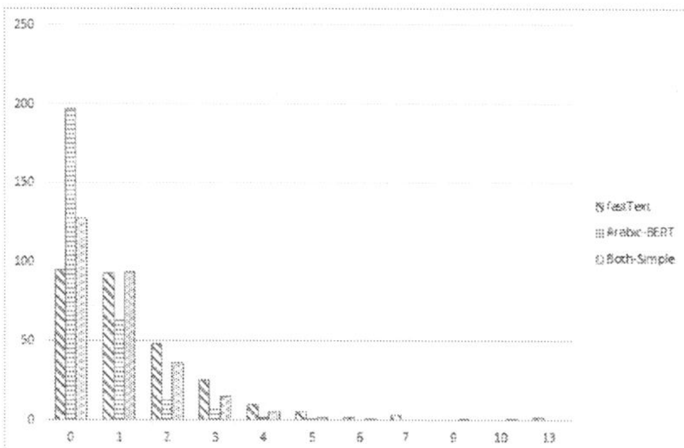

Figure 3: number of changed words using fastText-alone, Arabic-Bert-alone and combined

- Original/Target, considering it as a reference to the mT5 system.
- Generated/Original, comparing the newly generated sentence with the original complex sentence.
- Generated/Target, comparing the newly generated sentence with the target simple sentence.

To further illustrate these three models' performance, figure 4, represents the distribution of F-1 across the testing data instances using different BERT models. The default model F-1 plots skewed towards the right reflecting strong similarity across the three parallel sentences (Original/Target/Generated). Whereas, AraBERT plots Original/Target and Generated/Original skewed to the left indicating less similarity across the data. While, ARBERT's plots represent a normal distribution representing a more accurate similarity measure in the data. This findings suggests ARBERT that applying a WordPeice sentence tokeniser BERT model performed better in sentence representation.

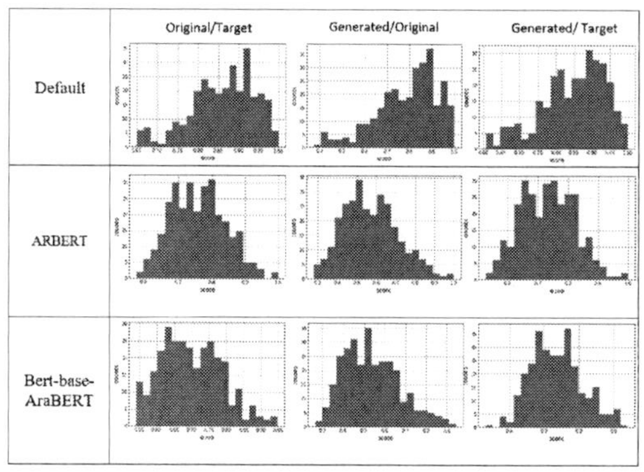

Figure 4: The F1 scores for each sentence pair, the scores are more spread out, which makes it easy to compare different methods

5.2 Manual Evaluation

Classification Approach - Manual Evaluation a manual analysis of the produced sentences of combined system has been performed. The results displayed in figure5 on a scale of good, useful, a bit useful, and useless simplification. 55% of the new simplified sentences were either good, useful or a bit useful as a majority. While 45% of the sentences were classified as useless simplification where the complex word was replaced either by a more complex word or its antonym. For example, a useful simplification from the combined system as in this sentence from "Saaq al-Bambuu",

كُنتُ أحدق فِي الطَبَق وَالصَمت يَكَادُ يَبتَلع المَكَان

Kuntu 'uḥaddiqu fī alṭabaqi wa-al-ṣamtu yakādu yabtali' al-makān.

[I was staring at the plate and the silence almost swallowed up the place.]

In this sentence, the word 'أحَدِق' (*uḥaddiqu*,' staring') was replaced by أتَأمَل ('ata'mmalu, 'muse'), that is more frequent and simpler and generate:

كُنتُ أتَأمَل فِي الطَبَق وَالصَمت يَكَادُ يَبتَلع المَكَان

Although, it is simpler it doesn't reach the exact target word أنظُر ('Anẓuru, 'look')

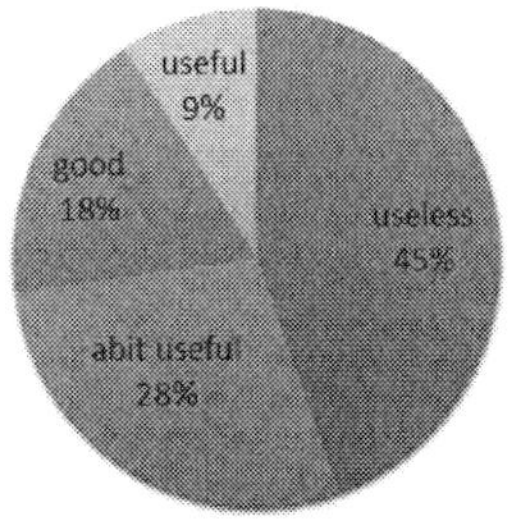

Figure 5: Simplified sentences analysis based on the usefulness of the lexical substitution processes.

Generative Approach-Manual Evaluation despite the initial automatic evaluation provided promising results, the manual evaluation of the generated text provides deeper insight into mT5's output for the Arabic simplification task. According to the manual error analysis as shown in figure 6 only 31 sentences were correctly simplified from 299 testing instances. In addition, about 120 generated sentences were incomplete and the system produced 64 meaningless or ill-formed sentences. A significant shortcoming that the produced sentences tends to have the same repeated phrase. Moreover, one of the generated sentences were more complex than the original sentence.

Otherwise, mT5 in some cases can produce a perfectly valid paraphrase, which is better than the target simple sentence.

طَلب مِنَا الجلُوس فِي صَالُونَه المَلي، بِالكُتُب

ṭalab minnā al-julūs fī ṣālwnahu almaly' bi-al-kutub

[He asked us to sit in his salon full of books.]

فِي صَالُونَه الصَغير المَلي، بِالكُتُب **طَلب مِنا الجلُوس** أمَام مَكتَب صَغير

Fī ṣālunahu al-ṣaghīr almali' bil-kutubi, ṭalaba minnā al-julūsi 'amāma maktabi ṣaghīri

[In his small salon full of books, he asked us to sit in front of a small desk.] In this case, the generated sentence was syntactically simpler than the target while focusing on the main information.

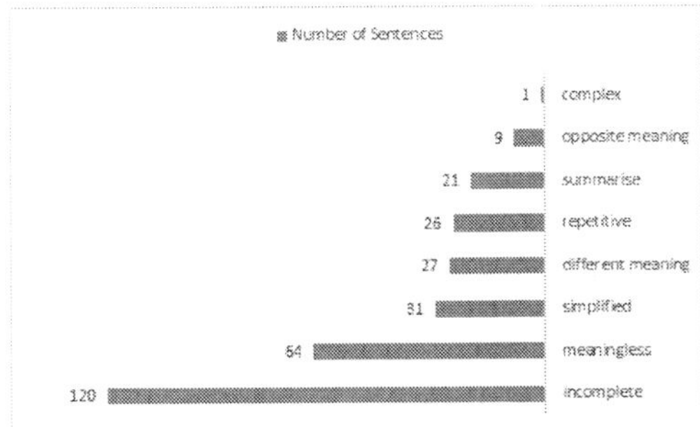

Figure 6: Manual error analysis distribution across testing data

6 Related Works

Blum and Levenston (1978) completed one of the first studies that introduce Lexical simplification for Teaching English as a Second Language (TESOL). Some of the following TS systems applied a rule-based approach (Petersen and Ostendorf, 2007; Evans et al., 2014). Most later carried out studies based on a monolingual parallel-aligned corpus of original and simplified texts by applying different machine-learning algorithms such as Aluísio et al. (2008) and Caseli et al. (2009) for Portuguese language, Collados (2013) for Spanish language and Glavaš and Štajner (2015) for English. Other researchers considered the TS problem as a monolingual translation problem that is best solved through applying the Statistical Machine Translation (SMT) framework (Specia, 2010; Zhu et al., 2010; Woodsend and Lapata, 2011; Wubben et al., 2012). Latest English TS studies start applying word embedding(Paetzold and Specia, 2016, 2017a) and BERT transformers for lexical simplification as presented in Qiang et al. (2020) proving its effectiveness in solving LS task.

Unlike English and Other Latin languages, only a few researchers have been tackling the problems of Arabic ATS. Al-Subaihin and Al-Khalifa (2011) a prototype unreleased system at King Saud University, they proposed Arabic Automatic Text simplification system (AATS) called Al-basset. The system architecture for AATS structured in the light of the state of the art of systems for other languages. Such as SYSTAR, a syntactic simplification system for the English aphasic or inarticulate population(Carroll et al., 1998). Another system, SIMPLIFICA, is a simplification tool for Brazilian Portuguese (BP) targeting those with low literacy levels (Scarton et al., 2010). The design of "Al-Basset" was constructed of four main stages: i) measuring complexity, in this stage they would adopt a statistical language model based on a machine learning technique called ARABILITY (Al-Khalifa and Al-Ajlan, 2010); ii) vocabulary (lexical) simplification by following the LS-pipeline and produce the synonyms either by building a new dictionary or using Arabic-WordNet(Rodríguez et al., 2008) while select the most common and possible synonym, by using the Google API; iii) syntactic simplification, they suggested identifying the complex structures by applying a look-up approach to a manually predefined list of Arabic complex structures; iv) diacratization using MADA(Habash et al., 2009) diacritizer task. The main limitation of implementing this system at this point is the unavailability of Arabic basic resources and tools. Such as dictionaries, corpora and parallel complex-simple structures which are the main components of any ATS system.

Al Khalil et al. (2017) provided the second attempt to build an AATS system at New York University in Abu-Dhabi. Their simplification system was designed to be semi-automatic to simplify Arabic modern fiction; it involved a linguist using a web-based application to apply ACTFL (American Council on the Teaching of Foreign Languages) language proficiency guidelines for simplification of five Arabic novels. They aimed to provide essential Arabic resources for building ATS and formulating manual simplification rules for Arabic fiction novels using TS stat-of-the-art. The first resource they expected to produce is a corpus consisting of 1M tokens of the 12-grade curriculum, 5M tokens of the adult novels (original and simplified counterparts), and 500K tokens of children's stories. Also, they provided a proposal to the SAMER (Simplification of Arabic Masterpieces for extensive reading) project based on the corpus analysis. Their guidelines invoke both the MADAMIRA (Pasha et al., 2014) and CAMAL dependency parser (Shahrour et al., 2016) for data analysis and classification of their corpus. They were aiming to build a readability measurement identifier to formulate a 4-levelled graded reader scale (GRS) by applying various machine-learning classifiers.

7 Conclusion

In this paper, we have presented the first Modern Standard Arabic sentence simplification system by applying both classification and generative approaches. On the one hand, the classification approach focuses on lexical simplification. We looked at the different classification methods and showed that a combined method generates well-formed simple sentences. In addition, using word embeddings and transformers prove to produce a reasonable set of substitutions for the complex word more accurately than traditional methods such as WordNet. Our interpretation of the limitation of the classification system arises from the fact that some of the generated sentence structures are not well-formed and that the system can misidentify what makes some complex words in the CWI step. Even though this limitation reveals the limitations of the Arabic CEFR vocabulary list in identifying the complex word, the list is shown to be more useful in the substitution replacement step.

On the other hand, while the generative Seq2Seq approach provides a less accurate simplified version in most cases, in some cases it outperforms the classification approaches by generating a simplified sentence, which can be even better than the target human simple sentence. Nevertheless, one of the limitations of the generative approach concerns the trend to repeat identical patterns, which can be partly controlled by post-processing.

8 Limitations

We have discussed the relative limitations of the two approaches in the paper. Overall, our paper relies on a single parallel resource. When other datasets become available, it will be important to experiment with them. With the use of pre-trained models, the requirements for training models from scratch are relatively low.

9 Ethics Statement

This paper is the authors' own original work, which has not been previously published elsewhere.

References

Muhammad Abdul-Mageed, AbdelRahim Elmadany, and El Moatez Billah Nagoudi. 2021. ARBERT &

MARBERT: Deep bidirectional transformers for Arabic. In *Proceedings of the 59th Annual Meeting of the Association for Computational Linguistics and the 11th International Joint Conference on Natural Language Processing (Volume 1: Long Papers)*, pages 7088–7105, Online. Association for Computational Linguistics.

Hend S Al-Khalifa and Amani A Al-Ajlan. 2010. Automatic readability measurements of the arabic text: An exploratory study. *Arabian Journal for Science and Engineering*, 35(2 C):103–124.

Muhamed Al Khalil, Nizar Habash, and Hind Saddiki. 2017. Simplification of arabic masterpieces for extensive reading: A project overview. *Procedia Computer Science*, 117:192–198.

Afnan A Al-Subaihin and Hend S Al-Khalifa. 2011. Albaseet: A proposed simplification authoring tool for the arabic language. In *2011 International Conference on Communications and Information Technology (ICCIT)*, pages 121–125. IEEE.

Sandra M Aluísio, Lucia Specia, Thiago AS Pardo, Erick G Maziero, and Renata PM Fortes. 2008. Towards brazilian portuguese automatic text simplification systems. In *Proceedings of the eighth ACM symposium on Document engineering*, pages 240–248.

Fernando Alva-Manchego, Joachim Bingel, Gustavo Paetzold, Carolina Scarton, and Lucia Specia. 2017. Learning how to simplify from explicit labeling of complex-simplified text pairs. In *Proceedings of the Eighth International Joint Conference on Natural Language Processing (Volume 1: Long Papers)*, pages 295–305.

Wissam Antoun, Fady Baly, and Hazem Hajj. 2020. Arabert: Transformer-based model for arabic language understanding. *arXiv preprint arXiv:2003.00104*.

Shoshana Blum and Eddie A Levenston. 1978. Universals of lexical simplification. *Language learning*, 28(2):399–415.

Stefan Bott and Horacio Saggion. 2011. An unsupervised alignment algorithm for text simplification corpus construction. In *Proceedings of the Workshop on Monolingual Text-To-Text Generation*, pages 20–26.

John Carroll, Guido Minnen, Yvonne Canning, Siobhan Devlin, and John Tait. 1998. Practical simplification of english newspaper text to assist aphasic readers. In *Proceedings of the AAAI-98 Workshop on Integrating Artificial Intelligence and Assistive Technology*, pages 7–10. Citeseer.

Helena M Caseli, Tiago F Pereira, Lucia Specia, Thiago AS Pardo, Caroline Gasperin, and Sandra Maria Aluísio. 2009. Building a brazilian portuguese parallel corpus of original and simplified texts. *Advances in Computational Linguistics, Research in Computer Science*, 41:59–70.

José Camacho Collados. 2013. *Syntactic Simplification for Machine Translation*. Ph.D. thesis, Wolverhampton, United Kingdom.

Jacob Devlin, Ming-Wei Chang, Kenton Lee, and Kristina Toutanova. 2018. Bert: Pre-training of deep bidirectional transformers for language understanding. *arXiv preprint arXiv:1810.04805*.

Richard Evans, Constantin Orasan, and Iustin Dornescu. 2014. An evaluation of syntactic simplification rules for people with autism. In *Online Open-source*. Association for Computational Linguistics.

Laila Familiar and Tanit Assaf. 2016. *Saud al-Sanousi's Saaq al-Bambuu: The Authorized Abridged Edition for Students of Arabic*. Georgetown University Press.

Mehrdad Farahani, Mohammad Gharachorloo, Marzieh Farahani, and Mohammad Manthouri. 2021. Parsbert: Transformer-based model for persian language understanding. *Neural Processing Letters*, 53(6):3831–3847.

Goran Glavaš and Sanja Štajner. 2015. Simplifying lexical simplification: Do we need simplified corpora? In *Proceedings of the 53rd Annual Meeting of the Association for Computational Linguistics and the 7th International Joint Conference on Natural Language Processing (Volume 2: Short Papers)*, pages 63–68.

Edouard Grave, Piotr Bojanowski, Prakhar Gupta, Armand Joulin, and Tomas Mikolov. 2018. Learning word vectors for 157 languages. *arXiv preprint arXiv:1802.06893*.

Nizar Habash, Owen Rambow, and Ryan Roth. 2009. Mada+ tokan: A toolkit for arabic tokenization, diacritization, morphological disambiguation, pos tagging, stemming and lemmatization. In *Proceedings of the 2nd international conference on Arabic language resources and tools (MEDAR), Cairo, Egypt*, volume 41, page 62.

Di Jin, Zhijing Jin, Zhiting Hu, Olga Vechtomova, and Rada Mihalcea. 2020. Deep learning for text style transfer: A survey. *arXiv preprint arXiv:2011.00416*.

Robert Östling and Jörg Tiedemann. 2016. Efficient word alignment with Markov Chain Monte Carlo. *Prague Bulletin of Mathematical Linguistics*, 106:125–146.

Gustavo Paetzold and Lucia Specia. 2016. Semeval 2016 task 11: Complex word identification. In *Proceedings of the 10th International Workshop on Semantic Evaluation (SemEval-2016)*, pages 560–569.

Gustavo Paetzold and Lucia Specia. 2017a. Lexical simplification with neural ranking. In *Proceedings of the 15th Conference of the European Chapter of the Association for Computational Linguistics: Volume 2, Short Papers*, pages 34–40.

Gustavo H Paetzold and Lucia Specia. 2017b. A survey on lexical simplification. *Journal of Artificial Intelligence Research*, 60:549–593.

Kishore Papineni, Salim Roukos, Todd Ward, and Wei-Jing Zhu. 2002. Bleu: a method for automatic evaluation of machine translation. In *Proceedings of the 40th annual meeting of the Association for Computational Linguistics*, pages 311–318.

Arfath Pasha, Mohamed Al-Badrashiny, Mona T Diab, Ahmed El Kholy, Ramy Eskander, Nizar Habash, Manoj Pooleery, Owen Rambow, and Ryan Roth. 2014. Madamira: A fast, comprehensive tool for morphological analysis and disambiguation of arabic. In *Lrec*, volume 14, pages 1094–1101.

Sarah E Petersen and Mari Ostendorf. 2007. Text simplification for language learners: a corpus analysis. In *Workshop on Speech and Language Technology in Education*. Citeseer.

Jipeng Qiang, Yun Li, Yi Zhu, Yunhao Yuan, and Xindong Wu. 2020. Lexical simplification with pretrained encoders. In *Proceedings of the AAAI Conference on Artificial Intelligence*, volume 34, pages 8649–8656.

Colin Raffel, Noam Shazeer, Adam Roberts, Katherine Lee, Sharan Narang, Michael Matena, Yanqi Zhou, Wei Li, and Peter J Liu. 2019. Exploring the limits of transfer learning with a unified text-to-text transformer. *arXiv preprint arXiv:1910.10683*.

Horacio Rodríguez, David Farwell, Javi Farreres, Manuel Bertran, Musa Alkhalifa, M Antonia Martí, William Black, Sabri Elkateb, James Kirk, Adam Pease, et al. 2008. Arabic wordnet: Current state and future extensions. In *Proceedings of The Fourth Global WordNet Conference, Szeged, Hungary*.

Ali Safaya, Moutasem Abdullatif, and Deniz Yuret. 2020. Kuisail at semeval-2020 task 12: Bert-cnn for offensive speech identification in social media. In *Proceedings of the Fourteenth Workshop on Semantic Evaluation*, pages 2054–2059.

Horacio Saggion. 2017. Automatic text simplification. *Synthesis Lectures on Human Language Technologies*, 10(1):1–137.

Carolina Scarton, Matheus Oliveira, Arnaldo Candido Jr, Caroline Gasperin, and Sandra Aluísio. 2010. Simplifica: a tool for authoring simplified texts in brazilian portuguese guided by readability assessments. In *Proceedings of the NAACL HLT 2010 Demonstration Session*, pages 41–44.

Anas Shahrour, Salam Khalifa, Dima Taji, and Nizar Habash. 2016. Camelparser: A system for arabic syntactic analysis and morphological disambiguation. In *Proceedings of COLING 2016, the 26th International Conference on Computational Linguistics: System Demonstrations*, pages 228–232.

Matthew Shardlow. 2014. A survey of automated text simplification. *International Journal of Advanced Computer Science and Applications*, 4(1):58–70.

Advaith Siddharthan. 2002. An architecture for a text simplification system. In *Language Engineering Conference, 2002. Proceedings*, pages 64–71. IEEE.

Punardeep Sikka and Vijay Mago. 2020. A survey on text simplification. *arXiv preprint arXiv:2008.08612*.

Lucia Specia. 2010. Translating from complex to simplified sentences. In *International Conference on Computational Processing of the Portuguese Language*, pages 30–39. Springer.

Kristian Woodsend and Mirella Lapata. 2011. Wikisimple: Automatic simplification of wikipedia articles. In *Proceedings of the AAAI Conference on Artificial Intelligence*, volume 25.

Sander Wubben, EJ Krahmer, and APJ van den Bosch. 2012. Sentence simplification by monolingual machine translation. *Proceedings of the 50th Annual Meeting of the Association for Computational Linguistics*.

Wei Xu, Courtney Napoles, Ellie Pavlick, Quanze Chen, and Chris Callison-Burch. 2016. Optimizing statistical machine translation for text simplification. *Transactions of the Association for Computational Linguistics*, 4:401–415.

Linting Xue, Noah Constant, Adam Roberts, Mihir Kale, Rami Al-Rfou, Aditya Siddhant, Aditya Barua, and Colin Raffel. 2020. mt5: A massively multilingual pre-trained text-to-text transformer. *arXiv preprint arXiv:2010.11934*.

Zhemin Zhu, Delphine Bernhard, and Iryna Gurevych. 2010. A monolingual tree-based translation model for sentence simplification. In *Proceedings of the 23rd International Conference on Computational Linguistics (Coling 2010)*, pages 1353–1361.

Generating Classical Arabic Poetry using Pre-trained Models

Maryam ElOraby*
Mohammed Abdelgaber*
Nehal Elkaref
Mervat Abu-Elkheir
German University in Cairo, Egypt
{maryam.eloraby,mohammed.abdelgaber,nehal.elkaref}@student.guc.edu.eg
mervat.abuelkheir@guc.edu.eg

Abstract

Poetry generation tends to be a complicated task given meter and rhyme constraints. Previous work resorted to exhaustive methods in-order to employ poetic elements. In this paper we leave pre-trained models, GPT-J and BERTShared to recognize patterns of meters and rhyme to generate classical Arabic poetry and present our findings and results on how well both models could pick up on these classical Arabic poetic elements.

1 Introduction

Arabic poetry dates back to the sixth century, making it the earliest form of Arabic literature. It's often divided into two categories; classical and modern poetry. The classical Arabic poetry refers to the poetry written before the 20th century, more specifically poetry that adheres to the rules of classical prosody (العروض *al-'arūd*); following meters or patterns of syllabic pulses, and a rhyme (القافية *al-qafiya*). Modern poetry, on the other hand, has liberated itself gradually from these rules.

Classical poetry is also called vertical poetry in reference to the vertical parallel structure of its two parts known as hemistichs. A classic poem is versified where each verse consists of two halves, each is called شطر *shatr* 'hemistich'. Each verse in a poem follows a meter. Meters fall into fifteen different categories collected by the grammarian and prosodist *Al-Farahidi*. Later, one of his students, *Al-Akhfash*, discovered one more meter making them sixteen.

2 Related Work

Generating poetry is not a straightforward task as there are rules that need to be maintained to ensure the presence of poetic elements such as rhythm and rhyme, whereby these constraints tend to be added as a part of the architecture of the model.

To model constraints during training, Hopkins and Kiela (2017) converted their training corpus into its corresponding phonetic encoding and trained a Long-Short Term Memory (LSTM) trained on these encodings. They also introduced another approach that had a character-level LSTM model trained on a generic corpus of poetry an upon outputting a word, it gets approved or rejected by a Finite State Acceptor (FSA) classifier which ensures that only meter abiding words can be a part of the final poem.

Ghazvininejad et al. (2016) created *Hafez*, a program trained to generate topical poetry. Their system relied on Recurrent Neural Networks (RNNs) for coherence and finite state machinery to constraint rhyme and rhythm. From prosaic text, Van de Cruys (2020) generated English and French poetry by having gated recurrent units (GRUs; Cho et al. (2014)) in an encoder-decoder setting and an added layer of general attention (Luong et al., 2015). To ingrain their output with poetic elements, they applied a prior probability distribution to their network's probability output, where probabilities relating to words abiding by rhyme and topic constraints were boosted.

RNNs have also been used without constrain, for example, to build on encoder-decoder architecture Yan (2016) created a network that constructs a poem during each iteration, which gets fed to the network during the following iteration, hence, each poem takes part in constructing the next. On the other hand, Zhang and Lapata (2014) reserved one RNN for building hidden representations for a current line of poetry which was then fed to another RNN that sequentially predicted words of the next line of poetry. Pre-trained models have been put to use to the same task as well. For instance, Beheitt and Hmida (2022) trained GPT-2 (Radford et al., 2019) on Arabic news then fine-tuned the model on Arabic poetry. Hämäläinen et al. (2022) made

* Contributed to the work equally.

Proceedings of the The Seventh Arabic Natural Language Processing Workshop (WANLP), pages 53 - 62
December 8, 2022 ©2022 Association for Computational Linguistics

use of an encoder-decoder architecture to generate modern French poetry, where the encoder is initialized from a pre-trained RoBERTa (Liu et al., 2019) checkpoint while the decoder is based on a pre-trained GPT-2 checkpoint. They scraped a corpus of French poems, and used it to train their model for sequence-to-sequence generation, where it predicts a verse given a previous verse in a poem. They also conditioned beam search on rhymes during the generation phase.

In our work we dedicate another two pre-trained models of different architectures to explore how effective they are at recognising patterns of classical Arabic poetry through the poems they are trained to generate.

3 Data

Initially, we compiled datasets of *ashaar*[1] and the *Arabic Poetry Dataset*[2]. Combined, each data sample was comprised of a poem's *era/country of origin*, *verses*, *author*, *meter* and a poem's *topic(s)*. Additional scraping was done from *al-diwan*[3] to fill in missing values and to add a new column to the dataset that is rhyme.
Furthermore, the dataset was tweaked to only contain poems from eight eras, the *Abbasid*, *Ayubi*, *Ottoman*, *Umayyad*, *Andalusian*, *Mamluk* eras and the *Pre-Islamic Period*. We target these eras as they have more structure compared to the Free Verse poetry which has no musical pattern or rhyme. We also chose to centralise our poems around 15 out of the main 16 meters of Arabic poetry and thus we removed meters variants from our corpus.

3.1 Meters

We depict meter frequency in Figure 1 and we can observe that the meters الطويل *al-Ṭawīl*, الكامل *al-Kāmil*, البسيط *al-Basīṭ*, and الوافر *al-Wāfir* are the most dominant, while the least frequent meters are المضارع *al-Muḍāri'* and المقتضب *al-Muqtaḍab*. Although such imbalance could be problematic but it is also reflective of the nature of classical Arabic poetry, where the aforementioned four most occurring meters were predominately utilised for writing poetry compared to other meters (Golston and Riad, 1997). Furthermore, المضارع *al-Muḍāri'* and المقتضب *al-Muqtaḍab* were rejected by most theoreticians, beginning with *Al-Akhfash*, who regarded them as artificial, fictitious, and not used in real poetry (Frolov, 1996). Each of the mentioned meters has its own unique sequence of *taf'īlāt 'feet'* where a line of poetry follows this pattern of feet in each of its' hemistich.

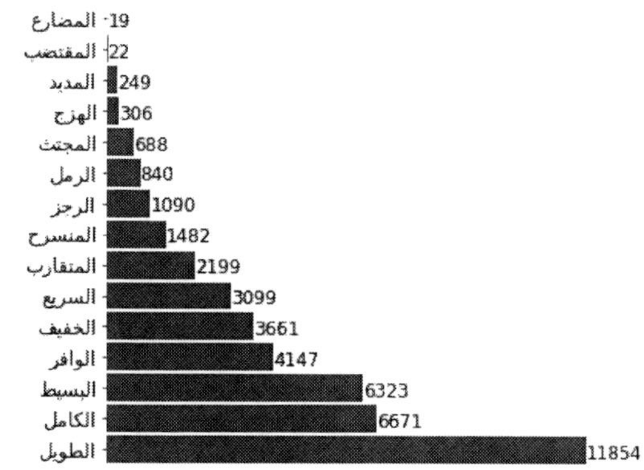

Figure 1: Meter Frequency

3.2 Topics

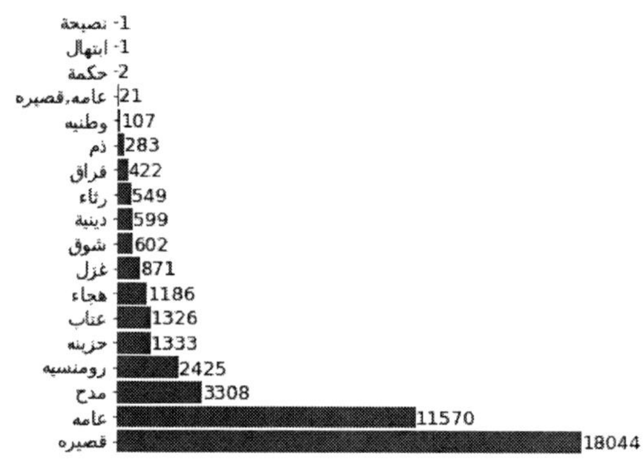

Figure 2: Topic Frequency

Poems in our targeted eras cover 17 different themes as shown in Figure 2. The most frequent topics are القصيرة *al-qṣyra* 'short' and العامة *al-'ama* 'generic'. As the the name of the former topic suggests, poems labelled as القصيرة *al-qṣyra* 'short' should have a small number of verses and accordingly we found that poems ranged from at least one verse to ten verses. However, we discovered that out of the entire 18K poems, 120 of them had more than 10 verses and four more had a substantially higher number of verses that reached over 50.

[1]https://huggingface.co/datasets/arbml/ashaar
[2]https://www.kaggle.com/datasets/ahmedabelal/arabic-poetry
[3]https://www.aldiwan.net

3.3 Rhymes

In vertical poems, a verse consists of two hemistichs. The second hemistichs of all verses within a poem are expected to end with the same letter. Figure 3 below contains present rhymes and their counts.

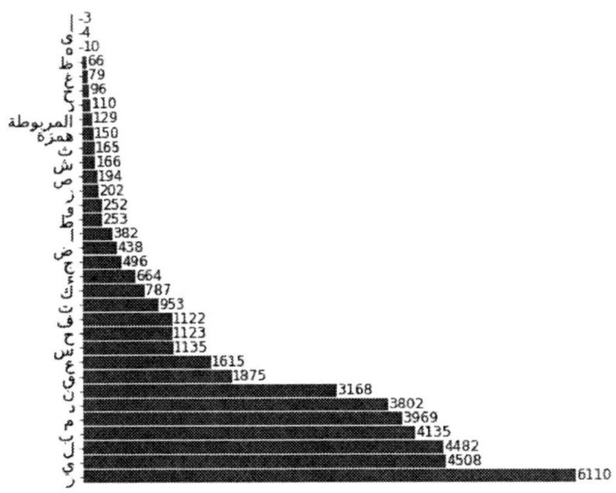

Figure 3: Rhyme Frequency

Rhymes could be consonants, short vowels or long vowels. Three of the Arabic short vowels written as diacritics have their long vowel version in letter form, and each pair is phonetically identical. In Table 1 we provide short vowels existing in our poems and their equivalent long vowel. In our dataset, a poem having a short vowel for a rhyme is labelled with its long vowel equivalent. Moreover, a short vowel and its corresponding long vowel could be used interchangeably within a poem. We can see an example of this in the following verses[4]:

وَلَمّا ابتَلى بِالحُبِ رَقَ لِشَكوَتي

وَما كانَ لَولا الحُبُ مِمَّن يَرِقُ لي

أُحِبُ الَّذي هامَ الحَبيبُ بِحُبِه

أَلا فَاعجَبوا مِن ذا الغَرامِ المُسَلسَلِ

The second and fourth lines constitute the second hemistichs of a verse. And as can be seen, the second half of the first verse ends with (ي) while the second half of the last verse ends with a consonant however preceded by the diacritic (اِ).

[4]Poem by Bulbul Gram Ahajery from the Ayubi era https://www.aldiwan.net/poem14884.html

Long Vowel	Short Vowel	Pronunciation
ي	اِ	/i/
ا	اَ	/a/
و	اُ	/u/

Table 1: Short vowels and their equivalent long vowels

4 Models

We experiment with training two different transformer-based architectures: encoder-decoder model and a decoder-only model to generate poetry based once on a prompted meter, and again on a prompted topic.

4.1 BERTShared

Transformer-based encoder-decoder models have shown to significantly boost performance on a variety of Seq2Seq (sequence-to-sequence) tasks (Lewis et al., 2020; Raffel et al., 2020). However, the pre-training of encoder-decoder models is highly costly (Zhang et al., 2020). Rothe et al. (2020) proved the efficacy of warm-starting the encoder-decoder models with the checkpoints of publicly available pre-trained language models, such as BERT and GPT-2, for various Seq2Seq tasks.

Adopting this approach, we used CAMelBERT-CA (Inoue et al., 2021), a BERT checkpoint pre-trained on classical Arabic text, to warm-start both the encoder and decoder. This checkpoint was chosen since the subset of poems we chose to work with is known a priori to be written in classical Arabic. We specifically experimented with BERTShared architecture, in which the parameters of the encoder and decoder are shared, reducing the model's memory footprint by half (Rothe et al., 2020).

The input to the encoder is a vector sequence $\mathbf{X}_{1:n_x}$ of length n_x and at the decoder the model generates an output sequence $\mathbf{Y}_{1:n_y}$ of length n_y. The model defines a conditional distribution of target vectors $\mathbf{Y}_{1:n_y}$ given the input sequence $\mathbf{X}_{1:n_x}$:

$$p_{\theta_{enc},\theta_{dec}}(\mathbf{Y}_{1:n_y}|\mathbf{X}_{1:n_x}) \tag{1}$$

where the BERT-based encoder part encodes the input sequence $\mathbf{X}_{1:n_x}$ to a contextualized encoded sequence $\overline{\mathbf{X}}_{1:n_x}$:

$$f_{\theta_{enc}} : \mathbf{X}_{1:n_x} \rightarrow \overline{\mathbf{X}}_{1:n_x} \tag{2}$$

and the BERT-based decoder part models the conditional probability distribution of the target sequence $\mathbf{Y}_{1:n_y}$ given the sequence of encoded sequence $\overline{\mathbf{X}}_{1:n_x}$:

$$p_{\theta_{dec}}(\mathbf{Y}_{1:n_y}|\overline{\mathbf{X}}_{1:n_x}) \quad (3)$$

To generate poems using this architecture, we adopted the beam search multinomial sampling scheme, with a set maximum generation length of 130.

4.2 GPT-J

The performance of the transformer-based language models goes up according to Power-law with the number of model parameters, the size of the dataset, and the amount of compute (Radford et al., 2019). We use GPT-J, an open-source decoder-only transformer language model with 6B parameters (Wang and Komatsuzaki, 2021) which is four times the size of the largest GPT-2 model and two times the size of the largest GPT-Neo model (Black et al., 2021) parameters-wise.

In uni-directional models like GPT-J, when given an input sequence of tokens $\mathbf{w} = [w_1, w_2, ..., w_n]$ a probability $p(\mathbf{w})$ is assigned by the model to the sequence by factorizing it as the product of conditional probabilities:

$$p(\mathbf{w}) = \prod_t p(w_t|w_{t\text{-}1}, ..., w_1) \quad (4)$$

so the task becomes predicting the next token given the previously generated/input tokens.
Initial experiments done on the pre-trained GPT-J model showed the model is capable of generating coherent and grammatically correct Arabic sentences. This motivated us to use the model in Arabic poetry generation, adopting the Top-p method of sampling.

5 Experiment Setup

5.1 BERTShared Setup

In both experiments implemented using the BERTShared architecture, we tokenized our text using CAMeLBERT-CA's pre-trained WordPiece tokenizer. We also added two new tokens to the tokenizer to outline the structure of the vertical poems; a token to separate the two *shatrs* 'hemistichs' of a verse and another token to mark the start of a verse and separate the verses from each other.
In the first experiment we used meters as inputs and in the second we used topics. The poems are passed as the targeted outputs in both experiments, and 512 is used as a maximum output length since BERT trains positional embeddings for up to 512 positions. Furthermore, we split each poem in our dataset into chunks of 23 verses each.

Both of the BERTShared models were developed using the HuggingFace transformers library[5] and trained on a 16GB T4 NVIDIA Tesla GPU on a Google Colab notebook[6], using a batch size of 16. Both models were fine-tuned using Adam with the default learning rate of 5e-5, and a linear-rate warm-up of 3k.

5.1.1 Meters as Prompts

In the first experiment where we trained a BERTShared model with meters as inputs, we worked with a sample of 15,000 poems from our dataset due to memory limitations. The meter frequencies after sampling are shown in Figure 4.

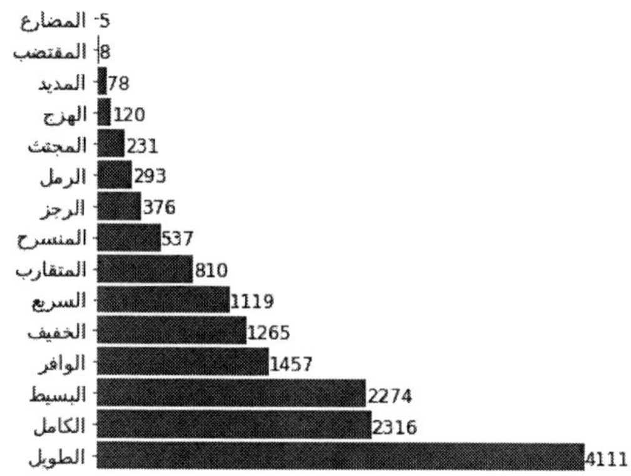

Figure 4: Meter frequency after sampling

Afterwards, we partitioned the dataset into 85% training and 15% validation using a seed of 42. Regarding the input length, we used 5 as a maximum length as we found that this length accounts for all meter labels.

5.1.2 Topics as Prompts

This experiment involved generating poems based on a prompted topic, thus topics were passed as inputs, with a maximum length of four. We excluded all samples tagged as العامة *al-'ama* 'generic' and القصيرة *al-qṣyra* 'short' to focus on the specific topics rather than the general, miscellaneous ones. Second, the poems in our dataset were originally

[5]https://huggingface.co/docs/transformers/
[6]https://colab.research.google.com/

Grouped Topics Label	Topic Labels
(Sad) حزينه	(Sad) حزينه (Lament) رثاء (Separation) فراق
(Romantic) رومنسيه	(Romantic) رومنسيه
(Religious) دينية	(Religious) دينية
(Reproach) عتاب	(Reproach) عتاب
(Love) غزل	(Love) غزل (Longing) شوق
(Praise) مدح	(Praise) مدح
(Invective) هجاء	(Blame) ذم (Invective) هجاء
(Patriotic) وطنيه	(Patriotic) وطنيه

Table 2: Adopted grouping of poetry topics in BERTShared experiments.

labelled with 17 different topics, but some data samples were scarce. In attempt to balance out the number of samples per class, we ignored ابتهال *ibthāl* 'supplication', حكمة *ḥikma* 'wisdom', and نصيحة *naṣiḥa* 'advice' topics for being the rarest. Then we grouped some of topics together, in a manner slightly inspired by a grouping suggested by Alyafeai et al. (2022). The grouping for this experiment is shown in Table 2.

5.2 GPT-J Setup

Influenced by how character tokenizers perform better compared to the BPE morphological tokenizer in Arabic poem-meter classification task (Alyafeai et al., 2021), two models were developed using a character tokenizer, one of which uses meters while the other uses topics as prompts. Additional two models were implemented where the rhyme is passed once along with the meter and another with the topic to exert more control over the generation process.

Google's V3-8 TPU [7] was used to run the GPT-J models. Pre-training the model on Arabic text was not possible, as it requires at least a v3-256 TPU. Therefore, the GPT-J model pre-trained on the English-dominated *Pile dataset* (Gao et al., 2020) was fine-tuned on our dataset. The models with the highest validation score on the partitioned 90% training and 10% validation dataset were picked. Partitioning was done using a seed of 2022.

[7] https://cloud.google.com/tpu/docs/regions-zones

Grouped Topics Label	Topic Labels
(Sad) حزينه	(Sad) حزينه (Lament) رثاء (Separation) فراق (Reproach) عتاب
(Romantic) رومنسيه	(Romantic) رومنسيه (Love) غزل (Longing) شوق
(Praise) مدح	(Praise) مدح
(Blame) ذم	(Blame) ذم (Invective) هجاء

Table 3: Adopted grouping of poetry topics in GPT-J experiments.

5.2.1 Data Preparation

Models fine-tuned on meters used 42,461 poems. However, models fine-tuned on topics used only 12,252 poems after going through a process of exclusion and grouping similar to what's done in BERTShared model.

All poems tagged as العامة *al-'ama* 'generic', القصيرة *al-qṣyra* 'short', ابتهال *ibthāl* 'supplication', حكمة *ḥikma* 'wisdom', and نصيحة *naṣiḥa* 'advice', were excluded. Then the rest of the poems were grouped as suggested by Alyafeai et al. (2022). Table 3 shows the final grouping used for GPT-J experiments.

The prompt format used to feed the poems to the model is:

```
[Tag]
Poem Text
<|endoftext|>
```

where *Tag* refers to the meter only, the topic only, the meter and rhyme or the topic and rhyme depending on which model is fine-tuned.

Each line of the poem *(bayt)* contains two verses separated by a forward slash (/) just like the following example:

وكاثرت متعة لذاته / فلم أر ذلك إلا متاعا

In the meter only and topic only models, rhyme was emphasized by inserting a hyphen (-) before

Hyperparameter	Value
lr	5e-5
end lr	1e-5
weight decay	0.1
batch size	16

Table 4: Hyperparameters set for all GPT-J models

Model Name	Total Steps	Warm up Steps
Meter only	1380	100
Topic only	300	30
Meter and Rhyme	1450	150
Topic and Rhyme	630	60

Table 5: Number of fine-tuning steps for each GPT-J model

the first letter of the rhyme.

5.2.2 Fine-tuning Hyperparameters

Table 4 shows the hyperparameters used for all the mentioned models. Higher and lower learning rates were used, but no sign of improvement was observed in the validation score. Table 5 shows the warm-up steps and the total steps for each model.

5.2.3 Inference Hyperparameters

To generate diverse poems, the inference hyperparameters used were:
Top-p = `0.9`, and Temperature = `0.9`

5.2.4 Omitted Models

Some initial model were implemented using AraGPT2 [8] BPE subword tokenizer. The poems showed a great tendency for repetition, as well as outputting invalid tokens and English letters.
An attempt was made to turn the AraGPT2 tokenizer into a character-level tokenizer by segmenting words into characters. This was done by inserting a hyphen (-) between every two letters. Another model was implemented using the new tokenizer and despite it achieving the best validation score of all models, the generated poems were incoherent and incomprehensible.

6 Evaluation

Some of the generated poems of our models are shown in Table 6. Because poems are essentially a form of art, no automated tool, or AI model could fully substitute the assessment of poetry by a human. Hence, we turned to four experts in classical Arabic poetry for an evaluation based on a number of dimensions as mentioned in 6.2. Additionally, we employed existing tools to test how much our model adheres to meters as will be explained in the following subsection.

6.1 Machine Evaluation

We first utilized the Arabic poetry classification model which Inoue et al. (2021) trained and made available on HuggingFace[9], to classify meters of the generated poems and assess the models' accuracy in capturing them.
We used each model to generate 10 poems per each of the 15 meters, consisting of a maximum of seven verses each. Then we passed the 300 poems to the poetry classification model, verse by verse. For each model and meter, we counted how many poems out of the 10 had all their verses adhering to their prompted meter. The results are presented in Figure 5. It shows that for الطويل *al-Ṭawīl* - the class with the most data samples - both models perform very well; the BERTShared model correctly captured the meter in the 10 poems it generated for this prompt, and the GPT-J model performed as equally for the 10 poems it generated for the same prompt. Both models could not capture the meters for any of المضارع *al-Muḍāriʻ* or المقتضب *al-Muqtaḍab*, the classes which had the least amount of samples in our dataset as shown in Figure 1. Furthermore, GPT-J model outputs display an overall linear correlation between the class size and the per-class accuracy. BERTShared, on the other hand, shows a good performance for some classes like الرمل *al-Ramal* that has 293 samples, but is under-performing, for instance, in السريع *al-Sarīʻ* meter of 1119 samples.

6.2 Human Evaluation

We sent out two surveys for our evaluators to assess the quality of poems with respect to meters and topics separately.

The survey analysing quality of topics of 16 poems, two poems from each topic group shown in Table 3 from each model. The evaluators were asked to answer the following questions from a scale of one to five, with one being the worst and five being the best:

[8] `https://huggingface.co/aubmindlab/aragpt2-base`

[9] `https://huggingface.co/CAMeL-Lab/bert-base-arabic-camelbert-ca-poetry`

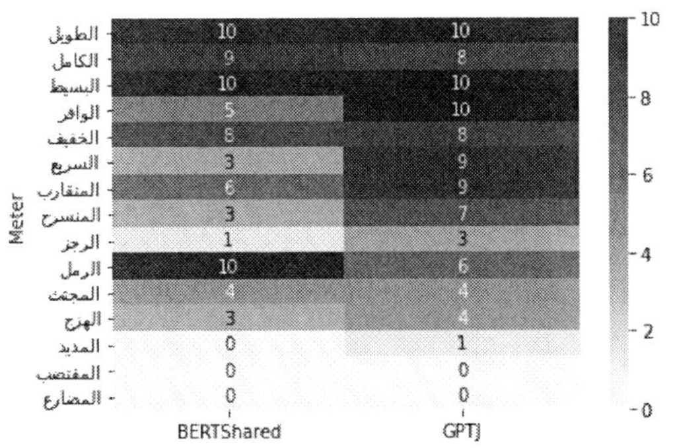

Figure 5: Per-meter accuracy of BERTShared and GPT-J. The y-axis is sorted by meter frequencies as in Figure 1.

1. How fluent is the generated poem?
2. How coherent is the poem with respect to as specified topic?
3. How consistent is the rhyme throughout the poem?
4. What meter does this poem follow?
5. How consistent is the meter throughout the poem?

Meanwhile, our second survey had a total of 18 poems, covering the following nine meters:

- الطويل *al-Ṭawīl*
- البسيط *al-Basīṭ*
- الوافر *al-Wāfir*
- الخفيف *al-Khafīf*
- المنسرح *al-Munsariḥ*
- الرمل *al-Ramal,*
- المتقارب *al-Mutaqārib*
- السريع *al-Sarī'*
- الكامل *al-Kāmil*

Our evaluators were required to answer the following questions and much like the first survey their answer should range from one to five:

1. How fluent is the generated poem?
2. How coherent is the poem with respect to as specified topic?
3. How consistent is the rhyme throughout the poem?
4. How much do verses follow the same rhythm?
5. How close are the verses to the specified meter?

Figure 6 shows each model's per-meter accuracy, how well the generated poems adhered to the prompted meter, as reported by the human evaluation. The results also vary between our models; GPT-J outperforms BERTShared in some meters but BERTShared does in some others. Overall, both models perform better the more data samples there are. Similarly, the per-topic accuracy for each model after averaging the evaluators' ratings is decipted in Figure 7.
Figure 8 reports the evaluators' ratings of the generated poems in terms of their fluency, thematic coherence, and rhyme consistency. On average, we see that BERTShared outperforms GPT-J in the fluency and grammatical correctness of the poems; and the coherency. However, GPT-J model shows a better ability of keeping the rhymes consistent throughout the verses of the poem.

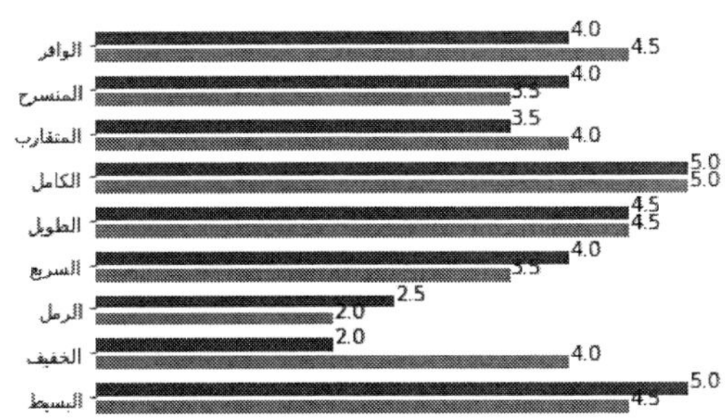

Figure 6: Per-meter accuracy of GPT-J (Red) and BERTShared (Grey) models as per human evaluation.

7 Conclusion & Future Work

We have presented two approaches to classical Arabic poetry generation. We have experimented with two transformer-based architectures: the encoder-decoder model initialized with BERT-based checkpoints, and the decoder-only architecture: GPT-J. We fine-tuned both models on a classical Arabic

Model	Prompt	Generated Poem
BERTShared	Meter: الوافر *al-Wāfir*	ألا من للموت أهون من حياة ومن لي أن أعيش بغير عيش عجبت لمن يموت وليس يدري وما في الموت موت بعد موت لعمرك ما الحياة وإن تناهت على ما قد مضى من الدنيا وعيش أرى الموت الشقاء لكل حي ولا خير الحياة لمن لحي
	Topic: (Romantic) رومنسيه	ألا أيها القلب الذي هو واجد على كل حال من سرورك موقد وإني لأرجو أن يدوم وصاله وما أنا إلا مغرم متزيد فيا ليت شعري ما الذي بي من الجوى إذا لم يكن لي في هواك مزيد أيا كبد حرى عليك تقطعت ويا لك من قلب عليك شديد فديتك لو كان الوصال بناظري إلى الله أشكو بعد ذاك الصدود ولو كنت أدري كيف أصغي لقولكم ولكن قلبي لا يزال يصيد
GPT-J	Meter: الطويل *al-Ṭawīl*	ومن جاءني بالخمس منه بحقه وكيف يحامي حاجب بالأجارب لقد حط في بعض اللقاء مكانه وما حط في بعض اللقاء مناسبي وقد جاءني بالخمس والجهل مذنب فما هو لي في بيت مجد وكاذب ولكن إذا ما أعطيت كف مجدها وليس لها غير الملاقاة ثاقب فلا برحت أيدي الليالي مخافة تقر لها عيني وتلوى الحواجب
	Topic: (Sad) حزينه	وعين على الأشجان بات ينيرها ومن دونه عود اللمى فيعيرها وحالف صبري في التجلد إنها إذا قام منها الوجد في الدهر حورها إذا نازحتها الدار بات يجودها بما جاد في الأيام منها أسيرها أتطلب دار لم ينل من بلادها ويعذب إلا في التراب بدورها إذا ما ارتدى بالماء لم يحو مقلة سوى ذلك الصافي ولا ذلك النورها

Table 6: Examples of generated poetry

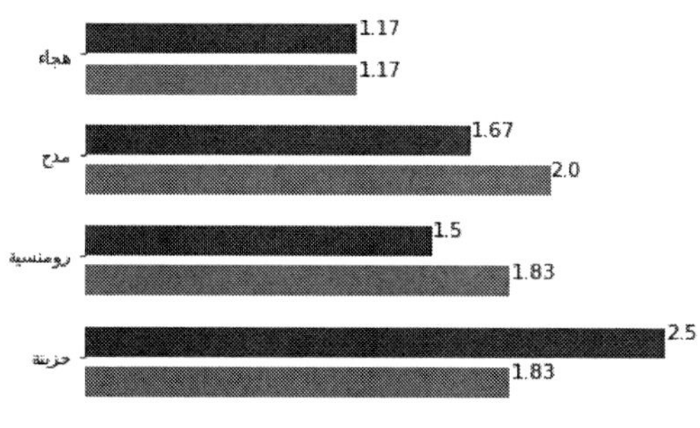

Figure 7: Per-topic accuracy of GPT-J (Red) and BERTShared (Grey) models as per human evaluation.

poems corpus for two prompt-based generation tasks, and made use of two evaluation methods: one machine-based that focused on the models' ability to adhere to the prompted meters, and one human-based that focused on assessing the quality of the generated poems. The evaluators regarded the poems as interesting human evaluation revealed that BERTShared model performed slightly better

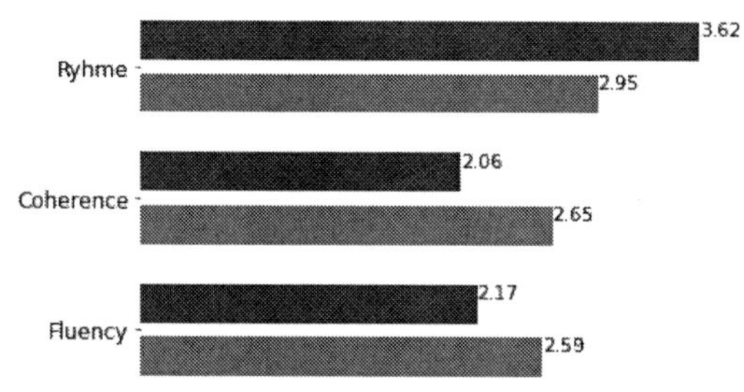

Figure 8: Rhyme consistency, fluency, and coherence ratings of the poems generated by GPT-J (Red) and BERTShared (Grey) models as per human evaluation.

in generating more fluent and coherent poems, but GPT-J model could capture the rhymes much better. In the future, we aim to incorporate human evaluation in the loop in a reinforcement learning environment, where the model should learn to generate the poetry based on corrected faulty poems.

Limitations

A limitation hindering both models are poems of topics labelled العامة *al-'ama* 'generic' and القصيرة *al-qṣyra* 'short' as they are the most occurring topics as show in Figure 2 yet they cover no distinct domain. Furthermore, we found no records online that could confirm that poets intended to write their poems following a certain theme, therefore we had to rely completely on *aldiwan*'s topic labelling not knowing what is based on or how accurate it is. Another is human evaluation, despite the presence of experts, there were too many poems to assess, and evaluators were not keen on the surveys especially meters evaluation as to them the number of meters to evaluate poems for is large.
In addition, GPT-J could not be pre-trained due to unavailability of the required hardware, so fine-tuning was used instead, which is suboptimal.

Acknowledgements

We gratefully acknowledge Google TRC program for providing the TPU machines that allowed us to train the GPT-J models. We are grateful, as well, to each of Abdel-Hamid Mohamed Taha, Mahmoud Salam Abo-Malek, Rayyan Mohamed and Mohamed Ashry for their contribution in evaluating this work.

References

Zaid Alyafeai, Maged Saeed AlShaibani, Mustafa Ghaleb, and Irfan Ahmad. 2021. Evaluating various tokenizers for arabic text classification. *CoRR*, abs/2106.07540.

Zaid Alyafeai, Maged Saeed AlShaibani, and Omar Hammad. 2022. Qawafi: Arabic poetry analysis using deep learning and knowledge based methods. https://github.com/ARBML/qawafi.

Mohamed El Ghaly Beheitt and Moez Ben Haj Hmida. 2022. Automatic arabic poem generation with gpt-2. In *Proceedings of the 14th International Conference on Agents and Artificial Intelligence (ICAART 2022)*, volume 2, pages 366–374.

Sid Black, Leo Gao, Phil Wang, Connor Leahy, and Stella Biderman. 2021. GPT-Neo: Large Scale Autoregressive Language Modeling with Mesh-Tensorflow.

Kyunghyun Cho, Bart Van Merriënboer, Caglar Gulcehre, Dzmitry Bahdanau, Fethi Bougares, Holger Schwenk, and Yoshua Bengio. 2014. Learning phrase representations using rnn encoder-decoder for statistical machine translation. *arXiv preprint arXiv:1406.1078*.

Dmitry Frolov. 1996. The circles of al-Khalil and the structure of luzumiyyat of Abu'l-'Ala' al-Ma'arri. *Studies in Near Eastern Languages and Literatures. Memorial Volume of Karel Petraček, Praha*, pages 223–236.

Leo Gao, Stella Biderman, Sid Black, Laurence Golding, Travis Hoppe, Charles Foster, Jason Phang, Horace He, Anish Thite, Noa Nabeshima, Shawn Presser, and Connor Leahy. 2020. The pile: An 800gb dataset of diverse text for language modeling. *arXiv preprint arXiv:2101.00027*.

Marjan Ghazvininejad, Xing Shi, Yejin Choi, and Kevin Knight. 2016. Generating topical poetry. In *Proceedings of the 2016 Conference on Empirical Methods in Natural Language Processing*, pages 1183–1191.

Chris Golston and Tomas Riad. 1997. The phonology of classical arabic meter. *Linguistics: An Interdisciplinary Journal of the Language Sciences*, 35(1):111–132.

Mika Hämäläinen, Khalid Alnajjar, and Thierry Poibeau. 2022. Modern French Poetry Generation with RoBERTa and GPT-2. In *Proceedings of the International Conference on Computational Creativity, ICCC'22*.

Jack Hopkins and Douwe Kiela. 2017. Automatically generating rhythmic verse with neural networks. In *Proceedings of the 55th Annual Meeting of the Association for Computational Linguistics*, volume 1, pages 168–178.

Go Inoue, Bashar Alhafni, Nurpeiis Baimukan, Houda Bouamor, and Nizar Habash. 2021. The interplay of variant, size, and task type in Arabic pre-trained language models. In *Proceedings of the Sixth Arabic Natural Language Processing Workshop*.

Mike Lewis, Yinhan Liu, Naman Goyal, Marjan Ghazvininejad, Abdelrahman Mohamed, Omer Levy, Veselin Stoyanov, and Luke Zettlemoyer. 2020. BART: Denoising sequence-to-sequence pre-training for natural language generation, translation, and comprehension. In *Proceedings of the 58th Annual Meeting of the Association for Computational Linguistics*, pages 7871–7880.

Yinhan Liu, Myle Ott, Naman Goyal, Jingfei Du, Mandar Joshi, Danqi Chen, Omer Levy, Mike Lewis, Luke Zettlemoyer, and Veselin Stoyanov. 2019. Roberta: A robustly optimized bert pretraining approach. *arXiv preprint arXiv:1907.11692*.

Thang Luong, Hieu Pham, and Christopher D. Manning. 2015. Effective approaches to attention-based neural machine translation. In *Proceedings of the 2015 Conference on Empirical Methods in Natural Language Processing*, pages 1412–1421. Association for Computational Linguistics.

Alec Radford, Jeffrey Wu, Rewon Child, David Luan, Dario Amodei, and Ilya Sutskever. 2019. Language models are unsupervised multitask learners. *OpenAI blog*, 1(8):9.

Colin Raffel, Noam Shazeer, Adam Roberts, Katherine Lee, Sharan Narang, Michael Matena, Yanqi Zhou, Wei Li, and Peter J. Liu. 2020. Exploring the limits of transfer learning with a unified text-to-text transformer. *Journal of Machine Learning Research*, 21(140):1–67.

Sascha Rothe, Shashi Narayan, and Aliaksei Severyn. 2020. Leveraging Pre-trained Checkpoints for Sequence Generation Tasks. *Transactions of the Association for Computational Linguistics*, 8:264–280.

Tim Van de Cruys. 2020. Automatic poetry generation from prosaic text. In *Proceedings of the 58th annual meeting of the association for computational linguistics*, pages 2471–2480.

Ben Wang and Aran Komatsuzaki. 2021. GPT-J-6B: A 6 Billion Parameter Autoregressive Language Model. `https://github.com/kingoflolz/mesh-transformer-jax`.

Rui Yan. 2016. i, poet: Automatic poetry composition through recurrent neural networks with iterative polishing schema. In *Proceedings of the Twenty-Fifth International Joint Conference on Artificial Intelligence*, pages 2238—2244.

Jingqing Zhang, Yao Zhao, Mohammad Saleh, and Peter Liu. 2020. PEGASUS: Pre-training with extracted gap-sentences for abstractive summarization. In *Proceedings of the 37th International Conference on Machine Learning*, volume 119, pages 11328–11339.

Xingxing Zhang and Mirella Lapata. 2014. Chinese poetry generation with recurrent neural networks. In *Proceedings of the 2014 Conference on Empirical Methods in Natural Language Processing (EMNLP)*, pages 670–680.

A Benchmark Study of Contrastive Learning for Arabic Social Meaning

Md Tawkat Islam Khondaker[†] **El Moatez Billah Nagoudi**[†] **AbdelRahim Elmadany**[†]
Muhammad Abdul-Mageed[†] **Laks V.S. Lakshmanan**

[†]Deep Learning & Natural Language Processing Group
The University of British Columbia

{tawkat@cs.,laks@cs.,muhammad.mageed@}ubc.ca

Abstract

Contrastive learning (CL) brought significant progress to various NLP tasks. Despite this progress, CL has not been applied to Arabic NLP to date. Nor is it clear how much benefits it could bring to particular classes of tasks such as those involved in Arabic social meaning (e.g., sentiment analysis, dialect identification, hate speech detection). In this work, we present a comprehensive benchmark study of state-of-the-art supervised CL methods on a wide array of Arabic social meaning tasks. Through extensive empirical analyses, we show that CL methods outperform vanilla finetuning on most tasks we consider. We also show that CL can be data efficient and quantify this efficiency. Overall, our work allows us to demonstrate the promise of CL methods, including in low-resource settings.

1 Introduction

Proliferation of social media resulted in unprecedented online user engagement. People around the world share their emotions, fears, hopes, opinions, etc. online on a daily basis (Farzindar and Inkpen 2015; Zhang and Abdul-Mageed 2022) on platforms such as Facebook and Twitter. Hence, these platforms offer excellent resources for social meaning tasks such as emotion recognition (Abdul-Mageed and Ungar 2017; Mohammad et al. 2018), irony detection (Van Hee et al. 2018), sarcasm detection (Bamman and Smith 2015), hate speech identification (Waseem and Hovy 2016), stance identification (Mohammad et al. 2016), among others. While the majority of previous social meaning studies were carried out on English, a fast-growing number of investigations focus on other languages. In this paper, we focus on Arabic.

Several works have been conducted on different Arabic social meaning tasks. Some of these focus on Modern Standard Arabic (MSA) (Abdul-Mageed et al. 2011, 2012), while others take Arabic dialects as their target (ElSahar and El-Beltagy 2015; Al Sallab et al. 2015). While many works have focused on sentiment analysis, e.g., (Abdul-Mageed et al., 2012; Nabil et al., 2015; ElSahar and El-Beltagy, 2015; Al Sallab et al., 2015; Al-Moslmi et al., 2018; Al-Smadi et al., 2019; Al-Ayyoub et al., 2019; Farha and Magdy, 2019) and dialect identification (Elfardy and Diab, 2013; Zaidan and Callison-Burch, 2011, 2014; Cotterell and Callison-Burch, 2014; Zhang and Abdul-Mageed, 2019; Bouamor et al., 2018; Abdul-Mageed et al., 2020b,a, 2021b), others focused on detection of user demographics such as age and gender (Zaghouani and Charfi 2018; Rangel et al. 2019), irony detection (Karoui et al. 2017; Ghanem et al. 2019), and emotion analysis (Abdul-Mageed et al. 2016; Alhuzali et al. 2018). Our interest in the current work is improving Arabic social meaning through representation learning.

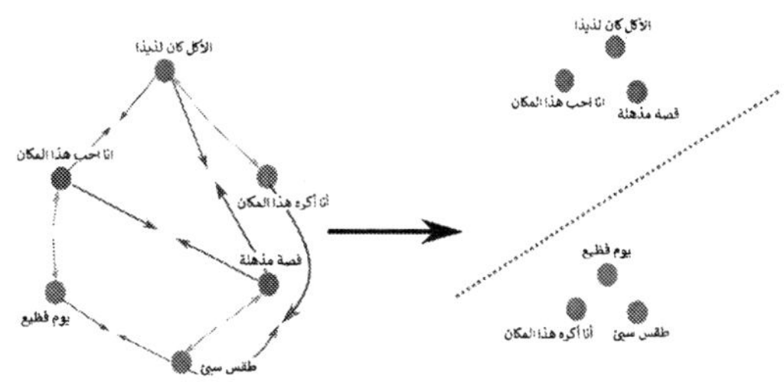

Figure 1: Visual illustration of how supervised contrastive learning works. Representations from the same class are *pulled* close to each other while representations from the different classes are *pushed* further apart.

In spite of recent progress in representation learning, most work in Arabic social meaning mostly focuses on finetuning language models such as AraT5 (Nagoudi et al., 2022), CamelBERT (Inoue et al., 2021), MARBERT (Abdul-Mageed et al., 2021a), QARIB (Abdelali et al., 2021), among others. In particular, Arabic social media processing has to date ignored the emerging sub-area of contrastive learning (CL) (Hadsell et al. 2006). Given a labeled dataset, CL (Khosla et al., 2020) attempts

Proceedings of the The Seventh Arabic Natural Language Processing Workshop (WANLP), pages 63 - 75
December 8, 2022 ©2022 Association for Computational Linguistics

to pull representations of the same class close to each other while pushing representations of different classes further apart (Figure 1). In this work, we investigate five different supervised contrastive learning methods in the context of Arabic social meaning. To the best of our knowledge, this is the first work that provides a comprehensive study of supervised contrastive learning on a wide range of Arabic social meanings. We show that performance of CL methods can be task-dependent. We attempt to explain this performance from the perspective of task specificity (i.e., how fine-grained the labels of a given task are). We also show that contrastive learning methods generally perform better than vanilla finetuning based on cross entropy (CE). Through an extensive experimental study, we also demonstrate that CL methods outperform CE finetuning under resource-limited constraints. Our work allows us to demonstrate the promise of CL methods in general, and in low-resource settings in particular.

To summarize, we offer the following contributions:

1. We study a comprehensive set of supervised CL methods for a wide range of Arabic social meaning tasks, including abusive language and hate speech detection, emotion and sentiment analysis, and identification of demographic attributes (e.g. age, gender).

2. We show that CL-based methods outperform generic CE-based vanilla finetuning for most of the tasks. To the best of our knowledge, this is the first work that provides an extensive study of supervised CL on Arabic social meaning.

3. We empirically find that improvements CL methods result in are task-specific and attempt to understand this finding in the context of the different tasks we consider with regard to their label granularity.

4. We demonstrate that CL methods can achieve better performance under limited data constraints, emphasizing and quantifying how well these can work for low-resource settings.

2 Related Works

2.1 Arabic Social Meaning

We use the term *social meaning* (SM) to refer to meaning arising in real-world communication in social media (Thomas, 2014; Zhang et al., 2022b). SM covers tasks such as sentiment analysis (Abdul-Mageed et al., 2012; Abu Farha et al., 2021; Saleh et al., 2022; Alali et al., 2022), emotion recognition (Alhuzali et al., 2018; Mubarak et al., 2022c; Abu Shaqra et al., 2022; Mansy et al., 2022), age and gender identification (Abdul-Mageed et al., 2020c; Abbes et al., 2020; Mubarak et al., 2022b; Mansour Khoudja et al., 2022), hate-speech and offensive language detection (Elmadany et al., 2020a; Mubarak et al., 2020, 2022a; Husain and Uzuner, 2022), and sarcasm detection (Farha and Magdy, 2020; Wafa'Q et al., 2022; Abdullah et al., 2022).

Most of the recent studies are transformers-based. They directly finetune pre-trained models such as mBERT (Devlin et al., 2018), MARBERT (Abdul-Mageed et al., 2021a), and AraT5 (Nagoudi et al., 2022) on SM datasets like (Abdul-Mageed et al., 2020c; Alshehri et al., 2020; Abuzayed and Al-Khalifa, 2021; Nessir et al., 2022), using data augmentation (Elmadany et al., 2020b), ensampling (Mansy et al., 2022; Alzu'bi et al., 2022), and multi-tasks (Abdul-Mageed et al., 2020b; Shapiro et al., 2022; AlKhamissi and Diab, 2022). However, to the best of our knowledge, there is no published research studying CL on Arabic language understanding in general nor social meaning processing in paticular.

2.2 Contrastive Learning

CL aims to learn effective embedding by pulling semantically close neighbors together while pushing apart non-neighbors (Hadsell et al. 2006). CL employs a CL-based similarity objective to learn the embedding representation in the hyperspace (Chen et al., 2017; Henderson et al., 2017). In computer vision, Chen et al. (2020a) propose a framework for contrastive learning of visual representations without specialized architectures or a memory bank. Khosla et al. (2020) shows that supervised contrastive loss can outperform CL loss on ImageNet (Russakovsky et al., 2015). In NLP, similar methods have been explored in the context of sentence representation learning (Karpukhin et al., 2020; Gillick et al., 2019; Logeswaran and Lee, 2018; Zhang et al., 2022a). Among the most notable works is Gao et al. (2021) who propose unsupervised CL framework, *SimCSE*, that predicts input sentence itself by augmenting it with dropout as noise.

Recent works have been studying CL extensively for improving both semantic text similarity (STS) and text classification tasks (Meng et al. 2021; Qu et al. 2020; Qiu et al. 2021; Janson et al. 2021). Fang et al. (2020) propose back-translation as a source of positive pair for NLU tasks. Klein and Nabi (2022) argue that feature decorrelation between high and low dropout projected representations improves STS tasks. Zhou et al. (2022) design an instance weighting method to penalize false negatives and generate noise-based negatives to guarantee the uniformity of the representation space. Su et al. (2022) propose a token-aware CL method by contrasting the token from the same sequence to improve the uniformity in the embedding space. We now formally introduce these CL methods and how we employ them in our work.

3 Methods

Given a set of training examples $\{x_i, y_i\}_{i=1,...,N}$ and an encoder based on a pre-trained language model (PLM), f outputs contextualized token representation of x_i,

$$H = \{\ h_{[CLS]},\ h_1,\ h_2,\ ...,\ h_{[SEP]}\ \} \quad (1)$$

Where $\boldsymbol{H}$ is the hidden representation of the final layer of the encoder.

The standard practice of finetuning PLMs passes the pooled representation $h_{[CLS]}$ of `[CLS]` to a softmax classifier to obtain the probability distribution for the set of classes $\mathbf{C}$ (Figure 2a).

$$p(y_c|h_{[CLS]}) = softmax\ (\mathbf{W}h_{[CLS]});\ \ c \in \mathbf{C} \quad (2)$$

Where $\mathbf{W} \in \mathcal{R}^{d_C \times d_h}$ are trainable parameters and d_h is hidden dimension. The model is trained with the objective of minimizing cross-entropy (CE) loss,

$$\mathcal{L}_{CE} = -\frac{1}{N}\sum_{i=1}^{N}\sum_{c=1}^{C} y_{i,c}\ log(p(y_{i,c}|h_{i_{[CLS]}}))^1 \quad (3)$$

3.1 Supervised Contrastive Loss (SCL)

The objective of supervised contrastive loss (Khosla et al. 2020) is to pull the representations of the same class close to each other while pushing the representations of different classes further apart. Following Gao et al. (2021), we adopt dropout-based data augmentation where for each representation h_i, we produce an equivalent dropout-based representation h_j and consider h_j as having the same label as h_i (Figure 2b). The model attempts to minimize NTXent loss (Chen et al., 2020a). The purpose of NTXent loss is to take each in-batch representation as an anchor and minimize the distance between the anchor(h_i) and the representations from the same class (P_i) while maximizing the distance between the anchor and the representation from different classes,

$$\mathcal{L}_{NTX} = \sum_{i=1}^{2N} \frac{-1}{P_i} \sum_{j \in P_i} \log \frac{e^{sim(h_i,h_j)/\tau}}{\sum_{k=1}^{2N} 1_{i \neq k} e^{sim(h_i,h_k)/\tau}} \quad (4)$$

Where τ is used to regulate the temperature. The final loss for SCL is

$$\mathcal{L}_{SCL} = (1-\lambda)\mathcal{L}_{CE} + \lambda\mathcal{L}_{NTX}$$

3.2 Contrastive Adversarial Training (CAT)

Instead of dropout-based augmentation, Pan et al. (2022) propose to generate adversarial examples applying *fast gradient sign method* (FGSM) (Goodfellow et al., 2015). Formally, *FGSM* attempts to maximize $\mathcal{L}_{CE}$ by adding a small perturbation r bounded by ϵ,

$$max\mathcal{L}_{CE} = arg\max_{r} \mathcal{L}(f(x_i + r, y_i)$$
$$s.t.\ ||r|| < \epsilon, \quad \epsilon > 0 \quad (5)$$

Goodfellow et al. (2015) approximate the perturbation r with a linear approximation around x_i and an *L2* norm constraint. However, Pan et al. (2022) propose to approximate r around the word embedding matrix $V \in \mathcal{R}^{d_V \times d_h}$ (Figure 2c), where d_V is the vocabulary size. Hence, the adversarial perturbation is computed as,

$$r = -\epsilon \frac{\nabla_V \mathcal{L}(f(x_i, y_i)}{||\nabla_V \mathcal{L}(f(x_i, y_i)||_2} \quad (6)$$

After receiving x_i, the perturbed encoder f^{V+r} outputs `[CLS]` representation h_j, which is treated as the positive pair of h_i. Both h_i and h_j are passed through a non-linear projection layer and the resulting representations are used to train the model with InfoNCE loss (Oord et al., 2018).

[1] $h_{i_{[CLS]}}$ and h_i are used interchangeably in the rest of the paper.

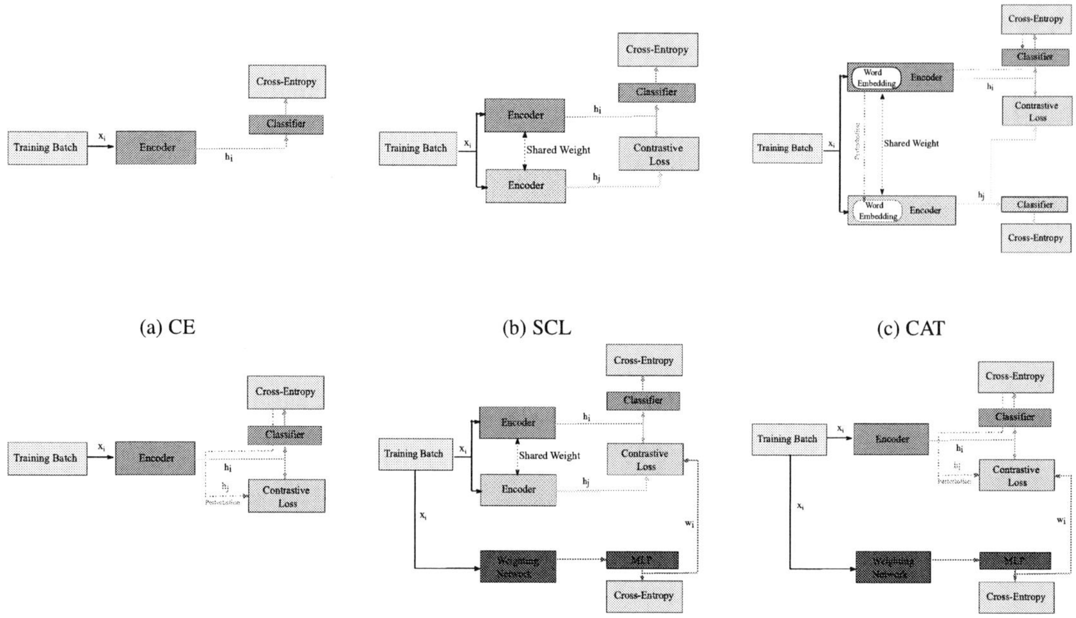

(a) CE (b) SCL (c) CAT

(d) TACT (e) LCL (f) TLCL

Figure 2: Illustration of supervised contrastive learning methods used in this work.

$$z_i = \mathbf{W_2} ReLU(\mathbf{W_1} h_i) \quad (7)$$

$$z_j = \mathbf{W_2} ReLU(\mathbf{W_1} h_j) \quad (8)$$

$$\mathcal{L}_{InfoNCE} = -\log \frac{e^{sim(z_i,z_j)/\tau}}{\sum_{k=1}^{2N} 1_{i \neq k} e^{sim(z_i,z_k)/\tau}} \quad (9)$$

The final loss is calculated as,

$$\mathcal{L}_{CAT} = \frac{1-\lambda}{2}(\mathcal{L}_{CE} + \mathcal{L}_{CE}^{V+r}) + \lambda \mathcal{L}_{InfoNCE}$$

3.3 Token-level Adversarial Contrastive Training (TACT)

We also study a variant of CAT where instead of perturbing the word embedding matrix V, we directly perturb the token representations h_i (Figure 2d),

$$r = -\epsilon \frac{\nabla_{h_i} \mathcal{L}(f(x_i, y_i)}{||\nabla_{h_i} \mathcal{L}(f(x_i, y_i))||_2} \quad (10)$$

$$h_j = h_i + r \quad (11)$$

Similar to CAT, we pass h_i and h_j through a non-linear projection layer and use the obtained representations to train the model to minimize InfoNCE loss (Eq. 9). We compute the final loss as,

$$\mathcal{L}_{CAT} = \frac{1-\lambda}{2}(\mathcal{L}_{CE} + \mathcal{L}_{CE}^{h+r}) + \lambda \mathcal{L}_{InfoNCE} \quad (12)$$

3.4 Label-aware Contrastive Loss (LCL)

Suresh and Ong (2021) propose to adapt contrastive loss for fine-grained classification tasks by incorporating inter-label relationships. The authors propose an additional weighting network (Figure 2e) to encode the inter-label relationships. First, both the encoder and the weighting network are optimised using cross-entropy loss ($\mathcal{L}_{CE}$), $\mathcal{L}_E$, and $\mathcal{L}_w$, respectively. The prediction probabilities obtained from the softmax layer of the weighting network are used to compute the confidence of the current sample for a given class c,

$$\mathbf{w}_{i,c} = \frac{e^{h_{i,c}}}{\sum_{k=1}^{C} e^{h_{i,k}}} \quad (13)$$

These weights are then used to train the model with NTXent loss.

$$\mathcal{L}_i = \sum_{j \in P_i} \log \frac{w_{i,y_i} \cdot e^{sim(h_i,h_j)/\tau}}{\sum_{k=1}^{2N} 1_{i \neq k} w_{i,y_k} \cdot e^{sim(h_i,h_k)/\tau}} \quad (14)$$

$$\mathcal{L}_f = \sum_{i=1}^{2N} \frac{-\mathcal{L}_i}{P_i} \quad (15)$$

Similar to Section 3.1, we use dropout-based data augmentation. Given a confusable sample, the weighting network will assign higher scores for

Dataset	Train	Dev	Test	No. of Classes
Abusive	4,677	584	585	3
Adult	33,690	5,000	5000	2
Age	5,000	5,000	5,000	3
AraNeT$_{\text{emo}}$	50,000	910	941	8
Dangerous	3,474	615	663	2
Dialect at BinaryLevel	50,000	5,000	5,000	2
Dialect at CountryLevel	50,000	5,000	5,000	21
Dialect at RegionLevel	38,271	4,450	5000	4
Gender	50,000	5,000	5,000	2
Hate Speech	6,839	1,000	2,000	2
Irony	3,621	403	805	2
Offensive	6,839	1,000	2,000	2
Sarcasm	7,593	844	2,110	2
SemEval$_{\text{emo}}$	3,376	661	1,563	4
Sentiment Analysis	49,301	4,443	4,933	3

Table 1: Statistics of datasets used in our experiments.

the classes that are more closely associated with the sample. Incorporating these high values back into the denominator of NTXent will steer the encoder toward finding more distinguishing patterns to differentiate between confusable samples. The final LCL loss is computed as follows:

$$\mathcal{L}_{LCL} = (1 - \lambda)(\mathcal{L}_E + \mathcal{L}_w) + \lambda \mathcal{L}_f \quad (16)$$

3.5 Token Adversarial LCL (TLCL)

Instead of dropout-oriented representation as an augmentation, we experiment with token adversarial representation for LCL (Figure 2f) described in Section 3.3. First, we compute the adversarial representation h_j using Eq. 10 and Eq. 11. Then, we compute NTXent loss (Eq. 14) for LCL to obtain the final token adversarial LCL loss, $\mathcal{L}_{TLCL}$. We now describe our datasets.

4 Datasets

In this section, we present the Arabic social meaning tasks and datasets used in our study. A summary of the datasets is presented in Table 1.

Abusive and Adult Content. For the abusive and adult content detection tasks, we use datasets from Mubarak et al. (2017) and Mubarak et al. (2021). These datasets consist of 1.1k and 43k tweets, respectively. For these datasets, the goal is to classify an Arabic tweet into one of the two classes in the set, i.e., *{obscene, clean}* for the abusive task, and *{adult, not-adult}* for the adult content detection task.

Age and Gender. For both tasks, we use the *Arap-Tweet* dataset (Zaghouani and Charfi, 2018) which consists of *1.3M, 160k, 160k* for the Train, Dev, and Test respecctively. The dataset covers 11 Arab regions. Zaghouani and Charfi (2018) assign age group labels from the set *{under-25, 25-to-34, above-35}* and gender from the set *{male, female}*.

Dangerous. We use the dangerous speech dataset from Alshehri et al. (2020). This dataset consists of $4,445$ manually annotated tweets labelled as either *safe* or *dangerous*.

Dialect Identification: Six datasets are used for this task: ArSarcasm$_{\text{Dia}}$ (Farha and Magdy, 2020), the Arabic Online Commentary (AOC) (Zaidan and Callison-Burch, 2014), NADI-2020 (Abdul-Mageed et al., 2020a), MADAR (Bouamor et al., 2019), QADI (Abdelali et al., 2020), and Habibi (El-Haj, 2020). The dialect identification task involves three dialect classification levels: (1) Binary-level (*MSA* vs. *DIA*), (2) Region-level (4 *regions*), and (3) Country-level (21 *countries*).

Emotion. For this task, we use two datasets: *AraNeT$_{emo}$* and *SemEval$_{emo}$*. The first one is proposed by Abdul-Mageed et al. (2020c). The dataset consists of 192K tweets labeled with the eight emotion classes from the set $\{$*anger, anticipation, disgust, fear, joy, sadness, surprise, trust*$\}$. *SemEval$_{emo}$* (Mohammad et al., 2018) consists of $5,603$ tweets labeled with four emotions from the set $\{$*anger, fear, joy, sadness*$\}$.

Offensive Language and Hate Speech. We use the dataset released by Mubarak et al. (2020) during an offensive and hate speech shared task.[2] This dataset consists of $10k$ manually annotated tweets with four tags *{offensive, not-offensive, hate, not-hate*

Irony. We use the irony identification dataset for Arabic tweets (IDAT) developed by Ghanem et al. (2019). This dataset contains $5,030$ MSA and dialectal tweets. It is labeled with *ironic* and *non-ironic* tags.

Sarcasm. We use the *ArSarcasm* dataset released by (Farha and Magdy, 2020). *ArSarcasm* contains $10,547$ tweets. The tweets are labeled with *sarcasm* and *not-sarcasm* tags.

Sentiment Analysis This task includes 19 sentiment datasets. We merge the 17 datasets benchmarked by Abdul-Mageed et al. (2021a) with two new datasets: Arabizi sentiment analysis dataset (Fourati et al., 2020) and AraCust (Almuqren and Cristea, 2021), a Saudi Telecom Tweets corpus for sentiment analysis. The data contains *190k, 6.5k, 44.2k* samples for Train, Dev and Test. The dataset is labeled with three tags from the set {*positive, negative, neutral*}.

5 Experimental Setup

We implement all the methods using MARBERT (Abdul-Mageed et al., 2021a) (`UBC-NLP/MARBERT`) from HuggingFace's Transformers library (Wolf et al., 2020), as the backbone architecture. We use MARBERT as it is reported to achieve SOTA on a wide range of Arabic language understanding tasks in Abdul-Mageed et al. (2021a). Our methods, however, can be applied to any other model. We use the same hyperparameters for all the methods to ensure fair comparisons. We set the maximum sequence length to 128 and use a batch size of 16 to train the models using Adam optimizer with a learning rate $5e-5$. The initial number of training epochs is set to 25 with an early stopping threshold of 5. For CL-based models, we set λ to 0.5 and τ to 0.3. For all the experiments, we consider the checkpoint with the best macro F_1 score on the development sets to evaluate performance on the respective test sets. To limit GPU usage during our experiments, we normalize all datasets considered by limiting the size of Train, Dev, and Test splits to *50k, 5k, 5k* samples respectively.[3]

[2]http://edinburghnlp.inf.ed.ac.uk/workshops/OSACT4/

[3]For example, for the *Age* and *Gender* datasets, Train, Dev, and Test splits have 1.3m, 160k, and 160k, respectively. So, we randomly pick 50k, 5k, and 5k samples respectively.

6 Results

As explained, we compare different methods on 15 different Arabic social media datasets involving binary and multiclass classification. We present performance of the methods in Table 2. Evidently, CL-based methods achieve better performance on majority of the tasks. On average, three out of five CL-based methods (LCL, SCL, and TACT) achieve better performance than CE-MARBERT. Overall, LCL achieves the best F_1-score averaging across all the tasks.

It is important to note that there is no unique superior method across the tasks. This shows that CL-based methods can be task-specific, depending on the nature of how they are formulated. For example, LCL performs well on multiclass datasets such as *Abusive* and $AraNeT_{emo}$, while TLCL performs well on $SemEval_{emo}$. LCL and TLCL adopt more fine-grained representations with the incorporation of the weighting network which consequently helps them distinguish confused classes. However, for *Dialect at RegionLevel*, we speculate that since the labels are already fine-grained, it is more important to improve the robustness rather than inter-label relationship. Therefore, CAT achieves best performance on this task, followed by TLCL. Similarly, on binary classification tasks such as *hate speech* and *Offensive language detection*, where a subtle semantic change in meaning can alter the labels, robust methods are expected to outperform others. Therefore, adversarial methods like CAT and TACT achieve better F_1-score.

For most of the tasks, F_1-scores obtained from different CL-methods are close to each other and the vanilla SCL achieves similar average score to the other models. This proves that although task-specific formulation may help the models to improve on a certain task, the most important factor evolves around the fundamental *minmax* nature of contrastive learning which is minimizing the distance among the representations of the same class while maximizing the distance among the representations of the different classes.

7 Analysis

7.1 Data Efficiency

To investigate how the methods perform with limited data, we train the models under different size constraints using three datasets (one binary and

	CE	SCL	CAT	TACT	LCL	TLCL
Abusive	77.15	78.09	76.48	75.69	**78.32**	75.26
Adult	88.16	**89.50**	86.54	89.13	88.85	89.48
Age	44.22	45.12	42.28	**46.45**	45.90	43.20
AraNeT$_{emo}$	62.47	61.49	59.31	57.99	62.56	**64.13**
Dangerous	61.44	63.76	67.83	66.00	65.76	**69.28**
Dialect at BinaryLevel	85.71	85.63	**86.67**	84.98	85.79	81.84
Dialect at CountryLevel	32.84	**33.63**	33.24	32.69	33.62	31.34
Dialect at RegionLevel	65.29	64.78	**65.54**	64.56	62.92	64.92
Gender	62.23	63.56	65.58	65.77	**65.90**	65.14
Hate Speech	80.91	80.00	71.06	**82.62**	81.00	75.26
Irony	**84.75**	84.30	84.72	84.18	84.29	83.43
Offensive	90.43	89.92	**91.37**	91.23	90.41	88.84
Sarcasm	70.67	71.09	72.09	74.14	**75.32**	69.40
SemEval$_{emo}$	79.25	77.22	77.08	77.85	**80.61**	78.59
Sentiment Analysis	**77.69**	77.32	76.89	76.68	75.61	74.82
Avg.	70.88	71.03	70.45	71.33	**71.79**	70.33

Table 2: Macro F1-score of the models on Arabic social media datasets. Here, *CE* = Cross-Entropy; *SCL* = Supervised Contrastive Learning; *CAT* = Contrastive Adversarial Training; *TACT* = Token-level Adversarial Contrastive Training; *LCL* = Label-aware Contrastive Loss; *TLCL* = Token Adversarial LCL.

	Dialect-Country				Dialect-Region				AraNeT$_{emo}$			
	10%	25%	50%	100%	10%	25%	50%	100%	10%	25%	50%	100%
CE	27.78	30.5	30.91	32.84	63.09	63.16	63.59	65.29	53.85	56.73	59.18	62.47
SCL	28.49	**31.87**	**32.89**	**33.63**	63.08	63.23	63.37	64.78	54.47	58.35	58.35	61.49
CAT	26.57	30.33	32.71	33.24	**64.32**	**65.3**	**65.42**	**65.54**	54.75	54.03	55.51	59.31
TACT	27.63	29.88	32.04	32.69	63.8	64.1	64.32	64.56	53.27	**59.3**	59.18	57.99
LCL	**28.97**	30.5	31.78	33.62	63.72	64.72	65.06	62.92	**55.47**	59.25	62.21	62.56
TLCL	27.69	30.44	32.18	31.34	62.71	64.53	64.6	64.92	54.62	59.31	**62.98**	**64.13**

Table 3: Model performance on varying dataset sizes. **Bold** values represent the best performance for a particular dataset and dataset size.

two multiclass). We present results of this set of experiments in Table 3. One interesting observation is that improvement in performance is not always monotonic with respect to data size. We believe that larger-sized training sets only aid models with test samples with idiosyncrasies and that small training sets sufficiently cover a wide range of data distributions. However, we observe that CE-MARBERT fails to outperform CL-based methods in any constraint. Specifically, for *Dialect at CountryLevel* dataset, 50% of the data is sufficient for SCL to outperform CE-MARBERT trained on the full dataset. Additionally, CAT achieves comparable performance to CE-MARBERT with 50% training data. For *Dialect at RegionLevel* dataset, only 10% training data is sufficient for CAT, TACT, and LCL to outperform CE-MARBERT with 50% training data. Moreover, CAT requires only 50% training data to outperform CE-MARBERT with full training data. Finally, for *AraNeT$_{emo}$* dataset, LCL, TACT, and TLCL with 25% training data outperform CE-MARBERT with 50% training data. TLCL with 50% data outperforms CE-MARBERT with full (i.e., 100%) training data while LCL with 50% data achieves similar performance. *This analysis shows that enhancing the representations of different classes via CL helps the model to produce more distinguishable clusters. As a result, the models require only smaller training data to project a sample to a particular class.*

7.2 Impact of Batch Size

We study how batch size affects model performance. We consider batch sizes of 4, 8, 16 on three datasets, showing performance in Figure 3. We observe that, with only a few exceptions, performance of the models increases along with the increase of batch size. Larger batch sizes contain more samples from different classes, which helps the model to learn better via comparing these samples. Our

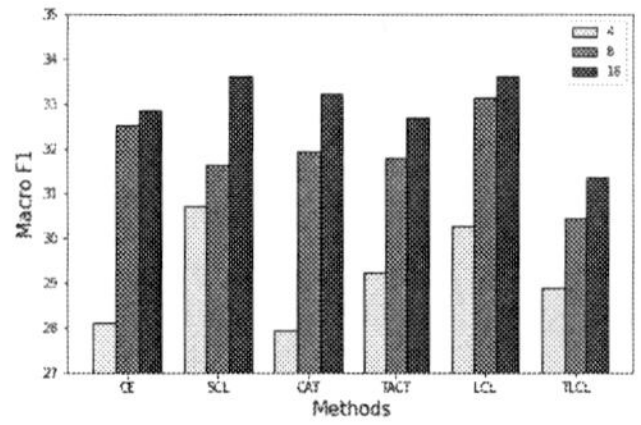

(a) Dialect at CountryLevel

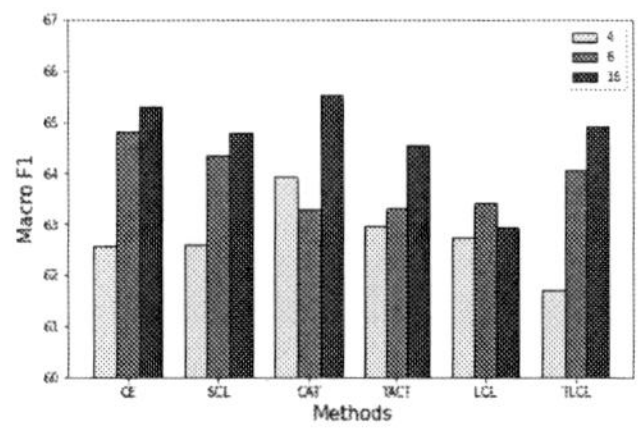

(b) Dialect at RegionLevel

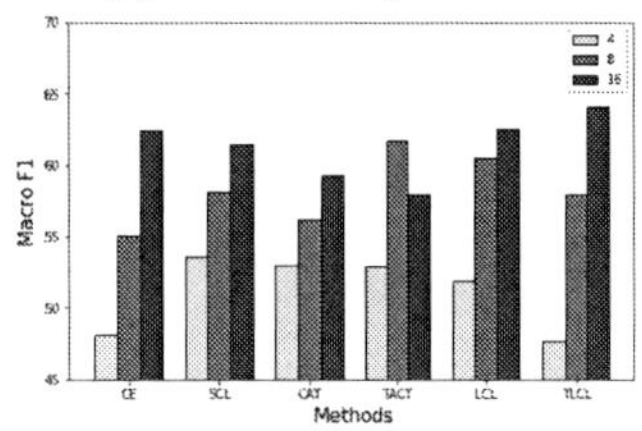

(c) $\text{AraNeT}_{\text{emo}}$

Figure 3: Ablation study on the impact of batch size on performance of the models.

(a) CE

(b) SCL

(c) CAT

(d) TACT

(e) LCL

(f) TLCL

Figure 4: t-SNE representations of the validation set of *abusive* dataset (green = normal, red = abusive, blue = hate).

analysis corroborates findings of prior works such as Chen et al. (2020b), Cao et al. (2022), and Qiu et al. (2021) that propose the incorporation of a separate memory bank to hold the negative samples for comparison.

7.3 Visualization of Representations

We plot t-SNE representations of the test samples from the *Abusive* dataset in Figure 4. The representations are colored with true labels. We notice that CL-based methods cluster *normal* and *abusive* samples far from each other, unlike CE-MARBERT. Since CL attempts to maximize the distance between different classes, it helps the models produce more distinct clusters. Additionally, LCL and TLCL methods cluster *abusive* and *hate* classes better than other methods. Since, they capture inter-label relations, the methods identify confusable examples of *abusive* and *hate* better than other methods.

8 Limitations

An inherent limitation of CL methods is their reliance on hyperparameters. In particular, they are sensitive to batch size. Larger batch sizes usually yield better performance. Other hyperparameters like τ and λ can also impact performance given a specific task. Lastly, the accommodation of larger batch size comes at the cost of higher computational resources.

9 Conclusion

In this work, we study various supervised contrastive learning methods for a wide range of Arabic social meaning tasks. We show that CL-based methods outperform generic cross entropy finetuning for majority of the tasks. Through empirical investigations, we find that improvements resulting from applying CL methods are task-specific. We interpret these results vis-a-vis different downstream tasks, with a special attention to the number of classes involved in each task. Finally, we demonstrate that CL methods can achieve better performance with limited training data and hence can be employed for low-resource settings.

In the future, we plan to extend our work beyond sentence classification by experimenting on tasks such as token-classification and question-answering. Our work stands as a comprehensive investigation of applying contrastive learning to Arabic social meaning. We hope this work will trigger further investigations of CL in Arabic NLP in general.

References

Ines Abbes, Wajdi Zaghouani, Omaima El-Hardlo, and Faten Ashour. 2020. Daict: A dialectal Arabic irony corpus extracted from twitter. In *Proceedings of The 12th Language Resources and Evaluation Conference*, pages 6265–6271.

Ahmed Abdelali, Sabit Hassan, Hamdy Mubarak, Kareem Darwish, and Younes Samih. 2021. Pre-training bert on arabic tweets: Practical considerations. *arXiv preprint arXiv:2102.10684*.

Ahmed Abdelali, Hamdy Mubarak, Younes Samih, Sabit Hassan, and Kareem Darwish. 2020. Arabic Dialect Identification in the Wild. *Proceedings of the Sixth Arabic Natural Language Processing Workshop*.

Muhammad Abdul-Mageed, Hassan AlHuzli, and Mona Diab DuaaAbu Elhija. 2016. Dina: A multi-dialect dataset for arabic emotion analysis. In *The 2nd workshop on Arabic corpora and processing tools*, page 29.

Muhammad Abdul-Mageed, AbdelRahim Elmadany, and El Moatez Billah Nagoudi. 2021a. ARBERT & MARBERT: Deep bidirectional transformers for Arabic. In *Proceedings of the 59th Annual Meeting of the Association for Computational Linguistics and the 11th International Joint Conference on Natural Language Processing (Volume 1: Long Papers)*, pages 7088–7105, Online. Association for Computational Linguistics.

Muhammad Abdul-Mageed, Mohammed Korayem, and Ahmed YoussefAgha. 2011. "Yes we can?": Subjectivity annotation and tagging for the health domain. In *Proceedings of the International Conference Recent Advances in Natural Language Processing 2011*, pages 666–671.

Muhammad Abdul-Mageed, Sandra Kübler, and Mona Diab. 2012. SAMAR: A system for subjectivity and sentiment analysis of arabic social media. In *Proceedings of the 3rd Workshop in Computational Approaches to Subjectivity and Sentiment Analysis*, pages 19–28. Association for Computational Linguistics.

Muhammad Abdul-Mageed and Lyle Ungar. 2017. EmoNet: Fine-grained emotion detection with gated recurrent neural networks. In *Proceedings of the 55th Annual Meeting of the Association for Computational Linguistics (Volume 1: Long Papers)*, volume 1, pages 718–728.

Muhammad Abdul-Mageed, Chiyu Zhang, Houda Bouamor, and Nizar Habash. 2020a. NADI 2020: The first nuanced Arabic dialect identification shared task. In *Proceedings of the Fifth Arabic Natural Language Processing Workshop*, pages 97–110, Barcelona, Spain (Online). Association for Computational Linguistics.

Muhammad Abdul-Mageed, Chiyu Zhang, AbdelRahim Elmadany, Houda Bouamor, and Nizar Habash. 2021b. NADI 2021: The second nuanced Arabic dialect identification shared task. In *Proceedings of the Sixth Arabic Natural Language Processing Workshop*, pages 244–259, Kyiv, Ukraine (Virtual). Association for Computational Linguistics.

Muhammad Abdul-Mageed, Chiyu Zhang, AbdelRahim Elmadany, and Lyle Ungar. 2020b. Toward micro-dialect identification in diaglossic and code-switched environments. In *Proceedings of the 2020 Conference on Empirical Methods in Natural Language Processing (EMNLP)*, pages 5855–5876, Online. Association for Computational Linguistics.

Muhammad Abdul-Mageed, Chiyu Zhang, Azadeh Hashemi, et al. 2020c. AraNet: A deep learning toolkit for arabic social media. In *Proceedings of the 4th Workshop on Open-Source Arabic Corpora and Processing Tools, with a Shared Task on Offensive Language Detection*, pages 16–23.

Malak Abdullah, Dalya Alnore, Safa Swedat, Jumana Khrais, and Mahmoud Al-Ayyoub. 2022. Sarcasmdet at semeval-2022 task 6: Detecting sarcasm using pre-trained transformers in english and arabic languages. In *Proceedings of the 16th International Workshop on Semantic Evaluation (SemEval-2022)*, pages 1025–1030.

Ibrahim Abu Farha, Wajdi Zaghouani, and Walid Magdy. 2021. Overview of the WANLP 2021 shared task on sarcasm and sentiment detection in Arabic. In *Proceedings of the Sixth Arabic Natural Language Processing Workshop*, pages 296–305, Kyiv, Ukraine (Virtual). Association for Computational Linguistics.

Ftoon Abu Shaqra, Rehab Duwairi, and Mahmoud Al-Ayyoub. 2022. A multi-modal deep learning system for arabic emotion recognition. *International Journal of Speech Technology*, pages 1–17.

Abeer Abuzayed and Hend Al-Khalifa. 2021. Sarcasm and sentiment detection in arabic tweets using bert-based models and data augmentation. In *Proceedings of the sixth Arabic natural language processing workshop*, pages 312–317.

Mahmoud Al-Ayyoub, Abed Allah Khamaiseh, Yaser Jararweh, and Mohammed N Al-Kabi. 2019. A comprehensive survey of arabic sentiment analysis. *Information Processing & Management*, 56(2):320–342.

Tareq Al-Moslmi, Mohammed Albared, Adel Al-Shabi, Nazlia Omar, and Salwani Abdullah. 2018. Arabic senti-lexicon: Constructing publicly available language resources for arabic sentiment analysis. *Journal of Information Science*, 44(3):345–362.

Ahmad Al Sallab, Hazem Hajj, Gilbert Badaro, Ramy Baly, Wassim El Hajj, and Khaled Bashir Shaban. 2015. Deep learning models for sentiment analysis in arabic. In *Proceedings of the second workshop on Arabic natural language processing*, pages 9–17.

Mohammad Al-Smadi, Bashar Talafha, Mahmoud Al-Ayyoub, and Yaser Jararweh. 2019. Using long short-term memory deep neural networks for aspect-based sentiment analysis of arabic reviews. *International Journal of Machine Learning and Cybernetics*, 10(8):2163–2175.

Muath Alali, Nurfadhlina Mohd Sharef, Masrah Azrifah Azmi Murad, Hazlina Hamdan, and Nor Azura Husin. 2022. Multitasking learning model based on hierarchical attention network for arabic sentiment analysis classification. *Electronics*, 11(8):1193.

Hassan Alhuzali, Muhammad Abdul-Mageed, and Lyle Ungar. 2018. Enabling deep learning of emotion with first-person seed expressions. In *Proceedings of the Second Workshop on Computational Modeling of People's Opinions, Personality, and Emotions in Social Media*, pages 25–35.

Badr AlKhamissi and Mona Diab. 2022. Meta AI at Arabic hate speech 2022: MultiTask learning with self-correction for hate speech classification. In *Proceedinsg of the 5th Workshop on Open-Source Arabic Corpora and Processing Tools with Shared Tasks on Qur'an QA and Fine-Grained Hate Speech Detection*, pages 186–193, Marseille, France. European Language Resources Association.

Latifah Almuqren and Alexandra Cristea. 2021. Aracust: a saudi telecom tweets corpus for sentiment analysis. *PeerJ Computer Science*, 7:e510.

Ali Alshehri, Muhammad Abdul-Mageed, et al. 2020. Understanding and detecting dangerous speech in social media. In *Proceedings of the 4th Workshop on Open-Source Arabic Corpora and Processing Tools, with a Shared Task on Offensive Language Detection*, pages 40–47.

Salaheddin Alzu'bi, Thiago Castro Ferreira, Lucas Pavanelli, and Mohamed Al-Badrashiny. 2022. aixplain at arabic hate speech 2022: An ensemble based approach to detecting offensive tweets.

David Bamman and Noah Smith. 2015. Contextualized sarcasm detection on twitter. In *proceedings of the international AAAI conference on web and social media*, volume 9, pages 574–577.

Houda Bouamor, Nizar Habash, Mohammad Salameh, Wajdi Zaghouani, Owen Rambow, Dana Abdulrahim, Ossama Obeid, Salam Khalifa, Fadhl Eryani, Alexander Erdmann, and Kemal Oflazer. 2018. The MADAR Arabic dialect corpus and lexicon. In *Proceedings of the Eleventh International Conference on Language Resources and Evaluation (LREC 2018)*, Miyazaki, Japan. European Language Resources Association (ELRA).

Houda Bouamor, Sabit Hassan, and Nizar Habash. 2019. The madar shared task on arabic fine-grained dialect identification. In *Proceedings of the Fourth Arabic Natural Language Processing Workshop*, pages 199–207.

Rui Cao, Yihao Wang, Yuxin Liang, Ling Gao, Jie Zheng, Jie Ren, and Zheng Wang. 2022. Exploring the impact of negative samples of contrastive learning: A case study of sentence embedding. In *Findings of the Association for Computational Linguistics: ACL 2022*, pages 3138–3152, Dublin, Ireland. Association for Computational Linguistics.

Ting Chen, Simon Kornblith, Mohammad Norouzi, and Geoffrey Hinton. 2020a. A simple framework for contrastive learning of visual representations. In *Proceedings of the 37th International Conference on Machine Learning*, volume 119 of *Proceedings of Machine Learning Research*, pages 1597–1607. PMLR.

Ting Chen, Yizhou Sun, Yue Shi, and Liangjie Hong. 2017. On sampling strategies for neural network-based collaborative filtering. In *Proceedings of the 23rd ACM SIGKDD International Conference on Knowledge Discovery and Data Mining*, KDD '17, page 767–776, New York, NY, USA. Association for Computing Machinery.

Xinlei Chen, Haoqi Fan, Ross Girshick, and Kaiming He. 2020b. Improved baselines with momentum contrastive learning. *arXiv preprint arXiv:2003.04297*.

Ryan Cotterell and Chris Callison-Burch. 2014. A multi-dialect, multi-genre corpus of informal written arabic. In *LREC*, pages 241–245.

Jacob Devlin, Ming-Wei Chang, Kenton Lee, and Kristina Toutanova. 2018. Bert: Pre-training of deep bidirectional transformers for language understanding. *arXiv preprint arXiv:1810.04805*.

Mahmoud El-Haj. 2020. Habibi-a multi dialect multi national arabic song lyrics corpus. In *Proceedings of the 12th Language Resources and Evaluation Conference*, pages 1318–1326.

Heba Elfardy and Mona T Diab. 2013. Sentence level dialect identification in arabic. In *ACL (2)*, pages 456–461.

AbdelRahim Elmadany, Chiyu Zhang, Muhammad Abdul-Mageed, and Azadeh Hashemi. 2020a. Leveraging affective bidirectional transformers for offensive language detection. In *Proceedings of the 4th Workshop on Open-Source Arabic Corpora and Processing Tools, with a Shared Task on Offensive Language Detection*, pages 102–108.

AbdelRahim Elmadany, Chiyu Zhang, Muhammad Abdul-Mageed, and Azadeh Hashemi. 2020b. Leveraging affective bidirectional transformers for offensive language detection. In *The 4th Workshop on Open-Source Arabic Corpora and Processing Tools (OSACT4), LREC.*

Hady ElSahar and Samhaa R El-Beltagy. 2015. Building large arabic multi-domain resources for sentiment analysis. In *International Conference on Intelligent Text Processing and Computational Linguistics*, pages 23–34. Springer.

Hongchao Fang, Sicheng Wang, Meng Zhou, Jiayuan Ding, and Pengtao Xie. 2020. Cert: Contrastive self-supervised learning for language understanding. *arXiv preprint arXiv:2005.12766.*

Ibrahim Abu Farha and Walid Magdy. 2019. Mazajak: An online arabic sentiment analyser. In *Proceedings of the Fourth Arabic Natural Language Processing Workshop*, pages 192–198.

Ibrahim Abu Farha and Walid Magdy. 2020. From Arabic Sentiment Analysis to Sarcasm Detection: The ArSarcasm Dataset. In *Proceedings of the 4th Workshop on Open-Source Arabic Corpora and Processing Tools, with a Shared Task on Offensive Language Detection*, pages 32–39.

Atefeh Farzindar and Diana Inkpen. 2015. Natural language processing for social media. *Synthesis Lectures on Human Language Technologies*, 8(2):1–166.

Chayma Fourati, Abir Messaoudi, and Hatem Haddad. 2020. Tunizi: a tunisian arabizi sentiment analysis dataset. In *AfricaNLP Workshop, Putting Africa on the NLP Map. ICLR 2020, Virtual Event*, volume arXiv:3091079.

Tianyu Gao, Xingcheng Yao, and Danqi Chen. 2021. SimCSE: Simple contrastive learning of sentence embeddings. In *Proceedings of the 2021 Conference on Empirical Methods in Natural Language Processing*, pages 6894–6910, Online and Punta Cana, Dominican Republic. Association for Computational Linguistics.

Bilal Ghanem, Jihen Karoui, Farah Benamara, Véronique Moriceau, and Paolo Rosso. 2019. Idat@fire2019: Overview of the track on irony detection in arabic tweets. In *Mehta P., Rosso P., Majumder P., Mitra M. (Eds.) Working Notes of the Forum for Information Retrieval Evaluation (FIRE 2019). CEUR Workshop Proceedings. In: CEUR-WS.org, Kolkata, India, December 12-15.*

Daniel Gillick, Sayali Kulkarni, Larry Lansing, Alessandro Presta, Jason Baldridge, Eugene Ie, and Diego Garcia-Olano. 2019. Learning dense representations for entity retrieval. In *Proceedings of the 23rd Conference on Computational Natural Language Learning (CoNLL)*, pages 528–537, Hong Kong, China. Association for Computational Linguistics.

Ian Goodfellow, Jonathon Shlens, and Christian Szegedy. 2015. Explaining and harnessing adversarial examples. In *International Conference on Learning Representations.*

Raia Hadsell, Sumit Chopra, and Yann LeCun. 2006. Dimensionality reduction by learning an invariant mapping. In *2006 IEEE Computer Society Conference on Computer Vision and Pattern Recognition (CVPR'06)*, volume 2, pages 1735–1742. IEEE.

Matthew Henderson, Rami Al-Rfou, Brian Strope, Yunhsuan Sung, Laszlo Lukacs, Ruiqi Guo, Sanjiv Kumar, Balint Miklos, and Ray Kurzweil. 2017. Efficient natural language response suggestion for smart reply.

Fatemah Husain and Ozlem Uzuner. 2022. Investigating the effect of preprocessing arabic text on offensive language and hate speech detection. *Transactions on Asian and Low-Resource Language Information Processing*, 21(4):1–20.

Go Inoue, Bashar Alhafni, Nurpeiis Baimukan, Houda Bouamor, and Nizar Habash. 2021. The interplay of variant, size, and task type in Arabic pre-trained language models. In *Proceedings of the Sixth Arabic Natural Language Processing Workshop*, pages 92–104, Kyiv, Ukraine (Virtual). Association for Computational Linguistics.

Sverker Janson, Evangelina Gogoulou, Erik Ylipää, Amaru Cuba Gyllensten, and Magnus Sahlgren. 2021. Semantic re-tuning with contrastive tension. In *International Conference on Learning Representations, 2021.*

Jihen Karoui, Farah Banamara Zitoune, and Veronique Moriceau. 2017. Soukhria: Towards an irony detection system for arabic in social media. *Procedia Computer Science*, 117:161–168.

Vladimir Karpukhin, Barlas Oguz, Sewon Min, Patrick Lewis, Ledell Wu, Sergey Edunov, Danqi Chen, and Wen-tau Yih. 2020. Dense passage retrieval for open-domain question answering. In *Proceedings of the 2020 Conference on Empirical Methods in Natural Language Processing (EMNLP)*, pages 6769–6781, Online. Association for Computational Linguistics.

Prannay Khosla, Piotr Teterwak, Chen Wang, Aaron Sarna, Yonglong Tian, Phillip Isola, Aaron Maschinot, Ce Liu, and Dilip Krishnan. 2020. Supervised contrastive learning. In *Advances in Neural Information Processing Systems*, volume 33, pages 18661–18673. Curran Associates, Inc.

Tassilo Klein and Moin Nabi. 2022. SCD: Self-contrastive decorrelation of sentence embeddings. In *Proceedings of the 60th Annual Meeting of the Association for Computational Linguistics (Volume 2: Short Papers)*, pages 394–400, Dublin, Ireland. Association for Computational Linguistics.

Lajanugen Logeswaran and Honglak Lee. 2018. An efficient framework for learning sentence representations. In *International Conference on Learning Representations*, volume abs/1803.02893.

Asmaa Mansour Khoudja, Mourad Loukam, and Fatma Zohra Belkredim. 2022. Towards author profiling from modern standard arabic texts: A review. In *Proceedings of Sixth International Congress on Information and Communication Technology*, pages 745–753. Springer.

Alaa Mansy, Sherine Rady, and Tarek Gharib. 2022. An ensemble deep learning approach for emotion detection in arabic tweets. *International Journal of Advanced Computer Science and Applications*, 13(4).

Yu Meng, Chenyan Xiong, Payal Bajaj, Paul Bennett, Jiawei Han, Xia Song, et al. 2021. Coco-lm: Correcting and contrasting text sequences for language model pretraining. *Advances in Neural Information Processing Systems*, 34:23102–23114.

Saif Mohammad, Felipe Bravo-Marquez, Mohammad Salameh, and Svetlana Kiritchenko. 2018. SemEval-2018 task 1: Affect in tweets. In *Proceedings of The 12th International Workshop on Semantic Evaluation*, pages 1–17, New Orleans, Louisiana. Association for Computational Linguistics.

Saif Mohammad, Svetlana Kiritchenko, Parinaz Sobhani, Xiaodan Zhu, and Colin Cherry. 2016. Semeval-2016 task 6: Detecting stance in tweets. In *Proceedings of the 10th international workshop on semantic evaluation (SemEval-2016)*, pages 31–41.

Hamdy Mubarak, Hend Al-Khalifa, and AbdulMohsen Al-Thubaity. 2022a. Overview of osact5 shared task on arabic offensive language and hate speech detection.

Hamdy Mubarak, Shammur Absar Chowdhury, and Firoj Alam. 2022b. Arabgend: Gender analysis and inference on arabic twitter. *arXiv preprint arXiv:2203.00271*.

Hamdy Mubarak, Kareem Darwish, and Walid Magdy. 2017. Abusive language detection on Arabic social media. In *Proceedings of the First Workshop on Abusive Language Online*, pages 52–56, Vancouver, BC, Canada. Association for Computational Linguistics.

Hamdy Mubarak, Kareem Darwish, Walid Magdy, Tamer Elsayed, and Hend Al-Khalifa. 2020. Overview of OSACT4 Arabic offensive language detection shared task. In *Proceedings of the 4th Workshop on Open-Source Arabic Corpora and Processing Tools, with a Shared Task on Offensive Language Detection*, pages 48–52, Marseille, France. European Language Resource Association.

Hamdy Mubarak, Sabit Hassan, and Ahmed Abdelali. 2021. Adult content detection on Arabic Twitter: Analysis and experiments. In *Proceedings of the Sixth Arabic Natural Language Processing Workshop*, pages 136–144, Kyiv, Ukraine (Virtual). Association for Computational Linguistics.

Hamdy Mubarak, Sabit Hassan, and Shammur Absar Chowdhury. 2022c. Emojis as anchors to detect arabic offensive language and hate speech. *arXiv preprint arXiv:2201.06723*.

Mahmoud Nabil, Mohamed Aly, and Amir F Atiya. 2015. Astd: Arabic sentiment tweets dataset. In *Proceedings of the 2015 Conference on Empirical Methods in Natural Language Processing*, pages 2515–2519.

El Moatez Billah Nagoudi, AbdelRahim Elmadany, and Muhammad Abdul-Mageed. 2022. AraT5: Text-to-text transformers for Arabic language generation. In *Proceedings of the 60th Annual Meeting of the Association for Computational Linguistics (Volume 1: Long Papers)*, pages 628–647, Dublin, Ireland. Association for Computational Linguistics.

Mohamed Aziz Ben Nessir, Malek Rhouma, Hatem Haddad, and Chayma Fourati. 2022. icompass at arabic hate speech 2022: Detect hate speech using qrnn and transformers.

Aaron van den Oord, Yazhe Li, and Oriol Vinyals. 2018. Representation learning with contrastive predictive coding. *arXiv preprint arXiv:1807.03748*.

Lin Pan, Chung-Wei Hang, Avirup Sil, and Saloni Potdar. 2022. Improved text classification via contrastive adversarial training. In *Proceedings of the AAAI Conference on Artificial Intelligence*, volume 36, pages 11130–11138.

Yao Qiu, Jinchao Zhang, and Jie Zhou. 2021. Improving gradient-based adversarial training for text classification by contrastive learning and auto-encoder. *arXiv preprint arXiv:2109.06536*.

Yanru Qu, Dinghan Shen, Yelong Shen, Sandra Sajeev, Jiawei Han, and Weizhu Chen. 2020. Coda: Contrast-enhanced and diversity-promoting data augmentation for natural language understanding. *arXiv preprint arXiv:2010.08670*.

Francisco Rangel, Paolo Rosso, Anis Charfi, Wajdi Zaghouani, Bilal Ghanem, and Javier Sánchez-Junquera. 2019. Overview of the track on author profiling and deception detection in arabic. *Working Notes of FIRE 2019. CEUR-WS. org, vol. 2517*, pages 70–83.

Olga Russakovsky, Jia Deng, Hao Su, Jonathan Krause, Sanjeev Satheesh, Sean Ma, Zhiheng Huang, Andrej Karpathy, Aditya Khosla, Michael Bernstein, Alexander C. Berg, and Li Fei-Fei. 2015. Imagenet large scale visual recognition challenge. *International Journal of Computer Vision*, 115(3).

Hager Saleh, Sherif Mostafa, Abdullah Alharbi, Shaker El-Sappagh, and Tamim Alkhalifah. 2022. Heterogeneous ensemble deep learning model for enhanced arabic sentiment analysis. *Sensors*, 22(10):3707.

Ahmad Shapiro, Ayman Khalafallah, and Marwan Torki. 2022. Alexu-aic at arabic hate speech 2022: Contrast to classify. *arXiv preprint arXiv:2207.08557*.

Yixuan Su, Fangyu Liu, Zaiqiao Meng, Tian Lan, Lei Shu, Ehsan Shareghi, and Nigel Collier. 2022. TaCL: Improving BERT pre-training with token-aware contrastive learning. In *Findings of the Association for Computational Linguistics: NAACL 2022*, pages 2497–2507, Seattle, United States. Association for Computational Linguistics.

Varsha Suresh and Desmond Ong. 2021. Not all negatives are equal: Label-aware contrastive loss for fine-grained text classification. In *Proceedings of the 2021 Conference on Empirical Methods in Natural Language Processing*, pages 4381–4394, Online and Punta Cana, Dominican Republic. Association for Computational Linguistics.

Jenny A Thomas. 2014. *Meaning in interaction: An introduction to pragmatics*. Routledge.

Cynthia Van Hee, Els Lefever, and Véronique Hoste. 2018. Semeval-2018 task 3: Irony detection in english tweets. In *Proceedings of The 12th International Workshop on Semantic Evaluation*, pages 39–50.

Al-Jamal Wafa'Q, Ahmad M Mustafa, and Mostafa Z Ali. 2022. Sarcasm detection in arabic short text using deep learning. In *2022 13th International Conference on Information and Communication Systems (ICICS)*, pages 362–366. IEEE.

Zeerak Waseem and Dirk Hovy. 2016. Hateful symbols or hateful people? predictive features for hate speech detection on twitter. In *Proceedings of the NAACL student research workshop*, pages 88–93.

Thomas Wolf, Lysandre Debut, Victor Sanh, Julien Chaumond, Clement Delangue, Anthony Moi, Pierric Cistac, Tim Rault, Remi Louf, Morgan Funtowicz, Joe Davison, Sam Shleifer, Patrick von Platen, Clara Ma, Yacine Jernite, Julien Plu, Canwen Xu, Teven Le Scao, Sylvain Gugger, Mariama Drame, Quentin Lhoest, and Alexander Rush. 2020. Transformers: State-of-the-art natural language processing. In *Proceedings of the 2020 Conference on Empirical Methods in Natural Language Processing: System Demonstrations*, pages 38–45, Online. Association for Computational Linguistics.

Wajdi Zaghouani and Anis Charfi. 2018. Arap-tweet: A large multi-dialect twitter corpus for gender, age and language variety identification. In *Proceedings of the Eleventh International Conference on Language Resources and Evaluation (LREC-2018)*.

Omar F Zaidan and Chris Callison-Burch. 2011. The arabic online commentary dataset: an annotated dataset of informal arabic with high dialectal content. In *Proceedings of the 49th Annual Meeting of the Association for Computational Linguistics: Human Language Technologies: short papers-Volume 2*, pages 37–41. Association for Computational Linguistics.

Omar F Zaidan and Chris Callison-Burch. 2014. Arabic dialect identification. *Computational Linguistics*, 40(1):171–202.

Chiyu Zhang and Muhammad Abdul-Mageed. 2019. No army, no navy: Bert semi-supervised learning of arabic dialects. In *Proceedings of the Fourth Arabic Natural Language Processing Workshop*, pages 279–284.

Chiyu Zhang and Muhammad Abdul-Mageed. 2022. Improving social meaning detection with pragmatic masking and surrogate fine-tuning. In *Proceedings of the 12th Workshop on Computational Approaches to Subjectivity, Sentiment & Social Media Analysis*, pages 141–156.

Chiyu Zhang, Muhammad Abdul-Mageed, and Ganesh Jawahar. 2022a. Infodcl: A distantly supervised contrastive learning framework for social meaning. *arXiv preprint arXiv:2203.07648*.

Chiyu Zhang, Muhammad Abdul-Mageed, and El Moatez Billah Nagoudi. 2022b. Decay no more: A persistent twitter dataset for learning social meaning. *Workshop Proceedings of the 16th International AAAI Conference on Web and Social Media*.

Kun Zhou, Beichen Zhang, Xin Zhao, and Ji-Rong Wen. 2022. Debiased contrastive learning of unsupervised sentence representations. In *Proceedings of the 60th Annual Meeting of the Association for Computational Linguistics (Volume 1: Long Papers)*, pages 6120–6130, Dublin, Ireland. Association for Computational Linguistics.

Adversarial Text-to-Speech for low-resource languages

Ashraf Elneima
African Institute for Mathematical Sciences
aelneima@aimsammi.org

Mikołaj Bińkowski
DeepMind
binek@deepmind.com

Abstract

In this paper we propose a new method for training adversarial text-to-speech (TTS) models for low-resource languages using auxiliary data. Specifically, we modify the MelGAN (Kumar et al., 2019) architecture to achieve better performance in Arabic speech generation, exploring multiple additional datasets and architectural choices, which involved extra discriminators designed to exploit high-frequency similarities between languages. In our evaluation, we used subjective human evaluation, MOS - Mean Opinion Score, and a novel quantitative metric, the Fréchet Wav2Vec Distance, which we found to be well correlated with MOS. Both subjectively and quantitatively, our method outperformed the standard MelGAN model.

1 Introduction

Text-to-speech (TTS) is the task of generating natural speech that corresponds to a given text. TTS systems play essential roles in a wide range of applications, ranging from human-computer interaction to assistance for people with vision or speech impairments.

In recent years the field of TTS has been dominated by the neural auto-regressive models for raw audio waveform such as WaveNet (Oord et al., 2016a), SampleRNN (Mehri et al., 2016) and WaveRNN (Kalchbrenner et al., 2018). However, inference with these models is inherently slow and inefficient given the high frequency of audio data; because of the auto-regressive behaviour and the sequential generation of the audio samples. Thus, auto-regressive models are usually impractical for real-time applications. Researchers put much effort into enabling parallelism of the TTS models, which resulted in a number of *non-auto-regressive* ones, such as Parallel WaveNet (Oord et al., 2018) which distils a trained auto-regressive decoder into a flow-based convolutional student model, WaveGlow (Prenger et al., 2019) which is a flow-based generative model based on Glow (Kingma and Dhariwal, 2018) as well as the Generative Adversarial Network (GAN (Yi et al., 2019))-based models such as MelGAN (Kumar et al., 2019) and GAN-TTS (Bińkowski et al., 2019). They are highly parallelizable and more suitable to run efficiently on modern hardware. However, those recent developments often came at the price of scale, and hence may be impractical for certain applications with limited compute or data budgets.

Deep neural networks have revolutionized the field of TTS achieving human-level performance on particular languages by leveraging massive collections of good-quality datasets, e.g. The LJ Speech Dataset[1]. However, these successes came at cost since creating these large datasets typically requires a great deal of human effort to manually record and label individual data samples. This cost can be particularly extreme when recording and labelling requires expert supervision (for example, recording high quality audio requires a professional studio and staff). For many languages we lack resources to create sufficiently large labelled datasets, which limits the widespread adoption of TTS techniques.

The lack of available resources makes it extremely valuable to study the relationship between the different languages. The high-frequency similarities between languages can be exploited to learn better speech synthesis models for low-resource languages. However, not much work has focused so far on exploring this direction. The notable exceptions include some multi-lingual TTS models (Do et al., 2021). In Lee et al. (2018) they pre-trained a speech synthesis network using datasets from both high-resource and low-resource languages, and fine-tuned the network using only low-resource data. The results showed that the learned phoneme embedding vectors are located closer if their pronunciations are similar across the languages.

[1] https://keithito.com/LJ-Speech-Dataset/

Proceedings of the The Seventh Arabic Natural Language Processing Workshop (WANLP), pages 76 - 84
December 8, 2022

In this work, we explore raw waveform generation for low-resource languages using auxiliary data, taking Arabic as our case study and MelGAN (Kumar et al., 2019) as our baseline model. This study examines the Arabic language since it has a large global population, it is a complex language to model,[2] and there is a scarcity of Arabic TTS datasets, making it a low-resource language. Our main contributions are as follows:

- We train a fast and efficient TTS system for the Arabic language using a publicly available speech dataset[3].
- We propose an extension to MelGAN (Kumar et al., 2019) model which makes it more amenable to knowledge transfer between languages and evaluate its efficiency for low-resource speech datasets, focusing on co-training between vastly different languages/dialects and learning from low-quality samples.
- We propose a quantitative metric for Arabic speech generation based on Fréchet distance (Eiter and Mannila, 1994), the metric inspired by the DeepSpeechDistance for English language (Bińkowski et al., 2019), where we replace the DeepSpeech network with the Wav2Vec2ForCTC Arabic audio recognition network[4].

2 Background

The generative Adversarial Networks (GANs) Goodfellow et al. (2014) are a class of implicit generative models trained by adversarial means between two networks: the generator and the discriminator. Generators attempt to produce data that resemble reference distributions, while the discriminator tries to distinguish real data from generated data, providing a useful training signal.

Due to the high temporal resolution of raw waveform, the presence of structure at different time scales, and the short- and long-term interdependencies among these structures, audio synthesis is a challenging task. Most approaches simplify the problem by modelling a lower-resolution intermediate representation that can be efficiently computed from the raw temporal signal and preserves enough amount of information to allow a faithful inversion back to audio. It is therefore common to decompose text-to-speech (TTS) systems into two stages: the first stage maps text into the intermediate representation, while the second stage transforms it into audio waveform. Among the most commonly used intermediate representations are aligned linguistic features (Oord et al., 2016b) and Mel-spectrograms (Shen et al., 2018; Gibiansky et al., 2017). In this work, we use Mel-spectrogram as an intermediate representation and focus on the second stage. Considering the Mel-spectrogram inversion stage, the TTS systems can be categorized into three distinct families: the pure signal processing techniques, the auto-regressive models and the non-auto-regressive models. The auto-regressive models like the WaveNet (Oord et al., 2016a) produced the state-of-the-art results in text-to-speech synthesis (Sotelo et al., 2017; Shen et al., 2018) but inference with these models is inherently slow and inefficient due to the sequential generation of audio. The non-auto-regressive models hence are highly parallelizable and can exploit modern deep learning hardware like GPUs and TPUs. Well known examples are the WaveGlow (Prenger et al., 2019) which is a flow-based generative model based on Glow (Kingma and Dhariwal, 2018), and GAN-based TTS models like MelGAN (Kumar et al., 2019) and GAN-TTS (Bińkowski et al., 2019).

MelGAN generator is a fully convolutional feed-forward network which takes Mel-spectrogram as input and outputs a raw waveform. The generator is trained adversarially against a multi-scale architecture comprised of three discriminators that have identical network structures but operate on different audio scales. On the other, End-to-end architectures like the Tacotron (Wang et al., 2017), EATS (Donahue et al., 2020) and WaveGrad 2 (Chen et al., 2021) are introduced in the field of TTS to reduce the compound error of two-stage TTS systems. Tacotron is a generative text-to-speech model based on a seq-to-seq model with an attention mechanism (Sutskever et al., 2014), whereas Tacotron 2 (Shen et al., 2018) is a follow-up work that eliminates the non-neural network elements used in the original Tacotron.

Many works covered Arabic TTS synthesis to generate human-like speech, such as Abdel-Hamid

[2]Worldwide there are more than 420 million native Arabic speakers who speak over 25 dialects of the language, each of which has its own unique characteristics and dialectal words.

[3]`http://en.arabicspeechcorpus.com/`

[4]`https://huggingface.co/docs/transformers/model_doc/wav2vec2#transformers.`

et al. (2006), Rebai and BenAyed (2016) and Fahmy et al. (2020), but none of them adopted the GAN-based TTS models for the Arabic language. Fahmy et al. (2020) describes how to use a modified deep architecture from Tacotron 2 (Shen et al., 2018) to generate Mel-spectrograms from Arabic diacritic text as an intermediate feature representation followed by a WaveGlow (Prenger et al., 2019) architecture acting as a vocoder to produce a high-quality Arabic speech. The proposed model is trained using a published pre-trained Tacotron 2 English model using a dataset with a total of 2.41 hours of recorded speech [3]. To the best of our knowledge, this is the best Arabic TTS available.

3 Methodology

In this section, we present the details of the architectures of our models, the datasets, and the evaluation metrics we used. In MelGAN's official repository[5], generator weights are publicly available, but discriminator weights are not. We use various methods of knowledge transfer between languages, including fine-tuning and co-training.

3.1 Model Architecture

In our analysis, we used the MelGAN architecture (Kumar et al., 2019) with an amended downsampling schedule that we found to perform better in our early experiments. With the proposed schedule, we ensure that there is no common divisor between downsampling factors to encourage focus on different frequencies across discriminators. We used factors 3 and 5 to downsample audio before passing it to the second and third discriminators. The downsampling is done by a strided average pooling layer.

MelGAN's multi-discriminator architecture incorporates an inductive bias that aims to exploit different structures at various temporal resolutions. In addition, we are interested in investigating another inductive bias that aims to exploit the considerable overlap between the phonemes of different languages and dialects, which may be helpful to improve the performance of low-resource languages. In the proposed approach we introduce auxiliary data to the model through an additional discriminator, designed to operate on short segments of speech to capture high-frequency similarities. We found optimal segment length for this extra discriminator to be 512-time steps. We consider two ways of feeding the extra data to the model:

- As part of first setting, the additional discriminator is fed a batch of 512-time step segments of two types, one generated directly by passing a small window of the auxiliary dataset mel-spectrogram to the generator, and another produced by sub-sampling the audio generated with the main dataset conditioning to pass to the main discriminators.
- While in the second setting, the additional discriminator accepted a batch of 512-time step segments both are sub-sampled from the audio generated with the main dataset conditioning to pass to the main discriminators, but to introduce the auxiliary dataset, part of the ground truth segments are replaced by random segments of the auxiliary dataset.

The mixing ratio between the two types of segments in both settings is a hyper-parameter that we optimise experimentally.

Passing the auxiliary data to the generator in the first setting provides a more complicated task for the generator to learn, while in the second setting the generator's task remains unchanged; however the additional discriminator is provided with more ground truth samples and hence enriches the adversarial signal passed back to the generator. Finally, the additional discriminator uses half of the standard MelGAN discriminators' capacity[6], which we found to perform roughly on par with the full capacity variant.

3.2 Datasets

We used the Arabic Speech Corpus dataset[3] as our main dataset. The training set contains 1813 spoken utterances of a standard Arabic dialect recorded by a single speaker, covering a duration of 2 hours; additional 100 samples form a test set. The data is labelled with diacritic Arabic text (Sweet, 1877). In addition to the main dataset, we used three auxiliary datasets as described in the table 1. The auxiliary datasets include LJSpeech[1], Tunisian_MSA[7] and AMMI_Speech datasets[8]. The AMMI_Speech dataset is gathered by AMMI[9] student. The

[5] https://github.com/descriptinc/melgan-neurips

[6] half the number of convolution filters

[7] https://www.openslr.org/46/

[8] https://github.com/besacier/AMMIcourse/tree/master/STUDENTS-RETURN/Arabic4

[9] African Master of Machine Intelligence - https://aimsammi.org

Name	Language	Dialect	Speakers	Quality	Hrs
LJSpeech	English	-	1	high	24
Tunisian_MSA train	Arabic	Tunisian	118	low	11
Tunisian_MSA test	Arabic	Tunisian/Libyans	4	average	2
AMMI_Speech	Arabic	Standard	3	low	6
Arabic Speech Corpus	Arabic	Standard	1	high	2

Table 1: The datails of the auxiliary datasets used.

Tunisian_MSA train and test set are separated into two auxiliary datasets due to their varying quality.

3.3 Evaluation Metrics

For evaluation, two metrics are employed: the Mean Opinion Score (MOS) and a novel quantitative metric, the Conditional Fréchet Wav2Vec Distance (cFWD).

Mean Opinion Score In order to compare the performance of our models, we carried out Mean Opinion Score (MOS) tests. We gathered 100 samples generated by the different models using the same conditioning, along with 100 original samples. All the generated samples were not seen during training. MOS scores were computed on a population of 53 individual raters; each of them had to evaluate blindly a subset of 150 samples drawn randomly from the overall pool and assign a score from 1 to 5. Our tests were crowdsourced over multimedia platforms and testers were asked to wear headphones and be Arabic speakers. Additionally, we computed the 95% confidence intervals for the scores:

$$\hat{\mu}_i = \frac{1}{N_i}\sum_{k=1}^{N_i} s_{i,k}$$

$$CI_i = \left[\hat{\mu}_i - 1.96\frac{\hat{\sigma}_i}{\sqrt{N_i}}, \hat{\mu}_i + 1.96\frac{\hat{\sigma}_i}{\sqrt{N_i}}\right]$$

Conditional Fréchet Wav2Vec Distance This metric is inspired by the DeepSpeech Distances (Bińkowski et al., 2019) and analogous to Fréchet Inception Distance (FID, Heusel et al., 2017) commonly used in generative modelling of images. In order to extract the high-level features from raw Arabic audio, the DeepSpeech2 model was replaced by the pre-trained Wav2Vec2ForCTC Arabic speech recognition model found in the HuggingFace Transformers library[4].

To obtain reasonable estimates of this metric it is preferred to use sufficiently large sets of samples. The original implementation used 50 thousand samples (Soloveitchik et al., 2021). However, as this would be too resource-intensive, we artificially expand the generated and real sets by randomly subsampling small windows from each audio.

The distribution for a set of waveforms is formed by sub-sampling thirty 2-second-long sub-samples from each audio; this way we construct fixed-length sub-samples from arbitrary-long ones, covering their whole length and putting equal weight to short and long samples. Finally, the features extraction is done by framing each sub-sample using a 40ms window of raw audio at 16kHz and stride of 20ms, passing the frames to the speech recognition model, and extracting the 512-dimensional output of the $feature\_projection$ layer, and then taking the average of the features along the temporal dimension. The Fréchet distance is calculated by comparing the distributions of such representations of real and generated samples from our test set, which has 100 samples, resulting in 3000 samples after subsampling. For representations $X \in \mathbb{R}^{m\times d}$ and $Y \in \mathbb{R}^{n\times d}$, where d is the representation dimension, and m is the number of samples, the (squared) Fréchet distance is obtained using the following estimator:

$$\widehat{\text{Fréchet}}^{\,2}(X,Y) =$$

$$\|x - \mu_Y\|_2^2 + Tr\left(\Sigma_X + \Sigma_Y - 2\left(\Sigma_X\Sigma_Y\right)^{1/2}\right)$$

An initial evaluation of the metric involved calculating the Fréchet distance between a reference sound and the same sound after adding multiple levels of Gaussian noise separately. The results are shown in figure 1.

4 Experiments

In this section we provide details on the experiments, including baselines and ablation study. We train our models using our main dataset, the Arabic Speech Corpus dataset[3], either with or without addition of the one of the auxiliary datasets described

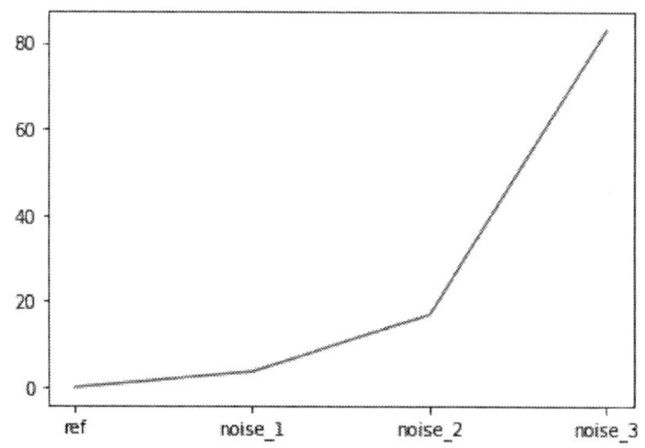

Figure 1: An initial evaluation for the Conditional Fréchet Wav2Vec Distance using different levels of Gaussian noise.

in table 1. In all experiments, unless stated otherwise, the English dataset[1] is used as an auxiliary dataset. The MelGAN model (Kumar et al., 2019) with an amended downsampling schedule was used in all experiments, and we added one additional discriminator when auxiliary datasets were analyzed. Currently, no clear strategies have been developed for GANs with auxiliary data; thus, fine-tuning and training from scratch using both the main and auxiliary datasets seems reasonable and we explored both here.

4.1 Baselines

We compare MelGAN model with a model described by Fahmy et al. (2020) to evaluate its effectiveness for Arabic language synthesis. Based on a modified deep architecture from Tacotron 2 (Shen et al., 2018), the model creates a mel-spectrogram of diacritical Arabic text as an intermediate feature representation, before using WaveGlow (Prenger et al., 2019) as a vocoder to synthesize high-quality Arabic speech. To develop the final model, Fahmy et al. (2020) started from English pre-trained model and fine-tuned using Arabic Speech Corpus dataset[3].

To examine the effectiveness of the additional discriminator (through which the auxiliary data is introduced), we compare the baseline MelGAN with the results obtained with different mixing ratios for the main and auxiliary segments that are passed to this additional discriminator.

4.2 Fine-tuning

In this experiment, we carry out transfer learning in its plain form, i.e. we start with a model pre-trained on an auxiliary dataset and then fine-tune using our main dataset. We use the standard MelGAN architecture (Kumar et al., 2019), with no additional discriminators. The initial pre-training is done on English data[1], followed by fine-tuning on 2 hours of Arabic data[3].

Transfer learning in our setting involves additional challenge that is specific to adversarial models: it seems crucially important to ensure that the min-max game between the generator and discriminator is balanced both during pre-training and fine-tuning. The latter becomes difficult e.g. in a situation when only one of the networks is avialable with pre-trained weights. This unfortunately happens to be the case with MelGAN, whose generator weights are publicly available from official repository[5], but discriminator weights are not shared. Of course pre-training both generator and discriminator from scratch using the English dataset is technically an option, however it is also computationally intensive, and was beyond capacity of our resources. In order to address this issue, we fine-tuned the discriminator alone with the main dataset for 2K steps while fixing the generator weights before fine-tuning the entire model. The discriminator was initially initialized either randomly or using the weights of a pre-trained Arabic discriminator.

4.3 Training GANs with auxiliary data

In this set of experiments we introduce an auxiliary dataset by developing a variant of MelGAN architecture with an additional discriminator. Original discriminators in MelGAN use longer segments than discriminators in GAN-TTS. In training the proposed architecture, we used both the main dataset and a range of auxiliary ones; including an English dataset[1], two Arabic dialect datasets[7], or a low-quality standard Arabic dataset[8]. According to how the auxiliary dataset is introduced to the model, the experiments can be divided into two parts as follows:

Generator with auxiliary segments In this setting, we send to the generator the mel-pectrogram of 512-time steps windows of the auxiliary dataset. The resulting segments are added to the discriminator along with 512-time steps segments subsampled from the audio generated given the main dataset conditioning. Mixing ratio refers to the ratio between these two types of segments.

Extra ground truths for discriminator In this setting, as illustrated in figure 2, we present a way

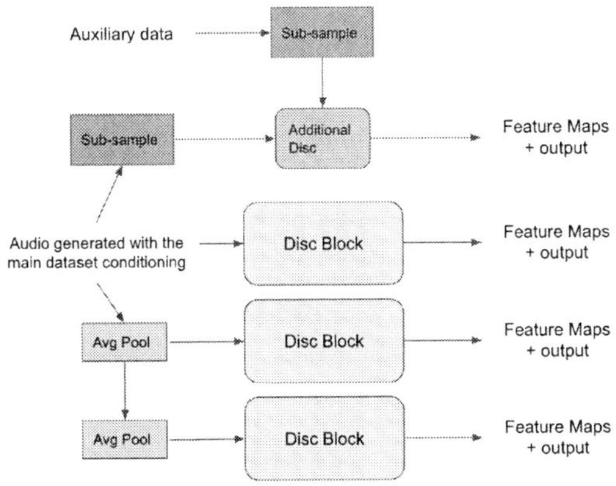

Figure 2: An illustration of the second part of training GANs with auxiliary data experiments, where we pass as extra ground truths for the discriminator.

to incorporate auxiliary data into the model without complicating the generator task. The additional discriminator batches are derived by subsampling 512-time steps segments from audios generated given the main dataset conditioning. The ground truths for part of this segment are replaced with random segments from the auxiliary datasets, but the rest remain fixed. Mixing ratio refers to the ratio between these two types of segments. Through this, we can improve the discriminator adversarial signal being fed back to the generator. A small window was used to concentrate on the high-frequency features. Different segments sizes were tested and 512 was found to perform the best.

4.4 Efficiency analysis of various speech datasets as auxiliary dataset

We present here a discussion of the effects of using various auxiliary datasets. For the comparison, each of the auxiliary datasets is introduced separately as additional ground truths for the extra discriminator with a mixing ratio of 1:1 between the main and the auxiliary datasets respectively.

4.5 Ablations

The proposed model combines several hyperparameters and we have two approaches to introducing auxiliary datasets to the model; we hence conduct an ablation study to understand how different choices impact the model. In light of our limited resources, the ablation study was carried out using English as the auxiliary dataset, which provided the best results compared to other auxiliary datasets. Our experiments examined different ratios for mixing the Arabic and English segments passed to the extra discriminator. Further, we compared how well the auxiliary dataset worked either as additional ground truths or as a generator input. Finally, we evaluated the effect of smaller segment lengths and the full capacity of the extra discriminator.

4.6 Training Details

All the training is performed on the Arabic Speech Corpus train-set[3] and one of the three additional datasets. The training settings is the same as described in the MelGAN paper (Kumar et al., 2019). The experiments ran on Google Cloud Virtual Machine with a 4-Core CPU and Nvidia T4 GPU. Each model is trained for 500000 steps.

5 Results

This section summarizes all the results of the experiments described in the Experiments section 4. We evaluated the performance on the test set of the Arabic Speech Corpus dataset3 using the MOS and the average of the last five Conditional Fréchet Wav2Vec Distance scores. It is worth noting that the mean of the best and the mean of the last five scores produced almost the same ordering. Also, in all tables and figures, the mixing ratio represents the ratio between main and auxiliary segments respectively we feed to the additional discriminator.

Table 2 presents the quantitative results of the proposed model incorporating the English dataset[1] as additional ground truths for the extra discriminator, as well as the MelGAN (Kumar et al., 2019) model and WaveGlow model (Prenger et al., 2019). The table shows the models that have 4 or less additional signals compared to the MelGAN model. The addition of one segment of the Arabic dataset would result in adding two additional signals: one to the generator's adversarial loss and one to the discriminator's adversarial loss, while the addition of one segment of the English dataset would result in one signal added to the discriminator's adversarial loss. The results show that MelGAN is able to achieve a performance that is comparable to WavGlow in the synthesis of Arabic speech. Furthermore, the study shows that MelGAN + Extra Disc outperforms both MelGAN and WaveGlow models, and adding auxiliary dataset increases the performance even further. MelGAN + Extra Disc and mixing ratio of 1:2 between Arabic and English data sets respectively provided the best performance across all models. Figure 3 shows the importance of adding a mixture of Arabic and English segments compared to the extreme cases.

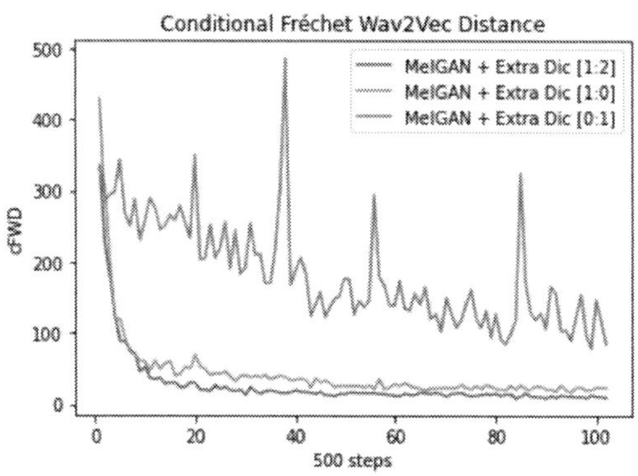

Figure 3: Conditional Fréchet Wav2Vec Distance reported every 500 steps during training of MelGAN + Extra Disc model with three different mixing ratios.

Table 3 represents the quantitative results of using different auxiliary datasets 1 as additional ground truths for the extra discriminator in the proposed model. The mixing ratio between the main and auxiliary datasets was 1:1. The results shows that different language auxiliary datasets (English[1]) with high quality produce better results than the same language or dialects (Standard[8], Tunisian[7] or Libyan Arabic[7]) auxiliary datasets with low or average quality.

FWD	Auxiliary Dataset
27.50	Tunisian_MSA trian
18.64	AMMI_Speech
18.56	Tunisian_MSA test
16.95	LJSpeech

Table 3: Average of the last five Conditional Fréchet Wav2Vec Distance for MelGAN + Extra Disc models trained with different auxiliary datasets fixed mixing ration if 1 : 1. The extra segments is added as an additional ground truths.

Tables 4, 5, 6 shows the results of the ablation study. According to the study, MelGAN + Extra Disc with 1:2 mixing ratio between Arabic[3] and English[1] data sets provided the best performance across all models. As well, adding auxiliary datasets as additional grounds truths in the extra discriminator is better than including the auxiliary dataset in the generator itself. Last but not least, by using full capacity extra discriminator and reducing segment lengths, we would achieve better results than with the current settings.

FWD	How Auxiliary Date Introduced
13.57	Generator with auxiliary segments
11.16	Extra ground truths for discriminator

Table 5: Average of the last five Conditional Fréchet Wav2Vec Distance for MelGAN + Extra Disc models with different ways of introducing the extra segments to the models and finxed mixing ratio of 1 : 2.

FWD	Capacity	Length
22.94	Half	512
18.85	Full	512
13.57	Full	256
10.46	Full	128

Table 6: Average of the last five Conditional Fréchet Wav2Vec Distance for MelGAN + Extra Disc models with different extra discriminator's capacity and segment length and mixing ratio of 1 : 1.

6 Ethical considerations

This paper aims to advance the field of text-to-speech and hence all considerations related to potential nefarious applications of such technology apply to this work. This includes the potential use of such systems to imitate voice of a certain individual in order to present a message that such person has never uttered. We also acknowledge that TTS systems carry a bias towards the dialect/accent of the population whose speech was used as a training data. However, we hypothesise our model might be suitable to counter such effects: as it has been designed for low-resource languages, it might well be used to improve TTS systems for underrepresented dialects or accents of otherwise well-modelled languages, in turn reducing geographical bias affecting certain populations.

Nevertheless, we believe that overall benefits of improved text-to-speech models outweight these and other ethical risks.

7 Conclusion

In this work, we have proposed an extension for MelGAN that utilizes information of auxiliary high-resource languages/dialects to help training of low resource language audio synthesis models. The proposed approach outperformed standard MelGAN

Model	Mixing Ratio	FWD	MOS	95%CI
WaveGlow	–	–	3.13	±0.061
MelGAN	–	18.01	3.10	±0.063
MelGAN + Extra Disc	1 : 0	22.94	3.29	±0.057
MelGAN + Extra Disc	2 : 0	12.15	3.40	±0.056
MelGAN + Extra Disc	1 : 1	16.95	3.55	±0.058
MelGAN + Extra Disc	1 : 2	**11.16**	**3.63**	±0.056
Original	–	–	3.88	±0.061

Table 2: Mean Opinion Score and average of the last five Conditional Fréchet Wav2Vec Distance scores for the MelGAN + Extra Disc models that have 4 or less additional signals compared to the MelGAN model. The extra segments is added as an additional ground truths. Note here, for MOS of WaveGlow model the samples are generated using the predicted mel-spectrogram not the ground truth mel-spectrogram.

Arabic \ English	0 segments	1 segments	2 segments	3 segments	4 segments
0 segments	18.01	105.51	–	–	–
1 segments	22.94	16.95	**11.16**	27.46	19.80
2 segments	12.15	11.68	17.30	18.27	17.37
3 segments	22.03	13.54	12.24	22.03	16.85
4 segments	13.07	18.59	16.84	18.73	15.41

Table 4: Average of the last five Conditional Fréchet Wav2Vec Distance for MelGAN + Extra Disc models with different mixing ratios. The extra segments is added as an additional ground truths.

model as well as the baseline WaveGlow in both the quantitative and subjective human evaluation. We demonstrated in an ablation study the importance of different components of the system to achieve good results. We hope to see how this approach can help training of the audio synthesis models in the future. Before that, we have trained the MelGAN model for conditional Arabic TTS using a publicly available dataset.

Furthermore, We have proposed a quantitative metric for generative models of Arabic speech that we called Conditional Fréchet Wav2Vec Distance, and demonstrated experimentally that it ranks models in line with Mean Opinion Scores obtained through human evaluation. The metric is based on the available Wav2Vec2ForCTC Arabic speech recognition model. Our quantitative results as well as subjective evaluation of the generated samples showcase the efficiency of our proposed approach for speech generation.

References

Ossama Abdel-Hamid, Sherif Mahdy Abdou, and Mohsen Rashwan. 2006. Improving arabic hmm based speech synthesis quality. In *Ninth International Conference on Spoken Language Processing*.

Mikołaj Bińkowski, Jeff Donahue, Sander Dieleman, Aidan Clark, Erich Elsen, Norman Casagrande, Luis C Cobo, and Karen Simonyan. 2019. High fidelity speech synthesis with adversarial networks. *arXiv preprint arXiv:1909.11646*.

Nanxin Chen, Yu Zhang, Heiga Zen, Ron J Weiss, Mohammad Norouzi, Najim Dehak, and William Chan. 2021. Wavegrad 2: Iterative refinement for text-to-speech synthesis. *arXiv preprint arXiv:2106.09660*.

Phat Do, Matt Coler, Jelske Dijkstra, and Esther Klabbers. 2021. A systematic review and analysis of multilingual data strategies in text-to-speech for low-resource languages. *Proc. Interspeech 2021*, pages 16–20.

Jeff Donahue, Sander Dieleman, Mikołaj Bińkowski, Erich Elsen, and Karen Simonyan. 2020. End-to-end adversarial text-to-speech. *arXiv preprint arXiv:2006.03575*.

Thomas Eiter and Heikki Mannila. 1994. Computing discrete fréchet distance.

Fady K Fahmy, Mahmoud I Khalil, and Hazem M Abbas. 2020. A transfer learning end-to-end arabic text-to-speech (tts) deep architecture. In *IAPR Workshop on Artificial Neural Networks in Pattern Recognition*, pages 266–277. Springer.

Andrew Gibiansky, Sercan Arik, Gregory Diamos, John Miller, Kainan Peng, Wei Ping, Jonathan Raiman, and Yanqi Zhou. 2017. Deep voice 2: Multi-speaker neural text-to-speech. *Advances in neural information processing systems*, 30.

Ian Goodfellow, Jean Pouget-Abadie, Mehdi Mirza, Bing Xu, David Warde-Farley, Sherjil Ozair, Aaron Courville, and Yoshua Bengio. 2014. Generative adversarial nets. *Advances in neural information processing systems*, 27.

Martin Heusel, Hubert Ramsauer, Thomas Unterthiner, Bernhard Nessler, and Sepp Hochreiter. 2017. Gans trained by a two time-scale update rule converge to a local nash equilibrium. In *Advances in Neural Information Processing Systems*, volume 30. Curran Associates, Inc.

Nal Kalchbrenner, Erich Elsen, Karen Simonyan, Seb Noury, Norman Casagrande, Edward Lockhart, Florian Stimberg, Aaron Oord, Sander Dieleman, and Koray Kavukcuoglu. 2018. Efficient neural audio synthesis. In *International Conference on Machine Learning*, pages 2410–2419. PMLR.

Durk P Kingma and Prafulla Dhariwal. 2018. Glow: Generative flow with invertible 1x1 convolutions. *Advances in neural information processing systems*, 31.

Kundan Kumar, Rithesh Kumar, Thibault de Boissiere, Lucas Gestin, Wei Zhen Teoh, Jose Sotelo, Alexandre de Brébisson, Yoshua Bengio, and Aaron C Courville. 2019. Melgan: Generative adversarial networks for conditional waveform synthesis. *Advances in neural information processing systems*, 32.

Younggun Lee, Suwon Shon, and Taesu Kim. 2018. Learning pronunciation from a foreign language in speech synthesis networks. *arXiv preprint arXiv:1811.09364*.

Soroush Mehri, Kundan Kumar, Ishaan Gulrajani, Rithesh Kumar, Shubham Jain, Jose Sotelo, Aaron Courville, and Yoshua Bengio. 2016. Samplernn: An unconditional end-to-end neural audio generation model. *arXiv preprint arXiv:1612.07837*.

Aaron Oord, Yazhe Li, Igor Babuschkin, Karen Simonyan, Oriol Vinyals, Koray Kavukcuoglu, George Driessche, Edward Lockhart, Luis Cobo, Florian Stimberg, et al. 2018. Parallel wavenet: Fast high-fidelity speech synthesis. In *International conference on machine learning*, pages 3918–3926. PMLR.

Aaron van den Oord, Sander Dieleman, Heiga Zen, Karen Simonyan, Oriol Vinyals, Alex Graves, Nal Kalchbrenner, Andrew Senior, and Koray Kavukcuoglu. 2016a. Wavenet: A generative model for raw audio. *arXiv preprint arXiv:1609.03499*.

AVD Oord, S Dieleman, H Zen, K Simonyan, O Vinyals, A Graves, N Kalchbrenner, A Senior, and K Kavukcuoglu. 2016b. A generative model for raw audio. *arXiv preprint arXiv:1609.03499*.

Ryan Prenger, Rafael Valle, and Bryan Catanzaro. 2019. Waveglow: A flow-based generative network for speech synthesis. In *ICASSP 2019-2019 IEEE International Conference on Acoustics, Speech and Signal Processing (ICASSP)*, pages 3617–3621. IEEE.

Ilyes Rebai and Yassine BenAyed. 2016. Arabic speech synthesis and diacritic recognition. *International Journal of Speech Technology*, 19(3):485–494.

Jonathan Shen, Ruoming Pang, Ron J Weiss, Mike Schuster, Navdeep Jaitly, Zongheng Yang, Zhifeng Chen, Yu Zhang, Yuxuan Wang, Rj Skerrv-Ryan, et al. 2018. Natural tts synthesis by conditioning wavenet on mel spectrogram predictions. In *2018 IEEE international conference on acoustics, speech and signal processing (ICASSP)*, pages 4779–4783. IEEE.

Michael Soloveitchik, Tzvi Diskin, Efrat Morin, and Ami Wiesel. 2021. Conditional frechet inception distance. *arXiv preprint arXiv:2103.11521*.

Jose Sotelo, Soroush Mehri, Kundan Kumar, Joao Felipe Santos, Kyle Kastner, Aaron Courville, and Yoshua Bengio. 2017. Char2wav: End-to-end speech synthesis.

Ilya Sutskever, Oriol Vinyals, and Quoc V Le. 2014. Sequence to sequence learning with neural networks. *Advances in neural information processing systems*, 27.

Henry Sweet. 1877. *A handbook of phonetics*, volume 2. Clarendon Press.

Yuxuan Wang, RJ Skerry-Ryan, Daisy Stanton, Yonghui Wu, Ron J Weiss, Navdeep Jaitly, Zongheng Yang, Ying Xiao, Zhifeng Chen, Samy Bengio, et al. 2017. Tacotron: A fully end-to-end text-to-speech synthesis model. *arXiv preprint arXiv:1703.10135*, 164.

Xin Yi, Ekta Walia, and Paul Babyn. 2019. Generative adversarial network in medical imaging: A review. *Medical image analysis*, 58:101552.

NADI 2022:
The Third Nuanced Arabic Dialect Identification Shared Task

Muhammad Abdul-Mageed, Chiyu Zhang, AbdelRahim Elmadany,
Houda Bouamor,[†] Nizar Habash[‡]
The University of British Columbia, Vancouver, Canada
[†]Carnegie Mellon University in Qatar, Qatar
[‡]New York University Abu Dhabi, UAE
{muhammad.mageed@,a.elmadany@,chiyuzh@mail}.ubc.ca
hbouamor@cmu.edu nizar.habash@nyu.edu

Abstract

We describe the findings of the third Nuanced Arabic Dialect Identification Shared Task (NADI 2022). NADI aims at advancing state-of-the-art Arabic NLP, including Arabic dialects. It does so by affording diverse datasets and modeling opportunities in a standardized context where meaningful comparisons between models and approaches are possible. NADI 2022 targeted both dialect identification (Subtask 1) and dialectal sentiment analysis (Subtask 2) at the country level. A total of 41 unique teams registered for the shared task, of whom 21 teams have participated (with 105 valid submissions). Among these, 19 teams participated in Subtask 1, and 10 participated in Subtask 2. The winning team achieved F_1=27.06 on Subtask 1 and F_1=75.16 on Subtask 2, reflecting that both subtasks remain challenging and motivating future work in this area. We describe the methods employed by the participating teams and offer an outlook for NADI.

1 Introduction

Arabic is a collection of languages and language varieties some of which are not mutually intelligible, although it is sometimes conflated as a single language. *Classical Arabic (CA)* is the variety used in old Arabic poetry and the Qur'an, the Holy Book of Islam. CA continues to be used to date, side by side with other varieties, especially in religious and literary discourses. CA is also involved in code-switching contexts with *Modern Standard Arabic (MSA)* (Abdul-Mageed et al., 2020b). In contrast, as its name suggests, MSA is a more modern variety (Badawi, 1973) of Arabic. MSA is usually employed in pan-Arab media such as AlJazeera network and in government communication across the Arab world.[1] *Dialectal Arabic (DA)* is the term used to collectively refer to

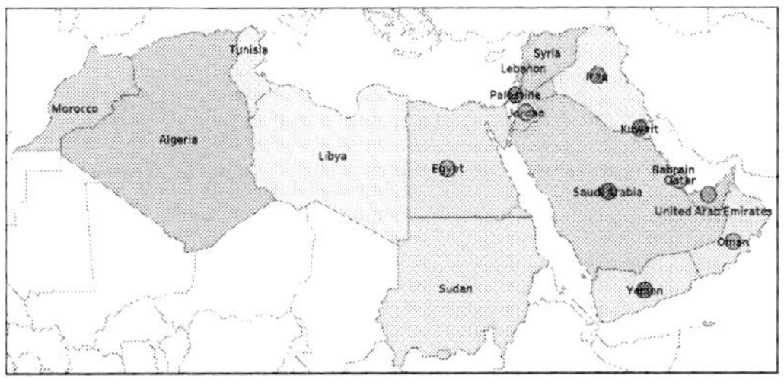

Figure 1: A map of the Arab World showing the 18 countries in the *Subtask 1* dataset and the 10 countries in the *Subtask 2* dataset. Each country is coded in a color different from neighboring countries. Subtask 2 countries are coded as circles with dark color.

Arabic dialects. DA is sometimes defined regionally into categories such as Gulf, Levantine, Nile Basin, and North African (Habash, 2010; Abdul-Mageed, 2015). More recent treatments of DA focus on more nuanced variation at the country or even sub-country levels (Bouamor et al., 2018; Abdul-Mageed et al., 2020b). Many of the works on Arabic dialects thus far have focused on dialect identification, the task of automatically detecting the source variety of a given text or speech segment.

In this paper, we introduce the findings and results of the third Nuanced Arabic Dialect Identification Shared Task (NADI 2022). NADI aims at encouraging research work on Arabic dialect processing by providing datasets and diverse modeling opportunities under a common evaluation setup. The first instance of the shared task, NADI 2020 (Abdul-Mageed et al., 2020a), focused on province-level dialects. NADI 2021 (Abdul-Mageed et al., 2021b), the second iteration of NADI, focused on distinguishing both MSA and DA according to their geographical origin at the country level. NADI 2022 extends on both editions and offers a richer context as it targets both Arabic dialect identification and *and* dialectal sentiment analysis.

NADI 2022 shared tasks proposes two subtasks:

[1]https://www.aljazeera.com/

Proceedings of the The Seventh Arabic Natural Language Processing Workshop (WANLP), pages 85 - 97
December 8, 2022 ©2022 Association for Computational Linguistics

Subtask 1 on dialect identification, and **Subtask 2** on dialect sentiment analysis. While we invited participation in either of the two subtasks, we encouraged teams to submit systems to *both* subtasks. By offering two subtasks, our hope was to receive systems that exploit diverse machine learning and other methods and architectures such as multi-task learning systems, ensemble methods, sequence-to-sequence architectures in single models such as the text-to-text Transformer, etc. Many of the submitted systems investigated diverse approaches, thus fulfilling our objective.

A total of 41 unique teams registered for NADI 2022. Of these, 21 unique teams actually made submissions to our leaderboard (n=105 valid submissions). We received 16 papers from 15 teams, of which we accepted 15 for publication. Results from participating teams show that both dialect identification at the country level and dialectal sentiment analysis from short sequences of text remain challenging even to complex neural methods. These findings clearly motivate future work on both tasks.

The rest of the paper is organized as follows: Section 2 provides a brief overview of Arabic dialect identification and sentiment analysis. We describe the two subtasks and NADI 2022 restrictions in Section 3. Section 4 introduces shared task datasets and evaluation setup. We present participating teams and shared task results and provide a high-level description of submitted systems in Section 5. We conclude in Section 6.

2 Literature Review

2.1 Arabic Dialects

Arabic can be categorized into CA, MSA, and DA. Although CA and MSA have been studied extensively (Harrell, 1962; Cowell, 1964; Badawi, 1973; Brustad, 2000; Holes, 2004), DA is has received more attention only in recent years. One major challenge for studying DA has been the lack of resources. For this reason, most pioneering DA works focused on creating resources, usually for only a small number of regions or countries (Gadalla et al., 1997; Diab et al., 2010; Al-Sabbagh and Girju, 2012; Sadat et al., 2014; Harrat et al., 2014; Jarrar et al., 2016; Khalifa et al., 2016; Al-Twairesh et al., 2018; El-Haj, 2020). A number of works introducing multi-dialectal datasets and regional level detection models followed (Zaidan and Callison-Burch, 2011; Elfardy et al., 2014; Bouamor et al., 2014; Meftouh et al., 2015).

Some of the earliest Arabic dialect identification shared tasks were offered as part of the VarDial workshop. These shared tasks used speech broadcast transcriptions (Malmasi et al., 2016), and later integrated acoustic features (Zampieri et al., 2017) and phonetic features (Zampieri et al., 2018) extracted from raw audio.

The Multi-Arabic Dialects Application and Resources (MADAR) project (Bouamor et al., 2018) was the first that introduced finer-grained dialectal data and a lexicon. The MADAR data was used for dialect identification at the country and city levels covering 25 cities in the Arab world (Salameh et al., 2018; Obeid et al., 2019). The MADAR data was commissioned rather than being naturally occurring, which might not be the best for dialect identification, especially when considering dialect identification in the social media context. Several larger datasets covering 10-21 countries were then introduced (Mubarak and Darwish, 2014; Abdul-Mageed et al., 2018; Zaghouani and Charfi, 2018; Abdelali et al., 2021; Issa et al., 2021; Baimukan et al., 2022). These datasets were mainly compiled from naturally-occurring posts on social media platforms such as Twitter. Some approaches for collecting dialectal data are unsupervised. A recent example is Althobaiti (2022) who describe an approach for automatically tagging Twitter posts with 15 country-level dialects and extracting relevant word lists. Some works also gather data at the fine-grained level of cities. For example, Abdul-Mageed et al. (2020b) introduced a Twitter dataset and a number of models to identify country, province, and city level variation in Arabic dialects. The NADI shared task (Abdul-Mageed et al., 2020a, 2021b) built on these efforts by providing datasets and common evaluation settings for identifying Arabic dialects. Althobaiti (2020) is a relatively recent survey of computational work on Arabic dialects.

2.2 Sentiment Analysis

Besides dialect identification, several studies investigate socio-pragmatic meaning (SM) exploiting Arabic data. SM refers to intended meaning in real-world communication and how utterances should be interpreted within the social context in which they are produced (Thomas, 2014; Zhang et al., 2022). Typical SM tasks include sentiment analysis (Abdul-Mageed et al., 2014; Abdul-Mageed, 2019), emotion recognition (Alhuzali et al., 2018), age and gender identification (Abbes et al., 2020), offensive language detection (Mubarak et al., 2020; Elmadany et al., 2020), and sarcasm detection (Abu Farha and Magdy, 2020). In NADI 2022, we focus on sentiment analysis of Arabic dialects in social media. Several studies of Arabic sentiment analysis are listed in surveys such as Elnagar et al. (2021) and Alhumoud and Wazrah (2022). Most of these studies target sentiment in MSA. Recently, there are some studies that target sentiment in Arabic dialects in social media sources such Twitter. Some of these studies create datasets (Guellil et al., 2020a; Al-Laith et al., 2021; Abo et al., 2021; Alowisheq et al., 2021; Hassan et al., 2021; Alwakid et al., 2022), focusing on one or more dialects or regions (Abdul-Mageed et al., 2020c; Fourati et al., 2020; Guellil et al., 2020b; Almuqren and Cristea, 2021; Guellil et al., 2021; Abu Farha and Magdy, 2021; Shamsi and Abdallah, 2022). Many of the previous sentiment analysis works, however, either do not distinguish dialects altogether or focus only on a few dialects such as Egyptian, Levantine, or Tunisian. This motivates us to introduce the dialectal sentiment analysis subtask as part of NADI 2022.

To the best of our knowledge, our work is the first to enable investigating sentiment analysis in 10 Arabic dialects. For our sentiment analysis subtask, we also annotate and release a novel dataset and facilitate comparisons in a standardized experimental setting.

2.3 The NADI Shared Tasks

NADI 2020 The first NADI shared task, (Abdul-Mageed et al., 2020a) was co-located with the fifth Arabic Natural Language Processing Workshop (WANLP 2020) (Zitouni et al., 2020). NADI 2020 targeted both country- and province-level dialects. It covered a total of 100 provinces from 21 Arab countries, with data collected from Twitter. It was the first shared task to target naturally occurring fine-grained dialectal text at the sub-country level.

NADI 2021 The second edition of the shared task (Abdul-Mageed et al., 2021b) was co-located with WANLP 2021 (Habash et al., 2021). It targeted the same 21 Arab countries and 100 corresponding provinces as NADI 2020, also exploiting Twitter data. NADI 2021 improved over NADI 2020 in that non-Arabic data were removed. In addition, NADI-2021 teased apart the data into MSA and DA and focused on classifying MSA and DA tweets into the countries and provinces from which they are collected. As such, NADI 2021 had four subtasks: MSA-country, DA-country, MSA-province, and DA-province.

NADI 2022 As introduced earlier, **this current edition** of NADI focuses on studying Arabic dialects at the country level as well as dialectal sentiment (i.e., sentiment analysis of data tagged with dialect labels). Our objective is that NADI 2022 can support exploring variation in social geographical regions that have not been studied before. We discuss NADI 2022 in more detail in the next section.

It is worth noting that NADI shared task datasets are starting to be used for various types of (e.g., linguistic) studies of Arabic dialects, For example, Alsudais et al. (2022) studies the effect of geographic proximity on Arabic dialects exploiting datasets from MADAR (Bouamor et al., 2018) and NADI (Abdul-Mageed et al., 2020a, 2021b).

3 Task Description

3.1 Shared Task Subtasks

The NADI 2022 shared task consists of two subtasks, both focused on dialectal Arabic at the country level. **Subtask 1** is about dialect identification and **Subtask 2** is about sentiment analysis of Arabic dialects. We now introduce each subtask.

Subtask 1 (Dialect Identification) The goal of Subtask 1 is to identify the specific country-level dialect of a given Arabic tweet. For this subtask, we reuse the training, development, and test datasets of 18 countries from NADI 2021 (Abdul-Mageed et al., 2021b). In addition to the test set of NADI 2021, we introduce a *new* test set manually annotated with k country-level dialects, where $k = 10$ but is kept unknown to teams. We ask participants to submit system runs on these two test sets.

Subtask 2 (Dialectal Sentiment Analysis) The goal of Subtask 2 is to identify the sentiment of a given tweet written in Arabic. Tweets are collected from 10 different countries during the year of 2018 and involve both MSA and DA. The data are manually labeled with sentiment tags from the set {*positive*, *negative*, *neutral*}. More information about our data splits and evaluation settings for both Subtask 1 and Subtask 2 is given in Section 4.

Figure 1 shows the countries covered in NADI 2022 for both subtasks.

3.2 Shared Task Restrictions

We follow the same general approach to managing the shared task we adopted in NADI 2020 and NADI 2021. This includes providing participating teams with a set of restrictions that apply to all subtasks, and clear evaluation metrics. The purpose of our restrictions is to ensure fair comparisons and common experimental conditions. In addition, similar to NADI 2020 and 2021, our data release strategy and our evaluation setup through the CodaLab online platform facilitated competition management, enhanced timeliness of acquiring results upon system submission, and guaranteed ultimate transparency. Once a team registered in the shared task, we directly provided the registering member with the data via a private download link. We provided the data in the form of the actual tweets posted to the Twitter platform, rather than tweet IDs. This guaranteed comparison between systems exploiting identical data.

For both subtasks, we provided clear instructions requiring participants not to use any external data. That is, teams were required to only use the data we provided to develop their systems and no other datasets regardless how these are acquired. For example, we requested that teams do not search nor depend on any additional user-level information such as geolocation. To alleviate these strict constraints and encourage creative use of diverse (machine learning) methods in system development, we provided an unlabeled dataset of 10M tweets in the form of tweet IDs. This dataset is provided in addition to our labeled Train and Dev splits for the two subtasks. To facilitate acquisition of this unlabeled dataset, we also provided a simple script that can be used to collect the tweets. We encouraged participants to use the 10M unlabeled tweets in whatever way they wished.

4 Shared Task Datasets and Evaluation

TWT-10 We collected $\sim 10K$ tweets covering 10 Arab countries (*Egypt*, *Iraq*, *Jordan*, *KSA*, *Kuwait*, *Oman*, *Palestine*, *Qatar*, *UAE*, and *Yemen*) via the Twitter API.[2] The tweets were collected during the year of 2018. We asked a total of three college-educated Arabic native speakers to annotate these tweets with three types of information: (1) *dialectness* (MSA vs. DA), (2) 10-*way country-level dialects*, and (3) *three-way sentiment labels* (i.e., $\{positive,\ negative,\ neutral\}$). For each of the 10 countries, 500 tweets were labeled by two different annotators. We calculated the inter-annotator agreement using Cohen's Kappa . We obtained a Kappa (K) of 0.85 for the sentiment labeling task and K of 0.41 for the 10-way dialect identification one. Table 1 also presents the distribution of dialect and sentiment classes. It also shows that MSA comprises 50.86% of TWT-10 (while DA is 49.14%). Table 2 shows tweet examples with sentiment labels randomly selected from a number of countries representing different regions in our annotated dataset.

[2]https://developer.twitter.com/en/docs/twitter-api

Country	**Dialect**		**Sentiment**			**Total**
	MSA	**DA**	**Pos**	**Neg**	**Neut**	
Egypt	137	363	176	187	137	500
Iraq	314	186	230	219	51	500
Jordan	257	243	169	253	78	500
KSA	300	200	194	152	154	500
Kuwait	170	330	203	227	70	500
Oman	340	160	166	179	155	500
Palestine	248	252	159	169	172	500
Qatar	181	319	288	194	18	500
UAE	270	230	232	112	156	500
Yemen	326	174	118	198	184	500
Total	**2,543**	**2,457**	**1,935**	**1,890**	**1,175**	**5,000**

Table 1: The TWT-10 dataset class distributions.

Subtask 1 (Dialect Identification) We use the dataset of Subtask 1.2 of NADI 2021 (i.e., country-level DA) (Abdul-Mageed et al., 2021b). This dataset was collected using tweets covering 21 Arab countries during a period of 10 months (Jan. to Oct.) during the year of 2019. It was heuristically labelled exploiting the users' geo-location feature and mobility patterns and automatically cleaned to exclude non-Arabic and MSA tweets. For the purpose of this shared task, we keep the same training, development, and test splits as NADI 2021 but we exclude data from Djibouti, Somalia, and Mauritania since these are poorly represented in the dataset. We call the resulting dataset **TWT-GEO**. TWT-GEO includes 18 country-level dialects, split into **Train** ($\sim 20K$ tweets), **Dev** ($\sim 5K$ tweets), and **Test-A** ($\sim 4.8K$ tweets). We refer to the test set of TWT-GEO as Test-A since we use an additional test split for evaluation, **Test-B**. Test-B contains 1.5K dialect tweets randomly sampled from the TWT-10 dataset described earlier. Table 3 presents the class distributions in Subtask 1 Train, Dev, and Test splits (Test-A and Test-B).

Country	Example	Sentiment
Egypt	محدش عنده فكة وجع !!	Negative
	مرتضى : معروف و كوفي ملهمش مليم عندي و من يمتلك عرضا يغور	Neutral
	كوباية شاي خيالية لدرجة أني عايز آكل الكوباية الفاضية تسلم أيدي اصلن	Positive
Jordan	وييننننك يا زووجي توخدني عبارريس	Negative
	منرجع منحكي: التعداد السكاني والمساكن، بدها تعرف الدولة وين ساكن	Neutral
	شفتو حق جلسات وناسة وش سوا هههههههها!!!!!!اي	Positive
KSA	لما تبي تحاكي احد بس ماتدري شتقول	Negative
	مادري ليش آذآ شفت احد نآيم احسه مسكين !!	Neutral
	الفجر يقيم خمس وعشر عشر ساعات بمديك توصل الشرقية تغطّ رجولك بالبحر وتتعشا وترجع	Positive
Kuwait	كالعاده الخشوف طاحسين بالتايم والسحوت يرضعون.	Negative
	احدٍ آذا مديتله طيبك .. يغيب ماتملي عيونه كبار الفعايل واحدٍ يموت إن كان سويت به طيب يخاف مايقدر يرد الجمايل	Neutral
	اي والله أغليه و نفسي فيه مفتونه.	Positive
UAE	ذا كنت تحبني صج ومن كل قلبك تعشقني ، حسسني بهالشي خلني أحس اني اهمك صج مابي كم كلمه حلوه وانتا طول يومك مو معاي ومشغول بغيري	Negative
	اقولك تدري منو سوالي فولو	Neutral
	يبيله احلى بوسه على الصبح ولحس الخبق	Positive

Table 2: Randomly picked dialectal tweets from select countries in our annotated data for Subtask 2.

Country	TRAIN	DEV	TEST-A	TEST-B
Algeria	1,809	430	379	—
Bahrain	215	52	50	—
Egypt	4,283	1,041	1,025	219
Iraq	2,729	664	648	117
Jordan	429	104	101	144
KSA	2,140	520	501	116
Kuwait	429	105	103	202
Lebanon	644	157	119	—
Libya	1,286	314	309	—
Morocco	8,58	207	210	—
Oman	1,501	355	360	91
Palestine	428	104	99	160
Qatar	215	52	51	190
Sudan	215	53	53	—
Syria	1,287	278	279	—
Tunisia	859	173	211	—
UAE	642	157	157	136
Yemen	429	105	103	99

Table 3: Distribution of classes for Subtask 1 data.

Subtask 2 (Sentiment Analysis) For this subtask, we use the manually annotated 5,000 tweets (including both MSA and dialects) in TWT-10. We randomly split the tweets into **Train** (1,500 tweets), **Dev** (500 tweets), and **Test** (3,000 tweets). We intentionally provide a small training dataset to encourage various approaches (e.g., *few-shot* learning). Figure 2 shows the distribution of sentiment classes across the data splits.

Unlabeled Dataset We provide participants with a total of 10M unlabeled Arabic tweets in the form of tweet IDs. We refer to this collection as **UNLABELED-10M**. We collected these tweets in

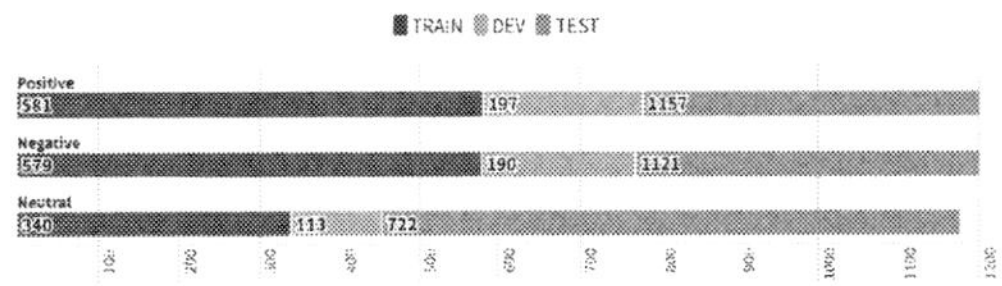

Figure 2: Subtask 2 class distributions across data splits.

2019. In UNLABELED-10M, Arabic was identified using Twitter language tag (`ar`). We included in our data package released to participants a simple script to collect these tweets. Participants were free to use UNLABELED-10M for any of the two subtasks.[3]

Evaluation Metrics The official evaluation metric for **Subtask 1** is Macro-Averaged F_1-score. We evaluate on Test-A and Test-B separately, and use the average score between these two test sets as the final score of Subtask 1. For **Subtask 2**, F_{NP}-score is the official metric, where we use the average of the F_1 scores of the *positive* and *negative* classes only while neglecting the neutral class. These metrics are obtained on blind test sets. We also report performance in terms of *macro-averaged precision*, *macro-averaged recall* and *accuracy* for systems submitted to each of the two subtasks.

Each participating team was allowed to submit

[3]Datasets for all the subtasks and UNLABELED-10M are available at `https://github.com/UBC-NLP/nadi`. More details about the data format can be found in the accompanying `README` file.

Team	Affiliation	Tasks
259 (Qaddoumi, 2022)	New York University, USA	1
Ahmed and Khalil (El-Shangiti and Mrini, 2022)	Independent Researcher, Morocco	1, 2
ANLP-RG (Fsih et al., 2022)	Faculty of Economics and Management of Sfax, Tunisia	2
BFCAI (Sobhy et al., 2022)	Benha University, Egypt	1
BhamNLP	King Abdulaziz University, KSA and Uni. of Birmingahm, UK	2
Elyadata	ELYADATA, Tunisia	1
Giyaseddin (Bayrak and Issifu, 2022)	Marmara University, Turkey	1, 2
GOF (Jamal et al., 2022)	University of Windsor, Canada	1
iCompass (Messaoudi et al., 2022)	iCompass, Tunisia	1
ISL-AAST	Arab academy for science and technology, Egypt	1, 2
MTU_FIZ (Shammary et al., 2022)	Munster Technological University, Ireland	1
NLP_DI (Kanjirangat et al., 2022)	Dalle Molle Institute for AI, Switzerland	1
Oscar_Garibo	Valencian International University, Spain	1, 2
Pythoneers (Attieh and Hassan, 2022)	Aalto University, Finland	1, 2
rematchka (Abdel-Salam, 2022)	Cairo University, Egypt	1, 2
RUTeam	Reichman University, Israel	1, 2
SQU (AAlAbdulsalam, 2022)	Sultan Qaboos University, Oman	1
SUKI (Jauhiainen et al., 2022)	University of Helsinki, Finland	1
UniManc (Khered et al., 2022)	The University of Manchester, UK	1, 2
XY (AlShenaifi and Azmi, 2022)	Kind Saud University, KSA	1
zTeam	British University in Dubai, UAE	1

Table 4: List of teams that participated in either one or the two of subtasks. Teams with accepted papers are cited.

up to five runs for each test set of a given subtask, and only the highest scoring run was kept for each team. Although official results are based only on a blind test set, we also asked participants to report their results on the Dev sets in their papers. We set up two CodaLab competitions for scoring participant systems.[4] We plan to keep the Codalab competition for each subtask live post competition for researchers who would be interested in training models and evaluating their systems using the shared task blind test sets. For this reason, we will not release labels for the test sets of any of the subtasks.

5 Shared Task Teams & Results

5.1 Participating Teams

We received a total of 41 unique team registrations. After the testing phase, we received a total of 105 valid submissions from 21 unique teams. The breakdown across the subtasks is as follows: 42 submission for Test-A of Subtask 1 from 19 teams, 41 submissions for Test-B of Subtask 1 from 19 teams, 22 submissions for Subtask 2 from 10 teams. Table 4 lists the 21 teams. A total of 15 teams submitted a total of 16 description papers from which we accepted 15 papers for publication. Accepted papers are given in Table 4.

[4]The different CodaLab competitions are available at the following links: Subtask 1; Subtask 2.

5.2 Baselines

We provide three baselines for each of the two subtasks. **Baseline-I** is based on the majority class in the Train data for each subtask. For Subtask 1, Baseline-I performs at F_1=1.97 on Test-A and F_1=2.59 on Test-B, hence it obtains an average F_1 of 2.28. For Subtask 2, Baseline-I performs at F_{NP}=27.83. **Baseline-mBERT**, **Baseline-XLMR**, and **Baseline-MARBERT** are fine-tuned multilingual BERT-Base model (mBERT) (Devlin et al., 2019), cross-lingual RoBERTa (XLMR) (Conneau and Lample, 2019), and MARBERT (Abdul-Mageed et al., 2021a), respectively. More specifically, we take checkpoints for these models from Hugginface Library (Wolf et al., 2020) and finetune each of them for 20 epochs with a learning rate of 2e-5 and batch size of 32. The maximum length of input sequence is set to 64 tokens. We evaluate each model at the end of each epoch and choose the best model based on performance on the respective Dev set. We then report performance of the best model on test sets. Baseline-MARBERT is our strongest baseline: it obtains F_1=31.39 on Test-A of Subtask 1, F_1=16.94 on Test-B of Subtask 1, average F_1=24.17 over Test-A and Test-B, and F_{NP}=72.36 on Subtask 2.

5.3 Shared Task Results

Table 5 presents the leaderboard of Subtask 1 and is sorted by the main metric of Subtask 1, i.e., average macro-F_1 score. As Tables 6 and 7 show, for each

Team	Avg. Macro-F_1
1 rematchka	27.06
2 UniManc	26.86
3 GOF	26.44
4 mtu_fiz	25.50
5 iCompass	25.32
6 ISL-AAST	24.59
7 Ahmed_and_Khalil	24.35
Baseline-MARBERT	24.17
8 Pythoneers	24.12
9 Giyaseddin	22.42
10 SQU	22.42
11 Elyadata	22.41
12 NLP_DI	21.28
13 RUTeam	17.28
14 259	16.89
15 zTeam	16.12
16 XY	15.80
Baseline-mBERT	15.70
17 BFCAI	15.48
18 SUKI	15.11
Baseline-XLMR	14.68
19 Oscar_Garibo	14.45
Baseline-I	2.28

Table 5: Results for Subtask 1 (Country-Level DA).

Team	Macro-F_1	Acc	Rec	Prec
1 UniManc	18.95	36.84	20.48	25.82
2 mtu_fiz	17.67	33.92	18.79	25.03
3 rematchka	17.64	36.50	19.62	23.59
4 GOF	17.19	34.60	18.56	22.12
5 Ahmed_and_Khalil	17.15	34.67	19.47	23.39
6 ISL-AAST	16.95	35.07	18.40	22.47
7 iCompass	16.94	34.94	19.52	19.01
Baseline-MARBERT	16.94	34.06	18.82	23.19
8 NLP_DI	16.44	27.68	18.49	20.28
9 Pythoneers	15.61	29.51	15.90	19.51
10 Elyadata	15.46	29.85	16.34	20.25
11 SQU	14.84	30.12	16.80	21.32
12 Giyaseddin	14.30	29.92	15.59	21.95
13 259	11.85	22.25	11.43	14.21
14 RUTeam	11.35	22.80	11.86	14.60
15 SUKI	10.58	20.56	10.11	12.98
Baseline-mBERT	10.53	22.05	11.42	14.06
16 zTeam	10.47	25.71	13.23	16.29
17 BFCAI	9.71	23.13	11.99	14.54
Baseline-XLMR	9.62	21.91	11.33	14.05
18 XY	9.25	23.74	11.73	17.57
19 Oscar_Garibo	8.40	19.40	9.80	11.74
Baseline-I	2.59	14.86	10.00	1.49

Table 7: Results on Test-B of Subtask 1.

Team	Macro-F_1	Acc	Rec	Prec
1 rematchka	36.48	53.05	35.22	41.89
2 GOF	35.68	52.10	34.91	39.18
3 UniManc	34.78	52.33	34.74	38.74
4 iCompass	33.70	51.91	33.71	35.86
5 mtu_fiz	33.32	51.18	32.42	38.87
6 Pythoneers	32.63	48.91	31.77	36.77
7 ISL_AAST	32.24	50.27	32.07	37.53
8 Ahmed_and_Khalil	31.54	50.34	32.04	34.00
Baseline-MARBERT	31.39	47.77	31.01	35.53
9 Giyaseddin	30.55	47.65	30.04	34.18
10 SQU	30.01	46.85	29.75	34.57
11 Elyadata	29.35	45.84	28.60	31.27
12 NLP_DI	26.12	42.08	25.75	28.29
13 RUTeam	23.20	36.61	22.84	24.00
14 XY	22.36	39.85	21.33	30.52
15 259	21.93	34.11	22.69	22.32
16 zTeam	21.76	39.43	20.77	27.25
17 BFCAI	21.25	38.63	20.47	25.25
Baseline-mBERT	20.88	35.22	20.67	21.82
18 Oscar_Garibo	20.50	36.80	20.06	22.15
Baseline-XLMR	19.74	36.22	19.83	21.00
19 SUKI	19.63	29.23	20.85	21.95
Baseline-I	1.97	21.54	5.55	1.20

Table 6: Results on Test-A of Subtask 1.

Team	F_1-PN	Acc	Rec	Prec
1 rematchka	75.16	69.70	66.22	67.57
2 UniManc	73.54	67.70	63.92	65.27
3 BhamNLP	73.46	67.33	62.83	65.24
4 Pythoneers	73.40	68.23	65.87	66.08
Baseline-MARBERT	72.36	66.66	63.92	64.50
5 Ahmed_and_Khalil	71.46	66.03	63.73	63.84
6 Giyaseddin	71.43	65.80	62.20	63.51
7 ISL_AAST	70.55	64.97	61.41	62.58
8 ANLP-RG	67.31	61.90	59.67	59.69
Baseline-XLMR	63.24	57.30	55.53	55.66
9 RUTeam	61.07	56.17	53.58	53.90
Baseline-mBERT	55.84	50.13	49.00	49.47
10 Oscar_Garibo	46.43	43.00	41.92	42.00
Baseline-I	27.83	38.57	33.33	12.86

Table 8: Results for Subtask 2 (Sentiment Analysis).

team, we take their best score of Test-A and Test-B and then calculate the average macro-F_1 score over the best scores of these two test sets (i.e., Test-A and Test-B). `Team rematchka` (Abdel-Salam, 2022) obtained the best performance on Subtask 1 with 27.06 average macro-F_1. We can observe that seven teams outperform our strongest baseline, Baseline-MARBERT. `Team rematchka` also achieved the best F_1 of 36.48 on Test-A of Subtask 1. `Team UniManc` (Khered et al., 2022) acquired the best F_1 of 18.95 on Test-B of Subtask 1. Results show that dialect identification based on text input is challenging. We note that there is a sizable discrepancy between test results on Test-A and Test-B: Test-B results are much lower. We believe the reason is that Test-B is derived from a different distribution (e.g., different collection time) as compared to training data of Subtask 1.

Table 8 shows the leaderboard of Subtask 2 and is sorted by the main metric of Subtask 2, F_{NP} score. Again, `Team rematchka` achieved the best F_{NP} score of 75.16. We observe that four and then eight teams outperformed our Baseline-MARBERT and Baseline-XLMR, respectively.

Team Name	# submit	Main Metric	Features: N-gram	TF-IDF	Linguistic	Word embeds	Sampling	Techniques: Classical ML	Neural nets	Transformer	Ensemble	Adapter	Multitask	Prompting	Distillation	Data Aug.	Use unlabeled: Pre-training
Subtask 1																	
rematchka	6	27.06							✓	✓	✓			✓			
UniManc	6	26.86					✓			✓							
GOF	4	26.44								✓							
mtu_fiz	8	25.50							✓	✓		✓				✓	
iCompass	2	25.32								✓							
ISL_AAST	5	24.59								✓		✓				✓	
Ahmed_and_Khalil	2	24.35								✓							
Pythoneers	4	24.12								✓	✓		✓		✓		
Giyaseddin	3	22.42								✓							
SQU	4	22.42	✓	✓		✓		✓	✓	✓							✓
NLP_DI	9	21.28	✓						✓	✓							✓
RUTeam	2	17.28			✓					✓							
259	2	16.89	✓					✓		✓							
zTeam	2	16.12				✓		✓	✓	✓							
XY	10	15.80						✓	✓	✓	✓						
BFCAI	6	15.48		✓		✓		✓	✓								
SUKI	2	15.11	✓					✓									
Subtask 2																	
rematchka	4	75.16			✓				✓	✓	✓			✓			
UniManc	3	73.54								✓							✓
BhamNLP	3	73.46	✓			✓			✓	✓							
Pythoneers	1	73.40								✓	✓		✓		✓		
Ahmed_and_Khalil	1	71.46								✓							
Giyaseddin	1	71.43								✓							
ISL_AAST	3	70.55								✓		✓				✓	
ANLP-RG	3	67.31								✓							
RUTeam	1	61.07			✓					✓							

Table 9: Summary of approaches used by participating teams who also submitted system descriptions. Teams are sorted by their performance on official metric, the average $Macro\text{-}F_1$ score over Test-A and Test-B for Subtask 1 and $F1_{NP}$ score over the positive and negative classes for Subtask 2. Classical machine learning (ML) refers to any non-neural machine learning methods such as naive Bayes and support vector machines. The term "neural nets" refers to any model based on neural networks (e.g., FFNN, RNN, and CNN) except Transformer models. Transformer refers to neural networks based on a Transformer architecture such as BERT. **Data Aug.**: Data Augmentation.

5.4 General Description of Submitted Systems

In Table 9, we provide a high-level summary of the submitted systems. For each team, we list their best score with the the main metric of each subtask and the number of their submissions. As shown in this table, most teams used Transformer-based pretrained language models, including mBERT (Devlin et al., 2019), ArabBERT (Antoun et al., 2020), MARBERT (Abdul-Mageed et al., 2021a).

The top team of Subtasks 1 and 2, i.e., `rematchka`, exploited MARBERT, AraBERT, and AraGPT2 (Antoun et al., 2021) with different prompting techniques and added linguistic features to their models.

The team placing first on Test-B of Subtask 1, i.e., `UniManc`, used MARBERT and enhanced the model on under-represented classes by introducing a sampling strategy.

Teams `mtu_fiz` (Shammary et al., 2022) and `ISL_AAST` used adapter modules to fine-tune MARBERT and applied data augmentation techniques.

`Team UniManc` found that further pretraining MARBERT on the 10M unlabelled tweets we released does not benefit Subtask 1 but improves performance on Subtask 2.

Six teams also utilized classical machine learning methods (e.g., SVM and Naive Bayes) to develop their systems.

6 Conclusion and Future Work

We presented the findings and results of the third Nuanced Arabic Dialect Identification shared task, NADI 2022. The shared task has two subtasks: Subtask 1 on country-level dialect identification (including 18 countries) and Subtask 2 on dialectal sentiment analysis (including 10 countries). NADI continues to be an attractive shared task, as reflected by the wide participation: 41 registered teams, 21 submitting teams scoring 105 valid models, and 15 published papers. Results obtained by the various teams show that both dialect identification and dialectal sentiment analysis of short text sequences remain challenging tasks. This motivates further work on Arabic dialects, and so we plan to run future iterations of NADI. Our experience from NADI 2022 shows that inclusion of additional subtasks, along with dialect identification, provides a rich context for modeling. Hence, we intend to continue adding at least one subtask (e.g., sentiment analysis covering more countries, emotion detection) to our main focus of dialect identification. We will also consider adding a data contribution track to NADI. In that track, teams may collect and label new datasets for public release.

Acknowledgements

MAM acknowledges support from Canada Research Chairs (CRC), the Natural Sciences and Engineering Research Council of Canada (NSERC; RGPIN-2018-04267), the Social Sciences and Humanities Research Council of Canada (SSHRC; 435-2018-0576; 895-2020-1004; 895-2021-1008), Canadian Foundation for Innovation (CFI; 37771), and Digital Research Alliance of Canada,[5] and UBC Advanced Research Computing-Sockeye.[6]

References

Abdulrahman AAlAbdulsalam. 2022. SQU-CS @ NADI 2022: Dialectal Arabic Identification using One-vs-One Classification with TF-IDF Weights Computed on Character n-grams. In *Proceedings of the Seventh Arabic Natural Language Processing Workshop (WANLP 2022)*. Association for Computational Linguistics.

Ines Abbes, Wajdi Zaghouani, Omaima El-Hardlo, and Faten Ashour. 2020. DAICT: A dialectal Arabic irony corpus extracted from Twitter. In *Proceedings of the 12th Language Resources and Evaluation Conference*, pages 6265–6271, Marseille, France. European Language Resources Association.

Reem Abdel-Salam. 2022. Dialect & sentiment identification in nuanced Arabic tweets using an ensemble of prompt-based, fine-tuned and multitask bert-based models. In *Proceedings of the Seventh Arabic Natural Language Processing Workshop (WANLP 2022)*. Association for Computational Linguistics.

Ahmed Abdelali, Hamdy Mubarak, Younes Samih, Sabit Hassan, and Kareem Darwish. 2021. QADI: Arabic dialect identification in the wild. In *Proceedings of the Sixth Arabic Natural Language Processing Workshop*, pages 1–10, Kyiv, Ukraine (Virtual). Association for Computational Linguistics.

Muhammad Abdul-Mageed. 2015. *Subjectivity and sentiment analysis of Arabic as a morophologically-rich language*. Ph.D. thesis, Indiana University.

Muhammad Abdul-Mageed. 2019. Modeling Arabic subjectivity and sentiment in lexical space. *Information Processing & Management*, 56(2):291–307.

Muhammad Abdul-Mageed, Hassan Alhuzali, and Mohamed Elaraby. 2018. You tweet what you speak: A city-level dataset of Arabic dialects. In *Proceedings of the Eleventh International Conference on Language Resources and Evaluation (LREC 2018)*, Miyazaki, Japan. European Language Resources Association (ELRA).

Muhammad Abdul-Mageed, Mona T. Diab, and Sandra Kübler. 2014. SAMAR: subjectivity and sentiment analysis for arabic social media. *Comput. Speech Lang.*, 28(1):20–37.

Muhammad Abdul-Mageed, AbdelRahim Elmadany, and El Moatez Billah Nagoudi. 2021a. ARBERT & MARBERT: Deep bidirectional transformers for Arabic. In *Proceedings of the 59th Annual Meeting of the Association for Computational Linguistics and the 11th International Joint Conference on Natural Language Processing (Volume 1: Long Papers)*, pages 7088–7105, Online. Association for Computational Linguistics.

Muhammad Abdul-Mageed, Chiyu Zhang, Houda Bouamor, and Nizar Habash. 2020a. NADI 2020: The first nuanced Arabic dialect identification shared task. In *Proceedings of the Fifth Arabic Natural Language Processing Workshop*, pages 97–110, Barcelona, Spain (Online). Association for Computational Linguistics.

Muhammad Abdul-Mageed, Chiyu Zhang, AbdelRahim Elmadany, Houda Bouamor, and Nizar Habash. 2021b. NADI 2021: The second nuanced Arabic dialect identification shared task. In *Proceedings of the Sixth Arabic Natural Language Processing Workshop*, pages 244–259, Kyiv, Ukraine (Virtual). Association for Computational Linguistics.

[5]https://alliancecan.ca

[6]https://arc.ubc.ca/ubc-arc-sockeye

Muhammad Abdul-Mageed, Chiyu Zhang, AbdelRahim Elmadany, and Lyle Ungar. 2020b. Toward micro-dialect identification in diaglossic and code-switched environments. In *Proceedings of the 2020 Conference on Empirical Methods in Natural Language Processing (EMNLP)*, pages 5855–5876, Online. Association for Computational Linguistics.

Muhammad Abdul-Mageed, Chiyu Zhang, Azadeh Hashemi, and El Moatez Billah Nagoudi. 2020c. AraNet: A deep learning toolkit for Arabic social media. In *Proceedings of the 4th Workshop on Open-Source Arabic Corpora and Processing Tools, with a Shared Task on Offensive Language Detection*, pages 16–23, Marseille, France. European Language Resource Association.

Mohamed Elhag Mohamed Abo, Norisma Idris, Rohana Mahmud, Atika Qazi, Ibrahim Abaker Targio Hashem, Jaafar Zubairu Maitama, Usman Naseem, Shah Khalid Khan, and Shuiqing Yang. 2021. A multi-criteria approach for Arabic dialect sentiment analysis for online reviews: Exploiting optimal machine learning algorithm selection. *Sustainability*, 13(18):10018.

Ibrahim Abu Farha and Walid Magdy. 2020. From Arabic sentiment analysis to sarcasm detection: The ArSarcasm dataset. In *Proceedings of the 4th Workshop on Open-Source Arabic Corpora and Processing Tools, with a Shared Task on Offensive Language Detection*, pages 32–39, Marseille, France. European Language Resource Association.

Ibrahim Abu Farha and Walid Magdy. 2021. Benchmarking transformer-based language models for Arabic sentiment and sarcasm detection. In *Proceedings of the Sixth Arabic Natural Language Processing Workshop*, pages 21–31, Kyiv, Ukraine (Virtual). Association for Computational Linguistics.

Ali Al-Laith, Muhammad Shahbaz, Hind F Alaskar, and Asim Rehmat. 2021. Arasencorpus: A semi-supervised approach for sentiment annotation of a large Arabic text corpus. *Applied Sciences*, 11(5):2434.

Rania Al-Sabbagh and Roxana Girju. 2012. YADAC: Yet another dialectal Arabic corpus. In *Proceedings of the Eighth International Conference on Language Resources and Evaluation (LREC'12)*, pages 2882–2889, Istanbul, Turkey. European Language Resources Association (ELRA).

Nora Al-Twairesh, Rawan N. Al-Matham, Nora Madi, Nada Almugren, Al-Hanouf Al-Aljmi, Shahad Alshalan, Raghad Alshalan, Nafla Alrumayyan, Shams Al-Manea, Sumayah Bawazeer, Nourah Al-Mutlaq, Nada Almanea, Waad Bin Huwaymil, Dalal Alqsair, Reem Alotaibi, Suha Al-Senaydi, and Abeer Alfutamani. 2018. SUAR: towards building a corpus for the saudi dialect. In *Fourth International Conference On Arabic Computational Linguistics, ACLING 2018, November 17-19, 2018, Dubai, United Arab Emirates*, volume 142 of *Procedia Computer Science*, pages 72–82. Elsevier.

Sarah Omar Alhumoud and Asma Ali Al Wazrah. 2022. Arabic sentiment analysis using recurrent neural networks: a review. *Artif. Intell. Rev.*, 55(1):707–748.

Hassan Alhuzali, Muhammad Abdul-Mageed, and Lyle Ungar. 2018. Enabling deep learning of emotion with first-person seed expressions. In *Proceedings of the Second Workshop on Computational Modeling of People's Opinions, Personality, and Emotions in Social Media*, pages 25–35, New Orleans, Louisiana, USA. Association for Computational Linguistics.

Latifah Almuqren and Alexandra I. Cristea. 2021. Aracust: a saudi telecom tweets corpus for sentiment analysis. *PeerJ Comput. Sci.*, 7:e510.

Areeb Alowisheq, Nora Al-Twairesh, Mawaheb Altuwaijri, Afnan AlMoammar, Alhanouf Alsuwailem, Tarfa Albuhairi, Wejdan Alahaideb, and Sarah Alhumoud. 2021. MARSA: multi-domain Arabic resources for sentiment analysis. *IEEE Access*, 9:142718–142728.

Nouf AlShenaifi and Aqil Azmi. 2022. Arabic dialect identification using machine learning and transformer-based models: Submission to the NADI 2022 Shared Task. In *Proceedings of the Seventh Arabic Natural Language Processing Workshop (WANLP 2022)*. Association for Computational Linguistics.

Abdulkareem Alsudais, Wafa Alotaibi, and Faye Alomary. 2022. Similarities between Arabic dialects: Investigating geographical proximity. *Information Processing & Management*, 59(1):102770.

Maha J Althobaiti. 2020. Automatic Arabic dialect identification systems for written texts: A survey. *arXiv preprint arXiv:2009.12622*.

Maha J. Althobaiti. 2022. Creation of annotated country-level dialectal Arabic resources: An unsupervised approach. *Nat. Lang. Eng.*, 28(5):607–648.

Ghadah Alwakid, Taha Osman, Mahmoud El Haj, Saad Alanazi, Mamoona Humayun, and Najm Us Sama. 2022. MULDASA: Multifactor lexical sentiment analysis of social-media content in nonstandard Arabic social media. *Applied Sciences*, 12(8):3806.

Wissam Antoun, Fady Baly, and Hazem Hajj. 2020. AraBERT: Transformer-based model for Arabic language understanding. In *Proceedings of the 4th Workshop on Open-Source Arabic Corpora and Processing Tools, with a Shared Task on Offensive Language Detection*, pages 9–15, Marseille, France. European Language Resource Association.

Wissam Antoun, Fady Baly, and Hazem Hajj. 2021. AraGPT2: Pre-trained transformer for Arabic language generation. In *Proceedings of the Sixth Arabic Natural Language Processing Workshop*, pages 196–207, Kyiv, Ukraine (Virtual). Association for Computational Linguistics.

Joseph Attieh and Fadi Abdulfattah Mohammed Hassan. 2022. Arabic Dialect Identification and Sentiment Classification using Transformer-based Models. In *Proceedings of the Seventh Arabic Natural Language Processing Workshop (WANLP 2022)*. Association for Computational Linguistics.

MS Badawi. 1973. Levels of contemporary Arabic in Egypt. *Cairo: Dâr al Ma'ârif.*

Nurpeiis Baimukan, Houda Bouamor, and Nizar Habash. 2022. Hierarchical aggregation of dialectal data for Arabic dialect identification. In *Proceedings of the Thirteenth Language Resources and Evaluation Conference, LREC 2022, Marseille, France, 20-25 June 2022*, pages 4586–4596. European Language Resources Association.

Gıyaseddin Bayrak and Abdul Majeed Issifu. 2022. Domain-Adapted BERT-based models for Nuanced Arabic Dialect Identification and Tweet Sentiment Analysis. In *Proceedings of the Seventh Arabic Natural Language Processing Workshop (WANLP 2022)*. Association for Computational Linguistics.

Houda Bouamor, Nizar Habash, and Kemal Oflazer. 2014. A multidialectal parallel corpus of Arabic. In *Proceedings of the Ninth International Conference on Language Resources and Evaluation (LREC'14)*, pages 1240–1245, Reykjavik, Iceland. European Language Resources Association (ELRA).

Houda Bouamor, Nizar Habash, Mohammad Salameh, Wajdi Zaghouani, Owen Rambow, Dana Abdulrahim, Ossama Obeid, Salam Khalifa, Fadhl Eryani, Alexander Erdmann, and Kemal Oflazer. 2018. The MADAR Arabic dialect corpus and lexicon. In *Proceedings of the Eleventh International Conference on Language Resources and Evaluation (LREC 2018)*, Miyazaki, Japan. European Language Resources Association (ELRA).

Kristen Brustad. 2000. *The Syntax of Spoken Arabic: A Comparative Study of Moroccan, Egyptian, Syrian, and Kuwaiti Dialects.* Georgetown University Press.

Alexis Conneau and Guillaume Lample. 2019. Cross-lingual language model pretraining. In *Advances in Neural Information Processing Systems 32: Annual Conference on Neural Information Processing Systems 2019, NeurIPS 2019, December 8-14, 2019, Vancouver, BC, Canada*, pages 7057–7067.

Mark W. Cowell. 1964. *A Reference Grammar of Syrian Arabic.* Georgetown University Press, Washington, D.C.

Jacob Devlin, Ming-Wei Chang, Kenton Lee, and Kristina Toutanova. 2019. BERT: Pre-training of deep bidirectional transformers for language understanding. In *Proceedings of the 2019 Conference of the North American Chapter of the Association for Computational Linguistics: Human Language Technologies, Volume 1 (Long and Short Papers)*, pages 4171–4186, Minneapolis, Minnesota. Association for Computational Linguistics.

Mona Diab, Nizar Habash, Owen Rambow, Mohamed Altantawy, and Yassine Benajiba. 2010. COLABA: Arabic dialect annotation and processing. In *LREC workshop on Semitic language processing*, pages 66–74.

Mahmoud El-Haj. 2020. Habibi - a multi dialect multi national Arabic song lyrics corpus. In *Proceedings of the 12th Language Resources and Evaluation Conference*, pages 1318–1326, Marseille, France. European Language Resources Association.

Ahmed Oumar El-Shangiti and Khalil Mrini. 2022. Ahmed and Khalil at NADI 2022: Transfer Learning and Addressing Class Imbalance for Arabic Dialect Identification and Sentiment Analysis. In *Proceedings of the Seventh Arabic Natural Language Processing Workshop (WANLP 2022)*. Association for Computational Linguistics.

Heba Elfardy, Mohamed Al-Badrashiny, and Mona Diab. 2014. AIDA: Identifying code switching in informal Arabic text. In *Proceedings of the First Workshop on Computational Approaches to Code Switching*, pages 94–101, Doha, Qatar. Association for Computational Linguistics.

AbdelRahim Elmadany, Chiyu Zhang, Muhammad Abdul-Mageed, and Azadeh Hashemi. 2020. Leveraging affective bidirectional transformers for offensive language detection. In *Proceedings of the 4th Workshop on Open-Source Arabic Corpora and Processing Tools, with a Shared Task on Offensive Language Detection*, pages 102–108.

Ashraf Elnagar, Sane Yagi, Ali Bou Nassif, Ismail Shahin, and Said A. Salloum. 2021. Sentiment analysis in dialectal Arabic: A systematic review. In *Advanced Machine Learning Technologies and Applications - Proceedings of AMLTA 2021, Cairo, Egypt, March 22-24, 2021*, volume 1339 of *Advances in Intelligent Systems and Computing*, pages 407–417. Springer.

Chayma Fourati, Abir Messaoudi, and Hatem Haddad. 2020. Tunizi: a tunisian arabizi sentiment analysis dataset. *arXiv preprint arXiv:2004.14303*.

Emna Fsih, Saméh Kchaou, Rahma Boujelbane, and Lamia Hadrich Belguith. 2022. Benchmarking Transfer Learning Approaches for Sentiment Analysis of Arabic Dialect. In *Proceedings of the Seventh Arabic Natural Language Processing Workshop (WANLP 2022)*. Association for Computational Linguistics.

Hassan Gadalla, Hanaa Kilany, Howaida Arram, Ashraf Yacoub, Alaa El-Habashi, Amr Shalaby, Krisjanis Karins, Everett Rowson, Robert MacIntyre, Paul Kingsbury, David Graff, and Cynthia McLemore. 1997. CALLHOME Egyptian Arabic transcripts LDC97T19. Web Download. Philadelphia: Linguistic Data Consortium.

Imane Guellil, Ahsan Adeel, Faiçal Azouaou, Fodil Benali, Ala-Eddine Hachani, Kia Dashtipour, Mandar

Gogate, Cosimo Ieracitano, Reza Kashani, and Amir Hussain. 2021. A semi-supervised approach for sentiment analysis of arab(ic+izi) messages: Application to the algerian dialect. *SN Comput. Sci.*, 2(2):118.

Imane Guellil, Faical Azouaou, and Francisco Chiclana. 2020a. Arautosenti: Automatic annotation and new tendencies for sentiment classification of arabic messages. *Social Network Analysis and Mining*, 10(1):1–20.

Imane Guellil, Marcelo Mendoza, and Faiçal Azouaou. 2020b. Arabic dialect sentiment analysis with ZERO effort. \\ case study: Algerian dialect. *Inteligencia Artif.*, 23(65):124–135.

Nizar Habash, Houda Bouamor, Hazem Hajj, Walid Magdy, Wajdi Zaghouani, Fethi Bougares, Nadi Tomeh, Ibrahim Abu Farha, and Samia Touileb, editors. 2021. *Proceedings of the Sixth Arabic Natural Language Processing Workshop*. Association for Computational Linguistics, Kyiv, Ukraine (Virtual).

Nizar Y Habash. 2010. *Introduction to Arabic natural language processing*, volume 3. Morgan & Claypool Publishers.

Salima Harrat, Karima Meftouh, Mourad Abbas, and Kamel Smaïli. 2014. Building resources for algerian arabic dialects. In *INTERSPEECH 2014, 15th Annual Conference of the International Speech Communication Association, Singapore, September 14-18, 2014*, pages 2123–2127. ISCA.

R.S. Harrell. 1962. *A Short Reference Grammar of Moroccan Arabic: With Audio CD*. Georgetown classics in Arabic language and linguistics. Georgetown University Press.

Sabit Hassan, Hamdy Mubarak, Ahmed Abdelali, and Kareem Darwish. 2021. ASAD: Arabic social media analytics and unDerstanding. In *Proceedings of the 16th Conference of the European Chapter of the Association for Computational Linguistics: System Demonstrations*, pages 113–118, Online. Association for Computational Linguistics.

Clive Holes. 2004. *Modern Arabic: Structures, Functions, and Varieties*. Georgetown Classics in Arabic Language and Linguistics. Georgetown University Press.

Elsayed Issa, Mohammed AlShakhori1, Reda Al-Bahrani, and Gus Hahn-Powell. 2021. Country-level Arabic dialect identification using RNNs with and without linguistic features. In *Proceedings of the Sixth Arabic Natural Language Processing Workshop*, pages 276–281, Kyiv, Ukraine (Virtual). Association for Computational Linguistics.

Salma Jamal, Aly M. Kassem, Omar Mohamed, and Ali Ashraf. 2022. On The Arabic Dialect. In *Proceedings of the Seventh Arabic Natural Language Processing Workshop (WANLP 2022)*. Association for Computational Linguistics.

Mustafa Jarrar, Nizar Habash, Faeq Alrimawi, Diyam Akra, and Nasser Zalmout. 2016. Curras: an annotated corpus for the Palestinian Arabic dialect. *Language Resources and Evaluation*, pages 1–31.

Tommi Jauhiainen, Heidi Jauhiainen, and Krister Lindén. 2022. Optimizing Naive Bayes for Arabic Dialect Identification. In *Proceedings of the Seventh Arabic Natural Language Processing Workshop (WANLP 2022)*. Association for Computational Linguistics.

Vani Kanjirangat, Tanja Samardzic, Ljiljana Dolamic, and Fabio Rinaldi. 2022. NLP_DI at NADI Shared Task Subtask-1: Sub-word Level Convolutional Neural Models and Pre-trained Binary Classifiers for Dialect Identification. In *Proceedings of the Seventh Arabic Natural Language Processing Workshop (WANLP 2022)*. Association for Computational Linguistics.

Salam Khalifa, Nizar Habash, Dana Abdulrahim, and Sara Hassan. 2016. A large scale corpus of Gulf Arabic. In *Proceedings of the Tenth International Conference on Language Resources and Evaluation (LREC'16)*, pages 4282–4289, Portorož, Slovenia. European Language Resources Association (ELRA).

Abdullah Khered, Ingy Abdelhalim, and Riza Batista-Navarro. 2022. Building an Ensemble of Transformer Models for Arabic Dialect Classification and Sentiment Analysis. In *Proceedings of the Seventh Arabic Natural Language Processing Workshop (WANLP 2022)*. Association for Computational Linguistics.

Shervin Malmasi, Marcos Zampieri, Nikola Ljubešić, Preslav Nakov, Ahmed Ali, and Jörg Tiedemann. 2016. Discriminating between similar languages and Arabic dialect identification: A report on the third DSL shared task. In *Proceedings of the Third Workshop on NLP for Similar Languages, Varieties and Dialects (VarDial3)*, pages 1–14, Osaka, Japan. The COLING 2016 Organizing Committee.

Karima Meftouh, Salima Harrat, Salma Jamoussi, Mourad Abbas, and Kamel Smaili. 2015. Machine translation experiments on PADIC: A parallel Arabic DIalect corpus. In *Proceedings of the 29th Pacific Asia Conference on Language, Information and Computation*, pages 26–34, Shanghai, China.

Abir Messaoudi, Chayma Fourati, Hatem Haddad, and Moez Ben HajHmida. 2022. iCompass Working Notes for the Nuanced Arabic Dialect Identification Shared task. In *Proceedings of the Seventh Arabic Natural Language Processing Workshop (WANLP 2022)*. Association for Computational Linguistics.

Hamdy Mubarak and Kareem Darwish. 2014. Using Twitter to collect a multi-dialectal corpus of Arabic. In *Proceedings of the EMNLP 2014 Workshop on Arabic Natural Language Processing (ANLP)*, pages 1–7, Doha, Qatar. Association for Computational Linguistics.

Hamdy Mubarak, Kareem Darwish, Walid Magdy, Tamer Elsayed, and Hend Al-Khalifa. 2020. Overview of OSACT4 Arabic offensive language detection shared task. In *Proceedings of the 4th Workshop on Open-Source Arabic Corpora and Processing Tools, with a Shared Task on Offensive Language Detection*, pages 48–52, Marseille, France. European Language Resource Association.

Ossama Obeid, Mohammad Salameh, Houda Bouamor, and Nizar Habash. 2019. ADIDA: Automatic dialect identification for Arabic. In *Proceedings of the 2019 Conference of the North American Chapter of the Association for Computational Linguistics (Demonstrations)*, pages 6–11, Minneapolis, Minnesota. Association for Computational Linguistics.

Abdelrahim Qaddoumi. 2022. Arabic Sentiment Ensemble NADI Shared Task 2. In *Proceedings of the Seventh Arabic Natural Language Processing Workshop (WANLP 2022)*. Association for Computational Linguistics.

Fatiha Sadat, Farzindar Kazemi, and Atefeh Farzindar. 2014. Automatic identification of Arabic language varieties and dialects in social media. In *Proceedings of the Second Workshop on Natural Language Processing for Social Media (SocialNLP)*, pages 22–27, Dublin, Ireland. Association for Computational Linguistics and Dublin City University.

Mohammad Salameh, Houda Bouamor, and Nizar Habash. 2018. Fine-grained Arabic dialect identification. In *Proceedings of the 27th International Conference on Computational Linguistics*, pages 1332–1344, Santa Fe, New Mexico, USA. Association for Computational Linguistics.

Fouad Shammary, Yiyi Chen, Zsolt T. Kardkovács, Haithem Afli, and Mehwish Alam. 2022. TF-IDF or Transformers for Arabic Dialect Identification? ITFLOWS participation in the NADI 2022 Shared Task. In *Proceedings of the Seventh Arabic Natural Language Processing Workshop (WANLP 2022)*. Association for Computational Linguistics.

Arwa A. Al Shamsi and Sherief Abdallah. 2022. Sentiment analysis of Emirati dialect. *Big Data Cogn. Comput.*, 6(2):57.

Mahmoud Sobhy, Ahmed H. Abu El Atta, Ahmed A. El-Sawy, and Hamada Nayel. 2022. Word Representation Models for Arabic Dialect Identification. In *Proceedings of the Seventh Arabic Natural Language Processing Workshop (WANLP 2022)*. Association for Computational Linguistics.

Jenny A Thomas. 2014. *Meaning in interaction: An introduction to pragmatics*. Routledge.

Thomas Wolf, Lysandre Debut, Victor Sanh, Julien Chaumond, Clement Delangue, Anthony Moi, Pierric Cistac, Tim Rault, Remi Louf, Morgan Funtowicz, Joe Davison, Sam Shleifer, Patrick von Platen, Clara Ma, Yacine Jernite, Julien Plu, Canwen Xu, Teven Le Scao, Sylvain Gugger, Mariama Drame, Quentin Lhoest, and Alexander Rush. 2020. Transformers: State-of-the-art natural language processing. In *Proceedings of the 2020 Conference on Empirical Methods in Natural Language Processing: System Demonstrations*, pages 38–45, Online. Association for Computational Linguistics.

Wajdi Zaghouani and Anis Charfi. 2018. Arap-tweet: A large multi-dialect Twitter corpus for gender, age and language variety identification. In *Proceedings of the Eleventh International Conference on Language Resources and Evaluation (LREC 2018)*, Miyazaki, Japan. European Language Resources Association (ELRA).

Omar F. Zaidan and Chris Callison-Burch. 2011. The Arabic online commentary dataset: an annotated dataset of informal Arabic with high dialectal content. In *Proceedings of the 49th Annual Meeting of the Association for Computational Linguistics: Human Language Technologies*, pages 37–41, Portland, Oregon, USA. Association for Computational Linguistics.

Marcos Zampieri, Shervin Malmasi, Nikola Ljubešić, Preslav Nakov, Ahmed Ali, Jörg Tiedemann, Yves Scherrer, and Noëmi Aepli. 2017. Findings of the VarDial evaluation campaign 2017. In *Proceedings of the Fourth Workshop on NLP for Similar Languages, Varieties and Dialects (VarDial)*, pages 1–15, Valencia, Spain. Association for Computational Linguistics.

Marcos Zampieri, Shervin Malmasi, Preslav Nakov, Ahmed Ali, Suwon Shon, James Glass, Yves Scherrer, Tanja Samardžić, Nikola Ljubešić, Jörg Tiedemann, Chris van der Lee, Stefan Grondelaers, Nelleke Oostdijk, Dirk Speelman, Antal van den Bosch, Ritesh Kumar, Bornini Lahiri, and Mayank Jain. 2018. Language identification and morphosyntactic tagging: The second VarDial evaluation campaign. In *Proceedings of the Fifth Workshop on NLP for Similar Languages, Varieties and Dialects (VarDial 2018)*, pages 1–17, Santa Fe, New Mexico, USA. Association for Computational Linguistics.

Chiyu Zhang, Muhammad Abdul-Mageed, and El Moatez Billah Nagoudi. 2022. Decay no more: A persistent twitter dataset for learning social meaning. *Workshop Proceedings of the 16th International AAAI Conference on Web and Social Media.*

Imed Zitouni, Muhammad Abdul-Mageed, Houda Bouamor, Fethi Bougares, Mahmoud El-Haj, Nadi Tomeh, and Wajdi Zaghouani, editors. 2020. *Proceedings of the Fifth Arabic Natural Language Processing Workshop*. Association for Computational Linguistics, Barcelona, Spain (Online).

The Shared Task on Gender Rewriting

Bashar Alhafni,[1] Nizar Habash,[1] Houda Bouamor,[2] Ossama Obeid,[1]
Sultan Alrowili,[3] Daliyah Alzeer,[4] Khawlah M. Alshanqiti,[5] Ahmed ElBakry,[6]
Muhammad ElNokrashy,[6] Mohamed Gabr,[6] Abderrahmane Issam,[7]
Abdelrahim Qaddoumi,[8] K. Vijay-Shanker,[3] Mahmoud Zyate[9]*
[1]New York University Abu Dhabi, [2]Carnegie Mellon University in Qatar,
[3]University of Delaware, [4]Taif University, [5]Umm Alqura University,
[6]Microsoft ATL Cairo, [7]Archipel Cognitive, [8]New York University, [9]Leyton
alhafni@nyu.edu

Abstract

In this paper, we present the results and findings of the Shared Task on Gender Rewriting, which was organized as part of the Seventh Arabic Natural Language Processing Workshop. The task of gender rewriting refers to generating alternatives of a given sentence to match different target user gender contexts (e.g., female speaker with a male listener, a male speaker with a male listener, etc.). This requires changing the grammatical gender (masculine or feminine) of certain words referring to the users. In this task, we focus on Arabic, a gender-marking morphologically rich language. A total of five teams from four countries participated in the shared task.

1 Introduction

The problem of gender bias in Natural Language Processing (NLP) systems has been receiving a lot of attention across a variety of tasks such as machine translation, co-reference resolution, and dialogue systems. Research has shown that NLP systems do not only have the ability to embed societal biases, but they also amplify and propagate them in ways that create representational harms and degrade users' experiences (Sun et al., 2019; Blodgett et al., 2020). The main cause of this problem is usually attributed to inherently biased data that is used to build these systems and which mirrors the inequalities of the world we live in. Therefore, many approaches were proposed to mitigate this problem by either using counterfactual data augmentation techniques (Lu et al., 2018; Hall Maudslay et al., 2019; Zmigrod et al., 2019) or by debiasing pretrained representation that is trained on biased data (Bolukbasi et al., 2016; Zhao et al., 2018; Manzini et al., 2019; Zhao et al., 2020). However, even the most balanced of models can still exhibit and amplify bias if they are designed to produce a single text output without taking their users' gender preferences into consideration (Habash et al., 2019; Alhafni et al., 2020, 2022b). Therefore, to provide the correct user-aware output, NLP systems should be designed to produce outputs that are as gender specific as the users preferences they have access to. Recently, Alhafni et al. (2022b) introduced the task of gender rewriting, which refers to generating alternatives of a given sentence to match different target user gender contexts. To encourage more researchers to work on this problem, we organized the Shared Task on Gender Rewriting. We focus on Modern Standard Arabic (MSA), a gender-marking morphologically rich language, in contexts involving two users.[1]

This shared task was organized as part of the Seventh Arabic Natural Language Processing Workshop (WANLP), collocated with EMNLP 2022. This is the first shared task at WANLP in seven years to target a language generation problem in Arabic. A total of five teams from four countries participated in the shared task. One team contributed to a system description paper which is included in the WANLP proceedings and cited in this paper. We provide a description of all submitted systems and the approaches they use. All of the datasets created for this shared task will be made publicly available to support further research on gender rewriting.

This paper is organized as follows. We first provide a description of the shared task (§2). We then describe the data used in the shared task, including a newly created set which we used for evaluation in §3. Next, we provide a description of all submitted systems in §4 and discuss the results in §5. Finally, we discuss the lessons we learned from running this shared task and provide recommendations to the (Arabic) NLP community in §6.

*The first four authors are the shared task organizers, listed in order of contribution. The remaining authors are the shared task participants in alphabetical order.

[1] http://gender-rewriting-shared-task.camel-lab.com/

Proceedings of the The Seventh Arabic Natural Language Processing Workshop (WANLP), pages 98 - 107
December 8, 2022 ©2022 Association for Computational Linguistics

Input Sentence	Target Speaker	Target Listener	Output Sentence
سعيدة حقا بمعرفتكن يا سيدات (Really glad to know you ladies)	Masculine	Masculine	سعيد حقا بمعرفتكم يا سادة (Really glad to know you gentlemen)
	Feminine	Masculine	سعيدة حقا بمعرفتكم يا سادة (Really glad to know you gentlemen)
	Masculine	Feminine	سعيد حقا بمعرفتكن يا سيدات (Really glad to know you ladies)
	Feminine	Feminine	سعيدة حقا بمعرفتكن يا سيدات (Really glad to know you ladies)

Table 1: Example of the gender rewriting task. The input sentence has four rewritten alternatives that match the different target user gender contexts. First person gendered words are in purple and second person gendered words are in red.

2 Task Description

The task of gender rewriting was introduced by Alhafni et al. (2022b) and it refers to generating alternatives of a given Arabic sentence to match different target user gender contexts. We focus on contexts involving two users (I and/or You) – first and second grammatical persons with independent grammatical gender preferences. This requires changing the grammatical gender (masculine or feminine) of certain words referring to the users (speaker/first person and listener/second person) in the input sentence. Therefore, given an Arabic sentence as an input, the goal is to generate four different gender rewritten alternatives to match the different target user gender contexts (i.e., female speaker with a male listener, a male speaker with a male listener, a male speaker with a female listener, and a female speaker with a female listener). Table 1 shows an example of the gender rewriting problem where the input sentence is rewritten to its four gender alternatives that match the four target user gender contexts.

Notation We use the notation that is defined by Alhafni et al. (2022b). Namely, we use four elementary symbols to facilitate the discussion of this task: 1M, 1F, 2M and 2F. The digit part of the symbol refers to the grammatical person (1st or 2nd) and the letter part refers to the grammatical gender (Masculine or Feminine). Additionally, we use B to refer to invariant/ambiguous gender.

2.1 Shared Task Restrictions

We provided the participants with a set of restrictions for building their systems to ensure a common experimental setup and fair comparison. Participants were asked not to use any external manually labeled datasets. However, the use of publicly available unlabeled data was allowed. Participants were also not allowed to use the publicly available development and test sets of the shared task corpus for training their systems. Moreover, we provided the participants with a new blind test set that was manually annotated for this shared task. The participants were provided with the input sentences and they did not have access to the gold references. We discuss the properties and statistics of this new test set in more detail in §3.2.

2.2 Evaluation Metrics

We follow Alhafni et al. (2022b) by treating the gender rewriting problem as a user-aware grammatical error correction task and use the MaxMatch (M^2) scorer (Dahlmeier and Ng, 2012) as our evaluation metric. The M^2 scorer computes the Precision (P), Recall (R), and $F_{0.5}$ by maximally matching phrase-level edits made by a system to gold-standard edits. The gold edits are computed by the M^2 scorer based on provided gold references. We also report BLEU (Papineni et al., 2002) scores which are obtained using SacreBLEU (Post, 2018). We report the gender rewriting results in a normalized space for Alif, Ya, and Ta-Marbuta (Habash, 2010).

3 Shared Task Data

In this section, we describe the data we use in the shared task.

3.1 The Arabic Parallel Gender Corpus

We use the publicly available Arabic Parallel Gender Corpus (APGC) – a parallel corpus of Arabic sentences with gender annotations and gender rewritten alternatives of sentences selected from

OpenSubtitles 2018 (Lison and Tiedemann, 2016). The corpus comes in three versions: APGC v1.0 (Habash et al., 2019), APGC v2.0 (Alhafni et al., 2022a), and APGC v2.1 (Alhafni et al., 2022b). In this shared task, we use APGC v2.1 which contains 80,326 gender-annotated parallel sentences (596,799 words) of contexts involving first and second grammatical persons covering singular, dual, and plural constructions.

Annotations Each sentence in APGC v2.1 has one of nine labels: 1M/2M, 1M/2F, 1F/2M, 1F/2F, 1M/B, B/2M, 1F/B, B/2F, and B. Each of these labels indicates the existence (or lack thereof) of first and/or second persons gendered references in the sentence. APGC v2.1 also contains two types of word-level gender labels: basic and extended. The basic schema labels each word as B, 1F, 2F, 1M, or 2M. The basic labels refer to the *primary* person-gender marking signal in the word, which could come from the base form if gendered or the pronominal enclitic if the base form is not gendered.[2] The extended schema marks the person-genders of both the base words and their pronominal enclitics. This results in 25 word-level gender labels (e.g., B+1F, 1F+2M, etc.). All sentences containing gender-specific words have gender-rewritten parallels. The parallels of B-labeled sentences are trivial copies. Out of the 80,326 sentences in APGC v2.1, 54% (43,346) contain gendered words. In terms of word-level statistics, only 9.7% (58,066) are gender specific.

APGC v2.1 is organized into five parallel corpora that are fully aligned (1-to-1) at the word level: Input, Target 1M/2M, Target 1F/2M, Target 1M/2F, and Target 1F/2F. All five corpora are balanced in terms of gender, i.e., the number of 1F and 1M words is the same; and the number of 2F and 2M words is the same. The Input corpus contains sentences with all possible word types (B, 1F, 2F, 1M, 2M). The Target 1M/2M corpus contains sentences that consist of B, 1M, 2M words; the Target 1F/2M corpus contains sentences that consist of B, 1F, 2M words; the Target 1M/2F corpus contains sentences that consist of B, 1M, 2F words; and the Target 1F/2F corpus contains sentences that consist of B, 1F, 2F words.

[2]Changing the grammatical gender of Arabic words involves either changing the form of the base word, changing the pronominal enclitics that are attached to the base word, or a combination of both (Alhafni et al., 2022b)

Splits We use Alhafni et al. (2022a)'s splits: 57,603 sentences (427,523 words) for training (TRAIN), 6,647 sentences (49,257 words) for development (DEV), and 16,076 sentences (120,019 words) for testing (TEST).

3.2 Blind Test Set

To ensure fair comparison between all participants, we manually annotated a new blind test set to evaluate their systems. We plan on making this new test set publicly available. We will refer to this set as *Blind Test* throughout the paper.

Data Selection We followed the same procedure that was used in (Habash et al., 2019) and (Alhafni et al., 2022a) to create the APGC. We selected sentences from the English-Arabic OpenSubtitles 2018 dataset (Lison and Tiedemann, 2016) by extracting sentence pairs that include first or second pronouns on the English side. We annotated 5,000 sentences such that 1,061 (21.2%) include first and second person pronouns, 2,116 (42.3%) include only first person pronouns, and 1,823 (36.5%) include only second person pronouns. The sentences were selected such: (a) they do not overlap with any of the sentences that are in APGC; and (b) their proportions approximate the distribution of the Arabic-English pairs in the OpenSubtitles 2018 dataset that have first or second persons pronouns on the English side (Alhafni et al., 2022a).

Data Annotation We conducted the annotation through a linguistic annotation firm that hired professional linguists to complete the task.[3] We provided them with the same annotation guidelines that were defined in Alhafni et al. (2022a) and used to annotate the APGC. That is, the annotators were asked to identify the genders of the first and second person references in each sentence. In the case a gendered reference exists, the annotators were asked to copy the sentence and modify it to obtain the opposite gender forms. As was done when creating the APGC, the modifications are strictly limited to morphological reinflections and word substitutions. Therefore, the total number of words is maintained along with a perfect alignment between each sentence and its parallel opposite gender forms. This allowed us to obtain basic and extended word-level gender annotations automatically as was done by Alhafni et al. (2022a,b).

[3]https://www.ramitechs.com/

(a)

	Original Test Set	
Sentences	Label	Rewriting Label
2,818 56.4%	B	
91 1.8%	1F/B	1M/B
172 3.4%	1M/B	1F/B
559 11.2%	B/2F	B/2M
1,292 25.8%	B/2M	B/2F
8 0.2%	1F/2F	1M/2F 1F/2M 1M/2M
21 0.4%	1F/2M	1M/2M 1F/2F 1M/2F
13 0.5%	1M/2F	1F/2F 1M/2M 1F/2M
26 1.4%	1M/2M	1F/2M 1M/2F 1F/2F
5,000		

(b)

Balanced Test Set					
Input	Target 1M/2M	Target 1F/2M	Target 1M/2F	Target 1F/2F	Sentences
B	B	B	B	B	2,818 38.5%
1F/B	1M/B	1F/B	1M/B	1F/B	263 3.6%
1M/B	1M/B	1F/B	1M/B	1F/B	263 3.6%
B/2F	B/2M	B/2M	B/2F	B/2F	1,851 25.3%
B/2M	B/2M	B/2M	B/2F	B/2F	1,851 25.3%
1F/2F	1M/2M	1F/2M	1M/2F	1F/2F	68 0.9%
1F/2M	1M/2M	1F/2M	1M/2F	1F/2F	68 0.9%
1M/2F	1M/2M	1F/2M	1M/2F	1F/2F	68 0.9%
1M/2M	1M/2M	1F/2M	1M/2F	1F/2F	68 0.9%
					7,318

Table 2: **Sentence-level** statistics of the original (a) and the balanced Blind Test set (b) with its five versions.

(a)

	Original Test Set	
Words	Label	Rewriting Label
32,548 91.8%	B	
138 0.4%	1F	1M
241 0.7%	1M	1F
738 2.1%	2F	2M
1,805 5.1%	2M	2F
35,470		

(b)

Balanced Test Set					
Input	Target 1M/2M	Target 1F/2M	Target 1M/2F	Target 1F/2F	Words
B	B	B	B	B	46,550 88.3%
1F	1M	1F	1M	1F	452 0.9%
1M	1M	1F	1M	1F	452 0.9%
2F	2M	2M	2F	2F	2,624 5%
2M	2M	2M	2F	2F	2,624 5%
					52,702

Table 3: **Word-level** statistics of the original (a) and the balanced Blind Test set (b) with its five versions.

Data Statistics Table 2(a) includes the statistics of the newly annotated sentences. This constitutes the Original Blind Test set. Out of all sentences in this set, 2,818 (56.4%) are labeled as B. There are 1,851 sentences (37%) that include only second-person gendered references (B/2F and B/2M). This is about five times more than sentences with only first-person gendered references (1F/B and 1M/B), which accounts for 5.3% (263 sentences) of all sentences. Moreover, the number of sentences including first or second person masculine references is more than the ones including feminine references (1,292 B/2M vs 559 B/2F, and 172 1M/B vs 91 1F/B). There are 68 (1.4%) sentences that have both first and second gendered references. These results are consistent with APGC v2.0 (Alhafni et al., 2022a). The basic word-level statistics of the Original Blind Test set are presented in Table 3(a). We evaluated inter-annotator agreement (IAA) on 500 sentences between two annotators. The IAA in terms of nine sentence-level labels (B, M, F, for 1st and for 2nd persons, e.g., 1M/2F or 1B/2M) was 98.0%. Agreement in exact match on gender rewriting alternatives was 96.2%.

Similarly to Habash et al. (2019) and Alhafni et al. (2022a), to ensure equal gender representation in our dataset, we force balance the corpus by adding the manually rewritten sentences to the test set and using their original forms as their rewritten forms. This constitutes the Balanced Blind Test set. The sentence-level statistics of the balanced set are presented in Table 2(b). This corpus has 7,318 sentences in total. Out of all sentences, 38.5% (2,818) are marked as B, whereas sentences with gendered references constituted 61.5% (4,500 sentences). Moreover, we organize the data into five balanced corpora as was done in APGC v2.0 (§3.1). The basic word-level statistics of the Balanced Blind Test set are presented in Table 3(b). The extended word-level statistics of the Balanced Blind Test set are in Table 4.

Word Gender Label		
Basic	Extended	Words
B	B	46,550 88.3%
1M	1M+B	445 0.8%
	B+1M	7 0.01%
1F	1F+B	445 0.8%
	B+1F	7 0.01%
2M	2M+B	2,464 4.7%
	B+2M	144 0.3%
	2M+2M	16 0.03%
2F	2F+B	2,464 4.7%
	B+2F	144 0.3%
	2F+2F	16 0.03%
		52,702

Table 4: Statistics of the extended word-level gender of the Blind Test set.

Team	Affiliation
Cairo Team	Microsoft ATL Cairo, Egypt
CasaNLP	Archipel Cognitive, and Leyton, Morocco
Distinguishers	Taif University, and Umm Alqura University, KSA
Qaddoumi	New York University, USA
UDEL-NLP	University of Delaware, USA

Table 5: List of the five teams who participated in the gender rewriting shared task.

Team	Gender ID	Special Preprocessing	Pretrained Models
Cairo Team	Word		CAMeLBERT MSA + AraT5-MSA
CasaNLP	Word	Word Side Constraints	CAMeLBERT MSA + AraT5-MSA
Distinguishers	Word	Morphological Features	CAMeLBERT MSA + AraBERT
Qaddoumi		Romanization	T5
UDEL-NLP		Sentence Side Constraints	ArabicT5

Table 6: Approaches and techniques used by the participants. Gender ID refers to gender identification. Special Preprocessing refers to any form of preprocessing done to modify the data (e.g., adding side-constraints, morphological processing, transliteration, etc.). Pretrained Models indicates the usage of pretrained models as part of the system.

4 Participants and Systems

Five teams from four countries participated in the shared task. Table 5 presents the names of the participating teams and their affiliations. Next, we describe the approaches the participants took to develop their gender rewriting systems.

4.1 Systems Descriptions

All participants leveraged pretrained language models such as AraBERT (Antoun et al., 2020), CAMeLBERT (Inoue et al., 2021), T5 (Raffel et al., 2020), and AraT5 (Nagoudi et al., 2022), when developing their systems. Some systems consisted of multiple components to do gender identification and then rewriting as was done in Alhafni et al. (2022b), while others treated the problem as a traditional sequence-to-sequence (Seq2Seq) task. Table 6 presents a summary of the different approaches used to develop the different systems.

Cairo Team The system developed by Cairo Team was a multi-step system consisting of the following components: (a) a word-level gender identification classifier; (b) a word-level person identification classifier; and (c) sentence-level gender rewriting Seq2Seq models. The word-level classifiers were built by fine-tuning CAMeLBERT MSA (Inoue et al., 2021), on the training data of APGC v2.1. Cairo Team used the *basic* word-level annotations in the corpus to build these two classifiers. Concretely, the gender identification component was trained to identify the gender of each word as M, F, or B, whereas the person identification component was trained to classify the person which the word refers to as 1st, 2nd, or none. For the sentence-level Seq2Seq models, Cairo Team built four different models, one for each target user gender context (i.e., 1M/2M, 1F/2M, 1M/2F, 1F/2F), by fine-tuning AraT5-MSA$_{\text{BASE}}$ (Nagoudi et al., 2022).

During inference, the input sentence is passed to the word-level classifiers to get the gender and person labels for each word. These predicted labels indicate which words need to be rewritten based on the compatibility between the labels and the target user gender contexts. Then, the same input sentence is passed to each Seq2Seq model to get its rewritten forms. After that, Cairo Team uses a simple heuristic to reduce the noise that could be generated in the outputs of the Seq2Seq models and to ensure that only the necessary gendered words are changed. To do so, Cairo Team generates all subsets of possible trigrams for each gendered word that needs to be changed in the input. Then, they search for partial matches of these trigrams in the Seq2Seq model generated sentences and pick the generated words that have the highest match. The intuition behind this approach is that: (a) the Seq2Seq model would benefit from seeing the entire sentence to apply in-context word gender rewriting; and (b) most of the gendered words in the APGC v2.1 (96.9%) are due to morphological inflections, which allows the matching heuristic to have a high coverage.

The fine-tuning of the models was done using Hugging Face's Transformers (Wolf et al., 2020). Both the word-level gender and person identification classifiers were fine-tuned on a single GPU for 10 epochs with a maximum sequence length of 128, a batch size of 32, and a learning rate of 1e-4. The sentence-level gender rewriting component was fine-tuned on a single GPU for 30 epochs with a maximum sequence length of 128, a batch size of 16, and a learning rate of 1e-3. Checkpoints were saved every 1000 steps and at the end of fine-tuning, the best checkpoint was picked based on the development set.

CasaNLP The system introduced by CasaNLP was also a multi-step system that consists of word-level gender identification and sentence-level gender rewriting. For gender identification, the team used the gender identification model that was developed and released by Alhafni et al. (2022b).[4] The gender identification component takes the input sentence and assigns an *extended* gender label to every word in the input. After that and based on the compatibility between the labels and the target user gender contexts, CasaNLP adds word-level target gender labels as *side-constraints* (Sennrich et al., 2016) to the words that need to be rewritten in the input sentence (e.g., أنا [2F] سعيد). They do this preprocessing step across all sentences in APGC v2.1. Then, they fine-tune AraT5-MSA$_{BASE}$ on the preprocessed sentences in TRAIN. The intuition here is that the model should learn to only rewrite the words that are marked in the input. The team follows the same procedure during inference to generate the gender rewritten alternatives.

The fine-tuning of the models was done using Hugging Face's Transformers. The sentence-level gender rewriting system was fine-tuned for 10 epochs with a maximum sequence length of 64, a batch size of 32, and a learning rate of 1e-3 with 4 gradient accumulation steps.

Distinguishers This team introduced a multi-step system that does word-level gender identification and out-of-context word-level gender rewriting. For gender identification, they used the model that was developed and released by Alhafni et al. (2022b).[4] For gender rewriting, the team developed an out-of-context word-level Seq2Seq model. The model followed the approach introduced in BERT-fused (Zhu et al., 2020), where they first use AraBERT (Antoun et al., 2020) to extract representations for the input word, and then the representations are fused with each layer of the encoder and decoder of a standard Transformer model (Vaswani et al., 2017). The model was trained on gendered words present in APGC v2.1. They also explored adding morphological features to their Seq2Seq model. They used CAMeLTools (Obeid et al., 2020) to do morphological tokenization on the words and get their part-of-speech tags. They added the tags as side-constraints to each word. During inference, they first run the gender-identification component over the input sentence to get predicted gender labels for each word. Then for each word that needs to be rewritten, they pass it to the Seq2Seq model to get its gender alternative.

The out-of-context word-level gender rewriting model was built using Simple Transformers.[5] The model was fine-tuned on a single GPU for 5 epochs with a maximum sequence length of 25, a learning rate of 1e-5, and a batch size of 32.

Qaddoumi The approach this team took to build their gender rewriting system relied on romanizing the Arabic text and using an *English* pre-trained model. The team preprocessed the data in APGC v2.1 by using the Safe Buckwalter transliteration scheme (Buckwalter, 2002; Habash, 2010). They continue fine-tuning a grammatical error correction model that was originally built by fine-tuning T5 (Raffel et al., 2020) on the JFLEG corpus (Napoles et al., 2017).[6] When producing the final outputs, they convert the text back to Arabic script.

The sentence-level gender rewriting system was fine-tuned using the Happy Transformer library on a single GPU for 5 epochs with a maximum sequence length of 1024, a batch size of 32, and a learning rate of 5e-5.[7]

UDEL-NLP The system developed by UDEL-NLP was at the sentence-level and based on T5. The team introduced a new Arabic T5 model called ArabicT5 (Alrowili and Vijay-Shanker, 2022),

[4] https://github.com/CAMeL-Lab/gender-rewriting/

[5] https://github.com/ThilinaRajapakse/simpletransformers

[6] https://huggingface.co/vennify/t5-base-grammar-correction

[7] https://github.com/EricFillion/happy-transformer

Team	Precision	Recall	$F_{0.5}$	BLEU
Cairo Team	**76.26 (1)**	72.27 (3)	**75.42 (1)**	**94.89 (1)**
CasaNLP	51.05 (4)	**84.60 (1)**	55.45 (4)	86.06 (4)
Distinguishers	20.93 (5)	19.03 (5)	20.52 (5)	84.89 (5)
Qaddoumi	56.49 (3)	77.06 (2)	59.68 (2)	88.53 (3)
UDEL-NLP	57.10 (2)	68.61 (4)	59.08 (3)	91.02 (2)
Alhafni et al. (2022b)	**88.50**	**84.98**	**87.78**	**97.62**

Table 7: Results on the Blind Test set. Numbers in parentheses are the ranks.

which was pretrained on MSA by using an efficient T5 implementation (Tay et al., 2021). They fine-tuned the ArabicT5 model by adding side-constraints to the beginning of each sentence to indicate the target users' gender, and appending an <eos> to each sentence. The team follows the same preprocessing steps during inference.

The sentence-level gender rewriting system was built by fine-tuning ArabicT5 using Hugging Face's Transformers on a single GPU for 70 epochs, a maximum sequence length of 512, a batch size of 32, and a learning of 1e-4.

(a)

Team	Word Δ
Cairo Team	0.80%
CasaNLP	-0.02%
Distinguishers	1.28%
Qaddoumi	-0.63%
UDEL-NLP	0.05%

(b)

Metric	Correl
Precision	-42.95%
Recall	-77.56%
$\mathbf{F_{0.5}}$	-50.86%
BLEU	-11.86%

Table 8: (a) The relative difference in the number of generated words for each team in comparison with the Blind Test reference. (b) The Pearson correlation of the shared task metrics in Table 7 with the *absolute* values of Word Δ.

5 Results

Table 7 presents the results on the newly annotated Blind Test set. The last row is for the state-of-the-art system by Alhafni et al. (2022b). The best result in terms of $F_{0.5}$ is achieved by the Cairo Team (75.42), the official winner of the shared task. This is mainly due to their high score in precision (76.26). Qaddoumi comes in second place achieving an $F_{0.5}$ of 59.68, followed by UDEL-NLP in third place with 59.08 in $F_{0.5}$. In fourth place, CasaNLP achieves an $F_{0.5}$ score of 55.45 with the highest recall of 84.60. Distinguishers comes in fifth place, achieving 20.52 in $F_{0.5}$. It is worth noting that none of the systems is able to beat the previously published system by Alhafni et al. (2022b) applied to the new Blind Test.

Error Analysis We conducted a simple error analysis over the outputs of all system on the Blind Test set. Given that most teams employed sentence-level Seq2Seq models when developing their gender rewriting systems, we suspected that the outputs will be noisy since sentence-level models will not guarantee that changes are only applied to gendered words, or maintain the word-level parallelism between the input and output. Table 8(a) presents the relative difference in the number of generated words for each team in comparison with the Blind Test reference; and Table 8(b) presents their correlation with the shared task metrics. None of the teams maintained the total number of words. We observe a strong negative correlation between the absolute value of relative word count differences and the evaluation metrics – almost -51% correlation with $F_{0.5}$, and -78% correlation with recall.

After inspecting the outputs of the submitted systems, we noticed that much of the noise was due to not handling punctuation correctly. We removed the punctuation from all the outputs and evaluated the systems in this space. Table 9 shows the results on the Blind Test set after removing the punctuation. The scores of all teams went up significantly, with the exception of Distinguishers. The highest increase of 31.6 points in $F_{0.5}$ is in the case of CasaNLP. In terms of the ranks of the systems in this unofficial evaluation space, CasaNLP is the best performer and they achieve 87.04 in $F_{0.5}$. They also have the highest precision, recall, and BLEU scores. The Cairo Team comes in second place with an $F_{0.5}$ of 83.76, followed by UDEL-NLP who achieves an $F_{0.5}$ of 70.22. Qaddoumi and Distinguishers are in fourth and fifth places, achieving 63.35 and 20.41 in $F_{0.5}$, respectively.

Team	Precision	Recall	$F_{0.5}$	BLEU
Cairo Team	87.34 (2)	71.98 (3)	83.76 (2)	95.74 (2)
CasaNLP	**87.72 (1)**	**84.45 (1)**	**87.04 (1)**	**97.18 (1)**
Distinguishers	20.81 (5)	18.96 (5)	20.41 (5)	84.11 (5)
Qaddoumi	60.68 (4)	76.90 (2)	63.35 (4)	89.06 (4)
UDEL-NLP	70.67 (3)	68.50 (4)	70.22 (3)	91.99 (3)
Alhafni et al. (2022b)	**88.38**	**84.87**	**87.65**	**97.30**

Table 9: Results on the Blind Test set of after removing the punctuation. Numbers in parentheses are the ranks.

6 Outlook and Lessons Learned

We organized this shared task on gender rewriting for Arabic to raise awareness in the Arabic NLP community of the problem of gender bias in Arabic NLP systems, and to encourage the community to come up with new approaches to alleviate this problem. Although the shared task received some interest from the community, the participation was limited[8] when compared to other shared tasks organized at recent editions of WANLP[9] or OSACT.[10] We believe that this is due to a couple of factors.

First is the **skewed interest towards sentence-level classification** tasks within the Arabic NLP community and the lack of novel open-vocabulary sequence transduction tasks. For instance, most of the shared tasks organized at WANLP over the past few years focused on sentence-level classification to tackle dialect identification: MADAR and NADI (Bouamor et al., 2019; Abdul-Mageed et al., 2020, 2021); or Arabic sarcasm detection: ArSarcasm (Abu Farha et al., 2021). The last shared task that featured a generation problem in Arabic was the QALB shared task on grammatical error correction (Rozovskaya et al., 2015).

We acknowledge the importance of working on sentence-level classification problems, but there are many natural language generation tasks where Arabic is still lagging behind compared to other languages. Examples of such tasks include dialectal machine translation, grammatical error correction, text simplification, and style transfer, to name a few. We envision that the development of resources and models for such tasks would re-spark the interest of the Arabic NLP community in a wide range of exciting, yet unsolved problems in Arabic NLP.

Second is the **novelty and difficulty** of the gender rewriting problem compared to other conventional sequence transduction tasks. Approaching the problem correctly requires developing controlled generation models that are able to make subtle, yet complex and grammatically correct, edits at the word level. In retrospect, we recognize that we could have organized this shared task as two subtasks: one on gender identification at the word or sentence levels, and the other on sentence-level gender rewriting. This could have served as a bridge between classification and generation tasks, too, and allowed more people to participate for part if not the whole of the task. As such, we recommend that organizers of novel and nontraditional tasks to break the problem into subtasks to encourage more participation.

Lastly, the main goal of participating in a shared task is to learn about a new problem by introducing an interesting solution, which could benefit the community as a whole, as a positive or negative result. Being on top of the leaderboard should not be the only motive; we encourage organizers within the community to echo this sentiment when running their shared tasks.

Limitations and Ethical Considerations

Our intention of organizing this shared task is to increase the inclusiveness of NLP applications that deal with gender-marking morphologically rich languages. However, we acknowledge that, like all NLP technologies, developing systems for gender identification and rewriting could be used in malicious ways to discriminate against, or erase, certain identities in certain contexts. We also acknowledge that by limiting the choice of gender expressions to grammatical gender, we exclude alternatives such as non-binary gender or no-gender expressions. We are not aware of any sociolinguistics published research that discusses such alternatives for Arabic. We stress on the importance of adapting Arabic NLP models to new gender alternative forms as they emerge as part of the language usage.

[8]While 15 teams registered for the shared task initially, only five of them ended up participating.

[9]http://www.arabic-nlp.net/

[10]https://osact-lrec.github.io/

References

Muhammad Abdul-Mageed, Chiyu Zhang, Houda Bouamor, and Nizar Habash. 2020. NADI 2020: The first nuanced Arabic dialect identification shared task. In *Proceedings of the Fifth Arabic Natural Language Processing Workshop*, pages 97–110, Barcelona, Spain (Online). Association for Computational Linguistics.

Muhammad Abdul-Mageed, Chiyu Zhang, AbdelRahim Elmadany, Houda Bouamor, and Nizar Habash. 2021. NADI 2021: The second nuanced Arabic dialect identification shared task. In *Proceedings of the Sixth Arabic Natural Language Processing Workshop*, pages 244–259, Kyiv, Ukraine (Virtual). Association for Computational Linguistics.

Ibrahim Abu Farha, Wajdi Zaghouani, and Walid Magdy. 2021. Overview of the WANLP 2021 shared task on sarcasm and sentiment detection in Arabic. In *Proceedings of the Sixth Arabic Natural Language Processing Workshop*, pages 296–305, Kyiv, Ukraine (Virtual). Association for Computational Linguistics.

Bashar Alhafni, Nizar Habash, and Houda Bouamor. 2020. Gender-aware reinflection using linguistically enhanced neural models. In *Proceedings of the Second Workshop on Gender Bias in Natural Language Processing*, pages 139–150, Barcelona, Spain (Online). Association for Computational Linguistics.

Bashar Alhafni, Nizar Habash, and Houda Bouamor. 2022a. The Arabic parallel gender corpus 2.0: Extensions and analyses. In *Proceedings of the Thirteenth Language Resources and Evaluation Conference*, pages 1870–1884, Marseille, France. European Language Resources Association.

Bashar Alhafni, Nizar Habash, and Houda Bouamor. 2022b. User-centric gender rewriting. In *Proceedings of the 2022 Conference of the North American Chapter of the Association for Computational Linguistics: Human Language Technologies*, pages 618–631, Seattle, United States. Association for Computational Linguistics.

Sultan Alrowili and K. Vijay-Shanker. 2022. Generative approach for gender-rewriting task with ArabicT5. In *Proceedings of the Seventh Arabic Natural Language Processing Workshop*, Abu Dhabi, UAE. Association for Computational Linguistics.

Wissam Antoun, Fady Baly, and Hazem Hajj. 2020. AraBERT: Transformer-based model for Arabic language understanding. In *Proceedings of the 4th Workshop on Open-Source Arabic Corpora and Processing Tools, with a Shared Task on Offensive Language Detection*, pages 9–15, Marseille, France. European Language Resource Association.

Su Lin Blodgett, Solon Barocas, Hal Daumé III, and Hanna Wallach. 2020. Language (technology) is power: A critical survey of "bias" in NLP. In *Proceedings of the 58th Annual Meeting of the Association for Computational Linguistics*, pages 5454–5476, Online. Association for Computational Linguistics.

Tolga Bolukbasi, Kai-Wei Chang, James Y Zou, Venkatesh Saligrama, and Adam T Kalai. 2016. Man is to computer programmer as woman is to homemaker? debiasing word embeddings. In *Advances in Neural Information Processing Systems*, volume 29. Curran Associates, Inc.

Houda Bouamor, Sabit Hassan, and Nizar Habash. 2019. The MADAR shared task on Arabic fine-grained dialect identification. In *Proceedings of the Fourth Arabic Natural Language Processing Workshop*, pages 199–207, Florence, Italy. Association for Computational Linguistics.

Tim Buckwalter. 2002. Buckwalter Arabic morphological analyzer version 1.0. Linguistic Data Consortium (LDC) catalog number LDC2002L49, ISBN 1-58563-257-0.

Daniel Dahlmeier and Hwee Tou Ng. 2012. Better evaluation for grammatical error correction. In *Proceedings of the 2012 Conference of the North American Chapter of the Association for Computational Linguistics: Human Language Technologies*, pages 568–572, Montréal, Canada.

Nizar Habash, Houda Bouamor, and Christine Chung. 2019. Automatic gender identification and reinflection in Arabic. In *Proceedings of the First Workshop on Gender Bias in Natural Language Processing*, pages 155–165, Florence, Italy.

Nizar Y Habash. 2010. *Introduction to Arabic natural language processing*, volume 3. Morgan & Claypool Publishers.

Rowan Hall Maudslay, Hila Gonen, Ryan Cotterell, and Simone Teufel. 2019. It's all in the name: Mitigating gender bias with name-based counterfactual data substitution. In *Proceedings of the 2019 Conference on Empirical Methods in Natural Language Processing and the 9th International Joint Conference on Natural Language Processing (EMNLP-IJCNLP)*, pages 5267–5275, Hong Kong, China.

Go Inoue, Bashar Alhafni, Nurpeiis Baimukan, Houda Bouamor, and Nizar Habash. 2021. The interplay of variant, size, and task type in Arabic pre-trained language models. In *Proceedings of the Sixth Arabic Natural Language Processing Workshop*, pages 92–104, Kyiv, Ukraine (Virtual). Association for Computational Linguistics.

Pierre Lison and Jörg Tiedemann. 2016. OpenSubtitles2016: Extracting Large Parallel Corpora from Movie and TV Subtitles. In *Proceedings of the Language Resources and Evaluation Conference (LREC)*, Portorož, Slovenia.

Kaiji Lu, Piotr Mardziel, Fangjing Wu, Preetam Amancharla, and Anupam Datta. 2018. Gender bias in neural natural language processing.

Thomas Manzini, Lim Yao Chong, Alan W Black, and Yulia Tsvetkov. 2019. Black is to criminal as caucasian is to police: Detecting and removing multiclass bias in word embeddings. In *Proceedings of the 2019 Conference of the North American Chapter of the Association for Computational Linguistics: Human Language Technologies, Volume 1 (Long and*

Short Papers), pages 615–621, Minneapolis, Minnesota. Association for Computational Linguistics.

El Moatez Billah Nagoudi, AbdelRahim Elmadany, and Muhammad Abdul-Mageed. 2022. AraT5: Text-to-text transformers for Arabic language generation. In *Proceedings of the 60th Annual Meeting of the Association for Computational Linguistics (Volume 1: Long Papers)*, pages 628–647, Dublin, Ireland. Association for Computational Linguistics.

Courtney Napoles, Keisuke Sakaguchi, and Joel Tetreault. 2017. JFLEG: A fluency corpus and benchmark for grammatical error correction. In *Proceedings of the 15th Conference of the European Chapter of the Association for Computational Linguistics: Volume 2, Short Papers*, pages 229–234, Valencia, Spain. Association for Computational Linguistics.

Ossama Obeid, Nasser Zalmout, Salam Khalifa, Dima Taji, Mai Oudah, Bashar Alhafni, Go Inoue, Fadhl Eryani, Alexander Erdmann, and Nizar Habash. 2020. CAMeL tools: An open source python toolkit for Arabic natural language processing. In *Proceedings of The 12th Language Resources and Evaluation Conference*, pages 7022–7032, Marseille, France. European Language Resources Association.

Kishore Papineni, Salim Roukos, Todd Ward, and Wei-Jing Zhu. 2002. BLEU: a Method for Automatic Evaluation of Machine Translation. In *Proceedings of the Conference of the Association for Computational Linguistics (ACL)*, pages 311–318, Philadelphia, Pennsylvania, USA.

Matt Post. 2018. A call for clarity in reporting BLEU scores. In *Proceedings of the Third Conference on Machine Translation: Research Papers*, pages 186–191, Brussels, Belgium.

Colin Raffel, Noam Shazeer, Adam Roberts, Katherine Lee, Sharan Narang, Michael Matena, Yanqi Zhou, Wei Li, and Peter J. Liu. 2020. Exploring the limits of transfer learning with a unified text-to-text transformer. *Journal of Machine Learning Research*, 21(140):1–67.

Alla Rozovskaya, Houda Bouamor, Nizar Habash, Wajdi Zaghouani, Ossama Obeid, and Behrang Mohit. 2015. The second QALB shared task on automatic text correction for Arabic. In *Proceedings of the Second Workshop on Arabic Natural Language Processing*, pages 26–35, Beijing, China. Association for Computational Linguistics.

Rico Sennrich, Barry Haddow, and Alexandra Birch. 2016. Controlling politeness in neural machine translation via side constraints. In *Proceedings of the 2016 Conference of the North American Chapter of the Association for Computational Linguistics: Human Language Technologies*, pages 35–40, San Diego, California. Association for Computational Linguistics.

Tony Sun, Andrew Gaut, Shirlyn Tang, Yuxin Huang, Mai ElSherief, Jieyu Zhao, Diba Mirza, Elizabeth Belding, Kai-Wei Chang, and William Yang Wang. 2019. Mitigating gender bias in natural language processing: Literature review. In *Proceedings of the 57th Annual Meeting of the Association for Computational Linguistics*, pages 1630–1640, Florence, Italy. Association for Computational Linguistics.

Yi Tay, Mostafa Dehghani, Jinfeng Rao, William Fedus, Samira Abnar, Hyung Won Chung, Sharan Narang, Dani Yogatama, Ashish Vaswani, and Donald Metzler. 2021. Scale efficiently: Insights from pre-training and fine-tuning transformers.

Ashish Vaswani, Noam Shazeer, Niki Parmar, Jakob Uszkoreit, Llion Jones, Aidan N. Gomez, Lukasz Kaiser, and Illia Polosukhin. 2017. Attention is all you need. *CoRR*, abs/1706.03762.

Thomas Wolf, Lysandre Debut, Victor Sanh, Julien Chaumond, Clement Delangue, Anthony Moi, Pierric Cistac, Tim Rault, Remi Louf, Morgan Funtowicz, Joe Davison, Sam Shleifer, Patrick von Platen, Clara Ma, Yacine Jernite, Julien Plu, Canwen Xu, Teven Le Scao, Sylvain Gugger, Mariama Drame, Quentin Lhoest, and Alexander Rush. 2020. Transformers: State-of-the-art natural language processing. In *Proceedings of the 2020 Conference on Empirical Methods in Natural Language Processing: System Demonstrations*, pages 38–45, Online. Association for Computational Linguistics.

Jieyu Zhao, Subhabrata Mukherjee, Saghar Hosseini, Kai-Wei Chang, and Ahmed Hassan Awadallah. 2020. Gender bias in multilingual embeddings and cross-lingual transfer. In *Proceedings of the 58th Annual Meeting of the Association for Computational Linguistics*, pages 2896–2907, Online. Association for Computational Linguistics.

Jieyu Zhao, Yichao Zhou, Zeyu Li, Wei Wang, and Kai-Wei Chang. 2018. Learning gender-neutral word embeddings. In *Proceedings of the 2018 Conference on Empirical Methods in Natural Language Processing*, pages 4847–4853, Brussels, Belgium.

Jinhua Zhu, Yingce Xia, Lijun Wu, Di He, Tao Qin, Wengang Zhou, Houqiang Li, and Tie-Yan Liu. 2020. Incorporating bert into neural machine translation.

Ran Zmigrod, Sabrina J. Mielke, Hanna Wallach, and Ryan Cotterell. 2019. Counterfactual data augmentation for mitigating gender stereotypes in languages with rich morphology. In *Proceedings of the 57th Annual Meeting of the Association for Computational Linguistics*, pages 1651–1661, Florence, Italy.

Overview of the WANLP 2022 Shared Task on Propaganda Detection in Arabic

Firoj Alam[1], **Hamdy Mubarak**[1], **Wajdi Zaghouani**[2], **Giovanni Da San Martino**[3], **Preslav Nakov**[4]

[1]Qatar Computing Research Institute, HBKU, Qatar
[2]Hamad Bin Khalifa University, Qatar
[3]University of Padova, Italy
[4]Mohamed bin Zayed University of Artificial Intelligence, UAE

{falam,hmubarak,wzaghouani}@hbku.edu.qa, dasan@math.unipd.it, preslav.nakov@mbzuai.ac.ae

Abstract

Propaganda is the expression of an opinion or an action by an individual or a group deliberately designed to influence the opinions or the actions of other individuals or groups with reference to predetermined ends, which is achieved by means of well-defined rhetorical and psychological devices. Propaganda techniques are commonly used in social media to manipulate or to mislead users. Thus, there has been a lot of recent research on automatic detection of propaganda techniques in text as well as in memes. However, so far the focus has been primarily on English. With the aim to bridge this language gap, we ran a *shared task on detecting propaganda techniques in Arabic tweets* as part of the WANLP 2022 workshop, which included two subtasks. Subtask 1 asks to identify the set of propaganda techniques used in a tweet, which is a multilabel classification problem, while Subtask 2 asks to detect the propaganda techniques used in a tweet together with the exact span(s) of text in which each propaganda technique appears. The task attracted 63 team registrations, and eventually 14 and 3 teams made submissions for subtask 1 and 2, respectively. Finally, 11 teams submitted system description papers.

1 Introduction

Social media platforms have become an important communication channel, where we can share and access information from a variety of sources. Unfortunately, the rise of this democratic information ecosystem was accompanied by and dangerously polluted with misinformation, disinformation, and malinformation in the form of propaganda, conspiracies, rumors, hoaxes, fake news, hyper-partisan content, falsehoods, hate speech, cyberbullying, etc. (Oshikawa et al., 2020; Alam et al., 2021; Pramanick et al., 2021; Rosenthal et al., 2021; Alam et al., 2022; Barnabò et al., 2022; Guo et al., 2022; Hardalov et al., 2022; Nguyen et al., 2022; Sharma et al., 2022)

Propaganda is conveyed through the use of diverse propaganda techniques (Miller, 1939), which range from leveraging on the emotions of the audience (e.g., using loaded language, appealing to fear, etc.) to using logical fallacies such as *straw men* (misrepresenting someone's opinion), *whataboutism*, *red herring* (presenting irrelevant data), etc. In the last decades, propaganda was widely used on social media to influence and/or mislead the audience, which became a major concern for different stakeholders, social media platforms, and policymakers. To address this problem, the research area of *computational propaganda* has emerged, and here we are particularly interested in automatically identifying the use of propaganda techniques in text, images, and multimodal content. Prior work in this direction includes identifying propagandistic content in an article based on writing style and readability level (Rashkin et al., 2017; Barrón-Cedeno et al., 2019), at the sentence and the fragment levels from news articles with fine-grained techniques (Da San Martino et al., 2019b), and in memes (Dimitrov et al., 2021a). These efforts focused on English, and there was no prior work on Arabic. Our shared task aims to bridge this gap by focusing on detecting propaganda in Arabic social media text, i.e., tweets.

2 Related Work

In the current information ecosystem, propaganda has evolved to *computational propaganda* (Woolley and Howard, 2018; Da San Martino et al., 2020b), where information is distributed on social media platforms, which makes it possible for malicious users to reach well-targeted communities at high velocity. Thus, research on propaganda detection has focused on analyzing not only news articles but also social media content (Rashkin et al., 2017; Barrón-Cedeno et al., 2019; Da San Martino et al., 2019b, 2020b; Nakov et al., 2021a,b; Hristakieva et al., 2022).

Proceedings of the The Seventh Arabic Natural Language Processing Workshop (WANLP), pages 108 - 118
December 8, 2022 ©2022 Association for Computational Linguistics

Rashkin et al. (2017) focused on article-level propaganda analysis. They developed the TSHP-17 corpus, which used distant supervision for annotation with four classes: *trusted*, *satire*, *hoax*, and *propaganda*. The assumption of their distant supervision approach was that all articles from a given news source should share the same label. They collected their articles from the English Gigaword corpus and from seven other unreliable news sources, including two propagandistic ones. Later, Barrón-Cedeno et al. (2019) developed a new corpus, QProp , with two labels: propaganda vs. non-propaganda, and also experimented on TSHP-17 and QProp corpora. For the TSHP-17 corpus, they binarized the labels: propaganda *vs.* any of the other three categories as non-propaganda. They investigated the writing style and the readability level of the target document, and trained models using logistic regression and SVMs. Their findings confirmed that using distant supervision, in conjunction with rich representations, might encourage the model to predict the source of the article, rather than to discriminate propaganda from non-propaganda. Similarly, Habernal et al. (2017, 2018) developed a corpus with 1.3k arguments annotated with five fallacies, including *ad hominem*, *red herring*, and *irrelevant authority*, which directly relate to propaganda techniques.

Recently, Da San Martino et al. (2019b), curated a set of persuasive techniques, ranging from leveraging on the emotions of the audience such as using *loaded language* and *appeal to fear*, to logical fallacies such as *straw man* (misrepresenting someone's opinion) and *red herring* (presenting irrelevant data). They focused on textual content, i.e., newspaper articles. In particular, they developed a corpus of news articles annotated with eighteen propaganda techniques. The annotation was at the fragment level, and could be used for two tasks: (*i*) binary classification —given a sentence in an article, predict whether any of the 18 techniques has been used in it, and (*ii*) multi-label classification and span detection task —given a raw text, identify both the specific text fragments where a propaganda technique is used as well as the specific technique. They further proposed a multi-granular deep neural network that captures signals from the sentence-level task and helps to improve the fragment-level classifier. Da San Martino et al. (2020a) also organized a shared task on Detection of Propaganda Techniques in News Articles.

Subsequently, Dimitrov et al. (2021b) organized the SemEval-2021 task 6 on Detection of Propaganda Techniques in Memes. It had a multimodal setup, combining text and images, and asked participants to build systems to identify the propaganda techniques used in a given meme. Yu et al. (2021) looked into interpretable propaganda detection.

Other related shared tasks include the FEVER task (Thorne et al., 2018) on fact extraction and verification, the Fake News Challenge (Hanselowski et al., 2018), the FakeNews task at MediaEval (Pogorelov et al., 2020), as well as the NLP4IF tasks on propaganda detection (Da San Martino et al., 2019a) and on fighting the COVID-19 infodemic in social media (Shaar et al., 2021a). Finally, we should mention the CheckThat! lab at CLEF (Elsayed et al., 2019a,b; Barrón-Cedeño et al., 2020; Shaar et al., 2020; Hasanain et al., 2020; Nakov et al., 2021c,d; Shaar et al., 2021b; Nakov et al., 2022a,b,c,d), which addresses many aspects of disinformation for different languages over the years such as fact-checking, verifiable factual claims, check-worthiness, attention-worthiness, and fake news detection.

The present shared task is inspired from prior work on propaganda detection. In particular, we adapted the annotation instructions and the propaganda techniques discussed in (Da San Martino et al., 2019b; Dimitrov et al., 2021b).

3 Tasks and Dataset

Below, we first formulate the two subtasks of our shared task, and then we discuss our datasets, including how we collected the data and what annotation guidelines we used.

3.1 Tasks

In the shared tasks, we offered the following two subtasks:

- **Subtask 1:** Given the text of a tweet, identify the propaganda techniques used in it.

- **Subtask 2:** Given the text of a tweet, identify the propaganda techniques used in it together with the span(s) of text in which each propaganda technique appears.

Note that Subtask 1 is formulated as a multilabel classification problem, while Subtask 2 is a sequence labeling task.

Figure 1: An example of tweet annotation with propaganda techniques *loaded language* and *name calling*.

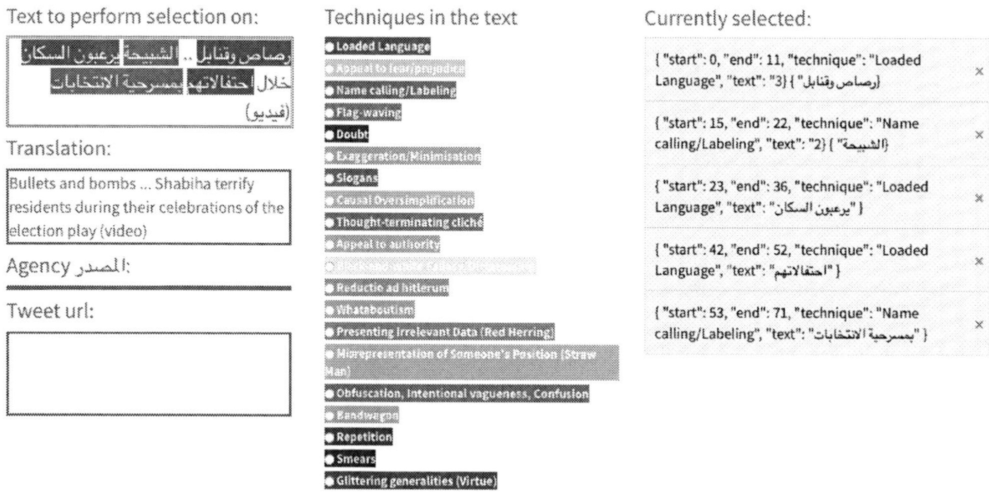

Figure 2: An example of tweet annotation with propaganda techniques *loaded language* and *slogan*.

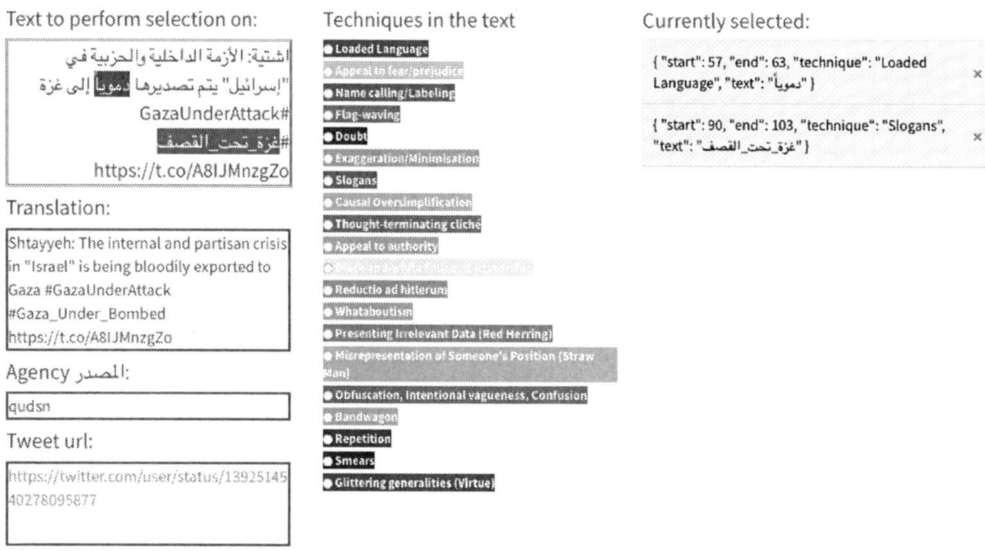

3.2 Dataset

We used Social Bakers[1] to obtain the top-2 news sources from each Arab country, e.g., Al Arabiya and Sky News Arabia from UAE, Al Jazeera and Al Sharq from Qatar, etc. We further added five international sources that broadcast Arabic news: Al-Hurra News, BBC Arabic, CNN Arabic, France 24, and Russia Today. We then extracted from Twitter their latest 3,200 tweets. To have a balanced dataset that covers a wide range of topics, we chose 100 random tweets from each source, and then we sampled 930 tweets for annotation.

[1] https://www.socialbakers.com/

We target emotional appeals (e.g., loaded language, appeal to fear, flag waving, exaggeration, etc.) and logical fallacies (e.g., whataboutism, causal oversimplification, red herring, band wagon, etc.). We adopted the same techniques studied in (Da San Martino et al., 2019b; Dimitrov et al., 2021b). Below we briefly summarize them:

1. **Appeal to authority:** Stating that a claim is true simply because a valid authority or expert on the issue said it was true. We also include here the special case where the reference is not an authority or an expert, which is referred to as *Testimonial* in the literature.

2. **Appeal to fear / prejudices:** Seeking to build support for an idea by instilling anxiety and/or panic in the population towards an alternative. In some cases, the support is built based on preconceived judgements.

3. **Bandwagon** Attempting to persuade the target audience to join in and take the course of action because "everyone else is taking the same action."

4. **Black-and-white fallacy or dictatorship:** Presenting two alternative options as the only possibilities, when in fact more possibilities exist. As an the extreme case, tell the audience exactly what actions to take, eliminating any other possible choices (ictatorship).

5. **Causal oversimplification:** Assuming a single cause or reason when there are actually multiple causes for an issue. This includes transferring blame to one person or group of people without investigating the complexities of the issue.

6. **Doubt:** Questioning the credibility of someone or something.

7. **Exaggeration / minimisation:** Either representing something in an excessive manner: making things larger, better, worse (e.g., *the best of the best*, *quality guaranteed*) or making something seem less important or smaller than it really is (e.g., saying that an insult was actually just a joke).

8. **Flag-waving:** Playing on strong national feeling (or to any group, e.g., race, gender, political preference) to justify or to promote an action or an idea.

9. **Glittering generalities (virtue)** These are words or symbols in the value system of the target audience that produce a positive image when attached to a person or issue. Peace, hope, happiness, security, wise leadership, freedom, "The Truth", etc. are virtue words. Virtue can be also expressed in images, where a person or an object is depicted positively.

10. **Loaded language:** Using specific words and phrases with strong emotional implications (either positive or negative) to influence an audience.

11. **Misrepresentation of someone's position (straw man):** Substituting an opponent's proposition with a similar one, which is then refuted in place of the original proposition.

12. **Name calling or labeling:** Labeling the object of the propaganda campaign as something that the target audience fears, hates, finds undesirable or loves, praises.

13. **Obfuscation, intentional vagueness, confusion:** Using words that are deliberately not clear, so that the audience may have their own interpretations. For example, when an unclear phrase with multiple possible meanings is used within an argument and, therefore, it does not support the conclusion.

14. **Presenting irrelevant data (red herring):** Introducing irrelevant material to the issue being discussed, so that everyone's attention is diverted away from the points made.

15. **Reductio ad hitlerum:** Persuading an audience to disapprove an action or an idea by suggesting that the idea is popular with groups hated in contempt by the target audience. It can refer to any person or concept with a negative connotation.

16. **Repetition:** Repeating the same message over and over again, so that the audience will eventually accept it.

17. **Slogans:** A brief and striking phrase that may include labeling and stereotyping. Slogans tend to act as emotional appeals.

18. **Smears** A smear is an effort to damage or call into question someone's reputation, by propounding negative propaganda. It can be applied to individuals or groups.

19. **Thought-terminating cliché:** Words or phrases that discourage critical thought and meaningful discussion about a given topic. They are typically short, generic sentences that offer seemingly simple answers to complex questions or that distract the attention away from other lines of thought.

20. **Whataboutism:** A technique that attempts to discredit an opponent's position by charging them with hypocrisy without directly disproving their argument.

Table 1: Statistics about the corpus. In parentheses, we show the number of tweets. *Total* represents the number of techniques in each set.

Prop Technique	Train (504)	Dev (52)	Dev-Test (51)	Test (323)
Appeal to authority	21	7	1	1
Appeal to fear/prejudice	48	7	4	25
Black-and-white Fallacy/Dictatorship	2	1	2	7
Causal Oversimplification	4	1	1	4
Doubt	29	1	2	19
Exaggeration/Minimisation	44	10	16	26
Flag-waving	5	2	2	9
Glittering generalities (Virtue)	25	7	2	1
Loaded Language	446	46	42	326
Name calling/Labeling	244	44	33	163
Obfuscation, Intentional vagueness, Confusion	9	3	1	6
Presenting Irrelevant Data (Red Herring)	1	0	0	0
Repetition	9	2	1	3
Slogans	44	1	1	6
Smears	85	12	15	50
Thought-terminating cliché	6	1	1	0
Whataboutism	3	1	1	0
Total	**1025**	**146**	**125**	**646**

The annotation is done in different stages: (*i*) three annotators independently annotate the same tweet, and (*ii*) they meet together with one consolidator to discuss each instance and to come up with gold annotations. Since the annotations are at the fragment level, it might happen that an annotation is spotted by only one annotator. The two phases ensure that each annotation is eventually discussed by all annotators. In order to train the annotators, we provide clear annotation instructions with examples and ask them to annotate a sample of tweets. Then, we revise their annotations and provide feedback. Figures 1 and 2 show example tweets with annotated propaganda techniques.

Table 1 shows the distribution of the propaganda techniques in our dataset for different data splits. Our annotation guidelines inclide twenty techniques, but in the annotated dataset, there were no instances of *bandwagon*, *straw man*, and *reductio ad hitlerum*. Overall, the distribution of the propaganda techniques in our dataset is very skewed, which made the task challenging.

4 Evaluation Framework

4.1 Evaluation Measures

To measure the performance of the systems, for both subtasks, we use micro-F1 and macro-F1, as these are multi-class multi-label problems, where the labels are imbalanced. The official evaluation measure for subtask 1 is micro-F1, but the scorer also reports macro-F1.

Subtask 2 is a multi-label sequence tagging problem. We modified the standard micro-averaged F1 to account for partial matching between the spans. More details about the modified macro-averaged F1 can be found in (Da San Martino et al., 2019b; Dimitrov et al., 2021b).

4.2 Task Organization

We ran the shared task in two phases:

Development Phase In the first phase, we provided the participants three subsets of the dataset: train, dev, and dev_test. The purpose of the dev set was to fine-tune the trained model, and the dev_test set was to evaluate the model performance on unseen dev_test set.

Test Phase In the second phase, we released the actual test set and the participants were given just a few days to submit their final predictions via the submission system on Codalab.[2] In this phase, the participants could again submit multiple runs, but they would not get any feedback on their performance. Only the latest submission of each team was considered as official and was used for the final team ranking. The final leaderboard on the test set was made publicly available after the system submission deadline.

5 Participants and Results

In this section, we provide a general description of the systems that participated in each subtask and their results. Table 2 shows the results for all teams for both subtasks, as well as a random baseline. We can see that subtask 1 was more popular, attracting submissions by 14 teams, while there were only three submissions for subtask 2.

5.1 Subtask 1

Table 3 gives an overview of the systems that took part in subtask 1. We can see that transformers were quite popular, most notably AraBERT, followed by BERT, and MARBERT. Some participants also used ensembles methods, data augmentation, and standard preprocessing.

The best-performing team NGU_CNLP (Samir et al., 2022) first explored various baselines models such as bag of words with SVM, Naïve Bayes, Stochastic Gradient Descent, Logistic Regression,

[2]https://codalab.lisn.upsaclay.fr/competitions/7274

Table 2: Results for subtask 1 on multilabel propaganda detection and subtask 2 on identifying propaganda techniques and their span(s) in the text. The results are ordered by the official score: Micro-F1. *Indicated that no system description paper was submitted.

Rank/Team	Macro F1	Micro F1
Subtask 1		
1. NGU_CNLP (Samir et al., 2022)	0.185	0.649
2. IITD (Mittal and Nakov, 2022)	0.183	0.609
3. CNLP-NITS-PP (Laskar et al., 2022)	0.068	0.602
3. AraBEM (Eshrag Ali et al., 2022)	0.068	0.602
3. Pythoneers (Attieh and Hassan, 2022)	0.177	0.602
4. AraProp (Singh, 2022)	0.105	0.600
5. iCompass (Taboubi et al., 2022)	0.191	0.597
6. SI2m & AIOX Labs (Gaanoun and Benelallam, 2022)	0.137	0.585
7. mostafa-samir*	0.186	0.580
8. Team SIREN AI (Sharara et al., 2022)	0.153	0.578
9. ChavanKane (Chavan and Kane, 2022)	0.111	0.565
10. mhmud.fwzi*	0.087	0.552
11. TUB (Mohtaj and Möller, 2022)	0.076	0.494
12. tesla*	0.120	0.355
13. *Baseline (Random)*	0.043	0.079
Subtask 2		
1. Pythoneers (Attieh and Hassan, 2022)		0.396
2. IITD (Mittal and Nakov, 2022)		0.355
3. NGU_CNLP (Samir et al., 2022)		0.232
4. *Baseline (Random)*		0.013

Random Forests and K-nearest Neighbor. Eventually, for their final submission, they used AraBERT with stacking-based ensemble (5-fold split). They further explored translation-based data augmentation using the English PTC corpus (Da San Martino et al., 2019b).

The second best system was IITD (Mittal and Nakov, 2022), and they used XLM-R and fine-tuned the model. They also explored data augmentation by translating ad adding the PTC corpus as training, but in their experiments this did not help improve the performance.

The third system was CNLP-NITS-PP (Laskar et al., 2022), and they used the AraBERT Twitter-base model along with data augmentation. Note that all systems outperformed the random baseline.

5.2 Subtask 2

In Table 3, we also present an overview of the systems that took part in Subtask 2. Once again, this subtask was dominated by transformer models. We can see in the table that transformers were quite popular, and among them, the most commonly used one was AraBERT, followed by BERT and MARBERT. The participants in this task also used data augmentation and standard pre-processing.

Table 2 shows the evaluation results: we report our random baseline, which is based on the random selection of spans with random lengths and a random assignment of labels.

Table 3: Overview of the approaches used for subtasks 1 and 2, for the teams that submitted a description paper. The systems are ordered by the official score: F1-micro.

Rank/Team	Models					Other		
	BERT	XML-R	AraBERT	ARBERT	MARBERT	Data augmentation	Preprocessing	NER
Subtask 1								
1. NGU_CNLP (Samir et al., 2022)			✓			✓	✓	
2. IITD (Mittal and Nakov, 2022)		✓						
3. CNLP-NITS-PP (Laskar et al., 2022)			✓			✓	✓	
3. AraBEM (Eshrag Ali et al., 2022)	✓							
3. Pythoneers (Attieh and Hassan, 2022)			✓				✓	
4. AraProp (Singh, 2022)					✓		✓	
5. iCompass (Taboubi et al., 2022)					✓		✓	
6. SI2m & AIOX Labs (Gaanoun and Benelallam, 2022)				✓		✓		✓
8. Team SIREN AI (Sharara et al., 2022)			✓				✓	
9. ChavanKane (Chavan and Kane, 2022)			✓		✓	✓	✓	
11. TUB (Mohtaj and Möller, 2022)	✓						✓	
Subtask 2								
1. Pythoneers (Attieh and Hassan, 2022)			✓					
2. IITD (Mittal and Nakov, 2022)	✓							
3. NGU_CNLP (Samir et al., 2022)						✓		

The best system for this subtask was Pythoneers (Attieh and Hassan, 2022). They used AraBERT with a Conditional Random Field (CRF) layer, which was trained on encoded data using the BIO schema.

The second-best system was IITD (Mittal and Nakov, 2022), which used a Multi-Granularity Network (Da San Martino et al., 2019b) with the mBERT encoder.

The third system was NGU_CNLP (Samir et al., 2022). They converted the data to BIO format and fine-tuned a token classifier based on Marefa-NER[3] (pretrained using XLM-RoBERTa).

5.3 Participants' Systems

NGU_CNLP (Samir et al., 2022)[`subtask 1:1`, `subtask 2:3`] team participated in both subtasks. For subtask 1, they used a combination of a data augmentation strategy with a transformer-based model. This model ranked first among the 14 systems that participated in this subtask. Their preliminary experiments for subtask 1 consist of using a bag-of-words model with different classical algorithms such as Support Vector Machines, Naïve Bayes, Stochastic Gradient Descent, Logistic regression, Random Forests, and simple K-nearest Neighbor. For subtask 2, they fine-tuned the Marefa-NER model, which is based on XLM-RoBERTa. The system ranked third among the three systems that participated in this subtask.

[3]`https://huggingface.co/marefa-nlp/marefa-ner`

Pythoneers (Attieh and Hassan, 2022)[subtask 1:3, subtask 2:1] also participated in both subtasks. For subtask 1, they trained a multi-task learning model that performs binary classification per propaganda technique. For subtask 2, they first converted the data into BIO format and then fine-tuned an AraBERT model with a Conditional Random Field (CRF) layer. Their subtask 1 system ranked third with a micro-averaged F1-Score of 0.602, and their subtask 2 system ranked first with a micro-averaged F1-Score of 0.396.

IITD (Mittal and Nakov, 2022)[subtask 1:2, subtask 2:2] . This team also participated in both subtasks. They used multilingual pretrained language models for both subtask s. For subtask 1, they used a pretrained XLM-R to estimate a Multinoulli distribution after projecting the CLS embedding to a 20-dimensional embedding (one per propaganda technique). For subtask 2, they used a multi-granularity network (Da San Martino et al., 2019b) with mBERT encoder. Even though both systems were trained on only the dataset released in this shared task, they also discussed several methods (zero-shot transfer, continued training, and translation of PTC (Da San Martino et al., 2019b) to Arabic) to study cross-lingual propaganda detection. This suggested interesting research challenges for future exploration, such as how to effectively use data from different domains and how to learn language-agnostic embeddings in propaganda detection systems.

CNLP-NITS-PP (Laskar et al., 2022)[subtask 1:3]. This team participated in subtask 1 and they used AraBERT Twitter-base model for multilabel propaganda classification. They further used data augmentation; in particular, they generated synthetic training data using root and stem substitution from the original train samples and prepared additional synthetic examples. They changed the input labels to the model to be one-hot encoded to indicate multiple labels and modified the macro-F1 scorer to give a score for multiple labels. To make predictions with the model, they used a sentiment analysis pipeline from HuggingFace Transformers and selected all the labels that yielded a score greater than or equal to 0.32. They observed the scores for the predictions on the validation test set and found that most correct labels had a score greater than 0.30. They also found that there was a large gap in the score for the label when the score was below 0.30.

AraBEM (Eshrag Ali et al., 2022)[subtask 1:3]. This team participated in subtask 1 and they fine-tuned BERT to perform multi-class binary classification. They used standard pre-processing including normalization (mapping letters with various forms, i.e., alef, hamza, and yaa to their representative characters), and removing special characters, diacritics, and repeated characters.

AraProp (Singh, 2022)[subtask 1:4]. This team participated in subtask 1. First, they tokenized the input and produced contextualized word embeddings for all input tokens. To get a fixed-size output representation, they simply averaged all contextualized word embeddings by taking attention mask into account for correct averaging. Then, they added a dropout layer with a dropout rate of 0.3, followed by a linear layer with a sigmoid activation function for the output. They experimented with multiple transformer-based language models: two multilingual models and six monolingual (Arabic) models. Their findings suggest that the MARBERTv2-based fine-tuned model outperforms other models in terms of F1-micro score.

iCompass (Taboubi et al., 2022)[subtask 1:5] team participated in subtask 1. Their system used standard pre-processing such as normalization and removing stopwords, emojis, special characters, and links. Then, they used pre-trained language models such as MARBERT and ARBERT. They further added global average and max pooling layers on top of the models. Finally, they used cross-validation to improve the model performance.

SI2M & AIOX Labs (Gaanoun and Benelallam, 2022)[subtask 1:6] team participated in subtask 1. They used data augmentation, named entity recognition (NER), and manual rules. For data augmentation, they combined the training and the dev sets, and randomly mixed the sequences to create new synthetic sequences, which they concatenated with the train and the dev sets. Their final system uses a mixed dataset of 2,000 examples. Next, they fine-tuned ARBERT on the augmented dataset, and they made predictions based on a defined threshold of the classifier's confidence. If no technique got a prediction probability greater than the threshold, the token was assigned the label *No technique*. Moreover, to detect the *Name Calling/Labelling* technique, they used a NER model based on AraBERT. Finally, to detect *Repetition*, they used manual rules, after removing the stopwords.

Team SIREN AI (Sharara et al., 2022)[subtask 1:8] participated in subtask 1 and used AraBERT for fine-tuning. Like other teams, they used standard pre-processing, e.g., removing HTML markup, diacritics, non-digit repetitions, etc.

ChavanKane (Chavan and Kane, 2022)[subtask 1:9] team participated in subtask 1 and experimented with AraBERT v1, v02 and v2, MARBERT, ARBERT, XLMRoBERTa, and AraELECTRA. They used a specific variant of DeHateBERT, which is initialized from multilingual BERT and fine-tuned only on Arabic datasets. They also tried creating an ensemble of all models, which consists of five models such as DeHateBERT, AraBERTv2, AraBERTv02, AraBERTv01, and MARBERT. For the final prediction from the ensembles, they used hard voting.

TUB (Mohtaj and Möller, 2022)[subtask 1:11]. This team participated in subtask 1 and used a semantic similarly detection approach based on conceptual word embedding. They converted all sentences in the train, dev, and test sets into vectors using the BERT model. For each sentence in the test set, they detected the five most similar instances from the train and the dev sets, with a cosine similarity above 0.4. Then, they assigned the three most frequent labels among the five instances as the label of the target sentence.

6 Conclusion and Future Work

We presented the WANLP'2022 shared task on *Propaganda Detection in Arabic*, as part of which we developed the first dataset for Arabic propaganda detection with focus on social media content. This was a successful task: a total of 63 teams registered to participate, and 14 and 3 teams eventually made an official submission on the test set for subtasks 1 and 2, respectively. Finally, 11 teams submitted a task description paper. Subtask 1 asked to identify the propaganda techniques used in a tweet, and subtask 2 further asked to identify the the span(s) of text in which each propaganda technique appears. For both subtasks, the majority of the systems fine-tuned pre-trained Arabic language models, and used standard pre-processing. Some systems used data augmentation and ensemble methods.

In future work, we plan to increase the data size and to add hierarchically structured propaganda techniques.

7 Acknowledgments

This publication was made possible by NPRP grant 13S-0206-200281 *Resources and Applications for Detecting and Classifying Polarized and Hate Speech in Arabic Social Media* from the Qatar National Research Fund.

Part of this work was also funded by Qatar Foundation's IDKT Fund TDF 03-1209-210013: *Tanbih: Get to Know What You Are Reading*.

This research is also carried out as part of the Tanbih mega-project,[4] developed at the Qatar Computing Research Institute, HBKU, which aims to limit the impact of "fake news", propaganda, and media bias, thus promoting digital literacy and critical thinking.

The findings herein are solely the responsibility of the authors.

References

Firoj Alam, Stefano Cresci, Tanmoy Chakraborty, Fabrizio Silvestri, Dimiter Dimitrov, Giovanni Da San Martino, Shaden Shaar, Hamed Firooz, and Preslav Nakov. 2022. A survey on multimodal disinformation detection. In *Proceedings of the 29th International Conference on Computational Linguistics*, COLING '22, pages 6625–6643, Gyeongju, Republic of Korea.

Firoj Alam, Shaden Shaar, Fahim Dalvi, Hassan Sajjad, Alex Nikolov, Hamdy Mubarak, Giovanni Da San Martino, Ahmed Abdelali, Nadir Durrani, Kareem Darwish, Abdulaziz Al-Homaid, Wajdi Zaghouani, Tommaso Caselli, Gijs Danoe, Friso Stolk, Britt Bruntink, and Preslav Nakov. 2021. Fighting the COVID-19 infodemic: Modeling the perspective of journalists, fact-checkers, social media platforms, policy makers, and the society. In *Findings of EMNLP 2021*, pages 611–649.

Joseph Attieh and Fadi Hassan. 2022. Pythoneers at WANLP 2022 shared task: Monolingual AraBERT for Arabic propaganda detection and span extraction. In *Proceedings of the Seventh Arabic Natural Language Processing Workshop*, Abu Dhabi, UAE.

Giorgio Barnabò, Federico Siciliano, Carlos Castillo, Stefano Leonardi, Preslav Nakov, Giovanni Da San Martino, and Fabrizio Silvestri. 2022. FbMultiLingMisinfo: Challenging large-scale multilingual benchmark for misinformation detection. In *Proceedings of the 2022 International Joint Conference on Neural Networks*, IJCNN '22', pages 1–8, Padova, Italy.

Alberto Barrón-Cedeño, Tamer Elsayed, Preslav Nakov, Giovanni Da San Martino, Maram Hasanain, Reem

[4]http://tanbih.qcri.org/

Suwaileh, Fatima Haouari, Nikolay Babulkov, Bayan Hamdan, Alex Nikolov, Shaden Shaar, and Zien Sheikh Ali. 2020. Overview of CheckThat! 2020 — automatic identification and verification of claims in social media. In *Proceedings of the 11th International Conference of the CLEF Association: Experimental IR Meets Multilinguality, Multimodality, and Interaction*, CLEF '2020, pages 215–236, Thessaloniki, Greece.

Alberto Barrón-Cedeno, Israa Jaradat, Giovanni Da San Martino, and Preslav Nakov. 2019. Proppy: Organizing the news based on their propagandistic content. *Information Processing & Management*, 56(5):1849–1864.

Tanmay Chavan and Aditya Kane. 2022. Chavankane at WANLP 2022 shared task: Large language models for multi-label propaganda detection. In *Proceedings of the Seventh Arabic Natural Language Processing Workshop*, WANLP '22, Abu Dhabi, UAE.

Giovanni Da San Martino, Alberto Barrón-Cedeño, and Preslav Nakov. 2019a. Findings of the NLP4IF-2019 shared task on fine-grained propaganda detection. In *Proceedings of the Second Workshop on Natural Language Processing for Internet Freedom: Censorship, Disinformation, and Propaganda*, NLP4IF '19, pages 162–170, Hong Kong, China.

Giovanni Da San Martino, Alberto Barrón-Cedeno, Henning Wachsmuth, Rostislav Petrov, and Preslav Nakov. 2020a. SemEval-2020 task 11: Detection of propaganda techniques in news articles. In *Proceedings of the fourteenth workshop on semantic evaluation*, SemEval '20, pages 1377–1414.

Giovanni Da San Martino, Stefano Cresci, Alberto Barrón-Cedeño, Seunghak Yu, Roberto Di Pietro, and Preslav Nakov. 2020b. A survey on computational propaganda detection. In *Proceedings of the Twenty-Ninth International Joint Conference on Artificial Intelligence*, IJCAI '20, pages 4826–4832.

Giovanni Da San Martino, Seunghak Yu, Alberto Barrón-Cedeño, Rostislav Petrov, and Preslav Nakov. 2019b. Fine-grained analysis of propaganda in news article. In *Proceedings of the 2019 Conference on Empirical Methods in Natural Language Processing and the 9th International Joint Conference on Natural Language Processing*, EMNLP-IJCNLP '19, pages 5636–5646, Hong Kong, China.

Dimitar Dimitrov, Bishr Bin Ali, Shaden Shaar, Firoj Alam, Fabrizio Silvestri, Hamed Firooz, Preslav Nakov, and Giovanni Da San Martino. 2021a. Detecting propaganda techniques in memes. In *Proceedings of the 59th Annual Meeting of the Association for Computational Linguistics and the 11th International Joint Conference on Natural Language Processing*, ACL-IJCNLP '21, pages 6603–6617.

Dimitar Dimitrov, Bishr Bin Ali, Shaden Shaar, Firoj Alam, Fabrizio Silvestri, Hamed Firooz, Preslav Nakov, and Giovanni Da San Martino. 2021b. SemEval-2021 task 6: Detection of persuasion techniques in texts and images. In *Proceedings of the 15th International Workshop on Semantic Evaluation*, SemEval '21, pages 70–98.

Tamer Elsayed, Preslav Nakov, Alberto Barrón-Cedeño, Maram Hasanain, Reem Suwaileh, Pepa Atanasova, and Giovanni Da San Martino. 2019a. CheckThat! at CLEF 2019: Automatic identification and verification of claims. In *Proceedings of the 41st European Conference on Information Retrieval*, ECIR '19, pages 309–315, Cologne, Germany.

Tamer Elsayed, Preslav Nakov, Alberto Barrón-Cedeño, Maram Hasanain, Reem Suwaileh, Giovanni Da San Martino, and Pepa Atanasova. 2019b. Overview of the CLEF-2019 CheckThat!: Automatic identification and verification of claims. In *Experimental IR Meets Multilinguality, Multimodality, and Interaction*, LNCS, pages 301–321.

Refaee Eshrag Ali, Ahmed Basem, and Saad Motaz. 2022. AraBEM at WANLP 2022 shared task: Propaganda detection in Arabic tweets. In *Proceedings of the Seventh Arabic Natural Language Processing Workshop*, WANLP '22, Abu Dhabi, UAE.

Kamel Gaanoun and Benelallam. 2022. SI2M & AIOX Labs at WANLP 2022 shared task: Propaganda detection in Arabic, a data augmentation and name entity recognition approach. In *Proceedings of the Seventh Arabic Natural Language Processing Workshop*, WANLP '22, Abu Dhabi, UAE.

Zhijiang Guo, Michael Schlichtkrull, and Andreas Vlachos. 2022. A survey on automated fact-checking. *Transactions of the Association for Computational Linguistics*, 10:178–206.

Ivan Habernal, Raffael Hannemann, Christian Pollak, Christopher Klamm, Patrick Pauli, and Iryna Gurevych. 2017. Argotario: Computational argumentation meets serious games. In *Proceedings of the 2017 Conference on Empirical Methods in Natural Language Processing: System Demonstrations*, pages 7–12, Copenhagen, Denmark.

Ivan Habernal, Patrick Pauli, and Iryna Gurevych. 2018. Adapting serious game for fallacious argumentation to German: Pitfalls, insights, and best practices. In *Proceedings of the Eleventh International Conference on Language Resources and Evaluation*, LREC '18, pages 3329–3335, Miyazaki, Japan.

Andreas Hanselowski, Avinesh PVS, Benjamin Schiller, Felix Caspelherr, Debanjan Chaudhuri, Christian M. Meyer, and Iryna Gurevych. 2018. A retrospective analysis of the fake news challenge stance-detection task. In *Proceedings of the 27th International Conference on Computational Linguistics*, COLING '18, pages 1859–1874, Santa Fe, New Mexico, USA.

Momchil Hardalov, Arnav Arora, Preslav Nakov, and Isabelle Augenstein. 2022. A survey on stance detection for mis- and disinformation identification. In

Findings of the Association for Computational Linguistics: NAACL 2022, NAACL '22, pages 1259–1277, Seattle, Washington, USA.

Maram Hasanain, Fatima Haouari, Reem Suwaileh, Zien Sheikh Ali, Bayan Hamdan, Tamer Elsayed, Alberto Barrón-Cedeño, Giovanni Da San Martino, and Preslav Nakov. 2020. Overview of CheckThat! 2020 Arabic: Automatic identification and verification of claims in social media. In *Working Notes of CLEF 2020—Conference and Labs of the Evaluation Forum*, CLEF '2020, Thessaloniki, Greece.

Kristina Hristakieva, Stefano Cresci, Giovanni Da San Martino, Mauro Conti, and Preslav Nakov. 2022. The spread of propaganda by coordinated communities on social media. In *Proceedings of the 14th ACM Web Science Conference*, WebSci '22, pages 191–201, Barcelona, Spain.

Sahinur Rahman Laskar, Rahul Singh, Abdullah Faiz Ur Rahman Khilji, Riyanka Manna, Partha Pakray, and Sivaji Bandyopadhyay. 2022. CNLP-NITS-PP at WANLP 2022 shared task: Propaganda detection in Arabic using data augmentation and AraBERT pre-trained model. In *Proceedings of the Seventh Arabic Natural Language Processing Workshop*, WANLP '22, Abu Dhabi, UAE.

Clyde R. Miller. 1939. The Techniques of Propaganda. From "How to Detect and Analyze Propaganda," an address given at Town Hall. The Center for learning.

Shubham Mittal and Preslav Nakov. 2022. Iitd at WANLP 2022 shared task: Multilingual multi-granularity network for propaganda detection. In *Proceedings of the Seventh Arabic Natural Language Processing Workshop*, WANLP '22, Abu Dhabi, UAE.

Salar Mohtaj and Sebastian Möller. 2022. TUB at WANLP 2022 shared task: Using semantic similarity for propaganda detection in Arabic. In *Proceedings of the Seventh Arabic Natural Language Processing Workshop*, WANLP '22, Abu Dhabi, UAE.

Preslav Nakov, Firoj Alam, Shaden Shaar, Giovanni Da San Martino, and Yifan Zhang. 2021a. COVID-19 in Bulgarian social media: Factuality, harmfulness, propaganda, and framing. In *Proceedings of the International Conference on Recent Advances in Natural Language Processing*, RANLP '21, pages 1001–1013, Online. INCOMA Ltd.

Preslav Nakov, Firoj Alam, Shaden Shaar, Giovanni Da San Martino, and Yifan Zhang. 2021b. A second pandemic? Analysis of fake news about COVID-19 vaccines in Qatar. In *Proceedings of the International Conference on Recent Advances in Natural Language Processing*, RANLP '21, pages 1014–1025, Online. INCOMA Ltd.

Preslav Nakov, Alberto Barrón-Cedeño, Giovanni Da San Martino, Firoj Alam, Rubén Míguez, Tommaso Caselli, Mucahid Kutlu, Wajdi Zaghouani, Chengkai Li, Shaden Shaar, Hamdy Mubarak, Alex Nikolov, Yavuz Selim Kartal, and Javier Beltrán. 2022a. Overview of the CLEF-2022 CheckThat! lab task 1 on identifying relevant claims in tweets. In *Working Notes of CLEF 2022—Conference and Labs of the Evaluation Forum*, CLEF '2022, Bologna, Italy.

Preslav Nakov, Alberto Barrón-Cedeño, Giovanni Da San Martino, Firoj Alam, Julia Maria Struß, Thomas Mandl, Rubén Míguez, Tommaso Caselli, Mucahid Kutlu, Wajdi Zaghouani, Chengkai Li, Shaden Shaar, Gautam Kishore Shahi, Hamdy Mubarak, Alex Nikolov, Nikolay Babulkov, Yavuz Selim Kartal, and Javier Beltrán. 2022b. The CLEF-2022 CheckThat! lab on fighting the COVID-19 infodemic and fake news detection. In *Proceedings of the 44th European Conference on IR Research: Advances in Information Retrieval*, ECIR '22, pages 416–428, Berlin, Heidelberg.

Preslav Nakov, Alberto Barrón-Cedeño, Giovanni Da San Martino, Firoj Alam, Julia Maria Struß, Thomas Mandl, Rubén Míguez, Tommaso Caselli, Mucahid Kutlu, Wajdi Zaghouani, Chengkai Li, Shaden Shaar, Gautam Kishore Shahi, Hamdy Mubarak, Alex Nikolov, Nikolay Babulkov, Yavuz Selim Kartal, Javier Beltrán, Michael Wiegand, Melanie Siegel, and Juliane Köhler. 2022c. Overview of the CLEF-2022 CheckThat! lab on fighting the COVID-19 infodemic and fake news detection. In *Proceedings of the 13th International Conference of the CLEF Association: Information Access Evaluation meets Multilinguality, Multimodality, and Visualization*, CLEF '2022, Bologna, Italy.

Preslav Nakov, Giovanni Da San Martino, Firoj Alam, Shaden Shaar, Hamdy Mubarak, and Nikolay Babulkov. 2022d. Overview of the CLEF-2022 CheckThat! lab task 2 on detecting previously fact-checked claims. In *Working Notes of CLEF 2022—Conference and Labs of the Evaluation Forum*, CLEF '2022, Bologna, Italy.

Preslav Nakov, Giovanni Da San Martino, Tamer Elsayed, Alberto Barrón-Cedeño, Rubén Míguez, Shaden Shaar, Firoj Alam, Fatima Haouari, Maram Hasanain, Nikolay Babulkov, Alex Nikolov, Gautam Kishore Shahi, Julia Maria Struß, and Thomas Mandl. 2021c. The CLEF-2021 CheckThat! lab on detecting check-worthy claims, previously fact-checked claims, and fake news. In *Proceedings of the 43rd European Conference on Information Retrieval*, ECIR '21, pages 639–649, Lucca, Italy.

Preslav Nakov, Giovanni Da San Martino, Tamer Elsayed, Alberto Barrón-Cedeño, Rubén Míguez, Shaden Shaar, Firoj Alam, Fatima Haouari, Maram Hasanain, Watheq Mansour, Bayan Hamdan, Zien Sheikh Ali, Nikolay Babulkov, Alex Nikolov, Gautam Kishore Shahi, Julia Maria Struß, Thomas Mandl, Mucahid Kutlu, and Yavuz Selim Kartal. 2021d. Overview of the CLEF-2021 CheckThat! lab on detecting check-worthy claims, previously fact-checked claims, and fake news. In *Proceedings of the 12th International Conference of the CLEF Association: Information Access Evaluation Meets Multiliguality, Multimodality, and Visualization*, CLEF '2021, Bucharest, Romania (online).

Van-Hoang Nguyen, Kazunari Sugiyama, Preslav Nakov, and Min-Yen Kan. 2022. FANG: Leveraging social context for fake news detection using graph representation. *Commun. ACM*, 65(4):124–132.

Ray Oshikawa, Jing Qian, and William Yang Wang. 2020. A survey on natural language processing for fake news detection. In *Proceedings of the 12th Language Resources and Evaluation Conference*, LREC '20, pages 6086–6093.

Konstantin Pogorelov, Daniel Thilo Schroeder, Luk Burchard, Johannes Moe, Stefan Brenner, Petra Filkukova, and Johannes Langguth. 2020. FakeNews: Corona virus and 5G conspiracy task at MediaEval 2020. In *Proceedings of the MediaEval 2020 Workshop*, MediaEval '20.

Shraman Pramanick, Dimitar Dimitrov, Rituparna Mukherjee, Shivam Sharma, Md. Shad Akhtar, Preslav Nakov, and Tanmoy Chakraborty. 2021. Detecting harmful memes and their targets. In *Findings of the Association for Computational Linguistics: ACL-IJCNLP 2021*, pages 2783–2796.

Hannah Rashkin, Eunsol Choi, Jin Yea Jang, Svitlana Volkova, and Yejin Choi. 2017. Truth of varying shades: Analyzing language in fake news and political fact-checking. In *Proceedings of the 2017 Conference on Empirical Methods in Natural Language Processing*, EMNLP '17, pages 2931–2937, Copenhagen, Denmark.

Sara Rosenthal, Pepa Atanasova, Georgi Karadzhov, Marcos Zampieri, and Preslav Nakov. 2021. SOLID: A large-scale semi-supervised dataset for offensive language identification. In *Findings of the Association for Computational Linguistics: ACL-IJCNLP 2021*, pages 915–928.

Ahmed Samir, Abo Bakr Soliman, Mohamed Ibrahim, Laila Hesham, and Samhaa ElBeltag. 2022. NGU_CNLP at WANLP 2022 shared task: Propaganda detection in Arabic. In *Proceedings of the Seventh Arabic Natural Language Processing Workshop*, WANLP '22, Abu Dhabi, UAE.

Shaden Shaar, Firoj Alam, Giovanni Da San Martino, Alex Nikolov, Wajdi Zaghouani, Preslav Nakov, and Anna Feldman. 2021a. Findings of the NLP4IF-2021 shared tasks on fighting the COVID-19 infodemic and censorship detection. In *Proceedings of the Fourth Workshop on NLP for Internet Freedom: Censorship, Disinformation, and Propaganda*, NLP4IF '21, pages 82–92.

Shaden Shaar, Maram Hasanain, Bayan Hamdan, Zien Sheikh Ali, Fatima Haouari, Alex Nikolov, Mucahid Kutlu, Yavuz Selim Kartal, Firoj Alam, Giovanni Da San Martino, Alberto Barrón-Cedeño, Rubén Míguez, Javier Beltrán, Tamer Elsayed, and Preslav Nakov. 2021b. Overview of the CLEF-2021 CheckThat! lab task 1 on check-worthiness estimation in tweets and political debates. Bucharest, Romania (online).

Shaden Shaar, Alex Nikolov, Nikolay Babulkov, Firoj Alam, Alberto Barrón-Cedeño, Tamer Elsayed, Maram Hasanain, Reem Suwaileh, Fatima Haouari, Giovanni Da San Martino, and Preslav Nakov. 2020. Overview of CheckThat! 2020 English: Automatic identification and verification of claims in social media. In *Working Notes of CLEF 2020—Conference and Labs of the Evaluation Forum*, CLEF '2020, Thessaloniki, Greece.

Mohamad Sharara, Wissam Mohamad, Ralph Tawil, Ralph Chobok, Wolf Assi, and Antonio Tannoury. 2022. Team SIREN AI at WANLP 2022 shared task: AraBERT model for propaganda detection. In *Proceedings of the Arabic Natural Language Processing Workshop*, WANLP '22, Abu Dhabi, UAE.

Shivam Sharma, Firoj Alam, Md. Shad Akhtar, Dimitar Dimitrov, Giovanni Da San Martino, Hamed Firooz, Alon Halevy, Fabrizio Silvestri, Preslav Nakov, and Tanmoy Chakraborty. 2022. Detecting and understanding harmful memes: A survey. In *Proceedings of the Thirty-First International Joint Conference on Artificial Intelligence*, IJCAI '22, pages 5597–5606, Vienna, Austria.

Gaurav Singh. 2022. AraProp at WANLP 2022 shared task: Leveraging pre-trained language models for Arabic propaganda detection. In *Proceedings of the Seventh Arabic Natural Language Processing Workshop*, WANLP '22, Abu Dhabi, UAE.

Bilel Taboubi, Bechir Brahem, and Hatem Haddad. 2022. iCompass at WANLP 2022 shared task: ARBERT & MARBERT for multilabel propaganda classification in Arabic tweets. In *Proceedings of the Seventh Arabic Natural Language Processing Workshop*, WANLP '22, Abu Dhabi, UAE.

James Thorne, Andreas Vlachos, Christos Christodoulopoulos, and Arpit Mittal. 2018. FEVER: a large-scale dataset for fact extraction and VERification. In *Proceedings of the Conference of the North American Chapter of the Association for Computational Linguistics: Human Language Technologies*, NAACL '18, pages 809–819, New Orleans, Louisiana, USA.

Samuel C Woolley and Philip N Howard. 2018. *Computational propaganda: political parties, politicians, and political manipulation on social media*. Oxford University Press.

Seunghak Yu, Giovanni Da San Martino, Mitra Mohtarami, James Glass, and Preslav Nakov. 2021. Interpretable propaganda detection in news articles. In *Proceedings of the International Conference on Recent Advances in Natural Language Processing*, RANLP '21, pages 1597–1605.

ArzEn-ST: A Three-way Speech Translation Corpus for Code-Switched Egyptian Arabic - English

Injy Hamed,[1,2] Nizar Habash,[1] Slim Abdennadher,[3] Ngoc Thang Vu[2]
[1]Computational Approaches to Modeling Language Lab, New York University Abu Dhabi
[2]Institute for Natural Language Processing, University of Stuttgart
[3]Computer Science Department, The German University in Cairo
injy.hamed@nyu.edu

Abstract

We present our work on collecting ArzEn-ST, a code-switched Egyptian Arabic - English Speech Translation Corpus. This corpus is an extension of the ArzEn speech corpus, which was collected through informal interviews with bilingual speakers. In this work, we collect translations in both directions, monolingual Egyptian Arabic and monolingual English, forming a three-way speech translation corpus. We make the translation guidelines and corpus publicly available. We also report results for baseline systems for machine translation and speech translation tasks. We believe this is a valuable resource that can motivate and facilitate further research studying the code-switching phenomenon from a linguistic perspective and can be used to train and evaluate NLP systems.

1 Introduction

Code-switching (CSW), defined as the alternation of language in text or speech, is a common linguistic phenomenon in multilingual societies. CSW can occur on the boundaries of sentences, words (within the same sentence), or morphemes (within the same word). While the worldwide prevalence of CSW has been met with increasing efforts in NLP systems trying to handle such mixed input, data sparsity remains one of the main bottlenecks hindering the development of such systems (Çetinoğlu et al., 2016).

In this paper, we present ArzEn-ST,[1] a speech translation (ST) corpus for code-switched Egyptian Arabic (Egy) - English. We extend the ArzEn Egyptian Arabic-English CSW conversational speech corpus (Hamed et al., 2020) with translations going to both directions; the primary (Egyptian Arabic) as well as secondary (English) languages. See Figure 1. This corpus is a valuable resource filling an important gap, given the naturalness and high

Audio: 

Transcription: بحس ان that's counter-productive يعني

Egy Translation: بحس ان ده بيعمل نتيجة عكسية يعني

English Translation: I feel that's counter-productive actually

Figure 1: An example from the corpus, showing the four representations for each utterance: audio, transcription, Egyptian Arabic translation, and English translation.

frequency of CSW in it. It can be used for the purpose of linguistic investigations as well as for building and evaluating NLP systems. We provide benchmark baseline results for the tasks of automatic speech recognition (ASR), machine translation (MT), and ST. We make the translation guidelines and full corpus available, as well as the experiments' scripts and data splits.[2]

The paper is organized as follows. In Section 2, we provide an overview of previous work done for code-switched ASR, MT, and ST tasks as well as corpora collection. In Section 3, we provide an overview of the ArzEn speech corpus. In Section 4, we elaborate on the translation guidelines used to create the three-way parallel ST corpus. Finally, in Section 5, we report the performance of the ASR, MT, and ST baseline systems.

2 Related Work

2.1 CSW Automatic Speech Recognition

CSW ASR has gained a considerable amount of research (Vu et al., 2012; Li and Vu, 2019; Ali et al., 2021; Hamed et al., 2022a; Hussein et al., 2022), where several CSW speech corpora have been collected, covering multiple language pairs, including Chinese-English (Lyu et al., 2015), Hindi-English (Ramanarayanan and Suendermann-Oeft, 2017), Spanish-English (Solorio and Liu, 2008), Arabic-

[1]Arz is the ISO 639-3 code for Egyptian Arabic.

[2]http://arzen.camel-lab.com/

Proceedings of the The Seventh Arabic Natural Language Processing Workshop (WANLP), pages 119 - 130
December 8, 2022 ©2022 Association for Computational Linguistics

Language	Citations
Translating CSW → monolingual	
Hindi-English → English	(Dhar et al., 2018; Srivastava and Singh, 2020; Tarunesh et al., 2021; Chen et al., 2022)
Sinhala-English → Sinhala	(Kugathasan and Sumathipala, 2021)
English-Spanish → English	(Chen et al., 2022)
MSA-Egyptian Arabic → English	(Chen et al., 2022)
English-Bengali → both	(Mahata et al., 2019)
Egyptian Arabic -English → both	ArzEn-ST (the corpus presented in this paper)
Translating monolingual → CSW	
Hindi → Hindi-English	(Tarunesh et al., 2021; Banerjee et al., 2018)
English → Bengali-English	(Banerjee et al., 2018)
English → Gujarati-English	(Banerjee et al., 2018)
English → Tamil-English	(Banerjee et al., 2018)
English, Hindi → Hindi-English	(Srivastava and Singh, 2021)

Table 1: Overview on available human-annotated CSW-focused parallel corpora.

English (Ismail, 2015; Hamed et al., 2018, 2020; Chowdhury et al., 2021), Arabic-French (Djegdjiga et al., 2018), Frisian-Dutch (Yilmaz et al., 2016), Mandarin-Taiwanese (Lyu et al., 2006), Turkish-German (Çetinoğlu, 2017), English-Malay (Ahmed and Tan, 2012), English-isiZulu (van der Westhuizen and Niesler, 2016) and Sepedi-English (Modipa et al., 2013). In this work, we build on our ArzEn speech corpus (Hamed et al., 2020), and enrich it with multiple translations.

2.2 CSW Machine Translation

While research in CSW MT has been gaining attention over the past years (Sinha and Thakur, 2005; Dhar et al., 2018; Mahata et al., 2019; Menacer et al., 2019; Song et al., 2019; Tarunesh et al., 2021; Xu and Yvon, 2021; Chen et al., 2022; Hamed et al., 2022b; Gaser et al., 2022), the collected CSW parallel corpora are limited. By looking into the reported corpora, we identify a number of dimensions in which they vary. First is synthetic or human-annotated data. Second, for human-annotated data, it can be either collected, or especially commissioned for MT/NLP. Third, for collected data, it can be obtained from textual or speech sources. And finally, the data set may include translations to one or more languages.

To circumvent the data scarcity issue, researchers investigated the use of synthetically generated CSW parallel data for training and testing (Gupta et al., 2020; Yang et al., 2020; Xu and Yvon, 2021). While this is acceptable for training purposes, synthetic data should not be used for testing, as it does not reflect real-world CSW distributions.

For collecting human-annotated parallel corpora, researchers have tried either asking bilingual speakers to translate naturally occurring CSW sentences into monolingual sentences, or as another solution to data scarcity, have commissioned annotators to translate monolingual sentences into CSW sentences. In Table 1, we present a summary of available human-annotated parallel corpora that are focused on CSW. For the latter approach, we note that generating CSW data in a human-commissioned fashion could differ from naturally-occurring CSW sentences. Such data could be biased to the grammatical structure of the monolingual sentences, and could be dominated by single noun switches, being the easiest CSW type to generate.

The former approach of translating naturally-occurring CSW sentences into monolingual sentences is the most optimal way to collect a CSW parallel corpus; however, most of the collected corpora rely on CSW sentences obtained from textual sources (mostly from social media platforms). The main concern here is that CSW phenomena occurring in text are more restricted than those occurring in natural speech. In text, people are usually dissuaded from changing scripts, and therefore either avoid switching languages, or switch languages without switching scripts. The latter issue was tackled by Shazal et al. (2020), where the authors used a sequence-to-sequence deep learning model to transliterate SMS/chat text collected by Chen et al. (2017) from Arabizi (where Arabic words are written in Roman script) to Arabic orthography. While this corpus is not focused on CSW, it contains CSW sentences.

Finally, we categorize the collected corpora in terms of the translation direction. As shown in Table 1, most of the corpora include translations for CSW sentences to the secondary language, which is most commonly English. A smaller number of researchers investigated translating CSW sentences into the primary language. And even fewer researchers included translations to both directions.

The work of Menacer et al. (2019) is also relevant to our work. The authors extracted Modern Standard Arabic (MSA)-English CSW sentences from the UN documents, to which English translations are available (Eisele et al., 2010). The Arabic translations were generated by translating the English segments using the Google Translate API. While this can be used for training purposes, these translations should not be used as gold reference. Moreover, given the nature of the corpus, it contained limited types of CSW, as opposed to the types that occur in conversational speech.

2.3 CSW Speech Translation

Work on CSW ST is still in its early stages, with little prior work (Nakayama et al., 2019; Weller et al., 2022; Huber et al., 2022). For CSW ST corpora, two corpora are available for Spanglish: Bangor Miami (Cieri et al., 2004) and Fisher (Deuchar et al., 2014). While the Fisher dataset is not a CSW-focused corpus, it contains a considerable amount of CSW (Weller et al., 2022). Similarly, for CSW Egyptian Arabic-English, the Callhome dataset also contains some amount of CSW (Gadalla et al., 1997; Kumar et al., 2014). A Japanese-English ST corpus (Nakayama et al., 2019) was also collected, however it includes read-speech and not spontaneous speech. Huber et al. (2022) collected a one-hour German-English code-switching speech translation corpus containing read-speech.

Our new corpus, ArzEn-ST, fills an important resource gap, providing an ST corpus for code-switched Egyptian Arabic-English. The corpus is human-annotated where the source sentences are collected through interviews with bilingual speakers, and contain naturally-generated CSW sentences; they are then translated in both directions: monolingual Egyptian Arabic and monolingual English.

3 Overview of the ArzEn Corpus

ArzEn is a conversational speech corpus that is collected through informal interviews. The interviews were held at the German University in Cairo, which is a private university where English is the instruction language. The topics discussed were general topics such as education, work and life experiences, career, technology, personal life, hobbies, and travelling experiences. No instructions were given to participants regarding code-switching; they were not asked to produce nor avoid code-switching. Interviews were held with 38 Egyptian Arabic-English bilingual speakers (61.5% males, 38.5% females), in the age range of 18-35, who are students (55%) and employees (45%) at the university. The speech corpus comprises of 12 hours of speech, containing 6,216 sentences.

3.1 Code-switching Types in ArzEn

The four main CSW types mentioned in the literature are present in ArzEn (Poplack, 1980; Stefanich et al., 2019). We present a corpus example for each of the types in Table 2.

Inter-sentential CSW This type of CSW is defined as switching languages from one sentence to another.

Extra-sentential CSW This type of CSW, also called **tag-switching**, is where tag elements from one language are inserted into a monolingual sentence in another language, without the need for grammatical considerations. It mostly involves the use of fillers, interjections, tags, and idiomatic expressions. This type of CSW requires only minimal knowledge of the grammar of the secondary language.

Intra-sentential CSW This type, also referred to as **code-mixing**, is defined as using multiple languages within the same sentence, where the CSW segments must conform to the underlying syntactic rules of both languages. This type of CSW requires a better understanding of the grammar of both languages, compared to extra-sentential CSW.

Intra-word CSW This type, also called **morphological CSW**, is where switching occurs at the level of morphemes. Given that Egyptian Arabic is a morphologically rich language (Habash et al., 2012b), morphological code-switching occurs where Egyptians attach Arabic clitics and affixes to English words.

CSW Type	Example
Inter-sentential CSW	It's very difficult making friends at work. عملت صحاب بس مش في الشغل. *I made friends, but not at work.* It's very difficult making friends at work.
Extra-sentential CSW	Okayأنا مولود في مصر في القاهرة Okay *I was born in Egypt, in Cairo.*
Intra-sentential CSW	كان في actually جزء related to research *There was* actually *a part* related to research
Intra-word CSW	ايه ال+*expectation* بتاعك لل+*project* ؟ *What is your* expectation *for the* project?
Explicatory CSW	Okay طيب في مثلا quote أو مقولة قريتها في كتاب وعجبتك؟ Okay *okay is there a* quote *or a quote* that you read in a book and liked?
Elaboratory CSW	لو ال novel دي يعني هي oriental أو هي شرقية فهقراها اه من .. من author عربي *If this* novel *is like* oriental *or it is [originally written] in Arabic then I will read it ah from .. from an Arab* author *[in its Arabic version].*

Table 2: Examples of different CSW types in ArzEn followed by their English translation. The originally Arabic phrases are italicized in the English translation. For Explicatory and Elaboratory CSW, the underlining marks the repeated phrases.

In addition to the above, and motivated by our interest in translation from CSW texts, we identify two types of repetitive CSW phenomena in terms of their communicative purposes.

Explicatory CSW This type of CSW is where the speaker simply repeats the same word in another language.

Elaboratory CSW This type of CSW is where the speaker code-switches to further elaborate on the meaning.

Both types are challenging in terms of handling the CSW repetitions when translating into a single language. We address these issues in Section 4.

3.2 Code-switching Statistics in ArzEn

ArzEn contains a considerable amount of CSW. On the sentence level, 33.2% of the sentences are monolingual Arabic, 3.1% are monolingual English, and 63.7% code-mixed. Among the code-mixed sentences, 46.0% have morphological CSW.

On the word level, in the code-mixed sentences, 81.3% of the words are Arabic, 15.2% are English, and 3.4% are morphologically CSW words. Morphological CSW in ArzEn involves the use of both Arabic clitics and affixes. A list of the clitics and affixes occurring in morphological code-switched words present in the ArzEn corpus and their frequencies are provided in Hamed et al. (2022a).

3.3 Input Transcription

The ArzEn collected interviews were manually transcribed by Egyptian Arabic-English bilingual speakers. The transcribers were requested to use Arabic script for Arabic words and Roman script for English words. For morphological CSW words, Arabic clitics and affixes are written in Arabic script and English words are written in Roman script, as follows: **Arabic prefixes/proclitics + English words # Arabic suffixes/enclitics**, for example ال+TASK#ات *Al+TASK#At*[3] 'the+task#s'. While the transcribers generally followed the rules in a strict manner, we observe script confusion in the case of borrowed words that have become strongly embedded in Egyptian Arabic. In such cases, transcriptions can contain occurrences of the same words in both scripts, such as *mobile* and موبايل *mwbAyl*, *film* and فيلم *fylm*, and *camera* and كاميرا *kAmyrA*.

Given the spontaneous nature of the corpus, disfluencies were found due to repetitions, corrections, and changing course/structure mid-sentence. Such disfluencies were marked with '..', which occurs in more than 26% of the corpus sentences. The following tags were also used for non-speech parts: [HES] for hesitation, [HUM] for humming, [COUGH], [LAUGHTER], and [NOISE].

[3]Transliteration in the HSB scheme (Habash et al., 2007).

4 ArzEnST Translation Guidelines

The transcriptions are translated to monolingual English and monolingual Egyptian Arabic sentences by human translators.[4] In this section, we discuss the translation guidelines. In general, our decisions are mainly guided by giving a higher priority to fluency over accuracy. We opt for producing as natural as possible outputs that reflect the style of the original sentence. Even though we acknowledge that some of our decisions can make the translation task harder for MT systems, our goal is to produce natural translations. The guidelines cover three categories, general translation rules (denoted by *GR*), conversational speech translation rules (denoted by *SR*), and code-switching translation rules (denoted by *CSWR*). In Table 3, we present translation examples covering some of the rules.

4.1 General Translation Rules (*GR*)

[*GR*$_{intended}$] Translators are requested to provide natural translations with the intended meaning rather than literal translations. This also covers the case of idiomatic expressions. See Table 3 (a).

[*GR*$_{difficult}$] Similar to the LDC Arabic-to-English Translation Guidelines (LDC, 2013), segments that are difficult to translate should be indicated using ((text)). Such cases usually contain highly dialectal Arabic words or Arabic idioms. See Table 3 (b).

[*GR*$_{abbrev}$] For all abbreviations, we made the decision to provide transliteration as pronounced instead of translation,[5] for example *NLP* is transliterated as ان ال بي *An Al by*, and *AIESEC* is transliterated as آيزيك *Āyzyk*.

[*GR*$_{propn}$] Non-abbreviated proper nouns should be transliterated, unless they have meaning. In that case, they should be translated as long as the meaning of the sentence remains coherent, otherwise, should be transliterated.[6] See Table 3 (c).

[4]English translations are performed by one translator, and the dev and test sets are revised by one of the authors. Egyptian Arabic translations are performed by one translator and revised by another.

[5]We plan to annotate these cases with full translations in the future, to assist in tasks interested in removing English/Arabic text.

[6]The translators were advised to refer to Wikipedia Arabic for the translations of titles of books and films.

4.2 Conversational Speech Translation Rules (*SR*)

[*SR*$_{style}$] Translations should capture the same fluency and style of the original text. This means that disfluencies such as repetitions should also be included in translations. See Table 3 (d).

[*SR*$_{punc+}$] Punctuation, non-speech tags, and disfluency marks '..' present in the source text should be kept the same and in the same relative position in the sentence in the target translation.

[*SR*$_{partial}$] Due to disfluencies, it is common to have partial Arabic words. We transliterate such partial words, and similar to LDC (2013), we mark them with a preceding '%' sign. See Table 3 (e).

4.3 Code-switching Translation Rules (*CSWR*)

[*CSWR*$_{borrowed}$] For English words that are commonly used in Arabic, an attempt should first be made to identify a commonly used reasonable translation, otherwise, translators are allowed to transliterate. Examples of the latter case, included loanwords such as *mobile* and *laptop* that have become strongly integrated in Arabic, as opposed to *online* and *presentation* which can be translated to عبر الأنترنت and عرض تقديمي, respectively.

[*CSWR*$_{rewrites}$] We allow modifications to CSW segments when translating into English for the purpose of achieving better fluency. Similarly, when translating into Arabic, we also allow slight modifications to the original Arabic words. We elaborate on such cases for both directions below.

CSW→En: We allow modification to the original English words. This is mainly needed to handle difference in grammatical structures across languages as well as morphological CSW. For example, ASK+بي *by+ASK* is translated as 'he asks'. See Table 3 (f-g).

CSW→Ar: It is allowed to slightly modify the original Arabic words for better fluency. The following are common cases where this is needed.

- Since Arabic makes heavy use of the definite article +ال *Al+* to mark different constructions such as adjectival modification and idafa (possessive construct), translators are given permission to drop/reassign the placement of definite articles for the purpose of maximizing fluency. For example, the adjectival construction

Rule category	Example		Text
General Translation Rules	(a)		**[GR*intended*] Provide intended meaning rather than literal translation**
		CSW:	لأنه ال+team ممكن أخش مع حد مابيشتغلش فاشيل أنا الليلة كلها
		Egy:	لأنه الفريق ممكن أخش مع حد مابيشتغلش فاشيل أنا الليلة كلها
		Eng:	Because in the team, I can be with someone that doesn't work and ((I will be responsible for everything)).
	(b)		**[GR*difficult*] Indicate segments that are hard to translate**
		CSW:	ففكست علي ال+internship و روحت ال+camp معاهم
		Egy:	ففكست علي التدريب و روحت المعسكر معاهم
		Eng:	((So, I declined)) the internship and I went to the camp with them.
	(c)		**[GR*propn*] Translate or transliterate proper nouns**
		CSW:	أكتر فيلم بحبه The Dark Knight, Batman's Dark Knight عشان بحس إن يعني الفيلم ده فيه كمية أفكار عبقرية مش طبيعية
		Egy:	أكتر فيلم بحبه فارس الظلام , باتمان فارس الظلام عشان بحس إن يعني الفيلم ده فيه كمية أفكار عبقرية مش طبيعية
		Eng:	The movie I like the most is The Dark Knight, Batman's Dark Knight because I feel that this movie has a lot of creative ideas.
Conversational Speech Translation Rules	(d)		**[SR*style*] Capture the same meaning, fluency, and naturalness**
		CSW:	سافرت برا مصر قبل كده غير ال .. ال+bachelor project؟
		Egy:	سافرت برا مصر قبل كده غير ال .. مشروع التخرج؟
		Eng:	Have you ever travelled abroad apart from the .. the bachelor project?
	(e)		**[SR*partial*] Transliterate and annotate partial words**
		CSW:	طيب و إزاي بت ..بت+overcome الموضوع ده؟ إزاي بتعدي ال .. ال+stress ده؟
		Egy:	طيب و إزاي بت ..بتتخطى الموضوع ده؟ إزاي بتعدي ال .. الضغط ده؟
		Eng:	Well, how do you %bt .. #overcome this issue?how do you overpass this .. this #stress?
Code-switching Translation Rules	(f)		**[CSWR*rewrites*] Modify English words in translation**
		CSW:	[HUM] و قعدت فى كذا city
		Egy:	[HUM] و قعدت فى كذا مدينة
		Eng:	[HUM] and I have stayed in multiple cities
	(g)		**[CSWR*rewrites*] Modify English words in translation**
		CSW:	فانا لو عندك كذا robot و كذا task المفروض يتعملوا, فأنا بكتب ال+code لل+robots إن هي تروح لل+task#ات دي، بس
		Egy:	فانا لو عندك كذا روبوت و كذا مهمة المفروض يتعملوا, فأنا بكتب الكود للروبوتات إن هي تروح للمهام دي، بس
		Eng:	So, if you have multiple robots and multiple tasks you should be working on, so I just write the code for the robots so that they should handle these tasks, that's it.
	(h)		**[CSWR*rewrites*] Modify Arabic words in translation**
		CSW:	يعنى بيبقى environment مختلف عن ال+environment بتاع ال+big city
		Egy:	يعنى بتبقى بيئة مختلفة عن البيئة بتاعة المدن الكبيرة
		Eng:	I mean the environment differs from the environment of the big city.
	(i)		**[CSWR*rewrites*] Modify Arabic words in translation**
		CSW:	[HES] هو ال+bachelor project بتاعى هو يعني related somehow لل+optical field
		Egy:	[HES] هو مشروع التخرج بتاعى هو يعني بشكل ما مرتبط بالمجال البصري
		Eng:	[HES] my bachelor project is actually somehow related to the optical field
	(j)		**[CSRW*reorder*] Modify the order between Arabic and English words**
		CSW:	لكن لو عندنا stereo camera في طرق معينة نقدر نستخدمها إن إحنا نقدر نحدد المسافة بين الكاميرا أو بين ال+two objects معينين بالطريقة دي تمام؟
		Egy:	لكن لو عندنا كاميرا ستيريو في طرق معينة نقدر نستخدمها إن إحنا نقدر نحدد المسافة بين الكاميرا أو بين جسمين معينين بالطريقة دي تمام؟
		Eng:	But if we have a stereo camera and in certain ways we can use it to estimate the distance between the camera and the specific two objects this way, okay?
	(k)		**[CSRW*style*] Handle repetitions in segments with syntactic divergence**
		CSW:	ماشي okay طيب ممكن تحكيلنا عن ال .. ال+bachelor project بتاعك؟
		Egy:	ماشي تمام طيب ممكن تحكيلنا عن ال .. مشروع التخرج بتاعك؟
		Eng:	Ok,well,can you tell us about your..your bachelor project?
		CSW:	اه [HES] أكتر .. من أكتر ال .. my favorite books يعني animal .. animal farm
		Egy:	اه [HES] أكتر .. من أكتر ال .. كتبي المفضلة يعني مزرعة .. مزرعة الحيوان
		Eng:	Yes [HES] the most .. one of the most .. my favourite books I mean .. animal animal farm.

Table 3: Translation examples following different guideline rules.

working life +ال gets translated to الحياة المهنية (with two definite article instances).

- Given that Arabic is a gender-marking language, gender reinflection is sometimes needed to guarantee fluent translation into Arabic. See Table 3 (h).
- Modifying Arabic prepositions following English words. See Table 3 (i).

[$CSWR_{reorder}$] We allow changing the order between the original Arabic and English words to handle syntactic divergences between the two languages and achieve better fluency. See Table 3 (j).

[$CSWR_{style}$] The SR_{style} rule gets further compounded in the case of CSW when repetition occurs at a location where there is syntactic divergence between both languages, such as adjectival phrases in our language pair. In this case, since the order of words changes during translation, the word to be repeated at that position could also change. Following our fluency preference, we prefer the translation that gives higher fluency over providing an accurate literal translation. See Table 3 (k).

[$CSWR_{disfluency}$] Another interesting translation challenge arises in the context of CSW when speakers repeat words using different languages. In the case of explicatory CSW, where the English and Arabic words have the exact same meaning, we allow translating the English word into the same present Arabic word, treating it as a case of repetition due to disfluency. In the case of elaboratory CSW, where CSW is used to further elaborate on meaning, we ask the translator to find another translation of the word that would better capture the subtle difference between both words. If that is not possible, we allow the repetition of the word.

5 Benchmarking Baseline Systems

In this section, we discuss the ASR, MT, and ST baseline systems. We describe the experimental setup for each and present the results in Table 4.

5.1 Experimental Setup

We follow the same train, dev, and test splits defined in Hamed et al. (2020). For all the experiments, we use ArzEn-ST dev set (1,402 sentences) for tuning and ArzEn-ST test set (1,470 sentences) for testing. For training, we use ArzEn-ST train set (3,344 sentences), in addition to other monolingual data which we mention below.

Automatic Speech Recognition We train a joint CTC/attention based E2E ASR system using ESPnet (Watanabe et al., 2018). The encoder and decoder consist of 12 and 6 Transformer blocks with 4 heads, feed-forward inner dimension 2048 and attention dimension 256. The CTC/attention weight (λ_1) is set to 0.3. SpecAugment (Park et al., 2019) is applied for data augmentation. For the Language Model (LM), the RNNLM consists of 1 LSTM layer with 1000 hidden units and is trained for 20 epochs. For decoding, the beam size is 20 and the CTC weight is 0.2.

In addition to using ArzEn-ST for training, we also train the ASR system and LM using Callhome (Gadalla et al., 1997), MGB-3 (Ali et al., 2017), a 5-hours subset from Librispeech (Panayotov et al., 2015), and a 5-hours subset from MGB-2 (Ali et al., 2016).[7] We perform Alif/Ya normalization (Arabic), remove punctuation and corpus-specific annotations, and lower-case English words.[8]

Machine Translation We train Transformer models using Fairseq (Ott et al., 2019) on a single GeForce RTX 3090 GPU. We use the hyperparameters from the FLORES benchmark for low-resource machine translation (Guzmán et al., 2019). The hyperparameters are given in Appendix A. For each MT model, we use a BPE model trained jointly on source and target sides. The BPE model is trained using Fairseq with character_coverage set to 1.0. We tune the vocabulary size for each experiment for the values of $1k, 3k, 5k, 8k$, and $16k$.

In addition to ArzEn-ST, we also train the MT system using $324k$ extra Egyptian Arabic-English parallel sentences obtained from the following parallel corpora: Callhome Egyptian Arabic-English Speech Translation Corpus (Kumar et al., 2014), LDC2012T09 (Zbib et al., 2012), LDC2017T07 (Chen et al., 2017), LDC2019T01 (Chen et al., 2019), LDC2020T05 (Li et al., 2020), and MADAR (Bouamor et al., 2018).[9] These extra corpora include $15k$ sentences with CSW instances. When translating into En, we use all these extra corpora as Arabic-English training. However, when translating into Egy, we use these extra corpora as English-Arabic training, but we exclude the $15k$ sentences producing CSW Arabic as our reference does not have CSW sentences. Data pre-

[7]We followed the setup used in (Hamed et al., 2022a).

[8]For the Callhome corpus, we removed partial words.

[9]For corpora with no defined data splits, we follow the guidelines provided in Diab et al. (2013).

	ASR		MT		ST	
			CSW→En	CSW→Egy	CSW→En	CSW→Egy
Training Set	**WER**	**CER**	**BLEU**	**BLEU**	**BLEU**	**BLEU**
ArzEn-ST	57.9	36.2	8.6	48.0	4.5	13.0
ArzEn-ST + Extra	34.7	20.0	34.3	79.8	16.5	31.1

Table 4: Summary of results for baseline systems evaluated on ArzEn-ST test set. We present baseline systems for both settings: (1) training using ArzEn-ST data only and (2) training using ArzEn-ST data with **Extra** monolingual speech corpora for the ASR system and **Extra** monolingual Egyptian Arabic-English parallel sentences for the MT systems. We report Word Error Rate (WER) and Character Error Rate (CER) for ASR systems, and BLEU score (Papineni et al., 2002) using SacrebleuBLEU (Post, 2018) for MT and ST systems.

processing involved removing all corpus-specific annotations, URLs and emoticons, lowercasing, running Moses' (Koehn et al., 2007) tokenizer, MADAMIRA (Pasha et al., 2014) simple tokenization (D0) and Alif/Ya normalization (Arabic).

Speech Translation We build a cascaded speech translation system, where we train an ASR system and use an MT system to translate the ASR system's outputs. We opt for a cascaded system over an end-to-end system due to the limitation of available resources to build an end-to-end system, in addition to the fact that cascaded systems have been shown to outperform end-to-end systems in low-resource settings (Denisov et al., 2021).

5.2 Results

Table 4 presents the results for the MT and ST baseline systems. We also report results for the ASR system used to build the cascaded ST system.[10] We report results for both settings: (1) when training only using ArzEn-ST corpus and (2) when training using ArzEn-ST corpus in addition to the extra monolingual data specified for each task (**Extra**). As expected, adding extra monolingual data greatly improves results. We observe that translating into Arabic achieves higher BLEU scores than translating into English. This is expected, as in the case of translating from CSW text, Arabic words (around 85% of words) remain mostly the same with possible slight modifications required. We also observe that for the ST models, the performance is nearly reduced by half compared to the MT results. This highlights the difficulty of the task. Given that CSW ST has only been slightly tackled by other researchers, we hope that this corpus will motivate further research on this task.

[10]ASR results are different than those reported in Hamed et al. (2022a) as we limit the data to publicly-available corpora, use different preprocessing, and different data splits.

6 Conclusion and Future Work

Code-switching has become a worldwide prevalent phenomenon. This created a need for NLP systems to be able to handle such mixed input. Code-switched data is typically scarce, which is evident in the limited number of available corpora for machine translation and speech translation tasks. In this paper, we extend the previously collected ArzEn speech corpus with translations to both its primary and secondary languages, providing a three-way code-switched Egyptian Arabic-English speech translation corpus. We have discussed the translation guidelines, particularly with regards to issues arising due to the spontaneous nature of the corpus as well as code switching. We reported benchmark results for baseline ASR, MT, and ST systems. We make this corpus available to motivate and facilitate further research in this area.

For future work, we plan on improving the corpus and using it for code-switching linguistic investigations as well as NLP tasks. With regards to corpus improvements, we plan on adding additional translation references and CODAfying (Habash et al., 2012a; Eskander et al., 2013) the corpus. From a linguistic perspective, having signals from the monolingual Arabic and English translations, we plan to further understand why code-switching occurs at the given points. Finally, we plan to use this corpus for NLP tasks, working on data augmentation for the purpose of improving machine translation and speech translation.

Acknowledgements

This project has benefited from financial support by DAAD (German Academic Exchange Service). We also thank the reviewers for their insightful comments and constructive feedback.

References

Basem HA Ahmed and Tien-Ping Tan. 2012. Automatic speech recognition of code switching speech using 1-best rescoring. In *Proceedings of the International Conference on Asian Language Processing*, pages 137–140.

Ahmed Ali, Peter Bell, James Glass, Yacine Messaoui, Hamdy Mubarak, Steve Renals, and Yifan Zhang. 2016. The mgb-2 challenge: Arabic multi-dialect broadcast media recognition. In *Proceedings of the Spoken Language Technology Workshop*, pages 279–284.

Ahmed Ali, Shammur Chowdhury, Amir Hussein, and Yasser Hifny. 2021. Arabic code-switching speech recognition using monolingual data. In *Proceedings of Interspeech.*

Ahmed Ali, Stephan Vogel, and Steve Renals. 2017. Speech recognition challenge in the wild: Arabic mgb-3. In *Proceedings of the Automatic Speech Recognition and Understanding Workshop*, pages 316–322.

Suman Banerjee, Nikita Moghe, Siddhartha Arora, and Mitesh M Khapra. 2018. A dataset for building code-mixed goal oriented conversation systems. In *Proceedings of the International Conference on Computational Linguistics.*

Houda Bouamor, Nizar Habash, Mohammad Salameh, Wajdi Zaghouani, Owen Rambow, Dana Abdulrahim, Ossama Obeid, Salam Khalifa, Fadhl Eryani, Alexander Erdmann, and Kemal Oflazer. 2018. The MADAR Arabic dialect corpus and lexicon. In *Proceedings of the International Conference on Language Resources and Evaluation.*

Özlem Çetinoğlu. 2017. A code-switching corpus of turkish-german conversations. In *Proceedings of the Linguistic Annotation Workshop*, pages 34–40.

Özlem Çetinoğlu, Sarah Schulz, and Ngoc Thang Vu. 2016. Challenges of computational processing of code-switching. In *Proceedings of the Workshop on Computational Approaches to Linguistic Code Switching.*

Shuguang Chen, Gustavo Aguilar, Anirudh Srinivasan, Mona Diab, and Thamar Solorio. 2022. Calcs 2021 shared task: Machine translation for code-switched data. *arXiv preprint arXiv:2202.09625.*

Song Chen, Dana Fore, Stephanie Strassel, Haejoong Lee, and Jonathan Wright. 2017. BOLT Egyptian Arabic sms/chat and transliteration LDC2017T07. Philadelphia: Linguistic Data Consortium.

Song Chen, Jennifer Tracey, Christopher Walker, and Stephanie Strassel. 2019. BOLT Egyptian Arabic parallel discussion forums data. Linguistic Data Consortium (LDC) catalog number LDC2019T01, ISBN 1-58563-871-4.

Shammur Absar Chowdhury, Amir Hussein, Ahmed Abdelali, and Ahmed Ali. 2021. Towards one model to rule all: Multilingual strategy for dialectal code-switching Arabic asr. In *Proceedings of Interspeech.*

Christopher Cieri, David Miller, and Kevin Walker. 2004. The fisher corpus: A resource for the next generations of speech-to-text. In *Proceedings of the International Conference on Language Resources and Evaluation*, pages 69–71.

Pavel Denisov, Manuel Mager, and Ngoc Thang Vu. 2021. IMS'systems for the IWSLT 2021 low-resource speech translation task. *Proceedings of the International Conference on Spoken Language Translation.*

Margaret Deuchar, Peredur Davies, Jon Herring, M Carmen Parafita Couto, and Diana Carter. 2014. Building bilingual corpora. *Advances in the Study of Bilingualism*, pages 93–111.

Mrinal Dhar, Vaibhav Kumar, and Manish Shrivastava. 2018. Enabling code-mixed translation: Parallel corpus creation and MT augmentation approach. In *Proceedings of the Workshop on Linguistic Resources for Natural Language Processing*, pages 131–140.

Mona Diab, Nizar Habash, Owen Rambow, and Ryan Roth. 2013. LDC Arabic treebanks and associated corpora: Data divisions manual. *arXiv preprint arXiv:1309.5652.*

Amazouz Djegdjiga, Martine Adda-Decker, and Lori Lamel. 2018. The French-Algerian code-switching triggered audio corpus (FACST). In *Proceedings of the International Conference on Language Resources and Evaluation.*

Andreas Eisele, Yu Chen, and UN Multi. 2010. a multilingual corpus from united nation documents. In *Proceedings of the International Conference on Language Resources and Evaluation*, pages 924–929.

Ramy Eskander, Nizar Habash, Owen Rambow, and Nadi Tomeh. 2013. Processing spontaneous orthography. In *Proceedings of the Conference of the North American Chapter of the Association for Computational Linguistics (NAACL)*, pages 585–595, Atlanta, Georgia.

Hassan Gadalla, Hanaa Kilany, Howaida Arram, Ashraf Yacoub, Alaa El-Habashi, Amr Shalaby, Krisjanis Karins, Everett Rowson, Robert MacIntyre, Paul Kingsbury, David Graff, and Cynthia McLemore. 1997. Callhome Egyptian Arabic transcripts. *Linguistic Data Consortium, Philadelphia.*

Marwa Gaser, Manuel Mager, Injy Hamed, Nizar Habash, Slim Abdennadher, and Ngoc Thang Vu. 2022. Exploring segmentation approaches for neural machine translation of code-switched Egyptian Arabic-English text. *arXiv preprint arXiv:2210.06990.*

Deepak Gupta, Asif Ekbal, and Pushpak Bhattacharyya. 2020. A semi-supervised approach to generate the code-mixed text using pre-trained encoder and transfer learning. In *Findings of the Association for Computational Linguistics: EMNLP 2020*, pages 2267–2280.

Francisco Guzmán, Peng-Jen Chen, Myle Ott, Juan Pino, Guillaume Lample, Philipp Koehn, Vishrav Chaudhary, and Marc'Aurelio Ranzato. 2019. The flores evaluation datasets for low-resource machine translation: Nepali-English and Sinhala-English. In *Proceedings of the Conference on Empirical Methods in Natural Language Processing*.

Nizar Habash, Mona Diab, and Owen Rambow. 2012a. Conventional orthography for dialectal Arabic. In *Proceedings of the International Conference on Language Resources and Evaluation*, pages 711–718.

Nizar Habash, Ramy Eskander, and Abdelati Hawwari. 2012b. A morphological analyzer for Egyptian Arabic. In *Proceedings of the meeting of the special interest group on computational morphology and phonology*, pages 1–9.

Nizar Habash, Abdelhadi Soudi, and Tim Buckwalter. 2007. On Arabic Transliteration. In A. van den Bosch and A. Soudi, editors, *Arabic Computational Morphology: Knowledge-based and Empirical Methods*, pages 15–22. Springer, Netherlands.

Injy Hamed, Pavel Denisov, Chia-Yu Li, Mohamed Elmahdy, Slim Abdennadher, and Ngoc Thang Vu. 2022a. Investigations on speech recognition systems for low-resource dialectal Arabic–English code-switching speech. *Computer Speech & Language*, 72:101278.

Injy Hamed, Mohamed Elmahdy, and Slim Abdennadher. 2018. Collection and analysis of code-switch Egyptian Arabic-English speech corpus. In *Proceedings of the International Conference on Language Resources and Evaluation*.

Injy Hamed, Nizar Habash, Slim Abdennadher, and Ngoc Thang Vu. 2022b. Investigating lexical replacements for Arabic-English code-switched data augmentation. *arXiv preprint arXiv:2205.12649*.

Injy Hamed, Ngoc Thang Vu, and Slim Abdennadher. 2020. Arzen: A speech corpus for code-switched Egyptian Arabic-English. In *Proceedings of the International Conference on Language Resources and Evaluation*, pages 4237–4246.

Christian Huber, Enes Yavuz Ugan, and Alexander Waibel. 2022. Code-switching without switching: Language agnostic end-to-end speech translation. *arXiv preprint arXiv:2210.01512*.

Amir Hussein, Shammur Absar Chowdhury, Ahmed Abdelali, Najim Dehak, and Ahmed Ali. 2022. Code-switching text augmentation for multilingual speech processing. *arXiv preprint arXiv:2201.02550*.

Manal A Ismail. 2015. The sociolinguistic dimensions of code-switching between Arabic and English by saudis. *International Journal of English Linguistics*, 5(5):99.

Philipp Koehn, Hieu Hoang, Alexandra Birch, Chris Callison-Burch, Marcello Federico, Nicola Bertoldi, Brooke Cowan, Wade Shen, Christine Moran, Richard Zens, et al. 2007. Moses: Open source toolkit for statistical machine translation. In *Proceedings of the Annual Meeting of the Association for Computational Linguistics Demo and Poster Sessions*, pages 177–180.

Archchana Kugathasan and Sagara Sumathipala. 2021. Neural machine translation for Sinhala-English code-mixed text. In *Proceedings of the International Conference on Recent Advances in Natural Language Processing*, pages 718–726.

Gaurav Kumar, Yuan Cao, Ryan Cotterell, Chris Callison-Burch, Daniel Povey, and Sanjeev Khudanpur. 2014. Translations of the callhome Egyptian Arabic corpus for conversational speech translation. In *Proceedings of International Workshop on Spoken Language Translation*.

Linguistic Data Consortium LDC. 2013. BOLT program: Arabic to English translation guidelines.

Chia-Yu Li and Ngoc Thang Vu. 2019. Integrating knowledge in end-to-end automatic speech recognition for Mandarin-English code-switching. In *International Conference on Asian Language Processing*, pages 160–165.

Xuansong Li, Stephen Grimes, and Stephanie Strassel. 2020. BOLT Egyptian Arabic-English word alignment – conversational telephone speech training. Linguistic Data Consortium (LDC) catalog number LDC2020T05, ISBN 1-58563-920-6.

Dau-Cheng Lyu, Ren-Yuan Lyu, Yuang-chin Chiang, and Chun-Nan Hsu. 2006. Speech recognition on code-switching among the Chinese dialects. In *Proceedings of the International Conference on Acoustics Speech and Signal Processing Proceedings*, volume 1, pages I–I.

Dau-Cheng Lyu, Tien-Ping Tan, Eng-Siong Chng, and Haizhou Li. 2015. Mandarin–English code-switching speech corpus in south-east asia: Seame. *Language Resources and Evaluation*, 49(3):581–600.

Sainik Kumar Mahata, Soumil Mandal, Dipankar Das, and Sivaji Bandyopadhyay. 2019. Code-mixed to monolingual translation framework. In *Proceedings of the Forum for Information Retrieval Evaluation*, pages 30–35.

Mohamed Amine Menacer, David Langlois, Denis Jouvet, Dominique Fohr, Odile Mella, and Kamel Smaïli. 2019. Machine translation on a parallel code-switched corpus. In *Proceedings of the Canadian Conference on Artificial Intelligence*, pages 426–432. Springer.

Thipe I Modipa, Marelie H Davel, and Febe De Wet. 2013. Implications of Sepedi/English code switching for ASR systems. In *Proceedings of Pattern Recognition Association of South Africa*.

Sahoko Nakayama, Takatomo Kano, Andros Tjandra, Sakriani Sakti, and Satoshi Nakamura. 2019. Recognition and translation of code-switching speech utterances. In *Proceedings of the Conference of the Oriental COCOSDA International Committee for the Coordination and Standardisation of Speech Databases and Assessment Techniques*, pages 1–6.

Myle Ott, Sergey Edunov, Alexei Baevski, Angela Fan, Sam Gross, Nathan Ng, David Grangier, and Michael Auli. 2019. Fairseq: A fast, extensible toolkit for sequence modeling. In *Proceedings of the Conference of the North American Chapter of the Association for Computational Linguistics*.

Vassil Panayotov, Guoguo Chen, Daniel Povey, and Sanjeev Khudanpur. 2015. Librispeech: an ASR corpus based on public domain audio books. In *Proceedings of the International Conference on Acoustics, Speech and Signal Processing*, pages 5206–5210.

Kishore Papineni, Salim Roukos, Todd Ward, and Wei-Jing Zhu. 2002. Bleu: a method for automatic evaluation of machine translation. In *Proceedings of the 40th annual meeting of the Association for Computational Linguistics*, pages 311–318.

Daniel S Park, William Chan, Yu Zhang, Chung-Cheng Chiu, Barret Zoph, Ekin D Cubuk, and Quoc V Le. 2019. Specaugment: A simple data augmentation method for automatic speech recognition. In *Proceeding of Interspeech*, pages 2613–2617.

Arfath Pasha, Mohamed Al-Badrashiny, Mona T Diab, Ahmed El Kholy, Ramy Eskander, Nizar Habash, Manoj Pooleery, Owen Rambow, and Ryan Roth. 2014. Madamira: A fast, comprehensive tool for morphological analysis and disambiguation of Arabic. In *Proceedings of the International Conference on Language Resources and Evaluation*, pages 1094–1101.

Shana Poplack. 1980. Sometimes i'll start a sentence in Spanish y termino en espanol: toward a typology of code-switching. *Linguistics*, 18:581–618.

Matt Post. 2018. A call for clarity in reporting BLEU scores. In *Proceedings of the Conference on Machine Translation: Research Papers*, pages 186–191.

Vikram Ramanarayanan and David Suendermann-Oeft. 2017. Jee haan, i'd like both, por favor: Elicitation of a code-switched corpus of Hindi-English and Spanish-English human-machine dialog. In *Proceedings of Interspeech*, pages 47–51.

Ali Shazal, Aiza Usman, and Nizar Habash. 2020. A unified model for Arabizi detection and transliteration using sequence-to-sequence models. In *Proceedings of the Arabic Natural Language Processing Workshop*, pages 167–177.

R Mahesh K Sinha and Anil Thakur. 2005. Machine translation of bi-lingual Hindi-English (Hinglish) text. In *Proceedings of the Machine Translation summit (MT Summit X)*, pages 149–156.

Thamar Solorio and Yang Liu. 2008. Learning to predict code-switching points. In *Proceedings of the Conference on Empirical Methods in Natural Language Processing*, pages 973–981.

Kai Song, Yue Zhang, Heng Yu, Weihua Luo, Kun Wang, and Min Zhang. 2019. Code-switching for enhancing NMT with pre-specified translation. In *Proceedings of the Conference of the North American Chapter of the Association for Computational Linguistics: Human Language Technologies, Volume 1 (Long and Short Papers)*, pages 449–459.

Vivek Srivastava and Mayank Singh. 2020. Phinc: A parallel Hinglish social media code-mixed corpus for machine translation. In *Proceedings of the Workshop on Noisy User-generated Text*.

Vivek Srivastava and Mayank Singh. 2021. Hinge: A dataset for generation and evaluation of code-mixed Hinglish text. In *Proceedings of the Workshop on Evaluation and Comparison of NLP Systems*.

Sara Stefanich, Jennifer Cabrelli, Dustin Hilderman, and John Archibald. 2019. The morphophonology of intraword codeswitching: Representation and processing. *Frontiers in Communication*, page 54.

Ishan Tarunesh, Syamantak Kumar, and Preethi Jyothi. 2021. From machine translation to code-switching: Generating high-quality code-switched text. In *Proceedings of The Joint Conference of the Annual Meeting of the Association for Computational Linguistics and the International Joint Conference on Natural Language Processing*.

Ewald van der Westhuizen and Thomas Niesler. 2016. Automatic speech recognition of English-isiZulu code-switched speech from South African soap operas. *Procedia Computer Science*, 81:121–127.

Ngoc Thang Vu, Dau-Cheng Lyu, Jochen Weiner, Dominic Telaar, Tim Schlippe, Fabian Blaicher, Eng-Siong Chng, Tanja Schultz, and Haizhou Li. 2012. A first speech recognition system for Mandarin-English code-switch conversational speech. In *Proceedings of the International Conference on Acoustics, Speech and Signal Processing*, pages 4889–4892. IEEE.

Shinji Watanabe, Takaaki Hori, Shigeki Karita, Tomoki Hayashi, Jiro Nishitoba, Yuya Unno, Nelson Enrique Yalta Soplin, Jahn Heymann, Matthew Wiesner, Nanxin Chen, et al. 2018. Espnet: End-to-end speech processing toolkit. In *Proceeding of Interspeech*, pages 2207–2207.

Orion Weller, Matthias Sperber, Telmo Pires, Hendra Setiawan, Christian Gollan, Dominic Telaar, and Matthias Paulik. 2022. End-to-end speech translation for code switched speech. *Findings of the Association for Computational Linguistics*.

Jitao Xu and François Yvon. 2021. Can you traducir this? machine translation for code-switched input. In *Proceedings of the Workshop on Computational Approaches to Linguistic Code-Switching*, pages 84–94.

Zhen Yang, Bojie Hu, Ambyera Han, Shen Huang, and Qi Ju. 2020. Csp: Code-switching pre-training for neural machine translation. In *Proceedings of the 2020 Conference on Empirical Methods in Natural Language Processing*, pages 2624–2636.

Emre Yilmaz, Maaike Andringa, Sigrid Kingma, Jelske Dijkstra, F Kuip, H Velde, Frederik Kampstra, Jouke Algra, H Heuvel, and David A van Leeuwen. 2016. A longitudinal bilingual Frisian-Dutch radio broadcast database designed for code-switching research. In *Proceedings of the International Conference on Language Resources and Evaluation*.

Rabih Zbib, Erika Malchiodi, Jacob Devlin, David Stallard, Spyros Matsoukas, Richard Schwartz, John Makhoul, Omar F. Zaidan, and Chris CallisonBurch. 2012. Machine translation of Arabic dialects. In *Proceedings of the Conference of the North American Chapter of the Association for Computational Linguistics*, pages 49–59.

A MT Hyperparameters

The following is the train command:
python3 fairseq_cli/train.py $DATA_DIR –source-lang src –target-lang tgt –arch transformer –share-all-embeddings –encoder-layers 5 –decoder-layers 5 –encoder-embed-dim 512 –decoder-embed-dim 512 –encoder-ffn-embed-dim 2048 –decoder-ffn-embed-dim 2048 –encoder-attention-heads 2 –decoder-attention-heads 2 –encoder-normalize-before –decoder-normalize-before –dropout 0.4 –attention-dropout 0.2 –relu-dropout 0.2 –weight-decay 0.0001 –label-smoothing 0.2 –criterion label_smoothed_cross_entropy –optimizer adam –adam-betas '(0.9, 0.98)' –clip-norm 0 –lr-scheduler inverse_sqrt –warmup-updates 4000 –warmup-init-lr 1e-7 –lr 1e-3 –stop-min-lr 1e-9 –max-tokens 4000 –update-freq 4 –max-epoch 100 –save-interval 10 –ddp-backend=no_c10d

Maknuune: A Large Open Palestinian Arabic Lexicon

Shahd Dibas,[†] Christian Khairallah,[‡] Nizar Habash[‡]
Omar Fayez Sadi,[*] Tariq Sairafy,[*] Karmel Sarabta,[*] Abrar Ardah[*]
[†]University of Oxford, [‡]New York University Abu Dhabi
[*]University College of Educational Sciences - UNRWA
shahd.dibas@ling-phil.ox.ac.uk, christian.khairallah@nyu.edu, nizar.habash@nyu.edu

Abstract

We present Maknuune مكنونة, a large open lexicon for the Palestinian Arabic dialect. Maknuune has over 36K entries from 17K lemmas, and 3.7K roots. All entries include diacritized Arabic orthography, phonological transcription and English glosses. Some entries are enriched with additional information such as broken plurals and templatic feminine forms, associated phrases and collocations, Standard Arabic glosses, and examples or notes on grammar, usage, or location of collected entry.

1 Introduction

Arabic is a collective of historically related variants that co-exist in a diglossic (Ferguson, 1959) relationship between a Standard variant and geographically specific dialectal variants. Standard Arabic (SA, العربية الفصحى) is typically used to refer to the older Classical Arabic (CA) used in Quranic texts and pre-islamic poetry, all the way to Modern SA (MSA), the official language of news and culture in the Arab World. Dialectal Arabic (DA) is classified geographically into regions such as Egyptian, Levantine, Maghrebi, and Gulf. The dialects, which differ among themselves and SA, are the primary mode of spoken communication, although increasingly they are dominating in written form on social media. That said, DA has no official prescriptive grammars or orthographic standards, unlike the highly standardized and regulated MSA. In the realm of natural language processing (NLP), MSA has relatively more annotated and parallel resources than DA; although there are many notable efforts to fill gaps in all Arabic variants (Alyafeai et al., 2022).

In this paper, we focus on Palestinian Arabic (PAL), which is part of the South Levantine Arabic dialect subgroup. PAL consists of several subdialects in the region of Historic Palestine that vary in terms of their phonology and lexical choice (Jarrar et al., 2016). PAL, like all other DA, has been historically influenced by many languages, specifically, in its case, Syriac, Turkish, Persian, English and most recently Modern Hebrew (Halloun, 2019), as well as other Arabic dialects that came in interaction with PAL after the Nakba. While this research effort was originally motivated by the need to document and preserve the cultural heritage and unique identities of the various PAL sub-dialects, it has expanded to cover PAL's ever-evolving nature as a living language, and provides a resource to support research and development in Arabic dialect NLP.

Concretely, we present **Maknuune** مكنونة,[1] a large open lexicon for PAL, with over 36K entries from 17K lemmas, and 3.7K roots.[2] All entries include diacritized Arabic orthography and phonological transcription following Habash et al. (2018), as well as English glosses. Important inflectional variants are included for some lemmas, such as broken plural and templatic feminine. About 10% of the entries are phrases (multiword expressions) indexed by their primary lemmas. And about 67% of the entries include MSA glosses, examples, and/or notes on grammar, usage, or location of collected entry. To our knowledge, Maknuune is the largest open machine-readable dictionary for PAL. Maknuune is publicly viewable and downloadable.[3]

We discuss some related work in Section 2, and highlight some PAL linguistic facts that motivated many of our design choices in Section 3. Section 4 presents our data collection process and annotation guidelines. We present statistics for our lexicon and evaluate its coverage in Section 5.

[1] مكنونة /maknūne/ is a PAL farming term that refers to an egg intentionally left behind in a specific location to encourage the chicken to lay more eggs in that location. We hope that the lexicon will encourage other researchers and citizen linguists to contribute to it.

[2] In this initial phase of Maknuune, we focus on the PAL sub-dialects spoken in the West Bank, an area with dialectal diversity across many dimensions such as *lifestyle* (urban, rural, bedouin), religion, gender, and social class.

[3] www.palestine-lexicon.org

Proceedings of the The Seventh Arabic Natural Language Processing Workshop (WANLP), pages 131 - 141
December 8, 2022 ©2022 Association for Computational Linguistics

2 Related Work

Linguistic Descriptions There are several linguistic references describing various aspects of PAL (Rice and Sa'id, 1979; Herzallah, 1990; Hopkins, 1995; Elihai, 2004; Talmon, 2004; Bassal, 2012; Cotter and Horesh, 2015). These are mostly targeting academics and language learners. We consulted many of these resources as part of developing our annotation guidelines.

Dialectal Corpora We can group DA corpora based on the degree of richness in their annotations. Some noteworthy examples of unannotated or lightly annotated corpora of relevance include the MADAR Corpus (Bouamor et al., 2018), comprising 2K parallel sentences spread across 25 dialects of Arabic, including PAL (Jerusalem variety) and the NADI corpus for nuanced dialect identification (Abdul-Mageed et al., 2021). The Shami Corpus (Abu Kwaik et al., 2018) includes 21K PAL sentences, and the Parallel Arabic Dialect Corpus (PADIC) contains 6.4K PAL sentences (Meftouh et al., 2015). In the spirit of genre diversification and wider coverage across dialects, El-Haj (2020) introduced the Habibi Corpus for song lyrics, which comprises songs from many Arab countries including all Levantine Arab countries.

Public and freely available morphologically annotated corpora are scarce for DA and often do not agree on annotation guidelines. A notable annotated dataset for PAL is the Curras corpus (Jarrar et al., 2016), a 56K-token morphologically annotated corpus. Other annotated Levantine dialect efforts include the Jordan Comprehensive Contemporary Arabic Corpus (JCCA) (Sawalha et al., 2019), the Jordanian and Syrian corpora by Alshargi et al. (2019), and the Baladi corpus of Lebanese Arabic (Al-Haff et al., 2022).

We consulted some of the public corpora as part of the development of Maknuune. However, most of the above datasets are based on web scrapes, which limits the amount of actual lemma coverage that they could attain.

Dialectal Lexicons Examples of machine-readable DA lexicons include the 36K-lemma lexicon used for the CALIMA EGY fully inflected morphological analyzer (Habash et al., 2012), based on the CALLHOME Egypt lexicon (Gadalla et al., 1997), and the 51K-lemma Egyptian Arabic Tharwa lexicon (Diab et al., 2014), which provides some morphological annotations.

The *Palestinian Colloquial Arabic Vocabulary* comprises 4.5K entries including expressions (Younis and Aldrich, 2021), and the MADAR Lexicon contains 2.7K entries dedicated to the Jerusalem variety of PAL, including lemmas, phonological transcriptions, and glosses in MSA, English and French (Bouamor et al., 2018).

In addition to the above there are a number of dictionaries for Levantine Arabic variants, e.g., Elihai (2004) (9K entries and 17K phrases for PAL), Halloun (2019) (for PAL), Freiha (1973) (ca. 5K entries for Lebanese Arabic), and Stowasser and Ani (2004) (15K entries for Syrian Arabic). These resources include base lemma forms, occasional plural forms, verb aspect inflections, and expressions; however, none of them are available in a machine-readable format, to the best of our knowledge.

The lexicon presented in this work strives to be a large-scale and open resource with rich entries covering phonology, morphology, and lexical expressions, and with a wide-ranging coverage of PAL sub-dialects. The lexicon may never be complete, but by making it open to sharing and contribution, we hope it will become central and useful to NLP researchers and developers, as well as to linguists working on Arabic and its dialects.

3 Linguistic Facts

In this section we present some general linguistic facts about PAL and highlight specific challenging phenomena that motivated many of our annotation decisions.

3.1 Phonology and Orthography

Like all other DA, and unlike MSA, PAL has no standard orthography rules (Jarrar et al., 2016; Habash et al., 2018). In practice, PAL is primarily written in Arabic script, and to a lesser extent in Arabizi style romanization (Darwish, 2014). Some of the variations in the written form reflect the words' phonology, morphology, and/or etymological connections to MSA. Orthogonal and detrimental to the orthography challenge, PAL has a high degree of variability within it sub-dialects in phonological terms. We highlight some below, noting that some also exist in other DA.

Consonantal Variables A number of PAL consonants vary widely within sub-dialects. For example, the voiceless velar stop */k/* is affricated to the palatal */tsh/* in many PAL rural varieties (Herzallah, 1990), e.g., كَيف *kayf* 'how' appears as */k ee f/* (urban) or */tsh ee f/* (rural).[4] Similarly, the MSA voiceless uvular stop */q/* in the word قَلْب *qal.b* 'heart' is realized either as glottal stop */2 a l b/* in urban dialects, as a voiceless velar stop */k a l b/* in rural dialects, or a voiced velar stop */g a l b/* in Bedouin dialects (Herzallah, 1990). It should be noted that there are some exceptions that do not conform to the above generalizations. For example, in Beit Fajjar,[5] the word قَهْوَة *qah.waħ* 'coffee' typically varying elsewhere as */{2,q,g,k} a h w e/* is realized as */tsh h ee w a/*. Moreover, some words do not have varying pronunciations such as عْقَال *ς.qaAl* */3 g aa l/* 'Egal headband'.

Monophthongization Some PAL diphthongs shift to different monophthongs in different locations. For example the */a y/* diphthong in شَيخ *šayx* */sh a y kh/* 'Sheikh' shifts often to */ee/* (*/sh ee kh/*), but also to */ii/* (*/sh ii kh/*).[6] Following the CODA* guidelines for diacritizing DA (Habash et al., 2018), we spell the */oo/* and */ee/* sounds using َو *aw* and َي *ay* (without a *sukun* on the و *w* or ي *y*), respectively, e.g., كَوم *kawm* */k oo m/* 'pile' and بَيت *bayt* */b ee t/* 'house'.

Metathesis In some rural dialects in villages near Tulkarem, Jenin and Ramallah, there are words with consonant pairs within a syllable that appear in a different order than is the norm in PAL, e.g., a word like كَهْرَبا *kah.rabaA* */k a h r a b a/* 'electricity' realizes as */k a r h a b a/*.

Epenthesis PAL exhibits systematic epenthesis of the */i/* or */u/* sounds producing paired word alternations such as */b a 3 d/* and */b a 3 i d/* for بعد 'still;after' or */kh u b z/* and */kh u b u z/* or */kh u b i z/* (in different sub-dialects) for خبز 'bread'. We opted to use the fully epenthesized forms in the lexicon, i.e., بَعِد *baςid*, خُبُز *xubuz*, and خُبِز *xubiz*, for the above mentioned examples.

[4]Arabic orthographic transliteration is presented in the HSB Scheme (italics) (Habash et al., 2007). Arabic script orthography is presented in the CODA* scheme, and Arabic phonology is presented in the CAPHI scheme (between /../) (Habash et al., 2018).

[5]A Palestinian town located 8 kilometers south of Bethlehem in the West Bank.

[6]In the Palestinian village of Ramadin, near Hebron in the West Bank.

3.2 Morphology

Like other DA, PAL has a complex morphology employing templatic and concatenative morphemes, and including a rich set of morphological features: gender, number, person, state, aspect, in addition to numerous clitics. We highlight some specific morphological phenomena that we needed to handle.

Ta Marbuta The so-called feminine singular suffix morpheme, or Ta Marbuta (ة *ħ*), is a morpheme that can be used to mark feminine singular nominals, but that also appears with masculine singular and plural nominals. Morphophonemically, it has a number of forms in PAL that vary contextually. First, in some PAL sub-dialects, the Ta Marbuta is pronounced as */a/* when preceded by an emphatic consonant, velars, and pharyngeal fricatives, e.g., بَطَّة *baT∼aħ* */b a t. t. a/* 'duck'; otherwise it realizes as */e/*, e.g., بِسَّة *bis∼iħ* */b i s s e/*. In some northern PAL dialects, the */e/* variant appears as */i/*; and in some southern PAL dialects, the distinction is gone and all Ta Marbutas are pronounced */a/*. Second, the Ta Marbuta turns into its allomorph */i t/* in *Idafa* constructions, e.g., */b i s s i t/* 'the/a cat of'. Finally, for some active participle deverbal nouns, the Ta Marbuta realizes as */aa/* or */ii t/* when followed by a pronominal object clitic, e.g., كاتْباه *kaAt.baAh* */k aa t b aa (h)/* or كاتْبِيْتُه *kaAt.biy.tuh* or */k a t b ii t u (h)/* 'she wrote it'.

Complex Plural Forms Besides the common use of broken plural (templatic plural) in DA, we encountered cases of *blocked* plurals where a typical sound plural or templatic plural is not generated because another word form is used in its place (Aronoff, 1976). One example from Ramadin, is the plural form of the word عَيِّل *ςay∼il* */3 a y y i l/* 'child [lit. dependent]', which is blocked by the word form ضْعُوف *D.ςuwf* */dh. 3 uu f/* 'children [lit. weaklings]'.

3.3 Syntax

Previous research on Arabic dialects reveals that the syntactic differences between these dialects are considered to be minor compared to the morphological ones (Brustad, 2000). One particular challenging phenomenon we encountered is a class of nouns used in adjectival constructions, but violating noun-adjective agreement rules, which involve gender, number and rationality (Alkuhlani and Habash, 2011). For instance, the word خيخة *xiyxah̄ /kh ii kh a/* 'weak/lame' does not typically agree with the nouns it modifies unlike a normal adjective such كبير *k.biyr /k b ii r/* 'old [human]/large [nonhuman]'. So, the words سيّارة *siy∼aArah̄* 'car [f.s.]', عُرس *ςurus* 'wedding [m.s.]', and ناس *naAs* 'people [m.p]' can all be modified by خيخة *xiyxah̄*; however, they need three different forms of كبير *k.biyr*: كبيرة *k.biyrih̄*, كبير *k.biyr*, and كبار *k.baAr*, respectively. We mark the POS of such nominals as ADJ/NOUN in our lexicon, as it is a class that deserves further study.

3.4 Figures of Speech and Multiword Expressions

PAL has a rich culture of figures of speech and multiword expressions (compounds, collocations, etc.) that has not been well documented. We highlight some phenomena that we cover in Maknuune.

Collocations As part of working on Maknuune, we encountered numeorus collocations (words that tend to co-occur with certain words more often than they do with others). For example, the verbs used for trimming off the tough ends of some vegetables vary based on the vegetable: يْقمّع بَامْيا */y Q a m m i 3 # b aa m y e/* 'trim off the tough ends of okra', يْقرّم فَاصُولْيا */y q a r r i m # f aa s. uu l y a/* 'trim off the tough ends of green beans', يْعَكّب عَكّوب */y 3 a k k i b # 3 a k k uu b/* 'remove the thorns from artichoke (Gundelia)', and يْطَرْطِف ذُرة */y t. a r t. i f # D u r a/* 'cut the blossom ends of the maize stalks'.

Compounds We encountered many compositional and non-compositional compounds. Examples include جَوَاز سَفَر *jawaAz safar /J a w aa z # s a f a r/* '[lit. permission-of-travel, passport]', which is also used in MSA. Some words appear in many compounds with a wide range of meaning, e.g., the word بَيت *bayt* '[lit. house]' appears in compounds referring to celebrations, funerals, bathrooms, and whether or not a family has children (see the examples in Table 3).

Synecdoches It has been widely observed that PAL speakers use synecdoches[7] in their dialects (Seto, 1999). Examples include the use of كَوم لَحِم */k oo m # l a 7 i m/* '[lit. a pile of meat]', and كَبَابِيش */k a b aa b ii sh/* '[lit. plural of hair]' to mean 'children'.

Euphemisms PAL speakers use many euphemistic expressions. For example, in some villages in Nablus, the expression يَوم تْهَنّى */y oo m # t h a n n a/* '[lit. the day he felt happy]' to mean 'the day he passed away'. In other areas in the West Bank, the phrase عَينُه كَريمة */3 ee n o # k a r ii m e/* '[lit. his eye is generous]' to mean 'one-eyed'; and the phrase بَيت خَالْتي */b ee t # kh aa l t i/* '[lit. my aunt's house]' means 'prison'.

4 Methodology

In this section, we discuss the methodology we adopted in data collection for Maknuune, as well as the guidelines we followed for creating the lexicon entries.

4.1 Data Sources

The current work spans over five years of effort, and a large number of volunteering informants, linguistics students, and citizen linguists (over 130 people). The data was collected from many different sources.

First are **interviews** with (mostly but not entirely) elderly people who live in rural areas such as villages and towns or in refugee camps in the West Bank. The researchers went to the field and met with several people. They attended several social gatherings and participated in different events, e.g. weddings, funerals, field harvests, traditional cooking sessions, sewing, etc. They asked the language users several questions pertaining to the following themes: weddings, funerals, occupations, illnesses, cooking traditional dishes, plants, animals, myths, games, weather terms, tools and utensils, etc. They were particularly interested in documenting terms and expressions that are used mainly by the old generation.

Secondly, to achieve the needed balance in the lexicon, the researchers consulted an in-house **balanced corpus**, that contains ∼40,000 words. The corpus comprises data that was transcribed from several recorded conversations that revolve around the same themes as above, written chats and texts, and some internet material (both written and spoken). Common words including verbs, adjectives,

[7] A figure of speech in which a term for a part of something is used to refer to the whole, or vice versa.

adverbs, and function words (e.g., prepositions, conjunctions, particles) were taken from the balanced corpus. At a later stage in the development of Maknuune, we consulted with the Curras Corpus (Jarrar et al., 2016) to identify additional missing lemmas, with limited yield. We compare to Curras in terms of coverage in Section 5. All of the above was also supplemented by methodical rounds of well-formedness checking to improve consistency across all fields, i.e., diacritization, transcription, root validity, etc.

Finally, in addition to the previous two methods, the researchers employed their **linguistic intuition** skills, knowledge of Palestinian Arabic (as native speakers) and the knowledge of the language users to provide additional word classes and multiword expressions that are associated with the existing lemmas.

It should be noted that whether an MSA lemma cognate of a PAL lemma (with similar or exact pronunciation, or meaning) exists was not considered a factor in including the PAL lemma in the lexicon. We focused on creating a representative sample of PAL including all its sub-dialects.

4.2 Lexical Entries

Each entry in the Maknuune lexicon consists of six required and three optional fields. The six required fields are the **Root**, **Lemma**, **Form**, **Transcription**, **POS & Features**, and **English Gloss**. The optional fields are the **MSA Gloss**, **Example** and **Notes**. Figure 1 presents an example of a number of entries coming from the same root.

4.2.1 Root, Lemma, and Form

The **Root**, **Lemma** and **Form** represent three degrees of morphological abstraction. The **root** in Arabic in general is a templatic morpheme that interdigitates with a pattern or template to form a word stem that can then be inflected further. Roots are very abstract representations that broadly define the morphological family a word belongs to at the derivational and inflectional level. **Lemmas** on the other hand are abstractions of the inflectional space that is limited by variations in the morphological features of person, gender, number, aspect, etc. Lemmas are the central entries of the lexicon. **Forms** are base words (i.e., without clitics) that are inflected in a specific way. We follow the same general guidelines of determining lemmas as used in large Arabic morphological analyzers (Graff et al., 2009; Habash et al., 2012; Khalifa et al., 2017). There are of course some constructions that have grammaticalized into new lemmas, e.g., عَشَان *ςašaAn* can be treated as the noun شَان *šaAn* 'situation;status' with a proclitic, or the subordinating conjunction meaning 'because'.

For nouns and adjectives, we provide the lemma in the masculine singular form, unless it is a feminine form that does not vary in gender, in which case it is provided in the feminine singular. Very infrequently, some nouns only appear in plural form, which become their lemma, e.g. أَوَاعِي *ÂawaAςiy* */2 a w aa 3 i/* 'clothes'. We do not list the sound plural and sound feminine inflections of nouns and adjectives. However, broken plurals and templatic feminine forms are provided and linked through the same lemma as the singular form.

For verbs, we provide the lemmas in the third masculine singular perfective form as is normally done in Arabic lexicography. We provide three forms linked to the lemma: the third masculine singular perfective, the third masculine singular imperfective, and the second person masculine imperative (command) forms. These are provided for completeness to identify the basic verbal inflectional paradigm (albeit, not completely).

These three representations are provided in Arabic script. Since PAL does not have an official standard orthography, we intentionally decided to follow the Conventional Orthography for Dialectal Arabic (CODA*) (Habash et al., 2018). In addition to being used in developing Curras (Jarrar et al., 2016), CODA* has been adopted by a website for teaching PAL to non-native speakers.[8]

4.2.2 Transcription with CAPHI++

One of CODA*'s limitations is that it abstracts over some of the phonological variations. As such, we follow the suggestions by Habash et al. (2018) to use a phonological representation, CAPHI, to indicate the specific phonology of the entries. CAPHI, which stands for Camel Phonetic Inventory is inspired by the International Phonetic Alphabet (IPA) and Arpabet (Shoup, 1980), and is designed to only use characters directly accessible on the common keyboard to ease the job of annotators.

Owing to the phonological variations that are found in PAL, we extended CAPHI's symbol set with *cover phonemes* that represent a number of possible interchangeable phones. We call our extended set CAPHI++. Table 2 presents the new 9

[8]https://www.palestinianarabic.com/

	Root	Lemma	Form	Transcription	POS:Features	English	MSA	Example	Notes
(a)	ت.ف.ح	تُفَّاح	تُفَّاح	t u f f aa 7	NOUN:MS	apples	تُفَّاح	كِلو تُفَّاح أقل شي رح يكلفك 8 شيقل	Collective Noun
(b)	ت.ف.ح	تُفَّاحَة	تُفَّاحَة	t u f f aa 7 a	NOUN:FS	apple	تُفَّاحَة	كان الصحن قدامي فتناوَلِت تُفَّاحَة بس طلعت مدودة	Unit Noun
(c)	ت.ف.ح	تُفَّاحَة	تَفَافِيح	t a f a f ii 7	NOUN:P	apple			
(d)	ت.ف.ح	تُفَّاحَة	تُفَّاحِة آدَم	t u f f aa 7 i t # 2 aa d a m	NOUN:PHRASE	Adam's apple		شايف تُفَّاحة آدم هاي؟ هاي يعني إني أرجل منكَ ومن كل عيلتك الخايخين	
(e)	ت.ف.ح	مْتَفَّح	مْتَفَّح	m t a f f i 7	ADJ:MS	reddish and healthy	مُحْمَر وصِحِّي	وجهها مْتَفّح وحليانة كثير اسم الله	
(f)	ت.ف.ح	تَفَّح	تَفَّح	t a f f a 7	VERB:P	turn reddish and healthy	يصبح مُحْمَر وصِحِّي	تَفّح وجهها بعد الجيزة. لاحظتوا؟	
(g)	ت.ف.ح	تَفَّح	يْتَفَّح	y t a f f i 7	VERB:I	turn reddish and healthy			
(h)	ت.ف.ح	تَفَّح	تَفَّح	t a f f i 7	VERB:C	turn reddish and healthy			

Table 1: Eight entries from Maknuune that share the same root, and are paired with four distinct lemmas.

CAPHI++	CAPHI	CAPHI Transcription	CODA	CAPHI++ Transcription
Q	k q 2 g	k aa l / q aa l / 2 aa l / g aa l	قَال	Q aa l
D	d dh	d ii b # dh ii b	دِيب	D ii b
J	j dj	r i j j aa l # r i dj dj aa l	رِجَّال	r i J J aa l
Z	z dh	z a n b / dh a n b	دَنْب	Z a n b
T	t th	t i m m / th i m m	ثِمّ	T i m m
S	s th	th a w r a / s a w r a	ثَوْرَة	S a w r a
Z.	z. dh.	2 a z. u n n / 2 a dh. u n n	أَظُنّ	2 a Z u n
D.	d. dh.	b ee d. / b ee dh.	بَيض	b ee D.
K	k tsh	k ee f / tsh ee f	كِيف	K ee f

Table 2: The CAPHI++ symbols set and its expanded CAPHI symbols, with examples.

symbols we introduced. All of these symbols are to be presented in upper case, while normal CAPHI symbols are in lower case. The new CAPHI++ symbols represent specific sets of mostly two variants in common use in different PAL sub-dialects. For example, instead of including four entries for the word قَلَم *qalam* (*/q a l a m/*, */k a l a m/*, */2 a l a m/*, */g a l a m/*), we only provide one form (*/Q a l a m/*). Exceptional usages that do not conform to the specific generalizations of the CAPHI++ cover symbols are listed independently, e.g., a second entry for the above example is provided for the Beit Fajjar pronunciation of */tsh a l a m/*.

We acknowledge that the transcriptions provided may not represent the full breadth of PAL sub-dialects. We make our resource open so that additional forms and variants can be added in the future, as needed.

4.2.3 POS and Features

The analysis cell in every entry indicates the POS and features of the word form. We use 35 POS tags based on a combination of previously used POS tagsets in Arabic NLP (Graff et al., 2009; Pasha et al., 2014; Khalifa et al., 2018). Our closest relative is the tagset used by (Khalifa et al., 2018) for work on Emirtai Arabic annotation. See the full list of POS tags in Table 6 in Appendix A. However, we extend their POS list with three tags: ADJ/NOUN (for adjectives with exceptional agreement), NOUN_ACT (active participle deverbal noun), and NOUN_PASS (passive participle deverbal noun).

For features, we use MS (masculine singular), FS (feminine singular), and P (plural) for nominals, and P (perfective), I (imperfective) and C (command) for third masculine singular verb forms only.

4.2.4 Phrases

In addition to basic word forms, we overload the use of the form cells to list phrases (multiword expressions, collocations, and figures of speech) that are paired with the lemma. In such cases, the POS:Features cell is given the POS of the lemma, with the extension **PHRASE**, e.g., line (d) in Table 1, and Table 3.

4.2.5 Glosses, Examples and Notes

We provided the English gloss equivalents of all the PAL words. The MSA gloss was provided for about a third of the entries at the time of writing. In cases where no single word in MSA or English can encode a culturally specific concept, the annotators translated the whole situation/concept. For example, in Ramadin, there are two words for

Root	Lemma	Form	Transcription	POS:Features	English	MSA	Example
ب.ي.ت	بَيت	بَيت مَضْوِي	b ee t # m a D. w i	NOUN:PHRASE	the parents have many children, especially males		
ب.ي.ت	بَيت	بَيت مَلْيَان	b ee t # m a l y aa n	NOUN:PHRASE	the parents have many children		
ب.ي.ت	بَيت	بَيت رُمَّان	b ee t # r u m m aa n	NOUN:PHRASE	the parents have many children		
ب.ي.ت	بَيت	بَيت مْعَتِّم	b ee t # m 3 a t t i m	NOUN:PHRASE	there are no children at all in the house # the parents did not give birth to any children		
ب.ي.ت	بَيت	بَيت خَرَاب	b ee t # kh a r aa b	NOUN:PHRASE	all of the children are females # there are no male children in the house		أخوك عادي مسخمط بَيتُه خَرَاب، الله ما طعمه ولاد
ب.ي.ت	بَيت	بَيت عَامِر	b ee t # 3 aa m i r	NOUN:PHRASE	a house that is full of gatherings and happy celebrations		
ب.ي.ت	بَيت	بَيت عَمْرَان	b ee t # 3 a m r aa n	NOUN:PHRASE	a house that is full of gatherings and happy celebrations		
ب.ي.ت	بَيت	بَيت أجِر	b ee t # 2 a J i r	NOUN:PHRASE	funeral	جَنَازَة	عملوله بَيت أجِر مسكين؟
ب.ي.ت	بَيت	يِفْتَح بَيت	y i f t a 7 # b ee t	NOUN:PHRASE	pay for the necessaties and needs of a family		هذا الراتب يا يابا ما بِيفتح بَيت بطولكرم
ب.ي.ت	بَيت	سِتّ بَيت	s i t t # b ee t	NOUN:PHRASE	housewife # the wife who can cook and clean the house very well	ربَّة منزِل	بِديش أتجوز وحدة موظفة. بدي إياها سِت بيت
ب.ي.ت	بَيت	بَيت الخَارِج	b ee t # 2 i l kh aa r i J	NOUN:PHRASE	bathroom	حمَّام	كنَّا نروح عشي اسمه بَيت الخارج ما بقى في حمامات زي هلا
ب.ي.ت	بَيت	بَيت المَيّ	b ee t # 2 i l m a. y y	NOUN:PHRASE	bathroom	حمَّام	ودِّي اخوتك عبَيت المي
ب.ي.ت	بَيت	بَيت خَالْتِي	b ee t # kh aa l t i	NOUN:PHRASE	prison	سِجن	كان عندي مشوار هيك لبَيت خَالْتِي هههههه
ب.ي.ت	بَيت	بَيت المُونة	b ee t # i l m oo n e	NOUN:PHRASE	pantry	مخزن طعام	جيبيلي قنينة زيت جديدة من بَيت المُونة

Table 3: Examples of NC compounds in Maknuune for the lemma بَيت 'house'.

'baby camel' depending on its age: ذَلُول *ðaluwl /dh a l uu l/*, 'barely a few days old' and حْوَيِّر *H.way∼ir /7 w a y y i r/* 'around 14-15 months old'. Another complex example is the word تَلْجِيم *tal.jiym /t a l J ii m/* '[lit. harnessing or bridling]' which can refer also to 'reciting some verses from the Quran (Surat Al-Takweer, Ayat Al-Kursi or Surat Al-Hashr) on a razor or a thread and closing the razor or tying the thread and leaving them aside until a lost or missing riding animal has returned home.'

Finally, we provide usage examples for some entries, as well as grammatical or collection notes. Notes vary in type from *Collective Noun* and *Collected near Nablus*, to *Vulgar*.

5 Coverage Evaluation

We approximate the coverage of our lexicon by comparing it with the Curras corpus (Jarrar et al., 2016), the largest resource available for PAL.[9] Since Curras is a corpus and our resource is a lexicon, the analysis is carried out in such a way to account for that difference. We present next some

POS Type	Unique lemma:POS	Entries	Forms	Phrases
Nominals	10,871	16,258	13,449	2,809
Verbs	6,179	19,622	18,982	640
Other	254	324	263	61
Proper & Foreign	65	98	65	33
Total	**17,369**	**36,302**	**32,759**	**3,543**

Table 4: POS type and entry statistics in Maknuune.

high-level corpus statistics and then a detailed comparison between Maknuune and Curras. Then, we provide some comparison between Maknuune and the lexicons of two morphological analyzers for MSA and EGY.

5.1 Maknuune & Curras Statistics

Maknuune POS Types Table 4 shows some basic statistics about Maknuune, dividing entries across four basic POS types (see Table 6). Maknuune has about three times more verb entries than verb lemmas, reflecting the fact that almost each verb appears in all three aspects (perfective, imperfective, and command) in third person masculine singular form. Similarly for nominals (nouns, adjectives, etc.), the ratio of 1.2 forms per lemma reflects the inclusion of plural entries for many

[9] Al-Haff et al. (2022) describe a revised version of that corpus, but it was not made available at the time of writing.

	Statistics	Maknuune	Curras Lexicon
All Entries	All entries	36,302	16,067
	Unique lemma:POS	17,369	8,448
	Unique lemma:POSType	17,083	8,161
	Unique lemmas	16,821	7,925
	Unique POS	35	33
	Unique roots	3,703	
	Entries per root	9.6	
	Unique lemma:POS per root	4.5	
Inflected Forms	All inflected forms	32,759	16,067
	Unique POS:features	76	224
Phrases	All phrase entries	3,543	
	Unique POS	25	

Table 5: Side-by-side view of the statistics of both Maknuune and the lexicon extracted from Curras.

nominals. Phrasal entries account for 10% of all Maknuune entries, and close to three quarters of them are associated with nominals (63% of all lemmas).

The Curras Lexicon In order to compare Maknuune with Curras, we extract a lexicon, henceforth Curras Lexicon, out of the Curras corpus by uniquing its entries based on lemma, inflected form, POS, and grammatical features (for Curras, aspect, person, gender, and number). We compare the Curras Lexicon to Maknuune in Table 5.

Firstly, Curras does not include roots; and although it is a corpus, it does not identify phrases in the way Maknuune does. As such, we do not compare them in those terms in Table 5.

Secondly, by virtue of being a lexicon, Maknuune possesses more unique lemmas, weighing in at 17,369 lemmas taking POS into account (lemma:POS), while the total number of inflected forms is at 32,759, both of which are about 50% more than in the Curras Lexicon. This clearly showcases Maknuune's richness in terms that go beyond the day-to-day language that one sees frequently in corpora like Curras. In contrast, Curras being a corpus, its extracted lexicon showcases a greater inflectional coverage with 224 unique word analyses as opposed to 76 for Maknuune.

Finally, as inferable from the difference between the number of unique lemmas and lemma:POS, 548 lemmas are associated to more than one POS in Maknuune.

5.2 Corpus Coverage Analysis

In the interest of estimating how well our lexicon would fare with real-world data, we perform an analysis between the Curras and Maknuune lemmas, to see how many of the Curras lemmas Maknuune actually covers. From an initial investigation, we note that there are numerous minor differences that need to be normalized to ensure a more meaningful evaluation. As such, we first pre-process all lemmas (in both lexicons) by stripping the سكون *sukun* diacritic, stripping all the فتحة diacritics that appear before a ا *A*, converting the همزة وصل ٱ *Ä* to ا *A*, and stripping the كسرة (*i*) and فتحة (*a*) diacritics if they appear before ة *ħ*. We then compare all the annotated lemma:POSType in Curras (56,004 tokens and 8,315 normalized types) to the lemmas in Maknuune.

We exclude 12,673 (23%) of the tokens pertaining to punctuation, digits and proper noun POS, none of which were especially targeted by Maknuune. Of the remaining 43,331 entries, 49% have exact match in Maknuune. We sample 10% of the unique entries with no exact match (433 types and 1,965 tokens), and manually annotate them for their mismatch class. We found that 74% of all the sampled types (80% in tokens) are actually present in Maknuune, but with slight differences in orthography mainly in the presence or absence of diacritics but also some spelling conventions. For about 20% of sampled types (17% in tokens), the lemma type is not one that we targeted such as foreign words and proper nouns that are differently labeled in Curras, or MSA words. Finally, 6% of sampled types (3% in tokens) are entries that are admittedly missing in Maknuune and can be added.

This suggests that we have very good coverage although the annotation errors and differences make it less obvious to see. A simple projected estimate assuming that our 10% sample is representative would suggest that Maknuune's coverage of Curras' lexical terms (other than proper nouns and punctuation) is close to 94% (97% in token space); however a full detailed classification would be needed to confirm this projection.

5.3 Overlap with MSA and EGY

In this section we conduct an evaluation similar to the one carried out in Section 5.2 but with an MSA lexicon (Calima$_{MSA}$), and an Egyptian Arabic lexicon (Calima$_{EGY}$).[10] The analysis reveals that 44% of Maknuune overlaps with Calima$_{MSA}$ at the lemma:POSType level (63% if all entries are dediacritized),[11] and that 49% of Maknuune overlaps similarly with Calima$_{EGY}$ (75% dediacritized). Taking into account that Maknuune spelling follows the CODA* guidelines, the analysis suggests that the 37% of Maknuune lemma:POSTypes, which do not exist in the MSA lexicon we used, are heavily dialectal. The overlap with EGY is predictably higher, and the 25% of Maknuune lemma:POSTypes (dediacritized) not existing in EGY highlights the differences between the two dialects despite their many similarities.

5.4 Observations on Lexical Richness and Diversity

The quantitative analyses we presented above allow us to see the big picture in terms of lexical richness and diversity in Maknuune and its complementarity to existing resources. However, we acknowledge that such an approach misses a lot of details that are collapsed or lost when ignoring subtle differences in semantics, phonology and morphology.

We first point at homonyms showing semantic changes and spread, such as آوَى /2 aa w a/ which is 'thread a needle' in PAL and 'shelter sb' in both MSA and PAL, بَطّ */b a t. t./* which means 'very small olives that people find hard to pick' in some villages in Palestine and 'ducks' in both MSA and PAL, and آخرة */2 aa kh r e/* which means 'desserts' in Nablus and 'the Day of the Judgment' in both MSA and PAL, albeit with a different pronunciation. Clearly, additional entries are needed to mark these difference.

Furthermore, the majority of the entries in Maknuune are actually pronounced differently from MSA even if spelled the same without diacritics and thus warrant entries of their own, with clear phonological specifications.

Finally, if we consider morphology (which is not modeled here per se), many PAL lemmas that have MSA lemma cognates are actually inflected differently, e.g., مَدّ *mad∼* 'extend;stretch' (in PAL and MSA), has different inflections for some parts of the paradigm: the 2nd person masculine plural is مَدّيتوا *mad∼aytuwA* in PAL and مَدَدْتُم *madad.tum* in MSA. Hence, each lemma in our lexicon heads a morphological paradigm which differs from its MSA counterpart.

6 Conclusion and Future Work

We presented Maknuune, a large open lexicon for the Palestinian Arabic dialect. Maknuune has over 36K entries from 17K lemmas, and 3.7K roots. All entries include Arabic diacritized orthography, phonological transcription and English glosses. Some entries are enriched with additional information such as broken plural and templatic feminine forms, associated phrases and collocations, Standard Arabic glosses, and examples or notes on grammar, usage, or location of collected entry.

In the future, we plan to continue to expand Maknuune to cover more PAL sub-dialects, more entries, and richer annotations, in particular for locations of usage, and morpholexical features such as rationality. We hope that by making it public, more researchers and citizen linguists will help enrich it and correct anything missing in it.

We also plan to make use of Maknuune as part of the development of larger resources and tools for Arabic NLP. The phonological transcriptions can be helpful for work in speech recognition and the morphological information for developing morphological analyzers and POS taggers. Furthermore, we plan to utilize Maknuune to develop pedagogical applications to help teach PAL to non-Arabic speakers and to children of Palestinians in the diaspora.

Acknowledgments

We would like to thank Prof. Jihad Hamdan, Muhammed Abu Odeh, Adnan Abu Shamma, Issra Ghazzawi and Kazem Abu-Khalaf for the helpful discussions.

References

Muhammad Abdul-Mageed, Chiyu Zhang, AbdelRahim Elmadany, Houda Bouamor, and Nizar Habash. 2021. NADI 2021: The second nuanced Arabic dialect identification shared task. In *Proceedings of the Sixth Arabic Natural Language Processing Workshop*, pages 244–259, Kyiv, Ukraine (Virtual). Association for Computational Linguistics.

[10]For MSA, we compared with the `calima-msa-s31_0.4.2.utf8.db` version (Taji et al., 2018) based on SAMA (Graff et al., 2009) and for EGY we only compared to the `calima-egy-c044_0.2.0.utf8.db` based on Habash et al. (2012). For EGY, only `CALIMA` analyses entries are selected.

[11]The *shadda* (∼) is not included in dediacritization.

Kathrein Abu Kwaik, Motaz Saad, Stergios Chatzikyriakidis, and Simon Dobnik. 2018. Shami: A corpus of Levantine Arabic dialects. In *Proceedings of the Eleventh International Conference on Language Resources and Evaluation (LREC 2018)*, Miyazaki, Japan. European Language Resources Association (ELRA).

Karim Al-Haff, Mustafa Jarrar, Tymaa Hammouda, and Fadi Zaraket. 2022. Curras + Baladi: Towards a Levantine Corpus. In *Proceedings of the Language Resources and Evaluation Conference*, pages 769–778, Marseille, France. European Language Resources Association.

Sarah Alkuhlani and Nizar Habash. 2011. A Corpus for Modeling Morpho-Syntactic Agreement in Arabic: Gender, Number and Rationality. In *Proceedings of the Conference of the Association for Computational Linguistics (ACL)*, Portland, Oregon, USA.

Faisal Alshargi, Shahd Dibas, Sakhar Alkhereyf, Reem Faraj, Basmah Abdulkareem, Sane Yagi, Ouafaa Kacha, Nizar Habash, and Owen Rambow. 2019. Morphologically annotated corpora for seven Arabic dialects: Taizi, sanaani, najdi, jordanian, syrian, iraqi and Moroccan. In *Proceedings of the Fourth Arabic Natural Language Processing Workshop*, pages 137–147, Florence, Italy. Association for Computational Linguistics.

Zaid Alyafeai, Maraim Masoud, Mustafa Ghaleb, and Maged S. Al-shaibani. 2022. Masader: Metadata sourcing for Arabic text and speech data resources. In *Proceedings of the Language Resources and Evaluation Conference*, Marseille, France.

Mark Aronoff. 1976. Word formation in generative grammar. *Linguistic Inquiry, Monograph one, The MIT press.*

Ibrahim Bassal. 2012. Hebrew and Aramaic Substrata in Spoken Palestinian Arabic. *Mediterranean Language Review*, 19:85–104.

Houda Bouamor, Nizar Habash, Mohammad Salameh, Wajdi Zaghouani, Owen Rambow, Dana Abdulrahim, Ossama Obeid, Salam Khalifa, Fadhl Eryani, Alexander Erdmann, and Kemal Oflazer. 2018. The MADAR Arabic Dialect Corpus and Lexicon. In *Proceedings of the Language Resources and Evaluation Conference (LREC)*, Miyazaki, Japan.

Kristen Brustad. 2000. *The Syntax of Spoken Arabic: A Comparative Study of Moroccan, Egyptian, Syrian, and Kuwaiti Dialects*. Georgetown University Press.

William Cotter and Uri Horesh. 2015. Sociolinguistics of Palestinian Arabic. *Encyclopedia of Arabic Language & Linguistics.*

Kareem Darwish. 2014. Arabizi Detection and Conversion to Arabic. In *Proceedings of the Workshop for Arabic Natural Language Processing (WANLP)*, pages 217–224, Doha, Qatar.

Mona T Diab, Mohamed Al-Badrashiny, Maryam Aminian, Mohammed Attia, Heba Elfardy, Nizar Habash, Abdelati Hawwari, Wael Salloum, Pradeep Dasigi, and Ramy Eskander. 2014. Tharwa: A Large Scale Dialectal Arabic-Standard Arabic-English Lexicon. In *Proceedings of the Language Resources and Evaluation Conference (LREC)*, pages 3782–3789, Reykjavik, Iceland.

Mahmoud El-Haj. 2020. Habibi - a multi dialect multi national Arabic song lyrics corpus. In *Proceedings of the 12th Language Resources and Evaluation Conference*, pages 1318–1326, Marseille, France. European Language Resources Association.

Yohanan Elihai. 2004. *The olive tree dictionary: A transliterated dictionary of conversational Eastern Arabic (Palestinian)*. Minerva Jerusalem.

Charles F Ferguson. 1959. Diglossia. *Word*, 15(2):325–340.

Anis Freiha. 1973. *Dictionary of Non-Classical Vocables in the Spoken Arabic of Lebanon*. Librairie du Liban.

Hassan Gadalla, Hanaa Kilany, Howaida Arram, Ashraf Yacoub, Alaa El-Habashi, Amr Shalaby, Krisjanis Karins, Everett Rowson, Robert MacIntyre, Paul Kingsbury, David Graff, and Cynthia McLemore. 1997. CALLHOME Egyptian Arabic transcripts LDC97T19. Web Download. Philadelphia: Linguistic Data Consortium.

David Graff, Mohamed Maamouri, Basma Bouziri, Sondos Krouna, Seth Kulick, and Tim Buckwalter. 2009. Standard Arabic Morphological Analyzer (SAMA) Version 3.1. Linguistic Data Consortium LDC2009E73.

Nizar Habash, Fadhl Eryani, Salam Khalifa, Owen Rambow, Dana Abdulrahim, Alexander Erdmann, Reem Faraj, Wajdi Zaghouani, Houda Bouamor, Nasser Zalmout, Sara Hassan, Faisal Al shargi, Sakhar Alkhereyf, Basma Abdulkareem, Ramy Eskander, Mohammad Salameh, and Hind Saddiki. 2018. Unified guidelines and resources for Arabic dialect orthography. In *Proceedings of the Language Resources and Evaluation Conference (LREC)*, Miyazaki, Japan.

Nizar Habash, Ramy Eskander, and Abdelati Hawwari. 2012. A Morphological Analyzer for Egyptian Arabic. In *Proceedings of the Workshop of the Special Interest Group on Computational Morphology and Phonology (SIGMORPHON)*, pages 1–9, Montréal, Canada.

Nizar Habash, Abdelhadi Soudi, and Tim Buckwalter. 2007. On Arabic Transliteration. In A. van den Bosch and A. Soudi, editors, *Arabic Computational Morphology: Knowledge-based and Empirical Methods*, pages 15–22. Springer, Netherlands.

Moïn Halloun. 2019. *An etymological lexicon of foreign words in Palestinian Arabic : Arabic-Arabic-English : the influence of Greek, Pahlavi, Latin, Persian Syriac, Ottoman language and modern languages in the Palestinian dialect.* Bethlehem: Bethlehem University, The Institute of Oral Cultural Heritage of the Palestinians.

Rukayyah S Herzallah. 1990. *Aspects of Palestinian Arabic phonology: A nonlinear approach.* Cornell University.

Simon Hopkins. 1995. sarār "pebbles" — A Canaanite Substrate Word in Palestinian Arabic. *Zeitschrift für arabische Linguistik*, (30):37–49.

Mustafa Jarrar, Nizar Habash, Faeq Alrimawi, Diyam Akra, and Nasser Zalmout. 2016. Curras: an annotated corpus for the Palestinian Arabic dialect. *Language Resources and Evaluation*, pages 1–31.

Salam Khalifa, Nizar Habash, Fadhl Eryani, Ossama Obeid, Dana Abdulrahim, and Meera Al Kaabi. 2018. A morphologically annotated corpus of Emirati Arabic. In *Proceedings of the Language Resources and Evaluation Conference (LREC)*, Miyazaki, Japan.

Salam Khalifa, Sara Hassan, and Nizar Habash. 2017. A morphological analyzer for Gulf Arabic verbs. In *Proceedings of the Workshop for Arabic Natural Language Processing (WANLP)*, Valencia, Spain.

Karima Meftouh, Salima Harrat, Salma Jamoussi, Mourad Abbas, and Kamel Smaili. 2015. Machine translation experiments on PADIC: A parallel Arabic dialect corpus. In *Proceedings of the Pacific Asia Conference on Language, Information and Computation.*

Arfath Pasha, Mohamed Al-Badrashiny, Mona Diab, Ahmed El Kholy, Ramy Eskander, Nizar Habash, Manoj Pooleery, Owen Rambow, and Ryan Roth. 2014. MADAMIRA: A fast, comprehensive tool for morphological analysis and disambiguation of Arabic. In *Proceedings of the Language Resources and Evaluation Conference (LREC)*, pages 1094–1101, Reykjavik, Iceland.

Frank Rice and Majed Sa'id. 1979. *Eastern Arabic.* Georgetown University Press.

Majdi Sawalha, Faisal Alshargi, Abdallah AlShdaifat, Sane Yagi, and Mohammad A. Qudah. 2019. Construction and annotation of the Jordan comprehensive contemporary Arabic corpus (JCCA). In *Proceedings of the Fourth Arabic Natural Language Processing Workshop*, pages 148–157, Florence, Italy. Association for Computational Linguistics.

Ken-ichi Seto. 1999. Distinguishing metonymy from synecdoche. *Metonymy in language and thought*, 4:91–120.

June E Shoup. 1980. Phonological aspects of speech recognition. *Trends in Speech Recognition*, pages 125–138.

K. Stowasser and M. Ani. 2004. *A Dictionary of Syrian Arabic: English-Arabic.* G - Reference, Information and Interdisciplinary Subjects Series. Georgetown University Press.

Dima Taji, Salam Khalifa, Ossama Obeid, Fadhl Eryani, and Nizar Habash. 2018. An Arabic Morphological Analyzer and Generator with Copious Features. In *Proceedings of the Fifteenth Workshop on Computational Research in Phonetics, Phonology, and Morphology (SIGMORPHON)*, pages 140–150.

Raphael Talmon. 2004. 19th century Palestinian Arabic: the testimony of Western travellers. *Jerusalem studies in Arabic and Islam*, (29):210–280.

A. Younis and M. Aldrich. 2021. *Palestinian Colloquial Arabic Vocabulary.* Arabic Vocabulary. Lingualism.

A POS Type Mapping and Examples

POS Type	POS	Examples
Nominals	ADJ	أَسْوَد، سُودَا، سُود
	ADJ_COMP	أَكْبَر، أَصْغَر
	ADJ/NOUN	نِيقَة، خُرْخُشَة، عُبْرَة، خِيخَة
	NOUN	وَلَد، وْلَاد، زَلَمِة، زْلَام، لِيرَة
	NOUN_ACT	بفيت بالروايات كَاتِب قصة قصيرة
	NOUN_PASS	كل شي مَكْتُوب عالكتاب تبعي؟
	NOUN_QUANT	بَعْض، نُص، كُل، أَغْلَب
Verbs	VERB	لِعِب، يِلْعَب، اِلْعَب
Proper	NOUN_PROP	نُور، عَائِشَة
Other	ABBREV	إلَخ
	ADJ_NUM	أَوَّل، ثَانِي، ثَالِث، رَابِع
	ADV	هَون، هَيك، هْنَاك، هَلَّا
	ADV_INTERROG	شْلَونَك؟
	ADV_REL	وَين ما يروح بلاقيه بوجهي
	CONJ	كنا قعدنا عنفس السفرة حَتَّى ولادهم الصغار
	CONJ_SUB	تعبت كثير لَمَّا وصلت الدار
	INTERJ	وَلّ، نَعَم، لَا
	NOUN_NUM	وَاحَد، اِثْنِين، ثَلَاثِة
	PART	طَبّ أنت هلا شو خصك فيي
	PART_DET	ال
	PART_FOCUS	أَمَّا بخصوص عمي هند، فاحنا مالازم نسكت
	PART_FUT	رَح، رَايِح
	PART_INTERROG	أنت خليلي شِي؟
	PART_NEG	مِش، مُو
	PART_PROG	أنت مش عَم تعطيني فرصة أحكي
	PART_RESTRICT	كلهم مناح إِلَّا الكبيرة
	PART_VOC	يَا ولد !
	PREP	مِن، عَن، لَ، فِي
	PRON	أَنَا، إِخْنَا، إِنْتِن
	PRON_EXCLAM	مَا احلاها!!
	PRON_DEM	هٰذَا، هَذَولَاك، هَرْعُو، هَرْعِيتُو، هَرْعَيتَا
	PRON_INTERROG	كِيف، مَتَى، وَين، لَيش، اَيش
	PRON_REL	اللِّي، أَكَم
	VERB_NOM	اِصْحى، أُوعَى
	VERB_PSEUDO	أَكِن، رَيت، كَأَنّ

Table 6: Mapping of part-of-speech (POS) types to POS tags used to annotate base words in Maknuune, and associated examples.

Developing a Tag-Set and Extracting the Morphological Lexicons to Build a Morphological Analyzer for Egyptian Arabic

Amany Fashwan a.fashwan@gmail.com

Sameh Alansary s.alansary@alexu.edu.egy

Linguistics and Phonetics Department, Faculty of Arts, Alexandria University, Egypt

Abstract

This paper sheds light on an in-progress work for building a morphological analyzer for Egyptian Arabic (EGY). To build such a tool, a tag-set schema is developed depending on a corpus of 527,000 EGY words covering different sources and genres. This tag-set schema is used in annotating about 318,940 words, morphologically, according to their contexts. Each annotated word is associated with its suitable prefix(s), original stem, tag, suffix(s), glossary, number, gender, definiteness, and conventional lemma and stem. These morphologically annotated words, in turns, are used in developing the proposed morphological analyzer where the morphological lexicons and the compatibility tables are extracted and tested. The system is compared with one of best EGY morphological analyzers; CALIMA.

1 Introduction

After the emergence of social media networks, and specially, after the Arab Spring revolutions, the data has become available everywhere. This led to have an increased attention in the field of Natural Language Processing (NLP) for Colloquial Arabic Dialects (CADs) where the adopted NLP tools for Modern Standard Arabic (MSA) are not suitable to process and understand them (Harrat, Meftouh, & Smaïli, 2017).

An important challenge for working on these dialects is to create morphological analyzers or tools that provide all possible analyses for a particular written word out of its context (Salloum & Habash, 2014) since it is an essential step in most NLP applications such as machine translation, information retrieval, text to speech, text categorization …etc. (Habash, Eskander, & Hawwari, 2012).

Morphological segmentation is the process of converting the surface form of a given word to its lexical form with additional grammatical information such as parts of speech, gender, and number (Joseph & Chang, 2012). In Morphological Analyzer (MA) tool, the morphemes along with their morphological information of a given word are provided for all its possible analyses out of its context.

This paper presents an in-progress work for building a morphological analyzer for Egyptian Arabic. To build such a tool, a Part-of-Speech (POS) tag-set schema is developed depending on different criteria to be used in annotating our corpus morphologically. The annotated data is used in detecting the different analysis solutions of each word, extracting the morphological lexicons and the compatibility tables to allow only valid morphological analysis solutions to be generated by the proposed morphological analyzer.

The rest of this paper is organized as follows. In Section 2, the related works are reviewed, then the used corpus and the process of developing the tag-set schema are discussed in Section 3. In Section 4, the proposed morphological analyzer and the prosses of the automatic extraction of the used morphological tables and the compatibility tables are discussed. The discussion of the system current status, coverage and evaluation are reviewed in Section 5. Finally, the discussion of conclusion and future work are listed in Section 6.

2 Related Works

Whereas there are many trials for defining tag-set schemas for MSA, for example, Khoja's Arabic Tag-set (Khoja, Garside, & Knowles, 2001; Khoja S. , 2003), ARBTAGS Tag-set (Alqrainy, 2008), and Penn Arabic Treebank (PATB) Part-of-Speech Tag-set (Maamouri & Bies, 2004), only few trials interested in EGY; (Maamouri, Krouna, Tabessi, Hamrouni, & Habash, 2012) who present a tag-set schema (ARZATB tag-set) that is based on the PATB guidelines (Maamouri M. , Bies, Krouna, Gaddeche, & Bouziri, 2009). They compare tags for Egyptian (ARZ) with those used in MSA. The

Proceedings of the The Seventh Arabic Natural Language Processing Workshop (WANLP), pages 142 - 160
December 8, 2022

tags specify the forms of the morphemes used in constructing a word, but do not address discrepancies between morpheme form and functions. For example, the broken plural nouns in this tag set are treated the same as singular nouns: 'رجالة' /riggɑːl+æh/ 'men' is tagged as NOUN+NSUFF_FEM_SG. A new POS tag-set (CAMEL POS) is opted to be used in (Khalifa, et al., 2018). It is inspired by the ARZATB tag-set and guidelines. It is designed as single tag-set for both MSA and the dialects to facilitate research on adaptation between MSA and the dialects, support backward compatibility with previously annotated resources and enforce a functional morphology analysis that is deeper and more compatible with Arabic morphosyntactic rules than form-based analysis.

The lexicon and rules are the core knowledge base of any morphological analysis/generation system (Habash, 2010). The trials for modeling dialectal Arabic (DA) morphology have followed one of two directions. The first direction interested in extending MSA tools to cover dialectal phenomena. Some trials built their Egyptian colloquial lexicon for morphological analyzer on the top of Buckwalter Arabic Morphological Analyzer (BAMA) Version 2.0 (Buckwalter, 2004); (Shaalan, Bakr, & Ziedan, 2007), (Abo Bakr, Shaalan, & Ziedan, 2008), (Salloum & Habash, 2011), (Habash, Roth, Rambow, Eskander, & Tomeh, 2013), (Habash & Rambow, 2005), (Al-Sabbagh & Girju, 2010), (Diab, et al., 2014), (Maamouri M. , et al., 2006) and (Al Ameri & Shoufan, 2021). The second direction interested in modeling DA morphology directly; (Kilany, et al., 2002), (Habash & Rambow, 2006), (Habash, Eskander, & Hawwari, 2012), (Habash, Diab, & Rambow, 2012), (Mohamed, Mohit, & Oflazer, 2012), (Eskander, Habash, & Rambow, 2013), (Maamouri M. , et al., 2014), (Samih & Kallmeyer, 2017), (Zalmout, Erdmann, & Habash, 2018) and (Habash, Marzouk, Khairallah, & Khalifa, 2022).

Handling the problem of lacking standard orthography for colloquial Arabic dialects is very important for building the morphological analyzers. There are few works proposed the EGY to offer a set of orthographic rules, standards, and conventions for dialectal Arabic varieties; (Darwish, et al., 2018) is an attempt to conventionalize the orthography close to the dialectal pronunciation as much as possible regardless of the way a word is typically written. (Habash, Diab, & Rambow, 2012) provides detailed description of Conventional Orthography for Dialectal Arabic (CODA) as applied to EGY. A unified common set of guidelines and meta-guidelines that help in creating dialect specific conventions is presented in (Habash, et al., 2018) applied to 28 Arab city dialects including Cairo, Alexandria, and Aswan.

Lacking annotated resources considered as the bottleneck for processing and building robust tools and applications. However, low-resource languages still lack datasets, such as the Arabic language and its dialects. EGY has received a growing attention for building corpora that may be useful for many purposes such as dialect identification or sentiment analysis, for example, but only (Abo Bakr, Shaalan, & Ziedan, 2008), (Maamouri M. , et al., 2014), (Al-Sabbagh & Girju, 2012), (Bouamor, et al., 2018), and (Darwish, et al., 2018) are interested in building multi-dialect, multi-genre, morphologically annotated corpora that include EGY.

However, these annotated corpora have few shortcomings: none of them are freely available for use; they also do not represent enough variety of resource. Moreover, some of them normalize the orthography to MSA-like standards which fail to grasp the dialectal orthography differences, e.g., 'كتير' /kitiːr/ normalized as 'كثير' /kaɵiːr/. Since MSA and the colloquials share a large proportion of their lexicon, the MSA tags are considered as much as possible as in (Maamouri, Krouna, Tabessi, Hamrouni, & Habash, 2012) and (Khalifa, et al., 2018). Nevertheless, we prefer to develop our own tag-set schema since we differ from (Maamouri, Krouna, Tabessi, Hamrouni, & Habash, 2012) in that we detect the tag according to its paradigmatic forms alongside its syntagmatic functions, as in (Khalifa, et al., 2018), as much as possible rather than depending on the morpheme form only. In addition, we opted to add more detailed tags in order to be more suitable to describe EGY, such as adverb of time, adverbs of place and adverbs of manner, and combine or split other tags that are described in the previously related-work tag-set schemas. Moreover, we feel the need to build a larger and more robust corpus, adding more various resources and genres. Consequently, this motivates us for building a new morphologically annotated resource for EGY to help in building the proposed morphological analyzer. It provides the conventional orthography guidelines and develops a more suitable POS tag set for the EGY. For accessing our corpus, follow the link in[1].

3 The Corpus

The corpus used in developing the tag-set schema and the morphological analyzer consists of about 527,000 words representing about 82,700 tokens. The texts were selected from different sources such as social media, books and other web articles written in EGY (From Jan 2011- June 2019). In addition, these selected texts cover more than one genre. Lack of the standard orthography form in dialectal Arabic is handled by assigning for each word the conventional EGY Lemma and the conventional stem to be close to the EGY pronunciation as much as possible regardless the way a word is typically written. To improve the speed and accuracy of the manual morphological annotation, an interface is developed that allows the annotators to concentrate on the task of providing the best morphological analysis of each word according to its context. Six skilled linguistic annotators are trained to morphologically annotate the corpus. The conventional orthography guidelines, the annotation process and the inter-annotation agreement are reviewed in (Fashwan & Alansary, 2021).

3.1 The Morphological Features

The morphological annotation process includes adding features to a word in context, including its morphology, semantics, and other aspects. In the current used corpus, each document is saved in a database where there are several features that are added to each word. These features are: Raw Word, Edited Word, EGY Conventional Lemma, MSA Lemma, Person, Gender, Number, Definiteness, Gloss, POS tags and Conventional Stem.

The EGY Conventional Lemma is detected depending on the conventional orthography guidelines discussed in (Fashwan & Alansary, 2021). It is undiacritized, in this stage, due to the difference in the pronunciation among EGY sub-dialects, which is reflected in how a word may be diacritized, but, in the next stage, it is planned to be diacritized depending on one variety.

Not all EGY Lemmas have a corresponding MSA Lemma. For example, the origin of the word /mæʕæliʃ/ 'معلش' 'sorry/excuse' is /mɑ: ʕælæjhi ʃæjʔ/ 'ما عليه شيء'. In this case, the MSA Lemma is assigned as combined 'CMB'. It is worth mentioning that not all combined words are handled in the same manner; some words are split into more than one word assigned with their suitable POS tags according to the conventional orthography guidelines. Another case is the loanwords that are adopted in EGY and do not have MSA Lemma, for example, the word /niʃæjjær/ 'نشير' 'we share'. In this case, the MSA Lemma is assigned as 'LNW'. In addition, there are some words that are used in EGY, but its linguistic source is unknow. These words may have a counterpart meaning in MSA, consequently, the MSA Lemma is assigned. For example, the counterpart MSA lemma of the word /ʔiddæ:/ 'إدى' 'give;provide' is /ʔæʕṭæ:/ 'أعطى'.

The Gender takes two values: **1) "M"** for Masculine, or **2) "F"** for Feminine. The number takes one of four values: **1) "S"** for Singular, **2) "D"** for Dual, **3) "P"** for Plural, or **3) "B"** for Broken Plural /jæmʕ ɑt-tæksi:r/ 'جمع التكسير'. The Definiteness takes one of three values: **1) "D"** for Definite, **2) "I"** for Indefinite, or **3) "E"** added through being the governor of an EDAFAH possessive construction /ʔiḍɑ:fæh/ 'إضافة'.

The following sub-section defines the tag-set design schema used in assigning the suitable pos tag for all prefixes, suffixes, and stems in the compiled corpus.

3.2 The Tag-Set

The used POS tag-schema, in this work, specifies the suitable tags and sub-tags for prefixes, suffixes and stem. The current representation treats affixes and stems as separate tokens. It resembles the BAMA's representation (Buckwalter, 2004; Habash, Eskander; Hawwari, 2012). Depending on the linguistic characteristics of EGY and general POS tag-set design criteria in (Atwell, 2008) such as mnemonic tag names, the underlying linguistic theory, classification by form or function, categorization problems, tokenization issues, ...etc., there are several decisions are considered while defining the current POS tag-set design criteria:

- Since MSA and the Colloquials share a large proportion of their lexicon (Parkinson,

[1] https://forms.gle/3cpu1orvy4ohrosB9

1981), the MSA tags are considered as much as possible.

- The tag is intended to remain readable by linguists.
- The tag is detected according to its paradigmatic forms alongside its syntagmatic functions as much as possible.
- No 'combined tags' are used. Consequently, some words are needed to be split into their component morphemes where each morpheme is tagged separately.
- Since not all tags in MSA are suitable for the linguistic characteristics in EGY, more detailed compatible tags are needed.

In what follows, the POS of stem, prefixes and suffixes of the word are detailed in addition to its attributes:

1. Stem:

Nouns: The three main classified tags of MSA, namely: Noun, Verb, and Particle are applied in the current POS tag design schema. In (Al-Dahah, 1989), nouns are classified into 21 sub-classes, and other classifications overlap. In the current design schema, the noun is classified into 16 sub-classes. Appendix A provides a description of noun types as classified in the current proposed schema with their examples. In noun POS tags, the only tag that does not follow the Traditional Arabic Grammar is the adverb of degree.

Verbs: The verbs in Arabic are of two types: inflected and non-inflected. The inflected verb is classified, depending on its voice, into two types: active and passive. While active verb is classified, depending on the tense and the morphological forms, into three groups: Perfect Verb **(PV)**, Imperfect Verb **(IV)** and Imperative Verb (RV), the passive verb is classified into two groups only: Perfect Verbs **(PV)** and Imperfect Verbs **(IV)**. The non-inflected verbs, also known as non-conjugated verbs, appear in perfect, imperfect, or imperative form. In the current design schema, the verbs are classified into four sub-classes as Appendix B shows. Three types are defined depending on the classical Arabic classification and only the Pseudo Verb tag is defined depending on the linguistic nature of EGY texts.

Particles: They are words that do not belong to nouns or verbs, but they add specific meaning to them in a sentence or connect two or more sentences. In traditional Arabic, the particles may also be classified into two groups according to their effect on nouns or verbs. The governing particles /ɑl-ħuru:f ɑl-ʕɑ:milæh/ 'الحروف العاملة' that affect the form of the following noun or verb; and the non-governing particles /ɑl-ħuru:f ɣæjr ɑl-ʕɑ:milæh/ 'الحروف غير العاملة' which do not affect the form of the following noun or verb (Al-Dahah, 1989). Appendix C indicates how particles are defined and classified in EGY.

Others (Residual): Others (residuals) include foreign words, non-Arabic words, punctuation marks, Emojis, abbreviations, numbers, in addition to words that express the speaker's reaction to a particular suggestion or sentence. E.g., /hhhh/ 'هههههه', /ti:t/ 'تيت' and /jöh/ 'يوه' as Appendix D shows.

2. Prefixes:

In the current design schema, the prefixes are defined depending on the previously described stems particles in addition to newly defined tags, as Appendix E indicates. As concerning to imperfect and imperative particles, information about verb person, gender, and number **(PGN)** of the verb subject are added since these particles are represented in prefixes for imperfect and imperative verbs only.

3. Suffixes:

Two types of suffixes tags are defined depending on the previously described tags of stem. In addition, the noun's suffix inflections are defined where the nouns may be inflected for suffixes of person, gender, definiteness, number such as 'ين' /i:n/, 'ات' /ɑ:t/, 'ة' /t/, etc. They are given the tag 'NSUF' alongside their gender, number, and definiteness **(GND)**. It is worth mentioning that the same suffix may be attached with different gender, number, or definiteness since we detect the tag according to its functions rather than its form. For example, the 'ة' /t/ 'taa marbouta' may be assigned 'NSUF_FS' as in 'مدرسة' /mædræsæ/ 'school', 'NSUF_MS' as in 'أسامة' /ʔusɑ:mæ/ 'Osama', 'NSUF_MB' 'رجالة' /riggɑ:læ/ 'men;people', etc. In case the noun is not inflected for suffix as in 'ولد' /wælæd/, a word is given 'null/NSUF' in POS annotation alongside its stem's **(GND)**.

The verb inflections are represented in suffixes for all verb tenses and information about verb person, gender, and number **(PGN)** of the verb subject are added.

Since the case endings are dropped out in EGY writing except the case morpheme 'ا' /ʔælif ɑttænwi:n/ 'ألف التنوين' 'Alif for nunnation' that may be written in some words, for example, /ʃukræn/ 'شكرا' 'thanks', /giddæn/ 'جدا' 'very much', and /mæsælæn/ 'مثلا' 'for example', there is a need to add a tag that represents this information, although it is a syntactic rather than morphological. Consequently, the tag 'CASE' is added to the previous enclitic tags. For more details about used suffixes in the current POS tag-set schema, check as Appendix F.

3.3 Corpus Annotation Current State

As a first step, about 318,940 words are annotated morphologically. These annotated words are the milestone for the automatic extraction of the morphological lexicons and the compatibility tables used for developing the proposed morphological analyzer. They are also planned to be used to extend the annotation to the remaining words of the EGY corpus, automatically. Table 1 shows the frequencies of POS tags in the currently annotated corpus. After the residuals that are annotated in the whole corpus data, the most frequent tags in the corpus are the nominals (NOU, NOU_NUM, NOU_SUP, and NOU_PRP).

Tag	Frequency
Others (Residuals)	72,330
Nouns (NOU, NOU_NUM, NOU_SUP and NOU_PRP)	81,981
Prepositions (PRP)	33,345
Pronouns (PRN, PRN_DEM and PRN_REL)	29,880
Verbs (VER_ACT, VER_PSV, VER_DFC and VER_SUD)	24,658
Other Particles (PRT_NEG, PRT_FUT, PRT_VER, PRT_INT, PRT_VOC, PRT_AUG, PRT_EXC and PRT_EMP)	18,629
Adverbs (ADV_PLC, ADV_TIM, ADV_TPL and ADV_DGR)	15,453
Adjectives (ADJ, ADJ_SUP and ADJ_NOM)	13,790
Conjunctions (CNJ and CNJ_SUB)	9,659
Interrogative Pronouns (PRN_INT)	4,847

Table 1: POS Tag Frequencies.

The annotated data contains about 12,100 unique conventional EGY lemmas representing about 18,400 MSA lemmas. Each EGY lemma is associated with different stems and each stem is associated with their different tags and conventional stems according to their contexts.

4 The Morphological Analyzer

EGY Arabic words are rarely written with diacritic marks; consequently, they may have many morphological analyses, and the number of these analyses differs from one word to another. Since the morphological analyzer deals with words out of their contexts, it should be able to produce all possible analyses of each form, identify the part-of-speech of each analysis solution of the word (i.e., noun, verb, and particle) and identify the morphological features (i.e., gender, number, time, and person). It is not an easy task to capture all analysis solutions of each word, but the annotated corpora one of the most important resources that can be helpful in detecting these solutions depending on the different contexts of the same word.

We follow a concatenative lexicon-driven approach for the annotation of our morphological corpus. The concatenation can be defined as a sequence of prefix(es), stem and suffix(es) or as a sequence of proclitic(s), word form and enclitic(s), where the morphological segments are recognized and processed as part of the annotation process. We adopt the former scheme, where the plan is to allow for the conversion between the two in our morphological analyzer.

The focus in this paper is on the prefix(es), stem and suffix(es) representation. Our approach resembles the adopted one in Buckwalter Version 2.0 (Buckwalter, 2004) who uses a simple prefix-stem-suffix representation where the stem is used as the base form and morphotactics and orthographic rules are built directly into the lexicon itself instead of being specified in terms of general rules that interact to realize the output. It has three components: the lexicon, the compatibility tables, and the analysis engine.

4.1 Extracting the Morphological Lexicons and Compatibility Tables

These lexicons need to meet certain specifications such as high coverage, high level of quality, directly reusable in NLP tools, and freely available to potential users (Sawalha, 2011). The morphological lexicons are essential for generating all possible combinations of morphemes. The wrong combinations of morphemes of lexicons are the major problem of generation. Consequently, the compatibility tables are needed for filtering out these wrong combinations.

The unique solutions of the morphologically annotated words in our corpus are used to automatically generate the morphological lexicons: the prefixes lexicon (dictPrefixes), the stems lexicon (dictStems), the suffixes lexicon (dictSuffixes) and the out of vocabulary (OOV) lexicon (dictOOV). In addition, the compatibility tables combAC, combAC and combBC are extracted to help in obtaining the valid concatenations among the different morphological categories of Prefixes, Stem and Suffixes lexicons.

For extracting these lexicons and the compatibility tables, we start with the unique annotated solutions in our corpus as a combination of (EGY lemma, MSA Lemma, conventional stem, [prefix+stem+suffix] and features). Figure 1 shows the process for extracting the features needed for building the lexicons from these solutions.

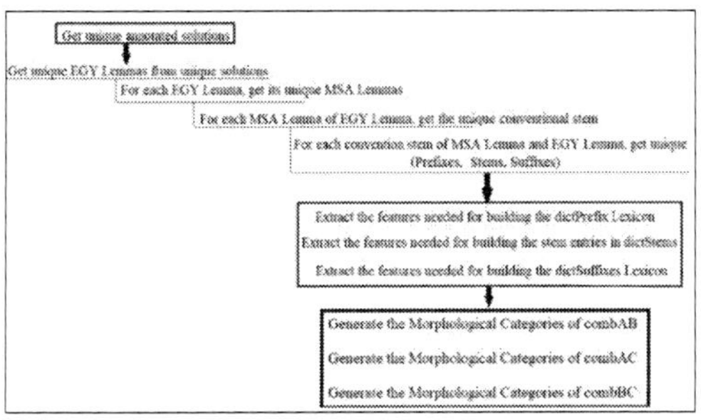

Figure 1: Lexicons and Compatibility Tables Extraction Process.

The extracted information in each Lexicon are as follows:

1. **Stems Lexicon (dictStem)**

In this lexicon, one of three keys appears at the beginning of each line to represent a specific morphological feature while parsing the stems lexicon. These keys are as follows:

- **';; '**: what follows this key represents the conventional EGY lemma for the subsequent lines till the next ';; ' key.
- **';;- '**: what follows this key represents the MSA diacritized lemma for the subsequent lines till the next ';;- ' key. The same EGY lemma may have a different MSA lemma due to the different diacritization of the MSA lemma.
- **';;-- '**: it is the default key for representing the stem entry and its conventional orthography. If it is the only written key, then the stem entry, the output stem, and the conventional stem are the same. If there are other keys found within the line after it, this means that there are more details while handling the stem and its conventional orthography. This helps in handling many processes such as transformation, omission, and assimilation that occur for the analyzed words. For Example, the '^' key may appear within the line after ';;-- ' key, then the word before it may represent different morphological information. For example, it could represent a stem's morpho-phonological changes due to the assimilation when the word is attached to an enclitic: (;;-عل^على /ʕæl^ʕælæ:/ 'on;above') as in the word 'عليّ' /ʕælæj+jæ/ 'on me' where the stem ends with /æ:/ 'ى' and the enclitic begins with /j/ 'ي', which leads to an assimilation process where the two conceding /æ:j/ 'يى' are transformed to /jj/ 'يّ'.
- When none of the previous keys appear at the beginning of the input line, a line is parsed as it consists of three tab-delimited fields: **1)** the morphological category that controls the compatibility of prefixes-stem-suffixes, **2)** the English gloss(es) of stem in addition to information about the number, gender, and definiteness (in case the stem is a noun, adjective or adverb), or the person of the stem (in case of verbs only and pronouns) and **3)** the selective POS tags that appear in the analysis output. The morphological category of each stem is extracted automatically depending on the suffixes that are attached to each solution. For example, the "N-ap-I" category refers to the indefinite nouns that are attached to "ة/NSUF_(GN)I" as in "مدرسة" /mædræsæ/ 'school' and the "IV-y-0" category refers to the "ي/IVSUF_2F" suffix that is not attached to another suffix as in "تبتسمي" /ti-btisim+i:/ 'you + smile'.

2. **Prefixes and Suffixes Lexicons (dictPrefixes) and (dictSuffixes)**

In these lexicons, all used prefixes and suffixes of the annotated words are listed. They consist of four tab-delimited fields: **1)** the prefix/suffix entry in Arabic orthography without any diacritics, **2)** the morphological category that controls the compatibility of prefixes-stems-suffixes, **3)** the English gloss(es) of each prefix/suffix part in the prefix/suffix entry, and **4)** the selective POS tags that appear in the analysis output. The morphological category of each prefix in the corpus is detected automatically depending on the prefixes' parts in addition to the tag of the stem that is attached to them. For example, the 'IVPrf-wa-bi-n' category represents the 'و/CNJ' prefix in addition to progressive particle 'ب/PRT_PRG' and 1st person plural prefix that are attached to Imperfect Verbs 'ن/IVPRF_1P' as in 'وبنرسم' /wibni-rsim/ 'and + we + draw;trace;sketch'. The morphological category of each suffix in the corpus is detected automatically depending on the suffixes' parts in addition to the tag of the stem that is attached to them. For example, the 'ADSuf-nl-h' category represents the 3rd person pronouns that may be attached to the adverbs as in 'بينه' /beɪn+uh/ 'between;among + him'.

3. **Out of Vocabulary Lexicon (dictOOV):**

This lexicon is created to be used in predicting the OOV words. It consists of three tab-delimited fields: **1)** the unique stem patterns, **2)** the morphological category that controls the compatibility of prefixes-stems-suffixes and **3)** the selective POS tags that appear in the analysis output. For detecting the stem patten of each stem, the consonants are represented by the placeholder "-", while weak letters 'حروف العلة' /ħuru:f ɑl-ʕillæh/ and hamazat ('أ', 'إ', 'ؤ', 'ئ', 'ء') are kept as they are. For example, the stem pattern of 'اعمل' /iʕmil/ 'do;act;make', 'اهرب' /ihrab/ 'run away' and 'اكتب' /iktib/ '' is '---ا'.

4. **The Compatibility Tables**

The compatibility table (combAB) lists the two compatible morphological categories of Prefixes and Stems. It consists of two tab-delimited fields: **1)** Prefix Morphological Category and **2)** Stem Morphological Category that appear together in the annotated data. The compatibility table (combAC) lists the two compatible morphological categories of Prefixes and Suffixes. It consists of two tab-delimited fields: **1)** Prefix Morphological Category and **2)** Suffix Morphological Category that appear together in the annotated data. The compatibility table (combBC) lists the two compatible morphological categories of Stems and Suffixes. It consists of two tab-delimited fields: **1)** Stem Morphological Category and **2)** Suffix Morphological Category that appear together in the annotated data. The morphological categories that are not listed in the compatibility tables are simply incompatible.

4.2 The Analyzer

The current morphological analyzer goes through four main steps to get all possible morphological analyses of the input words:

1) Text Preprocessing and Lexicons Parsing: in this step, it is important to detect the word boundaries of the input text since it is essential step for the word segmentation process. In addition, the 'dictPrefixes' and 'dictSuffixes' lexicons are parsed to get the four tab-delimited fields in dictionaries where the prefix/suffix entry is the default key for these dictionaries. Each line in 'dictStems' lexicon is parsed in different manner depending on the key used at the beginning of each line as mentioned above (section 4.1). The conventional stem in this lexicon is handled to get all possible stem variations of the input word. For example, the stem variations ('إلّي', 'إلي', 'إلى', 'آلى', 'ألي', 'ألى', ...etc.) are generated automatically from the conventional stem 'إلى' /ʔilæ:/ 'to;towards' to avoid writing all these expected stem variations in the lexicon. The stem variations that cannot be predicted automatically are added to the 'dictStems' lexicon with their suitable morphological category.

2) Word Segmentations and Compatibility Check: For suggesting different segmentations of the same word, the dictionaries of the parsed lexicons are used. The three morphological categories of the three components are checked in the compatibly tables as figure 2 shows. If they are found together, then they are compatible, and this is a valid solution. Else, they are incompatible, and this is not valid solution.

3) Dealing with OOV Words: For handling the OOV words, the analyzer tries, first, to split the input word depending on its beginning and end. For Example, it splits OOV word that begin with /jɑ:/ 'يا' since attaching it to another word is a common spelling mistake in EGY writings as in 'يارب' /jɑ: ræbb/ 'Oh, Lord' and 'ياسلام' /jɑ: sælɑ:m/ 'really'. To keep the original word and the split words in output analysis, another feature is added; normalized word 'norm_word'. All possible solutions for each part are detected regardless of the solutions of the two parts are compatible according to their context or not. In case there is no rule for splitting the OOV word or it is split but only one of its parts has analysis solution, the analyzer tries to detect the prefix and the suffix of the input word. If they are predicted, the stem is converted to its corresponding pattern as mentioned above. If the stem pattern is found in the 'dictOOV', the morphological categories of prefix, suffix, and the suggested stem pattern are checked in the compatibly tables. If they are found together, then they are compatible, and this is a valid solution, but no lemma or gloss are detected.

4) Output Solutions: After getting all possible solutions of the input text for all words and handling the OOV words, the output valid solutions are saved in XML format.

5 The Current Status

The extracted morphological stem lexicon contains 39K stems corresponding to about 12,100 EGY Lemmas and about 18,400 MSA lemmas. The extracted prefixes and suffixes lexicons contain

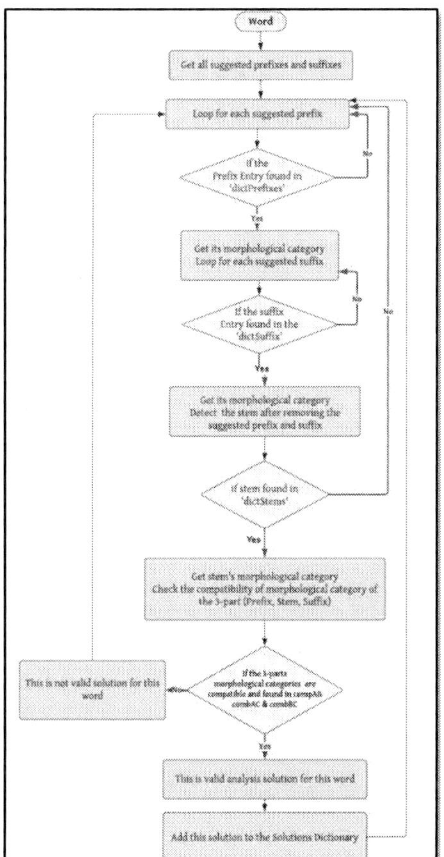

Figure 2: Workflow for Suggesting Words' Segmentations and Get Valid Solutions.

324 complex prefixes and 661 complex suffixes (unique undiacritized form and POS tag combinations). Since the annotation process of our corpus is still in progress, the covered stems, prefixes, suffixes and lemmas are still limited compared to CALIMA analyzer (Habash, Eskander, & Hawwari, 2012) that has 100K stems corresponding to 36K lemmas in addition to 2,421 complex prefixes and 1,179 complex suffixes (unique diacritized form and POS tag combinations).

5.1 Coverage Evaluation

We tested our analyzer against a sample of our manually annotated EGY corpus of 5,000 words which was not used as part of its development, i.e., a completely blind test. This evaluation is a POS recall evaluation. It is not about selecting the correct POS answer in context. We do not consider whether the EGY lemma or the MSA Lemma choice are correct or not. We compare our system results with CALIMA coverage. The results are reported in Table 2. The 'Correct Answer' column indicates the percentage of the test words whose correct analysis in context appears among the analyses returned by the analyzer. The 'No Correct Answer' column presents the percentage of time one or more analyses are returned, but none matching the correct answer. The 'No Analysis' column indicates the percentage of words returning no analyses.

	Correct Answer	**No Correct Answer**	**OOV**
Our System	66.9%	10.3%	22.8%
CLIMA	82.1%	9.6%	8.3%

Table 2: Comparing Results with CALIMA.

6 Conclusion and Future Work

The POS tag-set schema is developed and about 318,940 words are morphologically annotated, and the morphological lexicons and the compatibility tables are automatically extracted. The analyzer output is compared to CALIMA output. We plan to make this tool public so it can be used by other people working on EGY NLP tasks, from annotating corpora to building morphological disambiguation tools. To enhance our results, we plan to continue improving the coverage of our analyzer using a variety of methods. First, we are investigating techniques to automatically fill in the tag categories gaps using information from multiple entries in our annotated corpus belonging to different lemmas that share similar characteristics, e.g., hollow verbs. Another direction is to increase the stems entries by checking stems, in BAMA's stems lexicon, for those words that are common between EGY and MSA and adapting their morphological category to be more suitable for EGY. Furthermore, we plan to add additional features such as the diacritized EGY lemmas and the diacritized stems.

References

Abo Bakr, H. A., Shaalan, K., & Ziedan, I. (2008). A hybrid approach for converting written Egyptian colloquial dialect into diacritized Arabic. *In The 6th international conference on informatics and systems, infos2008.* Cairo. Retrieved 7 27, 2018, from https://www.researchgate.net/profile/Khaled_Shaalan/publication/206006074_A_Hybrid_Approach_for_Converting_Written_Egyptian_Colloquial_Dialect_into_Diacritized_Arabic/links/0912f505a298ee3308000000.pdf

Al Ameri, S. S., & Shoufan, A. (2021). Building Lexical Resources for Dialectical Arabic. In *Natural Language Processing for Global and Local Business* (pp. 332-364). IGI Global.

Al-Dahah, A. (1989). *A Dictionary of Arabic Grammer in Charts and Tables " معجم قواعد اللغة العربية في جداول ولوحات".* Beirut, Lebanon: Librairie du Liban publisher.

Alqrainy, S. (2008). A morphological-syntactical analysis approach for Arabic textual tagging. Leicester, UK: De Montfort University. Retrieved 11 8, 2021

Al-Sabbagh, R., & Girju, R. (2010). Mining the Web for the Induction of a Dialectical Arabic Lexicon. *In LREC.* Retrieved 6 23, 2019, from https://www.researchgate.net/profile/Rania_Al-Sabbagh/publication/220746429_Mining_the_Web_for_the_Induction_of_a_Dialectical_Arabic_Lexicon/links/02e7e51597e45d9c5d000000.pdf

Al-Sabbagh, R., & Girju, R. (2012). YADAC: Yet another Dialectal Arabic Corpus. *In LREC*, (pp. 2882-2889). Retrieved 6 23, 2019, from https://pdfs.semanticscholar.org/67ad/6967eb602c7416e8aaa138bb4c45a23b4e07.pdf

Atwell, E. (2008). Development of tag sets part-of-speech tagging. In A. Ludeling, & M. Kyto (Eds.), *Handbook, Corpus Linguistics: An International* (Vol. 1, pp. 501 - 526). Walter de Gruyter. Retrieved 7 5, 2019, from https://eprints.whiterose.ac.uk/81781/1/DevelopmentTagSetPOSTagging.pdf

Bouamor, H, Habash, N., Salameh, M., Zaghouani, W., Rambow, O., Abdulrahim, D., Obeid, O., Khalifa, S., Eryani, F., Erdmann, A., & Oflazer, K. (2018). The MADAR Arabic Dialect Corpus and Lexicon. *In Proceedings of the 11th International Conference on Language Resources and Evaluation.* Retrieved 8 7, 2018, from http://www.lrec-conf.org/proceedings/lrec2018/pdf/351.pdf

Buckwalter, T. (2004). *Buckwalter Arabic Morphological Analyzer Version 2.0.* Linguistic Data Consortium, University of Pennsylvania, 2004. LDC Catalog No.: LDC2004L02. Retrieved 11 20, 2019, from https://catalog.ldc.upenn.edu/LDC2004L02

Darwish, K., Mubarak, H., Abdelali, A., Eldesouki, M., Samih, Y., Alharbi, R., Attia, M., Magdy, W., & Kallmeyer, L. (2018). Multi-Dialect Arabic POS Tagging: A CRF Approach. *In Proceedings of the Eleventh International Conference on Language Resources and Evaluation (LREC.* Retrieved 6 19, 2019, from https://www.aclweb.org/anthology/L18-1015

Diab, M., Al-Badrashiny, M., Aminian, M., Attia, M., Dasigi, P., Elfardy, H., Eskander, E., Nizar, H., Hawwari, A., & Salloum, W. (2014). Tharwa: A Large Scale Dialectal Arabic-Standard Arabic-English Lexicon. *In LREC*, (pp. 3782-3789). Retrieved 7 28, 2018, from https://www.researchgate.net/profile/Mohammed_Attia2/publication/305489865_Tharwa_A_Large_Scale_Dialectal_Arabic-Standard_Arabic-English_Lexicon/links/582f14bb08ae138f1c034db8.pdf

Eldesouki, M., Samih, Y., Abdelali, A., Attia, M., Mubarak, H., Darwish, K., & Laura, K. (2017). Arabic multi-dialect segmentation: bi-LSTM-CRF vs. SVM. Retrieved 9 1, 2022, from https://arxiv.org/pdf/1708.05891.pdf

Eskander, R., Habash, N., & Rambow, O. (2013). Automatic Extraction of Morphological Lexicons from Morphologically Annotated Corpora. *In Proceedings of the 2013 conference on empirical methods in natural language processing*, (pp. 1032-

1043). Retrieved 7 4, 2019, from https://www.aclweb.org/anthology/D13-1105

Fashwan, A., & Alansary, S. (2021). A Morphologically Annotated Corpus and a Morphological Analyzer for Egyptian Arabic. Procedia Computer Science. *189*, pp. 203-210.

Habash, N. (2010). Introduction to Arabic natural language processing. *Synthesis Lectures on Human Language Technologies Journal, Vol. 3*, pp. 1-187.

Habash, N., & Rambow, O. (2005). Arabic Tokenization, Part-of-Speech Tagging and Morphological Disambiguation in One Fell Swoop. *In Proceedings of the 43rd annual meeting of the association for computational linguistics (ACL'05)*, (pp. 573-580). Retrieved 7 4, 2019, from https://www.aclweb.org/anthology/P05-1071

Habash, N., & Rambow, O. (2006). MAGEAD: A Morphological Analyzer and Generator for the Arabic Dialects. *In Proceedings of the 21st International Conference on Computational Linguistics and 44th Annual Meeting of the Association for Computational Linguistics*, (pp. 681-688). Retrieved 6 24, 2019, from https://www.aclweb.org/anthology/P06-1086

Habash, N., Diab, M., & Rambow, O. (2012). Conventional Orthography for Dialectal Arabic. *In LREC*, (pp. 711-718). Retrieved 6 19, 2019, from http://www.lrec-conf.org/proceedings/lrec2012/pdf/579_Paper.pdf

Habash, N., Eryani, F., Khalifa, S., Rambow, O., Abdulrahim, D., Erdmann, A., . . . Saddiki, H. (2018). Unified guidelines and resources for Arabic dialect orthography., (pp. In Proceedings of the Eleventh International Conference on Language Resources and Evaluation (LREC-2018)). Retrieved 6 19, 2019, from https://www.aclweb.org/anthology/L18-1574

Habash, N., Eskander, R., & Hawwari, A. (2012). A morphological Analyzer for Egyptian Arabic. *In Proceedings of the twelfth meeting of the special interest group on computational morphology and phonology* (pp. 1-9). Association for Computational Linguistics. Retrieved 7 29, 2018, from https://aclanthology.org/W12-2301.pdf

Habash, N., Marzouk, R., Khairallah, C., & Khalifa, S. (2022). Morphotactic Modeling in an Open-source Multi-dialectal Arabic Morphological Analyzer and Generator. *In Proceedings of the 19th SIGMORPHON Workshop on Computational Research in Phonetics, Phonology, and Morphology*, (pp. 92-102). Retrieved 7 1, 2022, from https://aclanthology.org/2022.sigmorphon-1.10.pdf

Habash, N., Roth, R., Rambow, O., Eskander, R., & Tomeh, N. (2013). Morphological analysis and disambiguation for dialectal Arabic. *In Proceedings of the 2013 Conference of the North American Chapter of the Association for Computational Linguistics: Human Language Technologies*, (pp. 426-432). Retrieved 7 3, 2019, from https://www.aclweb.org/anthology/N13-1044

Harrat, S., Meftouh, K., & Smaïli, K. (2017). Machine translation for Arabic dialects (survey). *Information Processing and Management.* Retrieved 7 28, 2018, from https://www.researchgate.net/profile/Kamel_Smaili/publication/319423437_Machine_translation_for_Arabic_dialects_survey/links/5a0a32f0a6fdcc2736dea63b/Machine-translation-for-Arabic-dialects-survey.pdf

Chang, J. Z., & Chang, J. S. (2012). Word root finder: a morphological segmentor based on CRF. *Proceedings of COLING 2012: Demonstration Papers.* Retrieved from 2012: https://aclanthology.org/C12-3007.pdf

Khalifa, S., Habash, N., Eryani, F., Obeid, O., Abdulrahim, D., & Al Kaabi, M. (2018). A morphologically annotated corpus of Emirati Arabic. *In Proceedings of the eleventh international conference on language resources and evaluation (LREC 2018).* Retrieved 5 29, 2021, from https://aclanthology.org/L18-1607.pdf

Khoja, S. (2003). APT: An automatic arabic part-of-speech tagger. *Doctoral dissertation.* Lancaster University. Retrieved 11 8, 2021

Khoja, S., Garside, R., & Knowles, G. (2001). An Arabic tagset for the morphosyntactic tagging of Arabic. *Doctoral dissertation, 13*, . Lancaster University (UK). Retrieved 8 11, 2021

Kilany, H., Gadalla, H., Arram, H., Yacoub, A., El-Habashi, A., & McLemore, C. (2002). *Egyptian Colloquial Arabic Lexicon.* LDC catalog number LDC99L22. Retrieved 8 5, 2019, from https://catalog.ldc.upenn.edu/LDC99L22

Maamouri, M., & Bies, A. (2004). Developing an Arabic treebank: Methods, guidelines, procedures, and tools. *In Proceedings of the Workshop on Computational Approaches to Arabic Script-based languages*, (pp. 2-9). Retrieved 11 8, 2021, from https://aclanthology.org/W04-1602.pdf

Maamouri, M., Bies, A., Buckwalter, T., Diab, M. T., Habash, N., Rambow, O., & Tabessi, D. (2006). Developing and Using a Pilot Dialectal Arabic Treebank. *In LREC*, (pp. 443-448). Retrieved 8 4, 2018, from https://www.ldc.upenn.edu/sites/www.ldc.upenn.edu/files/lrec2006-developing-using-dialectal-arabic-treebank.pdf

Maamouri, M., Bies, A., Krouna, S., Gaddeche, F., & Bouziri, B. . (2009). *Penn Arabic treebank guidelines.* Linguistic Data Consortium.

Maamouri, M., Bies, A., Kulick, S., Ciul, M., Habash, N., & Eskander, R. (2014). Developing an Egyptian Arabic Treebank: Impact of Dialectal Morphology on Annotation and Tool Development. *LREC*, (pp. 2348-2354). Retrieved 6 1, 2021, from http://www.lrec-conf.org/proceedings/lrec2014/pdf/1145_Paper.pdf

Maamouri, M., Krouna, S., Tabessi, D., Hamrouni, N., & Habash, N. (2012). *Arabic Treebanking Egyptian Arabic (ARZ) Morphological (ARZGM) Version 1.21 (With Permession).* Retrieved 08 21, 2022, from https://www.researchgate.net/publication/331315455_Egyptian_Arabic_Morphological_Annotation_Guidelines/stats

Mohamed, E., Mohit, B., & Oflazer, K. (2012). Annotating and Learning Morphological Segmentation of Egyptian Colloquial Arabic. *In LREC*, (pp. 873-877). Retrieved 7 4, 2019, from http://nlp.qatar.cmu.edu/papers/465_Paper.pdf

Parkinson, D. B. (1981). VSO to SVO in Modern Standard Arabic: A study in diglossia syntax. In *al-'Arabiyya* (Vol. 14, pp. 24-37). Georgetown University Press. Retrieved 5 15, 2021

Salloum, W., & Habash, N. (2011). Dialectal to standard Arabic paraphrasing to improve Arabic-English statistical machine translation. *In Proceedings of the first workshop on algorithms and resources for modelling of dialects and language varieties* (pp. 10-21). Association for Computational Linguistics. Retrieved 7 26, 2018, from http://delivery.acm.org/10.1145/2150000/2140535/p10-salloum.pdf?ip=196.204.161.40&id=2140535&acc=OPEN&key=4D4702B0C3E38B35%2E4D4702B0C3E38B35%2E4D4702B0C3E38B35%2E6D218144511F3437&__acm__=1560078805_b75acb510a9652c29cada891c1ec3bd2

Salloum, W., & Habash, N. (2014). ADAM: Analyzer for Dialectal Arabic Morphology. *Journal of King Saud University-Computer and Information Sciences, 26(4)*, 372-378. Retrieved 7 30, 2018, from https://www.sciencedirect.com/science/article/pii/S1319157814000342

Samih, Y., & Kallmeyer, L. (2017). Dialectal Arabic Processing Using Deep Learning. *Doctoral dissertation, Ph. D. thesis, Heinrich-Heine-Universität Düsseldorf, Düsseldorf.* Germany. Retrieved 8 5, 2018, from https://docserv.uni-duesseldorf.de/servlets/DerivateServlet/Derivate-47492/Dissertation_younes_samih.pdf

Sawalha, M. S. (2011). *Open-source resources and standards for Arabic word structure analysis: Fine grained morphological analysis of Arabic text corpora.* University of Leeds.

Shaalan, K., Bakr, H., & Ziedan, I. (2007). Transferring egyptian colloquial dialect into modern standard arabic. *In International Conference on Recent Advances in Natural Language Processing (RANLP–2007)*, (pp. 525-529). Borovets, Bulgaria. Retrieved 6 10, 2019, from http://www.linguisticsnetwork.com/wp-content/uploads/Transferring-Egyptian-Colloquial-Dialect-into-Modern-Standard-Arabic-2.compressed.pdf

Zalmout, N., Erdmann, A., & Habash, N. (2018). Noise-Robust Morphological Disambiguation for Dialectal Arabic. *In Proceedings of the 2018 Conference of the North American Chapter of the Association for Computational Linguistics: Human Language Technologies, (Long Papers), Volume 1* , pp. 953-964. Retrieved 7 4, 2019, from https://www.aclweb.org/anthology/N18-1087

A Nouns

Noun Sub Classes	Description and Example
Noun 'الاسم' /ɑl-ism/ **(NOU)**	It is the common noun that refers to entities and concepts that have a more general reference than sub-tags. والولد راح مدرسته مع مامته في أول يوم وكل المدرسين رحبوا بيه. wil-wælæd rɑ:ħ mædræstu mæʕæ mɑ:mtu fi: ʔæwwil jöm wi-kull ɑl-mudarrisi:n ræħæbu: bi:h
Proper Noun 'اسم العلم' /ism ɑl-ʕælæm/ **(NOU_PRP)**	It is a noun that has a unique referential meaning in a context that is mutually exclusive with other entities. It refers to names of people, geographical entities, months, and acronyms. محمد هو اللي قالي الكلام ده أول شهر مارس كدة وكنا وقتها في إسكندرية. mæħæmmæd huwwæ illi: ʔɑ:lli: ɑl-kælɑ:m dæh fi: ʔæwwil ʃæhr mɑ:ris kidæ wi-kunnɑ: wæʔtæhæ fi: ʔiskindirijjæ
Numeral Noun 'اسم العدد' /ism ɑl-ʕædæd/ **(NOU_NUM)**	It is a noun that indicates the quantity and order of countable nouns by transferring the numbers into the correct form of Arabic words. الأهلي غلب الزمالك واحد/صفر. ɑl-ʔæhli: ɣælæb ɑz-zæmɑ:lik wɑ:ħid/ṣifr
Adjective 'الصفة' /ɑṣ-ṣifæ/ **(ADJ)**	It is a noun that describes or clarifies the meaning of the immediately preceding noun. البنت الشاطرة تسمع كلام مامتها. ɑl-bint ɑʃ-ʃɑ:træ tismæʕ kælɑ:m mɑ:mithɑ:
Numeral Adjective 'الصفة العدد' /ɑṣ-ṣifæ ɑl-ʕædæd/ **(ADJ_NUM)**	It is an adjective that indicates the quantity and order of countable nouns by transferring the numbers into the correct form of Arabic words. الحكاية الحادية عشر. ɑl-ħikɑ:jæh ɑl-ħɑ:dijætæ ʕæʃær
Nominal Adjective 'الصفة الاسمية' /ɑṣ-ṣifæ ɑl-ismijjæ/ **(ADJ_NOM)**	It is a noun that describes or clarifies the meaning of a noun, but it appears as the main predicate of a nominal phrase in the sentence. كانت حقيقي جميلة وعمري ما شفت بنت في أخلاقها أبدا. kɑ:nit ħæʔi:ʔi: gæmi:læ wi-ʕumri: mɑ: ʃuft bint fi: ʔæχlɑ:ʔhɑ:
Superlative Adjective 'صفة تفضيل' /ṣifæt tæfḍi:l/ **(ADJ_SUP)**	It is a noun that is used for the comparative and superlative when comparing persons or things. It describes the immediately preceding noun. الحاجة الأحلى اللي تعملها إنك تسمع الكلام وإنت ساكت. ɑl-ħɑ:gæ ɑl-ʔæħlæ: illi: tiʕmilhɑ: ʔinnak tismæʕ ɑl-kælɑ:m wi-ʔintæ sɑ:kit
Superlative Noun 'اسم تفضيل' /ism tæfḍi:l/ **(NOU_SUP)**	It is a noun that is used for the comparative and superlative when comparing persons or things, but it appears as the main predicate of a nominal phrase in the sentence. والله دي كانت أجمل حاجة حصلتلي في حياتي. wɑl-læhi: di: kɑ:nt ʔægmæl ħɑ:gæ ħæṣælitli: fi: ħæjɑ:ti:
Adverb of Place 'اسم المكان' /ism ɑl-mækɑ:n/ **(ADV_PLC)**	It is a noun that indicates where the action of a verb is or was carried out. قعد جوة البيت طول اليوم. ʔæʕæd juwwæ ɑl-beɪt ṭu:l ɑl-jöm

Noun Sub Classes	Description and Example
Adverb of Time 'اسم الزمان' /ism ɑz-zæmɑ:n/ **(ADV_TIM)**	It is a noun that indicates when the action of a verb happened. It expresses a point in time, and it can also indicates how long something lasted or lasts. والله لسه شايفه إمبارح ومش عارف حقدر أشوفه تاني بكرة ولا لأ. wɑl-læhi: lissæ ʃɑ:jfuh ʔimbɑ:riħ wi-miʃ ʕɑ:rif ħæ-ʔdær ʔæʃu:fuh tɑ:ni: bukræ wællæ læʔ
Adverb of both Time and Place 'اسم زمان ومكان' /ism mækɑ:n wɑ-zæmɑ:n/ **(ADV_TPL)**	It is a noun that could be used as an adverb of time or place according to its context. كان رايح عند السوبر ماركت يجيب حاجات للبيت. kɑ:n rɑ:jiħ ʕænd ɑs-su:bær mɑ:rkit jigi:b ħɑ:gɑ:t lil-beɪt وعند اللحظة دي الوضع اتقلب خالص. wi-ʕænd ɑl-læħzˤæ di: ɑl-wæḍʕ itʔælæb ʁɑ:liʂ
Adverb of Manner 'حال' /ħɑ:l/ **(ADV_MNN)**	It is a noun that describes the circumstances under which an action takes place. كنت جاية تعبانة قوي ومن كتر التعب قعدت سرحانة. kunt gɑ:jjæ tæʕbɑ:næ ʔæwi: wi-min kutr ɑt-tæʕæb ʔæʕædt sarħɑ:næ
Adverb of Degree 'ظرف الحال أو درجة الحال' /zˤærf ɑl-ħɑ:l ʔæw dærægæt ɑl-ħɑ:l/ **(ADV_DGR)**	It is a noun that indicates the intensity of a verb, adjective, or another adverb. It is not found in MSA, but it is added to EGY in the current tag-set schema. أنا حقيقي بحبك جدا. ʔænɑ: ħæʔi:ʔi: bæħibbæk jiddæn كان نفسي أسمع منك كلمة واحدة بس kɑ:n nifsi: ʔæsmæʕ minnæk kilmæ wɑ:ħæ bæs
Pronoun 'الضمير' /ɑḍ-ḍæmi:r/ **(PRN)**	It is a word that acts as the subject of a sentence instead of a noun. The pronouns in this category are the disconnected pronouns. The pronouns in this category are: أنا ʔænɑ:, إحنا ʔiħnɑ:, إنت ʔintæ, إنتي ʔinti:, هو huwwæ, هي hijjæ, هما hummɑ:, and إنتو ʔintu:
Relative Pronoun 'الاسم الموصول' /ɑl-ism ɑl-mæwʂu:l/ **(PRN_DEM)**	It is a noun that introduces relative clauses. It connects two sentences to give a full meaning. الكلام اللي قولناه كان صح. ɑl-kælɑ:m illi: ʔulnɑ:h kɑ:n ʂæħħ
Demonstrative Pronoun 'اسم الإشارة' /ism ɑl- ʔiʃɑ:ræ/ **(PRN_REL)**	It is a noun that is used for proximal or distal reference. It is indicated by a tangible sign a person, an animal, a thing, or a place. اللي قولته ده مش عايزة أسمعه تاني والناس دول تنساهم خالص. illi: ʔultu: dæh miʃ ʕæjzæ ʔæsmæʕu: tɑ:ni: win-nɑ:s döl tinsɑ:hum ʁɑ:liʂ
Interrogative Pronouns 'اسم الاستفهام' /ism ɑl- istifhɑ:m/ **(PRN_INT)**	It is a noun that introduces a question about something or an action. أنا مش عارفة ده حصل إزاي وإمتى ومين الناس دول أصلا؟ ʔænɑ: miʃ ʕɑ:rfæ dæh ħæʂæl ʔizzɑ:j wi-ʔimtæ: wi-mi:n ɑn-nɑ:s döl ʔæʂlæn

B Verbs

Verb Sub Classes	Description and Example
Active Verb 'الفعل المبني للمعلوم' /ɑl-fiʕl ɑl-mæbni: lil-mæʕlu:m/ **(VER_ACT:<tense>)**	It indicates the subject of the verb is doing the action. **VER_ACT:PV** أنا سمعت الكلام ده من حد قريب ʔæna: sæmæʕt al-kælɑ:m dæh min ħædd ʔuræjjib **VER_ACT:IV** حسن هو اللي بيعمل كدة دايما ħæsæn huwwæ illi: bi-jiʕmil kidæ dɑ:jmæn **VER_ACT:RV** بالله عليك قول الحق bil-læh ʕæli:k ʔu:l ɑl-ħæʔ
Passive Verb 'الفعل المبني للمجهول' /ɑl-fiʕl ɑl-mæbni: lil-mæghu:l/ **(VER_PSV:<tense>)**	It indicates the subject of the verb undergoes the action rather than doing it. It is rarely used in EGY where the pattern /ʔinfæʕæl/ 'انفعل' or /ʔitfæʕʕæl/ 'اتفعل' is used instead. **VER_PSV:IV** البلدي يوكل ɑl-bælædi: ju:kæl **VER_PSV:PV** حاجة كدة على ما قسم ħɑ:gæ kidæ ʕælæ: mɑ: ʔusim Nevertheless, some passive verbs from MSA are used in some levels of EGY, for example, the passive /qi:læ/ 'قيل' 'be said'.
Non-Conjugated Verb 'الفعل غير المتصرف' /ɑl-fiʕl ɣæjr ɑl-mutaṣærrif/, also known as frozen verb **(VER_FRZ:<tense>)**	It indicates the non-inflected verbs, also known as **frozen verbs**, that are restricted to one tense only. Whereas non-conjugated verbs in MSA may be restricted to perfect, imperfect or imperative tenses, they may be restricted, in EGY, to the perfect or imperative tenses only: **VER_FRZ:PV** والله أنا قولتله الكلام ده قبل كدة لعل وعسى يعمل حاجة wal-læhi: ʔæna: ʔultilu ɑl-kælɑ:m dæh ʔæbl kidæh læʕæl wi-ʕæsæ: jiʕmil ħægæh **VER_FRZ:RV** هات اللي معاك ده hɑ:t illi: mæʕɑ:k dæh
Pseudo Verb 'شبيه الفعل' /ʃæbi:h ɑl-fiʕl/ **(VER_SUD)**	It is a word that has the same syntactic behavior as verbs in that they take a subject and a predicate, or a sentential complement. بس بقى كدة حرام عليك bæs bæʔæ: kidæh ħærɑ:m ʕæleık معلش يا حبيبي حصل خير mæʕæliʃʃ jɑ: ħæbi:bi: ħæṣæl xeır

C Particles

Particle Sub Classes	Description and Example
Conjunction 'حرف عطف' /ħærf ʕæṭf/ **(CNJ)**	A group of particles used to connect elements of equal status in pronunciation or in meaning. مش متأكدة مين قال كدة يا محمد يا أحمد miʃ mutæʔækkidæ mi:n ʔɑ:l kidæh jɑ: mæħæmmæd jɑ: ʔæħmæd الدخول في علاقة متبعة أو مش مريحة حاجة صعبة قوي ɑd-duxu:l fi: ʕælɑ:qæ mutʕibæh ʔæw miʃ muri:ħæh ħɑ:gæ ṣæʕbæ ʔæwi:
Subordinating Conjunction 'حرف ربط' /ħærf ræbṭ/ **(CNJ_SUB)**	A group of particles is used to link two clauses in the sentence or two sentences. Some of these articles are still used in EGY: شكلها مجنونة لكنها في منتهى العقل ʃæklæhɑ: mægnu:næh lækinnæhɑ: fi: muntæhæ: ɑl-ʕæʔl Others are found but are never used as subordinating conjunction: كان أمله ينجح بس للأسف محصلش kɑ:n ʔæmælu jingæħ bæs lil-ʔæsæf mæħæṣæʃ Others are not found in traditional Arabic: عشان تخليني ذكرى في دفترك ʕæʃɑ:n tixælli:ni: zikræ: fi: dæftærik

Particle Sub Classes	Description and Example
Vocative Particle 'حرف نداء' /ħærf nidɑ:ʔ/ **(PRT_VOC)**	A group of particles is used to call or alert a person addressed. A noun preceded by a vocative article is called a vocative noun. يا حبيبتي متعمليش في نفسك كدة بالراحة شوية jɑ: ħæbi:bti: mætiʕmili:ʃ fi: næfsik kidæh bir-rɑ:ħæ ʃiwæjjæh
Preposition 'حرف جر' /ħærf gærr/ **(PRP)**	A group of particles that is used with a noun, pronoun, or noun phrase to show direction, location, or time or introduce an object. حتلاقيني هناك من بدري ħætlɑ:ʔi:ni: hinɑ:k min badri: موجود على المكتب أو في الدرج mæwgu:d ʕælæ: ɑl-mæktæb ʔæw fi: ɑd-durg
Augment Particle 'حرف زائد' /ħærf zɑ:ʔid/ **(PRT_AUG)**	A group of particles that do not affect the meaning if removed from the sentence, but it is added to denote affirmation. ما أنا جبتها لك .. مش جبتها لك mɑ: ʔænɑ: gibtæhɑ: læ-k miʃ gibtæhɑ: læk
Exceptive Particle 'حرف استثناء' /ħærf istiθnɑ:ʔ/ **(PRT_EXC)**	A group of particles used to exclude the following noun from the scope of the words before it. كله إلا كدة والله حرام kulluh ʔillɑ: kidæh wɑl-læhi: ħærɑ:m وفي الآخر محدش جه غير نورين wi-fi: ɑl-ʔɑ:ʁir mæħæddiʃ jæh ɣeɪr nu:ri:n لقيتك أرض متضمش سوى المطاريد læʔeɪtik ʔærḍ mætḍummiʃ siwæ: ɑl-mæṭɑ:ri:d
Emphatic Particle 'حرف توكيد' /ħærf tæwki:d/ **(PRT_EMP)**	A group of particles that used to put emphasis on intention. أما سيدنا النبي ربه كافيه ʔæmmɑ: si:dnɑ: ɑn-nabi: ræbbuh kɑ:fi:h
Futurity Particle 'حرف استقبال' /ħærf istiqbɑ:l/ **(PRT_FUT)**	It is a particle that modifies the verb tense from the present tense to the future. It is not usually used in EGY. قبل أي شيء سوف أسقط الدستور الحالي ʔæbl ʔæjj ʃeɪʔ sæwfæ ʔusqiṭ ɑd-dustu:r ɑl-ħɑ:li:
Negative Particle 'حرف نفي' /ħærf næfj/ **(PRT_NEG)**	A group of particles is used to negate the proposition expressed after them, or to deny its affirmation. الموضوع بوخ ومش حلو خالص كدة ɑl-mæwḍu:ʕ kidæ bæwwæx wi-miʃ ħilw xɑ:liṣ الفلم ما كنش حلو خالص ɑl-film mɑ: kænʃ ħilw xɑ:liṣ لأ مش صح læʔ miʃ ṣæħħ أنا لا عايزة أشوفك ولا أسمع صوتك ʔænɑ: lɑ: ʕɑ:jzæ ʔæʃu:fæk wælɑ: ʔæsmæʕ ṣötæk
Explanation Particle 'حرف تفسير' /ħærf tæfsi:r/ **(PRT_XPL)**	A group of particles used to ask to explain the preceding word, phrase or sentence. It is not commonly used in EGY. في يوم عشرة من شوال أي بعد عيد الفطر fi: jöm_ʕæʃæræ min ʃæwwɑ:l ʔæj bæʕd ʕi:d ɑl-fiṭr
Interrogative Particle 'حرف استفهام' /ħærf istifhɑ:m/ **(PRT_INT)**	A group of particles is used to elicit understanding, conception, or approval. The noun that follows an interrogative particle is called an interrogative noun. هل ممكن حد فيكم يقولي إحنا وصلنا لهنا إزاي؟ hæl mumkin ħædd fi:kum jiʔulli: ʔiħnɑ: wæṣælnɑ: li-hinɑ: ʔizzɑ:j

Particle Sub Classes	Description and Example
Verb Particle 'حرف فعل' /ħærf fiʕl/ **(PRT_VER)**	A group of non-governing particles that precede the perfect or imperfect verbs and do not affect their mood. و<u>قد</u> أثبت الإرهاب فشله <u>wæ- qæd </u>ʔæθbætæ ɑl-ʔirhɑ:b fæʃæluh <u>قد</u> يكون الموضوع غريب حبتين <u>qæd</u> jiku:n ɑl-mæwḍu:ʕ ɣæri:b ħæbbitem

D Residuals

Residuals	Description and Example
Abbreviation **(ABR)**	It is a shortened form used in place of the whole word or phrase to save space and time, avoid repetition of long words and phrases, or simply to conform to conventional usage. For example, /d/ 'د' express the word /duktör/ 'دكتور' 'doctor'.
Emojis **(EMO)**	Any of various small images, symbols, or icons used in texts to express the emotional attitude of the writer, convey information concisely, convey a message playfully, without using words, etc. Examples: 😉 ☹ 👌 👍
Latin Words **(LTN)**	All non-Arabic words are written in other alphabets. 'good', 'responsibility', and 's'Joe'.
Foreign Words **(FRN)**	Non-Arabic words that are written in Arabic alphabets as spoken in another language with no morpholohical changes or adoptations. For example, /weır ʔær ju: gö/ 'وير أر يو جو'.
Numbers **(NUM)**	All alphanumeric numbers.
Punctuation Marks **(PNC)**	They include full stop, comma, colon, semicolon, parentheses, square brackets, quotation mark, dash, question mark … etc.
Interjections **(INJ)**	Words that express the speaker's reaction to a particular suggestion or sentence. For example, /hhhh/ 'هههههه', /ti:t/ 'تيت' and /jöh/ 'يوه'.

E Prefixes

Prefix	Description and Example
Conjunction 'حرف عطف' /ħærf ʕæṯf/ **(CNJ)**	A group of Prefixes that is attached to the beginning of another word to connect elements of equal status in pronunciation or meaning. رحت لحد عنده <u>و</u>**سألته** إيه اللي حصل <u>ف</u>**رفض** يقولي أي حاجة ruħt liħædd ʕænduh <u>wi</u>-sæʔltuh ʔeıh illi: ħæṣæl <u>fæ</u>-ræfæḍ jiʔu:lli: ʔæjj ħɑ:gæh
Definiteness Particle 'أداة تعريف' /ʔæda:t tæʕri:f' **(DET)**	It is a definite article that is attached to the beginning of another noun or adjective and makes them definite, rather than indefinite. <u>ال</u>**حكاية** وما فيها إن <u>ال</u>**بنت** دي كانت جميلة جدا وكل <u>ال</u>**شارع** بيحبها <u>ɑl</u>-ħikɑ:jæh wi-mɑ: fi:hɑ: ʔinn ɑl-bint di: kɑ:nit gæmi:læh giddæn wi-kull ɑʃ-ʃɑ:riʕ bijħibbæhɑ:
Causative Particle 'حرف تعليل' /ħærf tæʕli:l/	A group of particles that is attached to the beginning of an imperfect verb to express and confirm the logic of an argument. It is worth mentioning that it is not used in all levels of Arabic in Egypt.
(PRT_CST)	لازم نتفق إنه جاء <u>ل</u>**يحمينا** لا <u>ل</u>**يقهرنا** lɑ:zim nittifiʔ ʔinnuh jɑ:ʔ <u>li</u>-jæhmi:nɑ: lɑ: <u>li</u> jæqhærnɑ:

Prefix	Description and Example
Preposition 'حرف جر' /ħærf gærr/ **(PRP)**	A group of particles that is attached to the beginning of another noun, or pronoun to show direction, location, or time, or to introduce an object. In traditional Arabic, there are three prepositions that are still used in EGY: /ka:f/ 'ك', /ba:ʔ/ 'ب' and /la:m/ 'ل'. كان **كصديق** مقرب ليها وكانت دايما تحكي **له** كل حاجة **بالتفصيل**. ka:n kæ-ʂædi:q muqærræb li:ha: wi-ka:nt da:jmæn tiħki: lu-h kull ħa:gæh biat-tæfʂi:l In EGY, the prepositions /bi:/ 'بي' and /li:/ 'لي' are attached to pronouns: هي كانت **ليها** رموش طويلة hijjæ ka:nit li:-ha: rumu:ʃ ʈæwi:læh حاول يتصل **بيها** أكتر من مرة بس ما ردتش ħa:wil yittiʂil bi:-ha: ʔæktær min mærræh The prepositions /fi/ 'ف', /ʕæ/ 'ع' that are variations of /fi:/ 'في' and /ʕælæ:/ 'على', respectively, are now used, in EGY, as prefixes. مش فاكر كنت سايبه **عالمكتب** هنا ولا **فالعربية** miʃ fa:kir kunt sa:jbuh ʂal-mæktæb hina: wælla: fil-ʕæræbijjæh
Emphatic Particle 'حرف توكيد' /ħærf tæwki:d/ **(PRT_EMP)**	A group of particles that is attached to the beginning of a perfect or imperfect verb to put emphasis on intention. أوعى **لينسوك** يا ولدي مصر مين ʔiwʕæ: læ-jnæssu:k ja: wælædi: mæʂr mi:n والله لولا تدخل الجيش لحماية الثورة **لكنا** ليبيا جديدة wal-læhi: lölа: tædæxxul al-geɪʃ li-ħima:jit as-sæwræh la-kunna: li:bja: gidi:dæh
Futurity Particle 'حرف استقبال' /ħærf istiqba:l/ **(PRT_FUT)**	It is a particle that is attached to the beginning of an imperfect verb to represent the future tense. The traditional future particle /sæ/ 'س' is rarely used in EGY and the /ħæ/ 'ح', /ʕæ/ 'ع' and /hæ/ 'ه' are used instead. مش **حيكون** أكتر من اللي حصل miʃ ħæ-jku:n ʔæktær min illi: ħæʂæl وقاللي صدقيني مش **هتندمي** wi-ʔa:lli: ʂæddæʔi:ni: miʃ hæ-tindæmi: **عتسألني** ليه بلملم ف الخلـج ʕæ-tisʔæli:ni: leɪh bælæmlim fi: al-xælæg (*Example from Upper Egypt*)
Progressive Particle 'حرف للمضارع المستمر' /ħærf lil-muda:riʕ al-mustamirr/ **(PRT_PRG)**	A group of particles that is not used in traditional Arabic and is attached to the beginning of an imperfect verb to express the incomplete action or state in progress at a specific time. كان **بيعيد** ويزيد في الكلام كل شوية ka:n bi-jʕi:d wi-jzi:d fi: al-kæla:m kull ʃiwæjjæh
Jussive-governing Particle 'حرف جزم' /ħærf gæzm/ **(PRT_JSV)**	A group of particles that is attached to the beginning of an imperfect verb only to express a required action to do. It is rarely used in EGY. **ولنتابع** الأحداث الجارية بكل حرص wæl-nuta:biʕ al-ʔæħda:s al-ga:rijjæh bikull ħirʂ

Prefix	Description and Example
Negative Particle 'حرف نفي' /ħærf næfj/ **(PRT_NEG)**	A group of particles that is attached to the beginning of another word to negate it or deny its affirmation. This is newly added in EGY. It is not used in traditional Arabic. **محدش** في الدنيا يستاهل **ومفيش** حد الواحد يضحي بنفسه عشانه **ميستهلوشي** mæ-ħæddiʃ fi: ɑd-dunjɑ: jistɑ:hil wimæ-fi:ʃ ħædd ɑl-wɑ:ħid jiḍæħħi: binæfsuh ʕæʃɑ:nuh mæ-jistæhlu:ʃi:
Vocative Particle 'حرف نداء وتنبيه' /ħærf nidɑ:ʔ witænbi:h/ **(PRT_VOC)**	A group of particles that is attached to the beginning of a noun to call or alert a person addressed. **أحبيبتي – أصاحبي – أزميلي - آهو** ʔæ-ħæbi:bti: - ʔæ-ṣɑ:ħbi: - ʔæ-zmi:li: - ʔæ-hu:
Imperative Verb Particles 'حروف الأمر' /ħuru:f ɑl-ʔæmr/ **RVPRF_(PGN)**	A group of particles (أ، ن، ي، ت) that are attached to the beginning of the infinitive verb and change it to the present tense without changing its basic form. They are represented in word-form in proclitic-word-form-enclitic representation. RVPRF_2MS اعمل IVPRF_2FS اعملي IVPRF_2MP اعملوا
Imperfect Verb Particles 'حروف المضارعة' /ħuru:f ɑl-muḍɑ:riʕæh/ **IVPRF_(PGN)**	A group of particles (أ، ن، ي، ت) that are attached to the beginning of the infinitive verb and change it to the present tense without changing its basic form. They are represented in word-form in proclitic-word-form-enclitic representation. IVPRF_1S أقول IVPRF_3MS يقول IVPRF_3MP يقولوا (rarely used in EGY) IVPRF_3FP يقلن IVPRF_1P نقول IVPRF_2MS or IVPRF_3FS تقول IVPRF_2FS تقولي IVPRF_2MP تقولوا تقلن (rarely used in EGY) IVPRF_2FP

F Suffixes

Suffix	Description and Example
Negative Particle 'حرف نفي' /ħærf næfj/ **(PRT_NEG)**	A group of particles that is attached to the end of another word to negate it or deny its affirmation. This is newly added in EGY; it is not used in traditional Arabic. It is always accompanied with the prefix negative particle /mæ/ 'م' or the negative particle /mɑ:/ 'ما'. **محدش** في الدنيا يستاهل **ومفيش** حد الواحد يضحي بنفسه عشانه **ميستهلوشي** mæ-ħæddiʃ fi: ɑd-dunjɑ: jistɑ:hil wimæ-fi:ʃ ħædd ɑl-wɑ:ħid jiḍæħħi: binæfsuh ʕæʃɑ:nuh mæ-jistæhlu:ʃi:
Pronoun 'الضمير المتصل' /ɑḍ-ḍæmi:r ɑl-muttæṣil/ **(PRN)**	A group of pronouns that is attached to the end of a verb and represents its subject or object. It may also be attached to a noun or a preposition (stem or prefix preposition). أنا مش **نبهتكم** من إمبارح للموضوع ده أهو **موبايلها** مقفول ومحدش عارف **لها** طريق والحكاية دي **فيها** إن ʔænɑ: miʃ næbbihtu-kum min ʔimbɑ:riħ lil-mæwḍu:ʕ dæh ʔæhu: mubɑ:jil-hɑ: mæʔfu:l wi mæ-ħæddiʃ ʕɑ:rif læ-hɑ: ṭæri:ʔ wil-ħikɑ:jæ di: fi:-hɑ: ʔinnæ

Suffix	Description and Example
Noun Suffixes **NSUF_(GND)**	A letter or a group of letters (morphemes) that are added to the end of a stem and change the noun gender or number. They are represented in word-form in proclitic-word-form-enclitic representation. 'أمهات' /ʔummæha:t/ 'هات/NSUF_FP', أبهات /ʔæbbæha:t/ 'هات/NSUF_MP' 'علامات' /ʕæla:ma:t/ 'ات/NSUF_FP', 'كتبات' /kutuba:t/ 'ات/NSUF_MB' 'رحمة' /ræħmæh/ 'ة/NSUF_FS', 'خواجة' /χæwa:gæh/ 'ة/NSUF_MS' 'كتابين' /kita:beın/ 'ين/NSUF_MD', 'ممثلين' /mumæssili:n/ 'ين/NSUF_MP' 'مشاكل' /mæʃa:kil/ 'null/NSUF_FB', 'أرض' /ʔærḍ/ 'null/NSUF_FS', etc.
Perfect Verb Suffixes **PVSUF_(PGN)**	A letter or a group of letters (morphemes) that are added to the end of a stem and change the perfect verb gender, number or person. They are represented in word-form in proclitic-word-form-enclitic representation. 'شفت' /ʃuft/ 'ت/PVSUF_2MS' or 'ت/PVSUF_1S', 'شافت' /ʃa:fit/ 'ت/PVSUF_3FS' 'قالوا' /ʔa:lu:/ 'وا/PVSUF_3MP', 'عمل' /ʕæmæl/ 'null/PVSUF_2MS', etc.
Imperfect Verb Suffixes **IVSUF_(PGN)**	A letter or a group of letters (morphemes) that are added to the end of a stem and change the imperfect verb gender, number or person. They are represented in word-form in proclitic-word-form-enclitic representation. 'يكونوا' /jiku:nu:/ 'وا/PVSUF_3MP', 'تكتبو' /tiktibu:/ 'و/PVSUF_2MP' 'يهون' /jihu:n/ 'null/PVSUF_3MS', etc.
Imperative Verb Suffixes **RVPRF_(PGN)**	A letter or a group of letters (morphemes) that are added to the end of a stem and change the imperative verb gender, number or person. They are represented in word-form in proclitic-word-form-enclitic representation. 'قولي' /ʔu:li:/ 'ي/RVSUF_2FS', 'ارسم' /irsim/ 'null/RVSUF_2MS', 'روحوا' /ru:ħu:/ 'وا/ RVSUF_2MP', etc.

A Weak Supervised Transfer Learning Approach for Sentiment Analysis to the Kuwaiti Dialect

Fatemah Husain
Kuwait University
College of Life Sciences
Information Science Department
f.husain@ku.edu.kw

Hana Al-Ostad
Gulf University for Science & Technology
College of Arts & Sciences
Computer Science Department
alostad.h@gust.edu.kw

Halima Omar
Kuwait University
College of Life Sciences
Communication Disorders Science Department
halima.omar@cls.ku.edu.kw

Abstract

Developing a system for sentiment analysis is very challenging for the Arabic language due to the limitations in the available Arabic datasets. Many Arabic dialects are still not studied by researchers in Arabic sentiment analysis due to the complexity of annotators' recruitment process during dataset creation. This paper covers the research gap in sentiment analysis for the Kuwaiti dialect by proposing a weak supervised approach to develop a large labeled dataset. Our dataset consists of over 16.6k tweets with 7,905 negatives, 7,902 positives, and 860 neutrals that spans several themes and time frames to remove any bias that might affect its content. The annotation agreement between our proposed system's labels and human-annotated labels reports 93% for the pairwise percent agreement and 0.87 for Cohen's kappa coefficient. Furthermore, we evaluate our dataset using multiple traditional machine learning classifiers and advanced deep learning language models to test its performance. The results report 89% accuracy when applied to the testing dataset using the ARBERT model.

1 Introduction

Datasets are the foundation of the most significant innovation in the field of Natural Language Processing (NLP). The development of NLP algorithms and tools is dependent on the availability and quality of the datasets that serve their goals. While there are plenty of English language datasets, for some other natural languages, there are still minimal resources, such as the Arabic language (Husain and Uzuner, 2021). The Arabic language is considered among the low-resource languages for NLP, however, the number of people who speaks Arabic exceeds 353.6 million [1].

The Arabic language has multiple forms. The Classical Arabic Language (CAL) is the oldest form of Arabic and is often used in Islamic manuscripts (e.g., the Quran) (Habash, 2010; Husain and Uzuner, 2022). Modern Standard Arabic (MSA) is the official language for Arabic countries and it is used in official media resources, writing books, etc(Habash, 2010; Husain and Uzuner, 2021). The last and most dominant form of Arabic is the Arabic dialects, which are the native language form of daily communication. The Arabic dialects differ based on geographical and social classes(Habash, 2010). Moreover, Arabic dialects are often used in online user-generated content such as on Twitter, Facebook, and Instagram. This variation among Arabic dialects makes it very challenging to develop tools that can process Arabic social media content accurately.

In this study, we develop a dataset based on an innovative method to reduce the number of human annotators and propose a text classification model for sentiment analysis specifically for the Kuwaiti dialect. The Kuwaiti dialect has not been comprehensively covered and studied in previous computational linguistic research. According to our knowledge, only(Salamah and Elkhlifi, 2014) investigates some linguistic tools for the Kuwaiti dialect to develop an approach for unsupervised sentiment analysis, however, their dataset is not publicly available for researchers. This gap in research inspires us to further study the Kuwaiti dialect and

[1] https://www.worlddata.info/languages/arabic.php

Proceedings of the The Seventh Arabic Natural Language Processing Workshop (WANLP), pages 161 - 173
December 8, 2022 ©2022 Association for Computational Linguistics

to create linguistic resources to support research in this area. This initial step in studying the Kuwaiti dialect could also support the study of other under-represented Arabian Gulf dialects that might share some vocabularies with the Kuwaiti dialect, for example, it can help researchers in Bahraini or Qatari dialects.

The key contributions of this study are three-fold:

1. Introducing the first public Kuwaiti dataset for sentiment analysis with over 16.6K tweets covering various topics.

2. Implementing a unique data labeling system inspired by (Smith et al., 2022) for the **language model in a loop by incorporating prompting into weak supervision**, which combines the benefits of using weak supervised learning and zero-shot pre-trained transfer learning models.

3. Comparing the performance of multiple classical machine learning classifiers and several BERT models for sentiment analysis covering the Kuwaiti dialect.

This paper starts with some background information after the introduction that covers the Kuwaiti dialect, sentiment analysis resources, the latest approaches and software frameworks in labeling large datasets, the weak supervised techniques, and the zero-shot models applied in the experiments. The methodology is discussed in detail in the third section, including dataset construction, dataset labeling, classification model, and performance evaluation. In the third section, we present the results, error analysis, and discuss them thoroughly. The paper concludes with a conclusion and proposes directions for future works. The paper also includes an ethics statement at the end and appenedices.

2 Background

2.1 The State of Kuwait and the Kuwaiti Dialect

The state of Kuwait is a small country with a total area of 17,820 square kilometers located in the northwestern corner of the Persian Gulf (i.e. Arabian Gulf). Geographically, Kuwait was divided into four main areas; Sharq (East), Qibla (West), Hay al−Wasat (Middle Neighbourhood), and al−Mirqab (South)(Al-Qenaie et al., 2011). Kuwaitis have been exposed to continuous contact with several cultures, Arabic dialects, and languages; such as Cairene Arabic (i.e. Egyptian), dialects of Saudi Arabia, Turkish, Hindi, and Persian(Al-Qenaie et al., 2011). Furthermore, Kuwait was a protectorate of the British Empire for 62 years, which also create an effect on the Kuwaiti dialect(Hayat and AlBader, 2022). This complex structure of the Kuwaiti dialect makes it very difficult to create a linguistic system that can automatically process Kuwaiti text accurately.

2.2 Sentiment Analysis Datasets

The available research in sentiment analysis for the Kuwaiti dialect is very limited. Salamah and Elkhlifi(Salamah and Elkhlifi, 2014) create a dataset of 340,000 tweets related to the interrogation of ministers by the National Assembly of Kuwait. Other Arabian gulf dialects have also been recently targeted to develop sentiment analysis datasets. A parallel balanced dataset of English, MSA, and Bahrani dialect consisting of 5,000 product reviews and a dataset of 500 movie comments in Bahraini dialect were created for a sentiment analysis system(Omran et al., 2022). In (A. Al Shamsi and Abdallah, 2022), the authors introduced the first Emirati sentiment analysis dataset, which consists of 70,000 Instagram comments. Multiple sentiment analysis resources were developed for the Saudi dialect, such as: (1) (Rizkallah et al., 2018) develop 2010 tweets dataset for sentiment analysis; (2) (Alahmary et al., 2019) collect 32,063 Saudi tweets; (3) (Alruily and Shahin, 2020) construct a dataset of 11,764 tweets about Saudi universities; (4) in (Alharbi et al., 2022), the authors create a dataset of 22,433 reviews of tourist places.

2.3 Labeling Large Training Dataset

Data labeling is one of the most challenging tasks in creating datasets for text classification. The following points summarize the main challenges in NLP related to data labeling:

- Advanced deep learning and transfer learning algorithms require very large size labeled datasets.

- Subject Matter Experts (SMEs) have limitted time, thus its difficult to obtain labels for a large dataset from SMEs.

- In the case of crowd-sourcing, the labeling task will be very costly and raise some quality

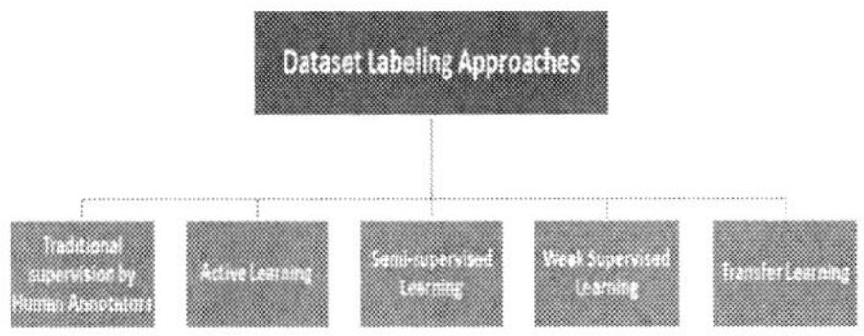

Figure 1: Summary of data labeling approaches

issues (e.g., proficiency in the subject, personal bias, background knowledge effects, and agreement among annotators).

- Privacy might be required in some projects, which might impact the annotation process and the recruitment of annotators.

Knowing the complexity behind the labeling process, researchers proposed many solutions to label data without human annotators. Fig.1 illustrates a summary of different approaches to labeling/annotating data, including both with and without help from SMEs.

Active learning is one of the advances in the traditional labeling by SMEs for supervised learning. It attempts to overcome the labeling bottleneck by asking queries in the form of unlabeled instances to be labeled by an oracle (e.g., a human annotator). In this way, the active learner aims to achieve high accuracy using as few labeled instances as possible, thereby minimizing the cost of obtaining labeled data(Settles, 2009).

The second approach of data labeling is **semi-supervised learning**, based on (Ratner et al.; Engelen and Hoos, 2020) in this approach a small dataset is labeled using an unsupervised algorithm, then the small dataset is used to label a much larger unlabeled dataset.

The third approach is **transfer learning**, based on (Pan and Yang, 2010); this approach aims to extract the knowledge from one or more source tasks (model pre-trained on a different dataset) and apply the knowledge to a target task (to label the dataset).

The above three approaches reduce the need for SMEs to annotate additional training datasets. However, using these approaches will not avoid the need to label some data; this will not be the case when using **weak supervised learning** or **Zero-Shot (ZS) learning**, where the first approach avoid human labeling by using labeling functions created with the help of the SMEs who provides supervision at a higher level than case-by-case labeling, and the ZS learning make use of pre-trained model to label the dataset without any additional fine-tuning on the new corpus (Tunstall et al., 2022).

2.3.1 Weak supervised learning

Weak supervised learning is defined by (Tok et al., 2021) as a collection of techniques in machine learning in which models are trained using sources of information that are easier to provide than hand-labeled data, where this information is incomplete, inexact, or otherwise less accurate.

The noisy, weak labels are combined using a generative model trained based on the accuracies of the labeling functions; the accuracies are derived from agreement and disagreement of the labeling functions and used to form the training data.

Weak supervision has received much attention in recent years, and several open-source software frameworks for weak supervision have been released to be used by data scientists in building real-world systems. Example software frameworks include Snorkel(Ratner et al., 2017), Swell-Shark(Biomedical NER)(Fries et al., 2017), and FlyingSquid(Fu et al., 2020).

Stanford researchers, found that when they compared to the productivity of teaching the SMEs Snorkle weak supervised framework, versus spending the equivalent time just hand-labeling data, the team was able to build models not only 2.8x faster but also with 45.5% better predictive performance on average(Ratner et al., 2017). Also, they found that using Snorkel leads to an average of 132% performance improvement over baseline techniques(Ratner et al., 2017).

Another research on weak supervised learning by MIT researchers found that the combination of a few "strong" labels and a larger "weak" label dataset resulted in a model that learned well and trained at a faster rate(Robinson et al., 2020).

2.3.2 Snorkel Open Source Weak Supervision Framework

Snorkel framework(Ratner et al., 2017) is a project proposed by researchers at Stanford AI Lab started in the year 2015. It is the oldest among the weak supervised learning software frameworks. Snorkel team published over 60+ peer-reviewed publications(AI). Besides the open-source library, the Snorkel research team built a commercial version called **Snorkel Flow**[2] by incorporating years of experience from applying weak supervision to real-world machine learning problems.

The following describes the steps of the Snorkel system:

1. The SME users write Labeling Functions (LFs) that express weak supervision sources like distant supervision, patterns, and heuristics.

2. Snorkel applies the LF on unlabeled data and learns a generative model to combine the LFs' outputs into probabilistic labels.

3. Snorkel uses these labels to train a discriminative classification model, such as a deep neural network.

2.3.3 Zero-Shot (ZS) Learning

Based on (Tunstall et al., 2022) ZS classification is suitable in a setting where no labeled data is provided. Using Natural Language Inference (NLI) the ZS model can predict the class of the unlabeled sample, even if the model was not trained on those classes. The ZS models leverage the semantic similarity between labels and the text context(Yildirim and Asgari-Chenaghlu, 2021). In this type of experiment setup, the text is treated as the premise, and the hypothesis is formed as "this example is about {label}". In addition, a set of expected labels is fed to the promise, and the entailment score tells if the promise is about that topic/label or not.

A good candidate to perform ZS classification on languages other than English is XLM-RoBERTA (XLM-R) model. It was trained on one hundred languages, including Arabic and many other low-resource languages. Based on the findings from (Conneau et al., 2020), applying the XLM-R model on the cross-lingual Natural Language Inference (XNLI) task, significantly outperforms multilingual BERT (mBERT) by +13.8% average accuracy. Moreover, it also performs exceptionally well on low-resource languages, improving 11.8% in XNLI accuracy for Swahili and 9.2% for Urdu over the previous XLM model.

Another State-Of-The-Art (SOTA) model in XNLI task is Multilingual mDeBERTa. As of December 2021, mDeBERTa-base is the best performing multilingual base-sized transformer model, it achieved a 79.8% ZS cross-lingual accuracy on XNLI and a 3.6% improvement over XLM-R Base (He et al., 2021).

2.4 Language Models in a Loop

In (Smith et al., 2022), the researchers proposed a framework incorporating ZS model prompting into programmatic weak supervision. The following is a detailed explanation of the steps:

1. The SMEs express their domain knowledge via prompts combined with unlabeled examples and given to a pre-trained ZS language model.

2. The ZS model's responses are interpreted with label maps to produce votes on the true label.

3. These votes are denoised with a label model, and the resulting estimated labels are used to train an end model.

4. The SMEs can refine their prompts throughout the process by inspecting unlabeled examples and evaluating with a small labeled development set.

Based on the findings from (Smith et al., 2022), using this approach which combines ZS models with weak supervised learning, can significantly improve performance over using the ZS model alone, with an average of 19.5% reduction in errors. They also found that this approach produces classifiers with comparable or superior accuracy to those trained from hand-engineered rules.

3 Methodology

3.1 Dataset

3.1.1 Dataset Extraction, Collection, and Filtering

The process used in collecting data spans over one year to ensure the diversity of data content, and to remove any bias or impacts that might be caused by social factors within the Kuwaiti society. We select four controversial events that happen in different time frames in Kuwait. These events create debatable and stressful content on the online Arabic Twitter-sphere. The followings are a short description of each event and the hashtags used to extract its tweets:

- Farah Akbar. These tweets were collected during April 2021. Farah Akbar is a Kuwaiti woman who was brutally murdered. Her

[2] https://snorkel.ai/

killer had threatened and harassed her after she rejected his marriage proposal. The hashtags used to extract these tweets related to Farah's event are:عزاء _النساء# and جريمة _قتل _صباح _السالم#.

- Dalal Al-Abd Al-Jader. These tweets were collected during October 2021. Dalal Al-Abd Al-Jader is a Kuwaiti girl who was killed by her mother and kept for five years inside the apartment without being buried. The hashtag used to extract these tweets is العدالة _لدلال _العبدالجادر#.

- Bideon. Bidoon or bedun refers to a stateless Arab minority in Kuwait. They do not have nationalities and are not allowed to obtain most official documents, which causes difficulties in finding employment, accessing healthcare, and education. We select tweets that were posted during February 2022 about the Bidoon because it coincides with the Moroccan child Rayan incident which received the attention of an overwhelming number of online users including Kuwaitis. This reaction from Kuwaitis toward Rayan incident increased the anger of people from the Bidoon community in Kuwait, which led them to go out to the streets and protest for their citizenship and other civil rights. The hashtags used to extract these tweets are البدون _اولويه# الطفل _البدون _عبدالعزيز#البدون#.

- Sheick Al-Hazem. These tweets were collected during April 2022. Sheikh Al-Hazem is a Kuwaiti Shia clergy who was assaulted while in the mosque by three government officials who try to confiscate money collected from people for Zakat (i.e. donation). The hashtag used to extract these tweets is محشوم _الشيخ _مهدي _الهزيم#.

3.1.2 Dataset Labeling

Tweets are categorized according to the feeling in which they are present, either to be positive; such as happiness, fun, and pride, or to be negative; such as sadness and contempt, or to be neutral in the sense that there is no expression of feelings. The followings are samples from the dataset from each label:

- Positive: وجود كل انسان اليوم بساحة الارادة حسسني بالامان

  "People's presence at the Will Square today makes me feel safe".

- Neutral: حملة مناهضة العنف ضد المرأة

  "The campaign against women's violence".

- Negative: لاشئ يؤلم اكثر من خيبة امل تاتيك من شخص ظننت انه لن يؤذيك ابدا

  "Nothing hurts more than disappointment comes from someone you thought would never hurt you".

Snorkel and Language Models in a Loop for Dataset Labeling:

We used Snorkel open-sourced software framework(Ratner et al., 2017, 2016) because the available alternative frameworks are not supporting our goal. For example, SwellShark is used for Biomedical NER, Skweak is tightly integrated with SpaCy which does not support Arabic, and FlyingSquid has limited documentation with a focus on video classification.

Fig.2 illustrates the steps we followed to label the training dataset. Our proposed labeling system differs from (Smith et al., 2022) system as for the LFs, we used several ZS pre-trained models and one promote instead of using one ZS model and changing the promote as in (Smith et al., 2022).

To select the ZS pre-trained models used in our experiments, firstly, we searched for the top ZS pre-trained models published in the Hugging Face repository[3]. The selection criteria were based on the list of top downloaded ZS models that either support multilingual or support the Arabic language and is fine-tuned on XNLI using either XLM-R or mDeBERTa models. We applied this selection criteria because any ZS model fine-tuned on one of those two models is expected to give good result with low-resource languages such as Arabic dialects as previous studied demonstrated(Conneau et al., 2020; He et al., 2021). Next, we tested the previously selected models using part of our dataset. We excluded the models that reported poor performance and did not support the Kuwaiti dialect.

After extensive experimenting, the final selected ZS models are the following:

1. joeddav/xlm-roberta-large-xnli(Davison) [4]

[3]https://huggingface.co/

[4]https://huggingface.co/joeddav/xlm-roberta-large-xnli

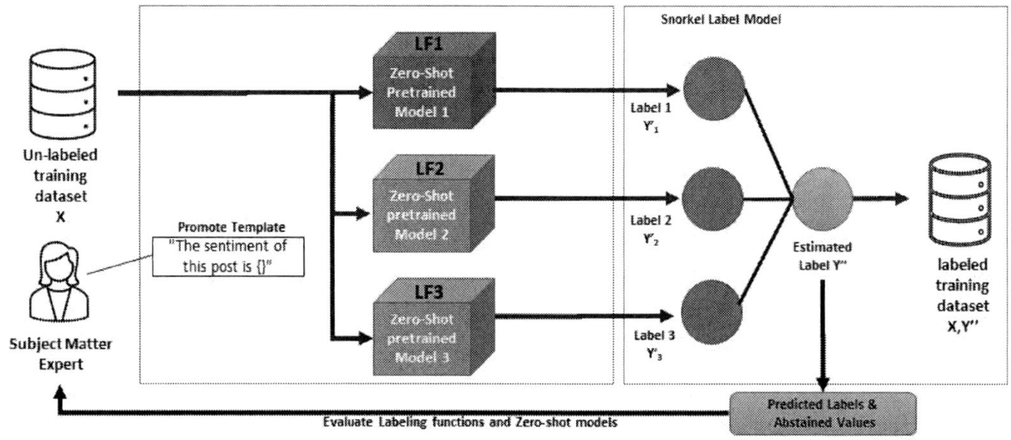

Figure 2: Snorkel weak supervised learning steps

2. MoritzLaurer/mDeBERTa-v3-base-mnli-xnli(Laurer et al., 2022) [5]
3. vicgalle/xlm-roberta-large-xnli-anli (Davison) [6]

Using the selected ZS models, we created three LFs, the LF either returns a sentiment label (positive, negative, neutral) or returns the "ABSTAIN" value in case the labeling function could not label the text. We also set the promote hypothesis template to "The sentiment of this post is { }".

Next, we applied the LF to the unlabeled training dataset. We iterated on this process several times. In each iteration, we checked the abstained tweets and samples of the predicted tweets to evaluate and refine the sentiment labels keywords and the ZS language models.

Then, we tested the performance of the Snorkel probabilistic labeling model based on the exact steps illustrated in Fig.2, but we applied it to the gold-labeled testing dataset. Finally, we retrieved the resulting labeled training dataset by removing the abstained tweets and keeping only the labeled tweets.

Gold-Labeled Dataset: In addition to Snorkel's labeled dataset, we hire 7 annotators between the age of 17 and 24 years who are Kuwaiti and proficient in the Kuwaiti dialect among other Arabic dialects to manually label a set of 2,100 tweets (300 tweets per annotator). A detailed labeling instruction including definitions and samples from each label along with a background survey and a pilot study were used to help the annotators to provide accurate labels. The pilot study consist of 15 tweets; 5 were labeled as samples from different labels and 10 were used to test the annotators. Annotators who accurately labeled the testing 10 tweets were presented with 300 tweets to label as part of the gold-labeled dataset.

We further check the human-labeled tweets for accuracy by reviewing them with an expert annotator and excluding all inexact tweets. The final version of the gold-labeled dataset consists of 1,534 tweets. This set of tweets was used to further examine our approach to data labeling using weak supervision techniques.

3.1.3 Dataset Cleaning and Preprocessing

We removed duplicated tweets, retweet keyword "RT", and user mentions. Previous studies highlighted the limited effects of preprocessing Arabic tweets when used with advanced classification models such as BERT-model(Husain and Uzuner, 2022; Husain, 2020). Thus, only hashtags were removed before applying feature extractions and using the text for the classification models.

The size of the resulting labeled dataset from our proposed labeling system, and after removing the abstained tweets is a total of 16,667 tweets; 7,905 negative, 7,902 positive, and 860 neutral. The resulting labeled dataset is nearly balanced on tweet counts between negative and positive labels, but not on the neutral labels. At this stage, the labeled dataset is ready for the next step to be used in baseline models and to fine-tune Arabic language

[5] https://huggingface.co/MoritzLaurer/mDeBERTa-v3-base-mnli-xnli

[6] https://huggingface.co/vicgalle/xlm-roberta-large-xnli-anli

models.

3.2 Classification Models

We randomly split the dataset into three parts; the train set with 60% of the total number of tweets, the validation set with 20%, and the test set is 20%. All sets have equal proportions of label distributions, Fig.3 shows the distribution of each set. Firstly, we train the classification models using the train set and evaluate them using the validation set, then we combine the validation set with the train set and train the classification models and evaluate them using the test set. As described in the following sections, multiple classifiers were applied to evaluate the dataset.

3.2.1 Baseline Models

We develop four baseline classification models; Logistic Regression (LR), Support Vector Machine (SVM), Multinomial Naive Bayes (M-NB), and Bagging with a 2-5 characters-based TF-IDF vectorizer. Previous studies emphasize the importance of applying a character-based feature when the dataset is extracted from user-generated content such as Twitter because character-based features are language-independent features that perform well with misspelling errors or obfuscating words, as is the case on most Twitter content(Bohra et al., 2018; Nobata et al., 2016). The feature and models were implemented using Python scikit-learn library.

3.2.2 BERT Models

The main classification models which we used in developing and evaluating the sentiment analysis system are sharing the same Bidirectional Encoder Representations from Transformers (BERT) architecture, however, they vary in the parameters and data used in creating them. The BERT model applies pre-trained language representations to downstream tasks through a fine-tuning approach. This approach is also called transfer learning, in which the pre-trained language representations are developed using a neural network model on a known task, and then fine-tuning is performed to use the same model for a new purpose-specific task such as sentiment analysis(Devlin et al., 2018). The following four BERT models are applied in our experiments:

- AraBERT Model(Antoun et al.). It is a monolingual Arabic BERT model. It has various versions with variations in the model architecture and training corpus. In this study, "bert-base-arabertv02-twitter" is applied, which is trained by continuing the pre-training process using the masked language model pipeline with around 60 million Arabic tweets. This version of AraBERT includes emoji in its vocabulary[7].
- ARBERT(Abdul-Mageed et al., 2021). It uses the same network architecture of the BERT base model with a large MSA dataset that has been collected from 6 various sources[8].
- MARBERT(Abdul-Mageed et al., 2021). This model has been developed by the same authors as ARBERT, however, it was developed using a larger dialectal dataset than ARBERT with more tokens that are collected from randomly selected tweets. It has the same architecture as ARBERT, but without the Next Sentence Prediction (NSP) objective as tweets are concise and short.
- Microsoft Multilingual Model (MiniLM)(Wang et al., 2020). It is a small and fast pre-trained model for language understanding and generation. It is distilled from the "XLM-RoBERTa" model, however, the transformer architecture of MiniLM is the same as that of the BERT model[9].

All BERT models used in this study were from the Hugging Face repository and the experiment was developed in Python using the PyTorch- Transformers library. The models were used with the same parameters settings; maximum length = 128 characters, patch size = 16, epoch = 2, epsilon = 1e-8, and learning rate = 2e-5. We did not use feature engineering because fine-tuning and deep learning do not need feature engineering, instead, we use the pool layer from the encoder and feed it into a simple Feed Forward Neural Network (FFNN) layer.

3.3 Model Performance Evaluation

We applied hyperparameter tuning via a stratified 5-fold cross-validation process on the training set to arrive at the most efficient hyperparameters. The

[7]https://huggingface.co/aubmindlab/bert-base-arabertv02-twitter

[8]https://github.com/UBC-NLP/marbert

[9]https://huggingface.co/microsoft/Multilingual-MiniLM-L12-H384

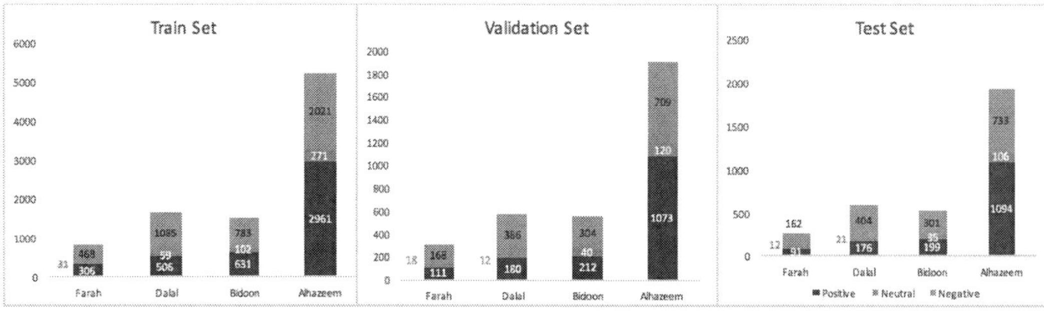

Figure 3: Classes distribution of each subset from the dataset

distribution of the sentiment classes is not equal in all sets, as can be seen from Fig.3. Thus, we depend on macro-averaged measurements to remove any bias toward a particular class. Macro F1 and accuracy were applied in most experiments. Models were evaluated using a stratified 5-fold cross-validation to remove any bias by averaging the results. The evaluation metrics were developed using the Scikit-Learn Python library. Google Colab was used to conduct the experiment. We further evaluate the results through manual inspection and error analysis.

4 Results and Discussion

Firstly, we evaluate the Snorkel annotated dataset to check for the annotation agreement between the Snorkle-labeled dataset and the gold-labeled dataset (human-labeled dataset). Thus, we consider pairwise percent agreement and Cohen's kappa coefficient metrics to evaluate annotation agreement. The result report 93% for the pairwise percent agreement and Cohen's kappa coefficient is a near-perfect agreement with a value equals to 0.87.

We also tested the performance of the Snorkel probabilistic labeling model by applying the same steps illustrated in Fig.2. Snorkel framework already provides a function to evaluate its performance in case gold labels are present in the dataset. Thus, we applied the steps to the gold-labeled testing dataset of size=1,534 tweets, and the final performance results of the labeling system were accuracy score of 93%, and F1-Macro of 84%.

Table 1 presents the results for the baseline models and Table 2 shows the results for the main classification models. As can be noticed, the SVM reports the best performance among the baseline models. However, after further training using both train and validate sets, it reports almost perfect performance with 0.99 and 1.00 for the macro-averaged F1 and accuracy scores respectively, which indicates a possibility of over-fitting. Investigating the result from the SVM model shows that only 3 positive tweets were misclassified as negative, 5 negative tweets were misclassified as positive, and for the neutral tweets, 1 tweet was misclassified as positive and 4 tweets were misclassified as negative. A similar finding is also applied to the bagging model.

The results of the BERT models highlight an important finding. Even though AraBERT includes in its pre-training dataset tweets and emoji, similar to our dataset, and MARBERT is developed using a large tweets dataset, they both were not performing as well as ARBERT. The ARBERT model reports 0.75 and 0.89 for the macro-averaged F1 and accuracy scores respectively on the test set.

	Datasets			
	Validation		**Test**	
	F1	**Acc.**	**F1**	**Acc.**
LR	0.66	0.81	0.78	0.91
SVM	**0.75**	**0.84**	**0.99**	**1.00**
M-NB	0.51	0.75	0.54	0.78
Bagging	0.67	0.76	0.98	0.99

Table 1: Baseline models results

	Datasets			
	Validation		**Test**	
	F1	**Acc.**	**F1**	**Acc.**
AraBERT	0.66	0.85	0.66	0.86
MiniLM	0.50	0.72	0.53	0.78
ARBERT	**0.72**	**0.87**	**0.75**	**0.89**
MARBERT	0.62	0.84	0.71	0.88

Table 2: Main models results

4.1 Error Analysis

Since the dataset consists of a large number of tweets, explicit sentiment tweets and more ambiguous ones were encountered. The explicit tweets were clear, easy to classify, and convey sentiments by both Snorkel and human annotators. On the other hand, various tweets were challenging to classify. Some were not clear in terms of the focus of the topic as the reader would find the meaning complicated to understand, and others were difficult to decide their suggested sentiment. Samples from the explicit sentiment and ambiguous tweets are presented in Appendix A.

Additionally, one noted observation while going through the tweets was that they contained foreign vocabularies that were borrowed from other languages (English in most cases), modified to fit the Kuwaiti dialect, or just written in Arabic alphabets like (بريك / *break* and اوفر تايم / over time), and used regularly among Kuwaitis, showing that the Kuwaiti dialect is constantly updating with new words added to it.

5 Conclusions

In this paper, we release the first open large-scale dataset focused on sentiment analysis for the Kuwaiti dialect using a semi-supervised approach. We created a semi-supervised model based on the Snorkel framework to reduce the need for human annotators and boost the size of the labeled data rapidly and accurately. To test the applicability of the dataset, we evaluated various traditional machine learning classifier baselines, as well as advanced BERT-based language model classifiers. The results showed that our approach generates high-performance scores in both macro-average F1 and accuracy results. We believe our approach will help foster research and development of NLP systems, which were previously little studied due to the challenges faced by human annotators.

6 Future Work

To further prove the validity and significance of our proposed weak supervised labeling system, we plan to test the labeling methodology on Arabian Gulf dialects other than the Kuwaiti dialect. Furthermore, for labeling functions in Snorkel, we plan to test various versions of the prompt text used in the zero-shot pre-trained models using different Arabic and English prompts and by testing the effect of combining rule-based and heuristic labeling functions with zero-shot pre-trained models on the accuracy of weak supervised labeling system.

7 Ethics Statement

We constructed the sentiment analysis Kuwaiti dataset using the public tweets that span several time-frames and themes, Snorkel open-sourced framework for automatic labeling, and human annotators for the annotation evaluation dataset. All sensitive and personalized content was removed from the tweets for users' privacy concerns. An SME who is an expert in NLP, Kuwaiti dialect, and Snorkel framework administrated the creation of labels using Snorkel to ensure the accuracy of the automatic annotation process. We only recruited Kuwaiti annotators that are fluent Kuwaiti speakers, with a very high approved task acceptance rate to label the evaluation dataset manually.

References

Arwa A. Al Shamsi and Sherief Abdallah. 2022. Sentiment analysis of emirati dialect. *Big Data and Cognitive Computing*, 6(2).

Muhammad Abdul-Mageed, AbdelRahim Elmadany, and El Moatez Billah Nagoudi. 2021. ARBERT & MARBERT: Deep bidirectional transformers for Arabic. In *Proceedings of the 59th Annual Meeting of the Association for Computational Linguistics and the 11th International Joint Conference on Natural Language Processing (Volume 1: Long Papers)*, pages 7088–7105, Online. Association for Computational Linguistics.

Snorkel AI. Advancing snorkel from research to production. Last accessed 02 September 2022.

Shamlan Al-Qenaie et al. 2011. *Kuwaiti Arabic: A socio-phonological perspective*. Ph.D. thesis, Durham University.

Rahma M. Alahmary, Hmood Z. Al-Dossari, and Ahmed Z. Emam. 2019. Sentiment analysis of saudi dialect using deep learning techniques. In *2019 International Conference on Electronics, Information, and Communication (ICEIC)*, pages 1–6.

Banan A. Alharbi, Mohammad A. Mezher, and Abdullah M. Barakeh. 2022. Tourist reviews sentiment classification using deep learning techniques: A case study in saudi arabia. *International Journal of Advanced Computer Science and Applications*, 13(6).

Meshrif Alruily and Osama R Shahin. 2020. Sentiment analysis of twitter data for saudi universities. *International Journal of Machine Learning and Computing*, 10(1).

Wissam Antoun, Fady Baly, and Hazem Hajj. Arabert: Transformer-based model for arabic language understanding. In *LREC 2020 Workshop Language Resources and Evaluation Conference 11–16 May 2020*, page 9.

Aditya Bohra, Deepanshu Vijay, Vinay Singh, Syed Sarfaraz Akhtar, and Manish Shrivastava. 2018. A dataset of hindi-english code-mixed social media text for hate speech detection. In *Proceedings of the second workshop on computational modeling of people's opinions, personality, and emotions in social media*, pages 36–41.

Alexis Conneau, Kartikay Khandelwal, Naman Goyal, Vishrav Chaudhary, Guillaume Wenzek, Francisco Guzmán, Edouard Grave, Myle Ott, Luke Zettlemoyer, and Veselin Stoyanov. 2020. Unsupervised cross-lingual representation learning at scale. In *Proceedings of the 58th Annual Meeting of the Association for Computational Linguistics*, pages 8440–8451, Online. Association for Computational Linguistics.

Joe Davison. xlm-roberta-large-xnli.

Jacob Devlin, Ming-Wei Chang, Kenton Lee, and Kristina Toutanova. 2018. Bert: Pre-training of deep bidirectional transformers for language understanding. *arXiv preprint arXiv:1810.04805*.

Jesper E. van Engelen and Holger H. Hoos. 2020. A survey on semi-supervised learning. *Machine Learning*, 109(2):373–440.

Jason Fries, Sen Wu, Alex Ratner, and Christopher Ré. 2017. Swellshark: A generative model for biomedical named entity recognition without labeled data. *arXiv preprint arXiv:1704.06360*.

Daniel Fu, Mayee Chen, Frederic Sala, Sarah Hooper, Kayvon Fatahalian, and Christopher Ré. 2020. Fast and three-rious: Speeding up weak supervision with triplet methods. In *International Conference on Machine Learning*, pages 3280–3291. PMLR.

Nizar Y. Habash. 2010. 1 edition, volume 3 of *Synthesis Lectures on Human Language Technologies*. Morgan Claypool Publishers. [link].

Noor A Hayat and Yousuf B AlBader. 2022. The mcchicken phenomenon: How has english become a prevalent language among kuwaiti youths? *World Journal of English Language*, 12(6).

Pengcheng He, Jianfeng Gao, and Weizhu Chen. 2021. DeBERTaV3: Improving DeBERTa using ELECTRA-Style Pre-Training with Gradient-Disentangled Embedding Sharing. *arXiv*.

Fatemah Husain. 2020. OSACT4 shared task on offensive language detection: Intensive preprocessing-based approach. In *Proceedings of the 4th Workshop on Open-Source Arabic Corpora and Processing Tools, with a Shared Task on Offensive Language Detection*, pages 53–60, Marseille, France. European Language Resource Association.

Fatemah Husain and Ozlem Uzuner. 2021. A survey of offensive language detection for the arabic language. *ACM Trans. Asian Low-Resour. Lang. Inf. Process.*, 20(1).

Fatemah Husain and Ozlem Uzuner. 2022. Investigating the effect of preprocessing arabic text on offensive language and hate speech detection. *ACM Trans. Asian Low-Resour. Lang. Inf. Process.*, 21(4).

Moritz Laurer, Wouter van Atteveldt, Andreu Casas, and Kasper Welbers. 2022. Less annotating, more classifying – addressing the data scarcity issue of supervised machine learning with deep transfer learning and bert-nli.

Chikashi Nobata, Joel Tetreault, Achint Thomas, Yashar Mehdad, and Yi Chang. 2016. Abusive language detection in online user content. In *Proceedings of the 25th international conference on world wide web*, pages 145–153.

Thuraya M Omran, Baraa T Sharef, Crina Grosan, and Yongmin Li. 2022. Transfer Learning and Sentiment Analysis of Bahraini Dialects Sequential Text Data using Multilingual Deep Learning Approach. *Chaos, Solitons and Fractals*.

Sinno Jialin Pan and Qiang Yang. 2010. A survey on transfer learning. *IEEE Transactions on Knowledge and Data Engineering*, 22(10):1345–1359.

A. Ratner, P. Varma, B. Hancock, and C. Ré. Weak supervision: A new programming paradigm for machine learning. Last accessed 02 September 2022.

Alexander Ratner, Stephen H Bach, Henry Ehrenberg, Jason Fries, Sen Wu, and Christopher Ré. 2017. Snorkel: rapid training data creation with weak supervision. *Proceedings of the VLDB Endowment*, 11(3):269–282.

Alexander J Ratner, Christopher M De Sa, Sen Wu, Daniel Selsam, and Christopher Ré. 2016. Data programming: Creating large training sets, quickly. *Advances in neural information processing systems*, 29.

Sandra Rizkallah, Amir Atiya, Hossam ElDin Mahgoub, and Momen Heragy. 2018. Dialect versus msa sentiment analysis. In *The International Conference on Advanced Machine Learning Technologies and Applications (AMLTA2018)*, pages 605–613, Cham. Springer International Publishing.

Joshua Robinson, Stefanie Jegelka, and Suvrit Sra. 2020. Strength from weakness: Fast learning using weak supervision. In *Proceedings of the 37th International Conference on Machine Learning*, volume 119 of *Proceedings of Machine Learning Research*, pages 8127–8136. PMLR.

Janan Ben Salamah and Aymen Elkhlifi. 2014. Microblogging opinion mining approach for kuwaiti dialect. In *The International Conference on Computing Technology and Information Management (ICCTIM)*, page 388. Citeseer.

Burr Settles. 2009. Active learning literature survey.

Ryan Smith, Jason A Fries, Braden Hancock, and Stephen H Bach. 2022. Language Models in the Loop: Incorporating Prompting into Weak Supervision. *arXiv*.

W.H. Tok, A. Bahree, and S. Filipi. 2021. *Practical Weak Supervision: Doing More with Less Data*. O'Reilly Media, Incorporated.

Lewis Tunstall, Leandro von Werra, and Thomas Wolf. 2022. *Natural language processing with transformers*. " O'Reilly Media, Inc.".

Wenhui Wang, Furu Wei, Li Dong, Hangbo Bao, Nan Yang, and Ming Zhou. 2020. Minilm: Deep self-attention distillation for task-agnostic compression of pre-trained transformers.

S. Yildirim and M. Asgari-Chenaghlu. 2021. *Mastering Transformers: Build state-of-the-art models from scratch with advanced natural language processing techniques*. Packt Publishing.

A Appendices

A.1 Explicit Tweets

Explicit tweets refer to tweets that contain some verbs or nouns expressing the feelings and opinions of the author clearly. These tweets were very easily classified based on the sentiment labels; negative, positive, or neutral, by the proposed Snorkel system and human annotators as well. Samples from these tweets are shown in Table 3.

A.2 Ambiguous Tweets

Ambiguous tweets refer to tweets that contain unclear text that is complicated in terms that it shows feelings and emotion but it is not clear whether this sentiment is negative, positive, or neutral. Thus, it is not factual or news, rather it illustrates some sentiment but the state if the sentiment is not stable. Table 4 shows some examples of ambiguous tweets from the dataset.

Sentiment	Tweet
Positive	الله موجود ،،، ما ورى هالشكول حلول ..! #كفى _استهتار _بمصير _البدون *God exists,,,there are no solutions for those people enough negligence of the Bidoon*
Negative	دائما فجر تظهر في هذا الموقف لتعطي انطباع الامان للجهاز المركزي فجر أنتي من أبواق الجهاز ومن اللاتي تعتاش على قضية البدون انسانة في غاية الخسة *Fajer always appears in this position to make an impression of the safety for the central control. Fajer, you are one of the horns of the central control, and among those who subsist on the issue of the Bidoon, a very mean person*
Neutral	الخدمة المدنية.. غير صحيح ما يتداول بشأن رفض الديوان صرف مكافأة #الصفوف _الأمامية لـ #البدون *The Civil Service.. incorrect rumors about the refusal of the Diwan to disburse a reward to the front rows of the Bidoon*

Table 3: Samples from the explicit tweets

Challenge	Tweet
Not direct. It could be sarcastic by referring to the amount of attention and empathy Rayan was getting, but could also be serious, free from sarcasm	لم نجد هذا الكم من التعاطف لأطفال البدون الذين يتساقطون يومياً في بئر الحرمان لم نجد أبداً هذا الكم من المشاعر لشباب #البدون *We did not find this amount of sympathy for the Bidoon children who fall daily into the well of deprivation. We have never found this amount of feelings for the Bidoon youth have never found this amount of feelings for the Bidoon youth*
The sentiment here was both positive and negative, as the idea of unity gave a positive feeling, but stating the issues they were facing gave a negative one.	وستبقى قضية الكويتيين #البدون _اولويه عند كل شريف في هذا الوطن الجمعة القادمه ٢٢٠٢ الساعة الواحدة بعد صلاة الجمعة في تيماء العزة والكرامة والحرية وقفة الكويتيين البدون جنسية ضد الظلم والإهانة والتسويف والتجاهل ولكي *The issue of Kuwaitis Bedoons will remain a priority for every honorable person in this country, next Friday 11/2/2022 one o'clock after Friday prayers in Taima, the pride, dignity and freedom. The stateless Kuwaitis stand against injustice, humiliation, procrastination and disregard, and for our message to reach everyone, we are a people who deserve to live with dignity.*

Table 4: Samples from the ambiguous tweets

MAWQIF: A Multi-label Arabic Dataset for Target-specific Stance Detection

Nora Alturayeif[1,2], **Hamzah Luqman**[1,3], **and Moataz Ahmed**[1,4]

[1]King Fahd University of Petroleum and Minerals, Saudi Arabia
[2]Imam Abdulrahman Bin Faisal University, Saudi Arabia
[3]SDAIA-KFUPM Joint Research Center for Artificial Intelligence, KFUPM
[4]Interdisciplinary Research Center of Intelligent Secure Systems (IRC-ISS), KFUPM
[1]{g201902190,hluqman,moataz}@kfupm.edu.sa

Abstract

Social media platforms are becoming inherent parts of people's daily life to express opinions and stances toward topics of varying polarities. Stance detection determines the viewpoint expressed in a text toward a target. While communication on social media (e.g., Twitter) takes place in more than 40 languages, the majority of stance detection research has been focused on English. Although some efforts have recently been made to develop stance detection datasets in other languages, no similar efforts seem to have considered the Arabic language. In this paper, we present MAWQIF, the first Arabic dataset for target-specific stance detection, composed of 4,121 tweets annotated with stance, sentiment, and sarcasm polarities. MAWQIF, as a multi-label dataset, can provide more opportunities for studying the interaction between different opinion dimensions and evaluating a multi-task model. We provide a detailed description of the dataset, present an analysis of the produced annotation, and evaluate four BERT-based models on it. Our best model achieves a macro-F_1 of 78.89%, which shows that there is ample room for improvement on this challenging task. We publicly release our dataset, the annotation guidelines, and the code of the experiments.[1]

1 Introduction

Currently, online forums and social media platforms are being inherent parts of people's daily life as a media of expressing their stances toward different targets (e.g., events, politics, services, or controversial news). Consequently, the demand for automatic solutions for stance detection significantly increases as the volume of unstructured data does.

Stance detection is the task of predicting whether the author of a written text is in favor of, against, or neutral toward a subject of interest (i.e., target), in which the stance is explicitly or implicitly stated in the text (Küçük and Fazli, 2020; AlDayel and Magdy, 2021). Automatic and high-performance solutions for stance detection can play a valuable role in decision-making for politicians, businesses, and authorities. The input to the stance detector is usually a pair of written text and a target. However, other inputs can be used to boost the model performance such as the user's social activity on the social media platforms (e.g., retweets and likes).

Existing stance detection datasets can be categorized based on the target dependency into *target-specific*, *cross-target*, and *target-independent*. In *target-specific* stance detection, a specific target (e.g., Donald Trump or BREXIT referendum) has to be given along with the user's text, and sometimes the user's information, in order to detect the stance toward the predefined target. In *cross-target* stance detection, the objective is to build a classifier that can transfer the learned knowledge between targets using a large dataset that comprise a wider range of different targets. In the *target-specific* and *cross-target* tasks, the target of the stance is an explicit entity (e.g., person, event, or controversial issue), whereas the target in *target-independent* tasks is a claim or a piece of fake news and the objective is to detect whether the comments are confirming the claim/news or denying its veracity.

A significant number of stance detection techniques have been proposed in the literature. However, most of these studies used an old public dataset, SemEval-2016 (Mohammad et al., 2016), including those published recently (Chen et al., 2021; Li et al., 2021b; Al-Ghadir et al., 2021; Allaway et al., 2021; Liang et al., 2021). We believe that more benchmarked stance detection datasets should be released under a common open license for public usage. Non-English data, multilingual data, and annotations of other opinion dimensions (e.g., sarcasm and emotions) should all be considered for establishing new stance detection datasets.

[1]https://github.com/NoraAlt/Mawqif-Arabic-Stance

Proceedings of the The Seventh Arabic Natural Language Processing Workshop (WANLP), pages 174 - 184

We aim to facilitate the research on target-specific stance detection of Arabic micro-blogs. To our knowledge, this problem has not been studied for the Arabic language and there is no publicly available dataset for Arabic that can be used for target-specific stance detection. Arabic is a challenging language for most natural language processing (NLP) applications due to its unique nature in the variety of dialectics and its rich and complex morphology (Badaro et al., 2020). Furthermore, different from media that use Modern Standard Arabic (MSA) with formal linguistic criteria, social media texts represent dialectal Arabic and contain an informal writing style (e.g., spelling errors, abbreviations, irregular grammar, emojis, and symbols). Thus, automatically detecting the user's stance on social media, specifically in Arabic, is a worthwhile and challenging task. In addition, the increase of Arabic content on social media, and the mobilized masses for political and economic changes in the Middle East have motivated us to search in this direction.

In this paper, we release MAWQIF, the first Arabic dataset that can be used for target-specific stance detection. This dataset consists of 4,121 tweets in multi-dialectal Arabic. Each tweet is annotated with a stance toward one of three targets: "COVID-19 vaccine," "digital transformation," and "women empowerment." In addition, this is a multi-label dataset where each data point is annotated for stance, sentiment, and sarcasm, which will provide a benchmark for the three tasks. It will also help in analyzing the interaction between the different opinion dimensions (i.e., stance, sentiment, and sarcasm).

Our contributions in this paper can, therefore, be summarized as follows. **1)** We construct and release MAWQIF, the first multi-label Arabic dataset for stance detection. The proposed dataset consists of 4,121 tweets covering three topics (i.e., targets) that are controversial in the Middle East. We also provide a detailed description of the dataset and an analysis of the produced annotation; **2)** The proposed dataset is annotated for stance, sentiment, and sarcasm. This provides more opportunities for studying the interaction between different opinion dimensions, and evaluating a model trained on different opinion dimensions in a multi-task paradigm to boost the performance of stance detection; **3)** We benchmark the proposed dataset on the stance detection task and evaluate the performance of four BERT-based models.

2 Related work

Stance detection is a relatively new field of study; however, considerable effort has been devoted into building datasets for stance detection tasks. From the definitions of the three stance detection tasks (presented in Section 1); the structure of the datasets used for target-independent tasks is different than the datasets used for target-specific or cross-target tasks. In target-independent stance detection, each input entry is usually in the form of a pair of textual claims and responses. Examples of target-independent datasets are: Emergent (Ferreira and Vlachos, 2016), IBM Debater (Bar-Haim et al., 2017), Pheme (Kochkina et al., 2017), RumourEval-17 (Derczynski et al., 2017), FNC-1 (Hanselowski et al., 2018), Args.me (Ajjour et al., 2019), Perspectrum (Chen et al., 2019), RumourEval-19 (Gorrell et al., 2019), Arabic News Stance (Khouja, 2020), and (Baly et al., 2018). Meanwhile, the input entry for target-specific and cross-target stance detection systems usually consists of a text and target pair.

Several datasets have been proposed for target-specific and cross-target stance detection. These datasets have been collected from different platforms such as social media (Mohammad et al., 2016; Xu et al., 2016; Sobhani et al., 2017; Taulé et al., 2017; Küçük and Can, 2018; Lai et al., 2018; Conforti et al., 2020; Lai et al., 2020; Cignarella et al., 2020; Grimminger and Klinger, 2021; Zotova et al., 2021), debate websites (Stab et al., 2018; Hosseinia et al., 2020; Vamvas and Sennrich, 2020), and news commentaries (Hercig et al., 2017; Allaway and Mckeown, 2020). With regard to language orientation, most of the available stance detection datasets are monolingual where their data are available in one language. The majority of these monolingual datasets are in English language (Mohammad et al., 2016; Sobhani et al., 2017; Stab et al., 2018; Allaway and Mckeown, 2020; Conforti et al., 2020; Lai et al., 2020; Hosseinia et al., 2020; Grimminger and Klinger, 2021). For Italian, Lai et al. (2018) and Cignarella et al. (2020) collected tweets targeting the Italian constitutional reform and the Sardines movement, respectively. Similarly, Küçük and Can (2018) collected Turkish tweets targeting football clubs. Furthermore, a dataset for Chinese language is presented in (Xu et al., 2016), and a Czech stance detection dataset is presented

Language	Dataset Name / Ref.	Targets	Annotation	Size
English	SemEval-2016 Task 6 (Mohammad et al., 2016)	Atheism, Climate change, Feminist movement, Hillary Clinton, Abortion legalization	Stance, Sentiment	4,163 Tweets
	Multi-target SD (Sobhani et al., 2017)	2016 US presidential electors	Stance	4,455 Tweets
	UKP (Stab et al., 2018)	8 controversial topics	Stance	25,492 Comments
	Procon20 (Hosseinia et al., 2020)	419 controversial issues	Stance	6,094 Comments
	VAST (Allaway and Mckeown, 2020)	Several topics	Stance	23,525 Comments
	WT-WT (Conforti et al., 2020)	Health insurance companies	Stance	51,284 Tweets
	TW-BREXIT (Lai et al., 2020)	BREXIT referendum	Stance	1,800 Triplets of tweets
	Election-2020 (Grimminger and Klinger, 2021)	2020 US presidential electors	Stance, Hate speech	3,000 Tweets
Italian	ConRef-STANCE-ita (Lai et al., 2018)	Italian constitutional reforms	Stance	963 Triplets (tweet, retweet, reply)
	SardiStance (Cignarella et al., 2020)	Sardines movement	Stance	3,242 Tweets
Chinese	NLPCC-2016 Task 4 (Xu et al., 2016)	5 topics	Stance	3,250 Weibo posts
Czech	Hercig et al. (2017)	Miloš Zeman, Smoking ban	Stance, Sentiment	5,423 Comments
Turkish	Küçük and Can (2018)	Football clubs	Stance	1,065 Tweets
Spanish, Catalan	IberEval 2017 (Taulé et al., 2017)	Catalan independence	Stance	5,400 Tweets (for each language)
	Zotova et al. (2021)	Catalan independence	Stance (automatic annotation)	Spanish: 10K Tweets, Catalan: 10K Tweets
German, French, Italian	X-stance (Vamvas and Sennrich, 2020)	150 political issues	Stance (automatic annotation)	German: 40,200, French: 14,129, Italy: 1,173

Table 1: Publicly available datasets for target-specific and cross-target stance detection.

in (Hercig et al., 2017). However, few datasets are multilingual where more than one language is considered in collecting the data. Vamvas and Sennrich (2020) proposed a multilingual dataset with French, German, and Italian languages. Two other datasets considered Catalan and Spanish languages in one dataset (Taulé et al., 2017; Zotova et al., 2021). Table 1 summarizes the publicly available datasets used for target-specific and cross-target stance detection.

In our dataset, we attempt to address two gaps; the language and the annotation of other opinion dimensions. Despite the growing interest in studying stance detection, no study, as far as we know, considered Arabic language for target-specific stance detection. In this paper, we release the first Arabic target-specific stance detection dataset. It is worthwhile noting that there are two stance detection datasets that target Arabic language (Khouja, 2020; Alhindi et al., 2021). However, these two datasets are dedicated to study claim verification, as they consist of claim/reference pairs to predict the stance of a claim toward the reference sentence. Thus, they cannot be used for building a target-specific stance detection model. In addition, the two datasets are comprising texts in modern standard Arabic, which is not the language used in social media debates where dialectal Arabic is quite prevalent.

Moreover, most of the existing datasets annotated each text with stance labels (Favor, Against, None). Other studies considered the sentiment polarity during data annotation. The aim of involving sentiment annotation was to analyze the interaction between stance and sentiment in order to boost the performance of stance detection (Mohammad et al., 2016; Hosseinia et al., 2020). However, there is no study to the best of our knowledge has considered sarcasm features for stance detection. According to the findings of a comparative empirical study by (Ghosh et al., 2019), the main source of misclassification in stance detection is texts with sarcastic content. Therefore, studying sarcasm could be beneficial for improving the performance of stance detection models. We thus proposed to annotate our dataset with sarcasm in addition to stance and sentiment polarities. Our dataset is established in order to create a novel Arabic linguistic resource for stance, sentiment, and sarcasm.

3 MAWQIF Dataset

In this section, we explain the procedure followed to collect a set of opinions (texts) toward selected targets for stance detection. We also present the crowdsourcing setup used for stance annotation and discuss the statistics of the proposed dataset.

3.1 Data Collection and Filtering

Most of the available stance detection datasets focus mainly on a narrow range of political topics, such as elections and referendums. In contrast, we extended the considered domains in our dataset to include other topics related to hot social issues in the Middle East. Similar to prior works (Li et al., 2021a; Conforti et al., 2020; Lai et al., 2020; Sobhani et al., 2016; Mohammad et al., 2016) that targeted multiple topics, we considered three targets: "COVID-19 vaccine," "digital transformation," and "women empowerment." The proposed dataset has been collected from Twitter platform. We crawled tweets using Snscrape[2] crawler which is a python library for social networking services.

A set of keywords and query hashtags were used as seeds to collect target-related tweets. This phase resulted in collecting around 400K tweets. It should be noted that a considerable number of collected tweets contain stance-indicative hashtags; however, this does not imply that the tweet will take the same stance as indicated by the hashtag. An example from our dataset:

#لا_للتطعيم_الاجباري لو تطعيم كورونا مضر كان حتى تطعيمات الأطفال مضره، توكل على الله وطعم
#No_to_compulsory_vaccination If the corona vaccine is harmful then even the vaccines for children are harmful, so put your trust in Allah and get it

The second phase in the data collection stage was to filter and prepare the collected data. We performed the following preprocessing steps: 1) We kept only the Arabic tweets, which include multi dialects, and removed tweets in other languages. 2) We removed duplicates and retweets. 3) Tweets from news media accounts were eliminated using the information contained in *user_description* attribute available in the Snscrape tweet object. 4) We defined a set of keywords and phrases that usually appear in advertisements and adult tweets to exclude these types of tweets. 5) Tweets were cleaned from URLs and user mentions. Applying these filters resulted in reducing the collected tweets to around 200K tweets for all three targets combined. Finally, we randomly sampled around 1,400 tweets for each target, obtaining 4,121 tweets in total for annotation.

3.2 Annotation

To annotate our data, we used Appen crowdsourcing platform[3] to hire native Arabic speakers who live in Arab countries for the annotation task. We asked the contributors (i.e., annotators) to perform stance, sentiment, and sarcasm annotations for each tweet of the proposed dataset. This will help in using the dataset for these three tasks.

To build our quality control step, we conducted the annotation process in multiple iterations. In each iteration, we used a batch of 100 tweets for evaluating annotation quality. Initially, we created an annotation form that provides instructions for annotating the three dimensions (i.e., stance, sentiment, and sarcasm), and asked the annotators to annotate each tweet with the three dimensions at the same time. We noticed that the assignment was quite challenging, resulting in a low score of inter-agreement between annotators. Therefore, we designed a separate annotation form for each dimension (i.e., we assigned three separate tasks for different annotators). We noticed that letting the annotator focus on one task at a time was much easier and resulted in a higher inter-agreement between the annotators. In addition, it resulted in greater consensus among the annotators. Therefore, rather than generating a single annotation form for all three dimensions, we picked the latter approach for our annotation process.

In the stance annotation form, we asked the annotators to read a tweet and identify its stance (i.e, Favor, Against, None) toward a predefined target. The annotators were also asked to determine if the target is mentioned explicitly or implicitly in the

[2]https://github.com/JustAnotherArchivist/snscrape

[3]https://appen.com

tweet. We designed similar annotation forms to determine the sentiment of a tweet (i.e, Positive, Negative, or Neutral), and to determine if the tweet contains sarcastic content or not. With regard to sarcasm, we define it, according to the Cambridge English dictionary, as: "*Sarcastic means the text expresses an evaluation whose literal polarity is different from the intended polarity to hurt someone emotionally or criticize something in a humorous way*". To ensure the consistency between the annotation of the proposed dataset and other similar datasets, we followed the stance and sentiment annotation guidelines formulated in (Mohammad et al., 2017). Our dataset release is accompanied by the annotation guidelines.

Each tweet–target pair was annotated by three to seven annotators. We require to stop collecting annotations on a row when the row's confidence score is above 0.7 or when a maximum of seven annotations is reached. Appen system provides a mechanism to compute the confidence score based on the level of agreement among multiple annotators, weighted by the trust scores of the annotators. We control the quality of the annotation by 420 test questions with correct labels for stance, sentiment, and sarcasm that were interleaved between the regular questions. An annotator's trust score was computed on these test questions; under-performers who got scores below 80% were eliminated and all their submitted annotations were also ignored.

3.3 Dataset Statistics

The distribution of the confidence in the annotations of the three dimensions (i.e., stance, sentiment, and sarcasm) is shown in Figure 1. Based on our analysis in evaluating the annotation quality using our test questions, the confidence threshold for high-confidence annotation was set to 0.7. We observed a lower inter-agreement on the sentiment annotation, with around 30% of annotations' confidence score below 0.7 (light red in Figure 1). This, in line with our beliefs, confirm the highly subjective nature of sentiment annotation. Meanwhile, stance annotations produced a higher agreement, with 15% were considered as low-confidence. The highest confidence annotations were achieved in sarcasm, with only 5.75% below 0.7 score.

The MAWQIF dataset contains 4,121 annotated tweets representing three targets: "COVID-19 vaccine" with 1,373 tweets, "digital transformation" with 1,348 tweets, and "women empowerment" with 1,400 tweets. This dataset is a multi-label

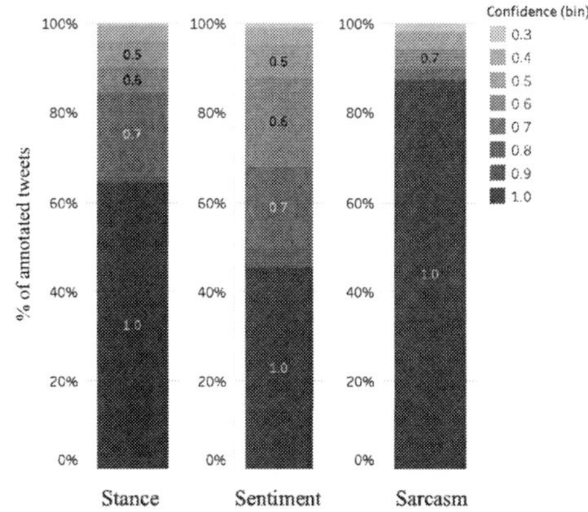

Figure 1: Distributions of the confidence in the stance, sentiment, and sarcasm annotations.

dataset where each tweet is annotated for stance, sentiment, and sarcasm. Table 2 show some examples from MAWQIF dataset. We split the dataset into training and testing sets with 85% and 15%, respectively. The data split statistics are shown in Table 3.

Figure 2 illustrates the labels' distribution across all targets, and the distribution per target. As observed from this figure, the percentage of tweets that do not have a clear stance and are labeled as *none* are low (9.51%) compared to the ones labeled as *neutral* sentiment (31%). This demonstrates that neutral tweets do not imply that they do not show any stance. Regarding sarcasm, most of the tweets were annotated as non-sarcasm (95.39%). This is expected, given that we were not targeting sarcastic text in our dataset.

The labels' distribution varies between the three targets. Tweets discussing digital transformation tend to lean toward a favorable stance compared to the other targets. Regarding sentiment polarity, positive content appears more frequently when discussing women empowerment or digital transformation, compared to the COVID-19 vaccine topic with only 25% positive tweets. Furthermore, sarcastic content appears more frequently in COVID-19 vaccine related tweets.

We also studied the association between stance and sentiment, and between stance and sarcasm through a co-occurrence heatmap (Figure 3). Examination of the stance-sentiment matrix reveals that stance is not always aligned with the sentiment for a target within a text. This implies that a tweet may have a negative polarity, but the stance is in favor, or vice versa (some examples are shown in

Target	Tweet	Stance	Sentiment	Sarcasm
COVID-19 Vaccine	حاشتنا كورونا وطبنا منها ولله الحمد ومانحتاج تطعيم ولاتحسفنا أبدا We were diagnosed with Corona and recovered from it, thank God, we do not need a vaccination and we will never regret it	Against	Positive	No
Digital Transformation	مليون كتاب!! اين التحول الالكتروني للمناهج؟كمية هدر سنوي للكتب مؤسفة نتمنى احلال الاجهزة اللوحية بدلاً من الكتب Million books!! Where is the digital transformation of curricula? The amount of annual waste of books is unfortunate. We wish to replace books with tablets	Favor	Negative	No
Women Empowerment	#القبض_على_مدعيه_النبوه فاهمة تمكين المرأة غلط 😂😂 #Arrest_of_the_prosecutor_of_prophecy she misunderstod women's empowerment 😂😂	None	Neutral	Yes

Table 2: Examples from MAWQIF dataset that show how stance may not align with sentiment polarity.

	Train				Test				Total
Target	#Tweets	%Favor	%Against	%None	#Tweets	%Favor	%Against	%None	
COVID-19 Vaccine	1167	43.62	43.53	12.85	206	43.69	43.69	12.62	1373
Digital Transformation	1145	76.77	12.40	10.83	203	76.85	12.32	10.84	1348
Women Empowerment	1190	63.87	31.18	4.96	210	63.81	30.95	5.24	1400
All	3502	61.34	29.15	9.51	619	61.39	29.08	9.53	4121

Table 3: Data split statistics of MAWQIF dataset.

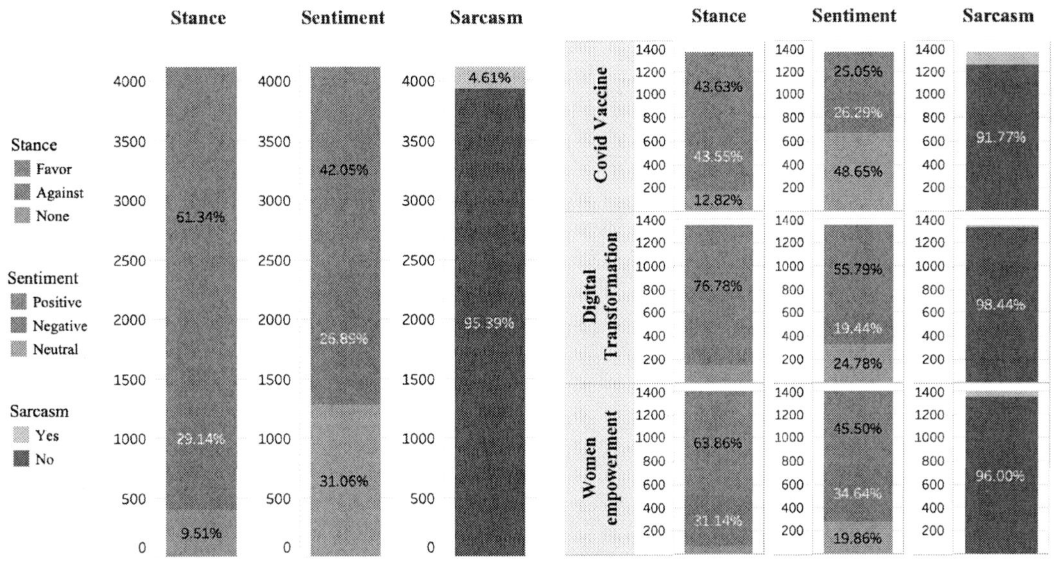

(a) Overall labels' distribution (b) Labels' distribution per target

Figure 2: Labels' distribution in MAWQIF dataset.

	Sentiment		
Stance	Positive	Negative	Neutral
Favor	66.22%	8.11%	25.67%
Against	2.25%	69.61%	28.14%
None	8.16%	17.09%	74.74%

	Sarcasm	
Stance	Yes	No
Favor	2.18%	97.82%
Against	7.58%	92.42%
None	11.22%	88.78%

0% 100%

Figure 3: Association between Stance and Sentiment, (a) Stance-Sentiment association, (b) Stance-Sarcasm association.

Table 2). Around 34% of favor tweets are actually not positive, and 31% of tweets with negative stances are annotated with a non-negative sentiment. From the stance-sarcasm matrix, we can observe that sarcastic content appears more in instances that are labeled as *against* compared to instances of favorable stance.

4 Benchmark Experiments

In this section, we present benchmarking experiments performed on the target-specific stance detection task. As mentioned earlier, the main purpose of MAWQIF dataset is stance detection. Therefore, we considered only the stance detection task for the benchmark experiments. However, the sentiment and sarcasm annotations could be used in further experiments (i.e, future studies) to analyze the interaction between the three dimensions.

Models BERT-based models have been shown to be effective in a variety of text classification tasks (González-Carvajal and Garrido-Merchán, 2020), including dialectical Arabic text (Alturayeif and Luqman, 2021). Thus, we chose to develop a BERT-based classifier that we fine-tuned for target-specific stance detection. Specifically, we fine-tuned the following four BERT-based models for stance detection:

1. CAMeLBERT-da, is a BERT-based model trained on 5.8 billion tokens from the Dialectal Arabic (DA) dataset (Inoue et al., 2021).
2. MARBERT, is a BERT-based model trained on 15.6 billion tokens from 1 billion Arabic tweets (Abdul-Mageed et al., 2020).
3. AraBERT, is trained on 8.6 billion tokens from five datasets consisting of Modern Standard Arabic (MSA) text (Antoun et al., 2020).
4. AraBERT-twitter, is trained by extending the training of AraBERT (v0.2) on 60 million Arabic tweets (Antoun et al., 2020).

We fine-tuned the four pre-trained models and built a standard pipeline under the PyTorch Lightning framework. The fine-tuning code is available online along with our dataset. The proposed system starts by preprocessing the Arabic texts by removing diacritics, tatweel, non-Arabic letters, and repeated characters. Then, a WordPiece (Wu et al., 2016) tokenizer is used to split the input text into tokens compatible with BERT-based models. For classification, the hidden representation of the [CLS] token is fed into a feed-forward layer along with a Softmax function. We set the maximum sequence length to 128 tokens, and the batch size to 32. Each of the four models is fine-tuned for 20 epochs; AdamW optimizer (Loshchilov and Hutter, 2017) is used with a learning rate of 2e-5. The hyper-parameters used in these experiments have been selected empirically.

Evaluation Metrics We evaluated our baseline models using F_{avg2} and F_{avg3} scores. F_{avg2} is the macro-average F1 over the "favor" and "against" stance labels (the "none" class was ignored since it was scarcely in the data). This score is computed as follows:

$$F_{avg2} = \frac{F_{favor} + F_{against}}{2} \tag{1}$$

where F_{favor} and $F_{against}$ are computed as follows:

$$F_{favor} = \frac{2Precision_{favor}Recall_{favor}}{Precision_{favor} + Recall_{favor}} \tag{2}$$

$$F_{against} = \frac{2Precision_{against}Recall_{against}}{Precision_{against} + Recall_{against}} \tag{3}$$

We selected F_{avg2} metric to align with other stance detection datasets that report their results using F_{avg2} metric (Mohammad et al., 2016). We are also reporting our results using F_{avg3} that considers all stances and it is computed as follows:

$$F_{avg3} = \frac{F_{none} + F_{favor} + F_{against}}{3} \tag{4}$$

Results Tables 4 and 5 present the obtained results of the proposed models with the development and test sets, respectively. The development set was obtained by dividing the training set into 5-folds and training the model with cross-validation. As shown in Tables 4 and 5, AraBERT-twitter model yields the best overall and per-target performance. This can be attributed to the type of the train data (i.e, dialectical Arabic tweets) that were used to train AraBERT-twitter model, which is similar to the type of Arabic tweets used in MAWQIF dataset. Furthermore, we can observe that the best performed model (i.e. AraBERT-twitter) and the other three models (CAMeLBERT-da, MARBERT, and AraBERT) generalized quite well to the test data, even achieving higher accuracies and macro-F_1 scores.

Although MARBERT was trained on dialectical Arabic tweets, its performance is low compared

Model	COVID-19 Vaccine F_{avg2}	COVID-19 Vaccine F_{avg3}	Digital Transformation F_{avg2}	Digital Transformation F_{avg3}	Women Empowerment F_{avg2}	Women Empowerment F_{avg3}	Overall F_{favor}	Overall $F_{against}$	Overall F_{none}	Overall F_{avg2}	Overall F_{avg3}	Overall Acc
CAMeLBERT-da	71.84	57.42	59.36	42.35	73.61	49.07	79.90	56.63	12.30	68.27	49.61	71.72
MARBERT	73.94	**63.96**	49.30	44.99	78.31	52.21	82.83	51.53	**26.79**	67.18	53.72	74.86
AraBERT	76.01	57.62	59.51	49.19	73.41	48.94	80.85	58.44	16.47	69.64	51.92	73.77
AraBERT-twitter	**76.77**	61.71	**62.25**	**56.31**	**84.91**	**56.60**	**83.78**	**65.51**	25.34	**74.64**	**58.21**	**76.56**

Table 4: Stance detection results on the development set.

Model	COVID-19 Vaccine F_{avg2}	COVID-19 Vaccine F_{avg3}	Digital Transformation F_{avg2}	Digital Transformation F_{avg3}	Women Empowerment F_{avg2}	Women Empowerment F_{avg3}	Overall F_{favor}	Overall $F_{against}$	Overall F_{none}	Overall F_{avg2}	Overall F_{avg3}	Overall Acc
CAMeLBERT-da	70.67	59.61	59.38	47.28	83.96	55.97	81.78	60.90	20.19	71.34	54.29	73.61
MARBERT	73.94	63.96	62.83	50.77	81.64	**59.98**	82.91	62.70	**29.11**	72.81	58.24	75.97
AraBERT	73.39	62.26	67.43	52.36	78.09	52.06	82.17	63.77	20.74	72.97	55.56	75.10
AraBERT-twitter	**80.05**	**65.49**	**70.86**	**63.03**	**85.77**	57.18	**86.54**	**71.25**	27.91	**78.89**	**61.90**	**79.78**

Table 5: Stance detection results on the test set.

to AraBERT-twitter. This may be explained by the fact that MARBERT was trained with masked-language modeling (MLM) objective only, whereas AraBERT was trained with both MLM and the next sentence prediction (NSP) objectives. While MLM aims to capture the relationship between words, NSP aims to understand longer-term dependencies between sentences. Thus, NSP objective could improve the ability to capture more information in the sentence–stance pairs that appear in our training dataset.

CAMeLBERT-da was trained on dialectical Arabic data collected from social media sites and other resources. However, CAMeLBERT-da has a lower performance due to the smaller size of its training data compared to the data used to train AraBERT-twitter. CAMeLBERT-da was trained on 5.8 billion words with a vocabulary size of 30K, while AraBERT-twitter was trained on 8.6 billion words with a vocabulary size of 60K in addition to 60M multi-dialect tweets.

It is also noticeable in the obtained results that the performance of all models in detecting the *none* stance is low compared with other stances. This can be attributed to the small number of tweets with *none* stance used in model training. However, *none* is a class that is not of interest as the ultimate goal is to infer if the author of a written text is in favor of or against a specific target. On other hand, the obtained results with the *favor* stance were high compared with the *against* stance in all experimented models. This indicates that there is room for improvement in all models, where a model can benefit from the techniques that mitigate the impact of class imbalance.

Furthermore, we can observe from Table 5 that the performance scores of all models were the highest with the "women empowerment" target. This might be an indication of strong signals appearing in the tweets discussing women empowerment that separate instances that are in favor and those that are against.

5 Conclusion

We introduced MAWQIF, the first multi-label Arabic dataset for target-specific stance detection. The proposed dataset consists of 4,121 multi-dialectal Arabic tweets targeting three topics that are controversial in the Middle East. MAWQIF is not limited to stance annotation, it is further annotated with sentiment and sarcasm polarity. Thus, MAWQIF can serve as a new benchmark for three tasks: stance detection, sentiment analysis, and sarcasm detection. In addition, it can enable future research in studying the interaction between different opinion dimensions, and evaluating multi-task models. We also presented a detailed description of the dataset and an analysis of the produced annotation. Lastly, we experimented on the target-specific stance detection task and establish strong baselines based on four BERT-based models.

Future work may improve upon the reported results by minimizing the effects of class imbalance, which can be accomplished by oversampling or undersampling techniques, or by training with weighted loss. Another interesting direction for further research is developing a joint neural architecture based on a multi-task learning paradigm that jointly models sentiment and sarcasm to boost the performance of stance detection.

To facilitate future research, we publicly release our dataset, the annotation guidelines, and the code that can be used to reproduce the presented evaluation results.

Acknowledgments

The authors would like to acknowledge the support received from the Saudi Data and AI Authority (SDAIA) and King Fahd University of Petroleum and Minerals (KFUPM) under the SDAIA-KFUPM Joint Research Center for Artificial Intelligence Grant JRC-AI-RFP-05.

References

Muhammad Abdul-Mageed, AbdelRahim Elmadany, and El Moatez Billah Nagoudi. 2020. Arbert & marbert: Deep bidirectional transformers for arabic. *arXiv*.

Yamen Ajjour, Henning Wachsmuth, Johannes Kiesel, Martin Potthast, Matthias Hagen, and Benno Stein. 2019. Data acquisition for argument search: The args.me corpus. volume 11793 LNAI of *Joint German/Austrian Conference on Artificial Intelligence (Künstliche Intelligenz)*, pages 48–59.

Abdulrahman I. Al-Ghadir, Aqil M. Azmi, and Amir Hussain. 2021. A novel approach to stance detection in social media tweets by fusing ranked lists and sentiments. *Information Fusion*, 67:29–40.

Abeer AlDayel and Walid Magdy. 2021. Stance detection on social media: state of the art and trends. *Information Processing and Management*, 58.

Tariq Alhindi, Amal Alabdulkarim, Ali Alshehri, Muhammad Abdul-Mageed, and Preslav Nakov. 2021. Arastance: A multi-country and multi-domain dataset of arabic stance detection for fact checking. pages 57–65.

Emily Allaway and Kathleen Mckeown. 2020. Zero-shot stance detection: A dataset and model using generalized topic representations. Proceedings of the 2020 Conference on Empirical Methods in Natural Language Processing, pages 8913–8931.

Emily Allaway, Malavika Srikanth, and Kathleen Mckeown. 2021. Adversarial learning for zero-shot stance detection on social media. pages 4756–4767.

Nora Alturayeif and Hamzah Luqman. 2021. Fine-grained sentiment analysis of arabic covid-19 tweets using bert-based transformers and dynamically weighted loss function. *Applied Sciences*, 11(22):10694.

Wissam Antoun, Fady Baly, and Hazem Hajj. 2020. Arabert: Transformer-based model for arabic language understanding. *arXiv*.

Gilbert Badaro, Ramy Baly, Hazem Hajj, Wassim El-hajj, Khaled Bashir Shaban, Nizar Habash, Ahmad Al-sallab, and A L I Hamdi. 2020. A survey of opinion mining in arabic : A comprehensive system perspective covering challenges and advances in tools , resources , models , applications , and visualizations. *ACM Transactions on Asian and Low-Resource Language Information Processing*, 18:1–52.

Ramy Baly, Mitra Mohtarami, James Glass, Alessandro Moschitti, and Preslav Nakov. 2018. Integrating stance detection and fact checking in a unified corpus. *arXiv*.

Roy Bar-Haim, Indrajit Bhattacharya, Francesco Dinuzzo, Amrita Saha, and Noam Slonim. 2017. Stance classification of context-dependent claims. volume 1 of *Proceedings of the 15th Conference of the European Chapter of the Association for Computational Linguistics: Volume 1, Long Papers*, pages 251–261.

Pengyuan Chen, Kai Ye, and Xiaohui Cui. 2021. Integrating n-gram features into pre-trained model: A novel ensemble model for multi-target stance detection. volume 12893 LNCS, pages 269–279. Springer Science and Business Media Deutschland GmbH.

Sihao Chen, Daniel Khashabi, Wenpeng Yin, Chris Callison-Burch, and Dan Roth. 2019. Seeing things from a different angle: Discovering diverse perspectives about claims. volume 1 of *NAACL HLT 2019 - 2019 Conference of the North American Chapter of the Association for Computational Linguistics: Human Language Technologies*.

Alessandra Teresa Cignarella, Mirko Lai, Cristina Bosco, Viviana Patti, and Paolo Rosso. 2020. Sardistance @ evalita2020: Overview of the task on stance detection in italian tweets. volume 2765 of *EVALITA 2020 Seventh Evaluation Campaign of Natural Language Processing and Speech Tools for Italian*, pages 1–10.

Costanza Conforti, Jakob Berndt, Mohammad Taher Pilehvar, Chryssi Giannitsarou, Flavio Toxvaerd, and Nigel Collier. 2020. Will-they-won't-they: A very large dataset for stance detection on twitter. *arXiv*.

Leon Derczynski, Kalina Bontcheva, Maria Liakata, Rob Procter, Geraldine Wong Sak Hoi, and Arkaitz Zubiaga. 2017. Semeval-2017 task 8: Rumoureval: Determining rumour veracity and support for rumours. Proceedings of the 11th International Workshop on Semantic Evaluation (SemEval-2017), pages 69–76.

William Ferreira and Andreas Vlachos. 2016. Emergent: a novel data-set for stance classification. Proceedings of the 2016 conference of the North American chapter of the association for computational linguistics: Human language technologies. ACL, pages 1163–1168.

Shalmoli Ghosh, Prajwal Singhania, Siddharth Singh, Koustav Rudra, and Saptarshi Ghosh. 2019. Stance detection in web and social media: A comparative study. International Conference of the Cross-Language Evaluation Forum for European Languages, pages 75–87.

Santiago González-Carvajal and Eduardo C. Garrido-Merchán. 2020. Comparing bert against traditional machine learning text classification. *arXiv e-prints*.

Genevieve Gorrell, Elena Kochkina, Maria Liakata, Ahmet Aker, Arkaitz Zubiaga, Kalina Bontcheva, and Leon Derczynski. 2019. Rumoureval 2019: Determining rumour veracity and support for rumours. Proceedings of the 13th International Workshop on Semantic Evaluation (SemEval-2019), pages 845–854.

Lara Grimminger and Roman Klinger. 2021. Hate towards the political opponent: A twitter corpus study of the 2020 us elections on the basis of offensive speech and stance detection. *arXiv*.

Andreas Hanselowski, Avinesh P.V.S., Benjamin Schiller, Felix Caspelherr, Debanjan * Chaudhuri, Christian M Meyer, and Iryna Gurevych. 2018. A retrospective analysis of the fake news challenge stance-detection task. Proceedings of the 27th International Conference on Computational Linguistics (COLING 2018).

Tomáš Hercig, Peter Krejzl, Barbora Hourová, Josef Steinberger, and Ladislav Lenc. 2017. Detecting stance in czech news commentaries. ITAT, pages 176–180.

Marjan Hosseinia, Eduard Dragut, and Arjun Mukherjee. 2020. Stance prediction for contemporary issues: Data and experiments. Proceedings of the Eighth International Workshop on Natural Language Processing for Social Media. Association for Computational Linguistics (ACL).

Go Inoue, Bashar Alhafni, Nurpeiis Baimukan, Houda Bouamor, and Nizar Habash. 2021. The interplay of variant, size, and task type in arabic pre-trained language models. pages 92–104.

Jude Khouja. 2020. Stance prediction and claim verification: An arabic perspective. Proceedings of the Third Workshop on Fact Extraction and VERification (FEVER), pages 8–17.

Elena Kochkina, Maria Liakata, and Isabelle Augenstein. 2017. Turing at semeval-2017 task 8: Sequential approach to rumour stance classification with branch-lstm. Proceedings of the 11th International Workshop on Semantic Evaluations (SemEval-2017), pages 475–480.

Dilek Küçük and Fazli Can. 2018. Stance detection on tweets: An svm-based approach. *arXiv*, pages 1–13.

Dilek Küçük and C. A.N. Fazli. 2020. Stance detection: A survey. *ACM Computing Surveys*, 53.

Mirko Lai, Viviana Patti, Giancarlo Ruffo, and Paolo Rosso. 2018. Stance evolution and twitter interactions in an italian political debate. volume 10859 LNCS of *International Conference on Applications of Natural Language to Information Systems*, pages 15–27.

Mirko Lai, Viviana Patti, Giancarlo Ruffo, and Paolo Rosso. 2020. #brexit: Leave or remain? the role of user's community and diachronic evolution on stance detection. *Journal of Intelligent and Fuzzy Systems*, 39:2341–2352.

Yingjie Li, Tiberiu Sosea, Aditya Sawant, Ajith Jayaraman Nair, Diana Inkpen, and Cornelia Caragea. 2021a. P-stance: A large dataset for stance detection in political domain. pages 2355–2365.

Yingjie Li, Chenye Zhao, and Cornelia Caragea. 2021b. Improving stance detection with multi-dataset learning and knowledge distillation. Proceedings of the 2021 Conference on Empirical Methods in Natural Language Processing, pages 6332–6345.

Bin Liang, Yonghao Fu, Lin Gui, Min Yang, Jiachen Du, Yulan He, and Ruifeng Xu. 2021. Target-adaptive graph for cross-target stance detection. Proceedings of the World Wide Web Conference, WWW 2021, pages 3453–3464. Association for Computing Machinery, Inc.

Ilya Loshchilov and Frank Hutter. 2017. Decoupled weight decay regularization. *arXiv preprint arXiv:1711.05101*.

Saif M. Mohammad, Svetlana Kiritchenko, Parinaz Sobhani, Xiaodan Zhu, and Colin Cherry. 2016. Semeval-2016 task 6: Detecting stance in tweets. 10th International Workshop on Semantic Evaluation (SemEval-2016), pages 31–41.

Saif M. Mohammad, Parinaz Sobhani, and Svetlana Kiritchenko. 2017. Stance and sentiment in tweets. *ACM Transactions on Internet Technology (TOIT)*, 17:1–23.

Parinaz Sobhani, Diana Inkpen, and Xiaodan Zhu. 2017. A dataset for multi-target stance detection. volume 2 of *15th Conference of the European Chapter of the Association for Computational Linguistics, EACL 2017*, pages 551–557.

Parinaz Sobhani, Saif M Mohammad, and Svetlana Kiritchenko. 2016. Detecting stance in tweets and analyzing its interaction with sentiment. Proceedings of the Fifth Joint Conference on Lexical and Computational Semantics (SEM 2016), pages 159–169.

Christian Stab, Tristan Miller, Benjamin Schiller, Pranav Rai, and Iryna Gurevych. 2018. Cross-topic argument mining from heterogeneous sources using attention-based neural networks. Proceedings of the 2018 Conference on Empirical Methods in Natural Language Processing, EMNLP 2018.

Mariona Taulé, M. Antónia Martín, Francisco Rangel, Paolo Rosso, Cristina Bosco, and Viviana Patti. 2017. Overview of the task on stance and gender detection in tweets on catalan independence at ibereval 2017. volume 1881 of *2nd Workshop on Evaluation of Human Language Technologies for Iberian Languages, IberEval 2017*, pages 157–177.

Jannis Vamvas and Rico Sennrich. 2020. X-stance: A multilingual multi-target dataset for stance detection. 5th SwissText & 16th KONVENS Joint Conference 2020.

Yonghui Wu, Mike Schuster, Zhifeng Chen, Quoc V Le, Mohammad Norouzi, Wolfgang Macherey, Maxim Krikun, Yuan Cao, Qin Gao, Klaus Macherey, et al. 2016. Google's neural machine translation system: Bridging the gap between human and machine translation. *arXiv preprint arXiv:1609.08144*.

Ruifeng Xu, Yu Zhou, Dongyin Wu, Lin Gui, Jiachen Du, and Yun Xue. 2016. Overview of nlpcc shared task 4: Stance detection in chinese microblogs. *Natural language understanding and intelligent applications*, pages 907–916.

Elena Zotova, Rodrigo Agerri, and German Rigau. 2021. Semi-automatic generation of multilingual datasets for stance detection in twitter. *Expert Systems with Applications*, 170:1–29.

Assessing the Linguistic Knowledge in Arabic Pre-trained Language Models Using Minimal Pairs

Wafa Alrajhi
King Saud University
wAAlrajhi@imamu.edu.sa

Hend Al-Khalifa
King Saud University
hendk@ksu.edu.sa

AbdulMalik Al-Salman
King Saud University
salman@ksu.edu.sa

Abstract

Despite the noticeable progress that we recently witnessed in Arabic pre-trained language models (PLMs), the linguistic knowledge captured by these models remains unclear. In this paper, we conducted a study to evaluate available Arabic PLMs in terms of their linguistic knowledge. BERT-based language models (LMs) are evaluated using Minimum Pairs (MP), where each pair represents a grammatical sentence and its contradictory counterpart. MPs isolate specific linguistic knowledge to test the model's sensitivity in understanding a specific linguistic phenomenon. We cover nine major Arabic phenomena from: Verbal sentences, Nominal sentences, Adjective Modification, and Idafa construction. The experiments compared the results of fifteen Arabic BERT-based PLMs. Overall, among all tested models, CAMeL-CA and GigaBERT outperformed the other PLMs by achieving the highest overall accuracy.

1 Introduction

Recently, tremendous pre-trained neural network models existed and are used effectively in different Natural language processing (NLP) tasks. This renaissance began roughly when Google launched the Transformers architecture in 2017 (Vaswani et al., 2017). Furthermore, different models are developed after the Transformers, such as Generative pre-training (GPT) (Radford et al., 2018), GPT-2 (Radford et al., 2019), GPT-3 (Brown et al., 2020), and Bidirectional Encoder Representations from Transformers (BERT) (Devlin et al., 2019). These models have proved their strength in many NLP tasks, such as machine translation, summarization, and sentiment analysis.

In 2019, several attempts appeared to train BERT models, specifically for the Arabic language. AraBERT was one of the first Arabic models that aimed to contribute to Arabic NLP in three different tasks: Sentiment Analysis (SA), Named Entity Recognition (NER), and Question Answering (QA) (Antoun et al., 2020). Furthermore, the end of 2020 has witnessed a race where several Arabic models were published, namely: Arabic-BERT (Safaya & Yuret, 2020), GigaBERT (Lan et al., 2020), ARBERT, and MARBERT (Abdul-Mageed & Elmadany, 2020). Also, 2021 was no less intense; several versions of AraBERT models (Antoun et al., 2020), as well as ARAELECTRA (Antoun et al., 2021), and QARiB (Abdelali et al., 2021), were published. Despite these developments, the vision remains blurred in terms of how these models analyze the language in regard to various linguistic phenomena such as syntax, semantics, and grammar, which is an open area for research.

Evaluating the linguistic knowledge of PLMs has gained popularity recently. Therefore, numerous methods were developed to test the model's linguistic competence and the acquisition of different linguistic phenomena. Humans develop the ability to distinguish between grammatical and ungrammatical sentences while they are growing. Thus, studies showed that PLMs could mimic human ability, whereas, despite having no formal grammar training, the models can distinguish between grammatical and ungrammatical sentences (Warstadt et al., 2019). Many of these studies are specified for exploring the models' linguistic knowledge in the English Language (Warstadt et al., 2020; Bouraoui et al., 2020) and Chinese Language (Xiang et al., 2021). Nevertheless, to the best of our knowledge, no study has been devoted to understanding the linguistic knowledge of Arabic pre-trained language models.

PLMs, such as BERT, assign a probability/score to a sequence of words (Xiang et al., 2021). Many studies have used these scores to rank a sentence's

Proceedings of the The Seventh Arabic Natural Language Processing Workshop (WANLP), pages 185 - 193
December 8, 2022 ©2022 Association for Computational Linguistics

correctness and evaluate the models' knowledge (Wang et al., 2019) (Shin et al., 2019). A common method to evaluate the model's linguistic knowledge is minimal pairs (MP). MP is a set of two-sentence pairs (grammatical and ungrammatical) that is used to test the model's preferences among them. Assigning a higher score for the grammatical sentence from the MP pair verifies the model's understanding of a specific phenomenon. Each pair of sentences provided by MP minimally differs by changing one word only. This change should ensure that the grammatical rule is contrasted, whereas, the grammatical and ungrammatical sentences are balanced. Example 1 illustrates a pair of MP sentences where we provided two verbal sentences; the first one is based on correct Arabic language grammar where the verb agrees with the subject in gender. The second sentence of Example 1 presents a contrast for the rule, as the verb does not agree in gender with the subject.

Furthermore, another example of Arabic language grammar is presented in Example 2. The first sentence in Example 2 (correct) provides a verb that does not agree with the subject in number, while the second sentence contrasts the rule. As we noticed from the examples, MPs are used to prompt the analysis and subsequent improvements of PLMs (Warstadt et al., 2019) (Bouraoui et al., 2020) (Xiang et al., 2021). In addition, each pair isolates a specific phenomenon, allowing the PLM to be tested separately for each linguistic phenomenon.

Example 1:

يزرع الفلاح الشجرة *(جملة صحيحة)*

yzrE AlflAH Al$jrp

The farmer (male) plants (masculine verb) the tree *(grammatical)*

تزرع الفلاح الشجرة *(جملة خاطئة)*

tzrE AlflAH Al$jrp

The farmer (male) plants (feminine verb) the tree *(ungrammatical)*

Example 2:

ذهب الولدان برحلة *(جملة صحيحة)*

**hb AlwldAn brHlp*

The boys went (single) on a trip *(grammatical)*

ذهبا الولدان برحلة *(جملة خاطئة)*

**hbA AlwldAn brHlp*

The boys went (dual) on a trip (ungrammatical)

In this study, we introduce a handcrafted Arabic minimal pair MPs consisting of around 3000 sentences[1]. As each MP contains both grammatical and ungrammatical sentences, the dataset is balanced and written in Modern Standard Arabic (MSA). Moreover, since the Arabic Language is extensive and complex, we limited this study to cover nine basic Arabic syntactic, semantic, and grammatical phenomena, including: verbal sentence, nominal sentence, adjective modification, and Idafa construction. Fifteen BERT-based LMs were tested using the models' sensitivity to detect the grammatical contrast. Therefore, our contributions in this paper can be listed as follows:

1- Building the first handcrafted Arabic minimal pair MPs dataset consisting of 3000 sentences.
2- Evaluating the linguistic knowledge of fifteen Arabic PLMs.

The remainder of the paper is organized as follows: the next section discusses the basic phenomena of Arabic syntax. Then, we present a description of the existing Arabic PLMs. Next, section 4 illustrates the conducted experiments, followed by their results and discussion. Finally, Section 6 concludes the paper with limitations and future work.

2 Arabic Linguistics

Arabic is a distinctive language with unique characteristics, rich morphology, and free word ordering (Habash, N.Y., 2010). The Arabic sentence is divided into two types: the verbal sentence and the nominal sentence. For each type, there are several forms that the sentence can take and remain linguistically correct. The following subsections cover a summary of these primary forms. Additionally, the relationship between nouns, case assignment, gender, and number agreement in the sentence structure are also covered. Table 1 shows acceptable and unacceptable examples of MPs for each linguistic phenomenon that we included in this study. In each example, the underlined word represents the word that we changed to contrast the grammar.

[1]https://github.com/wafa7d/AssessingArabicBERTs

Phenomenon			Accepted Example	Unaccepted Example
Verbal Sentence	1.	Agreement of the verb and subject in gender	يزرع الفلاح الشجرة yzrE AlflAH Al$jrp The farmer (male) plants (masculine) the tree	تزرع الفلاح الشجرة tzrE AlflAH Al$jrp The farmer (male) plants (feminine) the tree
	2.	Disagreement of the verb and subject in number	قطف الفلاحون الثمار qTf AlflAHwn AlvmAr Peasants (plural) harvested (single) fruits	قطفوا الفلاحون الثمار qTfwA AlflAHwn AlvmAr The peasants (plural) harvested (plural) the fruits
Nominal Sentence	3.	Agreement of the subject and predicate in number	الطالبتان مجدتان AlTAlbtAn mjdtAn The two students are good	الطالبة مجدتان AlTAlbp mjdtAn The student are good
	4.	Agreement of the subject and predicate in gender	هذا طالب نشيط h*A TAlb n$yT This (masculine) is an active student (male)	هذه طالب نشيط h*h TAlb n$yT This (masculine) is an active student (female)
Adjective Modifications	5.	Rational	المهندس البارع Almhnds AlbArE The brilliant (masculine) engineer (male)	المهندس البارعة Almhnds AlbArEp The brilliant (feminine) engineer (male)
	6.	Irrational	الات جديدة |lAt jdydp New (feminine) machines (feminine)	الات جدد ậlạt jdd New (masculine) machines (feminine)
Idafa Construction	7.	Adjective agrees with head noun in case	باب حديقة كبير bạb ḥdyqť kbyr Large (single) garden door (single)	أبواب حديقة كبير >bwAb Hdyqp kbyr Large (single) garden doors (plural)
	8.	Adjective agrees with second noun in definiteness	قراءة العلم النافع qrA'p AlElm AlnAfE Reading beneficial knowledge	قراءة علم النافع qrA'p Elm AlnAfE Reading beneficial knowledge
	9.	Adjective agrees with first noun in gender	قائد الفرقة القوي qA}d Alfrqp Alqwy Strong (masculine) squad leader(male)	قائد الفرقة القوية qA}d Alfrqp Alqwyp Strong (feminine) squad leader(male)

Table 1 Minimal Pairs (MPs) for nine linguistic phenomena of Arabic Language that were covered in this paper (the translitarion is done using Buckwalter)

2.1 Verbal Sentences

Verbal sentences can be expressed in several forms, where expressing the subject may vary in each of these forms (Habash, N.Y., 2010). In this paper, we covered the following forms of verbal sentences:

- Verbal sentence with non-pronominal subject where:
  a) The verb and subject agree in gender.
  b) The verb and subject do not agree in number.

The basic form of the verbal sentence is: Verb-Subject-Object(s), where the non-pronominal subject appears after the verb. In this case, the verb and the subject should agree in the gender, but not the number, i.e., singular, dual, and plural. Consequently, the male subject requires a male verb, e.g. (He wrote – ktb – كتب), likewise if the subject is feminine, the feminine sign should be attached to the verb, e.g. (She wrote – ktbt – كتبت).

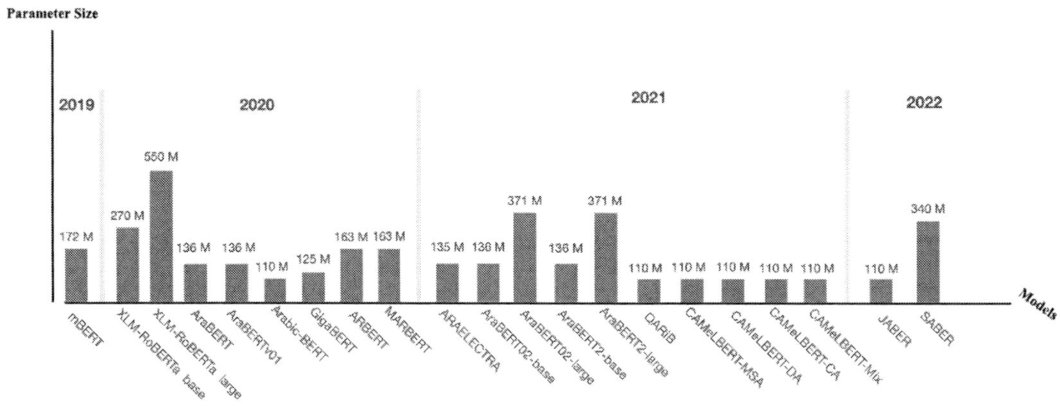

Figure 1 The Timeline of Arabic PLMs with Their Parameters

Table 1 demonstrates the different verbal sentence forms by providing acceptable and unacceptable examples for each of these forms.

2.2 Nominal Sentences

Similar to verbal sentences, nominal sentences can be expressed through different forms; the simplest form is the Subject-Predicate/Topic-Complement (Habash, N.Y., 2010). The subject can be a definite noun, proper noun, or pronoun, while the predicate is an indefinite noun, proper noun, or adjective. Two different cases are considered in the nominal sentence as follows:

1. Agreement of subject and predicate in number.
2. Agreement of subject and predicate in gender.

As mentioned above, the subject and predicate should agree in number and gender, as demonstrated by several examples in Table 1.

2.3 Adjective Modifications

Similar to English, adjectives in Arabic are nouns that describe other nouns or pronouns. The Arabic adjectives can describe rational and irrational nouns, which are the two adjective modification cases that we considered. Arabic adjectives agree in definiteness and case with nouns. However, the adjective of the rational nouns agrees in gender and number as well. Table 1 illustrates examples of the difference between rational and irrational adjectives (Habash, N.Y., 2010).

2.4 Idafa Construction

In the Idafa construction, two nouns are related; the first noun imposes the semantics and grammar on the second noun, such as: (squad leader / قائد الفرقة). It is considered a noun phrase and can be part of a second noun phrase. In this construction, an adjective might follow the Idafa construction describing the head noun, such as: (<u>strong</u> squad leader / قائد الفرقة <u>القوي</u>). This adjective agrees with the head noun in case and gender. Nevertheless, it agrees with the second noun in terms of definiteness (Habash, N.Y., 2010). The paper covers these three cases, and examples are illustrated in Table 1.

3 The Evolution of Arabic PLMs

Chronologically, the first multilingual BERT model that supported the Arabic language appeared in 2019; it was mxBERT (Pires et al., 2019). It was followed by the first monolingual Arabic model, i.e., AraBERT (Antoun et al., 2020), which appeared in early 2020. Figure 1 illustrates the evolution of Arabic PLMs, showing their parameter sizes and existence order. Moreover, Table 2 summarizes the configurations of the basic BERT-based Arabic model. Next, we provide a brief description of these PLMs.

3.1 AraBERT

AraBERT configurations followed BERT, which includes: 12 encoder blocks, 768 hidden dimensions, 12 attention heads, 512 maximum sequence lengths (Antoun et al., 2020). The masked language model task, which proves its efficiency in improving the pre-training task, was used as a pre-processing step. The total size of the pre-training dataset reached approximately 70 million sentences without any redundancy. Four empowered versions of the model were released at the beginning of 2021, where the data reached 77

Details / LM	Variants	Size	#Words	#Steps
AraBERT (Antoun et al., 2020)	MSA	23GB	2.7B	1.2M
AraBERTv01 (Antoun et al., 2020)	MSA	23GB	2.7B	1.2M
AraBERTv02-based (Antoun et al., 2019)	MSA	77GB	8.6B	3M
AraBERTv02-large (Antoun et al., 2020)	MSA	77GB	8.6B	550K
AraBERTv2-based (Antoun et al., 2020)	MSA	77GB	8.6B	550K
AraBERTv2-large (Antoun et al., 2020)	MSA	77GB	8.6B	550K
ArabicBERT (Safaya & Yuret, 2020)	MSA/DA	95GB	8.2B	4M
GigaBERT (Lan et al., 2020)	MSA	-	10.4B	1.47M
ARBERT (Abdul-Mageed & Elmadany , 2021)	MSA	61GB	6.5B	8M
MARBERT (Abdul-Mageed & Elmadany , 2021)	MSA/DA	128GB	15.6B	17M
CAMeLBERT-MSA (Inoue et al., 2021)	MSA	107GB	12.6B	1M
CAMeLBERT-DA (Inoue et al., 2021)	DA	45GB	5.8B	1M
CAMeLBERT-CA (Inoue et al., 2021)	CA	6GB	847M	1M
CAMeLBERT-Mix (Inoue et al., 2021)	MSA/ DA/CA	167GB	17.3B	1M

Table 2 BERT-based LMs Configurations

GB; AraBERT (136 million), AraBERTv01 (136 million), AraBERTv02-based (136 million), AraBERTv02-large (371 million), AraBERTv2-based (136 million), AraBERTv2-large (371 million). These versions vary in parameter size, and a more extensive dataset was used in the training process.

3.2 GigaBERT

GigaBERT is a cross-lingual model English-to-Arabic customized BERT that follows, as AraBERT, the same configuration of BERT (Antoun et al., 2020). It was trained using the fifth edition of the Gigaword English and Arabic corpora, which consists of 13 million articles. Wikipedia's data were added to manage the unbalance between English and Arabic datasets. Furthermore, the Arabic dataset was up-sampled by repeating Wikipedia's data five times and Gigaword three times.

3.3 ARBERT and MARBERT

The authors (Abdul-Mageed & Elmadany, 2021) introduced these two models, and both followed BERT architecture. ARBERT was trained on MSA only and the dataset reached 61 GB of text. MARBERT was trained on MSA and Arabic dialects, making the model more suitable for downstream tasks. Thus, almost 1 billion Arabic tweets were used to train MARBERT, which is around 128GB of text.

3.4 CAMeLBERT

The authors of (Inoue et al., 2021) proposed up to eight Arabic PLMs aiming to investigate the effect of the training data size/type variations on the behavior of these LMs. Mainly, CAMeLBERT-MSA was trained on 107 GB of Modern Standard Arabic (MSA) text, CAMeLBERT-DA was trained on 54 GB of Dialectal Arabic (DA) text, CAMeLBERT-CA was trained on 6 GB of Classical Arabic (CA) text, and CAMeLBERT-Mix is a mix of all the previous three, where its training data reached 167GB. Similar to the previous models, the authors followed the BERT model's architecture. The PLMs are evaluated on different NLP tasks: NER, POS tagging, Sentiment Analysis, dialect identification, and poetry classification. The authors elucidate the importance of the proximity of the subtask data training and pre-training data, compared to the size of the pre-training data.

4 Method

In the following subsections, we precisely describe the data coverage and the conducted experiment.

Phenomena/LMs	AraBERT (Antoun et al., 2020)	AraBERTv01 (Antoun et al., 2020)	AraBERTv02-based (Antoun et al., 2020)	AraBERTv02-large (Antoun et al., 2020)	AraBERTv2-based (Antoun et al., 2020)	AraBERTv2-large (Antoun et al., 2020)	ArabicBERT (Safaya & Yuret, 2020)	GigaBERT (Lan et al., 2020)	ARBERT (Abdul-Mageed & Elmadany, 2021)	MARBERT (Abdul-Mageed & Elmadany, 2021)	QARiB (Abdul-Mageed et al., 2021)	CAMeLBERT-MSA (Inoue et al., 2021)	CAMeLBERT-DA (Inoue et al., 2021)	CAMeLBERT-CA (Inoue et al., 2021)	CAMeLBERT-Mix (Inoue et al., 2021)
Overall accuracy	47.7%	51.3%	52.0%	51.1%	49.7%	53.2%	52.5%	**55.1%**	53.2%	54.4%	49.2%	51.0%	49.1%	**55.1%**	49.1%
Verbal sentence															
1. Agreement of the verb and subject in gender	55.3%	44%	46%	47.3%	65.3%	58%	48.6%	60%	41.3%	39.3%	42.6%	52%	47.3%	**76.5%**	42.6%
2. Disagreement of the verb and subject in number	66.5%	60.5%	58.5%	63%	57%	55.5%	64.5%	**76%**	59.5%	62%	72%	63%	57.5%	66%	63.5%
Nominal sentence															
3. Agreement of the subject and predicate in number	**56.9%**	43%	34.4%	45%	43.7%	54.9%	54.9%	54.3%	39%	45.6%	45%	50.3%	41.7%	**56.9%**	39%
4. Agreement of the subject and predicate in gender	**56.2%**	42.7%	44.7%	41.2%	46.7%	42.7%	46.7%	46.2%	53.7%	46.2%	36.6%	44.2%	44.2%	48.2%	37.6%
Adjective Modification															
5. Rational	49.3%	51.3%	46%	45.3%	46%	50%	54%	51.3%	48%	49.3%	39.3%	47.3%	44%	**56%**	37%
6. Irrational	26%	59%	73%	63%	43%	51%	56%	64%	66%	**75%**	49%	51%	51%	56%	54%
Idafa construction															
7. Adjective agrees with head noun in case	**58%**	57%	41%	47%	52%	51%	56%	51%	48%	47%	50%	48%	39%	56%	53%
8. Adjective agrees with second noun in definiteness	49.3%	44%	53.3%	53.3%	33.3%	45.3%	45.3%	50.6%	45.3%	41.3%	46%	50.6%	**56%**	54.6%	54.6%
9. Adjective agrees with first noun in gender	56%	45.3%	42.6%	53.3%	54.6%	**58.6%**	44%	50.6%	56%	46.6%	40%	57.3%	45.3%	44%	49.3%

Table 3 Accuracy results for Arabic PLMs; **Bold** numbers indicate the highest accuracy

4.1 Data

Following Arabic basic morphology, syntax, and semantics, we constructed a handcrafted dataset for this experiment. This dataset covers nine major Arabic linguistic phenomena that include the aforementioned grammars of verbal sentences, nominal sentences, adjective modification, and Idafa. The dataset comprised well-established contrasts in Arabic Minimal Pairs (MPs), which served as a stimulus for the models, allowing us to measure the linguistic knowledge of the model. Almost 3000 MPs were constructed; 1000 MPs for the verbal structure, 1000 MPs for the nominal structure, 500 MPs for the adjective modification sentences, and 500 MPs for the Idafa construction. The data is balanced between grammatical and ungrammatical sentences, so that 50% of the data is grammatically correct. The dataset was constructed by an Arabic language expert (Master's Degree in the Arabic Language) and reviewed by three Arabic-native speakers. Accordingly, each MP belonging to the same grammar is structurally analogous, verifying that the grammatical sentence fulfills the Arabic grammar and that the ungrammatical sentence

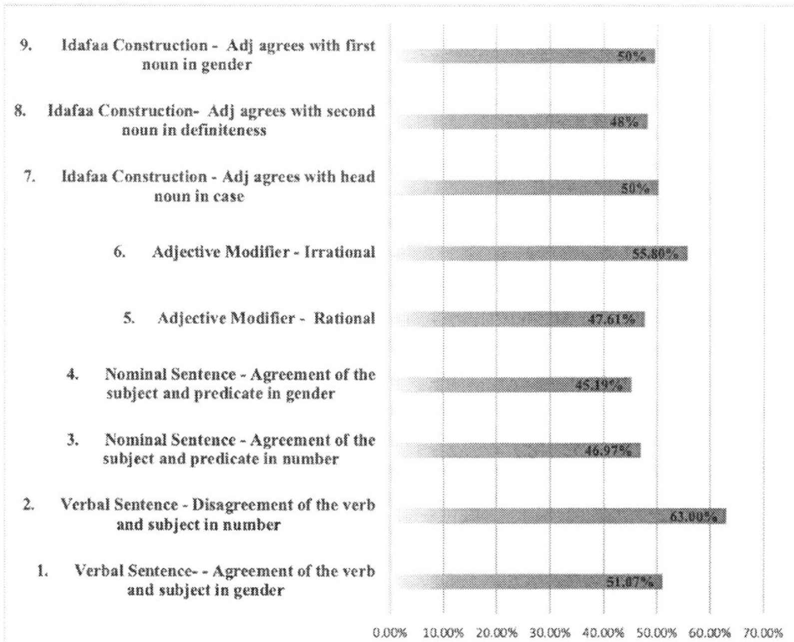

Figure 2 Arabic PLMs Average Performance on each of the Nine Arabic Phenomenon

contrasts the required grammar. All these sentences are in MSA.

4.2 Experiments

This study focuses on BERT-Based Arabic models, which allows us to examine the actual effect of different factors on the models' knowledge acquisition, such as parameter size and corpus size. As a result, we want to uncover the reasons behind the models' performance variations, if any exist. Given MPs to each model, the model should assign a higher probability to the correct grammatical sentence; in that case, the classification of MP is accepted.

In the conducted experiments, we covered fifteen Arabic PLMs. This includes six versions of AraBERT: AraBERT, AraBERTv01, AraBERTv02-base, AraBERTv02-large AraBERTv2-base, AraBERTv2-large. It also includes ArabicBERT, GigaBERT, QARiB, ARBERT, MARBERT, four versions of CAMeLBERT: CAMeLBERT-MSA, CAMeLBERT-CA, CAMeLBERTDA, and CAMeLBERT-Mix.

Table 2 illustrates the configurations of the models, highlighting the variations in terms of parameter size, corpus size, variant types of the Arabic language used in the pre-training process, and the number of training steps.

5 Results and Discussion

We evaluated each model using the accuracy metric. As shown in equation 1, the accuracy is the fraction of examples for which the model assigns a relatively higher probability for the correct sentence.

$$Accuracy = \frac{Correctly\ classified\ sentences}{Total\ number\ of\ sentences} \quad (1)$$

Table 3 illustrates the results of the Fifteen Arabic PLMs; surprisingly, even the highest accuracy did not exceed 60% in any of the covered Arabic linguistic phenomena. Overall, the performance of the models was similar, with accuracies ranging from 47% to 55%. As a result, unlike PLMs in other languages, such as English (Warstadt et al., 2020), these findings show an obvious deficiency in evaluating and understanding Arabic linguistic phenomena by PLMs.

CAMeL-CA and GigaBERT achieved the highest overall average accuracy (55.1%) in all of the Arabic phenomena we tested, including verbal, nominal, adjective, and Idafa. Unlike all models,

CAMeL-CA was exclusively pre-trained on Classical Arabic, indicating that the model has acquired a better understanding of Arabic linguistic knowledge than other models. On the other hand, GigaBERT was pre-trained on Modern Standard Arabic.

For verbal sentences, CAMeL-CA yielded the highest accuracy of 76.5% in the disagreement between the subject and verb in gender, and GigaBERT outperformed all models in the agreement of verb and subject in number, with an accuracy of 76%. On the other hand, for the nominal sentence, AraBERT and CAMeL-CA performed similarly and achieved the best accuracies, approximately 57% in the subject's agreement and predicate in number. Additionally, AraBERT also achieved the highest performance in the subject's agreement and predicate in gender.

Moreover, CAMeL-CA and MARBERT have achieved the highest accuracies for the rational and irrational adjective modifiers. Specifically, CAMeL-CA achieved the highest accuracy in rational adjective modifiers, reaching 56%, While MARBERT achieved 75% accuracy in irrational. Furthermore, although the sentences in the Idafa constructions are more comprehensive, covering verbal or nominal structures, the models' accuracy remained in the same range. AraBERT, CAMeLBERT-DA, and CAMeLBERT-MSA gave the highest accuracies in the Idafa constructions.

To summarize, Figure 2 shows the average accuracy of all the models for each Arabic phenomenon. The most notable phenomenon recognized by PLMs is the disagreement between the verb and the subject in number. Conversely, the models perform poorly in the nominal sentence agreement between subject and predicate in number.

6 Conclusion

This paper aims to comprehend the linguistic abilities conferred by Arabic PLMs. We present a study to understand the basic grammar concepts obtained by the current BERT-based Arabic PLMs using MPs. Each MP represents a distinct phenomenon; hence, it can reflect the model understanding to that phenomenon. Therefore, utilizing the grammatical/ungrammatical pairs of MPs, it is feasible to assess how well the model comprehends a particular phenomenon by assigning it a higher probability to the grammatical sentence. The experiments include evaluating nine basic Arabic phenomena on fifteen BERT-based Arabic PLMs. The findings indicate a clear lack of PLMs' understanding of most of the evaluated Arabic phenomena. However, the highest average accuracy was achieved by CAMeL-CA and GigaBERT reaching 55.1%, with CAMeL-CA outperforming in three linguistic phenomena. It is worth mentioning that CAMeL-CA has used classical Arabic in its pre-training process, which justifies its high scores in our evaluation.

Finally, the capacities targeted by our experiments are not exhaustive. Future research can build on this paper's findings to study other linguistic aspects of Arabic PLMs in depth and include other models.

7 References

Vaswani, A., Shazeer, N., Parmar, N., Uszkoreit, J., Jones, L., Aidan N. Gomez., Lukasz Kaiser. and Polosukhin, I., 2017. Attention is all you need. Advances in neural information processing systems, 30.

Radford, A., Narasimhan, K., Salimans, T. and Sutskever, I., 2018. *Improving language understanding by generative pre-training.*

Radford, A., Wu, J., Child, R., Luan, D., Amodei, D. and Sutskever, I., 2019. *Language models are unsupervised multitask learners.* OpenAI blog, 1(8), p.9.

Brown, T., et al. 2020. *Language models are few-shot learners.* Advances in neural information processing systems, 33, pp.1877-1901.

Devlin, J., Chang, M.W., Lee, K. and Toutanova, K., 2019, June. *BERT: Pre-training of Deep Bidirectional Transformers for Language Understanding.* In Proceedings of the 2019 Conference of the North American Chapter of the Association for Computational Linguistics: Human Language Technologies, Volume 1 (Long and Short Papers) (pp. 4171-4186).

Antoun, W., Baly, F. and Hajj, H., 2020, May. *AraBERT: Transformer-based Model for Arabic Language Understanding.* In Proceedings of the 4th Workshop on Open-Source Arabic Corpora and Processing Tools, with a Shared Task on Offensive Language Detection (pp. 9-15).

Safaya, A., Abdullatif, M. and Yuret, D., 2020. *BERT-CNN for Offensive Speech Identification in Social Media.* In Proceedings of the Fourteenth Workshop on Semantic Evaluation", Barcelona (online)", International Committee for Computational Linguistics.

Lan W, Chen Y, Xu W, Ritter A. *Gigabert: Zero-shot transfer learning from English to Arabic.* In Proceedings of The 2020 Conference on Empirical Methods on Natural Language Processing (EMNLP) 2020.

Abdul-Mageed, M. and Elmadany, A., 2021, August. *ARBERT & MARBERT: Deep Bidirectional Transformers for Arabic.* In Proceedings of the 59th Annual Meeting of the Association for Computational Linguistics and the 11th International Joint Conference on Natural Language Processing (Volume 1: Long Papers) (pp. 7088-7105). https://doi.org/10.18653/v1/2021.acl-long.551

Antoun, W., Baly, F. and Hajj, H., 2021, April. AraELECTRA: Pre-Training Text Discriminators for Arabic Language Understanding. In Proceedings of the Sixth Arabic Natural Language Processing Workshop (pp. 191-195).

Abdelali, A., Hassan, S., Mubarak, H., Darwish, K. and Samih, Y., 2021. *Pre-training bert on arabic tweets: Practical considerations.* arXiv preprint arXiv:2102.10684..

Warstadt, A., Singh, A. and Bowman, S., 2019. *Neural Network Acceptability Judgments*. Transactions of the Association for Computational Linguistics, 7, pp.625-641. https://doi.org/10.1162/tacl_a_00290

Warstadt, A., Parrish, A., Liu, H., Mohananey, A., Peng, W., Wang, S.F. and Bowman, S., 2020. *BLiMP: The Benchmark of Linguistic Minimal Pairs for English*. Transactions of the Association for Computational Linguistics, 8, pp.377-392. https://doi.org/10.1162/tacl_a_00321

Bouraoui, Z., Camacho-Collados, J. and Schockaert, S., 2020, April. *Inducing relational knowledge from BERT*. In Proceedings of the AAAI Conference on Artificial Intelligence (Vol. 34, No. 05, pp. 7456-7463). https://doi.org/10.1609/aaai.v34i05.6242

Xiang, B., Yang, C., Li, Y., Warstadt, A. and Kann, K., 2021, April. CLiMP: *A Benchmark for Chinese Language Model Evaluation*. In Proceedings of the 16th Conference of the European Chapter of the Association for Computational Linguistics: Main Volume (pp. 2784-2790). https://doi.org/10.18653/v1/2021.eacl-main.242

Wang, A. and Cho, K., 2019, June. *BERT has a Mouth, and It Must Speak: BERT as a Markov Random Field Language Model*. In Proceedings of the Workshop on Methods for Optimizing and Evaluating Neural Language Generation (pp. 30-36). https://doi.org/10.18653/v1/W19-2304

Shin, J., Lee, Y. and Jung, K., 2019, October. *Effective sentence scoring method using bert for speech recognition*. In Asian Conference on Machine Learning (pp. 1081-1093). PMLR.

Habash, N.Y., 2010. *Introduction to Arabic natural language processing*. Synthesis lectures on human language technologies, 3(1), pp.1-187. https://doi.org/10.2200/S00277ED1V01Y201008HLT010)

Pires, T., Schlinger, E. and Garrette, D., 2019, July. *How Multilingual is Multilingual BERT?*. In Proceedings of the 57th Annual Meeting of the Association for Computational Linguistics (pp. 4996-5001). https://doi.org/10.18653/v1/P19-1493

Inoue, G., Alhafni, B., Baimukan, N., Bouamor, H. and Habash, N., 2021, April. *The Interplay of Variant, Size, and Task Type in Arabic Pre-trained Language Models*. In Proceedings of the Sixth Arabic Natural Language Processing Workshop (pp. 92-104).

Identifying Code-switching in Arabizi

Safaa Shehadi and **Shuly Wintner**
Department of Computer Science
University of Haifa, Israel
safa.shehadi@gmail.com, shuly@cs.haifa.ac.il

Abstract

We describe a corpus of social media posts that include utterances in Arabizi, a Roman-script rendering of Arabic, mixed with other languages, notably English, French, and Arabic written in the Arabic script. We manually annotated a subset of the texts with word-level language IDs; this is a non-trivial task due to the nature of mixed-language writing, especially on social media. We developed classifiers that can accurately predict the language ID tags. Then, we extended the word-level predictions to identify sentences that include Arabizi (and code-switching), and applied the classifiers to the raw corpus, thereby harvesting a large number of additional instances. The result is a large-scale dataset of Arabizi, with precise indications of code-switching between Arabizi and English, French, and Arabic.

1 Introduction

Arabizi is a writing system for (primarily dialectal) Arabic that uses the Roman alphabet. It is ubiquitous on social media outlets, and has many characteristics of social media writings in other languages (e.g., slang, tendency towards the spoken register, spelling errors, abbreviations, character repetition, use of emoticons, etc.) The use of the Roman alphabet facilitates (and perhaps even encourages) *code-switching*: moving between Arabic (represented in Arabizi) and other languages, notably English and French, sometimes even within the same sentence.

Code-switching is becoming more and more prevalent as the world's population is becoming more multilingual (Grosjean, 1998). It is a natural phenomenon that is triggered by linguistic, sociolinguistic, psycholinguistic, demographic, and contextual prompts, and has been studied mainly in the spoken language until recently. With the ubiquity of text online, however, code-switching is beginning to be investigated also in the written language (e.g., Solorio and Liu, 2008; Solorio et al., 2014; Aguilar et al., 2018; Solorio et al., 2021). Such research has various practical applications, both for understanding and for generation of code-switched language (Sitaram et al., 2019; Doğruöz et al., 2021). Our main interest is in code-switching phenomena in Arabizi; in order to better understand them, a large dataset of Arabizi is required.

The main goal of this work is to construct a large-corpus of Arabizi utterances, potentially including instances of code-switching between Arabizi and English, French, or Arabic written in the Arabic script. The dataset is based on social media posts from two outlets: Twitter and Reddit. To collect the data, we implemented a classifier that can identify sentences containing words in Arabizi, Arabic, English, and French, and used it to filter out texts harvested from the two outlets.

We describe the dataset and the methods we used to curate it (Section 3). We then discuss the challenge of determining the language ID of words in multilingual texts, and describe classifiers that can accurately predict such language tags, based on a schema we developed for the task (Section 4). We extend the word-level classifiers to sentence-level ones, assigning a complex tag to each sentence that indicates the presence of words from various categories (i.e., languages) in it (Section 5). Finally, we use the classifiers to extract additional instances of sentences with Arabizi (and with code-switching) from our raw corpus (Section 6).

This paper makes several contributions: 1. We release a large-scale corpus of Twitter and Reddit posts that include Arabizi; 2. We introduce a novel annotation scheme that determines the language of words in multilingual utterances; specifically, we advocate a unique tag for words that can be included in more than one mental lexicon (and hence trigger code-switching); 3. We release a portion of the dataset, manually annotated according to this annotation scheme; and 4. We provide highly-accurate classifiers that can determine the language

Proceedings of the The Seventh Arabic Natural Language Processing Workshop (WANLP), pages 194 - 204

ID tags of words in this corpus; the classifiers were used to identify hundreds of thousands of additional sentences that are very likely to include Arabizi in general and code-switching with Arabizi in particular. We expect these resources, which are all publicly available,[1] to be instrumental for future research in code-switching and in Arabizi.

2 Related work

Arabizi has attracted some interest in recent years, and various works address the tasks of detecting it and converting Arabizi to the Arabic script. Darwish (2014) used word- and sequence-level features to identify Arabizi mixed with English and achieved 98.5% accuracy on the identification task. He argued that classifying a word as Arabizi or English has to be done *in context*, and thus employed sequence labeling using Conditional Random Fields (CRF) for classification. The data were selected from Twitter, by querying (three) commonly used Arabizi words and then extracting the user IDs of all the authors of the resulting tweets, obtaining all their tweets, under the assumption that authors who use Arabizi once may use it often. Then, tweets in which most of the words contained Arabic letters were filtered out. This resulted in 522 tweets consisting of 5207 tokens, of which 1203 were in Arabizi.

Cotterell et al. (2014) compiled a corpus of more than half a million pages from an Algerian newspaper website, from which they extracted almost 7M tokens which were annotated for language, using three tags: Arabic, French, or Other. More recently, Samih and Maier (2016) compiled a corpus of Arabic mixed with Moroccan Darija, in which tokens were assigned to seven categories: three for languages, and then mixed (morphemes from more than one language in the same token), named entity, ambiguous and other. In total, 223K tokens were annotated.

The task of transliterating Arabizi to Arabic was addressed by Al-Badrashiny et al. (2014), who employed finite-state transducers, a language model and morphological processors for Arabic. They used a dataset consisting of 1500 words only. This approach was then extended to the Tunisian dialect (Masmoudi et al., 2015). The transliteration task was applied to the Tunisian dialect in a more recent work (Younes et al., 2022), using contemporary machine-learning techniques, but the datasets remained relatively small. Shazal et al. (2020) addressed the joint task of identifying Arabizi and transliterating it to the Arabic script, reporting high word accuracy on a large (1M token) dataset.

Tobaili (2016) trained an SVM classifier to identify Arabizi in multilingual Twitter data. He assumed that in order to tag a tweet as Arabizi it should have more Arabizi words than English words. The best results were obtained using three features: (1) the languages as detected by *Langdetect*; (2) the language as detected by the twitter API; and (3) the count of word occurrences per tweet. The dataset used in this work is small, and has merely 465 Arabizi sentences from Lebanon and 955 from Egypt. Tobaili (2016) also found that the use of Arabizi differed between Egypt and Lebanon (for example, more omission of vowels in the former, and more mixed language in the latter).

Two Arabizi datasets were recently compiled and released (Baert et al., 2020): LAD, a corpus of 7.7M tweets written in Arabizi; and SALAD, a randomly-selected subset of LAD, containing 1700 tweets, manually annotated for sentiment analysis. The tweets were harvested using Twint: Twitter Intelligence Tool, by setting 48 common words in Egyptian as seeds. This work focused mainly on the Egyptian dialect, and the manually-annotated dataset is rather small.

Seddah et al. (2020) built the first North-African Arabizi treebank. It contains 1500 sentences, fully annotated with morpho-syntactic and Universal Dependency codes, with full translation at both the word and the sentence levels. It is also supplemented by 50K unlabeled sentences collected using web-crawling. The texts reflect the Algerian dialect, and contain 36% French tokens. Recently, this dataset was extended by adding transliterations of all the Arabizi tokens, as well as sentence-level annotations of sentiment and topic (Touileb and Barnes, 2021).

Adouane et al. (2016) focused on the task of identifying Arabizi (and Romanized Bereber) in social media texts, reporting near-perfect accuracy using very simple character-ngram features. The data were collected from North-African sources and reflect these dialects. More recently, Younes et al. (2020) used deep learning methods to identify the language of words in Tunisian social media texts. They defined five categories for the classification (Tunisian dialect words, foreign langauge words, punctuation, symbols, and emoticons) and

[1] Available from https://github.com/HaifaCLG/Arabizi.

reported almost perfect accuracy on this task.

One of our goals in this work is to create a large dataset of sentences containing Arabizi, potentially mixed with words in other languages, focusing on the Egyptian and Lebanese dialects. Unlike much existing work, we annotate our dataset at the word level, thereby yielding a richer annotation that clearly outlines sentences with code-switching. Our language ID annotation scheme acknowledges the difficulty of assigning language ID tags to words that may be shared by more than one mental lexicon; such words, which include proper names and cognates, are assumed to trigger code-switching (Clyne, 2003; Broersma and De Bot, 2006; Broersma, 2009; Soto et al., 2018; Soto and Hirschberg, 2019). We then use our annotated dataset to train classifiers that we employ to extract more code-switched Arabizi instances from Reddit and Twitter, thereby extending the scope of our dataset significantly.

3 Data collection

We conjectured that social media outlets, particularly Reddit and Twitter, would include a sizable amount of Arabizi utterances. To identify them, we modified the method suggested by Rabinovich et al. (2018), which has subsequently been used also to harvest code-switched data from Reddit (Rabinovich et al., 2019).

First, we identified some Reddit fora ('subreddits') where we expected to find Arabizi used. These included `r/arab`, `r/arabs`, `r/egypt`, `r/jordan`, `r/lebanon`, and `r/syria`. We downloaded the entire collection of the above subreddits. The resulting (raw) Reddit dataset consisted of 3,584,915 sentences, 59,593,594 words and 72,305 authors.

For twitter, we followed Darwish (2014) and defined a few dialectal Arabic seed words that we expected to occur with high frequency in Arabizi texts, focusing on the Egyptian dialect (where we expected to find code-switching with English) and the Lebanese dialect (where we expected mixed French). These seed terms are listed in Appendix A. We located and retained tweets that included any of the seed words in our list. We then extracted the user IDs of authors of such texts, under the assumption that authors that use Arabizi in some tweets are likely to use it elsewhere, too; and we included all tweets authored by these users in our corpus. The resulting (raw) Twitter dataset consisted of 2,466,642 sentences (22,530,044 words) authored by 1090 users: 936 Egyptians and 154 Lebanese.

We used NLTK (Bird et al., 2009) for sentence boundary detection and tokenization. As the tokenizer did not split emojis from other tokens, we added a simple post-processing step to make sure all emojis were standalone tokens. We removed extra spaces and separated Arabic letters from non-Arabic ones. We also shortened adjacent repeated letters to only two (e.g., we converted '*ahhhhh edaaa thankkk youuuu*' to '*ahh edaa thankk youu*').

Next, we aimed to identify sentences containing Arabizi in the raw dataset. We first utilized a number of language identification tools, including *Spacy* (Honnibal et al., 2020), Google's *LangDetect* (we used the Python port), *langid* (Lui and Baldwin, 2011, 2012), and *FastText* (Joulin et al., 2017). Unsurprisingly, they all failed to detect Arabizi with acceptable accuracy.

To evaluate the accuracy of existing language ID tools on Arabizi we selected 100 sentences from the annotated Arabizi dataset of Tobaili (2016): the first 50 sentences containing only Arabizi words from the Egypt dataset, and the first 50 from the Lebanon dataset. We applied the above-mentioned classifiers to these 100 sentences; since none of the tools was trained on Arabizi data, none predicted Arabizi. But they did not predict Arabic, either: instead, *Langdetect* defaulted to Somali 43 times, (and Indonesian 25 times); *Langid* detected English, Spanish-Castilian, Indonesian, and Swahili for 50 of the sentences; *Fasttext* preferred English and Spanish; and *Spacy* identified half of the sentences as Somali or Indonesian.

We therefore resorted to defining our own language ID detection model, which we specifically tuned to identifying Arabizi (in addition to English and French). We developed a dedicated scheme for tagging words in a mixed-language dataset (Section 4.1), manually tagged a sizeable number of sentences reflecting the various language combinations witnessed in the dataset (Section 4.2), and then used the manually annotated subset to train classifiers (Sections 4.3–4.4) that can assign language ID tags to words in unseen texts. Finally, we extended the annotation from words to sentences (Section 5) in order to devise an efficient extractor for more instances of code-switched Arabizi from our corpus. We now detail these stages.

4 Word level classification

Some existing work on Arabizi focused on identifying the language of a sentence, or a larger chunk of text. For example, Tobaili (2016) defined a tweet as Arabizi if it contained at least 50% Arabizi tokens. In contrast, we focus on identifying the language of each individual token in the corpus, as our main motivation is to prepare a dataset suitable for research on code-switching, which may of course be intra-sentential. As mentioned above, existing tools for word-level language ID fail miserably when Arabizi is concerned.

We begin by discussing the challenges involved in word-level annotation of multilingual texts (Section 4.1), detail the manual annotation (Section 4.2), and then discuss our classifiers, both statistical (Section 4.3) and neural (Section 4.4).

4.1 Annotation of language ID

Annotating multilingual data for language is challenging, especially where named entities are involved. Much work on code-switching assumes that a switch is defined when two consecutive words come from two different languages; and much cognitive linguistic work focuses on understanding what facilitate such switches. Specifically, it has been suggested that *cognates* (words in two languages that share a similar form and a similar meaning) facilitate code-switching (Clyne, 2003; Broersma and De Bot, 2006; Soto and Hirschberg, 2019). However, assigning a clear language tag to words in multilingual texts may not always be possible (Clyne, 2003, Chapter 3).

Consider the case of *borrowing*: a French word may be borrowed by Arabic, and sound like a foreign word initially, during which period its use in an otherwise Arabic sentence may be considered an insertional switch (e.g., `balcon` '*balcony*'). With time, this word may obtain properties of the borrowing language (its phonology might be adapted to Arabic, it may obtain Arabic morphological affixes, etc.), until finally it may be considered by native Arabic speakers, including monolinguals, a common Arabic word. How should such words be tagged during various stages of their assimilation?

Similarly, *culturally-specific words* in one language may be borrowed into another language simply because they have no translation equivalents in the borrowing language. For example, Arabic `alhamdulillah` '*thank God*' can be used verbatim in an otherwise English (or French) text. This may extend also to common nouns, for example `mjadara` '*mujadara, a lentil-based dish*'.

A particularly challenging case is *named entities* (which are often the extreme case of cognates). They can have identical forms in the two languages (e.g., '*Beirut*' in Arabic and in English); but they may also be adapted to the phonology of each language, and thus drift apart from each other (e.g., `Amreeca` '*America*', `Surya` '*Syria*', `Alqahirah` '*Cairo*'). The distance between the two forms may be significant (e.g., `al-Jazair` '*Algeria*'). Sometimes, proper names are translated rather than adapted (e.g., `al-welayat al-muttahida` '*United States*'), or use different words altogether (e.g., `masr` '*Egypt*'). What language ID tag should we assign to such tokens in multilingual texts?

Several decisions must be taken in order for the annotation to be consistent, and not all decisions can always be fully justified. Our motivation in devising the annotation scheme was to facilitate consistency by providing clear and easy-to-apply guidelines. We thus defined the following categories:

0: Arabizi including any form variant that may be considered Arabizi;

1: English including common social media variants of words such as spelling errors, shorthand (`Idk` '*I don't know*', `plz` '*please*'), letter repetition (`nooooo` '*no*', `Cuuute` '*cute*'), etc.;

2: French with similar social media accommodations;

3: Arabic written in the Arabic script;

4: Shared see below;

5: Other tokens that are either non-linguistic or common to several languages. These include punctuation marks, numbers, emoticons and emojis, etc. As we focus only on Arabic, English and French, we also mark tokens in other languages as 'other'. Examples include '*Bhag hindu ka baccha*', '*Eww!*', '*12k?*', and '*ahahahaha*'. Notice that morphological indications of language may change a token from 'Other' to that language; e.g., '*1st*' or '*3rd*' are considered English.

In light of our focus on code-switching, we defined the category *shared* to include words that we have reasons to believe may belong to more than one mental lexicon (or, alternatively, to a shared mental lexicon). In the linguistic literature, *trigger words* are defined as words that are positively associated with code-switching, either because they are cognates or because they increase the facilitation of the other language (Clyne, 2003; Broersma and De Bot, 2006). Our annotation guidelines were the following; notice that in all these cases, the annotation is context-independent: the same token will be tagged uniformly independently of where it occurs.

- Arabizi named entities which have different (translated) counterparts in English are tagged as Arabizi, and their translation equivalents are considered English; e.g., `Al-Emirat Al-Arabiya Al-mutahida` *'United Arab Emirates'*, `masr` *'Egypt'*, `al-maghrib` *'Morocco'*.
- Named entities in Arabizi and English that are *not* translated, and hence are written in a similar way in both languages, are considered as shared words; e.g., `al-ordon` *'Jordan'*, `alqahirah` *'Cairo'*, `Lubnan` *'Lebanon'*.
- Culturally-dependent terms that have no translation equivalent in the other language are tagged as shared; e.g., `mjadara` *'mujadara'*, `alhamdulillah` *'thank God'*, `ramadan` *'ramadan'*, `muezzin` *'muezzin'*.
- This also extends to loan words that do not have translation equivalents in the borrowing languages e.g., `video` *'video'*, or where the loan word is commonly used even if a translation exists; e.g., `taxi` *'taxi'*, `mobile` *'cellphone'*.

To demonstrate the word-level annotation, consider the following examples:

- `Ask for Mjadara Hamra`

Here, the first two tokens are obviously English ('1'), while the third token is tagged '4' for shared. The fourth token, `Hamra` *'red'*, raises a question: is it the adjective *'red'*, in which case it should be tagged '0' for Arabizi, or is it part of a named entity that includes `Mjadara` *'mujadara'*, in which case it should be '4' for shared? We opted for the former. In contrast, in

- `even the humble kibbe nayeh`

We tagged the first 3 tokens as English ('1'), and `kibbe nayeh` *'raw kibbe'*, where `kibbe` is a popular dish consisting of meat and bulgur, but `nayeh` *'raw'* changes its meaning to a different dish made from raw meat, were both tagged '4' for shared as we considered them part of a single named entity.

A particularly interesting example is

- `Nis-har youm el sabt 3al Balcon`

which means *'We stay up Saturday night on the balcony'*. The verb `nishar` *'we spend the evening'* was probably spelled with a dash in order to prevent the *'sh'* from being pronounced as English [sh]. We tagged all tokens '0' for Arabizi, except the last one which was tagged '4' for shared.

Finally, some cases involved intra-word code-switching. In

- `ma2darsh a subtweet u da mabda2yan` *'I can't subtweet you, this is tentative'*

the English *'subtweet'* is used as a verb, with the Arabic prefix *'a'* which is a derivational morpheme that converts nouns to verbs; the result is `asubtweet` *'to subtweet'*. In this case, the author introduced a space between the two mporphemes so we could tag *'a'* as Arabizi and *'subtweet'* as English. In another example, `ana ba-act` *'I act'*, the author used a dash between the Arabizi prefix *'ba'* and the English verb *'act'*, so again we could tag both morphemes separately. We do not have a special tag for tokens that involve morphemes in more than one language because no such case was witnessed in our dataset.

4.2 Manual annotation

From the raw datasets we described in Section 3, we initially manually annotated 1050 sentences (roughly 500 each from Reddit and Twitter) at the word level, assigning a tag of '0' to '5' to each token.[2] We then used the classifier described below (Section 4.3) to identify more "interesting" samples in the entire dataset (the vast majority of the sentences in the dataset are naturally plain English sentences). Of those, we manually selected more sentences that reflected as best as possible the diversity of sentence types in the dataset, and manually corrected the predictions of the classifier. This process resulted in 2643 manually annotated sentences, over 1000 of which including Arabizi words, which constitute the final word-level annotated dataset on which we train and evaluate our classifiers. The details are summarized in Table 1 (note that not all sentences in a given post were annotated).

4.3 Statistic classification

We begin with more conservative statistic classification. Since the tag of a given token is highly

[2]Manual annotation was performed by the first author, who is a native speaker of Palestinian Arabic and fluent in English. The main challenge was the identification of shared words, which required discussion between the two authors, as well as with colleagues.

Dataset	Posts	Sents.	Tokens
Reddit	922	980	13752
Twitter	1653	1663	16061
Total	2575	2643	29813

Table 1: Word-level annotated dataset.

depepndent on the tags of its predecessors, we used CRF (Lafferty et al., 2001) to train a sequence-to-sequence classifier. We used the following features to represent each instance (token):

- The word itself in lowercase;
- Are all the word's letters uppercase?;
- Is only the first letter uppercase?;
- Is the word in the (freely-available list of) 5050 most frequent English words, taken from the one billion word Corpus of Contemporary American English?;
- Is the word in the 930 most frequent French words?;
- Is it an Arabic word? We used CAMel tools (Obeid et al., 2020) in order to detect Arabic words;
- Does the word contain numerals? This is useful because digits are used to represent Arabic letters in Arabizi;
- All the features above, with respect to the previous word;
- Is it the first word in the sentence?;
- Is it the last word in the sentence?

Here and elsewhere, we used ten-fold cross-validation for evaluation. Table 2 lists the evaluation results (precision, recall and F1) for each category separately, as well as the number of words of each category in the test set ("support"). It also shows the total evaluation metrics, averaged over all categories (we report micro-, macro- and weighted averages). The total accuracy, over the entire test set, is 0.949.

Tag	Prc.	Rcl.	F1	Support
Arabizi	0.90	0.95	0.92	4865
English	0.96	0.98	0.97	16563
French	0.74	0.64	0.69	149
Arabic	0.99	0.99	0.99	2671
Shared	0.81	0.51	0.63	1401
Other	0.97	0.94	0.95	4164
Micro avg.	0.95	0.95	0.95	29813
Macro avg.	0.90	0.84	0.86	29813
Weighted avg.	0.95	0.95	0.95	29813

Table 2: Results: word-level statistic classification.

4.4 Neural classification

We also experimented with more contemporary neural classification. We defined a deep neural network consisting of three layers: (1) An embedding layer which is the concatenation of the last 4 layers of a BERT (Devlin et al., 2019) model (we used the multilingual uncased version); (2) A bidirectional LSTM (Hochreiter and Schmidhuber, 1997) layer: 2 hidden layers of size 400, and dropout of 0.5; (3) A CRF layer (Huang et al., 2015).

We used the BERT tokenizer, in the multilingual uncased version, to tokenize the text. As the tokenizer is different, the number of tokens differs slightly from the case of statistical classification (this explains the differences in the support size between Tables 2 and 3). More importantly, BERT's predictions are provided for units (sub-tokens) that we did not manually annotate. As is common in such cases, for each original token that was split by BERT we selected the tag of the first sub-token and induced it over the other sub-tokens to which the original token was split. Of course, this may harm the accuracy of the neural classifier.

We used the Adam optimizer with a learning rate of 0.001 and cross-entropy loss. We trained the model for four epochs and chose a batch size of 32. The results are listed in Table 3. The total accuracy, over the entire test set, is 0.952, almost identical to the accuracy of the statistic classifier.

Tag	Prec.	Rcl.	F1	Support
Arabizi	0.91	0.95	0.93	4869
English	0.97	0.98	0.97	16938
French	0.56	0.43	0.49	167
Arabic	0.98	0.99	0.98	2680
Shared	0.77	0.66	0.71	1406
Other	0.97	0.94	0.95	4385
Micro avg.	0.95	0.95	0.95	30445
Macro avg.	0.86	0.82	0.84	30445
Weighted avg.	0.95	0.95	0.95	30445

Table 3: Results: word-level neural classification.

5 Identifying code-switching

The word-level annotation immediately facilitates the identification of code-switching: a sentence with at least one word in Arabizi and one in either English or French necessarily includes a switch. To simplify this task, we now annotate full sentences: we assign complex tags to sentences that reflect the existence of each of our six word categories in a given sentence. The tags consist of six bits, each referring to the presence in the sentence of words categorized as Arabizi, English, French, Arabic, shared, and Other. This Table 4 lists the number of samples associated with each 6-bit tag in the annotated dataset.

For example, the sentence

- `good luck albi, have a nice dayy <3` '*good luck my love, have a nice day* ♡'

is associated with the tag 110001, reflecting the presence of English, Arabizi and an emoticon (note that we treat the misspelled '*dayy*' as a valid English word). More example sentences include:

- `"Khalas tamam , you know best"` '*Okay, you know best*' . (110000)
- `happiest birthday ya hussein :)` '*happiest birthday oh hussein :)*' (110011)
- `Take a flight to Jeddah w ishtiri al baik` '*Take a flight to Jeddah and buy the bike*' (110010, as '*Jeddah*' is shared)

Note that we do not commit on the precise location of the switch; when a sentence contains shared words, they may serve as wildcards for determining this location. For example, in the last sentence above, the switch may occur before or after the shared word '*Jeddah*'.

5.1 Direct classification

First, we trained a statistic classifier to directly predict the 6-bit tags. We experimented with various statistic classification models, including SVM, logistic regression, KNN, and random forest. The latter yielded the best accuracy, so the results we report below were obtained with random forest. We used the following features:

- Character uni-gram, bi-gram and tri-gram counts, normalized by the number of characters in the sentence. We only used the most frequent 250 n-grams;
- Number of English, Arabic and French words, all normalized by the number of tokens in the sentence (excluding emojis);
- The number of tokens that contain numeric digits, normalized by the number of tokens in the sentence;
- The normalized number of emojis, punctuation and numbers in the sentence, to help identify the category *Other*;

Arabizi	English	French	Arabic	Shared	Other	Occurrences
0	1	0	0	0	1	604
0	1	0	0	1	1	297
0	1	0	0	0	0	233
1	1	0	0	0	1	187
1	0	0	0	0	0	184
1	1	0	0	1	1	155
1	0	0	0	0	1	154
0	0	0	1	0	1	153
1	1	0	0	0	0	115
1	1	0	0	1	0	109
0	0	0	1	0	0	91
0	1	0	0	1	0	71
0	0	0	0	0	1	65
1	0	0	0	1	0	55
1	0	0	0	1	1	43
0	1	0	1	0	1	36
0	0	0	0	1	1	22
0	0	0	0	1	0	14
0	0	1	0	0	1	10
0	1	0	1	0	0	8
0	1	1	0	0	1	5
0	1	0	1	1	1	5
0	0	1	0	0	0	4
1	0	1	0	0	1	4
1	0	1	0	0	0	4
0	0	1	0	1	1	3
1	1	0	1	0	1	2
0	0	0	1	1	0	2
0	0	0	1	1	1	2
0	1	0	1	1	0	2
1	1	0	1	0	1	1
0	1	1	0	1	1	1
1	0	1	0	1	1	1
1	1	1	0	0	1	1
1	1	1	0	1	0	1
1	0	0	1	1	1	1
1	1	1	0	1	1	1
1	1	0	1	1	1	1

Table 4: Distribution of sentence-level tags in the annotated dataset.

- The number of English words detected by *fastText* with confidence score greater than 0.95;
- The number of French words detected by *fastText* with confidence score greater than 0.5;
- The number of words that do not belong to any of the previous categories, which helps detect *Arabizi* and *Other*;

- A binary flag which checks whether the whole sentence was detected by fastText as English with confidence score greater than 0.8. We observed that sentences with score greater than 0.8 tend to actually include English words, but pure Arabizi sentences are sometimes erroneously classified as English with lower confidence;
- A binary flag which checks whether the whole sentence was detected as French with confidence score greater than 0.3;
- A binary flag which checks whether the whole sentence was detected as some language other than French, English, or Arabic. This helps detecting *Arabizi* and other languages.

We used ten-fold cross-validation and evaluated the accuracy of the model in predicting each of the bits in the tag vector independently (i.e., predicting whether a given sentence includes words in English, Arabizi, French, etc.) The accuracy results on each category are listed in Table 5. The total accuracy of assigning the exact 6-bit tag to each sentence is 0.62.

Tag	Acc.	Prec.	Rcl.	F1
Arabizi	0.90	0.91	0.83	0.87
English	0.92	0.95	0.94	0.95
French	0.99	0.10	0.03	0.05
Arabic	1.00	1.00	1.00	1.00
Shared	0.75	0.67	0.34	0.45
Other	0.96	0.99	0.96	0.97

Table 5: Results: sentence-level direct classification.

5.2 Indirect classification

As an alternative to direct classification, it is possible to combine the predictions of the word-level classifiers (Section 4) and create 6-bit tags for each sentence. Recall that tags at the sentence level only indicate the existence of words from a given category in the sentence (rather than whether *all* words in the sentence are annotated correctly). The results of inducing sentence-level tags from the word-level ones (as obtained by the statistic classifier, Section 4.3) are listed in Table 6. The total accuracy of correctly identifying the complex, 6-bit tag is 0.78, much better than with the direct classifier.

Note that in both approaches, the identification of Arabic is perfect, most likely owing to the different character set of Arabic; and in both cases, shared words are the most challenging to identify (recall that they were also hard to manually annotated). The accuracy on French is low, probably because of the small number of sentences with French words in the training data.

Tag	Acc.	Prec.	Rcl.	F1
Arabizi	0.94	0.91	0.95	0.93
English	0.95	0.96	0.96	0.96
French	0.99	0.75	0.55	0.63
Arabic	1.00	1.00	1.00	1.00
Shared	0.86	0.89	0.62	0.73
Other	0.98	0.99	0.98	0.98

Table 6: Results: indirect sentence-level classification.

6 Harvesting more data

With the highly accurate classifiers described above, we set out to extend our corpus of Arabizi in general and Arabizi code-switching in particular. We applied the statistic word-level classifier (Section 4.3) to the entire dataset we collected from Reddit and Twitter (Section 3). We extracted all the sentences that included at least one Arabizi word, and associated each token in these sentences with its language ID tag; we also decorated the entire sentence with the complex 6-bit tag that indicates which languages are included in it. This resulted in a set of over 880K sentences, which constitutes our automatically-obtained dataset of Arabizi (see Table 7). This dataset, we trust, will be an invaluable resource for research in Arabizi and in code-switching.

	Reddit	Twitter	Total
With Arabizi	218619	668208	886827
Arabizi	67566	479317	546883
Ar–En CS	165982	277032	443014
Ar–Fr CS	1165	1913	3078

Table 7: The automatically-annotated dataset. Number of sentences with at least one Arabizi token (*With Arabizi*); with a majority of Arabizi tokens (*Arabizi*); and with code-switching between Arabizi and English (*Ar–En CS*) and between Arabizi and French (*Ar–Fr CS*).

As an additional verification of the dataset, we randomly chose 100 sentences (50 each from Reddit and Twitter) that were annotated as including at least two tokens each in both Arabizi and English (hence, that included code-switching) and manually inspected them. Of the 100, 77 (42 from Twitter, 35 from Reddit) indeed included code-switching between English and Arabizi.

A qualitative analysis of the errors revealed several cases in which a nonstandard spelling of English was erroneously considered Arabizi. For example, in the fully English `wtf yo where da love go`, our classifier identified '*da*' as Arabizi, probably because it is a common Egyptian word meaning '*this*'. Similarly, in `I ' m sorry 4 ya loss` the classifier unsurprisingly identified '*ya*' as Arabizi.

Some proper nouns that we tagged as *shared*, especially those whose origin is Arabic, were predicted as Arabizi. E.g., in `They also mentioned a new location ; somewhere in sin el fil`, the last three tokens were predicted Arabizi, but we tagged them as shared (the name of a suburb of Beirut). Finally, tokens that involve both letters and digits were sometimes erroneously tagged as Arabizi (e.g., `I have the 20GB 2Mbps plan`).

7 Conclusion

We described a classifier that identifies words in Arabizi, English, Arabic, and French in multilingual sentences from social media. We applied the classifier to a large set of sentences collected from Twitter and Reddit, and produced a huge dataset of more than 880K automatically-annotated Arabizi sentences, of which over 446K include code-switching with either English or French.

We are now ready to use this dataset for a large-scale corpus-based investigation of theoretical research questions in cognitive linguistics. Specifically, we are interested in the correlation between shared words, as defined in our annotation scheme, and code-switching. We leave such investigations for future work.

8 Ethical considerations and limitations

This research was approved by the University of Haifa IRB. We collected data from two social media outlets, Reddit and Twitter, in compliance with their terms of service (Reddit, Twitter). For the latter, we distribute tweet IDs and sentence IDs instead of the actual sentences, in line with Twitter's terms of use. For anonymity, we systematically replaced all user IDs (in both datasets) by unique IDs; we do not have, and therefore do not distribute, any personal information of the authors. With this additional level of anonymization, we anticipate very minimal risk of abuse or dual use of the data.

Like any other dataset, the corpus we report on here is not representative. In particular, it probably includes Arabizi as used mainly in Egypt and in Lebanon but not elsewhere in the Arab-speaking world. It is very likely unbalanced in terms of any demographic aspect of its authors. Clearly, the automatic annotation of language IDs is not perfect, and may introduce noise. Use of this corpus for linguistic research must therefore be done with caution. Nevertheless, we trust that the sheer size of the dataset would make it instrumental for research on code-switching in general and in Arabizi in particular.

Acknowledgements

We thank Melinda Fricke, Yulia Tsvetkov, Yuli Zeira, and the anonymous reviewers for their valuable feedback and suggestions. This work was supported in part by grant No. 2019785 from the United States-Israel Binational Science Foundation (BSF), and by grants No. 2007960, 2007656, 2125201 and 2040926 from the United States National Science Foundation (NSF).

A Lists of seed words

We collected data from Reddit and Twitter based on texts that included the following words.

Lebanese `bya3ref` '*he knows*', `ma3leh` '*never mind*', `be7ke` '*to say*', `halla2` '*now*', `ma32ool` '*reasonable*', `3shen` '*in order to*', `3am` (present tense particle) `mazboot` '*alright*' `kteer` '*many/much*' `3lay/3layki` '*on me/on* you_{fem}'.

Egyptian `awy` '*very/very much*', `kwayes` '*OK*', `ezai` '*how*', `5ales` '*never*', `7a2ee2y` '*really*', `m3lesh` '*never mind*', `howa–eh` '*what*'.

Interestingly, the word `mazboot` '*alright*' means '*strong*' in Hindi, so it yielded many false positives. However, since it also resulted in having many relevant Lebanese tweets, we manually scanned them and removed irrelevant users. Similarly, the world `awy` '*very*' is highly indicative of the Egyptian dialect, but it is also used as an abbreviation of the English word '*away*'. Attempting to use the seed words `baddi` '*I want*' and `balki` '*maybe*', both highly widespread in Lebanon, resulted in harvesting many irrelevant texts; upon inspection we revealed that these words are frequent proper names in India. They were therefore removed from the seed word list.

References

Wafia Adouane, Nasredine Semmar, and Richard Johansson. 2016. Romanized Berber and Romanized Arabic automatic language identification using machine learning. In *Proceedings of the Third Workshop on NLP for Similar Languages, Varieties and Dialects (VarDial3)*, pages 53–61, Osaka, Japan. The COLING 2016 Organizing Committee.

Gustavo Aguilar, Fahad AlGhamdi, Victor Soto, Mona Diab, Julia Hirschberg, and Thamar Solorio. 2018. Named entity recognition on code-switched data: Overview of the CALCS 2018 shared task. In *Proceedings of the Third Workshop on Computational Approaches to Linguistic Code-Switching*, pages 138–147.

Mohamed Al-Badrashiny, Ramy Eskander, Nizar Habash, and Owen Rambow. 2014. Automatic transliteration of Romanized dialectal Arabic. In *Proceedings of the Eighteenth Conference on Computational Natural Language Learning*, pages 30–38, Ann Arbor, Michigan. Association for Computational Linguistics.

Gaétan Baert, Souhir Gahbiche, Guillaume Gadek, and Alexandre Pauchet. 2020. Arabizi language models for sentiment analysis. In *Proceedings of the 28th International Conference on Computational Linguistics*, pages 592–603, Barcelona, Spain (Online). International Committee on Computational Linguistics.

Steven Bird, Ewan Klein, and Edward Loper. 2009. *Natural Language Processing with Python*. O'Reilly Media, Sebastopol, CA.

Mirjam Broersma. 2009. Triggered codeswitching between cognate languages. *Bilingualism: Language and Cognition*, 12(4):447–462.

Mirjam Broersma and Kees De Bot. 2006. Triggered codeswitching: A corpus-based evaluation of the original triggering hypothesis and a new alternative. *Bilingualism: Language and cognition*, 9(1):1–13.

Michael G. Clyne. 2003. *Dynamics of language contact: English and immigrant languages*. Cambridge approaches to language contact. Cambridge University Press, Cambridge.

Ryan Cotterell, Adithya Renduchintala, Naomi Saphra, and Chris Callison-Burch. 2014. An Algerian Arabic-French code-switched corpus. In *Proceedings of the First Workshop on Free/Open-Source Arabic Corpora and Corpora Processing Tools*. Association for Computational Linguistics.

Kareem Darwish. 2014. Arabizi detection and conversion to Arabic. In *Proceedings of the EMNLP 2014 Workshop on Arabic Natural Language Processing (ANLP)*, pages 217–224, Doha, Qatar. Association for Computational Linguistics.

Jacob Devlin, Ming-Wei Chang, Kenton Lee, and Kristina Toutanova. 2019. BERT: pre-training of deep bidirectional transformers for language understanding. In *Proceedings of the 2019 Conference of the North American Chapter of the Association for Computational Linguistics: Human Language Technologies, NAACL-HLT 2019*, pages 4171–4186. Association for Computational Linguistics.

A. Seza Doğruöz, Sunayana Sitaram, Barbara E. Bullock, and Almeida Jacqueline Toribio. 2021. A survey of code-switching: Linguistic and social perspectives for language technologies. In *Proceedings of the 59th Annual Meeting of the Association for Computational Linguistics and the 11th International Joint Conference on Natural Language Processing*, pages 1654–1666. Association for Computational Linguistics.

François Grosjean. 1998. Studying bilinguals: Methodological and conceptual issues. *Bilingualism: Language and Cognition*, 1(2):131 – 149.

Sepp Hochreiter and Jürgen Schmidhuber. 1997. Long short-term memory. *Neural computation*, 9(8):1735–1780.

Matthew Honnibal, Ines Montani, Sofie Van Landeghem, and Adriane Boyd. 2020. spaCy: Industrial-strength Natural Language Processing in Python.

Zhiheng Huang, Wei Xu, and Kai Yu. 2015. Bidirectional LSTM-CRF models for sequence tagging. *CoRR*, abs/1508.01991.

Armand Joulin, Edouard Grave, Piotr Bojanowski, and Tomas Mikolov. 2017. Bag of tricks for efficient text classification. In *Proceedings of the 15th Conference of the European Chapter of the Association for Computational Linguistics: Volume 2, Short Papers*, pages 427–431, Valencia, Spain. Association for Computational Linguistics.

John Lafferty, Andrew McCallum, and Fernando Pereira. 2001. Conditional random fields: Probabilistic models for segmenting and labeling sequence data. In *Proceedings of the 18th International Conference on Machine Learning (ICML-01)*, pages 282–289, San Francisco. Morgan Kaufmann.

Marco Lui and Timothy Baldwin. 2011. Cross-domain feature selection for language identification. In *Proceedings of 5th International Joint Conference on Natural Language Processing*, pages 553–561, Chiang Mai, Thailand. Asian Federation of Natural Language Processing.

Marco Lui and Timothy Baldwin. 2012. Langid.Py: An off-the-shelf language identification tool. In *Proceedings of the ACL 2012 System Demonstrations*, page 25–30, USA. Association for Computational Linguistics.

Abir Masmoudi, Nizar Habash, Mariem Ellouze, Yannick Estève, and Lamia Hadrich Belguith. 2015. Arabic transliteration of Romanized Tunisian dialect text: A preliminary investigation. In *Computational Linguistics and Intelligent Text Processing*, pages 608–619, Cham. Springer International Publishing.

Ossama Obeid, Nasser Zalmout, Salam Khalifa, Dima Taji, Mai Oudah, Bashar Alhafni, Go Inoue, Fadhl Eryani, Alexander Erdmann, and Nizar Habash. 2020. CAMeL tools: An open source python toolkit for Arabic natural language processing. In *Proceedings of the 12th Language Resources and Evaluation Conference*, pages 7022–7032, Marseille, France. European Language Resources Association.

Ella Rabinovich, Masih Sultani, and Suzanne Stevenson. 2019. CodeSwitch-Reddit: Exploration of written multilingual discourse in online discussion forums. In *Proceedings of the 2019 Conference on Empirical Methods in Natural Language Processing and the 9th International Joint Conference on Natural Language Processing (EMNLP-IJCNLP)*, pages 4776–4786, Hong Kong, China. Association for Computational Linguistics.

Ella Rabinovich, Yulia Tsvetkov, and Shuly Wintner. 2018. Native language cognate effects on second language lexical choice. *Transactions of the Association for Computational Linguistics*, 6:329–342.

Younes Samih and Wolfgang Maier. 2016. An Arabic-Moroccan Darija code-switched corpus. In *Proceedings of the Tenth International Conference on Language Resources and Evaluation (LREC'16)*, pages 4170–4175, Portorož, Slovenia. European Language Resources Association (ELRA).

Djamé Seddah, Farah Essaidi, Amal Fethi, Matthieu Futeral, Benjamin Muller, Pedro Javier Ortiz Suárez, Benoît Sagot, and Abhishek Srivastava. 2020. Building a user-generated content North-African Arabizi treebank: Tackling hell. In *Proceedings of the 58th Annual Meeting of the Association for Computational Linguistics*, pages 1139–1150, Online. Association for Computational Linguistics.

Ali Shazal, Aiza Usman, and Nizar Habash. 2020. A unified model for Arabizi detection and transliteration using sequence-to-sequence models. In *Proceedings of the Fifth Arabic Natural Language Processing Workshop*, pages 167–177, Barcelona, Spain (Online). Association for Computational Linguistics.

Sunayana Sitaram, Khyathi Raghavi Chandu, Sai Krishna Rallabandi, and Alan W. Black. 2019. A survey of code-switched speech and language processing.

Thamar Solorio, Elizabeth Blair, Suraj Maharjan, Steven Bethard, Mona Diab, Mahmoud Ghoneim, Abdelati Hawwari, Julia AlGhamdi, Fahadand Hirschberg, Alison Chang, et al. 2014. Overview for the first shared task on language identification in code-switched data. In *Proceedings of the First Workshop on Computational Approaches to Code Switching*, pages 62–72.

Thamar Solorio, Shuguang Chen, Alan W. Black, Mona Diab, Sunayana Sitaram, Victor Soto, Emre Yilmaz, and Anirudh Srinivasan, editors. 2021. *Proceedings of the Fifth Workshop on Computational Approaches to Linguistic Code-Switching*. Association for Computational Linguistics, Online.

Thamar Solorio and Yang Liu. 2008. Learning to predict code-switching points. In *Proceedings of the 2008 Conference on Empirical Methods in Natural Language Processing*, pages 973–981, Honolulu, Hawaii. Association for Computational Linguistics.

Victor Soto, Nishmar Cestero, and Julia Hirschberg. 2018. The role of cognate words, POS tags and entrainment in code-switching. In *Proceedings of Interspeech 2018, the 19th Annual Conference of the International Speech Communication Association*, pages 1938–1942. ISCA.

Victor Soto and Julia Hirschberg. 2019. Improving code-switched language modeling performance using cognate features. In *Proceedings of Interspeech 2019, the 20th Annual Conference of the International Speech Communication Association*, pages 3725–3729. ISCA.

Taha Tobaili. 2016. Arabizi identification in Twitter data. In *Proceedings of the ACL 2016 Student Research Workshop*, pages 51–57, Berlin, Germany. Association for Computational Linguistics.

Samia Touileb and Jeremy Barnes. 2021. The interplay between language similarity and script on a novel multi-layer Algerian dialect corpus. In *Findings of the Association for Computational Linguistics: ACL-IJCNLP 2021*, pages 3700–3712, Online. Association for Computational Linguistics.

Jihene Younes, Hadhemi Achour, Emna Souissi, and Ahmed Ferchichi. 2020. A deep learning approach for the Romanized Tunisian dialect identification. *The International Arab Journal of Information Technology*, 17(6):935–946.

Jihene Younes, Hadhemi Achour, Emna Souissi, and Ahmed Ferchichi. 2022. Romanized Tunisian dialect transliteration using sequence labelling techniques. *J. King Saud Univ. Comput. Inf. Sci.*, 34(3):982–992.

Authorship Verification for Arabic Social Media Texts Using Arabic Knowledge-Base Model (AraKB)

Fatimah Alqahtani[1] and Helen Yannakoudakis[2]
Department of Informatics, King's College London, UK
Fatimah.alqahtani@kcl.ac.uk[1] , Helen.yannakoudakis@kcl.ac.uk[2]

Abstract

The issue of verifying authorship has been a controversial and much disputed subject within the field of digital forensics and cyber investigations. Although extensive research has been carried out on authorship verification tasks, few studies have analyzed Arabic social media texts. This paper seeks to overcome this limitation and presents a new knowledge-based model to enhance Natural Language Understanding and thereby improve authorship verification performance. The proposed model provided promising results that would benefit research for different Natural Language Processing tasks for Arabic.

1 Introduction

Arabic has a very rich vocabulary; each word has many derivatives that describe the root meaning in more specific or nuanced ways. For example, the word (thirst /عطش) has up to 45 synonyms, including those alluding to different stages of thirst. Compared to other languages, Arabic's structure increases the complexity of pre-processing, whereby unnecessary characters must be removed or carefully replaced. Moreover, the complexity of Arabic morphology tends to increase the set of features, syntax, and semantic structures, which might not be effective for the purposes of authorship verification (AV), the process of determining whether or not two pieces of writing are written by the same author by comparing their writing styles (Abbasi & Chen, 2005).

Although extensive research has been carried out on AV in different languages, few studies have focused on the Arabic language. AV in Arabic entails numerous particular linguistic difficulties, including with regard to inflection, elongation, diacritics, word length (Abbasi & Chen, 2005), and other challenges, as described below:

- Inflection: In Arabic, one word can generate three or more different words with minor change, therefore orthographical properties result in lexical variation. When the number of features increases, then determining the right number of features may impact authorship analysis performance (Larkey & Connel, 2001).
- Elongation: Proper pre-processing is necessary to remove unnecessary characters, but this may lose word emphasis or stylometric features of writers (Shaalan & Raza, 2009).
- Diacritics: Less effective when using word-based syntactic features (Abbasi & Chen, 2005).
- Word length: Shorter word lengths in Arabic (e.g., compared to English) reduces the effectiveness of lexical features (Abbasi & Chen, 2005).
- Diglossia: May not provide significant features or an adequate ontology to provide proper mappings (Badawi, 1996).
- Grammatical structure: Arabic dialect analysis creates more challenges.
- Capitalisation and punctuation: Identifying patterns is challenging (Ryding, 2005).
- Agglutinative constructs: Difficult parts of speech tagging could degrade the stylometric features of AV (Shaalan & Raza, 2009).

Proceedings of the The Seventh Arabic Natural Language Processing Workshop (WANLP), pages 205 - 213
December 8, 2022

In addition to the previous challenges, as AV mostly depends on the style of writing, minimal data pre-processing is required. Unlike most NLP tasks, such as sentiment analysis and text classification, AV problems cannot undergo extensive data pre-processing, as stemming, normalization, diacritics removal, and other pre-processing techniques would eliminate the author's style of writing, and therefore make AV more challenging. The challenge becomes even greater with authorship analysis tasks for very short texts (Azarbonyad, 2015; Luyckx & Daelemans, 2011), such as those on social media platforms. Hence, a minimal number of Arabic AV studies have been conducted due to the inherent difficulty of such undertakings.

Consequently, there is a need to investigate different linguistic features that could help to improve performance of Arabic AV for Arabic short texts (particularly Twitter posts). This paper presents a novel method and a new presentation of data to verify the authorship of Arabic texts specifically on Twitter; however, the experiment in principle could be applicable to other social media platforms and any short Arabic texts.

The following section presents a brief overview of the recent work on Arabic AV, then Section 3 explains the research methodology used in this work. Section 4 presents the experimental setup and results, and Section 5 discusses the results of the experiments. Finally, Section 6 summarizes the main conclusions and identifies areas for future investigation.

2 Related Work

As mentioned earlier, there are few studies of Arabic AV, and those which have been undertaken mainly analyzed very long texts, such as novels (Kumar & Chaurasia, 2012) and other books (Ahmed, 2017, 2018). In the following we will review the ones conducted on medium to short texts, as they are more relevant to the current study (which pertains to tweets).

An extensive set of documents was collected from Dar Al-Ifta,[1] consisting of 3,000 balanced datasets and 4,686 documents from unbalanced datasets (Al-Sarem, Emara, Cherif, Kissi, & Wahab, 2018). The method is based on the frequency-based features of unigrams, bigrams, and trigrams, and on style-based features (character, lexical, syntactic, semantic, content-specific, structural, and language-specific). First, the data were filtered, and TFIDF vectors were created. A bootstrap aggregating learner was then used to estimate the classification based on a maximum number of votes technique. Several stylometric and frequency-based features were used, showing that combining the bigram model with style-based features achieved the highest accuracy. However, it was unclear whether authors' documents were used in training or chunking in such lengthy article datasets.

Two experiments by (Ahmed, 2019a) sought to find the best feature ensemble, using the features of tokens, stems, root, diacritics, and POS tags of n-grams (1 to 4) as features for Arabic author verification. The author used a dataset consisting of 253 documents written by different authors from five domains. The average document sizes for the studied domains were 802 for columnists, 820 for economics, 1159 for fiction, 1108 for nonfiction, and 850 for politics. The accuracy for each domain varied from 80-84.53%. It is important to note that domains with the smallest sample size achieved the worst results. The second experiment was to find the effect of training or testing sample size, and it revealed that the training dataset size did not correlate with improved accuracy for the AV method. In conclusion, the study found that a training set with a smaller number of documents outperformed one with a larger number of documents.

Arabic AV using 125 documents from five common genres in Modern Standard Arabic (MSA), including opinion columns, economics, fiction, nonfiction, and politics, was undertaken by evaluating SVM-calculated distance metrics of the Canberra, Manhattan, Cosine, and Jaccard measures using tokens, stems, and POS tags as features (Ahmed, 2019b). It was found that the Canberra distance measure was the best-performing distance measure in most genres, with an accuracy rate as high as 97.8%. However, the method omits digits, punctuation marks, and special characters in pre-processing, which limits the applicability of these findings to short texts.

In our recent work on Arabic AV (Alqahtani & Dohler, 2022a), we collected a dataset consisting

[1] https://www.dar-alifta.org/Foreign/default.aspx

of 100 Twitter users written in the Arabic language, whereby each user had 1000 to 3000 tweets. Firstly, we extracted a number of sylometric (content-free) features compatible with both the Arabic language and with Twitter posts. Comparing different classifiers, we found that Gradient Boosting, with an average accuracy of 0.75, outperformed Random Forest, Support Vector Machine, and k-Nearest Neighbor. In the second experiment, the effect of combining content-specific features (e.g., TF-IDF) with the extracted stylometric features was tested, which improved the accuracy by almost 2%. The performance of using a combination of stylometric and TF-IDF resulted in 0.77 average accuracy and F1-score.

In general, it can be concluded that authorship analysis tasks depend on the feature set, the number of authors, and the dataset genres that reflect the Arabic language type (Classical, MSA, or Colloquial). In addition, the changing behavior of authors is an inherent problem that affects solving authorship verification problems.

The root cause of the limited number of works on Arabic-language authorship analysis is the inherent characteristics of the Arabic language itself. Compared to other languages, Arabic-language structure increases the complexity of pre-processing, whereby unnecessary characters must be removed or carefully replaced. Moreover, the complexity of Arabic-language morphology tends to increase the set of features, syntax, and semantic structures, which is not germane to authorship analysis tasks. Therefore, although the language provides the flexibility of numerous features, most of them are either not used or are not enough for related tasks. One implication of this is the limited number of Arabic-language authorship identification studies and the minimal number of datasets that are available for the Arabic language (Alqahtani & Dohler, 2022b).

3 Methodology

The most recent work on Arabic AV using linguistic features (stylometric features and TF-IDF) gave promising results (Alqahtani & Dohler, 2022a), and this study seeks to build on this by investigating the effect of using other features that help to extract more tweets, and understand the context of tweets without being word-dependent. In this work, we will continue the work on the same dataset and use the same stylometric features to find the effect of the investigated features on verifying authorship.

The concept is creating a table of words (each in different rows) that carry specific values for each column/feature. The aim is to explain the words' meanings and identify their range of closeness or divergence from other words. We created an Arabic knowledge-base in the form of a large table, whereby each word in a row is described with a set of features (columns), each of which carries a number between 0 (if the column is the complete opposite of the word) and 1 (if the column is the exact meaning of the word). Other values are explained in more detail in section 3.2.

As stylometric features are considered to be essential features for AV tasks, we extend the work in (Alqahtani & Dohler, 2022a) in addition to using our novel AraKB model. The results give an indication about the effect of using this technique to verify authorship with special relevance to very brief texts (specifically tweets).

3.1 Dataset

As a part of our investigation, and in order to have comparable results from our experiments, we used the same dataset as in our previous work (Alqahtani & Dohler, 2022a). The dataset contains 100 Twitter users, tweeting in a mixture of Gulf dialect and MSA. The total number of tweets in the corpus is 375,428, with a maximum of 3000 and minimum of 1000 tweets per user. For the knowledge-based model, as this experiment is fully accredited on words, the first step was to prepare the words included in the knowledge-based table. Arabic language words for classical and MSA alone are counted in the millions (Jalaluddin Al-Suyuti, 1998), in addition to newly generated words in various forms of colloquial Arabic. Creating one table containing all Arabic words is impossible, thus we extracted the 1000 most-used words in the dataset to employ them in the experiment.

It is important to note that when extracting the most used words in the dataset we found many Arabic stop words; while used heavily in writing, stop words usually have a negligible impact on the meaning of sentences (Bouzoubaa, Baidouri, Loukili, & Yazidi, 2009). Although stop words are usually eliminated in the data processing phase in some NLP tasks, such as information retrieval, in order to reduce noise, we argue that some stop words some words are important to keep, and always make a difference in the sentence, particularly negation words.

Negation words play vital role in changing the sentence meaning completely. For example, the word (not/ليس) when added to any word will give the opposite or negation of it, and therefore change the whole meaning. Hence, we kept all the negation words, such as (ليس لا ,لم,) and any dialectical word that carries a negation meaning, such as (مو, ماني , مافي).

3.2 AraKB creation

After the words were extracted and the unimportant stop words were eliminated, the table was created for the top 1000 most-used words in the dataset. However, we found some words that could not be included, such as names, usernames, and English words, which were consequently ignored.

It is important to point out that we treated emojis and punctuation the same as words, because in this experiment we aim to not only determine their existence but also investigate the meaning that they carry. In tweet communication, such features assume a particular potency and relevance to particular authors' styles and sentiments, which can often be expressed more fully by an emoji or a particular punctuation mark. The total number of the actual words was 895 words, 15 punctuations, and 90 emojis.

Regarding the number of features (columns), we tried to create as many features as possible to describe the words in a detailed way. An insufficient number of descriptions would be insufficient to enable the model to predict meaning, while a greater number of describing words conversely yields more accurate results.

In this experiment, we created a big table which includes 1000 rows and 100 columns, wherein each row carries one word, and each column contains one feature. These 100 features were about common status, words, or adjectives that would describe the meaning of different words. When writing the features, the following issues were considered:

1. The features did not contain any word and its opposite, to avoid repetition. For example, we did not need to have two features **(Cold and Hot)**, because when we give the feature **Cold** the value 0, that would give the same meaning of the word **Hot**.

2. We wrote the feature names in English language in order to make the work readable and understandable by non-Arabic readers.

Each word is represented by a value that distinguishes it from other words. Each word in a row is described with a set of features (columns), each of which carries a number between 0 (if the column is the complete opposite of the word) and 1 (if the column is the exact meaning of the word). In addition, features that do not take the values 0 or 1 will take floating point numbers (between 0-1), based on the relatedness of the feature with the word. For features that are not applicable for the word, or which do not carry a yes/no answer, the value "NA" (not applicable) was assigned.

Features

Words	POS	FW	Negation	Emoji	Puncutation	Abbreviation	Word correctness	Formal
شكرا	Interjection	1	NA	0	NA	NA	0.4	0.5
الحب	N	0	NA	0	NA	NA	NA	0.5
الملك	N	0	NA	0	NA	NA	NA	0.5
كفووو	NA	0	NA	0	NA	NA	NA	0.4
كورونا	N	0	NA	0	NA	NA	NA	0.5

Figure 1: Sample of the AraKB data.

The purpose is to enable the model to recognize the approximate meaning of the word by having more description and the meaning of each word, rather than merely acknowledging the existence of the word itself. Figure 1 presents examples of the words each and their description (features). This method allows understanding the sentiment features and semantic relationships of the context, which might help to understand the user's pattern. Through the combination of the features' values in each tweet, the model predicted the context and the user's style of writing.

It is important to note that the process of entering this voluminous information was not random, but followed a specific method, as discussed in the next section.

3.3 AraKB annotation

This experiment aims to understand the meaning of words among Gulf Arabic speakers. Consequently, the AraKB table was created using words taken from the collected tweets and was compiled manually, to produce data that mimics real language on social media. The table was filled by the researcher and reviewed by an Arabic linguist to ensure an accurate description of the words, and that it was a reliable and realistic reference for the use of Gulf Arabic dialect words.

The linguist is an Arabic teacher who holds a Master's degree in Arabic language and literature. In addition, the linguist is active on different social media accounts (including Twitter), and is therefore familiar with the use of words and synonyms among Twitter users. More importantly, the linguist speaks the Gulf dialect (same dialect of the dataset), to ensure that they understand and describe the words and their full semantic and contextual implications as intended by Twitter users.

Regarding the features, a list was created to describe words from different aspects. For the sake of better explanation about the nature of features, they were divided into three categories, as explained in Appendix A.

3.4 Evaluation

During the creation of AraKB and annotating the words, some agreements and disagreements emerged between the researcher and the linguist on the values/description of the words. All the words themselves were kept as they are, and each produced a different table of values. Consequently, a method was needed to assess the level of agreement between the annotators in order to evaluate the quality of the data. As the data comprises nominal values, Cohen's kappa coefficient (for inter-rater reliability) was applied to measure the reliability of AraKB data.[2]

We calculated the number of complete agreements for all values. For each word, we counted how many features are identical in values between the annotators (agreement values). Any different values filled by the annotators were considered to be disagreements, regardless of the difference between values, such as different floating point numbers. For example, a field could carry the value 0.3 for Annotator #1, and 0.7 for Annotator #2. In that case, any difference was considered as a disagreement, and the same applied on all fields/values. Kappa is measured through the following equation:

$$k = \frac{p_0 - p_e}{1 - p_e} \quad (1)$$

Where p_o is the actual values of agreement among the annotators divided by the total number of values, and p_e it is probability of agreement between columnists, calculated as follows:

$$p_e = \sum_q \frac{n_{A1q}}{i} \times \frac{n_{A2q}}{i} = \frac{1}{i^2} \sum_q n_{A1q} \times n_{A2q} \quad (2)$$

After the value of k is calculated, the result is categorized to a specific level of agreement (McHugh, 2012), which is shown in Table 1

Cohen's kappa statistics	Level of agreement
≤ 0	No agreement
0.1 – 0.20	Poor agreement
0.21 – 0.40	Fair agreement
0.41 – 0.60	Moderate agreement
0.61 – 0.80	Substantial agreement
0.81 – 0.99	Almost perfect agreement
1	Perfect agreement

Table 1: Interpretation of Cohen's Kappa value.

The Kappa coefficient was measured for 100,000 values. In the case of our data, due to the large number of values, the level of agreement between the annotators was measured based on each column (feature). However, it is important to note that there were some columns that had 100% agreement (for the language-constant features), which therefore cannot carry different values (as described in Appendix A). In addition, 34 features of the second category also had 100% agreement.

The different values of the features and possible disagreements happened in the third category (60 features), which had the possibility to carry different values based on dialect, context, or different opinions of the annotators. In order to give more realistic and interpretable values, scales were agreed for some features to measure the relatedness of the word to the specific feature. For example, the feature Dangerous had a range of values based on how "dangerous" the word is, thus the value 1 was given for words like **Drugs, Kill**, and very dangerous things that could cause death. Values of 0.9-0.5 were assigned for other dangerous things that would not necessarily cause death, such as the words **Disease** and **Scorpion**. Values of 0.4-0.1 were given for things that may cause death if used wrongly, like **Car, Technology,** etc. Lastly, the value 0 was given for very safe things, such as the word **Shirt**.

The same process was applied for most of the features. It is important to note that there were

[2] Introduced by Jacob Cohen in 1960.

some words that carry a different meaning among Saudi users. For example, Thursday/الخميس is the beginning of the weekend at Saudi Arabia and most Gulf countries, so this word is usually used in semantic clouds connoting the status of fun and partying. Consequently, the word took the value 1 for the feature Interesting, based on its use in our data. Another example is for words used in informal contexts in different ways, such as the word بيض/egg. It is axiomatic that this word should be described as Food, but after an observation of its usage among the Saudi social media users, it was clearly used to express a state of boredom or something that is not interesting, thus it was given the value 0 for the feature Interesting.

After both annotators filled all fields of AraKB separately, we applied Kappa statistics only on the features of the third category (60 features), whose values could carry agreement and disagreement. For that a number of 60,000 features (60 features × 1000 words) were calculated by Cohen's kappa, which resulted in the findings reported in Table 2.

Total of fields	Agreement	Disagreement	Kappa Value
60,000	59,925	75	0.99

Table 2: Cohen's Kappa and inter-rater agreement.

Kappa value is 0.99, which is considered to be almost perfect based on the interpretation of Cohen's Kappa value, which gives the table more reliability, whereby it can be used in other works related to Gulf Arabic texts. This value was achieved as there is a specific measurement for each field, as explained earlier.

However, it is important to state that most of the fields had the NA value, because not all the features are applicable to describe the words, which explains the low number of disagreement values between the annotators. A total of 2,818 exact values were filled with numbers other than NA.

4 Experiments

4.1 Experimental setup

Unlike the use of TF-IDF features in the work of (Alqahtani & Dohler, 2022a), which depended on the existence of the words, the main purpose of AraKB is that the model will recognize the approximate meaning of the word by the set of features. Therefore, it can verify the users through the repeated status, emotions, and expressions reflected in their written texts.

Firstly, we needed to convert our AraKB Excel table into a form that would be usable in our code. A huge dictionary was created that contains all 1,000 words as keys (keys#1), whereby each word has its own smaller dictionary that has the set of features as keys (keys#2), each with their values (0, 0.1, 0.2, 0.3, 0.4, 0.5, 0.6, 0.7, 0.8, 0.9, 1, or NA). The dictionary was created for all columns except the POS column, as it has different values than the other columns (i.e., verb, noun, adjective, etc.), which was annotated manually and will be explained separately.

After that, we calculated the vectors by dividing the tweet into single words (tokens). A function was created that takes each word of the tweet and finds if it exists in one of the (keys #1). If the word exists, its dictionary with the key#2 is recalled, and their values are added. This process is repeated for every word in the tweet, then the values of all words in the tweet are calculated by taking the average of each feature's value of the words. If no word in the text exists in the table, the model will ignore the text.

We cannot take the average of the categorical values of the feature/column (POS), as this column has a different part of speech tags that represent words such as nouns, verbs, and adverbs, etc. Each value of the POS column has a separate column, so that each word will have a value in the related POS column (as previously set in the AraKB).

Another function was created related to the Negation feature, which contains the most used negation words that exist in the dataset (either MSA or Gulf dialect). The purpose of this feature is to reverse the meaning of the word following the negation. After calculating the vectors, the value of word coming after negation will be the opposite and will be with minus. For example, the word "صادق/honest" has the value 1 in the Honesty feature, but if it comes after the word "ليس/not" then the value for Honesty will be converted to -1. Lastly, the values of the Honesty feature will be averaged with other words existent in the tweet, therefore the level of "Honesty" will be reduced in the whole tweet.

To sum up, the values of each word of the tweet were extracted and averaged with other values. Figure 2 shows the concept of the calculation. The model scanned the tweet and found the words (المدرسة/المتعة/الطفل) that exist in our AraKB, thus it took each value for the column 1 (feature 1) and calculated the average values for all existent words, which gave the value 0.53. The same was repeated for all columns, until a list of vectors representing each tweet was compiled.

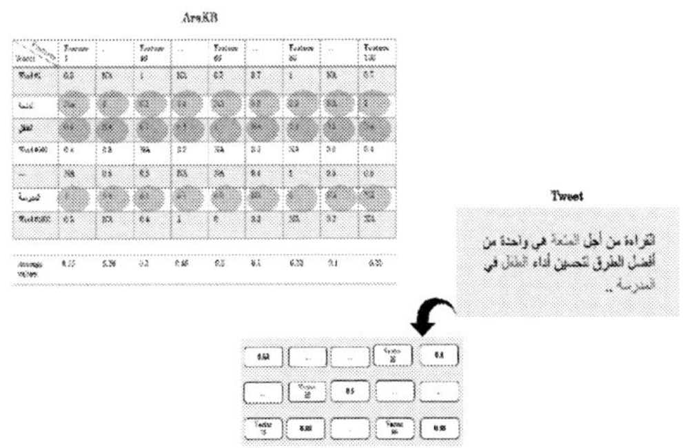

Figure 2: Process of converting the tweets to vectors.

Using this method might enable the model to ascertain the extent to which the tweet carries values of each feature written by each user, whereby it might be able to identify a pattern about how the user expresses their thoughts/emotions in their writing. In this experiment we used a previously tested stylometric feature (Alqahtani & Dohler, 2022a) in addition to our novel AraKB features.

4.2 Experimental results

As stated earlier, this experiment was based on the dataset used by (Alqahtani & Dohler, 2022a), and with same setting used in the previous experiments (train/test ration, the used classifier, CV 5-folds, etc.), in addition to conducting the same pre-processing steps in order to have comparable results.

Using the best performance algorithm (Gradient Boosting), our experiment showed a 2% improvement in performance (accuracy and F1-score) when adding the AraKB features to the previous stylometric features, as opposed to using the latter alone. Table 3 and Table 4 compare the results of using the stylometric features in the previous study (Alqahtani & Dohler, 2022a) and the results of the same tested dataset when using the AraKB features (respectively)

Feature	Avg F1	Avg recall	Avg precision	Avg accuracy
Stylometric	0.75	0.76	0.75	0.75
Stylometric + TF-IDF	0.77	0.75	0.79	0.77

Table 3: Results of using stylometric features by (Alqahtani & Dohler, 2022a).

Feature	Avg F1	Avg recall	Avg precision	Avg accuracy
Stylometric + AraKB	0.77	0.77	0.77	0.77

Table 4: Results of using AraKB and Stylometric features.

5 Discussion

Looking at the results of using a combination of stylometric and AraKB features shows a similarity in average results with the results of previous experiments that used a combination of stylometric and TF-IDF features. This indicates that using AraKB gives similar performance to using the TF-IDF features.

However, it is important to note that AraKB features contained only 1,000 Arabic words, due to the laborious and time-consuming individual efforts entailed. It is assumed that the outcomes would be substantially improved by adding many more words that an author would possibly write with. The purpose of this experiment is preliminary testing using AraKB features, to determine if these features enhance the performance of verifying authorship in short texts like Twitter posts.

One could argue that using AraKB is over-fitted to the dataset from which the list of words was derived. However, we have selected the thousand most prolifically used words of the whole dataset, which is actually far from being a reason of overfitting. This is because choosing the most repeated words entails that most of the users have used these words, therefore these words are not considered to be user-distinctive (i.e., they reflect homogenous use of language). In addition, our approach considers the meaning of words averaged with others in the same tweets, which means that it is not word-dependent like other content-dependent features, such as TF-IDF or BOW.

6 Conclusion

The limited work on Arabic AV texts shows the need to investigate more features that could enhance the verification process. In this experiment, we prove that creating features that represent the word's meaning, as in AraKB, does help to effectively verify the authorship, and might be helpful in other NLP tasks, such as sentiment analysis.

Future work on AraKB might extend the number of Arabic words, which will definitely improve its performance. In addition, further studies should investigate the influence of each of AraKB features, as we could focus only on the most influential ones.

Acknowledgments

The authors of this paper would like to thank the linguist Maha Alqahtani for taking the time and effort to manually review AraKB.

References

Ahmed Abbasi and Hsinchun Chen. 2005. Applying authorship analysis to extremist-group Web forum messages. *IEEE Intelligent Systems*, *20*(5), 67–75. https://doi.org/10.1109/MIS.2005.81

Bouzoubaa, K., Baidouri, H., Loukili, T., & Yazidi, T. El. (2009). Arabic stop words: Towards a generalisation and standardisation. In *Knowledge Management and Innovation in Advancing Economies: Analyses and Solutions - Proceedings of the 13th International Business Information Management Association Conference, IBIMA 2009*, *3*, 1844–1848.

El-Said Badawi. 1996. Understanding Arabic: essays in contemporary Arabic linguistics in honor of El-Said Badawi. American Univ in Cairo Press.

Fatimah Alqahtani and Mischa Dohler. 2022a. Investigating Predictive Features for Authorship Verification of Arabic Tweets. IJCSNS, 22(6), 115.

Fatimah Alqahtani and Mischa Dohler. 2022b. Survey of Authorship Identification Tasks on Arabic Texts. In *ACM Transactions on Asian and Low-Resource Language Information Processing.*

Hosein Azarbonyad, Mostafa Dehghani, Maarten Marx, and Jaap Kamps. 2015. Time-Aware Authorship Attribution for Short Text Streams. In *Proceedings of the 38th International ACM SIGIR Conference on Research and Development in Information Retrieval*, pages. 727-730.

Hossam Ahmed. 2017. Dynamic Similarity Threshold in Authorship Verification: Evidence from Classical Arabic. In *Procedia of The 3rd International Conference on Arabic Computational Linguistics*, pages 145–152. https://doi.org/10.1016/j.procs.2017.10.103

Hossam Ahmed. 2018. The Role of Linguistic Feature Categories in Authorship Verification. In *Procedia of The 4th International Conference on Arabic Computational Linguistics*, *142*, pages 214–221.

Hossam Ahmed. 2019a. Distance-Based Authorship Verification Across Modern Standard Arabic Genres. In *of the 3rd workshop on arabic corpus linguistics,* pages 89-96

Hossam Ahmed. 2019b. Sample Size in Arabic Authorship Verification. In *Proceedings of the 3rd International Conference on Natural Language and Speech Processing,* pages 84-91. Association for Computational Linguistics.

Jalaluddin Al-Suyuti. 1998. Al-Mazhar fi 'ulum al-lughat wa 'iwa'aha. Almaktabat aleasria.

Karin C. Ryding. 2005. A Reference Grammar of Modern Standard Arabic. Cambridge university press. https://doi.org/https://doi.org/10.1017/CBO9780511486975

Khaled Shaalan and Hafsa Raza. 2009. NERA: Named entity recognition for Arabic. In *Journal of the American Society for Information Science and Technology*, *60*(8), pages 1652–1663. https://doi.org/10.1002/asi.21090

Kim Luyckx and Walter Daelemans. 2011. The effect of author set size and data size in authorship attribution. *26*(1), pages 35-55 https://doi.org/10.1093/llc/fqq013

Leah S. Larkey and Margaret E. Connell. 2001. Arabic Information Retrieval at UMass in TREC-10. In *The Tenth Text REtrieval Conference*.

Mary L. McHugh. 2012. Interrater reliability : the kappa statistic. In *Biochemica Medica*, *22*(3), pages 276–282. Retrieved from https://hrcak.srce.hr/89395

Mohammad Al-Sarem, Walid Cherif, Ahmed Abdel Wahab, Abdel-Hamid Emara, and Mohamed Kissi. 2018. Combination of stylo-based features and frequency-based features for identifying the author of short Arabic text. In *of the 12th International Conference on Intelligent Systems: Theories and Applications*, pages 1-6. https://doi.org/10.1145/3289402.3289500

Sushil Kumar and Mousmi A. Chaurasia. 2012. Assessment on Stylometry for Multilingual Manuscript. In *IOSR Journal of Engineering*, *2*(9), pages 1–6. https://doi.org/10.9790/3021-02910106

A Appendices

Features specifications:

1. Language-constant features: Where we had six features that are considered to be constant in the language, which are known and cannot be considered in terms of personal opinion. These features are: Part of Speech, Function word, Negation, and Punctuation. Filling these words was based on previous knowledge of Arabic grammar. In addition, the features (Abbreviation and Emoji) took either the value 0 or 1 value based on the existence of the feature in the word. The following provide more details and examples about each feature and explanation of why they were considered as constant features.
2. Features that carry a yes/no answer. There were 34 features that only took values of 0, 1, or NA; the values cannot be a number in between 0-1. These features are: (Human, Alive, Female, Animal, Body-part, Food-related, Time-related, Place-related, Eaten, Past, Work/study, Question, Nationality, Weather, Prayer, Compare, Place, Time, Number, Many, Media-content, Listing, Quoting, Calling, Sport, Art, Policy, Literature, Religion, Science, Travel, Economy, Law, and Technology). These features are either applicable on the word or not, so they would take either the value 1 or 0.
3. The other features. The remaining 60 features may carry range of different values (e.g., 0, 0.1, 0.2, 0.3, 0.4, 0.5, 0.6, 0.7, 0.8, 0.9, 1, or NA) based on the word's relatedness to the features. These features are: (Formal, Word correctness, Long, Strong, Expensive, Dangerous, Ability, Shyness, Like, Peaceful, Loyalty, Excellence, Privacy, Necessity, Reality, Desire, Request, Rich, Big, Normal, Beautiful, Smart, Useful, Cause-death, Noisy, Cold, Heavy, Thankful, Youthful, Romantic, Agree, Happy, Angry, Welcome, Sarcastic ,Similar, Scary, Disgusting, Well-known, Crime, Childish, Optimism, Simple, Comfortable, Interesting, Healthy, Surprised, Wonder, Argue, Certainty, Emphasis, Honesty, Emotional , Laugh, Abusive, Racist, Shame, Wish, and Royal).

A Semi-supervised Approach for a Better Translation of Sentiment in Dialectical Arabic UGT

Hadeel Saadany
Centre for Translation Studies
University of Surrey
United Kingdom
hadeel.saadany@surrey.ac.uk

Constantin Orăsan
Centre for Translation Studies
University of Surrey
United Kingdom
c.orasan@surrey.ac.uk

Emad Mohamed
RGCL
University of Wolverhampton
Wolverhampton, UK
e.mohamed2@wlv.ac.uk

Ashraf Tantawy
School of Computer Science and Informatics
De Montfort University
Leicester, UK
ashraf.tantavy@dmu.ac.uk

Abstract

In the online world, Machine Translation (MT) systems are extensively used to translate User-Generated Text (UGT) such as reviews, tweets, and social media posts, where the main message is often the author's positive or negative attitude towards the topic of the text. However, MT systems still lack accuracy in some low-resource languages and sometimes make critical translation errors that completely flip the sentiment polarity of the target word or phrase and hence delivers a wrong affect message. This is particularly noticeable in texts that do not follow common lexico-grammatical standards such as the dialectical Arabic (DA) used on online platforms. In this research, we aim to improve the translation of sentiment in UGT written in the dialectical versions of the Arabic language to English. Given the scarcity of gold-standard parallel data for DA-EN in the UGT domain, we introduce a semi-supervised approach that exploits both monolingual and parallel data for training an NMT system initialised by a cross-lingual language model trained with supervised and unsupervised modeling objectives. We assess the accuracy of sentiment translation by our proposed system through a numerical 'sentiment-closeness' measure as well as human evaluation. We will show that our semi-supervised MT system can significantly help with correcting sentiment errors detected in the online translation of dialectical Arabic UGT.

1 Introduction

Incorporating automatic translation tools by websites such as Twitter, amazon.com and booking.com has become common practice to cater for their multilingual users. In this context, sentiment preservation is of great importance because decisions about purchasing a product or service, as well as analysis of public trends, are based on accurate translation of the user's affect message. Arabic UGT constitutes a significant challenge for MT systems because it is commonly a mix of Dialectical Arabic (DA) and Modern Standard Arabic (MSA) which differ significantly on the lexico-grammatical level. Research has shown that the code-switching between DA and MSA by online users can lead to a serious mistranslation of sentiment for several reasons (Saadany and Orasan, 2020).

First, there are lexical and structural differences between the two versions of the Arabic language which cause confusion to MT systems in choosing the correct sentiment-carrying word. On the lexical level, there are polysemous words used in both MSA and DA which can have exact opposite sentiment poles. To give one example, the word 'جامد' means 'rigid' in MSA, but in DA, within the UGT domain, it often means 'great or awesome'. Hence, we find the positive Goodreads review 'كتاب جامد جدا' (A very good book)[1] is mistranslated by the online MT tool into 'A very rigid book', incorrectly reflecting a negative sentiment. The same word, however, in another book review written in MSA – 'جامده جدا طريقه المؤلف في سرد الاحداث' – is correctly translated as 'The author's way of narrating events is very rigid', rightly reflecting the dissatisfaction of the author.

Second, the Arabic writing system does not have letters for short vowels; instead short vowels are realised as diacritic symbols on or below letters. UGT commonly lacks diacritics and hence it of-

[1] https://www.goodreads.com/book/show/16031620

Proceedings of the The Seventh Arabic Natural Language Processing Workshop (WANLP), pages 214 - 224
December 8, 2022 ©2022 Association for Computational Linguistics

ten contains words spelled alike in MSA and DA but different in meaning due to different pronunciation. An example of these homographs is in the DA tweet[2] 'كفايانا نصب' where the noun 'نصب' commonly means 'fraud' in DA with the diacritic 'fatha' (a short /a/ sound) on the first letter; the tweet should read 'Enough of the fraud'. The online MT system flips the negative polarity as it mistakes this word with its common homograph in MSA meaning 'monument', pronounced with 'damma' (a short /u/ sound) on its first and second letters. The mistranslation of the homograph produces a neutral statement, 'enough monument', which completely misses the negative polarity of the source.

The third problem is that the way sentiment is expressed by the DA used in UGT is different than the structured DA data that is commonly used to train DA-EN NMT systems (e.g. Zbib et al. (2012); Bouamor et al. (2014); Elmahdy et al. (2014); Meftouh et al. (2015); Bouamor et al. (2018)). Some of the main differences is that UGT typically contains profanity and aggressive words that are not to be found in the available dialectical data. Moreover, the DA used on online platforms such as Twitter usually contains unusual orthography to express emotions or to obfuscate aggression and, at times, nuanced words that are understood only within context. A review of the literature shows that the authentic parallel datasets for DA-EN consist mainly of hand-crafted structured data which significantly differ from this type of noisy DA used in UGT. On the other hand, there is a considerable number of large parallel MSA-EN datasets in various domains (e.g OPUS[3] open-source parallel MSA-EN datasets include UN documents, TEDx talks, subtitles, news commentary, etc.). Since DA in the UGT domain has peculiar qualities and since it differs on the lexico-grammatical level from Standard Arabic and, at times, same words can have opposite sentiment in the two versions, the freely available MSA datasets are not optimal for translating sentiment in UGT written in a dialectical version.

Given the scarcity of any substantial gold-standard DA-EN data within the UGT domain, we propose to improve the transfer of sentiment in Arabic UGT by training a semi-supervised NMT system where we leverage the relatively large gold-standard MSA-EN data with DA monolingual data from the UGT domain. We take advantage of pre-training a cross-lingual language model with both a Masked Language Modelling (MLM) objective and a Translation Language Modelling (TLM) objective for creating a shared embedding space for English, MSA and DA. We show that initialising our NMT model with these cross-lingual pretrained word representations has a significant impact on the translation performance in general and on the transfer of sentiment in particular. In this research, therefore, we make the following contributions:

- We introduce a semi-supervised AR-EN NMT system trained on both parallel and monolingual data for a better translation of sentiment in Arabic UGT.
- We introduce an empirical evaluation method for assessing the transfer of sentiment between Arabic and English in the UGT domain.
- We make our compiled dataset, crosslingual language models and semi-supervised NMT system publicly available[4].

To present our contributions, the paper is divided as follows: Section 2 provides a summary of relevant approaches to supervised and unsupervised MT as well as research attempts for the translation of DA. Section 3 describes our semi-supervised NMT system set up and its requirements. Section 4 presents the experiments we conducted on our compiled datasets as well as the assessment methods used to evaluate the improvement of sentiment translation in DA UGT. Finally, Section 5 presents our conclusions on the different experiments and the limitations of the study.

2 Related Work

The earliest attempt to solve the problem of translating DA has been introduced by Zbib et al. (2012). They created the largest existing parallel data for DA to English which is relied upon in most MT research for DA. The dataset consists of around 250k parallel sentences. They used Mechanical Turk to translate sentences from DA to EN. Most of the DA is in the Levantine and Egyptian dialects, but none of the texts used belong to the UGT domain. They show that when translating the dialectical test sets, the DA-EN MT system performs 6.3

[2] https://twitter.com/Abdullahehemidy/status/221985043793444865, Accessed: Aug 2022

[3] https://opus.nlpl.eu/

[4] https://tinyurl.com/bdfh8e4m

and 7.0 BLEU points higher than an MT system trained on a 150M-word MSA-EN parallel corpus. Another approach to solve the data scarcity problem was introduced by Salloum and Habash (2013) who propose pivoting to MSA instead of directly translating from DA to EN. They transform DA sentences into MSA by a large number of hand-written morphosyntactic transfer rules.

There have been other attempts to create DA-EN and DA-MSA parallel datasets such as the multi-dialectical MDC and MADAR datasets (Bouamor et al., 2014, 2018), the QCA speech corpus (Elmahdy et al., 2014), and the PADIC parallel corpus which includes five dialects and MSA, but not English (Meftouh et al., 2015). These datasets, however, are relatively too small (max 14.7k parallel sentences) and differ considerably from the UGT domain. Since the problem of DA-EN scarcity of data still exists up to the time of writing this research, the most recent attempts to improve the translation of DA to English have focused either on augmenting the available datasets by bootstrapping techniques (Abid, 2020) or on training with the large available MSA datasets and fine-tuning on the smaller DA datasets (Sajjad et al., 2020).

A recent research line in MT which has been introduced to overcome the sparsity of gold-standard parallel data for low-resource languages is unsupervised MT which relies solely on monolingual data of the source and target languages in training (Lample et al., 2017, 2018; Artetxe et al., 2017). The key idea is to build a common latent space for two languages (or more) which can be used to reconstruct a sentence in a given language from a noisy version of it (Vincent et al., 2008), or to obtain the translated sentence by using a back-translation procedure (Sennrich et al., 2015a). The use of high quality cross-lingual word embeddings pretrained by state-of-the-art cross-lingual language models to initialise the unsupervised MT systems has recently contributed to a significant improvement in their performance (Lample and Conneau, 2019; Artetxe et al., 2019; Conneau et al., 2020). In this research, we combine both methods of supervised and unsupervised MT to compensate for the sparsity of the DA-EN data from the UGT domain. Our semi-supervised system is explained in the following section.

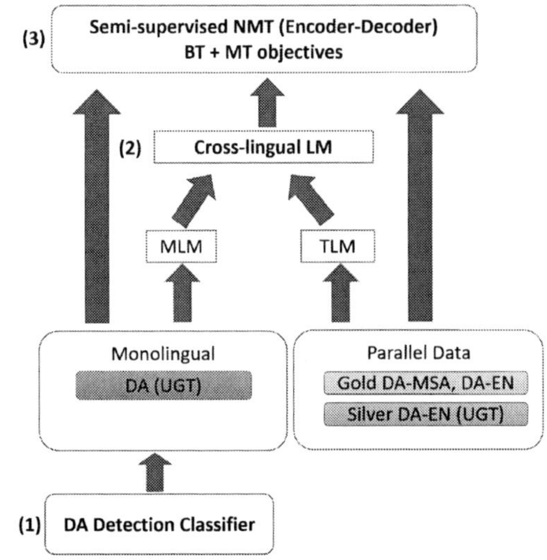

Figure 1: Semi-supervised NMT system

3 Semi-supervised NMT System Set Up

3.1 Cross-Lingual Language Model

Due to their lexico-grammatical differences, we treat dialectical and standard Arabic as two distinct languages. Hence, we construct a multi-directional NMT system between the permutations of DA-MSA-EN with the objective of obtaining the highest translation accuracy in the DA-EN direction. The setup of this system is shown in Figure 1. For constructing our semi-supervised NMT system we require the following data:

1. MSA-EN clean parallel data usually used for training NMT,
2. MSA-DA clean parallel data from any domain,
3. DA-EN silver-standard parallel data from the UGT domain with sentiment lexicon infused, and
4. DA monolingual data from the UGT domain.

It should be noted that the Arabic UGT is not written in DA per se, it is usually a mix of DA and MSA. Since we are treating DA and MSA as two distinct languages, we need to extract only the DA instances from the UGT dataset. For this purpose, we build our own DA detection classifier as per step (1) in Figure 1.

In step (2), we pretrain a cross-lingual language model to initialise our NMT system. We follow Lample and Conneau (2019) approach to train a cross-lingual language model with the combination of the following two objectives:

Masked Language Model (MLM): The MLM we train has a similar objective to BERT (Devlin et al., 2018) masking technique but adopting Lample and Conneau (2019)'s approach by including the use of text streams of an arbitrary number of sentences (truncated at 200 tokens) instead of pairs of sentences. We optimise the MLM objective on the MSA and EN source data as well as the DA monolingual data mentioned in data requirements 1, 2, and 4 above.

Translation Language Model (TLM): We use the TLM objective to improve cross-lingual training where the language model is trained on the gold-standard parallel sentences (i.e MSA-EN and MSA-DA in data requirements 1 and 2 above). The training is achieved by randomly masking words in both the source and target sentences. Thus, to predict a word masked in a DA sentence, for example, the model can either attend to surrounding DA words or to the EN/MSA side of the parallel data if the DA context is not sufficient to infer the masked DA word. By relying on the parallel data, the TLM objective helps in the alignment of embedding spaces across the three languages.

3.2 Semi-Supervised Machine Translation

To maximally exploit the similarity between the DA and MSA, we use the embeddings from the cross-lingual model we trained in step (2) of the experiment to initialise the encoder and decoder of the NMT system instead of random initialisation (step (3) in Figure 1). We train our system with both supervised and unsupervised NMT objectives. The unsupervised objective is achieved by a back-translation (BT) objective optimised by a round-trip translation of the UGT monolingual data. So a sentence s in DA monolingual data is translated to EN, and then back-translated with the objective of generating s. As for the supervised objective, we use the normal Machine Translation (MT) objective on our gold and silver parallel data. The compilation of the data requirements for our model is explained in the next section.

4 Experiment and Results

4.1 Data Compilation

As explained in Section 3.1, we need gold and silver standard parallel data for DA, MSA and EN as well as DA from the UGT domain. For the gold standard DA-EN data, we use the MDC (Bouamor et al., 2014) and the MADAR (Bouamor et al., 2018) corpora which consist of $\approx 33k$ parallel sentences where the DA side comprises Egyptian, Syrian, Palestinian, Jordanian and Tunisian dialects. Although this corpus has diverse dialects, it differs from the noisy DA used in UGT as it contains handcrafted sentences written for a traveler's guide. We, therefore, use two other gold DA-EN datasets that are closer to the UGT domain. The first is compiled by Abid (2020) consisting of 18k sentences created for the evaluation of the DA-EN translation by native speakers of Egyptian and Levantine dialects. The second is the Sentiment After Translation (SAT) corpus (Salameh et al., 2015) which consists of 1200 manually translated tweets from Levantine. The latter is the only gold-standard DA-EN UGT data we are aware of. As for the MSA-EN gold-standard data, we opt for diversifying the domain. Thus, we use 2M sentences from the Opus UN multilingual, and 1M from mixed Opus which is extracted from TEDx talks and subtitles (Tiedemann, 2012).

For the monolingual data, we compiled UGT datasets that were used as benchmarks for Arabic sentiment detection tasks to guarantee that they have a sentiment content. The monolingual datasets comprise tweets (Gamal et al., 2019), Goodreads reviews (LABR dataset) (Aly and Atiya, 2013) and the Arabic Online Commentary (AOC) (Zaidan and Callison-Burch, 2011). To extract the DA instances from these datasets, we build a DA detection classifier by fine-tuning a Roberta-XLM (Conneau et al., 2019) model on the Arabic Online Commentary (AOC) dataset (Zaidan and Callison-Burch, 2011). The AOC is composed of 3M MSA and dialectal comments created by extracting reader commentary from the online versions of three Arabic newspapers which have a high degree (about half) of dialectal content. From the 3M comments in this dataset, only 108,173 comments are labelled via crowdsourcing. We use the labelled comments for training our DA classifier. We randomly shuffle the labelled dataset and split it into 80% training (Train), 10% validation (Dev), and 10% test (Test). The accuracy of the model on the test set reached 92% which assured a satisfactory extraction of the DA instances from the monolingual dataset.

As for the silver-standard dataset, we have noticed that Google Translate, which is the ad hoc MT

Data Type	Corpus	Domain	No. Sentences
Gold MSA-EN	Multi-UN Mixed OPUS	UN Documents TEDx, Subtitles	2M 1M
Gold DA-MSA	MADAR MDC	Traveler's Guide	60K
Gold DA-EN	MADAR MDC (Abid, 2020)	Traveler's Guide Subtitles Wiki Fables	90K
Silver DA-MSA	AOC LABR SAT + NileULEX lexicon	(Back translation) Tweets Goodreads reviews Online comments	166K
Silver DA-EN	AOC LABR SAT + NileULex lexicon	(Automatic Translation) Tweets Goodreads reviews Online Comments	166K
Monolingual DA	AOC LABR SAT + NileULex lexicon	Tweets Goodreads reviews Online Comments	166K
Total Sentences			**3.648M**

Table 1: Distribution of the datasets used for training and their particular domains

system on different UGT platforms such as Twitter, translates English into standard Arabic. We leveraged this feature by translating our monolingual Arabic dialectical dataset into English and then back translated it into Arabic. This round-trip translation produced a synthetic parallel data of DA-EN-MSA. We expected that this synthetic dataset would contain a large number of mistranslated sentiment-carrying dialectical expressions and idioms that are commonly used in Arabic UGT. To alleviate the effect of these errors, we opted for correcting these DA expressions by infusing a lexicon of DA positive/negative phrases commonly used in UGT. For this purpose, we manually translated into MSA and English the NileULex (El-Beltagy, 2016) sentiment lexicon which consisted of DA phrases and idioms extracted from DA tweets. The lexicon consisted of 1000 positive and negative phrases that were found to be frequently used in tweets. We replaced these idioms with their correct translations in the MSA and EN side of the data. The sentence distribution of our datasets is shown in Table 1.

4.2 Training Details

4.3 Semi-supervised NMT system

Lample and Conneau (2019) have shown that the alignment of embedding spaces across languages that share the same alphabet and a significant fraction of vocabulary proves to be effective in cross-lingual tasks such as MT. Since this precisely applies to DA and MSA in our experiment, we use the synthesised and gold parallel datasets as well as the monolingual datasets described in the previous section to build the crosslingual language model for DA, MSA and EN. We use both the monolingual and the parallel data to train our model with a Translation objective (TLM) used in combination with a masking objective (MLM). Before training, the data is preprocessed by Moses tokeniser (Koehn et al., 2007). We use fastBPE[5] to learn BPE codes and split words into subword units. Since shared vocabulary has also proved to improve the performance of multilingual models on downstream cross-lingual tasks (Lample and Conneau, 2019; Conneau et al., 2020), we chose to have a shared subword vocabulary for all datasets. The BPE codes are learned on the concatenation of sentences sampled by applying a BPE model (Sennrich et al., 2015b) directly on raw text data for all languages. We apply the BPE coding on a network vocabulary size of 20000. We remove sentence pairs which contain empty lines or lines with a length longer than 200 tokens.

For training our cross-lingual model, we use a transformer architecture with 1024 hidden units, 8 heads, and a dropout rate of 0.1. We use the Adam optimiser (Kingma and Ba, 2014) for optimisation, a linear warm-up (Vaswani et al., 2017) and learning rates varying from 10^{-4} to 5.10^{-4}. For the MLM and TLM objectives, we use streams of 200 tokens and train on mini-batches of size 32. For the TLM objective, we also sample mini-batches of 32 tokens composed of sentences with similar lengths.

[5] https://github.com/glample/fastBPE

We use the averaged perplexity over languages as a stopping criterion for training the cross-lingual models.

We then use the pretrained embedding vectors in our crosslingual language model to initiate the semi-supervised NMT system trained on our gold and synthetic parallel datasets as well as the larger monolingual datasets. As explained in Section 3.2, the NMT system is trained with an MT objective for the three languages, DA-EN-MSA, simultaneously. We use the permutations of the three languages DA, EN, MSA taken two at a time. It is also trained with an unsupervised BT objective by maximising the back translation accuracy of the monolingual UGT dataset. For machine translation, we train on a 6 layer transformer and we increase the maximum token length to 200 to accommodate for MSA relatively long sentences. For the semi-supervised NMT system, we use the BLEU score of the DA-EN direction as the stopping criteria. We train for 100 epochs with an epoch size of 100k sentences. The training of the language model and the semi-supervised NMT system was conducted on 3 24GB GeForce RTX 3090 GPUs for a period of 9 days.

4.3.1 Baseline Models

We aimed to experiment with two alternative set ups where the monolingual UGT data is not included in training. The first is a supervised baseline model trained on the gold-standard MSA-EN and DA-EN datasets as well as the silver DA-EN dataset. We also concatenated our manually translated sentiment lexicon to the training data. For this baseline, DA and MSA are indiscriminately treated as one source language. We aimed to see how far concatenating DA and MSA data can improve the sentiment translation of DA into English in the UGT dataset. In the second set up, we followed similar research approaches (Salloum and Habash, 2013; Sajjad et al., 2020) which overcome the sparsity of DA data by pivoting to MSA as an intermediary step in the DA-EN MT pipeline. Thus, we build a DA-MSA MT system trained on the gold-standard DA-MSA datasets and then translated the MSA output into English. For translating into English, we used Marian open-source pretrained AR-EN MT model[6]. We call this latter model the Pivoting model. For both the baseline and the Pivoting model, we trained two NMT systems by replicating the same preprocessing technique of our semi-supervised model. Thus, we trained an unsupervised BPE encoding model for source and target data and split words into subword units. We set the maximum vocabulary size to 20000. The two models were trained using a transformer for both the encoding and decoding layers with 8 heads of self-attention and with an inner feed-forward layer of size 2048 and a batch size of 4096 sentences. We used the Adam optimiser with learning rate 2 and initialised training with 4000 warm up steps. We trained for 100k steps.

4.4 Results

For evaluation, we aimed to assess our proposed models' ability not only to produce quality translations but more importantly to transfer the UGT sentiment correctly from DA to EN. Therefore, we conducted different types of evaluation techniques on two test sets: a held-out DA-EN test set (180 parallel sentences) and a hand-crafted test set (50 sentences) selected from the monolingual DA dataset of tweets and book reviews. The hand-crafted dataset contained carefully chosen tweets and reviews with DA negative and positive expressions which constitute a challenge for available MT systems such as Google API (see Appendix A for some examples). A professional translator created a reference to the hand-crafted set. Both evaluation sets were translated by our baseline, the Pivoting model, the semi-supervised system proposed in this paper and Google Translate. We devised both human and automatic sentiment evaluation measures to assess how far the model is capable of maintaining the correct polarity of the source text for both test sets. The sacrebleu metric (Post, 2018) was also used as to assess whether the quality of the translation is balanced with the preservation of sentiment by our proposed models. Details of the experiment evaluations are presented in the next sections and examples of the semi-supervised DA-EN model output as compared to the ad hoc online MT tool for Twitter are included in Appendix A of this paper.

4.5 Translation Quality

Although there are benchmark datasets for the translation of DA into English (Bouamor et al., 2018; Meftouh et al., 2015; Sajjad et al., 2020), none belongs to the UGT domain. Accordingly, due to discrepancy in domain for our test data, we could not compare our results to any of these research experiments. We compare the BLEU scores

[6] https://nlp.johnsnowlabs.com/2021/01/03/translate_ar_en_xx.html

Model	SAM Score Test Set	Average SAM Score Test Set	Human Evaluation Hand-crafted Set H1	H2	H3	BLEU Test Set
Baseline	10.52	0.18	1.53	1.38	1.51	12.12
Pivoting MS-DA-EN	10.95	0.14	2.26	2.5	3	11.87
Google Translate	9.14	0.16	3.32	**3.28**	3.33	26.98
Semi-supervised MT	**5.26**	**0.10**	**4**	3.26	**4.35**	**32.29**

Table 2: Evaluation results for sentiment-closeness measure, human evaluation, and BLEU on test sets. The best scores are in bold.

of the held-out test set for outputs of the baseline, the Pivoting model, Google API and the semi-supervised MT model. As can be seen in Table 2, the BLEU score of the semi-supervised system is 5.31 points higher than Google Translate system and both the baseline and the Pivoting model fall far behind. This indicates that the quality of translation improves with our semi-supervised approach. However, despite the higher scores achieved by our system, research has shown that the BLEU metric may not be optimal for assessing how far the MT models transfer the sentiment correctly (Saadany and Orasan, 2021). The reason is that due to its restrictive exact matching to the reference, BLEU does not accommodate for importance n-gram weighting which may be essential in assessing sentiment-critical n-grams. For this reason, we conduct two types of sentiment-focused measures, automatic and manual, on our test sets. The sentiment assessment is explained in the next section.

4.5.1 Sentiment Quality

The first method is a Sentiment-Aware Measure (SAM) which evaluates the sentiment distance between the MT output (the hypothesis) and the reference translation in English. SAM is calculated by using the SentiWord dictionary of prior polarities (Gatti et al., 2015). SentiWord is a sentiment lexicon that combines the high precision of manual lexica and the high coverage of automatic ones (covering 155,000 words). It is based on assigning a 'prior polarity' score for each lemma-POS in both SentiWordNet and a number of human-annotated sentiment lexica (Baccianella et al., 2010; Warriner et al., 2013). The prior polarity is the out-of-context positive or negative score which a lemma-POS evokes.

We assume that SAM is proportional to the distance between the sentiment scores of the unmatched words in the system translation of the DA source and the reference in English, the higher the distance the greater the SAM score. To calculate the SAM score, we designate the number of remaining mismatched words in the hypothesis and reference translation by m and n, respectively. We calculate the total SentiWord sentiment score for the lemma-POS[7] of the mismatched words in the translation and reference sentences using a weighted average of the sentiment score of each mismatched lemma-POS. The weight of a hypothesis mismatched word w_h and a reference mismatched word w_r is calculated based on the sentiment score of its lemma-POS, s, as follows:

$$w_h^i = |s_i| \qquad i = 1, 2, \ldots, m. \tag{1}$$

$$w_r^i = |s_i| \qquad i = 1, 2, \ldots, n. \tag{2}$$

Then the total sentiment score for hypothesis S_h and reference S_r is given by:

$$S_h = \sum_{i=1}^{m} \alpha_i s_i, \quad \alpha_i = \frac{w_h^i}{\sum_{i=1}^{m} w_h^i} \tag{3}$$

$$S_r = \sum_{i=1}^{n} \beta_i s_i, \quad \beta_i = \frac{w_r^i}{\sum_{i=1}^{n} w_r^i} \tag{4}$$

The normalised SAM score is given by:

$$p = \frac{|S_r - S_h|}{2} \tag{5}$$

As seen from equation (5), SAM is interpreted as a translation cost. Thus, a lower SAM score indicates a shorter distance from the sentiment score of the source, and hence a better translation. As illustrated by Table 2, the semi-supervised NMT system maintains the lowest sentiment distance as it records the lowest total SAM score for the test set (5.26). Moreover, the average SAM score between the hypothesis of the semi-supervised model and

[7] We use spaCy V3.1 library to assign the lemma-POS of each token.

reference is also the lowest (0.10). Compared to the other models, the lower SAM scores indicate that the semi-supervised model is more capable of maintaining the sentiment polarity of the individual tokens of the source DA tweet or review as it shows the least sentiment discrepancy between its hypothesis and the reference translation.

For the second evaluation, we aimed to conduct a focused assessment of the ability of each model to transfer sentiment in challenging examples. We, therefore, conducted a human evaluation on the smaller hand-crafted dataset that consisted of UGT DA examples that constitute a challenge to online MT systems. We asked three native speakers of Arabic, who are also near native in English, to scale from 1 to 5 how far the sentiment expressed in the source DA tweet or the online review is preserved. We provided each human annotator with four translations of the source produced by the baseline, the Pivot model, the semi-supervised system and Google Translate. The average scores of the three annotators (H1, H2, H3) for each output is recorded in Table 2. As can be seen from the scores, the average performance of the semi-supervised model is slightly higher than Google Translate for Annotator H1 and H3, but lower for annotator H2. The baseline and the Pivoting model, however, are performing around 2 scales below the average according to all annotators. Overall, the automatic and manual sentiment evaluation of the four systems indicate that the semi-supervised MT system is more competent in preserving the sentiment of the source DA text.

4.6 Error Analysis

We conducted an error analysis on the mistranslation of sentiment by extracting the translations that received the lower scores by the human annotators in the hand-crafted dataset. It was observed that the aggressive DA examples in tweets were generally missed by Google API, the baseline as well as the Pivoting model. For example, the aggression in the DA tweet 'يخرب بيتك يا سعد الدين' (Go to hell Saadu-deen) is missed in the output of the Google API – *'your house will be destroyed, Saadu-deen'* – as it provides a literal meaning to the DA offensive curse 'يخرب بيتك' (Go to hell). The semi-supervised model output, on the other hand, correctly transfers the offensive message as it translates the tweet with a similarly aggressive curse: *'Damn you Saadu-deen'* (See Ex3 and Ex4 in Appendix A for similar aggressive tweets).

Moreover, the UGT monolingual data used for training the semi-supervised model had a positive effect in improving the translation of problematic structures such as negation particles which were realised as clitics added to the stem of the word. For example, the negation in the tweet 'منصحش اي حد يشتريها' (I would not advise anyone to buy it) is correctly transferred by the hypothesis of the semi-supervised model whereas Google API produces the wrong translation: *'I advise anyone to buy it'*, and the Pivoting model produces a similarly wrong meaning: *'Anybody buys it'* (See also Ex3 in Appendix A). It was also noticed that the baseline performed well on structured DA-EN data but the translation quality was significantly degraded with the DA test data of tweets and online reviews. This substantiates our hypothesis that the available DA-EN structured data are not optimum for building a robust DA-EN system capable of translating the UGT domain.

Finally, it was noticed that are several examples where the sentiment gist of the source is transferred despite structural errors. For example, the human annotators marked the hypothesis of the semi-supervised model *'We are backwardness in us'* as correctly transferring the negative sentiment despite the ill-formed structure. The correct reference of this tweet is *'Backwardness is in us'*. This trade-off between sentiment accuracy and translation fluency is evident in a number of hypotheses produced by the semi-supervised model (See Ex4, Ex5, Ex6 in Appendix A for similar examples).

5 Conclusion

In this research, we tackled the intricate problem of translating sentiment in different Arabic dialects in the UGT domain such as tweets and online reviews. We overcome the problem of the scarcity of gold-standard parallel data by training an NMT model with both a supervised and an unsupervised objective functions using monolingual as well as parallel data. We compared this model to a baseline that was trained solely on parallel data and a DA-EN MT model where we pivoted on MSA as an intermediary step. Our semi-supervised model showed improved performance over these two models not only in terms of translation quality but specifically in the preservation of the sentiment polarity of the source. We also conducted automatic and manual evaluation of the models' performance and proposed a lexicon-based metric that takes into account the sentiment distance between the source and the MT output. Overall, our error analysis has revealed that despite some structural inaccuracies the semi-supervised model is more capable of transferring the correct sentiment specifically in aggressive tweets. Future research will address the challenge of trading off translation fluency for sentiment accuracy to improve the translation of sentiment-oriented Arabic online content.

References

Wael Abid. 2020. The SADID Evaluation Datasets for Low-Resource Spoken Language Machine Translation of Arabic Dialects. In *Proceedings of the 28th International Conference on Computational Linguistics*, pages 6030–6043.

Mohamed Aly and Amir Atiya. 2013. Labr: A large scale Arabic book reviews dataset. In *Proceedings of the 51st Annual Meeting of the Association for Computational Linguistics (Volume 2: Short Papers)*, pages 494–498.

Mikel Artetxe, Gorka Labaka, and Eneko Agirre. 2019. An effective approach to unsupervised machine translation. *arXiv preprint arXiv:1902.01313*.

Mikel Artetxe, Gorka Labaka, Eneko Agirre, and Kyunghyun Cho. 2017. Unsupervised neural machine translation. *arXiv preprint arXiv:1710.11041*.

Stefano Baccianella, Andrea Esuli, and Fabrizio Sebastiani. 2010. Sentiwordnet 3.0: an enhanced lexical resource for sentiment analysis and opinion mining. In *LREC*, volume 10, pages 2200–2204.

Houda Bouamor, Nizar Habash, and Kemal Oflazer. 2014. A Multidialectal Parallel Corpus of Arabic. In *LREC*, pages 1240–1245.

Houda Bouamor, Nizar Habash, Mohammad Salameh, Wajdi Zaghouani, Owen Rambow, Dana Abdulrahim, Ossama Obeid, Salam Khalifa, Fadhl Eryani, Alexander Erdmann, et al. 2018. The MADAR Arabic dialect corpus and lexicon. In *Proceedings of the eleventh international conference on language resources and evaluation (LREC 2018)*.

Alexis Conneau, Kartikay Khandelwal, Naman Goyal, Vishrav Chaudhary, Guillaume Wenzek, Francisco Guzmán, Edouard Grave, Myle Ott, Luke Zettlemoyer, and Veselin Stoyanov. 2019. Unsupervised cross-lingual representation learning at scale. *arXiv preprint arXiv:1911.02116*.

Alexis Conneau, Kartikay Khandelwal, Naman Goyal, Vishrav Chaudhary, Guillaume Wenzek, Francisco Guzmán, Édouard Grave, Myle Ott, Luke Zettlemoyer, and Veselin Stoyanov. 2020. Unsupervised Cross-lingual Representation Learning at Scale. In *Proceedings of the 58th Annual Meeting of the Association for Computational Linguistics*, pages 8440–8451.

Jacob Devlin, Ming-Wei Chang, Kenton Lee, and Kristina Toutanova. 2018. Bert: Pre-training of deep bidirectional transformers for language understanding. *arXiv preprint arXiv:1810.04805*.

Samhaa R. El-Beltagy. 2016. NileULex: A phrase and word level sentiment lexicon for Egyptian and Modern Standard Arabic. In *Proceedings of the Tenth International Conference on Language Resources and Evaluation (LREC'16)*, pages 2900–2905, Portorož, Slovenia. European Language Resources Association (ELRA).

Mohamed Elmahdy, Mark Hasegawa-Johnson, and Eiman Mustafawi. 2014. Development of a tv broadcasts speech recognition system for Qatari Arabic. In *Proceedings of the Ninth International Conference on Language Resources and Evaluation (LREC'14)*, pages 3057–3061.

Donia Gamal, Marco Alfonse, El-Sayed M El-Horbaty, and Abdel-Badeeh M Salem. 2019. Twitter benchmark dataset for Arabic sentiment analysis. *Int J Mod Educ Comput Sci*, 11(1):33.

Lorenzo Gatti, Marco Guerini, and Marco Turchi. 2015. Sentiwords: Deriving a high precision and high coverage lexicon for sentiment analysis. *IEEE Transactions on Affective Computing*, 7:409–421.

Diederik P Kingma and Jimmy Ba. 2014. Adam: A method for stochastic optimization. *arXiv preprint arXiv:1412.6980*.

Philipp Koehn, Hieu Hoang, Alexandra Birch, Chris Callison-Burch, Marcello Federico, Nicola Bertoldi, Brooke Cowan, Wade Shen, Christine Moran, Richard Zens, et al. 2007. Moses: Open source toolkit for statistical machine translation. In *Proceedings of the 45th annual meeting of the association for computational linguistics companion volume proceedings of the demo and poster sessions*, pages 177–180.

Guillaume Lample and Alexis Conneau. 2019. Cross-lingual language model pretraining. *arXiv preprint arXiv:1901.07291*.

Guillaume Lample, Alexis Conneau, Ludovic Denoyer, and Marc'Aurelio Ranzato. 2017. Unsupervised machine translation using monolingual corpora only. *arXiv preprint arXiv:1711.00043*.

Guillaume Lample, Myle Ott, Alexis Conneau, Ludovic Denoyer, and Marc'Aurelio Ranzato. 2018. Phrase-based & neural unsupervised machine translation. *arXiv preprint arXiv:1804.07755*.

Karima Meftouh, Salima Harrat, Salma Jamoussi, Mourad Abbas, and Kamel Smaili. 2015. Machine translation experiments on PADIC: A parallel Arabic dialect corpus. In *The 29th Pacific Asia conference on language, information and computation*.

Matt Post. 2018. A call for clarity in reporting BLEU scores. *arXiv preprint arXiv:1804.08771*.

Hadeel Saadany and Constantin Orasan. 2020. Is it Great or Terrible? Preserving Sentiment in Neural Machine Translation of Arabic Reviews. In *Proceedings of the Fifth Arabic Natural Language Processing Workshop*, pages 24–37.

Hadeel Saadany and Constantin Orasan. 2021. BLEU, METEOR, BERTScore: Evaluation of Metrics Performance in Assessing Critical Translation Errors in Sentiment-oriented Text. *TRITON 2021*, page 48.

Hassan Sajjad, Ahmed Abdelali, Nadir Durrani, and Fahim Dalvi. 2020. AraBench: Benchmarking Dialectal Arabic-English Machine Translation. In *Proceedings of the 28th International Conference on Computational Linguistics*, pages 5094–5107.

Mohammad Salameh, Saif Mohammad, and Svetlana Kiritchenko. 2015. Sentiment after translation: A case-study on Arabic social media posts. In *Proceedings of the 2015 conference of the North American chapter of the association for computational linguistics: Human language technologies*, pages 767–777.

Wael Salloum and Nizar Habash. 2013. Dialectal Arabic to English machine translation: Pivoting through modern standard Arabic. In *Proceedings of the 2013 Conference of the North American Chapter of the Association for Computational Linguistics: Human Language Technologies*, pages 348–358.

Rico Sennrich, Barry Haddow, and Alexandra Birch. 2015a. Improving neural machine translation models with monolingual data. *arXiv preprint arXiv:1511.06709*.

Rico Sennrich, Barry Haddow, and Alexandra Birch. 2015b. Neural machine translation of rare words with subword units. *arXiv preprint arXiv:1508.07909*.

Jörg Tiedemann. 2012. Parallel data, tools and interfaces in opus. In *LREC*, volume 2012, pages 2214–2218. Citeseer.

Ashish Vaswani, Noam Shazeer, Niki Parmar, Jakob Uszkoreit, Llion Jones, Aidan N Gomez, Łukasz Kaiser, and Illia Polosukhin. 2017. Attention is all you need. In *Advances in neural information processing systems*, pages 5998–6008.

Pascal Vincent, Hugo Larochelle, Yoshua Bengio, and Pierre-Antoine Manzagol. 2008. Extracting and composing robust features with denoising autoencoders. In *Proceedings of the 25th international conference on Machine learning*, pages 1096–1103.

Amy Beth Warriner, Victor Kuperman, and Marc Brysbaert. 2013. Norms of valence, arousal, and dominance for 13,915 English lemmas. *Behavior research methods*, 45(4):1191–1207.

Omar Zaidan and Chris Callison-Burch. 2011. The Arabic online commentary dataset: an annotated dataset of informal Arabic with high dialectal content. In *Proceedings of the 49th Annual Meeting of the Association for Computational Linguistics: Human Language Technologies*, pages 37–41.

Rabih Zbib, Erika Malchiodi, Jacob Devlin, David Stallard, Spyros Matsoukas, Richard Schwartz, John Makhoul, Omar Zaidan, and Chris Callison-Burch. 2012. Machine translation of Arabic dialects. In *Proceedings of the 2012 conference of the north american chapter of the association for computational linguistics: Human language technologies*, pages 49–59.

A Appendix

Ex1	Source	سحلنى
	Google Translate	slay me
	Our System	pissed me off
	Reference	He made me quite angry
Ex2	Source	اسفين جدا
	Google Translate	very wedged
	Our System	very sorry
	Reference	We are very sorry
Ex3	Source	الله يحفظك مبحبش اكدب انا
	Google Translate	May God protect you, I love you
	Our System	May God protect you, I don't like to lie
	Reference	May God protect you, I don't like to lie
Ex4	Source	الله لايوفقه
	Google Translate	God doesn't help him
	Our System	God does not grant him success
	Reference	May God not grant him success.
Ex5	Source	معليش خلينا شوي نتكلم يعني يسرق احسن هيك؟
	Google Translate	OK let's talk a little, I mean steal the best heck?
	Our System	Sorry, let's talk a little he steals the best like this?
	Reference	Let's just talk a bit, so does he better steal like this?
Ex6	Source	بدون زعل فكونا من الكلام
	Google Translate	Without getting upset, let's talk
	Our System	Without getting upset, so be from talking
	Reference	Without getting upset, so be it from talking

Cross-lingual transfer for low-resource Arabic language understanding

Khadige Abboud[1], **Olga Golovneva***[1,2], **Christopher DiPersio**[1]

[1]Alexa AI, Amazon, Cambridge, MA
[2]FAIR Labs, Meta, Washington, DC

abboudk@amazon.com, olggol@meta.com, dipersio@amazon.com

Abstract

This paper explores cross-lingual transfer learning in natural language understanding (NLU), with the focus on bootstrapping Arabic from high-resource English and French languages for domain classification, intent classification, and named entity recognition tasks. We adopt a BERT-based architecture and pretrain three models using open-source Wikipedia data and large-scale commercial datasets: monolingual:Arabic, bilingual:Arabic-English, and trilingual:Arabic-English-French models. Additionally, we use off-the-shelf machine translator to translate internal data from source English language to the target Arabic language, in an effort to enhance transfer learning through translation. We conduct experiments that finetune the three models for NLU tasks and evaluate them on a large internal dataset. Despite the morphological, orthographical, and grammatical differences between Arabic and the source languages, transfer learning performance gains from source languages and through machine translation are achieved on a real-world Arabic test dataset in both a zero-shot setting and in a setting when the models are further finetuned on labeled data from the target language.

1 Introduction

The fast growing interest in conversational AI-based voice assistants has increased the importance of finding ways to efficiently and rapidly expand these services to multiple new languages. One of the core components of virtual assistants is Natural Language Understanding (NLU), which is usually composed of three main tasks: domain classification (DC), intent classification (IC), and named entity recognition (NER). NLU tasks are responsible for classifying the domain and intent from the user's utterance and identifying and extracting entities from their requests through slot-filling.

*Work done during the author's tenure at Amazon.

Training an NLU model to support a new language requires a large amount of labeled utterances, which is costly and time-inefficient, particularly for low-resource languages. In recent years, a lot of success was shown through cross-lingual knowledge transfer on various NLU tasks for zero-shot transfer and few-shot transfer (Johnson et al., 2019; Ponti et al., 2021; Wang et al., 2021; Pires et al., 2019; Muller et al., 2021). This is made possible with the availability of multilingual pretrained language models such as mBERT (Devlin et al., 2019) and XLM-R (Conneau et al., 2020). However, cross-lingual transfer was shown to be more effective among similar languages (e.g., English to French) as opposed to distant languages (e.g., English to Arabic), especially for languages that differ in their script (Muller et al., 2021; Conneau et al., 2020; Johnson et al., 2019; Wu and Dredze, 2019). Efforts to reduce the distance between source and target languages include transliteration/romanization to Latin script (Muller et al., 2021; Johnson et al., 2019), and machine translation (Wang et al., 2021; Ponti et al., 2021). Although romanization was shown to be beneficial for languages that are not included in pretraining, it degraded performance on languages that are included in these large multilingual models like Arabic and Japanese (Muller et al., 2021). Driven by some of the shortcomings of pretrained multilingual models, several monolingual models have been trained and released in the past couple of years for multiple languages like Arabic (Antoun et al., 2020; Abdul-Mageed et al., 2021; Inoue et al., 2021), German (de Vries et al., 2019), and French (Martin et al., 2020). Whether multi-lingual or monolingual models are adopted, task-specific labeled data is still required for finetuning.

In this paper, we experiment with cross-lingual transfer from English and French, two high-resource languages with rich NLU labeled datasets for bootstrapping NLU model for the low-resource

Proceedings of the The Seventh Arabic Natural Language Processing Workshop (WANLP), pages 225 - 237
December 8, 2022

Arabic language, specifically for virtual assistant (VA) systems. To this end, we train three BERT models on a mix of open-source data and machine translated user inquiries: a monolingual - Arabic only, a bilingual Arabic-English and a trilingual Arabic - English - French models. Particulars of Arabic language such as orthographic inconsistencies in diacritized script and inflectional affixation are mitigated by preprocessing the data before training. We distill each of the BERT models to a smaller student model that better fit memory and latency requirements of commercial VA systems. We present experimental results on internally gathered real-world Arabic dataset that illustrate cross-lingual transfer through NLU knowledge transfer and machine translation (MT). Gains from transfer learning (TL) are achieved on the target Arabic dataset in both DC and joint IC-NER tasks in a zero-shot setting, few-shot setting, and in a setting with non-production Arabic labeled data included in finetuning.

2 Related Work

Cross-lingual transfer for low-resource language: There is a large body of research that shows successful cross-lingual transfer for a variety of tasks in both zero-shot setting, when the model is finetuned on data from the source language only, and in a regular setting, when the model is finetuned on the target language. (Johnson et al., 2019) explores cross-lingual transfer from English to Japanese, not only a morphologically dissimilar language, but also fundamentally different on the character and token level. Authors use a Bi-LSTM based model with word and character embeddings and finetune it for NER task. To increase the benefit of transfer learning, the authors propose to romanize Japanese characters to unify the character embedding space between the target and source languages.

The introduction of pretrained multilingual language models like mBERT (Devlin et al., 2019) and XLM-R (Conneau et al., 2020) has opened the doors for wider exploration of cross-lingual transfer learning (Wang et al., 2021; Libovický et al., 2019; Muller et al., 2021; Wu and Dredze, 2019). (Muller et al., 2021) has shown that the reason why some languages do not benefit from these massive multilingual models is largely related to script differences; particularly for languages that have not been seen by mBERT. Experiments in (Muller et al., 2021) show that transliteration to Latin script for low-resource languages with different script does improve performance for part-of-speech tagging, dependency parsing, and NER tasks, however not for languages that are included in mBERT like Arabic and Japanese. Such findings are also echoed in (Wu and Dredze, 2019). Another way to bring distant languages closer is through machine translation. (Wang et al., 2021) introduces a step before finetuning on IC-NER task by retraining pretrained multilingual models (mBERT and XLM-R) for MT task. Authors show that performance gain with the proposed approach is larger between distant languages than that between similar languages. (Ponti et al., 2021) proposes an integrated translation – monolingual classifier system that exploits cross-lingual transfer through setting the translation as a latent variable between the target text and the labels (a translate-test approach). Using reinforcement learning, (Ponti et al., 2021) trains the integrated translation-classifier system with classification accuracy as the reward. This approach however, can be only applied to DC and IC tasks where the whole utterance is labeled with one class.

NLU models for Arabic: Non-deterministic NLU models for Arabic have not been extensively explored until recently; largely due to a lack of rich labeled datasets for the various NLU tasks. (Soliman et al., 2017) proposed Arabic specific word2vec embeddings. (Al-Smadi et al., 2020) utilized pretrained Multilingual Universal Sentence Encoder (MUSE) embedding and trained a bidirectional-gated recurrent neural network with a mix of average and max pooling layer for Arabic NER task using the WikiFANEGold dataset (Alotaibi and Lee, 2014) which classifies entities into eight classes only (person, location, organization, geopolitical, etc.).

Although mBERT includes Arabic, cross-lingual transfer did not show performance gains for Arabic as it did on Indo-European languages (Muller et al., 2021; Wu and Dredze, 2019). Motivated by the monolingual BERT models, (Antoun et al., 2020) trained AraBERT, a monolingual BERT-based language representation model for Arabic language on data that includes Arabic Wikipedia dumps, in addition to two publicly available large Arabic corpora: 5M (El-Khair, 2016) and 3.5M (Zeroual et al., 2019) articles, both extracted from Arabic news sources. Authors in (Antoun et al., 2020) also introduced a preprocessing step on the data prior to using it for pre-training BERT, which used off-the-shelf Arabic Farasa tokenizer (Abdelali et al., 2016) for subword unit segmentation. Building on AraBERT, ArBERT (Abdul-Mageed et al., 2021) and CAMeLBERT (Inoue et al., 2021) have added additional Arabic datasets to pretraining a monolingual BERT that cover more topics and dialects. Because of the lack of rich labeled Arabic dataset, the NER task in (Helwe et al., 2020; Inoue et al., 2021; Abdul-Mageed et al., 2021) is limited to classifying nouns into three main classes only (person, location, organization)[1], a much simpler NER task than that needed to power a virtual assistant system, where user requests can span hundreds of entity labels.

In this paper, we propose a multilingual NLU model for Arabic language, targeted for commercial virtual assistant system. We explore cross-lingual transfer through MT and task-specific learning transfer from rich source languages (English and French) to Arabic. Despite the languages not being closely related, we show that multilingual models outperforms the monolingual model on large-scale Arabic traffic for both DC and IC-NER tasks. To our knowledge, this is the first Arabic model trained and evaluated for such complex NLU tasks required for virtual assistants which involves classifying 18 domains, 333 intents, and 268 entity labels.

3 Arabic NLU

3.1 Challenges in Arabic

Arabic differs from English and French morphologically, orthographically, and grammatically. Some of the differences can hinder cross-lingual transfer learning. These differences include:

- **Script**: Arabic script has opposite writing direction and does not use the Latin alphabet, instead it is written from right to left using the distinct *Abjad* writing system;
- **Inflectional morphology**: Unlike English, inflections in Arabic can be suffixes or prefixes (Shamsan and Attayib, 2015), and Arabic inflections have far more person, number, and gender distinctions than that in English;
- **Diacritics**: Some short vowels are included on Arabic text as diacritics, which are optional written symbols.

These are only a few of the differences that can complicate transfer learning to Arabic from resource-rich languages, usually Indo-European like English, Spanish, and French. The language complexity is further inflated in dialectal Arabic, due to the lack of writing standards resulting in orthographic inconsistencies (Kwaik et al., 2018). Modern standard Arabic (MSA) is only used for writing and is spoken mostly in official settings like news broadcasts and government announcements. In households, the common location for virtual assistants, dialectal Arabic is more likely to be used. Furthermore, to globalization and historical reasons, some of dialectal Arabic's loan-words and phrases come from other languages, particularly English and French[2].

Arabic has templatic and concatenative morphology where verbs and nouns are derived from 3,000 roots (El-Kishky et al., 2019) by applying templates to the roots to generate stems and then adding prefixes and suffixes. In Arabic, inflectional affixation is very common; the definite article ("the"), prepositions ("to", "in", "for"), conjunctions ("and", "then"), and pronouns ("you", "my", "our", etc.) are represented as affixes on words they modify. This poses a challenge for NER. For example, in the utterance "order **two** boxes of apples", the quantity to be ordered can be inferred from token "**two**". In Arabic, however, the quantity "**two**" would be a suffix to token "**box**", "اطلبي صندوقين من التفاح" (literal: "order box**Two** of apples"). Table 1 shows a few examples that illustrate the challenges of inflectional affixation in Arabic. In an effort to address this, we add a rule-based normalization step that splits affixes; however, we limit this to affixes that make a functional difference to the meaning (e.g., pronouns and quantity) as opposed to non-functional ones, e.g., definite article, and prepositions.

Although diacritics are used to disambiguate meaning, especially in the absence of context, we have decided to strip diacritics [3] from open-source data due to the following three reasons:

[1]The popular ANERcorp dataset (Benajiba and Paolo, 2008) has a total of 9 labels: the 3 main classes in addition to Other and IOB tagging.

[2]Although TL from French and English can particularly help dialectal Arabic due to natural code-switching, the specific impact on code-switching is out of scope of this paper.

[3]With the exception of Shadda diacritic.

- We conducted a study on internally localized and diacritized data that showed that diacritics in fact harm NLU model performance more than they help disambiguate words, and this is mainly due to inconsistencies in the use of diacritics when transcribing data. Details are in Appendix: A.2;
- Relying on diacritized text for NLU will further limit the available resources for Arabic, as most open-source datasets (e.g., Wikipedia) are not diacritized; and
- The use of DNN-based language models such as BERT heavily relies on context for predictions, which can help disambiguate words without the need for diacritics, similar to how Arabic speakers would use the surrounding context to infer the meanings of words.

would you turn it off?	*call my mum*	*play a song in the room*
أتطفئيها؟	إتصلي بأمي	شغلي أغنية بالغرفة
wouldYouTurnOffIt	call mumMy	play song InTheRoom

Table 1: Examples of inflectional affixation in Arabic. On the right, a 5-token English utterance can be written with a single token in Arabic, pronouns ("it", "my") are attached as a suffix, and the definite article ("the") and preposition ("in") can be attached as prefixes.

3.2 Data

For training BERT models, we use two main sources of unlabeled data: internal data from a commercial VA system[4] and external open-source data from Wikipedia. For the latter, we collect Wikipedia dumps for Arabic (ar), English (en), and French (fr) and extract their content using WikiExtractor package (Attardi, 2015). For ar-Wikipedia data, in addition to the preprocessing described in the previous section, we split sentences based on full stop, along with semicolon and comma if the sentence length is greater than 25 tokens, because commas are commonly used in Arabic as a sentence delimiter, and the full stop is used at the end of a paragraph. The extracted Wikipedia data accounts for ≈ 6.3M, 98.5M, 34.2M sentences for ar, en, and fr, respectively, as listed in Table 2. Wikipedia and other open-source data are different from the nature of user inquiries to virtual assistants. We have found this to be particularly true for Arabic Wikipedia data, which overwhelmingly covers political and historical vocabulary and topics. To overcome this bias, we have opted to mix the data with commercial dataset from an NLU system. We use the rich and resource-heavy English and French data, accounting for 36.2M and 14.6M, respectively, and corresponding to users requests, i.e., unannotated utterance text. All user utterances have been de-identified and anonymized. We used AWS translate to translate English user requests into Arabic, and obtained an unannotated Arabic MT dataset of equal size to the English dataset (≈ 3.2M). For pretraining, we split the data randomly into 85:15 train:validation sets, and to balance the data across languages for the multilingual models, we follow (Conneau and Lample, 2019) and we sample sentences according to a multinomial distribution with probabilities $q_i = \sqrt{p_i}/(\sum_j^N \sqrt{p_j})$, $p_i = n_i/\sum_j^N n_j$ in which N is the total number of languages in the model and $n_i$is the total number of utterances in language i. For finetuning, we use annotated NLU data from a commercial VA system, representing user inquiries in English and French, two mature and high-resource languages. We sample equally 418,477 utterances from the two languages for finetuning the pretrained bilingual and trilingual models for DC and IC-NER tasks. In a zero-shot setting, only English and French labeled datasets are used in finetuning the models. Note that the bilingual model is pretrained on unlabeled Arabic and English datasets, it is finetuned only on labeled English data in a zero-shot setting. For comparison, we finetune a second set of models that we refer to as pre-production (pre-prod) models with an additional 369,485 annotated Arabic utterances added during finetuning. This dataset (forth row in Table3) is collected using Mechanical Turk (mTurk). We use the mTurk data to train a third set of few-shot models, by sampling only 10 utterances per intent and using that in training.We also explore transfer learning for NLU task through translation; we translate labeled English traffic using AWS Translate into Arabic. In order to enhance the quality of the MT dataset, we post-process the translated utterances automatically to reproject labels and recombine affix when split incorrectly, e.g.,

- **input**: <CallType> call </CallType> <ContactName>Ali</ContactName>
- **MT**: <CallType>الإتصال بـ</CallType> <ContactName>علي</ContactName>

[4]Details about the commercial virtual assistant system and the internal data are omitted to maintain authors anonymity.

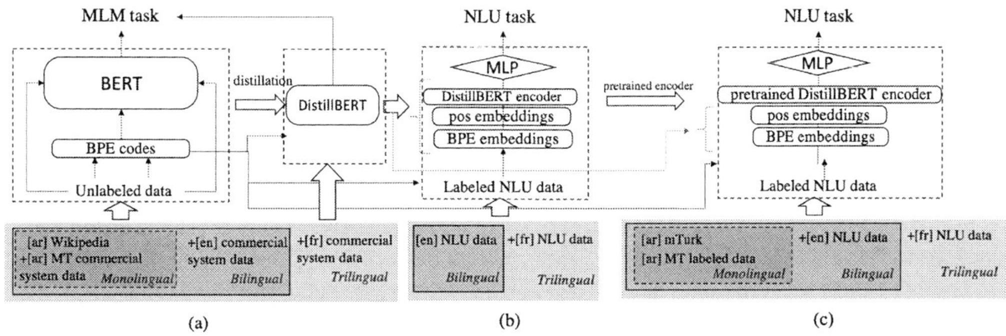

Figure 1: Schematic of monolingual and multilingual BERT training and distillation for Arabic NLU tasks: (a) BERT pretraining and distillation on unlabeled data; (b) Task-specific pretraining DistillBERT for NLU task on labeled data from resource rich source languages, English and French; (c) Finetuning on mix of Arabic, English, and French labeled data in addition to MT Arabic data.

- **postprocessed**: <CallType>الإتصال</CallType> <ContactName>بعلي</ContactName>
- **input**: Call </UserTrigger>my</UserTrigger> <NumberType>Phone</NumberType>
- **MT**: اتصل</UserTrigger> <NumberType>بهاتفي</NumberType></NumberType>
- **postprocessed**: اتصل</NumberType> بهاتف<NumberType> <UserTrigger>ي</UserTrigger>

We finetune another set of models for each of the zero-shot, few-shot, and pre-prod setting by adding a total of 417,895 utterances sampled from the MT labeled data during finetuning[5]. Having the MT labeled dataset enables the evaluation of the monolingual model in a zero-shot setting by finetuning only on the MT dataset. All models are tested on the same Arabic dataset consisting of a total 864,127 Arabic utterances annotated from real-world VA commercial system. This test dataset spans 18 domains, 333 intents, and 268 entity labels[6]

3.3 Model Training

3.3.1 Pretraining

We pretrain three BERT models, monolingual (Mono), bilingual (Bi) and trilingual (Tri), models using open-source Wikipedia data and unlabeled inquires to a commercial VA system together with the corresponding MT ones. We use **BERTbase** setting (Devlin et al., 2019) with 12 encoder layers, 768 hidden dimensions, 3072 hidden size, and 12 attention heads, and pretrain for a Masked Language Model (MLM) task for 40 epochs with 15% of tokens masked. We adopt Byte Pair Encoding (BPE) for subword tokenization of BERT pretraining in an effort to deal with inflectional affixation in Arabic. We use FastBPE (Sennrich et al., 2016; et al., 2015) for BPE extraction, learning 30K, 80K, 90K codes[7] from Wikipedia data for the monolingual, bilingual, and trilingual models, respectively. For run-time efficiency and inference speed, we further distill each model to a smaller student model during pretraining. The student model architecture is composed of 4 layers, 768 hidden dimensions, 1200 hidden size, and 12 attention head. This architecture, DistillBERT, is a slightly bigger model than TinyBERT (Jiao et al., 2020) but is 3x smaller and 4.7x faster than the original BERT. For knowledge distillation we use the same dataset used for training the teacher model and adopt logit matching method between teacher and student from (Hinton et al., 2015), where the student is trained to minimize two losses during training; the standard cross-entropy loss and the cross-entropy loss between the teacher and the student. We use the same datasets and BPE codes for distillation on the same MLM task. The pretraining step is illustrated in Figure 1(a).

[5]During finetuning, all data is mixed, with no particular order.

[6]Our evaluation data contains only 32.86% of the tokens labeled as *Other*. The combined training data in Table3 covers all 18 domains and a total of 235 intents out of which 225 intents are in the testset, and the remaining uncovered test intents are part of the tail 0.64% of the testsets.

[7]The reason we vary BPE code number across the three models is to account for the additional vocabulary from the added languages. Otherwise, either the smaller monolingual model will suffer from codes not generalizing to new vocabulary, or the larger trilingual model will suffer from codes being too granular.

Table 2: Unlabeled data for extracting BPE codes and BERT model pretraining and distillation.

Data source	Language	Size (sentence)
Wikipedia	Arabic (ar)	6,377,443
Wikipedia	English (en)	98,524,407
Wikipedia	French (fr)	34,248,312
VA system	English (en)	36,288,990
VA system	French (fr)	14,609,950
VA system	Machine-translated Arabic (ar-MT)	36,288,980

3.3.2 Task-specific Pretraining

Before the final-finetuning on NLU tasks, we leverage the rich English and French labeled data for a pre-finetuning step, in which we pretrain the encoders for the bilingual and trilingual models specifically on NLU tasks.In this task-specific pretraining, illustrated in Figure 1(b), we do not include any labeled data for the target language, Arabic, as we are testing how much of the NLU learning can be transferred from the source languages. Consequently, this step is excluded from the monolingual model.

Table 3: Labeled data for finetuning and evaluating NLU models for DC and IC-NER tasks. Only the first three datasets are used for the zero-shot experiments, the forth dataset is used for the few-shot experiment, the fifth dataset is added for finetuning the pre-prod models, and the last dataset is only used for evaluation.

Dataset	Language	Size (utterance)	
		Train	Test
en traffic	en	418,477	0
fr traffic	fr	418,477	0
ar-MT dataset	ar-MT	417,895	0
ar mTurk few shot	ar	2,547	0
ar mTurk data	ar	369,485	0
ar traffic	ar	0	864,127

3.3.3 Finetuning

In the final step, the three pretrained DistillBERT models are finetuned for NLU tasks on labeled internal data listed in Table 3 and illustrated in Figure 1(c). For each of the three models, we train three sets of models: zero-shot, few-shot, and pre-prod models. The only difference is the inclusion of the mTurk labeled data from the target Arabic language for the latter two experiments. In the few-shot setting we sample 10 utterances randomly per intent while maintaining a minimum of 40 utterances per domain. For each of these set of experiments, we also train a model with and without MT data, as a result we have a total of 17 models. We select the monolingual model with few-shots to be our baseline, and compare it to the bilingual and trilingual models[8].

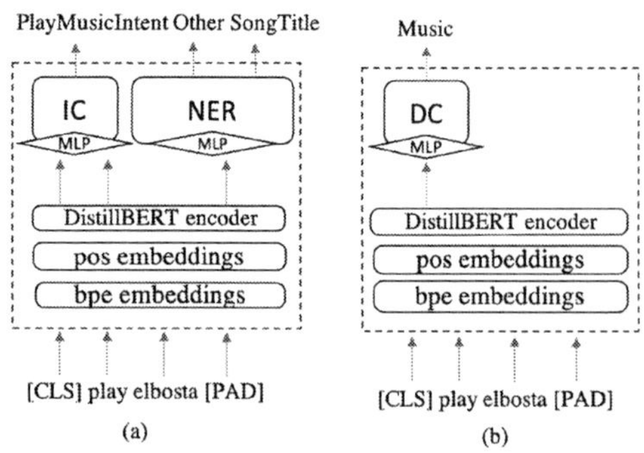

Figure 2: Schematics of the finetuning step for DC and IC-NER tasks.

- **BASELINE**: a monolingual DistillBERT model distilled from **BERTbase** model pretrained on Arabic unlabeled data
- **Bilingual**: a DistillBERT model distilled from BERTbase model pretrained on mix of unlabeled Arabic and English with task-specific pretraining on NLU labeled data from high-resource English language
- **Trilingual**: a DistillBERT model distilled from BERTbase model pretrained on mix of unlabeled Arabic, English, and French with task-specific pretraining on NLU labeled data from high-resource languages: English and French

The IC-NER model is trained for a joint-task objective with two-layer MLP for the IC task and two-layer MLP plus a CRF layer for the NER task as illustrated in Figure 2. For the DC task, we have the same DistillBERT architecture with the exception of the final two MLP layers for one-vs-all classification task.

4 Results and Discussion

We measure the performance of our models for DC and IC-NER tasks in terms of domain classification error rate (DCER) and semantic error

[8]Because the pretraining objective is targeted for MLM task, a different objective than the target NLU tasks, we do not have a monolingual zero-shot model, and therefore use the monolingual few-shot model as our baseline.

Table 4: Results relative to baseline (% change) for Monolingual (**Mono**) Bilingual (**Bi**) and Trilingual (**Tri**) models on IC-NER and DC tasks evaluated on 864,127 Arabic utterances. Average performance is across domains. Bold values indicate best performance for each setting (zero/few-shot/pre-prod).

Δ%SemER		Zero-shot Mono	Zero-shot Bi	Zero-shot Tri	Few-shot Mono	Few-shot Bi	Few-shot Tri	Pre-prod Mono	Pre-prod Bi	Pre-prod Tri
Overall	w/o MT	-	0.29	-7.50	0	-15.06	-20.76	-49.32	-55.24	-52.49
	with MT	-10.64	-12.49	**-19.20**	-14.24	-20.47	**-23.21**	-56.60	**-57.85**	-57.31
Average	w/o MT	-	4.09	-6.16	0	-13.28	-22.55	-41.46	-44.49	-44.68
	with MT	-6.30	-11.80	**-17.88**	-8.69	-18.51	**-24.03**	-47.42	-46.48	**-47.76**
Δ%DCER										
Overall	w/o MT	-	-8.89	**-22.65**	0	-27.33	**-30.21**	-53.61	-61.59	-59.48
	with MT	-12.93	-18.12	-21.53	-14.73	-28.03	-29.25	-58.99	**-62.92**	-61.63
Average	w/o MT	-	-2.48	-24.15	0	-23.50	-32.70	-47.53	-53.44	-51.71
	with MT	-13.32	-18.90	**-24.31**	-15.62	-30.08	**-33.20**	-51.33	-53.88	**-53.91**

rate (SemER), respectively. DCER is calculated by $\frac{\#domain\ errors}{\#total\ utterances}$. The semantic error measures how many mistakes are done in entity recognition and slot filling, and is calculated by $SemER = \frac{D+I+S}{C+D+S}$ (Su et al., 2018), where D=deletion, I=insertion, S=substitution and C=correct-slots. An IC error is counted as a substitution. All models are evaluated on the same testset and performance is reported as a percentage difference (%Δ) to the baseline few-shot monolingual model.

Table 4, shows the zero-shot and the few-shot performance for the three models with and without MT Arabic data added to finetuning. The multilingual models outperform the baseline monolingual model with the exception of slight 0.29% in SemER in Bi zero-shot model. In the few-shot models, NLU models benefit from a reduction of 15.06% SemER from English alone, and an additional 5.7% reduction from French data with respect to baseline. Table 4, to the right, compares the overall performance of pre-prod models. The impact of cross-lingual transfer learning does not fade even when development Arabic labeled data is added to the model, both multilingual models still outperform the monolingual one. However, adding the mTurk data to finetuning overshadows the impact of French data and the Bi model slightly outperfroms the Tri model. Notice for pre-prod models the benefit of cross-lingual transfer reduces significantly with the addition of MT data. Table 4 demonstrates the transfer learning through translation. By simply using an off-the-shelf machine translator, we can boost the NLU performance on a low-resource target language by 12.79% and 11.7% for the bilingual and the trilingual models, respectively. Adding few-shots and full MTurk data reduces the benefit of MT data to 2-4.8% and 2.7-5.4% for the Bi and Tri models, respectively. For the sake of comparison, we repeat the Bi and Tri experiments on a distilled version of mBERT: distilmBERT (Sanh et al., 2019) (details in Appendix A.3). Results in Table A.2 illustrate the importance of utilizing unlabeled utterances from VA system in pretraining, particularly in early stages of bootstrapping NLU model for a new language, where our model achieves up to 25.1 SemER improvement over distilmBERT in zero-shot setting. Nevertheless, similar TL gains are obtained on distilmBERT with the Tri model outperforming the monolingual model in all settings.

In addition to the overall, i.e., where all utterances have equal contribution to performance (micro-average), Table 4 also reports the average performance per domain, where each domain has equal weight despite its size (macro-average). Considering the average performance and the overall performance, the best performing model in terms of SemER is the trilingual model finetuned on a mix of labeled English, French and Arabic MT data in all zero-shot, and few-shot setting. Although the Bi model beats the Tri model overall in pre-prod setting, the Tri model is still better on average per domain. This suggests that the trilingual model is improving performance for the smaller domains on the target Arabic language. In fact, the Tri model outperforms on average all other models in zero-shot, few-shot, and pre-prod setting. For the latter model setting, we further investigated whether adding English/French data hurt specific domains. We looked at top large domains that did not benefit from adding English and French in Table A.4: AlarmsAndNotifications, SmartHome, and CallingAndCommunication domains with performance reduction of 2.94%, 0.53% and 9.93%.

CallingAndCommunication domain consistently under performed in the Tri model when compared to the Mono model, in all zero-shot, few-shot, and pre-prod models. In these domains, there were issues related to language differences. For example, the top failing utterances in SmartHome were requests to turn off/on appliances. In Arabic turn off/on is a single token (طفّي/أضيئي/شغّلي/سكّري), while in English it is two tokens. Similarly, utterances in the CallingAndCommunication domain are related to finishing the call, in English that would be "hang up", but in Arabic it is again a single token (اقطعي/سكّري/أنهي/أقفلي). This causes imbalance in carrier phrases and a change in the distribution of label sequence for these domains, e.g., compare the two label sequence in the two languages: "turn|Action on|Action light|Device" with "شغّلي|Action الإضاءة|Device". This can be mitigated by down-sampling English data for these domains, which is left for future experimentation. Overall, even without MT data, the multilingual pre-prod models beat the monolingual model 14 out of 18 domains on the DC task and in 13 out of 18 domains for IC-NER task, clearly showing the effect of cross-lingual transfer of NLU learning from rich English and French source languages to the low-resource Arabic language, despite being linguistically very different.

5 Conclusion

In this paper, we addressed the problem of bootstrapping an NLU model for Arabic from two high-resource Indo-European languages. We presented two multilingual BERT-based models, pretrained and distilled in-house, and compared them to a monolingual Arabic baseline model to explore cross-lingual transfer learning. In an effort to tackle the unique challenges in Arabic language, we adopted a preprocessing step in which we dediacritize the text to reduce the variance and inconsistencies in the data for an already low-resource language. We also split functional affixes and adopt BPE encoding to deal with inflectional affixation in Arabic. Furthermore, in order to reduce the distance between the target language and the source languages we used off-the-shelf machine translator to pretrain and finetune the models, in addition to large-scale open-source Wikipedia and internal datasets. Transfer learning performance gains on the target Arabic language showed a reduction of up to 20.76% in semantic error rate for the IC-NER task and 30.21% in classification error for the DC task for the trilingual model in few-shot setting. Similar cross-lingual learning gains were achieved in a zero-shot setting and pre-prod setting with the improvement gap between monolingual and multilingual models narrowing as data from MT and the Arabic target language is added to finetuning the models.

References

Ahmed Abdelali, Kareem Darwish, Nadir Durrani, and Hamdy Mubarak. 2016. Farasa: A fast and furious segmenter for Arabic. In *Proceedings of the 2016 Conference of the North American Chapter of the Association for Computational Linguistics: Demonstrations*, pages 11–16. ACL.

Muhammad Abdul-Mageed, AbdelRahim Elmadany, and El Moatez Billah Nagoudi. 2021. ARBERT & MARBERT: Deep bidirectional transformers for Arabic. In *Proceedings of the 59th Annual Meeting of the Association for Computational Linguistics and the 11th International Joint Conference on Natural Language Processing (Volume 1: Long Papers)*, pages 7088–7105. ACL.

Mohammad Al-Smadi, Saad Al-Zboon, Yaser Jararweh, and Patrick Juola. 2020. Transfer learning for Arabic named entity recognition with deep neural networks. *IEEE Access*, 8:37736–37745.

Fahd Alotaibi and Mark Lee. 2014. A hybrid approach to features representation for fine-grained Arabic named entity recognition. In *Proceedings of COLING 2014, the 25th International Conference on Computational Linguistics: Technical Papers*, pages 984–995. Dublin City University and Association for Computational Linguistics.

Wissam Antoun, Fady Baly, and Hazem Hajj. 2020. AraBERT: Transformer-based model for arabic language understanding. In *Proceedings of the 4th Workshop on Open-Source Arabic Corpora and Processing Tools, with a Shared Task on Offensive Language Detection*, pages 9–15.

Giuseppe Attardi. 2015. Wikiextractor. `https://github.com/attardi/wikiextractor`.

Yassine Benajiba and Rosso Paolo. 2008. Anercorpdataset. `https://camel.abudhabi.nyu.edu/anercorp/`.

Alexis Conneau, Kartikay Khandelwal, Naman Goyal, Vishrav Chaudhary, Guillaume Wenzek, Francisco Guzmán, Edouard Grave, Myle Ott, Luke Zettlemoyer, and Veselin Stoyanov. 2020. Unsupervised cross-lingual representation learning at scale. In *Proceedings of the 58th Annual Meeting of the Association for Computational Linguistics*, pages 8440–8451. ACL.

Alexis Conneau and Guillaume Lample. 2019. Cross-lingual language model pretraining. *Advances in Neural Information Processing Systems*, 32:7059–7069.

Wietse de Vries, Andreas van Cranenburgh, Arianna Bisazza, Tommaso Caselli, Gertjan van Noord, and Malvina Nissim. 2019. Bertje: A dutch BERT model. *arXiv preprint arXiv:1912.09582*.

Jacob Devlin, Ming-Wei Chang, Kenton Lee, and Kristina Toutanova. 2019. BERT: Pre-training of deep bidirectional transformers for language understanding. In *Proceedings of NAACL HLT*, pages 4171–4186.

Ibrahim Abu El-Khair. 2016. 1.5 billion words Arabic corpus. *arXiv preprint arXiv:1611.04033*.

Ahmed El-Kishky, Xingyu Fu, Aseel Addawood, Nahil Sobh, Clare Voss, and Jiawei Han. 2019. Constrained sequence-to-sequence semitic root extraction for enriching word embeddings. In *Proceedings of the Fourth Arabic Natural Language Processing Workshop*, pages 88–96.

Guillaume Lample et al. 2015. C++ implementation of Neural Machine Translation of Rare Words with Subword Units, with Python API. `https://github.com/glample/fastBPE`.

Chadi Helwe, Ghassan Dib, Mohsen Shamas, and Shady Elbassuoni. 2020. A semi-supervised BERT approach for Arabic named entity recognition. In *Proceedings of the Fifth Arabic NLP Workshop*, pages 49–57. ACL.

Geoffrey Hinton, Oriol Vinyals, and Jeff Dean. 2015. Distilling the knowledge in a neural network. *arXiv preprint arXiv:1503.02531*.

Go Inoue, Bashar Alhafni, Nurpeiis Baimukan, Houda Bouamor, and Nizar Habash. 2021. The interplay of variant, size, and task type in Arabic pre-trained language models. In *Proceedings of the Sixth Arabic Natural Language Processing Workshop*, pages 92–104. ACL.

Xiaoqi Jiao, Yichun Yin, Lifeng Shang, Xin Jiang, Xiao Chen, Linlin Li, Fang Wang, and Qun Liu. 2020. TinyBERT: Distilling BERT for natural language understanding. In *Proceedings of the 2020 Conference on Empirical Methods in Natural Language Processing: Findings*, pages 4163–4174.

Andrew Johnson, Penny Karanasou, Judith Gaspers, and Dietrich Klakow. 2019. Cross-lingual transfer learning for Japanese named entity recognition. In *Proceedings of NAACL HLT (Industry Papers)*, pages 182–189.

Kathrein Abu Kwaik, Motaz Saad, Stergios Chatzikyriakidis, and Simon Dobnika. 2018. A lexical distance study of Arabic dialects. *Procedia computer science*, 142:2–13.

Jindřich Libovický, Rudolf Rosa, and Alexander Fraser. 2019. How language-neutral is multilingual BERT? *arXiv preprint arXiv:1911.03310*.

Louis Martin, Benjamin Muller, Pedro Javier Ortiz Suárez, Yoann Dupont, Laurent Romary, Éric de la Clergerie, Djamé Seddah, and Benoît Sagot. 2020. CamemBERT: a tasty French language model. In *Proceedings of the 58th Annual Meeting of the Association for Computational Linguistics*, pages 7203–7219. ACL.

Benjamin Muller, Antonios Anastasopoulos, Benoît Sagot, and Djamé Seddah. 2021. When being unseen from mBERT is just the beginning: Handling new languages with multilingual language models. In *Proceedings of the 2021 Conference of the North American Chapter of the Association for Computational Linguistics: Human Language Technologies*, pages 448–462. ACL.

Telmo Pires, Eva Schlinger, and Dan Garrette. 2019. How multilingual is multilingual BERT? In *Proceedings of the 57th Annual Meeting of the Association for Computational Linguistics*, pages 4996–5001. ACL.

Edoardo Maria Ponti, Julia Kreutzer, Ivan Vulić, and Siva Reddy. 2021. Modelling latent translations for cross-lingual transfer. *arXiv preprint arXiv:2107.11353*.

Victor Sanh, Lysandre Debut, Julien Chaumond, and Thomas Wolf. 2019. Distilbert, a distilled version of bert: smaller, faster, cheaper and lighter. *ArXiv*, abs/1910.01108.

Rico Sennrich, Barry Haddow, and Alexandra Birch. 2016. Neural machine translation of rare words with subword units. In *Proceedings of the 54th Annual Meeting of the ACL*, pages 1715–1725. ACL.

Muayad Abdul-Halim Ahmad Shamsan and Abdulmajeed Attayib. 2015. Inflectional morphology in arabic and english: a contrastive study. *International Journal of English Linguistics*, 5(2):139.

Abu Bakr Soliman, Kareem Eissa, and Samhaa R El-Beltagy. 2017. Aravec: A set of Arabic word embedding models for use in Arabic NLP. *Procedia Computer Science*, 117:256–265.

Chengwei Su, Rahul Gupta, Shankar Ananthakrishnan, and Spyros Matsoukas. 2018. A re-ranker scheme for integrating large scale nlu models. In *2018 IEEE Spoken Language Technology Workshop (SLT)*, pages 670–676. IEEE.

Chao Wang, Judith Gaspers, Thi Ngoc Quynh Do, and Hui Jiang. 2021. Exploring cross-lingual transfer learning with unsupervised machine translation. In *ACL IJCNLP 2021*, pages 2011–2020. ACL.

Shijie Wu and Mark Dredze. 2019. Beto, bentz, becas: The surprising cross-lingual effectiveness of BERT. In *Proceedings of the 2019 Conference on*

Empirical Methods in Natural Language Processing and the 9th International Joint Conference on Natural Language Processing (EMNLP-IJCNLP), pages 833–844. ACL.

Imad Zeroual, Dirk Goldhahn, Thomas Eckart, and Abdelhak Lakhouaja. 2019. OSIAN: Open source international arabic news corpus-preparation and integration into the CLARIN-infrastructure. In *Proceedings of the 4th Arabic NLP Workshop*, pages 175–182.

A Appendix

A.1 Limitations

The task-specific knowledge transfer proposed in this paper is dependent on the availability of annotated data in high-resource languages for the same NLU tasks: domain/intent classification and NER. That is, although the training data is not in the target language, it still covers the same domains and majority of the intents in the test sets. The ability of the model to generalize to new domains and intents (out-of-domain) in the target language needs further assessment and experimentation. The affix-splitting and de-diacritization preprocessing step proposed in this paper works only for languages with templatic and concatenative morphology, like Arabic and other Semitic languages (e.g., Hebrew). Additionally, the transfer learning gains obtained with machine translation can be limited by the quality of the adopted translator itself. The experiments conducted in this paper uses only a single machine translator for both pretraining and finetuning. Exploring different off-the-shelf machine translators and the impact of the translation quality on NLU tasks needs further experimentation and requires large GPU resources, particularly for pretraining.

Table A.1: Average performance difference (Δ) between models with and without diacritics in 5-fold experiments on NLU tasks (+ve values in favor of model without diacritics).

Δ	DC accuracy	IC accuracy	Slot F1	Frame accuracy
Avg.	0.07	0.38	0.97	2.91
fold1	2.59	1.45	1.34	3.44
fold2	-0.99	1.69	0.24	2.07
fold3	-0.92	0.46	0.86	3.37
fold4	-0.23	-0.31	0.23	1.46
fold5	-0.08	-1.38	2.17	4.21

A.2 Diacritics harm NLU model

In Arabic, short vowels are indicated on letters as diacritics and are used to disambiguate the meaning of the word. Full diacritization is used in classical Arabic, but are often omitted from written texts in MSA. As a result, Arabic has many homographs, that can be distinguished from the context. We conducted a limited-scope study to assess the impact of diacritics on NLU model performance using a set of 1,306 utterances fully diacritized and annotated internally, the utterances cover 12 of the 18 domains used in this paper. We performed a 5-fold cross-validation experiment on the 1,306 set with and without diacritics. We created 5 folds of train-test splits, stratified per domain. Then we duplicate these sets and strip the diacritics. Finally for each of these 10 sets we train a statistical NLU model and evaluate its performance. In addition to training 10 models corresponding to 5 folds of data splits with and without diacritics, each fold was trained and tested 5 times to average the variations in stochastic model performance.

Table A.1 above represents performance averaged across 25 runs for each of the models (with and without diacritics). T-test on domain accuracy, overall intent accuracy and slot F1 showed no significant difference in the means. Overall frame accuracy is slightly better in the model without diacritics, with p=0.01 in two-sample two-tailed t-Tests. To investigate the difference in performance, we further looked at the tokens in the broken utterances in the model with diacritics with respect to the model without diacritics (i.e., utterances that are correctly recognized in the model without diacritics but not in the model with diacritics). We found that on average, the coverage percentage of the tokens in the broken utterances by the training data reduced by 6.59% when adding diacritics. This suggests that diacritics is adding noise through annotation inconsistencies and increasing out-of-vocabulary data, thus reducing model performance.

A.3 Comparison to open-source distilmBERT (Sanh et al., 2019)

We repeat the multilingual experiments on distilmBERT (Sanh et al., 2019), a distilled version of mBERT pretrained and distilled on concatenation of Wikipedia data from 104 languages including English, French, and our target language Arabic. distilmBERT is slightly larger than our distilled model with 6 layers, 768 dimension and 12 heads, compared to our 4-layer distillBERT described in Subsection3.3.1. Because distilmBERT is multilingual, we only run the bilingual and trilingual ver-

Table A.2: SemER and DCER performance of DistilmBERT (Sanh et al., 2019) relative to our monolingual baseline (% change) for Bilingual (**Bi**) and Trilingual (**Tri**) on IC-NER and DC tasks evaluated on 864,127 Arabic utterances. Average performance is across domains. Bold represents best performance within the same setting (zero-shot/few-shot/pre-prod).

Δ% SemER		**Zero-shot** Bi	Tri	**Few-shot** Bi	Tri	**Pre-prod** Bi	Tri
Overall	w/o MT	19.8	17.6	3.3	-3.6	-52.1	-55.2
	with MT	-8.5	**-11.3**	-18.4	**-20.5**	-59.4	**-59.9**
Average	w/o MT	34.8	22.1	-0.5	-10.8	-42.1	-44.2
	with MT	-11.9	**-16.3**	-20.9	**-24.1**	-50.0	**-50.9**
Δ%Overall DCER							
Overall	w/o MT	59.7	41.8	10.8	3.4	-55.7	-55.4
	with MT	-8.3	**-11.1**	**-17.4**	**-17.4**	-61.2	**-61.7**
Average	w/o MT	74.3	46.1	-9.0	-16.0	-48.5	-48.3
	with MT	-19.6	**-24.6**	-30.0	**-32.8**	-54.9	**-55.2**

sions of it, i.e., models finetuned on task-specific annotated data from English, French, and/or MT data. For each model, we finetune different versions of the model one with MT data and one without (w/o) MT data in each of the settings: zero-shot, few-shot, and pre-prod using the same data described in Table3, resulting a total of 12 models. TableA.2 shows the performance of Bi and Tri models using pretrained distilmBERT evaluated on our internally gathered real-world Arabic dataset. The reported SemER and DCER error rates in are relative to our baseline model, so that the values can be compared to our results reported in Table 4. The zero-shot performance w/o MT shows the power of pretraining our in-house models on unlabeled data from a VA system combined with Wikipedia data. Overall, our Tri model beats the corresponding distilmBERT model by 25.1 SemER reduction and 64.45 DCER reduction relative to baseline. However, the gap in performance reduces to 2.71 SemER point reduction in few-shot setting to Tri distilmBERT slightly beating our model with 2.59 SemER in pre-prod setting. This could be attributed to the larger model distilmBERT uses. Nevertheless, a similar trend in the gains obtained from transferring the NLU task-specific knowledge and through MT from English and French in distilmBERT, this generalizes our conclusion that a multilingual model, and particularly the Tri one, outperforms a monolingual model for early stage bootstrapping NLU model for Arabic as seen in Zero-shot, Few-shot and Pre-prod setting.

Table A.3: Zero- and few-shot performance relative (%Δ) to baseline for DC and IC-NER tasks on Arabic.

ΔSemER		Zero-shot					Few-shot				
Domain	**# Test Utterances**	**Bi**	**Tri**	**Mono + MT**	**Bi + MT**	**Tri + MT**	**Bi**	**Tri**	**Mono + MT**	**Bi + MT**	**Tri + MT**
Overall	864127	0.29	-7.5	-10.64	-12.49	**-19.2**	-15.06	-20.76	-14.24	-20.47	**-23.21**
Average	48007	4.09	-6.16	-6.3	-11.8	**-17.88**	-13.28	-22.55	-8.69	-18.51	**-24.03**
Music	202589	-3.48	-19.67	-25.17	-16.91	**-35.63**	-15.8	-26.54	-28.3	-25.28	**-32.25**
Knowledge	137882	**-79.26**	-64.66	-48.69	-56.14	-53.56	**-61.13**	-47.94	-45.02	-55.02	-54.02
General	131709	42.24	35.17	18.08	16.18	**12.14**	-0.04	**-8.5**	20.11	0.66	-2.7
AlarmsAndNotifications	110817	64.82	57.91	27.87	**13.99**	19.95	5.44	**-2.84**	9.59	**-2.84**	-1.06
SmartHome	68787	14.58	-1.24	14.34	3.7	**-6.69**	2.7	**-17.38**	9.03	-5.7	-14.24
CallingAndCommunication	56787	4.66	6.72	-3.65	**-5.22**	-1.72	-6.04	2.07	-4.18	**-10.36**	-1.05
ToDos	42428	35.44	26.58	14.4	22.41	**13.68**	21.51	**7.41**	8.45	11.58	9.63
Weather	23422	-22.14	-15.67	-14.31	-13.4	**-23.93**	**-33.79**	-28.13	-10.24	-20.31	-23.62
Calendar	23157	-7.79	-27.53	-38.56	-36.95	**-40.68**	-22.35	-31.9	-45.92	-43.44	**-45.93**
Video	17285	-0.68	-12.74	-3.43	-21.46	**-25.45**	-24.2	**-27.1**	-6.05	-21.12	-27.0
AssistantGeneratedContent	16870	174.99	99.59	**71.06**	87.71	85.94	**41.32**	75.49	66.07	72.19	75.58
Apps	8887	-17.85	**-47.81**	24.54	7.35	-29.67	-12.66	**-48.93**	19.05	-33.62	-47.69
Books	8748	-7.76	-28.27	-27.99	**-34.83**	-30.8	-24.33	-36.41	-31.51	-33.24	**-38.33**
Help	7727	31.02	28.79	**5.34**	13.58	6.06	13.91	**1.61**	4.28	10.39	3.33
News	4448	-25.07	-25.07	-42.05	-44.85	**-45.29**	-27.98	-37.12	-43.79	-30.13	**-49.08**
Shopping	2121	12.82	1.09	-10.69	**-17.54**	-15.86	-9.44	-14.71	-8.95	-18.03	**-18.89**
MovieShowTimes	374	-39.31	-48.25	-42.18	**-50.3**	-49.83	-40.82	**-56.11**	-47.51	-44.51	-51.94
Sports	89	21.16	-21.16	**-34.61**	23.08	7.7	30.78	-25.01	**-30.76**	13.48	-28.83
ΔDCER											
Overall	864127	-8.89	**-22.65**	-12.92	-18.13	-21.52	-27.32	**-30.21**	-14.73	-28.04	-29.25
Average	48007	-2.48	-24.15	-13.32	-18.9	**-24.31**	-23.5	-32.7	-15.62	-30.08	**-33.2**
Music	202589	-0.07	-25.45	-28.71	4.3	**-36.43**	-39.98	-57.1	-60.82	**-68.58**	-67.29
Knowledge	137882	**-82.25**	-71.46	-54.14	-61.49	-58.45	-61.96	-59.44	-79.83	-78.99	**-80.83**
General	131709	67.37	39.34	-10.9	**-23.51**	15.14	-74.88	**-82.13**	-76.33	-76.81	-75.85
AlarmsAndNotifications	110817	266.49	229.82	193.52	**139.7**	201.5	11.9	18.81	37.92	**10.89**	21.11
SmartHome	68787	-11.36	**-32.1**	33.32	-14.94	-16.44	3.02	-3.31	-7.96	-4.75	**-29.93**
CallingAndCommunication	56787	26.82	**26.5**	48.31	37.22	28.65	-22.6	**-62.32**	12.77	-51.95	-61.02
ToDos	42428	157.05	57.58	**46.96**	77.85	59.61	-19.11	**-25.62**	32.78	-12.45	13.47
Weather	23422	0.54	-1.5	7.89	6.46	**-13.89**	10.9	**-2.32**	1.05	4.82	-1.83
Calendar	23157	-58.25	**-84.35**	-81.31	-67.32	-76.38	-27.47	**-30.26**	22.14	-21.85	-25.23
Video	17285	7.34	-17.83	-5.47	-19.97	**-22.64**	**-62.12**	-51.18	-50.89	-59.94	-58.97
AssistantGeneratedContent	16870	314.18	120.79	116.59	115.87	**114.9**	-0.02	-27.45	-34.02	-2.87	**-35.15**
Apps	8887	-31.77	**-63.78**	11.48	-14.4	-42.7	40.72	45.03	112.88	**16.99**	88.94
Books	8748	-19.04	-52.47	-62.12	**-72.2**	-65.31	**77.01**	100.26	109.78	113.02	108.13
Help	7727	22.6	21.17	5.12	9.18	**3.79**	-8.97	-8.97	0.11	**-20.8**	-12.13
News	4448	8.3	16.78	-6.95	-18.85	**-23.74**	6.67	**-56.67**	**-56.67**	-16.67	**-56.67**
Shopping	2121	24.14	9.78	0.11	**-13.97**	-9.99	33.23	**22.08**	34.89	29.25	31.19
MovieShowTimes	374	-67.63	-68.6	-71.5	**-75.85**	-69.57	**-31.32**	-27.03	-4.02	-16.72	-24.68
Sports	89	3.33	**-56.67**	-50.0	6.67	-26.67	-19.84	**-29.11**	10.73	-4.84	-16.08

Table A.4: Pre-prod DCER and SemER performance relative (%Δ) to baseline for DC and IC-NER tasks on Arabic.

ΔSemER Domain	**# Test Utterances**	**Mono**	**Bi**	**Tri**	**Monol + MT**	**Bi + MT**	**Tri + MT**
Overall	864127	-49.32	-55.24	-52.49	-56.6	**-57.85**	-57.31
Average	48007	-41.46	-44.49	-44.68	-47.42	-46.48	**-47.76**
Music	202589	-46.72	-58.09	-51.21	-58.67	-60.5	**-62.93**
Knowledge	137882	-42.29	-55.68	-57.66	-52.81	**-61.29**	-59.64
General	131709	-50.01	-47.1	**-55.04**	-50.54	-46.71	-53.02
AlarmsAndNotifications	110817	-68.49	-66.66	-67.28	**-69.93**	-66.64	-66.99
SmartHome	68787	-54.05	-68.49	-56.93	-60.1	**-69.29**	-59.57
CallingAndCommunication	56787	-55.56	-45.78	-41.64	**-56.86**	-53.13	-46.93
ToDos	42428	-43.56	-41.27	-34.58	**-52.05**	-40.41	-39.96
Weather	23422	-58.86	-52.36	-56.84	**-63.35**	-45.63	-52.72
Calendar	23157	-57.59	-54.83	-60.57	-63.86	-62.73	**-64.23**
Video	17285	-15.78	-31.34	-31.09	-25.94	-33.63	**-35.72**
AssistantGeneratedContent	16870	**-65.39**	-63.49	-51.95	-55.44	-61.86	-43.44
Apps	8887	-64.95	-67.54	-72.14	-69.82	-67.88	**-74.16**
Books	8748	-10.65	-18.31	-16.92	-16.18	-21.07	**-21.65**
Help	7727	5.86	10.24	5.17	**2.6**	7.91	3.29
News	4448	-47.58	-51.96	-49.69	-49.77	-52.32	**-54.26**
Shopping	2121	-8.83	-21.15	-18.89	-18.28	-24.94	**-27.57**
MovieShowTimes	374	-57.75	-59.38	**-63.89**	-61.71	-60.0	-60.89
Sports	89	-19.23	-9.6	-21.16	**-38.46**	-9.6	-32.68
ΔDCER							
Overall	864127	-53.6	-61.58	-59.48	-58.99	**-62.91**	-61.62
Average	48007	-47.53	-53.44	-51.71	-51.33	-53.88	**-53.91**
Music	202589	-66.53	-70.47	-67.01	-69.06	-68.77	**-73.53**
Knowledge	137882	-48.61	-61.49	-62.96	-58.19	**-65.64**	-65.11
General	131709	-30.69	-27.65	-41.26	-34.41	-35.52	**-42.22**
AlarmsAndNotifications	110817	-71.58	-75.34	-66.29	-73.34	**-77.13**	-68.65
SmartHome	68787	-63.99	**-80.65**	-64.55	-70.78	-78.4	-64.69
CallingAndCommunication	56787	-64.15	**-69.59**	-52.2	-67.32	-68.56	-49.49
ToDos	42428	-17.45	**-28.54**	-26.88	-20.87	-20.15	-26.9
Weather	23422	-67.58	-64.27	-65.91	**-70.16**	-50.76	-57.58
Calendar	23157	-89.16	-88.84	-89.53	-89.58	-90.47	**-91.34**
Video	17285	-6.21	-18.02	-20.16	-8.84	-17.7	**-22.75**
AssistantGeneratedContent	16870	**-75.52**	-63.42	-45.24	-39.51	-72.86	-27.67
Apps	8887	-76.62	-77.19	**-83.24**	-79.24	-77.12	-82.92
Books	8748	-8.17	-17.89	-19.55	-14.96	-23.41	**-26.38**
Help	7727	-5.92	-0.44	-5.46	-7.8	-3.83	**-9.63**
News	4448	-29.78	-48.92	-35.68	-46.33	-54.39	**-56.69**
Shopping	2121	-6.32	**-22.32**	-11.11	-9.79	-16.0	-19.67
MovieShowTimes	374	-80.19	-86.47	-85.02	-84.06	**-87.92**	-84.06
Sports	89	-56.67	-56.67	-56.67	**-63.33**	-53.33	**-63.33**

Improving POS Tagging for Arabic Dialects on Out-of-Domain Texts

Noor Abo Mokh
Indiana University*
noorabom@iu.edu

Daniel Dakota
Indiana University
ddakota@iu.edu

Sandra Kübler
Indiana University
skuebler@indiana.edu

Abstract

We investigate part of speech tagging for four Arabic dialects (Gulf, Levantine, Egyptian, and Maghrebi), in an out-of-domain setting. More specifically, we look at the effectiveness of 1) upsampling the target dialect in the training data of a joint model, 2) increasing the consistency of the annotations, and 3) using word embeddings pre-trained on a large corpus of dialectal Arabic. We increase the accuracy on average by about 20 percentage points.

1 Introduction

Although POS tagging has achieved high results across languages and benchmarks (Bohnet et al., 2018; Heinzerling and Strube, 2019; Wang et al., 2021), there are still challenges, particularly across different domains and for languages with rich morphology, especially in terms of handling rare and unknown words (Plank et al., 2016; Yasunaga et al., 2018). For languages such as Arabic, their diglossic nature adds additional complexity, as POS tagging models must capture a plethora of lexical and syntactic variation plus orthographic differences. For Arabic, the majority of available POS taggers are trained on Modern Standard Arabic (MSA), such as MADAMIRA (Pasha et al., 2014) and Farasa (Darwish and Mubarak, 2016). There is however a growing interest in developing tools specifically for dialectal Arabic (described in Shoufan and Alameri (2015) and Elnagar et al. (2021)), given its preferred use in daily communication, especially on social media platforms and integrated into voice systems.

Our ultimate goal is the computational analysis of syntactic differences across Arabic dialects, which requires syntactically annotated parallel data. However, the existing dialectal parallel corpus, MADAR (Bouamor et al., 2018), does not provide any linguistic annotation. Thus we need access to a POS tagger (and ultimately a parser) that provides reliable analyses across different dialects, in an out-of-domain settings, since all existing POS tagged corpora are from domains different from that of MADAR. In this challenging setting, we investigate methods to improve POS tagging accuracy for the dialects. We investigate solutions that create a single tagger across all dialects as well as individual taggers for each of the four dialects of interest.

The paper is organized as follows: Section 2 gives a short description of dialectal differences, section 3 explains our research questions, section 4 provides a survey of related work. Section 5 describes the corpora and the experimental setup, in sections 6–9, we present the results and an error analysis. We conclude in section 10.

2 Arabic Dialects

Dialects of Arabic show a wide range of linguistic differences, within the dialects themselves and compared to MSA. MSA is mostly used in formal writing such as books and news articles while dialects are used for most other daily communications. Arabic dialects are interesting because much of the variation involves function words, providing strong signals of the presence of syntactic differences.

In Table 1 we provide an example sentence in four dialects that exhibit three instances of syntactic variation. The first example is the complementizer أن 'that'. أن is used in MSA, Levantine (LEV) and Egyptian (EGY) but not in Maghrebi (MAG). In MAG, the complementizer is optional, resulting in different syntactic structures. Another example is found in the use of the interrogatives across dialects. MSA and MAG use an interrogative pronoun (the hamza-alef أ in أتظن in MSA

*The work was done prior to joining Amazon.

Proceedings of the The Seventh Arabic Natural Language Processing Workshop (WANLP), pages 238 - 248
December 8, 2022

Dialect	Sentence	Buckwalter[1]
MSA	مرَاد اتظن ان المشكلة ستحل هنَاك	mrAd AtZn An Alm$klp stHl hnAk
LEV	مرَاد انت مفكر انه المشكلة رح تنحل هنَاك	mrAd Ant mfkr Anh Alm$klp rH tnHl hnAk
EGY	مرَاد فَاكر ان المشكلة هتنحل هنَاك	mrAd fAkr An Alm$klp htnHl hnAk
MAG	مرَاد وَاش كتظن المشكلة غَادي تحل تمَاك	mrAd wA$ ktZn Alm$klp gAdy tHl tmAk
Eng.	Do you think (that) this is the solution for the problem Murad?	

Table 1: A parallel sentence selected from MADAR

and وَاش in MAG) while no question word is used in the other dialects. A final difference concerns the future marking. While in all dialects, future marking is obligatory and precedes the verb تحل, each dialect uses a different marker (سَ in MSA, غادي in MAG, هَ in EGY (in هتنحل), and رح in LEV). Note that in EGY, the particle is realized as a clitic variant as opposed to a separate word in MAG and LEV. Additionally, for MAG, the future marker غَادي, is inflected and carries agreement, unlike in EGY and LEV.

3 Research Questions

Our main question is how we can improve POS tagging for dialectal Arabic when testing on out-of-domain data. To address this question, we break it down into four sub-questions: 1) Does the POS tagger profit more from having access to a large training set even though the majority of training examples are from a different dialect, or is a smaller, dialect specific training set more appropriate? 2) Does upsampling help mitigate the data imbalance in a joint dialectal model? 3) Can we increase consistency in annotations, using minimal effort? And will increased consistency yield an increased accuracy? 4) Can using pre-trained embeddings improve POS tagging performance?

4 Related Work

4.1 Arabic POS Tagging

Many of the currently available POS taggers are trained on MSA, such as MADAMIRA and Farasa (Pasha et al., 2014; Abdelali et al., 2016) (MADAMIRA also supports Egyptian). Recently, more attention has been given to POS tagging for dialectal Arabic. One approach for dialectal Arabic has been to adapt an MSA model. For example, Zribi et al. (2017) adapted an MSA morphological analyzer, which includes a POS tagger, to Tunisian Arabic by integrating a Tunisian-based lexicon, containing roots and patterns. While they report the system's accuracy as 87.3%, such adaptation methods are less effective than dialect-specific taggers. Alharbi et al. (2018); Alharbi and Lee (2020), e.g., found that a tagger designed for a specific dialect, in this case Gulf, performed better than an adapted MSA tagger. Other dialect specific taggers include the tagger by Al-Shargi et al. (2016) for Moroccan and Sanaani and the one by Khalifa et al. (2018) for Emirati[2]. The difficulty of adaption can be attributed to the diglossic nature of Arabic, which makes it challenging for such systems to process colloquial Arabic (Farghaly and Shaalan, 2009; Diab and Habash, 2007). Arabic has the standard form (MSA), and the spoken forms of Arabic (in addition to other varieties such as Classical Arabic), which coexist and are used by speakers in distinct situations. Each of those varieties has its own linguistic features.

A problem concerning dialect specific taggers is that they do not use uniform annotation schemes. Thus, they may be ineffective in a cross-dialectal setting. Darwish et al. (2018) approach this problem by introducing a multi-dialectal POS tagger for the dialects of Gulf, Levantine, Egyptian and Maghrebi by developing a CRF tagger, which is extended by Darwish et al. (2020) to using bi-LSTM layers as input. Their system provided state-of-the-art performance for POS tagging of dialectal Arabic.

4.2 Domain Adaptation for POS Tagging

Domain adaptation has been pivotal in attempts to handle the differences in data distributions between a source and target domain. Kübler and Baucom (2011) use an ensemble of three POS taggers

[1] http://www.qamus.org/transliteration.htm

[2] See Duh and Kirchhoff (2005); Habash et al. (2013) for overviews of dialect specific POS taggers and NLP tools.

Dialect	No. words: train	No. words: test
Gulf	74 162	21 208
Levantine	80 940	23 090
Egyptian	83 908	23 986
Maghrebi	71 090	20 234

Table 2: Size of the Darwish corpus per dialect.

trained on the source corpus to annotate sentences in the target domain; they then select identically predicted sentences and add them to the training data. These data selection techniques yielded improvements when POS tagging target domain data.

Kuncham et al. (2014) adapt a Hindi morphological analyzer for a domain specific use by adding domain specific words to the lexicon. Another approach is creating POS tagging experts. Mukherjee et al. (2017) create genre experts for POS tagging by using topic modeling in both the training and test set, where they train an expert for each topic and then use the expert to POS tag the same topic. They then assign new test sentences to the genre expert by using similarity metrics.

The importance of including small amounts of target data is attested by Attia and Elkahky (2019). This is further supported by Behzad and Zeldes (2020) who find that a tagger trained on a small amount of Reddit data can outperform taggers trained on much larger out-of-domain corpora.

5 Experimental Setup

5.1 Multidialectal POS-Tagged Corpus

For training, we use the multi-dialectal POS-tagged corpus by Darwish et al. (2018, henceforth the Darwish corpus) since, to the best of our knowledge, it is the only publicly available, POS tagged multi-dialectal corpus for Arabic. The sentences in this corpus are selected from a large collection of Arabic tweets. The corpus includes four major dialects (350 sentences each): Gulf, Levantine, Egyptian, and Maghrebi (representing sub-varieties spoken in Morocco, Algeria and Tunisia). To extract dialectal sentences without code-switching with MSA, Samih et al. (2017b) used a list of exclusively dialectal words such as Maghrebi كيفما (Eng.: like/as) and Levantine هيك (Eng.: like this). A detailed description of the tweet selection methodology is provided by Eldesouki et al. (2017); Samih et al. (2017b). Table 2 gives an overview of the corpus. Since the sentences are taken from Twitter, they are mostly comments on events, conversations, and attitudes. The corpus was morphologically analyzed using a dialectal morphological analyzer (Samih et al., 2017b).

The POS tagset is derived from the MSA corpus described by Darwish et al. (2017), it includes 18 MSA POS tags, plus two additional dialect specific tags: Prog_Part (tense marker) and Neg_Part (negation marker). A native speaker of each dialect annotated the corpus for POS.

5.2 MADAR

For testing, we use MADAR (Bouamor et al., 2018). The corpus is based on the (English) Basic Traveling Expression Corpus (BTEC) by Takezawa et al. (2007). The English text was translated into dialects of Arabic. This means that we have a significant difference in domains between MADAR and the Darwish corpus.

MADAR is a collection of parallel sentences from different dialects representing the Arabic varieties of 25 cities[3] in addition to MSA, i.e., the information in MADAR is more fine-grained. For compatibility with the Darwish corpus, we group the MADAR data into four major dialects: Egyptian (EGY), Gulf (GLF), Levantine (LEV), and Maghrebi (MAG).

Our initial preprocessing consists of normalizing all Hamzas in all dialects to Alifs and Yaas and then converting to Buckwalter transliteration[4]. Additionally, we removed all hashtags, URLs, and handles from the data since (1) they are not necessary for the purposes of this study (2) this was necessary since the POS tagger does not seem to be able to handle URLs, etc.

5.3 Designing the Gold Standard

Since MADAR is not annotated for POS tags, we selected 100 sentences per dialect to annotate manually. Since we have several translations of each original sentence per dialect (one per city), we ensure that only one version of an original sentence is chosen for a dialect, thus ensuring lexical and syntactic variation in the test sentences. Table 3 shows an overview of the test set.

[3]The following cities are covered: Aleppo, Alexandria, Algiers, Amman, Aswan, Baghdad, Basra, Beirut, Benghazi, Cairo, Damascus, Doha, Fes, Jeddah, Jerusalem, Khartoum, Mosul, Moscut, Rabat, Riyadh, Sanaa, Salt, Sfax, Trupoli, Tunis.

[4]We use the conversion to Buckwalter transliteration from `https://github.com/KentonMurray/Buckwalter/blob/master/buckwalter.py`

Dialect	No. words
GLF	699
LEV	666
EGY	754
MAG	727
Total	2 846

Table 3: Size of our MADAR test set per dialect

In order to obtain a segmentation close to the one in the Darwish corpus, we used the multi-dialectal Arabic morphological analyzer by Samih et al. (2017b); Eldesouki et al. (2017); Samih et al. (2017a). This morphological analyzer uses a unified segmentation model for the four major dialects Gulf, Levantine, Egyptian, Maghrebi.

We then used the multi-dialectal Arabic POS tagger by Darwish et al. (2018) to automatically POS tag the sentences. Each dialect was corrected by two speakers of Arabic. We then examined inter-annotator agreement: Across all dialects, the annotators showed high agreement (95% for Egyptian, 90% for Levantine, 90% for Gulf, and 85% for Maghrebi). This was followed by an additional pass to resolve differences between annotators. We used the Camel POS tagging guidelines[5] to guide our decisions[6]. For instance, some negation markers were marked as PART, when they are supposed to be marked as NEG_PART.

5.4 Part-of-Speech Tagger

We train the POS tagger using the Bi-LSTM architecture introduced by Darwish et al. (2018, 2020); Alharbi et al. (2018)[7] for tagging dialects of Arabic.

A sentence is fed into the bi-LSTM with a final forward LSTM layer. The neural network of the tagger by Darwish et al. (2018) uses embeddings of stems and affixes trained on the training data, rather than pretrained models. For example, for the word مدخلتوش, the vector represents the stem and the clitics: م, دخل, تو, and ش.

6 First Experiments

6.1 Reproducing Prior Results

We first reproduce the results reported by Darwish et al. (2018) for the joint dialectal experimental setup[8]. Following Darwish et al. (2018), we train on the Darwish corpus using the concatenation of the training sets of all dialects. We then test on each dialect separately using the dialect's test section from the same corpus. Results are shown in Table 4. The first row reports the results by Darwish et al. (2018), and the second row are our results using our preprocessing (see section 5.2). Our results show a higher accuracy than the results reported by Darwish et al. (2018). This may be due to improvements in the POS tagger or the additional preprocessing step, in which we removed Twitter specific tags: hashtags, URLs, and handles.

6.2 Testing on MADAR

We now train the POS tagger using the training sections from the Darwish corpus for all dialects (the joint model)[9] and test on each dialect from MADAR separately. In this setup, target and source data are from the same dialects[10], but different in terms of domains. The results are shown in row 3 in Table 4. The accuracy is lower for all dialects than for the in-domain data in row 2. For instance, the accuracy for GLF is 59.5% for MADAR, but 97.7% when tested on Darwish. We expected the accuracy to be lower for the out-of-domain test data, but the drop in accuracy is rather extreme, between 27.3 and 38.2 percent points. The OOV rates between the Darwish corpus and the MADAR test set range from 36% to 44%, which at least partly explains the results.

These results lead to the question whether training a joint dialectal model is the best solution. The joint model has the advantage of a large training size, but 3/4 of the training data are from dialects other than the one that we are testing on. For this reason, we experiment with training and testing on each dialect separately, to see whether a smaller but dialectally more similar training set results in higher accuracies. In this experiment, we train, e.g., on the Egyptian dialect training data from Darwish and test on Egyptian from MADAR. The results are

[5] https://camel-guidelines.readthedocs.io/en/latest/morphology/

[6] Camel uses a different tagset from that in the Darwish corpus, but it offers guidelines on how to annotate specific phenomena.

[7] Available from `https://github.com/qcri/dialectal_arabic_pos_tagger`.

[8] Note that the currently available version is different from the one used by Darwish et al. (2018, 2020); Alharbi et al. (2018).

[9] We experimented with adding the MSA section to the training set. Results were considerably lower.

[10] Or as close as possible based on the two corpora.

	Model	Train	Test set	GLF	LEV	EGY	MAG
1)	(Darwish et al., 2018)	Darwish joint	Darwish	87.2	88.6	93.2	87.7
2)	ours + preprocessing	Darwish joint	Darwish	97.7	96.6	95.6	94.4
3)	ours + preprocessing	Darwish joint	MADAR	59.5	61.3	68.3	61.4
4)	ours + preprocessing	Darwish single dialect	MADAR	66.3	67.6	74.4	67.4
5)	ours + preprocessing	Darwish joint upsampled	MADAR	72.8	75.0	81.1	74.2

Table 4: Summary of POS tagging results.

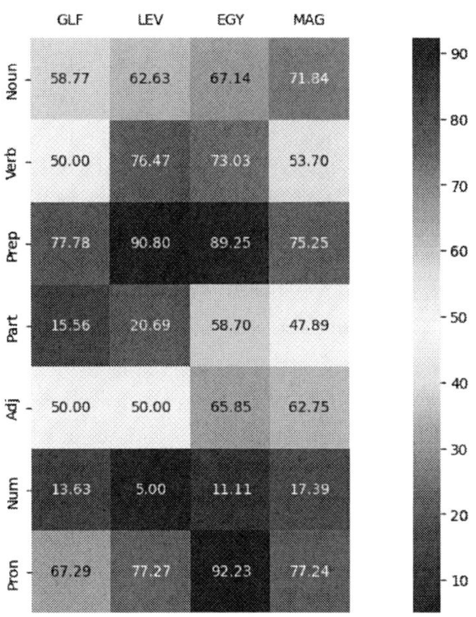

Figure 1: Results per dialect (precision) for MADAR.

reported in row 4 of Table 4. This setting performs worse than testing in-domain (row 2) but improves over the results of using the joint model. For instance, the accuracy for Gulf (GLF) increases to 66.30%, compared to 59.5% for the joint model. The accuracy gain is similar across all dialects. The increase in accuracy despite the smaller training set may be due to the fact that the Darwish corpus focuses on highly dialectal data, which maximizes dialectal differences.

6.3 Error Analysis

We further examine the tagging errors for each dialect: In Figure 1, we show a heatmap for tagging quality for MADAR; we show precision per tag and dialect for the experiment in row 3 in Table 4 (e.g., PREP was correct 75.25%). We focus on the tags which produced the majority of the errors: Pronouns (PRON), Nouns, Numbers (NUM), Adjectives (ADJ), Particles (PART), Prepositions (PREP), Verbs.

Numbers have the lowest tagging precision rate across all dialects, it ranges from 17.39% for MAG to 5.00% for LEV. This low accuracy is due to inconsistencies in annotations in the training set, where numbers sometimes are tagged as nouns and in other cases as NUM. For instance, the number three in the phrase ثلَاث دقَايق (Eng.: 'three minutes') and in ثلَاث سنَوَات (Eng.: 'three years') are assigned NUM and NOUN respectively. Another issue, which also applies to other POS tags, is the inconsistency in spelling across speakers, for instance, تَاني is sometimes spelled with ت, but in other instances with ث. This is an issue for LEV and EGY, where variation in spelling is more likely to occur due to phonetic variation.

Spelling variation may also result in ambiguity in POS tagging. For example, particles (PART) show a remarkably low accuracy for GLF and LEV because of homographic words shared across dialects, resulting in ambiguity. As an example, the word وش, (Eng.: which) in GLF is a particle, the same orthographic form is a noun in LEV وِشّ (Eng.: face). Since the model is trained on all dialects, the LEV وِشّ is incorrectly assigned the tag PART.

We also notice that future and negation markers show different performance across dialects. For LEV, for instance, the system fails to assign the future marker to any future clitic. A closer examination shows that the same future marker (رح) is marked as FUT_PART in the LEV training data but marked as PART in the MAG data, indicating annotation inconsistency across dialects. Such inconsistencies will be addressed in section 8.

7 Addressing the Data Imbalance

One drawback of using a joint model of the four dialects is that it is trained on only 25% examples of the target dialect, which means that dialect specific, correct decisions may be overruled by other dialects. In section 6.2, we showed that creating

Word	Original POS	New POS
Negation markers	PART	NEG_PART
Interrogatives	PART	ADV
Rel. Pronouns	PART	PRON
FUT and PROG markers	inconsistent	fixed
unmarked CONJ	PART/NOUN	CONJ
Adverbs	NOUN	ADV
Verbal suffixes	PRON	concatenated Verb and suffix
Nominal suffixes	NSUFF	concatenated Noun and suffix

Table 5: Annotation changes

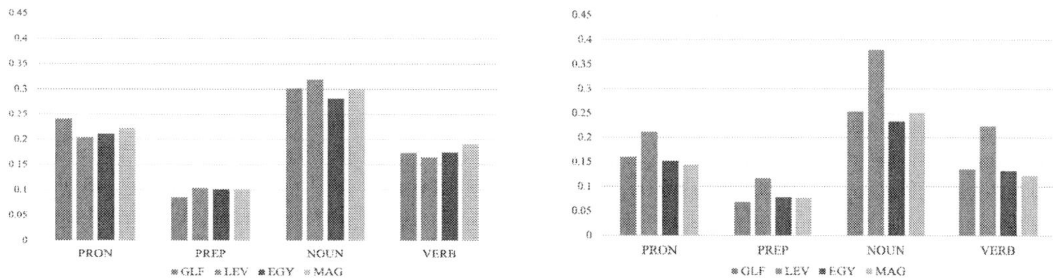

Figure 2: Distribution of POS tags across dialects before (left) and after (right) annotation changes. For instance, EGY has 16% PRON of all POS tags.

individual POS tagger models per dialect improves results. Here, we investigate whether we can use upsampling to further improve results. Upsampling is a standard method for handling data imbalance, for example in shared tasks on Arabic dialect identification (Zitouni et al., 2020; Habash et al., 2021) and for POS tagging non-standardized web data (Neunerdt et al., 2014; Horsmann and Zesch, 2015). For this approach, we duplicate instances of the target domain in the training data. For example, if the target domain is Egyptian, then in the training data (consisting of the four dialects), we duplicate the Egyptian examples, creating a more balanced training set by increasing the number of examples of the target class.

The results of this experiment are shown in Table 4, row 5. These results show an improvement overall across all dialects in comparison to the joint model (row 3) and the single dialect model. The best performance was achieved for LEV, its accuracy increased by 13.7 percent points over the joint model; for EGY, it increased by 12.8 percent points.

This shows that upsampling can successfully combine the advantages of having a large training set and a focused one.[11]

8 Annotation Changes

A closer examination of the POS tagger errors shows that in some cases, the problems derive from the gold annotations of the training data. Apart from the expected annotation errors due to lack of attention, which are mostly random, we also find more systematic inconsistencies, partly across dialects.

One such inconsistency concerns dialect-specific POS tags, such as negation, progressive, and future markers. For instance, in the GLF data, none of the negation markers were annotated with the negation-specific POS tag.

Systematic inconsistencies can potentially be corrected semi-automatically. To address the annotation inconsistencies, we further experiment with annotation changes on the Darwish corpus (our training data; Darwish et al. (2018)). We created a list of annotation inconsistencies, focusing on those which can be found and corrected automatically. We used the Camel Lab guidelines[12] as a reference since they provide specific and consistent POS tagging guidelines for dialects of Arabic. We performed systematic changes on the corpus while maintaining consistency across dialects. A list of

[11] We also explored tripling the number of samples for the target dialect, but this was less effective.

[12] https://camel-guidelines.readthedocs.io/en/latest/

Dialects	GLF	LEV	EGY	MAG
our baseline	59.5	61.3	68.3	61.4
baseline upsampled	72.8	75.0	81.1	74.2
on new annotation	82.3	75.2	80.2	73.8
new annotation upsampled	73.6	73.8	80.7	73.8

Table 6: Summary of POS tagging accuracy per dialect before and after annotation changes.

the targeted annotations in shown in Table 5.

For the distribution of POS tags in each dialect before and after the corrections, see Figure 2, focusing on the four most frequent POS tags. The plots show that in the original annotations, the ratios per POS tag are similar across dialects; after the corrections, there are more differences, showing that we model differences between dialects better. Note that the size of the corpus has changed due to the annotation changes, resulting in differences in POS tag distributions within dialects: We reattached the verb suffixes (previously tagged as PRON), for example, the verb يظهر (V) and the suffix وَا (PRON) are reattached into a single word يظهروَا. We also reattached nominal suffixes (previously tagged as NSUFF), such as صيدلي (Noun) and ة (NSUFF) into the single word صيدلية. As a consequence, the number of words decreases (e.g., the word count for Levantine decreases by 6%). Reattaching verbal suffixes also causes a decrease in pronouns across all dialects but Levantine shown in Figure 2. In LEV, relative pronouns which were originally tagged as PART are now categorized as PRON.

We then perform experiments training a joint model on all dialects after annotation modification, and test on each dialect separately to check whether the annotation changes boost the tagging performance.

Results are reported in Table 6. When comparing the results after modifying the annotations, we notice a considerable improvement in results over the baseline for all dialects, with increases ranging from 11.9% (EGY) to 22.8% (GLF). For GLF and LEV, the results on the improved annotations without upsampling even increase over the upsampled baseline (i.e., from 72.8% to 82.32% for GLF). We attribute this improvement to a higher consistency in the annotations. A comparison of the results on the improved annotations with and without upsampling shows that given the improved annotations, upsampling is less relevant or even harmful: The accuracy for EGY increases from 80.2% to 80.7% while the accuracy for GLF and LEV decreases (GLF: from 82.3% to 73.6%), and the accuracy for MAG remains stable. One explanation is that some words became more ambiguous as a result of the annotation changes. The word مَا, for example, was annotated inconsistently across dialects. It is ambiguous between a pronoun and a particle reading. However, in the original annotations, it was mostly annotated as particle. Another example is the negation marker: This POS tag was originally used in all dialects but Gulf. Additionally, the dialects use different words for negation, but not all were annotated as such. Now they are annotated consistently across dialects, which has changed the majority reading from pronoun or particle to negation marker.

9 Using Pretrained Word Embeddings

Next we investigate whether word embeddings can be beneficial and have a positive impact on the quality of POS tagging. The assumption is that the pre-trained word embeddings derived from large corpora of dialectal Arabic can help mitigate problems with lexical coverage in the randomly initialized embeddings in the out-of-domain setting.

The choice of the pretrained embeddings is important. We use the word embeddings trained on a large corpus of dialectal Arabic (Erdmann et al., 2019).

To train the embeddings, Erdmann et al. (2018) collected data for four major dialects of Arabic: Gulf, Levantine, Egyptian, and Maghrebi, which cover the four dialects of our test data. The corpora are a mix of crawled data from a variety of forums and blogs, including comments on posts (Almeman and Lee, 2013; Khalifa et al., 2016; Zbib et al., 2012), MADAR (Bouamor et al., 2018), news commentary corpus (Zaidan and Callison-Burch, 2011), tweets from the corpus of Palestinian Arabic (Jarrar et al., 2014), with the number of sentences per dialect ranging between 1.1M and 1.7M. The model was trained using fastText (Bojanowski

	original	+ embeddings
vectors	1 998	2 134 625
dimension	300	400
window size	10	10
batch size	128	128

Table 7: Embedding layer parameters

	GLF	LEV	EGY	MAG
Without embeddings	82.3	75.2	80.2	73.8
With embeddings	83.2	84.3	87.9	78.9

Table 8: Accuracy of POS tagging with and without using pre-trained embeddings using improved annotations.

et al., 2017)[13]. Since MADAR is part of the training data for the embeddings, we can expect a higher lexical coverage for the test data.

Table 8 shows the results for POS tagging with and without using the pre-trained embedding and the improved annotations. The results show that the performance on all dialects increases, and for all but GLF the gains are considerable, LEV gains the most: For this dialect, the accuracy increases from 75.2% to 84.3%. For GLF, we see a moderate increase from 82.3% to 83.2%. This dialect had the highest accuracy before embeddings, as it has the highest lexical overlap with the training corpus.

We also had a look at the tagging errors for the model using the pre-trained embeddings. A heatmap of POS tag precision is provided in Figure 3. We see that numbers are still the most difficult POS tag, similar to the results in Figure 1. However, for all dialects but MAG, the accuracies are considerably higher. For MAG, most of the numbers were mistagged as NOUN. This seems to be due to inconsistencies in the training data. Since the spelling of numbers tends to differ between dialects, the POS tagger cannot learn from the other dialects. The same pattern of gains holds for particles, previously the second most difficult category, except for MAG. The current second most difficult POS tag are adjectives. Here we see a decrease over all dialects in comparison to Figure 1. This can be explained by the systematic ambiguity between nouns and adjectives. The POS tagger seems to favor annotating these ambiguous words as adjectives, which leads to a high precision for nouns,

[13]We do not use BERT embeddings since they cannot be easily integrated into the POS tagger architecture. See Table 7 for embedding parameters.

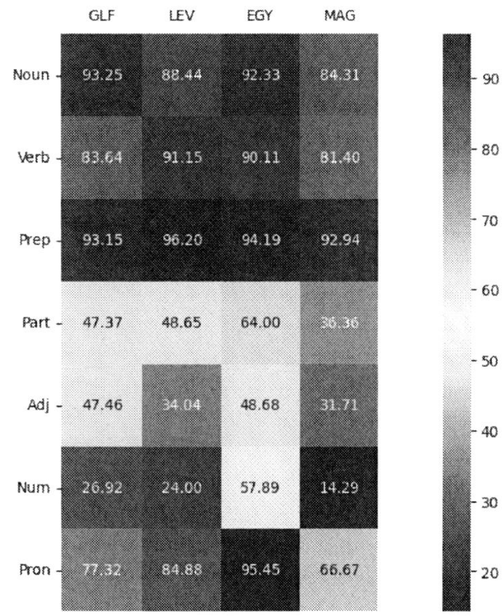

Figure 3: Results per dialect (precision) when using pre-trained embeddings.

and a low one for adjectives.

For instance, the adjective آسف (Eng.: sorry) is tagged as NOUN because of its alternative interpretation 'regret'.

10 Conclusion and Future Work

We have investigated POS tagging for Arabic dialects when the test set is out-of-domain. This setting has proven to be difficult, originally resulting in a low accuracy. Our work shows that we can improve the POS tagger's accuracy by upsampling the target dialect in the training data, by increasing consistency of annotations, and by using word embeddings pre-trained on a large corpus of dialectal Arabic. On average we have seen improvements of about 20 percent points.

Our overarching goal is the investigation of morpho-syntactic and syntactic differences between Arabic dialects. Our next step is to experiment with the granularity of POS tags. The current small POS tagset may not provide enough information for an investigation of syntactic differences. We also plan to develop a parsing model for Arabic dialects.

References

Ahmed Abdelali, Kareem Darwish, Nadir Durrani, and Hamdy Mubarak. 2016. Farasa: A fast and furious segmenter for Arabic. In *Proceedings of the 2016 Conference of the North American Chapter of the Association for Computational Linguistics: Demonstrations*, pages 11–16, San Diego, CA.

Faisal Al-Shargi, Aidan Kaplan, Ramy Eskander, Nizar Habash, and Owen Rambow. 2016. Morphologically annotated corpora and morphological analyzers for Moroccan and Sanaani Yemeni Arabic. In *Proceedings of the 10th Language Resources and Evaluation Conference (LREC)*, Portorož, Slovenia.

Abdullah I. Alharbi and Mark Lee. 2020. BhamNLP at SemEval-2020 task 12: An ensemble of different word embeddings and emotion transfer learning for Arabic offensive language identification in social media. In *Proceedings of the Fourteenth Workshop on Semantic Evaluation*, pages 1532–1538, Barcelona (online). International Committee for Computational Linguistics.

Randah Alharbi, Walid Magdy, Kareem Darwish, Ahmed Abdelali, and Hamdy Mubarak. 2018. Part-of-speech tagging for Arabic Gulf dialect using Bi-LSTM. In *Proceedings of the Eleventh International Conference on Language Resources and Evaluation (LREC)*, Miyazaki, Japan.

Khalid Almeman and Mark Lee. 2013. Automatic building of Arabic multi dialect text corpora by bootstrapping dialect words. In *1st International Conference on Communications, Signal Processing, and their Applications (ICCSPA)*, pages 1–6, Sharjah, UAE.

Mohammed Attia and Ali Elkahky. 2019. Segmentation for domain adaptation in Arabic. In *Proceedings of the Fourth Arabic Natural Language Processing Workshop (WANLP)*, pages 119–129, Florence, Italy.

Shabnam Behzad and Amir Zeldes. 2020. A cross-genre ensemble approach to robust Reddit part of speech tagging. In *Proceedings of the 12th Web as Corpus Workshop*, pages 50–56, Marseille, France. European Language Resources Association.

Bernd Bohnet, Ryan McDonald, Goncalo Simoes, Daniel Andor, Emily Pitler, and Joshua Maynez. 2018. Morphosyntactic tagging with a meta-BiLSTM model over context sensitive token encodings. In *Proceedings of the 56th Annual Meeting of the Association for Computational Linguistics*, pages 2642–2652, Melbourne, Australia.

Piotr Bojanowski, Edouard Grave, Armand Joulin, and Tomas Mikolov. 2017. Enriching word vectors with subword information. *Transactions of the Association for Computational Linguistics*, 5:135–146.

Houda Bouamor, Nizar Habash, Mohammad Salameh, Wajdi Zaghouani, Owen Rambow, Dana Abdulrahim, Ossama Obeid, Salam Khalifa, Fadhl Eryani, Alexander Erdmann, and Kemal Oflazer. 2018. The MADAR Arabic dialect corpus and lexicon. In *Proceedings of the Eleventh International Conference on Language Resources and Evaluation (LREC)*, Miyazaki, Japan.

Kareem Darwish, Mohammed Attia, Hamdy Mubarak, Younes Samih, Ahmed Abdelali, Lluís Màrquez, Mohamed Eldesouki, and Laura Kallmeyer. 2020. Effective multi-dialectal Arabic POS tagging. *Natural Language Engineering*, 26(6):677–690.

Kareem Darwish and Hamdy Mubarak. 2016. Farasa: A new fast and accurate Arabic word segmenter. In *Proceedings of the Tenth International Conference on Language Resources and Evaluation (LREC)*, pages 1070–1074, Portorož, Slovenia.

Kareem Darwish, Hamdy Mubarak, Ahmed Abdelali, and Mohamed Eldesouki. 2017. Arabic POS tagging: Don't abandon feature engineering just yet. In *Proceedings of the Third Arabic Natural Language Processing Workshop*, pages 130–137, Valencia, Spain.

Kareem Darwish, Hamdy Mubarak, Ahmed Abdelali, Mohamed Eldesouki, Younes Samih, Randah Alharbi, Mohammed Attia, Walid Magdy, and Laura Kallmeyer. 2018. Multi-dialect Arabic POS tagging: A CRF approach. In *Proceedings of the Eleventh International Conference on Language Resources and Evaluation (LREC)*, Miyazaki, Japan.

Mona Diab and Nizar Habash. 2007. Arabic dialect processing tutorial. In *Proceedings of the Human Language Technology Conference of the NAACL*, pages 5–6, New York, NY.

Kevin Duh and Katrin Kirchhoff. 2005. POS tagging of dialectal Arabic: A minimally supervised approach. In *Proceedings of the ACL Workshop on Computational Approaches to Semitic Languages*, pages 55–62, Ann Arbor, MI.

Mohamed Eldesouki, Younes Samih, Ahmed Abdelali, Mohammed Attia, Hamdy Mubarak, Kareem Darwish, and Laura Kallmeyer. 2017. Arabic multi-dialect segmentation: bi-LSTM-CRF vs. SVM. *arXiv preprint arXiv:1708.05891*.

Ashraf Elnagar, Sane M Yagi, Ali Bou Nassif, Ismail Shahin, and Said A Salloum. 2021. Systematic literature review of dialectal Arabic: Identification and detection. *IEEE Access*, 9:31010–31042.

Alexander Erdmann, Salam Khalifa, Mai Oudah, Nizar Habash, and Houda Bouamor. 2019. A little linguistics goes a long way: Unsupervised segmentation with limited language specific guidance. In *Proceedings of the 16th Workshop on Computational Research in Phonetics, Phonology, and Morphology*, pages 113–124, Florence, Italy.

Alexander Erdmann, Nasser Zalmout, and Nizar Habash. 2018. Addressing noise in multidialectal word embeddings. In *Proceedings of the 56th Annual Meeting of the Association for Computational Linguistics*, pages 558–565, Melbourne, Australia.

Ali Farghaly and Khaled Shaalan. 2009. Arabic natural language processing: Challenges and solutions. *ACM Transactions on Asian Language Information Processing (TALIP)*, 8(4):1–22.

Nizar Habash, Houda Bouamor, Hazem Hajj, Walid Magdy, Wajdi Zaghouani, Fethi Bougares, Nadi Tomeh, Ibrahim Abu Farha, and Samia Touileb, editors. 2021. *Proceedings of the Sixth Arabic Natural Language Processing Workshop*. Association for Computational Linguistics, Kyiv, Ukraine (Virtual).

Nizar Habash, Ryan Roth, Owen Rambow, Ramy Eskander, and Nadi Tomeh. 2013. Morphological analysis and disambiguation for dialectal Arabic. In *Proceedings of theConference of the North American Chapter of the Association for Computational Linguistics: Human Language Technologies*, pages 426–432, Atlanta, GA.

Benjamin Heinzerling and Michael Strube. 2019. Sequence tagging with contextual and non-contextual subword representations: A multilingual evaluation. In *Proceedings of the 57th Annual Meeting of the Association for Computational Linguistics*, pages 273–291, Florence, Italy.

Tobias Horsmann and Torsten Zesch. 2015. Effectiveness of domain adaptation approaches for social media PoS tagging. In *Proceeding of the Second Italian Conference on Computational Linguistics*, pages 166–170, Trento, Italy.

Mustafa Jarrar, Nizar Habash, Diyam Akra, and Nasser Zalmout. 2014. Building a corpus for Palestinian Arabic: A preliminary study. In *Proceedings of the EMNLP 2014 Workshop on Arabic Natural Language Processing (ANLP)*, pages 18–27, Doha, Qatar.

Salam Khalifa, Nizar Habash, Dana Abdulrahim, and Sara Hassan. 2016. A large scale corpus of Gulf Arabic. *arXiv preprint arXiv:1609.02960*.

Salam Khalifa, Nizar Habash, Fadhl Eryani, Ossama Obeid, Dana Abdulrahim, and Meera Al Kaabi. 2018. A morphologically annotated corpus of Emirati Arabic. In *Proceedings of the Eleventh International Conference on Language Resources and Evaluation (LREC 2018)*, Miyazaki, Japan.

Sandra Kübler and Eric Baucom. 2011. Fast domain adaptation for part of speech tagging for dialogues. In *Proceedings of the International Conference on Recent Advances in NLP (RANLP)*, Hissar, Bulgaria.

Prathyusha Kuncham, Chandu Khyathi Raghavi, Kovida Nelakuditi, and Dipti Misra Sharma. 2014. Domain adaptation in morphological analysis. *International Journal of Languages, Literature and Linguistics*, 1(2).

Atreyee Mukherjee, Sandra Kübler, and Matthias Scheutz. 2017. Creating POS tagging and dependency parsing experts via topic modeling. In *Proceedings of Fifteenth Conference of the European Chapter of the ACL (EACL)*, Valencia, Spain.

Melanie Neunerdt, Michael Reyer, and Rudolf Mathar. 2014. Efficient training data enrichment and unknown token handling for POS tagging of non-standardized texts. In *Conference on Natural Language Processing (KONVENS)*, pages 186–192, Hildesheim, Germany.

Arfath Pasha, Mohamed Al-Badrashiny, Mona Diab, Ahmed El Kholy, Ramy Eskander, Nizar Habash, Manoj Pooleery, Owen Rambow, and Ryan Roth. 2014. MADAMIRA: A fast, comprehensive tool for morphological analysis and disambiguation of Arabic. In *Proceedings of the Language Resources and Evaluation Conference (LREC)*, Reykjavik, Iceland.

Barbara Plank, Anders Søgaard, and Yoav Goldberg. 2016. Multilingual part-of-speech tagging with bidirectional long short-term memory models and auxiliary loss. In *Proceedings of the 54th Annual Meeting of the Association for Computational Linguistics (Volume 2: Short Papers)*, pages 412–418, Berlin, Germany. Association for Computational Linguistics.

Younes Samih, Mohammed Attia, Mohamed Eldesouki, Ahmed Abdelali, Hamdy Mubarak, Laura Kallmeyer, and Kareem Darwish. 2017a. A neural architecture for dialectal Arabic segmentation. In *Proceedings of the Third Arabic Natural Language Processing Workshop*, pages 46–54, Valencia, Spain.

Younes Samih, Mohamed Eldesouki, Mohammed Attia, Kareem Darwish, Ahmed Abdelali, Hamdy Mubarak, and Laura Kallmeyer. 2017b. Learning from relatives: Unified dialectal Arabic segmentation. In *Proceedings of the 21st Conference on Computational Natural Language Learning (CoNLL 2017)*, pages 432–441, Vancouver, Canada.

Abdulhadi Shoufan and Sumaya Alameri. 2015. Natural language processing for dialectical Arabic: A survey. In *Proceedings of the Second Workshop on Arabic Natural Language Processing*, pages 36–48, Beijing, China.

Toshiyuki Takezawa, Genichiro Kikui, Masahide Mizushima, and Eiichiro Sumita. 2007. Multilingual spoken language corpus development for communication research. *International Journal of Computational Linguistics & Chinese Language Processing: Special Issue on Invited Papers from ISCSLP 2006*, 12(3):303–324.

Xinyu Wang, Yong Jiang, Nguyen Bach, Tao Wang, Zhongqiang Huang, Fei Huang, and Kewei Tu. 2021. Automated concatenation of embeddings for structured prediction. In *Proceedings of the 59th Annual Meeting of the Association for Computational Linguistics and the 11th International Joint Conference on Natural Language Processing*, pages 2643–2660, Online.

Michihiro Yasunaga, Jungo Kasai, and Dragomir Radev. 2018. Robust multilingual part-of-speech tagging via adversarial training. In *Proceedings of the 2018 Conference of the North American Chapter of the Association for Computational Linguistics: Human Language Technologies, Volume 1 (Long Papers)*, pages 976–986, New Orleans, Louisiana. Association for Computational Linguistics.

Omar Zaidan and Chris Callison-Burch. 2011. The Arabic online commentary dataset: An annotated dataset of informal Arabic with high dialectal content. In *Proceedings of the 49th Annual Meeting of the Association for Computational Linguistics: Human Language Technologies*, pages 37–41, Portland OR.

Rabih Zbib, Erika Malchiodi, Jacob Devlin, David Stallard, Spyros Matsoukas, Richard Schwartz, John Makhoul, Omar Zaidan, and Chris Callison-Burch. 2012. Machine translation of Arabic dialects. In *Proceedings of the 2012 Conference of the North American Chapter of the Association for Computational Linguistics: Human Language Technologies*, pages 49–59, Montréal, Canada.

Imed Zitouni, Muhammad Abdul-Mageed, Houda Bouamor, Fethi Bougares, Mahmoud El-Haj, Nadi Tomeh, and Wajdi Zaghouani, editors. 2020. *Proceedings of the Fifth Arabic Natural Language Processing Workshop*. Association for Computational Linguistics, Barcelona, Spain (Online).

Inès Zribi, Mariem Ellouze, Lamia Hadrich Belguith, and Philippe Blache. 2017. Morphological disambiguation of Tunisian dialect. *Journal of King Saud University - Computer and Information Sciences*, 29(2):147–155.

Domain Adaptation for Arabic Crisis Response

Reem ALRashdi
University of Ha'il, Ha'il, KSA
University of York, York, UK
reem.alreshede@uoh.edu.sa
rmma502@york.ac.uk

Simon O'Keefe
University of York, York, UK
simon.okeefe@york.ac.uk

Abstract

Deep learning algorithms can identify related tweets to reduce the information overload that prevents humanitarian organisations from using valuable Twitter posts. However, they rely heavily on human-labelled data, which are unavailable for emerging crises. Because each crisis has its own features, such as location, time and social media response, current models are known to suffer from generalising to unseen disaster events when pre-trained on past ones.Tweet classifiers for low-resource languages like Arabic has the additional issue of limited labelled data duplicates caused by the absence of good language resources. Thus, we propose a novel domain adaptation approach that does not rely on human-labelled data to automatically label tweets from emerging Arabic crisis events to be used to train a model along with available human-labelled data. We evaluate our work on data from seven 2018–2020 Arabic events from different crisis types (flood, explosion, virus and storm). Results show that our method outperforms self-training in classifying crisis-related tweets in real-time scenarios.

1 Introduction

Arabic represents the world's fifth most spoken language and Arabic language users are the fastest-growing language group on the web (Lane, 2019). In February 2011, protestors in Egypt used Twitter as their main communication platform (Tufekci and Wilson, 2012). This emphasises that Twitter is an important and rich source of real-time and useful information during crises in Arabic countries. People share their statuses and post information about injured or dead people and infrastructural damage (Vieweg, 2012). They also tweet to ask for help or to offer help to others. Although humanitarian organisations could use these information to significantly improve crisis response with regard to reducing human and financial losses, they do not due to the information overload issue (George et al., 2021). To solve this problem, deep learning algorithms have been utilised to identify Arabic tweets from unseen crises to support disaster management and enhance situational awareness in the Middle East (Adel and Wang, 2020; Alharbi and Lee, 2021). However, they did not consider the domain-shift between source and target tweets posted during these events, which prevents the models from reaching a good generalisation level. As a result, semi-supervised approaches that automatically generate new labelled training data from an unlabelled corpus to reduce the gaps between the two domains are desirable.

Distant supervision has been applied to automatically generate new labelled training data for event extraction task (Chen et al., 2017; Zeng et al., 2018). Moreover, semi-supervised domain adaptation techniques have been successfully adopted to incorporate unlabelled target data to labelled source data to reduce the domain-shift between the two domains. Our work here is motivated by the success of applying distant supervision and domain adaptation methods to high-resource English-language tweets presented in our previous works (ALRashdi and O'Keefe, 2019; Alrashdi and O'Keefe, 2020). However and unlike English, Arabic is considered a low-resource language, with several notable issues highlighted in the crisis literature. First is the lack of labelled Arabic tweets for crisis response (Adel and Wang, 2020). Second, the lack of good supporting resources for Arabic, such as external knowledge bases or language dictionaries (Alharbi and Lee, 2019). Finally, Arabic tweets are informal and regional in nature, and Arabic regions have unique dialects which differ in syntax, phonology and morphology (Chiang et al., 2006).

In this paper, we propose an adaptive domain adaptation method from our previous work for English crisis response in (Alrashdi and O'Keefe, 2020) to overcome all these challenges for Arabic

Proceedings of the The Seventh Arabic Natural Language Processing Workshop (WANLP), pages 249 - 259
December 8, 2022

crisis response. Our work, here, aims at minimising the domain shift between the target and the source Arabic tweets. We use a distant supervision-based framework to label the unlabelled target data (pseudo-labelling), whereby an initial keyword list is established using clusters from past events. The most related keywords are then selected using a statistical method. The selected keyword list is then expanded by employing distant supervision via an external source (Almaany[1]), and those tweets with a bigram of keywords are labelled as positive tweets, while tweets with none of the keywords are labelled as negative tweets. The generated labelled data is then mixed with the available source data to train a new target model. Unlike self-training in (Win and Aung, 2018; Li, 2021), our method does not replicate the label noise that exists in the current dataset. In addition, crisis data that cannot be detected using existing keyword alert systems, as in (Sakaki et al., 2010), will be detected by our method because of the new crisis keywords derived from Almaany. To the best of our knowledge, this is the first attempt to use distant supervision under the umbrella of domain adaptation techniques to classify unseen crisis-related Arabic data from current events. The experimental results show that the proposed method can be seen as a robust approach to classifying unseen Arabic tweets from an emerging event regardless of the crisis types used to create the keyword list. Furthermore, it extends our framework's abilities from our prior work to automatically label data from low-resource languages with limited capabilities.

2 Related work

Distant supervision (DS). Recent NLP studies have shown the effectiveness of using DS to generate training data via external sources. The researchers in (Chen et al., 2017) employ DS to automatically generate a large-scale dataset using a linguistic knowledge base (FrameNet) for event extraction tasks, where triggers and arguments are extracted from Wikipedia data. Zeng et al. (2018) argue that detecting key argument is enough for determining the event type for event extraction tasks. They extract the most related arguments that best describe the event from existing structured knowledge (FreeBase). However, we use an Arabic dictionary (Almaany) for Arabic ill-formed texts, tweets, based on the existence of essential keywords in the synonyms of a related form.

Domain adaptation (DA). Li et al. (2018b) introduce a semi-supervised DA approach that does not require limited labelled data from the target domain. They use a pre-trained model on one crisis dataset to classify tweets from an emerging event – to be added to the training data in the retrained stage. Their iterative self-training method shows good results, particularly when classifying tweets related to a specific crisis. This method outperforms expectation-maximisation when combined with naive Bayes (Li et al., 2018a). Self-training has been also combined with deep learning models and findings indicate that using unlabelled target data resulted in better adaptation performance (Li et al., 2021). Alharbi and Lee (2022) preform similar study by applying data selection with pre-trained learning models on tweets related to Arabic crises. Another work extends domain adaptation with adversarial training to include a graph-based semi-supervised learning (Alam et al., 2018). F1 score on only two datasets (Queensland Floods and Nepal Earthquake) improves the performance with 5%–7% absolute gain.

To contribute to this line of research, we propose an adaptive yet novel semi-supervised DA that uses DS to give pseudo-labels to unlabelled data from target event to be then incorporated to labeled source data from past disasters to build a robust Arabic crisis-related classifier. We compare our method to the widely used labeling technique in the literature, self-training. We also explore using keyword sets from different crisis type to the target event.

3 Proposed Method

The method consists of two stages as described in algorithm 1.

3.1 Distant supervision-based labelling framework

The proposed labelling framework is described by the steps shown in Figure 1.

Step one: Creating the initial keyword list. We use K-means to classify several Arabic corpora from different events. K-means has been successfully applied to different Arabic Twitter data (Sangaiah et al., 2019; Saeed et al., 2022). For cluster optimisation, elbow method was uncertain for our data because the results shown in the figures are not clear. Because of

[1] available on: https://www.almaany.com

Algorithm 1 Robust domain adaptation approach with pseudo-labelled target data.

1. Given: Clusters of tweets related to several crisis events from different time intervals and locations (CLS); manually Labelled tweets of source data (MLS); unlabelled tweets from target domain (UT) retrieved using Twitter API and publicly available tweet IDs; and manually labelled test data from target domain (MLTT).
2. DS-based labelling stage: Use our framework to label UT based on CLS and employing distant supervision via external knowledge base (giving them pseudo-labels).
3. Adaptation stage: Build a target model using MLS with the pseudo-labelled data from the target domain.
4. Evaluate the model on MLTT.

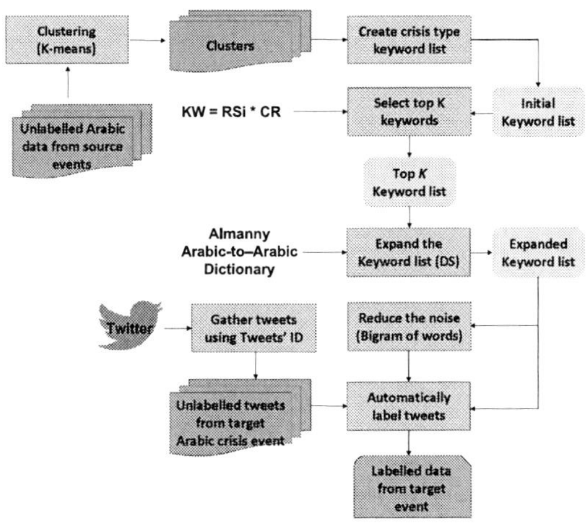

Figure 1: The proposed labelling framework.

that, we use silhouette score measurements to determine the optimal number of clusters to apply K-means to the data for every crisis event from the unlabelled corpora. After that, we assign profiles as labels for each cluster. The reason behind labelling the clusters is that assigning profiles that describe the tweets within the clusters is another way to decide whether the cluster is related to the crisis and informative. To do so, we follow the centroid approach: we pick the centre data point of each cluster to extract the cluster's features. This approach is suitable for our work because the variance within the clusters is slight, and the centre data point of the cluster is the closest one to represent it. Our data are similar in that the tweets are all posted during a crisis and different in providing information about it. Therefore, other approaches can be misleading for our data. To ensure the effectiveness of the centroid approach, we select the closest three data points instead of one. We then extract the features for each cluster and use them to assign profiles from these data points. Our data represents many crisis topics, including: advertisements; political opinions; irrelevant to the crisis; emotional support; infrastructural and utility damage; dead, injured or affected people; and providing help and caution advice. For example, the closest three data points for cluster #3 in the Beirut Explosion corpus (3,445 tweets) are: "حصيلة قتلى انفجار ميناء # بيروت ترتفع إلى ٥٣١. https://t.co/Hbah7vFFKi.https://t.co/HLYVLF7zco" , "أشبه ما يكون بما حدث في هيروشيما وناجاساكي أعداد كبيرة من القتلى والجرحى #انفجار_بيروت # انفجار_مرفأ_بيروت" and "اوضح فيديو للانفجار الهائل الذي هز العاصمة اللبنانية # بيروت الانفجار نتج عنه دمار كبير وانباء عن سقوط عشرات الجرحى https://t.co/uwD2JWpyF4". These tweets contain the words "قتلى", which mean (dead people), "انفجار" (explosion) and "جرحى" (injured people). It is obvious that the most represented tweets of the cluster talk about dead and injured people during the Beirut Explosion incident. As a result, this topic is assigned to cluster #3. After assigning topics to clusters, we divide the clusters into two classes: related and informative and irrelevant or not informative. In particular, infrastructure and utility damages, dead, injured or affected people, and providing help and caution advice are classified as related and informative. On the other hand, advertisements, political opinions, and emotional support are labelled as irrelevant or not informative. While doing this, we observe that all the crisis events have a cluster with a vast number of tweets advertising for specific products or services. We decide to label the tweets expressing political opinions and emotional support as not informative because the information in the posted tweets offers no benefits to humanitarian organisations. Finally, the initial keyword list is created based on the chosen clusters (related and informative) from different collections related to the same crisis type. We stem each word to its root by utilising ISIRI Stemmer, as in (Al-Horaibi et al., 2017; Abuaiadah et al., 2017), to avoid word redundancy and reduce the amount of linguistically similar words. We also use NLTK libraries to remove stop words such as "في، من، هذا", hashtags such as "#انفجار", places such as "حفر الباطن" and useless Twitter-specific words such as "RT" and "via" from the initial keyword list. To conduct fair experiments, at this point, we eliminate the test event data.

Step two: Selecting top K keywords. The top K keywords are then chosen based on an intrinsic filtering method. To select the top K keyword list for Arabic crisis events, we calculate the keyword (KW) value, inspired by (Chen et al., 2017), for each keyword in the initial keyword list. In a tweet, a word that describes a given crisis type can be a verb, a noun or an adverb. For instance, for the Floods crisis type, the top K keyword list contains "غرق", "سيل",and "مطر", which have the highest KW values compared to the other words in the initial Floods list. Intuitively, a word describing a crisis type appears more than other words in the related tweets. In addition, if the same word appears in both related and unrelated tweets, it has a low probability to be a keyword of this crisis type. Thus, KW is calculated as follows:

$$RS_i = \frac{Count(W_i, CT)}{Count(CT)} \quad (1)$$

$$CR_i = \log \frac{3}{(Count(CTC_i)} \quad (2)$$

$$KW_i = RS_i * CR_i, \quad (3)$$

where RS_i (role saliency) represents the saliency of *i*-th keyword to identify a specific word of a given crisis type, $Count(W_i, CT)$ is the number of a word W_i that occurs in all the tweets related to the crisis type *CT*, and *Count(CT)* is the count of times that all words occur in all the tweets related to the crisis type. CR_i (crisis relevance) represents the ability of the *i*-th keyword to distinguish between the tweets related to the crisis type and irrelevant tweets, and $Count(CTC_i)$ equals 1 if the *i*-th keyword occurs only in the related tweets and 2 if the *i*-th keyword occurs in both related and irrelevant tweets. We compute KW_i for all the words in the initial keyword list from step one and sort them according to their KW values to select the top K keywords for a given crisis type. Table 1 shows that crisis-related and flood-related words

Ranking	Keyword	KW Value
1	مطر	0.00371
2	غرق	0.00130
32	كسر	0.00065
98	رادار	0.00019

Table 1: KW values of some words from the initial Floods keyword list.

have higher KW values than the unrelated ones. Other statistical methods such as pointwise mutual information (PMI; (Church and Hanks, 1990)) or term frequency-inverse document frequency (TF-IDF; (Jones, 1972)) have not been used here for solid reasons. Calculating PMI for positive and negative examples to give the final PMI score is not a fair metric in our case because of the imbalanced data problem in Kawarith dataset. On the other hand, this problem does not affect our formula as *Count(CT)* accounts for the total number of words in the related tweets only. TF-IDF is not suitable in our case because IDF has more impact on the final result than TF; in our case, they should be equally important since tweets are short and full of noise. If we used TF-IDF on our data, rare words such as misspelled words would have higher TF-IDF than essential keywords. Additionally, an important keyword may appear in both related and not related tweets. For instance, in earthquake crisis-type data, the word "earthquake" may appear very frequently in related earthquake event tweets but only once or twice in unrelated earthquake event tweets. On the other hand, our method does not discard the impact of word frequency if the word appears in both related and unrelated tweets.

Step three: Applying distant supervision. The list containing top K keywords is then expanded to include similar semantic words from the Almaany Arabic-to-Arabic dictionary. Almaany is an online dictionary that provides corresponding meanings with similar semantic words for each term in Arabic and has been widely used by in Arabic researches (Touahri and Mazroui, 2021; Al-Matham and Al-Khalifa, 2021). We retrieve all the synonyms provided by Almaany for each crisis keyword if the corresponding meaning of the top keyword is related to the crisis type. For example, the top keyword "سيل" exists in the Almaany dictionary but with two corresponding meanings based on the shape and the signs of the word: " سَيْل " and " سِيل".The meaning of " سَيْل" is the water of the rain that rushes over the earth's surface, whereas "سيّل " refers to converting material from a solid state to a liquid state. According to their meanings, " سيْل " is related to the Floods crisis type, but " سيّل" is not. Thus, all the synonyms associated with " سيْل ", such as " فيضان " and " طوفان " can be mapped to " سيْل ", which is a crisis keyword gathered from the first step and selected in the second step as one of the top K keywords based on its high KW value. In other words, if one of the top crisis type keywords exists in the Almaany dictionary and its meaning relates to a given crisis type (Floods or Explosion), then distant supervision assumes that all the synonyms related to the given word express that crisis type. As a result, the number of keywords increases in the final list. For instance, the number of keywords rises from 10 to 78 in the keyword list for the Floods crisis type. This list contains two types of keywords: strong keywords (top K keywords) and weak keywords (extracted from Almaany). If a word exists in the top K keywords and is a synonym associated with another top K keyword at the same time, then we consider it a strong keyword. Weak keywords may bring noise to the data, which we try to reduce in step five. As a result, 7 final keyword lists are generated according to the test event and the crisis type of the test event.

Step four: Gathering unlabelled tweets from prior crisis events. These tweets are obtained using Twitter API by their IDs provided by an Arabic twitter corpus (Kawarith) (Alharbi and Lee, 2021).

Step five: Noise reduction. We filter the unlabelled corpus gathered from step four after deleting duplicated and non-Arabic tweets by applying a specific lexical feature (bigram of keywords). After cleaning the unlabelled tweets, only the examples with two keywords from the final keyword list remain. This step reduces the effect of a powerful hashtag when the hashtag without the "#" symbol is one of the keywords. For example, if we use "# كورونا" as one of our hashtags in the previous step, and "كورونا" is one of the keywords in the final keyword list, then tweets like "ناس خايفين من # كورونا و ناس تشل و تحط خطبات و ملكات برويد برويد ان شاء الله لاحقين ماهو ذا الشغل خطبات و ملكات بالله عندكم و الا بس عندنا ؟؟" will not be selected for the Covid'19 event. On the other hand, the tweet "@RT @masrawy: #عاجل مصرع ٥ إصابة ٥١ آخرين الداخلية تكشف تفاصيل انفجار معهد الأورام" will be selected for the Cairo Bombing event because of the appearance of at least two keywords from the final Explosion keyword list: "إصابة" (derived from "اصاب" and "انفجار" (derived from "فجّر" in this case. This process also eliminates several tweets that contain only one weak keyword expanded from Almaany, which decreases most of the noise caused by step three. For instance, the tweet "@3ashoouur: إن شاء الله العاصفه الجايه نكون محبوسين انا و إنتي في بيت واحد " will not be chosen for the Dragon Storm event since " عاصفه" is a weak keyword derived from Almaany using "عصف" which is associated with one of the top K keywords for the Floods crisis type, "اعصار".

Step six: Labelling the corpus as related and not related examples. A collection of data from the new crisis event is automatically generated by labelling tweets from step five as relevant (positive) examples and tweets with no keywords from the expanded keyword list as not related (negative) examples. For instance, the tweet " RT @ww6223ww6: بالتوفيق بإذن الله لابناء العم في انتخابات الغرفة التجارية في فئة الصناعيين و فئة التجار #حفر_الباطن" will be labeled as not related because of the absence of keywords from the final Floods crisis-type list.

3.2 Adaptation stage

We add the pseudo-labelled target data created in the first stage to the available manually labelled source data from the same crisis type as the target crisis (from Kawarith) to build a new target model to classify the unseen tweets from the emerging event. Pseudo-labelled target data generated by our distant supervision-based framework provides new keywords than those existed in the source data. Adding these data to the manually labelled tweets brings target-related features to the training data, including location and crisis nature. By mixing the source and target data in training the target model, we increase the ability of the target classifier to identify related target tweets, including any type of information during the target event lifetime (Sit et al., 2019). For example, tweets containing advice, warnings and alerts start to appear at the beginning of the event onset and decrease thereafter while tweets containing reports on damage and affected individuals reach their peak in the middle of the disaster.

4 Experiments

To determine the effectiveness of using pseudo-labelled target data generated by our framework in domain adaptation settings, we compare two labelling with three adaptation methods. To automatically give labels to the unlabelled target data we apply Distant Supervision (DS) – using our distant supervision-based framework; and Self-Labelling (SelfL; (Li et al., 2018b)) – using a pre-trained model on MLS.

To incorporate target labelled data, we use three adaptation methods: Target Model (TM) – building a model following the source architecture as described in the above section; Finetuning (FT) – modifying all the weights of the pre-trained model using the pseudo-labelled or self-labelled target data; and Feature extraction (FX) – treating the pre-trained model as a feature extractor. Here, we only train a linear classifier using pseudo-labelled or self-labelled data on the top of the extracted features.

As a result, we compare 8 classifiers on 14 settings (keyword sets from the same or different crisis type of the target event - both from Kawarith, as shown in Table 2): (1) SL-LT, supervised learning model trained on MLTT (upper limit); (2) SL-LS, supervised learning model pre-trained on MLS (lower limit); (3) DS-TM; (4) SelfL-TM; (5) DS-FX; (6) SelfL-FX; (7) DS-FT; and (8) SelfL-FT. All the models are tested on MLTT. To train SL-LT, we split MLTT into training (70%) and testing sets (30%). The same testing set is then used to evaluate all the models on the given events. We consider the lower limit model to be our baseline, while the upper limit model is our ideal case.

We follow (Alharbi and Lee, 2021) in cleaning Arabic input tweets. We substitute hyperlinks with the Arabic word "رابط", which means HTTP address or URL. Similarly, we replace user mentions with "مستخدم", hashtags with "هاشتاق", and numbers with "رقم". Four types of letter normalizations are performed: (1) "أ ، آ ، إ", the different forms of *alef* are normalized to " ا "; (2) "ى ، ئ", forms of *elaf maqsora*, to "ي ", (3) "ؤ", a form of *waw*, to " و"; and (4) *ta marboutah* "ة ، ه" to "ه".We also eliminate stop words, special characters, punctuation, Twitter-specific words such as "RT", elongation, emojis, non-Arabic characters, diacritics and short vowels. We use ConvBiLSTM (Tam et al., 2021) as the tweet classifier which contains two sub-models: the CNN model for feature extraction and the BiLSTM model for interpreting the features across time steps in both directions. We define a sequential model and add various layers to it. The first is the embedding layer, which represents fastText Arabic embedding as it has been pre-trained using Arabic Wikipedia articles and outperforms other embeddings in Arabic text classification (DHARMA et al., 2022; Habib et al., 2021). The pre-trained embedding has been also fine-tuned in our work using tweets from Kawarith. The embedding layer converts tweets into numerical values and feature embedding. Feature embedding is then fed into the CNN layer with 64 filters and max pooling of size 4. The output of the CNN layer (reduced dimensions of features) is received by the BiLSTM layer with 100 neurons, followed by dropout layers with a rate of 0.5 for regulating the network. The final dense layer is the output layer with two cells representing categories along with a sigmoid activation function to produce classification results. To obtain the best parameter for our model, we utilise Adam as an optimiser and binary cross-entropy loss and set the maximum length to 100. In the end, our model with 25 epochs and a batch size of 32 yields better results. And due to the stochastic nature of the learning algorithm, we repeat every experiment 30 times and take the mean as the final score.

Setting	Keyword Set	Target Set
S1	Explosion	Cairo Bombing
S2	Explosion	Beirut Explosion
S3	Floods	Jordan Floods
S4	Floods	Kuwait Floods
S5	Floods	Hafer-albatin Floods
S6	Floods	Covid'19
S7	Explosion	Covid'19
S8	Floods	Dragon Storm
S9	Explosion	Dragon Storm
S10	Floods	Cairo Bombing
S11	Floods	Beurit Explosion
S12	Explosion	Jordan Floods
S13	Explosion	Kuwait Floods
S14	Explosion	Hafer-albatin Floods

Table 2: Source, keywords and target set for each setting (S) in our experiments.

5 Results and Discussion

Results from the first column in Table 3 show that SL-LS can be useful when classifying target Arabic

S/M	SL-LS	DS-TM	SelfL-TM	DS-FX	SelfL-FX	DS-FT	SelfL-FT	SL-LT
S1	0.753	**0.833**	0.608	0.683	0.784	0.628	0.795	**0.945**
S2	0.768	**0.831**	0.589	0.618	0.584	0.635	0.592	**0.881**
S3	0.798	**0.822**	0.687	0.804	0.647	0.803	0.625	**0.924**
S4	0.746	0.803	0.653	0.708	**0.819**	0.725	0.802	**0.929**
S5	0.717	0.747	**0.757**	0.754	0.679	0.754	0.670	**0.839**
S6	0.744	**0.846**	0.741	**0.850**	0.757	0.842	0.757	**0.954**
S7	0.744	**0.831**	0.741	0.730	0.757	0.729	0.757	**0.954**
S8	0.658	**0.741**	0.560	**0.742**	0.647	0.725	0.640	**0.852**
S9	0.658	**0.734**	0.560	0.651	0.647	0.612	0.640	**0.852**
S10	0.753	**0.843**	0.608	0.694	0.784	0.689	0.795	**0.945**
S11	0.768	**0.771**	0.589	0.682	0.584	0.687	0.592	**0.881**
S12	0.798	**0.810**	0.687	0.640	0.647	0.644	0.625	**0.924**
S13	0.746	0.767	0.653	0.719	**0.819**	0.753	0.802	**0.929**
S14	0.717	0.737	**0.757**	0.505	0.679	0.532	0.670	**0.839**

Table 3: Results in F1 score for 8 models tested on 5 crisis events from the same crisis type and 9 crisis events from different crisis type as the keywords set. Note that S is the setting and M is the model. Best results are in bold.

data. F1 scores for most settings are above 0.70, except for settings 8 and 9 (0.658), which represent the same target data (Dragon Storm). This outcome suggests that crisis data from other crisis types of the target event can be used to train a model for identifying Arabic tweets for crisis response. This result is consistent with prior studies (Nguyen et al., 2017; Li et al., 2018a). On the other hand, Dragon Storm in settings 8 and 9 does not share any of the common features, such as crisis type, location, occurrence time or dialects, with the source events or the keyword sets. This is not the case for the Covid'19 event, since dialects used to post tweets about Covid'19 have been used in the data of the source event, including Saudi and Kuwaiti. This observation clarifies the gap in F1 scores between Dragon Storm and Covid'19 (0.658 < 0.744).

5.1 Keyword and target sets share crisis types

From Table 3, we find out that at least one of the domain adaptation models outperforms SL-LS in all the settings. The highest scores are recorded by DS-TM for all the settings except settings 4 (SelfL-FX) and 5 (SelfL-TM). In contrast, it is clear that DA techniques are not always better than SL-LS. For example, SelfL-FX causes the Beirut Explosion model's performance to decrease by 18%, while SelfL-FT causes the Hafer-albatin Floods model's performance to fall by 4%. This is based on the level of similarity between source and target data and the nature of the adaptation methods. In FX, the high-level features of the source data are transferred to the target data; in FT, more specific target features are incorporated through changing the weights of some layers. Having said that, the Beirut Explosion data differs from the source data even with the existence of another explosion event (Cairo Explosion). The Cairo and Beirut Explosion data are written in different dialects and have dissimilar characteristics: Cairo Explosion was a terrorist act, whereas Beirut Explosion was caused by mismanagement on the part of the Lebanese government. On the other hand, the two Floods events in the source data used to train the model make the Hafer-albatin Floods data very similar. To summarise, DS-TM can be seen as the best general approach among the other 5 domain adaptation classifiers – regardless of the similarity between source and target domains – as it reports the best results in 3 out of 5 settings and a very minor gap compared to the best score in the other two (< 1%). An interesting finding, from columns 2 and 3 for settings (1-5) in Table 3, is that DS performs better as a labelling method than SelfL when TM is used as an adaptation method in 4 out of 5 settings. For setting 5, SelfL-TM is better than DS-TM with a gap of 1% in model performance. However, it is clear from the results that DS-TM always improves the performance by an average of 5.5%. In contrast, SelfL-TM causes a decline in performance for 4 out of 5 target events (average of 12.2%). The model performance when FX is used to adopt pseudo labelled target outperforms that with self-labelled data in 3 settings (2, 3 and 5). The same scenario is replicated for the last adaptation method, finetuning (FT). These outcomes suggest that the impact of the labelling method is greater than the impact of the adaptation method when pre-trained models are used due to the nature of the labeling method. DS produces pseudo-labelled target data with important keywords extracted from the keyword set with the same type and new keywords derived from Almaany. This can be very useful if the test set includes these initial or derived keywords. However, if the source and target data are alike in terms of having similar event features (e.g., location, infrastructure damage, people response and dialects), then SelfL can produce accurate self-labelled target data. On review, we observe that 5 out of the 10 top keywords are present in tweets from setting 3, the Jordan Floods incident. Additionally, 62.5% (50 out of 80) of the expanded keyword list occur in the target data. This increases the ability of the DS labelling method to accurately label tweets from this event to the extent that building a target model along with the source data performs better than other models. In setting 5, SelfL-TM outperforms other domain adaptation methods. The reason behind this result is that Hafer-albatin is very similar to the other two Floods events, especially Kuwait Floods. Hafer-albatin and Kuwait are proximal locations and share dialects. Another reason is that the incident data contain 5 out of the top 10 Floods keywords, yet the percentage of the expanded keywords from Almaany is low (38%). Although SelfL-TM should report better results for Kuwait floods than DS-TM because of the similarity level with Hafer-albatin Floods and the small number of common top keywords (3 out of 10), it does not. This can be explained by the nature of the Arabic language, any root word in Arabic has more than 10 shapes regardless of the language signs. This increases the ability of our framework to retrieve more related tweets where most of the expanded keywords occurring in the target data are shapes from root words such as " تحذير، حذر، يحذرون، يحذر" from " حذر ". This represents a significant advantage in using our framework to automatically label Arabic crisis tweets from emerging events. We also note that, in setting 2, both labelling methods cause a substantial drop in model performance when FT or FX is used as the adaptation method, unlike in the other settings. This is because of the high level of divergence between the source and target domains – to the extent that using a pre-trained model in the domain adaptation method always inhibits model performance.

5.2 Keyword and target sets from different crisis types

As stated in column 2 for settings (6-14) from Table 3, and as expected, DS-TM results slightly decrease when using crisis data from different crisis types as the target data to create the keyword set. We find that the number of the shared top or expanded keywords occurring in the target data decreases. Evidently, when the number of shared keywords decreases, the performance of DS labelling method also declines. However, this is not the case in settings 1 and 10. Our results are better in classifying the Cairo Explosion data when the Floods keyword set is used in place of the Explosion keyword set. This is because the number of the top Floods keywords exist in tweets related to Cairo Explosion event is higher than that of the top Explosion keywords (6 > 5). The high divergence level between the Cairo and Beirut Explosion data helps in producing such an outcome. For the Kuwait Floods event, the performance of DS-TM drops from 0.803 to 0.767 in F1 score. It is worth noting that the top keyword list changes from the previous list and does not include " حذر", which gives DS-TM an advantage in the previous section. For the Covid'19 and Dragon Storm events, Table 3 shows that the results of DS-TM change when using different crisis types to build the keyword sets for Floods and Explosion- settings 6 to 9. It seems that the framework with the Floods keyword set generates better pseudo-labelled data from Covid'19 and Dragon Storm than with the Explosion keyword set. This is definitely caused by the number of shared top or expanded keywords. The Dragon Storm data includes 6 top keywords and 55% of the expanded keywords from the Floods keyword set. On the other hand, only 2 top keywords and 16% of the expanded keywords are shared with the Explosion keyword set. The performance of our standalone model supports this finding: for example, its F1 score for tweets related to Covid'19 in setting 6 is higher than in setting 7. This is because setting 6 uses the Floods keyword set, while setting 7 uses the Explosion keyword set. Based on these observations, we can posit that Arabic tweets from an event of any crisis type can be used to generate keyword sets for any emerging disaster. However, the performance of DS-TM can be improved by using crisis data from the same or similar crisis type to establish the initial keyword list for the given emerging Arabic event. We note that using tweets from different crisis types to pre-train a model to classify target events presents several problems. The main issue is that keywords from related tweets in the source data can be remarkable keywords in the irrelevant target data. An example of this case is setting 9, where the Explosion crisis type included in the source data features terrorism-associated words due to the nature of bombings and explosions, while unrelated tweets from the Dragon Storm target event contain these words due to the crisis locations (Palestine and Syria), where people often post about terrorist acts. Using DS to automatically label the Arabic target corpus – before merging with the manually labelled source tweets to build DS-TM – dramatically reduces this problem. DS-TM does not use models pre-trained on source data, and the DS labels the tweet as related and informative only if it contains two keywords from the expanded keyword set; it is rare to find two terrorist words in one tweet posted during the Dragon Storm crisis. Thus, the DS outperforms SelfL in the three adaptation methods. Another issue is that the number of shared top or expanded keywords can be reduced when tweets from crisis events belonging to different crisis types to the target data are used to generate the keyword sets. This is the case in settings 11, 12, 13 and 14. Although this issue restricts the capacity of DS to produce good target pseudo-labelled data, the best reported domain adaptation model for setting 11 is DS-TM. This is because of the divergence level between the source and target events, which leads SelfL to produce noisy self-labelled data related to Beirut Explosion incident. In contrast, DS-TM does not outperform SelfL-FX for the Kuwait Floods event – even in setting 13 with the increased number of common top keywords. Nevertheless, this number is still too small (4 > 3) to change the performance of DS-TM. We also observe that DS-TM remains the best reported domain adaptation model for the Jordan Floods disaster in setting 12. Here, the length and content of the keyword set change when using incidents from another crisis type. Although the number decreases, the list becomes richer by including words with multiple shapes present in the Jordan Floods data: "انقاذ" and " كارثة". This is because of the powerful nature of the Arabic language in having multiple shapes on one root as discussed above. For setting 14 (Hafer-albatin), the number of common keywords decreases from 5 to 2, with no words with multiple shapes like "صوت ". Thus, SelfL-TM produces the best results among the 6 domain adaptation models. In general, DS-TM is the most robust tweet classifier among all the mentioned domain adaptation models. In all cases, it improves model performance after incorporating the pseudo-labelled data, unlike the alternatives.

The last column in Table 3 show that the best recorded DA models for all settings are very far from the results for the upper limit, LT. One possible explanation is that the source data are collected from events from various crisis types. In general, therefore, the results of these Arabic domain adaptation models show much room for improvement.

6 Conclusion

We introduced a domain adaptation method to automatically label Arabic tweets from emerging disasters. Our goal is to overcome the issues of low-resource languages in applying solutions to domain shifts between source and target data. We use clusters instead of manually labelled tweets along with Almaany to extend the initial keyword list. Results showed that our method always improves the model performance (average of 3.7% absolute gain in F1 score) if the keyword sets share the crisis type of the target events.We also ran experiments to use keyword sets from different crisis types to the target incident. As a result, we found out that our framework can classify unseen tweets from a given disaster using a keyword set from different disasters and DS-TM always improves model performance (average of 5.5% absolute gain in F1 score). To this end, we can say that that DS-TM represents robust models to classify tweets from emerging events for languages with limited resources. It also expands our approach's ability to use corpora from other crisis types of the target data to create keyword sets that suit the situation of Arabic tweets. We hope that leveraging automatically labelled data will accelerate the current research on classifying Arabic tweets in crisis response. In the future, we want to extend our method to other low-resource languages like Spanish. We also believe that tweets share features with ill-formed texts, which points to the potential of our method to identify specific events, behaviors or feelings expressed on other communication platforms.

References

Diab Abuaiadah, Dileep Rajendran, and Mustafa Jarrar. 2017. Clustering arabic tweets for sentiment analysis. In *2017 IEEE/ACS 14th International Conference on Computer Systems and Applications (AICCSA)*, pages 449–456. IEEE.

Ghadah Adel and Yuping Wang. 2020. Detecting and classifying humanitarian crisis in arabic tweets. In *2020 3rd International Conference on Artificial Intelligence and Big Data (ICAIBD)*, pages 269–274. IEEE.

Lamia Al-Horaibi, M Badruddin Khan, and L Al-Horaibi Muhammad Badruddin Khan. 2017. Sentiment analysis of arabic tweets using semantic resources. *Int. J. Comput. Inf. Sci*, 13(1).

Rawan N Al-Matham and Hend S Al-Khalifa. 2021. Synoextractor: a novel pipeline for arabic synonym extraction using word2vec word embeddings. *Complexity*, 2021.

Firoj Alam, Shafiq Joty, and Muhammad Imran. 2018. Domain adaptation with adversarial training and graph embeddings. *arXiv preprint arXiv:1805.05151*.

Alaa Alharbi and Mark Lee. 2019. Crisis detection from arabic tweets. In *Proceedings of the 3rd workshop on arabic corpus linguistics*, pages 72–79.

Alaa Alharbi and Mark Lee. 2021. Kawarith: an arabic twitter corpus for crisis events. In *Proceedings of the Sixth Arabic Natural Language Processing Workshop*, pages 42–52.

Alaa Alharbi and Mark Lee. 2022. Classifying arabic crisis tweets using data selection and pre-trained language models. In *Proceedinsg of the 5th Workshop on Open-Source Arabic Corpora and Processing Tools with Shared Tasks on Qur'an QA and Fine-Grained Hate Speech Detection*, pages 71–78.

Reem Alrashdi and Simon O'Keefe. 2020. Automatic labeling of tweets for crisis response using distant supervision. In *Companion Proceedings of the Web Conference 2020*, pages 418–425.

Reem ALRashdi and Simon O'Keefe. 2019. Robust domain adaptation approach for tweet classification for crisis response. In *International Conference Europe Middle East & North Africa Information Systems and Technologies to Support Learning*, pages 124–134. Springer.

Yubo Chen, Shulin Liu, Xiang Zhang, Kang Liu, and Jun Zhao. 2017. Automatically labeled data generation for large scale event extraction. In *Proceedings of the 55th Annual Meeting of the Association for Computational Linguistics (Volume 1: Long Papers)*, pages 409–419.

David Chiang, Mona Diab, Nizar Habash, Owen Rambow, and Safiullah Shareef. 2006. Parsing arabic dialects. In *11th Conference of the European Chapter of the Association for Computational Linguistics*, pages 369–376.

Kenneth Church and Patrick Hanks. 1990. Word association norms, mutual information, and lexicography. *Computational linguistics*, 16(1):22–29.

EDDY MUNTINA DHARMA, FORD LUMBAN GAOL, HARCO LESLIE HENDRIC SPITS WARNARS, and BENFANO SOEWITO. 2022. The accuracy comparison among word2vec, glove, and fasttext towards convolution neural network (cnn) text classification. *Journal of Theoretical and Applied Information Technology*, 100(2).

Yasmeen George, Shanika Karunasekera, Aaron Harwood, and Kwan Hui Lim. 2021. Real-time spatio-temporal event detection on geotagged social media. *Journal of Big Data*, 8(1):1–28.

Maria Habib, Mohammad Faris, Alaa Alomari, and Hossam Faris. 2021. Altibbivec: A word embedding model for medical and health applications in the arabic language. *IEEE Access*, 9:133875–133888.

Karen Sparck Jones. 1972. A statistical interpretation of term specificity and its application in retrieval. *Journal of documentation*.

James Lane. 2019. The 10 most spoken languages in the world. *Babbel Magazine*, 6.

Hongmin Li. 2021. *Domain adaptation approaches for classifying social media crisis data*. Kansas State University.

Hongmin Li, Doina Caragea, and Cornelia Caragea. 2021. Combining self-training with deep learning for disaster tweet classification. In *The 18th International Conference on Information Systems for Crisis Response and Management (ISCRAM 2021)*.

Hongmin Li, Doina Caragea, Cornelia Caragea, and Nic Herndon. 2018a. Disaster response aided by tweet classification with a domain adaptation approach. *Journal of Contingencies and Crisis Management*, 26(1):16–27.

Hongmin Li, Oleksandra Sopova, Doina Caragea, and Cornelia Caragea. 2018b. Domain adaptation for crisis data using correlation alignment and self-training. *International Journal of Information Systems for Crisis Response and Management (IJISCRAM)*, 10(4):1–20.

Dat Tien Nguyen, Kamela Ali Al Mannai, Shafiq Joty, Hassan Sajjad, Muhammad Imran, and Prasenjit Mitra. 2017. Robust classification of crisis-related data on social networks using convolutional neural networks. In *Eleventh international AAAI conference on web and social media*.

Radwa MK Saeed, Sherine Rady, and Tarek F Gharib. 2022. An ensemble approach for spam detection in arabic opinion texts. *Journal of King*

Saud University-Computer and Information Sciences, 34(1):1407–1416.

Takeshi Sakaki, Makoto Okazaki, and Yutaka Matsuo. 2010. Earthquake shakes twitter users: real-time event detection by social sensors. In *Proceedings of the 19th international conference on World wide web*, pages 851–860.

Arun Kumar Sangaiah, Ahmed E Fakhry, Mohamed Abdel-Basset, and Ibrahim El-henawy. 2019. Arabic text clustering using improved clustering algorithms with dimensionality reduction. *Cluster Computing*, 22(2):4535–4549.

Muhammed Ali Sit, Caglar Koylu, and Ibrahim Demir. 2019. Identifying disaster-related tweets and their semantic, spatial and temporal context using deep learning, natural language processing and spatial analysis: a case study of hurricane irma. *International Journal of Digital Earth*.

Sakirin Tam, Rachid Ben Said, and Ö Özgür Tanriöver. 2021. A convbilstm deep learning model-based approach for twitter sentiment classification. *IEEE Access*, 9:41283–41293.

Ibtissam Touahri and Azzeddine Mazroui. 2021. Deep analysis of an arabic sentiment classification system based on lexical resource expansion and custom approaches building. *International Journal of Speech Technology*, 24(1):109–126.

Zeynep Tufekci and Christopher Wilson. 2012. Social media and the decision to participate in political protest: Observations from tahrir square. *Journal of communication*, 62(2):363–379.

Sarah Elizabeth Vieweg. 2012. *Situational awareness in mass emergency: A behavioral and linguistic analysis of microblogged communications*. Ph.D. thesis, University of Colorado at Boulder.

Si Si Mar Win and Than Nwe Aung. 2018. *Automated text annotation for social media data during natural disasters*. Ph.D. thesis, MERAL Portal.

Ying Zeng, Yansong Feng, Rong Ma, Zheng Wang, Rui Yan, Chongde Shi, and Dongyan Zhao. 2018. Scale up event extraction learning via automatic training data generation. In *Proceedings of the AAAI Conference on Artificial Intelligence*, volume 32.

Weakly and Semi-Supervised Learning for Arabic Text Classification using Monodialectal Language Models

Reem AlYami[2, 3] and **Rabeah Al-Zaidy**[1, 3]
[1]Center for Integrative Petroleum Research (CIPR), [2]Preparatory Year Program,
[3]Information and Computer Science Department
King Fahd University of Petroleum and Minerals
Saudi Arabia
reem.yami@kfupm.edu.sa, rabeah.alzaidy@kfupm.edu.sa

Abstract

The lack of resources such as annotated datasets and tools for low-resource languages is a significant obstacle to the advancement of Natural Language Processing (NLP) applications targeting users who speak these languages. Although learning techniques such as semi-supervised and weakly supervised learning are effective in text classification cases where annotated data is limited, they are still not widely investigated in many languages due to the sparsity of data altogether, both labeled and unlabeled. In this study, we deploy both weakly, and semi-supervised learning approaches for text classification in low-resource languages and address the underlying limitations that can hinder the effectiveness of these techniques. To that end, we propose a suite of language-agnostic techniques for large-scale data collection, automatic data annotation, and language model training in scenarios where resources are scarce. Specifically, we propose a novel data collection pipeline for under-represented languages, or dialects, that is language and task agnostic and of sufficient size for training a language model capable of achieving competitive results on common NLP tasks, as our experiments show. The models will be shared with the research community [1].

1 Introduction

In recent years, the emergence of social media platforms allowed the increased use of the informal form of a language in online user-generated content. As a result, more languages are present in online content, introducing a challenge to language processing tools that are developed to improve user experience. This is evident in the discrepancy in the levels of support for many tasks in language technologies for different languages, such as the lack of keyboard support and spell checking extensions for low resource languages, even those with a large online user base (Soria et al., 2018).

Supervised learning models for text classification are ubiquitous in natural language processing tasks (Minaee et al., 2021). For high-resource languages such as English, Chinese, and German, a variety of annotated datasets are constantly made available by both industry and academia (Wang et al., 2019a; Xu et al., 2020; Schabus et al., 2017). On the other hand, low-resource languages such as many Asian languages still suffer from a shortage of annotated datasets for fundamental NLP tasks, including text classification (Joshi et al., 2020). Given that many NLP applications, whether speech or text, heavily rely on classification, this shortage can negatively impact the accessibility of AI-enabled services to speakers of these languages (Minaee et al., 2020). To assist in reducing this gap of opportunity, a large body of studies in the NLP community is dedicated to facing challenges with low-resource languages using several approaches.

One approach is to focus on developing multilingual models that are capable of learning language-agnostic representations of data (Wang et al., 2020). Another approach uses meta-learning and few-shot learning models to improve results on tasks with small sets of annotated data (Pires et al., 2019; Artetxe et al., 2017). Adapting to small sets of data can also be achieved using semi-supervised models where a seed of annotated data is used to bootstrap a supervised model using only a relatively small set of labeled data (Van Engelen and Hoos, 2020). Weakly supervised models fall into this class of approaches as well, where primary external knowledge sources are incorporated to provide larger sets of annotated data for the model (Elnagar et al., 2019; Guellil et al., 2020). For extremely low-resourced languages, these techniques are difficult to apply due to the lack representative datasets whether labeled or unlabeled (Joshi et al., 2020).

In this work, we address the challenges facing incorporating learning techniques designed for scenarios where annotated data is scarce. Specifically,

[1]https://huggingface.co/reemalyami

Proceedings of the The Seventh Arabic Natural Language Processing Workshop (WANLP), pages 260 - 272
December 8, 2022 ©2022 Association for Computational Linguistics

for Arabic dialects, the main challenge is that in data sources where dialectal data in a raw form is abundant, it is rarely distinguished from other Arabic dialects, posing a challenge when the goal is to target a specific dialect. To that end, we curate and construct datasets and dictionaries, develop an automatic annotation scheme, develop multiple Pre-trained Language Models (PLMs) and conduct an empirical study to examine the performance of the text classification task under the learning paradigms of semi, weak and full supervision. Although Arabic is a widely spoken language, with over 400 million speakers, it still remains a low-resource language, especially in terms of the availability of annotated datasets for emerging NLP tasks (Althobaiti, 2020). Thus, the approaches proposed in this work, although testing on Arabic, are applicable to any similarly low-resourced language.

In summary, the contributions of this paper are:

1. Propose a novel data collection pipeline from Twitter that is language and task agnostic.
2. Construct seven Arabic dialect-specific dictionaries.
3. Develop an automatic annotation technique for Arabic dialects.
4. Train seven Arabic dialect-specific language models.
5. Propose a novel technique for Arabic dialect classification that improves over conventional semi-supervised methods.
6. Evaluate the performance of Arabic dialect identification in supervised, weakly supervised, and semi-supervised settings.

The remainder of this paper is organized as follows. In the next section we present related work. Section 3 presents the data collection and annotation pipeline. In Section 4 we describe the proposed language models. Section 5 describes the classification models. In Section 6 we describe the experimental setup and evaluation. In Section 7 we provide a discussion. In Section 8 we conclude and describe future directions for the work.

2 Related Work

2.1 Arabic Dialect Datasets

Arabic belongs to the group of *diglossic* languages, where different variations of the language are spoken in the community sharing the language. Arabic has two general forms, Modern Standard Arabic (MSA) the form used in written and formal communication among all speakers, and dialectal Arabic (DA), which are local variants of the language used in day-to-day communication varying based on region. In Arabic, there are multiple dialects in different regions of the Arab world: Gulf, Levantine and North Africa. Users commonly communicate in informal contexts using their local dialect rather than the formal MSA, more so in spoken than written. This introduces a challenge for Arabic-based applications. As a consequence of the scarcity of dialectal resources for Arabic, many studies focus on building Arabic dialectal corpora to investigate various NLP tasks in Arabic (Einea et al., 2019; Abdul-Mageed et al., 2020; Bouamor et al., 2018; Haouari et al., 2020; Elnagar et al., 2018; Hasanain et al., 2018) (Alyami and Olatunji, 2020; Al-Twairesh et al., 2018; Baly et al., 2019; Abdul-Mageed et al., 2018a; Abidi et al., 2017; Itani et al., 2017; Elnagar and Einea, 2016). Several of these datasets are publicly available (Haouari et al., 2020; Bouamor et al., 2018; Abdul-Mageed et al., 2020; Elnagar et al., 2018; Einea et al., 2019) and have greatly assisted both the research community and industry in tackling Arabic NLP challenges.

Datasets for the Arabic Dialect Identification (ADI) task vary in size, variety, granularity level, and the domain of the text. As seen in early work, datasets that investigate specific dialects on a specific domain, namely, news domain, do so on a certain granularity level that is the regional level (Zaidan and Callison-Burch, 2011, 2014; Malmasi et al., 2016). Other work developed dialectal datasets at the city and country levels. The first focuses on the dialects in specific cities in a country (Bouamor et al., 2018, 2019a; Abdul-Mageed et al., 2018b). Country-level studies focus on a specific country and all the sub-dialects spoke in that country. More recent works on the country level dialect focus on a specific task (Yang et al., 2020; Farha and Magdy, 2019; Habash et al., 2019) or investigate the combination of MSA data with other dialects (AlYami and AlZaidy, 2020; Alshargi et al., 2019; Khalifa et al., 2016). In many works, the collected data is based on crawling data from user-profile content, resulting in data samples that, semantically, represent the content discussed by specific users around a specific set of *seed words* (Abdul-Mageed et al., 2020; Bouamor et al., 2018, 2019a). In regards to automatic annotation of Arabic datasets, the existing tools focus specifically on linguistic annotation for limited Arabic varieties, especially MSA, which in turn cannot readily be used to annotate other dialects (Habash et al., 2009).

2.2 Arabic Dialect Identification

In many cases, it is beneficial to identify the specific dialect prior to performing core NLP tasks such as parsing, tokenizing or other downstream tasks such as semantic inference (Abdelali et al., 2016). For this reason, we conduct our study on the specific problem of Arabic dialect classification. Many ADI studies use n-gram based Language Model (LM) where they adopt different character level n-gram representations due to the Out Of Vocabulary (OOV) problem (Malmasi and Zampieri, 2017; Mishra and Mujadia, 2019; Ragab et al., 2019). Other features for classification such as Term Frequency — Inverse Document Frequency (TF-IDF) are used as well (Ragab et al., 2019; Bouamor et al., 2019b; Abdelali et al., 2021; Talafha et al., 2020; Gaanoun and Benelallam, 2020). Since many of these techniques lead to producing sparse representations, other work proposed utilizing static dense vectors (Elaraby and Abdul-Mageed, 2018; Meftouh et al., 2019).

Although dense vectors tend to improve classification performance in general, their adaptations in ADI yield results comparable to those of the n-gram models (Abu Farha and Magdy, 2019). Additionally, a key aspect to consider in Arabic dialects is *polysemous* words due to Arabic dialects having a shared vocabulary among them, yet the words in many cases have different meanings from one specific dialect to another (Zampieri and Nakov, 2021). Recent studies building on contextual features demonstrated promising results on a range of token and sequence classification tasks, including the dialect identification task (Zhang and Abdul-Mageed, 2019; Abdelali et al., 2021; Gaanoun and Benelallam, 2020; Abdelali et al., 2021).

Due to the shortage in datasets for many individual Arabic dialects, few efforts have utilized semi-supervised learning (SSL) in classifying Arabic dialects that showed promising results and some outperformed supervised learning approach (Zhang and Abdul-Mageed, 2019; Beltagy et al., 2020; Althobaiti, 2021). In recent years weak-supervision is utilized in text classification problems such as Arabic dialect identification, sentiment analysis and document classification as seen in the case of clinical text classification (Huang, 2015; Deriu et al., 2017; Meng et al., 2018; Wang et al., 2019b).

3 Data collection and annotation for low-resource languages

In this section we describe our proposed approaches for large data collection for specific languages and dialects and our automatic annotation approach for large data.

3.1 Large Data Collection

In order to build large datasets for low-resource languages we propose two approaches used to develop two datasets, Arabic Dialect Short Text dataset (ADST) and the Arabic Dialect Dictionary dataset (ADD). The collection approach for each is described below.

Arabic Dialect Short Text (ADST) is collected from Twitter, since many Arab countries are among the top 20 countries to use Twitter (Twi), in addition to the Twitter's feature that allows retrieving tweets given specific keywords. We use Tweepy API that permits data collection for research purposes under the digital millennium copyright act [2]. Our approach for language or dialect specific data, defines two parameters: keywords and the location of the dialect, defined using country geo-coordinates (latitude and longitude) via Free map online tool [3] (loc).

In contrast to studies where keywords are static, which limits dialect diversity and coverage (Bouamor et al., 2019a; Abdul-Mageed et al., 2020), we propose to collect keywords *dynamically*, i.e. collected from Twitter on a daily basis. Keyword are obtained from the *trending keywords* feature in Twitter for each of the targeted countries to capture words related to the speakers of a given dialect.

In order to collect country coordinates for Twitter Data Collection we divide this into two subcomponents. These components are as follows:

1. **Country Centric Point:** To ensure collecting dialectal tweets from the specified countries. One of the parameters that can be passed to the Twitter query is the latitude and longitude of the targeted point to collect tweets from

[2] https://help.twitter.com/en/rules-and-policies/copyright-policy

[3] https://www.freemaptools.com/radius-around-point.htm

the selected geographical location on the map. Since Twitter permits that a geometric centering point on the country's map is specified using latitude and longitude and curating all the tweets in the circle radius inside each country using an online tool to obtain these data points as illustrated in the Figure 1.

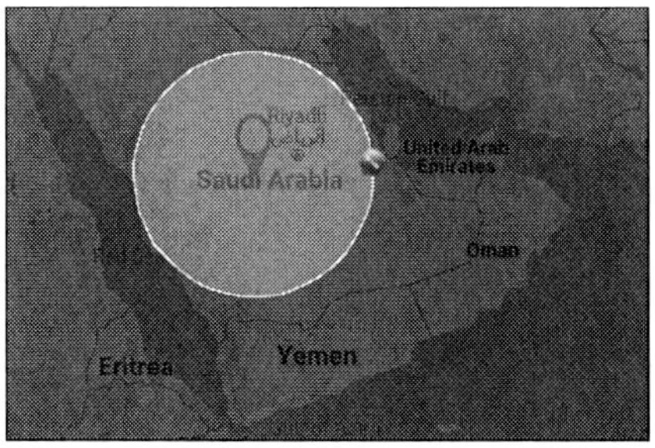

Figure 1: Specifying a centring geographical point in Saudi Arabia.

2. **Coordinates:** After defining a centring point the countries coordinates were retrieved along with area of the circle radius. In order to verify the retrieved coordinates another online tool is utilized were it yielded identical results [4].

Data Preprocessing

The preprocessing step includes de-duplication, Arabic letter normalization, removal of digits, character elongation, and samples with less than seven tokens in order to have richer representation. The effect of preprocessing on ADST size is shown in Table 1.

Country	Retrieved Tweets	Unique Tweets	7+ Tokens Tweets
Saudi Arabia (SA)	4,693,533	3,614,590	**2,415,622**
Egypt (EG)	5,677,800	3,313,610	**2,099,977**
Kuwait (KU)	4,047,308	823,546	**477,973**
Oman (OM)	665,463	316,500	**200,384**
Lebanon (LB)	670,715	294,275	**204,430**
Jordan (JO)	657,472	232,124	**97,400**
Algeria (DZ)	245,480	115,564	**103,488**

Table 1: ASTD size and the effect of the preprocessing on the tweets

Arabic Dialect Dictionary (ADD)

In this study a dictionary refers to a list of words and symbols that is usually used to automatically label data in case human annotation is unavailable as it is a cost effective method (Jurafsky and Martin, 2009). In our work seven Arabic dialectal dictionaries are built from different Arabic dialect sources. A dictionary for each country is built by collecting popular dialect-specific terms from public websites *Mo3jam* [5] and *Atlas Allhajaat* [6], where both sources provide a list of dialectal terms. The ADD is normalized using a similar process to ASTD in addition to stopword removal. Stopwords are collected from an online linguistic repository (El-Khair, 2017; ASW) of **1,614** stopwords. Finally, the ADD is reviewed by a human reviewer for final cleaning; the resulting dictionary description is shown in Table 2.

Country	SA	DZ	EG	JO	LB	KU	OM
#ADD	7,045	3,869	2,227	1,453	1,195	2,066	1,550

Table 2: The ADD Size

3.2 Automatic Data Annotation

Annotating a large dataset of Arabic dialects for the ADI task manually is costly, which introduces the need for an automatic annotation approach.

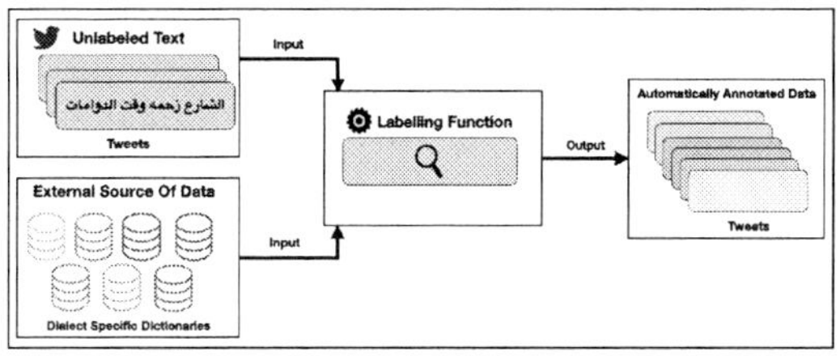

Figure 2: Tweets Automatic Annotation Process.

Our proposed automatic annotation process is shown in Figure 2. The annotation is performed through a labeling function that utilizes ADD as an external source to generate automatic labels. The data is annotated automatically using the dialect-specific dictionary (ADD), where the tweets curated from a particular country are labeled as a positive sample of the country dialect only if the tweet contains n or more tokens from the corresponding country's dictionary, as illustrated in Figure 3. In our work we set $n = 2$ after an empirical assessment. After annotating the dialect, each dialect has its own automatically annotated dataset. Each dataset contains the positive dialect instances, and for the negative samples, the other automatically labeled dialect samples from other dialects are incorporated, producing a balanced dataset. The size of the resulting dataset is shown in Table 3.

[4]https://latitude.to/lat/23.48690/lng/44.82030

[5]https://ar.mo3jam.com/

[6]http://www.atlasallhajaat.com/

Tweet	Identified Words
خوش حظر والله قاعدين يلعبون هالحزه	['خوش', 'هالحزه']

Figure 3: Sample tweet that is automatically labeled

Dialect	SA	DZ	EG	JO	LB	KU	OM
Total	104,976	61,860	104,976	17,496	20,304	53,052	29,664

Table 3: Automatically Annotated Data

4 AraRoBERTa

This section provides a description of the dialect-specific language models developed using the large datasets we collected. To obtain the Arabic RoBERTa (AraRoBERTa) models, we train 7 BERT-based models using the RoBERTa-base configuration with Masked Language Modeling (MLM) pre-training objective (Devlin et al., 2018; Liu et al., 2019). It consists of *12* encoder layers/blocks, *768* hidden dimensions, *12* attention heads, and *512* maximum sequence length (Devlin et al., 2018; Wolf et al., 2020). The batch size is 32 with 10 epochs after initial experimentation based on the loss. Although initial experimentation is done on the hyperparameter, the adopted values are similar to the literature.

The optimization is similar to the adopted BERT optimization (Liu et al., 2019), using the Adam optimizer (Kingma and Ba, 2017) with similar parameters. The collected tweets described in Section 3.1 from each dialect are utilized for pre-training the corresponding AraRoBERTa dialectal language model as shown in Table 4. We use the Byte Per Encoding (BPE) tokenizer using HuggingFace implementation [7]. BPE resolves the OOV problem, making it simpler, more efficient, and provides a small vocabulary size that is 52K (Sennrich et al., 2016). The developed AraRoBERTa models and the selected contextual baselines are described in Table 4 in term of the Arabic training data, the vocabulary size and the model configuration. In this work AraRoBERTa is built using HuggingFace Transformers API (Wolf et al., 2020) on (1x16GB NVIDIA Tesla P100) GPU.

Also, other contextual baselines are used to compare the performance of AraRoBERTa variations against as shown in Table 4. These models are: 1) **mBERT**: The multilingual version of BERT that is trained on 100 languages including Arabic (Devlin et al., 2018). 2) **XLM-R** The multilingual version of RoBERTa that is trained on 100 languages (Conneau et al., 2020). 3) **AraBERT** A monolingual model developed on Arabic specifically MSA (Antoun et al., 2020).

[7] https://huggingface.co/docs/transformers/tokenizer_summary#byte-pair-encoding

5 ADI Models

The ADI task is formed as a classification task. We adopt three classification models using semi and weak supervision paradigms. In these models, we build on a transformer-based classifier. In this section, we provide an overview of our proposed models.

5.1 Dialect Classification Problem

The Arabic dialect classification problem is defined as follows. Given a set of short texts,

$$D = \{(t_1, y_1), (t_2, y_2), ...(t_n, y_n)\}$$

where t denotes the short text instances, n denotes the number of instances and the label is denoted by $Y = \{P, N\}$ where P represent a specific Arabic dialect and N represent the negative samples that does not belong to the dialect, the model performs binary classification to assign each t_i a y_j label.

5.2 Semi-Supervised Model

The conventional SSL approach known as *self-training* illustrated in Figure 4 does not ensure having negative samples in the training data since the data is collected from a specific country affecting the performance of the model. Hence, another semi-supervised approach is proposed to mitigate the limitation of the conventional SSL approach.

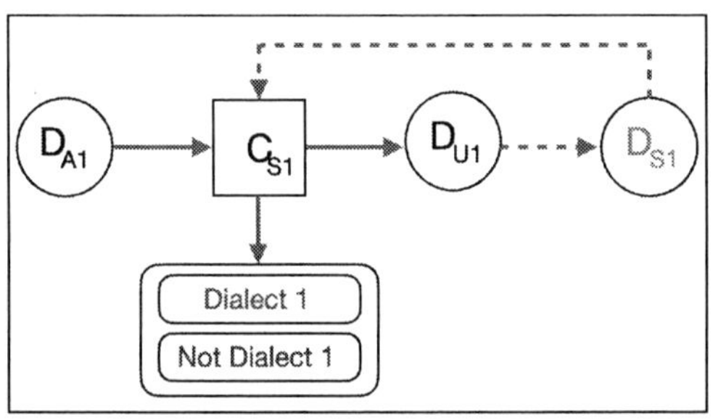

Figure 4: The pipeline for conventional semi-supervised classification model.

The proposed SSL task learns from both the labeled and unlabeled data. For the labeled data, we manually annotated dataset as follows. A human expert labels each tweet as belonging to one of

Model	Training Data			Vocabulary		Configuration	
	Source	Variant	#Tokens	Tokenizer	Size	Arch.	#Params.
mBERT	Wikipedia	MSA/Multi-Lang	Ar(153M)/All(1.5B)	WP	Ar(5K)/All(110K)	base	110M
XLM-R_B	CommonCrawl	MSA/Multi-Lang	Ar(2.9B)/All(295B)	SP	Ar(14K)/All(250K)	base	270M
AraBERT	Several (3 sources)	MSA	2.5B	SP	Ar(60K)/All(64K)	base	135M
AraRoBERTa-SA	Arabic Twitter	SA DA	45.4M	BPE	52K	base	126M
AraRoBERTa-EG		EG DA	37.2M	BPE	52K	base	126M
AraRoBERTa-KU		KU DA	8.9M	BPE	52K	base	126M
AraRoBERTa-OM		OM DA	3.8M	BPE	52K	base	126M
AraRoBERTa-LB		LB DA	3.6M	BPE	52K	base	126M
AraRoBERTa-JO		JO DA	2.6M	BPE	52K	base	126M
AraRoBERTa-DZ		DZ DA	1.9M	BPE	52K	base	126M

Table 4: Configurations of existing models and AraRoBERTa models. WP is WordPiece and SP is SentencePiece tokenizers.

seven pre-defined dialects which is then reviewed by another expert. Both annotators are either native speakers or closely familiar with the dialect. The seven dialects we consider are: Saudi Arabia, Kuwait, Oman, and Egypt, Algeria, Jordan, and Lebanon. For the last 3 countries, native speakers are recruited to label the data from a freelance service website [8]. The annotators are compensated based on their offer in the platform. A request explaining the required task is raised, then each freelancer offers her/his services with the price defined by the freelancer. If a mutual agreement is reached, the freelancer is paid before performing the task.

Only annotators with the location corresponding to the needed dialect were hired. A meeting with each freelancer is conducted to explain the task then an initial sample of 10 tweets is annotated by the annotator to ensure the task is understood by the annotator. In addition to this data, the dataset from the NADI shared task, released under the creative commons license, is used (Abdul-Mageed et al., 2020). The proposed semi-supervised model is illustrated in Figure 5. For dialect i the classifier C_{Si} takes as an input the annotated data D_A and after initial training it is utilized to produce the pseudo-labels: $Y_S = \{P_S, N_S\}$ on the unlabeled data D_U. In the pseudo-labeled data D_{Si} the negative samples are denoted by $N_{S_i} = P_{S_1}, \ldots P_{S_{m-1}}$ where $P_{S_i} \notin N_{S_i}$ and $|P_{S_i}| == |N_{S_i}|$ as illustrated in the figure where the colors denote the negative sample that corresponds to the positive sample for each dialect. That is then augmented with the labeled data for the model to train on both data until the defined termination criteria is reached.

[8] `https://khamsat.com/`

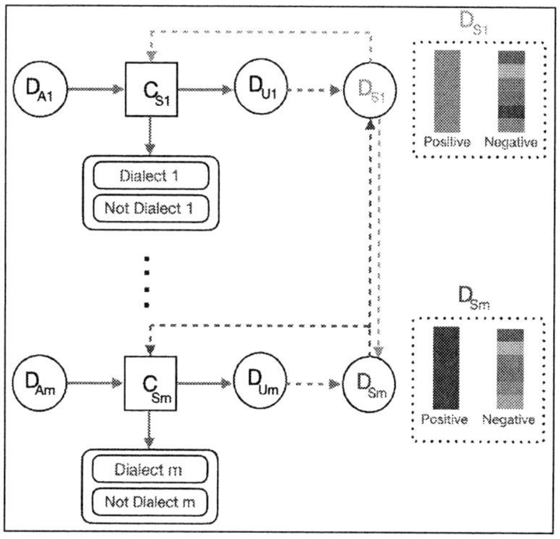

Figure 5: The pipeline for the proposed semi-supervised classification model.

5.3 Weakly-Supervised Model

This learning task learns from unlabeled data by providing an approximate label. The set of weak labels (class) are assigned using a labelling function g that utilizes an external source of information to annotate the unlabeled instances D_U producing Y_W, where $Y_W = \{P_w, N_w\}$, denoting a weak label. This is performed on all unlabeled data to create a new training set $D_W = \{(t_{w1}, y_{w1}), (t_{w2}, y_{w2}), ...(t_{wm}, y_{wm})\}$, where m denotes the number of samples and $w_i \in Y_W$. Here the labels Y_W are produced automatically, as illustrated in Figure 6. The weakly labeled data D_W produced by the automatic annotator for dialect i is subsequently used to train a binary classifier C_{Wi} to predict dialect i.

6 Experiments and Evaluation

Here we describe the evaluation experiments for fully, semi and weakly supervised learning models

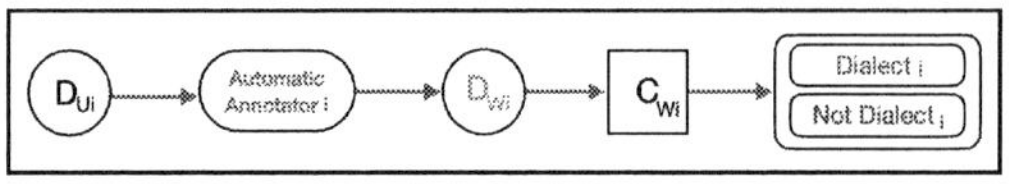

Figure 6: The pipeline for the weakly-supervised classification model.

for the ADI task. The performance is evaluated using the F-1 measure, following existing literature.

6.1 Supervised ADI

We follow an experimental setup similar to the pre-training task as described in Section 4 except for the number of epochs, which is five. This experiment evaluates the performance of AraRoBERTa variations on the dialect classification task using the manually annotated data described earlier with a train/validation/test split of 70/10/20 respectively. Additionally, the results are compared with other contextual baselines described earlier and with a traditional machine learning model, namely, Logistic Regression (LR) as it yielded the best results on the same task in a previous study (AlYami and AlZaidy, 2020). The training data for LR is similar to the ones described above and TF-IDF is used to represent text. The experiment is preformed with 10-fold cross validation and a train/test split of 80/20.

Experimental Results The results for the supervised experiments are shown in Table 5. Larger AraRoBERTa models, namely, AraRoBERTa-SA and AraRoBERTa-EG, outperform other models. AraRoBERTa-KU model outperforms its multilingual counterparts and is slightly lower than AraBERT. In other cases, both AraRoBERTa and AraBERT yielded similar results, and the other multilingual models outperformed them. Except for AraRoBERTa-OM yielding the lowest performance among other models. Although AraRoBERTa models are trained on maximum 1.8% of the data that AraBERT is trained on, it yields very competitive results. In five out of seven AraRoBERTa flavors, it outperformed the contextual baseline models as shown in Table 5.

For the remaining two, although trained an even smaller fraction, it yielded a similar performance to AraBERT and multilingual models. This encourages training other models on a specific content even if the available data size is smaller compared to other training data in the literature. Additionally, when comparing AraRoBERTa against LR the two largest AraRoBERTa models outperform it. Also, AraRoBERTa-KU yields a slightly lower result. However, from the results, when having access to small dataset size, traditional ML performs better.

Dialect	AraRoBERTa	AraBERT	mBERT	XLMR	LR
SA	**0.836**	0.806	0.823	0.784	0.791
EG	**0.934**	0.898	0.872	0.879	0.862
KU	0.916	0.913	0.883	0.886	**0.921**
OM	0.718	0.845	0.839	**0.896**	0.883
LB	0.849	0.849	0.879	0.866	**0.892**
JO	0.848	0.856	0.872	0.833	**0.881**
DZ	0.859	0.855	0.873	0.908	**0.923**

Table 5: The supervised classification results. The best results are in bold.

6.2 Semi-supervised ADI

The performance of semi-supervised classifiers is evaluated on the same test set used in the supervised baseline. Then, it is compared against it. The sample size for the unlabeled data is reduced due to computational limitations where a random sample of 16,000 training samples are selected to perform the semi-supervised experiments with a 0.95 threshold for the prediction confidence for the pseudo-labeled instances. The training stops when the remaining unlabeled data points are less than 5% .

Experimental Results The results of the SSL classifier are shown in Table 6. We can notice it outperforms the performance of the supervised models in multiple dialects. Also, we can notice that AraRoBERTa-Om and AraRoBERTa-LB that were built on the lower end in terms of training data, yield better performance than its supervised AraRoBERTa counterparts.

Dialect	Supervised	SSL
SA	**0.84**	0.83
EG	**0.93**	**0.93**
KU	**0.92**	0.89
OM	0.72	**0.80**
LB	0.85	**0.88**
JO	**0.85**	0.83
DZ	0.86	**0.87**

Table 6: The semi-supervised classification results. The best results are in bold.

6.3 Weak-supervised Dialect Classification

The performance of weak-supervised classifiers is evaluated on the same test set used in the supervised baseline. Then, it is compared against it. This setup follows the supervised setup, however, the number of epochs is different since initial experiments showed that three epochs are suitable as the training data is larger and the training loss flattens before reaching three epochs.

Experimental Results The results for the weak-supervised experiments are shown in Table 7 in general for all models across dialects yield lower performance compared to AraRoBERTa supervised classifiers as shown by the performance change. Although the classification data size is larger by around *6x* for the Jordan dialect and up to *33x* for Saudi dialect. However, the degrade in performance is noticeable in AraRoBERTa models trained on smaller data size like AraRoBERTa-JO rather than larger models like AraRoBERTa-SA.

Dialect	Supervised	WSL
SA	**0.84**	0.81
EG	**0.93**	0.86
KU	**0.92**	0.61
OM	**0.72**	0.40
LB	**0.85**	0.78
JO	**0.85**	0.71
DZ	**0.86**	0.78

Table 7: The weak-supervised classification results. The best results are in bold.

7 Discussion

This section provides an analysis for the experimental results and discusses the significant findings.

7.1 Supervised Classification Model

As shown in the experiments above, we note that the least performing model on the supervised classification task is AraRoBERTa-OM. The model has a false-negative rate of 20.75%, whereas the false-positive rate is only 2.25%, indicating a bias towards rejecting Omani texts although the model is balanced for positive and negative samples. To probe this further, the model was tested again on a slightly-modified version of the test set, where we replaced positive samples that were misclassified by the model, with different positive samples that contained more Omani-specific terms. The amount of replaced samples is around 10% of the test data. As a result, the ability of the model to identify the Oman dialect increased, reflected by an 3% increase in the true-positive rate and a decrease in the false-negatives from the previous 20.75% to 18.12%. This can be due to the training set of AraRoBERTa-OM, which could have contained a larger portion of utterances with majority of tokens are Omani specific terms and did not account for ones with majority of tokens that are common with other dialects.

In other cases, the classification inaccuracies may not be a result of the training set for the language model but rather be due to the dialect itself. For instance, AraRoBERTa-SA and AraRoBERTa-LB both exhibit a more inclusive bias, i.e. labeling other dialects as positive, with false-positive rates of 11.38% and 11.62%, respectively, compared to low false-negatives of around 4% for each. To probe this further we examine missclassified samples in the test set, where we show some examples in Figures 7 and 8. For the examples in Figure 7 , although the full tweet belongs to another dialect, Jordan dialect, we can see all of the words in the tweet can be used by Saudi speakers in regions near the Saudi/Jordan border.

On the other hand, in Figure 8, the first sample is Egyptian dialect where the second is Saudi, using words that are specific to these dialects. This contrast indicates that a bias towards false-positives can be attributed to either a training set for the language model that is not sufficiently representative of the dialect, or to the approach with which Arabic dialects are generally defined, i.e. by country. Typically, regions along the borders of countries commonly share a similar dialect, which in certain datasets becomes more pronounced in cases of large and centrally located countries such as Saudi Arabia.

اخوي جاب ايفون برو حكالي بطاريته احسن من الايفونات الي قبل
علي الاقل هي خلصت توجيهي معها حق شوي انتي بشو مريتي

Figure 7: A sample of the misclassified tweets by AraRoBERTa-SA, these samples are negative samples. However, the model classified them as Saudi.

7.2 Semi-supervised Learning

The results of the SSL classifier are shown in Table 8. Note that the performance at iteration-0 is supervised and semi-supervised at iteration 1 and 2.

اذا بفتح كمان سناب حد ويلاقيه حاطط لقيت الطيطبه رح اسويله ديليت ماصارت اغنيه ترا
تو جالسين نتقق ف سناب انتي اول وحده تروحي

Figure 8: A sample of the misclassified tweets by AraRoBERTa-LB, these samples are negative samples. However, the model classified them as Lebanese.

The performance in later iterations outperforms the model's performance at iteration-0 in the majority of the models. Indicating the effectiveness of the proposed approach.

LM	Iteration	Training	F-1	Remaining %
AraRoBERTa-SA	0	2,800	0.818	9%
	1	28,528	**0.834**	7%
	2	30,028	0.83	<1%
AraRoBERTa-EG	0	2,800	0.933	63%
	1	17,020	**0.925**	34%
	2	23,608	0.911	2%
AraRoBERTa-KU	0	2,800	0.902	68%
	1	17,416	0.882	28%
	2	22,420	**0.886**	2%
AraRoBERTa-OM	0	2,800	0.84	51 %
	1	17,284	**0.802**	43%
	2	22,564	0.784	3%
AraRoBERTa-LB	0	2,800	0.876	72%
	1	23,440	**0.883**	25%
	2	27,928	0.864	1%
AraRoBERTa-JO	0	2,800	0.839	65%
	1	20,488	**0.832**	32%
	2	27,016	0.812	<1%
AraRoBERTa-DZ	0	2,800	0.859	84%
	1	27,016	0.854	13%
	2	29,608	**0.873**	<1%

Table 8: The semi-supervised classifiers results. The *Remaining %* equals the *remaining samples/original sample size (16K)*.

7.3 Weak-supervised Classification Model

In order to understand the results obtained by the AraRoBERTa models in weak-supervised setup, we looked at the performance of the models on the validation data as shown in Table 9. We can see the results obtained indicate the model learned from the automatically labeled data and obtained high results. However, the performance on the test data indicates that the models with lower results have learned from noisy samples, which can be one of the downsides of utilizing this approach. Here we can see this when comparing supervised AraRoBERTa-KU and the weak-supervised AraRoBERTa-KU, we can see the model is predicting the automatic positive sample as a negative sample. Indicating that these samples are noisy since the supervised version can identify the positive samples easily. On the other hand, we can see the effectiveness of weak-supervised on the same task but in different dialects like SA and EG. Providing a promising way of automatically labeling the dialect given a model trained on large data like SA and EG.

Dialect	Validation	Test	Performance Change
SA	0.9	0.812	-8.8%
EG	0.955	0.857	-9.8%
KU	0.948	0.744	-20.4%
OM	0.915	0.404	-51.1%
LB	0.966	0.783	-18.3%
JO	0.884	0.708	-17.6%
DZ	0.929	0.776	-15.3%

Table 9: The performance of AraRoBERTa in the weak-supervised setting on both the validation and test phases in all dialects based on the F-1 score.

8 Conclusion

This paper proposed different approaches for Arabic dialect text classification as a low-resource scenario and conducted an empirical study to evaluate the performance of the adopted approaches. The paper proposed a novel data collection pipeline from Twitter that is language and task agnostic.

Also, developed dialect-specific contextual language models to learn from unlabeled data that yield effective and stable performance across dialects, as seen in supervised classification. While AraRoBERTa models were pretrained on a fraction of the data size that other contextual baselines were trained on, the results showed that most of the supervised AraRoBERTa models outperformed these models. In addition, when compared to the traditional ML model, larger AraRoBERTa models outperform it as well.

Additionally, to the best of our knowledge, we constructed the first dialectal dictionary to utilize it in the automatic annotation in scenarios where labeled data are not available and then utilized in a weak-supervised task. Although the automatic function contains one hand-crafted rule, this approach is a promising technique for annotating large data and utilizing it in a text classification task. Also, the proposed SSL model can be adopted when only a few labeled examples are available where it shows its effectiveness and stability.

References

Arabic stop words. http://www.abuelkhair.net/index.php/en/arabic/arabic-stop-words. (Accessed on 10/22/2021).

Filtering tweets by location | docs | twitter developer platform. https://developer.twitter.com/en/docs/tutorials/filtering-tweets-by-location. (Accessed on 01/02/2022).

Twitter: most users by country | statista. https://www.statista.com/statistics/242606/\number-of-active-twitter-users-in\-selected-countries/. (Accessed on 07/28/2021).

Ahmed Abdelali, Kareem Darwish, Nadir Durrani, and Hamdy Mubarak. 2016. Farasa: A fast and furious segmenter for arabic. In *Proceedings of the 2016 conference of the North American chapter of the association for computational linguistics: Demonstrations*, pages 11–16.

Ahmed Abdelali, Hamdy Mubarak, Younes Samih, Sabit Hassan, and Kareem Darwish. 2021. QADI: Arabic dialect identification in the wild. In *Proceedings of the Sixth Arabic Natural Language Processing Workshop*, pages 1–10, Kyiv, Ukraine (Virtual). Association for Computational Linguistics.

Muhammad Abdul-Mageed, Hassan Alhuzali, and Mohamed Elaraby. 2018a. You tweet what you speak: A city-level dataset of arabic dialects. In *Proceedings of the Eleventh International Conference on Language Resources and Evaluation (LREC 2018)*.

Muhammad Abdul-Mageed, Hassan Alhuzali, and Mohamed Elaraby. 2018b. You tweet what you speak: A city-level dataset of Arabic dialects. In *Proceedings of the Eleventh International Conference on Language Resources and Evaluation (LREC 2018)*, Miyazaki, Japan. European Language Resources Association (ELRA).

Muhammad Abdul-Mageed, Chiyu Zhang, Houda Bouamor, and Nizar Habash. 2020. NADI 2020: The First Nuanced Arabic Dialect Identification Shared Task. In *Proceedings of the Fifth Arabic Natural Language Processing Workshop (WANLP 2020)*, Barcelona, Spain.

Karima Abidi, Mohamed Amine Menacer, and Kamel Smaili. 2017. Calyou: A comparable spoken algerian corpus harvested from youtube. In *18th Annual Conference of the International Communication Association (Interspeech)*.

Ibrahim Abu Farha and Walid Magdy. 2019. Mazajak: An online Arabic sentiment analyser. In *Proceedings of the Fourth Arabic Natural Language Processing Workshop*, pages 192–198, Florence, Italy. Association for Computational Linguistics.

Nora Al-Twairesh, Rawan Al-Matham, Nora Madi, Nada Almugren, Al-Hanouf Al-Aljmi, Shahad Alshalan, Raghad Alshalan, Nafla Alrumayyan, Shams Al-Manea, Sumayah Bawazeer, et al. 2018. Suar: Towards building a corpus for the saudi dialect. *Procedia computer science*, 142:72–82.

Faisal Alshargi, Shahd Dibas, Sakhar Alkhereyf, Reem Faraj, Basmah Abdulkareem, Sane Yagi, Ouafaa Kacha, Nizar Habash, and Owen Rambow. 2019. Morphologically annotated corpora for seven Arabic dialects: Taizi, sanaani, najdi, jordanian, syrian, iraqi and Moroccan. In *Proceedings of the Fourth Arabic Natural Language Processing Workshop*, pages 137–147, Florence, Italy. Association for Computational Linguistics.

Maha J. Althobaiti. 2020. Automatic arabic dialect identification systems for written texts: A survey.

Maha J Althobaiti. 2021. Country-level arabic dialect identification using small datasets with integrated machine learning techniques and deep learning models. In *Proceedings of the Sixth Arabic Natural Language Processing Workshop*, pages 265–270.

R. AlYami and R. AlZaidy. 2020. Arabic dialect identification in social media. In *2020 3rd International Conference on Computer Applications Information Security (ICCAIS)*, pages 1–2.

Sarah N Alyami and Sunday O Olatunji. 2020. Application of support vector machine for arabic sentiment classification using twitter-based dataset. *Journal of Information & Knowledge Management*, 19(01):2040018.

Wissam Antoun, Fady Baly, and Hazem Hajj. 2020. AraBERT: Transformer-based model for Arabic language understanding. In *Proceedings of the 4th Workshop on Open-Source Arabic Corpora and Processing Tools, with a Shared Task on Offensive Language Detection*, pages 9–15, Marseille, France. European Language Resource Association.

Mikel Artetxe, Gorka Labaka, and Eneko Agirre. 2017. Learning bilingual word embeddings with (almost) no bilingual data. In *Proceedings of the 55th Annual Meeting of the Association for Computational Linguistics (Volume 1: Long Papers)*, pages 451–462, Vancouver, Canada. Association for Computational Linguistics.

Ramy Baly, Alaa Khaddaj, Hazem Hajj, Wassim El-Hajj, and Khaled Bashir Shaban. 2019. Arsentd-lev: A multi-topic corpus for target-based sentiment analysis in arabic levantine tweets. *arXiv preprint arXiv:1906.01830*.

Ahmad Beltagy, Abdelrahman Wael, and Omar ElSherief. 2020. Arabic dialect identification using bert-based domain adaptation. *arXiv preprint arXiv:2011.06977*.

Houda Bouamor, Nizar Habash, Mohammad Salameh, Wajdi Zaghouani, Owen Rambow, Dana Abdulrahim, Ossama Obeid, Salam Khalifa, Fadhl Eryani, Alexander Erdmann, et al. 2018. The madar arabic dialect corpus and lexicon. In *Proceedings of the eleventh international conference on language resources and evaluation (LREC 2018)*.

Houda Bouamor, Sabit Hassan, and Nizar Habash. 2019a. The MADAR shared task on Arabic fine-grained dialect identification. In *Proceedings of the Fourth Arabic Natural Language Processing Workshop*, pages 199–207, Florence, Italy. Association for Computational Linguistics.

Houda Bouamor, Sabit Hassan, and Nizar Habash. 2019b. The MADAR shared task on Arabic fine-grained dialect identification. In *Proceedings of the Fourth Arabic Natural Language Processing Workshop*, pages 199–207, Florence, Italy. Association for Computational Linguistics.

Alexis Conneau, Kartikay Khandelwal, Naman Goyal, Vishrav Chaudhary, Guillaume Wenzek, Francisco Guzmán, Edouard Grave, Myle Ott, Luke Zettlemoyer, and Veselin Stoyanov. 2020. Unsupervised cross-lingual representation learning at scale. In *Proceedings of the 58th Annual Meeting of the Association for Computational Linguistics*, pages 8440–8451, Online. Association for Computational Linguistics.

Jan Deriu, Aurélien Lucchi, Valeria De Luca, Aliaksei Severyn, Simon Müller, Mark Cieliebak, Thomas Hofmann, and Martin Jaggi. 2017. Leveraging large amounts of weakly supervised data for multi-language sentiment classification. *Proceedings of the 26th International Conference on World Wide Web*.

Jacob Devlin, Ming-Wei Chang, Kenton Lee, and Kristina Toutanova. 2018. Bert: Pre-training of deep bidirectional transformers for language understanding. *arXiv preprint arXiv:1810.04805*.

Omar Einea, Ashraf Elnagar, and Ridhwan Al Debsi. 2019. Sanad: Single-label arabic news articles dataset for automatic text categorization. *Data in brief*, 25:104076.

Ibrahim Abu El-Khair. 2017. Effects of stop words elimination for arabic information retrieval: A comparative study.

Mohamed Elaraby and Muhammad Abdul-Mageed. 2018. Deep models for Arabic dialect identification on benchmarked data. In *Proceedings of the Fifth Workshop on NLP for Similar Languages, Varieties and Dialects (VarDial 2018)*, pages 263–274, Santa Fe, New Mexico, USA. Association for Computational Linguistics.

Ashraf Elnagar and Omar Einea. 2016. Brad 1.0: Book reviews in arabic dataset. In *2016 IEEE/ACS 13th International Conference of Computer Systems and Applications (AICCSA)*, pages 1–8. IEEE.

Ashraf Elnagar, Omar Einea, and Ridhwan Al-Debsi. 2019. Automatic text tagging of arabic news articles using ensemble deep learning models. In *Proceedings of the 3rd International Conference on Natural Language and Speech Processing*, pages 59–66.

Ashraf Elnagar, Yasmin S Khalifa, and Anas Einea. 2018. Hotel arabic-reviews dataset construction for sentiment analysis applications. In *Intelligent natural language processing: Trends and applications*, pages 35–52. Springer.

Ibrahim Abu Farha and Walid Magdy. 2019. Mazajak: An online arabic sentiment analyser. In *Proceedings of the Fourth Arabic Natural Language Processing Workshop*, pages 192–198.

Kamel Gaanoun and Imade Benelallam. 2020. Arabic dialect identification: An Arabic-BERT model with data augmentation and ensembling strategy. In *Proceedings of the Fifth Arabic Natural Language Processing Workshop*, pages 275–281, Barcelona, Spain (Online). Association for Computational Linguistics.

Imane Guellil, Faical Azouaou, and Francisco Chiclana. 2020. Arautosenti: automatic annotation and new tendencies for sentiment classification of arabic messages. *Social Network Analysis and Mining*, 10(1):1–20.

Nizar Habash, Houda Bouamor, and Christine Chung. 2019. Automatic gender identification and reinflection in arabic. In *Proceedings of the First Workshop on Gender Bias in Natural Language Processing*, pages 155–165.

Nizar Habash, Owen Rambow, and Ryan Roth. 2009. Mada+ tokan: A toolkit for arabic tokenization, diacritization, morphological disambiguation, pos tagging, stemming and lemmatization. In *Proceedings of the 2nd international conference on Arabic language resources and tools (MEDAR), Cairo, Egypt*, volume 41, page 62.

Fatima Haouari, Maram Hasanain, Reem Suwaileh, and Tamer Elsayed. 2020. Arcov-19: The first arabic covid-19 twitter dataset with propagation networks. *arXiv preprint arXiv:2004.05861*.

Maram Hasanain, Reem Suwaileh, Tamer Elsayed, Mucahid Kutlu, and Hind Almerekhi. 2018. Evetar: building a large-scale multi-task test collection over arabic tweets. *Information Retrieval Journal*, 21(4):307–336.

Fei Huang. 2015. Improved arabic dialect classification with social media data. In *Proceedings of the 2015 Conference on Empirical Methods in Natural Language Processing*, pages 2118–2126.

Maher Itani, Chris Roast, and Samir Al-Khayatt. 2017. Corpora for sentiment analysis of arabic text in social media. In *2017 8th international conference on information and communication systems (ICICS)*, pages 64–69. IEEE.

Pratik Joshi, Sebastin Santy, Amar Budhiraja, Kalika Bali, and Monojit Choudhury. 2020. The state and fate of linguistic diversity and inclusion in the NLP world. In *Proceedings of the 58th Annual Meeting of the Association for Computational Linguistics*, pages 6282–6293, Online. Association for Computational Linguistics.

D. Jurafsky and J.H. Martin. 2009. *Speech and Language Processing: An Introduction to Natural Language Processing, Computational Linguistics, and Speech Recognition*. Prentice Hall series in artificial intelligence. Pearson Prentice Hall.

Salam Khalifa, Nizar Habash, Dana Abdulrahim, and Sara Hassan. 2016. A large scale corpus of Gulf Arabic. In *Proceedings of the Tenth International Conference on Language Resources and Evaluation (LREC'16)*, pages 4282–4289, Portorož, Slovenia. European Language Resources Association (ELRA).

Diederik P. Kingma and Jimmy Ba. 2017. Adam: A method for stochastic optimization.

Yinhan Liu, Myle Ott, Naman Goyal, Jingfei Du, Mandar Joshi, Danqi Chen, Omer Levy, Mike Lewis, Luke Zettlemoyer, and Veselin Stoyanov. 2019. Roberta: A robustly optimized bert pretraining approach. *arXiv preprint arXiv:1907.11692*.

Shervin Malmasi and Marcos Zampieri. 2017. Arabic dialect identification using iVectors and ASR transcripts. In *Proceedings of the Fourth Workshop on NLP for Similar Languages, Varieties and Dialects (VarDial)*, pages 178–183, Valencia, Spain. Association for Computational Linguistics.

Shervin Malmasi, Marcos Zampieri, Nikola Ljubešić, Preslav Nakov, Ahmed Ali, and Jörg Tiedemann. 2016. Discriminating between similar languages and Arabic dialect identification: A report on the third DSL shared task. In *Proceedings of the Third Workshop on NLP for Similar Languages, Varieties and Dialects (VarDial3)*, pages 1–14, Osaka, Japan. The COLING 2016 Organizing Committee.

Karima Meftouh, Karima Abidi, Salima Harrat, and Kamel Smaili. 2019. The SMarT classifier for Arabic fine-grained dialect identification. In *Proceedings of the Fourth Arabic Natural Language Processing Workshop*, pages 259–263, Florence, Italy. Association for Computational Linguistics.

Yu Meng, Jiaming Shen, Chao Zhang, and Jiawei Han. 2018. Weakly-supervised neural text classification. In *Proceedings of the 27th ACM International Conference on Information and Knowledge Management*, pages 983–992.

Shervin Minaee, Nal Kalchbrenner, Erik Cambria, Narjes Nikzad, Meysam Chenaghlu, and Jianfeng Gao. 2020. Deep learning based text classification: A comprehensive review. *CoRR*, abs/2004.03705.

Shervin Minaee, Nal Kalchbrenner, Erik Cambria, Narjes Nikzad, Meysam Chenaghlu, and Jianfeng Gao. 2021. Deep learning–based text classification: A comprehensive review. *ACM Comput. Surv.*, 54(3).

Pruthwik Mishra and Vandan Mujadia. 2019. Arabic dialect identification for travel and Twitter text. In *Proceedings of the Fourth Arabic Natural Language Processing Workshop*, pages 234–238, Florence, Italy. Association for Computational Linguistics.

Telmo Pires, Eva Schlinger, and Dan Garrette. 2019. How multilingual is multilingual BERT? In *Proceedings of the 57th Annual Meeting of the Association for Computational Linguistics*, pages 4996–5001, Florence, Italy. Association for Computational Linguistics.

Ahmad Ragab, Haitham Seelawi, Mostafa Samir, Abdelrahman Mattar, Hesham Al-Bataineh, Mohammad Zaghloul, Ahmad Mustafa, Bashar Talafha, Abed Alhakim Freihat, and Hussein Al-Natsheh. 2019. Mawdoo3 AI at MADAR shared task: Arabic fine-grained dialect identification with ensemble learning. In *Proceedings of the Fourth Arabic Natural Language Processing Workshop*, pages 244–248, Florence, Italy. Association for Computational Linguistics.

Dietmar Schabus, Marcin Skowron, and Martin Trapp. 2017. One million posts: A data set of german online discussions. In *Proceedings of the 40th International ACM SIGIR Conference on Research and Development in Information Retrieval*, SIGIR '17, page 1241–1244, New York, NY, USA. Association for Computing Machinery.

Rico Sennrich, Barry Haddow, and Alexandra Birch. 2016. Neural machine translation of rare words with subword units. In *Proceedings of the 54th Annual Meeting of the Association for Computational Linguistics (Volume 1: Long Papers)*, pages 1715–1725, Berlin, Germany. Association for Computational Linguistics.

Claudia Soria, Valeria Quochi, and Irene Russo. 2018. The DLDP survey on digital use and usability of EU regional and minority languages. In *Proceedings of the Eleventh International Conference on Language Resources and Evaluation (LREC 2018)*, Miyazaki, Japan. European Language Resources Association (ELRA).

Bashar Talafha, Mohammad Ali, Muhy Eddin Za'ter, Haitham Seelawi, Ibraheem Tuffaha, Mostafa Samir, Wael Farhan, and Hussein T Al-Natsheh. 2020. Multi-dialect arabic bert for country-level dialect identification. *arXiv preprint arXiv:2007.05612*.

Jesper E Van Engelen and Holger H Hoos. 2020. A survey on semi-supervised learning. *Machine Learning*, 109(2):373–440.

Alex Wang, Yada Pruksachatkun, Nikita Nangia, Amanpreet Singh, Julian Michael, Felix Hill, Omer Levy, and Samuel R. Bowman. 2019a. SuperGLUE: A stickier benchmark for general-purpose language understanding systems. *arXiv preprint 1905.00537.*

Yanshan Wang, Sunghwan Sohn, Sijia Liu, Feichen Shen, Liwei Wang, Elizabeth J Atkinson, Shreyasee Amin, and Hongfang Liu. 2019b. A clinical text classification paradigm using weak supervision and deep representation. *BMC medical informatics and decision making*, 19(1):1–13.

Zihan Wang, Karthikeyan K, Stephen Mayhew, and Dan Roth. 2020. Extending multilingual BERT to low-resource languages. In *Findings of the Association for Computational Linguistics: EMNLP 2020*, pages 2649–2656, Online. Association for Computational Linguistics.

Thomas Wolf, Lysandre Debut, Victor Sanh, Julien Chaumond, Clement Delangue, Anthony Moi, Pierric Cistac, Tim Rault, Rémi Louf, Morgan Funtowicz, Joe Davison, Sam Shleifer, Patrick von Platen, Clara Ma, Yacine Jernite, Julien Plu, Canwen Xu, Teven Le Scao, Sylvain Gugger, Mariama Drame, Quentin Lhoest, and Alexander M. Rush. 2020. Huggingface's transformers: State-of-the-art natural language processing.

Liang Xu, Hai Hu, Xuanwei Zhang, Lu Li, Chenjie Cao, Yudong Li, Yechen Xu, Kai Sun, Dian Yu, Cong Yu, Yin Tian, Qianqian Dong, Weitang Liu, Bo Shi, Yiming Cui, Junyi Li, Jun Zeng, Rongzhao Wang, Weijian Xie, Yanting Li, Yina Patterson, Zuoyu Tian, Yiwen Zhang, He Zhou, Shaoweihua Liu, Zhe Zhao, Qipeng Zhao, Cong Yue, Xinrui Zhang, Zhengliang Yang, Kyle Richardson, and Zhenzhong Lan. 2020. CLUE: A Chinese language understanding evaluation benchmark. In *Proceedings of the 28th International Conference on Computational Linguistics*, pages 4762–4772, Barcelona, Spain (Online). International Committee on Computational Linguistics.

Qiang Yang, Hind Alamro, Somayah Albaradei, Adil Salhi, Xiaoting Lv, Changsheng Ma, Manal Alshehri, Inji Jaber, Faroug Tifratene, Wei Wang, Takashi Gojobori, Carlos M. Duarte, Xin Gao, and Xiangliang Zhang. 2020. Senwave: Monitoring the global sentiments under the covid-19 pandemic.

Omar F. Zaidan and Chris Callison-Burch. 2011. The Arabic online commentary dataset: an annotated dataset of informal Arabic with high dialectal content. In *Proceedings of the 49th Annual Meeting of the Association for Computational Linguistics: Human Language Technologies*, pages 37–41, Portland, Oregon, USA. Association for Computational Linguistics.

Omar F Zaidan and Chris Callison-Burch. 2014. Arabic dialect identification. *Computational Linguistics*, 40(1):171–202.

M. Zampieri and P. Nakov. 2021. *Similar Languages, Varieties, and Dialects: A Computational Perspective*. Studies in Natural Language Processing. Cambridge University Press.

Chiyu Zhang and Muhammad Abdul-Mageed. 2019. No army, no navy: BERT semi-supervised learning of Arabic dialects. In *Proceedings of the Fourth Arabic Natural Language Processing Workshop*, pages 279–284, Florence, Italy. Association for Computational Linguistics.

Event-Based Knowledge MLM for Arabic Event Detection

Asma Yamani[2], **Amjad Alsulami**[2] and **Rabeah Al-Zaidy**[1, 2]
[1]Center for Integrative Petroleum Research (CIPR)
[2] Information and Computer Science Department
King Fahd University of Petroleum and Minerals
Saudi Arabia
{g201906630,g202101130,rabeah.alzaidy}@kfupm.edu.sa

Abstract

With the fast pace of reporting around the globe from various sources, event extraction has increasingly become an important task in NLP. The use of pre-trained language models (PTMs) has become popular to provide contextual representation for downstream tasks. This work aims to pre-train language models that enhance event extraction accuracy. To this end, we propose an Event-Based Knowledge (EBK) masking approach to mask the most significant terms in the event detection task. These significant terms are based on an external knowledge source that is curated for the purpose of event detection for the Arabic language. The proposed approach improves the classification accuracy of all the 9 event types. The experimental results demonstrate the effectiveness of the proposed masking approach and encourage further exploration.

1 Introduction

Our lives are a sequence of events. Some of them concern the individual, some have their effect extended to a greater population, where others can even have a global effect. As the sources of news about events vary and the speed of the reporting has increased dramatically, event extraction has become an important challenge for governments and different agencies to have appropriate responses to the concerning events. Event extraction composes mainly of 2 tasks. The first is *event detection*, in which the event is detected, usually by a trigger, and then classified. A subsequent task is *event argument extraction*. It aims to identify different semantic entities related to the detected and classified event. There are several challenges related to event extraction and annotation, such as having multiple event types for the same piece of news, i.e. *Multi-label* problem. Also, multiple roles for the same entity, commonly referred to as the *role overlap* problem. In addition, similar sentences that contain the event trigger and the same entities may be classified as being an event or not based on the *tense*, whether it is an event that happened or something that is planned for in the future. All these challenges contribute to the complexity of the event extraction problem.

As with many downstream tasks, a sophisticated text representation, through contextual representation and attention mechanisms, was able to improve the performance of event detection models as shown in various studies related to events in the English language (Yang et al., 2019; Wang et al., 2019; Caselli et al., 2021). However, this has not been widely explored yet in event extraction for events reported in the Arabic Language. Event detection studies related to Arabic Language mainly focus on feature extraction using statistical approaches such as TF-IDF (Chouigui et al., 2018) and N-gram along with Part-of-Speech (POS) and Named Entity Recognition (NER) (Smadi and Qawasmeh, 2018; Alsaedi and Burnap, 2015) or using rule-based approaches as in (Mohammad and Qawasmeh, 2016).

In addition, domain adaptation through continuing to pre-train a contextual model, such as Bidirectional Encoder Representations from Transformers (BERT) (Devlin et al., 2018), on domain-specific corpora such as events (Caselli et al., 2021), or modifying the masked language modeling (MLM) learning task to focus on entities have shown significant effect on the performance of the downstream task that they are catered towards (e.g., NER, medical domain NLP tasks, stance detection tasks) (Lin et al., 2021; Kawintiranon and Singh, 2021). As imposing an inductive bias to the MLM learning task has yet to be explored for the event extraction task, or when modeling the Arabic Language, we propose Event-Based Knowledge Masked Language Model (EBK-MLM) for the purpose of better detection and classification of events reported in the Arabic Language.

The contribution of this work is as follows: (1) We collect and annotate an Arabic Event dataset

Proceedings of the The Seventh Arabic Natural Language Processing Workshop (WANLP), pages 273 - 286

namely AraEvent[1] which consists of 2 sub-datasets AraEvent(November) and AraEvent(July) that is sourced from 4 popular Twitter news accounts. (2) We customize the MLM learning task to have an inductive bias towards the most significant terms in events, which achieves an average of 3.67% accuracy improvement in the event detection and classification task when tested on a non-homogeneous dataset, with up to 6.25% improvement in some event types[2].

The rest of this paper is structured as follows: in Section 2, we present some related work to our study. Then in Section 3, we propose the pre-training method. In Section 4, we present our fine-tuning experiments, whose results we discuss in Section 5. In section 6, we list the limitations of our work. Finally, in Section 7, we conclude and set some future directions.

2 Related Work

2.1 Event Extraction

Event detection, the first component of event extraction, usually starts by identifying the trigger, which is the word that most clearly identifies an event type, then the event classification task would follow (Chen et al., 2015; Nguyen and Grishman, 2015; Liu et al., 2016; Chen et al., 2017). However, more recent work (Liu et al., 2019) focuses on detecting the event without identifying the trigger as some events do not contain triggers. In addition, annotating the clearest trigger is a time-consuming task. The study proposed Type-aware Bias Neural Network with Attention Mechanisms that takes as an input a tokenized sentence with NER tags coupled with the event type then builds the representation based on the target event type. The output is 1 if the sentence conveys the event type, $zero$ otherwise. The attention mechanism gave more weight to the trigger words when developing the representation. The resulting model had similar performance on the ACE2005 event extraction dataset to SOTA event detection models (Sun et al., 2019; Chen et al., 2015; Nguyen and Grishman, 2015; Liu et al., 2016; Chen et al., 2017) that started with identifying the trigger, however, without using attention.

Using the representation of pre-trained contextual language models such as BERT for different downstream tasks, and more specifically here the event extraction task, have been gaining attraction recently. In (Yang et al., 2019; Wang et al., 2019) fine-tuned BERT is used for event argument extraction. The first study (Yang et al., 2019) identifies the trigger first via multiple fine-tuned BERT models for sentence classification, then based on the class(es) of events triggered, the arguments are extracted via a second BERT component fine-tuned for token classification to extract the arguments. In (Wang et al., 2019), a hierarchical approach is applied, in which the instance embedding from the BERT module for each token is concatenated with a rule-oriented embedding generated by hierarchical modular attention to classify Person, Time, Organization and Location. The result from this classification is finally fed to the Argument Role Classifier. The study (Caselli et al., 2021) follows a domain adaptive retraining approach, in which it continues pre-training BERT from the *'bert-base-uncased'* checkpoint on 79, 515 articles containing news about past or ongoing protest-related events. This improves the Trigger detection $F1$ score from 0.41, when using $BERT$, to 0.73 when using the $PROTEST-ER$ model that is pre-trained on protest-related articles. It also improves the argument extraction $F1$ score from 0.20, when using $BERT$, to 0.42 when using the $PROTEST-ER$ model. Our work aims to adapt the MLM task to give higher significance to words related to the events of our interest.

2.2 Arabic Event Extraction

In recent years, event detection and extraction systems that support the Arabic Language have evolved gradually. In a study, an event detection framework is introduced, which aims to detect disruptive events using temporal, textual, and spatial features (Alsaedi and Burnap, 2015). First, to differentiate between event and non-events tweets, a Naive Bayes classifier is trained and tested on a dataset that consists of 1200 tweets. The words composing the tweet are taken into account as features with the attributes: Unigrams, Bigrams, POS, NER. Compared to SVM and Logistic Regression, Naive Bayes performed the best, achieving an $F1$ score of 0.80. An unsupervised rules-based approach is proposed to extract events from Arabic tweets (Mohammad and Qawasmeh, 2016). Extracting the event, demystifying the NER and the Temporal resolution are all the three stages mentioned to extract the event. Focusing on event detec-

[1] https://huggingface.co/datasets/Asma/AraEvent
[2] https://huggingface.co/Asma/EBK-BERT

tion phase, Automatic Content Extraction (ACE) guidelines are mapped into syntax rules that use POS tags to extract event statements, event triggers, event time, and event type. For evaluation, $1,000$ Arabic tweets are used to evaluate the proposed approach, which maintained a 75.9% accuracy for extracting event triggers using Naive Bayes. Another study (Smadi and Qawasmeh, 2018) extracts a set of features from tweets for the events extraction task. Morphological features are used to analyze the structure of the text. POS, semantic features like NER, and word features such as Unigrams and their TF-IDF represents the different sets of features extracted by the system. To evaluate the proposed approach, a dataset of 2k Arabic tweets is utilized, and three classifiers are used: SVM, Naive Bayes, and Decision Tree. Results shows SVM scoring the highest F1 score for the event trigger extraction task scores with 92.6%.The study (Chouigui et al., 2018) presents statistical approaches for the event extraction task.

Focusing on Arabic news articles' titles, keywords are extracted by calculating the term weight for each word utilizing TF-IDF and comparing it with a threshold. For each keyword extracted, the event is defined using the POS co-occurrence rule. To evaluate the system, another news site is used for the events extraction task. The results shows that the performance of the approach is class-based and works well for domain-specific events such as the economy. As for datasets, EveTAR (Almerekhi et al., 2016) is the first publicly-available Arabic event detection dataset. In total, there are 590M tweets covering 66 significant events (eight categories). Using Wikipedia's Current Events Portal, it was collected over a one-month period. Tweets related to an event are grouped according to their time period of occurrence in order to represent that event. After cleaning and removing inaccessible tweets belonging to inaccessible accounts, the second version of the dataset comprised of 355M tweets (Hasanain et al., 2017). A recent study (Alharbi and Lee, 2021) presents a multi-dialect Arabic Twitter corpus for crisis events that include more than a million Arabic tweets from 22 crises and hazards between 2018 and 2020. To benchmark the dataset, AraBERT base model is fine-tuned by using annotated data from the same event to categorize tweets according to different labels. Despite limited task-specific training data, BERT-based models perform well on this task. Transformer-based models have yet to be used or evaluated for the detection and extraction of Arabic events of various types.

2.3 Arabic Pre-Trained Language Models (PTMs)

Pre-trained contextual representation models are known to be well suited for tasks that require understanding a given text, such as sentiment analysis, NER, and extractive question answering. One of the first Arabic PTMs with BERT_{base} architecture is AraBERT(Antoun et al., 2020). It uses the BERT_{base} configuration (Devlin et al., 2018) and is trained on both the MLM and Next sentence prediction tasks (NSP). Other Arabic PTMs trained on the BERT configurations are QARiB(Abdelali et al., 2021), MARBERT, ARBERT(Abdul-Mageed et al., 2021), and CAMeLBERT(Inoue et al., 2021). They mainly differ in the pre-training data source, such as whether they included Dialectal Arabic (DA), e.g., QARiB, MARBERT, CAMeLBERT-DA, CAMeLBERT-Mix or used only Modern Standard Arabic (MSA), e.g., AraBERT, ARBERT. Other differences include the size of the pre-training data and the ratio of DA to MSA, e.g. CAMeLBERT and QARiB. However, changing the masking procedure for the MLM training task has not been, to the best of our knowledge, investigated for Arabic Language.

Also, although multiple studies utilize PTMs in various tasks and applications, the use of contextual representation for event extraction in Arabic, has not been investigated yet.

2.4 Variations in the MLM learning task for PTMs

Masked Language Modeling (MLM) is a training task in which a model tries to learn the masked token representation using the surrounding unmasked words. It is adopted by BERT (Devlin et al., 2018) to train Language models by masking 15% of the tokens in pre-training. In BERT, 80% of the masked tokens are masked by $[Mask]$, 10% by the original token, and 10% by a random token (Devlin et al., 2018). Several studies have varied the masked token selection for the MLM training objective. A study proposed BERTSpan that masks contiguous random spans (Joshi et al., 2019). BERTSpan outperforms BERT on the extractive question answering tasks, coreference resolution, and 9 GLUE tasks. In (Sun et al., 2019), Enhanced Representation through kNowledge IntEgration (ERINE) is proposed to mask phrases and entities rather than random tokens. ERNIE is applied to 5 Chinese NLP tasks, including natural language inference, semantic similarity, named entity recognition, sentiment analysis, and question answering and it improved NER and natural Language inference the most.

In Sentiment Knowledge Enhanced Pre-training for Sentiment Analysis (SKEP)(Tian et al., 2020), Pointwise Mutual Information is used to identify the most important words for the sentiment analysis task. It outperforms RoBERTa on sentence-level sentiment classification, Aspect-level sentiment classification, and opinion role labeling. Knowledge Enhanced Masked Language Model (KE-MLM) is proposed for Stance Detection (Kawintiranon and Singh, 2021). It uses log-odds-ratio to identify key stance tokens then used them for selecting the mask. It outperforms SKEP and other BERT variations on the Stance Detection task. Another specific application for knowledge-based masking is in the medical domain, in which Medical Entities are masked (Lin et al., 2021). It outperforms random masking and other baseline models on three clinical NLP tasks, TLINK temporal relation extraction, DocTimeRel classification, and negation detection, and one biomedical task, PubMedQA. Using cloze-like masking is proposed to provide indirect supervision to downstream tasks in a self supervised setting (Zhang and Hashimoto, 2021). The approach is evaluated on three text-classification tasks by masking words that exhibit a strong indication for the classes of the downstream task during a second stage pre-training of BERT. The results showed improved performance of models using cloze-like masking over other contextual models not masked using cloze-like masking. As knowledge-based masking is not addressed for the purpose of event extraction, in this work, we aim to leverage the knowledge related to certain types of events in the masking process in order to improve the representation of word related to our downstream task.

3 Pre-training EBK-BERT

We propose Event Knowledge-Based BERT (EBK-BERT), which leverages knowledge extracted from events-related sentences to mask words that are significant to the events detection task (Section 3.1). This approach aims to produce a language model that enhances the performance of the down-stream event detection task, which is later trained during the fine-tuning process. The BERT-base configuration is adopted which has 12 encoder blocks, 768 hidden dimensions, 12 attention heads, 512 maximum sequence length, and a total of $110M$ parameters. The details of the implementation is in the following subsections.

3.1 EBK Token Masking

As previous studies have shown, contextual representation models that are pre-trained using the MLM training task benefit from masking the most significant words, using whole word masking. To select the most significant words we use odds-ratio (Szumilas, 2010). Only words with greater than 2 odds-ratio are considered in the masking, which means the words included are at least twice as likely to appear in one event type than the other. Calculating the odds-ratio for event detection is calculated as:

$$logodds(w, e) = \frac{\|e \text{ and } w\| \times \|!e \text{ and } !w\|}{\|!e \text{ and } w\| \times \|e \text{ and } !w\|} \quad (1)$$

were w is the word we are calculating the log-odds ratio for, with respect to a particular event e. Top 5 significant words are presented in Table 1

In order to mitigate the effect of noise generated by rare words, we perform word lemmatization using the Farasa lemmatizer (Abdelali et al., 2016), which combines, to a great extent, different word surfaces to their lemma. As presented in Appendix A Table 9, the vocabulary size shrinks after lemmatization. It combines words such as الفيضان, فيضانات, and فيضان, into one word فيضان, which helps focus the mask later on the most significant part of the word and avoid inflated odds-ratio values due to the infrequent terms. It is worth noting that there are words that appear in 2 or, at maximum, 3 event types. Event types *Contact*, followed by *Personnel* and *Nature* most significant words have the highest presence in the pre-training corpus based on 8 million sentences drawn randomly. The density of the frequency of the words is: 78.7% of the words are composed of one token, 19.7% of the words are composed of two tokens, and less than %2 words compose of more than 2 tokens.

3.2 Pre-training Data

The pre-training data consists of news articles from the 1.5 billion words corpus by (El-Khair, 2016). Due to computation limitations, we only use articles from Alittihad, Riyadh, Almasryalyoum, and

top	Personnel	Transaction	Contact	Nature	Movement	Life	Justice	Conflict	business
1	استقال	راجحي	التقى	ارضي	اجلاء	مقتل	قبض	اشتباك	انشاء
2	اقال	توصيل	نظير	فيضان	غادر	قتيل	اتهم	معركة	نسخ
3	رشح	استحواذ	لقاء	درجة	مغادر	اصاب	أطاح	قصف	اختار
4	ترشح	تمويل	خادم	درج	هجر	حالة	ضبط	معرك	شراء
5	مهمة	نيوكاسل	بحث	اعصار	نزوح	تسجيل	ايقاف	نفاية	تسلا

Table 1: Top 5 significant words (after Farasa's lemmatization) using odds-ratio

Alqabas, which amount to $10GB$ of text and about 8M sentences after splitting the articles to approximately 100 word sentences to accommodate the 128 max_sentence length used when training the model. The average number of tokens per sentence is 105. The normalization is performed as described in Section 4.1.1.

3.3 Preparing Data for BERT Pre-training

A WordPiece (Schuster and Nakajima, 2012) tokenizer is trained on the entire dataset ($10GB$ text) with a vocabulary size of 30522 using Hugging Face's tokenizers. For the baseline model, 15% of the tokens, are randomly masked with $[MASK]$. For the EBK-BERT model, 10% of the tokens are masked randomly and the remaining 5% are masked by considering the top $80 - 100$ words from each event type ordered by the odds-ratio.

3.4 Pre-training Setup

Google Cloud GPU is used for pre-training the model. The selected hyperparameters are: learning rate=1$e - 4$, batch size =16, maximum sequence length = 128 and average sequence length = 104. In total, we pre-trained our models for $500,000$ steps, completing 1 epoch. Pre-training a single model took approximately 2.25 days.

3.5 Pre-training Results

Due to computation limitations, the model is trained for 1 epoch. We notice from Figure 1 that *EBK-BERT* has lower training loss than the *RandMask* model. This, however, cannot be an indicator to the performance of the model as $1/3$ of the masked words, which the model is learning the representation for, focus on about 3000 words from the 9 event types, whilst for the *RandMask* all the 15% masked words are random which adds complexity to the training process.

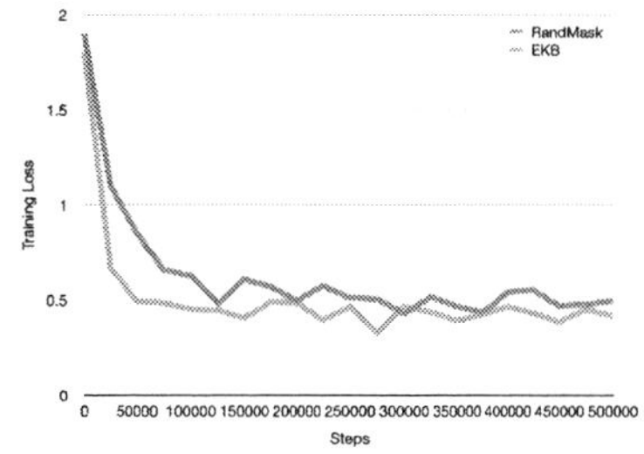

Figure 1: Training loss of *EBK-BERT* and *RandMask* model.

4 Fine-tuning Experiment

4.1 Event Data

The events dataset construction process is comprised of three steps: (1) Scrape tweets from four well-known Arabic news accounts on Twitter. (2) Conduct cleaning and filtering procedures on the collected tweets by applying text normalization. (3) Perform the annotation task by labeling the tweets according to their content.

4.1.1 Tweet Collection

Tweets are collected from well-known Arabic news accounts, which are: Al-Arabiya, Sabq, CNN Arabic, and BBC Arabic. These accounts belong to television channels and online newspapers, where they use Twitter to broadcast news related to real-world events. The first collection process tracks tweets from the news accounts for 20 days period, between November 2, 2021, and November 22, 2021 and we call this dataset AraEvent(November). We also pull test-specific data from different times to minimize the impact of bias due to the period in which we collected the data and we name it AraEvent(July). The retrieval process of the AraEvent(July) covers 6 days between July 6, 2022, and July 12, 2022, from the same news accounts and utilizing Twitter Streaming API [3]. As a first pre-processing step, each retweet by these accounts is filtered and excluded during the collection process. The AraEvent(November) and AraEvent(July) tweets datasets consist of around $12,095$ and 813 tweets, respectively. To ensure the quality of the datasets, text normalization is applied to convert tweets to a more standard form by eliminating noise from the data. The tweet normalization process removes the following: diacritics, punctuation marks, emoticons, URLs, user men-

[3] https://developer.twitter.com/en/docs/twitter-api

tions, emails. In addition, different surface forms of character Alif (أآإ) normalized to plain Alif (ا), and Taa Marbouta (ة) normalized to Haa (ه). Furthermore, we constrain the number of times the character is repeated to a maximum of two repetitions and replace successive spaces and newlines with one space separation. Non-Arabic characters are preserved as they might contain technical or scientific details related to the event. Hashtags are converted to plain text by separating the text into words as some hashtags may retain significant information about the event. However, Hashtags that contain the news account name in Arabic or English and also the Breaking hashtag both are removed because they are considered as redundant information, for example, #العربيه, ترندينغ_ سي_ بي_ #بي, and #عاجل. Finally, tweets containing words less than 7 in total are filtered out along with duplicate tweets. Tables 5 and 6 in the Appendix show statistics for the final AraEvent(November) dataset and AraEvent(July) datasets, respectively, after the pre-processing steps conducted above.

4.1.2 Annotation

The annotation process is performed after the text normalization and filtering steps and is conducted manually by two of the authors and a volunteer, disagreement was resolved by discussion. To specify the annotation rules and conditions, we follow the "Automatic Content Extraction (ACE) Arabic annotation events guidelines" (ACE, 2005), ACE2005. Based on the definition from (ACE, 2005), an event is considered to be an action involving a connection between participants. Therefore, a special collection of events' types and subtypes are labeled and considered while annotating the events dataset. Accordingly, a set of unclassified news tweets written in Arabic are given, and after applying the annotation guidelines, the results are broken down into types and subtypes of events.

To start the annotation process, first, we consider and focus on eight event types mentioned in (ACE, 2005): "Life, Movement, Transaction, Business, Conflict, Contact, Personnel, and Justice events", and the corresponding sub-type for every main type. Tweet examples of types and sub-types of events following the (ACE, 2005), are presented in Table 10, Appendix A. Second, based on our data, we made some adjustments to the (ACE, 2005) guidelines to accommodate as many events as possible which are published on the Arabic news accounts. The modifications are either to expand the definition of a particular event type and make it include a larger segment of acts or to add a new subtype to the main event type. Furthermore, Table 11 in Appendix A summarizes the key modifications this study introduces, including defining the changes, why we perform them, and also present illustrative examples.

Additionally, the frequent occurrence of natural events, especially the natural disaster, in the dataset inspired us to propose a main event type, Nature, and a subtype of this event, namely Natural Disasters. Floods, earthquakes, volcanoes, pollution from volcanoes that cause a loss of life or property are labeled as natural disasters. The following tweet is an example of Nature type event with subtype as Natural-disaster:

- Arabic: "اطلق اعمده دخان وسحب رماد الى ارتفاع ٣٥٠٠ مترلحظه انفجار بركان جبل اسو في اليابان"
- Translation: "Smoke plumes and ash clouds were released to an altitude of 3,500 meters at the moment of the eruption of Mount Aso volcano in Japan"

In this work, we do not include fires as natural disasters due to the lack of information on the cause of the fire. There are also two types of events to consider: 'None' and 'Other'. The label 'None' is used if there is no identified event in the tweet. On the other hand, 'Other' type is used to label any event that is not from the pre-defined list of types that the system considers and if the constructions of the event are not clearly defined or ambiguous. Examples of tweets labeled in Twitter Event dataset with 'None' and 'Other' types respectively are:

- Arabic: "استشاري لهذا السبب العلاقه وثيقه بين سمنه الاطفال والميكروبات المعويه الضاره"
- Translation: "consultant, for this reason, the close relationship between childhood obesity and harmful intestinal microbes"

- Arabic: "الشريف القابضه تعلن شراكتها مع كيوبك ارت لانشاء محطات الشحن للسيارات الكهربائيه في المملكه"

Type1	Subtype1	Type2	Subtype2	Type3	Subtype3	Tweet
Life	Die	Life	Injure	Conflict	Attack	Arabic: الشرطه الاوغنديه مقتل ٣ اشخاص واصابه ٣٣ اخرين في هجومي كامبالا الانتحاريين Translation: "Uganda police 3 killed, 33 injured in Kampala suicide bombings"
Conflict	Attack	Life	Die	-	-	Arabic: في هجوم بالقوس والسهم مقتل عده اشخاص على يد مهاجم ب النرويج Translation: "In a bow and arrow attack, several people were killed by an attacker in Norway"

Table 2: Examples of more than on event type labels

- Translation:" Al-Sharif Holding announces its partnership with Cubic Art to establish charging stations for electric cars in the Kingdom"

A tweet can have one, two, or three main types associated with a subtype based on the occurrence of the event as the examples show in Table 2. As a consequence of the annotation approach described above, for the AraEvent(November) dataset, we end up with 2,146 annotated events each with their corresponding type and subtype. In addition, 858 tweets contain 'Other' events, and a total of 8,069 tweets are of the 'None' type. The AraEvent(July) dataset contains 110 annotated events, each with a type and subtype with 257 tweets of the 'Other' type and 446 of the 'None' type.

4.1.3 Annotation Results

In this section, we present the statistics of the types of events that exist on the AraEvent(November) and AraEvent(July) datasets at the level of one event or the set of events that took place simultaneously. The AraEvent(November) statistics are present in Appendix A Table 7 in terms of individual or paired events only. The individual event type with the highest frequency based on the data we have is the Justice event with 527 tweets. The Conflict type comes as the next highest event with 449 tweets. The Life type ranked third with 304 tweets. The least accounted event type in the data is the Transaction type with 41 tweets. Regarding the paired events, the two highest events that occur concurrently are Life and Conflict as they record 203 tweets. Second, Conflict and Justice events happen at once in 37 tweets. Nature and Life event types occurred 11 times as the third most overlapped event. On the other hand, Personnel and Business types overlap with one event type only as following: Personnel and Conflict, Justice and Business. In addition, a set of Life, Justice, and Conflict events occur at the same time in 9 tweets. Table 2 shows an example of Life and Conflict paired events. The following is an example of paired events between Nature and Life:

- Arabic: شعر به في السعوديه مصرع شخص واصابه ٣ اخرين في زلزال قوي جنوب ايران
- Translation: "It was felt in Saudi Arabia, one person was killed and 3 others injured in a strong earthquake in southern Iran."

Regarding the AraEvent(July) dataset, individual and paired event type statistics are present in Appendix A Table 8. In terms of the lowest individual event types recorded in the data are Transaction and Nature events with 2 tweets each. Moreover, no business events are accounted for in the data. The individual event type with the highest frequency, based on the data we have, is the Justice event with 24 tweets. With 23 tweets, the Life type is ranked second, and lastly, the Conflict type is ranked third with 20 tweets.

4.2 Evaluation Experimental Setup

The event detection problem is a *Multi-Label problem*. The same sentence can contain multiple events. We follow (Liu et al., 2019) approach, in which we convert the multi-label problem to *multiple binary classification* problems. As we have 9 event types, from Section 4.1, we fine-tuned *EBK-BERT* per event type. This fine-tuning is performed to the *RandMask* model, too. To evaluate the models, four experiments are conducted.

1. The first experiment aims to evaluate the models when applied to test data from the same duration. Train-test split is used with an 80:20 ratio of the AraEvent(November) dataset.
2. The second experiment aims to evaluate the models when applied to test data from the same duration, but with limited training samples. Training samples in this experiment were limited to 100 balanced samples, and testing varies between event types as it constituted the balanced remaining samples not consumed in training.
3. The third experiment aims to evaluate the models when applied to test data from a different

duration. The AraEvent(November) dataset is used for training, and AraEvent(July) dataset is used for testing. Business, Transaction, and Nature types were not considered in this experiment due to having less than 10 samples each.

4. The fourth experiment aims to evaluate the models when applied to test data from a different duration, and with limited training samples. This experiment is considered to be the strongest form of testing of the four setups. Training samples in this experiment are limited to 100 balanced samples from the AraEvent(November) dataset, and testing is done on the AraEvent(July) data.

In all the experiments, we balance the positive class of an event type with a mixture of the other 8 types that do not overlap with the positive class, in addition to sentences that do not contain any events. Therefore, the final dataset of an event type includes: 50% sentences from the positive class of the event, 25% sentences from the other event types, and 25% sentences that do not contain events, the total amount of records for each class is presented in Tables 3 and 4. To initiate the fine-tuning step, AutoModelForSequenceClassification class from the transformers library of Huggingface [4] is used. All models are fine-tuned on 3 epochs with a learning rate of $5e-5$, batch size of 8, and a maximum sequence length of 128. For evaluation, As the datasets are balanced, we only report the mean of the accuracy per event type with a confidence interval of 95%. The fine-tuning is repeated 10 times with random initial seeds.

5 Evaluation Results and Discussion

To evaluate the proposed approach, we compare between the classification results of the fine-tuning of both the baseline *RandMask* and our proposed approach *EBK-BERT*. Starting with the first and second experiment, as presented in Table 3, *EBK-BERT* performs better than *RandMask* in all types. The Business type had the most improvement with about 3.5% improvement in accuracy. Then comes Personnel, Movement, and Contact with $2-3\%$ improvement in accuracy. The remaining events show an improvement of less than $1.6-0\%$. When limiting the training data, the Business type still shows the highest improvement with 4.2%, The remaining types show an improvement of $0.4-3\%$ except for Nature, which is affected negatively by the EBK Masking. The average improvement is 2.13% and 1.4% for the two experiments respectively. We conclude from this that, for most of the types, EBK Masking did amplify the fine-tuning process to produce more accurate predictions for homogeneous datasets.

As for the third and fourth experiments, where the test set is from a different time period, the results are presented in Table 4. The average improvement of the third experiment is at 1.74% with 5 out of the 6 datasets scoring more than 1% improvement. The fourth experiment which limits the training size to 100 shows the promising results of EBK Masking when capturing the masks correctly. The average improvement from the EBK Masking is at 3.67%. However, this average comes from two opposite responses to EBK Masking when testing on non-homogeneous datasets. Conflict and Contact had an improvement of 0.6% and -0.9%, which is an indication of a bias in the selection of significant words which did not generalize well when tested in a different period with a different event. Emphasizing that the models perform much better when training on the entire training dataset. Whereas for the remaining four event types, more than $5-6.25\%$ improvement is archived by *EBK-BERT*. This indicates that *EBK-BERT* generalizes well for different time periods even with limited fine-tuning data. Still, it cannot be ascertained whether this is the reason for the varying performance between the types since there are a lot of variables that may play a role, such as the data size, the difficulty of the event, the bias in the most significant words, and the percentage of the presence of the most significant words in the pre-training text.

6 Limitations

AraEvent is drawn from a short period, introducing some bias towards events happening in that period such as راجحي and نيوكسل. Also, errors from the lemmatization tool propagate to the ED task, as shown in the Table 1 ترشح, رشح are both present in the most significant words. In addition, as the models were trained on MSA Arabic corpus, we cannot generalize the results to dialectal Arabic as it may impose its own challenges.

[4] https://huggingface.co

		80:20 training to test ratio			Training size set to 100 balanced samples		
Event type	**Training size**	**Testing size**	**Random**	**EBK-BERT**	**Testing size**	**Random**	**EBK-BERT**
Personnel	189	47	0.862±0.014	**0.891±0.013**	136	0.866±0.013	**0.862±0.013**
Transaction	71	17	0.733±0.039	**0.750±0.047**	-	-	-
Contact	347	86	0.934±0.007	**0.955±0.004**	333	0.903±0.006	0.913±0.008
Nature	123	30	0.917±0.010	0.923±0.012	53	**0.942±0.007**	0.930±0.010
Movement	148	37	0.858±0.009	**0.882±0.023**	85	0.800±0.023	**0.811±0.018**
Life	858	214	0.880±0.006	**0.917±0.003**	972	0.796±0.008	**0.825±0.009**
Justice	393	234	0.910±0.006	**0.927±0.003**	1073	0.798±0.012	**0.824±0.011**
Conflict	1134	283	0.897±0.002	0.904±0.005	1317	0.807±0.004	0.811±0.001
Business	103	25	0.869±0.023	**0.904±0.017**	28	0.911±0.016	**0.954±0.015**

Table 3: Event classification accuracy results for AraEvent(November) based on an average of 10 runs per event type and a confidence interval of 95%

	Testing Dataset	Full training set size			Training size set to 100 balanced samples	
Event type	**Testing size**	**Training size**	**Random**	**EBK-BERT**	**Random**	**EBK-BERT**
Personnel	**32**	236	0.913 ± 0.018	**0.93125 ± 0.020**	0.853± 0.024	**0.903 ± 0.006**
Contact	**21**	433	0.967 ± 0.014	0.962 ± 0.012	0.919 ± 0.020	0.910 ± 0.026
Movement	**24**	185	0.788 ± 0.0191	**0.804 ± 0.017**	0.746 ± 0.0284	**0.808 ± 0.030**
Life	**45**	1137	0.985 ± 0.006	**0.990 ± 0.003**	0.901 ± 0.0197	**0.952 ± 0.00762**
Justice	**23**	627	0.833 ± 0.016	**0.86 ± 0.0113**	0.769 ± 0.019	**0.829 ± 0.023**
Conflict	**39**	1417	0.827 ± 0.009	**0.869 ± 0.013**	0.770± 0.019	0.777 ± 0.017

Table 4: Event classification accuracy results of AraEvent(July) based on an average of 10 runs per event type and a confidence interval of 95%

7 Conclusion and Future Work

This work aims to propose using the Event-Based Knowledge *(EBK)* approach for selecting the Mask for the MLM training task in order to improve the model's performance for the event detection task. In this *(EBK)*, the most significant words are extracted from an AraEvent(November) using odds ratio. This dataset is pulled from news channels' Twitter accounts and then annotated manually to 9 event types, inspired by ACE2005 Event Extraction dataset, with some modifications. The event classification experiment results show improvement over random masking by $0.56 - 3.645\%$ across all event types when tested on a homogeneous dataset, an average of 3.67% when tested on a non-homogeneous dataset with limited fine-tuning data. This shows the effectiveness of the proposed masking technique for event detection. The classification results, although higher than random masking, raise several questions on the reasons for the varying performance across the types. Running the experiment with different data sizes may asssist to answer the question of whether the data size plays a role in narrowing the effect of the proposed masking, in other words: Is *(EBK)* or similar masking approaches more suitable to perform tasks with small annotated datasets? Another improvement to be made to the approach is constructing the event datasets gradually over an expanded period of time to mitigate the bias towards the data collection period. Also, following the log-odds-ratio with Dirichlet prior approach should help us mitigate the bias of the collection period and rare words, in general. We consider this study as preliminary work as a proof of concept that mask approaches catered to a certain downstream task are beneficial to the downstream task for language models built for the Arabic Language. This is illustrated in this study on a language model built on a considerably limited amount of data. It is interesting to see if this approach can be applied to pre-train large-scale Arabic Language models for different downstream tasks.

Acknowledgements

The authors would like to acknowledge the support of King Fahd University of Petroleum and Minerals to complete this work. We would like to thank also Reem Alyami and Ebtehal Alsulami for the valuable discussion and support.

References

Ahmed Abdelali, Kareem Darwish, Nadir Durrani, and Hamdy Mubarak. 2016. Farasa: A fast and furious segmenter for Arabic. In *Proceedings of the 2016 Conference of the North American Chapter of the Association for Computational Linguistics: Demonstrations*, pages 11–16, San Diego, California. Association for Computational Linguistics.

Ahmed Abdelali, Sabit Hassan, Hamdy Mubarak, Kareem Darwish, and Younes Samih. 2021. Pre-training BERT on arabic tweets: Practical considerations. *CoRR*, abs/2102.10684.

Muhammad Abdul-Mageed, AbdelRahim Elmadany, and El Moatez Billah Nagoudi. 2021. ARBERT & MARBERT: Deep bidirectional transformers for Arabic. In *Proceedings of the 59th Annual Meeting of the Association for Computational Linguistics and the 11th International Joint Conference on Natural Language Processing (Volume 1: Long Papers)*, pages 7088–7105, Online. Association for Computational Linguistics.

ACE. 2005. (automatic content extraction) arabic annotation guidelines for events. *Linguistic Data Consortium.*

Alaa Alharbi and Mark Lee. 2021. Kawarith: an arabic twitter corpus for crisis events. In *Proceedings of the Sixth Arabic Natural Language Processing Workshop*, pages 42–52.

Hind Almerekhi, Maram Hasanain, and Tamer Elsayed. 2016. Evetar: A new test collection for event detection in arabic tweets. In *Proceedings of the 39th International ACM SIGIR conference on Research and Development in Information Retrieval*, pages 689–692.

Nasser Alsaedi and Pete Burnap. 2015. Arabic event detection in social media. In *Computational Linguistics and Intelligent Text Processing*, pages 384–401, Cham. Springer International Publishing.

Wissam Antoun, Fady Baly, and Hazem Hajj. 2020. AraBERT: Transformer-based model for Arabic language understanding. In *Proceedings of the 4th Workshop on Open-Source Arabic Corpora and Processing Tools, with a Shared Task on Offensive Language Detection*, pages 9–15, Marseille, France. European Language Resource Association.

Tommaso Caselli, Osman Mutlu, Angelo Basile, and Ali Hürriyetoğlu. 2021. Protest-er: Retraining bert for protest event extraction. In *Proceedings of the 4th Workshop on Challenges and Applications of Automated Extraction of Socio-political Events from Text (CASE 2021)*, pages 12–19.

Yubo Chen, Shulin Liu, Xiang Zhang, Kang Liu, and Jun Zhao. 2017. Automatically labeled data generation for large scale event extraction. In *Proceedings of the 55th Annual Meeting of the Association for Computational Linguistics (Volume 1: Long Papers)*, pages 409–419.

Yubo Chen, Liheng Xu, Kang Liu, Daojian Zeng, and Jun Zhao. 2015. Event extraction via dynamic multipooling convolutional neural networks. In *Proceedings of the 53rd Annual Meeting of the Association for Computational Linguistics and the 7th International Joint Conference on Natural Language Processing (Volume 1: Long Papers)*, pages 167–176.

Amina Chouigui, Oussama Ben Khiroun, and Bilel Elayeb. 2018. A tf-idf and co-occurrence based approach for events extraction from arabic news corpus. In *International Conference on Applications of Natural Language to Information Systems*, pages 272–280. Springer.

Jacob Devlin, Ming-Wei Chang, Kenton Lee, and Kristina Toutanova. 2018. Bert: Pre-training of deep bidirectional transformers for language understanding. Cite arxiv:1810.04805Comment: 13 pages.

Ibrahim Abu El-Khair. 2016. 1.5 billion words arabic corpus. *CoRR*, abs/1611.04033.

Maram Hasanain, Reem Suwaileh, Tamer Elsayed, Mucahid Kutlu, and Hind Almerekhi. 2017. Evetar: Building a large-scale multi-task test collection over arabic tweets.

Go Inoue, Bashar Alhafni, Nurpeiis Baimukan, Houda Bouamor, and Nizar Habash. 2021. The interplay of variant, size, and task type in Arabic pre-trained language models. In *Proceedings of the Sixth Arabic Natural Language Processing Workshop*, Kyiv, Ukraine (Online). Association for Computational Linguistics.

Mandar Joshi, Danqi Chen, Yinhan Liu, Daniel S. Weld, Luke Zettlemoyer, and Omer Levy. 2019. Spanbert: Improving pre-training by representing and predicting spans. *CoRR*, abs/1907.10529.

Kornraphop Kawintiranon and Lisa Singh. 2021. Knowledge enhanced masked language model for stance detection. In *Proceedings of the 2021 Conference of the North American Chapter of the Association for Computational Linguistics: Human Language Technologies*, pages 4725–4735, Online. Association for Computational Linguistics.

Chen Lin, Timothy Miller, Dmitriy Dligach, Steven Bethard, and Guergana Savova. 2021. EntityBERT: Entity-centric masking strategy for model pretraining for the clinical domain. In *Proceedings of the 20th Workshop on Biomedical Language Processing*, pages 191–201, Online. Association for Computational Linguistics.

Shulin Liu, Yang Li, Feng Zhang, Tao Yang, and Xinpeng Zhou. 2019. Event detection without triggers. In *Proceedings of the 2019 Conference of the North American Chapter of the Association for Computational Linguistics: Human Language Technologies, Volume 1 (Long and Short Papers)*, pages 735–744.

Shulin Liu, Kang Liu, Shizhu He, and Jun Zhao. 2016. A probabilistic soft logic based approach to exploiting latent and global information in event classification. In *AAAI*.

AS Mohammad and Omar Qawasmeh. 2016. Knowledge-based approach for event extraction from arabic tweets. *International Journal of Advanced Computer Science & Applications*, 1(7):483–490.

Thien Huu Nguyen and Ralph Grishman. 2015. Event detection and domain adaptation with convolutional neural networks. In *Proceedings of the 53rd Annual Meeting of the Association for Computational Linguistics and the 7th International Joint Conference on Natural Language Processing (Volume 2: Short Papers)*, pages 365–371.

Mike Schuster and Kaisuke Nakajima. 2012. Japanese and korean voice search. In *2012 IEEE International Conference on Acoustics, Speech and Signal Processing (ICASSP)*, pages 5149–5152. IEEE.

Mohammad Smadi and Omar Qawasmeh. 2018. A supervised machine learning approach for events extraction out of arabic tweets. In *2018 Fifth International Conference on Social Networks Analysis, Management and Security (SNAMS)*, pages 114–119. IEEE.

Yu Sun, Shuohuan Wang, Yu-Kun Li, Shikun Feng, Xuyi Chen, Han Zhang, Xin Tian, Danxiang Zhu, Hao Tian, and Hua Wu. 2019. ERNIE: enhanced representation through knowledge integration. *CoRR*, abs/1904.09223.

M. Szumilas. 2010. Explaining odds ratios. *J Can Acad Child Adolesc Psychiatry*, 19(3):227–229.

Hao Tian, Can Gao, Xinyan Xiao, Hao Liu, Bolei He, Hua Wu, Haifeng Wang, and Feng Wu. 2020. SKEP: Sentiment knowledge enhanced pre-training for sentiment analysis. In *Proceedings of the 58th Annual Meeting of the Association for Computational Linguistics*, pages 4067–4076, Online. Association for Computational Linguistics.

Xiaozhi Wang, Ziqi Wang, Xu Han, Zhiyuan Liu, Juanzi Li, Peng Li, Maosong Sun, Jie Zhou, and Xiang Ren. 2019. Hmeae: Hierarchical modular event argument extraction. In *Proceedings of the 2019 Conference on Empirical Methods in Natural Language Processing and the 9th International Joint Conference on Natural Language Processing (EMNLP-IJCNLP)*, pages 5777–5783.

Sen Yang, Dawei Feng, Linbo Qiao, Zhigang Kan, and Dongsheng Li. 2019. Exploring pre-trained language models for event extraction and generation. In *Proceedings of the 57th Annual Meeting of the Association for Computational Linguistics*, pages 5284–5294.

Tianyi Zhang and Tatsunori Hashimoto. 2021. On the inductive bias of masked language modeling: From statistical to syntactic dependencies. *arXiv preprint arXiv:2104.05694*.

A Appendix

Source	No. of tweets before cleaning	No. of duplicates	No. of tweets after cleaning
Al-Arabiya	2945	170	2775
Sabq	2837	143	2694
CNN Arabic	3192	574	2618
BBC Arabic	3121	135	2986
Total	12095	1022	11073

Table 5: AraEvent(November) data statistics

Source	No. of tweets before cleaning	No. of duplicates	No. of tweets after cleaning
Al-Arabiya	382	195	187
Sabq	394	199	195
CNN Arabic	400	181	219
BBC Arabic	400	188	212
Total	1576	763	813

Table 6: AraEvent(July) data statistics

Type	Personnel	Transaction	Contact	Nature	Movement	Life	Justice	Conflict	Business
Personnel	116	-	-	-	-	-	-	1	-
Transaction	-	41	-	-	1	1	1	-	-
Contact	-	-	216	-	1	-	-	-	-
Nature	-	-	-	60	1	11	1	4	-
Movement	-	1	1	1	80	1	3	6	-
Life	-	1	-	11	1	304	7	203	-
Justice	-	1	-	1	3	7	527	37	2
Conflict	2	-	-	4	6	203	37	449	-
Business	-	-	-	-	-	-	2	-	62
Total	118	44	217	77	93	527	578	700	64

Table 7: AraEvent(November) event types statistics

Type	Personnel	Transaction	Contact	Nature	Movement	Life	Justice	Conflict	Business
Personnel	16	-	-	-	-	-	-	-	-
Transaction	-	2	-	-	-	-	-	-	-
Contact	-	-	11	-	-	-	-	-	-
Nature	-	-	-	2	-	-	-	-	-
Movement	-	-	-	-	12	-	-	1	-
Life	-	-	-	-	-	23	-	7	-
Justice	-	-	-	-	-	-	24	-	-
Conflict	-	-	-	-	1	7	-	20	-
Business	-	-	-	-	-	-		-	-
Total	16	2	11	2	13	30	24	28	-

Table 8: AraEvent(July) event types statistics

	$\|words\|$ before lemmatization	Odds ratio >2 (Before lemmatization)	$\|words\|$ after lemmatization	Odds ratio >2 (After lemmatization)	Presence of the words in the pre-training corpus
Personnel	1017	445	798	272	11.40%
Transaction	470	283	404	375	8.31%
Contact	1328	447	975	447	14.69%
Nature	519	260	415	237	11.57%
Movement	766	413	637	363	9.72%
Life	2890	347	1922	305	6.08%
Justice	3619	371	2316	353	7.94%
Conflict	3700	455	2232	393	7.68%
business	648	303	532	289	10.48%
Total	14957	3324	10231	3034	-

Table 9: Statistics related to the significant words calculated by the odds-ratio

Type	Subtype	Tweet
Life	Be-Born	Arabic: في مثل هذا اليوم ولد احد اشهر ادباء روسيا والتاريخ هل قرات سيرته او بعضا من اعماله Translation:" On this day, one of the most famous writers of Russia and history was born. Have you read his biography or some of his works"
	Marry	Arabic: اميره يابانيه تتزوج من صديقها وتتنازل عن صفتها الملكيه Translation:"Japanese princess marries her boyfriend and relinquishes her royal status"
	Divorce	Arabic: علمت من مواقع التواصل فاتن موسى تكشف تفاصيل صادمه عن طلاقها من الفنان مصطفى فهمي Translation:"She knew from social media Faten Moussa reveals shocking details about her divorce from the artist Mustafa Fahmy"
	Injure	Arabic: النطقه الخضراء في بغداد اصابه ١٢٥ شخصا من القوات الامنيه والمتظاهرين المحتجين على نتائج الانتخابات Translation:"Baghdad' S Green Zone injured 125 security forces and protesters protesting the election results"
	Die	Arabic: قتل مالكولم اكس بالرصاص في قاعه رقص في مدينه نيويورك امام عائلته قبل ٥٦ عاما وكان يبلغ وقتها من العمر ٣٩ عاما Translation:"Malcolm X has shot dead in a New York City dance floor in front of his family 56 years ago at the time at the age of 39"
Movement	Transport	Arabic: الامير عبدالعزيز بن سعود يصل مملكه البحرين Translation:"Prince Abdulaziz bin Saud arrives in Bahrain"
Transaction	Transfer-Ownership	Arabic: السعوديه صندوق الاستثمارات السيادي يعلن استحواذه على ١٠٠ بالمائه من نادي نيوكاسل يونايتد Translation:"Saudi Sovereign Investment Fund announces acquisition of 100 percent of Newcastle United club"
	Transfer-Money	Arabic: الربيعه اكثر من مليار و٩٥٨ مليون دولار حجم المساعدات المقدمه من المملكه لبرنامج الاغذيه العالمي Translation:"Al- Rabiah more than one billion and 958 million dollars in aid from the Kingdom to the world food program"
Business	Start-Org	Arabic: اسواق عبدالله العثيم تفتتح احدث فروعها بحي النسيم ب سيهات Translation:"Abdullah Al-Othaim Markets opens its newest branches in Al-Naseem neighborhood in Sihat"
	End-Org	Arabic: امانه العاصمه المقدسه تغلق ٦ منشات تجاريه مخالفه للانظمه البلديه Translation:"Holy capital municipality closes 6 commercial establishments contrary to municipal regulations"
Conflict	Demonstrate	Arabic: احتجاجات في اصفهان على جفاف نهر زاينده بعد تحويل مجراه والسلطات الايرانيه تقطع الانترنت عن المنطقه Translation:"Protests in Isfahan over the drought of the Ziande River after the diversion of its course and the Iranian authorities cut off the Internet from the region."
	Attack	Arabic: ارمينيا و اذربيجان تتبادلان اطلاق النار على الحدود قرب اقليم ناغورنو كاراباخ الذي شهد العام الماضي حربا بين هذين البلدين وكل طرف يتهم الثاني بالتسبب بالواقعه Translation:"Armenia and Azerbaijan exchanged fire on the border near Nagorno-Karabakh, which last year witnessed a war between these two countries and each side accuses the second of causing the incident."
Contact	Meet	Arabic: الاسد التقى بوزير الخارجيه الاماراتي في دمشق Translation:"Assad met with UAE Foreign Minister in Damascus"
	Phone-Write	Arabic: الامير محمد بن سلمان يجري اتصالا هاتفيا للاطمئنان على صحه رئيس وزراء العراق مصطفى الكاظمي Translation:"Prince Mohammed bin Salman makes a phone call to check on the health of Iraqi Prime Minister Mustafa Al-Kadhimi"
Personnel	Start-Position	Arabic: اللبنانيه ساره منقاره تنضم لاداره بايدن كمستشاره خاصه لشؤون حقوق ذوي الاحتياجات الخاصه وهذا ما قالته ل حول ذلك Translation:"Lebanese Sarah Manqara joins Biden'S administration as a special adviser on special needs rights and that's what she said about that"
	End-Position	Arabic: المجلس الرئاسي الليبي يوقف وزيره الخارجيه نجلاء المنقوش عن العمل ويمنعها من السفر Translation:"Libyan Presidential Council suspends foreign minister Najla alManoush from work and prevents her from traveling"
	Nominate	Arabic: مرشح الجزائر محمد هامل امينا عاما جديدا لمنتدى الدول المصدره للغاز Translation:"Algeria's Candidate Mohamed Hamel as New Secretary-General of the Forum of Gas Exporters"
Justice	Arrest-Jail	Arabic: السلطات التركيه تعتقل العشرات بعد احتجاجات عنيفه ضد اللاجئين السوريين في انقره Translation:"Turkish authorities arrest dozens after violent protests against Syrian refugees in Ankara"
	Release-Parole	Arabic: مصر الافراج عن الناشطه اسراء عبد الفتاح Translation:"Egypt releases activist Israa Abdel Fattah"
	Trial-Hearing	Arabic: بدء محاكمه المغني الامريكي كيلي الحائز على جائزه غرامي بتهم ممارسه الابتزاز وتضليل العداله والاعتداء الجنسي على قاصرات Translation:"American Grammy award-winning singer Kelly begins trial on charges of abusing, misleading justice, and sexually assaulting minors"
	Charge-Indict	Arabic: على خلفيه مخطط لاغتيال مواطنين اسرائيليين في الجزيره السلطات القبرصيه توجه اتهامات جنائيه لسته اشخاص Translation:"Regarding assassinate Israeli citizens on the island, the Cypriot authorities are pressing criminal charges against six people"
	Sue	Arabic: فتاه ترفع دعوى في الولايات المتحده على الامير اندرو بتهمه الاعتداء الجنسي Translation:"Girl sues Prince Andrew in U.S. for sexual assault"
	Convict	Arabic: النيابه العامه صدور حكم ابتدائي باداته احد المتهمين ظهر في مقطع فيديو يتضمن قيامه بالتحرش بامراه Translation:"The public prosecution issued a preliminary verdict in the conviction of one of the accused appeared in a video clip that includes him harassing a woman"
	Sentence	Arabic: محكمه تركيه تقضي بسجن زوجه رئيس حزب معارض ل اردوغان عامين ونصف بسبب تقرير طبي Translation:" Turkish court sentences wife of the president of the opposition party to Erdogan with two and a half years in prison for medical report"
	Fine	Arabic: الف دولار قيمه الغرامات بحق نائبه رفضت ارتداء الكمامه بمبنى الكونغرس ٤٨ Translation:"$48, 000 worth of fines for a deputy who refused to wear the mask in the Capitol"
	Execute	Arabic: الاعدام لقاتل مدير بلديه كربلاء واستمرار الجدل على اداته عناصر حمايته Translation:" Execution of the killer of the mayor of Karbala and the continuing controversy over the condemnation of his protection elements"
	Extradite	Arabic: اليكس صعب تسليم المساعد البارز لرئيس فنزويلا نيكولاس مادورو الى الولايات المتحده Translation:"Alex Saab delivers Venezuela's top aide Nicolas Maduro to the United States"
	Acquit	Arabic: انهار امام المحكمه واجهش في البكاء القضاء الاميركي يبرئ الاميركي كايل ريتنهاوس من جريمه قتل Translation:"He collapsed in front of the court and faced in tears the American judiciary cleared American Kyle Rittenhouse of murder"
	Appeal	موفد الى انتويرب نور الدين الفريضي محكمه بلجيكيه تنظر الاستئناف المقدم من خليه اسد الله اسدي واحد المتهمين يتعاون مع المحققين Translation:"A Belgian court is hearing the appeal filed by Assadullah Asadi'S cell, one of the accused is cooperating with the investigators"
	Pardon	Arabic: ملك الاردن يعفو عن ١٥٥ محكوما باطاله اللسان عليه Translation:"King of Jordan pardons 155 convicted of Offensive Speech"

Table 10: Examples of Labeling Results Following Guidelines from (ACE, 2005).

Type		Subtype			
Name	Changes from ACE2005 Description if any	Name	Exist in ACE2005	Reason for Adding/changing	Example
Business	No changes	Buy	No	Transfer-Ownership sub-type restricted the buying and selling events for artifacts such as vehicles or weapons and organizations or facilities. Thus, we label the event as Buy or Sell when any physical item is purchased or sold respectively. (excluding items from Transfer-Ownership).	Arabic: تهافت الدول الغنية على شراء سلاح كورونا الجديد هل يصل إلى الفقيرة منها Translation:"Rich countries are eager to buy a new corona weapon will it reach the poor ones?
		Sell	No		Arabic: لوحه بانكسي المرقه تباع مجددا برقم قياسي قدره ٢٥٤ مليون دولار Translation:"Banksy torn painting is selling again for a record $254 million"
Justice	In contrast with ACE2005, we label the JUSTICE event subtypes based on actions by any entity that holds authority or dominance and not only the government, because the governing authority in a state that is experiencing aggression and wars might not have the authority over the conflict zones where the event occurs or it might be an occupation authority.	Accusation	No	The Accusation event occurs when a person, country, entity, president, or government speaker claims and accuses another state, person, or entity without evidence or a trial. In contrast with the Charge-Indict sub-type, which happen when there's a person or organization accused of a crime by a government actor.	Arabic: اثينا تتهم انقره بتوجيه زورق مهاجرين الى المياه اليونانيه Translation:"Athens accuses Ankara of directing migrant boats into Greek waters"
		Condemnation	No	The Condemnation event takes place when a state, official, organization, or persons condemn an act or attack by another country or organization , or people without any trial. In contrast with the Convict sub-type which occurs when the court conviction the accused.	Arabic: الخارجيه الالمانيه تدين استيلاء الحوثي على السفاره الاميركيه في صنعاء Translation:"German Foreign Affairs condemns the Houthi takeover of the US embassy in Sana'a.
Conflict	No changes	Attack	Yes	The attack sub-type event will be expanded from its original definition which includes "Conflict, clashes, fighting, and shooting" to cover other important attacks such as sexual harassment, rape, burglary, Cyberattack, and takeover a facility.	Arabic: عصابه برازيليه تسطو على بنك وتهرب بالرهائن مقيدين فوق اسطح السيارات Translation:"Brazilian gang robs a bank and escapes hostages tied up on car roofs"
Movement	No changes	Transport	Yes	The sub-type event Transport will expand to cover the transportation of physical items and not the items will not be limited to a weapon, vehicle, or even a person as defined in ACE2005.	Arabic: مركب الشمس نقل مركب الفرعون خوفو الى المتحف المصري الكبير Translation: "The sun boat transported Pharaoh Khufu's boat to the Great Egyptian Museum"
Contact	No changes	Meet	Yes	We modified the definition of the sub-type event Meet to happen when two or more entities meet and interact with each other regardless of whether they're in the same location or not which is the constraint that was identified by ACE2005.	Arabic: لبحث سبل اداره التنافس بين البلدين بشكل مسؤول البيت الابيض بايدن ونظيره الصيني يعقدان اجتماعا افتراضيا الاثنين المقبل Translation: "White House Biden and His Chinese Counterpart Hold Virtual Meeting next Monday to discuss ways to manage competition between the two countries responsibly"
Personnel	No changes	Nominate	Yes	The event will occur when a person has run or become a candidate in a race for either a party or presidential nomination and is not limited to a proposed person for a specific position by organizations.	Arabic: الدبيبه يرشح نفسه رسميا للانتخابات الرئاسيه الليبيه Translation:"Aldebiba officially nominates himself for Libyan Presidential elections "

Table 11: Examples of Labeling Results After modifying the Guidelines

Establishing a Baseline for Arabic Patents Classification: A Comparison of Twelve Approaches

Taif Al-Omar[1], Hend Al-Khalifa[2] and Rawan Al-Matham[3]
iWAN Research Group, King Saud University
[1]taifalomar@gmail.com, [2]hendk@ksu.edu.sa, [3]r.almatham@gmail.com

Abstract

Nowadays, the number of patent applications is constantly growing and there is an economical interest on developing accurate and fast models to automate their classification task. In this paper, we introduce the first public Arabic patent dataset called ArPatent and experiment with twelve classification approaches to develop a baseline for Arabic patents classification. To achieve the goal of finding the best baseline for classifying Arabic patents, different machine learning, pre-trained language models as well as ensemble approaches were conducted. From the obtained results, we can observe that the best performing model for classifying Arabic patents was ARBERT with F1 of 66.53%, while the ensemble approach of the best three performing language models, namely: ARBERT, CAMeL-MSA, and QARiB, achieved the second best F1 score, i.e., 64.52%.

1 Introduction

Over the past few years, there has been an increased focus on improving patent classification systems. This is due to the growing recognition of the importance of classification in improving the efficiency of patent examination and in providing better access to information for users of patent databases.

Currently, patent examiners manually classify patents, which is a time-consuming process. If a method could be developed for automatically classifying patents, it would greatly reduce the amount of time needed to examine a patent application. This is an important area of research because it has the potential to significantly improve the efficiency of patent examination.

Current research efforts in patent classification are focusing on improving the efficiency and accuracy of the classification process. One area of research is exploring the use of machine learning algorithms to automatically classify patents (Aristodemou & Tietze, 2018). Another area of research is looking at ways to improve the use of prior art information in the classification process (Harris et al., 2010).

While classifying patent text is applied widely for some languages, such as, English. The Arabic version of the problem requires the availability of Arabic patent annotated corpus with considerable size as well as experimenting with different classification models. Therefore, the contributions of this paper include:

1- Constructing the first Arabic Patent dataset (called ArPatent) labeled with the International Patent Classification (IPC).
2- Evaluating twelve classification approaches in order to achieve a baseline for Arabic patents classification.

The rest of the paper is organized as follows: sections 2 and 3 provide background and related work on patents and their classification; section 4 presents the data collection and preprocessing process. Sections 5 and 6 discuss the used methods and the obtained results. Finally, section 7 concludes the paper with limitation and research outlook.

2 Background

A patent is a form of intellectual property that gives its owner the legal right to exclude others from making, using, or selling an invention for a limited period of time.

Proceedings of the The Seventh Arabic Natural Language Processing Workshop (WANLP), pages 287 - 294
December 8, 2022 ©2022 Association for Computational Linguistics

A patent document typically includes a title, an abstract, a classification, a background section, a brief summary of the invention, a detailed description of the invention, one or more claims and drawings.

There are two schemes used for patent classification: (1) International Patent Classification (IPC) (International Patent Classification (IPC), n.d.) and (2) Cooperative Patent Classification (CPC) (Office, n.d.).

IPC scheme is a hierarchical patent classification system used in over 100 countries to classify the content of patents in a uniform manner; hence it is usually used for Arabic patents classification. It was established by the World Intellectual Property Organization (WIPO) in 1971.

Each patent publication is given one classification Section (see Table 1) identifying the topic to which the invention relates [1]. Further classification sections and indexing codes may be given to provide further information about the contents.

Section (Class)	Topic
A	Human Necessities
B	Performing Operations, Transporting
C	Chemistry, Metallurgy
D	Textiles, Paper
E	Fixed Constructions
F	Mechanical Engineering, Lighting, Heating, Weapons
G	Physics
H	Electricity

Table 1: IPC eight classification sections and topics

3 Related Work

There are many studies in the literature that tackled automated patent classification. The earliest studies employed classical Natural Language Processing (NLP) and Machine Learning (ML) approaches with feature engineering. For instance, (Fall et al., 2003) did many experiments in two levels, classes and subclasses. They compared the precision of using many classifiers, Naïve Bayes (NB), Support Vector Machine (SVM), Spars Network of Windows (SNoW) and K-Nearest Neighbor (KNN) classifiers on their self-collected WIPO [2] dataset named WIPO-alpha, with performing stop words removal, stemming, and term selection using information gain as a preprocessing step. The best result in classes-level experiments was obtained with NB classifier (79%). While in the subclasses-level the best result was with KNN (62%).

Similarly, (Tikk et al., 2008) used stemming, dimensionality reduction, stop word removal and removal of rare terms with a neural network called HITEC which was evaluated on WIPO-alpha corpus and Espace A/B [3] corpora. there results outperform other state-of-the art classifiers significantly (by 6.5~14.5%). Additionally, (Lim & Kwon, 2016) created a list of stop words specifically for the patent domain and used a TF-IDF weighing system to choose their feature set. The patent document classification was examined using a multi-label model and 564,793 registered Korean patents at the IPC subclass level. They achieved a precision rate of 87.2% when using titles, abstracts, claims, technical fields, and backgrounds.

Around 2017, the focus of automated patent classification research changed to Deep Learning (DL) approaches. (Grawe et al., 2017) trained Espace A/B patent dataset with Word2Vec and fed it to LSTM classifier. At the level of subclasses, they achieved an accuracy rate of 63%. Likewise, (Xiao et al., 2018) applied similar approach (Word2Vec and LSTM) with their self-collected domain-specific patent datasets for security. Their approach achieved 93.48% of accuracy. On the other hand, (Risch & Krestel, 2019) employed bi-directional GRUs (another type of RNN) to improve classification performance compared to Word Embeddings trained with Word2Vec on Wiki pages and the FastText embedding that was trained on different datasets (WIPO-alpha ,USPTO[4]-2M and USPTO-5M). Their approach increased the average precision for patent classification by 17 percent compared to state-of-the-art approaches.

Moreover, (Sofean, 2021) created a self-trained Word Embedding that was trained on a million patents collected from multiple patents datasets (European, German, Japanese and Chinese patents), and then classified them using LSTM

[1] https://ipcpub.wipo.int/

[2] https://www.wipo.int/

[3] https://www.epo.org/

[4] https://bulkdata.uspto.gov/

network. He obtained an accuracy of 67%. Another paper by (S. Li et al., 2018) developed DeepPatent algorithm for patent classification by combining Word Embeddings with CNN. It was tested on USPTO-2M dataset. Their approach achieved precision of 73.88%. Similarly, (Zhu et al., 2020) experiments were applied to classify Chinese short text patent using Word Embedding with CNN. Their results outperformed traditional RNN.

However, using CNNs alone has gained the best results in patent classification task. In (Abdelgawad et al., 2020), they achieved an accuracy of 52.02% at the subclass level with the WIPO-alpha dataset.

(Lee & Hsiang, 2020) fine-tuned a pre-trained BERT model on a their self-collected patent dataset which contains three million patents. They focused on patent claims without other parts and the best results they achieved was 66.83% for F1.

Ensemble techniques were also among the used approaches in patent classifications. (Eleni Kamateri et al., 2022) experimented with CLEF-IP 2011 test collection to compare the accuracy of classifying English patents using different individuals' classifiers (CNN, Bi-LSTM, Bi-GRU, LSTM, and GRU) and using ensemble approach with three classifiers. Their highest accuracy (64.85%) was gained by using ensemble approach that combined three of their best performing classifiers.

From the previous studies we noticed that there is a huge interest in the community for patent classification in languages such as English and Korean. Furthermore, the best results were obtained with fine-tuning BERT language models and ensemble approach. Therefore, in this paper we created the first Arabic patent dataset and applied the best classification approaches mentioned previously in the literature.

4 Data Acquisition and Preprocessing

4.1 Data Acquisition

Delivering an Arabic patent dataset is one of the contributions in this paper. The dataset was acquired by scraping the granted Arabic patents at the Saudi Authority of Intellectual Property (SAIP)[5] website using Selenium[6]. All the available patents at the website were retrieved, mainly 9772 patents. All patents were typically composed of the following sections: title, abstract, applicant, the International Patent Classification (IPC) and other details (see Figure 1). The size of the acquired data was approximately 413 MB with 1.58M tokens — words. We named our dataset "ArPatent" and it is publicly available through our Github repository[7].

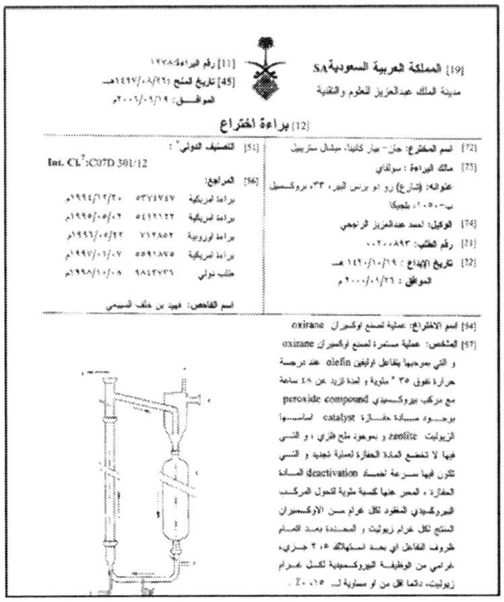

Figure 1: A screenshot of an Arabic patent document from SAIP[5]

4.2 Preprocessing

We chose to classify the patents into one of the eight IPC sections by training the models using titles and abstracts onlybelow; as they are the common sections among almost all patents. Nevertheless, six patents had no abstract hence were removed from the dataset. Moreover, one patent had no accurate IPC section and was excluded, so the remaining patents reached 9765. To explore and understand the dataset, we calculated the unigram and bigram frequencies after the data has been preprocessed as shown in Table 2 and Table 3.

The preprocessing steps consisted of removing Arabic and English punctuations or digits, removing elongation and normalizing Arabic letters by replacing different forms of alif "ا،أ،إ،آ" into the simple form "ا", replacing "ة" into "ه", and finally replacing any "ى" into "ي". It is noteworthy to mention that words with English letters were

[5] https://www.saip.gov.sa/en

[6] https://www.selenium.dev/

[7] https://github.com/iwan-rg/Arabic-Patents

	Word	Count		Word	Count
1	الاختراع	9726	7	ماده	2479
2	الحالي	6557	8	يكون	2384
3	الاقل	5073	9	مجموعه	2131
4	يمكن	2893	10	جزء	2062
5	تشتمل	2558	11	باستخدام	1910
6	بواسطه	2517	12	تتضمن	1904

Table 2: The top 15 bigram words in the Arabic patent dataset along with their frequencies.

	Word	Count		Word	Count
1	الاختراع, الحالي	6095	7	الاختراع, الراهن	458
2	يتعلق, الاختراع	1175	8	اكسيد, الكربون	399
3	درجه, حراره	815	9	الحالي, بجهاز	362
4	واحده, الاقل	788	10	الحالي, بنظام	342
5	الحالي, بطريقه	621	11	الحالي, بتوفير	332
6	الحالي, بعمليه	459	12	الاختراع, بطريقه	332

Table 3: The top 15 bigram words in the Arabic patent dataset along with their frequencies.

preserved as they might represent scientific or technical terms, therefore keeping them might enhance the classification performance and prevent information loss.

Furthermore, the min/max/average of number of words in titles and abstracts were computed and resulted in 4/237/53 for titles, and 10/35371/681 for abstracts. We can say that our dataset is considered an imbalanced since the number of patents in each IPC section was far from equal, see Table 4.

Section (Class)	No. of Patents
A	2169
B	2038
C	2783
D	61
E	733
F	741
G	764
H	476

Table 4: Number of patents in each IPC section

5 Methodology

To achieve the goal of finding the best baseline for classifying Arabic patents, different machine learning approaches were considered. First, from the traditional approaches, SVM were implemented with different word Embeddings techniques; namely: TF-IDF, and Skip-Gram Word2Vec. For Word2Vec, we used the pre-trained Embeddings AraVec (Soliman et al., 2017), and we also trained our own Word2Vec version, named ArPatent-Word2vec[8], on the entire preprocessed Arabic patent text.

Moreover, since BERT-based models have shown state-of-the-art performance at language understanding, we fine-tuned multiple Arabic BERT-based models on the unprocessed titles and abstracts of ArPatent for the task of patent classification. The used fine-tuning hyperparameters were: learning rate of 2e-5 using Adam's optimizer, A dropout layer of 0.1 at the feed-forward classifier, a batch size of 32 and 3 epochs. Moreover, the max length of tokens was set to 350 tokens for the tokenizer, truncating any input beyond that length. Furthermore, stratified split was used for splitting the data into 10/10/80 for testing, validation, and training respectively. The evaluation metrics used are accuracy, macro-precision, macro-recall and macro-F1 score, having the last as the primary metric since the dataset is highly imbalanced.

The following subsections give a summary of the used pre-trained models.

5.1 CAMeL-MSA

CAMeL-MSA (Inoue et al., 2021) is a pre-trained BERT model on Modern Standard Arabic (MSA) corpus that is comprised of the following public Arabic corpora: Abu El-Khair Corpus, dump of the Arabic Wikipedia on February 01, 2019[9], The unshuffled version of the Arabic OSCAR corpus, the Arabic Gigaword Fifth Edition and lastly the OSIAN corpus. The resulting dataset consisted of 107GB of text, yielding 12.6B tokens. It is worth

[8] https://github.com/iwan-rg/Arabic-Patents

[9] https://archive.org/details/arwiki-20190201

mentioning that the authors removed lines that had no Arabic characters from the text.

5.2 CAMeL-MIX

Same authors of CAMeL-MSA have contributed to releasing a model that was pre-trained on different Arabic variants, i.e., the same MSA corpus mentioned earlier, a range of dialectal Arabic corpora and a classical Arabic corpus from OpenITI. The model was pre-trained on text size of 167GB with 17.3B tokens, which is the largest number of tokens among all other BERT variants mentioned in this paper.

5.3 ARBERT

ARBERT (Abdul-Mageed et al., 2021) is also a BERT-based model pre-trained on 61GB of MSA text with 6.5B tokens, gathered from 1,800 Arabic books, the fifth edition of GigaWord, Abu El-Khair Corpus, OSCAR, OSIAN, and the December 2019 dump of Arabic Wikipedia.

5.4 MARBERTv2

MARBERT (Abdul-Mageed et al., 2021) was pre-trained to be best suited for dialectical Arabic using 1B tweets. The dataset makes up 128GB of text —15.6B tokens. For MARBERTv2, they further pre-trained MARBERT on the same dataset of ARBERT in addition to AraNews dataset. New MARBERTv2 dataset makes up 29B of tokens.

5.5 AraBERTv2

AraBERTv2 (Antoun et al., 2020), is a pre-trained BERT model for MSA NLP tasks. It was pre-trained on 77GB or 200M sentences of Arabic content resulting in 8.6B tokens. The corpus consisted of manually scraped Arabic news websites and four publicly available corpora: Arabic Wikipedia dump from 2020/09/01 [10], OSCAR unshuffled and filtered, The 1.5B words Arabic Corpus, and lastly the OSIAN Corpus. The authors noted that words with Latin characters were preserved during the training.

5.6 QARiB

QARiB (Ahmed Abdelali et al., 2021) was pre-trained on a collection of 420M tweets and 180M sentences of text. For the sentences, it was a combination of Arabic GigaWord Fourth Edition, Abu El-Khair Corpus and OpenSubtitles corpus. It resulted in 14B tokens

5.7 Max Voting Ensemble

An ensemble is a collection of models designed to exceed the performance of every single base-model by combining their predictions. Max voting —or majority vote— ensemble is one of the simplest methods of combining predictions. In max voting, each base-model makes a prediction and votes for each instance. In addition to fine-tuning the models, we considered designing an ensemble of the highest performing models. Since weighted sum ensembles presume that some models in the ensemble are more efficient compared to others; we considered applying both weighted and unweighted summing for predictions and reporting the highest.

Models	Acc.	P_{Macro}	R_{Macro}	$F1_{Macro}$
SVM-SG-ARAVEC	60.55	50.33	51.06	50.46
SVM-ArPatent-Word2vec	63.42	50.64	54.37	51.80
SVM-TF-IDF	63.83	54.11	**67.28**	56.62
CAMeL-MSA	68.03	59.10	59.73	59.27
CAMeL-MIX	66.39	57.07	56.72	56.81
ARBERT	70.18	72.60	64.91	**66.53**
MARBERTv2	62.40	52.37	51.36	51.68
AraBERTv2	63.11	53.01	51.40	51.74
QARiB	67.83	58.26	57.84	57.95
ENSEMBLE-1	**70.49**	**73.36**	63.54	64.52
ENSEMBLE-2	62.91	54.16	51.95	52.46
ENSEMBLE-3	68.24	59.60	57.66	58.10

Table 2: Experimental Results with the following metrics: accuracy (Acc.), macro precision (P), macro recall (R) and macro F1 score (F1).

[10] https://archive.org/details/arwiki-20200901

6 Results and Discussions

Table 5 shows our experimental results. We can see that the BERT-based models that were pre-trained on MSA text only, namely ARBERT and CAMeL-MSA, had a superior performance with an F1 measure of 66.53 and 59.27 respectively. Moreover, among the SVM classifiers, the SVM with TF-IDF word Embeddings achieved a significantly higher performance (F1= 56.62). Although ArPatent-Word2vec embeddings was trained on the ArPatent text, yet it did not improve the classification task, this might be attributed to the models being trained on the title and abstract of a patent rather than the complete patent dataset.

On the other hand, the accuracy of ENSEMBLE-1 results outperformed all other models with 70.49%. ENSEMBLE-1 consists of the three best performing models namely: ARBERT, CAMeL-MSA and QARiB, with weighted sum of 1, 0.5 and 0.5, giving ARBERT the priority in voting. We also combined the SVM models in ENSEMBLE-2 with the same weighted sum, giving the priority to SVM-TF-IDF.

The last ensemble, ENSEMBLE-3, was a combination of all SVMs and ARBERT, giving ARBERT and TF-IDF the twice weight of other SVMs.

From the results, we can observe that the best performing model in terms of F1 score was ARBERT. Although we tried to ensemble different models; but due to little diversity in base-models' predictions; the performance could not get improved, for example, refer to the confusion matrices in Figure 2, Figure 3 and Figure 4 for the models participating in ENSEMBLE-1 and notice the similarity in predictions. Moreover, due to the little number of samples for some classes, the overall performance was low, especially for class D where most of its instances were not classified correctly even with ARBERT.

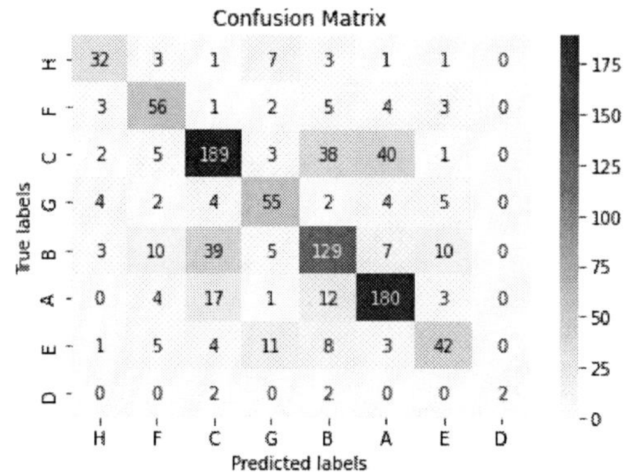

Figure 2: Confusion matrix of the best performing model ARBERT.

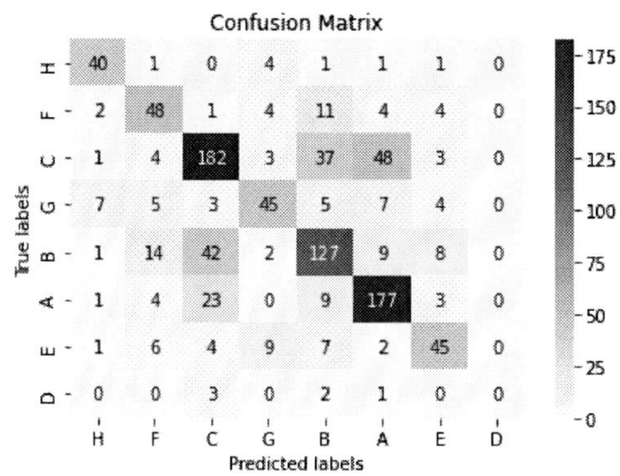

Figure 3: Confusion matrix of CAMeL-MSA.

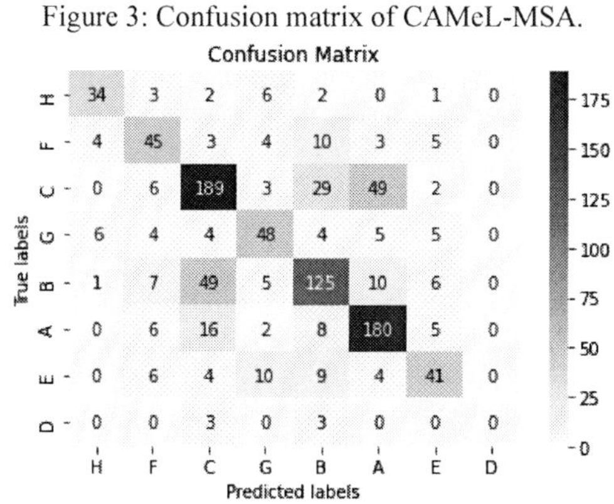

Figure 4: Confusion matrix of QARiB.

7 Conclusion

Classification of patents is a crucial part of the patent system, as it allows for the efficient and effective management of patent information. In this paper, we constructed the first Arabic patent dataset called ArPatent and experimented with twelve different classification approaches to develop a baseline for Arabic patent classification.

Our results show that the ARBERT model had the best performance in classifying patents. We can say that our results are comparable to those found in the literature, even with our small sized dataset.

One limitation of this work resides in the imbalanced dataset, this affected the performance of patent classification. Also, using only the patent's title and abstract for the purpose of classification did not yield good results. Therefore, as a future plan we intend to repeat the experiments while considering the whole text for classification also we need to increase the size of the dataset to obtain more successful results.

Finally, we believe that our paper has produced some preliminary knowledge and useful results that will help support the task of Arabic patent classification.

References

Abdelgawad, L., Kluegl, P., Genc, E., Falkner, S., & Hutter, F. (2020). c In U. Brefeld, E. Fromont, A. Hotho, A. Knobbe, M. Maathuis, & C. Robardet (Eds.), Machine Learning and Knowledge Discovery in Databases (pp. 688–703). Springer International Publishing. https://doi.org/10.1007/978-3-030-46133-1_41

Abdul-Mageed, M., Elmadany, A., & Nagoudi, E. M. B. (2021). ARBERT & MARBERT: Deep Bidirectional Transformers for Arabic. Proceedings of the 59th Annual Meeting of the Association for Computational Linguistics and the 11th International Joint Conference on Natural Language Processing (Volume 1: Long Papers), 7088–7105. https://doi.org/10.18653/v1/2021.acl-long.551

Ahmed Abdelali, Sabit Hassan, Hamdy Mubarak, Kareem Darwish, & Younes Samih. (2021). Pre-Training BERT on Arabic Tweets: Practical Considerations. https://arxiv.org/abs/2102.10684

Antoun, W., Baly, F., & Hajj, H. (2020). AraBERT: Transformer-based Model for Arabic Language Understanding. Proceedings of the 4th Workshop on Open-Source Arabic Corpora and Processing Tools, with a Shared Task on Offensive Language Detection, 9–15. https://aclanthology.org/2020.osact-1.2

Aristodemou, L., & Tietze, F. (2018). The state-of-the-art on Intellectual Property Analytics (IPA): A literature review on artificial intelligence, machine learning and deep learning methods for analysing intellectual property (IP) data. World Patent Information, 55, 37–51. https://doi.org/10.1016/j.wpi.2018.07.002

Eleni Kamateri, Vasileios Stamatis, Konstantinos Diamantaras, & Michail Salampasis. (2022). Automated Single-Label Patent Classification using Ensemble Classifiers. https://arxiv.org/abs/2203.03552

Fall, C. J., Törcsvári, A., Benzineb, K., & Karetka, G. (2003). Automated categorization in the international patent classification. ACM SIGIR Forum, 37(1), 10–25. https://doi.org/10.1145/945546.945547

Grawe, M. F., Martins, C. A., & Bonfante, A. G. (2017). Automated Patent Classification Using Word Embedding. 2017 16th IEEE International Conference on Machine Learning and Applications (ICMLA), 408–411. https://doi.org/10.1109/ICMLA.2017.0-127

Gomez, J. C., & Moens, M.-F. (2014). A Survey of Automated Hierarchical Classification of Patents. Professional Search in the Modern World, 215–249. https://doi.org/10.1007/978-3-319-12511-4_11

Harris, C. G., Arens, R., & Srinivasan, P. (2010). Comparison of IPC and USPC classification systems in patent prior art searches. Proceedings of the 3rd International Workshop on Patent Information Retrieval, 27–32. https://doi.org/10.1145/1871888.1871894

Inoue, G., Alhafni, B., Baimukan, N., Bouamor, H., & Habash, N. (2021). The Interplay of Variant, Size, and Task Type in Arabic Pre-trained Language Models. Proceedings of the Sixth Arabic Natural Language Processing Workshop, 92–104. https://aclanthology.org/2021.wanlp-1.10

International Patent Classification (IPC). (n.d.). Retrieved September 9, 2022, from https://www.wipo.int/classifications/ipc/en/index.html

Lee, J.-S., & Hsiang, J. (2020). Patent classification by fine-tuning BERT language model. World Patent Information, 61, 101965. https://doi.org/10.1016/j.wpi.2020.101965

Li, S., Hu, J., Cui, Y., & Hu, J. (2018). DeepPatent: Patent classification with convolutional neural networks and word embedding. Scientometrics, 117(2), 721–744. https://doi.org/10.1007/s11192-018-2905-5

Lim, S., & Kwon, Y. (2016). IPC Multi-label Classification Based on the Field Functionality of Patent Documents. In J. Li, X. Li, S. Wang, J. Li, & Q. Z. Sheng (Eds.), Advanced Data Mining and Applications (pp. 677–691). Springer International Publishing. https://doi.org/10.1007/978-3-319-49586-6_48

Office, E. P. (n.d.). Cooperative Patent Classification (CPC). Retrieved September 9, 2022, from https://www.epo.org/searching-for-patents/helpful-resources/first-time-here/classification/cpc.html#:~:textThe%20Cooperative%20Patent%20Classification%20(CPC,%2C%20groups%20and%20sub%2Dgroups

Risch, J., & Krestel, R. (2019). Domain-specific word embeddings for patent classification. Data Technologies and Applications, 53(1), 108–122. https://doi.org/10.1108/DTA-01-2019-0002

Sofean, M. (2021). Deep learning based pipeline with multichannel inputs for patent classification. World Patent Information, 66, 102060. https://doi.org/10.1016/j.wpi.2021.102060

Soliman, A. B., Eissa, K., & El-Beltagy, S. R. (2017). AraVec: A set of Arabic Word Embedding Models for use in Arabic NLP. Procedia Computer Science, 117, 256–265. https://doi.org/10.1016/j.procs.2017.10.117

Tikk, D., Biro, G., & Törcsvári, A. (2008). A Hierarchical Online Classifier for Patent Categorization [Chapter]. Emerging Technologies of Text Mining: Techniques and Applications; IGI Global. https://doi.org/10.4018/978-1-59904-373-9.ch012

Xiao, L., Wang, G., & Zuo, Y. (2018). Research on Patent Text Classification Based on Word2Vec and LSTM. 2018 11th International Symposium on Computational Intelligence and Design (ISCID), 01, 71–74. https://doi.org/10.1109/ISCID.2018.00023

Zhu, H., He, C., Fang, Y., Ge, B., Xing, M., & Xiao, W. (2020). Patent Automatic Classification Based on Symmetric Hierarchical Convolution Neural Network. Symmetry, 12(2), 186; https://doi.org/10.3390/sym12020186

Towards Learning Arabic Morphophonology

Salam Khalifa, Jordan Kodner, and Owen Rambow
Department of Linguistics, and
Institute for Advanced Computational Science (IACS)
Stony Brook University
{first.last}@stonybrook.edu

Abstract

One core challenge facing morphological inflection systems is capturing language-specific morphophonological changes. This is particularly true of languages like Arabic which are morphologically complex. In this paper, we learn explicit morphophonological rules from morphologically annotated Egyptian Arabic and corresponding surface forms. These rules are human-interpretable, capture known morphophonological phenomena in the language, and are generalizable to unseen forms.

1 Introduction

Much progress has been made in tasks such as morphological (re-)inflection and morphological analysis in recent years (e.g., Narasimhan et al., 2015; Kirov and Cotterell, 2018; Belth et al., 2021). However, low-resource languages still prove to be a significant challenge, despite growing interest, as the recent SIGMORPHON shared task reveals (Kodner et al., 2022; Kodner and Khalifa, 2022). Arabic dialects present a specific challenge in that there is an almost continual variation between dialects, mainly along the geographical dimension, and most dialects are low-resource. Cairene Arabic morphology is related to that of the dialects of (for example) Alexandria, Sohag, Aswan, and Khartoum. So from an NLP point of view, if we have knowledge of Cairene and need a morphological tool for one of the other dialects, we should be able to leverage our knowledge of Cairene. We propose to address the challenge by modeling morphophonological rules explicitly. Such rules provide an *explainable* representation of morphophonology. Once we have those rules, we can create NLP tools while leveraging rules from adjacent dialects. Having a standalone model of morphology, in terms of morphophonology or morphosyntax, improves the per formance of many downstream NLP tasks such as machine translation (Sennrich and Haddow, 2016; Erdmann et al., 2019; Alhafni et al., 2020), speech synthesis (Halabi, 2016) and morphological disambiguation (Khalifa et al., 2020; Inoue et al., 2022). Morphological resources provide explicit linguistic knowledge that is not necessarily captured by learning models.

In this paper we present a preliminary study on automatically learning morphophonological rules for Cairene Egyptian Arabic (henceforth, EGY). We choose EGY because it is well-studied and has many resources. The learning process relies on the rule representation inspired by the notion of *phonological rules*, where a phonological alternation is explicitly represented via an input, an output, and the phonemic context. We evaluate our approach based the accuracy of the generated forms and the genralizability of the learned rules. Additionally, we describe the dataset preparation process as there is no suitable dataset for our task. To the best of our knowledge, this task of rule-learning to specifically model morphophonology has not been studied before in the context of Arabic NLP. This study will help us investigate to what degree can we learn explicit linguistic properties from simple representations.

2 Related Work

There have been many efforts on morphological modeling for Arabic. Precompiled tabular morphological analyzers (Buckwalter, 2002, 2004; Graff et al., 2009; Habash et al., 2012; Khalifa et al., 2017; Taji et al., 2018) became the standard in many Arabic NLP pipelines. While they provide rich morphological analysis, they are directly encoded into the lexicon and do not explicitly model descriptive linguistic phenomena such as morphophonological interactions. In contrast, earlier efforts that modeled morphology using finite-state technology (e.g., Beesley, 1998; Habash and Rambow, 2006) used explicit rules leveraging roots and patterns. However, they were manually built and were abstracted to a high degree. More re-

Proceedings of the The Seventh Arabic Natural Language Processing Workshop (WANLP), pages 295 - 301
December 8, 2022 ©2022 Association for Computational Linguistics

Dialect	Realization
Egyptian	kitabha
Sudanese	kitaaba
Hijazi	kitaabaha
Emirati	kitaabha

Table 1: Different realizations of the same underlying form /kitaab+haa/ 'her book' كتابها in four dialects.

cently, Habash et al. (2022) focused on modeling allomorphy through linguistically descriptive rules. However, the rules are manually created and do not model phonological representations. Other efforts adopting neural approaches to modeling morphological inflections (Wu et al., 2021; Dankers et al., 2021; Batsuren et al., 2022) perform well for many languages, however, those models do not provide insightful general rules or descriptions of linguistic phenomena. In this effort we take a generative view on morphophonology and we aim to learn morphophonological rules and apply them automatically.

3 Background

Morphophonology and Arabic Morphophonology is the study of the interaction between morphological and phonological processes. In particular, morphophonemic analysis aims at discovering the set of underlying forms and ordered rules that are consistent with the data it analyzes (Hayes, 2008).

Arabic morphophonology is especially interesting as its complex morphology is both templatic and concatenative. Morphophonological changes occur on the stem pattern and on stem and word boundaries. In the case of concatnative morphology, adding morphemes around the stem may trigger phonological changes. Most of these reinterpret the syllabic structure of utterances, and Arabic varieties may employ different processes to maintain such structures (Broselow, 2017). Table 1 shows how different varieties realize the same underlying representation: Egyptian, Sudanese, and Hijazi all employ different strategies to avoid a super-heavy syllable /-taab/, while Emirati permits it.

Rule Representation The transformation rules that we aim to extract are inspired by the *Sound Pattern of English* (SPE; Chomsky and Halle, 1968), where a hypothetical underlying representation (UR) is transformed into a surface form (SF) by the application of a series of rules. Below is an example of a phonological rule representing *r-dropping* in many dialects of British English, where r is dropped when it falls between a vowel and a syllable boundary $]_\sigma$.

$$r \rightarrow \emptyset \,/\, V \_\_ \,]_\sigma$$
$$\text{UR} \rightarrow \text{SF} \,/\, \text{(context)} \_\_ \text{(context)}$$

Our work takes inspiration from the main three components of a rule, which are the UR, SF, and the context. The exact notion of rule, however, differs in order to make it machine-friendly. To this end, we take additional inspiration from two-level phonology (Antworth, 1991), which compresses stacks of SPE rules into a single UR and SF without intermediate steps.

4 Data

Our focus is on developing an *explainable* learning approach. Therefore, we control our experimental setup by having a few assumptions: a) we deal with whole words out of context, b) the data is in a broad phonetic transcription, c) SF is the word produced and UR is the morphologically segmented underlying representation, and d) the phonemic and morphemic inventories are assumed to be acquired beforehand (for example, by observing words in which the segmentation task is trivial).

Though EGY is resource-rich relative to many other varieties, there is no dataset that has been annotated for the task of morphophonological learning. To build such a dataset we need to create pairs of UR and SF to learn and evaluate morphophonological rules. In this work, we employ two existing resources created specifically for EGY: ECAL, and CALIMA_{EGY}.

4.1 Resources

The Egyptian Colloquial Arabic Lexicon (ECAL; Kilany et al., 2002) is a pronunciation dictionary primarily based on CALLHOME Egypt (Gadalla et al., 1997). Each entry in ECAL includes an orthographic, phonological, and morphological representation (Table 2(a)). Phonological forms represent SF. The orthography is undiacritized, and ECAL does not provide a full morphological segmentation. Therefore, we cannot use ECAL alone to extract URs, and we employ a separate resource in order to generate a hypothesized UR with morpheme boundaries.

CALIMA_{EGY} (Habash et al., 2012) is a morphological analyzer that generates a set of possible analyses for a given input token out of context. Each analysis includes a diacritized orthographic

(a)	ECA	Arabic	Pronunciation	lemma:morph
	mafatIHu	مفاتيحه	m@f@tIHu	muftAH:noun+masc-inan-plural+gen-3rd-masc-sg

(b)	diac	lemma	BW	POS	gen	num	enc0
	مَفاتِيحُه	مِفْتاح	POSS_PRON_3MS/ه+NOUN/مَفاتِيح	noun	m	s	3ms_poss

Table 2: An example of a partial entry from ECAL in (a). An example of a partial entry from CALIMA$_{EGY}$ in (b).

form, morphological segmentation, and morphological features. We leverage the segmentation provided through CALIMA$_{EGY}$ as the starting point for a UR to the SF extracted from ECAL.

4.2 Dataset Creation

We generate a UR from CALIMA$_{EGY}$ for every SF extracted from ECAL. We use the CamelTools (Obeid et al., 2020) analyzer engine. We feed in the ECAL orthographic form to generate all the possible analyses. We then automatically choose the best matching analysis based on the orthography, lemma, part-of-speech (POS), and morphological features from both resources. Tables 2(a,b) show the necessary information used from both resources for the word /mafatiiħu/ 'his keys' مفاتيحه. Once the best analysis is chosen, the segmentation is extracted from the Buckwalter fine-grained POS tag (Buckwalter, 2002) generated as part of the CALIMA$_{EGY}$ analysis.

Forms are normalized to approximate UR forms. Only *stem-bound* morphophonological sound changes, i.e., entirely predictable changes, are normalized. These included changes such as unconditioned /q/ > /ʔ/ and the distinction between emphatic and non-emphatic vowels. Another aspect to take into consideration is the hypothesized underlying representation of the affixes and clitics. Some morphemes, such as the 2.fem.sg clitic /ik/, can have two forms, [ik] or [kii] depending on the last segment in the stem. In such cases, we remained faithful to the form provided by CALIMA$_{EGY}$ which is always consistent.

Finally, we enrich the segmentation provided by the analyzer, delimiting prefixes with -, suffixes with =, and word boundaries with #.[1] Table 3(a) shows an example of the final (UR,SF) pair. When generating the final set of UR and SF pairs, we only picked entries that belong to the open-class POS, i.e., verbs, nouns, and adjective.

[1]We do not make a distinction between affixes and clitics boundaries because we discovered that it does not significantly affect the learning process.

Data

(a)	UR	SF	
	#mafAtIH=uh#	#mafatIHu#	مَفاتِيحُه

Locate alternations in UR

(b) #mafAtIH=uh#

Fit to smallest context

(c) afAtIH=uh#

Generalize

(d) aCACIC=uh#

Rule

(e)	LHS	RHS
	aCACIC=uh# → aCaCICu#	

Table 3: This figure shows process of rule extraction starting from (UR,SF) pairs. An entry from the dataset in (a). In (b), different alternations are located through Levenshtein distance, morpheme boundary changes are in blue, and phonemic changes are in red to visualize the changes. We then reduce UR to the smallest context in (c). Followed by generalizing the stem consonants in (d). In (e) we see the final form of the rule.

4.3 Splits

ECAL was based on a continuous text corpus and indicates the occurrences of the entries in each of the three splits in the original corpus, namely, TRAIN, DEV, and EVAL. Because the splits are based on running text, words may re-occur in each of the splits. So in addition to DEV and EVAL, we also create DEV-OOV and EVAL-OOV by removing any overlap with TRAIN as shown in Table 4(a).

5 Learning Approach

We frame the learning problem as learning simple transformation rules that capture morphophonological interactions in a given dataset of (UR,SF) pairs.

5.1 Rule Extraction

We employ a simple rule learning mechanism that consists of extracting string transformations and converting those transformations into *rules* learned from TRAIN. In the first round, the string transformations are captured by calculating Levenshtein distance on every (UR,SF) to extract edit operations. Those edit operations are then used to locate the positions of where alternations are happening. Alternations to both the morpheme boundaries and phonemes are being considered. Levenshtein edits return whole word contexts. In order to improve generalizability, we choose a window of 2 around an alternation, if more than one alternation occur, then the window will be around the smallest substring that contains all alternations. And to further generalize, all consonants of the stem are replaced with a generic *C* character. The vowels and all other morphemes remain fully specified. Note that in the original notion of rules mentioned in §3, the rule always corresponds to a single change, so several rules may have to apply in sequence to yield the appropriate SF. However, in our adaptation, a single rule captures all changes simultaneously.

A rule in our definition consists of two components: the left-hand side (LHS) of the rule which represents the UR and context, and the right-hand side (RHS) of the rule which represents the SF. In case no change occurs, i.e., UR and SF are identical, in other words, the only alternations are deletions of morpheme boundaries, then the rule is reduced to UR→*copy*. Every rule has an accompanying frequency which is the number of (UR,SF) pair types that generated this rule. Table 3(e) shows an example of a rule. After rule extraction and generalization we ended up with 4,661 rules, which is 35.4% of the size of TRAIN.

5.2 Rule Selection

Since rules are specified by a limited context, it is often the case that more than one rule could apply to a given UR. Finding a rule that matches a given UR and produces the correct SF is not a trivial task. At this stage of our study, we employ a simple heuristic to select the most fitting rule. For a new UR, the longest and the most *specific* LHS is chosen. Specificity is determined by the least amount of unspecified consonants in the stem, i.e., the least number of *C*s. If the chosen LHS is found to participate in multiple rules, then the most frequent rule is applied.

(a)

	TRAIN	DEV	EVAL
All	13,170	5,180	6,974
OOV	–	2,189	2,271

(b)

	TRAIN	DEV	EVAL
All	90.1%	80.5%	82.3%
OOV	–	69.4%	68.9%

Table 4: Accuracy on each data split in (a). **All** represents all the types belonging to the respective splits as indicated in ECAL. **OOV** represents the same splits excluding types which also occur in TRAIN in (b).

6 Evaluation

To evaluate our current rule learning approach, we compute the accuracy of the generated SF for every UR, reported in Table 4(b). TRAIN accuracy is reported for the purpose of validating the generalizability of the rules. Performance is under 100% because of the rule abstraction process and rule selection heuristic. Even in TRAIN, there are words to which multiple rules can apply.

Two numbers are provided for both DEV and EVAL. The numbers in the **All** group indicate performance on the full splits. These indicate likely performance in future downstream tasks applied to running text, however, these contain words which were also present in TRAIN, so they are not in themselves a good indicator of our model's ability to generalize to unseen words. The out-of-vocabulary (**OOV**) numbers only report accuracy on types that were unseen during training. They retain most of their performance, indicating that the rules that our model learns do apply to new types.

7 Discussion and Error Analysis

The results discussed in §6 are good indicators of the generalizability of all the components of our approach, including rule representation, extraction, and selection heuristics. We performed a qualitative error analysis to further verify the generalizability and linguistic validity of the acquired rules.

Sources of Errors We investigated sources of errors in the SF production by comparing the rules the were selected with the ground-truth rules of the 31% of DEV-OOV forms that were incorrectly produced. The ground-truth rules were classified as either *in-vocabulary* rules (INV-rules) which exist in the acquired rule inventory or *out-of-vocabulary* rules (OOV-rules) which do not. Of the errors, 32% misproduced words had INV-rules. The selection heuristic is the driving source of this error: in the overwhelming majority of cases, the most specific LHS was selected. On the other hand, 68% of the errors had OOV-rules, which means that those rules were never seen before. We investigated 100 of those rules (30%). We found that all phenomena that those rules capture are in fact already captured in existing rules, but the context of the alternation is new, and therefore, the LHS is deemed unseen. This investigation emphasizes the crucial roles of the rule search heuristic and choice of the context.

Linguistic Phenomena To reaffirm the value of learning morphophonology through rules, we analyzed the top 60 (*non-copy*) most frequent rules. The most frequent rule in this sample had a frequency of 166 and the lowest was 15. We describe the captured phenomena in the following points:

- Word-final long vowel shortening.
- Assimilation of determiner-final /l/ to a stem-initial coronal. The "sun" and "moon" letter rule.
- Shortening of stem /aa/ in certain patterns.
- Epenthetic /u/ and /a/ to break *CCC* clusters.
- Deletion of stem-initial glottal stop after a prefix.
- Lengthening of the feminine suffix marker /a/ when it attaches to some pronominal suffixes in active participles.
- Deletion of word-final /h/ in the 3.masc.sg /-uh/.
- Deletion of /i/ in the active participles of the pattern /CACiC/ before a pronominal suffix.

Those findings mirror descriptive phonology for EGY (Abdel-Massih et al., 1979; Broselow, 2017). The small number of phenomena we found in the rules highlights once again the importance of determining the optimal context. This is a matter we are currently investigating.

8 Conclusion and Future work

In this paper we presented a morphophonological learning approach for Egyptian Arabic. The main goal was to learn morphophonological rules from pairs of underlying representations and surface forms. We achieved this goal with a production accuracy of 82% on the evaluation set and 68% on completely unseen tokens from the same set. Additionally, the linguistic phenomena captured through the rules align with the descriptive grammars of Egyptian Arabic. This effort also resulted in a new dataset designed specifically for this task. The dataset was generated by combining relevant information from a pronunciation lexicon and an orthography-based morphological analyzer.

In ongoing work, we continue to develop the crucial components of our rule learning approach. We are focusing on developing a more dynamic approach to determine the context of a change and the degree of phone abstraction. We will validate our approach by applying it to more dialects, including dialects with very scarce resources. Additionally, in low resource simulated settings, we plan to investigate the cognitive plausibility of the rules which will give insights to child acquisition of morphophonological phenomena.

Acknowledgements

This project is part of a larger effort taking place at the Department of Linguistics at Stony Brook, we would like to thank the members of the research group Ellen Broselow, Robert Hoberman, Jeff Heinz, and Daniel Greeson for their feedback. The authors of this paper were partially funded by a Stony Brook University research seed grant. Some experiments were performed on the SeaWulf HPC cluster maintained by RCC, and IACS at Stony Brook University and made possible by NSF grant #1531492.

References

Ernest T. Abdel-Massih, Zaki N. Abdel-Malek, and El-Said M. Badawi. 1979. *A Reference Grammar of Egyptian Arabic*. Georgetown University Press.

Bashar Alhafni, Nizar Habash, and Houda Bouamor. 2020. Gender-aware reinflection using linguistically enhanced neural models. In *Proceedings of the Second Workshop on Gender Bias in Natural Language Processing*, pages 139–150, Barcelona, Spain (Online). Association for Computational Linguistics.

Evan L Antworth. 1991. Introduction to two-level phonology. *Notes on Linguistics*, 53:4–18.

Khuyagbaatar Batsuren, Gábor Bella, Aryaman Arora, Viktor Martinovic, Kyle Gorman, Zdeněk Žabokrtský, Amarsanaa Ganbold, Šárka Dohnalová, Magda Ševčíková, Kateřina Pelegrinová, Fausto Giunchiglia, Ryan Cotterell, and Ekaterina Vylomova. 2022. The SIGMORPHON 2022 Shared Task on Morpheme Segmentation. In *Proceedings of the 19th SIGMORPHON Workshop on Computational Research in Phonetics, Phonology, and Morphology*, pages 103–116,

Seattle, Washington. Association for Computational Linguistics.

Kenneth Beesley. 1998. Arabic morphology using only finite-state operations. In *Proceedings of the Workshop on Computational Approaches to Semitic Languages (CASL)*, pages 50–7, Montereal.

Caleb A Belth, Sarah RB Payne, Deniz Beser, Jordan Kodner, and Charles Yang. 2021. The greedy and recursive search for morphological productivity. In *Proceedings of the Annual Meeting of the Cognitive Science Society*, volume 43.

Ellen Broselow. 2017. Syllable Structure in the Dialects of Arabic. *The Routledge handbook of Arabic linguistics*, pages 32–47.

Tim Buckwalter. 2002. Buckwalter Arabic morphological analyzer version 1.0. Linguistic Data Consortium (LDC) catalog number LDC2002L49, ISBN 1-58563-257-0.

Tim Buckwalter. 2004. Buckwalter Arabic Morphological Analyzer Version 2.0. LDC catalog number LDC2004L02, ISBN 1-58563-324-0.

Noam Chomsky and Morris Halle. 1968. *The Sound Pattern of English*. Harper & Row New York.

Verna Dankers, Anna Langedijk, Kate McCurdy, Adina Williams, and Dieuwke Hupkes. 2021. Generalising to German plural noun classes, from the perspective of a recurrent neural network. In *Proceedings of the 25th Conference on Computational Natural Language Learning*, pages 94–108, Online. Association for Computational Linguistics.

Alexander Erdmann, Salam Khalifa, Mai Oudah, Nizar Habash, and Houda Bouamor. 2019. A Little Linguistics Goes a Long Way: Unsupervised Segmentation with Limited Language Specific Guidance. In *Proceedings of the 16th Workshop on Computational Research in Phonetics, Phonology, and Morphology*, pages 113–124, Florence, Italy. Association for Computational Linguistics.

Hassan Gadalla, Hanaa Kilany, Howaida Arram, Ashraf Yacoub, Alaa El-Habashi, Amr Shalaby, Krisjanis Karins, Everett Rowson, Robert MacIntyre, Paul Kingsbury, David Graff, and Cynthia McLemore. 1997. CALLHOME Egyptian Arabic transcripts LDC97T19. Web Download. Philadelphia: Linguistic Data Consortium.

David Graff, Mohamed Maamouri, Basma Bouziri, Sondos Krouna, Seth Kulick, and Tim Buckwalter. 2009. Standard Arabic Morphological Analyzer (SAMA) Version 3.1. Linguistic Data Consortium LDC2009E73.

Nizar Habash, Ramy Eskander, and Abdelati Hawwari. 2012. A Morphological Analyzer for Egyptian Arabic. In *Proceedings of the Workshop of the Special Interest Group on Computational Morphology and Phonology (SIGMORPHON)*, pages 1–9, Montréal, Canada.

Nizar Habash, Reham Marzouk, Christian Khairallah, and Salam Khalifa. 2022. Morphotactic modeling in an open-source multi-dialectal Arabic morphological analyzer and generator. In *Proceedings of the 19th SIGMORPHON Workshop on Computational Research in Phonetics, Phonology, and Morphology*, pages 92–102, Seattle, Washington. Association for Computational Linguistics.

Nizar Habash and Owen Rambow. 2006. MAGEAD: A morphological analyzer and generator for the Arabic dialects. In *Proceedings of the International Conference on Computational Linguistics and the Conference of the Association for Computational Linguistics (COLING-ACL)*, pages 681–688, Sydney, Australia.

Nawar Halabi. 2016. *Modern standard Arabic phonetics for speech synthesis*. Ph.D. thesis, University of Southampton.

Bruce Hayes. 2008. *Introductory Phonology*. Blackwell Textbooks in Linguistics. Wiley.

Go Inoue, Salam Khalifa, and Nizar Habash. 2022. Morphosyntactic Tagging with Pre-trained Language Models for Arabic and its Dialects. In *Findings of the Association for Computational Linguistics: ACL 2022*, pages 1708–1719, Dublin, Ireland. Association for Computational Linguistics.

Salam Khalifa, Sara Hassan, and Nizar Habash. 2017. A morphological analyzer for Gulf Arabic verbs. In *Proceedings of the Workshop for Arabic Natural Language Processing (WANLP)*, Valencia, Spain.

Salam Khalifa, Nasser Zalmout, and Nizar Habash. 2020. Morphological Analysis and Disambiguation for Gulf Arabic: The Interplay between Resources and Methods. In *Proceedings of the 12th Language Resources and Evaluation Conference*, pages 3895–3904, Marseille, France. European Language Resources Association.

Hanaa Kilany, Hassan Gadalla, Howaida Arram, Ashraf Yacoub, Alaa El-Habashi, and Cynthia McLemore. 2002. Egyptian Colloquial Arabic Lexicon. LDC catalog number LDC99L22.

Christo Kirov and Ryan Cotterell. 2018. Recurrent neural networks in linguistic theory: Revisiting pinker and prince (1988) and the past tense debate. *Transactions of the Association for Computational Linguistics*, 6:651–665.

Jordan Kodner and Salam Khalifa. 2022. SIGMORPHON–UniMorph 2022 shared task 0: Modeling inflection in language acquisition. In *Proceedings of the 19th SIGMORPHON Workshop on Computational Research in Phonetics, Phonology, and Morphology*, pages 157–175, Seattle, Washington. Association for Computational Linguistics.

Jordan Kodner, Salam Khalifa, Khuyagbaatar Batsuren, Hossep Dolatian, Ryan Cotterell, Faruk Akkus,

Antonios Anastasopoulos, Taras Andrushko, Aryaman Arora, Nona Atanalov, Gábor Bella, Elena Budianskaya, Yustinus Ghanggo Ate, Omer Goldman, David Guriel, Simon Guriel, Silvia Guriel-Agiashvili, Witold Kieraś, Andrew Krizhanovsky, Natalia Krizhanovsky, Igor Marchenko, Magdalena Markowska, Polina Mashkovtseva, Maria Nepomniashchaya, Daria Rodionova, Karina Scheifer, Alexandra Sorova, Anastasia Yemelina, Jeremiah Young, and Ekaterina Vylomova. 2022. SIGMORPHON–UniMorph 2022 shared task 0: Generalization and typologically diverse morphological inflection. In *Proceedings of the 19th SIGMORPHON Workshop on Computational Research in Phonetics, Phonology, and Morphology*, pages 176–203, Seattle, Washington. Association for Computational Linguistics.

Karthik Narasimhan, Regina Barzilay, and Tommi Jaakkola. 2015. An unsupervised method for uncovering morphological chains. *Transactions of the Association for Computational Linguistics*, 3:157–167.

Ossama Obeid, Nasser Zalmout, Salam Khalifa, Dima Taji, Mai Oudah, Bashar Alhafni, Go Inoue, Fadhl Eryani, Alexander Erdmann, and Nizar Habash. 2020. CAMeL tools: An open source python toolkit for Arabic natural language processing. In *Proceedings of The 12th Language Resources and Evaluation Conference*, pages 7022–7032, Marseille, France. European Language Resources Association.

Rico Sennrich and Barry Haddow. 2016. Linguistic input features improve neural machine translation. In *Proceedings of the First Conference on Machine Translation: Volume 1, Research Papers*, volume 1, pages 83–91.

Dima Taji, Jamila El Gizuli, and Nizar Habash. 2018. An Arabic dependency treebank in the travel domain. In *Proceedings of the Workshop on Open-Source Arabic Corpora and Processing Tools (OSACT)*, Miyazaki, Japan.

Shijie Wu, Ryan Cotterell, and Mans Hulden. 2021. Applying the transformer to character-level transduction. In *Proceedings of the 16th Conference of the European Chapter of the Association for Computational Linguistics: Main Volume*, pages 1901–1907, Online. Association for Computational Linguistics.

AraDepSu: Detecting Depression and Suicidal Ideation in Arabic Tweets Using Transformers

Mariam Hassib **Nancy Hossam** **Jolie Sameh** **Marwan Torki**
Faculty of Engineering, Alexandria University, Egypt
{mariamhassib1990,nancyhossam441999,joliesameh99}@gmail.com
mtorki@alexu.edu.eg

Abstract

Among mental health diseases, depression is one of the most severe, as it often leads to suicide which is the fourth leading cause of death in the Middle East. In the Middle East, Egypt has the highest percentage of suicidal deaths; due to this, it is important to identify depression and suicidal ideation.[1] In Arabic culture, there is a lack of awareness regarding the importance of diagnosing and living with mental health diseases. However, as noted for the last couple of years people all over the world, including Arab citizens, tend to express their feelings openly on social media. Twitter is the most popular platform designed to enable the expression of emotions through short texts, pictures, or videos. This paper aims to predict depression and depression with suicidal ideation. Due to the tendency of people to treat social media as their personal diaries and share their deepest thoughts on social media platforms. Social media data contains valuable information that can be used to identify users' psychological states. We create the AraDepSu dataset by scrapping tweets from Twitter and manually labeling them. We expand the diversity of user tweets, by adding a neutral label ("neutral") so the dataset includes three classes ("depressed", "suicidal", and "neutral"). Then we train our AraDepSu dataset on 30+ different Transformer-based models. We find that the best-performing model is MARBERT with accuracy, macro-average precision, macro-average recall, and macro-average F1-score values of 91.20%, 88.74%, 88.50%, and 88.75%.

1 Introduction

The well-being of a person comprises physical health and mental health. The mental health of a person shows the individual's state of mind. Mental disorders are a worldwide health problem affecting a large number of people and causing numerous deaths every year (Musleh et al., 2022).

Depression is one of the most well-known mental health disorders and it is considered a major issue for mental health practitioners. Depression is a mood disorder that causes a persistent feeling of sadness and loss of interest. Also called a major depressive disorder or clinical depression. It affects how you feel, think and behave and can lead to a variety of emotional and physical problems. Fortunately, it is also treatable especially if we identify it in the early stage.[2] In Arabic culture, early diagnosis of mental illness is difficult, because of the stigma of mental illness and lack of awareness in the field of psychiatry.[3] Depression has become a silent killer as it increases suicide risk. [4]

People tend to express their feelings openly on social media, especially on Twitter. Twitter provides a platform where users share their thoughts, emotions, feelings, and expressions. These tweets can aid in determining a person's thought process, mental health, and behavioral traits.

In this paper, our objective is to come up with a methodology to accurately classify and analyze Arabic tweets. We classify whether they are suffering from depression or depression with suicidal ideation which can help prevent suicidal deaths. We focus on the potential of Natural language processing (NLP) and machine learning techniques that can be utilized in the mental health field. NLP is very helpful when it comes to understanding the context of natural human language. As a result, it extracts latent meaning from text and creates AI-based solutions using text data available on social

[1]Suicide: The Fourth Cause of Death Among Young People. URL: https://www.bbc.com/arabic/59568886.

[2]What is Depression? URL: https://psychiatry.org/patients-families/depression/what-is-depression.

[3]Egypt: Mental health barriers URL: https://english.ahram.org.eg/NewsContent/50/1209/422608/AlAhram-Weekly/Focus/Egypt-Mental-health-barriers.aspx.

[4]Mental Health and Substance Abuse: Does Depression Increase The Risk For Suicide? URL: https://www.hhs.gov/answers/mental-health-and-substance-abuse/does-depression-increase-risk-of-suicide/index.html.

Proceedings of the The Seventh Arabic Natural Language Processing Workshop (WANLP), pages 302 - 311
December 8, 2022 ©2022 Association for Computational Linguistics

media platforms.

2 Background

Depression is considered a global concern. It is a very common illness, as it affects people across all nations. Approximately 280 million people have recently been afflicted with depression in the world.[5] Depression can cause the affected person to suffer greatly and function poorly at work, at school, and in the family. At its worst, depression can lead to suicide. Over 700,000 people die due to suicide every year.

Depression is different from usual mood fluctuations and short-lived emotional responses to challenges in everyday life.[6] It comes in many forms, each accompanied by its own symptoms. The most common and known form is major depressive disorder (MDD), which influences the ability of individuals to do daily tasks (Aldarwish and Ahmad, 2017). Depression does not have a target age, as it may begin at a young age. Curbing depression is essential to saving people's lives (Marcus et al., 2012).

In Arabic culture, the stigma on mental illness is deeply entrenched, and there is a lack of awareness regarding this issue. The review reveals that beyond society and culture, the persistence of mental illness stigma. In the Arab world may be explained by inefficient monitoring mechanisms of mental health legislation and policies within the healthcare setting (Merhej, 2019).

3 Related Work

This section presents a summary of prior studies that have been conducted on the prediction and monitoring of depression and suicide using social media.

Various related data have been in the literature for the prediction of depression via various approaches. Two main strategies were reported in the literature to collect data and detect depression through social media.

The first strategy is crowd-sourcing data collection from social media publicly available. This allows researchers to cheaply outsource simple tasks or questionnaires, and gather data in real-time. It also helps to obtain far more numerous and widespread observations than in traditional data collection given its relatively low cost. The crowd-sourcing strategy is mainly conducted in two stages (De Choudhury et al., 2013a,b). First, responses from an online clinical depression survey are gathered. Then, contents are collected by accessing the Twitter data of the consented participants. This main strategy limitation is time-consuming.

The second alternative strategy is characterized by gathering data quickly and cheaply (Coppersmith et al., 2014). As such, the data is collected directly from social media that are publicly available for participants with self-identified mental illnesses. The disadvantage of this strategy is its low reliability. Unfortunately, very few of these collected data and applied models were found in Arabic.

Conducting a sentiment analysis of texts in the Arabic language is more complex than that directed toward English texts. That is because the Arabic language is characterized by more forms than other languages. The formal variant of Arabic is Modern Standard Arabic (MSA), but this is rarely used in spoken interactions. The most frequently used informal variant is Dialectal Arabic (DA), especially for communication purposes. A total of 30 major Arabic dialects differ from MSA, the approaches used to translate difficult MSA terms are ineffective when applied to DA translation. Recently, Arabic researchers have developed solutions for different dialects, but these remain minimally inaccurate and cover only a few dialects (Al-Twairesh et al., 2017). Our work mainly focuses on Egyptian Dialectal with it the most studied and widely spoken DA.

A common challenge that faces most depression detection trials is to identify the symptoms of mental illness in online health communities. This is due to the symptom overlapping between multiple mental illnesses. To the best of our knowledge, no previous trials went deeply into the Arabic Twitter data for detecting whether a user's tweet is depressed or depressed with suicidal ideation. To fill this literature gap, our solution helps in detecting signs relevant to depression using Arabic language tweets. To avoid the limitations related to data collection we faced in the beginning, we combine low-cost and reliable data collection strategies. We collected more than 20k tweets data from public tweets and labeled them manually.

[5]Institute of Health Metrics and Evaluation. Global Health Data Exchange. URL: http://ghdx.healthdata.org/gbd-results-tool?params=gbd-api-2019-permalink/d780dffbe8a381b25e1416884959e88b.

[6]World Health Organization: Depression. URL: https://www.who.int/news-room/fact-sheets/detail/depression.

Dataset	Number of examples
ArTwitter (Abdulla et al., 2013)	3,543
TEAD (Abdellaoui and Zrigui, 2018)	2,000
BRAD (Elnagar et al., 2018)	2,000
ASTD (Nabil et al., 2015)	1,590
Total	**9,133**

Table 1: Number of examples from different datasets.

Figure 1: Word clouds for different classes in the AraDepSu dataset. Top: Depression words. Middle: Suicidal ideation words. words. Bottom: Non-depression words

4 Data

4.1 Data Collection

We extracted more than 10k tweets from different users with special keywords to get tweets with depression and suicidal ideation, posted between 2016 and 2022. We added to our dataset 1,230 records from the available data of the Modern Standard Arabic mood changing and depression dataset (Maghraby and Ali, 2022). Table 2 shows some of the depression keywords and Table 3 shows some of the depression with suicidal ideation keywords. Tweets in this study were a mixture of Modern Standard Arabic and Arabic dialects. Similar to the previous work on depression detection on English datasets (Babu and Kanaga, 2022), we collected data from different sentiment analysis datasets as shown in Table 1.

4.2 Cleaning and Pre-Processing Data

Our dataset annotation procedure includes two phases. In the first phase, we sanitized each tweet so that they do not contain irrelevant text, so they would be suitable input for our various models. First, we removed hyperlinks because they do not add much to the actual content of the tweet. Then, we removed empty columns and duplicate records.

4.3 Manually Labeling Process

In the second phase, each record is labeled by one category name, whether it is depression, depression with suicidal ideation, or non-depression. The annotators followed the authors' instructions in labeling the data. Each record was labeled by a single annotator. Then, the authors revised the annotated data sample by sample. In case of disagreement, the authors' decision is favored. Finally, we obtained a dataset with 20,213 tweets 5,472 classified with depression, 2,167 with suicidal ideation, and 12,574 as non-depression as shown in Table 4

In Figure 1 we show the word clouds for the different classes in AraDepSu dataset. The keywords for the depression class are highlighted in the depression words such as "life is hard", "I want to cry" and similar keywords. We observe the same kind of keywords for the suicidal ideation class such as " kill my self", "I wan to die" and similar keywords. For the non-depression class, the highlighted keywords are not relevant to a specific

Keyword	Example
تعبت Exhausted	تعبت و زهقت و جبت اخري من كل حاجة I am exhausted and fed up with everything.
مكتئب Depressed	انا مكتئب أكتئاب حاد و بحاول افضل واقف على رجلي عشان اهلي بس I am severely depressed, just trying to withstand it for my family's sake
منهارة Broken	قد يُخيل لكم إني قوية وثابتة بينما أنا في الحقيقة منهارة و بعيط You might think I'm strong and steady when in fact I'm broken and weeping.
حزينة Miserable	أنا حزينة ومقهورة أوي والله حتي مش عارفه اهرب من كل ده وانام I'm so miserable and defeated,I do not even know how to escape from all this and just sleep
اكتئاب Depression	فيني اكتئاب حاد I have severe depression
محدش بيحبني No one loves me	كنت عايزة اعرف بس انا ليه محدش بيحبني زي مابحبه ولا بفرق مع حد؟ I just want to know, why no one loves me as much as I do and I do not matter to anyone?
عايزه اعيط Want to Cry	انا عايزه اعيط او انام I want to cry or sleep

Table 2: Examples for depression from the annotated corpus.

Keyword	Example
عايز انتحر I want to commit suicide	عايز انتحر و اموت نفسي و اخلص I want to commit suicide and just end my life
اقتل نفسي kill myself	اقتل نفسي او اقتل نفسي مافيه خيار ثالث It is either killing myself or killing myself there is no other option.
ودي انتحر I want to commit suicide	ودي انتحر صراحه تعبت والله I want to commit suicide, honestly I'm tired, I swear
عايز اموت I want to die	لا ماضي ولا حاضر عايز اموت No past no future, I want to die.
مش عايزة اعيش I don't want to live	موتني يا رب أنا مش عايزة اعيش كفاية كدة Just kill me God, I do not want to live anymore that is enough.
بفكر انتحر Thinking about committing suicide	قاعدة بعيط وبفكر انتحر Crying and thinking about committing suicide
يارب خدني Just take me God	يارب خدني من العيلة دي في اقرب وقت Just take me God from this family as soon as possible

Table 3: Examples for depression with suicidal ideation from the annotated corpus.

topic.

5 Experiments and Results

5.1 Dataset

The final dataset consists of 20,213 tweets divided into 15,159 training tweets and 5,054 testing tweets. Table 4 provides the statistical details of the dataset.

5.2 Models

In our experiments, we use the following models:

5.2.1 mBERT

Multilingual BERT model (Devlin et al., 2018), is a single language model pre-trained from monolingual corpora on data from the Wikipedia dumps of 104 languages.

5.2.2 GigaBERT

GigaBERT is a customized bilingual BERT for English and Arabic. We use two variants of this model, GigaBERT-v3 and GigaBERT-v4. GigaBERT-v3 is a customized bilingual BERT for English and Arabic. It is pre-trained on a large-scale corpus with 10B tokens. GigaBERT-v4 is a continued pre-training of GigaBERT-v3 on code-switched data (Lan et al., 2020).

5.2.3 XLM-RoBERTa

XLM-RoBERTa is an Unsupervised Cross-lingual Representation Learning at Scale (Conneau et al., 2019). This model is pre-trained on 2.5TB of filtered data containing 100 languages. We use two variants of this model, XLM-RoBERTa-base, and

Set	Non-depression	Depression	Depression With Suicidal Ideation	Total
Training	9,408	4,117	1,634	15,159
Testing	3,166	1,355	533	5,054
Total	12,574	5,472	2,167	20,213

Table 4: Distribution of depression and depression with suicidal ideation.

Model	Precision	Recall	F1-Score	Accuracy
mBERT	84.25	87.04	85.55	87.93
GigaBERT(v3)	86.21	87.44	86.80	88.90
GigaBERT(v4)	87.05	87.59	87.32	89.35
XLM-RoBERTa-base	86.32	87.31	86.79	89.06
XLM-RoBERTa-large	85.95	87.28	86.59	88.88
AraBERT-base(v01)	86.23	86.39	86.30	88.66
AraBERT-base(v1)	85.78	86.78	86.27	88.29
AraBERT-base(v02)	87.42	87.75	87.58	89.73
AraBERT-base(v02)-twitter	87.02	88.66	87.81	89.73
AraBERT-base(v2)	86.36	86.15	86.25	88.68
AraBERT-large(v02)-twitter	87.48	88.33	87.90	89.93
AraELECTRA(discriminator)	86.36	87.97	87.14	89.24
AraELECTRA(generator)	82.82	87.27	84.78	87.34
Arabic BERT-base	86.05	86.78	86.41	88.52
Arabic BERT-mini	83.80	86.23	84.94	87.67
Arabic BERT-medium	84.97	84.82	84.89	87.57
Arabic BERT-large	86.64	86.91	86.76	88.74
Arabic ALBERT-base	85.86	86.38	86.12	88.43
Arabic ALBERT-large	86.43	86.01	86.20	88.48
Arabic ALBERT-xlarge	86.82	85.62	86.21	88.70
MARBERT	**88.74**	88.50	**88.75**	**91.20**
MARBERT(v2)	87.75	88.50	88.12	90.07
ARBERT	86.42	86.21	86.31	88.60
QARiB	88.20	88.26	88.23	90.13
AraGPT2-base	83.34	85.70	84.45	86.94
AraGPT2-medium	81.08	83.57	82.31	83.83
AraGPT2-large	83.97	84.60	84.26	84.67
AraT5-base	84.44	88.68	86.35	88.70
AraT5-msa-base	82.74	88.66	85.26	87.73
AraT5-tweet-base	86.06	**88.93**	87.40	89.65
AraT5-msa-small	74.90	82.77	77.74	81.58
AraT5-tweet-small	80.47	85.95	82.12	85.26

Table 5: Performance comparison of different models on our dataset.

XLM-RoBERTa-large.

5.2.4 AraBERT

AraBERT is an Arabic pretrained language model based on Google's BERT architecture and uses the same BERT-Base config (Antoun et al.). There are many versions of the model. AraBERTv0.1 and AraBERTv1, with the difference being that AraBERTv1 uses Farasa Segmenter (Durrani and Mubarak). AraBERT(v01/1) was trained on 23GB of text while AraBERT(v02/2) was trained on 77GB of text. AraBERTv0.2-Twitter-base/large are two new models for Arabic dialects and tweets.

They are trained on 60M Arabic tweets with emojis in their vocabulary in addition to common words that were not present at earlier versions. We use many variants of this model, AraBERT-base(v01/1/02/2) and AraBERT-base/large(v02)-twitter.

5.2.5 AraELECTRA

ELECTRA is a method for self-supervised language representation learning. AraELECTRA was trained on the same 77GB of text used for AraBERT (Antoun et al., 2021a). We use two variants of this model, AraELECTRA generator and AraELECTRA discriminator.

5.2.6 Arabic BERT

Arabic BERT Base model was pretrained on 8.2 Billion words of the Arabic version of OSCAR (Suárez et al., 2020) filtered from Common Crawl and a recent dump of Arabic Wikipedia and other Arabic resources which sum up to 95GB of text (Safaya et al., 2020). We use four variants of this model, Arabic BERT-base/mini/medium/large.

5.2.7 Arabic ALBERT

An Arabic edition of ALBERT model which was pretrained on 4.4 Billion words from the Arabic version of the unshuffled OSCAR corpus (Suárez et al., 2020) and the Arabic Wikipedia (Safaya, 2020). We use three variants of this model, Arabic ALBERT-base/large/xlarge.

5.2.8 ARBERT and MARBERT

ARBERT and MARBERT are based on the BERT-base architecture. ARBERT is a language model that is focused on Modern Standard Arabic (MSA) and was trained on 61GB of text from news articles. MARBERT is a language model that is focused on both Dialectal Arabic (DA) and MSA. MARBERT was trained on randomly sampled 1B Arabic tweets from a dataset of about 6B tweets, the dataset makes up 128GB of text. (Abdul-Mageed et al., 2021). MARBERTv2 was further trained on the same data as ARBERT in addition to AraNews dataset (Ali et al., 2021).

5.2.9 QARiB

QARiB is a QCRI Arabic and Dialectal BERT model, which was trained on 420 Million tweets and 180 Million sentences of text (Abdelali et al., 2021).

5.2.10 AraGPT2

AraGPT2 is an advanced Arabic language generation model, trained from scratch on a large Arabic corpus of internet text and news articles (Antoun et al., 2021b). We use three variants of this model, AraGPT2-base/medium/large.

5.2.11 AraT5

AraT5 Text-to-Text Transformers for Arabic Language Generation that is focused on both Dialectal Arabic (DA) and MSA. AraT5-MSA was trained on 70GB of text. AraT5-Tweet was trained on 178GB of text (Nagoudi et al., 2022).

5.3 Hyper-parameters Setting and Evaluation

In our experiments, we use the implementation provided by HuggingFace Transformers library (Wolf et al., 2019). We train our models for 5 epochs with a learning rate of 2e–5 and a maximum sequence length set to 128 tokens. Table 5 shows the results of different models on our dataset. The best-performing model is MARBERT with a macro-average F1-score of 88.75%.

6 Discussion

Models pre-trained on multiple languages
Table 6 compares the models pre-trained on multiple languages. GiagBERT outperforms mBERT and XLM-RoBERTa on AraDepSu dataset. We think the reason is that AraDepSu contains Arabic dialectic tweets and GiagBERT is trained only on English and Arabic data.

Models pre-trained on tweets
Table 7 compares the models pre-trained on tweets with the nWords of the pre-trained dataset and the f1-score results. MARBERT outperforms AraT5 even though it is trained on more data. We think the reason is that the majority of AraT5-tweet data is MSA according to the analyses done by (Nagoudi et al., 2022), and the majority of our dataset is from dialect tweets.

Models pre-trained on Modern Standard Arabic
Table 8 compares the models pre-trained on MSA with the size of the pre-trained dataset. AraBERT-base(v02) outperforms models pre-trained on larger datasets. In these models, the performance relies more on the architecture than on the dataset size.

Qualitative Evaluation As shown in the study, pre-trained models produced reliable results and accuracy. However, there were some drastic differences in their training circumstances. As stated

Model	Pre-trained languages	F1-Score
mBERT	104	85.55
GigaBERT(v3)	En-Ar	86.80
GigaBERT(v4)	En-Ar	**87.32**
XLM-RoBERTa-base	100	86.79
XLM-RoBERTa-large	100	86.59

Table 6: Comparison of different models pre-trained on multiple languages.

Model	Pre-trained tweets	F1-Score
AraBERT-base(v02)-twitter	60M	87.81
AraBERT-large(v02)-twitter	60M	87.90
MARBERT	1B	**88.75**
QARiB	420M	88.23
AraT5-tweet-base	1.5B	87.40
AraT5-tweet-small	1.5B	82.12

Table 7: Comparison of different models pre-trained on tweets.

Model	**DataSet Size**	**F1-Score**
AraBERT-base(v01)	23GB	86.30
AraBERT-base(v1)	23GB	86.27
AraBERT-base(v02)	77GB	**87.58**
AraBERT-base(v2)	77GB	86.25
AraELECTRA(discriminator)	77GB	87.14
AraELECTRA(generator)	77GB	84.78
Arabic BERT-base	95GB	86.41
Arabic BERT-mini	95GB	84.94
Arabic BERT-medium	95GB	84.89
Arabic BERT-large	95GB	86.76
Arabic ALBERT-base	35GB	86.12
Arabic ALBERT-large	35GB	86.20
Arabic ALBERT-xlarge	35GB	86.21
AraGPT2-base	77GB	84.45
AraGPT2-medium	77GB	82.31
AraGPT2-large	77GB	84.26

Table 8: Comparison of different models pre-trained on MSA.

previously, the core difference is that MARBERT focuses on Dialectic data in its training, while AraBERT focuses on Modern Standard Arabic (MSA) data. Since AraDepSu dataset is mainly composed of scraped tweets, there were many different dialects. This justifies why MARBERT produced the best accuracy and is considered the best model for this study.

We show in Table 9 the predictions of MARBERT and AraBERT-base(v02) on some test tweets. We observe that MARBERT excels with different dialects and tricky tweets. Those tricky tweets may address depression or suicidal depression in general, but can not be used as evidence that the user is depressed, or define their current state. This may result in a conflict between the prediction and the ground truth. The main reason for this error was believed to be that the pattern the model was searching for to label the string, as depression, for example, was found successfully but the human

Sentence	Ground Truth	Prediction	Pre-trained Data	Model
حاسس ان انا بحب الصيف لوحدي والله	Non-depression	Non-depression	Dialectic	MARBERT
I feel that I love summer alone, I swear to God.		Depression	MSA	AraBERT-base(v02)
شكلي كدا هفضل لغاية ما اموت مش عارفة انا عايزة ايه	Non-depression	Depression	Dialectic	MARBERT
It looks like I will not know what I want until I die.		Depression	MSA	AraBERT-base(v02)
ترا النهايه ليلى بتموت مبنشوف غير بهار حزينه	Non-depression	Non-depression	Dialectic	MARBERT
At the end Layla will die and you will only see Bahar sad.		Depression	MSA	AraBERT-base(v02)
انا اجذب ناس مدمره نفسيا وهالشيء مزعج	Depression	Depression	Dialectic	MARBERT
I attract psychologically destructive people and this is annoying.		Non-depression	MSA	AraBERT-base(v02)
احس يدي بتنكسر ابي احمل التيك توك قبل اموت خلاص طفشت	Depression	Depression	Dialectic	MARBERT
I feel my hand breaking, want to download Tik Tok before I die, I am so bored.		Non-depression	MSA	AraBERT-base(v02)
مليت وانا اتضايق روحي حد يتضايق وياي	Depression	Depression	Dialectic	MARBERT
I am bored of being upset, I want someone to be upset with me.		Depression	MSA	AraBERT-base(v02)
انتحر و اموت نفسي و اخلص	Suicidal Ideation	Suicidal Ideation	Dialectic	MARBERT
Is the only resort to commit suicide and end my life.		Suicidal Ideation	MSA	AraBERT-base(v02)
بصراحة الحياة صعبه اوي .. انا مش عايز اكمل	Suicidal Ideation	Suicidal Ideation	Dialectic	MARBERT
Life is too hard I do not want to continue with it.		Suicidal Ideation	MSA	AraBERT-base(v02)
اتمنى اني اموت ولا احس ب الي احسه الحين يارب مو قادره ولله	Suicidal Ideation	Suicidal Ideation	Dialectic	MARBERT
I wish to die and not feel what I am feeling now, Lord I just cannot anymore.		Suicidal Ideation	MSA	AraBERT-base(v02)

Table 9: Qualitative Evaluation: Predictions of different models on sample tweets from the test data.

common sense factor was missing.

7 Conclusion

This study enables intelligent instruments to identify and predict depression symptoms and suicide ideation from Arabic text based on depression-related words. This paper proposed computational approaches for the utilization of Arabic tweets. We scraped data from tweeter with keywords that act as depression triggers and labeled them manually.

In conclusion and based on the results discussed above, Arabic people do share their feelings on Twitter. The results prove that depressed people show specific behaviors within their tweets. They often use negative words to describe their symptoms, like suicidal thoughts or sleeping disorders.

We built a predictive model to predict whether a user's tweet is depressed or depressed with suicidal ideation. We examined the performance of all the above classifiers using a dataset collected from Twitter and labeled manually with truth labels ("depressed", "suicidal", "neutral"). We found the best accuracy with the MARBERT classifier at 91.20%.

Acknowledgement

We thank many volunteers at Alexandria University for their help in labeling and cleaning our dataset, in particular, Maram Attia, Amina Mohamed, Sara Khaled, Khlod Mohamed, Hagar Abouroumia, Ziyad Mohamed and Karim Elsayed.

References

Ahmed Abdelali, Sabit Hassan, Hamdy Mubarak, Kareem Darwish, and Younes Samih. 2021. Pre-training bert on arabic tweets: Practical considerations.

Houssem Abdellaoui and Mounir Zrigui. 2018. Using tweets and emojis to build tead: an arabic dataset for sentiment analysis. *Computación y Sistemas*, 22(3):777–786.

Muhammad Abdul-Mageed, AbdelRahim Elmadany, and El Moatez Billah Nagoudi. 2021. ARBERT & MARBERT: Deep bidirectional transformers for Arabic. In *Proceedings of the 59th Annual Meeting of the Association for Computational Linguistics and the 11th International Joint Conference on Natural Language Processing (Volume 1: Long Papers)*, pages 7088–7105, Online. Association for Computational Linguistics.

Nawaf Abdulla, N Mahyoub, M Shehab, and Mahmoud Al-Ayyoub. 2013. Arabic sentiment analysis: Corpus-based and lexicon-based. In *Proceedings of The IEEE conference on Applied Electrical Engineering and Computing Technologies (AEECT)*.

Nora Al-Twairesh, Hend Al-Khalifa, AbdulMalik Al-Salman, and Yousef Al-Ohali. 2017. Arasenti-tweet: A corpus for arabic sentiment analysis of saudi tweets. *Procedia Computer Science*, 117:63–72.

Maryam Mohammed Aldarwish and Hafiz Farooq Ahmad. 2017. Predicting depression levels using social media posts. In *2017 IEEE 13th international Symposium on Autonomous decentralized system (ISADS)*, pages 277–280. IEEE.

Zien Sheikh Ali, Watheq Mansour, Tamer Elsayed, and Abdulaziz Al-Ali. 2021. Arafacts: the first large arabic dataset of naturally occurring claims. In *Proceedings of the Sixth Arabic Natural Language Processing Workshop*, pages 231–236.

Wissam Antoun, Fady Baly, and Hazem Hajj. Arabert: Transformer-based model for arabic language understanding. In *LREC 2020 Workshop Language Resources and Evaluation Conference 11–16 May 2020*, page 9.

Wissam Antoun, Fady Baly, and Hazem Hajj. 2021a. AraELECTRA: Pre-training text discriminators for Arabic language understanding. In *Proceedings of the Sixth Arabic Natural Language Processing Workshop*, pages 191–195, Kyiv, Ukraine (Virtual). Association for Computational Linguistics.

Wissam Antoun, Fady Baly, and Hazem Hajj. 2021b. AraGPT2: Pre-trained transformer for Arabic language generation. In *Proceedings of the Sixth Arabic Natural Language Processing Workshop*, pages 196–207, Kyiv, Ukraine (Virtual). Association for Computational Linguistics.

Nirmal Varghese Babu and E Kanaga. 2022. Sentiment analysis in social media data for depression detection using artificial intelligence: A review. *SN Computer Science*, 3(1):1–20.

Alexis Conneau, Kartikay Khandelwal, Naman Goyal, Vishrav Chaudhary, Guillaume Wenzek, Francisco Guzmán, Edouard Grave, Myle Ott, Luke Zettlemoyer, and Veselin Stoyanov. 2019. Unsupervised cross-lingual representation learning at scale. *CoRR*, abs/1911.02116.

Glen Coppersmith, Mark Dredze, and Craig Harman. 2014. Quantifying mental health signals in twitter. In *Proceedings of the workshop on computational linguistics and clinical psychology: From linguistic signal to clinical reality*, pages 51–60.

Munmun De Choudhury, Scott Counts, and Eric Horvitz. 2013a. Social media as a measurement tool of depression in populations. In *Proceedings of the 5th annual ACM web science conference*, pages 47–56.

Munmun De Choudhury, Michael Gamon, Scott Counts, and Eric Horvitz. 2013b. Predicting depression via social media. In *Seventh international AAAI conference on weblogs and social media*.

Jacob Devlin, Ming-Wei Chang, Kenton Lee, and Kristina Toutanova. 2018. Bert: Pre-training of deep bidirectional transformers for language understanding. *arXiv preprint arXiv:1810.04805*.

Ahmed Abdelali Kareem Darwish Nadir Durrani and Hamdy Mubarak. Farasa: A fast and furious segmenter for arabic.

Ashraf Elnagar, Leena Lulu, and Omar Einea. 2018. An annotated huge dataset for standard and colloquial arabic reviews for subjective sentiment analysis. *Procedia computer science*, 142:182–189.

Wuwei Lan, Yang Chen, Wei Xu, and Alan Ritter. 2020. An empirical study of pre-trained transformers for arabic information extraction. *arXiv preprint arXiv:2004.14519*.

Ashwag Maghraby and Hosnia Ali. 2022. Modern standard arabic mood changing and depression dataset. *Data in Brief*, 41:107999.

Marina Marcus, M Taghi Yasamy, Mark van van Ommeren, Dan Chisholm, and Shekhar Saxena. 2012. Depression: A global public health concern.

Rita Merhej. 2019. Stigma on mental illness in the arab world: beyond the socio-cultural barriers. *International Journal of Human Rights in Healthcare*.

Dhiaa A Musleh, Taef A Alkhales, Reem A Almakki, Shahad E Alnajim, Shaden K Almarshad, Rana S Alhasaniah, Sumayh S Aljameel, and Abdullah A Almuqhim. 2022. Twitter arabic sentiment analysis to detect depression using machine learning. *CMC-COMPUTERS MATERIALS & CONTINUA*, 71(2):3463–3477.

Mahmoud Nabil, Mohamed Aly, and Amir Atiya. 2015. Astd: Arabic sentiment tweets dataset. In *Proceedings of the 2015 conference on empirical methods in natural language processing*, pages 2515–2519.

El Moatez Billah Nagoudi, AbdelRahim Elmadany, and Muhammad Abdul-Mageed. 2022. AraT5: Text-to-text transformers for Arabic language generation. In *Proceedings of the 60th Annual Meeting of the Association for Computational Linguistics (Volume 1: Long Papers)*, pages 628–647, Dublin, Ireland. Association for Computational Linguistics.

Ali Safaya. 2020. Arabic-albert.

Ali Safaya, Moutasem Abdullatif, and Deniz Yuret. 2020. KUISAIL at SemEval-2020 task 12: BERT-CNN for offensive speech identification in social media. In *Proceedings of the Fourteenth Workshop on Semantic Evaluation*, pages 2054–2059, Barcelona (online). International Committee for Computational Linguistics.

Pedro Javier Ortiz Suárez, Laurent Romary, and Benoît Sagot. 2020. A monolingual approach to contextualized word embeddings for mid-resource languages. *arXiv preprint arXiv:2006.06202*.

Thomas Wolf, Lysandre Debut, Victor Sanh, Julien Chaumond, Clement Delangue, Anthony Moi, Pierric Cistac, Tim Rault, Rémi Louf, Morgan Funtowicz, et al. 2019. Huggingface's transformers: State-of-the-art natural language processing. *arXiv preprint arXiv:1910.03771*.

Appendix

In figure 2, we show the confusion matrices for the best model MARBERT and AraBERT. MARBERT is the best model based on Dialectal Arabic and AraBERT is the best model based on MSA. Both models produce close results for the depression class. However, the confusion between the non-depression and suicidal ideation is more present in the AraBERT confusion matrix.

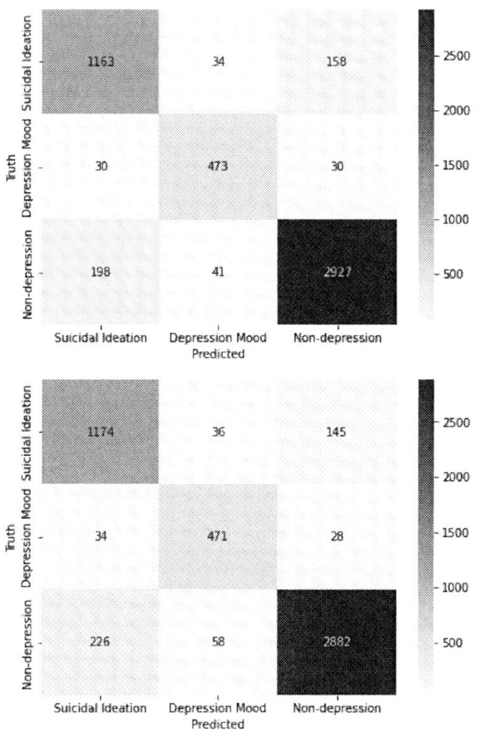

Figure 2: Top: MARBERT confusion matrix. Bottom: AraBERT-base(v02) confusion matrix.

End-to-End Speech Translation of Arabic to English Broadcast News

Fethi Bougares
Le Mans Université - France
fethi.bougares@univ-lemans.fr

Salim Jouili
Elyadata - Tunisia
salim.jouili@elyadata.com

Abstract

Speech translation (ST) is the task of directly translating acoustic speech signals in a source language into text in a foreign language. ST task has been addressed, for a long time, using a pipeline approach with two modules : first an Automatic Speech Recognition (ASR) in the source language followed by a text-to-text Machine translation (MT). In the past few years, we have seen a paradigm shift towards the end-to-end approaches using sequence-to-sequence deep neural network models. This paper presents our efforts towards the development of the first Broadcast News end-to-end Arabic to English speech translation system. Starting from independent ASR and MT LDC releases, we were able to identify about 92 hours of Arabic audio recordings for which the manual transcription was also translated into English at the segment level. These data was used to train and compare pipeline and end-to-end speech translation systems under multiple scenarios including transfer learning and data augmentation techniques.

1 Introduction

End-to-end approach to speech translation is gradually replacing the cascaded approach which consists of transcribing the speech inputs with an ASR system, and translating the obtained transcription using a text-to-text MT system. For instance, and for the first time, the winning system in the IWSLT 2020 TED English-to-German speech translation shared task was an end-to-end system (Ansari et al., 2020). Despite this positive result, the end-to-end approach is used on a limited scale due to the lack of labeled data. Indeed, data scarcity is today the major blocker for the widespread adoption of the end-to-end models. Taking this into consideration, recent works have focused on developing speech translation corpora. Joint efforts in this direction have allowed us to collect a significant quantity and good quality of speech translation corpora. Not surprisingly, speech translation corpus development has started for well-resourced languages including English and some European languages. In (Kocabiyikoglu et al., 2018), the 236 hours English→French ST Augmented LibriSpeech were released. Shortly after, (Di Gangi et al., 2019) released the MUST-C corpus including few hundreds (385 to 504 hours) of parallel ST data of TED talks translations from English to eight European languages. At the same time, the Europarl-ST (Iranzo-Sánchez et al., 2019) was released with translations between 6 European languages, with a total of 30 translation directions. While all the previous resource development effort has focused on well-resourced languages, the most recent published corpora CoVoST (Wang et al., 2020a) and CoVoST2 (Wang et al., 2020b). These latter works released a large-scale Multilingual Speech-To-Text Translation Corpus covering translations from 21 languages to English and from English to 15 languages. Although the Arabic-English is one of the language pairs covered by the CoVoST2 corpus, the authors consider it as a low-resource pair. In fact, CoVoST2 corpus contained only 6 hours of prepared speech uniformly splitted between train, dev and test sets. In this paper, we conduct a series of experiments to present the first results of Arabic to English End-to-End Broadcast News Speech translation.

This paper is organized as follows: section 2 presents Arabic-to-English speech translation related works. Section 3 gives details about the source of our training data and the method we have used to extract theses data. In section 4, we present our experimental setup as well as the used toolkits to train ou models. Sections 5 and 6 provides details about the pipeline and end-to-end speech translation systems, respectively. Section 7, gives a brief discussion and results analysis. Finally, section 8 concludes the findings of this study and discusses future work.

Proceedings of the The Seventh Arabic Natural Language Processing Workshop (WANLP), pages 312 - 319
December 8, 2022 ©2022 Association for Computational Linguistics

2 Related works

Arabic-English (AR-EN) is one of the most studied language pair in the context of Speech Recognition and Machine Translation. For instance, this language pair was integrated in several evaluation campaigns and projects including the International Workshop on Spoken Language Translation (IWSLT) and DARPA's Babylon project. These earlier projects have built on the traditional pipelined architecture integrating speech recognition system in the source language followed by machine translation from the transcript to the target language. In IWSLT, the speech translation task was introduced for the first time in 2006. The IWSLT06 (Paul, 2006) translation campaign was carried using either the manual or the automatic transcription of speech input in the travel domain. This translation task was renewed for several years using always the pipeline approach.

Pipeline architecture was also used by BBN in the context Babylon project (Stallard et al., 2011). They developed the TransTalk system including a pipeline of ASR and MT systems in both directions (AR↔EN). More recently, but still with the same approach, QCRI presented their live Arabic-to-English speech translation system in (Dalvi et al., 2017). The system is a pipeline of a Kaldi-based Speech Recognition followed by a Phrase-based/Neural MT system. Recently, there has been a shift to the most recent end-to-end approach without the intermediate step of transcribing the source language. Indeed, IWSLT 2018 was the first time where organizers drooped the ASR task and participants needed to develop an end-to-end speech translation systems. End-to-end speech translation has shown its effectiveness for multiple languages and in multiple scenarios. It becomes now a well-established task in IWSLT evaluation campaign were multiple shared taks are proposed to assess Spoken Language Translation (SLT) systems for many language pair in several settings. Despite the great interest being shown to the end-to-end approach for speech translation task, we were able to identify only one recent work by (Wang et al., 2020b) including Arabic-English language pair limited to a corpus of 6 hours. We are also aware of the IWSLT 2022 Dialectal Speech Translation[1] task which, unlike this work, focuses on Tunisian-to-English speech translation (Zanon Boito et al., 2022; Yan et al., 2022; Yang et al., 2022).

[1]https://iwslt.org/2022/dialect

3 Training Data

Whatever the chosen architecture for Speech translation system (pipeline or end-to-end), it requires a large amount of manually annotated training data that might be hard to obtain for multiple language pairs. For the Arabic-English language pair, a large amount of training data for ASR and MT was manually annotated in the framework of the DARPA's Global Autonomous Language Exploitation (GALE) project (Cohen, 2007). This huge amount of work was done for the purpose of making foreign languages speech and text accessible to English-only speakers through the development of automatic speech recognition and machine translation systems.

In this respect, Arabic broadcast news and conversation speech were collected from multiple sources, then annotated under the supervision of Linguistic Data Consortium (LDC). Audio corpora and their transcripts are separately released in three phases : GALE Phase 2, 3 and 4. In addition to the speech audio corpora and transcripts released to train Arabic ASR systems, LDC also made available multiple Arabic to English parallel corpora.The latter are intended to be used for training and evaluating Arabic to English MT systems. They have been developed by manually translating from a number of different sources including Arabic news-wire, discussion groups and broadcast news and conversation.

Upon closer inspection of these parallel corpora, we have found that part of the broadcast news and conversation parallel corpora were built by translating the manual transcripts released for the ASR task. Following the discovery we dug deep in the GALE speech recognition and machine translation LDC related releases and, as illustrated in Figure 1, we parsed all GALE speech recognition and machine translation corpora in order to extract a 3-way parallel corpus consisting of Arabic audio along with their Arabic transcriptions and English translation. As shown in Figure 1, for each transcribed audio file part of the GALE corpus, we extract only segments for which we were able to find an exact match between the manual transcription, from ASR training data, and the source side of parallel corpora. Table 1 shows the amount of speech audio for which we were able to find the corresponding translation in the LDC MT related releases. We report, for each phase: 2, 3 and 4, the original size of the speech corpus in hours and the extracted subset for which the English translation had been found.

GALE Phase	Hours	#Segments
Phase 2	436h 11 min	190.510
Phase 2 ST.	59h 12 min	24.519
Phase 3	419h 03 min	195.143
Phase 3 ST.	28h 50 min	13.261
Phase 4	96h 18 min	54.787
Phase 4 ST.	4.0h 08 min	1.855
Phase 2/3/4	951h 32 min	440.440
Extracted ST.	92h 10 min	39.635

Table 1: Statistics of the original GALE Arabic to English Speech Transcription corpus and the extracted subsets for which translations are available.

All the extracted segments were afterwards aligned using timestamps information from ASR transcript and translation from MT target side. As table 1 shows, an overall Arabic to English speech translation corpus of around 92 hours was extracted. This corpus was then cleaned out by removing all the back-channel and incomplete speech segments. The final corpus is then splitted into training, development and test sets. Development and test contain segments from randomly selected broadcast audio programs. Their size is respectively 1188 and 987 segments. Development set contain broadcast News and Conversation recordings from Abu Dhabi TV, Al Alam News Channel, based in Iran and Al Arabiya. Test set is made up of broadcast News and Conversation recordings from Abu Dhabi TV, Aljazeera, Al Arabiya and Syria TV. The remaining material was used as training data for ASR, MT and ST systems.

Table 2 gives a detailed statistics of the extracted Arabic to English Speech Translation corpus, including speech duration as well as token counts for both transcripts and translations.

	Train	dev.	test
Hours	83h54	3h05	2h38
Sentences	32.099	1188	987
#AR words	606.465	22.537	18.598
#EN words	945.801	35.180	27.880

Table 2: Statistics and splits of the extracted Arabic to English Speech Translation corpus extracted from LDC ASR and MT independent releases.

4 Experimental Setup

All our experiments are built using open source toolkits with the following settings: ASR models were built using the End-to-End Speech Processing Toolkit ESPnet (Watanabe et al., 2018b). We trained an attention-based encoder-decoder architecture with an encoder of 4 VGGBLSTM layers including 1024 cells in each layer. The second and third bottom BLSTM layers of the encoder reduced the utterance length by a factor of two. We used a decoder of one 1024-dimensional BLSTM layer. For both ASR and ST speech utterance, we extracted 40 Melfilterbank energy features with a step size of 10ms and a window size of 25ms. The extracted features, we applied mean and variance normalization. MT models were built using the FAIRSEQ package (Ott et al., 2019a). We trained end-to-end word and *bpe-based* translation systems using the *"lstm_luong_wmt_en_de"* model template. This template is a standard LSTM Encoder-Decoder architecture composed of 4 stacked BLSTM layers, each with 1000 cells, and 1000-dimensional embeddings (Luong et al., 2015). Translation tasks (AST and MT) evaluation was carried out using case-sensitive BLEU metric (Papineni et al., 2002). Scores are calculated using one human reference with Moses'mteval-v14.pl script [2] applied to de-tokenized and punctuated translation output. As for ASR, systems were evaluated using Word Error Rate (WER).

5 Pipeline Speech Translation

In this section, we evaluate the pipeline approach for speech translation in two different scenarios, plausible for many language pairs, depending on the amount and the type of training data used for the development of the Speech Translation task.

1. **Constrained Scenario** : Under this scenario

[2]https://github.com/moses-smt/mosesdecoder/blob/master/scripts/generic

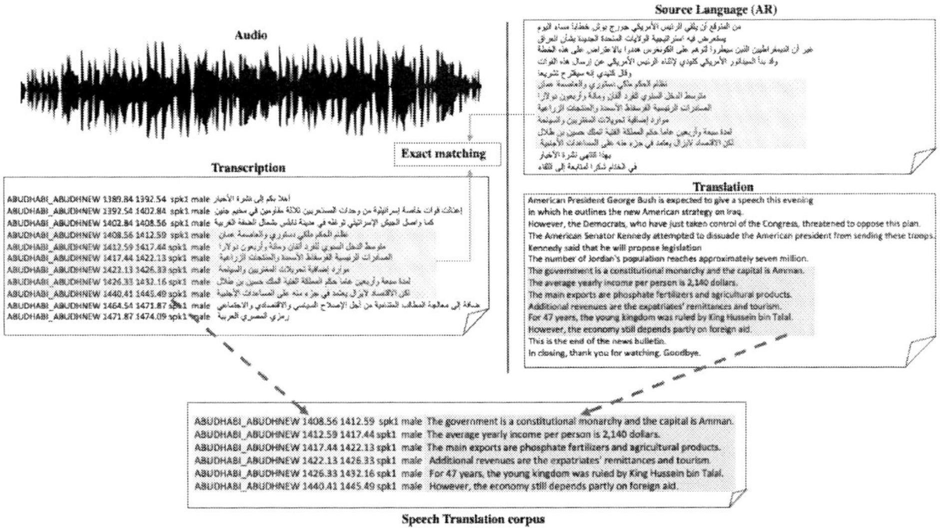

Figure 1: Extraction Arabic to English speech translation corpus from LDC ASR and MT independent releases.

we have access to a 3-way limited training data. This data includes speech audio files in source language their transcriptions in the source language and translations to the target language.

2. **Unconstrained Scenario** : In addition to resources from the constrained scenario, we have access to a large ASR and MT-specific resources.

As to the first scenario of the pipeline approach we only used the 3-way parallel data reported in table 2. In this instance, an end-to-end ASR module was trained using ESPnet (Watanabe et al., 2018a) toolkit on the speech audio files from Table 2 and their corresponding transcripts. In the Unconstrained Scenario, however, ASR module was trained using the totality of the GALE Phase 2, 3 and 4 ASR data reported in Table 1.

ASR System	dev	test
ASR_*Const*	20.90	21.90
ASR_*UnConst*	13.10	14.60

Table 3: ASR WER (in %) on the dev and test sets.

Table 3 presents the results of ASR system under both constrained and unconstrained scenarios. As shown in the Table 3, using a training set of around 84h of manually transcribed broadcast news and conversation, we obtained a WER of 20.90% and 21.90% on dev and test sets, respectively. Not surprisingly, WER has been significantly improved with the use of the complete GALE training data[3] (row ASR_*UnConst*) to achieve **13.10%** and **14.60%** on dev and test sets, respectively.

As previously stated, within the pipeline ST framework, the output of the ASR module is automatically translated to the target language using the MT module. The MT module is also an end-to-end system trained using Fairseq toolkit (Ott et al., 2019b) under both constrained (MT_*Const*) and unconstrained (MT_*UnCons*) scenarios. Table 4 reports the BLEU scores of the translation output by varying ASR module condition while fixing MT module constrained to speech translation data composed of the transcripts along with their corresponding English translation from Table 2.

Pipeline ST System	dev	test
MT_*Const_ASR*_Const	19.03	15.96
MT_*Const_ASR_UnConst*	20.69	16.58
MT_*Const_ref_Transc*	22.31	18.30

Table 4: Case-sensitive tokenized and single-reference BLEU scores (in %) of the pipeline speech translation system with the constrained MT module.

The first row in table 4 (MT_*Const_ASR*_Const) gives the BLEU

[3]We have taken particular care to remove dev and test data before using GALE corpora to train the ASR system.

score when the MT constrain module translates the output of a constrained ASR system (row ASR_*Const* from Table 3). In this case, a BLEU score of 19.03% and 15.96% is respectively achieved on dev and test sets. The second row in the same table (MT_*Const_ASR_UnConst*) shows the BLEU score when the ASR module is under the unconstrained condition, i.e. output from the system ASR_*UnConst* in Table 3 are used as input to the MT system. As expected, when it comes to translating a higher transcription quality, the translation quality is better and the BLEU score is increased by 1.66 and 0.62 BLEU points on dev and test sets, respectively. The last row of table 4 (MT_*Const_ref_Transc*) simulates the situation where we have access to a perfect transcripts in the source language. In this case, translation quality is further improved reaching 22.31 BLEU points on dev set and 18.30 points on test set.

In a similar vein, table 5 presents results in settings where MT module is no longer constrained to speech translation data. Indeed, additional Arabic to English Bilingual text from GALE LDC releases are used to train the unconstrained MT module [4]. This unconstrained MT module, was used to run several experiments using various input conditions similar to what we did within the constrained condition. The results of these experiments are presented in Table 5. The first row (MT_*UnConst_ASR_Const*) sets out the BLEU score when the unconstrained MT module translates the output of the constrained ASR (first row in table 3). Compared to using the constrained MT system, a considerable improvement of 12.84 (from 19.03 to 31.87) and 8.26 (from 15.96 to 24.22) BLEU points is achieved on dev and test sets, respectively.

As we have seen above, translation quality is further improved when the input to the translation module is of a higher quality generated by the unconstrained ASR system (row MT_*UnConst_ASR_UnConst*). This allows to reach a dev and test BLEU scores of 36.48 and 25.80 respectively. As expected, the BLEU score is even better when it comes to translate the reference transcription (MT_*UnConst_ref_Transc*) as shown in the last row of Table 5. In the latter case, we achieved a dev set BLEU score of 39.51 and a test set BLEU score of 30.60.

[4]Unconstrained MT system was trained using all GALE Arabic-English Parallel Text from 2007 to 2016.

Pipeline ST System	**dev**	**test**
MT_*UnConst_ASR_Const*	31.87	24.22
MT_*UnConst_ASR_UnConst*	36.48	27.51
MT_*UnConst_ref_Transc*	39.51	30.60

Table 5: Case-sensitive tokenized and single-reference BLEU scores (in %) of the pipeline speech translation system with Unconstrained MT module.

6 End-to-End Speech Translation

In this section, we present and evaluate the end-to-end approach for Arabic to English speech translation task. The End-to-End system is built using the ESPnet toolkit (Watanabe et al., 2018b). We used an attention-based encoder-decoder architecture. The encoder has two VGG-like CNN blocks followed by five stacked 1024-dimensional BLSTM layers. The decoder is composed of two 1024-dimensional LSTM layers. Each VGG block contains two 2D-convolution layers followed by a 2D-maxpooling layer whose aim is to reduce both time and frequency dimension of the input speech features by a factor of 2. All our experiments are conducted using characters as target tokens.

Table 6 shows the performance of the end-to-end ST model with different training configurations.

End2End ST system	**dev**	**test**
Baseline (1)	2.58	2.23
(1) + Enc. init	12.44	9.57
(1) + Unsup ph234	23.23	18.97
(1) + Enc. Init + Unsup ph234	**24.95**	**19.09**

Table 6: Case-sensitive tokenized and single-reference BLEU score (in %) of the End-to-end AR→EN Speech Translation system with Encoder initialization and data augmentation

The first row from Table 6 shows the baseline results obtained when the end-to-end model is trained under the constrained scenario, that is when the training data is restricted to the 83h54 minutes from table 2. We can clearly see that the end-to-end model is not strong enough to compete with the cascaded model trained using the same amount of data. Indeed, the BLEU score of the end-to-end system on the dev set is 2.58, compared to the 19.03 points of the pipeline model. The same goes for test set where end-to-end system BLEU score is 2.23 compared to 15.96 which is obtained with cascade translation approach.

From this initial baseline and with the aim of improving the end-to-end system translation quality, we employed the well established transfer learning technique (Bansal et al., 2018) commonly referred as encoder pre-training. Indeed, using the ASR encoder of the Unconstrained ASR system (row ASR_*UnConst* in 3) to initialize the parameters of the ST encoder greatly improves the performance of end-to-end ST networks. The results of the encoder pre-training are shown in the second row ((1) + Enc. init) of table 6. As a result, we observed a strong effect reflected by the substantial improvement in the BLEU score: +9.86 and +7.34 BLEU score for dev and test sets, respectively.

Just like the transfer learning via encoder pre-training approach, data augmentation is proven to enhance end-to-end speech translation quality. It is carried out using synthetic data which is generated by automatically translating the transcripts of an ASR corpora in the source language. Herein, we used the unconstrained NMT system (MT_*UnConst*) of table 5 in order to translate the Arabic GALE transcripts provided in table 1. Incomplete and back-channel speech segments were filtered out from the generated translations. All in all, we were able to create the synthetic corpus of 795 hours of Arabic to English speech translation corpus detailed in table 7.

	Hours	**#Sent.**	**#AR**	**#EN**
Gale Synth.	795	314.167	6.1M	9.1M

Table 7: Statistics of the synthetic Ar-En ST corpus.

These synthetic data are thereafter used as additional data to train the end-to-end ST system. The results of this data augmentation experiment are highlighted in Table 6 (row (1) + unsup ph234). As we can see from the obtained results synthetic training data boosts up the end-to-end ST system to achieve a BLEU scores of **23.23** points and **18.97** points for dev and test sets, respectively.

Both encoder pre-training and data augmentation are shown to be helpful improving significantly the ST baseline. We also experimented using both methods at the same time. The last row of the same table presents the results of the end-to-end speech translation trained with data augmentation using synthetic data from Table 7, and encoder hyperparameters initialization from the ASR_*UnConst* system presented in Table 3. By applying these two methods together, we were able to reach a BLEU scores of **24.95** and **19.09** points for dev and test sets, respectively. These end-to-end speech translation results are to be compared to pipeline results shown in row MT_*UnConst*_*ASR*_*UnConst* of table 5.

7 Discussion and analysis

Despite the improvements brought by transfer learning and data augmentation technics, the best results are still obtained using cascade architecture. We believe that this performance gap can be partly explained by the fact that end-to-end system was trained using only a small amount ($\sim$ 84 hours) of real speech translation corpus.

Based on the results of previous works from (Liu et al., 2019), the end-to-end ST models are known as an effective means of circumventing the error-propagation problem faced by the conventional pipeline system. Indeed, every involved component in the traditional pipeline approach produces errors, which are propagated through the cascade and lead to compounding follow-up errors. In order to assess the ability of our end-to-end system to overcome this error-propagation pattern, we selected some translation examples where pipeline system fails due to this problem and we checked the translation output of the end-to-end system. Example from table 8 shows a translation error caused by the propagation of transcription errors occurred at the end of the segment (text in bold ASR output row). The end-to-end system, however, relies on the source speech signal and translates correctly the same part of the input.

In addition to this error-propagation problem we have found that end-to-end system is sometimes penalized although its translation is correct. Table 9 presents and example where both systems out put correct translation but BLEU score is better with pipeline system. The thing might happen for pipeline system as well, but we believe that end-

ASR output	أنا قلت أنا قلت بشكل واضح إنه هناك بعض الإتجهات **المتصاعدة في العراق**
ASR reference	أنا قلت أنا قلت بشكل واضح إنه هناك بعض الإتجهات المتطرفة داخل فتح
Pipeline MT	I said, I said clearly that there are some escalating trends in Iraq.
E2E MT	And now I said I said that there are some interpretations of the institutions of the Fatah movement.
MT reference	I said, I clearly said that there are, there are some extremist currents within the Fatah movement.

Table 8: Example of error-propagation problem with pipeline speech translation system.

ASR output	إسرائيل هي التي ترفض الأعتراف بحماس أليس كذلك
ASR reference	إسرائيل هي التي ترفض الأعتراف بحماس أليس كذلك
Pipeline MT	Israel is the one that refuses to recognize Hamas, isn't it?
E2E MT	Israel refuses to recognize Hamas, isn't it?
MT reference	Israel is the one that refuses to recognize Hamas, right?

Table 9: Comparison of End-to-End and pipeline translation outputs.

to-end systems are more affected as the translation references are obtained by translated from a textual input, not from speech audio in the source language. This trend must be probed further in order to quantify its impact on the end-to-end ST system performance. We leave such investigations as future work.

8 Conclusions

In this paper, we presented the first results on Arabic-to-English end-to-end Automatic Speech Translation system. Arabic-English language pairs is one of the well-studied language pair in Natural Language Processing. Therefore, large quantities of data are made available in a wide variety of domains including ASR and MT. Starting from independent LDC releases for MT and ASR systems, we were able to extract around 92 hours of speech translation corpus composed of Arabic audio and their source transcriptions and English translation. We used this corpus to conduct speech translation experiments using a pipeline and an end-to-end Speech Translation architecture. Both methods were tested under a constrained and an unconstrained conditions. We showed that the performance gap, which is too big between the two considered approaches under the constrained condition, can be narrowed under unconstrained condition through the use of transfer learning and data augmentation techniques. In spite of considerable improvement obtained by applying these techniques, the gap remains important and we plan to reduce it in several ways including decoder pre-training, spectrogram augmentation and Self-Supervised Learning.

9 Acknowledge

This work was funded by the ESPERANTO project. ESPERANTO project has received funding from the European Union's Horizon 2020 research and innovation programme under the Marie Skłodowska-Curie grant agreement No 101007666.

References

Ebrahim Ansari, Amittai Axelrod, Nguyen Bach, Ondřej Bojar, Roldano Cattoni, Fahim Dalvi, Nadir Durrani, Marcello Federico, Christian Federmann, Jiatao Gu, Fei Huang, Kevin Knight, Xutai Ma, Ajay Nagesh, Matteo Negri, Jan Niehues, Juan Pino, Elizabeth Salesky, Xing Shi, Sebastian Stüker, Marco Turchi, Alexander Waibel, and Changhan Wang. 2020. FINDINGS OF THE IWSLT 2020 EVALUATION CAMPAIGN. In *Proceedings of the 17th International Conference on Spoken Language Translation*, pages 1–34, Online. Association for Computational Linguistics.

Sameer Bansal, Herman Kamper, Karen Livescu, Adam Lopez, and Sharon Goldwater. 2018. Pre-training on high-resource speech recognition improves low-resource speech-to-text translation. *CoRR*, abs/1809.01431.

J. Cohen. 2007. The gale project: A description and an update. In *2007 IEEE Workshop on Automatic Speech Recognition Understanding (ASRU)*, pages 237–237.

Fahim Dalvi, Yifan Zhang, Sameer Khurana, Nadir Durrani, Hassan Sajjad, Ahmed Abdelali, Hamdy Mubarak, Ahmed Ali, and Stephan Vogel. 2017. QCRI live speech translation system. In *Proceedings of the Software Demonstrations of the 15th Conference of the European Chapter of the Association for Computational Linguistics*, pages 61–64, Valencia, Spain. Association for Computational Linguistics.

Mattia A. Di Gangi, Roldano Cattoni, Luisa Bentivogli, Matteo Negri, and Marco Turchi. 2019. MuST-C: a Multilingual Speech Translation Corpus. In *Proceedings of the 2019 Conference of the North American Chapter of the Association for Computational Linguistics: Human Language Technologies, Volume 1 (Long and Short Papers)*, pages 2012–2017, Minneapolis, Minnesota. ACL.

Javier Iranzo-Sánchez, Joan Albert Silvestre-Cerdà, Javier Jorge, Nahuel Roselló, Adrià Giménez, Albert Sanchís, Jorge Civera, and Alfons Juan. 2019. Europarl-st: A multilingual corpus for speech translation of parliamentary debates. In *CoRR*, volume abs/1911.03167.

Ali Can Kocabiyikoglu, Laurent Besacier, and Olivier Kraif. 2018. Augmenting librispeech with french translations: A multimodal corpus for direct speech translation evaluation. In *CoRR*, volume abs/1802.03142.

Yuchen Liu, Hao Xiong, Zhongjun He, Jiajun Zhang, Hua Wu, Haifeng Wang, and Chengqing Zong. 2019. End-to-end speech translation with knowledge distillation. In *CoRR*, volume abs/1904.08075.

Thang Luong, Hieu Pham, and Christopher D. Manning. 2015. Effective approaches to attention-based neural machine translation. In *Proceedings of the 2015 Conference on Empirical Methods in Natural Language Processing*, pages 1412–1421, Lisbon, Portugal. ACL.

Myle Ott, Sergey Edunov, Alexei Baevski, Angela Fan, Sam Gross, Nathan Ng, David Grangier, and Michael Auli. 2019a. fairseq: A fast, extensible toolkit for sequence modeling.

Myle Ott, Sergey Edunov, Alexei Baevski, Angela Fan, Sam Gross, Nathan Ng, David Grangier, and Michael Auli. 2019b. fairseq: A fast, extensible toolkit for sequence modeling. In *Proceedings of the 2019 Conference of the North American Chapter of the Association for Computational Linguistics (Demonstrations)*, pages 48–53, Minneapolis, Minnesota. Association for Computational Linguistics.

Michael Paul. 2006. Overview of the IWSLT 2006 evaluation campaign. In *2006 International Workshop on Spoken Language Translation, IWSLT 2006, Keihanna Science City, Kyoto, Japan, November 27-28, 2006*, pages 1–15. ISCA.

David Stallard, Rohit Prasad, Prem Natarajan, Fred Choi, Shirin Saleem, Ralf Meermeier, Kriste Krstovski, Shankar Ananthakrishnan, and Jacob Devlin. 2011. The bbn transtalk speech-to-speech translation system. In Ivo Ipsic, editor, *Speech and Language Technologies*, chapter 3. IntechOpen, Rijeka.

Changhan Wang, Juan Pino, Anne Wu, and Jiatao Gu. 2020a. Covost: A diverse multilingual speech-to-text translation corpus. In *CoRR*.

Changhan Wang, Anne Wu, and Juan Pino. 2020b. Covost 2 and massively multilingual speech-to-text translation. In *CoRR*.

Shinji Watanabe, Takaaki Hori, Shigeki Karita, Tomoki Hayashi, Jiro Nishitoba, Yuya Unno, Nelson Enrique Yalta Soplin, Jahn Heymann, Matthew Wiesner, Nanxin Chen, Adithya Renduchintala, and Tsubasa Ochiai. 2018a. ESPnet: End-to-end speech processing toolkit. In *Proceedings of Interspeech*, pages 2207–2211.

Shinji Watanabe, Takaaki Hori, Shigeki Karita, Tomoki Hayashi, Jiro Nishitoba, Yuya Unno, Nelson Enrique Yalta Soplin, Jahn Heymann, Matthew Wiesner, Nanxin Chen, Adithya Renduchintala, and Tsubasa Ochiai. 2018b. Espnet: End-to-end speech processing toolkit. *CoRR*, abs/1804.00015.

Brian Yan, Patrick Fernandes, Siddharth Dalmia, Jiatong Shi, Yifan Peng, Dan Berrebbi, Xinyi Wang, Graham Neubig, and Shinji Watanabe. 2022. CMU's IWSLT 2022 dialect speech translation system. In *Proceedings of the 19th International Conference on Spoken Language Translation*, pages 298–307, Dublin, Ireland (in-person and online). Association for Computational Linguistics.

Jinyi Yang, Amir Hussein, Matthew Wiesner, and Sanjeev Khudanpur. 2022. JHU IWSLT 2022 dialect speech translation system description. In *Proceedings of the 19th International Conference on Spoken Language Translation*, pages 319–326, Dublin, Ireland (in-person and online). ACL.

Marcely Zanon Boito, John Ortega, Hugo Riguidel, Antoine Laurent, Loïc Barrault, Fethi Bougares, Firas Chaabani, Ha Nguyen, Florentin Barbier, Souhir Gahbiche, and Yannick Estève. 2022. ON-TRAC consortium systems for the IWSLT 2022 dialect and low-resource speech translation tasks. In *Proceedings of the 19th International Conference on Spoken Language Translation*, pages 308–318, Dublin, Ireland (in-person and online). Association for Computational Linguistics.

Arabic Keyphrase Extraction: Enhancing Deep Learning Models with Pre-trained Contextual Embedding and External Features

Randah Alharbi and **Husni Al-Muhtaseb**
King Fahd University of Petroleum
Minerals (KFUPM)
Dhahran-Saudi Arabia
g201907330, muhtaseb@kfupm.edu.sa

Abstract

Keyphrase extraction is essential to many Information retrieval (IR) and Natural language Processing (NLP) tasks such as summarization and indexing. This study investigates deep learning approaches to Arabic keyphrase extraction. We address the problem as sequence classification and create a Bi-LSTM model to classify each sequence token as either part of the keyphrase or outside of it. We have extracted word embeddings from two pre-trained models, Word2Vec and BERT. Moreover, we have investigated the effect of incorporating linguistic, positional, and statistical features with word embeddings on performance. Our best-performing model has achieved 0.45 F1-score on ArabicKPE dataset when combining linguistic and positional features with BERT embedding.

1 Introduction

Keyphrases are the phrases that best represent a document. They play an essential role in many Natural Language Processing (NLP) and Information Retrieval (IR) tasks, such as indexing, summarization, categorization, and opinion mining (Merrouni et al., 2020) (Hasan and Ng, 2014). Manual extraction of keyphrases is time-consuming and requires experts' knowledge; thus, the extraction needs to be automated (Merrouni et al., 2020). Although many studies have been proposed to address automatic keyphrase extraction and generation, the performance is still moderate due to the task's difficulty (Merrouni et al., 2020). Several approaches have been proposed; one of the earliest approaches is the two-step ranking, in which candidate phrases are extracted with several heuristics and then ranked using supervised or un-supervised methods (Hasan and Ng, 2014). Another approach is the classification approach, in which candidate phrases are classified as keyphrases or not (Papagiannopoulou and Tsoumakas, 2020). A more recent approach is formulating keyphrase extraction as a sequence labeling task in which each word in the documents is labeled as part of a keyphrase or not (Alzaidy et al., 2019). Another recent approach is to consider formulating the task as a generation task utilizing sequence-to-sequence models in order to be able to generate keyphrases that are not available in the source text, i.e., keyphrase generation (Meng et al., 2017).

Word embeddings prove their effectiveness in many NLP tasks. Several word embeddings are proposed, such as Word2Vec (Mikolov et al., 2013) and FastText (Bojanowski et al., 2017). The earliest proposed word embeddings generate the same vector for the word regardless of the word context hence called static word embeddings (Pilehvar and Camacho-Collados). Recently, several word embeddings generate different embeddings for the word depending on its context hence called contextualized word embeddings (Pilehvar and Camacho-Collados) such as BERT (Devlin et al., 2019), and ELMo (Peters et al., 2018). Several studies have utilized various types of word embeddings into supervised and unsupervised keyphrase extraction, and they positively affect performance.

Arabic has its own characteristics that pose many challenges on any IR or NLP task (Darwish and Magdy, 2014) (Habash, 2010). Thus, it is crucial to investigate the performance of state-of-the-art techniques of keyphrase extraction on Arabic, which might differ in terms of performance from other languages. Several datasets are available for Arabic keyphrase extraction; The Arabic keyphrase extraction Corpus (AKEC) (Helmy et al., 2016), Arabic Dataset proposed by (Al-Logmani and Al-Muhtaseb), WikiAll [1] from Arabic Wikipedia documents, and ArabicKPE (Helmy et al., 2018) .

During our investigation of the keyphrase extraction studies, we have found that studies on

[1] https://github.com/anastaw/Arabic-Wikipedia-Corpus

Proceedings of the The Seventh Arabic Natural Language Processing Workshop (WANLP), pages 320 - 330
December 8, 2022 ©2022 Association for Computational Linguistics

Arabic keyphrase extraction are falling behind in applying state-of-the-art technologies. For example, only a few studies have utilized word embeddings; Suleiman et al. 2019a have investigated using Word2Vec and semantic similarity to generate keyphrases for three documents only. Helmy et al. 2018 have investigated using Word2Vec and Bidirectional-Long Short Term Memory (Bi-LSTM) in keyphrase extraction. To fill this gap, we aim to apply deep learning approaches to keyphrase extraction utilizing the static and contextualized word embeddings for Arabic keyphrase extraction. Thus, we have formulated the task as a sequence labeling task and have used a Bi-LSTM classifier with token representation extracted from two types of pre-trained word embeddings. Additionally, we aim to investigate the effect of incorporating statistical, positional, and linguistic features with static and contextual embeddings.

In this study, we have used Bidirectional Encoder Representations from Transformers (BERT) in Arabic keyphrase extraction and have compared it to Word2Vec embedding. Additionally, we have investigated three ways of utilizing BERT for Arabic keyphrase extraction; extracting the output of the last encoder of the BERT model and using it as a feature, concatenating the output of the last four encoder layer of BERT, and Fine-tuning BERT. To the best of our knowledge, this is the first study incorporating contextualized word embedding from BERT into the Arabic keyphrase extraction task. We have found that utilizing contextual embeddings vastly enhances the performance of Arabic keyphrase extraction model. Moreover, adding features to the Arabic keyphrase extraction Bi-LSTM model, in general, has a positive effect on the model performance. The rest of the paper is organized as follows: we present the related works in section 2, Section 3 presents our methodology, and section 4 presents experiments results and discussion. Our conclusion is presented in section 5.

2 Related Work

Keyphrase extraction has two general approaches: unsupervised and supervised (Papagiannopoulou and Tsoumakas, 2020). Supervised approaches are powerful and perform better than unsupervised approaches. However, the unsupervised approaches are less expensive (Papagiannopoulou and Tsoumakas, 2020). Several unsupervised keyphrase extraction studies have been conducted. (Campos et al., 2020) have proposed YAKE!, an unsupervised keyphrase extraction system based on statistical features extracted from a single document. Their approach depends on six features; term frequency within the document, normalized term frequency, term relative position (sentence index), term relatedness to context, term case, and how often a term appears in different sentences (term different sentence). They have evaluated the system on 20 datasets in five languages. YAKE! proved its effectiveness generally compared to other systems with large text and performed well with shorter text on different domains and different document types. Moreover, the frequency feature has a more positive impact while removing term relatedness from the context and term different sentence features improves performance. Meanwhile, the term frequency feature is more useful when the document size increases, while the position feature is more beneficial in shorter texts. The case feature is more useful with mid to larger documents, while the term different sentence feature is better with short to mid documents. (Zhang et al., 2020) have leveraged word embedding for unsupervised graph-based keyphrase extraction. Their model selects candidate words based on their Part-Of-Speech (POS) tag; they have only selected nouns and adjectives. They have built three graphs; a word-word graph based on the word co-occurrence, a word-topic graph that connects words to their topics, and a topic-topic graph that is constructed when the same word appears in different topics. They have also proposed a modified random-walk model to rank candidate words and a new scoring model for candidate phrases based on the cosine similarity of the generated word embedding and the modified page rank score. The top scoring phrases are considered document keyphrases. Evaluating the type of word embeddings used shows that their embedding outperforms other embeddings on this task. They have reported that their model performs the best on all the tested datasets compared to other baselines. (Zu et al., 2020) have utilized word embedding with graph-based unsupervised keyphrase extraction along with document embedding. They have used a pre-trained Sent2Vec (Pagliardini et al., 2018) model trained on Wikipedia to create word embedding. The embedding vector is created by averaging all document words and n-gram embeddings. They have found that using the word as a node is better when dealing with a short text dataset and using a phrase as a node is better when dealing with a long text dataset.

Several studies have formulated the keyphrase extraction task as a sequence labeling task. (Basaldella et al., 2018) have proposed a deep learning model for automatic keyphrase extraction using Bi-LSTM and pre-trained GloVeembedding (Pennington et al., 2014). Their model outperforms CopyRNN (Meng et al., 2017) model on the same dataset. (Alzaidy et al., 2019) have utilized Bi-LSTM and CRF for keyphrase extraction from scientific documents using 100-dimension pre-trained GloVeembedding for embedding initialization. They have studied the role of each model layer on the performance and have compared CRF only, forward-LSTM, and Bi-LSTM. They have found that removing the Bi-LSTM layer negatively affects the recall, while removing the CRF layer increases the recall and decreases the precision. Hence, it indicates that Bi-LSTM can capture long-distance semantics and cause extraction of more gold-standard keyphrase. They have also found that CRF can capture the dependencies between labels leading to higher model precision. Combining Bi-LSTM and CRF has the best performance among the three created models. Additionally, the model outperforms CopyRNN (Meng et al., 2017). Many studies have used encoder-decoder architecture to generate absent and present keyphrases. The most popular study is the work by (Meng et al., 2017). They have proposed a generative model for keyphrase generation based on encoder-decoder architecture. They have used Bidirectional Gated Recurrent Units (Bi-GRU) for the encoder and forward-GRU for the decoder and incorporated attention mechanism (Bahdanau et al., 2015) (RNN-model) and copy mechanism (Gu et al., 2016) (CopyRNN-model) to deal with out-of-vocabulary words. CopyRNN model outperforms all the models they have compared by an average of almost 20% (Meng et al., 2017). Moreover, the CopyRNN model outperforms RNN in predicting both present and absent keyphrases. (Kehua Yang, 2019) encoder-decoder model is entirely based on the self-attention mechanism. They have incorporated semantic similarity between keyphrases. The model outperforms all baselines in predicting the present keyphrase. Additionally, it outperforms CopyRNN in predicting absent keyphrases. Targeting the problem of overlapping phrases generated by sequence-to-sequence models, (Zhao and Zhang, 2019) have proposed (ParaNet). The model consists of two parallel encoders; one to encode the text and the other to encode the linguistic constraints introducing coverage attention. They have used multi-task learning on two parallel decoders to generate the keyphrase and POS tag for each word in the keyphrase. They have tested different settings for combining the vector of the words and their syntactic tags, using the hyperbolic tangent function, using tree-LSTM, and adding coverage attention to the previous two. On the evaluation of present keyphrases, all their model settings outperform the extraction and generation methods baselines, including CopyRNN (Meng et al., 2017). Their best performing setting is when using tree-LSTM to combine vectors along with coverage attention.

Several studies have used BERT contextualized word embedding in two strategies; feature-based strategy or fine-tuning-based strategy. Word feature is extracted from the pre-trained BERT in the feature-based strategy. In fine-tuning based strategy, BERT model parameters are fine-tuned with the new smaller dataset for the downstream task adding one fully connected layer on top of it (Devlin et al., 2019). (Sun et al., 2020) have utilized BERT embedding in multi-task learning for keyphrase extraction. (Lim et al., 2020) have fine-tuned BERT and SciBERT (Beltagy et al., 2019) for keyphrase extraction. They have found that the best performance happens within the first three epochs of fine-tuning and that SciBERT performs better than BERT on scientific datasets. (Dascalu and Trăuşan-Matu, 2021) have experimented with four neural network architectures based on Bi-LSTM and multi-head attention on top of the transformer models BERT and SciBERT. A recent study has combined graph embedding and BERT embedding for keyphrase extraction is PhraseFormer (Nikzad-Khasmakhi et al., 2021). They have concatenated the resulting graph embedding and word embedding for each word and have used the resulting encoding as input. Another way of utilizing BERT for keyphrase extraction using a feature-based technique is using it in ranking candidate phrases (Mu et al., 2020). (Ding et al., 2021) have incorporated different types of features with BERT extracted features for the Chinese medical keyphrase extraction. The task is considered as a character-level labeling task. They have incorporated POS feature and lexicon feature using two techniques: concatenation and feature embedding. They have used the model without feature as a baseline and have tested the effect of features (POS only, lexicon only, and their combination) and the effect of different feature incorporation techniques (concatenation, embedding, and their combination). Their results show that incorporating the lexicon feature has a more positive impact than the POS feature, regardless of the incorporation techniques. Furthermore, the best incorporation technique is the embedding technique. (Sahrawat et al., 2020) have utilized contextualized word embeddings and compared them to static word embedding in sequence labeling keyphrase extraction. They have used Bi-LSTM-CRF and Bi-LSTM architectures with several embeddings; BERT, SciBERT, ELMo, TransformerXL (Dai et al., 2019), OpenAI-GPT (Radford and Narasimhan, 2018), OpenAI-GPT2 (Radford et al., 2019), RoBERTa (Liu et al., 2019), Glove, FastText, and Word2Vec. They have found that contextualized embeddings are better than static embedding, and BERT is the best among them since it uses bi-directional training.

Studies on Arabic keyphrase extraction followed several approaches. Rule-based approaches (El-Beltagy and Rafea, 2009) (Rammal et al., 2015)(Najadat et al., 2016)(Loukam et al., 2019) (Alotaibi and Ahmad, 2019) (Musleh et al., 2019), ranking approachs (Basaldella et al., 2017) (Amer and Foad, 2017), using a graph-based model as a base for ranking (Halabi and Awajan, 2019) (Al Hadidi et al., 2019), utilizing bag-of-concept (Awajan, 2015) (Suleiman and Awajan, 2017) (Suleiman et al., 2019b), machine learning approachs (Ali and Omar, 2015) (Armouty and Tedmori, 2019) (Al Etaiwi et al., 2019) and deep learning approachs (Helmy et al., 2018). (Ali and Omar, 2015) have combined statistical and machine learning methods and have formulated the keyphrase extraction task as a classification task. They have used term frequency, first occurrence, sentence count, c-value for multi-word nested terms, and TF-IDF statistical features to construct a feature vector. They have trained linear logistic regression, linear discriminant analysis, and support vector machine (SVM) classifiers. (Armouty and Tedmori, 2019) have used TF-IDF and the first occurrence weight of the term with Support Vector Machine (SVM), Naïve Bayes, and Random Forest classifiers. (Al Etaiwi et al., 2019) have used graph centrality measures along with term frequency and POS tags as input features to multi-layer perceptron, Naïve Bayes, Random Forest, and OneR algorithms. (Helmy et al., 2018) have proposed a deep learning-based model and a large-scale dataset for keyphrase extraction task. They have used AraVec (Soliman et al., 2017) to represent each token and a Bi-LSTM model.

3 Methodology

3.1 Data Preprocessing

The text is tokenized using Stanford Stanza neural pipeline for Arabic[2] and processed to remove punctuation, normalize all forms of Alef [إآأا] into plain Alef [ا] and decorated kaf [گ] to kaf [ك], and replace numbers' digits with a token to represent numbers which is [رقم] (number). Moreover, three types of features are extracted to be incorporated with the embeddings; linguistic feature (part-of-speech for each token), positional features (first occurrence and the sentence order of the first occurrence), and statistical feature (Term Frequency-Inverse Document Frequency-TFIDF). The part-of-speech tags are extracted using the MLE disambiguator of Camel tool (Obeid et al., 2020) and the TFIDF using TFIDF vectorizer from the scikit-learn library[3]. The actual value of the positional features and statistical feature and the one-hot encoding vector of the linguistic feature are concatenated to the end of the word embedding. Finally, the data is processed to be suitable for the sequence labeling task by converting the document into a sequence of tokens labeled with 1 if it is part of a keyphrase and with 0 if it is out of the keyphrase. Moreover, the maximum document length considered is 512 tokens for all models.

3.2 Models' specifications

A Bi-LSTM token classifier is built with one bidirectional LSTM layer that accepts input from the embedding layer and has one dense layer to generate the output label. There are two settings for the model input; the first is word embedding only, and the other is word embedding concatenated with different individual features or combined features. Figure 1 shows the model architecture. Two types of pre-trained word embeddings are used; static word embedding and contextualized word embedding, which are AraVec pre-trained embedding (Soliman et al., 2017) and AraBERT v2 (Antoun

[2]https://stanfordnlp.github.io/stanza/

[3]https://scikit-learn.org/stable/

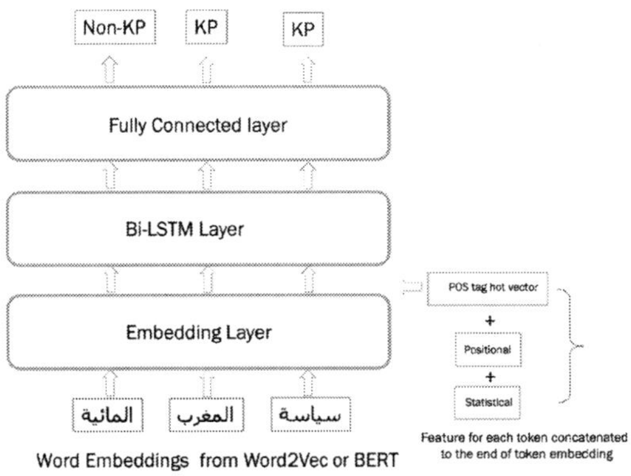

Figure 1: Proposed Model Architecture

Word2vec Embedding dimension	100
BERT Embedding dimension	768
Bi-LSTM hidden unit	150
POS tag embedding dimension	26
Learning rate	1.00E-05
Loss function	Cross entropy loss
Batch Size	1
Optimizer	SGD
Epoch for BERT	5
Epoch for Word2Vec	10
AraBERT pretrained Model	bert-base-arabertv02
Word2vec pretrained model	full_uni_sg_100_wiki
Maximum Document length	512

Table 1: Models Specifications

et al., 2020), respectively. We have used precision, recall, and F1-score metrics to evaluate the model performance on the level of extracted keywords and the extracted keyphrases. We have rewarded the model for each correctly extracted keyword at the keyword level, even if the model has generated part of the keyphrase. In contrast, at the keyphrase level, we have rewarded the model if it has generated the entire exact keyphrase. We have not stemmed the keywords before testing.

3.3 Experiments setup

The used dataset is ArabicKPE (Helmy et al., 2018) with the same splits provided by the authors; 4887 documents for training, 944 for model validation, and 941 for testing. In addition, Word2Vec and BERT have been used with Bi-LSTM and different features combinations. Further experiments with BERT include concatenating the last four hidden layers of BERT used as inputs to Bi-LSTM and fine-tuning BERT for keyphrase extraction on the used dataset. We have tested each feature independently and have combined two, three, and four features. Pytorch library[4] is used to build the models. The same hyper-parameters are used for all experiments as specified in Table 1. The Experiments are conducted using Google Colab Pro+ with GPU. Due to memory constraints and the large model size, the batch size is set to 1.

4 Results and Discussion

4.1 Using no features experiments

Table 2 and 3 present the results of using AraVec (Soliman et al., 2017) and AraBERT (Antoun et al., 2020) without features and our baseline of using no pre-trained embedding and no features. The results clearly show the benefit of using pre-trained word embedding compared to the baseline. Using pre-trained word embeddings enhances the model performance over the baseline in terms of F1-score for keyphrase level by 0.03 and 0.23 for Word2Vec and BERT, respectively. Moreover, Contextualized word embedding (BERT) has vastly enhanced the performance compared to static word embedding (Word2Vec) by 0.20.

4.2 Results of different BERT settings

In Table 3, we present the results of different settings of using BERT. The results show that using Bi-LSTM with embedding extracted from BERT has a slightly better F1-score than fine-tuning the BERT model for keyphrase extraction. This might be due to the ability of the model to learn more context utilizing Bi-LSTM. Moreover, unlike (Devlin et al., 2019) suggestion, using the output of the last encoder layer has a slightly better effect on performance than concatenating the output of the last four layers. This might be attributed to the difference in the language used to train the BERT model; different languages might have different behavior regarding choosing the best layer from the twelve encoder layers. Another possible reason is the difference in the tested downstream task as they test for the Named Entity Recognition (NER) task. Hence, for our task and language choice, it is better to use the output of the last encoder layer only to reduce the dimensionality of the input vector.

[4]https://pytorch.org/

Word2Vec Model Name	Keyword-Wise			Keyphrase-Wise		
	Precision	**Recall**	**F1-Score**	**Precision**	**Recall**	**F1-Score**
Bi-LSTM-Baseline	0.50	0.38	0.43	0.20	0.21	0.20
No added feature	0.64	0.33	0.44	0.28	0.19	0.23
POS	0.63	0.33	0.43	0.29	0.19	0.23
TFIDF	0.65	0.38	0.48	0.24	0.20	0.22
First Occurrence	0.57	0.41	0.47	0.30	0.25	0.27
Sentence Order	0.64	0.42	0.51	0.28	0.25	0.27
POS + TFIDF	**0.69**	0.34	0.45	0.28	0.18	0.22
POS + First occurrence	0.68	0.39	0.50	**0.31**	0.23	0.27
POS + Sentence order	0.60	**0.49**	**0.54**	0.28	**0.30**	**0.29**
TFIDF+ First occurrence	0.63	0.43	0.51	0.26	0.25	0.26
TFIDF+ sentence order	0.66	0.37	0.47	0.24	0.19	0.21
First occurrence + sentence order	0.68	0.40	0.50	0.29	0.24	0.26
TFIDF+ First occurrence + First sentence order	0.65	0.42	0.51	0.26	0.23	0.25
POS+ First occurrence + First sentence order	0.65	0.43	0.51	0.29	0.26	0.27
POS+ TFIDF+ First occurrence	0.67	0.38	0.48	0.26	0.21	0.23
POS+ TFIDF+ Sentence order	0.65	0.44	*0.52*	0.30	0.26	*0.28*
POS+ TFIDF+ First occurrence + First sentence order	0.64	0.41	0.50	0.27	0.24	0.25

Table 2: Word2Vec Experiments' results

4.3 Results of adding features:

We have tested the effect of incorporating the raw positional and statistical features' values to the embedding of each token and the one-hot 26 dimensions vector of the POS feature to the end of each word embedding.Table 2 and Table 3 show the results of adding each feature to Word2Vec and BERT embeddings respectively.

4.3.1 Independent features

In Word2Vec experiments, the results show that the positional features have the most impact on the performance in terms of the F1-score for the keyphrase level. Moreover, TFIDF has decreased the performance by 0.01 for the keyphrase level. Meanwhile, TFIDF has increased the performance over the no-feature model at the keyword level by 0.04. Adding POS tag features unexpectedly has no effect on the keyphrase level's performance and has decreased the keyword level's performance. In contrast, in BERT experiments, all features have a slightly positive impact on performance over the no-features model in terms of F1-score and recall of keyphrase level and recall of keyword level. Meanwhile, all features have not impacted performance regarding the F1-score of the keyword level. This slight improvement or no improvement in performance might be attributed to the fact that BERT already learned that information during the pr-training phase.

4.3.2 Combination of features

- **Combing two features**: In Word2Vec experiments, the best features combined with POS are the sentence order and the first occurrence. Combining TFIDF with POS has decreased the performance in terms of F1-score and recall for keyphrase level evaluation. However, it has increased the performance in terms of F1-score and recall at the keyword level. Combining numerical features reveals that combining TFIDF with sentence order has decreased the performance of the F1-score at the keyphrase level but has increased it on the keyword level. The best combination of two features in BERT experiments is when combining the POS feature with the first occurrence. Like Word2Vec, adding TFIDF to POS features has decreased the F1-score performance for the keyphrase level. Combining numerical features does not improve the performance, unlike when each independent numerical feature is used. That might result from combining features without normalizing them to have the same mean leading to some noise. Moreover, we can notice that in the context of keyword level evaluation, all F1-score results can be rounded to 0.60.

BERT Model Name	Keyword-Wise			Keyphrase-Wise		
	Precision	Recall	F1-Score	Precision	Recall	F1-Score
Bi-LSTM-Baseline	0.50	0.38	0.43	0.20	0.21	0.20
No added feature	**0.60**	0.59	0.59	**0.43**	0.43	0.43
Fine-Tuned	0.51	0.67	0.58	0.37	0.49	0.42
No-feature -4layer	0.56	0.59	0.58	0.41	0.44	0.42
POS	0.56	0.63	0.59	0.42	0.46	0.44
TFIDF	0.55	0.64	0.59	0.41	0.48	0.44
First Occurrence	0.53	0.67	0.59	0.40	0.51	**0.45**
Sentence Order	0.51	**0.69**	0.59	0.39	**0.52**	**0.45**
POS + TFIDF	0.56	0.60	0.58	0.42	0.43	0.42
POS + First occurrence	0.53	**0.69**	**0.60**	0.41	0.51	**0.45**
POS + Sentence order	0.51	**0.69**	0.59	0.38	**0.52**	0.44
TFIDF+ First occurrence	0.58	0.60	0.59	0.42	0.43	0.43
TFIDF+ sentence order	0.55	0.62	0.58	0.41	0.45	0.43
First occurrence + sentence order	0.55	0.64	0.59	0.40	0.46	0.43
TFIDF+ First occurrence + First sentence order	0.58	0.59	0.59	0.42	0.42	0.42
POS+ First occurrence + First sentence order	0.56	0.62	0.59	0.41	0.46	0.43
POS+ TFIDF+ First occurrence	0.56	0.62	0.59	0.42	0.45	0.44
POS+ TFIDF+ Sentence order	0.56	0.62	0.59	0.41	0.45	0.43
POS+ TFIDF+ First occurrence + First sentence order	0.54	0.65	0.59	0.39	0.47	0.43

Table 3: BERT Experiments' results

- **Combining three features**: In Word2Vec experiments, all three features combination has improved the performance in terms of F1-score for keyphrase level except for (POS+TFIDF+first occurrence) combination, which does not change the performance of keyphrase level but increases the performance of the keyword level. In contrast, BERT experiments show that the models have the same performance in terms of F1-score of the keyword level. While in keyphrase level performance, combining (POS+TFIDF+ First Occurrence) has slightly increased the performance, and combining (TFIDF+First occurrence+First sentence order) has slightly decreased the performance in terms of F1-score.
- **Combining four features**: BERT model has the same results as using no features on both keyphrase and keyword levels. On the other hand, Word2Vec has benefited by 0.02 and 0.06 F1-score for keyphrase level and keyword level, respectively, compared to using no features experiments.

4.4 Comparison with others' work

Table 4 shows our results compared to (Helmy et al., 2018). They have used deep learning with AraVec pre-trained word embedding (Soliman et al., 2017). Additionally, they have reported their results on the same dataset at the top 5, 10, and 15 retrieved keyphrases. They have compared the lemmatized version of the gold keyphrase with the lemmatized version of the predicted keyphrase. We have chosen to compare our results to their top 15 results since the maximum number of keyphrases available on the test set is 13 keyphrases for the document, and all of them will be included in our and their results. Moreover, they have not mentioned the used stemmer, and we have used ISRIStemmer from the NLTK library[5] to stem keywords. The results show that using no feature on Word2Vec has a similar F1-score to their model and that the best performing model on our Word2Vec experiments has outperformed their model due to incorporating features to Word2Vec embedding. Moreover, using BERT embedding without features and BERT's best performing model has vastly outperformed their model by 0.21 and 0.24, respectively.

4.5 Discussion

The best performing model on both level keyword level and keyphrase level for Word2Vec is when combining POS with the sentence order feature fol-

[5]https://www.nltk.org/

Model Name	Keyword-wise			Keyphrase-wise		
	Precision	Recall	F1-score	Precision	Recall	F1-score
(Helmy et al., 2018)@15KP	-	-	-	0.16	**0.67**	0.26
Word2Vec-no feature	**0.68**	0.35	0.46	0.30	0.21	0.25
BERT-no feature	0.63	0.62	0.63	**0.48**	0.47	0.47
Word2Vec -Best	0.63	0.52	0.57	0.32	0.34	0.33
BERT-Best	0.57	**0.71**	**0.64**	0.45	0.56	**0.50**

Table 4: Comparing the results with previous work

lowed by combining POS with TFIDF and sentence order. Conversely, the model with the least performance at the keyphrase level is when combining TFIDF with sentence order features. In general, it seems that using the TFIDF feature or combining it with other features degraded the model learning. In contrast, the model that has the least performance on the keyword level is when using the POS feature. In General, all BERT experiments have similar performance in both keyphrase and keyword levels. The keyphrase level scores differ by 0.03 only and range between 0.42 to 0.45, and all keyword level scores can be rounded to 0.60. The best performing models on BERT are when using first occurrence features alone, sentence order features alone, and when combining POS feature with first occurrence. While the least performing models are when combining TFIDF, first occurrence, and sentence order features and combining POS and TFIDF features. We can notice that the performance on the keyphrase level is not affected on 6 features combinations experiments out of 11, i.e., it is the same as no feature model. This might prove that BERT can encode linguistic and statistical features during pre-training. Further investigation and model propping are needed to confirm this finding. Generally, the improvements for both evaluation levels are aligned in BERT experiments. On the other hand, some Word2Vec experiments, which are TFIDF, POS+TFIDF, and TFIDF+Sentence order, have different behavior; the increased performance at the keyword level might be accompanied by a decreased performance at the keyphrase level. We can notice that TFIDF feature is available in all these experiments, which suggests that this feature might be beneficial to identifying the keyword more than the keyphrase. Comparing the gap between the scores of keyword level and keyphrase level on both Word2Vec and BERT, we notice that the difference between the two levels on BERT is smaller than the difference between the two levels on Word2Vec. This can be attributed to BERT's ability to generate the correct entire keyphrase due to more contextual information considered when giving context-dependent embedding compared to Word2Vec, which gives the same embedding for the word in different contexts. It seems that using Word2Vec enables models to recognize that the word is part of the keyphrase but could not present these words in the correct order. Additionally, we have noticed that different features combinations have different effects on performance depending on the embedding type. For example, BERT embedding based models are positively affected by the combination that includes the first occurrence feature more than the sentence order feature. In contrast, Word2Vec embedding based models are positively affected by the sentence order feature more than the first occurrence.

5 Conclusion

This study uses two types of pre-trained word embeddings for Arabic keyphrase extraction task: static and contextualized word embedding (Word2Vec and BERT). Several features are incorporated into the models to test their effect on performance. We have found that contextualized word embedding has vastly enhanced the performance of Arabic keyphrase extraction. Moreover, incorporating features with static embedding has more effect than incorporating features with contextualized embedding. Different features and features combinations affect the performance differently depending on the used embeddings. For future work, we consider trying the effect of adding more features to the models. Moreover, investigate the best combination of layers to select from BERT for keyphrase extraction.

Limitations

First, we have adopted a strict evaluation metric at the keyphrase level, which only rewards the correct keyphrase with the same keyword order and keyword numbers, i.e., we do not reward the model if it over generates a word in the middle of the keyphrase. This might affect the reported performance. Therefore, less strict metrics that consider stemming or word similarity might be helpful. Second, we broadcast the value of the POS for the unknown words that BERT decides to segment into sub-words which might introduce some noise to the training that might affect the performance. Nevertheless, trying not to broadcast the value does not affect the performance. Third, the randomness introduced on PyTorch run time execution with GPU setting might affect the ability to reproduce the same results when repeating the experiments. The model size and the time needed to model training have been challenging. Although we are using a GPU subscription with google colab, the run has taken a long time, and we have run out of drive space.

References

Wael Al Etaiwi, Arafat A. Awajan, and Dima Suleiman. 2019. Keywords extraction from arabic documents using centrality measures. In *2019 Sixth International Conference on Social Networks Analysis, Management and Security (SNAMS)*, pages 237–241.

Meran M. Al Hadidi, Muath Alzghool, and Hasan Muaidi. 2019. Keyword extraction from arabic text using the page rank algorithm. *International Journal of Innovative Technology and Exploring Engineering*, 8(12):3495–3504.

Mohammed Al-Logmani and Husni Al-Muhtaseb. Arabic dataset for automatic keyphrase extraction. In *Second International Conference on Software Engineering (SOEN-2017)*, pages 217–222.

Nidaa Ghalib Ali and Nazlia Omar. 2015. A hybrid of statistical and machine learning methods for Arabic keyphrase extraction. *Asian Journal of Applied Sciences*, 8(4):269–276.

Fahad Mazaed Alotaibi and Shakeel Ahmad. 2019. Keywords Extraction from the Text of Holy Quran Using Linguistic and Heuristic Rules. *International Journal of Computer Science and Network Security*, 19(2):82–87.

Rabah Alzaidy, Cornelia Caragea, and C. Lee Giles. 2019. Bi-lstm-crf sequence labeling for keyphrase extraction from scholarly documents. In *The World Wide Web Conference*, WWW '19, page 2551–2557, New York, NY, USA. Association for Computing Machinery.

Eslam Amer and Khaled Foad. 2017. Akea: An arabic keyphrase extraction algorithm. In *Proceedings of the International Conference on Advanced Intelligent Systems and Informatics 2016*, pages 137–146, Cham. Springer International Publishing.

Wissam Antoun, Fady Baly, and Hazem Hajj. 2020. AraBERT: Transformer-based model for Arabic language understanding. In *Proceedings of the 4th Workshop on Open-Source Arabic Corpora and Processing Tools, with a Shared Task on Offensive Language Detection*, pages 9–15, Marseille, France. European Language Resource Association.

Batool Armouty and Sara Tedmori. 2019. Automated keyword extraction using support vector machine from arabic news documents. In *2019 IEEE Jordan International Joint Conference on Electrical Engineering and Information Technology (JEEIT)*, pages 342–346.

Arafat Awajan. 2015. Keyword extraction from arabic documents using term equivalence classes. *ACM Trans. Asian Low-Resour. Lang. Inf. Process.*, 14(2).

Dzmitry Bahdanau, Kyunghyun Cho, and Yoshua Bengio. 2015. Neural machine translation by jointly learning to align and translate. In *3rd International Conference on Learning Representations, ICLR 2015, San Diego, CA, USA, May 7-9, 2015, Conference Track Proceedings*.

Marco Basaldella, Elisa Antolli, Giuseppe Serra, and Carlo Tasso. 2018. Bidirectional lstm recurrent neural network for keyphrase extraction. In *Digital Libraries and Multimedia Archives*, pages 180–187, Cham. Springer International Publishing.

Marco Basaldella, Muhammad Helmy, Elisa Antolli, Mihai Horia Popescu, Giuseppe Serra, and Carlo Tasso. 2017. Exploiting and evaluating a supervised, multilanguage keyphrase extraction pipeline for under-resourced languages. *International Conference Recent Advances in Natural Language Processing, RANLP*, 2017-Septe(1998):78–85.

Iz Beltagy, Kyle Lo, and Arman Cohan. 2019. SciBERT: A pretrained language model for scientific text. In *Proceedings of the 2019 Conference on Empirical Methods in Natural Language Processing and the 9th International Joint Conference on Natural Language Processing (EMNLP-IJCNLP)*, pages 3615–3620, Hong Kong, China. Association for Computational Linguistics.

Piotr Bojanowski, Edouard Grave, Armand Joulin, and Tomas Mikolov. 2017. Enriching word vectors with subword information. *Transactions of the Association for Computational Linguistics*, 5:135–146.

Ricardo Campos, Vítor Mangaravite, Arian Pasquali, Alípio Jorge, Célia Nunes, and Adam Jatowt. 2020. Yake! keyword extraction from single documents using multiple local features. *Information Sciences*, 509:257–289.

Zihang Dai, Zhilin Yang, Yiming Yang, Jaime Carbonell, Quoc Le, and Ruslan Salakhutdinov. 2019. Transformer-XL: Attentive language models beyond a fixed-length context. In *Proceedings of the 57th Annual Meeting of the Association for Computational Linguistics*, pages 2978–2988, Florence, Italy. Association for Computational Linguistics.

Kareem Darwish and Walid Magdy. 2014. Arabic Information Retrieval. *Foundations and Trends® in Information Retrieval*, 7(4):239–342.

Cristian Dascalu and Ştefan Trăuşan-Matu. 2021. Experiments with contextualized word embeddings for keyphrase extraction. In *2021 23rd International Conference on Control Systems and Computer Science (CSCS)*, pages 447–452.

Jacob Devlin, Ming-Wei Chang, Kenton Lee, and Kristina Toutanova. 2019. BERT: Pre-training of deep bidirectional transformers for language understanding. In *Proceedings of the 2019 Conference of the North American Chapter of the Association for Computational Linguistics: Human Language Technologies, Volume 1 (Long and Short Papers)*, pages 4171–4186, Minneapolis, Minnesota. Association for Computational Linguistics.

Liangping Ding, Zhixiong Zhang, and Yang Zhao. 2021. Bert-based chinese medical keyphrase extraction model enhanced with external features. In *Towards Open and Trustworthy Digital Societies: 23rd International Conference on Asia-Pacific Digital Libraries, ICADL 2021, Virtual Event, December 1–3, 2021, Proceedings*, page 167–176, Berlin, Heidelberg. Springer-Verlag.

Samhaa R. El-Beltagy and Ahmed Rafea. 2009. Kp-miner: A keyphrase extraction system for english and arabic documents. *Information Systems*, 34(1):132–144.

Jiatao Gu, Zhengdong Lu, Hang Li, and Victor O.K. Li. 2016. Incorporating copying mechanism in sequence-to-sequence learning. In *Proceedings of the 54th Annual Meeting of the Association for Computational Linguistics (Volume 1: Long Papers)*, pages 1631–1640, Berlin, Germany. Association for Computational Linguistics.

Nizar Y. Habash. 2010. Introduction to arabic natural language processing. *Synthesis Lectures on Human Language Technologies*, 3(1):1–187.

Dana Halabi and Arafat Awajan. 2019. Graph-Based Arabic Key-phrases Extraction. In *2019 2nd International Conference on new Trends in Computing Sciences (ICTCS)*, Amman, Jordan. IEEE.

Kazi Saidul Hasan and Vincent Ng. 2014. Automatic keyphrase extraction: A survey of the state of the art. In *Proceedings of the 52nd Annual Meeting of the Association for Computational Linguistics (Volume 1: Long Papers)*, pages 1262–1273, Baltimore, Maryland. Association for Computational Linguistics.

Muhammad Helmy, Marco Basaldella, Eddy Maddalena, Stefano Mizzaro, and Gianluca Demartini. 2016. Towards building a standard dataset for arabic keyphrase extraction evaluation. In *2016 International Conference on Asian Language Processing (IALP)*, pages 26–29.

Muhammad Helmy, R.M. Vigneshram, Giuseppe Serra, and Carlo Tasso. 2018. Applying deep learning for arabic keyphrase extraction. *Procedia Computer Science*, 142:254–261. Arabic Computational Linguistics.

Wei Zhang Jiqing Yao Yuquan Le Kehua Yang, Yaodong Wang. 2019. Keyphrase generation based on self-attention mechanism. *Computers, Materials & Continua*, 61(2):569–581.

Yeonsoo Lim, Deokjin Seo, and Yuchul Jung. 2020. Fine-tuning bert models for keyphrase extraction in scientific articles. *JOURNAL OF ADVANCED INFORMATION TECHNOLOGY AND CONVERGENCE*, 10:45–56.

Yinhan Liu, Myle Ott, Naman Goyal, Jingfei Du, Mandar Joshi, Danqi Chen, Omer Levy, Mike Lewis, Luke Zettlemoyer, and Veselin Stoyanov. 2019. Roberta: A robustly optimized bert pretraining approach. *ArXiv*, abs/1907.11692.

Mourad Loukam, Djamila Hammouche, Freha Mezzoudj, and Fatma Zohra Belkredim. 2019. Keyphrase extraction from modern standard arabic texts based on association rules. In *Arabic Language Processing: From Theory to Practice*, pages 209–220, Cham. Springer International Publishing.

Rui Meng, Sanqiang Zhao, Shuguang Han, Daqing He, Peter Brusilovsky, and Yu Chi. 2017. Deep keyphrase generation. In *Proceedings of the 55th Annual Meeting of the Association for Computational Linguistics (Volume 1: Long Papers)*, pages 582–592, Vancouver, Canada. Association for Computational Linguistics.

Zakariae Alami Merrouni, Bouchra Frikh, and Brahim Ouhbi. 2020. Automatic keyphrase extraction: a survey and trends. *Journal of Intelligent Information Systems*, 54(2):391–424.

Tomas Mikolov, Ilya Sutskever, Kai Chen, Greg Corrado, and Jeffrey Dean. 2013. Distributed representations of words and phrases and their compositionality. In *Proceedings of the 26th International Conference on Neural Information Processing Systems - Volume 2*, NIPS'13, page 3111–3119, Red Hook, NY, USA. Curran Associates Inc.

Funan Mu, Zhenting Yu, LiFeng Wang, Yequan Wang, Qingyu Yin, Yibo Sun, Liqun Liu, Teng Ma, Jing Tang, and Xing Zhou. 2020. Keyphrase extraction with span-based feature representations.

Dhiaa Musleh, Rashad Ahmed, Atta Rahman, and Fahd Al-Haidari. 2019. A novel approach to arabic keyphrase extraction. *ICIC Express Letters*, 10:875–884.

Hassan Najadat, Ismail Hmeidi, Mohammed N. Al-Kabi, and Maysa Mahmoud Bany Issa. 2016. Automatic keyphrase extractor from arabic documents. *International Journal of Advanced Computer Science and Applications*, 7.

Narjes Nikzad-Khasmakhi, Mohammad-Reza Feizi-Derakhshi, Meysam Asgari-Chenaghlu, Mohammad-Ali Balafar, Ali-Reza Feizi-Derakhshi, Taymaz Rahkar-Farshi, Majid Ramezani, Zoleikha Jahanbakhsh-Nagadeh, Elnaz Zafarani-Moattar, and Mehrdad Ranjbar-Khadivi. 2021. Phraseformer: Multimodal key-phrase extraction using transformer and graph embedding.

Ossama Obeid, Nasser Zalmout, Salam Khalifa, Dima Taji, Mai Oudah, Bashar Alhafni, Go Inoue, Fadhl Eryani, Alexander Erdmann, and Nizar Habash. 2020. CAMeL tools: An open source python toolkit for Arabic natural language processing. In *Proceedings of the 12th Language Resources and Evaluation Conference*, pages 7022–7032, Marseille, France. European Language Resources Association.

Matteo Pagliardini, Prakhar Gupta, and Martin Jaggi. 2018. Unsupervised learning of sentence embeddings using compositional n-gram features. In *Proceedings of the 2018 Conference of the North American Chapter of the Association for Computational Linguistics: Human Language Technologies, Volume 1 (Long Papers)*, pages 528–540, New Orleans, Louisiana. Association for Computational Linguistics.

Eirini Papagiannopoulou and Grigorios Tsoumakas. 2020. A review of keyphrase extraction. *Wiley Interdisciplinary Reviews: Data Mining and Knowledge Discovery*, 10(2):1–45.

Jeffrey Pennington, Richard Socher, and Christopher Manning. 2014. GloVe: Global vectors for word representation. In *Proceedings of the 2014 Conference on Empirical Methods in Natural Language Processing (EMNLP)*, pages 1532–1543, Doha, Qatar. Association for Computational Linguistics.

Matthew E. Peters, Mark Neumann, Mohit Iyyer, Matt Gardner, Christopher Clark, Kenton Lee, and Luke Zettlemoyer. 2018. Deep contextualized word representations. In *Proceedings of the 2018 Conference of the North American Chapter of the Association for Computational Linguistics: Human Language Technologies, Volume 1 (Long Papers)*, pages 2227–2237, New Orleans, Louisiana. Association for Computational Linguistics.

Mohammad Taher Pilehvar and Jose Camacho-Collados. *Embeddings in Natural Language Processing: Theory and Advances in Vector Representations of Meaning*. Springer Cham.

Alec Radford and Karthik Narasimhan. 2018. Improving language understanding by generative pre-training.

Alec Radford, Jeff Wu, Rewon Child, David Luan, Dario Amodei, and Ilya Sutskever. 2019. Language models are unsupervised multitask learners.

Mahmoud Rammal, Zeinab Bahsoun, and Mona Jabbour. 2015. Keyword extraction from arabic legal texts. *Interactive Technology and Smart Education*, 12:62–71.

Dhruva Sahrawat, Debanjan Mahata, Haimin Zhang, Mayank Kulkarni, Agniv Sharma, Rakesh Gosangi, Amanda Stent, Yaman Kumar, Rajiv Ratn Shah, and Roger Zimmermann. 2020. Keyphrase extraction as sequence labeling using contextualized embeddings. In *Advances in Information Retrieval*, pages 328–335, Cham. Springer International Publishing.

Abu Bakr Soliman, Kareem Eissa, and Samhaa R. El-Beltagy. 2017. Aravec: A set of arabic word embedding models for use in arabic nlp. *Procedia Computer Science*, 117:256–265. Arabic Computational Linguistics.

Dima Suleiman and Arafat Awajan. 2017. Bag-of-concept based keyword extraction from Arabic documents. *ICIT 2017 - 8th International Conference on Information Technology, Proceedings*, pages 863–869.

Dima Suleiman, Arafat A. Awajan, and Wael al Etaiwi. 2019a. Arabic text keywords extraction using word2vec. In *2019 2nd International Conference on new Trends in Computing Sciences (ICTCS)*, pages 1–7.

Dima Suleiman, Arafat A. Awajan, and Wael Al Etaiwi. 2019b. Arabic Text Keywords Extraction using Word2vec. *2019 2nd International Conference on New Trends in Computing Sciences, ICTCS 2019 - Proceedings*.

Si Sun, Chenyan Xiong, Zhenghao Liu, Zhiyuan Liu, and Jie Bao. 2020. Joint keyphrase chunking and salience ranking with bert. *CoRR 2020*, abs/2004.13639.

Yuxiang Zhang, Huan Liu, Suge Wang, W.H. Ip, Fan Wei, and Chunjing Xiao. 2020. Automatic keyphrase extraction using word embeddings. *Soft Computing*, 24:1–16.

Jing Zhao and Yuxiang Zhang. 2019. Incorporating linguistic constraints into keyphrase generation. In *Proceedings of the 57th Annual Meeting of the Association for Computational Linguistics*, pages 5224–5233, Florence, Italy. Association for Computational Linguistics.

Xian Zu, Fei Xie, and Xiaojian Liu. 2020. Graph-based keyphrase extraction using word and document em beddings. In *2020 IEEE International Conference on Knowledge Graph (ICKG)*, pages 70–76.

ArabIE: Joint Entity, Relation and Event Extraction for Arabic

Niama El Khbir, Nadi Tomeh, Thierry Charnois
LIPN, Université Sorbonne Paris Nord - CNRS UMR 7030
Villetaneuse, France
{elkhbir,tomeh,charnois}@lipn.fr

Abstract

Previous work on Arabic information extraction has mainly focused on named entity recognition and very little work has been done on Arabic relation extraction and event recognition. Moreover, modeling Arabic data for such tasks is not straightforward because of the morphological richness and idiosyncrasies of the Arabic language. We propose in this article the first neural joint information extraction system for the Arabic language.

1 Introduction

Information extraction (IE) is the task of identifying and classifying information of interest in a textual document. IE is an important area of research in NLP since it has many practical applications. In this article, we are interested in *joint modeling* of three IE tasks: named entity recognition (NER), relation extraction (RE), and event recognition (ER). A joint multi-tasking system, in comparison to a pipeline system, has the advantage of avoiding the propagation of errors among tasks.

This area of research is well explored in many languages such as English, Chinese, and Spanish. Nguyen and Nguyen (2018) proposed a model that jointly extracts entity mentions, event triggers and event arguments using shared hidden representations in a deep learning framework. Wadden et al. (2019) provided a framework for extracting entities, relations, and triggers using BERT embeddings and graph propagation to capture context relevant for these tasks. Lin et al. (2020) proposed a joint neural framework that extracts entities, relations and events from an input sentence as a globally optimal graph.

For Arabic, however, most proposed models are restricted to NER (Oudah and Shaalan, 2012; Benajiba et al., 2008b). Limited efforts have been dedicated to RE and ER (Taghizadeh et al., 2018; AL-Smadi and Qawasmeh, 2016), and no previous work has addressed them jointly. We attempt to fill this gap in the present work.

Similar to Lin et al. (2020), the model we propose in §2 extracts a graph from an input sequence in two steps: (a) two CRFs (Lafferty et al., 2001) with BIO-based tags are used to identify spans (subsequences of tokens) corresponding to *entities* and *event triggers* (graph nodes); then (b) greedy decoding is used to obtain the output graph.

Since Arabic is morphologically rich (Habash, 2010), entities are not limited to sequences of words like English for instance. Some entities correspond to affixes and some words carry multiple entities. Therefore, modeling on the subword level is necessary. To address this issue, we compare two approaches which we describe in detail in §3. In the first approach, we resort to word tokenization as a preprocessing step. We aim to split morphologically complex words into tokens, each of which corresponds to (or is a part of) one entity at most. An entity can thus be modeled as a sequence of tokens using the standard BIO tags. In the second approach, we augment the BIO tags to encode multiple entities per word, eliminating the need for prior tokenization.

Our contribution in this article is twofold:

- First, we present ArabIE (§2), the first neural joint IE model for Arabic, establishing state-of-the-art results (§4.2) on the ACE 2005 dataset (Walker and Consortium, 2005) (§4.1). We show that the performance of our model is comparable to that of other languages (§4.2).
- Second, we provide an empirical study of the interplay between tokenization (§3) and NER performance and its consequences on RE and ER (§4.2).

2 Multitask Joint Extraction Model

Given a text document as input, we aim at extracting, from each sentence, entities and binary

Proceedings of the The Seventh Arabic Natural Language Processing Workshop (WANLP), pages 331 - 345
December 8, 2022 ©2022 Association for Computational Linguistics

relations between them, event triggers, and their arguments. Formally, for an input sequence **x** of length L, the information extraction task is the operation that yields, as an output, a graph $G = (V, E)$ whose nodes V are spans of tokens of the input sequence representing identified entities and triggers, and whose edges E represent relations between two entities or event roles (relations between event triggers and their arguments entities). Each node and edge in the graph has a type. Similar to (Lin et al., 2020), our model performs end-to-end IE in four stages.

Token encoding Several combinations of representations from BERT's layers are inspected for encoding the input sequence, as done by Lin et al. (2020) for English data. Ultimately, the input sequence is encoded using the concatenation of BERT's last and third last layers to obtain an embedding for each token, as using these layers improves the performance on most subtasks. Jawahar et al. (2019) showed that BERT last layers contain semantic information about the text, which is beneficial for the processing of Arabic texts. Input sequences are optionally tokenized in a preprocessing step (§3).

Identification Token embeddings are passed to a network composed of a Feed-Forward Network (FFN) layer followed by a Conditional Random Field (CRF) layer. The network labels the sequence using the BIO scheme to identify spans of tokens that correspond to entities or event triggers. We use separate CRF taggers for entities and triggers so that each one specializes in one task. The sequence of labels produced by the CRF encodes a segmentation of the input sequence so that identified entities cannot overlap, the same applies for triggers. On the other hand, entities can overlap with triggers in some cases. The verb أوقفت *(Awqft; she arrested)* is for example a trigger of type `Justice` and the pronoun ت *(t)* is an entity of type `PER`.

Classification At this stage, entities and triggers are identified, but their types are not yet assigned. A fixed-size representation for each span is computed as the average of its first and last token's BERT embeddings. The output is passed to an FFN to obtain a score for each possible type. Again, we use separate FFNs for entities and triggers.

Scoring relations and event roles is performed in a similar manner. An edge between two spans is represented by concatenating their vectors. A relation edge links two entities while a role edge links a trigger to an entity. Representations of edges are passed to an FFN to compute a score for each relation or role type. A special *none* label to indicate the absence thereof. We also use a separate FFN is used for relations and roles.

Decoding We use unconstrained greedy decoding to obtain the output graph: for each node and edge of the graph, we select the highest-scoring type. In our experiments, we tried adding to the graph score a penalty on invalid graph configurations and decode with beam search similar to Lin et al. (2020) but didn't get any improvements.

Training The parameters of all networks are jointly trained end-to-end to minimize the sum of individual task losses. We use the negative log-likelihood of gold BIO paths as a loss function for the CRFs and of the gold label for the FFN classifiers.

3 Subword Entities

As discussed earlier in (§1), a word in Arabic can hold two or more entities anchored on its root or affixes. For example, the word مراسلتنا *(mrAsltnA; our reporter)* comprises two entities: مراسلة *(mrAslp; reporter)* of type person (`PER`) and نا *(nA; our)* of type organisation (`ORG`).[1] This example cannot be handled by our model, which assigns one label to each token in the sequence. Such a mismatch has been considered an anomaly in previous work using sequence labeling approaches (Benajiba et al., 2008a), and subword entities were simply discarded. We propose two solutions to this problem. Figure 1 summarizes the different approaches adopted on the example of the word مراسلتنا.

Word tokenization Subword entities typically correspond to *morphemes*. We, therefore, use a morphological analyzer to tokenize words in context. The probability that each resulting token corresponds to multiple entities decreases dramatically. In practice, we use the analyzer provided by CamelTools (Obeid et al., 2020) and refer to this tokenization scheme by `tok_morph`. The word in the

[1]This example is taken from the ACE 2005 corpus. We use the Buckwalter (Buckwalter) transliteration scheme for Romanization. Note that the taa' marbuuTa (ة; p) transforms to taa' (ت; t) when attached to the suffix (نا; nA).

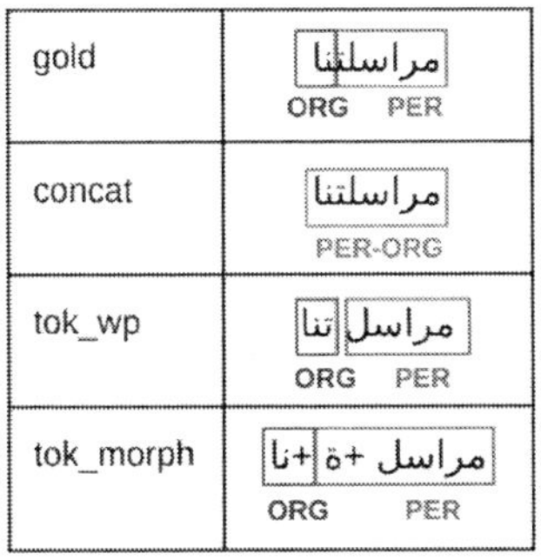

Figure 1: An example of the adopted approaches. Entities are framed in different colors w.r.t their label types. `PER: Person, ORG: Organization.`

above example is tokenized into three morphemes مراسل +ة +نا *(mrAsl +p +nA)*, the first two tokens correspond to the entity PER, the third one to ORG.

To obtain supervised training data for tokenized sequences, we align each word with its tokens (morphemes) at the character level and use the alignment to project gold entities onto the tokens. An entity is projected onto a token if the majority of its characters align with the token. If multiple entities are projected onto one token, only one of them is randomly selected.

To validate our hypotheses that morphemes are the right level for modeling entities, we compare the morphological analyzer to Word Pieces (Wu et al., 2016), a statistical tokenizer which does not necessarily produce valid affixes. This tokenizer produces مراسل تنا *(mrAsl tnA)* for the example word where the second token is not a morphologically valid suffix and does not exactly match the gold entity نا *(nA; our)*. We refer to this tokenization scheme by tok_wp.

Projection of entities onto tokens is not always perfect either because an entity doesn't correspond to a morpheme in gold data; the tokenizer doesn't produce a valid morpheme; or both. This results in some data loss that we later quantify and take into account during the evaluation phase.

An example of the data loss in tok_wp is that of the sentence سألتها عن الجيران *(s>lthA En AljyrAn; she asked her about the neighbours)*, with ت *(t)* being an entity of type PER, ها *(hA)* an entity of type PER, and الجيران *(AljyrAn)* an entity of type PER, with a relation of type PER-SOC between ها and الجيران. The tok_wp approach yields the following tokens: سأل تها عن الجيران. There is no way to project the two entities ها and ت onto the unique token تها. We therefore randomly project one of the two entities onto this token. If it happens to be ت, then ها is discarded and the PER-SOC relation between ها and الجيران is discarded too. We quantify this data loss in Table 3 for both tokenization schemes.

Label concatenation Instead of tokenization then projection, we concatenate labels of subword entities into one *complex* entity. The example word is thus labeled PER-ORG. This approach is appealing because of its simplicity, but it results in a much larger label set, as some words contain up to four entities. In practice, we restrict the label set to the labels seen in training data. We refer to this tokenization scheme by concat.

4 Experiments and Results

4.1 Experimental setup

Dataset and preprocessing We use the Arabic corpus provided by ACE05[2], which contains different document types annotated with entities, relations and events.

Source	Files	Words	Entities
NW	221	53026	17105
BN	127	26907	9099
WL	55	20181	6234
Total	403	100114	32438
Source	**Relations**	**Triggers**	**Roles**
NW	2674	1270	2957
BN	1606	870	1762
WL	439	130	256
Total	4719	2270	4975

Table 1: General statistics of raw ACE05 data. NW: newswires, BN: broadcast news, WL: weblogs.

The ACE05 data was published in 2006, but very little work has been carried out on it for entity extraction, and no work has been done on relation or event extraction. These previous works are discussed in details in §3.

We randomly split the data into 80% train, 10% dev, and 10% test, as no official split is provided. We will make our splits and our code publicly available.

[2]https://catalog.ldc.upenn.edu/LDC2006T06

Entities	Relations	Triggers	Roles	
FAC: 1427	ART: 338	Business: 24	Adjudicator: 91	Origin: 112
GPE: 7165	GEN-AFF: 1142	Conflict: 550	Agent: 282	Organization: 17
LOC: 1215	ORG-AFF: 1379	Contact: 274	Artifact: 378	Person: 302
ORG: 4885	PART-WHLE: 903	Justice: 379	Attacker: 303	Place: 351
PER: 17150	PER-SOC: 643	Life: 398	Beneficiary: 22	Plaintiff: 12
VEH: 418	PHYS: 314	Movement: 435	Buyer: 6	Prosecutor: 22
WEA: 481		Personnel: 152	Defendant: 135	Recipient: 17
		Transaction: 58	Destination: 275	Seller: 1
			Entity: 584	Target: 310
			Giver: 36	Vehicle: 50
			Instrument: 266	Victim: 364

Table 2: Entity, relation, trigger and event role gold ACE05 statistics by label types.

Segmentation We segment each document into sentences using punctuation marks, except for the broadcast news (BN) subcorpus, which we segment into fixed-length sentences due to lack of punctuation. Document segmentation may result in the loss of some entities and triggers (and their associated relations and roles) if a sentence boundary happens to be inside it. Comparing train rows of `gold` and `segm` in Table 3 allows to quantify the data loss after the segmentation phase.

Tokenization Tokenization described in §3 may result in data loss which we quantify in Table 3. However, we use the gold data for dev and test sets for all experiments without discarding any instance.

Dataset Statistics In Table 1, we present statistics done on raw ACE05 files. Note that the difference between role numbers here and gold role numbers of Table 3 is explainable by the fact that we don't handle time roles; arguments that refer to time. We made this choice following Wadden et al. (2019) and Zhang et al. (2019). Thus we also consider that "time" and "value" event arguments are not technically named entities.

In Table 2, we present statistics of entities, relations, triggers and event arguments by label types. Additional statisctis by label subtypes are presented in Tables 9, 10 and 11 of the appendices. In Table 4, we present occurrences of the top 10 most frequent entities of ACE05. The total number of gold entities being 32420, we can easily see that the pronominal entities which are in most cases subwords, are numerous. Hence the need for tokenization to manage them. Note that 21.88% of entities are one-character tokens and 10.18% are two-character tokens.

Tokenization	Split	Entities	Relations	Triggers	Roles
gold	train	26178	3801	1831	3346
	dev	3296	508	235	418
	test	2946	400	204	352
segm	train	26065	3727	1831	3181
concat	train	26065	3727	1831	3181
tok_wp	train	25554	3416	1831	3176
tok_morph	train	25833	3675	1829	3168

Table 3: Statistics on ACE05 train, dev, and test splits. The train, dev, and test sets are identical for all approaches. Comparison of rows `gold` and `segm` show data loss due to document segmentation into sentences, a common pre-tokenization step for all approaches. Comparison of rows `concat`, `tok_wp` and `tok_morph` with row `segm` quantifies data loss due to each tokenization approach.

Training Hyperparameters We trained our model for 80 epochs with a batch size of 6, using BertAdam optimizer, a learning rate of 5e-5 and weight decay of 1e-5 for BERT, and a learning rate of 1e-3 and weight decay of 1e-3 for other parameters.

We used `bert-large-arabertv2` model (Antoun et al., 2020) to conduct all experiments except for `tok_wp` experiments, where we used the `bert-large-arabertv02` tokenizer. Note that the tokenization schemes `tok_morph` do not match the vocabulary of the used BERT model and that there is not yet a BERT adapted to this tokenization procedure. In future works, we aim to solve this mismatch problem by training a BERT language model on the output of the morphological analyzer.

We ran our experiments on an Ubuntu machine, with a GPU Nvidia GEForce RTX 2080 with 8 GB of RAM. We estimated the needed computational budget to 6 GPU hours for each run of each experiment in Table 5.

Entity	Occurrences
ت (t)	2420
ه (h)	1823
ي (y)	1690
ها (hA)	933
هم (hm)	560
وا (wA)	459
نا (nA)	374
الرئيس (Alr}ys; the president)	307
ن (n)	282
أ (>)	279

Table 4: Occurrences of the top 10 most frequent entities of ACE05 gold data.

Evaluation We use precision, recall, and F1 measure for evaluating each task independently. We also combine the individual scores F_1^t of all tasks t into a global (macro) score F_g, where each task is weighted by N_t its number of instances:

$$F_g = \frac{1}{\sum_{t \in \mathcal{T}} N_t} \sum_{t \in \mathcal{T}} N_t F_1^t$$

We consider an entity (resp. trigger) correct if its span and label match those of a gold entity (resp. trigger). Subword entities (§3), however, are allowed not to match exactly their gold span inside the word, they are penalized only if their order inside the word is incorrect. If we take as an example the word of Figure 1, using the `tok_wp` approach, if the model predicts مراسل *(mrAsl)* as an entity of type PER, and تنا *(tnA)* as an entity of type ORG, the prediction is considered correct. The same evaluation is applied for the `tok_morph` and `concat` approaches.

We consider a relation correct if the participating entities match the gold ones and the relation label matches the gold label. We consider an event role correct if its span and label match the gold one.

While strict evaluation is also possible, we use this approximate approach to emphasize a fair comparison between the tokenization and the concatenation approaches. Both approaches are penalized for the data loss they engender.

4.2 Results

Tables 5 and 6 show results using labels of types (7 entities, 6 relations, 8 triggers, and 22 roles) and subtypes (44 entities, 18 relations, 32 triggers, and 22 roles), for each tokenization scheme. We average the scores across three runs and report numbers

	concat	tok_wp	tok_morph
Ent.	P: 83.66 ± 0.05 R: 82.26 ± 0.11 F: 82.96 ± 0.03	P: 84.42 ± 0.32 R: 84.05 ± 0.12 F: 84.23 ± 0.22	**P: 85.04 ± 0.25** **R: 85.07 ± 0.2** **F: 85.05 ± 0.12**
Rel.	P: 59.88 ± 1.29 R: 56.88 ± 0.62 F: 58.34 ± 0.94	P: 57.92 ± 1.38 R: 53.0 ± 3.02 F: 55.29 ± 1.67	**P: 62.3 ± 0.42** **R: 63.5 ± 0.61** **F: 62.9 ± 0.51**
Trigg.	P: 67.56 ± 2.38 R: 58.58 ± 0.73 F: 62.74 ± 1.45	**P: 69.49 ± 0.36** R: 57.68 ± 1.89 F: 63.02 ± 1.1	P: 66.32 ± 0.51 **R: 61.11 ± 1.62** **F: 63.59 ± 0.81**
Role	P: 55.8 ± 1.09 R: 43.75 ± 0.85 F: 49.04 ± 0.95	P: 52.75 ± 0.46 R: 40.15 ± 0.81 F: 45.59 ± 0.35	**P: 57.38 ± 1.5** **R: 47.25 ± 0.94** **F: 51.82 ± 0.98**
F_g	76.31	76.66	**78.65**

Table 5: Results on ACE05 data using type labels.

	concat	tok_wp	tok_morph
Ent.	P: 81.86 ± 0.18 R: 80.54 ± 0.32 F: 81.19 ± 0.25	P: 81.74 ± 0.22 R: 80.85 ± 0.13 F: 81.3 ± 0.18	**P: 83.05 ± 0.44** **R: 83.0 ± 0.45** **F: 83.02 ± 0.44**
Rel.	P: 58.61 ± 1.56 R: 55.33 ± 1.33 F: 56.92 ± 1.41	P: 56.62 ± 0.48 R: 51.25 ± 1.0 F: 53.8 ± 0.77	**P: 60.7 ± 0.44** **R: 57.5 ± 0.5** **F: 59.05 ± 0.06**
Trigg.	P: 64.93 ± 2.34 R: 55.88 ± 1.44 F: 60.06 ± 1.76	**P: 66.97 ± 0.68** **R: 56.61 ± 0.25** **F: 61.36 ± 0.14**	P: 64.32 ± 1.38 R: 54.41 ± 1.96 F: 58.96 ± 1.73
Role	P: 53.06 ± 1.07 R: 42.05 ± 1.39 F: 46.9 ± 1.03	P: 50.46 ± 2.45 R: 38.35 ± 0.57 F: 43.56 ± 1.28	**P: 55.48 ± 2.2** **R: 42.61 ± 1.14** **F: 48.2 ± 1.55**
F_g	74.50	74.03	**76.16**

Table 6: Results on ACE05 data using subtype labels.

for the model with the best average F-score over the four tasks on the dev set.

Existing work on Arabic NER for ACE05 did not address nominal and pronominal entities (Benajiba et al., 2008a) to avoid the tokenization problem, while we handle all grammatical categories of entity mentions.

`tok_morph` results The `tok_morph` approach gets the best F-score on each of the four tasks and has the best F_g score. We suppose that morphological information introduced by the tokenizer helps the model to improve the recognition of relations and roles.

`concat` results The `concat` approach gets the lowest F_g score. We can notice that its performance on triggers using type labels is quite close to that of `tok_morph`, but its performance on entities is poor compared to `tok_wp` and `tok_morph` approaches. We explain this by the increase in the number of labels to classify in this approach; 24 entity type labels (resp. 127 entity subtype labels), such as PER-VEH, ORG-VEH, VEH-VEH (resp. PER:Group-VEH:Air,

PER:Individual-VEH:Air), instead of 7 entity type labels (resp. 44 entity subtype labels), such as PER, LOC, VEH... (resp. PER:Group, PER:Individual, VEH:Air...) for the other approaches.

Relations (resp. roles) F-score is degraded by 4.56 (resp. 2.78) points compared to that of tok_morph even if the relation labels number is the same for these two approaches. We explain this by the fact that when the classification and identification of entities become more complex, the part of the loss specific to entities becomes difficult to minimize, which forces the model to prioritize this task over the others, thus degrading relation and role performance.

tok_wp results Entity and relation performance of tok_wp is close to that of tok_morph and better than that of concat. However, this approach gets the lowest F-score for relation and role tasks. This is partly due to a larger number of discarded entities in this approach than in the other approaches. More discarded entities leads to more discarded relations, and since we penalize each model with respect to discarded instances, this explains the discrepancy in performance.

Type labels experiments details We present in this subsection score details of the experiments of Table 5. Table 7 shows entity, relation, trigger, and role scores by type labels.

We do not report scores details of the subtype label experiments (Table 6) because they are too numerous, and in general the behavior and the performance of the subtype labels experiments follow that of the type label experiments.

We notice that among the entity types, PER has the best F-score. Likewise, among the relation types, ORG-AFF has the best F-score. PER and ORG-AFF represent respectively 52.87% and 29.22% of the total number of entities and relations.

Imbalanced Data Problem We notice furthermore that Business events have an F-score of 0; they represent only 0.5% (of the total number of events), which is a limited amount of data to train the model to recognize this class. The same behavior (with an F-score of 0) is observed for role types Beneficiary, Buyer, Organization, Prosecutor, Recipient, and Seller as they represent respectively 0.14%, 0.41%, 0.53%, 0.41%, and 0.02% of the total number of roles. For example, the Recipient role is always incorrectly predicted by the model as the Beneficiary role, since these two roles are very close semantically in the context of a Transaction event.

Comparison to other languages Table 8 show state-of-the-art F-scores of joint IE with ACE05 dataset for different languages. English, Chinese, and Spanish experiments were borrowed from Lin et al. (2020), who trained their model with type labels for entity, relation, and roles, and with subtype labels for triggers. We thus give scores of Arabic following this pattern.

Overall results Unless using concat tokenization procedure, our model assigns one label to each input token, which establishes an upper bound on its performance since multi-label tokens are out of its reach. For example, p+drop experiments could at most reach a recall of 97.31 for entities, 90.75 for relations, and 93.46 for roles; i.e., at most an F-score of 98.63 for entities, 95.15 for relations, and 96.71 for roles.

Importantly, the performance of our three systems of Table 5 is comparable to other languages (Lin et al., 2020) (details in Table 8).

Since there was no baseline addressing the entirety of ACE05 entities, nor a system for RE and ER, we propose tok_morph as a baseline.

5 Error Analysis

Error analysis is important to understand the model's weaknesses and to attempt to fix them in future work. Thus, we examined a sample of 32 sentences where we found 110 remaining errors from experiments with tok_morph tokenization and type labels.

Entity Errors About 23% are errors related to pronominal entities; these errors either come from entities predicted by the model and not annotated in the gold data or vice-versa or from correctly identified entities but incorrectly classified. For example, in the word صادرتها (*SAdrthA; confiscated it*), the pronoun ت (*t*) is annotated in gold data as a PER entity that the model does not predict. These errors are most likely due to the lack of labeling of a considerable number of pronominal entities of the gold data. As example, for the word المسلحين (*AlmslHyn; armed*), the model predicts the pronoun ين (*yn*) as a PER entity but it's not annotated in the gold data, although this pronoun was annotated

Entities	Relations	Triggers	Roles	
FAC: 0.82 ± 0.0	ART: 0.58 ± 0.02	Business: 0.0 ± 0.0	Adjudicator: 0.37 ± 0.03	Origin: 0.42 ± 0.0
GPE: 0.85 ± 0.0	GEN-AFF: 0.62 ± 0.02	Conflict: 0.67 ± 0.01	Agent: 0.44 ± 0.04	Organization: 0.0 ± 0.0
LOC: 0.66 ± 0.02	ORG-AFF: 0.73 ± 0.01	Contact: 0.39 ± 0.02	Artifact: 0.6 ± 0.04	Person: 0.57 ± 0.04
ORG: 0.76 ± 0.0	PART-WHLE: 0.56 ± 0.01	Justice: 0.62 ± 0.02	Attacker: 0.55 ± 0.02	Place: 0.49 ± 0.03
PER: 0.9 ± 0.0	PER-SOC: 0.63 ± 0.02	Life: 0.84 ± 0.0	Beneficiary: 0.0 ± 0.0	Plaintiff: 0.11 ± 0.16
VEH: 0.78 ± 0.01	PHYS: 0.31 ± 0.07	Movement: 0.42 ± 0.06	Buyer: 0.0 ± 0.0	Prosecutor: 0.0 ± 0.0
WEA: 0.81 ± 0.03		Personnel: 0.57 ± 0.03	Defendant: 0.22 ± 0.06	Recipient: 0.0 ± 0.0
		Transaction: 0.71 ± 0.02	Destination: 0.58 ± 0.05	Seller: 0.0 ± 0.0
			Entity: 0.41 ± 0.0	Target: 0.5 ± 0.05
			Giver: 0.35 ± 0.11	Vehicle: 1.0 ± 0.0
			Instrument: 0.69 ± 0.04	Victim: 0.67 ± 0.04

Table 7: Entity, Relation, Trigger and Role F-score details of experiment of Table 5 using `tok_morph` approach and type labels.

Language	Ent.	Rel.	Trigg.	Role
English	89.6	58.6	72.8	54.8
Chinese	88.5	62.4	65.6	52.0
Spanish	81.3	48.1	56.8	40.3
Arabic	85.05	62.9	58.96	51.82

Table 8: State-of-the-art F-scores of joint IE for different languages. Arabic scores are those of `tok_morph` experiments.

167 times in words like المتقاعدين (*AlmtqAEdyn; retirees*), الآخرين (*AlAxryn; the others*), and الراغبين (*AlrAgbyn; willing to*). Note that pronominal entities represent 31% of the total gold entities.

Relation Errors About 14% of the remaining errors are multiple relation entities, i.e., relations incorrectly predicted because their entities are involved in multiple relations. For example, in the gold annotations of the sentence وزير العدل المصري (*wzyr AlEdl AlmSry; Egyptian Minister of Justice*), the word وزير (*wzyr; Minister*) is involved in two relations of types `ORG-AFF` (resp. `GEN-AFF`) with the word العدل (*AlEdl; Justice*) (resp. المصري (*AlmSry; Egyptian*)). The model only predicts the first `ORG-AFF` relation between the two first words.

At least 6% are correctly identified and incorrectly classified relations, i.e., the model correctly predicts the two participating entities of the relation but incorrectly predicts the relation type. This error is usually due to the ambiguity induced by the existing semantic proximity between some relation types, such as `PART-WHOLE` and `ORG-AFF`.

Events Errors Nearly 23.5% are annotation errors, particularly related to triggers and roles. Specifically, out of the 35 remaining event errors, 67% are related to annotation omissions. As an example, in the sentence اتصل به شقيقيه (*AtSl bh $qyqyh; his brothers called him*), the model predicts the verb اتصل (*AtSl; called*) as a trigger of type `Contact`. This trigger is not annotated in the gold data but the model's prediction seems correct because an event of type `Contact` is defined in the annotation guide by: explicit phone or written communication between two or more parties. In the annotation guide the verb called in the sentence "John called Jane last night" is given as an example of a trigger of type `Contact`. Figure 2 presents a recurring example of a long sentence containing several omitted roles. In this sentence, we distinguish three errors: (1) the word المتهمين (*Almthmyn; The accused*) is predicted as an `Agent` argument by the model, which is intuitively correct as an `Agent` is defined in the annotation guide by "the attacking agent or the one that enacts the harm". This word is incorrectly annotated in the gold sentence as an argument of type `Victim`. (2) The word رفاق (*rfAq; companions*) is predicted as an argument of type `Agent` which is intuitively correct. This word is not annotated in the gold sentence as an argument. (3) The word الصائغ (*AlSAg; the jeweler*) is predicted as arguments of type `Victim` which is intuitively correct as a `Victim` is defined in the annotation guide by: the person who died. This word is not annotated in the gold sentence.

6 Related work

Entity Extraction Most Arabic IE work focuses on NER. We cite (Naji, 2012), who used artificial neural networks for NER. (Oudah and Shaalan, 2012) tested a hybrid approach, including both rule-

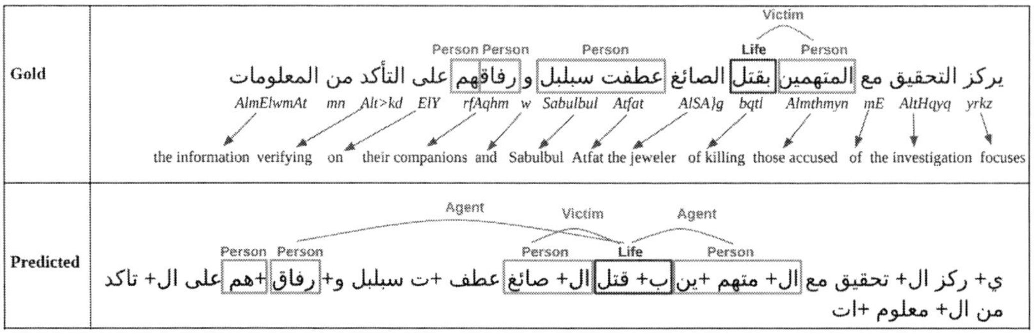

Figure 2: An example of remaining event errors (annotation omissions), using `tok_morph` tokenization and type labels. Entities are framed in green, triggers are framed in blue, event arguments (roles) are represented by red edges. `ORG: Organization, GPE: Geo-Political Entity, PER: Person.`

based and machine learning approaches. (Benajiba et al., 2008b) proposed an SVM-based model with a combination of language-dependent and language-dependent features, showing the relevance of morphological features for rich languages like Arabic. (Benajiba et al., 2010) built a system augmented by deeper lexical, syntactic, and morphological features that were extracted from noisy data obtained via projection from an Arabic-English parallel corpus. (Helwe et al., 2020) proposed a semi-supervised learning approach to train a BERT-based NER model using labeled and semi-labeled datasets. The works that deal with NER using ACE05, ACE04, or ACE03 either preprocess the data differently from ours, which results in a very different number of entities than ours or use different entity types than the one we used. For example, Benajiba et al. (2008b) evaluate their model separately for each data type of ACE05 (NW, BN, WL). In addition, they remove all annotations that they consider not oriented to the entity detection and recognition tasks, such as the nominal and pronominal entities, and only keep the named ones, which leads them to a total number of entities in the training and test corpora of 10218. This makes their performance incomparable to ours because we evaluate the model with almost 32000 entities for all our proposed approaches. Other work (Benajiba et al., 2010, 2009, 2008a) same preprocessing of Benajiba et al. (2008b). Oudah and Shaalan (2012) tested their model performance on `Date, Time, Price, Measurement, and Percent` entities of ACE05, while we test our model on the principal entity types (`PER, LOC, ORG, FAC, VEH...`).

Relation Extraction Arabic RE works include (Mohamed et al., 2015), who proposed a distant supervised learning model with specific features that characterize Arabic relations. (Sarhan et al., 2016) presented a semi-supervised pattern-based bootstrapping technique for RE using stemming and semantic expansion. (Taghizadeh et al., 2018) used a combination of kernel functions and the universal dependency parsing for supervised relation extraction. We can't compare our work to these as relation extremities (entities) are already recognized in a NER pre-processing, while we extract all information jointly.

Event Extraction Very little work has been done on ER; (AL-Smadi and Qawasmeh, 2016) proposed a knowledge-based approach for ER on Arabic tweets. And (Alsaedi and Burnap, 2015) proposed a classification/ clustering-based framework to detect real-world events from Twitter. (Ahmad et al., 2020) developed a Graph Attention Transformer Encoder to generate structured contextual representations for cross-lingual relation and event extraction working on ACE05. Yet, they haven't addressed the problem of the mismatch between the tokenization and the annotations; problematic entities were simply discarded.

7 Conclusion

We presented the first joint IE model for Arabic and showed a comparable performance to other languages. We also proposed two approaches to address subword entities, a situation specific to morphologically rich languages including Arabic, and showed that morphological information is important to their recognition. Our hope is that our work will provide a strong baseline for further research and increase interest in IE tasks which remain understudied by the Arabic NLP community.

Acknowledgements

This work is partially supported by a public grantoverseen by the French National Research Agency (ANR) as part of the program Investissements d'Avenir (ANR-10-LABX-0083).

References

Wasi Uddin Ahmad, Nanyun Peng, and Kai-Wei Chang. 2020. GATE: graph attention transformer encoder for cross-lingual relation and event extraction. *CoRR*, abs/2010.03009.

Mohammad AL-Smadi and Omar Qawasmeh. 2016. Knowledge-based approach for event extraction from arabic tweets. *International Journal of Advanced Computer Science and Applications*, 7(6).

Nasser Alsaedi and Pete Burnap. 2015. Arabic event detection in social media. In *Computational Linguistics and Intelligent Text Processing*, pages 384–401, Cham. Springer International Publishing.

Wissam Antoun, Fady Baly, and Hazem Hajj. 2020. AraBERT: Transformer-based model for Arabic language understanding. In *Proceedings of the 4th Workshop on Open-Source Arabic Corpora and Processing Tools, with a Shared Task on Offensive Language Detection*, pages 9–15, Marseille, France. European Language Resource Association.

Yassine Benajiba, Mona Diab, and Paolo Rosso. 2008a. Arabic named entity recognition using optimized feature sets. In *Proceedings of the Conference on Empirical Methods in Natural Language Processing*, EMNLP '08, page 284–293, USA. Association for Computational Linguistics.

Yassine Benajiba, Mona Diab, and Paolo Rosso. 2009. Using language independent and language specific features to enhance arabic named entity recognition. *Int. Arab J. Inf. Technol.*, 6:463–471.

Yassine Benajiba, Mona T. Diab, and P. Rosso. 2008b. Arabic named entity recognition: An svm-based approach.

Yassine Benajiba, Imed Zitouni, Mona Diab, and Paolo Rosso. 2010. Arabic named entity recognition: Using features extracted from noisy data. pages 281–285.

Tim Buckwalter. *Arabic Morphological Analyzer Version 2.0 LDC2004L02*. Linguistic Data Consortium, 2004.

Nizar Y. Habash. 2010. *Introduction to Arabic natural language processing*, 1 edition, volume 3 of *Synthesis Lectures on Human Language Technologies*. Morgan and Claypool Publishers.

Chadi Helwe, Ghassan Dib, Mohsen Shamas, and Shady Elbassuoni. 2020. A semi-supervised BERT approach for Arabic named entity recognition. In *Proceedings of the Fifth Arabic Natural Language Processing Workshop*, pages 49–57, Barcelona, Spain (Online). Association for Computational Linguistics.

Ganesh Jawahar, Benoît Sagot, and Djamé Seddah. 2019. What does BERT learn about the structure of language? In *Proceedings of the 57th Annual Meeting of the Association for Computational Linguistics*, pages 3651–3657, Florence, Italy. Association for Computational Linguistics.

John D. Lafferty, Andrew McCallum, and Fernando C. N. Pereira. 2001. Conditional random fields: Probabilistic models for segmenting and labeling sequence data. In *Proceedings of the Eighteenth International Conference on Machine Learning*, ICML '01, pages 282–289, San Francisco, CA, USA. Morgan Kaufmann Publishers Inc.

Ying Lin, Heng Ji, Fei Huang, and Lingfei Wu. 2020. A joint neural model for information extraction with global features. In *Proceedings of The 58th Annual Meeting of the Association for Computational Linguistics*.

Reham Mohamed, Nagwa M. El-Makky, and Khaled Nagi. 2015. Arabrelat: Arabic relation extraction using distant supervision. In *Proceedings of the International Joint Conference on Knowledge Discovery, Knowledge Engineering and Knowledge Management*, IC3K 2015, page 410–417, Setubal, PRT. SCITEPRESS - Science and Technology Publications, Lda.

Nazlia Naji. 2012. Arabic named entity recognition using artificial neural network. *Journal of Computer Science*, 8:1285–1293.

Trung Minh Nguyen and Thien Huu Nguyen. 2018. One for all: Neural joint modeling of entities and events.

Ossama Obeid, Nasser Zalmout, Salam Khalifa, Dima Taji, Mai Oudah, Bashar Alhafni, Go Inoue, Fadhl Eryani, Alexander Erdmann, and Nizar Habash. 2020. CAMeL tools: An open source python toolkit for Arabic natural language processing. In *Proceedings of the 12th Language Resources and Evaluation Conference*, pages 7022–7032, Marseille, France. European Language Resources Association.

Mai Oudah and Khaled Shaalan. 2012. A pipeline Arabic named entity recognition using a hybrid approach. In *Proceedings of COLING 2012*, pages 2159–2176, Mumbai, India. The COLING 2012 Organizing Committee.

Injy Sarhan, Yasser El-Sonbaty, and Mohamad Abou El-Nasr. 2016. Semi-supervised pattern based algorithm for arabic relation extraction. *2016 IEEE 28th International Conference on Tools with Artificial Intelligence (ICTAI)*, pages 177–183.

Nasrin Taghizadeh, Heshaam Faili, and Jalal Maleki. 2018. Cross-language learning for arabic relation extraction. *Procedia Computer Science*, 142:190–197.

David Wadden, Ulme Wennberg, Yi Luan, and Hannaneh Hajishirzi. 2019. Entity, relation, and event extraction with contextualized span representations. In *Proceedings of the 2019 Conference on Empirical Methods in Natural Language Processing and the 9th International Joint Conference on Natural Language Processing (EMNLP-IJCNLP)*, pages 5784–5789, Hong Kong, China. Association for Computational Linguistics.

C. Walker and Linguistic Data Consortium. 2005. *ACE 2005 Multilingual Training Corpus*. LDC corpora. Linguistic Data Consortium.

Yonghui Wu, Mike Schuster, Zhifeng Chen, Quoc V. Le, Mohammad Norouzi, Wolfgang Macherey, Maxim Krikun, Yuan Cao, Qin Gao, Klaus Macherey, Jeff Klingner, Apurva Shah, Melvin Johnson, Xiaobing Liu, Lukasz Kaiser, Stephan Gouws, Yoshikiyo Kato, Taku Kudo, Hideto Kazawa, Keith Stevens, George Kurian, Nishant Patil, Wei Wang, Cliff Young, Jason Smith, Jason Riesa, Alex Rudnick, Oriol Vinyals, Greg Corrado, Macduff Hughes, and Jeffrey Dean. 2016. Google's neural machine translation system: Bridging the gap between human and machine translation. *CoRR*, abs/1609.08144.

Tongtao Zhang, Heng Ji, and Avirup Sil. 2019. Joint Entity and Event Extraction with Generative Adversarial Imitation Learning. *Data Intelligence*, 1(2):99–120.

A Additional Dataset Statistics

We present here additional statistics of ACE05 subtype labels used in experiments of Table 6. We provide statistics of time roles even if we do not handle them. Note that event arguments (roles) do not have subtype labels.

Entity types	Number	Number by subtype	Percentage
Person	17150	Group: 6572 Individual: 10523 Indeterminate: 55	52.87%
Organization	4885	Media: 821 Commercial: 591 Government: 1432 Non-Governmental: 1171 Sports: 649 Educational: 135 Medical-Science: 22 Religious: 29 Entertainment: 36	15.06%
Location	1215	Boundary: 147 Celestial: 79 Region-General: 597 Region-International: 211 Land-Region-Natural: 89 Water-Body: 74 Address: 18	37.45%
Geographical/Social/Political	7165	Population-Center: 1328 Nation: 4560 Continent: 112 Special: 718 GPE-Cluster: 141 County-or-District: 146 State-or-Province: 160	22.09%
Facility	1127	Path: 176 Building-Grounds: 727 Airport: 23 Subarea-Facility: 117 Plant: 84	3.47%
Vehicle	418	Land: 185 Subarea-Vehicle: 2 Water: 76 Air: 155	12.87%
Weapon	481	Projectile: 179 Underspecified: 105 Sharp: 5 Shooting: 111 Blunt: 16 Exploding: 45 Chemical: 10 Nuclear: 10	14.83%
Total	32438	32438	100%

Table 9: Statistics of ACE05 entity types and subtypes.

Relation types	Number	Number by subtype	Percentage
Gen-Affiliation	1142	Org-Location: 561 Citizen-Resident-Religion-Ethnicity: 581	24.20%
Org-Affiliation	1379	Employment: 1136 Sports-Affiliation: 24 Membership: 195 Student-Alum: 13 Ownership: 6 Founder: 3 Investor-Shareholder: 2	29.22%
Part-Whole	903	Geographical: 607 Subsidiary: 291 Artifact: 5	19.13%
Personal-Social	643	Business: 306 Lasting-Personal: 81 Family: 256	13.62%
Physical	314	Located: 263 Near: 51	6.65%
Agent-Artifact	338	User-Owner-Inventor-Manufacturer: 338	7.16%
Total	4719	4719	100%

Table 10: Statistics of ACE05 relation types and subtypes.

Event types number	Event subtypes number	Roles number	Total Roles
Life: 398	Be-Born: 6	Person: 6 Place: 1 Time-Before: 1 Time-Within: 2	10
	Marry: 16	Place: 2 Person: 20 Time-Within: 2 Time-Holds: 1 Time-After: 1	26
	Divorce: 5	Person: 7 Place: 1	8
	Injure: 127	Victim: 125 Place: 52 Instrument: 46 Agent: 32 Time-At-Beginning: 1 Time-Within: 23 Time-After: 1	280
	Die: 244	Victim: 239 Agent: 83 Place: 78 Instrument: 53 Time-Within: 55 Time-Starting: 6 Time-Ending: 1 Time-At-Beginning: 1 Time-At-End: 3 Time-Holds: 1 Time-Before: 2	522
Movement: 435	Transport: 435	Artifact: 369 Origin: 111 Destination: 271 Agent: 96 Vehicle: 51 Time-Before: 5 Time-After: 2 Time-Within: 83 Time-Starting: 12 Time-Ending: 3 Time-At-Beginning: 3 Time-At-End: 1 Time-Holds: 6	1013
Transaction: 58	Transfer-Ownership: 10	Buyer: 6 Seller: 1 Beneficiary: 3 Artifact: 9 Price: 1 Place: 1 Time-Holds: 2 Time-Within: 3	26
	Transfer-Money: 48	Money: 33 Giver: 36 Recipient: 17 Beneficiary: 19 Place: 7 Time-Starting: 1 Time-Within: 11 Time-Holds: 1	125

Event types number	Event subtypes number	Roles number	Total Roles
Business: 24	Start-Org: 14	Org: 11 Agent: 14 Place: 3 Time-Before: 1 Time-Within: 1	30
	Merge-Org: 1	Org: 1	1
	Declare-Bankruptcy: 1	Org: 1	1
	End-Org: 8	Org: 4 Agent: 1 Place: 2 Time-Starting: 1 Time-Within: 1 Time-Holds: 1	10
Conflict: 550	Attack: 477	Attacker: 304 Target: 313 Instrument: 168 Place: 174 Time-Starting: 10 Time-At-Beginning: 2 Time-Within: 88 Time-After: 3 Time-Holds: 5 Time-Before: 2	1069
	Demonstrate: 73	Entity: 57 Place: 35 Time-Before: 1 Time-Starting: 1 Time-Within: 17 Time-Holds: 3	114
Contact: 274	Meet: 217	Entity: 362 Place: 91 Time-Starting: 7 Time-At-Beginning: 1 Time-Before: 1 Time-Within: 69 Time-Holds: 6 Time-Ending: 1 Time-After: 1	539
	Phone-Write: 57	Entity: 97 Place: 5 Time-Within: 8 Time-After: 1	111
Personnel: 152	Start-Position: 46	Entity: 12 Person: 44 Position: 7 Place: 12 Time-Before: 1 Time-Starting: 2 Time-Holds: 1 Time-Within: 9	88
	End-Position: 58	Entity: 6 Person: 55 Position: 3 Place: 9 Time-Within: 9 Time-Holds: 3 Time-Ending: 2	87
	Nominate: 7	Person: 7 Agent: 4 Position: 1 Place: 1 Time-Within: 1	14
	Elect: 41	Entity: 15 Person: 27 Position: 4 Place: 9 Time-Starting: 2 Time-Within: 10	67

Event types number	Event subtypes number	Roles number	Total Roles
Justice: 379	Arrest-Jail: 109	Person: 99 Agent: 49 Place: 32 Crime: 15 Time-Before: 3 Time-Starting: 8 Time-Within: 26 Time-Holds: 6 Time-Ending: 1 Time-After: 1 Time-At-End: 1	241
	Release-Parole: 31	Entity: 13 Person: 31 Place: 5 Time-Before: 1 Time-Within: 13	63
	Trial-Hearing: 65	Crime: 8 Defendant: 41 Adjudicator: 21 Prosecutor: 10 Place: 4 Time-Before: 1 Time-Starting: 5 Time-Within: 13 Time-Holds: 1 Time-After: 1	105
	Charge-Indict: 52	Defendant: 47 Prosecutor: 12 Adjudicator: 15 Crime: 21 Place: 4 Time-Before: 1 Time-Starting: 1 Time-At-Beginning: 1 Time-Within: 9 Time-Holds: 1 Time-Ending: 1	113
	Sue: 2	Adjudicator: 2 Time-Within: 1	3
	Convict: 5	Defendant: 5 Crime: 4 Place: 1 Adjudicator: 3 Time-Within: 2	15
	Sentence: 51	Adjudicator: 22 Defendant: 36 Sentence: 37 Crime: 20 Place: 4 Time-Starting: 5 Time-Within: 9 Time-Holds: 5 Time-Ending: 5	143
	Fine: 33	Entity: 28 Adjudicator: 12 Money: 41 Crime: 5 Place:1 Time-Within: 4	91
	Extradite: 7	Person: 7 Origin: 1 Destination: 4 Agent: 3	15
	Acquit: 3	Defendant: 3 Adjudicator: 1	4
	Appeal: 19	Adjudicator: 16 Plaintiff: 12 Crime: 2 Defendant: 1 Place: 1 Time-Within: 5 Time-Ending: 1	38
	Pardon: 2	Defendant: 2 Place:1	3

Table 11: Statistics of ACE05 trigger types and subtypes and role types.

Emoji Sentiment Roles for Sentiment Analysis: A Case Study in Arabic Texts

Shatha Ali A. Hakami
University of Birmingham &
Jazan University
United Kingdom / Saudi Arabia
sahakami@jazanu.edu.sa

Robert Hendley
University of Birmingham,
School of Computer Science
United Kingdom
r.j.hendley@cs.bham.ac.uk

Phillip Smith
University of Birmingham
School of Computer Science
United Kingdom
p.smith.7@cs.bham.ac.uk

Abstract

Emoji (the digital pictograms) are crucial features for textual sentiment analysis. However, analysing the sentiment roles of emoji is very complex. This is due to its dependency on different factors, such as textual context, cultural perspective, interlocutor's personal traits, interlocutors' relationships or a platforms' functional features. This work introduces an approach to analysing the sentiment effects of emoji as textual features. Using an Arabic dataset as a benchmark, our results confirm the borrowed argument that each emoji has three different norms of sentiment role (negative, neutral or positive). Therefore, an emoji can play different sentiment roles depending upon context. It can behave as an emphasizer, an indicator, a mitigator, a reverser or a trigger of either negative or positive sentiment within a text. In addition, an emoji may have neutral effect (i.e., no effect) on the sentiment of the text.

1 Introduction

Human social interaction consists not only of verbal exchanges, but also of non-verbal signals such as head-nods, facial expressions, gestures, posture, eye-movements or tone of voice. In text-based communication, it has been argued that many of these nonverbal cues are missed, which potentially makes the communication ambiguous and leads to misunderstandings (Kiesler et al., 1984). To mitigate this issue in textual messages, people tend to use many kinds of surrogates, such as emoticons (e.g. ":)" or ":("), and emoji (like 😊 and 😞). Carey (1980) categorized these nonverbal cues in text-based communication into five types: vocal spelling, lexical surrogates, spatial arrays, manipulation of grammatical markers, and minus features. Among these, emoticons and emoji are considered as examples of spatial arrays, that make a significant contribution to the interpretation of the textual contents' sentiment.

Sentiment analysis is used to discover opinions, emotions and attitudes in textual contents. Accordingly, Evans (2017) defined emoji as a form of developed punctuation (the way of encoding nonverbal prosody cues in writing systems) that supplements the written language to facilitate the writer's articulation of their emotions in text-based communication. Also, Miller et al. (2017) considered the use of emoji to be understood as analogically encoded symbols that are sensitive to a sender-receiver relationship, and that are fully integrated with the accompanying words (i.e., visible acts of meaning (Bavelas and Chovil, 2000)).

The view adopted in this work is that the visual representation of an emoji is a feature that influences the writer's choice of emoji (Wicke and Bolognesi, 2020; Hakami et al., 2022). As a result, it can affect wider stretches of text and so the emoji often tend to co-occur with 'negative' ('bad', 'unpleasant'), neutral ('non-emotional', 'mixed-emotional'), or 'positive' ('good', 'pleasant') collocates. These collocates can be either words or other emoji. This is similar to what discourse analysts call the "contextual valence shifters" (Polanyi and Zaenen, 2006). Contextual valence shifters are factors which assess a writer's attitude towards an event being described. This assessment relies on the lexical choice of the writer (i.e., the roles of the chosen words in the expressed texts), and the organization of the text. For example, Polanyi and Zaenen (2006) state that words often shift the valence of evaluative terms through their presuppositions. The adverb "barely", for instance, when it comes with the word "Sufficient" changes it sentiment from positive "Sufficient" into negative "barely sufficient". The later presupposes that better was expected.

Thus, in order to discover the sentiment roles of emoji within the body of a text, we need to investigate their general emoji-sentiment co-existence behaviors. To this end, we started our study by in-

Proceedings of the The Seventh Arabic Natural Language Processing Workshop (WANLP), pages 346 - 355
December 8, 2022 ©2022 Association for Computational Linguistics

vestigating all of the possible sentiment states that might occur when comparing the same text with and without emoji. Accordingly, we defined a set of emoji roles in the sentiment analysis of the accompanying texts. Then, we analyzed the results to verify the existence of opposite sentiment roles for each emoji considered in the study – represented by means of visible acts of meaning.

The rest of this paper is organized as follows. Section 2 reviews related work upon which we build; Section 3 presents the study's design; Section 4 presents the results analysis and discussion. Finally, in Section 5 we draw conclusions from this work along with highlighting its limitations as well as some recommendations for future work.

2 Related Work

Walther and D'addario (2001) studied the sentiment impacts of emoticons in computer-mediated communication (CMC). For the first time, they proposed to study emoticons and plain verbal messages as a whole. They studied the impacts of positive and negative emoticons on positive and negative verbal messages. In the paper, it is reported that positive emoticons increase the positivity of positive verbal messages, but negative emoticon do not increase the negativity of negative messages. They found that while the emotional valence of text (e.g., "I am happy") tends to be more important than any accompanying emoticons with respect to interpretation, a negative emoticon (e.g., the *Frowning Face*: ) can significantly change the interpretation of the message. Following the same approach, Derks et al. (2008, 2007) studied the sentiment impacts of more types of emoticons in various social contexts, and reported similar results. By applying similar approaches, the influences of emoticons on a person's perception (Ganster et al., 2012), and the effects of emoticons in task-oriented communication (Luor et al., 2010) were also studied. Lo (2008) provided additional evidence that emoticons affect interpretation, showing that the same text can be perceived as either happy or sad depending on which emoticon accompanies it.

Regarding emoji, Herring and Dainas (2017) identified eight mutually exclusive pragmatic functions of graphicons (i.e., emoticons, emoji, stickers, GIFs, images, and videos) use (reaction, action, tone modification, mention, riff, narrative sequence, ambiguous, and other) in comments on Facebook groups, taking the discourse context into account. The results of their analysis showed that emoji were the most used graphicon and also expressed the widest range of pragmatic functions, especially reaction and tone modification. On the other hand, Hu et al. (2017) identified seven intentions underlying emoji use (expressing sentiment, strengthening messages, adjusting tone, expressing humour, expressing irony, expressing intimacy, and describing content) and had respondents rate how likely they were to use 20 individual emoji to express each intention. According to (Hakami et al., 2020), an emoji when used in an Arabic language context, and perhaps in other langauges as well, can be a true sentiment indicator, a multi-sentiment indicator, an ambiguous sentiment indicator, or a no-sentiment indicator.

3 Study Design

The objective of this work is to construct an approach to the analysis of the sentiment effects of emoji in textual content. We intended to analyse these effects through the differentiation in the sentiment labels of texts with and without emoji. Besides the labels, we also intended to investigate the nuance impact of emoji on the sentiment, like negativity mitigation or positivity emphasis, by analysing the sentiment intensity of the texts (i.e., their sentiment scores). Generally, the change in a text's sentiment with and without emoji inclusion implies the impact of that emoji on that text. We refer to this as an emoji sentiment state. For example, if the text with and without emoji is annotated as positive, then the sentiment state will be ***Keep-positive***. However, if the sentiment of the text changes after adding emoji from positive to negative, then the sentiment state will be ***Reverse-to-negative***. We assumed that there are seven possible emoji sentiment states that might occurs in such a comparison. Comparing these states with the sentiment of the emoji itself will lead us to know the emoji sentiment role in a text. Presumably, there are eleven possible sentiment roles that an emoji can have within a text. Figure 1 summaries our model used in this study. A detailed description of how we obtained these states and roles and how the result analysis has been done follows.

3.1 Dataset Benchmark

Our consideration was on data that is from a social media platform, containing emoji, written in the Arabic language, multi-dialect and multi-aspect.

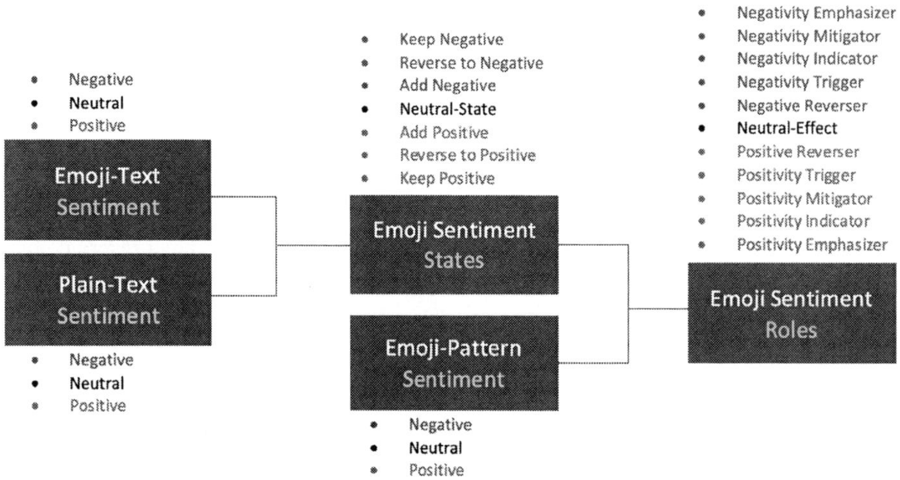

Figure 1: Model of analysis.

Collecting, cleaning and preparing a great deal of raw data for sentiment annotation in a short time is impossible. Thus, we targeted 14 different public datasets of Arabic social media containing 144,196 tweets from the Twitter platform that meet our criteria. The data details are stated comprehensively in Hakami et al. (2021). We refer to the resulting dataset as the Emoji-Text dataset. Then, we extracted and remove all of the emoji from the Emoji-Text dataset to get the same texts without the emoji. We refer to this as the Plain-Text dataset. From Emoji-Text dataset, we extracted 1034 unique emoji forming a total of 24,364 different emoji patterns.

3.2 Sentiment Annotation Process

Manual annotation is complex and expensive. We utilized four automatic Arabic sentiment classifiers as follows. The mechanism of preparing Arabic texts containing emoji for automatic sentiment annotation by some of these tools (i.e., Mazajak, CAMeL and ASAD) was adopted from Hakami et al. (2021).

3.2.1 Mazajak Sentiment Classifier

Mazajak (Abu Farha and Magdy, 2019) is the first online Arabic sentiment analyser, it is based on a deep learning model built on a convolutional neural network (CNN) followed by a long short-term memory (LSTM). This analyser provides different functionalities for Arabic sentiment analysis including two modes for raw text processing: the batch mode and the online API, which is what we used. The results were one of the sentiment annotations: positive, negative or neutral.

3.2.2 CAMeL Sentiment Tool

CAMeL Tools (Obeid et al., 2020) is a collection of open-source tools for Arabic NLP in Python. It provides utilities for many NLP tasks, including sentiment analysis. The system has two sentiment analysis models. We used the default model that was generated by fine-tuning the AraBERT language model (Antoun et al., 2020). This sentiment model returns one of the three sentiment labels: positive, negative, or neutral as an output for Arabic text annotation.

3.2.3 ASAD Sentiment Classifier

Arabic Social media Analysis and unDerstanding (ASAD) toolkit (Hassan et al., 2021) is an online tool of seven individual modules, one of which is for sentiment analysis. This toolkit is made available through a web API and a web interface where users can enter text or upload files. We used the sentiment web API via the Python programming language. Similar to the previous tools, this model annotates Arabic texts with sentiment labels: positive, negative or neutral.

3.2.4 Lexicon-based Sentiment Classifier

All of the above mentioned tools classify the texts with sentiment labels not scores. Therefore, we adopted the lexicon-based Logit-scale sentiment scoring technique (Lowe et al., 2011) as a fourth automatic sentiment annotator used in this analysis

	Plain-Text Sentiment (PT)	Emoji-Text Sentiment (ET)	Emoji Sentiment State
Negative Norm	Negative	Negative	Keep Negative
	Positive	Negative	Reverse to Negative
	Neutral	Negative	Add Negative
Neutral Norm	Neutral	Neutral	Neutral-State
Positive Norm	Positive	Positive	Keep Positive
	Negative	Positive	Reverse to Positive
	Neutral	Positive	Add Positive

Table 1: Summary of all possible emoji sentiment states within texts.

model.

Any lexicon-based approach involves calculating sentiment polarity of a text from positively, neutrally, and negatively weighted tokens within the text. These tokens (in our case) are words and emoji. Thus, we needed two Arabic-language-based sentiment lexicons: one for words, and one for emoji. The word sentiment lexicon used was based on the Ar-SeLn (Badaro et al., 2014) lexicon, a publicly available, large-scale Arabic word sentiment lexicon, where each word is annotated with a sentiment score. We augmented this by adding a set of words (with their sentiment scores) from our dataset that was not in the Ar-SeLn lexicon. The sentiment scores of the added words were calculated using the same approach that was applied by Kralj Novak et al. (2015) for emoji. We ended up with a word sentiment lexicon with 178,620 unique words, each with their corresponding sentiment score. For emoji, we used Arab-ESL[1] (Hakami et al., 2021), a publicly available Arabic emoji sentiment lexicon (i.e., extracted from Arabic texts), where each emoji is annotated with sentiment score and label. This lexicon contains 1,034 unique emoji.

To calculate the sentiment scores, we computed an index for the sentence from the scored sentiment components (i.e., words and emoji) using the Logit scale approach, as follows: $S = log(\sum Pos + 0.5) - log(\sum Neg + 0.5)$, where, Pos is the list of the positive components' scores; Neg is the list of the negative components' scores; and 0.5 is a smoother to prevent log(0). This formula tends to have the smoothest properties and is symmetric around zero (Lowe et al., 2011).

The approach of Hakami et al. (2021) was followed to convert the resulting sentiment scores into sentiment labels. We classified three scaled-groups of sentiment scores under three sentiment norms (negative, neutral and positive). Text with sentiment score i, where $-\infty \leq i < -0.0625$, was classified as negative. Text with sentiment score i, where $\infty \geq i > 0.0625$, was classified as positive. Lastly, a text was classified as neutral when its sentiment score i was in the range $-0.0625 \leq i \leq 0.0625$.

Separately, we calculated the sentiment score and label of each emoji pattern in each text using the same approach of calculating scores and labels for the sentences.

3.3 Annotation Reliability and Agreement Test

The majority voting approach was used to ensure that the data was annotated reliably by the algorithms. First, we only considered those texts where the sentiment matched for all the annotations on both positive and negative norms, both for texts with and without emoji. Then, for neutrality agreement, we considered the texts where their sentiment was produced by the lexicon-based statistical approach and was agreed by at least one of the other annotations. This resulted in 35,668 texts reliably annotated with sentiment.

To test the agreement between the aggregated sentiment annotation results by the machines and a manual annotation, we used Cohen's Kappa agreement tests (McHugh, 2012) on a sample of 2,567 texts. These texts were annotated manually. The test resulted in κ = 0.8601 which is a high consensus degree. Further, we used the same sample to check the accuracy of the annotation and it was 0.93.

3.4 Emoji Sentiment States and Roles

Based on the sentiment annotation of the texts (with and without emoji), our model of analysis consists

[1] https://github.com/ShathaHakami/Arabic-Emoji-Sentiment-Lexicon-Version-1.0

Emoji Sentiment State	Text Sentiment Scores	Emoji Pattern Sentiment	Emoji Sentiment Role
	ETs > PTs	Negative	Negativity Emphasizer
	ETs > PTs	Neutral	Negativity Emphasizer
	ETs > PTs	Positive	Negativity Mitigator
	ETs = PTs	Negative	Negativity Indicator
Keep Negative	ETs = PTs	Neutral	Negativity Indicator
	ETs = PTs	Positive	Negativity Mitigator
	ETs < PTs	Negative	Negativity Indicator
	ETs < PTs	Neutral	Negativity Indicator
	ETs < PTs	Positive	Negativity Mitigator
		Negative	Negativity Trigger
Add Negative	N/A	Neutral	Negativity Trigger
		Positive	Negativity Mitigator
		Negative	Negative Reverser
Reverse to Negative	N/A	Neutral	Negative Reverser
		Positive	Negativity Mitigator
		Negative	Negativity Trigger
Neutral-State	N/A	Neutral	Neutral-Effect
		Positive	Positivity Trigger
		Negative	Positivity Mitigator
Reverse to Positive	N/A	Neutral	Positive Reverser
		Positive	Positive Reverser
		Negative	Positivity Mitigator
Add Positive	N/A	Neutral	Positivity Trigger
		Positive	Positivity Trigger
	ETs > PTs	Negative	Positivity Mitigator
	ETs > PTs	Neutral	Positivity Emphasizer
	ETs > PTs	Positive	Positivity Emphasizer
	ETs = PTs	Negative	Positivity Mitigator
Keep Positive	ETs = PTs	Neutral	Positivity Indicator
	ETs = PTs	Positive	Positivity Indicator
	ETs < PTs	Negative	Positivity Mitigator
	ETs < PTs	Neutral	Positivity Indicator
	ETs < PTs	Positive	Positivity Indicator

Table 2: Summary of all possible emoji sentiment roles in the three sentiment norms: negative, neutral and positive. **ETs** means emoji-text sentiment score and **PTs** means plain-text sentiment score.

of seven sentiment states in which an emoji can occur. These states are: *Keep-positive*, *Keep-negative*, *Neutral-State*, *Add-positive*, *Add-negative*, *Reverse-to-positive* or *Reverse-to-negative*, as described in Table 1. These states are considered to be an intermediate phase in our model, transferring the analysis into exploring the emoji sentiment roles.

Knowing these intermediate sentiment states along with the sentiment of the emoji pattern leads to the identification of eleven possible sentiment roles that an emoji can have within a text. These roles are emphasis, indication, mitigation, reversing and triggering under each of the positive and negative sentiment norms. Furthermore, emoji could have a *no-effect* role reflecting the neutrality sentiment norm. Note that for the identification of some roles (i.e., emphasis, mitigation, and indication), knowing the sentiment scores of the texts (with and without emoji) was mandatory. Table 2 summarizes all of the possible emoji sentiment roles based on all of the possible cases between each of the sentiment states, along with the emoji sentiments.

		Negative					Neutral	Positive				
Emoji	Freq.	Emphasizer	Indicator	Mitigator	Reverser	Trigger	Neutral-Effect	Trigger	Reverser	Mitigator	Indicator	Emphasizer
	3692	0.065276	0.043879	0.455309	0	0.003792	0.000271	0.06961	0.014355	0.000542	0.024919	0.322048
	1045	0.180861	0.048804	0.461244	0	0.007656	0	0.055502	0.000957	0	0.004785	0.240191
	695	0.01983	0.082153	0.243626	0.001416	0.007082	0.001416	0.147309	0.021246	0.001416	0.008499	0.466006
	362	0.08311	0.093834	0.246649	0.002681	0.002681	0.002681	0.0563	0.010724	0.005362	0.016086	0.479893
	232	0.00823	0.069959	0.407407	0.004115	0.004115	0.004115	0.106996	0.004115	0.004115	0.016461	0.37037
	229	0.179167	0.3375	0.095833	0.004167	0.0125	0.033333	0.0375	0.004167	0.004167	0.083333	0.208333
	219	0.004348	0.056522	0.408696	0.004348	0.008696	0.004348	0.082609	0.004348	0.004348	0.013043	0.408696
	207	0.366972	0.03211	0.009174	0.004587	0.03211	0.009174	0.004587	0.004587	0.252294	0.247706	0.036697
	201	0.283019	0.033019	0.226415	0.004717	0.037736	0.009434	0.080189	0.014151	0.004717	0.023585	0.283019
	176	0.208556	0.048128	0.02139	0.005348	0.037433	0.005348	0.026738	0.005348	0.385027	0.106952	0.149733
	158	0.017751	0.12426	0.491124	0.005917	0.011834	0.005917	0.118343	0.017751	0.005917	0.011834	0.189349
	129	0.071429	0.014286	0.521429	0.007143	0.007143	0.007143	0.071429	0.007143	0.007143	0.028571	0.257143
	100	0.036036	0.099099	0.234234	0.009009	0.018018	0.009009	0.081081	0.009009	0.009009	0.027027	0.468468
	91	0.009804	0.058824	0.254902	0.009804	0.019608	0.019608	0.186275	0.009804	0.009804	0.009804	0.411765
	80	0.021978	0.032967	0.241758	0.010989	0.010989	0.010989	0.032967	0.032967	0.010989	0.010989	0.582418
	72	0.012048	0.084337	0.204819	0.012048	0.012048	0.012048	0.024096	0.012048	0.012048	0.024096	0.590361
	70	0.012346	0.111111	0.506173	0.012346	0.012346	0.012346	0.037037	0.024691	0.012346	0.012346	0.246914
	56	0.014925	0.164179	0.119403	0.014925	0.029851	0.014925	0.164179	0.014925	0.014925	0.014925	0.432836

Figure 2: Example of the probability distribution of eleven emoji sentiment roles for eighteen emoji from our data-set.

3.5 Emoji Roles Probability Distribution

After identifying the emoji sentiment role in each text in our dataset, we calculate the frequency distribution of all of the sentiment roles for each emoji. We start by identifying the frequency with which each emoji is associated with each sentiment role. The following equation captures the distribution of the set of sentiment roles for an emoji across the dataset, as follows: $N(c), \sum N(c) = N$. Where **N** denotes the number of times an emoji has been annotated with one of these labels: *negative*, *neutral*, or *positive*. **N(c)** are the occurrences of an emoji with the sentiment label **c**, where **c** is either *negative emphasizer, negative indicator, negative mitigator, negative reverser, negative trigger, no-effect, positive trigger, positive reverser, positive mitigator, positive indicator*, or *positive emphasizer*. From the above we form a discrete probability distribution: $\sum p_c = 1$; where $\mathbf{p_c}$ are the probabilities for each sentiment role that are estimated from relative frequencies as follows: $p_c = \frac{N(c)}{N}$. Since we were dealing with small samples, we used the Laplace estimate (also known as the rule of succession) (Good, 1965) as it is recommended to estimate the probability: $p_c = \frac{N(c)+1}{N+k}$, where **k** is the cardinality of the sentiment roles ($k = 11$ sentiment roles in our case). Figure 2 shows examples of the probability distribution $\mathbf{p_c}$ of the sentiment roles for some emoji.

Emoji Sentiment Role	Occurrence Freq.
Positivity Emphasizer	16,589
Negativity Emphasizer	12,451
Negativity Mitigator	3,091
Positivity Trigger	888
Negativity Indicator	750
Negativity Trigger	668
Positivity Mitigator	617
Positivity Indicator	449
Positive Reverser	111
Negative Reverser	27
Neutral-Effect	27
Total	35,668

Table 3: Summary of the resulted emoji sentiment roles in our data-set.

4 Results Analysis and Discussion

In the analysis, we found eleven of the defined sentiment roles within the dataset, as shown in Table 3. Due to the space limitations, we present a detailed analysis only for the case of the "Face With Tears of Joy" emoji (i.e., 😂). Results were analyzed based on three criteria: the emoji load (i.e., the number of the emoji in each text); the sentiment of the co-occurring emoji (emoji pattern) and the sentiment intensity (sentiment score) of the emoji pattern. The "Face With Tears of Joy" emoji (i.e., 😂) is defined as a positive emoji in Arab-ESL.

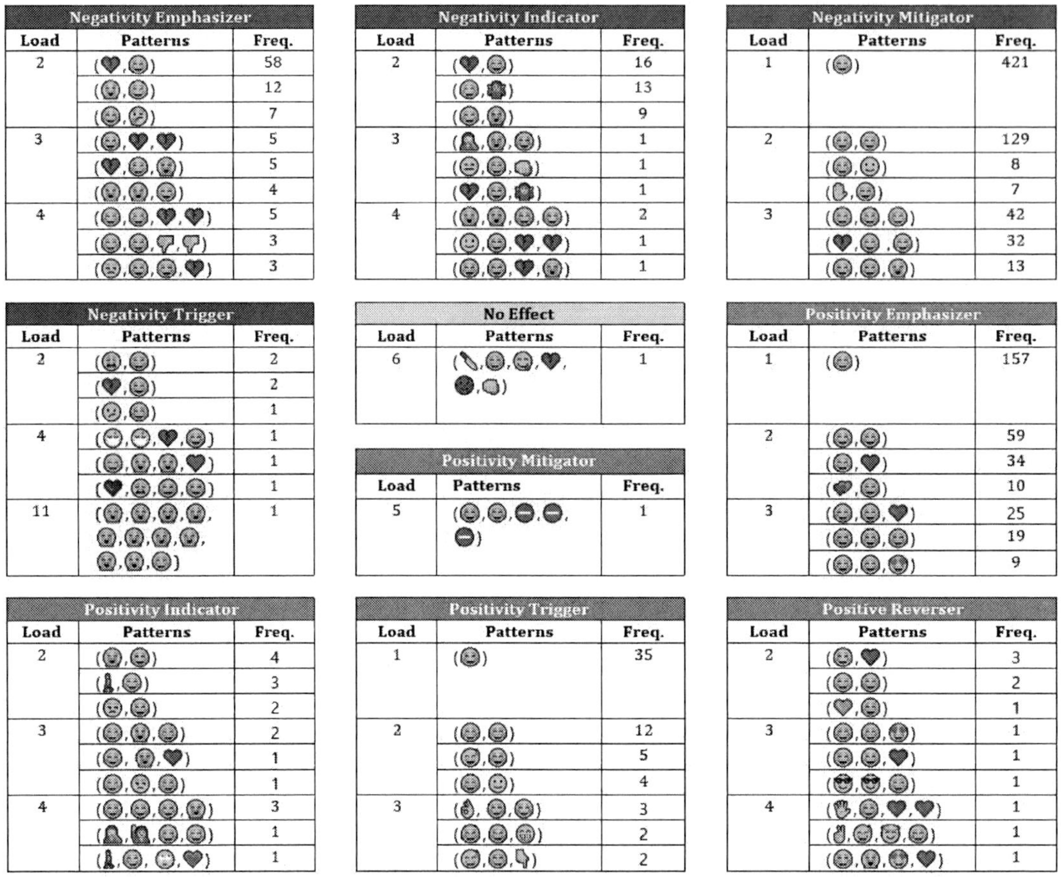

Figure 3: Examples of the emoji loads and patterns of the different sentiment roles that are played by the "Face With Tears of Joy" emoji (i.e., 😂).

However, our observations reveal that this emoji plays different sentiment roles including each of the three sentiment norms: positive, negative and neutral.

In the positive norm, the "Face With Tears of Joy" emoji is found, in some cases by itself (i.e., the emoji load = 1), playing roles such as: *positivity emphasizer* and *positivity trigger*, as shown in Figure 3. Besides the mentioned positive roles, this emoji also co-occurs with other positive emoji (e.g., [emoji]) to play roles such as: *positivity indicator* and *positive reverser*. Examples 6, 7, 8, 9 and 10 in Figure 4 illustrate this emoji acting as a *positivity emphasizer*, *positivity indicator*, *positivity mitigator*, *positive reverser* and *positivity trigger*, respectively. In these examples, we could conclude some positive meanings from the stated texts, like encouragement, complement, humour, and positive response; based on the positive sentiment roles of the co-existing emoji.

The "Face With Tears of Joy" emoji has been found 421 times by itself playing a *negativity mitigator* role within negative text (which has a sense of positivity)(see Figure 3) but it has not been found, when standing alone, playing any other roles in the negative sentiment norm. For behaving negatively, this emoji was always found co-occuring with other negative emoji (like [emoji]). Examples 1, 2, 3 and 4 in Figure 4 illustrate this emoji taking the role of a *negativity emphasizer*, *negativity indicator*, *negativity mitigator* and *negativity trigger*, respectively. In these examples, we could infer some negative meanings from the relevant texts, like sarcasm, bullying, complaining and regret, based on the negative sentiment roles of the co-occuring emoji.

Moreover, we found one case where this emoji played the *Neutral-effect* sentiment role. This is shown in Example 5 in Figure 4. The combination of the mixed sentiments of the text and the emoji used within it, makes the message become neutral. Thus, none of the contained emoji has a

Example No. (Sentiment)	Text	Emoji Role	Text Meaning
Example 1 (negative)	انا مش عارف الناس ال عماله تنزل صور الكليه والدنيا بتمطر وتقولك ما احلاها وكم انتي جميله متروح تتجوزها يا متخلف😒😂؟ I don't know why everybody is taking pictures and flirting the college in such a rainy day and say: "How lovely it looks". Why don't you go and marry it, idiot 😒😂?	Negativity Emphasizer	Sarcasm
Example 2 (negative)	مني طنشيها لو فيها خير كان سكتت علي طول جابت حرب البسوس 😂 توقع هي من قبيله جحدر الله يستر عليها 😂. Mona, ignore her. If she is wise enough, she could have remained silent, but she immediately mentioned the Al-Basus war 😂 I think she is from the Jahdar tribe 😂.	Negativity Indicator	Bullying
Example 3 (negative)	مش كفايا طول الصيف متبهدلين 😒؟ بطلو قر بقي😂😂. Wasn't enough that we had been working all the summer 😒? Stop mention it 😂😂.	Negativity Mitigator	Complaint
Example 4 (negative)	ماهو انا الي كتبت😂😂 It was me who wrote it 😂😂.	Negativity Trigger	Regret
Example 5 (neutral)	كل شوي القي متابعه من شيخ روحاني وتخسيس الوزن مدري من قايلهم اني دبه مسحووره😂💔🌚🔪😒😂 Every minute I receive a following request from either a spiritual sheikh account or a weight losing account. I don't know who tells them that I am fat and bewitched 😂💔🌚🔪😒😂	Neutral-Effect	Mixed Emotions
Example 6 (positive)	افضل تغريده لك منذ ولادتك بالتويتر 😂👌 This is the best tweet that you have written since you born in Twitter 😂👌	Positivity Emphasizer	Encouragement
Example 7 (positive)	كل شي منك جميل يا جميل 😂😂😂😂 Everything from you is beautiful 😂😂😂😂	Positivity Indicator	Complement
Example 8 (positive)	بسرعه محمد صلاح 😂😂 بنوزع فولوباك يومي 😑😑😑 عاده عايز تبطلها Hurry up Mohammed Salah 😂😂 We daily provide follow requests 😑😑😑 a habit you want to get rid of.	Positivity Mitigator	Random
Example 9 (positive)	تخوفي وبس رعب اللهم ياكافي💔😂 Not only you are scary, but you are also terrifying; Oh, my dear God💔😂.	Positive Reverser	Humor
Example 10 (positive)	سنوات 😂😂😂😂 Years 😂😂😂😂	Positivity Trigger	Positive Response

Figure 4: Examples of the different sentiment roles that are played by the "Face With Tears of Joy" emoji (i.e., 😂).

distinguished sentiment effect on this text.

Note that, in our model, the sentiment intensity of the co-existing emoji is an important factor in determining an emoji's sentiment role in a text. Furthermore, emoji sentiment intensity is affected by the emoji load in a text. For instance, in Figure 4, Example 1 has two emoji (😂 and 😒), while Example 3 has the same emoji with different load (i.e., three emoji) (😂, 😂 and 😒). The intensity of the 😒 emoji is -0.6879562 (the minus sign represent the negativity not the score value), which is higher than the intensity of the 😂 (0.2724255). Therefore, the emoji with higher intensity dominates the one with lower intensity, making the 😂 emoji become a *negativity emphasizer* through this pattern with (-0.0404245) sentiment intensity [2]. On the other hand, because of the duplication of the 😂 emoji in Example 3 (i.e., a negative text), its positive intensity in this specific text becomes higher than the negative intensity of the 😒 emoji in a way that makes the 😂 emoji play a *negativity mitigator* sentiment role via this emoji pattern [3].

[2] Log[(0.2724255+0.5) - (-0.6879562+0.5)] = -0.0404245
[3] Log[(0.5448510+0.5) - (-0.68795620+0.5)] = 0.2092938

5 Conclusions and Future Work

This study objectively depicts all the possible emoji sentiment roles that researchers interested in sentiment analysis might encounter when they are dealing with emoji within textual contents. We have investigated the sentiment roles of emoji within textual content, by investigating their general emoji-sentiment co-occurence behaviours. Accordingly, we defined a set of emoji roles in the sentiment analysis of the accompanying texts. Then, we analyzed the results to confirm the existence of opposing sentiment roles for each emoji considered in the study. To this end, we concluded that an emoji can be an emphasizer, an indicator, a mitigator, a reverser or a trigger of negative or positive sentiments; in addition, each emoji might have a sense of no-sentiment-effect that reflects the neutral sentiment norm. Nevertheless, investigating, deeply, the impact of the emoji sentiment roles stated here, on the semantics of texts should be considered in the future. In addition, an extended and detailed analysis is needed for the other common emoji rather than just for the "Face With Tears of Joy" emoji. Besides, a study on how the presence of emoji might affect the performance of fine-tuned sentiment classification models for Arabic can be one of the future considerations. Finally, we recommend reproducing this work with different languages in order to understand the similarities and differences of the emoji sentiment roles across different cultures and languages.

References

Ibrahim Abu Farha and Walid Magdy. 2019. Mazajak: An online Arabic sentiment analyser. In *Proceedings of the Fourth Arabic Natural Language Processing Workshop*, pages 192–198, Florence, Italy. Association for Computational Linguistics.

Wissam Antoun, Fady Baly, and Hazem Hajj. 2020. AraBERT: Transformer-based model for Arabic language understanding. In *Proceedings of the 4th Workshop on Open-Source Arabic Corpora and Processing Tools, with a Shared Task on Offensive Language Detection*, pages 9–15, Marseille, France. European Language Resource Association.

Gilbert Badaro, Ramy Baly, Hazem Hajj, Nizar Habash, and Wassim El-Hajj. 2014. A large scale arabic sentiment lexicon for arabic opinion mining. In *Proceedings of the EMNLP 2014 workshop on arabic natural language processing (ANLP)*, pages 165–173.

Janet Beavin Bavelas and Nicole Chovil. 2000. Visible acts of meaning: An integrated message model of language in face-to-face dialogue. *Journal of Language and social Psychology*, 19(2):163–194.

John Carey. 1980. Paralanguage in computer mediated communication. In *18th Annual Meeting of the Association for Computational Linguistics*, pages 67–69.

Daantje Derks, Arjan ER Bos, and Jasper Von Grumbkow. 2007. Emoticons and social interaction on the internet: the importance of social context. *Computers in human behavior*, 23(1):842–849.

Daantje Derks, Arjan ER Bos, and Jasper Von Grumbkow. 2008. Emoticons and online message interpretation. *Social Science Computer Review*, 26(3):379–388.

Vyvyan Evans. 2017. *The emoji code: The linguistics behind smiley faces and scaredy cats*. Picador USA.

Tina Ganster, Sabrina C Eimler, and Nicole C Krämer. 2012. Same same but different!? the differential influence of smilies and emoticons on person perception. *Cyberpsychology, Behavior, and Social Networking*, 15(4):226–230.

Irving John Good. 1965. The estimation of probabilities: An essay on modern bayesian methods, vol. 30.

Shatha Ali A. Hakami, Robert Hendley, and Phillip Smith. 2020. Emoji as sentiment indicators: An investigative case study in arabic text. In *The Sixth International Conference on Human and Social Analytics*, pages 26–32. IARIA.

Shatha Ali A. Hakami, Robert Hendley, and Phillip Smith. 2021. Arabic emoji sentiment lexicon (Arab-ESL): A comparison between Arabic and European emoji sentiment lexicons. In *Proceedings of the Sixth Arabic Natural Language Processing Workshop*, pages 60–71, Kyiv, Ukraine (Virtual). Association for Computational Linguistics.

Shatha Ali A. Hakami, Robert Hendley, and Phillip Smith. 2022. A context-free Arabic emoji sentiment lexicon (CF-Arab-ESL). In *Proceedinsg of the 5th Workshop on Open-Source Arabic Corpora and Processing Tools with Shared Tasks on Qur'an QA and Fine-Grained Hate Speech Detection*, pages 51–59, Marseille, France. European Language Resources Association.

Sabit Hassan, Hamdy Mubarak, Ahmed Abdelali, and Kareem Darwish. 2021. Asad: Arabic social media analytics and understanding. In *Proceedings of the 16th Conference of the European Chapter of the Association for Computational Linguistics: System Demonstrations*, pages 113–118.

Susan Herring and Ashley Dainas. 2017. "nice picture comment!" graphicons in facebook comment threads. In *Proceedings of the 50th Hawaii International Conference on System Sciences*.

Tianran Hu, Han Guo, Hao Sun, Thuy-vy Thi Nguyen, and Jiebo Luo. 2017. Spice up your chat: the intentions and sentiment effects of using emojis. In *Eleventh international aaai conference on web and social media*.

Sara Kiesler, Jane Siegel, and Timothy W McGuire. 1984. Social psychological aspects of computer-mediated communication. *American psychologist*, 39(10):1123.

Petra Kralj Novak, Jasmina Smailović, Borut Sluban, and Igor Mozetič. 2015. Sentiment of emojis. *PloS one*, 10(12):e0144296.

Shao-Kang Lo. 2008. The nonverbal communication functions of emoticons in computer-mediated communication. *Cyberpsychology & behavior*, 11(5):595–597.

Will Lowe, Kenneth Benoit, Slava Mikhaylov, and Michael Laver. 2011. Scaling policy preferences from coded political texts. *Legislative studies quarterly*, 36(1):123–155.

Tainyi Ted Luor, Ling-ling Wu, Hsi-Peng Lu, and Yu-Hui Tao. 2010. The effect of emoticons in simplex and complex task-oriented communication: An empirical study of instant messaging. *Computers in Human Behavior*, 26(5):889–895.

Mary L McHugh. 2012. Interrater reliability: the kappa statistic. *Biochemia medica: Biochemia medica*, 22(3):276–282.

Hannah Miller, Daniel Kluver, Jacob Thebault-Spieker, Loren Terveen, and Brent Hecht. 2017. Understanding emoji ambiguity in context: The role of text in emoji-related miscommunication. In *Proceedings of the International AAAI Conference on Web and Social Media*, volume 11.

Ossama Obeid, Nasser Zalmout, Salam Khalifa, Dima Taji, Mai Oudah, Bashar Alhafni, Go Inoue, Fadhl Eryani, Alexander Erdmann, and Nizar Habash. 2020. Camel tools: An open source python toolkit for arabic natural language processing. In *Proceedings of the 12th language resources and evaluation conference*, pages 7022–7032.

Livia Polanyi and Annie Zaenen. 2006. Contextual valence shifters. In *Computing attitude and affect in text: Theory and applications*, pages 1–10. Springer.

Joseph B Walther and Kyle P D'addario. 2001. The impacts of emoticons on message interpretation in computer-mediated communication. *Social science computer review*, 19(3):324–347.

Philipp Wicke and Marianna Bolognesi. 2020. Emoji-based semantic representations for abstract and concrete concepts. *Cognitive processing*, 21(4):615–635.

Gulf Arabic Diacritization: Guidelines, Initial Dataset, and Results

Nouf Alabbasi[1], Mohamed AlBadrashiny[2], Maryam Aldahmani[3], Ahmed AlDhanhani[4], Abdullah Saleh Alhashmi[4], Fawaghy Alhashmi[3], Khalid Al Hashemi[4], Rama Alkhobbi[5], Shamma AlMaazmi[6], Mohammed Alyafeai[7], Mariam M. Alzaabi[4], Mohamed Alzaabi[4], Fatma Badri[5], Kareem Darwish[2], Ehab Mansour Diab[8], Muhammad Elmallah[2], Amira Elnashar[9], Ashraf Elneima[2], MHD Tameem Kabbani[9], Nour Rabih[10], Ahmad Saad[11], Ammar Mamoun Sousou[5]

[1] New York University Abu Dhabi, UAE, [2] aiXplain Inc., CA, USA,
[3] United Arab Emirates University, AD, UAE, [4] Khalifa University, AD, UAE,
[5] Independent, [6] University of Sharjah, SH, UAE,
[7] Cyber Gate Defense, AD, UAE, [8] Invent Technology, AD, UAE,
[9] American University of Sharjah, SH, UAE, [10] King's College London, LDN, UK
[11] Mohammed Bin Rashid Space Centre, Dubai, UAE

naa475@nyu.edu, mohamed@aixplain.com, Maryam.aldahmani21@hotmail.com, ahmed.aldhanhani@ku.ac.ae, nnh3@hotmail.com, 201800838@uaeu.ac.ae, 1000052995@ku.ac.ae, Ramaalkhobbi@gmail.com, shammaalmazmi@hotmail.com, mohamed@cybergate.tech, 100044533@ku.ac.ae, m7mdz3abii@gmail.com, fatmakbadri@gmail.com, kareem.darwish@aiXplain.com, ehab@invent-technology.net, muhammad.elmallah@aiXplain.com, g00082075@aus.edu, ashraf.hatim@aixplain.com, b00088948@aus.edu, noor_rabie@hotmail.com, ahmadateejuae@gmail.com, ammar13ma@gmail.com

Abstract

Arabic diacritic recovery is important for a variety of downstream tasks such as text-to-speech. In this paper, we introduce a new Gulf Arabic diacritization dataset composed of 19,850 words based on a subset of the Gumar corpus. We provide a comprehensive set of guidelines for diacritization to enable the diacritization of more data. We also report on diacritization results based on the new corpus using a word-based Hidden Markov Model and a character-based sequence to sequence model.

1 Introduction

Arabic has two types of vowels, namely long and short vowels. Although long vowels are explicitly written, short vowels, which take the form of diacritic marks, are typically omitted in written Arabic, and readers need to infer these diacritics to properly pronounce words. Thus, diacritic recovery, also referred to as diacritization, is important for downstream tasks such as text-to-speech and language learning. Most previous efforts pertaining to Arabic diacritic recovery have focused on Modern Standard Arabic (MSA) and Classical Arabic (CA). The focus on these Arabic varieties has been aided by the availability of large training corpora such as the Penn Arabic Treebank (Maamouri et al., 2004) and Tashkeela (Zerrouki and Balla, 2017) and relatively stable diacritization standards. There has been some efforts related to diacritizing different Arabic dialects such as Egyptian (Zalmout and Habash, 2020), Palestinian (Jarrar et al., 2017), Morrocan, and Tunisian (Mubarak et al., 2019). Many challenges face dialectal diacritization, mostly related to the availability of large consistent data. While MSA/CA corpora may be composed of millions of words, dialectal datasets have been capped at tens of thousands of words (Mubarak et al., 2019; Zalmout and Habash, 2020). Furthermore, diacritization of the same dialect may differ from town to town, complicating data standardization and consistency. For example, the word سخن (sxn[1] – hot) is diacritized in the Egyptian dialect as سُخُنْ (suxuno) in Alexandria and سُخْنْ (suxono) in Cairo. Variations in pronunciation of words are rather common within the same dialect in locales of close geographical proximity.

In this paper, we present a new public diacritized dataset for Gulf Arabic in accordance to the pronunciation of the city of Dubai in the United Arab Emirates (UAE). The dataset is a 19,850 words subset of the Gumar corpus (Khalifa et al., 2018), which is composed of roughly 200 thousand words from Emirati internet novels. To diacritize the cor-

[1] Buckwalter transliteration is used exclusively in the paper.

Proceedings of the The Seventh Arabic Natural Language Processing Workshop (WANLP), pages 356 - 360
December 8, 2022 ©2022 Association for Computational Linguistics

pus, we conducted a workshop that included two senior computational linguists and 15 native speakers of the Emirati dialect to codify the diacritization guidelines and to actually diacritize the corpus. We split the corpus into training and test sentences, and we proceeded to build two different Emirati diacritizers using a word-based Hidden Markov Model (HMM) and a character-based sequence to sequence mapping architecture.

The contributions of this paper is as follows:

- We present a new dataset for Gulf Arabic diacritization based on the sub-dialect spoken in Dubai, UAE.
- We formalize guidelines for the diacritization of the dialect.
- We present initial results using 2 different diacritization models.

2 Related Work

Many approaches have been used for Arabic diacritization such as HMMs (Gal, 2002; Darwish et al., 2017), finite state transducers (Nelken and Shieber, 2005), character-based maximum entropy based classification (Zitouni et al., 2006), and a variety of deep learning approaches (Abandah et al., 2015; Belinkov and Glass, 2015; Mubarak et al., 2019; Rashwan et al., 2015). For MSA, most approaches tend to handle core word diacritics, which disambiguate a word in context, separately from case-endings, which typically appear at end of a word and specify the syntactic role of words. However, more recent approaches have resorted to guessing both types of diacritics jointly (Fadel et al., 2019; Mubarak et al., 2019) by either casting the problem as a character sequence labeling problem or as a character sequence to sequence (seq2seq) mapping respectively. Since the seq2seq models have a tendency to hallucinate, Mubarak et al. (2019) used a combination of limited context and voting to overcome the problem.

Unlike MSA, Arabic dialects generally omit case-endings and tend to apply *sukun* (o) on the last letter. Prior work on dialectal diacritization is rather scant. For dialectal Egyptian, Zalmout and Habash (2020) developed a morphological analyzer that also performs diacritization using sequence to sequence modeling. They reported a diacritization accuracy of 85.0%. For dialectal Gulf, Khalifa et al. (2017) developed a morphological analyzer for dialectal Gulf verbs, but diacritization was not the focus of their work. Khalifa et al. (2018) morphologically tagged an Emirati subset of the Gumar corpus including the diacritization of lemmas. However, mapping the diacritics from lemmas to words is non-trivial. For dialectal Palestinian, Jarrar et al. (2017) annotated a corpus of containing 43k words and diacritized all words. Abdelali et al. (2018); Darwish et al. (2018); Mubarak et al. (2019) used diacritized translations of the bible into dialectal Moroccan (151K words) and Tunisian (142K words) to train biLSTM over CRF, CRF only, and seq2seq models respectively for diacritizing both dialects. Of all three approaches, the seq2seq model led to the lowest word error rate (Moroccan: 1.4% and Tunisian: 2.5%).

3 Dataset

As mentioned earlier, we diacritized a subset of the Gumar corpus (Khalifa et al., 2018). The Gumar corpus is a collection of Internet novels composed of roughly 100 million words. A 200 thousand words subset of Gumar was in the Emirati dialect and was manually morphologically tagged. Though the lemmas were diacritized, their diacritization often did not correspond directly to the diacritization of words. Thus, we proceeded to diacritize a 19,850 word subset of the tagged Emirati portion of Gumar. We used the CODAfied version of the text, as opposed to the raw text, to have greater consistency in spelling. CODA, or Conventional Orthography for Dialectal Arabic, is an attempt at standardizing the spelling of different Arabic dialects (Habash et al., 2012).

For diacritization, we conducted a workshop that included two senior computational linguists and 15 native speakers of the Emirati dialect to codify the diacritization guidelines.

Diacritization Standards: After lengthy discussions, we settled on the following guidelines:

- All diacritization must be consistent with the accent spoken in Dubai, UAE.
- Leading *Hamza* in a closed set of words, such as ابو (>bw – father of) is not pronounced and hence undiacritized.
- Consecutive letters can have sukun, such as شِفْتْها ($ifotohA – I saw her)
- Words can start with *sukun*, such as بْيِلْعَب (boyiloEab – he plays). To ascertain if a word starts

with *sukun*, we use the *w* test, where the leading letter gets a *sukun* if it has a *sukun* when the letter *w* is added as a prefix.

- All words end with either *sukun*, which is assumed and subsequently dropped, or *shadda* (~).
- In ambiguous cases, *kasra* (i) is prioritized over *fatha* (a), which is prioritized over *dammah* (u).
- *Sukun* over *Lam Alaqamrya* does not need to be explicitly put. Ex. القَمَر (Alqamar – the moon).
- The question word شُ ($) always has a *dammah* (u).
- Coordinating conjunction letter و (w) in most cases has a *kasra* (i). Ex. وِقال (wiqAl – and he said).
- In ambiguous cases, plurality is prioritized over duality and that's because plurality occurs more, and the duality is a subset of the plurality.
- The singular masculine present tense marker ي (y) can only have *kasra* or *sukun*. Ex. يِلْعَب (yiloEab – he plays).
- Three letter past tense verbs are diacritized as فِعَل (fiEal), Except for verbs that start with ا (A). Ex. سِبَح (sibah – he swam).
- Some colors have specific diacritized forms, namely: حَمَر (Hamar – red) and خَضَر (xaDar – green).
- Default diacritics (*fatHa* followed by *alef*, *kasra* followed by *ya*, and *damma* followed by *wa*) are omitted.
- There is no need for a *kasra* for *hamza below alef* إ (<).
- *tanween fatha* (F) should come before the letter *alef* ا (A). Ex. طَبْعًا (TaboEFA – of course).
- For plural verbs that end with (وا) (wA), the و (w) mostly has *sukun* and the letter before it has *fatha*. Ex. لِعْبَوْا (liEobawoA – they played).
- We used the MSA diacritics and did not introduce any new diacritic marks.

Diacritization Process: We used a three step diacritization process designed to increase speed and improve accuracy. The steps are as follows:

- We diacritized the most frequent 1,300 words in the annotated Emirati Gumar corpus out of context. Our intuition was that most words have either one diacritized form or one diacritized form that is more dominant, and the most common words would cover a large proportion of the text in the corpus. Some example words that we diacritized in this manner are: أَرْمِس (>aromis – I speak), غالْيَة (gAloyap – precisous), and ليش (ly$ – why)[2]. We used the word list to automatically diacritize the corpus.
- We split the native speakers in the workshop into 4 groups, and each group was responsible to diacritize a different subset of the corpus. The groups were instructed to work together and to resolve disagreements. Each group was given sentences that were roughly 5,000 words.
- A senior computational linguist who is well versed in the Gulf dialect performed two rounds of review over the work of all the groups with frequent consultations with members of the groups.

Table 1 shows three sample sentences after review. The newly diacritized portion of Gumar is 2,953 sentences, which is composed of 19,850 words. For subsequent experiments, we split the dataset into training and test splits. Table 2 shows the breakdown of the dataset.

4 Experiments

We trained two different diacritization models based on our new dataset. Prior to training the models, we tokenized all the text to separate all punctuation. The data did not have any emojis, URLs, or emails. The models were as follows:

HMM Model: As the name suggests, we used a Hidden Markov Model to find the best diacritization of words in context. We used KenLM[3] to train a word trigram language model and an in-house implementation of A-star search to ascertain the best path in the lattice.

Seq2seq Model: We re-implemented the setup that was suggested by Mubarak et al. (2019). The model used the RNN-based sequence to sequence model that is implemented in OpenNMT (Klein

[2]As can be seen from the example, we removed default diacritics

[3]https://github.com/kpu/kenlm

Sentence	Buckwalter transliteration	Translation
سيف : سَمَعْتيها شو قالَت لِج ؟	syf : samaEotyhA $w qAlat lij	Saif: Did you hear what he she told you ?
وِقال خَليفَة : وِسَلْمِى عَليها بَعِد . . .	wiqAl xalyfap : wisalomaY EalyhA baEid	and Khalifa said: and Salma what about her.
جَزّوي : شو . . خَبْروني . .	jaz∼wy : $w ... xaborwny	Jazouy: what ... tell me.

Table 1: Example diacritized sentences.

split	Words	Sentences
Train	18,174	2,700
Test	1,676	253
Total	19,850	2,953

Table 2: Breakdown of diacritized dataset

Model	WER
HMM	6.7%
Seq2Seq	8.6%

Table 3: Diacritization results: Word Error Rate (WER)

et al., 2017), which is a neural machine translation toolkit, to translate undiacritized characters to diacritized characters. Since seq2seq models may hallucinate, we restricted contexts to 5 words instead of attempting to diacritize entire sentences and implemented voting across multiple contexts (Mubarak et al., 2019). The underlying model uses 2 unidirectional LSTM layers with 512 states and a dropout rate of 0.3. We also used 200 sentences from the training set as a validation set.

Table 3 shows the diacritization results of both models. As can be seen, the HMM model performed slightly better than the seq2seq model with 6.7% and 8.6% WER respectively. To understand the results, we proceeded to classify all the errors resulting from both approaches. We found that the most dominant errors for the HMM model were due to out of vocabulary words (OOVs), accounting for 73.3% of the errors. Given that we were using the CODAfied version of the Gumar corpus, we suspect that the OOV problem would be more pronounced for dialectal Gulf in the wild, where creative spellings would be more common. Conversely, hallucinations accounted for 34.6% of the errors for the seq2seq model. An example of hallucination is the word أُسْبوع (AusobwE – week) resulting in the misspelled version أَسْبِعوع (AasobiwE). We suspect that hallucination errors would be less pronounced if we had more training data. The results and error types seem to suggest that the dataset is relatively small, and more data is required to build more robust diacritizers. We hope that the newly annotated corpus with the associated diacritization standards can pave the way to building larger datasets.

5 Conclusion

In this paper we introduced a new dataset for Gulf Arabic diacritization based on the sub-dialect spoken in Dubai, UAE. The diacritization was based on formalized diacrtization guidelines that was developed by two senior computational linguists along with 15 native speakers, who were also instrumental in performing the actual diacritization. We plan to release the dataset publicly under an open source license. We also presented initial results using 2 different diacritization models. Though the dataset is relatively small (19,850 words), we were able to build two diacritization models that achieved less than 9% word error rate. We plan to expand the size of the corpus, particularly for non-CODAfied Gulf text. We hope that models trained on our data can help significantly speed up the diactization process.

6 Limitations

Some of the limitations include: 1) the corpus is based on one genre, namely Internet novels, that have limited linguistic diversity; 2) diacritization was done on the CODAfied subset of the Gumar corpus, while much naturally appearing text may not be CODA compliant; and 3) the dataset is relatively small and more data is required to train robust diacritization models (particularly deep learning models).

7 Ethics Statement

All the data that we annotated is in the public domain, and private data was used.

References

Gheith A Abandah, Alex Graves, Balkees Al-Shagoor, Alaa Arabiyat, Fuad Jamour, and Majid Al-Taee. 2015. Automatic diacritization of arabic text using recurrent neural networks. *International Journal on Document Analysis and Recognition (IJDAR)*, 18(2):183–197.

Ahmed Abdelali, Mohammed Attia, Younes Samih, Kareem Darwish, and Hamdy Mubarak. 2018. Diacritization of maghrebi arabic sub-dialects. *arXiv preprint arXiv:1810.06619*.

Yonatan Belinkov and James Glass. 2015. Arabic diacritization with recurrent neural networks. In *Proceedings of the 2015 Conference on Empirical Methods in Natural Language Processing*, pages 2281–2285, Lisbon, Portugal.

Kareem Darwish, Ahmed Abdelali, Hamdy Mubarak, Younes Samih, and Mohammed Attia. 2018. Diacritization of moroccan and tunisian arabic dialects: A crf approach. *OSACT*, 3:62.

Kareem Darwish, Hamdy Mubarak, and Ahmed Abdelali. 2017. Arabic diacritization: Stats, rules, and hacks. In *Proceedings of the Third Arabic Natural Language Processing Workshop*, pages 9–17.

Ali Fadel, Ibraheem Tuffaha, Mahmoud Al-Ayyoub, et al. 2019. Arabic text diacritization using deep neural networks. In *2019 2nd international conference on computer applications & information security (ICCAIS)*, pages 1–7. IEEE.

Ya'akov Gal. 2002. An hmm approach to vowel restoration in arabic and hebrew. In *Proceedings of the ACL-02 workshop on Computational approaches to Semitic languages*, pages 1–7. Association for Computational Linguistics.

Nizar Habash, Mona Diab, and Owen Rambow. 2012. Conventional orthography for dialectal Arabic. In *Proceedings of the Eighth International Conference on Language Resources and Evaluation (LREC'12)*, Istanbul, Turkey. European Language Resources Association (ELRA).

Mustafa Jarrar, Nizar Habash, Faeq Alrimawi, Diyam Akra, and Nasser Zalmout. 2017. Curras: an annotated corpus for the palestinian arabic dialect. *Language Resources and Evaluation*, 51(3):745–775.

Salam Khalifa, Nizar Habash, Fadhl Eryani, Ossama Obeid, Dana Abdulrahim, and Meera Al Kaabi. 2018. A morphologically annotated corpus of emirati arabic. In *Proceedings of the eleventh international conference on language resources and evaluation (LREC 2018)*.

Salam Khalifa, Sara Hassan, and Nizar Habash. 2017. A morphological analyzer for gulf arabic verbs. In *Proceedings of the Third Arabic Natural Language Processing Workshop*, pages 35–45.

Guillaume Klein, Yoon Kim, Yuntian Deng, Jean Senellart, and Alexander Rush. 2017. OpenNMT: Open-source toolkit for neural machine translation. In *Proceedings of ACL 2017, System Demonstrations*, pages 67–72, Vancouver, Canada. Association for Computational Linguistics.

Mohammed Maamouri, Ann Bies, Tim Buckwalter, and Wigdan Mekki. 2004. The penn arabic treebank: building a large-scale annotated arabic corpus. In *NEMLAR Conference on Arabic Language Resources and Tools*, pages 102—-109.

Hamdy Mubarak, Ahmed Abdelali, Kareem Darwish, Mohamed Eldesouki, Younes Samih, and Hassan Sajjad. 2019. A system for diacritizing four varieties of arabic. In *Proceedings of the 2019 Conference on Empirical Methods in Natural Language Processing and the 9th International Joint Conference on Natural Language Processing (EMNLP-IJCNLP): System Demonstrations*, pages 217–222.

Rani Nelken and Stuart M Shieber. 2005. Arabic diacritization using weighted finite-state transducers. In *Proceedings of the ACL Workshop on Computational Approaches to Semitic Languages*, pages 79–86. Association for Computational Linguistics.

Mohsen Rashwan, Ahmad Al Sallab, M. Raafat, and Ahmed Rafea. 2015. Deep learning framework with confused sub-set resolution architecture for automatic arabic diacritization. In *IEEE Transactions on Audio, Speech, and Language Processing*, pages 505–516.

Nasser Zalmout and Nizar Habash. 2020. Joint diacritization, lemmatization, normalization, and fine-grained morphological tagging. In *Proceedings of the 58th Annual Meeting of the Association for Computational Linguistics*, pages 8297–8307.

Taha Zerrouki and Amar Balla. 2017. Tashkeela: Novel corpus of arabic vocalized texts, data for auto-diacritization systems. *Data in brief*, 11:147–151.

Imed Zitouni, Jeffrey S Sorensen, and Ruhi Sarikaya. 2006. Maximum entropy based restoration of arabic diacritics. In *Proceedings of the 21st International Conference on Computational Linguistics and the 44th annual meeting of the Association for Computational Linguistics*, pages 577–584. Association for Computational Linguistics.

Learning From Arabic Corpora But Not Always From Arabic Speakers: A Case Study of the Arabic Wikipedia Editions

Saied Alshahrani **Esma Wali** **Jeanna Matthews**
Department of Computer Science
Clarkson University, Potsdam, NY, USA
alshahsf,walie,jnm@clarkson.edu

Abstract

Wikipedia is a common source of training data for Natural Language Processing (NLP) research, especially as a source for corpora in languages other than English. However, for many downstream NLP tasks, it is important to understand the degree to which these corpora reflect representative contributions of native speakers. In particular, many entries in a given language may be translated from other languages or produced through other automated mechanisms. Language models built using corpora like Wikipedia can embed history, culture, bias, stereotypes, politics, and more, but it is important to understand whose views are actually being represented. In this paper, we present a case study focusing specifically on differences among the Arabic Wikipedia editions (Modern Standard Arabic, Egyptian, and Moroccan). In particular, we document issues in the Egyptian Arabic Wikipedia with automatic creation/generation and translation of content pages from English without human supervision. These issues could substantially affect the performance and accuracy of Large Language Models (LLMs) trained from these corpora, producing models that lack the cultural richness and meaningful representation of native speakers. Fortunately, the metadata maintained by Wikipedia provides visibility into these issues, but unfortunately, this is not the case for all corpora used to train LLMs.

1 Introduction

Natural Language Processing (NLP) is increasingly used as a key ingredient in critical decision-making systems, such as resume parsers used in sorting a list of job candidates. These NLP systems often ingest large corpora of human text, attempting to learn from past human behavior to produce systems that will make recommendations about our future world (Wali et al., 2020). The corpora of human text, which are the main ingredients in NLP systems, convey many social concepts (Cho et al., 2021), including culture, heritage, and even historic biases (Bolukbasi et al., 2016; Caliskan et al., 2017; Babaeianjelodar et al., 2020). Google News, Books Corpora, Wikipedia, and the GLUE (The General Language Understanding Evaluation) dataset (Mittermeier et al., 2021; Wang et al., 2018) are all examples of the many digital text corpora that have been used in NLP research.

Many languages are substantially under-represented in both corpus development and NLP toolchain support. For example, there are more than 7000 spoken languages around the globe, and only 300 have Wikipedia corpora. Among these 300, there is wide variation in raw corpus size as well as the ratio of articles to the number of speakers. These differences are further amplified throughout the NLP toolchain (Wali et al., 2020). Languages without large corpora also often face a lack of support in common NLP tools and unexpected errors in other tools due to a lack of testing and use. This under-represents the culture and heritage of speakers of those languages in NLP-guided decision-making.

In addition, simply having a corpus of text in a language does not necessarily represent the culture of native speakers of that language. While some corpora are originally written by native speakers, others may be written by non-native speakers or even translated from other languages (Nisioi et al., 2016). It has also been observed that some Wikipedia corpora have been developed/created through bots or automated scripts, often involving translation from other languages (Baker, 2022). This paper highlights this less discussed yet important issue of the differences between text corpora written by native speakers and those translated and generated by automated systems. We also discuss their potential effects on downstream NLP systems. As a case study, we document discrepancies between Arabic Wikipedia editions and Egyptian Arabic Wikipedia.

Proceedings of the The Seventh Arabic Natural Language Processing Workshop (WANLP), pages 361 - 371
December 8, 2022

In Section 2, we discuss some related work, and in Section 3, we study Wikipedia and its Arabic editions, using English as a benchmark. Lastly, in Sections 4 and 5, we discuss our findings with a focus on the representativeness of NLP corpora, provide a few recommendations, and conclude with a short conclusion and pitch future work ideas.

2 Related Work

Bender et al. (2021) in an influential paper, shed light on the possible risks associated with using big data and the mitigation strategies to deal with this risk. They strongly recommend working on designing and carefully documenting datasets, as creating larger datasets and using them without having insight into their metadata could not only create documentation debt but also harm marginalized communities by introducing various kinds of biases in the results of LLMs. Without having metadata associated with the datasets, it is not possible for someone to understand training data characteristics and find ways to mitigate some of these attested issues or even unknown ones. Evaluating the approach regarding the applicability of LLMs (e.g., BERT or GPT-3) on the tasks like Natural Language Understanding (NLU) and misdirected research regarding it is another factor discussed and emphasized in this paper. Moreover, the authors advocate prioritizing LLMs' environmental and financial costs by having their costs and resources consumed adequately reported; these costs affect the communities being least benefited by them. Lastly, a suggestion was made regarding research directions to pursue the goals of creating language technology while avoiding some of the risks and harms identified in the paper.

To help with issues related to exclusion and bias, Bender and Friedman (2018) presented the approach of including data statements in all publications and documentation for NLP systems. The approach aims to yield various short-term and long-term benefits, including unfolding how data represents the people and the world, enabling research addressing issues of bias and exclusion, promoting the development of more representative datasets, and making it convenient for researchers to consider stakeholder values as they work.

Holland et al. (2020) raised the concern about the quality of data analysis methods before model development related to the cost and standardization. They presented the Dataset Nutrition Label, a diagnostic framework to aid standardized data analysis, making it more adaptable across domains. They also explored the limitations of the Label, including the challenges of generalizing across diverse datasets and guidelines for future research and policy agendas for the project. Likewise, to clarify the intended use cases of ML models and limit their usage in a context not well suited for them, Mitchell et al. (2019) suggested a framework named Model Cards to promote transparency in model reporting using short documents. Corry et al. (2021) studied dataset deprecation in ML and proposed a data deprecation framework focusing on risk, impact mitigation, appeal mechanisms, timeline, post-deprecation protocols, and publication checks that can be adapted and implemented by the ML community. They also advocate for a centralized, sustainable repository system for archiving datasets, tracking dataset deprecations, and helping to enable practices that can be integrated into research and publication processes.

To fill the gap in the standardization process in documenting datasets, Gebru et al. (2021) proposed datasheets for datasets, i.e., each dataset should be accompanied by a datasheet explaining its motivation, composition, collection process, recommended uses, etc. It aims to bridge the gap between creators and users of datasets and establish a communication channel taking a step toward ensuring transparency and accountability in datasets and ML systems. Arnold et al. (2019) proposed FactSheets to help increase trust in AI services and envisioned such documents to contain purpose, performance, safety, security, and provenance information to be completed by AI service providers for consumer examination. Denton et al. (2020) outlined a research program – a genealogy of machine learning data – for investigating how and why datasets have been created, what and whose values influence the data collection choices, and the contextual and contingent conditions of their creation. Hutchinson et al. (2021) introduced a framework for dataset development transparency that supports decision-making and accountability. The framework uses dataset development's cyclical, infrastructural, and engineering nature to draw on best practices from the software development lifecycle.

Wikipedia is used frequently in NLP research, including multilingual NLP (Yang and Roberts, 2021; Peters et al., 2018; Devlin et al., 2018; Petroni et al., 2019; Brown et al., 2020; Wali et al., 2020; Beytía et al., 2022; Hsu et al., 2021; Wong et al., 2021; Valentim et al., 2021; Johnson, 2020; Johnson and Lescak, 2022; Chen et al., 2021). For example, Beytía et al. (2022) documented a gender gap in Wikipedia biographical articles over a dataset of almost 6.2 million Wikipedia biographical articles across the 10 most spoken languages. The analysis was performed by proposing 4 multimodal metrics of the amount and quality of visual and written content. They found that text content favors female biographies, while the image quantity favors males, and the multilingual article coverage is biased slightly towards women. Similarly, a dataset by Valentim et al. (2021), covering 309 language editions and 33M Wikipedia articles, was presented to explore inter-language knowledge propagation by tracking the full propagation history of concepts in Wikipedia. This allows follow-up research on building predictive models with the help of aligned Wikipedia articles in a language-agnostic manner according to the concept they cover, resulting in 13M propagation instances.

Johnson and Lescak (2022) provide background about what differences might arise between different language editions of Wikipedia and how that might affect their models. The authors discuss three major ways content differences between language editions arise (local context, community and governance, and technology), recommend good practices when using multilingual and multimodal data for research and modeling, and suggest researchers expand the models available to Wikipedians for translating articles into their language.

In the space of the Arabic NLP, many researchers have studied the translation of the English language content to the Arabic language or its dialects back and forth using Machine Translation models (MTs); especially the Statistical Machine Translation models (SMTs) and the Neural Machine Translation models (NMTs), which achieved an excellent quality of translation (Al-Mannai et al., 2014; Badr et al., 2008; El-Kholy and Habash, 2010; Salloum and Habash, 2013; Sajjad et al., 2013a,b; Zbib et al., 2012). Several studies have utilized the MTs to translate the Egyptian dialect to Modern Standard Arabic (MSA) or vice versa. For example, Abo-Bakr et al. (2008) was the first work in this domain where the authors introduced a hybrid approach to translating an Egyptian sentence into its corresponding sentence in the MSA. In Mohamed et al. (2012), the author presented the opposite way, where they introduced a translator from the MSA to the Egyptian dialect. The recent work of Jeblee et al. (2014) presented many SMT systems to translate from English to Dialectal Arabic (DA) – the Egyptian Arabic dialect, using MSA as a pivot.

3 The Case of Wikipedia

Wikipedia corpora (i.e., content pages of Wikipedia) are used to train LLMs. For example, ELMo (Embeddings from Language Models) has been trained on the English Wikipedia and news crawl data (Peters et al., 2018), BERT (Bidirectional Encoder Representations from Transformers) has been trained on the BookCorpus (Zhu et al., 2015) with a crawl of the English Wikipedia (Devlin et al., 2018; Petroni et al., 2019), and GPT-3 (Generative Pre-trained Transformer) has been trained on five large datasets including the English Wikipedia as well (Brown et al., 2020).

NLP researchers find Wikipedia corpora attractive because of its large collection of multilingual content and its vast array of metadata that can be quantified and compared across the multilingual content pages (Mittermeier et al., 2021). Yet, recent works have underlined that those pre-trained LLMs embed bias, stereotypes, or even politics. Unlike many corpora, Wikipedia maintains rich metadata that allows researchers to assess the source of its contents, but little work has shown explicitly how different Wikipedia corpora impact these models (Bolukbasi et al., 2016; Caliskan et al., 2017; Yang and Roberts, 2021; Chen et al., 2021). At the same time, other recent works have also reported that the current pre-trained LLMs still under-represent the human languages despite being trained with hundreds of billions of parameters and trained on enormous datasets (Bender et al., 2021).

In the following subsections, we compare the Arabic Wikipedia editions (Modern Standard Arabic, Egyptian, and Moroccan) regarding pages to date, new pages, and top editors, besides English Wikipedia as a benchmark.[1] We also specifically study the impact of problems in Egyptian Arabic Wikipedia, including large-scale auto-generation and poor translation of content pages from English.

[1]We took a data snapshot of the four Wikipedia editions' statistics in July 2022 using the online Wikimedia Statistics service (`https://stats.wikimedia.org`). We contribute to the research community with our implementation of the online Wikimedia Statistics service as a Python package and command line interface. Wikistats-to-CSV (`wikistats2csv`) is accessible here: `https://github.com/SaiedAlshahrani/Wikistats-to-CSV`. See Appendix A for more details.

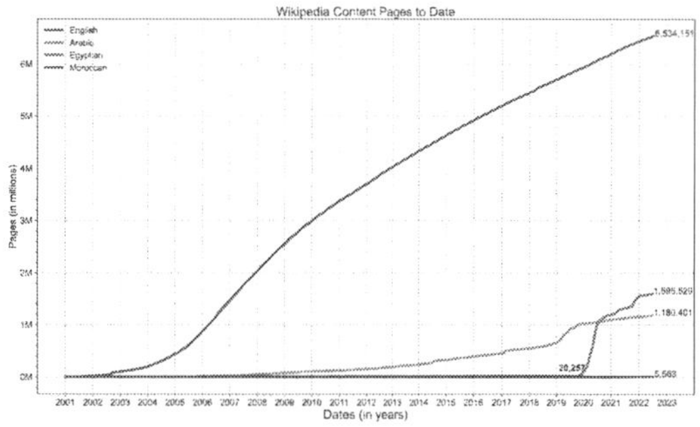

Figure 1: The total number of Wikipedia content pages to date for the four Wikipedia editions over the timeline of the Wikipedia project.

3.1 Arabic Wikipedia Editions

The free online encyclopedia, Wikipedia, was launched 20 years ago, in 2001, and released primarily in English (Wikipedia, 2022c). The Arabic language was one of the earliest languages added to Wikipedia. In 2004, the Arabic language content pages crossed the line of 1000 articles written by Arabic speakers to contribute to Wikipedia's Arabic content. By 2019, Arabic content pages exceeded 1 million articles (Wikimedia Foundation, 2022b). Many Arabic Wikipedia editions appeared in the project, such as the Egyptian Arabic in 2008 and Moroccan Arabic in 2019. These are two of many dialects of the Arabic language, like Gulf Arabic, Levantine Arabic, Tunisian Arabic, and other different Arabic dialects (Habash et al., 2013).

Table 1 compares some high-level statistics of the Arabic Wikipedia editions to English Wikipedia in terms of the total number of articles (content pages), total number of pages (both content and non-content pages)[2], total number of edits (including edits on redirects), the total number of administrators, the total number of registered users, and lastly, the total number of active users. Interestingly, Egyptian Arabic Wikipedia has a larger number of articles (content pages) than Arabic Wikipedia despite its later appearance.

3.1.1 Pages to Date

The content of Egyptian Arabic has recently grown rapidly and exponentially in the last two years. Whereas English, Arabic, and Moroccan Arabic show normal growth in their content pages (articles) over the timeline of Wikipedia.

[2]Wikipedia non-content pages include all redirects, images, categories, templates, user pages, project pages, and talk pages (Wikipedia, 2022d).

Figure 1 shows that there were approximately 20,000 Egyptian Arabic content pages in the middle of 2019, and presently, in the middle of 2022, the Egyptian Arabic content in Wikipedia crossed the 1 million and 1/2 content articles. Almost 1.6 million content pages were created in less than 3 years, which means over 50,000 articles were created monthly, or almost 2000 pages daily. In contrast, the Arabic language content pages are currently around 1.2 million pages created in 19 years, with an average of over 5000 articles created monthly, or around 200 content pages created daily (Wikimedia Foundation, 2022b). If we associate the total number of monthly created content pages of the Egyptian Arabic Wikipedia with its latest statistics of its active users, we find that each active user would create, on average, 280 articles per month. This exponential growth of the content pages in the Egyptian Arabic Wikipedia in only 30 months is the result of the large-scale automated creation of the content pages, where one of the most active contributors confirmed this in a book (Baker, 2022); we will discuss it in detail later.

We also visualize the percentage of all page types (content and non-content) to date for the four Wikipedia editions, displaying the difference in percentage between page types to study the characteristics of each Wikipedia within itself. Figure 2 shows that all English, Arabic, and Moroccan Arabic Wikipedia have approximately 15% to 21% of content pages and approximately 79% to 85% of non-content pages of their total number of all page types. These ratios are reasonable because that is the definition of having an online free encyclopedia that aims to enable and involve people all over the globe in the creation and dissemination of knowledge. To do so effectively, users, editors, or contributors must interact with each other through talk pages, user pages, project pages, and discussion pages, generating a massive number of non-content pages in a specific Wikipedia. However, Egyptian Arabic Wikipedia opposes expected percentages, where it has approximately 20% of non-content pages and 80% of content pages, and that is a consequence of the large-scale automation of content creation.

3.1.2 New Pages

To further examine this large-scale automated creation of the content pages in the Egyptian Arabic Wikipedia and to confirm our earlier hypothesis, we studied the timeline of the three Arabic Wikipedia

Language	Code	Articles	Total Pages	Edits	Admins	Registered Users	Active Users
English	en	6,543,738	56,401,668	1,101,698,546	1,032	44,056,435	114,504
Arabic	ar	1,183,778	7,815,021	58,966,845	26	2,293,115	4,820
Egyptian Arabic	arz	**1,596,851**	2,010,972	7,343,259	7	189,191	190
Moroccan Arabic	ary	5,744	43,714	188,790	3	6,415	31

Table 1: General statistics of the three Arabic Wikipedia editions besides the English Wikipedia regarding the number of articles (content pages), total pages (both content and non-content pages), edits, admins, registered users, and active users.

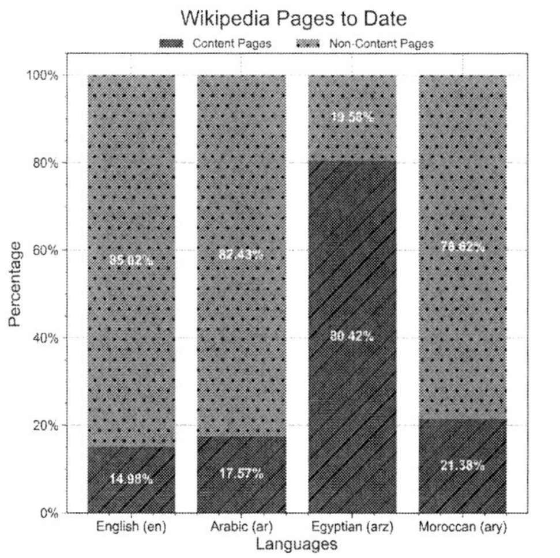

Figure 2: The percentage of all page types (content and non-content) to date for the four Wikipedia editions, displaying the difference in percentage between page types within each Wikipedia.

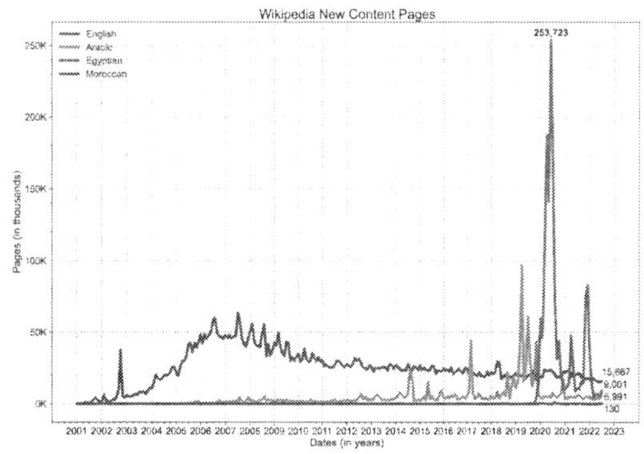

Figure 3: The total number of Wikipedia new content pages for the four Wikipedia editions over the timeline of the Wikipedia project.

editions besides the English Wikipedia. We found that in the middle of 2020, specifically June 2020, approximately 253,000 new content pages were created in the Egyptian Arabic Wikipedia. On the other hand, nearly 23,700 new content pages were created on English Wikipedia, nearly 4,280 were created on Arabic Wikipedia, and nearly 50 on Moroccan Arabic Wikipedia, all in the same period.

Figure 3 clearly shows that the total articles (content pages) of the Egyptian Arabic Wikipedia had multiple massive spikes over the timeline of the Wikipedia project, starting from late 2019 to the beginning of 2022. Still, the most significant spike was in June 2020, when approximately 253,000 new articles (content pages) were created in one month. This is not the same as the organic creation of content pages that reflect the Egyptian people and represent their culture, beliefs, traditions, perspectives, or even dialect.

This kind of practice also appears to be inconsistent with the main purpose of the Wikipedia project; which is, according to Jimmy Wales, a co-founder of Wikipedia, "*to create and distribute a free encyclopedia of the highest possible quality to every single person on the planet in their own language*" (Cohen, 2008; Wikipedia, 2022a). Wikipedia should only be written, contributed to, edited, and maintained by the people. This lack of representativeness and cultural richness holds in its fold many potential problems that could impact society negatively through using deployed AI systems or NLP tools like the LLMs that have been trained on inorganic corpora (Bender et al., 2021).

3.1.3 Top Editors

Wikipedia has four types of editors: registered users (logged-in users but not in group-bot nor name-bot sets), group-bots (logged-in users who are part of a bot group), name-bots (logged-in users whose name contains 'bot'), and anonymous users (users not logged-in but tracked by IP address) (Wikimedia Foundation, 2022c). To study the activity levels and contributions of each editor type, we visualize the percentage of all pages to date for the four Wikipedia editions by displaying the difference in percentage between editor types to study the characteristics of each Wikipedia within itself.

Figure 4 shows that Arabic and Moroccan Arabic Wikipedia editions have approximately 22% to 37% of their total number of pages created by registered users. At the same time, Egyptian Arabic

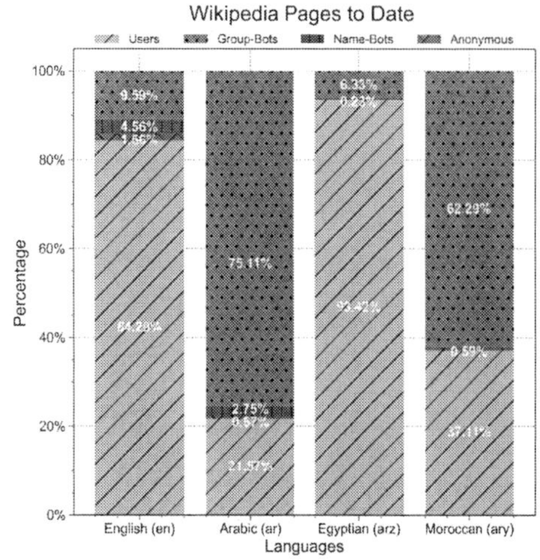

Figure 4: The percentage of all pages to date grouped by all editor types (registered users, group-bots, name-bots, and anonymous users) for the four Wikipedia editions, displaying the difference in percentage between editor types within each Wikipedia.

Wikipedia has approximately 94% of its total pages created by registered users, and English Wikipedia has 84% of its total pages created by registered users. However, as we see in the next section, this apparent high activity level from registered users can be misleading. Important differences between English Wikipedia and Egyptian Arabic Wikipedia include the high degree of automated activity by individual registered users and the considerable gap in the total number of registered users, meaning that one registered user in Egyptian Arabic Wikipedia could create the same number of pages as hundreds or even thousands of registered users in the English Wikipedia.

3.2 Egyptian Arabic Wikipedia Problems

We investigated Egyptian Arabic Wikipedia's top 'registered user' editors. We found that over 1 million articles, a surprising 63% of the total articles, in Egyptian Arabic Wikipedia have been created by one registered user called "HitomiAkane". This user has made more than 1,562,615 new creations (between articles, categories, templates, etc.), made nearly 1,615,216 edits, and created thousands of thousands of automatically generated content pages without human revision of the produced articles (Wikipedia, 2022b).

This large-scale content creation process was described by Maher Baker in his published book: *How I Wrote a Million Wikipedia Articles* (Baker, 2022). He used the English Wikipedia as a corpus and used Wikidata[3], which stores briefs of the articles in the form of items, each item consisting of properties and values, to generate a list of data (items) that share the same properties and values using the Wikidata Query Service[4] (a query engine to perform queries on Wikidata database). After generating these data lists, he developed an article template where he only filled in blanks for each line of the results (data lists), which eventually became the core content of these articles. We quote the example of *football player* that he used to demonstrate the automation process in the book:

> **[label] [date of birth]**, **[gender]** is a football player from **[citizenship]**, **[gender]** was born at **[date of birth]** in **[place of birth]**.

The user also reported that he added the missing extra information required by Wikipedia using PHP, translated the English content to Modern Standard Arabic (MSA) using PHP's Google Translate API, and boosted the process of creating and publishing the articles on Wikipedia using the MediaWiki Action API[5], a web service that allows access to a few Wiki features like page operations (create, edit, etc.) (Baker, 2022; Wikimedia Foundation, 2022a). He did not explicitly describe how he converted the MSA articles from the English translation to the Egyptian dialect. We hypothesize that the user maintained a lexicon of the most frequently used MSA words with their corresponding in the Egyptian dialect and replaced the MSA words with their Egyptian corresponding to make it look like it was produced organically by native speakers. We further suspect that many of these content articles may not have required any specific conversion to the Egyptian dialect of Arabic and thus could be considered to still be in MSA.[6] Overall, the process used represents a relatively shallow, template-based translation of content.

According to Wikipedia's bot policy, mass automated creation of content pages must be approved

[3]Wikidata: https://www.wikidata.org.

[4]Wikidata Query: https://query.wikidata.org.

[5]MediaWiki Action API: https://www.mediawiki.org.

[6]We plan to perform a representative analysis of randomly chosen articles from Arabic and Egyptian Wikipedia editions. Yet, to demonstrate our suspicions about this issue, we randomly chose two examples that discuss the same topic in Arabic and Egyptian Wikipedia (Nabq Protected Area – محمية نبق) to show that these two articles are mostly written in MSA:
∗ https://ar.wikipedia.org/wiki?curid=1107706.
∗ https://arz.wikipedia.org/wiki?curid=95486.

first, and when a user or bot operates without approval, the administrators have the right to block that user or bot (Wikipedia, 2022e). Unlike many digital corpora, Wikipedia maintains clear metadata that allows researchers to assess the source of content additions. This is an important step toward allowing researchers and users to assess whether a given corpus fits a specific use case.

Given the metadata about the Egyptian Arabic corpora, we can see that it would not be suitable corpora to learn the perspective of native speakers. Even when a Wikipedia article is a factual entry, the choice to write an article on one topic over another reflects the author's perspective and values. Similarly, the facts chosen to add to an article vs. other possible facts not included reflect the perspective and values of the authors. It matters whether these choices are made by native speakers or by translation from other languages. We recommend that when registered users employ automated translation processes, their contributions should be marked differently than "registered user"; perhaps "registered user (automation-assisted)".

4 Discussion

The Arabic language, in general, poses many challenges in NLP that prevent simply translating from another language like the English language due to it is morphological richness and high ambiguity (Shaalan et al., 2018; Farghaly and Shaalan, 2009). Additionally, the Arabic language has many dialectal variants, like Egyptian and Moroccan Arabic, that are different from MSA. These dialects are primarily spoken, do not have written standards, and have very few resources (Habash et al., 2013; Al-Mannai et al., 2014). Despite all these challenges the Arabic NLP faces, translating English content, especially from Wikipedia, to enrich low-resource languages' content like the Arabic language or any of its dialects like Egyptian is a common practice, which is mainly done using Machine Translation models (MTs) that existed in the 1950s and have evolved since then until today (El-Kholy and Habash, 2010).

Recently, Wikimedia Foundation has encouraged users, editors, and contributors to use MTs to translate and create the initial content of articles on the Wikipedia project using their content translation tool. This tool is a product of collaboration between Google (Google Translate) and the Wikimedia Foundation, and this tool has been used to translate more than 400,000 articles on Wikipedia (Bhattacharjee and Giner, 2022; Wikimedia Foundation, 2022). Without a doubt, the foundation seeks to improve the quality of the multilingual content of Wikipedia via article translation using translation tools like Google Translator. Still, it is important to consider the quality of these translation tools, the quality of the translation work conducted by non-expert Wikipedia users or bots, and what they could bring to the multilingual content of Wikipedia from potential serious issues, such as religious, political, or gender biases. Another serious problem is the unrepresentativeness of the content, especially when users or bots could create shallow content automatically (like what we saw in the Egyptian Arabic Wikipedia) using templates and translation tools that do not profoundly understand the targeted language (Ullmann and Saunders, 2021; Lopez-Medel, 2021; Hautasaari, 2013; Baker, 2022).

The heart of the lack of representativeness problem, specifically in the Arabic language, can be discussed from two different perspectives: the large-scale unsupervised automated generation of content, especially in Wikipedia, and the translation of content from English to other low-resource languages like Arabic using direct translation methods or tools like Google Translator. We have analyzed the Egyptian Arabic Wikipedia and found that more than 1 million articles have shallow content and are translated poorly from English to MSA. Until now, no one knows how the responsible user converted the translated MSA content to the Egyptian dialect. We suspect that most of these content articles have not truly converted to the Egyptian dialect and are still in MSA. It would be easy for users to assume that the Egyptian Arabic Wikipedia corpus was genuinely representative of the Egyptian people, their culture, heritage, or traditions. However, the many documented reasons indicate otherwise.

The other face of the lack of representativeness problem is when users or bots translate the content of the English language, for example, to other low-resource languages like Arabic using direct translation or off-the-shelf translation tools. Most of these translations done on Wikipedia content, in general, are done using direct translation, meaning that we are translating from language A to language B. The bottleneck for this kind of translation is the quality of the translation tool. The quality of the translation is likely superior if the tool is sophisticated, uses state-of-the-art technologies, and is trained on large parallel corpora of A and B languages. However, the existing off-the-shelf translation tools like Google Translator perform well, but not perfectly, and have many ethical problems like sexism and a few biases that could badly affect the translated content (Ullmann and Saunders, 2021; Lopez-Medel, 2021). It would also likely retain the sentiment, culture, and biases from the origin/source corpora rather than represent the society of native speakers of the targeted language.

Jeblee et al. (2014) designed three different translation systems: baseline MT system, where they directly translated English to Egyptian Arabic; one-step adoption MT system, where they directly translated English to MSA, used domain and dialect adoption, and translated the results to the Egyptian Arabic; and two-step adoption MT system, where they directly translated English to MSA, then used domain adoption, then in-domain MSA to dialect adoption to lastly translated the results to Egyptian Arabic. Such a complex work is what we meant by performing a sophisticated translation. We do not doubt such systems will produce a significantly accurate translation between English and Egyptian Arabic and could solve the problem of the lack of representativeness of the Egyptian Arabic Wikipedia content if it has been used. Nevertheless, the selection of which articles to write or translate and which aspects to highlight in an article would still not reflect the choices of native speakers.

As a big concern, a few researchers have studied the implications of using corpora that are automatically created, poorly translated using direct translation, automatically generated by advanced LLMs like ELMo, BERT, or GPT-3, or even the textual content of the assembled corpora using text augmentation techniques (Peters et al., 2018; Zhu et al., 2015; Brown et al., 2020; Baker, 2022; Bhattacharjee and Giner, 2022; Şahin, 2022). We believe that those LLMs, MTs, automation, and augmentation procedures will likely produce corpora full of serious issues. These corpora do not only embed bias, stereotypes, or even politics (Bolukbasi et al., 2016; Caliskan et al., 2017; Yang and Roberts, 2021; Cho et al., 2021; Chen et al., 2021), but they also do not echo the complex structure of the Arabic language and its dialects, do not express the views of the Arabic speakers, and do not represent the cultural richness and historical heritage of the Arabic language and its people.

5 Conclusion and Future Work

We studied, in this work, the Arabic Wikipedia editions (Modern Standard Arabic, Egyptian, and Moroccan) besides English Wikipedia in terms of their pages to date, new pages, and top editors, and shed light brightly on the problem of the Egyptian Arabic Wikipedia, where we found that one registered user has automated the creation of over 1 million content pages in less than 3 years and used shallow, template-based translation method that does not represent speakers of Egyptian Arabic.

We recommend that NLP practitioners avoid the inorganic, unauthentic, unrepresentative corpora in their applications (e.g., pipelines) when the goal is to learn from past human behavior and to thoroughly investigate how the corpora they do use were created, generated, or assembled; it is especially important to corpora that are produced by native speakers when the point is to examine culturally sensitive issues such as religious bias or gender bias, or political sentiment, etc. We have shown that currently, in Wikipedia, it is important to look beyond simply the "registered user" vs. "bot" distinction to recognize automated contributions, e.g., adding a "registered user (automation-assisted)" category will help us to distinguish between organically and automatically produced contributions by registered users.

In the future works, we plan to study the implications of using such unrepresentative corpora that are naively auto-created, shallowly translated, or automatically generated on the downstream applications of the NLP. We are compiling a list of alternative Egyptian Arabic corpora that have been introduced to the research community and are most likely to be organic, authentic, and representative corpora of the Egyptian Arabic dialect and its speakers. We also plan to introduce a representativeness metric that could assist in identifying the auto-generated content pages on the Wikipedia project. Lastly, we plan to design a neural network classifier that could aid in classifying the corpora in terms of representativeness.

Acknowledgments

We would like to thank the Clarkson Open Source Institute (COSI) for their support with infrastructure and hosting of our experiments. We also thank Abdullah Alshamsan and Norah Alshahrani for their help in collecting representative Arabic and Egyptian Arabic corpora for our future work.

Reproducibility

Code and data of our high-level analysis of Arabic Wikipedia editions are available on GitHub at `https://github.com/Clarkson-Accountability-Transparency/Analysis-of-Arabic-Wikipedias`.

References

Hitham Abo-Bakr, Khaled Shaalan, and Ibrahim Ziedan. 2008. A Hybrid Approach for Converting Written Egyptian Colloquial Dialect into Diacritized Arabic. In *The 6th International Conference on Informatics and Systems (INFOS2008)*, Cairo, Egypt. Faculty of Computers and Information, Faculty of Computers and Information.

Kamla Al-Mannai, Hassan Sajjad, Alaa Khader, Fahad Al Obaidli, Preslav Nakov, and Stephan Vogel. 2014. Unsupervised Word Segmentation Improves Dialectal Arabic to English Machine Translation. In *Proceedings of the EMNLP 2014 Workshop on Arabic Natural Language Processing (ANLP)*, pages 207–216, Doha, Qatar. Association for Computational Linguistics.

M. Arnold, R. K. E. Bellamy, M. Hind, S. Houde, S. Mehta, A. Mojsilović, R. Nair, K. Natesan Ramamurthy, A. Olteanu, D. Piorkowski, D. Reimer, J. Richards, J. Tsay, and K. R. Varshney. 2019. FactSheets: Increasing trust in AI services through supplier's declarations of conformity. *IBM Journal of Research and Development*, 63(4/5):6:1–6:13.

Marzieh Babaeianjelodar, Stephen Lorenz, Josh Gordon, Jeanna Matthews, and Evan Freitag. 2020. Quantifying Gender Bias in Different Corpora. In *Companion Proceedings of the Web Conference 2020*, WWW '20, page 752–759, New York, NY, USA. Association for Computing Machinery.

Ibrahim Badr, Rabih Zbib, and James Glass. 2008. Segmentation for English-to-Arabic Statistical Machine Translation. In *Proceedings of ACL-08: HLT, Short Papers*, pages 153–156, Columbus, Ohio. Association for Computational Linguistics.

Maher Asaad Baker. 2022. *How I Wrote a Million Wikipedia Articles*, 2 edition. BookRix GmbH Co. KG., Munich, Germany.

Emily M. Bender and Batya Friedman. 2018. Data Statements for Natural Language Processing: Toward Mitigating System Bias and Enabling Better Science. *Transactions of the Association for Computational Linguistics*, 6:587–604.

Emily M. Bender, Timnit Gebru, Angelina McMillan-Major, and Shmargaret Shmitchell. 2021. On the Dangers of Stochastic Parrots: Can Language Models Be Too Big? In *FAccT '21*, page 610–623, New York, NY, USA. Association for Computing Machinery.

Pablo Beytía, Pushkal Agarwal, Miriam Redi, and Vivek K Singh. 2022. Visual Gender Biases in Wikipedia: A Systematic Evaluation across the Ten Most Spoken Languages. In *Proceedings of the International AAAI Conference on Web and Social Media*, volume 16, pages 43–54.

Runa Bhattacharjee and Pau Giner. 2022. You can now use Google Translate to translate articles on Wikipedia. Last accessed on 2022-09-11.

Tolga Bolukbasi, Kai-Wei Chang, James Y Zou, Venkatesh Saligrama, and Adam T Kalai. 2016. Man is to Computer Programmer as Woman is to Homemaker? Debiasing Word Embeddings. *Advances in neural information processing systems*, 29.

Tom B. Brown, Benjamin Mann, Nick Ryder, Melanie Subbiah, Jared Kaplan, Prafulla Dhariwal, Arvind Neelakantan, Pranav Shyam, Girish Sastry, Amanda Askell, Sandhini Agarwal, Ariel Herbert-Voss, Gretchen Krueger, Tom Henighan, Rewon Child, Aditya Ramesh, Daniel M. Ziegler, Jeffrey Wu, Clemens Winter, Christopher Hesse, Mark Chen, Eric Sigler, Mateusz Litwin, Scott Gray, Benjamin Chess, Jack Clark, Christopher Berner, Sam McCandlish, Alec Radford, Ilya Sutskever, and Dario Amodei. 2020. Language Models are Few-Shot Learners. In *Proceedings of the 34th International Conference on Neural Information Processing Systems*, NIPS'20, Red Hook, NY, USA. Curran Associates Inc.

Aylin Caliskan, Joanna J Bryson, and Arvind Narayanan. 2017. Semantics derived automatically from language corpora contain human-like biases. *Science*, 356(6334):183–186.

Yan Chen, Christopher Mahoney, Isabella Grasso, Esma Wali, Abigail Matthews, Thomas Middleton, Mariama Njie, and Jeanna Matthews. 2021. Gender Bias and Under-Representation in Natural Language Processing Across Human Languages. In *Proceedings of the 2021 AAAI/ACM Conference on AI, Ethics, and Society*, AIES '21, page 24–34, New York, NY, USA. Association for Computing Machinery.

Won Ik Cho, Jiwon Kim, Jaeyeong Yang, and Nam Soo Kim. 2021. Towards Cross-Lingual Generalization of Translation Gender Bias. In *Proceedings of the 2021 ACM Conference on Fairness, Accountability, and Transparency*, FAccT '21, page 449–457, New York, NY, USA. Association for Computing Machinery.

Noam Cohen. 2008. Open-Source Troubles in Wiki World. The New York Times. Last accessed on 2022-09-11.

Frances Corry, Hamsini Sridharan, Alexandra Sasha Luccioni, Mike Ananny, Jason Schultz, and Kate Crawford. 2021. The Problem of Zombie Datasets: A Framework For Deprecating Datasets. *ArXiv*, abs/2111.04424.

Emily Denton, Alex Hanna, Razvan Amironesei, Andrew Smart, Hilary Nicole, and Morgan Klaus Scheuerman. 2020. Bringing the People Back In: Contesting Benchmark Machine Learning Datasets. *CoRR*, abs/2007.07399.

Jacob Devlin, Ming-Wei Chang, Kenton Lee, and Kristina Toutanova. 2018. BERT: Pre-training of Deep Bidirectional Transformers for Language Understanding. *arXiv preprint arXiv:1810.04805*.

Ahmed El-Kholy and Nizar Habash. 2010. Orthographic and morphological processing for English–Arabic statistical machine translation. *Machine Translation*, 26:25–45.

Ali Farghaly and Khaled Shaalan. 2009. Arabic Natural Language Processing: Challenges and Solutions. *ACM Transactions on Asian Language Information Processing*, 8(4).

Timnit Gebru, Jamie Morgenstern, Briana Vecchione, Jennifer Wortman Vaughan, Hanna Wallach, Hal Daumé III, and Kate Crawford. 2021. Datasheets for Datasets. *Communications of the ACM*, 64(12):86–92.

Nizar Habash, Ryan Roth, Owen Rambow, Ramy Eskander, and Nadi Tomeh. 2013. Morphological Analysis and Disambiguation for Dialectal Arabic. In *Proceedings of the 2013 Conference of the North American Chapter of the Association for Computational Linguistics: Human Language Technologies*, pages 426–432, Atlanta, Georgia. Association for Computational Linguistics.

Ari Hautasaari. 2013. "Could someone please translate this?": activity analysis of wikipedia article translation by non-experts. In *Proceedings of the 2013 Conference on Computer Supported Cooperative Work*, CSCW '13, page 945–954, New York, NY, USA. Association for Computing Machinery.

Sarah Holland, Ahmed Hosny, Sarah Newman, Joshua Joseph, and Kasia Chmielinski. 2020. The Dataset Nutrition Label: A Framework to Drive Higher Data Quality Standards. *Data Protection and Privacy, Volume 12: Data Protection and Democracy*.

Cheng-Mao Hsu, Cheng te Li, Diego Sáez-Trumper, and Yi-Zhan Hsu. 2021. WikiContradiction: Detecting Self-Contradiction Articles on Wikipedia. *2021 IEEE International Conference on Big Data (Big Data)*, pages 427–436.

Ben Hutchinson, Andrew Smart, Alex Hanna, Emily Denton, Christina Greer, Oddur Kjartansson, Parker Barnes, and Margaret Mitchell. 2021. Towards Accountability for Machine Learning Datasets: Practices from Software Engineering and Infrastructure. In *Proceedings of the 2021 ACM Conference on Fairness, Accountability, and Transparency*, FAccT '21, page 560–575, New York, NY, USA. Association for Computing Machinery.

Serena Jeblee, Weston Feely, Houda Bouamor, Alon Lavie, Nizar Habash, and Kemal Oflazer. 2014. Domain and Dialect Adaptation for Machine Translation into Egyptian Arabic. In *Proceedings of the EMNLP 2014 Workshop on Arabic Natural Language Processing (ANLP)*, pages 196–206, Doha, Qatar. Association for Computational Linguistics.

Isaac Johnson. 2020. Analyzing Wikidata Transclusion on English Wikipedia. *CoRR*, abs/2011.00997.

Isaac Johnson and Emily A. Lescak. 2022. Considerations for Multilingual Wikipedia Research. *ArXiv*, abs/2204.02483.

Maria Lopez-Medel. 2021. Gender bias in machine translation: an analysis of Google Translate in English and Spanish. *Academia.edu*.

Margaret Mitchell, Simone Wu, Andrew Zaldivar, Parker Barnes, Lucy Vasserman, Ben Hutchinson, Elena Spitzer, Inioluwa Deborah Raji, and Timnit Gebru. 2019. Model Cards for Model Reporting. In *Proceedings of the Conference on Fairness, Accountability, and Transparency*, FAT* '19, page 220–229, New York, NY, USA. Association for Computing Machinery.

John Mittermeier, Ricardo Correia, Rich Grenyer, Tuuli Toivonen, and Uri Roll. 2021. Using wikipedia to measure public interest in biodiversity and conservation. *Conservation Biology*, 35.

Emad Mohamed, Behrang Mohit, and Kemal Oflazer. 2012. Transforming Standard Arabic to Colloquial Arabic. In *Proceedings of the 50th Annual Meeting of the Association for Computational Linguistics (Volume 2: Short Papers)*, pages 176–180, Jeju Island, Korea. Association for Computational Linguistics.

Sergiu Nisioi, Ella Rabinovich, Liviu P. Dinu, and Shuly Wintner. 2016. A Corpus of Native, Non-native and Translated Texts. In *Proceedings of the Tenth International Conference on Language Resources and Evaluation (LREC'16)*, pages 4197–4201, Portorož, Slovenia. European Language Resources Association (ELRA).

Matthew E. Peters, Mark Neumann, Mohit Iyyer, Matt Gardner, Christopher Clark, Kenton Lee, and Luke Zettlemoyer. 2018. Deep Contextualized Word Representations. In *Proceedings of the 2018 Conference of the North American Chapter of the Association for Computational Linguistics: Human Language Technologies*, pages 2227–2237, New Orleans, Louisiana. Association for Computational Linguistics.

Fabio Petroni, Tim Rocktäschel, Patrick S. H. Lewis, Anton Bakhtin, Yuxiang Wu, Alexander H. Miller, and Sebastian Riedel. 2019. Language Models as Knowledge Bases? *CoRR*, abs/1909.01066.

Gözde Gül Şahin. 2022. To Augment or Not to Augment? A Comparative Study on Text Augmentation Techniques for Low-Resource NLP. *Computational Linguistics*, 48(1):5–42.

Hassan Sajjad, Kareem Darwish, and Yonatan Belinkov. 2013a. Translating Dialectal Arabic to English. In *Proceedings of the 51st Annual Meeting of the Association for Computational Linguistics (Volume 2: Short Papers)*, pages 1–6, Sofia, Bulgaria. Association for Computational Linguistics.

Hassan Sajjad, Francisco Guzmán, Preslav Nakov, Ahmed Abdelali, Kenton Murray, Fahad Al Obaidli, and Stephan Vogel. 2013b. QCRI at IWSLT 2013: experiments in Arabic-English and English-Arabic spoken language translation. In *Proceedings of the 10th International Workshop on Spoken Language Translation: Evaluation Campaign*, Heidelberg, Germany.

Wael Salloum and Nizar Habash. 2013. Dialectal Arabic to English machine translation: Pivoting through Modern Standard Arabic. In *Proceedings of the 2013 Conference of the North American Chapter of the Association for Computational Linguistics: Human Language Technologies*, pages 348–358, Atlanta, Georgia. Association for Computational Linguistics.

Khaled Shaalan, Sanjeera Siddiqui, Manar Alkhatib, and Azza Monem. 2018. *Challenges in Arabic Natural Language Processing*. World Scientific.

Stefanie Ullmann and Danielle Saunders. 2021. Google Translate is sexist. What it needs is a little gender-sensitivity training. Last accessed on 2022-09-11.

Rodolfo V Valentim, Giovanni Comarela, Souneil Park, and Diego Sáez-Trumper. 2021. Tracking Knowledge Propagation Across Wikipedia Languages. In *ICWSM*, pages 1046–1052.

Esma Wali, Yan Chen, Christopher Mahoney, Thomas Middleton, Marzieh Babaeianjelodar, Mariama Njie, and Jeanna Neefe Matthews. 2020. Is Machine Learning Speaking my Language? A Critical Look at the NLP-Pipeline Across 8 Human Languages. *arXiv preprint arXiv:2007.05872*.

Alex Wang, Amanpreet Singh, Julian Michael, Felix Hill, Omer Levy, and Samuel Bowman. 2018. GLUE: A Multi-Task Benchmark and Analysis Platform for Natural Language Understanding. In *Proceedings of the 2018 EMNLP Workshop BlackboxNLP: Analyzing and Interpreting Neural Networks for NLP*, pages 353–355, Brussels, Belgium. Association for Computational Linguistics.

Wikimedia Foundation. 2022. Content Translation - Mediawiki. Last accessed on 2022-09-11.

Wikimedia Foundation. 2022a. Mediawiki Action API. Last accessed on 2022-09-11.

Wikimedia Foundation. 2022b. Wikimedia Statistics. Last accessed on 2022-09-11.

Wikimedia Foundation. 2022c. Wikistats Metrics Definition. Last accessed on 2022-09-11.

Wikipedia. 2022a. Founder of Wikipedia. Last accessed on 2022-09-11.

Wikipedia. 2022b. User: Hitomiakane. Last accessed on 2022-09-11.

Wikipedia. 2022c. Wikipedia – The Free Encyclopedia. Last accessed on 2022-09-11.

Wikipedia. 2022d. Wikipedia Article Depth. Last accessed on 2022-09-11.

Wikipedia. 2022e. Wikipedia: Bot Policy. Last accessed on 2022-09-11.

KayYen Wong, Miriam Redi, and Diego Sáez-Trumper. 2021. Wiki-Reliability: A Large Scale Dataset for Content Reliability on Wikipedia. *Proceedings of the 44th International ACM SIGIR Conference on Research and Development in Information Retrieval*.

Eddie Yang and Margaret E. Roberts. 2021. Censorship of Online Encyclopedias: Implications for NLP Models. In *Proceedings of the 2021 ACM Conference on Fairness, Accountability, and Transparency*, FAccT '21, page 537–548, New York, NY, USA. Association for Computing Machinery.

Rabih Zbib, Erika Malchiodi, Jacob Devlin, David Stallard, Spyros Matsoukas, Richard Schwartz, John Makhoul, Omar F. Zaidan, and Chris Callison-Burch. 2012. Machine Translation of Arabic Dialects. In *Proceedings of the 2012 Conference of the North American Chapter of the Association for Computational Linguistics: Human Language Technologies*, pages 49–59, Montréal, Canada. Association for Computational Linguistics.

Yukun Zhu, Ryan Kiros, Rich Zemel, Ruslan Salakhutdinov, Raquel Urtasun, Antonio Torralba, and Sanja Fidler. 2015. Aligning Books and Movies: Towards Story-Like Visual Explanations by Watching Movies and Reading Books. In *2015 IEEE International Conference on Computer Vision*, pages 19–27.

A Wikistats-to-CSV (wikistats2csv)

Wikistats-to-CSV (`wikistats2csv`) downloads Wikipedia statistics for a given Wikipedia in a CSV file format to make the online Wikimedia Statistics (Wikistats) service more accessible than it is. AI and NLP researchers and practitioners mostly use Python programming language as their first choice, and bringing this service to them as a package or command line tool saves them time and ease downloading more than one statistical CSV file in a few lines of code. We have implemented Wikistats' three major metrics and their sub-metrics. Wikistats-to-CSV currently supports 20 queries or functions, 76 time periods, 144 filters, and 40 time intervals. We also added extra features, such as listing all Wikipedia languages with their codes, and we plan to add more features in future releases.

A Pilot Study on the Collection and Computational Analysis of Linguistic Differences Amongst Men and Women in a Kuwaiti Arabic WhatsApp Dataset

Hesah Aldihan[1,2] and **Robert Gaizauskas**[1] and **Susan Fitzmaurice**[1]
[1] University of Sheffield, UK
[2]University of Kuwait, Kuwait
{haldihan1,r.gaizauskas,s.fitzmaurice}@sheffield.ac.uk

Abstract

This study focuses on the collection and computational analysis of Kuwaiti Arabic, which is considered a low resource dialect, to test different sociolinguistic hypotheses related to gendered language use. In this paper, we describe the collection and analysis of a corpus of WhatsApp Group chats with mixed gender Kuwaiti participants. This corpus, which we are making publicly available, is the first corpus of Kuwaiti Arabic conversational data. We analyse different interactional and linguistic features to get insights about features that may be indicative of gender to inform the development of a gender classification system for Kuwaiti Arabic in an upcoming study. Statistical analysis of our data shows that there is insufficient evidence to claim that there are significant differences amongst men and women with respect to number of turns, length of turns and number of emojis. However, qualitative analysis shows that men and women differ substantially in the types of emojis they use and in their use of lengthened words.

1 Introduction

A wide range of sociolinguistic gender studies have been carried out in English speaking cultures and in the Arab world too. However, there is a lack of research on Gulf Arabic (GA) dialects, and especially the Kuwaiti dialect, from a sociolinguistic perspective. The GA dialects vary tremendously with regards to morpho-phonological features, lexical structures and the effect of language borrowing from different languages (Khalifa et al., 2016). There are some interesting linguistic phenomena in the Kuwaiti dialect. The way men and women speak is different and this can be noticed in their choice of words when communicating or expressing feelings or reacting to situations. It can be noticed that there are some words which men would refrain from using because they represent femininity. For example, the word اينن "eyanen", which means "amazing" is a word used to convey a positive sentiment towards an entity and is usually only used by women. This word can for example be used to describe a movie by Kuwaiti women, whereas men might use the word جبار "jbar" which is a polysemous adjective that in this context means "amazing", to describe the movie. Moreover, يا حافظ "ya hafeth" is a phrase that is only used by women. It can be translated into "Oh saviour (God)" to convey dissatisfaction or disappointment. If a man uses this expression, he would be described as someone who is feminine in the way he speaks.

Advances in the field of Arabic Natural Language Processing (ANLP) have made it possible to study such variation in lexical usage between genders as well to explore other features that are indicative of gender. However, the lack of KA textual resources and preprocessing tools make it a challenging task.

This study contributes to the field of ANLP in two ways. First, we have compiled and made publicly available a new, gender-labelled KA dataset, which can be used by researchers interested in the Kuwaiti dialect or gender studies. This dataset consists of textual book club conversations conducted on the WhatsApp online instant messaging mobile application. To the best of our knowledge this is the first published dataset of mixed gender KA conversational data. Second, we have carried out an analysis of interactional and linguistic features that may inform the development of a gender classification system for KA.

This paper is structured as follows. In the next section we review related work. In section 3 we first discuss how we have collected the raw data, then describe how this raw data has been preprocessed to prepare the dataset for analysis and finally discuss the features that will be explored and analysed. In section 4 we present our results and analysis. Finally, we conclude and discuss future work, as well as pointing out some of the limitations of

Proceedings of the The Seventh Arabic Natural Language Processing Workshop (WANLP), pages 372 - 380
December 8, 2022 ©2022 Association for Computational Linguistics

our work.

2 Related Work

Language is a rich source for analysis and many studies have been conducted to infer the relationship between different social variables and the language they construct (Holmes and Meyerhoff, 2008; Eckert and McConnell-Ginet, 2013). One of the social variables that is studied in relation to language is gender. Traditional studies of language and gender that have been conducted in the humanities and social sciences have had inconsistent findings and have received some criticism. For example, Wareing (1996) criticised conclusions drawn about the relationship between language and gender that are dependent on small samples of data. The implication of this criticism is that gender and language studies should be improved by using larger samples of data and different contexts (Litosseliti and Sunderland, 2002). However, now that we are in the era of 'big data', extracting large amounts of data for gender analysis has become possible. Moreover, sociolinguistic studies of gender have mostly been explored using qualitative methods such as interviews, surveys, recordings and manual observations. Bamman et al. (2014) argue that qualitative and quantitative analysis of sociolinguistic gender studies are complementary as qualitative analysis may shed light on phenomena and quantitative analysis provides the opportunity to explore phenomena through large scale studies and also identify cases that can be analysed qualitatively. Litosseliti and Sunderland (2002) explain:

> Language and gender may, then, legitimately be viewed from different perspectives: a pragmatic combination of methods and approaches, along with an acknowledgment of their possibilities and limitations, might allow us to focus on different aspects of the relationship between language and gender, or have a wider range of things to say about this.

In the context of studies that have explored gender differences in language use, Rosenfeld et al. (2016) looked into gender differences in language usage of WhatsApp groups. They analysed over 4 million WhatsApp messages from more than 100 users to find and understand differences between different age and gender demographic groups. In analysing the data, they relied on metadata only such as message lengths, size of the WhatsApp groups, time, average number of sentences sent per day, time between messages. In relation to gender, analysing the length of messages sent by both genders showed that women send and receive more messages than men. They also concluded that women are more active in small WhatsApp groups, whereas men are more active in larger WhatsApp groups. These differences were then employed in building age and gender prediction models. They performed a 10-fold cross validation for these tasks using decision trees and a Bayesian network. For the gender prediction task, using users' metadata with decision trees achieved 70.27% accuracy and 73.87% accuracy when used with a Bayesian network.

Other studies have looked into differences amongst genders in the use of emojis. Chen et al. (2018) compiled a large dataset of 401 million smartphone messages in 58 different languages and labelled them according to the gender of users. They used emojis from the dataset to study how they are used by males and females in terms of emoji frequency, emoji preference and sentiment conveyed by the emojis. They also studied the extent in which emojis are indicative of gender when used in a gender classification system. The results obtained from this study showed that not only are there considerable differences in the use of emojis between males and females, but also that a gender classification system that uses emojis alone as features can achieve an accuracy of 81%.

Shared NLP tasks that are organized for the research community have started off by tackling problems with the English language and in recent years have added Arabic datasets, reflecting the increasing interest in Arabic NLP. For example, the PAN 2017 Author Profiling Shared Task included two tasks: gender identification and language variety identification of Twitter users. Arabic, English, Portuguese, and Spanish datasets consisting of tweets were provided for training and testing. The system that achieved the highest accuracy result on gender identification in the Arabic dataset was the system developed by Basile et al. (2017). They used an SVM classifier in combination with word unigrams and character 3- to 5-grams and achieved an accuracy of 0.80.

As for studies that have targeted the Arabic language, Alsmearat et al. (2014) studied gender text classification of Arabic articles using the Bag-of-

Words (BoW) approach. They collected and manually labelled 500 Arabic articles from different Arabic news websites. The number of articles was distributed equally across both genders. They wanted to explore the result of performing feature reduction techniques such as PCA and correlation analysis on the high-dimensional data in combination with different machine learning algorithms for the gender classification task. Results showed that Stochastic Gradient Descent (SGD), Naive Bayes Multinomial (NBM) and Support Vector Machines (SVM) were the classifiers that performed best on the original dataset where the accuracy results surpassed 90%.

Furthermore, Mubarak et al. (2022) compiled a dataset of 166K Arabic tweets and labelled them with gender and geo location labels. They used this dataset for gender analysis and to build a gender classification system using SVMs that was tested on different features such as usernames of the twitter users, the profile pictures of the users, tweets and gender distribution of users' friends. Their study showed that using usernames alone as features for gender prediction achieved the highest F1 score of 82.1 %. In addition, Hussein et al. (2019) attempted to build a gender classification system for Egyptian Arabic. They created a dataset of 140K tweets that were retrieved from famous Egyptian influencers and active Egyptian users of Twitter. They labelled the dataset according to the gender of the Twitter users by referring to the users' profile image and names. They experimented with different features such as gender discriminative emojis, female suffixes, manually created dictionaries of swear words, emotion words, political words, flirting words, technological words and word embeddings. They used ensemble weighted average on a mixed feature vector fed into a Random Forest classifier and an N-gram feature vector fed into a Logistic Regression classifier. They achieved an accuracy score of 87.6%.

Not many gender studies in NLP have provided much insight into linguistic characteristics of gendered language, especially those related to dialectal Arabic. Furthermore, the field of ANLP still lacks enough dialectal arabic datasets to help inform the development of Arabic natural language processing tools. Khalifa et al. (2016) compiled Gumar corpus which consists of 100 million GA words from 1200 forum novels annotated according to the dialect, novel name and writer name. The corpus was also used to develop dialectal Arabic orthography. However, although Gumar corpus contains some KA text, the text is not naturally occuring conversational KA. Therefore, there is still a need to compile conversational KA resources. We aim to address this gap by contributing towards providing resources for the KA dialect and analysing sociolinguistic features of that dialect that can be used to inform NLP applications, such as gender classification systems.

3 Methodology

3.1 Data Collection

Since we are interested in studying the features of conversational data of Kuwaiti men and women, we chose to collect textual data from WhatsApp reading club groups.

As part of the data collection process, we applied for ethical approval before conducting the study. This involved ensuring that all participants were aware of the nature and purpose of the study and their role in it. We obtained informed consent from all participants.

The dataset was collected from three Kuwaiti reading club WhatsApp groups. These were already existing WhatsApp reading club groups that have been running for years and are managed by Kuwaiti admins. All participants were native Kuwaiti speakers whose first language is KA. The researcher was added to the groups to be able to export the chat after 9 months of being added. The chats were then exported from the mobile phone and saved in the researcher's computer for processing.

The dataset consists of 4479 turns (2623 turns by females and 1856 turns by males). The dataset will be made publicly available for researchers in the research field.[1]

3.2 Preprocessing

A number of steps were taken prior to exporting the chats from the researcher's mobile. This involved anonymising the names of the WhatsApp members. The usernames were replaced with the word "USER" concatenated with a number and a letter to represent the gender of the user (e.g, USER1F). The chats were then exported to the researcher's computer to prepare the data for computational pro-

[1] Interested parties can contact the first author for dataset access.

Gender		Emoji Count	Word Count	Num of Turns
Women (28 participants)	Total Number	2144	17388	2623
	Mean	76	621	94
	Median	23	163	29
	Std. Deviation	123	1132	144
	Minimum	2	6	2
	Maximum	506	5611	655
Men (14 participants)	Total Number	801	14005	1856
	Mean	57	1000	133
	Median	36	432	102
	Std. Deviation	68	1197	134
	Minimum	1	5	3
	Maximum	249	3941	444

Table 1: Descriptive Statistics of the Features Analysed

cessing. The following preprocessing steps were performed:

1. All sensitive and personal information was removed.
2. Real names that were mentioned in the chat were replaced with fictitious names.
3. URL links were removed.
4. Two versions of the dataset were created using the CAMel tools, built by Obeid et al. (2020), for preprocessing: one that involves tokenisation, removal of digits, diacritics and punctuation and changing alef variants to ا and alef maksura to ي and teh marbuta to ه; and another version that involves tokenisation and punctuatation removal. Depending on the type of textual analysis required, the dataset version was chosen.

3.3 Feature Analysis

We were interested in exploring interactional features and lexical features pertaining to the KA dialect. We chose to study how the following features were used amongst men and women participating in the study:

- Number of turns per gender.
- Length of turns per gender (word count).
- Use of emojis amongst females and males, especially in the context of the view that certain emjois are considered too feminine and others too masculine in the Kuwaiti society.
- Whether there are KA words or expressions that are exclusive to each gender.
- Most frequently used words.
- Lengthened or elongated words.

Table 1. presents the descriptive statistics of the first three features.

4 Results and Analysis

To analyse the results of this study, two approaches were taken: a quantitative statistical approach and a qualitative linguistic approach. As for the statistical approach, the Mann Whitney U test was used for analysis due to it being suitable for data, like ours, which is not normally distributed. It was done using SPSS [2]. One limitation of using a statistical approach in analysing the data is that it does not take into account the contextual information and meanings embedded within the text. Therefore, it was important to perform an in-depth manual analysis of the data to be able to describe the patterns found and provide interpretations for points that the statistical analysis could not capture.

4.1 Quantitative Analysis

We tested the distribution of each feature using normality tests, namely Shapiro-Wilk test (sample size less than 50) which indicated that the features were not normally distributed P values: (< 0.01). The Mann Whitney U test was used to test if there are significant differences between men and women

[2]Statistical Package for the Social Sciences: a statistical analysis software package. https://www.ibm.com/products/spss-statistics

with regards to three features: number of emojis used in the chat, number of turns taken, and total number of words (word count) for each user. This test is based on two hypotheses; a null hypothesis (H_0):

> H_0: states that there is no significant difference between men and women with regards to the features mentioned above.

and an alternative hypothesis (H_1):

> H_1 : states that there is a significant difference between men and women with regards to the features tested.

The hypotheses are accepted or rejected after comparing the P values to the threshold (0.05).

As can be seen in Table.2, all the P - values for all the features are larger than 0.05. This means that we lack enough evidence to suggest that there are significant differences between men and women in terms of number of emojis used, number of turns taken and word count.

In the following subsections, we look into the analysis of each feature in detail.

4.1.1 Number of Turns

We were interested in analysing the number of turns used by each user and gender. We were also interested in computing the percentage of turns for men and women from the total number of turns. We noticed that 59% of the total number of turns were by women, and the remaining 41% of turns were by men. However, the ratio of women to men in the corpus is 2:1 and based on the results we obtained from Mann Whitney U test: (women: median= 29, IQR = 105), (men: median= 102, IQR = 198), P - value > 0.05 as shown in Table 1, we lack enough evidence to suggest that there is a significant difference amongst men and women in terms of number of turns.

4.1.2 Length of Turns/ Word Count

The length of turns was computed to test the hypothesis that women speak more than men. This was done by counting the total number of words used in the chats for each user and the total word counts for each gender. Details are shown in Table 1.

On average, men speak more than woman (1000 words per male participant vs 621 words per female participant). However, Mann Whitney U test results for word counts (women: median= 163, IQR = 582), (men: median= 432, IQR = 1778), P - value > 0.05 as shown in Table 1, suggest that we lack enough evidence to claim that there is a significant difference amongst men and women in word usage.

We were also interested in comparing the average number of words per turn for women as compared with men. Referring to Table 1 we can see that for women the average number of words per turn is 17388/2623 = 6.62 while for men the average words per turn is 14005/1856 = 7.55. The difference here does not appear to be that great, but we have not carried out statistical analysis to see if that difference is significant.

4.1.3 Emoji Usage

We were interested in analysing how likely it is for men and women to use emojis when interacting in the chat groups. We noticed that on average women used .82 emojis per turn, while men used on average .43 emojis per turn. Therefore, the odds of using emojis amongst women compared to men is 1.9:1, indicating that women were almost 2 times more likely to use emojis than men. However, based on the results we retrieved from Mann Whitney U test: (women: median= 23, IQR = 84), (men: median= 36, IQR = 95), P - value > 0.05 as shown in Table 1, we lack enough evidence to suggest that there is a significant difference amongst men and women in emoji usage.

Nonetheless, it was important to explore the types of emojis, exclusivity of emojis and patterns of emojis used by men and women to achieve a better understanding of emoji usage amongst genders. This is discussed in the following section.

4.2 Qualitative Analysis

4.2.1 Frequency and Types of Emojis

Emojis were significant features observed in the group chats and were commonly used by both men and women. Women used a total of 2144 emojis, while men used a total of 801 emojis. As for the types of emojis used, various differences were observed. Emojis used by women are from a wide range of emoji categories and are colorful, whereas men used a limited set of emojis from certain categories. 68% of women used heart emojis, whereas only 29% of men used heart emojis. It was also noticed that women used different types and colors of heart emojis. However, men used limited heart emojis ❤️, 💔, 💕. Further more, women used a large variety of flowers and plants 🌷, 🌺, 🌻, 💐,

Features	P Value	U Value	Median of Females	Median of Males
Num of Emojis	0.779	185.500	23.00	35.50
Num of Turns	0.298	157.00	29.00	101.50
Word Count	0.350	161.00	163.00	431.50

Table 2: Mann-Whitney Test Results for Emojis, Number of Turns and Word Count Features

	Women		Men	
Rank	Emoji	Count	Emoji	Count
1	👏	218	👍	156
2	🙏	211	😂	143
3	😍	193	🌹	43
4	👍	140	🤣	42
5	🌸	116	😄	28
6	❤️	95	😊	26
7	😂	91	💕	20
8	🌹	85	😜	18
9	💐	75	☺️	17
10	🌷	75	😍	15

Table 3: Top Ten Emojis Used by Kuwaiti Men and Women

🌸, 🌹, 🌱, 🌿, whereas men used only two types of flowers 🌷 and 🌹.

The analysis also involved computing the 10 most frequently used emojis by men and women as shown in Table 3. As it can be seen, the top used emojis for both men and women are (👏 and 👍) which shows that both men and women are encouraging and applauding each other. It was observed that men used (😂 and 👍) significantly more than all the other emojis extracted, which were mainly smileys. In comparing the top 10 lists of emojis by men and women, it was noticed that women used 😍 (193 times) notably higher than men (15 times) and used flowers more than smileys as opposed to men.

4.2.2 Exclusivity of Emojis

There are some stereotypes regarding emoji usage such as that there are certain emojis that are not used by men due to them implying a feminine sense and other emojis not used by women because they are masculine. This study examined this stereotype to explore if this can be considered a feature indicative of gender. The emojis that were exclusively used by each gender were extracted and compared. It was noticed that men refrained from using certain emojis that are stereo-typically considered feminine and were used by women in the group chats such as 💋, 😚, 😻, 😌, 💖, 💜, 💕, 💕, 💜, 🦋. This observation also supports the hypothesis that women are more emotionally expressive than men (Goldshmidt and Weller, 2000). The emojis that were exclusively used by men mainly consisted of male character emojis such as 👨, 👨‍💻, 👨, 🚶, 🏃.

4.2.3 Patterns of Emoji Usage

A number of observations were made related to patterns of emoji usage. Women used a larger variety of emojis across different categories (smileys and people, activity, travel and places, food and drink , nature .. etc) than men to express themselves. Men used limited types of emojis from certain categories (smileys and people, nature) and very limited use of hearts or emojis that express emotions.

A pattern was also noticed regarding the number of emojis used per turn. Most users used one or two emojis in a turn and this lead to interest in analysing bigrams of emojis used by men and women to explore if there are any patterns of use or certain emoji combinations used. The most frequently used bigrams consisted of the same emoji repeated rather than a combination of two different emojis. It was observed that certain combinations were used significantly more by each gender. For example, 😂😂 was used 70 times by men and 38 times by women, 😍😍 was used 3 times by men and 64 times by women, and 👏👏 was used 4 times by men and 80 times by women. This showed certain emoji combinations may be used with different frequencies amongst men and women.

4.2.4 KA Lexical choices and Features

Other exploratory data analysis was conducted to analyse the lexical choices amongst men and women in the WhatsApp groups. Features such as the most frequently used words, the exclusively used words and other lexical features were analysed.
Analysis regarding the most frequently used words showed that the word "Allah", "الله" was one of

the highly repeated words amongst both men (262 times) and women (325 times). "Allah" means "God" and could appear in a sentence as a separate word or part of a phrase such as "masha'Allah",ماشاءالله which is an expression used to express appreciation when someone hears good news, and "inshaAllah", ان شاءالله which is an expression used to convey willingness to do something. The high repetition of these phrases could indicate cooperativeness and politeness in the conversations. The word "alketab" الكتاب which means "book" was also amongst the highest repeated words amongst men (32 times) and women (99 times). This is due to the conversations mainly revolving around reading books. Figure 1 and Figure 2 show the most frequent words in both the women's and men's chats.

Analysis was also done on the exclusively used words amongst both men and women. One aim of extracting the gender exclusive words was to find KA gendered words that denote femininity or masculinity to inform the development of a gender classification system. However, due to the formal nature of the reading club WhatsApp groups, only a few examples of this phenomenon were captured and they were mostly in women's messages. Some of the examples of female exclusive words found are: "shatoora" شطورة , meaning "smart girl", "b'khatri" بخاطري meaning "I really want ..", "habeebty" حبيبتي , meaning "my dear", "s'ghairoona" صغيروووونه, meaning "very small", "katkoota" كتكوووته , meaning "so cute" and "please" بليز.

Analysis of the chat also showed high occurrence of lengthened or elongated words which are words that include repeated letters to emphasise different meanings such as هههههههه "hhhhhhhhh" expressing laughter and واااااو "wooooow" expressing amazement. Lengthened words can be indicators of expressing feelings which is stereotypically attached to women's speech, and therefore we wanted to test this hypothesis by determining the number of lengthened words used by men and women per turn on average. There were some interesting observations. Women used 0.057 lengthened words per turn on average (so about once per 18 turns), whereas men used 0.037 (about once in 28 turns). This indicates that women tend to lengthen words roughly 1.5 times as often as men. After performing further inspection to the lengthened words, it was observed that women tend to perform this with a large variety of words when laughing هههههه "hhhhhh" , complimenting جمممميله"beautifuuuul", congratulating مبروووك "congraaatulations" , encouraging برااافووووو "bravooooo" , agreeing ايي "yeees" , greeting صباح النوووور "good mooorning" and expressing feelings such as missing the members مشتاقيين "miiis you". However, men's use of lengthened words were less diverse. They mostly used lengthening when laughing هههههههههه "hhhhhhhhhhh" and greeting هلاا "hiii".

Figure 1: Most Frequent Words Used by Women

Figure 2: Most Frequent Words Used by Men

5 Conclusion

We have described the first publicly available dataset of conversational Kuwaiti Arabic that is labelled by gender. We analysed the dataset by looking into interactional and linguistic features that are performed in mixed gender WhatsApp groups. We described the WhatsApp data collection process and analysed features such as number of turns, length of turns, emoji counts and Kuwaiti Arabic lexical features. Statistical analysis shows that our dataset does not allow us to conclude that significant differences between men's and women's language exist with respect to the features number of turns, length of turns, and number of emojis used. However, substantial differences in these features are observed. Furthermore, qualitative analysis of other features such as the range and specific types of emojis used, certain lexical choices and the phenomenon of word lengthening revealed considerable differences between women and men's language use.

Going forward we intend to build a gender classification system for Kuwaiti Arabic trained and tested on the dataset reported here. We intend to use insights gained in the study reported here to inform our feature selection, with the longer term aim of better understanding differences in men and women's language use in Kuwaiti Arabic.

Limitations

Our study is limited in several ways. The first relates to the dataset as a basis for studying differences in men and women's language differences in conversational KA. The compiled dataset is of limited size and unbalanced in gender labels. Since we wanted to study KA conversational data, it was only possible to get ethical approval for formal WhatsApp groups. This had an impact on both size and type of data collected. The size of data was subject to participants' level of interaction in the WhatsApp groups. Furthermore, the type of conversational data collected tends to have a formal tone due to the groups conversation revolving around discussing books. This means there may be a lack of certain sociolinguistic phenomena being present in the conversations. Moreover, the language usage of participants who are book club readers may not be representative of the KA dialect more generally. The second sort of limitations pertain to the restricted amount of analysis carried out as yet on our dataset. To date we have not built a gender classification system using this dataset to see, for example, how well word or emoji unigrams or bigrams might serve as a basis for predicting gender. As noted above in section 5, this is next on our agenda.

Ethics Statement

To gather the data we submitted an application to the University of Sheffield Ethics Review process and had this application approved. Participants were provided with an information sheet describing the aims and objectives of our research, what they would be expected to do, what data we would collect, how that data would be used and how it would be stored. We then obtained informed consent from each participant for our proposed work. Regarding potential use of our work we see both potential benefits and potential harms. On the benefits side, better understanding of the differences in language use between genders may help us identify and better understand the causes of these differences. Insights from this could lead to change in perception of gender roles and positive change in gender equality. On the negative side, ability to predict gender from language use could lead to targeting of individuals in various ways including advertising, political messaging or even persecution for expressing certain beliefs.

Acknowledgements

The authors would like to thank the reading club group members that participated in the study. We would also like to thank the statisticians who helped out with the analysis and the University of Kuwait for funding this work.

References

Kholoud Alsmearat, Mahmoud Al-Ayyoub, and Riyad Al-Shalabi. 2014. An extensive study of the bag-of-words approach for gender identification of arabic articles. In *2014 IEEE/ACS 11th International Conference on Computer Systems and Applications (AICCSA)*, pages 601–608. IEEE.

David Bamman, Jacob Eisenstein, and Tyler Schnoebelen. 2014. Gender identity and lexical variation in social media. *Journal of Sociolinguistics*, 18(2):135–160.

Angelo Basile, Gareth Dwyer, Maria Medvedeva, Josine Rawee, Hessel Haagsma, and Malvina Nissim. 2017. N-gram: New groningen author-profiling model. *arXiv preprint arXiv:1707.03764*.

Zhenpeng Chen, Xuan Lu, Wei Ai, Huoran Li, Qiaozhu Mei, and Xuanzhe Liu. 2018. Through a gender lens: Learning usage patterns of emojis from large-scale android users. In *Proceedings of the 2018 World Wide Web Conference*, pages 763–772.

Penelope Eckert and Sally McConnell-Ginet. 2013. *Language and gender*. Cambridge University Press.

Orly Turgeman Goldshmidt and Leonard Weller. 2000. talking emotions: Gender differences in a variety of conversational contexts. *Symbolic Interaction*, 23(2):117–134.

Janet Holmes and Miriam Meyerhoff. 2008. *The handbook of language and gender*, volume 25. John Wiley & Sons.

Shereen Hussein, Mona Farouk, and ElSayed Hemayed. 2019. Gender identification of egyptian dialect in twitter. *Egyptian Informatics Journal*, 20(2):109–116.

Salam Khalifa, Nizar Habash, Dana Abdulrahim, and Sara Hassan. 2016. A large scale corpus of gulf arabic. *arXiv preprint arXiv:1609.02960*.

Lia Litosseliti and Jane Sunderland. 2002. *Gender identity and discourse analysis*, volume 2. John Benjamins Publishing.

Hamdy Mubarak, Shammur Absar Chowdhury, and Firoj Alam. 2022. Arabgend: Gender analysis and inference on arabic twitter. *arXiv preprint arXiv:2203.00271*.

Ossama Obeid, Nasser Zalmout, Salam Khalifa, Dima Taji, Mai Oudah, Bashar Alhafni, Go Inoue, Fadhl Eryani, Alexander Erdmann, and Nizar Habash. 2020. CAMeL tools: An open source python toolkit for Arabic natural language processing. In *Proceedings of the 12th Language Resources and Evaluation Conference*, pages 7022–7032, Marseille, France. European Language Resources Association.

Avi Rosenfeld, Sigal Sina, David Sarne, Or Avidov, and Sarit Kraus. 2016. Whatsapp usage patterns and prediction models. In *ICWSM/IUSSP Workshop on Social Media and Demographic Research*.

Shan Wareing. 1996. What do we know about language and gender. In *eleventh sociolinguistic symposium, Cardiff, September*, pages 5–7.

Beyond Arabic: Software for Perso-Arabic Script Manipulation

Alexander Gutkin[†] **Cibu Johny**[†] **Raiomond Doctor**[‡*] **Brian Roark**[○] **Richard Sproat**[⊛]
Google Research
[†]United Kingdom [‡]India [○]United States [⊛]Japan
{agutkin,cibu,raiomond,roark,rws}@google.com

Abstract

This paper presents an open-source software library that provides a set of finite-state transducer (FST) components and corresponding utilities for manipulating the writing systems of languages that use the Perso-Arabic script. The operations include various levels of script normalization, including visual invariance-preserving operations that subsume and go beyond the standard Unicode normalization forms, as well as transformations that modify the visual appearance of characters in accordance with the regional orthographies for eleven contemporary languages from diverse language families. The library also provides simple FST-based romanization and transliteration. We additionally attempt to formalize the typology of Perso-Arabic characters by providing one-to-many mappings from Unicode code points to the languages that use them. While our work focuses on the Arabic script diaspora rather than Arabic itself, this approach could be adopted for any language that uses the Arabic script, thus providing a unified framework for treating a script family used by close to a billion people.

1 Introduction

While originally developed for recording Arabic, the Perso-Arabic script has gradually become one of the most widely used modern scripts. Throughout history the script was adapted to record many languages from diverse language families, with scores of adaptations still active today. This flexibility is partly due to the core features of the script itself which over the time evolved from a purely consonantal script to include a productive system of diacritics for representing long vowels and optional marking of short vowels and phonological processes such as gemination (Bauer, 1996; Kurzon, 2013). Consequently, many languages productively evolved their own adaptation of the Perso-Arabic script to better suit their phonology by not only augmenting the set of diacritics but also introducing new consonant shapes.

This paper presents an open-source software library designed to deal with the ambiguities and inconsistencies that result from representing various regional Perso-Arabic adaptations in digital media. Some of these issues are due to the Unicode standard itself, where a Perso-Arabic character can often be represented in more than one way (Unicode Consortium, 2021). Others are due to the lack or inadequacies of input methods and the instability of modern orthographies for the languages in question (Aazim et al., 2009; Liljegren, 2018). Such issues percolate through the data available online, such as Wikipedia and Common Crawl (Patel, 2020), negatively impacting the quality of NLP models built with such data. The script normalization software described below goes beyond the standard language-agnostic Unicode approach for Perso-Arabic to help alleviate some of these issues.

The library design is inspired by and consistent with prior work by Johny et al. (2021), introduced in §2, who provided a suite of finite-state grammars for various normalization and (reversible) romanization operations for the Brahmic family of scripts.[1] While the Perso-Arabic script and the respective set of regional orthographies we support – Balochi, Kashmiri, Kurdish (Sorani), Malay (Jawi), Pashto, Persian, Punjabi (Shahmukhi), Sindhi, South Azerbaijani, Urdu and Uyghur – is significantly different from those Brahmic scripts, we pursue a similar finite-state interpretation,[2] as described in §3. Implementation details and simple validation are provided in §4.

[*] On contract from Optimum Solutions, Inc.

[1] https://github.com/google-research/nisaba

[2] https://github.com/google-research/nisaba/tree/main/nisaba/scripts/abjad_alphabet

Proceedings of the The Seventh Arabic Natural Language Processing Workshop (WANLP), pages 381 - 387
December 8, 2022

2 Related Work

The approach we take in this paper follows in spirit the work of Johny et al. (2021) and Gutkin et al. (2022), who developed a finite-state script normalization framework for Brahmic scripts. We adopt their taxonomy and terminology of low-level script normalization operations, which consist of three types: Unicode-endorsed schemes, such as NFC; further visually-invariant transformations (*visual* normalization); and transformations that modify a character's shape but preserve pronunciation and the overall word identity (*reading* normalization).

The literature on Perso-Arabic script normalization for languages we cover in this paper is scarce. The most relevant work was carried out by Ahmadi (2020) for Kurdish, who provides a detailed analysis of orthographic issues peculiar to Sorani Kurdish along with corresponding open-source script normalization software used in downstream NLP applications, such as neural machine translation (Ahmadi and Masoud, 2020). In the context of machine transliteration and spell checking, Lehal and Saini (2014) included language-agnostic minimal script normalization as a preprocessing step in their open-source n-gram-based transliterator from Perso-Arabic to Brahmic scripts. Bhatti et al. (2014) introduced a taxonomy of spelling errors for Sindhi, including an analysis of mistakes due to visually confusable characters. Razak et al. (2018) provide a good overview of confusable characters for Malay Jawi orthography. For other languages the regional writing system ambiguities are sometimes mentioned in passing, but do not constitute the main focus of work, as is the case with Punjabi Shahmukhi (Lehal and Saini, 2012) and Urdu (Humayoun et al., 2022). The specific Perso-Arabic script ambiguities that abound in the online data are often not exhaustively documented, particularly in work focused on multilingual modeling (N. C., 2022; Bapna et al., 2022). As one moves towards lesser-resourced languages, such as Kashmiri and Uyghur, the NLP literature provides no treatment of script normalization issues and the only reliable sources of information are the proposal and discussion documents from the Unicode Technical Committee (e.g., Bashir et al., 2006; Aazim et al., 2009; Pournader, 2014). A forthcoming paper by Doctor et al. (2022) covers the writing system differences between these languages in more detail than we can include in this short paper.

Op. Type	FST	Language-dep.	Includes
NFC	$\mathcal{N}$	no	–
Common Visual	$\mathcal{V}_c$	no	$\mathcal{N}$
Visual	$\mathcal{V}$	yes	$\mathcal{V}_c$
Reading	$\mathcal{R}$	yes	–
Romanization	$\mathcal{M}$	no	$\mathcal{V}_c$
Transliteration	$\mathcal{T}$	no	–

Table 1: Summary of script transformation operations.

One area particularly relevant to this study is the work by the Internet Corporation for Assigned Names and Numbers (ICANN) towards developing a robust set of standards for representing various Internet entities in Perso-Arabic script, such as domain names in URLs. Their particular focus is on *variants*, which are characters that are visually confusable due to identical appearance but different encoding, due to similarity in shape or due to common alternate spellings (ICANN, 2011). In addition, they developed the first proposal to systematize the available Perso-Arabic Unicode code points along the regional lines (ICANN, 2015). These studies are particularly important for cybersecurity (Hussain et al., 2016; Ginsberg and Yu, 2018; Ahmad and Erdodi, 2021), but also inform this work.

This software library is, to the best our knowledge, the first attempt to provide a principled approach to Perso-Arabic script normalization for multiple languages, for downstream NLP applications and beyond.

3 Design Methodology

The core components are implemented as individual FSTs that can be efficiently combined together in a single pipeline (Mohri, 2009). These are shown in Table 1 and described below.[3]

Unicode Normalization For the Perso-Arabic string encodings which yield visually identical text, the Unicode standard provides procedures that normalize text to a conventionalized normal form, such as the well-known Normalization Form C (NFC), so that visually identical words are mapped to a conventionalized representative of their equivalence class (Whistler, 2021). We implemented the NFC standard as an FST, denoted $\mathcal{N}$ in Table 1, that handles three broad types of transformations: compositions, re-orderings and

[3]When referring to names of Unicode characters we lowercase them and omit the common prefix *arabic* (*letter*).

FST	Letter	Variant (source)	Canonical
$\mathcal{V}_l^*$	⟨ڗ⟩	*reh + small high tah*	*rreh*
$\mathcal{V}_l^{\mathrm{n}}$	⟨ک⟩	*kaf*	*keheh*
$\mathcal{V}_l^{\mathrm{f}}$	⟨ى⟩	*alef maksura*	*farsi yeh*
$\mathcal{V}_l^{\mathrm{i}}$	⟨ه⟩	*heh*	*heh goal*

Table 2: Example FST components of $\mathcal{V}_l$ for Urdu.

combinations thereof.

As an example of a first type, consider the *alef with madda above* letter ⟨آ⟩ that can be composed in two ways: as a single character (U+0622) or by adjoining *maddah above* to *alef* ({ U+0627, U+0653 }). The FST $\mathcal{N}$ rewrites the adjoined form into its equivalent composed form. The second type of transformation involves the canonical re-ordering of the Arabic combining marks, for example, the sequence of *shadda* (U+0651) followed by *kasra* (U+0650) is reversed by $\mathcal{N}$. More complex transformations that combine both compositions and re-orderings are possible. For example, the sequence { *alef* (U+0627), *superscript alef* (U+0670), *maddah above* (U+0653) } normalizes to its equivalent form { *alef with madda above* (U+0622), *superscript alef* (U+0670) }.

Crucially, $\mathcal{N}$ is language-agnostic because the NFC standard it implements does not define any transformations that violate the writing system rules of respective languages.

Visual Normalization As mentioned in §2, Johny et al. (2021) introduced the term *visual* normalization in the context of Brahmic scripts to denote visually-invariant transformations that fall outside the scope of NFC. We adopt their definition for Perso-Arabic, implementing it as a single language-dependent FST $\mathcal{V}$, shown in Table 1, which is constructed by FST composition: $\mathcal{V} = \mathcal{N} \circ \mathcal{V}_c \circ \mathcal{V}_l$, where $\circ$ denotes the composition operation (Mohri, 2009).[4]

The first FST after NFC, denoted $\mathcal{V}_c$, is language-agnostic, constructed from a small set of normalizations for visually ambiguous sequences found online that apply to all languages in our library. For example, we map the two-character sequence *waw* (U+0648) followed by *damma* (U+064F) or *small damma* (U+0619) to *u* (U+06C7).

The second set of visually-invariant transformations, denoted $\mathcal{V}_l$, is language-specific and additionally depends on the position within the word. Four special cases are distinguished that are represented as FSTs: position-independent rewrites ($\mathcal{V}_l^*$), isolated-letter rewrites ($\mathcal{V}_l^{\mathrm{i}}$), rewrites in the word-final position ($\mathcal{V}_l^{\mathrm{f}}$), and finally, rewrites in "non-final" word positions, which include visually-identical word-initial and word-medial rewrites ($\mathcal{V}_l^{\mathrm{n}}$). The FST $\mathcal{V}_l$ is composed as $\mathcal{V}_l^{\mathrm{i}} \circ \mathcal{V}_l^{\mathrm{f}} \circ \mathcal{V}_l^{\mathrm{n}} \circ \mathcal{V}_l^*$. Some examples of these transformations for Urdu orthography are shown in Table 2, where the variants shown in the third column are rewritten to their canonical Urdu form in the fourth column.

[4] See Johny et al. (2021) for details on FST composition and other operations used in this kind of script normalization.

Op. Type	FST	# states	# arcs	# Kb
NFC	$\mathcal{N}$	156	1557	28.10
Roman.	$\mathcal{M}$	32 546	52 257	1487.10
Translit.	$\mathcal{T}$	340	518	15.15

Table 3: Language-agnostic FSTs over UTF-8 strings.

Reading Normalization This type of normalization was introduced for Brahmic scripts by Gutkin et al. (2022), who noted that regional orthographic conventions or lack thereof, which oftentimes conflict with each other, benefit from normalization to some accepted form. Whenever such normalization preserves visual invariance, it falls under the rubric of visual normalization, but other cases belong to *reading* normalization, denoted $\mathcal{R}$ in Table 1. Similar to visual normalization, $\mathcal{R}$ is compiled from language-specific context-dependent rewrite rules. One example of such a rewrite is a mapping from *yeh* ⟨ي⟩ (U+064A) to *farsi yeh* ⟨ی⟩ (U+06CC) in Kashmiri, Persian, Punjabi, Sorani Kurdish and Urdu. For Malay, Sindhi and Uyghur, the inverse transformation is implemented as mandated by the respective orthographies.

For efficiency reasons $\mathcal{R}$ is stored independently of visual normalization $\mathcal{V}$. At run-time, the reading normalization is applied to an input string s as $s' = (s \circ \mathcal{V}) \circ \mathcal{R}$, which is more efficient than $s' = s \circ \mathcal{R}'$, where $\mathcal{R}' = \mathcal{V} \circ \mathcal{R}$.

Romanization and Transliteration We also provide language-agnostic romanization ($\mathcal{M}$) and transliteration ($\mathcal{T}$) FSTs. The FST $\mathcal{M}$ converts Perso-Arabic strings to their respective Latin representation in Unicode and is defined as $\mathcal{M} = \mathcal{N} \circ \mathcal{V}_c \circ \mathcal{M}_c$, where $\mathcal{N}$ and $\mathcal{V}_c$ were described above, and $\mathcal{M}_c$ implements a one-to-one mapping from 198 Perso-Arabic characters to their respective romanizations using our custom romanization scheme derived from language-specific Library of Congress rules (LC, 2022) and various ISO standards (ISO, 1984, 1993, 1999). For example, in

Language Information		Visual Normalization ($\mathcal{V}$)			Reading Normalization ($\mathcal{R}$)		
Code	Name	# states	# arcs	# Mb	# states	# arcs	# Mb
azb	South Azerbaijani	315 933	635 647	16.49	21	735	0.012
bal	Balochi	620 226	1 244 472	32.31	24	738	0.013
ckb	Kurdish (Sorani)	1 097 937	2 199 732	57.15	39	753	0.013
fa	Persian	940 436	1 884 347	48.96	36	750	0.013
ks	Kashmiri	1 772 494	3 547 448	92.21	44	794	0.014
ms	Malay	199 777	403 373	10.45	21	735	0.012
pa	Punjabi	2 050 154	4 105 465	106.69	24	738	0.013
ps	Pashto	291 564	587 552	15.23	24	738	0.013
sd	Sindhi	1 703 726	3 403 283	88.53	34	748	0.013
ug	Uyghur	1 255 054	2 513 231	65.31	24	738	0.013
ur	Urdu	2 071 139	4 138 950	107.65	31	745	0.013

Table 4: Summary of FSTs over UTF-8 strings for visual and reading normalization.

our scheme the Uyghur *yu* ⟨ۈ⟩ (U+06C8) maps to ⟨ü⟩. The transliteration FST $\mathcal{T}$ converts the strings from Unicode Latin into Perso-Arabic. It is smaller than $\mathcal{M}$ and is defined as $\mathcal{T} = \mathcal{M}_c^{-1}$.

Character-Language Mapping The geography and scope of Perso-Arabic script adaptations is vast. To document the typology of the characters we developed an easy-to-parse mapping between the characters and the respective languages and/or macroareas that relate to a group of languages building on prior work by ICANN (2015). For example, using this mapping it is easy to find that the letter *beh with small v below* ⟨ࢠ⟩ (U+08A0) is part of the orthography of Wolof, a language of Senegal (Ngom, 2010), while *gaf with ring* ⟨ڰ⟩ (U+06B0) belongs to Saraiki language spoken in Pakistan (Bashir and Conners, 2019). This mapping can be used to auto-generate the orthographic inventories for lesser-resourced languages.

4 Software Details and Validation

Our software library is implemented using Pynini, a Python library for constructing finite-state grammars and for performing operations on FSTs (Gorman, 2016; Gorman and Sproat, 2021). Each FST is compiled from the collections of individual context-dependent letter rewrite rules (Mohri and Sproat, 1996) and is available in two versions: over an alphabet of UTF-8 encoded bytes and over the integer Unicode code points. The FSTs are stored uncompressed in binary FST archives (FARs) in OpenFst format (Allauzen et al., 2007).

The summaries of language-agnostic and language-dependent FSTs over UTF-8 strings are shown in Table 3 and Table 4, respectively. As can be seen from the tables, the language-agnostic and reading normalization FSTs are relatively uncomplicated and small in terms of number of states, arcs and the overall (uncompressed) size on disk. The visual normalization FSTs are significantly larger, which is explained by the number of composition operations used in their construction (see §3). The reading normalization FSTs for South Azerbaijani and Malay shown in Table 4 implement the identity mapping. This is because we could not find enough examples requiring reading-style normalization in online data (see the Limitations section for more details).

Lang.	$s' = s \circ \mathcal{V}$		$s' = (s \circ \mathcal{V}) \circ \mathcal{R}$	
	% tokens	% types	% tokens	% types
ckb	18.27	25.84	30.07	41.26
sd	17.32	14.83	21.74	17.31
ur	0.09	1.16	0.10	1.23

Table 5: Percentage of tokens and types changed.

As an informal sanity check we validate the prevalence of normalization on word-frequency lists for Sorani Kurdish (ckb), Sindhi (sd) and Uyghur (ug) from project Crúbadán (Scannell, 2007). Table 5 shows the percentages of tokens and types changed ($s' \neq s$) by visual normalization on one hand and the combined visual and reading normalization on the other. Urdu has the fewest number of modifications compared to Sorani Kurdish and Sindhi, most likely due to a more regular orthography and stable input methods manifest in the crawled data. Significantly more extensive analysis and experiments in statistical language modeling and neural machine translation for the languages covered in this paper are presented in a forthcoming study (Doctor et al., 2022).

Example The use of the library is demonstrated by the following Python example that implements a simple command-line utility for performing reading normalization on a single string using Pynini APIs. The program requires two FAR files that

Lang.	Input	Output	Correct Output
bal	دئیٹ	دئیت	*teh*
ckb	لەشڪر	لەشکر	*keheh*
fa	مؤسسه	موسسه	*waw*
ks	هی‌تک	هؠتک	*kashmiri yeh*
pa	کئي	کئی	*farsi yeh*
sd	ڳوهه	ڳوہہ	*heh goal*
ug	سای	ساي	*yeh*
ur	صورة	صورۃ	*teh marbuta goal*

Table 6: Some examples of reading normalization.

store compiled visual and reading normalization grammars, the upper-case BCP-47 language code for retrieving the FST for a given language, and an input string:[5]

example.py

```
from absl import app
from absl import flags
from collections.abc import Iterable, Sequence
import pynini as pyn

flags.DEFINE_string("input", None, "Input string.")
flags.DEFINE_string("lang", None, "Language code.")
flags.DEFINE_string("reading_grm", None, "Reading FAR.")
flags.DEFINE_string("visual_grm", None, "Visual FAR.")
FLAGS = flags.FLAGS

def load_fst(grammar_path: str, lang: str) -> pyn.Fst:
  """Loads FST for specified grammar and language."""
  return pyn.Far(grammar_path)[lang]

def apply(text: str, fsts: Iterable[pyn.Fst]) -> str:
  """Applies sequence of FSTs on an input string."""
  try:
    composed = pyn.escape(text)
    for fst in fsts:
      composed = (composed @ fst).optimize()
    return pyn.shortestpath(composed).string()
  except pyn.FstOpError as error:
    raise ValueError(f"Error for string `{text}`")

def main(argv: Sequence[str]) -> None:
  # ... initializing FLAGS
  visual_fst = load_fst(FLAGS.visual_grm, FLAGS.lang)
  reading_fst = load_fst(FLAGS.reading_grm, FLAGS.lang)
  out = apply(FLAGS.input, [visual_fst, reading_fst])
  print(f"=> {out}")

if __name__ == "__main__":
  app.run(main)
```

The visual and reading FSTs for a given language are retrieved from the relevant FAR files using `load_fst` function. The input string is first converted to a linear FST. The visual and reading normalization FSTs are then sequentially composed with the input FST and a shortest path algorithm is applied on the result, which is then converted from a linear FST back to a Python string in `apply` function to yield the final normalized output.

Some examples of reading normalization produced using the `example.py` utility above for some of the supported languages are shown in Table 6. For each language, the input string in the second column of the table is normalized to a string shown in the third column. The final column shows the name of a particular letter in the output string that replaced the original letter from the input string, e.g., for Sorani Kurdish (`ckb`) the following rewrite occurs: *swash kaf* (`U+06AA`) $\rightarrow$ *keheh* (`U+06A9`), while for Punjabi (`pa`), *yeh* (`U+064A`) $\rightarrow$ *farsi yeh* (`U+06CC`).

5 Conclusion and Future Work

We have presented a flexible FST-based software package for low-level processing of orthographies based on Perso-Arabic script. We described the main components of the architecture consisting of various script normalization operations, romanization/transliteration, and character-language index. We expect to increase the current language coverage of eleven languages to further relatively well-documented orthographies, but also provide treatment for resource-scarce orthographies, such as the Ajami orthographies of Sub-Saharan Africa (Mumin, 2014).

Limitations

When developing the visual and reading normalization rules for the eleven languages described in this paper we made use of publicly available online data consisting of the respective Wikipedias, Wikipron (Lee et al., 2020), Crúbadán (Scannell, 2007) and parts of Common Crawl (Patel, 2020). The latter corpus is particularly noisy and requires non-trivial filtering (Kreutzer et al., 2022). Furthermore, many Wikipedia and Common Crawl documents contain code-switched text in several languages that are recorded in Perso-Arabic. Robust language identification (LID) is required to distinguish between tokens in such sentences (for example, Kashmiri vs. Pashto or Balochi) in order not to confuse between the respective orthographies. Since we did not have access to robust LID models for the languages under study, for lesser-resourced languages such as Kashmiri, Malay in Jawi orthography, South Azerbaijani and Uyghur, it is likely that some of the words we used as examples requiring normalization may have been misclassified resulting in normalizations that should not be there.

[5]The infrastructure for compiling the Pynini grammars is described in Johny et al. (2021).

References

Muzaffar Aazim, Kamal Mansour, and Roozbeh Pournader. 2009. Proposal to add two Kashmiri characters and one annotation to the Arabic block. Technical Report L2/09-176, Unicode Consortium.

Humza Ahmad and Laszlo Erdodi. 2021. Overview of phishing landscape and homographs in Arabic domain names. *Security and Privacy*, 4(4):1–14.

Sina Ahmadi. 2020. KLPT – Kurdish language processing toolkit. In *Proceedings of Second Workshop for NLP Open Source Software (NLP-OSS)*, pages 72–84, Online. Association for Computational Linguistics.

Sina Ahmadi and Maraim Masoud. 2020. Towards machine translation for the Kurdish language. In *Proceedings of the 3rd Workshop on Technologies for MT of Low Resource Languages*, pages 87–98, Suzhou, China. Association for Computational Linguistics.

Cyril Allauzen, Michael Riley, Johan Schalkwyk, Wojciech Skut, and Mehryar Mohri. 2007. OpenFst: A general and efficient weighted finite-state transducer library. In *International Conference on Implementation and Application of Automata*, pages 11–23. Springer.

Ankur Bapna, Isaac Caswell, Julia Kreutzer, Orhan Firat, Daan van Esch, Aditya Siddhant, Mengmeng Niu, Pallavi Baljekar, Xavier Garcia, Wolfgang Macherey, Theresa Breiner, Vera Axelrod, Jason Riesa, Yuan Cao, Mia Xu Chen, Klaus Macherey, Maxim Krikun, Pidong Wang, Alexander Gutkin, Apurva Shah, Yanping Huang, Zhifeng Chen, Yonghui Wu, and Macduff Hughes. 2022. Building machine translation systems for the next thousand languages. *arXiv preprint arXiv:2205.03983*.

Elena Bashir and Thomas J. Conners. 2019. Phonology and orthography. In *A Descriptive Grammar of Hindko, Panjabi, and Saraiki*, volume 4 of *Mouton-CASL Grammar Series [MCASL]*. De Gruyter Mouton.

Elena Bashir, Sarmad Hussain, and Deborah Anderson. 2006. Proposal for characters for Khowar, Torwali, and Burushaski. Technical Report L2-06/149, Unicode Consortium.

Thomas Bauer. 1996. Arabic writing. In Peter Daniels and William Bright, editors, *The World's Writing Systems*, chapter 50, pages 559–563. Oxford University Press, Oxford.

Zeeshan Bhatti, Imdad Ali Ismaili, Asad Ali Shaikh, and Waseem Javaid. 2014. Spelling error trends and patterns in Sindhi. *arXiv preprint arXiv:1403.4759*.

Raiomond Doctor, Alexander Gutkin, Cibu Johny, Brian Roark, and Richard Sproat. 2022. Graphemic normalization of the Perso-Arabic script. In *Proceedings of Grapholinguistics in the 21st Century (G21C)*, Paris, France. In press.

Avi Ginsberg and Cui Yu. 2018. Rapid homoglyph prediction and detection. In *Proceedings of the 1st International Conference on Data Intelligence and Security (ICDIS)*, pages 17–23, South Padre Island, TX, USA. IEEE.

Kyle Gorman. 2016. Pynini: A Python library for weighted finite-state grammar compilation. In *Proceedings of the SIGFSM Workshop on Statistical NLP and Weighted Automata*, pages 75–80, Berlin, Germany. Association for Computational Linguistics.

Kyle Gorman and Richard Sproat. 2021. *Finite-State Text Processing*, volume 14 of *Synthesis Lectures on Human Language Technologies*. Morgan & Claypool Publishers.

Alexander Gutkin, Cibu Johny, Raiomond Doctor, Lawrence Wolf-Sonkin, and Brian Roark. 2022. Extensions to Brahmic script processing within the Nisaba library: new scripts, languages and utilities. In *Proceedings of the Thirteenth Language Resources and Evaluation Conference*, pages 6450–6460, Marseille, France. European Language Resources Association.

Muhammad Humayoun, Harald Hammarström, and Aarne Ranta. 2022. Urdu morphology, orthography and lexicon extraction. *arXiv preprint arXiv:2204.03071*.

Sarmad Hussain, Ahmed Bakhat, Nabil Benamar, Meikal Mumin, and Inam Ullah. 2016. Enabling multilingual domain names: addressing the challenges of the Arabic script top-level domains. *Journal of Cyber Policy*, 1(1):107–129.

ICANN. 2011. Arabic case study team: Arabic case study team issues report. Internationalized Domain Names (IDN) Variant Issues project, Internet Corporation for Assigned Names and Numbers (ICANN).

ICANN. 2015. Task force on Arabic script IDN (TF-AIDN): Proposal for Arabic script Root Zone LGR. ICANN Internationalized Domain Names (IDN) program: Proposal documentation, Internet Corporation for Assigned Names and Numbers (ICANN). Version 2.7.

ISO. 1984. ISO 233:1984: Transliteration of Arabic characters into Latin characters. `https://www.iso.org/standard/4117.html`. International Organization for Standardization.

ISO. 1993. ISO iso 233-2:1993: Transliteration of Arabic characters into Latin characters — Part 2: Arabic language — Simplified transliteration. `https://www.iso.org/standard/4118.html`. International Organization for Standardization.

ISO. 1999. ISO iso 233-3:1999: Transliteration of Arabic characters into Latin characters — Part 3: Persian language — Simplified transliteration. `https://www.iso.org/standard/4118.html`. International Organization for Standardization.

Cibu Johny, Lawrence Wolf-Sonkin, Alexander Gutkin, and Brian Roark. 2021. Finite-state script normalization and processing utilities: The Nisaba Brahmic library. In *Proceedings of the 16th Conference of the European Chapter of the Association for Computational Linguistics: System Demonstrations*, pages 14–23, Online. Association for Computational Linguistics.

Julia Kreutzer, Isaac Caswell, Lisa Wang, Ahsan Wahab, Daan van Esch, Nasanbayar Ulzii-Orshikh, Allahsera Tapo, Nishant Subramani, Artem Sokolov, Claytone Sikasote, Monang Setyawan, Supheakmungkol Sarin, Sokhar Samb, Benoît Sagot, Clara Rivera, Annette Rios, Isabel Papadimitriou, Salomey Osei, Pedro Ortiz Suarez, Iroro Orife, Kelechi Ogueji, Andre Niyongabo Rubungo, Toan Q. Nguyen, Mathias Müller, André Müller, Shamsuddeen Hassan Muhammad, Nanda Muhammad, Ayanda Mnyakeni, Jamshidbek Mirzakhalov, Tapiwanashe Matangira, Colin Leong, Nze Lawson, Sneha Kudugunta, Yacine Jernite, Mathias Jenny, Orhan Firat, Bonaventure F. P. Dossou, Sakhile Dlamini, Nisansa de Silva, Sakine Çabuk Ballı, Stella Biderman, Alessia Battisti, Ahmed Baruwa, Ankur Bapna, Pallavi Baljekar, Israel Abebe Azime, Ayodele Awokoya, Duygu Ataman, Orevaoghene Ahia, Oghenefego Ahia, Sweta Agrawal, and Mofetoluwa Adeyemi. 2022. Quality at a glance: An audit of web-crawled multilingual datasets. *Transactions of the Association for Computational Linguistics*, 10:50–72.

Dennis Kurzon. 2013. Diacritics and the Perso-Arabic script. *Writing Systems Research*, 5(2):234–243.

LC. 2022. ALA-LC romanization tables. `http://loc.gov/catdir/cpso/roman`. The Library of Congress. Updated: 08/24/2022.

Jackson L. Lee, Lucas F.E. Ashby, M. Elizabeth Garza, Yeonju Lee-Sikka, Sean Miller, Alan Wong, Arya D. McCarthy, and Kyle Gorman. 2020. Massively multilingual pronunciation modeling with WikiPron. In *Proceedings of the Twelfth Language Resources and Evaluation Conference*, pages 4223–4228, Marseille, France. European Language Resources Association.

Gurpreet Singh Lehal and Tejinder Singh Saini. 2012. Conversion between scripts of Punjabi: Beyond simple transliteration. In *Proceedings of COLING 2012: Posters*, pages 633–642, Mumbai, India. The COLING 2012 Organizing Committee.

Gurpreet Singh Lehal and Tejinder Singh Saini. 2014. Sangam: A perso-Arabic to indic script machine transliteration model. In *Proceedings of the 11th International Conference on Natural Language Processing*, pages 232–239, Goa, India. NLP Association of India.

Henrik Liljegren. 2018. Supporting and sustaining language vitality in Northern Pakistan. In Leanne Hinton, Leena Huss, and Gerald Roche, editors, *The Routledge Handbook of Language Revitalization*, pages 427–437. Routledge.

Mehryar Mohri. 2009. Weighted automata algorithms. In Manfred Droste, Werner Kuich, and Heiko Vogler, editors, *Handbook of Weighted Automata*, Monographs in Theoretical Computer Science, pages 213–254. Springer.

Mehryar Mohri and Richard Sproat. 1996. An efficient compiler for weighted rewrite rules. In *34th Annual Meeting of the Association for Computational Linguistics*, pages 231–238, Santa Cruz, California, USA. Association for Computational Linguistics.

Meikal Mumin. 2014. The Arabic script in Africa: Understudied literacy. In Meikal Mumin and Kees Versteegh, editors, *The Arabic Script in Africa*, volume 71 of *Studies in Semitic Languages and Linguistics*, pages 41–76. Brill, Leiden, The Netherlands.

Gokul N. C. 2022. Unified NMT models for the Indian subcontinent, transcending script-barriers. In *Proceedings of the Third Workshop on Deep Learning for Low-Resource Natural Language Processing*, pages 227–236, Hybrid. Association for Computational Linguistics.

Fallou Ngom. 2010. Ajami scripts in the Senegalese speech community. *Journal of Arabic and Islamic Studies*, 10:1–23.

Jay M. Patel. 2020. Introduction to Common Crawl datasets. In *Getting Structured Data from the Internet*, pages 277–324. Springer.

Roozbeh Pournader. 2014. The right HEHs for Arabic script orthographies of Sorani Kurdish and Uighur. Technical Report L2/14-136, Unicode Consortium.

Sitti Munirah Abdul Razak, Muhamad Sadry Abu Seman, Wan Ali Wan Yusoff Wan Mamat, and Noor Hasrul Nizan Mohammad Noor. 2018. Transliteration engine for union catalogue of Malay manuscripts in Malaysia: E-Jawi Version 3. In *2018 International Conference on Information and Communication Technology for the Muslim World (ICT4M)*, pages 58–63. IEEE.

Kevin P. Scannell. 2007. The Crúbadán Project: Corpus building for under-resourced languages. In *Building and Exploring Web Corpora (WAC3-2007): Proceedings of the 3rd Web as Corpus Workshop*, volume 4, pages 5–15. Presses universitaires de Louvain. `http://crubadan.org/`.

Unicode Consortium. 2021. Arabic. In *The Unicode Standard (Version 14.0.0)*, chapter 9.2, pages 373–398. Unicode Consortium, Mountain View, CA.

Ken Whistler. 2021. Unicode normalization forms. Technical Report TR15-51, Unicode Consortium. Version 14.0.0.

Coreference Annotation of an Arabic Corpus using a Virtual World Game

Wateen Aliady [1,2], Abdulrahman Aloraini[1,3], Christopher Madge[1], Juntao Yu[4], Richard Bartle[4], and Massimo Poesio[1]

[1]Queen Mary University of London, United Kingdom
[2]Imam Mohammad Ibn Saud Islamic University, Saudi Arabia
[3]Qassim University, Saudi Arabia
[4]University of Essex, United Kingdom
{w.a.a.aliady, a.aloraini, c.j.madge, m.poesio}@qmul.ac.uk
{j.yu, rabartle}@essex.ac.uk

Abstract

Coreference resolution is a key aspect of text comprehension, but the size of the available coreference corpora for Arabic is limited in comparison to the size of the corpora for other languages. In this paper we present a Game-With-A-Purpose called *Stroll with a Scroll* created to collect from players coreference annotations for Arabic. The key contribution of this work is the embedding of the annotation task in a virtual world setting, as opposed to the puzzle-type games used in previously proposed Games-With-A-Purpose for coreference.

1 Introduction

Coreference resolution is the task of clustering the mentions in a text that refer to the same real world entity. In the following example of coreference resolution, bold phrases are said to corefer as they point to the same discourse entity, a person named Ibn Sina.

> **ابن سينا** عالم وطبيب اشتهر بالطب والفلسفة.
>
> **Ibn Sina** is a scientist and doctor who was known for philosophy and medicine.
>
> من أهم أعمال **العلامة** كتاب القانون في الطب.
>
> One of the most famous writings of **the scientist** is The Canon of Medicine.

Coreference resolution is a key element of text comprehension (Poesio et al., 2016; Wu et al., 2021). Identifying references to entities in the context is essential for meaning interpretation. In addition, anaphoric references are an important aspect of textual cohesion, as they connect different parts of the text to ensure its unity. Resolving anaphoric references is essential for most Natural Language Processing (NLP) applications, including automatic translation, information extraction and topic detection (Bouzid and Zribi, 2020).

Collecting coreference annotations from experts can be expensive, so crowdsourcing is often employed (Snow et al., 2008). This can be done using a crowdsourcing platform (Poesio et al., 2008) or by embedding the annotation task in a game in a seamless manner. Such games are referred to as Games-With-A-Purpose (GWAP) (Von Ahn and Dabbish, 2005; Von Ahn, 2006; Von Ahn et al., 2006a,b; Chamberlain et al., 2008; Poesio et al., 2013a; Lafourcade et al., 2015). GWAPs are games designed to collect judgments from players using their gaming skills and language competence; the main reward for players is entertainment. GWAPs have been used e.g., for biological data collection (Kleffner et al., 2017), and, in AI, for image processing (Von Ahn and Dabbish, 2005) and natural language processing (Chamberlain et al., 2008; Krause et al., 2010; Venhuizen et al., 2013; Fort et al., 2014; Dziedzic, 2016; Kicikoglu et al., 2019; Madge et al., 2019b,a; Bonetti and Tonelli, 2020). Using GWAPs for manual annotation is particularly well-suited when the aim is to collect large corpora, that would be too expensive to create using other forms of crowdsourcing (Poesio et al., 2013b).

The objective of this research is to create a GWAP called *Stroll with a Scroll* for Arabic coreference annotation. The motivations for our work are:

- The fact that the available Arabic coreference corpora are limited in size. In the CoNLL-2012 shared task the Arabic portion is about 1/3 of the Chinese and English subsets, comprising about 300k tokens. This is considered a barrier to improving the coreference resolution models accuracy (Pradhan et al., 2012).
- More in general, there is limited work on GWAPs for Arabic language annotation in comparison with English. To our knowledge

Proceedings of the The Seventh Arabic Natural Language Processing Workshop (WANLP), pages 388 - 393
December 8, 2022 ©2022 Association for Computational Linguistics

there is no game with the purpose of collecting Arabic coreference annotation.

Our main contributions are:

- To start a path towards using gamification to attract public engagement to contribute to the creation of larger Arabic coreference corpora, and more in general Arabic NLP corpora;
- The adoption of a virtual world setting, which we expect would increase the chances of attracting players but whose use is still limited in GWAPs for corpus annotation;

2 Related Work

2.1 Games with a Purpose for NLP

The first examples of Games-With-A-Purpose in AI are the well-known *ESP game* for image labelling and other games from Luis von Ahn's lab (Von Ahn and Dabbish, 2005; Von Ahn et al., 2006a,b; Seemakurty et al., 2010). Among the first GWAPs for NLP are *Jeux-de-Mots* for French lexical acquisition (Lafourcade, 2007) and, for English coreference, *Phrase Detectives* (Chamberlain et al., 2008). Other examples are *OnTo-Galaxy* to populate an ontology in English and collect synonyms for German verbs (Krause et al., 2010), *Wordrobe* for English word sense labelling (Venhuizen et al., 2013), *Zombilingo* for French dependency syntax annotation (Fort et al., 2014), *RoboCorp* for Polish named entities annotation (Dziedzic, 2016), *WordClicker* for English part of speech annotation (Madge et al., 2019b), *High School SuperHero* for Italian abusive language annotation (Bonetti and Tonelli, 2020) and *NameThatLanguage* for language recognition (Cieri et al., 2021).

There are some GWAPs for Arabic NLP, including *tashkeelWAP* for digitizing Arabic diacritics (Kassem et al., 2016), *3arosty* for Arabic named entities annotation (Sabty et al., 2016), *3ammeya* to build a corpus for Arabic dialects (Osman et al., 2015) and a GWAP to map Modern Standard Arabic to Arabic regional dialects (Nasser et al., 2013). However, to the best of our knowledge, this is the first GWAP for Arabic coreference and the first GWAP to embed the task of collecting Arabic annotations in a 3D virtual game.

Many of the early NLP GWAPs were essentially gamified versions of annotation tools. Attempts to produce more engaging games include *Puzzle Racer* and *Ka-boom!* for word sense disambiguation (Jurgens and Navigli, 2014). More recently, an engaging game design was developed for *WordClicker*, a part of speech tagging game where players take the role of a baker who fills jars with the part of speech it represents (Madge et al., 2019b).

2.2 GWAPs for Coreference

Phrase Detectives is an online interactive active game to collect English coreference annotation released in 2008. The game has two modes to participate in annotation. The first mode to select a markable that corefers to another highlighted markable and the second mode to validate other players' submitted answers. By 2019, the game had collected over 5 million annotations from more than 50,000 players; the 2nd release of the corpus was the largest crowdsourced corpus for coreference and one of the largest crowdsourced corpora for NLP (Poesio et al., 2019).

Wormingo is an online game to collect English coreference annotation. It creates a novel technique called motivation-annotation paradigm. That highlights the importance of text comprehension in producing accurately coreferenced corpora and making the annotation task easier. Text comprehension is essential in the motivational part of the game that is demonstrated by linguistic puzzles. The annotation part comes after the motivational part and follows the design of *Phrase Detectives* (Kicikoglu et al., 2019).

2.3 GWAPs Embedded in Virtual Worlds

One approach to making games more engaging is to embed them in the virtual world scenarios familiar from most video games. One example of GWAPs adopting this approach is *High School Superhero* (Bonetti and Tonelli, 2020, 2021), a 3D role-playing game is created for abusive language annotation in a sentence level.

Other example is *LingoTowns* (Althani et al., 2022), an isometric world consisting of towns. It hosts three mini-games: *PhraseFarm*, *CafeClicker* and *Lingotoruim*.

The more recent *Borderlands Science* (Waldispühl et al., 2020) is an integration of citizen science game named *Phylo* (Kawrykow et al., 2012) into a massively multiplayer online game called *Borderlands*. In three months, they have collected 50 million puzzle solutions.

3 Stroll with a Scroll

In this paper we introduce *Stroll with a Scroll*, a GWAP for (Arabic) coreference annotation in which the player is an agent embedded in a 3D world.

3.1 Game Design

In *Stroll with a Scroll*, players find themselves in an ancient middle eastern fictional town located in the desert. They roam around this town being represented by an avatar that is dressed in an ancient middle eastern garment as shown in Figure 1.

The game has a treasure hunt theme, with puzzles hidden in the text. To motivate players, we follow the motivation-annotation paradigm introduced by *Wormingo* that uses puzzles and gamification techniques to motivate the players (Kicikoglu et al., 2019). The inclusion of linguistic puzzles increases players' comprehension of text thus, understanding is required to perform coreference annotation.

There are plenty of chests scattered around the town which the player has to find. Only one chest is presented at a given moment; the player is guided to chest location through a navigation system that is displayed on the top right corner presented in Figure 1. The navigation system has three colours: red, yellow, and green to show how far is the avatar from the chest.

The player starts by opening a chest that has a scroll within it. The scroll has textual content with missing parts of information as these pieces were torn because these scrolls are old. The player must guess the lost parts by solving puzzles.

If the player guesses the right word, 10 puzzle points will be added. If a player fails to guess the word, no points will be added.

3.2 Coreference Annotation

The annotation task is presented as questions following the approach used in *Phrase Detectives* (Chamberlain et al., 2008) and *Wormingo* (Kicikoglu et al., 2019). Two types of questions are presented to the player: annotation questions, and validation questions. In the annotation, the player is asked to decide if a mention, colored by red, is discourse new, discourse old (If the player decides that a mention is discourse old, they must select the nearest antecedent from suggested antecedents highlighted in blue) or skip answering as in Figure 2. On the other hand, in the validation, the player is asked to validate the model (Aloraini et al., 2020) or other players.

3.3 Preprocessing

In earlier games such as *Phrase Detectives* , the preprocessing of documents to annotate only involved mention identification (Poesio et al., 2017). However, if a coreference resolver is available, carrying out a preliminary coreference annotation increases

Figure 1: A screenshot of the game.

the potential of a game to collect larger number of annotated documents, as annotation by human players can be driven by uncertainty about the annotation, as in an active learning setting (Li et al., 2020).

The input to *Stroll with a Scroll* is pre-annotated to extract mentions and coreference links using the first neural coreference resolver for Arabic (Aloraini et al., 2020) that achieved higher results than than the existing state-of-the-art system (Björkelund and Kuhn, 2014) on Arabic coreference resolution.

3.4 Aggregation

Stroll with a Scroll follows *Phrase Detectives* (Chamberlain et al., 2008) by using Mention Pair Annotation (Paun et al., 2018) to aggregate user annotations.

4 Discussion

We introduced *Stroll with a Scroll* , a new GWAP for annotating coreference in Arabic. Our GWAP is based on the motivation-annotation paradigm from *Wormingo* in having two disjoint parts: the puzzles part and the annotation part. This division ensures that the orthogonal game design mechanics e.g., aiming, driving and dropping that are the main contributors to most of the popular video games are separated from the annotation task. Video games are separated from the annotation task, so as not to negatively impact the annotation accuracy (Tuite, 2014; Madge et al., 2019a). However, the motivation and the annotation are both embedded in a virtual world scenario: document search involves finding chests in an old town, and filling gaps in the document is naturally presented as reconstructing the scroll. We expect that this novel setting will make the game more attractive to certain types of players who are more interested in 3D games than in puzzles.

5 Limitations

The future based rewards of the annotation part might discourage the players to continue. Furthermore, in the current development stage, the player does not have the option to select antecedents outside of the suggested ones.

6 Conclusion

Games-With-A-Purpose for collecting text annotations are an increasingly popular alternative to crowdsourcing platforms. Even so, to our knowledge there is no GWAP of collecting Arabic coreference annotation. We present a 3D virtual world GWAP of collecting coreference annotations for Arabic corpus. We expect the adoption of a virtual world setting would increase the chances of attracting players.

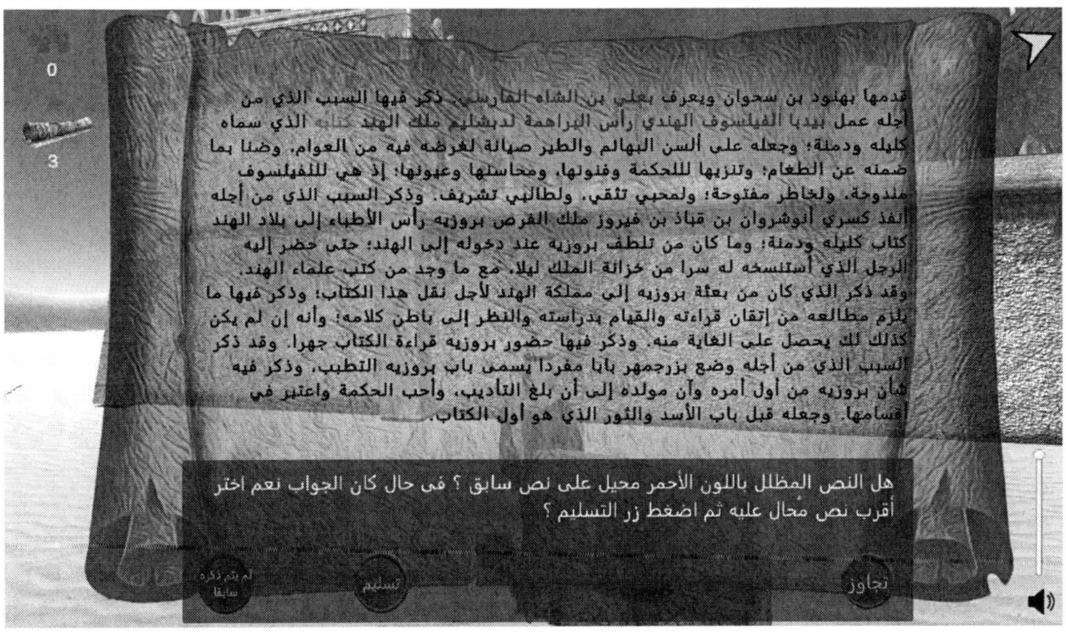

Figure 2: The annotation task embedded in a 3D game.

References

Abdulrahman Aloraini, Juntao Yu, and Massimo Poesio. 2020. Neural coreference resolution for Arabic. In *Proceedings of the Third Workshop on Computational Models of Reference, Anaphora and Coreference.*

Fatima Althani, Chris Madge, and Massimo Poesio. 2022. Less text, more visuals: Evaluating the onboarding phase in a GWAP for NLP. In *Proceedings of the 9th Workshop on Games and Natural Language Processing within the 13th Language Resources and Evaluation Conference*, pages 17–27, Marseille, France. European Language Resources Association.

Anders Björkelund and Jonas Kuhn. 2014. Learning structured perceptrons for coreference resolution with latent antecedents and non-local features. In *Proceedings of the 52nd Annual Meeting of the Association for Computational Linguistics (Volume 1: Long Papers)*, pages 47–57, Baltimore, Maryland. Association for Computational Linguistics.

Federico Bonetti and Sara Tonelli. 2020. A 3D role-playing game for abusive language annotation. In *Workshop on Games and Natural Language Processing*, pages 39–43.

Federico Bonetti and Sara Tonelli. 2021. Challenges in designing games with a purpose for abusive language annotation. In *Proceedings of the First Workshop on Bridging Human–Computer Interaction and Natural Language Processing*, pages 60–65.

Saoussen Mathlouthi Bouzid and Chiraz Ben Othmane Zribi. 2020. A generic approach for pronominal anaphora and zero anaphora resolution in arabic language. *Procedia Computer Science*, 176:642–652.

Jon Chamberlain, Massimo Poesio, and Udo Kruschwitz. 2008. Phrase detectives: A web-based collaborative annotation game. In *in Proceedings of the International Conference on Semantic Systems (I-Semantics 08)*, pages 42–49.

Christopher Cieri, James Fiumara, and Jonathan Wright. 2021. Using games to augment corpora for language recognition and confusability. In *Proc. of Interspeech: 22nd Annual Conference of the International Speech Communication.*

Dagmara Dziedzic. 2016. Use of the free to play model in games with a purpose: the robocorp game case study. *Bio-Algorithms and Med-Systems*, 12(4):187–197.

Karën Fort, Bruno Guillaume, and Hadrien Chastant. 2014. Creating zombilingo, a game with a purpose for dependency syntax annotation. In *Proceedings of the First International Workshop on Gamification for Information Retrieval*, pages 2–6.

David Jurgens and Roberto Navigli. 2014. It's all fun and games until someone annotates: Video games with a purpose for linguistic annotation. *Transactions of the Association for Computational Linguistics*, 2:449–464.

Lin Kassem, Caroline Sabty, Nada Sharaf, Menna Bakry, and Slim Abdennadher. 2016. tashkeelwap: A game with a purpose for digitizing arabic diacritics.

Alexander Kawrykow, Gary Roumanis, Alfred Kam, Daniel Kwak, Clarence Leung, Chu Wu, Eleyine Zarour, Luis Sarmenta, Mathieu Blanchette, and Jérôme Waldispühl. 2012. Phylo: A citizen science approach for improving multiple sequence alignment. *PloS one*, 7:e31362.

Doruk Kicikoglu, Richard Bartle, Jon Chamberlain, , and Massimo Poesio. 2019. Wormingo: a'true gamification'approach to anaphoric annotation. In *Proceedings of the 14th International Conference on the Foundations of Digital Games*, pages 1–7.

Robert Kleffner, Jeff Flatten, Andrew Leaver-Fay, David Baker, Justin B Siegel, Firas Khatib, and Seth Cooper. 2017. Foldit standalone: a video game-derived protein structure manipulation interface using rosetta. *Bioinformatics*, 33(17):2765–2767.

Markus Krause, Aneta Takhtamysheva, Marion Wittstock, and Rainer Malaka. 2010. Frontiers of a paradigm: exploring human computation with digital games. In *Proceedings of the ACM SIGKDD workshop on human computation*, pages 22–25.

Mathieu Lafourcade. 2007. Making people play for lexical acquisition with the jeuxdemots prototype. In *SNLP'07: 7th international symposium on natural language processing*, page 7.

Mathieu Lafourcade, Alain Joubert, and Nathalie Le Brun. 2015. *Games with a Purpose (GWAPs)*. Wiley.

Belinda Z. Li, Gabriel Stanovsky, and Luke Zettlemoyer. 2020. Active learning for coreference resolution using discrete annotation. In *Proceedings of the 58th Annual Meeting of the Association for Computational Linguistics*, pages 8320–8331, Online. Association for Computational Linguistics.

Chris Madge, Richard Bartle, Jon Chamberlain, Udo Kruschwitz, and Massimo Poesio. 2019a. The design of a clicker game for text labelling. In *2019 IEEE Conference on Games (CoG)*, pages 1–4. IEEE.

Chris Madge, Richard Bartle, Jon Chamberlain, Udo Kruschwitz, and Massimo Poesio. 2019b. Incremental game mechanics applied to text annotation. In *in Proceedings of the Annual Symposium on Computer-Human Interaction in Play*, pages 545–558.

Sara Nasser, Nada Sharaf, Mohamed Khamis, Slim Abdennadher, and Caroline Sabty. 2013. Collecting arabic dialect variations using games with a purpose: A case study targeting the egyptian dialect. In *Proceedings of the 2nd Workshop on Games and Natural Language Processing (GAMNLP 2013).*

Maya Osman, Caroline Sabty, Nada Sharaf, and Slim Abdennadher. 2015. Building a corpus for arabic dialects using games with a purpose. In *in 2015 First International Conference on Arabic Computational Linguistics (ACLing), IEEE*, pages 21–25.

Silviu Paun, Jon Chamberlain, Udo Kruschwitz, Juntao Yu, and Massimo Poesio. 2018. A probabilistic annotation model for crowdsourcing coreference. *http://aclweb. org/anthology/D18-1000*, pages 1926–1937.

Massimo Poesio, Jon Chamberlain, and Udo Kruschwitz. 2017. *Phrase Detectives*, pages 1149–1176.

Massimo Poesio, Jon Chamberlain, Udo Kruschwitz, Livio Robaldo, and Luca Ducceschi. 2013a. Phrase detectives: Utilizing collective intelligence for internet-scale language resource creation. *ACM Transactions on Interactive Intelligent Systems (TiiS)*, 3(1):1–44.

Massimo Poesio, Jon Chamberlain, Udo Kruschwitz, Livio Robaldo, and Luca Ducceschi. 2013b. Phrase detectives: Utilizing collective intelligence for internet-scale language resource creation. *ACM Transactions on Interactive Intelligent Systems (TiiS)*, 3(1):1–44.

Massimo Poesio, Jon Chamberlain, Silviu Paun, Juntao Yu, Alexandra Uma, and Udo Kruschwitz. 2019. A crowdsourced corpus of multiple judgments and disagreement on anaphoric interpretation. In *Proceedings of the 2019 Conference of the North American Chapter of the Association for Computational Linguistics: Human Language Technologies, Volume 1 (Long and Short Papers)*, volume 1, pages 1778–1789. Association for Computational Linguistics.

Massimo Poesio, Udo Kruschwitz, and Jon Chamberlain. 2008. ANAWIKI: Creating anaphorically annotated resources through web cooperation. In *Proceedings of the Sixth International Conference on Language Resources and Evaluation (LREC'08)*, Marrakech, Morocco. European Language Resources Association (ELRA).

Massimo Poesio, Roland Stuckardt, and Yannick Versley. 2016. *Anaphora resolution*. Springer.

Sameer Pradhan, Alessandro Moschitti, Nianwen Xue, Olga Uryupina, and Yuchen Zhang. 2012. Conll-2012 shared task: Modeling multilingual unrestricted coreference in ontonotes. pages 1–40.

Caroline Sabty, Mirna Yacout, Mohamed Sameh, and Slim Abdennadher. 2016. Gamified collection of arabic named entity recognition data.

Nitin Seemakurty, Jonathan Chu, Luis von Ahn, and Anthony Tomasic. 2010. Word sense disambiguation via human computation. In *Proceedings of the ACM SIGKDD Workshop on Human Computation*, HCOMP '10, page 60–63, New York, NY, USA. Association for Computing Machinery.

Rion Snow, Brendan O'Connor, Daniel Jurafsky, and Andrew Y. Ng. 2008. Cheap and fast - but is it good? evaluating non-expert annotations for natural language tasks. In *Proceedings of the Conference on Empirical Methods in Natural Language Processing (EMNLP)*, pages 254–263.

Kathleen Tuite. 2014. Gwaps: Games with a problem. In *FDG*.

Noortje J. Venhuizen, Valerio Basile, Kilian Evang, and Johan Bos. 2013. Gamification for word sense labeling. In *Proceedings of the 10th International Conference on Computational Semantics (IWCS 2013) – Short Papers*, pages 397–403, Potsdam, Germany. Association for Computational Linguistics.

Luis Von Ahn. 2006. Games with a purpose. *Computer*, 39(6):92–94.

Luis Von Ahn and Laura Dabbish. 2005. Esp: Labeling images with a computer game. In *AAAI spring symposium: Knowledge collection from volunteer contributors*, volume 2.

Luis Von Ahn, Mihir Kedia, and Manuel Blum. 2006a. Verbosity: a game for collecting common-sense facts. In *Proceedings of the SIGCHI conference on Human Factors in computing systems*, pages 75–78.

Luis Von Ahn, Ruoran Liu, and Manuel Blum. 2006b. Peekaboom: a game for locating objects in images. In *Proceedings of the SIGCHI conference on Human Factors in computing systems*, pages 55–64.

Jérôme Waldispühl, Attila Szantner, Rob Knight, Sébastien Caisse, and Randy Pitchford. 2020. Leveling up citizen science. *Nature Biotechnology*, 38:1124–1126.

Mingzhu Wu, Nafise Sadat Moosavi, Dan Roth, and Iryna Gurevych. 2021. Coreference reasoning in machine reading comprehension. In *Proceedings of the 59th Annual Meeting of the Association for Computational Linguistics and the 11th International Joint Conference on Natural Language Processing (Volume 1: Long Papers)*, pages 5768–5781, Online. Association for Computational Linguistics.

NatiQ: An End-to-end Text-to-Speech System for Arabic

Ahmed Abdelali[1], Nadir Durrani[1], Cenk Demiroglu[2],
Fahim Dalvi[1], Hamdy Mubarak[1], Kareem Darwish[3]
[1]Qatar Computing Research Institute - Hamad Bin Khalifa University, Doha, Qatar
[2]Özyeğin University, Istanbul, Türkiye [3]aiXplain Inc. Los Gatos, CA, USA
[1]aabdelali,ndurrani,fdalvi,hmubarak@hbku.edu.qa
[2]cenk.demiroglu@ozyegin.edu.tr [3]kareem.darwish@aixplain.com

Abstract

NatiQ is end-to-end text-to-speech system for Arabic. Our speech synthesizer uses an encoder-decoder architecture with attention. We used both tacotron-based models (tacotron-1 and tacotron-2) and the faster transformer model for generating mel-spectrograms from characters. We concatenated Tacotron1 with the WaveRNN vocoder, Tacotron2 with the WaveGlow vocoder and ESPnet transformer with the parallel wavegan vocoder to synthesize waveforms from the spectrograms. We used in-house speech data for two voices: 1) neutral male "Hamza"- narrating general content and news, and 2) expressive female "Amina"- narrating children story books to train our models. Our best systems achieve an average Mean Opinion Score (MOS) of 4.21 and 4.40 for Amina and Hamza respectively.The objective evaluation of the systems using word and character error rate (WER and CER) as well as the response time measured by real-time factor favored the end-to-end architecture ESPnet.NatiQ demo is available online at https://tts.qcri.org.

1 Introduction

Text to speech (TTS) is among the technologies that enables many solutions across different sectors. In the current pandemic time, education system is challenged with the new norm of distance and remote education. Teachers are not able to provide needed attention and support for every student; more precisely for lower elementary schools where students are very dependent on the teacher's guidance to follow the instructions. TTS can elevate some of this burden by allowing the young children to hear the content and have it read to them in a very fluent and pleasing voice. Advances in Neural technology allow achieving more natural voice compared to previous technologies (Kons et al., 2019).

We present **NatiQ**, an end-to-end speech system for Arabic. The system is composed of two independent modules: i) the web application and ii) the speech synthesizer. The web application uses *React Javascript* framework to handle dynamic User Interface and *MangoDB* to handle session related information. The system is built upon modern web technologies, allowing it to run cross-browsers and platforms. Figure 1 presents a screenshot of the interface.

Our best synthesizer is based on ESPnet Transformer TTS (Li et al., 2019) architecture that takes input characters in an encoder-decoder framework to output mel-spectograms. The intermediate form is then converted into wav form using the Generative Adversarial Networks vocoder WaveGAN (Donahue et al., 2019; Yamamoto et al., 2020). We explored additional architecture including Tacotron1 (Wang et al., 2017) and 2 (Shen et al., 2018) and for vocoders WaveRNN (Kalchbrenner et al., 2018) and WaveGlow (Prenger et al., 2018) to synthesize waveforms from the decoded mel-spectograms.

We built two in-house speech corpora *Amina* – a female speaker with expressive narration and *Hamza* – a male speaker with neutral narration. The former is targeted towards education and the latter is more suitable to broadcast media.

Given that Arabic is typically written with no short vowels, this required to include additional processing to the text before exploiting it in the training. In addition to the short vowels restoration, diacritization, the pre-processing steps involves segmentation, transcript matching, voice normalization and silence reduction. We will further describe the pipeline and the architecture in detail. The resulting systems were evaluated using both objective and subjective approaches employing automatic metrics such as CER and WER; and using MOS.

This works was done while Kareem Darwish was at Qatar Computing Research Institute.

Proceedings of the The Seventh Arabic Natural Language Processing Workshop (WANLP), pages 394 - 398
December 8, 2022

Lastely, the systems were assessed with Real-time Factor to evaluated decoding speed of each model.

Figure 1: NatiQ system in action

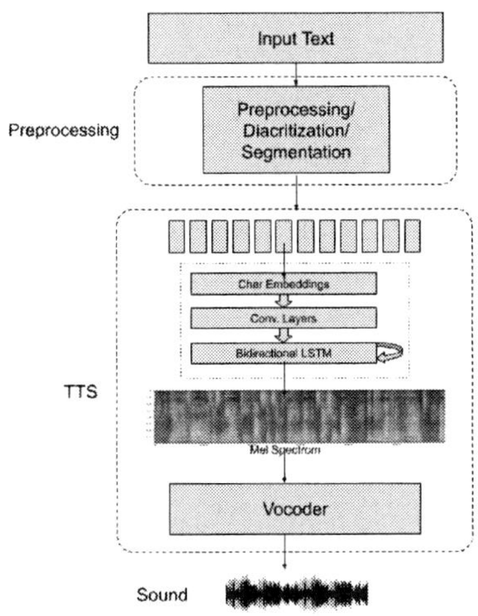

Figure 2: NatiQ Architecture.

2 System Architecture

Our NatiQ system is a web-based demonstration that is composed of two main components:

2.1 Web Application

The web application has two major components; the frontend and the backend. The frontend is created using the React Javascript framework to handle the dynamic User Interface (UI) changes such updates in generation. The backend is built using NodeJS and MongoDB to handle sessions, data associated with these sessions, communication with models, request inference and authentication. The frontend presents the user with an input text box and choice of speakers to choose from. Figure 1 shows a screenshot for the frontend. The responses from the backend will be presented to the user in a wave form that the user can listen to or download.

2.2 Speech Synthesis

Now we will describe the overall architecture of our synthesis model. Figure 2 shows the system architecture. The preprocessing module involves converting the numbers, abbreviations and dates into their vocalized form using linguistic and custom rules. Next the text is vowelized using Farasa (Abdelali et al., 2016), which diacritize and restore short vowels using the syntactic structure of the sentence.

The synthesizer is an encoder-decoder model cascaded with a vocoder to generate the waveforms. The former converts the preprocessed text into a mel-spectrum. The latter convert the mel-spectogram representation into a wave form. Below we describe different components of our model:

2.2.1 Data

We acquired high quality speech data recorded at a sampling rate of 44kHz from two speakers. A female speaker *Amina* was recorded reading selected passages mainly from children books in Modern Standard Arabic. The data contains 3964 segments and 50,714 words in total. The style for this recording is expressive. The second data *Hamza* was recorded by a male speaker and in neutral style. This data contains 6005 segments and 80,409 words in total. Figure 3 shows the segments length distribution for each of the speakers. For both of the speakers, the average length of the segments is around 7 seconds or around 12 words per segment.

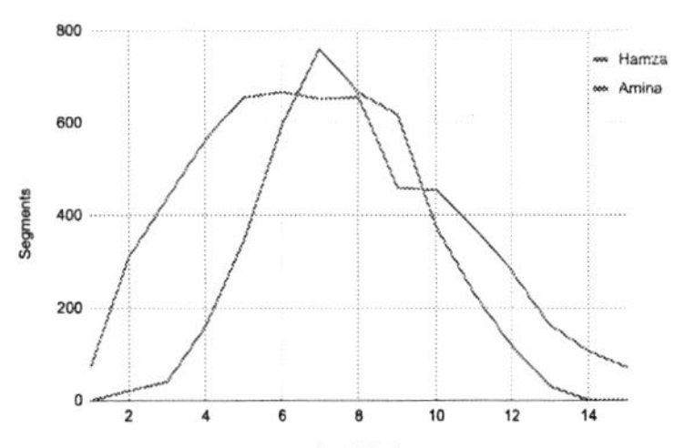

Figure 3: Distribution of segments lengths per speakers

2.2.2 Preprocessing

Data preprocessing steps involve: i) diacritization, ii) speech transcript matching, iii) segmentation, and iv) vowel normalization and silence reduction.

Diacritization Arabic has two types of vowels; namely long vowels, which are explicitly written in the text, and short vowels (aka diacritics) which are typically omitted in modern writings as native speakers can infer them based on contextual information. In order to read Arabic words properly, readers need to restore the missing diacritics and this is important for machines to pronounce the text correctly. We diacritized the text using `Farasa` (Abdelali et al., 2016). Although Farasa gives an accuracy above 94% the automatic diacritized data was, neverthless, reviewed by a language expert to ensure the accuracy of the annotations. This is important as some cases (for example named entities and foreign words) are often even challenging for a native speaker let alone for the automatic system. It's worth mentioning that we built a text normalization layer to convert digits, abbreviations, and special symbols to words to be fully diacritized by Farasa. Due to Arabic complexity and ambiguity, this conversion was not trivial in many cases.

Speech Transcript Matching Although native speakers don't require short vowels to correctly pronounce a word, in some rare cases they may make mistake of pronouncing a word with a wrong vowel. Rather than correcting the speaker which might require going back to the studio and re-record the segment again, we opted to change the transcript in such cases to reflect what was spoken. This will save both time and efforts required from the speaker and the recording studio.

Segmentation Due to the limitation of neural architectures to handle long audio samples (Shen et al., 2018), the data is sampled into frames of 10 seconds in average. The segmentation has to consider the sentence boundaries and not to break nor the context or the prosody. In general cases, long silences between segments is a good indicator but exception were found when related context or supplemental material that is still considered a part of the sentence still comes after a long pause.

Text Normalization This includes spelling out numbers, fractions, abbreviations and titles into their textual format such as "16.43" to "ستة عشر وأربعة وثلاثين جزء من المئة" (stp Ecr wOrbEp wvlAvyn jzC mn AlmQp)[1] or "وقال أ. د. ماجد" (wqAl O. d. mAjd) to "وقال الأستاذ الدكتور ماجد" (wqAl AlOstAV Aldktwr mAjd).

[1]Using Safe Buckwalter Arabic encoding

2.2.3 Models

We trained three models based on Tacotron-1 (Wang et al., 2017), Tacotron-2 (Shen et al., 2018) and Transformer TTS (Li et al., 2019) recipes. The choice of these models was driven mainly by: Real-time decoding and high-quality voice.

Model Tacotron1 builds on top of RNN sequence-to-sequence architecture. It includes an encoder, an attention-based decoder, and a post-processing module. The former takes text as characters and generates a mel-spectrogram. The post-processing module then generates waveform from the mel-spectogram. Tacotron1 uses a CBHG-based encoder which consists of a bank of 1-D convolutional filters, followed by highway networks and a bidirectional gated recurrent unit (GRU). The decoder is a content-based tanh attention decoder that generates an 80-band mel-scale spectrogram as the target. Finally we use **WaveRNN** (Kalchbrenner et al., 2018) on top to generate waveforms from the generated mel-spectograms. WaveRNN is a single layered RNN network that generates raw audio samples.

Model Tacotron2 follows the same recipe as Tacotron1 i.e. RNN-based sequence-to-sequence encoder-decoder architecture, it consists of a bi-directional LSTM-based encoder and a unidirectional LSTM-based decoder with location sensitive attention (Zhang et al., 2018). Additionally, the models employs different vocoder to generate waveforms. We used the **WaveGlow** (Prenger et al., 2018), a flow-based network capable of generating high quality speech from melspectograms. WaveGlow is a generative model that generates audio by sampling from zero mean spherical Gaussian distribution. It uses 12 coupling layers and 12 invertible 1×1 convolutions.

Model ESPnet Transformer TTS Inspired by Neural Machine Translation, Transformer TTS (Li et al., 2019) adapts multi-head self-attention mechanism and feed forward strategy to build an encoder-decoder model that would convert a sequence of inputs characters into an output sequence of acoustic features (log Mel-filter bank features), the model provide an adventage over the former models in the training speed as it uses a feed forward network compared to recurrent network based-models. Similarly to Tacotron1 and Tacotron2 models, Transformer TTS requires a vocoder to further convert the Mel features into wave form. We used Parallel WaveGAN (Yamamoto et al., 2020) a non-autoregressive WaveNet that uses generative adversarial network to convert the Mel-filter bank sequences to a waveform.

3 Evaluation

To evaluate the performance of each of the models, We built an evaluation test set composed of 100 sentences of varying lengths, collected from six domains including: Culture, Economy, Literature, Politics, Sports, and Technology. The sentences were collected between Jan 1st to Jan 20th, 2022. They include excerpts from current topics and news. We decoded each sentence using the models and for each of the voices. This resulted in a pool of 600 audio files to evaluate. We carried automatic and manual (subjective) evaluations described below:

3.1 Automatic Evaluation

We used state-of-the-art Arabic ASR system (Hussein et al., 2022) to decode the audio files generated by our TTS models. The ASR system gives state of the art performance on a number of standard data sets such as MGB-3 (Ali et al., 2017) and MGB-5 (Ali et al., 2019). We then compare the generated transcripts against the input sentences for which TTS outputs are generated. As the ASR system generates unvowelized text, we strip short vowels from the reference original text to allow a fair comparison. We used standard evaluation metrics Word Error Rate (WER) and Charecter Error Rate (CER). Table 1 shows the results using the automatic approach. The system built using ESPnet2 gave the lowest WER and CER. Additionally, the neutral voice "Hamza" achieved a lower error rate when compared to the expressive "Amina". This highlights the challenges dealing with non-monotonic voices which are typically richer and has more features that the network needs to capture (Valle et al., 2019). For Amina, Tacotron1 results are not worse than the leading ESPnet2 system; which potentially means that Tacotron1 is better at handling richer features. Tacotron2 suffers more from deletion, and substitution errors, this is the main cause for the CER/WER to be higher than other models.

	Amina		Hamza	
	CER	WER	CER	WER
ESPnet2	**17.47**	**40.42**	**8.01**	**24.87**
Tacotron1	22.51	43.98	27.48	46.12
Tacotron2	40.76	64.80	82.38	93.62

Table 1: CER and WER evaluation results.

	Amina	Hamza
ESPnet2	3.57	4.40
Tacotron1	4.21	4.38
Tacotron2	3.49	2.34

Table 2: MOS evaluation results for the three systems.

3.2 Qualitative Evaluation

We recruited 14 individuals (7 females and 7 males) to carry the manual subjective evaluation. The participants were instructed to listen to the audio and give their opinion on the speech quality using a scale from 1 to 5; The five-category MOS scale (Guski, 1997): 5 = excellent, 4 = good, 3 = fair, 2 = poor, 1 = bad. Each participants was presented with a set of 15 random samples from the pool. The overall results presented in Table 2 shows that the participants favored ESPNet:Hamza and Tacotron1:Amina. The results of ESPNet:Hamza are very comparable to the Tacotron1:Hamza. The results also shows that participants preferred the neutral voice over expressive one. Literature also reports that typically evaluators prefer neutral over expressive and expressivity is better perceived when the samples have a high quality (Tahon et al., 2017). The qualitative results are closely aligned with automatic evaluation, the differences in CER/WER between ESPNet:Amina and Tacotron1:Amina are less pronounced when compared to Hamza.

3.3 Speed

Lastly, another metric to evaluate the system, we used Real-time Factor (RTF): the ratio of the speech generation time to the utterance duration. Such measure is very crucial and essential in the deployment of any system, especially for real-time use. For a system to be considered real-time, RTF should be <= 1 (Pratap et al., 2020). Having a low RTF, will ensure that the system latency is reasonable and acceptable and indicate that the system can be used in real-time applications. Table 3 shows the average RTF for the three systems running on a 4 Cores Intel(R) Xeon(R) CPU E5-2640 v4 @ 2.40GHz and 32Gb of RAM and powered by NVIDIA Tesla V100 SXM2 32Gb GPU. The end-to-end ESPnet2 system, is the clear winner with a an RTF equal to 0.09 which is 1.5 and 17 times faster than Tacotron2 and Tacotron1 respectively. None of the systems run real-time on CPU. Our fastest system ESPnet2 runs at a speed of 4.24xRT.

	RTF	
Model	GPU	CPU
ESPnet2	**0.09**	4.24
Tacotron1	1.66	-
Tacotron2	0.14	-

Table 3: Realtime Factor evaluation results.

4 Conclusion

We presented NatiQ Arabic text-to-speech system, a system based on end-to-end framework that combines Transformer encoder-decoder and WaveGAN vocoder. The system was evaluated using subjective metric, Mean Opinion Score and objective Speed, WER and CER. The system achieved a MOS of 4.35 and 4.72 for Amina and Hamza respectively. Such performance is very comparable to English systems (Wang et al., 2017; Shen et al., 2018) . For the expressive speaker, the performance of the system still lags behind the neutral one. This is due to the complex and rich features encoded in expressive voice. We plan to explore different techniques that exploits the additional features in the voice such as (Liu et al., 2020) which aim to combine frames and style information as two objective functions to optimize while training the model.

References

Ahmed Abdelali, Kareem Darwish, Nadir Durrani, and Hamdy Mubarak. 2016. Farasa: A fast and furious segmenter for Arabic. In *Proceedings of the 2016 NAACL: Demonstrations*, pages 11–16, San Diego, California. ACL.

Ahmed Ali, Suwon Shon, Younes Samih, Hamdy Mubarak, Ahmed Abdelali, James Glass, Steve Renals, and Khalid Choukri. 2019. The mgb-5 challenge: Recognition and dialect identification of dialectal arabic speech. In *2019 IEEE (ASRU)*, pages 1026–1033.

Ahmed Ali, Stephan Vogel, and Steve Renals. 2017. Speech recognition challenge in the wild: Arabic mgb-3. In *2017 IEEE ASRU*, pages 316–322.

Chris Donahue, Julian McAuley, and Miller Puckette. 2019. Adversarial audio synthesis.

Rainer Guski. 1997. Psychological methods for evaluating sound quality and assessing acoustic information. *Acta Acustica united with Acustica*, 83:765–774.

Amir Hussein, Shinji Watanabe, and Ahmed Ali. 2022. Arabic speech recognition by end-to-end, modular systems and human. *Computer Speech & Language*, 71:101272.

Nal Kalchbrenner, Erich Elsen, Karen Simonyan, Seb Noury, Norman Casagrande, Edward Lockhart, Florian Stimberg, Aaron van den Oord, Sander Dieleman, and Koray Kavukcuoglu. 2018. Efficient neural audio synthesis.

Zvi Kons, Slava Shechtman, Alex Sorin, Carmel Rabinovitz, and Ron Hoory. 2019. High quality, lightweight and adaptable tts using lpcnet.

Naihan Li, Shujie Liu, Yanqing Liu, Sheng Zhao, and Ming Liu. 2019. Neural speech synthesis with transformer network. In *Proceedings of the AAAI Conference on Artificial Intelligence*, AAAI'19/IAAI'19/EAAI'19. AAAI Press.

Rui Liu, Berrak Sisman, Guanglai Gao, and Haizhou Li. 2020. Expressive tts training with frame and style reconstruction loss.

Vineel Pratap, Qiantong Xu, Jacob Kahn, Gilad Avidov, Tatiana Likhomanenko, Awni Hannun, Vitaliy Liptchinsky, Gabriel Synnaeve, and Ronan Collobert. 2020. Scaling up online speech recognition using convnets.

Ryan Prenger, Rafael Valle, and Bryan Catanzaro. 2018. Waveglow: A flow-based generative network for speech synthesis.

Jonathan Shen, Ruoming Pang, Ron J. Weiss, Mike Schuster, Navdeep Jaitly, Zongheng Yang, Zhifeng Chen, Yu Zhang, Yuxuan Wang, RJ Skerry-Ryan, Rif A. Saurous, Yannis Agiomyrgiannakis, and Yonghui Wu. 2018. Natural tts synthesis by conditioning wavenet on mel spectrogram predictions.

Marie Tahon, Gwénolé Lecorvé, Damien Lolive, and Raheel Qader. 2017. Perception of expressivity in TTS: linguistics, phonetics or prosody? In *Statistical Language and Speech Processing*, volume 10583, pages 262–274, Le Mans, France.

Rafael Valle, Jason Li, Ryan Prenger, and Bryan Catanzaro. 2019. Mellotron: Multispeaker expressive voice synthesis by conditioning on rhythm, pitch and global style tokens.

Yuxuan Wang, RJ Skerry-Ryan, Daisy Stanton, Yonghui Wu, Ron J. Weiss, Navdeep Jaitly, Zongheng Yang, Ying Xiao, Zhifeng Chen, Samy Bengio, Quoc Le, Yannis Agiomyrgiannakis, Rob Clark, and Rif A. Saurous. 2017. Tacotron: Towards end-to-end speech synthesis.

Ryuichi Yamamoto, Eunwoo Song, and Jae-Min Kim. 2020. Parallel wavegan: A fast waveform generation model based on generative adversarial networks with multi-resolution spectrogram. *ICASSP 2020 - 2020 IEEE (ICASSP)*, pages 6199–6203.

Jing-Xuan Zhang, Zhen-Hua Ling, and Li-Rong Dai. 2018. Forward attention in sequence- to-sequence acoustic modeling for speech synthesis. In *2018 IEEE ICASSP*, pages 4789–4793.

The Effect of Arabic Dialect Familiarity on Data Annotation

Ibrahim Abu Farha[1] **and Walid Magdy**[1,2]
[1] School of Informatics, The University of Edinburgh, Edinburgh, UK
[2] The Alan Turing Institute, London, UK
{i.abufarha,wmagdy}@ed.ac.uk

Abstract

Data annotation is the foundation of most natural language processing (NLP) tasks. However, data annotation is complex and there is often no specific correct label, especially in subjective tasks. Data annotation is affected by the annotators' ability to understand the provided data. In the case of Arabic, this is important due to the large dialectal variety. In this paper, we analyse how Arabic speakers understand other dialects in written text. Also, we analyse the effect of dialect familiarity on the quality of data annotation, focusing on Arabic sarcasm detection. This is done by collecting third-party labels and comparing them to high-quality first-party labels. Our analysis shows that annotators tend to better identify their own dialect and they are prone to confuse dialects they are unfamiliar with. For task labels, annotators tend to perform better on their dialect or dialects they are familiar with. Finally, females tend to perform better than males on the sarcasm detection task. We suggest that to guarantee high-quality labels, researchers should recruit native dialect speakers for annotation.

1 Introduction

Many natural language processing (NLP) tasks rely on training machine learning (ML) models on labelled data. The labels are assigned in different approaches, amongst the most common ones is human annotation. These labels are sometimes highly subjective and might be affected by annotators' backgrounds and beliefs. Such subjectivity would have minimal effects for objective tasks where people have consensus (Plank et al., 2014). However, these differences can be disruptive when considering subjective tasks such as sentiment analysis (Medhat et al., 2014; Abu Farha and Magdy, 2021), sarcasm detection (Abu Farha et al., 2022a), hate speech (MacAvaney et al., 2019) and many others. This applies to all languages, but for Arabic, it is more important due to the large dialectal variety amongst Arab annotators. Arabic has three variants; the first is classical Arabic (CA), which is the language of Quran and early literature. The second is modern standard Arabic (MSA), which is standardized and mainly used in news and books. The third is dialectal Arabic (DA), which is the colloquial language spoken in everyday life and it varies from one region to another. DA differs from MSA in the sense that these dialects are not standardized. Arabic dialects substantially differ from MSA and each other in terms of phonology, morphology, lexical choice and syntax (Habash, 2010). These variations affect how speakers of different dialects understand each other; where some words or maybe complete sentences can be incomprehensible.

Previous works on Arabic dialects focused on dialect identification either in text or speech such as the works of (Zaidan and Callison-Burch, 2014; Elfardy et al., 2014; Bouamor et al., 2014; Salameh et al., 2018; Elaraby and Abdul-Mageed, 2018; Bouamor et al., 2019; Abdul-Mageed et al., 2020, 2021). Other works focused on higher level tasks exploiting dialectal data such as sentiment analysis (Abdul-Mageed et al., 2014), emotion (Alhuzali et al., 2018), offensive language (Mubarak et al., 2020), and sarcasm (Abu Farha and Magdy, 2020). Most of these datasets are created through manual data annotation. Those annotations are collected by either recruiting designated annotators or through crowd-sourcing platforms. Especially in the case of crowd-sourced annotations, the annotators are usually from different regions and speak different dialects.

In this paper, we argue that dataset creators should take into consideration the effects of annotators' native dialect and dialect familiarity on the annotation process. Due to the differences between Arabic dialects, annotators might be assigning inaccurate labels to texts written in dialects they do not fully understand. In our work, we aim to analyse

Proceedings of the The Seventh Arabic Natural Language Processing Workshop (WANLP), pages 399 - 408
December 8, 2022

how a speaker of one dialect understands another. Also, we study the effect of dialect familiarity on the data annotation process, taking Arabic sarcasm as a case study of a highly subjective task.

In our paper, we investigate the following research questions:

- **RQ1**: How do speakers of different dialects understand text written in other dialects?
- **RQ2**: How do speakers of different dialects perform on the sarcasm detection task?
- **RQ3**: Is there a correlation between gender and the performance of an annotator on the sarcasm detection task?

In this paper, we answer these questions through collecting third-party annotations for SemEval's 2022 task 6 (iSarcasmEval) dataset (Abu Farha et al., 2022a). This dataset has first-party labels for both sarcasm and dialect, where the text authors provided the labels. Thus, we argue that those labels are of a higher quality compared to traditional third-party labels. In our work, we collect both sarcasm and dialect labels from third-party annotators, and we analyse the variation of performance based on annotators' mother dialect, familiarity with other dialects, and gender. Our analysis shows that: (1) annotators tend to better understand and identify their own dialect; (2) annotators are prone to confuse dialects with each other; (3) Egyptian dialect and MSA are the easiest to identify in written text; (4) sarcasm annotations are more trustworthy if they are provided by native dialect speakers; and (5) females tend to perform better than males on the sarcasm detection task. We hope that our findings in this study would work as guidelines for future work on labelling Arabic datasets. Data used for this work with all labels are made publicly available[1].

2 Related Work

2.1 Data Annotation and Subjectivity

Most NLP applications rely on manually annotated data. These annotations are collected from annotators from different cultures and backgrounds. Previous works acknowledged the effects of subjectivity on the quality of datasets. However, the literature lacks in-depth analyses or attempts to mitigate this issue. (Rottger et al., 2022) tried to approach this issue through suggesting new paradigms for data annotation. In their work, they suggest that dataset creators follow either descriptive or the prescriptive paradigm. Descriptive paradigm encourages annotator subjectivity, whereas prescriptive paradigm discourages it. They also argue that dataset creators should explicitly aim for one or the other. For Arabic, dialect intelligibility and understanding can be one of the subjective factors affecting the data annotation process. The literature of Arabic NLP lacks in-depth analyses on the effects of dialect familiarity on the quality of data annotations or how people understand different dialects. Habash et al. (2008) approached the dialectal variety focusing on creating standard annotation guidelines identifying dialect switching between MSA and at least one dialect. Zaidan and Callison-Burch (2014) mentioned that annotators tend to over-identify their dialect. We add to this line of work by exploring how annotators understand different dialects. We also analyse the quality of their labels on one of the most subjective tasks, sarcasm detection.

2.2 Dialectal Arabic NLP

One of the major challenges when studying dialectal Arabic (DA) was the lack of resources. For this reason, early works focused on creating resources that cover a few regions or countries (Jarrar et al., 2017; Khalifa et al., 2016; Sadat et al., 2014; Harrat et al., 2014; Al-Twairesh et al., 2018), while others focused on creating multi-dialect resources (Zaidan and Callison-Burch, 2011; Elfardy et al., 2014; Bouamor et al., 2014; Mubarak and Darwish, 2014; Cotterell and Callison-Burch, 2014) In addition, some previous works on Arabic dialects focused on dialect identification either in text or speech (Zaidan and Callison-Burch, 2014; Salameh et al., 2018; Abdul-Mageed et al., 2021, 2020; Bouamor et al., 2019; Elaraby and Abdul-Mageed, 2018; Elfardy et al., 2014; Bouamor et al., 2014).

Most of the works targeted the five major Arabic dialects: Egyptian (Nile Basin), Levantine, North African (Maghrebi), Gulf, and modern standard Arabic (MSA). However, in recent years, there has been an interest in a more fine-grained categorisation. Some of the significant works in this area are NADI shared tasks (Abdul-Mageed et al., 2020, 2021). The organisers provided data annotated on country and provenance levels, covering 21 countries and 100 provenances. Other works focused on higher level tasks exploiting dialectal data such as sentiment analysis (Abdul-Mageed et al., 2014),

[1] https://github.com/iabufarha/arabic-dialect-familiarity

emotion (Alhuzali et al., 2018), offensive language (Mubarak et al., 2020), and sarcasm (Abu Farha and Magdy, 2020). Most of the multi-dialectal resources were annotated either by designated annotators or crowd-sourced annotations. In most cases, annotators' familiarity with the dialects at hand is not taken into consideration. In our work, we aim to show that such information is necessary and should be one of the considerations when creating dialectal resources.

2.3 Sarcasm Detection

Sarcasm is a form of verbal irony that is often used to express ridicule or contempt. It is usually correlated with expressing an opinion in an indirect way where there would be a discrepancy between the literal and intended meaning of an utterance (Wilson, 2006). Sarcasm is one of the most subjective tasks that relies heavily on cultural references and the cultural background of the author. To understand sarcasm, a person needs to understand the context in which it is used, and language/dialect is part of that (Oprea and Magdy, 2019; Abercrombie and Hovy, 2016; Wallace et al., 2014). Most of previous work on sarcasm detection falls into one of two branches: creating datasets (Ptáček et al., 2014; Khodak et al., 2018; Barbieri et al., 2014; Filatova, 2012; Riloff et al., 2013; Abercrombie and Hovy, 2016; Oprea and Magdy, 2020a; Abu Farha and Magdy, 2020; Abu Farha et al., 2021) or creating detection models (Campbell and Katz, 2012; Riloff et al., 2013; Joshi et al., 2016; Wallace et al., 2015; Rajadesingan et al., 2015; Bamman and Smith, 2015; Amir et al., 2016; Hazarika et al., 2018; Oprea and Magdy, 2019). A few works focused on analysing the effect of including context in sarcasm detection models (Oprea and Magdy, 2019; Abercrombie and Hovy, 2016; Wallace et al., 2014). Wallace et al. (2014) showed that annotators tend to need context to provide judgements about ironic content. They showed that there is a correlation between that and the misclassified cases. Oprea and Magdy (2019) explored the effect of contextual information to detect sarcasm, and Oprea and Magdy (2020b) analysed the effect of cultural background and age on sarcasm understanding. Their analysis indicates that age, English language nativeness, and country are significantly influential on sarcasm understanding and should be considered in the design of sarcasm detection systems. Similar results were confirmed in the case of spoken sarcasm, where Puhacheuskaya and Järvikivi (2022) found that having a foreign accent had a negative impact on irony understanding.

Recently, Abu Farha et al. (2022b) compared human and machine performance on sarcasm detection for both English and Arabic. In their work, they compared human and machine performance on iSarcasmEval's dataset (Abu Farha et al., 2022a), a first-party annotated sarcasm dataset, where labels were provided by the authors of text themselves. Their analysis shows that sarcasm detection is challenging for humans, who perform nearly as well as state-of-the-art models. They also analysed error patterns for both humans and machine models. Based on their analysis they suggest avoiding third-party annotations for subjective tasks, building models and datasets that are better able to represent and utilise contextual information, and building better representations for proverbs and idioms which are heavily used to express sarcasm.

Our study adds to this line of work by focusing on Arabic and its dialects. In our work, we study how dialectal variation and familiarity affect human's ability to understand sarcasm.

3 Methodology

In this section, we describe our methodology for the analysis of dialects comprehension during data annotation tasks. We initially discuss the dataset we used and its ground-truth labels. Then we explain collecting third-party labels from annotators of different dialects, which will be compared later to the ground-truth labels for the analysis process.

3.1 Dataset

We use SemEval-2022 Task 6, iSarcasmEval, datasets (Abu Farha et al., 2022a). The shared-task includes three subtasks: sarcasm detection (subtask A), sarcasm category classification (subtask B), and pairwise sarcasm identification (subtask C). Subtasks A and C cover both English and Arabic, while subtask B is English only. The reason we chose iSarcasmEval's dataset is that the labels were provided by the authors themselves, which would make them more reliable than if they were provided by third-party annotators. For this work, we use the test set of Arabic subtask A (sarcasm detection). The test set consists of 1400 sentences, 200 of which are sarcastic and 1200 non-sarcastic. Each of the sentences has two labels provided by the author of the sentence: the dialect of the sentence (out of five dialects) and whether the sentence is meant to be sarcastic or not. Table 1 shows the statistics over the available dialects.

Dialect	Total	Sarcastic	Non-sarcastic
Nile Basin	520	131	389
MSA	482	16	466
Gulf	176	10	166
Levant	168	22	146
Maghreb	54	21	33

Table 1: Distribution of the dataset over the dialects.

3.2 Third-party Annotations

To analyse the performance of speakers of different dialects, we collected third-party annotations using Appen[2] platform. For each sentence, we collected *five annotations*. We allowed only native Arabic speakers to participate. Before starting the annotation process, each annotator is presented with test questions and only those who answer all the questions correctly would be allowed to participate in the annotation process. The test questions were sampled from a set of sentences that are clearly sarcastic/non-sarcastic. We used this approach to make sure that the annotators are not giving random answers and to avoid introducing any bias before the annotation. For each sentence, we asked annotators to provide the following:

- Sarcasm label indicating whether the text is sarcastic or not.
- Dialect label out of five: MSA, Egyptian (Nile), Gulf, Levantine, and Maghrebi.
- Mother dialect, which is the dialect the annotator grew up speaking.
- Known dialects, which are the dialects the annotator is familiar with.
- Gender of the annotator (either male or female).

A total of 22 annotators participated in our survey, 15 males and 7 females. Table 2 provides the distribution of the annotators according to their mother dialect and the dialects they are familiar with.

In the following sections, we provide an in-depth analysis of how each group of annotators of a given dialect performed in the labelling task of dialects and sarcasm.

[2]https://appen.com

Dialect	Mother dialect	Known by
Nile Basin	11	21
Levant	6	10
Gulf	1	7
Maghreb	4	5
MSA	-	16

Table 2: Annotators' details. The table shows the number of annotators who speak a specific dialect as a mother tongue and the number of annotators who mentioned that they know a specific dialect.

4 Results and Analysis

4.1 Dialect Identification

Figure 1 shows the accuracy of annotators in identifying the dialects. From the figure, it is clear the annotators, except Egyptian speakers, were able to identify MSA. Egyptian and Gulf speakers performed best on their dialect. Levantine and Maghrebi speakers performed better on dialects other than their own. Figure 2 shows the distribution of assigned dialect labels compared to the original ones. The results show that Egyptian and MSA are the easiest to identify. However, the annotators seem to confuse other dialects, especially Levantine and Maghrebi. Figure 3 provides a clearer picture of how speakers of one dialect identified other dialects. As shown in Figures 3a and 3c, Egyptian and Gulf speakers excel at identifying texts in their dialect. Figure 3d shows that Maghrebi speakers seem to confuse their dialect with MSA. Levantine speakers (Figure 3b) seem to confuse their dialect with the Gulf dialect. Similar to Figure 2, most annotators tend to easily identify MSA, except for Egyptian speakers who confuse it for Egyptian dialect. Gulf speakers seem to confuse Levantine and Maghrebi for the Gulf dialect.

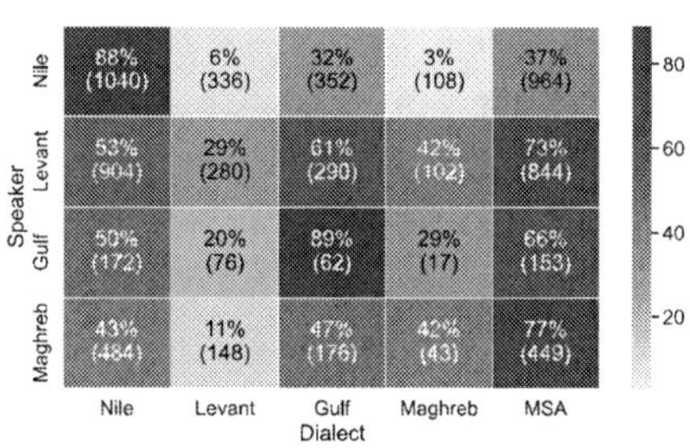

Figure 1: Dialect identification accuracy of annotators speaking different dialects. Annotation counts are indicated in brackets.

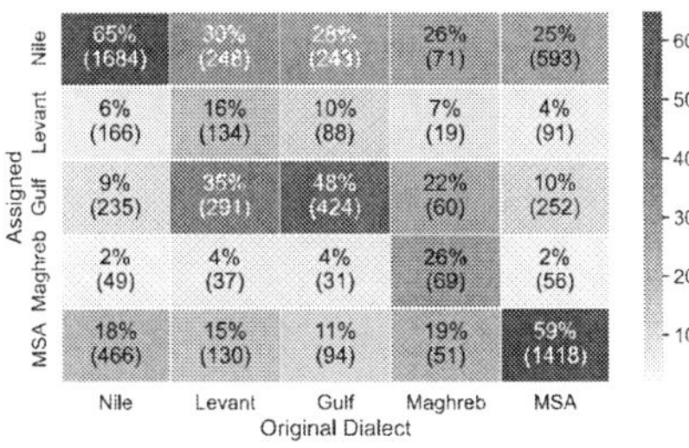

Figure 2: Assigned dialect labels vs the original ones. Annotation counts are indicated in brackets.

4.2 Sarcasm Detection

The effect of identifying dialects might be mild on the task of annotation itself. Thus, we examined the annotators' performance on the subjective task of sarcasm detection, which requires annotators to be able to understand the text to provide correct labels and is found to be a highly challenging task for annotators in different languages (Abu Farha et al., 2022b). Table 3 shows the annotators' performance on sarcasm detection. From the table, Levantine speakers seem to perform better on this task, followed by Gulf speakers. In order to have a better understanding, we analyse the performance over each dialect. Figure 4 shows the performance of speakers of a specific dialect on all the dialects. The figure shows $F1^{sarcastic}$ score and the number of annotations for the respective dialect. The results show that speakers of the Egyptian (Nile) dialect struggle to detect sarcasm written in MSA. Also, speakers of Maghrebi and Egyptian dialects struggle to identify sarcasm expressed using the Gulf's dialect. The results show that Levantine and Gulf speakers perform relatively well on all the dialects. Generally, the annotators achieved the highest score when the text was in Egyptian or their mother dialect.

Speaker's dialect	F1-sarcastic
Nile Basin	0.50
Gulf	0.53
Levant	0.58
Magreb	0.48

Table 3: Sarcasm detection performance (F1-sarcastic) of speakers of different dialects.

4.3 Sarcasm Detection - Dialect Familiarity

Figures 5a and 5b show the performance of annotators in two cases: when the text's dialect is one that they are familiar with and when it is not. When considering the case when the text's dialect is one that the annotators are familiar with (Figure 5a), the annotators have the highest performance on the Egyptian (Nile) dialect. These scores indicate that the annotators are truly familiar with the Egyptian (Nile) dialect. When looking at the cases where people are unfamiliar with the dialect, the performance is inconsistent. For example, the performance of Maghrebi speakers on texts in Levantine is higher for annotators who indicated that they are not familiar with the Levantine dialect. Another example is Levanbine speakers' performance on Maghrebi texts. Such inconsistencies indicate that some annotators might have provided a guess regarding the sarcasm label or that they underestimated their familiarity with the respective dialect.

Figures 6a and 6b show the performance when the annotators identified the dialects either correctly or incorrectly. The figures show that the performance is generally higher when the annotators identify the dialect correctly. This goes along with the previous observation that the annotators performed better on dialects they are familiar with. The exceptions are the performance of Levantine speakers on Maghrebi dialect, Maghrebi speakers on Levantine, and Nile speakers on Gulf dialect. Levantine speakers performed slightly better on MSA when they incorrectly identified the dialect. This goes along with the previous observation that indeed some annotators might be guessing the labels.

4.4 Sarcasm and Gender

We further analysed the performance of annotators based on their gender. Figure 7 shows the performance over dialects based on the annotators' gender. From the figure, it is noticeable that females perform better than males at detecting sarcasm. Females performed better than males on all dialects except MSA where the performance is quite comparable.

5 Discussion

In this section, we provide a discussion of the results mentioned in Section 4. We also revisit and answer our research questions as follows:

RQ1: How do speakers of different dialects understand other dialects? There are some similarities between dialects and, to some extent, people speaking different dialects can understand each other.

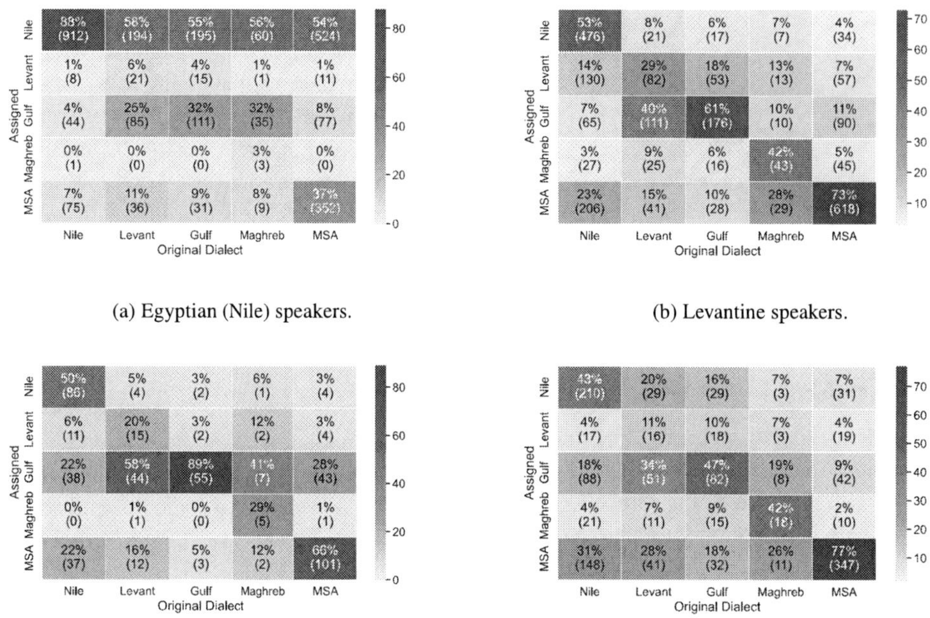

(a) Egyptian (Nile) speakers.

(b) Levantine speakers.

(c) Gulf speakers.

(d) Maghrebi speakers.

Figure 3: Dialect identification performance of speakers of different dialects. The table shows the assigned dialect labels vs the original ones for speakers of each dialect. Annotation counts are indicated in brackets.

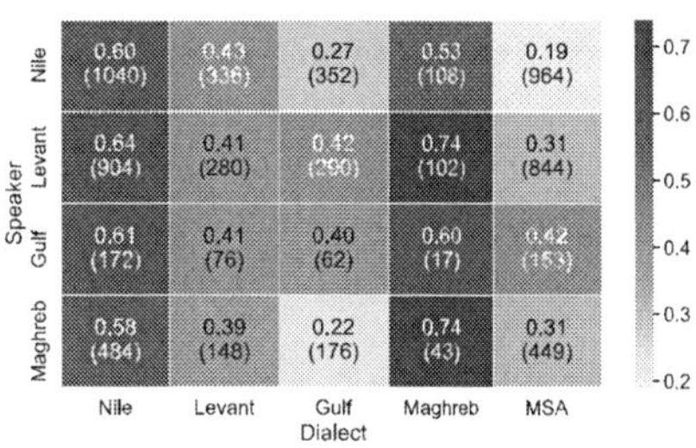

Figure 4: Sarcasm detection performance (F1-sarcastic) of different dialects speaker on each dialect. Original dialect labels were used. Annotation counts are indicated in brackets.

However, as shown in Section 4.1, annotators tend to confuse some dialects for different ones. For example, Egyptian speakers tend to over-identify their own dialect, assuming that more than 50% of other dialects to be Egyptian. This observation is similar to the behaviour observed in (Zaidan and Callison-Burch, 2014). Similar behaviour is observed with Gulf speakers towards Levantine. Such over-identification behaviour, and given the large number of Egyptian annotators, might introduce bias into datasets. Egyptian, Gulf, and Maghrebi speakers tend to perform better on their dialect. Levantine speakers' performance was inconsistent and they seemed to confuse Levantine for Gulf. This could be due to the spectrum of variation within the Levant countries from north to south, where the southern Levantine dialect is closer to the Gulf dialect.

The confusion between the dialects might be due to the fact that these dialects share many words or the differences are mostly phonological. Also, due to the slight differences between dialects' orthography, annotators might confuse sentences in dialects they are unfamiliar with and assign them to a different one. This phenomenon is clear in section 4.3, where Levantine speakers had better performance on MSA for sarcasm detection, but they assigned an incorrect dialect label.

RQ2: How do speakers of different dialects perform on the sarcasm detection task? As discussed in Sections 4.2 and 4.3, annotators tend to better understand sarcasm expressed in their dialect. This is due to the fact that annotators unfamiliar with a dialect would struggle to grasp the complete meaning of a sentence. Also, the fact that sarcasm usually relies on cultural references that can be specific to

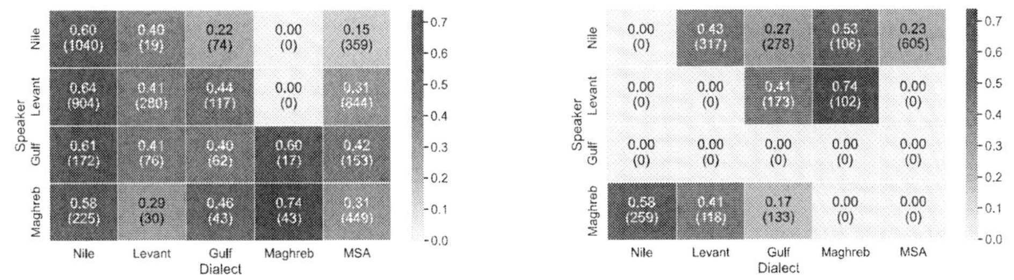

(a) Dialect is known.

(b) Dialect is unknown.

Figure 5: Sarcasm detection performance (F1-sarcastic) of speakers of different dialects. Annotation counts are indicated in brackets.

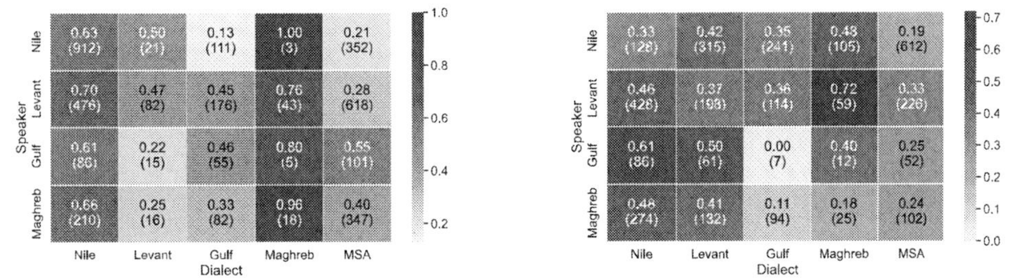

(a) Correctly identified the dialect.

(b) Incorrectly identified the dialect.

Figure 6: Sarcasm detection performance (F1-sarcastic) when based on their prediction of the dialect. Annotation counts are indicated in brackets.

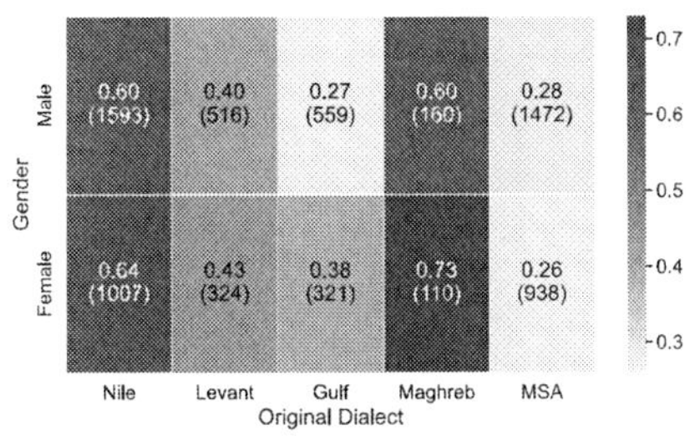

Figure 7: Sarcasm detection performance (F1-sarcastic) based on the annotators' gender. Annotation counts are indicated in brackets.

a region/dialect means that people unfamiliar with the dialect would not be able to understand such references. This observation aligns with the findings in (Oprea and Magdy, 2020b), where the authors found that English language nativeness and country are significantly influential on sarcasm understanding. Indeed, these factors should be considered when collecting third-party annotations for Arabic data. Although there are many shared linguistic and cultural aspects among Arabic speakers, there are still some local differences. Those are embodied in culture, traditions, and dialects. Thus, it is necessary to have native speakers, who are aware and familiar with these differences, annotating subjective and linguistically complex data like sarcasm.

RQ3: Is there a correlation between gender and the performance of an annotator on the sarcasm detection task? Based on the results in Section 4.4, female annotators seem to detect sarcasm better than male annotators. With the small number of annotators and the available data, we cannot provide an explanation for this observation. Future works should consider studying this in a better-designed setup that considers other factors such as educational background and personality traits.

We hope the findings of our study here will be of large benefits for researchers who work in the field of Arabic NLP, especially when applying data annotations. We have shown that dataset creators need to be careful when appointing annotators for labelling Arabic data. Our findings can act as a guide to appoint annotators with the suitable dialectal background for annotating data in each dialect.

6 Conclusions

In this paper, we analyse how Arabic speakers understand and identify other dialects in written text. We also analyse human performance on sarcasm detection and compare it across different dialects. We use SemEval's 2022 task 6 dataset, which has first-party sarcasm and dialect labels. Our analysis shows that the performance of annotators varies based on the annotators' familiarity with the text's dialect. Also, our analysis shows that annotators might not be familiar with the text's dialect and would confuse it with a different one. Our results also show that females are more likely to understand sarcasm compared to males. Based on the analysis, it is clear that dialect familiarity affects how annotators understand texts and their performance on a specific task. Consequently, we recommend that Arabic dataset creators should consider collecting annotations from native dialect speakers, which would guarantee higher-quality labels.

Limitations

The main limitation of our work is the number of annotators. In our work, we had only one speaker of the Gulf dialect. Future works should consider a larger sample size with a uniform distribution over the dialects. Another limitation is that we used the five major dialects. However, there are dialectal variations within these regions which should be considered. Finally, we only analysed the quality of the labels on sarcasm detection; future works should consider other tasks.

Acknowledgements

This work was partially supported by the Defence and Security Programme at the Alan Turing Institute, funded by the UK Government.

References

Muhammad Abdul-Mageed, Mona Diab, and Sandra Kübler. 2014. Samar: Subjectivity and sentiment analysis for arabic social media. *Computer Speech Language*, 28(1):20–37.

Muhammad Abdul-Mageed, Chiyu Zhang, Houda Bouamor, and Nizar Habash. 2020. NADI 2020: The first nuanced Arabic dialect identification shared task. In *Proceedings of the Fifth Arabic Natural Language Processing Workshop*, pages 97–110, Barcelona, Spain (Online). Association for Computational Linguistics.

Muhammad Abdul-Mageed, Chiyu Zhang, AbdelRahim Elmadany, Houda Bouamor, and Nizar Habash. 2021. NADI 2021: The second nuanced Arabic dialect identification shared task. In *Proceedings of the Sixth Arabic Natural Language Processing Workshop*, pages 244–259, Kyiv, Ukraine (Virtual). Association for Computational Linguistics.

Gavin Abercrombie and Dirk Hovy. 2016. Putting Sarcasm Detection into Context: The Effects of Class Imbalance and Manual Labelling on Supervised Machine Classification of Twitter Conversations. In *Proceedings of the ACL 2016 Student Research Workshop*, pages 107–113. ACL.

Ibrahim Abu Farha and Walid Magdy. 2020. From Arabic sentiment analysis to sarcasm detection: The ArSarcasm dataset. In *Proceedings of the 4th Workshop on Open-Source Arabic Corpora and Processing Tools, with a Shared Task on Offensive Language Detection*, pages 32–39, Marseille, France. European Language Resource Association.

Ibrahim Abu Farha and Walid Magdy. 2021. A comparative study of effective approaches for arabic sentiment analysis. *Information Processing Management*, 58(2):102438.

Ibrahim Abu Farha, Silviu Vlad Oprea, Steven Wilson, and Walid Magdy. 2022a. SemEval-2022 task 6: iSarcasmEval, intended sarcasm detection in English and Arabic. In *Proceedings of the 16th International Workshop on Semantic Evaluation (SemEval-2022)*, pages 802–814, Seattle, United States. Association for Computational Linguistics.

Ibrahim Abu Farha, Steven R. Wilson, Silviu Vlad Oprea, and Walid Magdy. 2022b. Sarcasm Detection is way too easy! An Empirical Comparison of Human and Machine Sarcasm detection. In *Findings of the Association for Computational Linguistics: EMNLP 2022*, Abu Dhabi, United Arab Emirates. Association for Computational Linguistics.

Ibrahim Abu Farha, Wajdi Zaghouani, and Walid Magdy. 2021. Overview of the WANLP 2021 shared task on sarcasm and sentiment detection in Arabic. In *Proceedings of the Sixth Arabic Natural Language Processing Workshop*, pages 296–305, Kyiv, Ukraine (Virtual). Association for Computational Linguistics.

Nora Al-Twairesh, Rawan Al-Matham, Nora Madi, Nada Almugren, Al-Hanouf Al-Aljmi, Shahad Alshalan, Raghad Alshalan, Nafla Alrumayyan, Shams Al-Manea, Sumayah Bawazeer, Nourah Al-Mutlaq, Nada Almanea, Waad Bin Huwaymil, Dalal Alqusair, Reem Alotaibi, Suha Al-Senaydi, and Abeer Alfutamani. 2018. Suar: Towards building a corpus for the saudi dialect. *Procedia Computer Science*, 142:72–82. Arabic Computational Linguistics.

Hassan Alhuzali, Muhammad Abdul-Mageed, and Lyle Ungar. 2018. Enabling deep learning of emotion with first-person seed expressions. In *Proceedings of the Second Workshop on Computational Modeling of People's Opinions, Personality, and Emotions in Social Media*, pages 25–35, New Orleans, Louisiana, USA. Association for Computational Linguistics.

Silvio Amir, Byron C. Wallace, Hao Lyu, Paula Carvalho, and Mario J. Silva. 2016. Modelling context with user embeddings for sarcasm detection in social media. In *CoNLL*, pages 167–177. ACL.

David Bamman and Noah A. Smith. 2015. Contextualized sarcasm detection on twitter. In *ICWSM*, pages 574–577. AAAI Press.

Francesco Barbieri, Francesco Ronzano, and Horacio Saggion. 2014. Italian irony detection in twitter: a first approach. In *CLiC-it*, page 28. AILC.

Houda Bouamor, Nizar Habash, and Kemal Oflazer. 2014. A multidialectal parallel corpus of Arabic. In *Proceedings of the Ninth International Conference on Language Resources and Evaluation (LREC'14)*, pages 1240–1245, Reykjavik, Iceland. European Language Resources Association (ELRA).

Houda Bouamor, Sabit Hassan, and Nizar Habash. 2019. The MADAR shared task on Arabic fine-grained dialect identification. In *Proceedings of the Fourth Arabic Natural Language Processing Workshop*, pages 199–207, Florence, Italy. Association for Computational Linguistics.

John D Campbell and Albert N Katz. 2012. Are there necessary conditions for inducing a sense of sarcastic irony? *Discourse Processes*, 49(6):459–480.

Ryan Cotterell and Chris Callison-Burch. 2014. A multi-dialect, multi-genre corpus of informal written Arabic. In *Proceedings of the Ninth International Conference on Language Resources and Evaluation (LREC'14)*, pages 241–245, Reykjavik, Iceland. European Language Resources Association (ELRA).

Mohamed Elaraby and Muhammad Abdul-Mageed. 2018. Deep models for Arabic dialect identification on benchmarked data. In *Proceedings of the Fifth Workshop on NLP for Similar Languages, Varieties and Dialects (VarDial 2018)*, pages 263–274, Santa Fe, New Mexico, USA. Association for Computational Linguistics.

Heba Elfardy, Mohamed Al-Badrashiny, and Mona Diab. 2014. AIDA: Identifying code switching in informal Arabic text. In *Proceedings of the First Workshop on Computational Approaches to Code Switching*, pages 94–101, Doha, Qatar. Association for Computational Linguistics.

Elena Filatova. 2012. Irony and sarcasm: Corpus generation and analysis using crowdsourcing. In *LREC*. ELRA.

Nizar Habash, Owen Rambow, Mona Diab, and Reem Kanjawi-Faraj. 2008. Guidelines for annotation of arabic dialectness. In *Proceedings of the LREC Workshop on HLT & NLP within the Arabic world*, pages 49–53.

Nizar Y Habash. 2010. Introduction to Arabic Natural Language Processing. *Synthesis Lectures on Human Language Technologies*, 3(1):1–187.

Salima Harrat, Karima Meftouh, Mourad Abbas, and Kamel Smaïli. 2014. Building Resources for Algerian Arabic Dialects. In *15th Annual Conference of the International Communication Association Interspeech*, Singapour, Singapore. ISCA.

Devamanyu Hazarika, Soujanya Poria, Sruthi Gorantla, Erik Cambria, Roger Zimmermann, and Rada Mihalcea. 2018. Cascade: Contextual sarcasm detection in online discussion forums. In *COLING*, pages 1837–1848. ACL.

Mustafa Jarrar, Nizar Habash, Faeq Alrimawi, Diyam Akra, and Nasser Zalmout. 2017. Curras: an annotated corpus for the palestinian arabic dialect. *Language Resources and Evaluation*, 51(3):745–775.

Aditya Joshi, Vaibhav Tripathi, Kevin Patel, Pushpak Bhattacharyya, and Mark Carman. 2016. Are word embedding-based features useful for sarcasm detection? In *EMNLP*, pages 1006–1011. ACL.

Salam Khalifa, Nizar Habash, Dana Abdulrahim, and Sara Hassan. 2016. A large scale corpus of Gulf Arabic. In *Proceedings of the Tenth International Conference on Language Resources and Evaluation (LREC'16)*, pages 4282–4289, Portorož, Slovenia. European Language Resources Association (ELRA).

Mikhail Khodak, Nikunj Saunshi, and Kiran Vodrahalli. 2018. A large self-annotated corpus for sarcasm. In *Proceedings of the Eleventh International Conference on Language Resources and Evaluation (LREC 2018)*, Miyazaki, Japan. European Language Resources Association (ELRA).

Sean MacAvaney, Hao-Ren Yao, Eugene Yang, Katina Russell, Nazli Goharian, and Ophir Frieder. 2019. Hate speech detection: Challenges and solutions. *PLOS ONE*, 14(8):1–16.

Walaa Medhat, Ahmed Hassan, and Hoda Korashy. 2014. Sentiment analysis algorithms and applications: A survey. *Ain Shams Engineering Journal*, 5(4):1093–1113.

Hamdy Mubarak and Kareem Darwish. 2014. Using Twitter to collect a multi-dialectal corpus of Arabic. In *Proceedings of the EMNLP 2014 Workshop on Arabic Natural Language Processing (ANLP)*, pages 1–7, Doha, Qatar. Association for Computational Linguistics.

Hamdy Mubarak, Kareem Darwish, Walid Magdy, Tamer Elsayed, and Hend Al-Khalifa. 2020.

Overview of OSACT4 Arabic offensive language detection shared task. In *Proceedings of the 4th Workshop on Open-Source Arabic Corpora and Processing Tools, with a Shared Task on Offensive Language Detection*, pages 48–52, Marseille, France. European Language Resource Association.

Silviu Oprea and Walid Magdy. 2019. Exploring author context for detecting intended vs perceived sarcasm. In *Proceedings of the 57th Annual Meeting of the Association for Computational Linguistics*, pages 2854–2859, Florence, Italy. Association for Computational Linguistics.

Silviu Oprea and Walid Magdy. 2020a. iSarcasm: A dataset of intended sarcasm. In *Proceedings of the 58th Annual Meeting of the Association for Computational Linguistics*, pages 1279–1289, Online. Association for Computational Linguistics.

Silviu Vlad Oprea and Walid Magdy. 2020b. The effect of sociocultural variables on sarcasm communication online. *Proc. ACM Hum.-Comput. Interact.*, 4(CSCW1).

Barbara Plank, Dirk Hovy, and Anders Søgaard. 2014. Linguistically debatable or just plain wrong? In *Proceedings of the 52nd Annual Meeting of the Association for Computational Linguistics (Volume 2: Short Papers)*, pages 507–511, Baltimore, Maryland. Association for Computational Linguistics.

Tomáš Ptáček, Ivan Habernal, and Jun Hong. 2014. Sarcasm detection on czech and english twitter. In *COLING*, pages 213–223. ACL.

Veranika Puhacheuskaya and Juhani Järvikivi. 2022. I was being sarcastic!: The effect of foreign accent and political ideology on irony (mis) understanding. *Acta Psychologica*, 222:103479.

Ashwin Rajadesingan, Reza Zafarani, and Huan Liu. 2015. Sarcasm detection on twitter: A behavioral modeling approach. In *WSDM*, pages 97–106. ACM.

Ellen Riloff, Ashequl Qadir, Prafulla Surve, Lalindra De Silva, Nathan Gilbert, and Ruihong Huang. 2013. Sarcasm as contrast between a positive sentiment and negative situation. In *EMNLP*, pages 704–714. ACL.

Paul Rottger, Bertie Vidgen, Dirk Hovy, and Janet Pierrehumbert. 2022. Two contrasting data annotation paradigms for subjective NLP tasks. In *Proceedings of the 2022 Conference of the North American Chapter of the Association for Computational Linguistics: Human Language Technologies*, pages 175–190, Seattle, United States. Association for Computational Linguistics.

Fatiha Sadat, Farzindar Kazemi, and Atefeh Farzindar. 2014. Automatic identification of Arabic language varieties and dialects in social media. In *Proceedings of the Second Workshop on Natural Language Processing for Social Media (SocialNLP)*, pages 22–27, Dublin, Ireland. Association for Computational Linguistics and Dublin City University.

Mohammad Salameh, Houda Bouamor, and Nizar Habash. 2018. Fine-grained Arabic dialect identification. In *Proceedings of the 27th International Conference on Computational Linguistics*, pages 1332–1344, Santa Fe, New Mexico, USA. Association for Computational Linguistics.

Byron C. Wallace, Do Kook Choe, and Eugene Charniak. 2015. Sparse, contextually informed models for irony detection: Exploiting user communities, entities and sentiment. In *Proceedings of the 53rd Annual Meeting of the Association for Computational Linguistics and the 7th International Joint Conference on Natural Language Processing (Volume 1: Long Papers)*, pages 1035–1044, Beijing, China. Association for Computational Linguistics.

Byron C. Wallace, Do Kook Choe, Laura Kertz, and Eugene Charniak. 2014. Humans require context to infer ironic intent (so computers probably do, too). In *Proceedings of the 52nd Annual Meeting of the Association for Computational Linguistics (Volume 2: Short Papers)*, pages 512–516, Baltimore, Maryland. Association for Computational Linguistics.

Deirdre Wilson. 2006. The pragmatics of verbal irony: Echo or pretence? *Lingua*, 116(10):1722–1743.

Omar F. Zaidan and Chris Callison-Burch. 2011. The Arabic online commentary dataset: an annotated dataset of informal Arabic with high dialectal content. In *Proceedings of the 49th Annual Meeting of the Association for Computational Linguistics: Human Language Technologies*, pages 37–41, Portland, Oregon, USA. Association for Computational Linguistics.

Omar F. Zaidan and Chris Callison-Burch. 2014. Arabic Dialect Identification. *Computational Linguistics*, 40(1):171–202.

Optimizing Naive Bayes for Arabic Dialect Identification

Tommi Jauhiainen, Heidi Jauhiainen, Krister Lindén
Department of Digital Humanities, University of Helsinki, Finland
tommi.jauhiainen@helsinki.fi

Abstract

This article describes the language identification system used by the SUKI team in the 2022 Nuanced Arabic Dialect Identification (NADI) shared task. In addition to the system description, we give some details of the dialect identification experiments we conducted while preparing our submissions. In the end, we submitted only one official run. We used a Naive Bayes-based language identifier with character n-grams from one to four, of which we implemented a new version, which automatically optimizes its parameters. We also experimented with clustering the training data according to different topics. With the macro F1 score of 0.1963 on test set A and 0.1058 on test set B, we achieved the 18th position out of the 19 competing teams.

1 Introduction

This paper describes the system used by the SUKI team at the Nuanced Arabic Dialect Identification (NADI) shared task 2022 (Abdul-Mageed et al., 2022). The task was the third in a series of language identification shared tasks focusing on Arabic languages (Abdul-Mageed et al., 2020, 2021b). In 2020, the first subtask of country-level classification was won by Talafha et al. (2020) using multi-dialect Arabic BERT model (Devlin et al., 2019) and the second subtask of province-level classification by El Mekki et al. (2020) using an ensemble of a BERT-based and a stochastic gradient descent (SGD) based (Zhang, 2004) identifiers. The various subtasks of the 2021 edition were won by AlKhamissi et al. (2021) using MARBERT-based systems (Abdul-Mageed et al., 2021a). A recent literature review of language identification for dialectal Arabic was conducted by Elnagar et al. (2021) and a more general survey of language identification techniques by Jauhiainen et al. (2019d). Deep learning, specifically BERT-based, systems dominated the two previous NADI shared tasks.

As the SUKI team, we have participated in various language identification (LI) related shared tasks throughout the years with our shallow HeLI or Naive Bayes-based systems. In 2016, we participated in the Arabic dialect sub-task of the 3rd edition of the Discriminating Between Similar Languages (DSL) shared task, which featured four Arabic dialects in addition to Modern Standard Arabic (MSA) (Jauhiainen et al., 2016). Using the HeLI LI method, we arrived at the seventh position, which was poor in contrast to the shared first place we reached in the first sub-task of DSL that year. The experiments described in this paper are the first time we have returned to the identification of various Arabic languages after that. In these experiments, we use a Naive Bayes (NB) based identifier instead of one based on the HeLI method. We implemented it and used it as a baseline in the 2019 Cuneiform Language Identification (CLI) shared task (Jauhiainen et al., 2019a). During the same year, we adapted our language model adaptation scheme (Jauhiainen et al., 2019c) to work with the NB implementation and won one of the two tracks in the Discriminating between the Mainland and Taiwan variation of Mandarin Chinese (DMT, Zampieri et al. (2019)) shared task (Jauhiainen et al., 2019b). More recently, we also won the Romanian Dialect Identification (RDI, Chakravarthi et al. (2021)) 2021 (Jauhiainen et al., 2021) and the Identification of Languages and Dialects of Italy (ITDI, Aepli et al. (2022)) 2022 (Jauhiainen et al., 2022a) shared tasks using the adaptive version of the NB identifier.

For the NADI shared task, we set out to find out whether our current NB implementation would be more competitive when distinguishing between close Arabic languages than our HeLI-based identifier in 2016. Additionally, we were trying to develop a way to use unlabeled data to improve the identifier results. The experiments to utilize unlabeled data were inconclusive and did not improve

Proceedings of the The Seventh Arabic Natural Language Processing Workshop (WANLP), pages 409 - 414
December 8, 2022

the identification results on the development set, so we did not end up using them in the one run we submitted. Also, as the language identification accuracy was already relatively low, using language model adaptation did not prove advantageous with the development data. Thus we submitted our only run using the non-adaptive NB identifier.

2 Shared Task Evaluation Setting

The third NADI shared task[1] featured 18 country-level dialects of Arabic. The official ranking metric was the macro-averaged F1 score. The shared task participants were given separate training and development sets consisting of tweets labeled with their respective country-level dialects. The training set was the same as in the NADI 2021 shared task (Abdul-Mageed et al., 2021b). According to the shared task instructions, the provided development set was not to be used as training data for the identifier used for the test data. The set sizes are seen in Table 1.

The participants were also given the tweet IDs of 10 million additional unlabeled Arabic tweets that could be used in training and developing the language identification system. The organizers provided a Python script that could be used to download the corresponding tweets using a Twitter API and their credentials. Currently, Twitter allows Academic users to download 10 million monthly tweets for research purposes. Due to the Twitter service being repeatedly over capacity and terminating the connection, the download had to be made in 16 parts, which took almost a week. Of the 9,999,998 downloaded tweets, 2,005,682 were tagged as **<UNAVAILABLE>**.

The participants were expected to provide results on two test sets; test set A featuring new unseen tweets for each of the 18 dialects and test set B featuring tweets from a subset of unknown size from the 18 languages.

We only used the NADI-labeled training and development sets for the submitted run. We did not use the development set for training the final identifier; we used it only to determine the method's optimal parameters.

3 System

The system uses a Naive Bayes-based method using the observed relative frequencies of multiple-size character n-grams as probabilities. As described by Jauhiainen et al. (2022a), the Naive Bayes type method adds together logarithms of the relative frequencies of character n-gram combinations f_i in the training data C_g as defined in Equation 1:

$$R(g, M) = -lg_{10} \prod_{i=1}^{\ell_{MF}} v_{C_g}(f_i) = \sum_{i=1}^{\ell_{MF}} -lg_{10}(v_{C_g}(f_i)) \tag{1}$$

where ℓ_{MF} is the number of individual features in the mystery text M to be identified, and f_i is M's ith feature. The relative frequency, $v_{C_g}(f)$, is calculated as in Equation 2:

$$v_{C_g}(f) = \begin{cases} \frac{c(C_g, f)}{\ell_{C_g^F}}, \text{ if } c(C_g, f) > 0 \\ \frac{1}{\ell_{C_g^F}} pm, \text{ otherwise} \end{cases} \tag{2}$$

where $c(C_g, f)$ is the count of feature f in the training corpus C_g of the language g. $\ell_{C_g^F}$ is the length of the corpus C_g when it has been transformed into a collection of features F, e.g., features of the same type as f. The pm is the penalty modifier, which is optimized using the development data.

The exact range of the used character n-grams is optimized using the development data. In previous versions of the identifier, we have semi-manually identified the optimal character n-gram ranges and the penalty modifier. However, on this occasion, we decided to implement an automatic optimizer to streamline experimentation. The automatic optimizer is first given initial character n-gram and penalty modifier ranges which it then uses to populate a todo-table. The parameters in the todo-table are evaluated, and the results are stored in a master results list. An additional top ten list of macro F1 scores is created with the parameters used to obtain them. The parameter instances used in the top ten list are checked, and nearby parameter combinations are added to a new todo-table if they are not found in the master results list. In the case of n-gram ranges, the optimizer tries one higher and one lower for both the minimum and maximum n-gram sizes. For the penalty modifier, it adds and subtracts 0.5 from the current one if there are no other penalty modifiers for the respective n-gram range in the master results list. If a "neighboring" penalty modifier exists in the results list, the halfway between the penalty modifiers is tried if the distance between modifiers is larger than 0.1. The cycle of evaluating the todo-table, creating a top ten list, and creating a new todo-table is continued as long as the top ten list changes between cycles. An ex-

[1] http://nadi.dlnlp.ai

Country	# tweets train	# tweets dev.	# tweets test A	# tweets test B
Egypt	4,283	1,041	?	?
Iraq	2,729	664	?	?
Saudi Arabia	2,140	520	?	?
Algeria	1,809	430	?	?
Oman	1,501	355	?	?
Syria	1,287	278	?	?
Libya	1,286	314	?	?
Tunisia	859	173	?	?
Morocco	858	207	?	?
Lebanon	644	157	?	?
United Arab Emirates	642	157	?	?
Yemen	429	105	?	?
Kuwait	429	105	?	?
Jordan	429	104	?	?
Palestine	428	104	?	?
Sudan	215	53	?	?
Qatar	215	52	?	?
Bahrain	215	52	?	?
Total	20,398	4,871	4,758	1,474

Table 1: The number of tweets of each Arabic dialect in the training and development sets of the NADI 2022 shared task.

n-gram range	penalty modifier
1 – 4	1.3
2 – 4	1.3
1 – 5	1.5
1 – 5	1.8

Table 2: An example of a master results list for the automatic optimizer.

n-gram range	penalty modifier
1 – 3	1.3
1 – 5	1.3
1 – 4	1.8
1 – 4	0.8
2 – 5	1.3
3 – 4	1.3
2 – 4	0.8
2 – 4	1.8
1 – 6	1.5
1 – 4	1.5
2 – 5	1.5
1 – 5	1.0
1 – 5	1.65
1 – 6	1.8
2 – 5	1.8
1 – 5	2.3

Table 3: An example todo-table generated on basis of master results list in Table 2.

ample of creating a todo-table from a top ten list is given in Tables 2 and 3.

We have published the code of the version used in the NADI shared task on GitHub.[2]

The only external part of our language identification pipeline was the Farasa morphological segmentation tool (Abdelali et al., 2016).[3] It had been successfully used in the NADI shared task before by El Mekki et al. (2020) and Wadhawan (2021), and by Alrifai et al. (2017) already in the 5th Author Profiling Task at PAN 2017 (Rangel et al., 2017). When the tweets are run through Farasa, it adds "+" characters between morphemes.

[2]https://github.com/tosaja/TunPRF-NADI

[3]https://farasa.qcri.org/segmentation/

# splits	Macro F1
1	0.2049
2	0.2038
4	0.2011
8	0.2011
16	0.1980

Table 4: The results of the adaptation experiments on the development data.

4 Experiments

Manually optimizing the parameters for the NB system, we arrived at the Macro F1 score of 0.2046 with n-grams from two to four and the penalty modifier of 1.40. After this, we did some experiments with language model adaptation using the same parameters, but adding more splits to adaptation worsened the results, as seen in Table 4. There was a slight increase in the F1 score, which indicated that some form of adaptation might be beneficial. However, it was clear that the accuracy of the identifier was too low for adaptation to have any meaningful effect, which is why we decided to leave adaptation experiments until our non-adaptive identification system would produce considerably better results.

The implemented automatic optimizer arrived at the macro F1 score of 0.2070 using character

Macro F1	n-gram range	penalty modifier
0.2119	1 – 4	1.375
0.2111	2 – 4	1.375
0.2106	2 – 5	1.5
0.2104	1 – 5	1.5
0.2094	1 – 5	1.5625
0.2087	1 – 4	1.4375
0.2082	2 – 4	1.3125
0.2078	1 – 5	1.625
0.2077	2 – 5	1.5625
0.2072	1 – 4	1.3125

Table 5: The final top 10 scores with their parameters on the development set. Farasa segmenter was used on both the training and the development data.

n-grams from one to four with a penalty modifier of 1.4375. The 0.002 score difference, when compared with the manual optimization results, was due to adding a space character at the beginning and the end of each tweet in the training data–a trick we had already done to the tweets being tested. We arrived at slightly better results using the optimizer with the Farasa-treated training and development sets. The top ten combinations with their macro F1 scores after running the automatical optimizer on the Farasa-treated training and development data can be seen in Table 5. We have not used any morphological segmentation with the NB identifier in our previous language identification experiments and cannot say whether using such segmentation is generally advantageous. The observed 2,4% macro F1 score improvement in this dataset could actually be a random effect.

Clustering Experiments Dividing languages into topic- or dialect-based clusters has proven fruitful in our earlier experiments (Jauhiainen et al., 2022b). We expected the training data to contain Tweets on many different topics and hypothesized that dividing the training data into several clusters might be advantageous. Each dialect would then be divided into several language models based on these clusters.

We created a custom clustering software based on the Naive Bayes identifier. It chose a random tweet among all the tweets and created language models from it. Then every other tweet was scored using those language models, and the one furthest from the original tweet was selected. Additional language models were also created from the second tweet, and then again, all the tweets were identified using both models. If the model claimed only one tweet, e.g., itself, the model was dropped out of the repertoire as an outlier. Then the tweet being as far as possible from both models was selected as the material for the third model. And again, all the tweets were re-scored, one chosen for new models, and so on until none of the models claimed more than half of all the tweets (max 10k tweets). This resulted in 214 clusters for all the dialects, as seen in Table 6. The displayed F1 scores are the best results on the development set after all the clusters on the corresponding row and above were combined into one cluster. The results of the clustering experiments were not good enough for the clustering to be used in an actual submission to the shared task. We still had some further ideas of how to try to improve the results but were unable to continue due to limited time.

# tweets in cluster	# clusters	# lang. combinations	Macro F1
2	61	1,119	0.1733
3	44	1,037	0.1682
4	15	935	0.1632
5	10	891	0.1607
6–9	19	858	0.1597
10–19	25	767	0.1540
20–39	16	588	0.1476
40–99	10	408	0.1378
100–199	4	263	0.1361
200–399	5	197	0.1413
400–999	2	108	0.1550
2,485	1	72	0.1748
3,674	1	54	0.1834
8,933	1	36	0.1964

Table 6: The results of the clustering experiments on the development data. The total number of clusters in the "# clusters" column is 214. The "# lang. combinations" column indicates the total number of the cluster – language combinations after all the clusters on the corresponding row and above were combined into one cluster.

5 Results

We ended up submitting only one run on each of the test sets using the non-adaptive version of the language identifier. First, we treated both the training and the test data with the Farasa segmenter and then ran them through the Naive Bayes language identifier using character n-grams from one to four with a penalty modifier of 1.375. With the macro F1 score of 0.1963 on test set A and 0.1058 on test set B, our submissions reached the 19/19 and 15/19 positions for the respective test sets. The final ranking for the whole shared task combined the results of the two test sets. We were ranked 18th out of the 19 participating teams, which shows that our results were not competitive against most other submitted results. As of this writing, we have not received the gold-standard labels for the test set.

6 Discussion

There are still several avenues worth exploring when using the NB-based identifier in classifying Arabic tweets. We intend to continue exploring different kinds of topic clustering methods to divide the training data into different models. Currently, we have no efficient means to utilize additional unannotated data, and developing such means remains a high priority.

7 Conclusion

We have presented the experiments we conducted when participating in the NADI 2022 shared task. Many of the experiments provided interesting results for further research. We were successful in implementing a new version of the NB identifier, which automatically optimizes its parameters, thus leaving more time to explore ideas to improve the identification accuracy. We reached the 19th and 15th places in the shared task.

Limitations

As seen from the results of the shared task, using a shallow NB identifier with character n-grams is not currently competitive against BERT-based deep learning systems in classifying Arabic tweets according to their origin countries. These experiments serve well in pointing out the limitations of a system that has won several other language identification shared tasks (Jauhiainen et al., 2019b, 2021, 2022a).

Acknowledgements

The research was conducted within the Language Identification of Speech and Text project funded by the Finnish Research Impact Foundation from its Tandem Industry Academia funding in cooperation with Lingsoft.

References

Ahmed Abdelali, Kareem Darwish, Nadir Durrani, and Hamdy Mubarak. 2016. Farasa: A fast and furious segmenter for Arabic. In *Proceedings of the 2016 Conference of the North American Chapter of the Association for Computational Linguistics: Demonstrations*, pages 11–16, San Diego, California. Association for Computational Linguistics.

Muhammad Abdul-Mageed, AbdelRahim Elmadany, and El Moatez Billah Nagoudi. 2021a. ARBERT & MARBERT: Deep bidirectional transformers for Arabic. In *Proceedings of the 59th Annual Meeting of the Association for Computational Linguistics and the 11th International Joint Conference on Natural Language Processing (Volume 1: Long Papers)*, pages 7088–7105, Online. Association for Computational Linguistics.

Muhammad Abdul-Mageed, Chiyu Zhang, Houda Bouamor, and Nizar Habash. 2020. NADI 2020: The first nuanced Arabic dialect identification shared task. In *Proceedings of the Fifth Arabic Natural Language Processing Workshop*, pages 97–110, Barcelona, Spain (Online). Association for Computational Linguistics.

Muhammad Abdul-Mageed, Chiyu Zhang, AbdelRahim Elmadany, Houda Bouamor, and Nizar Habash. 2021b. NADI 2021: The second nuanced Arabic dialect identification shared task. In *Proceedings of the Sixth Arabic Natural Language Processing Workshop*, pages 244–259, Kyiv, Ukraine (Virtual). Association for Computational Linguistics.

Muhammad Abdul-Mageed, Chiyu Zhang, AbdelRahim Elmadany, Houda Bouamor, and Nizar Habash. 2022. NADI 2022: The Third Nuanced Arabic Dialect Identification Shared Task. In *Proceedings of the Seventh Arabic Natural Language Processing Workshop (WANLP 2022)*.

Noëmi Aepli, Antonios Anastasopoulos, Adrian Chifu, William Domingues, Fahim Faisal, Mihaela Găman, Radu Tudor Ionescu, and Yves Scherrer. 2022. Findings of the VarDial evaluation campaign 2022. In *Proceedings of the Ninth Workshop on NLP for Similar Languages, Varieties and Dialects*, Gyeongju, Republic of Korea.

Badr AlKhamissi, Mohamed Gabr, Muhammad El-Nokrashy, and Khaled Essam. 2021. Adapting MARBERT for improved Arabic dialect identification: Submission to the NADI 2021 shared task. In *Proceedings of the Sixth Arabic Natural Language Processing Workshop*, pages 260–264, Kyiv, Ukraine (Virtual). Association for Computational Linguistics.

Khaled Alrifai, Ghaida Rebdawi, and Nada Ghneim. 2017. Arabic Tweeps Gender and Dialect Prediction – Notebook for PAN at CLEF 2017. In *Working Notes Papers of CLEF 2017 Evaluation Labs and Workshop*, Dublin, Ireland. CEUR-WS.org.

Bharathi Raja Chakravarthi, Mihaela Gaman, Radu Tudor Ionescu, Heidi Jauhiainen, Tommi Jauhiainen, Krister Lindén, Nikola Ljubešić, Niko Partanen, Ruba Priyadharshini, Christoph Purschke, Eswari Rajagopal, Yves Scherrer, and Marcos Zampieri. 2021. Findings of the VarDial evaluation campaign 2021. In *Proceedings of the Eighth Workshop on NLP for Similar Languages, Varieties and Dialects*, pages 1–11, Kyiv, Ukraine. Association for Computational Linguistics.

Jacob Devlin, Ming-Wei Chang, Kenton Lee, and Kristina Toutanova. 2019. BERT: Pre-training of deep bidirectional transformers for language understanding. In *Proceedings of the 2019 Conference of the North American Chapter of the Association for Computational Linguistics: Human Language Technologies, Volume 1 (Long and Short Papers)*, pages 4171–4186, Minneapolis, Minnesota. Association for Computational Linguistics.

Abdellah El Mekki, Ahmed Alami, Hamza Alami, Ahmed Khoumsi, and Ismail Berrada. 2020. Weighted combination of BERT and n-GRAM features for nuanced Arabic dialect identification. In *Proceedings of the Fifth Arabic Natural Language Processing Workshop*, pages 268–274, Barcelona, Spain (Online). Association for Computational Linguistics.

Ashraf Elnagar, Sane M. Yagi, Ali Bou Nassif, Ismail Shahin, and Said A. Salloum. 2021. Systematic Literature Review of Dialectal Arabic: Identification and Detection. *IEEE Access*, 9:31010–31042.

Tommi Jauhiainen, Heidi Jauhiainen, Tero Alstola, and Krister Lindén. 2019a. Language and Dialect Identification of Cuneiform Texts. In *Proceedings of the Sixth Workshop on NLP for Similar Languages, Varieties and Dialects*, pages 89–98, Ann Arbor, Michigan. Association for Computational Linguistics.

Tommi Jauhiainen, Heidi Jauhiainen, and Krister Lindén. 2019b. Discriminating between Mandarin Chinese and Swiss-German varieties using adaptive language models. In *Proceedings of the Sixth Workshop on NLP for Similar Languages, Varieties and Dialects*, pages 178–187, Ann Arbor, Michigan. Association for Computational Linguistics.

Tommi Jauhiainen, Heidi Jauhiainen, and Krister Lindén. 2021. Naive Bayes-based experiments in Romanian dialect identification. In *Proceedings of the Eighth Workshop on NLP for Similar Languages, Varieties and Dialects*, pages 76–83, Kyiv, Ukraine. Association for Computational Linguistics.

Tommi Jauhiainen, Heidi Jauhiainen, and Krister Lindén. 2022a. Italian language and dialect identification and regional French variety detection using adaptive naive bayes. In *Proceedings of the Ninth Workshop on NLP for Similar Languages, Varieties and Dialects*, Gyeongju, Republic of Korea.

Tommi Jauhiainen, Krister Lindén, and Heidi Jauhiainen. 2016. HeLI, a word-based backoff method for language identification. In *Proceedings of the Third Workshop on NLP for Similar Languages, Varieties and Dialects (VarDial3)*, pages 153–162, Osaka, Japan. The COLING 2016 Organizing Committee.

Tommi Jauhiainen, Krister Lindén, and Heidi Jauhiainen. 2019c. Language model adaptation for language and dialect identification of text. *Natural Language Engineering*, 25(5):561–583.

Tommi Jauhiainen, Marco Lui, Marcos Zampieri, Timothy Baldwin, and Krister Lindén. 2019d. Automatic Language Identification in Texts: A Survey. *Journal of Artificial Intelligence Research*, 65:675–782.

Tommi Jauhiainen, Jussi Piitulainen, Erik Axelson, and Krister Lindén. 2022b. Language identification as part of the text corpus creation pipeline at the language bank of finland. In *Digital Humanities in Nordic and Baltic Countries conference (DHNB 2022)*.

Francisco Rangel, Paolo Rosso, Martin Potthast, and Benno Stein. 2017. Overview of the 5th Author Profiling Task at PAN 2017: Gender and Language Variety Identification in Twitter. In *Working Notes Papers of CLEF 2017 Evaluation Labs and Workshop*, Dublin, Ireland. CEUR-WS.org.

Bashar Talafha, Mohammad Ali, Muhy Eddin Za'ter, Haitham Seelawi, Ibraheem Tuffaha, Mostafa Samir, Wael Farhan, and Hussein Al-Natsheh. 2020. Multi-dialect Arabic BERT for country-level dialect identification. In *Proceedings of the Fifth Arabic Natural Language Processing Workshop*, pages 111–118, Barcelona, Spain (Online). Association for Computational Linguistics.

Anshul Wadhawan. 2021. Dialect identification in nuanced Arabic tweets using farasa segmentation and AraBERT. In *Proceedings of the Sixth Arabic Natural Language Processing Workshop*, pages 291–295, Kyiv, Ukraine (Virtual). Association for Computational Linguistics.

Marcos Zampieri, Shervin Malmasi, Yves Scherrer, Tanja Samardžić, Francis Tyers, Miikka Silfverberg, Natalia Klyueva, Tung-Le Pan, Chu-Ren Huang, Radu Tudor Ionescu, Andrei M. Butnaru, and Tommi Jauhiainen. 2019. A report on the third VarDial evaluation campaign. In *Proceedings of the Sixth Workshop on NLP for Similar Languages, Varieties and Dialects*, pages 1–16, Ann Arbor, Michigan. Association for Computational Linguistics.

Tong Zhang. 2004. Solving large scale linear prediction problems using stochastic gradient descent algorithms. In *Proceedings of the twenty-first international conference on Machine learning*, page 116.

iCompass Working Notes for the Nuanced Arabic Dialect Identification Shared task.

Abir Messaoudi **Chayma Fourati** **Hatem Haddad** **Moez Ben HajHmida**
iCompass, Tunisia
{abir,chayma,hatem,moez}@icompass.digital

Abstract

We describe our submitted system to the Nuanced Arabic Dialect Identification (NADI) shared task. We tackled only the first subtask (Subtask 1). We used state-of-the-art Deep Learning models and pre-trained contextualized text representation models that we fine-tuned according to the downstream task in hand. As a first approach, we used BERT Arabic variants: MARBERT with its two versions MARBERT v1 and MARBERT v2, then we combined MARBERT embeddings with a CNN classifier, and finally, we tested the Quasi-Recurrent Neural Networks (QRNN) model. The results found show that version 2 of MARBERT outperforms all of the previously mentioned models on Subtask 1.

1 Introduction

Nowadays, social media is spread all over Arabic countries where people tend to express themselves in their own local dialect. Since it has different variants and dialects across the world, Arabic dialect identification presents a challenging task. Even if some dialects share some vocabulary, they still differ according to countries, where each dialect has its own specifications. Because of the massive amount of such content, automatic identification of Arabic dialects becomes crucial. Following the first (Abdul-Mageed et al., 2020b) and second (Abdul-Mageed et al., 2021) Nuanced Arabic Dialect Identification (NADI 2020 and NADI 2021), NADI 2022 subtask 1 focuses on identifying the Arabic dialect of a given text, especially on social media sources where there is no established standard orthography like Modern Standard Arabic (MSA) (Abdul-Mageed et al., 2022). The first attempts to tackle this challenge identified different Arabic dialects categories in addition to MSA: Maghrebi, Egyptian, Levantine, Gulf, and Iraqi (Zaidan and Callison-Burch, 2011). In (El-Haj et al., 2018) authors proposed 4 Arabic dialects categories by merging the Iraqi with the Gulf.

The paper is structured as follows: Section 2 provides a concise description of the used dataset, its statistics, and pre-processing techniques. Section 3 describes the used systems and the experimental setup to build models for Country-level dialect identification. Section 4 presents and discusses the obtained results. Finally, section 5 concludes and points to possible directions for future work.

2 Data Description

The provided training dataset of the competition (Abdul-Mageed et al., 2022) dedicated for the first subtask consists of around 25k tweets written in eighteen Arabic dialects including: Egypt, Iraq, KSA, Algeria, Oman, Syria, Libya, Tunisia, Morocco, Lebanon, UAE, Jordan, Kuwait, Yemen, Palestine, Bahrain, Qatar, and Sudan. Figure 1 presents the distribution of the tweets over the eighteen labels. In fact, the training dataset is imbalanced and presents skewed class proportions. We notice the domination of Egypt and Iraq tweets compared to the other countries.

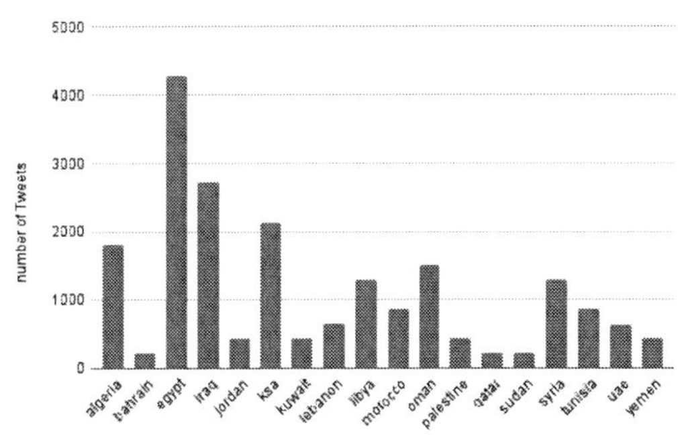

Figure 1: The distribution of tweets according to the 18 classes.

2.1 Data pre-processing

In order to normalize the dataset, we managed to do several strategies of cleaning. In fact, we remove

Proceedings of the The Seventh Arabic Natural Language Processing Workshop (WANLP), pages 415 - 419
December 8, 2022 ©2022 Association for Computational Linguistics

all non Arabic tokens, including ones like USER, URL, < LF >. Emojis were also removed. We normalize all the hashtags by simply decomposing them and we ended by removing successive white spaces.

In order to validate our models, we use the training and development datasets provided by NADI 2022 competition. Table 1 presents statistics of the training and development datasets for Subtask 1.

Data	# Sentences
Training	20398
Development	4871

Table 1: Training and development datasets statistics for Subtask 1.

3 System Description

Different deep learning architectures and pretrained language models were used in order to achieve the best results.

3.1 MARBERT

MARBERT, also by (Abdul-Mageed et al., 2020a) is a large-scale pretrained language model using BERT base's architecture and focusing on the various Arabic dialects. It was trained on 128 GB of Arabic tweets. The authors chose to keep the tweets that have at least 3 Arabic words. Therefore, tweets that have 3 or more Arabic tokens without removing non-Arabic (foreign languages) ones (15.6 billion Arabic and non-Arabic tokens). This is because dialects are often times mixed with other foreign languages. MARBERT enhances the language variety as it focuses on representing the previously underrepresented dialects and Arabic variants. MARBERT v2 is the second version of MARBERT pre-trained on the same MSA data as ARBERT in addition to AraNews dataset but with a bigger sequence length of 512 tokens for 40 epochs.

3.2 Convolutional Neural Network

The dataset was tokenized using both versions of MARBERT (v1 and v2) tokenizer, mapping words to their indexes. MARBERT embedding matrix was used at the embedding layer level. Then, Convolutional Neural Network (CNN) model was used as classifier and a fully connected layer with a softmax activation function in order to predict label's probabilities with the following hyper-parameters: batch size of 32, max sequence length of 64, and 4 epochs.

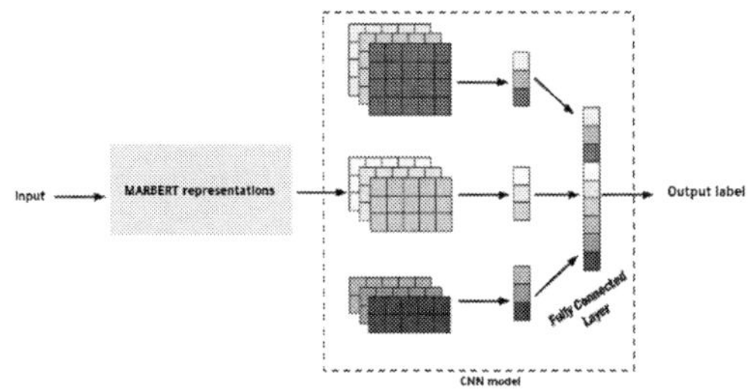

Figure 2: MARBERT + CNN architecture.

3.3 Quasi-recurrent Neural Network

Quasi-recurrent neural network (QRNN) (Bradbury et al., 2016) represents an architecture that combines the sequential manner of treating the input tokens from Recurrent Neural Networks (RNNs) and the parallel processing fashion of Convolutional Neural Networks (CNNs) to allow a longer term dependency window while also addressing several issues faced when using both architectures separately. Stacked QRNNs are reported to have a better predictive accuracy than stacked LSTMs of the same hidden size (Bradbury et al., 2016). MARBERT v2 was used as the embedding layer, followed by the QRNN model. Hyper-parameters used are: batch size of 32, max sequence length of 64, and 8 epochs.

Figure 3 represents details of the QRNN architecture.

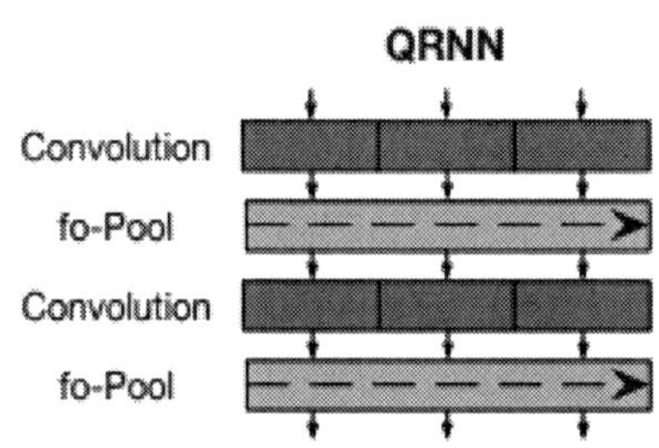

Figure 3: QRNN architecture.(Bradbury et al., 2016)

3.4 System submission

As an approach, we used the Arabic BERT (Devlin et al., 2019) variant MARBERT (Abdul-Mageed et al., 2020a) (second version) since it was trained mostly on dialectal Arabic which was underrepresented in previous pretrained models. Since this task's data is multi-dialectal, this model is expected to achieve the best performance. We used the training dataset provided by the NADI 2022 shared task that covers 18 dialects (total of 20K tweets, the same as NADI 2021) (Abdul-Mageed et al., 2022). We trained our model on a Google Cloud GPU of 8 cores using Google Colaboratory. The final model hyper-parameters that we used to make the submission are:

- Model name: MARBERT v2
- Number of epochs: 4
- Learning rate: 2e-5
- Batch size: 32
- Max sequence length: 64

4 Results and Discussion

We submitted one run to subtask 1: trained on the provided training dataset. This subtask is a multi-class classification problem, including eighteen labels.

Model	Macro-F1	Accuracy
MARBERT v1 + CNN	0.12	0.39
MARBERT v2 + CNN	0.14	0.40
MARBERT v2 + QRNN	0.26	0.41
MARBERT v2	**0.33**	**0.50**

Table 2: Results of different models on the development dataset.

Table 2 presents the results of experiments performed for this subtask. Preliminary results on the development dataset showed that a fine-tuned MARBERT v2 achieved the best performances compared to the other three models in term of Accuracy and marco-F1.

Using MARBERT v2 as the embedding layer followed by the QRNN outperforms MARBERT v2 as the embedding layer followed CNN. Fine-tuning the pre-trained model MARBERT with QRNN looks very promising for small sized annotated Arabic dialects data as mentioned in (Bennessir et al., 2022) but further experiments are needed to substantiate this assumption.

We notice that the data imbalance decreased the model performance in terms of macro-F1. Figures 4 and 5 show confusion matrices where the classes most correctly classified are: 2 for Egypt, 3 for Iraq and 5 for KSA, which are the countries with

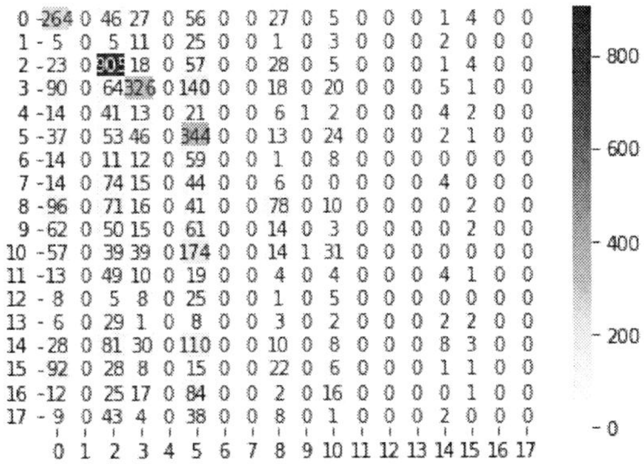

Figure 4: Confusion matrix of the MARBERT v2 + CNN model. ('0:alg','1:bah', '2:egy', '3:irq', '4:jor', '5:ksa', '6:kuw', '7:leb', '8:lib', '9:mor' ,'10:om', '11:pal', '12:qatar' ,'13:sud', '14:syr', '15:tun', '16:uae', '17:yem')

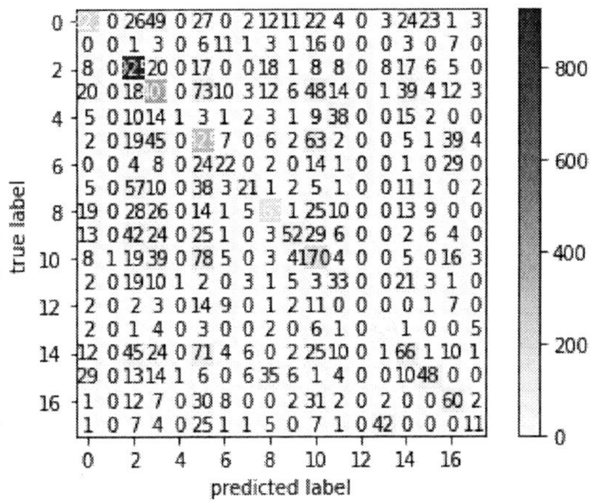

Figure 5: Confusion matrix of the MARBERT v2 model. ('0:alg','1:bah', '2:egy', '3:irq', '4:jor', '5:ksa', '6:kuw', '7:leb', '8:lib', '9:mor' ,'10:om', '11:pal', '12:qatar' ,'13:sud', '14:syr', '15:tun', '16:uae', '17:yem')

higher presence in the training dataset. The model trained with MARBERT + CNN architecture, in Figures 4, tends to always predict the oversampled classes, which explains the low Macro-F1 score. In fact, most of Omanian (10), Syrian (17) and Bahrainian (16) sentences are predicted as Saudian (5). Most of Moroccan (9) sentences are predicted as Algerians (0).

4.1 Official submission results

NADI provides two test sets: Test-A and Test-B. TEST-A covers 18 country-level dialects, containing 4,758 tweets, whereas the second test set

(TEST-B) covers an unknown country-level dialects. Then, the subtask score is calculated using the average score between the two test sets. Tables 3, 4 and 5 review the official results of iCompass system for NADI (resp. Test-A and Test-B) on the test dataset against the top three ranked systems.

Team	Rank	Macro-F1	Accuracy
rematchka	1	36.4807	53.0475
GOF	2	35.6825	52.1017
UniManc	3	34.7780	52.3329
iCompass	**4**	**33.7000**	**51.9126**

Table 3: Leaderboard of Test-A of Subtask 1.

Team	Rank	Macro-F1	Accuracy
UniManc	1	18.9481	36.8385
mtu_fiz	2	17.6715	33.9213
rematchka	3	17.6361	36.49936
iCompass	**7**	**16.937**	**34.9389**

Table 4: Leaderboard of Test-B of Subtask 1.

Team	Rank	Average Macro-F1
rematchka	1	27.06
UniManc	2	26.86
GOF	3	26.44
iCompass	**5**	**25.32**

Table 5: Leaderboard of Subtask 1.

5 Conclusion

In this work, MARBERT (Abdul-Mageed et al., 2020a) in its second version was used to identify Country-level dialect. The best results were obtained by MARBERT v2 with specific hyperparameters, which was selected for the final submission. Future work would involve building a multi-script Arabic dialects language model including Arabic script and Latin script based characters. Taking as example, Tunisians, who tend to express themselves using an informal way called TUNIZI (Fourati et al., 2021) that represents the Tunisian text written using Latin characters and numbers instead of Arabic letters.

References

Muhammad Abdul-Mageed, AbdelRahim Elmadany, and El Moatez Billah Nagoudi. 2020a. Arbert & marbert: deep bidirectional transformers for arabic. *arXiv preprint arXiv:2101.01785*.

Muhammad Abdul-Mageed, Chiyu Zhang, Houda Bouamor, and Nizar Habash. 2020b. NADI 2020: The first nuanced Arabic dialect identification shared task. In *Proceedings of the Fifth Arabic Natural Language Processing Workshop*, pages 97–110, Barcelona, Spain (Online). Association for Computational Linguistics.

Muhammad Abdul-Mageed, Chiyu Zhang, AbdelRahim Elmadany, Houda Bouamor, and Nizar Habash. 2021. NADI 2021: The second nuanced Arabic dialect identification shared task. In *Proceedings of the Sixth Arabic Natural Language Processing Workshop*, pages 244–259, Kyiv, Ukraine (Virtual). Association for Computational Linguistics.

Muhammad Abdul-Mageed, Chiyu Zhang, AbdelRahim Elmadany, Houda Bouamor, and Nizar Habash. 2022. NADI 2022: The Third Nuanced Arabic Dialect Identification Shared Task. In *Proceedings of the Seven Arabic Natural Language Processing Workshop (WANLP 2022)*.

Mohamed Aziz Bennessir, Malek Rhouma, Hatem Haddad, and Chayma Fourati. 2022. icompass at arabic hate speech 2022: Detect hate speech using qrnn and transformers. In *Proceedinsg of the 5th Workshop on Open-Source Arabic Corpora and Processing Tools with Shared Tasks on Qur'an QA and Fine-Grained Hate Speech Detection*, pages 176–180.

James Bradbury, Stephen Merity, Caiming Xiong, and Richard Socher. 2016. Quasi-recurrent neural networks. *arXiv preprint arXiv:1611.01576*.

Jacob Devlin, Ming-Wei Chang, Kenton Lee, and Kristina Toutanova. 2019. BERT: Pre-training of deep bidirectional transformers for language understanding. In *Proceedings of the 2019 Conference of the North American Chapter of the Association for Computational Linguistics: Human Language Technologies, Volume 1 (Long and Short Papers)*, pages 4171–4186.

Mahmoud El-Haj, Paul Rayson, and Mariam Aboelezz. 2018. Arabic dialect identification in the context of bivalency and code-switching. In *Proceedings of the 11th International Conference on Language Resources and Evaluation, Miyazaki, Japan.*, pages 3622–3627. European Language Resources Association.

Chayma Fourati, Hatem Haddad, Abir Messaoudi, Moez BenHajhmida, Aymen Ben Elhaj Mabrouk, and Malek Naski. 2021. Introducing a large Tunisian Arabizi dialectal dataset for sentiment analysis. In *Proceedings of the Sixth Arabic Natural Language Processing Workshop*, pages 226–230, Kyiv, Ukraine (Virtual). Association for Computational Linguistics.

Omar Zaidan and Chris Callison-Burch. 2011. The arabic online commentary dataset: an annotated dataset of informal arabic with high dialectal content. In *Proceedings of the 49th Annual Meeting of the Association for Computational Linguistics: Human Language Technologies*, pages 37–41.

TF-IDF or Transformers for Arabic Dialect Identification? ITFLOWS participation in the NADI 2022 Shared Task

Fouad Shammary[1], **Yiyi Chen**[2,3], **Zsolt T. Kardkovács**[1], **Haithem Afli**[1], **Mehwish Alam**[2,3]
[1] Department of Computer Science, Munster Technological University, Cork, Ireland
[2] FIZ-Karlsruhe - Leibniz Institute for Information Infrastructure, Karlsruhe, Germany
[3] Karlsruhe Institute of Technology, Karlsruhe, Germany
{firstname.lastname}@mtu.ie, {firstname.lastname}@fiz-karlsruhe.de

Abstract

This study targets the shared task of Nuanced Arabic Dialect Identification (NADI) organized with the Workshop on Arabic Natural Language Processing (WANLP). It further focuses on Subtask 1: the identification of the Arabic dialects at the country level. More specifically, it studies the impact of a traditional approach such as TF-IDF and then moves on to study the impact of advanced deep learning based methods. These methods include fully fine-tuning MARBERT as well as adapter based fine-tuning of MARBERT with and without performing data augmentation. The evaluation shows that the traditional approach based on TF-IDF scores the best in terms of accuracy on TEST-A dataset, while, the fine-tuned MARBERT with adapter on augmented data scores the second on Macro F1-score on the TEST-B dataset. This led to the proposed system being ranked second on the shared task on average.

1 Introduction

Arabic is a Semitic language spoken in more than 26 countries by more than 350 million people with at least 30 dialects[1]. Some previous studies attempted to use hierarchical deep learning for a fine-grained dialect classification (de Francony et al., 2019). Arabic has its own, letter based writing system which is used mostly for only those consonants which could denote a wide range of pronunciation alternatives. A single letter in this alphabet can have various forms depending on the context, and its position within the word which are encoded by different characters. There are also single character ligatures which are formed by two or more characters (e.g., from this corpus: `U+FEFB` ("AL") denotes `U+0627` (A) and (`U+0644` (L), or words like `U+FD71` ("aspired") or `U+FDF2` ("Allah") are also represented by a single character). Similarly to the Latin alphabet, Arabic letters can denote, e.g., Urdu, Ottoman Turkish, Sindhi, Malay, Uyghur, or even English and French words which are not uncommon.

This article targets the Nuanced Arabic Dialect Identification (NADI) 2022 Shared Task (Abdul-Mageed et al., 2022). It more specifically focuses on Subtask 1 aimed at identifying country-level dialects by providing ~20k Twitter data which are labeled by geo-location (i.e. country) from where the tweets were posted. In this Shared Task no external *labeled* data sources were allowed to be used, however, a large unlabeled dataset was also provided. The training set remains relatively small to encourage competitors to use few or zero-shot learning models. Solutions were tested on two datasets using macro-averaged F1-score:

- TEST-A: ~5k tweets with all previously provided dialects,
- TEST-B: ~1.5k tweets with an undisclosed number of country-level dialects.

According to the systems developed and presented in this work, dialect identification can be modeled at the character, word, expression, or phrase level. Each of these levels was modeled by the traditional TF-IDF method, a pre-trained transformer called MARBERT (Abdul-Mageed et al., 2021), and by using MARBERT with word level augmentation. These methods were analyzed individually as well as by using their combination in order to find the most informative parameter regarding the dialects. On TEST-A dataset the traditional approach produced the best accuracy, while on TEST-B dataset our approach won the runner-up award on macro-averaged F1-score.

2 Data

The NADI 2022 Shared Task Subtask 1 dataset contained a total of 20,398 tweets in the training set,

[1]ISO 639-3 identified dialects: `https://iso639-3.sil.org/code/ara`

Proceedings of the The Seventh Arabic Natural Language Processing Workshop (WANLP), pages 420 - 424
December 8, 2022

4,872 validation samples from 18 dialects, while unlabeled test sets, TEST-A and TEST-B contained 4,758 and 1,473 tweets respectively. Dialects are identified based on geolocation data where the tweets were originated instead of the linguistic analysis. This in itself leads to the contamination of the data since people might reside in a country other than their country of origin. Moreover, sometimes the words are used in or borrowed from other languages, e.g., English or Urdu. Additionally, there is an imbalance in the class distribution in the training dataset (see Table 1).

3 System

Three models were proposed for this subtask out of which the first model was a *traditional approach* without using any language models or deep neural network architecture, i.e., TF-IDF based. In the second approach, the data augmentation was performed with fine-tuned MARBERT (Abdul-Mageed et al., 2021) with and without adapters (Pfeiffer et al., 2020a).

3.1 System 1: Traditional Approach

In order to capture relevant differences between dialects, one can look for particular linguistic alterations of similar characters, words, phrases, or expressions. TF-IDF method has a long history in detecting such meaningful differences in texts, especially for detecting topics in large texts. This study considers all the texts with the same label as a single document. This way, dialects can be identified as common sub-word patterns (in our case 1 to 7-grams) which are frequent enough (i.e. $f(w) > t_f$) within a document (dialect), but they are not universal, i.e. at least $k > 0$ documents shall not contain this pattern at all. Since the dataset had the same topic for all dialects TF-IDF method most likely identifies dialects rather than topics. These (t_f, k)-patterns could be used as fingerprints for dialects. The most likely fingerprint using maximum likelihood determines the outcome of the prediction. The best accuracy was achieved using $(3, 9)$-patterns as fingerprints.

However, using N-grams could lead to a wide variety of errors. The appearance of words and encoding could be misleading using Arabic enabled, modern operating systems. For example, حاجه and حاجه appear to be the same, however, their underlying Unicode characters are completely different (e.g. the first letter is U+FEA3 with respect to U+062D). To avoid such a problem, one can introduce a transliteration module that maps these differences into a common alphabet. While it sometimes helps differences between words like السلامه and السلامۂ which are hardly noticeable in transliteration (both translate to "AlslAmh", the latter is Urdu and means "peace be upon you", the former is Arabic (means "safety"). Both appear in the NADI 2022 corpus. In the current study, it was noticed that the transliteration based approach tends to over-perform traditional character-based approaches when using (t_f, k)-fingerprints.

Since the training dataset was small and unbalanced, this approach favors more sampled dialects over small ones. A randomly sampled balanced set worsened the overall accuracy because of the small training samples.

3.2 Data Augmentation based Approach

Data augmentation is a technique where the amount of data is increased by adding slightly modified copies of the existing data. Several kinds of data augmentation techniques are generally used in NLP such as word level, and sentence level. This paper uses the word insertion technique from (Wei and Zou, 2019) combined with Transformers by inserting a word randomly based on context. This technique is performed on all tweets from the countries that represent less than 10% of the data. Each tweet is augmented by inserting one or two words randomly based on the contextualized embeddings from MARBERT. The entire dataset, which is comprised of both the newly augmented tweets dataset and the original tweets dataset, is checked for any duplicates which are then removed. For instance, there were 642 tweets from the UAE (labeled as "uae"), which increased to 1284 after augmentation and removing duplicates Table 1.

3.3 System 2: Fine-tuning MARBERT

The data was tokenized in the preprocessing step no other preprocessing was used. In this system, MARBERT embeddings were fed into the max pooling layer, and then dense layers. MARBERT was fine-tuned for 5 epochs. Early stopping was employed when there was no improvement in the validation metric (balanced accuracy).

3.4 System 3: Adapter-based Approach

In order to leverage the multilinguality and improve the transferability of MARBERT, while at the same

Table 1: Distribution of dialects within the NADI 2022 Shared Task Subtask 1 challenge training dataset before and after applying augmentation techniques.

Label	Nr. Samples (%)		Label	Nr. Samples (%)	
	Original	Augmented		Original	Augmented
egypt	4,283 (20.99%)	4,283 (13.55%)	libya	1,286 (6.31%)	2,571 (8.13%)
kuwait	429 (2.10%)	857 (2.71%)	iraq	2,729 (13.38%)	2,719 (8.60%)
tunisia	859 (4.21%)	1,715 (5.43%)	yemen	429 (2.10%)	858 (2.71%)
ksa	2,140 (10.49%)	2,139 (6.77%)	morocco	858 (4.21%)	1,715 (5.43%)
palestine	428 (2.10%)	855 (2.70%)	algeria	1,809 (8.86%)	3,606 (11.41%)
lebanon	644 (3.16%)	1,287 (4.07%)	bahrain	214 (1.05%)	430 (1.36%)
oman	1,501 (7.35%)	3,002 (9.50%)	uae	642 (3.15%)	1,284 (4.06%)
qatar	215 (1.05%)	430 (1.36%)	syria	1,287 (6.31%)	2,573 (8.14%)
jordan	429 (2.10%)	858 (2.71%)	sudan	215 (1.05%)	430 (1.36%)

time, being more computationally efficient, the fine-tuning strategy Adapter (Houlsby et al., 2019) is used. Transformer layers are connected using skip-connections with adapter layers, which are composed of a down-projection and an up-projection. For fine-tuning the model, only the parameters of the adapter layers are trained, while the pre-trained transformer layers are frozen. In (Pfeiffer et al., 2020b), the authors propose an adapter-based framework for multi-task cross-lingual transfer (MAD-X), in which the language adapters and task adapters are trained separately. Task adapters can be trained with datasets for specific tasks, while language adapters are task-agnostic. For country-level dialect detection, the augmented dataset was used to train task adapters based on MARABERT, using the configuration of PfeifferConfig[2] by leaving out the adapter in the last transformer layer (MAD-X 2.0), which proves to be superior than original MAD-X in zero-shot transfer (Pfeiffer et al., 2021). The hyper-parameters used for training are learning rate $1e-4$, batch size 16, and training epoch 6. The fine-tuned model performs the best at step 4500, which is used for testing.

4 Results

As shown in Table 2, the model that performs the best on the DEV dataset in every metric is MARBERT fine-tuned on the augmented dataset using adapters, i.e. Fine-tuned-Adapter-MARBERT (AUG). Surprisingly, the regarding model performs the worst on the TEST-A dataset. In comparison, the TF-IDF approach scores the best in all metrics other than the Macro-F1 score. Since MARBERT-based models are pre-trained on a much larger corpus, and fined-tuned for this specific task, one would expect the contrary. On the DEV dataset, it can be clearly seen that TF-IDF cannot model properly small sampled dialects which leads to poor macro-F1 performance. That is, the TF-IDF based solution can capture enough information for some dialects for which transformers can't. The only reasonable explanation is that information on dialects is most likely encoded at a sub-word level which MARBERT by design could not see.

On the TEST-B dataset, where the number of country-level dialects is unknown, Fine-tuned-Adapter-MARBERT (AUG) performs the best in every metric. However, the performance difference among transformer-based approaches with or without augmented data tested on either TEST-A or TEST-B dataset is not as noticeable as the difference between the traditional approach and the transformer-based approaches tested on TEST-B. This indicates the superiority of zero-shot transfer of the pre-trained transformer.

5 Discussion

Results show noticeably high variance in precision and overall accuracy between development and test data sets, regardless of which submitted model one cross-references. Under-sampling could explain that because in small samples words can either be interpreted as dialectal use of another, more common concept or simply another topic, stance, or key communication element which focuses the attention. In both cases, the word embedding, and TF-IDF could see clear alternatives for the same concept which is the basis of the classification.

Moreover, the traditional approach suffers sig-

[2] https://tinyurl.com/c6vwrmyt

Table 2: Results on DEV and TEST datasets. Aug indicates that the model trained on the augmented training dataset. Digits in bold indicate the best results for the corresponding dataset.

Dataset	**DEV**		**TEST-A**		**TEST-B**	
Models	Macro-F1	Accuracy	Macro-F1	Accuracy	Macro-F1	Accuracy
Traditional TF-IDF	0.1275	0.3437	0.0466	0.1642	0.0555	0.1906
Full Fine-tuned MARBERT	0.3329	0.5272	**0.1862**	**0.3218**	0.1668	0.3338
Fine-tuned MARBERT (Aug)	0.3192	0.5066	0.0495	0.1127	0.1702	0.3372
Fine-tuned-Adapter-MARBERT (Aug)	**0.3462**	**0.5293**	0.0485	0.1152	**0.1767**	**0.3392**

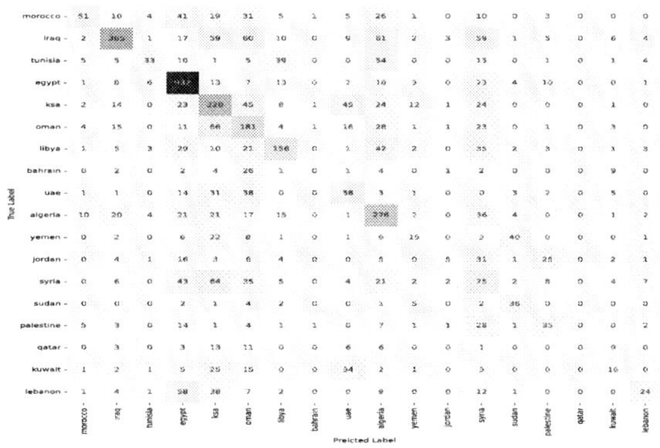

Figure 1: Confusion matrix of Fine-tuned-Adapter-MARBERT on the DEV set

nificantly less in accuracy in comparison with transformers-based models, and its performance is relatively consistent between the two differently sampled test sets. While TF-IDF models have no background knowledge of the language, there is no pretraining available, it still can outperform transformers in terms of accuracy, especially for dialects with large samples. In that sense, the TF-IDF approach is more stable, and therefore its power for generalization is stronger which means it can grab some important features of dialectal Arabic. There is a strong indication to improve or to create a sub-word based, or a transliteration and sub-word based transformer for Arabic.

Further analysis of predictions made be the best performing model show an expected over prediction of dialects with higher presence within the training data Figure 1. The over prediction showed a tendency towards dialects that are more similar. For instance, UAE was predicted more as Oman or KSA rather than Egypt. On the other hand, countries with small presence such as Qatar and Bahrain had no correct predictions on the DEV set.

6 Conclusion

This paper targets the problem of Arabic dialect detection based on a traditional approach as well as the pre-trained transformers in a dataset where few-shot learning was encouraged, and no large training set was provided. While the TF-IDF based approach performs less than the pre-trained transformer based approach on the NADI 2022 corpus which was expected, the accuracy of the TF-IDF approach surprisingly remained competitive on the whole (TEST-A) test set. TF-IDF obviously underperforms as compared to the MARBERT-based approach for low sampled dialects due to a lack of enough data for stable fingerprinting which explains TEST-B results. Since TF-IDF and MARBERT target different levels of the written language, so the most reasonable explanation is that dialect is more likely determined at the sub-word level. This hypothesis, however, needs further investigation.

Acknowledgements

This work is a part of the ITFLOWS project funded by the EU's Horizon 2020 research and innovation program under Grant Agreement No 882986 and the Science Foundation Ireland research Centre ADAPT through Grant 13/RC/2106_P2.

References

Muhammad Abdul-Mageed, AbdelRahim A. Elmadany, and El Moatez Billah Nagoudi. 2021. ARBERT & MARBERT: deep bidirectional transformers for arabic. In *Proceedings of the 59th Annual Meeting of the Association for Computational Linguistics and the 11th International Joint Conference on Natural Language Processing, ACL/IJCNLP 2021, (Volume 1: Long Papers), Virtual Event, August 1-6, 2021*, pages 7088–7105. Association for Computational Linguistics.

Muhammad Abdul-Mageed, Chiyu Zhang, AbdelRahim Elmadany, Houda Bouamor, and Nizar Habash. 2022. NADI 2022: The Third Nuanced Arabic Dialect Identification Shared Task. In *Proceedings of the Seven Arabic Natural Language Processing Workshop (WANLP 2022)*.

Gael de Francony, Victor Guichard, Praveen Joshi, Haithem Afli, and Abdessalam Bouchekif. 2019. Hierarchical deep learning for Arabic dialect identification. In *Proceedings of the Fourth Arabic Natural Language Processing Workshop*, pages 249–253, Florence, Italy. Association for Computational Linguistics.

Neil Houlsby, Andrei Giurgiu, Stanislaw Jastrzebski, Bruna Morrone, Quentin De Laroussilhe, Andrea Gesmundo, Mona Attariyan, and Sylvain Gelly. 2019. Parameter-efficient transfer learning for nlp. In *International Conference on Machine Learning*, pages 2790–2799. PMLR.

Jonas Pfeiffer, Andreas Rücklé, Clifton Poth, Aishwarya Kamath, Ivan Vulic, Sebastian Ruder, Kyunghyun Cho, and Iryna Gurevych. 2020a. Adapterhub: A framework for adapting transformers. In *Proceedings of the 2020 Conference on Empirical Methods in Natural Language Processing: System Demonstrations, EMNLP 2020 - Demos, Online, November 16-20, 2020*, pages 46–54. Association for Computational Linguistics.

Jonas Pfeiffer, Ivan Vulić, Iryna Gurevych, and Sebastian Ruder. 2020b. MAD-X: An Adapter-Based Framework for Multi-Task Cross-Lingual Transfer. In *Proceedings of the 2020 Conference on Empirical Methods in Natural Language Processing (EMNLP)*, pages 7654–7673, Online. Association for Computational Linguistics.

Jonas Pfeiffer, Ivan Vulić, Iryna Gurevych, and Sebastian Ruder. 2021. UNKs everywhere: Adapting multilingual language models to new scripts. In *Proceedings of the 2021 Conference on Empirical Methods in Natural Language Processing*, pages 10186–10203, Online and Punta Cana, Dominican Republic. Association for Computational Linguistics.

Jason Wei and Kai Zou. 2019. EDA: Easy data augmentation techniques for boosting performance on text classification tasks. In *Proceedings of the 2019 Conference on Empirical Methods in Natural Language Processing"*.

Domain-Adapted BERT-based Models for Nuanced Arabic Dialect Identification and Tweet Sentiment Analysis

Gıyaseddin Bayrak
Marmara University / Istanbul - Turkey
giyaseddinalfarkh@marun.edu.tr

Abdul Majeed Issifu
Marmara University / Istanbul - Turkey
abdul.majeed@marun.edu.tr

Abstract

This paper summarizes the solution of the Nuanced Arabic Dialect Identification (NADI) 2022 shared task. It consists of two subtasks: a country-level Arabic Dialect Identification (ADID) and an Arabic Sentiment Analysis (ASA). Our work shows the importance of using domain-adapted models and language-specific pre-processing in NLP task solutions. We implement a simple but strong baseline technique to increase the stability of fine-tuning settings to obtain a good generalization of models. Our best model for the Dialect Identification subtask achieves a Macro F-1 score of 25.54% as an average of both Test-A (33.89%) and Test-B (19.19%) F-1 scores. We also obtained a Macro F-1 score of 74.29% of positive and negative sentiments only, in the Sentiment Analysis task[1].

1 Introduction

The Arabic language is one of the rich languages in the world, spoken in large geographical regions. It is officially spoken by people from the Middle East and North Africa (MENA) countries, covering a population of approximately 400 million people. It's a culturally and grammatically rich language, with a complex morphological structure. Arabic is one of the Semitic languages and has a widely varying collection of more than 30 different dialects (according to the Summer Institute of Linguistics a.k.a. SIL International). These dialects are affected by geopolitical and religious influence. The question of how to classify the different varieties of spoken Arabic is a long-standing problem in the fields of Arabic and Semitic linguistics. Researchers still develop tools and systems to keep the language in the race of Natural Language Processing (NLP) tasks on both Modern Standard Arabic (MSA) and its Dialects (DA).

[1]The code of the implementation is available at https://github.com/giyaseddin/NADI

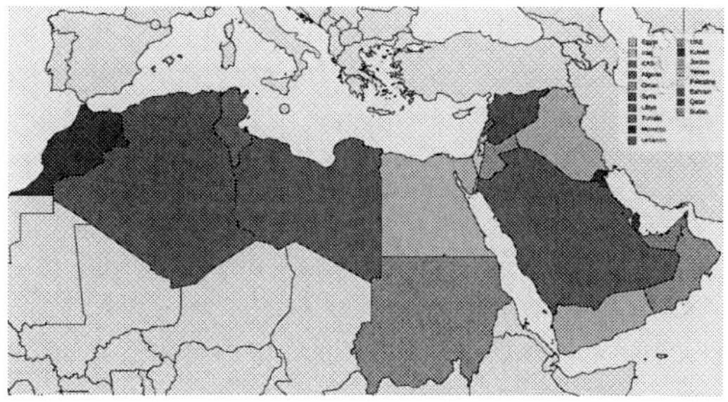

Figure 1: Geographical distribution of the countries listed in Subtask 1.

A dialect of the Arabic language can have a different meaning of a word or a vernacular dialect can differ syntactically, morphological, and orthographically in the choice of vocabulary and pronunciation. Each of these variations of dialects is distinct enough to make users resort to formal Arabic to understand each other. This prompts the need to develop a system that can automatically detect the source, region, and/or specific dialect of a given sequence of tokens or text segments. The NADI shared task series .... (Abdul-Mageed et al., 2020b) (Abdul-Mageed et al., 2021) (Abdul-Mageed et al., 2022) is one of the prominent competitions that provides datasets and modeling opportunities for researchers to improve NLP work in Arabic. Social media provides an environment for the use of both formal and informal language. This makes it more difficult when Arabic is used on social media since both dialects and the formality of the language will be taken into consideration when processing text data from social media like Twitter. This variety of dialects can be classified and used for more semantic and linguistic findings and work using machine learning and deep learning models.

Language Models (LM) have evolved over the years from the birth of the NLP domain, starting with simple n-gram LMs, with many computational and performance limitations. After the introduc-

Proceedings of the The Seventh Arabic Natural Language Processing Workshop (WANLP), pages 425 - 430
December 8, 2022 ©2022 Association for Computational Linguistics

Subset	Training			Dev	Test-A	Test-B	Test
	Total	Train	Validation				
Subask 1	20398	18358	2040	4758	4758	500	-
Subask 2	1500	1425	75	500	-	-	3000

Table 1: Data subset sizes for Task 1 and Task 2

tion of Deep Learning (DL), language modeling switched to language modeling using Recurrent Neural Networks (RNN), Gated Recurrent Unit (GRU), and Long-Short Term Memory (LSTM) with chronologically better deployability than the earlier methods. The drastic improvement was after introducing the Transformer architecture for language modeling (Vaswani et al., 2017) using the self-attention mechanism.

Transformer-based LM like Bidirectional Encoder Representations from Transformers (BERT) (Devlin et al., 2018), are currently widely used in the NLP field to achieve state-of-the-art (SOTA) results in various tasks. BERT and its variations (RoBERTa, DistilBERT, ALBERT, etc.) are outstanding models, and they are close to becoming a de facto baseline for almost all NLP tasks, especially for Natural Language Understanding (NLU) downstream tasks. This is because of the capability of these general models to be fine-tuned on narrower tasks in different domains with high accuracy and low cost.

In this paper, we develop a system for the classification of Arabic dialects at the country level. Arabic Dialect Identification (ADID) problem is challenging because adjacent countries influence each other, with the present intermediate dialects (Abdul-Mageed et al., 2021). Our system also provides Arabic Sentiment Analysis (ASA) of given tweet texts. We improve both ADID and ASA tasks using AraBERT (Antoun et al., 2020) and MARBERT (Abdul-Mageed et al., 2020a), Arabic language-specific pre-trained BERT models.

The rest of this paper is organized as follows. In section 2, we provide a detailed explanation of the problem and datasets provided by NADI-2022(Abdul-Mageed et al., 2022). Section 3 talks about the methodology and general system development. We provide the results in section 4 and discuss the results and model limitations in section 5. The paper is concluded in section 6.

2 Data

The NADI-2022 shared task provides two problem definitions of country-level dialect identification and sentiment analysis in Arabic, posted as Subtask 1 and 2 respectively. The geographical distribution of the countries covered in the dataset of Subtask 1 is shown in the map in Fig 1. Dialect distributions in the training and development sets vary based on the countries. In the datasets, for each country, we present the count of tweets included in both training and development sets, as seen in Fig 2. In the general collections of the tweets, there was no MSA taken into consideration in both datasets provided, rather just spoken dialects in the various countries as used in NADI-2021 (Abdul-Mageed et al., 2021). In Subtask 1, the test set is divided into TEST-A which includes 18 dialects on the country level, and TEST-B which covers *k* country-level dialects, where *k* is kept unknown. In Subtask 2 there's only one set for the test as shown in Table 1.

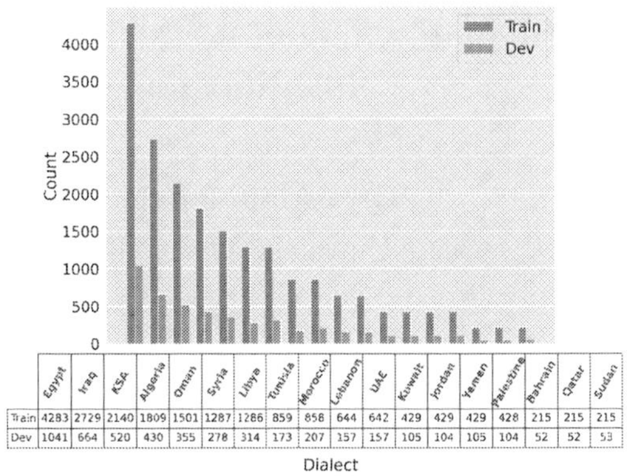

Figure 2: Country-level dialect distribution for the TRAIN and DEV data subsets of Subtask 1.

2.1 Subtask 1: Arabic Dialect Identification Dataset

The country-level dialect identification task is a multi-class classification problem that aims to identify and categorize which country, province, or dialect an Arabic tweet comes from. This task has a training dataset covering about 18 dialects of Arabic tweets summing up to 20K tweets. Subsets of both Subtasks data are in Table 1.

2.2 Subtask 2: Sentiment Analysis Dataset

The second task (subtask2) is a sentiment analysis problem aimed at determining whether an Arabic tweet is either positive, negative, or neutral. NADI-2022 provided a total of 5,000 tweets covering 10 Arab countries involving both MSA and DA. These tweets are manually labeled with tags from the set positive, negative, neutral.

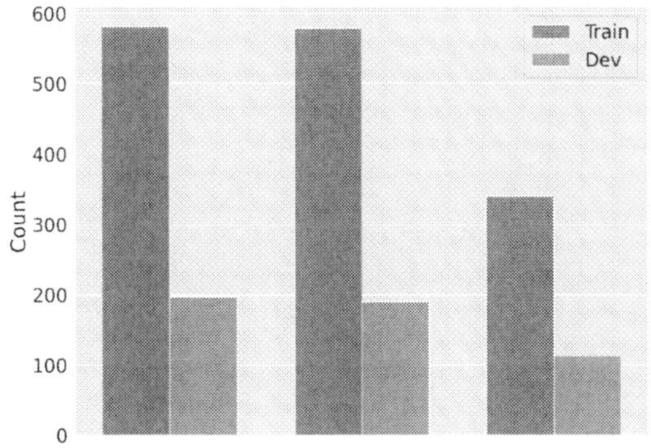

	Positive	Negative	Neutral
Train	581	579	340
Dev	197	190	113

Sentiment

Figure 3: Sentiment distribution for the TRAIN and DEV data subsets of Subtask 2.

3 System Development

In recent advancements of NLP, models with state-of-the-art (SOTA) results like SMART-RoBERTa Large (Jiang et al., 2019) have shown that using transformer models, it is reasonable to expect SOTA performance in tasks such as sentiment analysis (Aghajanyan et al., 2021) and question answering (Yamada et al., 2020). The SOTA leaderboard of SST-2 dataset (Socher et al., 2013) shows clearly that transformer models are currently the best for text classification with almost the top 50 models using transformer architecture[2]. We use the same approach in solving both Subtask 1 and Subtask 2 of the shared task. We used pre-trained transformer models in all experiments.

Domain-specific transfer learning and fine-tuning of transformer models is proven to be more robust by Issifu et al. (Çelkmasat et al., 2022) and Bayrak et al. (Akça et al., 2022), (Bayrak et al., 2022). They fine-tuned transformer models on Biomedical and Turkish law datasets respectively to achieve results better than their original general transformer models. Better performance obtained in these works are accredited to

- General domain pre-training: when the transformer model is being trained on a huge corpus collected from various sources.
- Domain-specific LM fine-tuning: a continuation of the pre-training but with a relevant domain corpus instead of the general one for getting more accurate token representations.
- Task-specific fine-turning: done using a supervised training dataset.

For a more robust performance of the system, we adopt Arabic language domain-specific pre-trained transformer models, AraBERT and MARBERT. These pre-trained models gained SOTA in SA on AJGT,HARD,LABR (2-class, unbalanced) datasets.

3.1 Pre-processing

Since social media is a platform where everyone can showcase their opinions, text data from Twitter (especially in Arabic) comes in raw, unclean, and with variations. Noise in tweets commonly comes from the use of slang words, non-ASCII characters like emoji, spelling mistakes, URLs, etc. (Wadhawan, 2021).

The measures we took to clean and prepossessed the data are adopted from AraBERT [3] as follows; 1) Removing HTML markup tags, eliminating non-text and out-of-context tokens. 2) Replacing URLs, Emails and user mentions in Twitter with the tokens: [رابط], [بريد], and [مستخدم] respectively [4]. 3) Stripping Tashkeel (diacritics) and Tatweel (elongation). Tashkeel is the use of short vowel/consonant marks that manifest a word's pronunciation. E.g. the word العَرَبِيّة becomes العربية. Tatweel is adding horizontal stroke between two Arabic letters to elongate its visual appearance. For example, the word كـــــلمة becomes كلمة after striping tatweel. We stripped these two (Tashkeel and Tatweel) to reduce the lexical sparsity of the words. They do not constitute the actual word's body and are not usually used in tweets. 4) For the same reasons mentioned, we insert white space before and after all non-Arabic digits. 5) Mapping all the Hindi numbers (٠ ١ ٢ ٣ ...) to Arabic numbers (0 1 2 3 ...). 6) Similarly, we reduced the repetition of characters to 2 characters by replacing the repeated characters with 2 of its kind. For example, the word مررررررررة becomes مررة. This helps normalize the words used in the tweets. 7) Replacing the slash / with a dash – since it is absent in the vocabulary of AraBERT. 8) We do not cancel out

[2]Papers with code SOTA models https://paperswithcode.com/sota/sentiment-analysis-on-sst-2-binary. 2014 -2022 results

[3]https://github.com/aub-mind/arabert

[4]Steps 1 and 2 of the pre-processing are redundant in our setting, they're already replaced in Subtask 1 and 2 data.

all the emojis; instead, we apply a normalization used in AraBERT, this helps eliminate the sparsity of the emojis.

3.2 Arabic BERT-based Model

Arabic transformer language models MARBERT and AraBERT are based on the original BERT architecture (Devlin et al., 2018). AraBERT is trained on 23GB of Arabic text, making ~70M sentences and 3B words, from Arabic Wikipedia, the Open Source International dataset (OSIAN) (Zeroual et al., 2019). MARBERT, however, is trained on 1B Arabic tweets, each tweet with at least 3 words. In our work we use AraBERT v0.2 Twitter-base [5] which is a further pre-training of AraBERT v02 on additional 60M Multi-Dialect tweets. We refer to this model in the result tables as *AraBERTtw*. We trained our models to classify Arabic language tweets into their various dialects on the country level using very selective hyper-parameters. To avoid local minima, overfitting, and related training issues, we adopt the setup and the hyper-parameters from the work of (Mosbach et al., 2020). We trained the model for 4 *epochs* with *batch size* of 16, and using ADAMW optimizer (Loshchilov and Hutter, 2017) with *learning rate* of $2e-5$, and *weight decay* $\lambda = 0.01$. The bias correction terms are set as $\beta_1 = 0.9$, $\beta_2 = 0.999$ and $\epsilon = 1e-6$ with the use of gradient clipping and a *warmup ratio* of 10% of the total training data.

We use the same setting for training the model for Subtask 2. The difference in ASA model is the number of neurons in the last classification layers is changed to 3, the number of classes in the problem.

4 Results

To evaluate the results, we use the official metrics defined by the shared task: Macro-Averaged F-score for Dialect ID (Subtask 1) and Macro-F1-PN score -neglecting the neutral class- over the positive and negative for the sentiment classification (Subtask 2).

In Table 2 we report the baseline model in the first row that is trained using similar hyper-parameters except the arbitrarily chosen: *5 epochs*, *batch size* of 32 *warmup steps=500*, *learning rate=5e-5* and optimizer's $\epsilon = 1e-8$. The results are also reported in the shared task's leader-board

Model		Dev		Test-A		Test-B	
	PP	F-1	Acc.	F-1	Acc.	F-1	Acc.
AraBERTtw$_{init}$	Yes	30.47	48.49	30.55	47.65	14.30	29.92
AraBERTtw	No	30.16	49.13	30.71	48.17	14.98	30.46
AraBERTtw	Yes	30.80	49.56	31.30	48.57	15.35	30.19
MARBERT	No	32.56	50.30	32.20	49.41	16.04	32.56
MARBERT	Yes	32.86	50.03	31.66	49.18	**17.51**	**35.14**
MARBERTv2	No	**33.18**	**52.27**	33.40	51.24	17.08	34.33
MARBERTv2	Yes	32.19	51.22	**33.89**	**51.66**	17.19	34.87

Table 2: F-1 Macro and Accuracy results of different models on Subtask 1. PP column indicates using pre-processing before training.

Model		Dev		Test	
	PP	F1-PN	Acc.	F1-PN	Acc.
AraBERTtw$_{init}$	Yes	72.24	67.00	71.43	65.80
AraBERTtw	No	**72.58**	**67.60**	71.21	65.80
AraBERTtw	Yes	72.07	66.80	71.43	65.80
MARBERT	No	71.44	66.00	**74.29**	**69.00**
MARBERT	Yes	72.14	67.20	73.14	67.60
MARBERTv2	No	71.91	65.80	74.25	68.70
MARBERTv2	Yes	68.42	62.40	74.06	68.53

Table 3: Accuracy and Macro F-1 of Negatives and Positives results of different models on Subtask 2. PP column indicates using pre-processing before training.

as *giyaseddin* team. In the same table, we show the macro F-1 score with the accuracy for the experimented models against each of the DEV, TEST-A, and TEST-B set provided by the shared-task for Subtask 1. Similarly, the test results of Subtask 2 are presented in Table 3. Our best-performing model (MARBERTv2) achieved 33.89% F-1 score in Subtask 1 TEST-A for Dialect ID with pre-processing. This is also the best-performing model in the average scores of both test sets with 25.54%. The model with the best generalization on TEST-B with a *k* number of countries, is MARBERT with pre-processing with F-1 score of 17.51%. For ASA in Subtask 2, MARBERT trained without the use of pre-processing performed better on the test set than other models with the best Macro-F1-PN score of 74.29%. We see from the confusion matrix of the best model on DEV subset of Subtask 1 in Fig 2 that dialects with a high number of examples are classified better than dialects with a lower number.

5 Discussion and Future Work

According to our experiments, we see that the pre-processing we used has a positive impact on Dialect Identification, unlike Sentiment Analysis. Initial results say that tokens and expressions that identify

[5] Model names on HuggingFace hub are *aubmindlab/bert-base-arabertv02-twitter* and *UBC-NLP/MARBERT*.

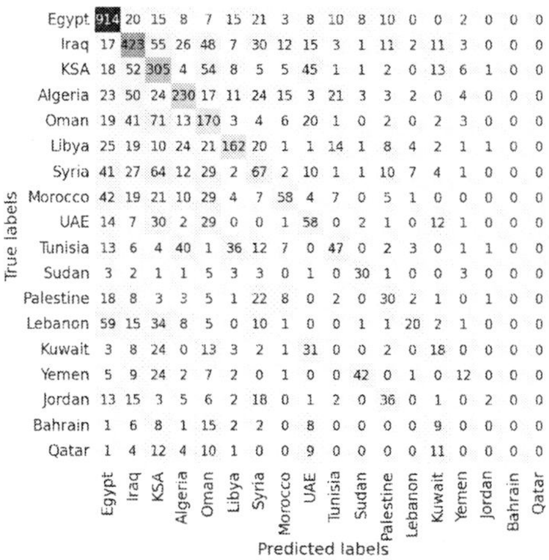

Figure 4: Confusion matrix of the predictions of the best performing MARBERT with no pre-processing against DEV subset of Subtask 1.

a dialect are not correlated with the processed (replaced or removed tokens like emojis, repetitions, etc.) so we see better results with them processed. In ASA, on the other hand, we see that they have an opposite effect on the classification. In general, MARBERT performs better on both subtasks even though its 2nd version performs better on the ARLUE benchmark (Abdul-Mageed et al., 2020a). In Fig 5 we see the Kernel Density Estimation (KDE) line of failing predictions of the model on ADID lies slightly to the left of the line of the successful predictions. This means that the probability to make correct predictions is higher when the sentence is longer.

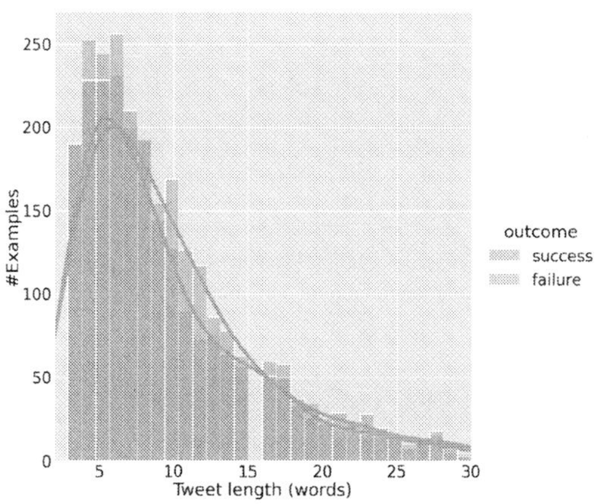

Figure 5: An overlapping histogram for both successful and failing predictions with respect to the word count (window from 1 to 30) taken from MARBERT with no pre-processing against DEV set of Subtask 1.

	Text	Label	Prediction	#Words	Comment
0	مين مدايجك بس	Egypt	Iraq	3	Mislabelled
1	الجو حلو لي درجة ودي أقل شعري	Syria	KSA	7	Mislabelled
2	احسن عدنان فالدنيا	Tunisia	Oman	3	Unclear / both
3	تعالي خاص اذا ممكن	KSA	Iraq	4	Unclear / both
4	يستاهل ابو ماجد	Syria	Oman	3	Mislabelled
5	يارب الامتحانات تخلص ! ! زهقت : (: (	Palestine	Egypt	10	Mislabelled

Table 4: Examples of instances that are mislabelled or unclear in Subtask 1.

In our analysis, we focus more on ADID, in which we still have to face the challenge of the highly correlated dialects such as Palestinian with Jordanian, or Saudi Arabian with Emirati or Omani. Combining MSA with the dialects makes the problem harder and it is out of the scope of Subtask 1. Moreover, labeling such a dataset is hard to achieve without any confusion in the labels, even a human-level baseline might not be purely reliable. We present some of the examples that are either mislabelled or unclear in Table 4. Collecting more data can help in this problem, but focusing on increasing the quality of the data, e.g. using active learning methods. Platform bias is clear in the tweet nature, which could be considered as a limitation for the model in different use cases. The models experimented on are not bias-free, even though the used model is pre-trained on multi-source corpus keeps they're still prone to social biases (Garrido-Muñoz et al., 2021). To increase the performance of our classifier models, we intern to leverage new models from different architectures like (Nagoudi et al., 2022), since it achieved SOTA on Arabic NLU tasks. We also plan to use an ensemble model like (AlKhamissi et al., 2021), for it has a potential improvement gap in the overall performance.

6 Conclusion

This study is focused on two main tasks: Arabic Dialect Identification and Arabic Sentiment Analysis based only on the text of the tweets. We demonstrate the nuanced variations between the models before and after applying language-specific pre-processing, besides using domain-adapted models pre-trained on Arabic corpus. Understanding these variations requires knowledge of the nature of different data collections that should be considered. We conclude that it is important to choose the set of hyper-parameters of fine-tuning carefully to obtain a more stable and better generalization. Finally, we found that MARBERT outperforms other models in the generalization capability in both subtasks.

References

Muhammad Abdul-Mageed, AbdelRahim Elmadany, and El Moatez Billah Nagoudi. 2020a. Arbert & marbert: deep bidirectional transformers for arabic. *arXiv preprint arXiv:2101.01785*.

Muhammad Abdul-Mageed, Chiyu Zhang, Houda Bouamor, and Nizar Habash. 2020b. NADI 2020: The first nuanced Arabic dialect identification shared task. In *Proceedings of the Fifth Arabic Natural Language Processing Workshop*, pages 97–110, Barcelona, Spain (Online). Association for Computational Linguistics.

Muhammad Abdul-Mageed, Chiyu Zhang, AbdelRahim Elmadany, Houda Bouamor, and Nizar Habash. 2021. NADI 2021: The second nuanced Arabic dialect identification shared task. In *Proceedings of the Sixth Arabic Natural Language Processing Workshop*, pages 244–259, Kyiv, Ukraine (Virtual). Association for Computational Linguistics.

Muhammad Abdul-Mageed, Chiyu Zhang, AbdelRahim Elmadany, Houda Bouamor, and Nizar Habash. 2022. NADI 2022: The Third Nuanced Arabic Dialect Identification Shared Task. In *Proceedings of the Seven Arabic Natural Language Processing Workshop (WANLP 2022)*.

Armen Aghajanyan, Anchit Gupta, Akshat Shrivastava, Xilun Chen, Luke Zettlemoyer, and Sonal Gupta. 2021. Muppet: Massive multi-task representations with pre-finetuning. *arXiv preprint arXiv:2101.11038*.

Onur Akça, Gıyaseddin Bayrak, Abdul Majeed Issifu, and Murat Can Ganz. 2022. Traditional machine learning and deep learning-based text classification for turkish law documents using transformers and domain adaptation. In *2022 International Conference on INnovations in Intelligent SysTems and Applications (INISTA)*, pages 1–6. IEEE.

Badr AlKhamissi, Mohamed Gabr, Muhammad El-Nokrashy, and Khaled Essam. 2021. Adapting marbert for improved arabic dialect identification: Submission to the nadi 2021 shared task. *arXiv preprint arXiv:2103.01065*.

Wissam Antoun, Fady Baly, and Hazem Hajj. 2020. Arabert: Transformer-based model for arabic language understanding. *arXiv preprint arXiv:2003.00104*.

Gıyaseddin Bayrak, Muhammed Şakir Toprak, Murat Can Ganiz, Halife Kodaz, and Ural Koç. 2022. Deep learning-based brain hemorrhage detection in ct reports. In *Challenges of Trustable AI and Added-Value on Health*, pages 866–867. IOS Press.

Gökberk Çelkmasat, Muhammed Enes Aktürk, Yunus Emre Ertunç, Abdul Majeed Issifu, and Murat Can Ganz. 2022. Biomedical named entity recognition using transformers with bilstm+ crf and graph convolutional neural networks. In *2022 International Conference on INnovations in Intelligent SysTems and Applications (INISTA)*, pages 1–6. IEEE.

Jacob Devlin, Ming-Wei Chang, Kenton Lee, and Kristina Toutanova. 2018. Bert: Pre-training of deep bidirectional transformers for language understanding. *arXiv preprint arXiv:1810.04805*.

Ismael Garrido-Muñoz, Arturo Montejo-Ráez, Fernando Martínez-Santiago, and L Alfonso Ureña-López. 2021. A survey on bias in deep nlp. *Applied Sciences*, 11(7):3184.

Haoming Jiang, Pengcheng He, Weizhu Chen, Xiaodong Liu, Jianfeng Gao, and Tuo Zhao. 2019. Smart: Robust and efficient fine-tuning for pretrained natural language models through principled regularized optimization. *arXiv preprint arXiv:1911.03437*.

Ilya Loshchilov and Frank Hutter. 2017. Decoupled weight decay regularization. *arXiv preprint arXiv:1711.05101*.

Marius Mosbach, Maksym Andriushchenko, and Dietrich Klakow. 2020. On the stability of fine-tuning bert: Misconceptions, explanations, and strong baselines. *arXiv preprint arXiv:2006.04884*.

El Moatez Billah Nagoudi, AbdelRahim Elmadany, and Muhammad Abdul-Mageed. 2022. AraT5: Text-to-text transformers for Arabic language generation. In *Proceedings of the 60th Annual Meeting of the Association for Computational Linguistics (Volume 1: Long Papers)*, pages 628–647, Dublin, Ireland. Association for Computational Linguistics.

Richard Socher, Alex Perelygin, Jean Wu, Jason Chuang, Christopher D Manning, Andrew Y Ng, and Christopher Potts. 2013. Recursive deep models for semantic compositionality over a sentiment treebank. In *Proceedings of the 2013 conference on empirical methods in natural language processing*, pages 1631–1642.

Ashish Vaswani, Noam Shazeer, Niki Parmar, Jakob Uszkoreit, Llion Jones, Aidan N Gomez, ukasz Kaiser, and Illia Polosukhin. 2017. Attention is all you need. *Advances in neural information processing systems*, 30.

Anshul Wadhawan. 2021. Dialect identification in nuanced arabic tweets using farasa segmentation and arabert. *arXiv preprint arXiv:2102.09749*.

Ikuya Yamada, Akari Asai, Hiroyuki Shindo, Hideaki Takeda, and Yuji Matsumoto. 2020. Luke: deep contextualized entity representations with entity-aware self-attention. *arXiv preprint arXiv:2010.01057*.

Imad Zeroual, Dirk Goldhahn, Thomas Eckart, and Abdelhak Lakhouaja. 2019. Osian: Open source international arabic news corpus-preparation and integration into the clarin-infrastructure. In *Proceedings of the fourth arabic natural language processing workshop*, pages 175–182.

Benchmarking transfer learning approaches for sentiment analysis of Arabic dialect

Emna Fsih, Saméh Kchaou, Rahma Boujelbane and **Lamia Hadrich Belguith**
ANLP Research Group / Sfax, Tunisia
{emnafsih, samehkchaou4, rahma.boujelbane}@gmail.com
lamia.belguith@fsegs.usf.tn

Abstract

Arabic has a widely varying collection of dialects. With the explosion of the use of social networks, the volume of written texts has remarkably increased. Most users express themselves using their own dialect. Unfortunately, many of these dialects remain under-studied due to the scarcity of resources. Researchers and industry practitioners are increasingly interested in analyzing users' sentiments. In this context, several approaches have been proposed, namely: traditional machine learning, deep learning transfer learning and more recently few-shot learning approaches. In this work, we compare their efficiency as part of the NADI competition to develop a country-level sentiment analysis model. Three models were beneficial for this sub-task: The first based on Sentence Transformer (ST) and achieve 43.23% on DEV set and 42.33% on TEST set, the second based on CAMeLBERT and achieve 54.00% on DEV set and 43.11% on TEST set and the third based on multi-dialect BERT model and achieve 66.72% on DEV set and 39.69% on TEST set.

1 Introduction

Digital connectivity among Arab population has remarkably grown in the last few years. Apart from technological progress, the COVID-19 pandemic has been a factor for the increase of the penetration rate and consequently the increase in dialectal textual content in social networks. The dialect forms that differ from one region to another, have been considered for a long time to oral conversations of everyday life. They have neither standard nor sufficient resources for computational processing, unlike the mother language: MSA. As a result, there is a growing interest in dealing with this type of content. In this work we focus on developing a sentiment analysis model in the framework of shared task: Sentiment analysis of country-level Arabic. Several approaches have been proposed in the literature to build sentiment analysis models for poorly endowed languages. Deep learning has been proved as a very effective paradigm to classify sentiments in large data sets. However, this approach was not effective on small data sets and most of the time traditional machine learning algorithms get better scores.

In recent time transfer learning approaches has been shown to be beneficial to train a small data set and this by fine tuning a neural network model trained on a large data-set. BERT model (Devlin et al., 2018) based on transformer architecture is one of the effective transfer learning model. Indeed, (Moudjari et al., 2020) have used it to classify if an Algerian tweets is positive, negative or neutral. The model achieved an accuracy of 68%. Also, (Abdul-Mageed et al., 2020) have proposed another variant of BERT model baptized MARBERT that focused on both Dialectal Arabic (DA) and Modern Standard Arabic (MSA). The sentiment analysis model achieved an F-score of 71.50%. Using the same model, (Abuzayed and Al-Khalifa, 2021) have explored the effectiveness of augmenting data techniques proposed by (Abu Farha et al., 2021) to analyse the sentiments among a tweets corpus, the authors obtained an F1-score of 86%. Moreover, the Few-Shot Learning (FSL) approach has also been exploited in sentiment analysis. It is a sub-area of transfer learning which allows to classify new data when there is only a few training samples with supervised information which is the case in the present work. FSL is adapted with some success to NLP tasks, such text classification: (Bao et al., 2019) have proposed a meta-learning based method by using distributional signatures for few-shot text classification. (Luo et al., 2021) have presented few-shot text classification system upgraded by Label semantic augmented meta-learner (LaSAML) uses of label semantics.

Proceedings of the The Seventh Arabic Natural Language Processing Workshop (WANLP), pages 431 - 435
December 8, 2022 ©2022 Association for Computational Linguistics

	Num-Tweets	Num-Words	Num-Vocab	Num-Emojis
TRAIN positive	581	7934	4448	86
TRAIN negative	579	7900	4767	72
TRAIN neutral	340	4935	3064	49
DEV positive	179	2552	1696	42
DEV negative	190	2754	1897	40
DEV neutral	113	1670	1207	20
TEST positive	1179	16206	8477	139
TEST negative	1142	15963	8184	122
TEST neutral	679	9453	5357	85

Table 1: Data set statistics.

In order to build our system for NADI shared Task: Country-level sentiment analysis, we opted for transfer learning approach. In fact, we compared the effectiveness of three transfer learning models on different configurations of the corpus proposed by the organizers, this paper is structured as follows: Section 2 describes the NADI shared task's data set. Section 3 details the pre-processing and normalisation applied to the data set. Section 4 describes the data augmentation. Section 5 presents our proposed Sentiment analysis model for country-level Arabic. Finally, the conclusion is given in section 6.

2 Data

Three labeled data sets have been provided by the organizers (Abdul-Mageed et al., 2022) to build a sentiment analysis model:

TRAIN set for model training: it contains 1500 tweets, 23889 words and 10422 different words (including 207 emojis).

DEV set to adjust the model parameters: it contains 500 tweets, 7893 words and 4290 different words (including 102 emojis).

TEST set for evaluation: it contains 3000 tweets, 47293 words and 17926 different words (including 346 emojis).

More statistics on word distribution in each class are given in Table 1.

3 Data Pre-processing and Normalisation

In order to enhance the quality of the tweets corpus before feeding them as an input to the classification models, we apply the following pre-processing treatments:

- Eliminate all useless units such as website links and superfluous characters between words for example "©", "®", "@".
- Remove redundant letters and punctuation's marks.

Normalisation: We used in this phase the set of CAMeL tools for Arabic Language Processing (Obeid et al., 2020) that allows to apply the following alterations: Normalization of few Arabic characters and spelling errors in order to unify them into one form. In fact, there are some letters in Arabic that can be described as confusing in some cases. We normalize words containing such letters having one representative letter. For example, the different representations of HAMZA (أ, آ, and إ) were converted into the letter Alif (ا). We remove unnecessary characters including those with no phonetic value, such as (. . . , ‹, ›).

4 Data augmentation

Different data augmentation techniques were proved to be useful to efficiently augment the corpus. Thus, due to the small size of the competition corpus, we propose to augment the corpus with other versions of the corpus generated by different augmentation method and test their effectiveness to improve the quality of the sentiment classification model.

Contextual augmentation: The first augmentation method consists on applying the contextual embeddings method to tweets. We use the BERT model of the library NLPAug tool in order to insert (aug-insert) or replace words using word embedding (aug-subst). For that, we use the multi-dialect-bert-base-arabic language model (Talafha et al., 2020). The chosen words for words substitution or insertion are selected randomly. This method allows to obtain 3000 sentences in addition to 1500 existing tweets. Table 2 describes a few examples after and before contextual augmentation method.

Sentences before augmentation	Sentences after augmentation
لجل حبه كلشي يهون. انسي الناس وانسي الكون	واللي حبه كلشي بعيد. له الدنيا و الكون بعينه
عسي موب هو اللي ساحب علي امك يا مسفر	عسي انك انت اللي ساحب لنا الخير يا مسفر
بعون الله هنكمل حلمنا :)	بعون الله هنكمل حلمنا :) ♥
ومن يتوكل على الله فهو حسبه ☺	ومن يتوكل على الله فهو حسبه ♥ ☺

Table 2: Examples of sentences before and after contextual augmentation.

Emojis exploration: The second augmentation method is based on the exploration of emojis (aug-emoj). We adapt several techniques. Firstly, we drop all emojis with the demoji package Python.

Conversely to the first technique, we choose to augment the tweets with emojis. We fix a list of positive emojis for positive tweets such as ♥, ☺. We adapt a manual passage on the corpus to select the emojis used only for positive tweets.

Subsequently, we add emojis attached to positive tweets that do not contain emojis. We also fix a list of emojis for negative tweets such as ☹, :'(. These emojis are only used to express negative comments.

Then, we add them to negative tweets without emojis. This method of exploring emojis makes it possible to obtain 1000 sentences added to the corpus.

5 Sentiment analysis model for country-level Arabic

5.1 Transformer models

Among transformer models language modeling architectures:

Multi-dialect BERT model: We have explored in this work a Multi-dialect Arabic BERT pre-trained language model (M1_Bashar). The latter, used the weights of the Arabic-BERT model (Safaya et al., 2020) trained on 10M Arabic tweets have been developed by (Talafha et al., 2020) for the task of Arabic dialect identification problem.

CAMeLBERT model for dialectal Arabic: CAMeLBERT developed by (Inoue et al., 2021), is a collection of BERT models pretrained on the dialectal Arabic (DA) data sets. It is intended to be fine-tuned on an NLP tasks, such as NER, POS tagging, sentiment analysis and dialect identification. In this work, we exploit it to build a sentiment analysis model (M2_CAMeL).

Sentence Transformer (ST): Is a very popular approach deployed for semantic similarity and clustering (Reimers and Gurevych, 2019). ST is a simple and efficient alternative for few-shot text classification. In this work, we adapt Sentence Transformer Fine-Tuning (SetFit) to solve Sentiment classification on NADI-2022 tweets (M3_SetFit).

5.2 Experiments

5.2.1 Baseline

We investigated at first the efficiency of transformer architecture on Baseline tweets for training and testing steps. We pretrained at first on the corpus proposed by the organizers, the models mentioned in the previous section. M1_Bashar model achieves greater F1-score of 66.72% on DEV set compared to other models. However, M3_SetFit achieved the highest F1-sore on testing data. Table 3 presents the obtained results.

	DEV	TEST
M1_Bashar	**66.72%**	39.69%
M2_CAMeL	47.85%	41.72%
M3_SetFit	43.23%	**42.33%**

Table 3: MACRO F1-PN SCORE for transformer models.

5.2.2 Impact of augmentation techniques

In order to test the effectiveness of each proposed augmentation method, we associated each one separately with the baseline corpus. Table 6 shows the obtained results. The augmentation based on the exploration of emojis achieves the greater result with an F1-score equal to 65.33% on DEV and 43.11% on TEST.

5.3 Discussion

To analyse the strengths and weaknesses of our model, we provide the confusion matrix for its performance on the NADI test set in Figure 1. The matrix highlights a number of issues stemming

Tweet	Actual	Predicted	Correct-Label
احبك و ابيك و اباك و ابغاك جمعتها لرضاك و اختار فيها ♥	Neutral	Positive	Positive
ثقلا تجبر احدا على محبتك ولو كنت تحبه	Negative	Positive	Positive
ثق في نفسك ثم لا احد	Negative	Positive	Positive
يسلمو على ذوقك	Negative	Positive	Positive
انت راحتي فهل لك ان تبقى معي الى الابد	Negative	Positive	Positive

Table 4: Examples of mislabeled tweets (1).

Tweet	Actual	Predicted	Correct-Label
وعليك مالسلام ورحمه الله وبركاته	Positive	Negative	Neutral
وعليكم السلام ورحمه الله وبركاته	Neutral	Positive	Neutral

Table 5: Examples of mislabeled tweets (2).

from the training data set itself. For instance, it can be clearly seen that the model is moderately effective in terms of positive and negative classes. The model predicts the true classes in almost 50% of cases.

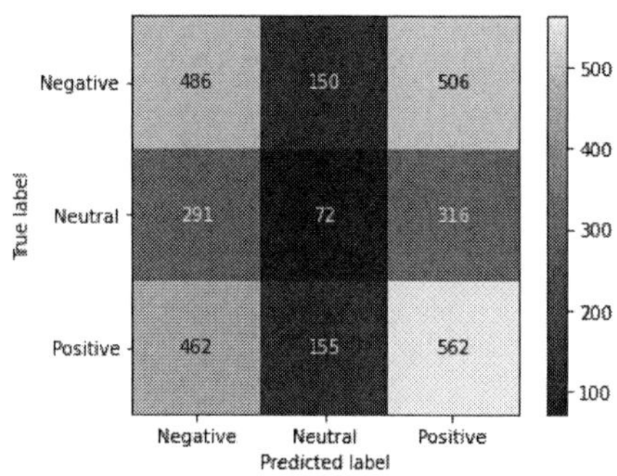

Figure 1: The confusion matrix of our SetFit model on NADI test set

However, the model is not at all efficient at the level of the neutral class this is expected given the number of neutral instances in the train. Some of the results shown in the confusion matrix have also led us to further investigate the data sets themselves. This resulted in finding that our model does in fact predict the correct class for certain tweets, which were somehow originally mislabeled. Some of these examples can be seen in Table 4. Another type of error was noticed possibly linked to spelling errors made by Internet users: for example the tweets cited in the Table 5 are two equivalent sentences but they are annotated differently in the test corpus. There is a small difference in the word وعليكم due to a typing error.

	DEV	TEST
M1_aug_insert	63.70%	39.04%
M1_aug_subst	64.16%	39.80%
M1_aug_emoj	**65.33%**	39.38%
M2_aug_insert	49.44%	39.78%
M2_aug_subst	47.13%	40.54%
M2_aug_emoj	54.00%	**43.11%**
M3_aug_insert	43.98%	40.84%
M3_aug_subst	48.21%	41.62%
M3_aug_emoj	46.09%	42.06%

Table 6: MACRO F1-PN SCORE for transformer models with augmentation.

6 Conclusion

In this paper, we presented our submitted method to the third NADI shared task. We proposed a transformer models for Sentiment analysis of country level Arabic. The experimental results shows that CAMeLBERT and SetFit models achieved an F1-score of 43.11% and 42.33% respectively on testing data set better than multi-dialect BERT model, while the latter achieved the best F1-score of 66.72% on development data-set.

References

Muhammad Abdul-Mageed, AbdelRahim Elmadany, and El Moatez Billah Nagoudi. 2020. Arbert & marbert: deep bidirectional transformers for arabic. *arXiv preprint arXiv:2101.01785*.

Muhammad Abdul-Mageed, Chiyu Zhang, Abdelrahim Elmadany, Houda Bouamor, and Nizar Habash. 2022. The nuanced arabic dialect identification shared task. In *Proceedings of the Seventh Workshop for Arabic Natural Language Processing at EMNLP 2022*, Abu Dhabi.

Ibrahim Abu Farha, Wajdi Zaghouani, and Walid Magdy. 2021. Overview of the WANLP 2021 shared task on sarcasm and sentiment detection in Arabic. In *Proceedings of the Sixth Arabic Natural Language Processing Workshop*, pages 296–305, Kyiv, Ukraine (Virtual). Association for Computational Linguistics.

Abeer Abuzayed and Hend Al-Khalifa. 2021. Sarcasm and sentiment detection in arabic tweets using bert-based models and data augmentation. In *Proceedings of the sixth Arabic natural language processing workshop*, pages 312–317.

Yujia Bao, Menghua Wu, Shiyu Chang, and Regina Barzilay. 2019. Few-shot text classification with distributional signatures. *arXiv preprint arXiv:1908.06039*.

Jacob Devlin, Ming-Wei Chang, Kenton Lee, and Kristina Toutanova. 2018. Bert: Pre-training of deep bidirectional transformers for language understanding. *arXiv preprint arXiv:1810.04805*.

Go Inoue, Bashar Alhafni, Nurpeiis Baimukan, Houda Bouamor, and Nizar Habash. 2021. The interplay of variant, size, and task type in Arabic pre-trained language models. In *Proceedings of the Sixth Arabic Natural Language Processing Workshop*, Kyiv, Ukraine (Online). Association for Computational Linguistics.

Qiaoyang Luo, Lingqiao Liu, Yuhao Lin, and Wei Zhang. 2021. Don't miss the labels: Label-semantic augmented meta-learner for few-shot text classification. In *Findings of the Association for Computational Linguistics: ACL-IJCNLP 2021*, pages 2773–2782, Online. Association for Computational Linguistics.

Leila Moudjari, Karima Akli-Astouati, and Farah Benamara. 2020. An Algerian corpus and an annotation platform for opinion and emotion analysis. In *Proceedings of the 12th Language Resources and Evaluation Conference*, pages 1202–1210, Marseille, France. European Language Resources Association.

Ossama Obeid, Nasser Zalmout, Salam Khalifa, Dima Taji, Mai Oudah, Bashar Alhafni, Go Inoue, Fadhl Eryani, Alexander Erdmann, and Nizar Habash. 2020. CAMeL tools: An open source python toolkit for Arabic natural language processing. In *Proceedings of the 12th Language Resources and Evaluation Conference*, pages 7022–7032, Marseille, France. European Language Resources Association.

Nils Reimers and Iryna Gurevych. 2019. Sentence-bert: Sentence embeddings using siamese bert-networks. In *Proceedings of the 2019 Conference on Empirical Methods in Natural Language Processing*. Association for Computational Linguistics.

Ali Safaya, Moutasem Abdullatif, and Deniz Yuret. 2020. KUISAIL at SemEval-2020 task 12: BERT-CNN for offensive speech identification in social media. In *Proceedings of the Fourteenth Workshop on Semantic Evaluation*, pages 2054–2059, Barcelona (online). International Committee for Computational Linguistics.

Bashar Talafha, Mohammad Ali, Muhy Eddin Za'ter, Haitham Seelawi, Ibraheem Tuffaha, Mostafa Samir, Wael Farhan, and Hussein T. Al-Natsheh. 2020. Multi-dialect arabic bert for country-level dialect identification.

SQU-CS @ NADI 2022: Dialectal Arabic Identification using One-vs-One Classification with TF-IDF Weights Computed on Character n-grams

Abdulrahman AAlAbdulsalam
Department of Computer Science
Sultan Qaboos University, Oman
a.aalabdulsalam@squ.edu.om

Abstract

In this paper, I present an approach using one-vs-one classification scheme with TF-IDF term weighting on character n-grams for identifying Arabic dialects used in social media. The scheme was evaluated in the context of the third Nuanced Arabic Dialect Identification (NADI 2022) shared task for identifying Arabic dialects used in Twitter messages. The approach was implemented with logistic regression loss and trained using stochastic gradient decent (SGD) algorithm. This simple method achieved a macro F1 score of 22.89% and 10.83% on TEST A and TEST B, respectively, in comparison to an approach based on AraBERT pretrained transformer model which achieved a macro F1 score of 30.01% and 14.84%, respectively. My submission based on AraBERT scored a macro F1 average of 22.42% and was ranked 10 out of the 19 teams who participated in the task.

1 Introduction

Arabic is well known for its rich morphology and complex system of inflectional forms (Habash et al., 2005). While a word in English may have few inflections, a word in Arabic contains many more inflectional forms depending on tense, number, person, mood, gender and voice (Neme and Laporte, 2013). Arabs mostly communicate informally using a continuum of dialects that vary from the east in the Arabian peninsula to the west in the North African region. These dialects add another layer of complexity since they differ at the phonological, morphological, lexical and syntactic levels (Abdul-Mageed et al., 2018). Despite dialects are predominantly used in spoken form, heavy usage of the written form is becoming very popular especially in social media platforms (Mubarak and Darwish, 2014).

Most of past research on Arabic Natural Language Processing (ANLP) have mainly focused on Modern Standard Arabic (MSA), the formal language of communication used in the Arab world. However, recently, Arabic dialects have gained more attention by researchers especially the Egyptian dialect (Guellil et al., 2021). Research on Arabic dialects involved improving parts-of-speech tagging (Alharbi et al., 2018), named entity recognition (Zirikly and Diab, 2015), parsing & grammar (Albogamy et al., 2017) and machine translation (Harrat et al., 2019). One key finding is that higher-level language tasks on Arabic dialects benefit substantially from the application of low-level pre-processing techniques that focus on better segmentation and word morphology analysis (El Kah and Zeroual, 2021; Duwairi and El-Orfali, 2014).

Arabic is considered a low-resource language when compared to other languages (Sajjad et al., 2020). This makes it challenging to utilize pre-existing approaches based on supervised machine learning (El Mekki et al., 2020). Recent works have focused on the use of few-shot or zero-shot learning techniques for Arabic dialects with promising results (Khalifa et al., 2021b,a).

The subtask of identifying Arabic dialect at the country-level was conducted as part of the third Nuanced Arabic Dialect Identification shared task: NADI 2022 (Abdul-Mageed et al., 2022). Similar subtask was organized in prior years during NADI 2020 (Abdul-Mageed et al., 2020) and NADI 2021 (Abdul-Mageed et al., 2021) shared tasks. Past attempts used a variety of approaches ranging from classical machine learning, to ensemble-based classification, and deep learning mutli-task transformer-based neural networks. The best performing methods reported for this subtask utilized the transformer-based models trained with multi-task prediction (Abdul-Mageed et al., 2021).

The current paper describes an approach based on one-vs-one classifiers trained with TF-IDF term weights on character n-grams for identifying Arabic dialects. The motivation for this approach is

Proceedings of the The Seventh Arabic Natural Language Processing Workshop (WANLP), pages 436 - 441
December 8, 2022 ©2022 Association for Computational Linguistics

the success of recent methods that exploit subword units for learning as opposed to the individual word tokens (Baniata et al., 2021; Alyafeai et al., 2022). The subword units representation work better in practice especially for Arabic and help reduce out-of-vocabulary (OOV) tokens; a common problem in natural language processing tasks. The proposed approach can be used as a baseline performance on the task of Arabic dialect identification.

2 Data

Shared task organizers have prepared and distributed two datasets with country-level labels for the task participants that can be utilized for system development as shown in Table 1. Each sample in the datasets is a single tweet message containing the original text with user mentions and website links replaced with the 'USER' and 'URL' tokens, respectively. In addition, two datasets TEST-A (4,758 samples) and TEST-B (1,474 samples) were distributed without labels and were used for final evaluation of participating teams submissions.

Country Label	TRAIN	DEV
egypt	4283	1041
iraq	2729	664
ksa	2140	520
algeria	1809	430
oman	1501	355
syria	1287	278
libya	1286	314
tunisia	859	173
morocco	858	207
lebanon	644	157
uae	642	157
jordan	429	104
kuwait	429	105
yemen	429	105
palestine	428	104
bahrain	215	52
qatar	215	52
sudan	215	53
TOTAL	20398	4871

Table 1: Country-level label counts for the shared task TRAIN and DEV datasets.

3 System Description

3.1 Data Preprocessing

The text in the datasets was preprocessed as follows:

- Remove all non-Arabic printable ASCII characters (hexdecimal codes `21` to `7E`).
- Remove any Arabic diacritic marks (Unicode ranges `0617-061A` and `064B-0652`).
- Normalize by replacing three or more repetitions of the same letter with two occurrences. For instance, the word مرررحباااا will be normalized to مررحباا in which many repetitions of the letters ا and ر were reduced to two occurrences only.
- Normalize by replacing variants of the letter Alif آ إ أ with the letter ا, the letter ة with the letter ه, and the letter ى with letter ي.

3.2 Algorithms & Implementations

Two submissions were sent to the task organizers for evaluation. First submission (henceforth will be referred to as `OVO-LR`) used one-vs-one binary classifiers implementing the Logistic Regression (LR) loss function defined in the equation below and trained with stochastic gradient descent (SGD) algorithm.

$$\sum_i (-y_i \log(h) \; + \; 1 - y_i \log(1-h)) \qquad (1)$$

Where h is the predicted probability of the true class label obtained with the sigmoid function ($\sigma(z) = \frac{1}{1-e^{(-z)}}$) and y_i is the true binary label (0 or 1).

A vocabulary consisting of character n-grams where $2 \leq n \leq 5$ (see table 2 for an example) was generated from all the text in TRAIN, DEV and TEST sets for the shared task. If the length of a particular word in the input text is less than 2 or greater than 5 then it was appended to the vocabulary. The Term Frequency-Inverted Document Frequency (TF-IDF) weights were computed for each word in the resulting vocabulary where each sample (a single Twitter message) in the dataset is considered a document. Each sample in the input was represented as a vector of TF-IDF weights using the one-hot enconding scheme. Eventually a collection of input samples in a dataset were presented for the classifier in a sparse matrix format containing the "bag of character n-grams" as input features.

The one-vs-one LR classifiers were trained using SGD algorithm with the L2 regularization penalty. Due to the skewed distribution of the class labels in both TRAIN and DEV sets, the class weights were set to be inversely proportional to label counts distribution found in the training data.

input text	character n-grams
الطرحه في النفر جنيه	ال لط طر رح حه الط لطر طرح رحه الطر لطرح طرحه الطرح لطرحه في ال لن نف فر الن لنف نفر النف لنفر النفر جن ني يه جني نيه جنيه

Table 2: Sample input text converted into character n-gram representation ($2 \leq n \leq 5$).

This submission was implemented using the following python `scikit-learn` packages using the default settings for other parameters:

- `SGDClassifier(loss='log', class_weights='balanced')`
- `OneVsOneClassifier()`
- `TfIdfVectorizer(analyzer='char', ngram_range=(2, 5))`

The second submission (`AraBERT-NADI`) used pretrained AraBERT transformer model (`bert-base-arabertv02-twitter`) which was trained on 60 millions tweets containing various Arabic dialects (Antoun et al., 2020). The model was adapted for the dialect identification task by retraining the prediction layer using the TRAIN set only for 10 epochs (learning rate = 2×10^{-5}, adam epsilon = 1×10^{-8}, training batch size = 16).

4 Results

Table 3 lists the results obtained for my official submissions on the DEV, TEST A and TEST B sets including the best scores for TEST A and TEST B in the task. The official metric used for ranking submissions in the task is the macro-averaged F1 scores. The final official scores show that `AraBERT-NADI` achieved better F1 score with +7.12% higher than `OVO-LR` for TEST A. The best overall F1 score for TEST A in the task is +6.47% higher than `AraBERT-NADI`. In addition, `AraBERT-NADI` scored +4.01% percentage points higher than `OVO-LR` for TEST B. The best F1 score obtained for TEST B is +4.11% percentage points higher than `AraBERT-NADI`. The reason for the sharp difference in performance between TEST A and TEST B could be explained by the fact that TEST B only contains a subset of the total 18 country labels in TEST A[1]. Another possible explanation is possible mismatch of label distribution between the training data (TRAIN and DEV) and TEST B. This will affect the performance of classification models which were trained to place significant weight on feature terms for the majority class labels and, therefore, become biased towards making positive predictions for the majority class label (Padurariu and Breaban, 2019). The difference in label distributions could justify the drastic drop in performance obtained in TEST B set in comparison to TEST A set (-12.06%, -15.17% and -17.53% points drop in F1 scores for `OVO-LR`, `AraBERT-NADI` and `BEST*`, respectively).

Table 4 lists the per-country label breakdown of the scores obtained on the DEV set for the submitted models. Overall, the `AraBERT-NADI` model performed better on most of country labels than the `OVO-LR` classifier. Both models performed worse on country labels with low distribution in the training data especially for the GULF dialects: Bahrain, Qatar and Yemen. An exception to this is the Arabic dialect of Sudan in which both models performed in-par or better than other dialects with much more training samples (e.g., Omani dialect). This maybe due to the fact that Sudanese dialect contain unique phrases not shared by many other Arabic dialects (see table 5). The `OVO-LR` scored better on Qatari and Kuwaiti dialects than `AraBERT-NADI` classifier. This may be because `OVO-LR` model was trained to increase the weight of low distribution class labels (i.e., assign more weight to samples from lower represented class labels). Both models obtained zero score on Bahraini dialect which is spoken in the GULF region. After manually inspecting the samples of Bahraini dialect in the TRAIN and DEV sets, it is clearly that there is a major difference in discourses between the two sets. Most of the samples in the TRAIN set include topics of sports genre and predominantly contain masculine pronouns. On the other hand, most of samples in the DEV set include topics of social genre with predominantly feminine pronouns.

Table 5 shows the top n-gram features used by `OVO-LR` model to classify each dialect. Many features are shared across dialects especially bi-grams such as شو, هه, وش and في. Notable discriminating features are n-grams that indicate country names such as تونس for Tunisia, لبنان for Lebanon, عراق for Iraq, and لمغ for Morocco. Country names are not good features for identifying dialects per se, which indicate one of the limitations of bag of words ap-

[1]According to the task organizers, TEST-B covers k country-level dialects, where k is unknown.

Submission	Dataset	Acc.	Rec.	Prec.	Macro-F1
OVO-LR	TEST A	36.34	22.97	23.18	22.89
	TEST B	20.69	11.18	15.03	10.83
	DEV	35.04	22.99	22.29	21.89
AraBERT-NADI	TEST A	46.85	29.75	34.57	30.01
	TEST B	30.12	16.80	21.32	14.84
	DEV	47.32	29.12	34.57	29.16
BEST*	TEST A	53.05	35.22	41.89	36.48
	TEST B	36.97	20.48	25.82	18.95

Table 3: Official task submissions results; BEST* are the top scores obtained in the task.

Country label	AraBERT-NADI			OVO-LR		
	Prec.	Rec.	F1	Prec.	Rec.	F1
algeria	63.21	41.16	49.86	42.89	43.49	43.19
bahrain	0.00	0.00	0.00	0.00	0.00	0.00
egypt	62.41	89.15	73.42	60.30	66.09	63.06
iraq	61.55	56.17	58.74	47.84	46.69	47.26
jordan	33.33	6.73	11.20	9.35	12.50	10.70
ksa	36.17	55.58	43.82	34.25	21.54	26.45
kuwait	20.59	6.67	10.07	10.16	18.10	13.01
lebanon	44.44	12.74	19.80	16.06	14.01	14.97
libya	47.26	43.95	45.54	39.66	29.94	34.12
morocco	46.25	17.96	25.87	19.01	11.17	14.07
oman	25.71	33.24	28.99	27.87	19.15	22.70
palestine	20.33	24.04	22.03	13.45	15.38	14.35
qatar	0.00	0.00	0.00	3.49	5.77	4.35
sudan	33.33	52.83	40.88	16.38	35.85	22.49
syria	24.51	22.66	23.55	19.77	12.59	15.38
tunisia	36.11	22.54	27.76	19.62	23.70	21.47
uae	27.06	29.30	28.13	16.10	33.12	21.67
yemen	40.00	9.52	15.38	5.15	4.76	4.95

Table 4: Breakdown of scores obtained on the DEV set for each country label in the dataset.

proach used in OVO-LR and the nature of the data used in the task.

5 Conclusion

In this paper, I presented my attempt to identify country-level Arabic dialects used in Twitter messages. The approach based on simple one-vs-one classifiers using logistic regression loss showed good baseline performance on the testing sets for the shared task in comparison to BERT-based transformer model (AraBERT) that was pretrained on 60 million Arabic tweets.

Acknowledgements

I would like to thank NADI 2022 shared task organizers for their efforts in preparing Arabic dialect datasets and releasing them to the research community. Such resources facilitate objective comparison of different methods and advance our knowledge of state-of-the-art in the field of Arabic Natural language Processing.

References

Muhammad Abdul-Mageed, Hassan Alhuzali, and Mohamed Elaraby. 2018. You tweet what you speak: A city-level dataset of arabic dialects. In *Proceedings of the Eleventh International Conference on Language Resources and Evaluation (LREC 2018)*.

Muhammad Abdul-Mageed, Chiyu Zhang, Houda Bouamor, and Nizar Habash. 2020. NADI 2020: The first nuanced Arabic dialect identification shared task. In *Proceedings of the Fifth Arabic Natural Language Processing Workshop*, pages 97–110,

algeria	هذ نت صح في ربي تاع ربي واش ران كي اك اش را
bahrain	الأ أن إت الأ حاد طو هه أبو وش تحاد إل وش لأ
egypt	ربنا ان بت كد دي بقي هت بق يا ده مش
iraq	يم عر نو ريد نه كول جي مو ار كو ج يج هاي اي اني عراق اكو
jordan	حدا حلو هيك حكي اشي رب له ابو اي سطي بد له زم طب دا نور بح
ksa	ره ون كث ما عط يال كذا مو لك سوي صي يال دري اب در ها لك ني الا وش ذا
kuwait	بخ مو لجو الجو حين لج ابي يت اق بعد بي يال حي حين هلا ني هل لحين حي ما نج صج
lebanon	ساح انو هي رح عم يدي ما كر حق هيد دا يل نان ار رح يا لبنا هيك عم لبنان شو يا
libya	ات هك ليب ليبي نح هلب خوي هكي ربي هذ توا في نق دير شن
morocco	هه داك لمغ ال غا لي فال اد ديال شي هاد
oman	ابا بع شي ما يد عاد سوي تو هاا ترا بعد هيه بو هال
palestine	بك لله حدا سي هد يسع ير حد يا شو هيك ها يسعد بت اشي مش
qatar	لج جي سنك لى نك واو لق عسى لج كم مب ما
sudan	بي ساي شن يهو لي شنو نو دي ياخ دا
syria	يكي عال بدي ما كت لك شو نو بع بدي عم هال اي انو
tunisia	با تونس تش اش كا وش في كان انت قال تو موش في
uae	حظ وي ول بي بك شو يت به تب حبه الي لب ني غل تك يال تك
yemen	لج سقط نك ردي يمن سقط جوو بت حبيش بيش لس ايش زول لي جو

Table 5: Selected subset of top character n-gram features used by the OVO-LR model to classify Arabic dialects.

Barcelona, Spain (Online). Association for Computational Linguistics.

Muhammad Abdul-Mageed, Chiyu Zhang, Abdel-Rahim Elmadany, Houda Bouamor, and Nizar Habash. 2021. NADI 2021: The second nuanced Arabic dialect identification shared task. In *Proceedings of the Sixth Arabic Natural Language Processing Workshop*, pages 244–259, Kyiv, Ukraine (Virtual). Association for Computational Linguistics.

Muhammad Abdul-Mageed, Chiyu Zhang, Abdel-Rahim Elmadany, Houda Bouamor, and Nizar Habash. 2022. NADI 2022: The Third Nuanced Arabic Dialect Identification Shared Task. In *Proceedings of the Seven Arabic Natural Language Processing Workshop (WANLP 2022)*.

Muhammad Abdul-Mageed, Chiyu Zhang, Abdel-Rahim A. Elmadany, Houda Bouamor, and Nizar Habash. 2021. NADI 2021: The second nuanced arabic dialect identification shared task. *CoRR*, abs/2103.08466.

Fahad Albogamy, Allan Ramsay, and Hanady Ahmed. 2017. Arabic tweets treebanking and parsing: A bootstrapping approach. In *Proceedings of the Third Arabic Natural Language Processing Workshop*, pages 94–99.

Randah Alharbi, Walid Magdy, Kareem Darwish, Ahmed Abdelali, and Hamdy Mubarak. 2018. Part-of-speech tagging for arabic gulf dialect using bi-lstm. In *Proceedings of the Eleventh International Conference on Language Resources and Evaluation (LREC 2018)*.

Zaid Alyafeai, Maged S Al-shaibani, Mustafa Ghaleb, and Irfan Ahmad. 2022. Evaluating various tokenizers for arabic text classification. *Neural Processing Letters*, pages 1–23.

Wissam Antoun, Fady Baly, and Hazem Hajj. 2020. Arabert: Transformer-based model for arabic language understanding. In *Proceedings of the 4th Workshop on Open-Source Arabic Corpora and Processing Tools, with a Shared Task on Offensive Language Detection*, pages 9–15.

Laith H Baniata, Isaac KE Ampomah, and Seyoung Park. 2021. A transformer-based neural machine translation model for arabic dialects that utilizes subword units. *Sensors*, 21(19):6509.

Rehab Duwairi and Mahmoud El-Orfali. 2014. A study of the effects of preprocessing strategies on sentiment analysis for arabic text. *Journal of Information Science*, 40(4):501–513.

Anoual El Kah and Imad Zeroual. 2021. The effects of pre-processing techniques on arabic text classification. *Int. J*, 10(1):1–12.

Abdellah El Mekki, Ahmed Alami, Hamza Alami, Ahmed Khoumsi, and Ismail Berrada. 2020. Weighted combination of bert and n-gram features for nuanced arabic dialect identification. In *Proceedings of the Fifth Arabic Natural Language Processing Workshop*, pages 268–274.

Imane Guellil, Houda Saâdane, Faical Azouaou, Billel Gueni, and Damien Nouvel. 2021. Arabic natural language processing: An overview. *Journal of King Saud University - Computer and Information Sciences*, 33(5):497–507.

Nizar Habash, Owen Rambow, and George Anton Kiraz. 2005. Morphological analysis and generation for arabic dialects. In *Proceedings of the ACL Workshop on Computational Approaches to Semitic Languages*, pages 17–24.

Salima Harrat, Karima Meftouh, and Kamel Smaili. 2019. Machine translation for arabic dialects (survey). *Information Processing & Management*, 56(2):262–273.

Muhammad Khalifa, Muhammad Abdul-Mageed, and Khaled Shaalan. 2021a. Self-training pre-trained language models for zero-and few-shot multi-dialectal arabic sequence labeling. *arXiv preprint arXiv:2101.04758*.

Muhammad Khalifa, Hesham Hassan, and Aly Fahmy. 2021b. Zero-resource multi-dialectal arabic natural language understanding. *arXiv preprint arXiv:2104.06591*.

Hamdy Mubarak and Kareem Darwish. 2014. Using twitter to collect a multi-dialectal corpus of arabic. In *Proceedings of the EMNLP 2014 Workshop on Arabic Natural Language Processing (ANLP)*, pages 1–7.

Alexis Amid Neme and Eric Laporte. 2013. Pattern-and-root inflectional morphology: the arabic broken plural. *Language Sciences*, 40:221–250.

Cristian Padurariu and Mihaela Elena Breaban. 2019. Dealing with data imbalance in text classification. *Procedia Computer Science*, 159:736–745.

Hassan Sajjad, Ahmed Abdelali, Nadir Durrani, and Fahim Dalvi. 2020. Arabench: Benchmarking dialectal arabic-english machine translation. In *Proceedings of the 28th International Conference on Computational Linguistics*, pages 5094–5107.

Ayah Zirikly and Mona Diab. 2015. Named entity recognition for arabic social media. In *Proceedings of the 1st workshop on vector space modeling for natural language processing*, pages 176–185.

Ahmed and Khalil at NADI 2022: Transfer Learning and Addressing Class Imbalance for Arabic Dialect Identification and Sentiment Analysis

Ahmed Oumar El-Shangiti
Independent Researcher
Marrakesh, Morocco
ahmedmohamedlemin@gmail.com

Khalil Mrini
Meta AI
Seattle, United States
khalil@meta.com

Abstract

In this paper, we present our findings in the two subtasks of the 2022 NADI shared task. First, in the Arabic dialect identification subtask, we find that there is heavy class imbalance, and propose to address this issue using focal loss. Our experiments with the focusing hyperparameter confirm that focal loss improves performance. Second, in the Arabic tweet sentiment analysis subtask, we deal with a smaller dataset, where text includes both Arabic dialects and Modern Standard Arabic. We propose to use transfer learning from both pre-trained MSA language models and our own model from the first subtask. Our system ranks in the 5th and 7th best spots of the leaderboards of first and second subtasks respectively.

1 Introduction

The 2022 **N**uanced **A**rabic **D**ialect **I**dentification (NADI) shared task (Abdul-Mageed et al., 2022) is comprised of two subtasks: Arabic dialect identification, and sentiment analysis for Arabic dialects. The aim of the shared task is to alleviate the lack of resources in NLP for Arabic dialects, amid growing interest in Arabic dialect language models (Elgezouli et al., 2020; Abdaoui et al., 2021; Issam and Mrini, 2022). The 2022 edition is the third NADI shared task. The 2021 (Abdul-Mageed et al., 2021b) and 2020 NADI shared tasks (Abdul-Mageed et al., 2020) focus on country- and province-level Arabic (sub-)dialect identification. These two editions also tackled tweets in Arabic dialects, gathering dialects from 100 provinces in 21 Arab countries.

In this paper, we tackle both subtasks, using both transfer learning from pre-trained language models, and transfer learning from one subtask to the other, as well as loss functions adapted to the class imbalance in the dataset.

The first subtask tackles country-level Arabic dialect identification in tweets. We first analyse the data, and find that there is a high class imbalance between the 18 countries represented in the tweets. We find that the largest class has nearly 20 times as many samples as the smallest one. We try multiple pre-trained Arabic language models, and find that the highest-performing model is MarBERT (Abdul-Mageed et al., 2021a). We try different loss functions, and find that focal loss (Lin et al., 2017) performs the best, as it applies a modulating term to the cross-entropy loss, enabling the training process to focus on wrongly classified samples. We fine-tune the *focusing* hyperparameter γ, and observe how performance fluctuates accordingly.

The second subtask deals with sentiment analysis for tweets in various Arabic dialects, as well as in Modern Standard Arabic. There are three classes: positive, negative, and neutral sentiment. In our data analysis, we find that there is less class imbalance in the second subtask, especially between the positive and negative classes. However, this second subtask has a much smaller training set, and therefore needs a supplement of knowledge from other sources. Given that external labeled data is not allowed, we decide to employ transfer learning, by fine-tuning the best model from the first subtask on this second one. As the dataset of the second subtask contains both Arabic dialects and Modern Standard Arabic, we hypothesize that performance will benefit from language models trained on Modern Standard Arabic, as well as from data in Arabic dialects. Finally, we show that our system ranks in the 5th and 7th best spots of the leaderboards in the first and second subtasks respectively, and propose suggestions for improving performance.

2 Data

In this section, we describe the data used for training our system in both subtasks.

The first subtask deals with Arabic Dialect Identification. The training data contains 18 classes. Each class corresponds to the national vernacular

Proceedings of the The Seventh Arabic Natural Language Processing Workshop (WANLP), pages 442 - 446
December 8, 2022 ©2022 Association for Computational Linguistics

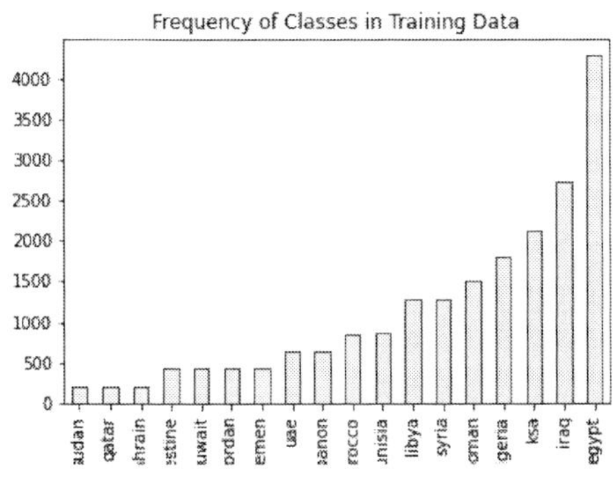

Figure 1: Distribution of country labels for training samples for the first subtask.

Subtask	F1	Acc.	Prec.	Recall
1	0.3305	0.5231	0.3629	0.3411
Subtask	F1	Acc.	Prec.	Recall
2	0.7334	0.6860	0.6658	0.6483

Table 1: Validation set results for our team in both subtasks. Results are computed by the online platform.

of a distinct Arab country. There are 20,398 training samples – all are tweets. We plot the distribution of country labels for training samples in Figure 1. The dataset is unbalanced, as we notice Egypt has 4,283 samples, whereas the smallest classes (Bahrain, Sudan, Qatar) have only 215 samples each.

We perform a similar analysis for validation data, and find that the distribution is similar, as shown in Figure 2. The validation dataset has 4,871 samples. The class with the most samples is again Egypt with 1,041 datapoints, whereas the smallest ones are Qatar and Bahrain with 52 samples each.

The second subtask is Sentiment Analysis over tweets in various Arabic dialects. This is a three-way classification problem, where the goal is to predict whether a tweet – regardless of the arabic dialect – has positive, neutral or negative sentiment. This subtask has fewer datapoints than the first one. The training set contains 1,500 samples, whereas the validation set contains 500 samples. There is roughly the same distribution over the sentiment classes between the two sets, as shown in Figures 3 and 4.

3 System Description

For both subtasks, we investigate the potentials of transfer learning for different Arabic BERT-based models. Specifically, we compared the follow-

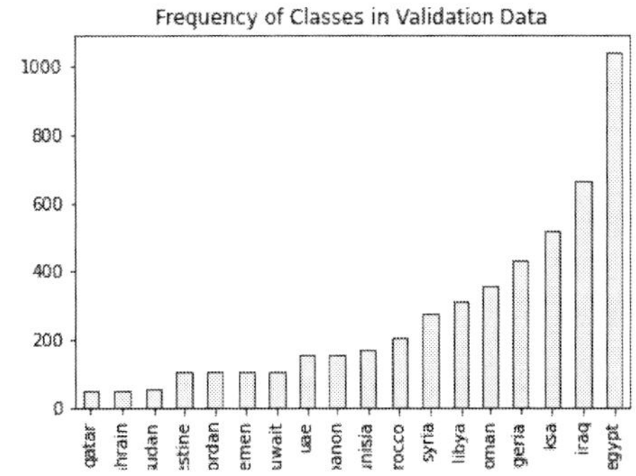

Figure 2: Distribution of country labels for validation samples for the first subtask.

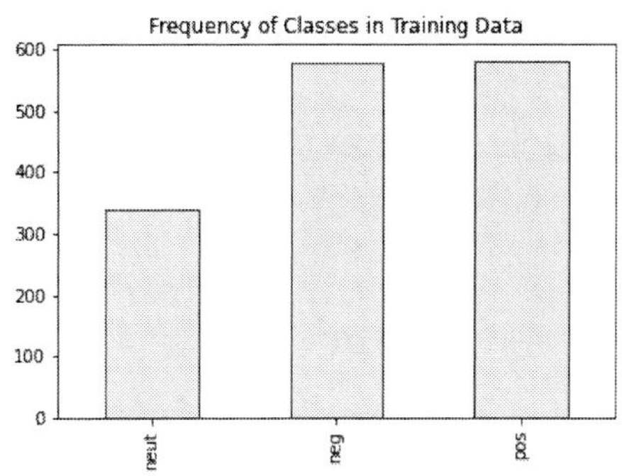

Figure 3: Distribution of sentiment labels for training samples for the second subtask.

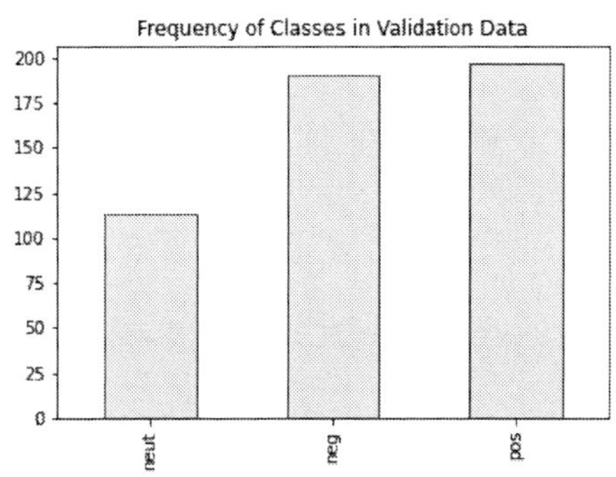

Figure 4: Distribution of sentiment labels for validation samples for the second subtask.

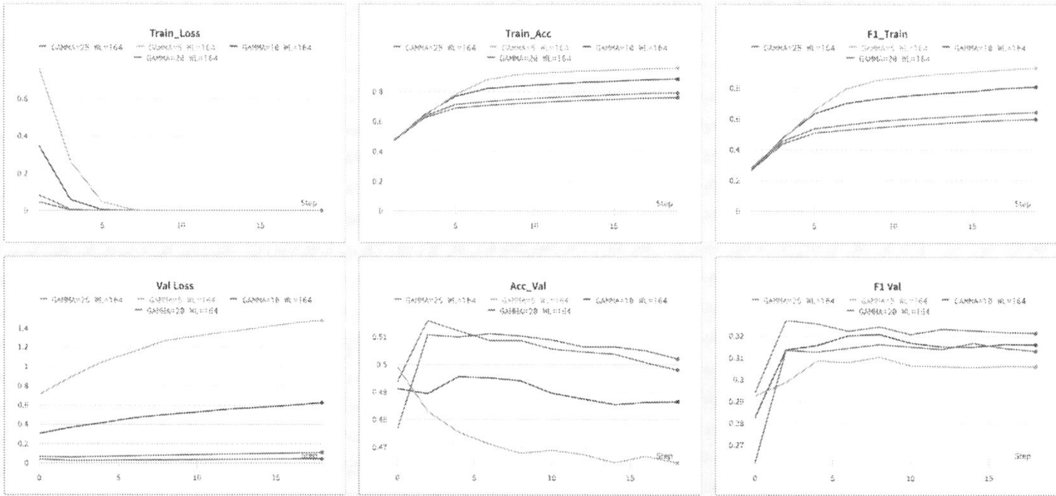

Figure 5: Graphs showing the progression of the loss, accuracy, and F1 scores for the training and validation sets of the first subtask on Arabic Dialect Identification. We change the values of the γ of the Focal Loss, varying them from 5 to 25.

ing pre-trained BERT-based models: MarBERT (Abdul-Mageed et al., 2021a), CamelBERT (Inoue et al., 2021) and AraBERT (Antoun et al., 2020).

Our experiments consist of fine-tuning a pre-trained BERT model, plus one or more fully connected layers. It turns out that the best performance is achieved using only the pre-trained model plus a classification layer.

For all experiments, we use the following hyper-parameters: a learning rate of $4 * 10^{-5}$, 10 training epochs, an Adam optimizer with weight decay regularization. The batch size is set to 32 for the first subtask, and 8 for the second subtask.

We implement our models using Pytorch. For the loss functions, we experiment with self-adjusting Dice Loss (`SelfAdjDiceLoss`) (Li et al., 2020), Negative Log-Likelihood Loss (`NLLLoss`), Cross-Entropy Loss (`CrossEntropyLoss`) with and without weighted classes, and Focal Loss (`FocalLoss`) (Lin et al., 2017). The latter has shown the best performance for both sub tasks. This could be due to the fact that the first subtask's dataset is imbalanced, and Focal Loss is designed to alleviate class imbalance. In order to focus on hard, wrongly classified samples, Focal Loss applies a modulating term to the cross-entropy loss. Given the cross-entropy loss formula:

$$\text{CEL}(p_t) = -log(p_t) \quad (1)$$

the focal loss formula is as follows:

$$\text{FL}(p_t) = (1 - p_t)^{\gamma} * [-log\,(p_t)] \quad (2)$$

where γ is the *focusing* hyperparameter. The higher the hyperparameter, the more the focal loss function will focus on wrongly classified samples.

Among the three pre-trained models considered, we found that MarBERT performs the best, in a fair evaluation with fixed hyperparameters. During our experiments, we found that the best configuration is a pre-trained MarBERT model, with a single classification layer, and a Focal Loss function.

Participants of the shared task were not allowed to use external labeled data for training. However, the second subtask has a substantially smaller training set than the first one. We decide to leverage the knowledge learned by the model during the first subtask, and fine-tune the model on the training set of the second subtask.

4 Results and Discussion

For the first subtask, we experiment with the γ hyperparameter of the Focal Loss. We try the following values: 5, 10, 20 (default value), and 25. We show the results on the validation and training sets in Figure 5. We see that the lowest validation loss is achieved with $\gamma = 25$, but the highest accuracy and F1 scores are achieved with $\gamma = 20$. So we use $\gamma = 20$ for the remainder of the experiments. This confirms that performance is higher when class imbalance is addressed during training. The accuracy and F1 scores seem to peak for the

TABLE 4. Leaderboard of Subtask 2

Rank	Team	Macro-F1-PN	Accuracy	Recall	Precision
1	rematchka	75.1555	69.7000	66.2230	67.5684
2	UniManc	73.5443	67.7000	63.9228	65.2702
3	BhamNLP	73.4566	67.3333	62.8315	65.2415
4	pythoneers	73.3959	68.2333	65.8708	66.0751
5	Ahmed_and_Khalil	71.4569	66.0333	63.7342	63.8411
6	giyaseddin	71.4278	65.8000	62.1962	63.5143
7	ISL_AAST	70.5527	64.9667	61.4095	62.5844
8	ANLP-RG	67.3106	61.9000	59.6697	59.6920
9	RUTeam	61.0675	56.1667	53.5776	53.8966
10	Oscar_Garibo	46.4261	43.0000	41.9179	41.9985

Figure 6: All 10 teams in the leaderboard for the second subtask on Sentiment Analysis for Arabic Dialects.

TABLE 1. Leaderboard of Subtask 1

Rank	Team	Average Macro-F1
1	rematchka	27.06
2	UniManc	26.86
3	GOF	26.44
4	mtu_fiz	25.50
5	iCompass	25.32
6	ISL-AAST	24.59
7	Ahmed_and_Khalil	24.35
8	pythoneers	24.12
9	giyaseddin	22.42
10	SQU	22.42

Figure 7: Top 10 teams in the leaderboard for the first subtask on Arabic Dialect Identification.

validation set at the second epoch, whereas they increase for the training set as the training epochs progress. This indicates that overfitting occurs after the second epoch, in particular for $\gamma = 20$.

We show our dev set results in Table 1. For both subtasks, the results are computed by the Codalab online platform based on the predictions of our system. The metrics are macro-F1, accuracy, precision, and recall. Macro-F1 gives equal weight to each class, which matters for the first subtask where there is heavy class imbalance.

For the test set results, our system scores in the 7th best spot in the first subtask, out of 19 participants, and the 5th best spot out of 10 participants in the second subtask. The leaderboards and test results for the first and second subtasks are shown in Figures 7 and 6 respectively. For the first subtask, there are two test subsets: Test-A is a subset containing all 18 classes, whereas Test-B is a subset containing k classes, where k is unknown. The results shown in Figure 7 are the Average of the Macro-F1 scores between both test subsets. We notice that the results of the second through fifth rows in the leaderboard of the first subtask are close. For the second subtask, the shared task organizers evaluate using "*Macro-F1-PN*", which is a Macro-F1 score computed for the Positive and Negative classes, ignoring the Neutral cases.

If we had more time, we would investigate Domain Adversarial learning and Multi-Task Learning. As transfer learning proved useful in the second subtask, this suggests that a multi-task learning setting could benefit both subtasks. Moreover, in the second subtask, there are tweets from different countries, but it is a feature that does not matter in the sentiment analysis task. The model would benefit from learning to not distinguish between Arabic dialects, as it would learn *dialect-agnostic* sentiment features that enable easy knowledge transfer between tweets in different Arabic dialects.

5 Conclusions

In this paper, we presented our team's approach to the two subtasks of the 2022 NADI shared task. We first analysed the data, and find that there is class imbalance between the 18 classes of the Arabic dialect identification subtask. In the Arabic tweet sentiment analysis subtask, we find that classes are relatively more balanced, but there are fewer datapoints to train on.

We propose to train on MarBERT, and we find that Focal Loss is the loss function that performs best, as it addresses class imbalance. Our experiments with the γ focusing hyperparameter show that we need a large γ value for high F1 scores, confirming that focal loss alleviates class imbalance.

Finally, our system scores favorably in the leaderboards in both subtasks. We suggest for the second subtask that domain-adversarial training could benefit performance, as it would make the model learn dialect-agnostic features about the sentiment classes.

References

Amine Abdaoui, Mohamed Berrimi, Mourad Oussalah, and Abdelouahab Moussaoui. 2021. Dziribert: a pre-trained language model for the algerian dialect. *arXiv preprint arXiv:2109.12346*.

Muhammad Abdul-Mageed, AbdelRahim Elmadany, et al. 2021a. Arbert & marbert: Deep bidirectional transformers for arabic. In *Proceedings of the 59th Annual Meeting of the Association for Computational Linguistics and the 11th International Joint Conference on Natural Language Processing (Volume 1: Long Papers)*, pages 7088–7105.

Muhammad Abdul-Mageed, Chiyu Zhang, Houda Bouamor, and Nizar Habash. 2020. NADI 2020: The first nuanced Arabic dialect identification shared task. In *Proceedings of the Fifth Arabic Natural Language Processing Workshop*, pages 97–110, Barcelona, Spain (Online). Association for Computational Linguistics.

Muhammad Abdul-Mageed, Chiyu Zhang, AbdelRahim Elmadany, Houda Bouamor, and Nizar Habash. 2021b. Nadi 2021: The second nuanced arabic dialect identification shared task. In *Proceedings of the Sixth Arabic Natural Language Processing Workshop*, pages 244–259.

Muhammad Abdul-Mageed, Chiyu Zhang, AbdelRahim Elmadany, Houda Bouamor, and Nizar Habash. 2022. NADI 2022: The Third Nuanced Arabic Dialect Identification Shared Task. In *Proceedings of the Seven Arabic Natural Language Processing Workshop (WANLP 2022)*.

Wissam Antoun, Fady Baly, and Hazem Hajj. 2020. Arabert: Transformer-based model for arabic language understanding. *arXiv preprint arXiv:2003.00104*.

Mukhtar Elgezouli, Khalid N Elmadani, and Muhammed Saeed. 2020. Sudabert: A pre-trained encoder representation for sudanese arabic dialect. In *2020 International Conference on Computer, Control, Electrical, and Electronics Engineering (ICCCEEE)*, pages 1–4. IEEE.

Go Inoue, Bashar Alhafni, Nurpeiis Baimukan, Houda Bouamor, and Nizar Habash. 2021. The interplay of variant, size, and task type in arabic pre-trained language models. In *Proceedings of the Sixth Arabic Natural Language Processing Workshop*, pages 92–104.

Abderrahmane Issam and Khalil Mrini. 2022. Goud.ma: a news article dataset for summarization in moroccan darija. In *3rd Workshop on African Natural Language Processing*.

Xiaoya Li, Xiaofei Sun, Yuxian Meng, Junjun Liang, Fei Wu, and Jiwei Li. 2020. Dice loss for data-imbalanced nlp tasks. In *Proceedings of the 58th Annual Meeting of the Association for Computational Linguistics*, pages 465–476.

Tsung-Yi Lin, Priya Goyal, Ross Girshick, Kaiming He, and Piotr Dollár. 2017. Focal loss for dense object detection. In *Proceedings of the IEEE international conference on computer vision*, pages 2980–2988.

Arabic Sentiment Ensemble NADI Shared Task 2

Abdelrahim Qaddoumi
New York University / amq259@nyu.edu

Abstract

This paper presents the 259 team's BERT ensemble designed for the NADI 2022 Subtask 2 (sentiment analysis) (Abdul-Mageed et al., 2022). Twitter Sentiment analysis is one of the language processing (NLP) tasks that provides a method to understand the perception and emotion of the public around specific topics. The most common research approach focuses on obtaining the tweet's sentiment by analyzing its lexical and syntactic features. We used multiple pretrained Arabic-Bert models with a simple average ensembling and then chose the best-performing ensemble on the training dataset and ran it on the development dataset. This system ranked 3rd in Subtask 2 with a Macro-PN-F1-score of 72.49%.

1 Introduction

Sentiment analysis (SA) is a process of computationally categorizing opinions expressed in a piece of text, especially in order to determine whether the attitude towards a particular product by labeling it positive, negative, or neutral. Sentiment analysis is a process of computationally categorizing opinions expressed in a piece of text, especially in order to determine whether the attitude towards a particular product by labeling it positive, negative, or neutral (Liu, 2012). As the world becomes increasingly digitized, sentiment analysis is becoming increasingly important. With the vast majority of people now using the internet and social media to communicate, NLP methods can help us analyze this massive amount of data to understand public opinion on various issues. Sentiment analysis can be extremely useful for businesses and governments, using sentiment analysis to track how the public's opinion (Liu, 2012).

One of the basic sentiment analysis approaches is a lexicon-based approach. This approach uses a list of words associated with neutral, positive, or negative sentiment. Then we use the generated list to score the sentiment of a text similar to what is done in (Neviarouskaya et al., 2010) and (Moreo et al., 2012). Another common approach is to use a machine learning algorithm to learn the sentiment of a text. However, this approach requires a training dataset of texts manually labeled with their sentiment for the machine learning algorithm to predict the sentiment of new texts such as (Chen and Tseng, 2011). Recently, transformers have been used for sentiment analysis, a deep learning method that learns the representation of text data for sentiment classification. This approach has been shown to outperform traditional machine learning methods such as support vector machines or deep learning models like long short-term memory or convolutional neural networks. In addition, the transformer approach can also handle a large amount of data, making it a scalable method for sentiment analysis like (Munikar et al., 2019).

While the accuracy of sentiment analysis in Arabic is still far from perfect, the current state of the art is much better than it was even a few years ago. The progress of sentiment analysis in Arabic has been significant in recent years. With the increasing availability of Arabic text data, there has been a corresponding increase in the development of methods and tools for sentiment analysis in Arabic. This progress will likely continue as more Arabic-specific data, and sophisticated methods become available (Al-Ayyoub et al., 2019).

There are a few reasons why sentiment analysis is complex with Arabic dialects. First, many variations in Arabic dialects make it difficult to identify patterns. Second, Arabic is a highly inflected language; words can have multiple meanings depending on their context in a sentence. This can make it difficult to determine the sentiment. Finally, Arabic dialects often use a lot of idiomatic expressions, which can also be challenging to interpret, as shown in (Laoudi et al., 2018).

The paper is structured as follows: Section 2

Proceedings of the The Seventh Arabic Natural Language Processing Workshop (WANLP), pages 447 - 451
December 8, 2022 ©2022 Association for Computational Linguistics

concisely describes the used dataset. Section 3 describes the models used for the ensemble for Sentiment Analysis. Section 4 presents the results obtained for each combination. Section 5 presents related works. Section 6 presents a general discussion. Finally, section 7 contains the conclusion and points for future work.

2 Data

The competition provided a dataset of 5,000 tweets split into a training dataset of 1500 tweets, a development dataset of 500 tweets, and 3000 for the testing dataset. The tweets are labeled 'pos' for positive, 'neg' for negative, and 'neut' for neutral. We used the training dataset to decide on the best ensemble combination of models.

Class	Train	Development
pos	581	197
neg	579	190
neut	340	113

Table 1: Dataset description for Subtask 2 - Sentiment Analysis

3 System Description

We used Arabic pretrained language models that were fine-tuned for sentiment analysis publicly available on HuggingFace. There was no extra fine-tuning or preprocessing done after that. Instead, these models were used in a simple average ensemble by adding the logit values of the models' combination, using the maximum value for prediction, and then looping over the different combinations of the available models.

3.1 CAMeLBERT

While pre-trained language models such as ArarBERT have shown significant success in many NLP tasks in various languages, including Arabic, it is unclear what these multilingual models learn in Arabic and their most important features. Thus, Inoue et al. (2021) worked on an experiment to see how different sized pre-training data sets and language variants affected the performance of pre-trained language models. The paper culminated with nine different models, but four models that are trained for sentiment analysis CAMeLBERT-MSA, CAMeLBERT-DA, CAMeLBERT-CA, and CAMeLBERT-Mix. For a full-list off the dataset (Inoue et al., 2021).

The main difference between the models is the different Arabic languages used in the dataset and there are three different types of Arabic: Modern Standard Arabic (MSA), Classical Arabic (CA), and Dialectical Arabic (DA) (Al-Saidat and Al-Momani, 2010). MSA is the Arabic form used in most written documents and media today, it is based on the grammar and vocabulary of the Qur'an, and is the language of Arab countries' governments and schools, Classical Arabic is the Arabic form used in the Qur'an and other early Islamic literature, Dialectical Arabic is the form of Arabic spoken in everyday life in Arab countries, and each dialect differs based on region, social class, and religion (Al-Saidat and Al-Momani, 2010).

3.1.1 CAMeLBERT MSA SA Model

The model is trained on dataset for Modern Standard Arabic. The size of the model is 107GB with 12.6 Billion words.

3.1.2 CAMeLBERT DA SA Model

The model is trained on dataset for Dialectal Arabic. The size of the model is 54GB with 5.8 Billion words.

3.1.3 CAMeLBERT CA SA Model

The model is trained on dataset for Classical Arabic. The size of the model is 6GB with 0.847 Billion words.

3.1.4 CAMeLBERT Mix SA Model

The model is the combination of the three models CAMeLBERT CA SA Model, CAMeLBERT DA SA Model, and CAMeLBERT MSA SA Model. The size of the model is 167GB with 17.3 Billion words.

3.2 Arabic-MARBERT-Sentiment Model

The model is the result of fine-tuning MARBERT (Abdul-Mageed et al., 2020a) on KAUST dataset (Alharbi et al., 2020) which contains 95,000 tweets.The size of the model is 0.655GB. This work is done by Ammar Alhaj Ali on Huggingface but unfortunately was not able to cite the model as the researcher did not add a way to cite it.

4 Results

We have validated the different ensemble combinations models on the training dataset. The ensemble with model CAMeLBERT Mix SA Model and CAMeLBERT MSA (Modern Standard Arabic) SA model based on BERT achieved the best results. We believe this is because the combination of different dialects in the Mix model with the modern standard Arabic version has the majority of text features among all other models. This ensemble probably achieved the best results because the task's data contains both MSA and dialects.

4.1 Submission Results

The final results that we achieved on the NADI Shared Task Subtask 2 - Sentiment Analysis:

1. Development Sentiment Analysis: Macro-F1-PN equal to 72.49%

2. Test Sentiment Analysis: Macro-F1-PN equal to 69%

4.2 Subtask 2 - Sentiment Analysis

Model	Precision	Recall	F1-PN
MSA	62.61%	61.92%	70.18%
Mix	60.65%	60.08%	69.70%
DA	57.91%	57.82%	67.07%
CA	52.97%	52.76%	61.92%

Table 2: Single Model Results for Subtask 2 - Sentiment Analysis

Models Ensemble	Dataset	Precision	Recall	F1-PN
Mix_MSA	Dev	63.31%	63.21%	72.49%
Mix_MSA	Test	61.80%	61.33%	69.86%
Mix_CA_MSA	Dev	62.50%	62.35%	71.94%
DA_MSA	Dev	63.14%	62.99%	71.63%
Mix_CA_DA_MSA	Dev	62.28%	62.11%	71.36%
Mix_DA_CA	Dev	62.07%	62.01%	70.98%

Table 3: Results for Subtask 2 - Sentiment Analysis

5 Related Work

Arabic Sentiment Analysis received more attention recently, with many approaches showing effectiveness on the task; however, while some surveys have summarised some of the approaches for Arabic SA in literature, most of these are reported on different datasets, making it challenging to identify the most effective approaches among them (Farha and Magdy, 2021). Therefore, the researchers Farha and Magdy (2021) present a comprehensive comparative study of the most effective approaches for Arabic sentiment analysis.

The paper (Abdul-Mageed et al., 2011) kicked off the work to partially fill this gap of the lack of work on sentiment analysis in Arabic. They present a newly developed manually annotated Modern Standard Arabic (MSA) corpus with a new polarity lexicon, and investigate the impact of different levels of preprocessing settings on the classification task (Abdul-Mageed et al., 2011).

The newly generated data from Internet users on social media can be processed to extract useful information, such as users' opinions, by two main approaches: corpus-based and lexicon-based; (Abdulla et al., 2013) addresses both approaches to SA for the Arabic language using social media data. In (Abdul-Mageed et al., 2014), the researchers presented SAMAR, a system that uses lemma and the two parts of speech tagsets for sentiment analysis of Arabic social media, and addresses four issues: lexical representation, standard features for Arabic, handling of Arabic dialects, and genre-specific features.

Following the current trend of using transformers in English sentiment analysis, the introduction of AraBERT also promoted the usage of transformers for Arabic sentiment analysis. In (Wadhawan, 2021), the researchers present a strategy to identify the sentiment of the Arabic tweet. Their approach was two steps, the first step involved preprocessing using Farasa Segmentation, and the second step involved transformer-based models, AraELECTRA and AraBERT. This trend was also accompanied by a few tasks that work on cultivating the work of Arabic sentiment analysis such as (Abdul-Mageed et al., 2020b), (Abdul-Mageed et al., 2021), and lastly, (Abdul-Mageed et al., 2022).

6 Discussion

It is interesting to see that the models alone can achieve good results. However, the model with just classical Arabic was able to achieve no trivial result with only 5% of the size of the Mix model, which is worth investigating to understand the reason behind the result. The current pretraining models available freely have a relatively good performance on this task even with such a limited dataset and no training, which shows researchers' quality and hard work in the Arabic NLP field.

Future work would involve fine-tuning these models on the training dataset, trying different ensemble methods, and trying few-shot learning. Another thing to explore would be to try AraT5, the most recent state-of-the-art Arabic natural language understanding system (Nagoudi et al., 2022). The paper (Nagoudi et al., 2022) proposed a simple and effective transfer learning approach and evaluated the approach on Arabic, finding that the approach outperforms the state-of-the-art on all tasks in the benchmark.

7 Conclusion

Tables 2 and 3 show the results obtained over development data for the NADI task (Pos being positive, Neg being negative, and Neut being neutral) for the single model and ensemble model. Five language models were used to classify sentiment (mix, ca, da, MSA, and MARBERT). A simple two models ensemble (Mix and MSA) obtained the best results for the task and was selected for the final submission.

References

Muhammad Abdul-Mageed, Mona Diab, and Mohammed Korayem. 2011. Subjectivity and sentiment analysis of modern standard arabic. In *Proceedings of the 49th Annual Meeting of the Association for Computational Linguistics: Human Language Technologies*, pages 587–591.

Muhammad Abdul-Mageed, Mona Diab, and Sandra Kübler. 2014. Samar: Subjectivity and sentiment analysis for arabic social media. *Computer Speech & Language*, 28(1):20–37.

Muhammad Abdul-Mageed, AbdelRahim Elmadany, and El Moatez Billah Nagoudi. 2020a. Arbert & marbert: deep bidirectional transformers for arabic. *arXiv preprint arXiv:2101.01785*.

Muhammad Abdul-Mageed, Chiyu Zhang, Houda Bouamor, and Nizar Habash. 2020b. NADI 2020: The first nuanced Arabic dialect identification shared task. In *Proceedings of the Fifth Arabic Natural Language Processing Workshop*, pages 97–110, Barcelona, Spain (Online). Association for Computational Linguistics.

Muhammad Abdul-Mageed, Chiyu Zhang, AbdelRahim Elmadany, Houda Bouamor, and Nizar Habash. 2021. NADI 2021: The second nuanced Arabic dialect identification shared task. In *Proceedings of the Sixth Arabic Natural Language Processing Workshop*, pages 244–259, Kyiv, Ukraine (Virtual). Association for Computational Linguistics.

Muhammad Abdul-Mageed, Chiyu Zhang, AbdelRahim Elmadany, Houda Bouamor, and Nizar Habash. 2022. NADI 2022: The Third Nuanced Arabic Dialect Identification Shared Task. In *Proceedings of the Seven Arabic Natural Language Processing Workshop (WANLP 2022)*.

Nawaf A Abdulla, Nizar A Ahmed, Mohammed A Shehab, and Mahmoud Al-Ayyoub. 2013. Arabic sentiment analysis: Lexicon-based and corpus-based. In *2013 IEEE Jordan conference on applied electrical engineering and computing technologies (AEECT)*, pages 1–6. IEEE.

Mahmoud Al-Ayyoub, Abed Allah Khamaiseh, Yaser Jararweh, and Mohammed N Al-Kabi. 2019. A comprehensive survey of arabic sentiment analysis. *Information processing & management*, 56(2):320–342.

Emad Al-Saidat and Islam Al-Momani. 2010. Future markers in modern standard arabic and jordanian arabic: a contrastive study. *European journal of social sciences*, 12(3):397–408.

Basma Alharbi, Hind Alamro, Manal Alshehri, Zuhair Khayyat, Manal Kalkatawi, Inji Ibrahim Jaber, and Xiangliang Zhang. 2020. Asad: A twitter-based benchmark arabic sentiment analysis dataset. *arXiv preprint arXiv:2011.00578*.

Chien Chin Chen and You-De Tseng. 2011. Quality evaluation of product reviews using an information quality framework. *Decision Support Systems*, 50(4):755–768.

Ibrahim Abu Farha and Walid Magdy. 2021. A comparative study of effective approaches for arabic sentiment analysis. *Information Processing & Management*, 58(2):102438.

Go Inoue, Bashar Alhafni, Nurpeiis Baimukan, Houda Bouamor, and Nizar Habash. 2021. The interplay of variant, size, and task type in arabic pre-trained language models. *arXiv preprint arXiv:2103.06678*.

Jamal Laoudi, Claire Bonial, Lucia Donatelli, Stephen Tratz, and Clare Voss. 2018. Towards a computational lexicon for moroccan darija: Words, idioms, and constructions. In *Proceedings of the Joint Workshop on Linguistic Annotation, Multiword Expressions and Constructions (LAW-MWE-CxG-2018)*, pages 74–85.

Bing Liu. 2012. Sentiment analysis and opinion mining. *Synthesis lectures on human language technologies*, 5(1):1–167.

Alejandro Moreo, M Romero, JL Castro, and Jose Manuel Zurita. 2012. Lexicon-based comments-oriented news sentiment analyzer system. *Expert Systems with Applications*, 39(10):9166–9180.

Manish Munikar, Sushil Shakya, and Aakash Shrestha. 2019. Fine-grained sentiment classification using bert. In *2019 Artificial Intelligence for Transforming Business and Society (AITB)*, volume 1, pages 1–5. IEEE.

El Moatez Billah Nagoudi, AbdelRahim Elmadany, and Muhammad Abdul-Mageed. 2022. AraT5: Text-to-text transformers for Arabic language generation. In *Proceedings of the 60th Annual Meeting of the Association for Computational Linguistics (Volume 1: Long Papers)*, pages 628–647, Dublin, Ireland. Association for Computational Linguistics.

Alena Neviarouskaya, Helmut Prendinger, and Mitsuru Ishizuka. 2010. Recognition of affect, judgment, and appreciation in text. In *Proceedings of the 23rd international conference on computational linguistics (Coling 2010)*, pages 806–814.

Anshul Wadhawan. 2021. Arabert and farasa segmentation based approach for sarcasm and sentiment detection in arabic tweets. *arXiv preprint arXiv:2103.01679*.

Dialect & Sentiment Identification in Nuanced Arabic Tweets Using an Ensemble of Prompt-based, Fine-tuned and Multitask BERT-Based Models

Reem Abdel-Salam
Cairo University, Faculty of Engineering, Computer Engineering / Giza, Egypt
reem.abdelsalam13@gmail.com

Abstract

Dialect Identification is important to improve the performance of various application as translation, speech recognition, etc. In this paper, we present our findings and results in the Nuanced Arabic Dialect Identification Shared Task (NADI 2022) for country-level dialect identification and sentiment identification for dialectical Arabic. The proposed model is an ensemble between fine-tuned BERT-based models and various approaches of prompt-tuning. Our model secured first place on the leaderboard for subtask 1 with an 27.06 F1-macro score, and subtask 2 secured first place with 75.15 F1-PN score. Our findings show that prompt-tuning-based models achieved better performance when compared to fine-tuning and Multi-task based methods. Moreover, using an ensemble of different loss functions might improve model performance.

1 Introduction

Arabic, spoken by over 500 million people worldwide, is the most populous member of the semitic language family. In general, Arabic can be divided into three categories: (1) Classical Arabic, the language of early literature; (2) Modern Standard Arabic (MSA), which is commonly used in school and formal settings; and (3) Dialectal Arabic (DA), a collection of geopolitically defined varieties. The existence of several dialects and complicated morphology are two distinguishing features of the Arabic language. Furthermore, the casual nature of social media chats, as well as the variations between MSA and DA, add to the complexity. Arabic dialects are not standardized. There are no formal grammar rules or formalism to guide the speakers. This makes various tasks such as machine translation and speech recognition challenging. Several works have been proposed to improve dialect identification as the recent shared-task NADI series (2020 and 2021) (Abdul-Mageed et al., 2021b, 2020). Several teams have used traditional methods as SVM with TF-IDF (Touileb, 2020; Nayel et al., 2021), others customized Bert-based models. AlKhamissi et al. (2021) added an adapter layer on top of MARBERT model. The authors of (El Mekki et al., 2021) used multi-task learning to predict dialect on provenance and country level. This paper presents our work in the Nuanced Arabic Dialect Identification (NADI) shared task (Abdul-Mageed et al., 2022). The NADI shared task (2022) consists of two subtasks. The first subtask is a country-level dialect identification, while the second subtask is sentiment analysis based on different Arabic dialects. Given that a key challenge in this task is the unbalanced distribution and the hard nature of the problem. We follow best practices from recent work on enhancing model generalization and robustness. The rest of the papers goes as follow: section 3 discusses the proposed methods, section 4 shows experimental results, and section 5 concludes the paper. The code has been made open-source and available on GitHub [1].

2 Data

Subtask	Train-set	Dev-set	Test-set	
1	20,398	4,871	4,758 test A	1,474 test B
2	1,500	500	3,000	

Table 1: Train-validation distribution for subtask 1 and 2.

The NADI dataset provided by the organizers consists of 2 datasets for each subtask. Table 1 shows the train-set, dev-set, and test-set distribution for both subtasks. Subtask 1 covers 18 country levels dialects: Algeria, Bahrain, Egypt, Iraq, Jordan,

[1] https://github.com/rematchka/Dialect-and-Sentiment-Identification-in-Nuanced-Arabic-Tweets

Proceedings of the The Seventh Arabic Natural Language Processing Workshop (WANLP), pages 452 - 457
December 8, 2022 ©2022 Association for Computational Linguistics

Kuwait, Lebanon, Libya, Morocco, Oman, Palestine, Qatar, Saudi Arabia, Sudan, Syria, Tunisia, United Arab Emirates, and Yemen. However, the data is extremely unbalanced. The train-set consists of 20,398 tweets, while the dev-set consists of 4,871 tweets. Subtask 2 covers 3 labels positive, negative, and neutral for dialectal sentiment analysis. The tweets span different ten Arab dialects. The dataset does not suffer from class imbalance.

3 System Description

This section presents the various approaches used while developing the final models: a voting classifier, a weighted ensemble of BERT-based models, and a prompt-BERT-based model.

Experimental setup for the fine-tuned models the learning rate was set to 4e-5 or 4e-6, cosine-annealing learning rate scheduler was used, the model's weight decay was set to 1e-8 and the length of the sentence for tokenization was set to 128 or 256. During training, batch size was set to 32, and at the end of each epoch, the model was evaluated on dev-set. The best-performing model in terms of F1-macro is saved.

3.1 Subtask 1 models

In subtask 1, the goal was to identify 18 different Arabic dialects, in an unbalanced dataset. In order to tackle this problem, we have experimented with several approaches. Most of the models used were BERT-based models such as MARBERT (Abdul-Mageed et al., 2021a), AraBERT (Antoun et al.), QARiB (Abdelali et al., 2021), AraELECTRA discriminator (Antoun et al., 2021a). Two methods Were used: 1) Fine-tuning, 2) Prompting-tuning. Table 2 shows a summary for models and techniques used. For MARBERT with prompt-tuning, openprompt library was used (Ding et al., 2021), which used P-tuning. In P-tuning (Lester et al., 2021) prompts are only inserted into the input embedding sequence, and this embedding is fed to the language model head and output is output to the linear classification head. One of the challenges in promoting is the design of the prompt and the output of the model. For the prompt we have used اللغة هي[MASK] (**"language is [MASK]"**), and for the output, we have used countries' names translated into Arabic.

Submitted systems for this subtask 3 systems were submitted, the first system was the prediction of MARBERT with prompting. The second is a weighted ensemble between all models listed in table 2. The weights were determined by using optimization, where the goal is to find weights that improve the prediction score in dev-set. As a result, some of the weights assigned to models were chosen to be zero. These models were Araecltra discriminator, AraBERT v2 twitter and AraGPT2 (Antoun et al., 2021b). The third system was a hard voting between MARBERT fine-tuned version and the prompt version.

3.2 Subtask 2 models

In subtask 2 the goal was to analyze sentiments in dialectal tweets. Several model experiments has been done as shown in table 3. In this subtask three approaches have been explored: 1) Multi-task learning (MTL), 2) Fine-tuning 3) Prompt-tuning.

3.2.1 MTL

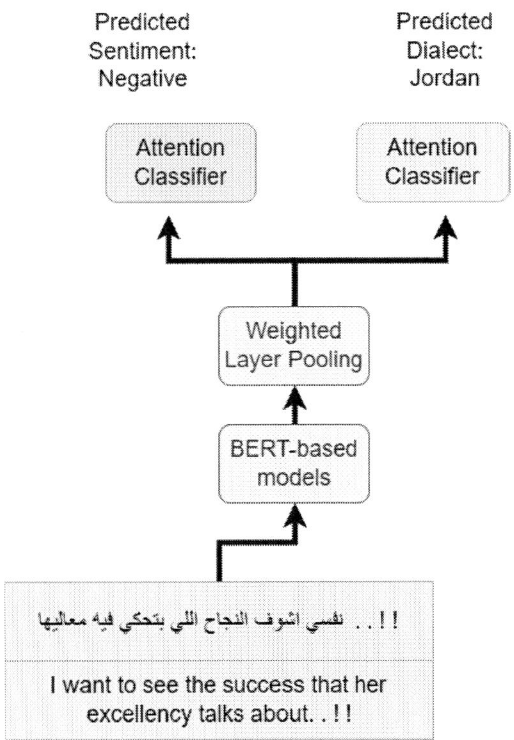

Figure 1: MTL architecture.

In MTL single-input multi-output approach was used, where we have two task-specific attention classifier layers, which help with the classification of the dialect and correspondent sentiment for a tweet. These layers work on top of the weighted pooling that used the output of the last 4 layers of

Models	Methods	Classification head	Loss Function	Macro-F1
MARBERT	Fine-tuning	Attention classifier	F1-CrossEntropy	33
Arabelectra Discriminator	Fine-tuning	Weighted pooling with Attention Classifier	Ensemble of F1-CrossEntropy and Focal Loss	22
AraBERT V2 twitter	Fine-tuning	Weighted pooling with Attention Classifier	Ensemble of F1-CrossEntropy and Focal Loss	29
AraGPT2	Fine-tuning	Attention classifier	Ensemble of F1-CrossEntropy and Focal Loss	22
QARiB	Fine-tuning	Weighted pooling with Attention Classifier and multi-sample dropout	Ensemble of F1-CrossEntropy and Focal Loss	25
MARBERT	**Prompt-tuning**	-	**CrossEntropy**	**37**

Table 2: Models and techniques developed during the experimental phase for subtask 1 and the F1-macro on the dev-set.

BERT-based-model, as shown in figure 1. In order to get the dialect and sentiment of a corresponding tweet, we have used a fine-tuned model to provide pseudo-labels for both datasets (subtasks 1 and 2). The train-set of both subtasks was concatenated and used for training MTL model.

3.2.2 Prompt-tuning

For prompt-based tuning, several approaches have been explored as prefix prompting (Li and Liang, 2021), OpenPrompt library, and P-tuning V2 with and without LSTM encoder. For prefix prompting, language model generation versions of BERT-base models were used. For the prompt, we have used تحليل المشاعر [MASK] (**"sentiment analysis is [MASK]"**), and for the output, we limited the model to generate three labels corresponding to sentiments, which are سعيد، سلبي، محايد (**"neutral, negative, happy"**). Figure 2 shows the architecture. During experiments, we tried to make the model generate the synonyms for these three labels. However, it turns out that limiting model generation to generate only 3 labels text was the best option in this task in terms of dev-set score. For OpenPrompt library, P-tuning V2 with and without LSTM, several prompts were used as ما هو شعور الكاتب؟[MASK] (**" what is the Sentiment of the writer? [MASK]"**) , تحليل المشاعر [MASK] (**"sentiment analysis is [MASK]"**), and المشاعر [MASK] (**"Sentiment is [MASK]"**).

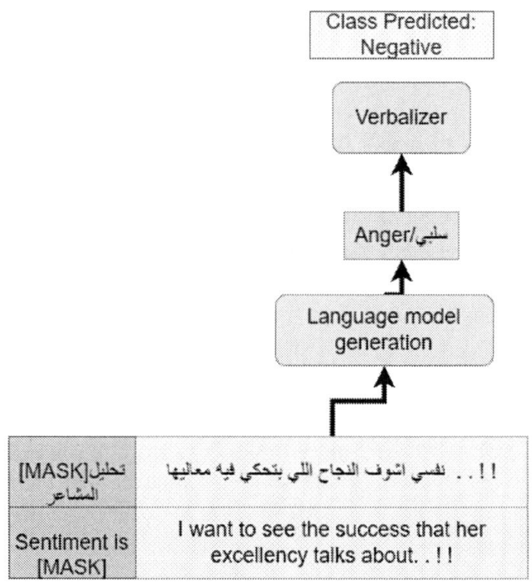

Figure 2: Prefix prompting architecture.

3.2.3 Submitted systems

for this subtask four different systems were submitted. The first system is an ensemble of the last 7 models in table 3. For determining weights we used the optimization method, where the goal is to find the best weight that improves overall pre-

Models	Methods	Classification head	Loss Function	Macro F1-PN
AraELECTRA-base-discriminator	Multi-task learning	Weighted layer pooling with Attention Classifier	FocalLoss (Lin et al., 2017)	66.5
MARBERT	Fine-tuning	Weighted layer pooling with Attention Classifier	Ensemble of F1-CrossEntropy and Focal Loss	71.5
MARBERT	Feature Engineering and Fine-tuning	LSTM with Classifier	CrossEntropy	72
AraBERT	Fine-tuning	Weighted layer pooling with Attention Classifier	F1-CrossEntropy	63.5
AraELECTRA-base-discriminator	Fine-tuning	Attention Classifier	CrossEntropy	58
AraBERT	p-tuning v2	Classifier	CrossEntropy	67.5
AraELECTRA-base-discriminator	p-tuning v2	Classifier	CrossEntropy	61.5
MARBERT	**p-tuning V2**	**LSTM to encode prompt and Classifier**	**CrossEntropy**	**73.5**
MARBERT	Prefix-Prompt tuning	-	CrossEntropy	72.5
AraBERT V2 twitter	Prompt-tuning	-	CrossEntropy	72.5
MARBERT	Prompt-tuning	-	CrossEntropy	73
AraBERT Large V2 twitter	Prompt-tuning	-	CrossEntropy	71.5
GigaBERT-v3 (Lan et al., 2020)	Prompt-tuning	-	CrossEntropy	62.5
AraGPT2	Prompt-tuning	-	CrossEntropy	60
CAMeLBERT (Inoue et al., 2021)	Prompt-tuning	-	CrossEntropy	67.5

Table 3: Models and techniques developed during the experimental phase for subtask 2 and macro F1-PN on dev-set.

diction on the dev-set. It turns out, that the best weight chosen is uniform $1/7$. The second and third submissions were hard and soft voting based on the prediction of the last 7 models in table 3. The fourth submission was based on a weighted ensemble between the first four models in the table. Similarly, optimization has been carried out to choose the best weights. It turns out that the third model (MARBERT with feature engineering and LSTM) was not important, and its weight was set to zero.

4 Results

In this section, The performance of the model is reported based on the official metric during dev-phase and test-phase. Moreover, error analysis is conducted to identify weaknesses of the proposed models. For subtask 1 the official metric is the macro average F1-score, while for subtask 2 the official metric is the macro-F1-PN score (macro f1-score for the negative and positive classes only).

4.1 Dev-phase results

The table 2 illustrates our model's dev-phase scores for subtask 1 using the macro F1-score metrics. It is clear that the low results reflect the difficulty of the task. The key problem, we believe, is the dataset's unbalanced nature. To improve performance, we tried a variety of ways. We tried oversampling, undersampling, batch-sampler, and balanced sam-

System Submission	Macro-F1	
	Test A	Test B
System 1: MARBERT with Prompt	36.3556	17.5
System 2: Weighted Ensemble	36.4807	17.6
System 3: Hard Voting	36.3291	17.17
Over All Performance	**27.06**	

Table 4: Performance of the submitted models on the leaderboard in subtask 1.

pling, but none of these produced satisfactory results. Table 3 shows results on dev-set for subtask 2. It can be concluded that prompt-based model performance was better than fine-tuning methods.

4.2 Test-phase results

Table 4 and 5 show performance the submitted model in the test-phase. For subtask 1, in test A the best-performing model was the weighted ensemble voting. For the second place, the MARBERT with prompt comes in place. For test B, the best performing model was the weighted ensemble, while the best second model was MARBERT with a prompt which achieved a good results (0.1) error difference compared to the weighted ensemble. In Subtask 2 the best performing model was system 4 which was an ensemble of fine-tuned models, MTL, and different versions of prompting.

4.3 Error analysis

As seen in Figure 3, our model performs well when predicting Egyptian, Saudi Arabian, Algerian, Oman, Libyan, and Iraqi languages. According to the confusion matrix, most dialects were incorrectly classified as these five dialects. We assume this is due in part to a large number of tweets from each dialect in the training-set. Further examination of the output revealed that our model performs very poorly on the less common dialects. Our approach is unable to reliably fore-

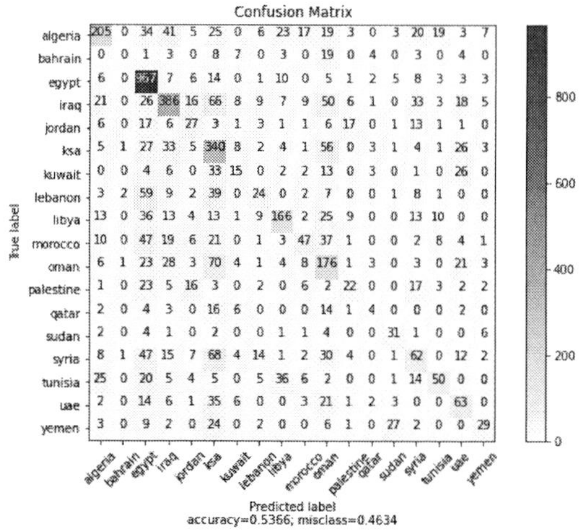

Figure 3: Confusion matrix of the predictions of the MARBERT Prompt model in subtask 1 on the dev-set.

cast the dialects of Palestine, Qatar, Bahrain, and the United Arab Emirates. We believe this is due to the skewed nature of the data once again, but also to the difficulty in distinguishing various dialects in general.

System Submission	F1-PN
System 1: Weighted Ensemble	72.77
System 2: Hard Voting	72.224
System 3: Soft Voting	72.224
System 4: Weighted Ensemble	**75.155**

Table 5: Performance of the submitted models on the leaderboard in subtask 2.

5 Conclusion

In this paper, we have presented our work submitted to NADI shared task. Our proposed solution is an ensemble of different BERT-base models. These Models are developed differently, some are MTL models, fine-tuned models, or prompt-based models. The obtained results have shown that our proposed models achieve good results in both subtasks, by achieving first place in subtask 1 and first place in subtask 2. future work will focus more on building a robust model to improve recognition of some dialects. Furthermore to investigate and find features that best discriminate dialects.

References

Ahmed Abdelali, Sabit Hassan, Hamdy Mubarak, Kareem Darwish, and Younes Samih. 2021. Pre-training bert on arabic tweets: Practical considerations.

Muhammad Abdul-Mageed, AbdelRahim Elmadany, and El Moatez Billah Nagoudi. 2021a. ARBERT & MARBERT: Deep bidirectional transformers for Arabic. In *Proceedings of the 59th Annual Meeting of the Association for Computational Linguistics and the 11th International Joint Conference on Natural Language Processing (Volume 1: Long Papers)*, pages 7088–7105, Online. Association for Computational Linguistics.

Muhammad Abdul-Mageed, Chiyu Zhang, Houda Bouamor, and Nizar Habash. 2020. NADI 2020: The first nuanced Arabic dialect identification shared task. In *Proceedings of the Fifth Arabic Natural Language Processing Workshop*, pages 97–110, Barcelona, Spain (Online). Association for Computational Linguistics.

Muhammad Abdul-Mageed, Chiyu Zhang, AbdelRahim Elmadany, Houda Bouamor, and Nizar Habash. 2021b. NADI 2021: The second nuanced Arabic dialect identification shared task. In *Proceedings of the Sixth Arabic Natural Language Processing Workshop*, pages 244–259, Kyiv, Ukraine (Virtual). Association for Computational Linguistics.

Muhammad Abdul-Mageed, Chiyu Zhang, AbdelRahim Elmadany, Houda Bouamor, and Nizar Habash. 2022. NADI 2022: The Third Nuanced Arabic Dialect Identification Shared Task. In *Proceedings of the Seven Arabic Natural Language Processing Workshop (WANLP 2022)*.

Badr AlKhamissi, Mohamed Gabr, Muhammad El-Nokrashy, and Khaled Essam. 2021. Adapting marbert for improved arabic dialect identification: Submission to the nadi 2021 shared task. *arXiv preprint arXiv:2103.01065*.

Wissam Antoun, Fady Baly, and Hazem Hajj. Arabert: Transformer-based model for arabic language understanding. In *LREC 2020 Workshop Language Resources and Evaluation Conference 11–16 May 2020*, page 9.

Wissam Antoun, Fady Baly, and Hazem Hajj. 2021a. AraELECTRA: Pre-training text discriminators for Arabic language understanding. In *Proceedings of the Sixth Arabic Natural Language Processing Workshop*, pages 191–195, Kyiv, Ukraine (Virtual). Association for Computational Linguistics.

Wissam Antoun, Fady Baly, and Hazem Hajj. 2021b. AraGPT2: Pre-trained transformer for Arabic language generation. In *Proceedings of the Sixth Arabic Natural Language Processing Workshop*, pages 196–207, Kyiv, Ukraine (Virtual). Association for Computational Linguistics.

Ning Ding, Shengding Hu, Weilin Zhao, Yulin Chen, Zhiyuan Liu, Hai-Tao Zheng, and Maosong Sun. 2021. Openprompt: An open-source framework for prompt-learning. *arXiv preprint arXiv:2111.01998*.

Abdellah El Mekki, Abdelkader El Mahdaouy, Kabil Essefar, Nabil El Mamoun, Ismail Berrada, and Ahmed Khoumsi. 2021. Bert-based multi-task model for country and province level msa and dialectal arabic identification. In *Proceedings of the Sixth Arabic Natural Language Processing Workshop*, pages 271–275.

Go Inoue, Bashar Alhafni, Nurpeiis Baimukan, Houda Bouamor, and Nizar Habash. 2021. The interplay of variant, size, and task type in Arabic pre-trained language models. In *Proceedings of the Sixth Arabic Natural Language Processing Workshop*, Kyiv, Ukraine (Online). Association for Computational Linguistics.

Wuwei Lan, Yang Chen, Wei Xu, and Alan Ritter. 2020. Gigabert: Zero-shot transfer learning from english to arabic. In *Proceedings of The 2020 Conference on Empirical Methods on Natural Language Processing (EMNLP)*.

Brian Lester, Rami Al-Rfou, and Noah Constant. 2021. The power of scale for parameter-efficient prompt tuning. *arXiv preprint arXiv:2104.08691*.

Xiang Lisa Li and Percy Liang. 2021. Prefix-tuning: Optimizing continuous prompts for generation. *arXiv preprint arXiv:2101.00190*.

Tsung-Yi Lin, Priya Goyal, Ross Girshick, Kaiming He, and Piotr Dollár. 2017. Focal loss for dense object detection. In *Proceedings of the IEEE international conference on computer vision*, pages 2980–2988.

Hamada Nayel, Ahmed Hassan, Mahmoud Sobhi, and Ahmed El-Sawy. 2021. Machine learning-based approach for arabic dialect identification. In *Proceedings of the Sixth Arabic Natural Language Processing Workshop*, pages 287–290.

Samia Touileb. 2020. Ltg-st at nadi shared task 1: Arabic dialect identification using a stacking classifier. In *Proceedings of the Fifth Arabic Natural Language Processing Workshop*, pages 313–319.

On The Arabic Dialects' Identification: Overcoming Challenges of Geographical Similarities Between Arabic dialects and Imbalanced Datasets

Salma Jamal
School of Information Technology
and Computer Science, Nile University
Giza, Egypt
sagamal@nu.edu.eg

Aly M. Kassem
School of Computer Science
University of Windsor, Canada
kassem6@uwindsor.ca

Omar Mohamed and **Ali Ashraf**
Faculty of Computers and Artificial Intelligence
Helwan University
Helwan, Egypt
{omar_20170353, aliashraf}@fci.helwan.edu.eg

Abstract

Arabic is one of the world's richest languages, with a diverse range of dialects based on geographical origin. In this paper, we present a solution to tackle subtask 1 (Country-level dialect identification) of the Nuanced Arabic Dialect Identification (NADI) shared task 2022 achieving third place with an average macro F1 score between the two test sets of 26.44%. In the preprocessing stage, we removed the most common frequent terms from all sentences across all dialects, and in the modeling step, we employed a hybrid loss function approach that includes Weighted cross entropy loss and Vector Scaling(VS) Loss. On test sets A and B, our model achieved 35.68% and 17.192% Macro F1 scores, respectively.

1 Introduction

The Arabic language is spoken in many regions of the world, including North Africa, Asia, and the Middle East. It is the official language of over 25 nations and one of the most widely used languages on the internet, with 164 million and 121 million internet users from the Middle East and North Africa, respectively. The expansion of the Arabic language over the centuries formed widely dispersed groups, which in turn transformed the language through time and separated it into different dialects, which are a specialized form of the Arabic language that is specific to a given region or social group, such as Egyptian, Jordanian, Lebanese, and Palestinian, etc. The closer the countries are geographically, the less variance between their dialects. Furthermore, in formal situations such as the media and education, all Arab nations use Modern Standard Arabic (MSA), but Arabic dialects are used in informal everyday life communication. Due to the intricacy of the language morphology and the scarcity of relevant datasets as the majority of the available datasets are data imbalanced, Arabic research received little attention in its early phases, particularly in the Arabic dialect identification task, because of the many challenges posed by the high similarity of dialects, especially in short phrases, as the same words are all commonly used in all dialects, in fact, the same word can have different meanings in the same dialect. However, it is a significant problem in many applications since being able to recognize the dialect effectively helps enhance specific applications and services, such as Automatic Speech Recognition, remote access, e-health, and e-learning. The majority of the research is focused on classifying the language into four regions: Gulf, Egyptian, Maghrebi, and Levantine, because it's less challenging than country-level dialect identification. Recent studies, however, have concentrated on classifying the language into finer-grained variants such as country-level dialects. In this paper, we present our approach to solving Nuanced Arabic Dialect Identification (NADI) shared task 2022 subtask-1 (Country-level dialect identification) (Abdul-Mageed et al., 2022). Our approach is divided into two main phases. The first step is in the prepossessing phase, where we removed the most frequent terms from all sentences across dialects to decrease the model confusion as the

Proceedings of the The Seventh Arabic Natural Language Processing Workshop (WANLP), pages 458 - 463
December 8, 2022 ©2022 Association for Computational Linguistics

same word can appear in different dialects. The second step is in the modeling phase, where we employed a hybrid loss function technique combining Weighted Cross Entropy loss and VS loss (Kini et al., 2021) to overcome the imbalanced data problem. The rest of the paper is organized as follows: section 2 provides a review of previous Arabic Dialect Identification literature, section 3 describes the proposed dataset, section 4 proposes the model of Arabic Dialect Identification, in section 5 and section 6 we show the results of the proposed model and discuss the experiments of the different parameter settings and various loss functions. Finally, we conclude in section 7.

2 Related Work

This section discusses previous research addressing Arabic Dialect Identification challenges in the Arabic language, the methodologies, strengths, and drawbacks. (Zaidan and Callison-Burch, 2011) labeled the Arabic Online Commentary Dataset (AOC) through crowd-sourcing by collecting reader's comments from three Arabic newspapers: Al-Ghad, Al-Youm Al-Sabe, and Al-Riyadh each of which represents one of the three dialects Egyptian, Gulf, and Levantine. The final dataset is composed of 108,173K comments. They built a model to classify even more crawled data and achieved an accuracy of 82.45%. (Abdelali et al., 2021) gathered dialectal Arabic tweets and labeled them based on account descriptions. The resulting dataset comprises 540k tweets from 2,525 users spread over 18 Arab nations. (Talafha et al., 2020) present a solution that won the 2020 NADI shared task (Subtask 1.2) (Abdul-Mageed et al., 2020) by adapting to the task's unlabeled data (task-adaptive pretraining), then fine-tuning the dialect identification task using AraBERT on 10M unlabeled tweets. (El Mekki et al., 2020) the solution that won Subtask 2.2 employed a hierarchical classifier with a combination of TF-IDF and AraBERT features to classify the country at the first level then at the second level to classify the province. (AlKhamissi et al., 2021) the solution that won the 2021 NADI shared (Abdul-Mageed et al., 2021b) employed an ensemble learning model by fine-tuning the MARBERT model with adapters and Vertical Attention (VAtt). Embedding two additional layers at each transformer block at the MARBERT model allows for preserving the pre-trained embedded knowledge in the MARBERT layers. At NADI-2021, an

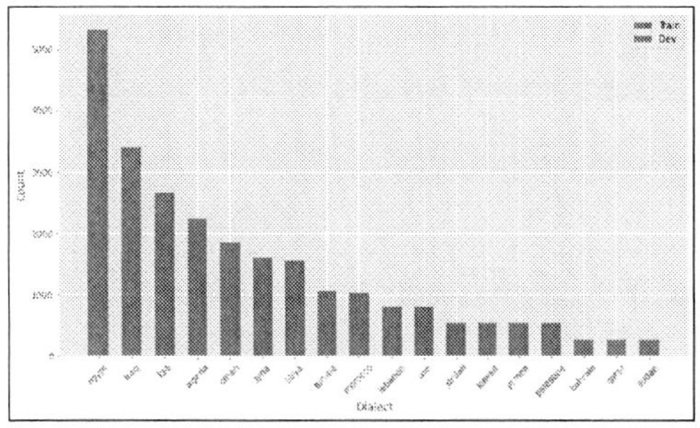

Figure 1: Train/Dev Sizes per Country

end-to-end deep Multi-Task Learning (MTL) approach (El Mekki et al., 2021) was used to address both country-level and province-level identification. The MTL model combines the contextualized word embedding of MARBERT with two task-specific attention layers that extract task-discriminative characteristics. The results of this study show that most studies relied on the robustness of the model to solve the issue of high word similarity in different dialects rather than conducting additional research to address the issue. In order to reduce the likelihood of model confusion between the different dialects, this study aims to overcome past limitations by adopting a strategy to exclude the most common phrases from the tweets in the dataset. In the modeling phase, we also employed a hybrid loss function combining VS loss and Weighted Cross Entropy loss to solve the issue of data imbalance, which is a common issue in most Arabic datasets.

3 Dataset

The proposed NADI-2022 dataset - Country-level dialect identification (sub-task 1) (Abdul-Mageed et al., 2022) has 18 distinct dialects with a total of 20k tweets for training, 4871 tweets for development, and two test sets for testing, test-A with 18 dialects and 4758 tweets, and test-b with an unknown number of dialects and 1474 tweets. However, the dataset's distribution is significantly uneven and skewed (see Figure 1), with Egypt being the most common dialect with a total of 4283 tweets and Sudan, Qatar, and Bahrain being the least common classes with a total of 215 tweets for each dialect. Arabic Dialect Identification has two major challenges. First, there is a significant degree of similarity between dialects in short words; numerous short phrases are utilized in all dialects. Second, there is an imbalance in data distribution. To overcome these issues, we eliminated the most frequently occurring phrases from the corpus and used a hybrid loss function composed of Weighted cross-entropy and VS loss.

4 System Description

This section will outline the methods we followed in developing our approach to solving subtask 1, starting with data pre-processing to the model's experiments with different loss functions.

4.1 Data Pre-Processing

4.1.1 Text cleaning

In this step, we focused on text cleaning by removing certain irrelevant letters and symbols from the tweets:

- We eliminated any non-Arabic characters, numbers, or Arabic diacritics.
- Each word in the tweet was normalized to its base form.
- Since the dataset is made up of Arabic dialect tweets, certain users have a tendency to repeat certain characters within words (text elongation). These extra characters were removed from each word.
- We eliminated the emojis from the tweets because they don't provide any additional context for classifying the tweets into their dialects.

4.1.2 Common Terms Removal

The removal of the most prevalent terms from each tweet is one of the key components of the proposed method. All Arabic dialects are derived from Modern Standard Arabic (MSA), as we previously stated. Additionally, the closer geographically located countries are, the less variance there is between their dialects. For these reasons, we noticed that many terms overlap between Arabic dialects, which could potentially confuse the model during the learning phase. Therefore, we decided to remove the most frequently occurring words in the dataset from all tweets.

Counting the number of times each term appeared in the whole dataset, the results varied from "1" occurrences, which we regarded as distinct terms from a particular dialect, to "4529" occurrences, which we regarded as words that confuse the model. As anticipated, words that can be used in multiple dialects are the most frequently occurring words outside of stop words. For example,

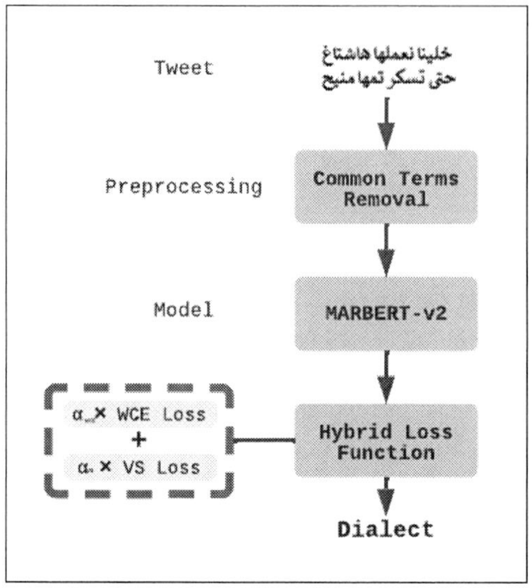

Figure 2: Pipeline of the proposed method

the word "قلبي" was repeated "347" times in the dataset and can have various meanings depending on the dialect it is used in, such as "my love" in the Egyptian dialect, "heart (the organ)" in UAE, etc. Another illustration is the term "طيب" which appeared "286" times and may signify either "ok" in the Egyptian dialect or "delicious" in Lebanon. Setting a hyperparameter that is the removal threshold to regard the term as common or distinct; if the count of the term exceeds the threshold, we remove it from the whole corpus.

4.2 Loss Functions

In this subsection, we discuss the two main loss functions and the hybrid approach between them.

4.2.1 Weighted Cross-Entropy Loss

Weighted Cross-Entropy loss is a variant of regular Cross-Entropy loss that differs by assigning sample weights inversely proportional to class frequency rather than treating all classes equally.

$$\text{CE} = -\frac{1}{N}\sum_{i}\sum_{j\in\{0,1\}} y_{ij}\log p_{ij} \qquad (1)$$

Equation 1, demonstrates that each x_i contributes equally to the overall objective When we don't want all x_i to be treated equally, the standard approach is to assign different weighting factors to different classes. Adding α_i as a weighting factor modifies the standard cross-entropy(Equation 1) as follows:

Data Pre-Processing	Loss Function	Macro-F1(%)
Cleaning only	Weighted CE	28.315
	VS loss	34.207
	Hybrid Loss	34.274
Frequent Removal	VS loss	34.461
	Hybrid Loss	35.8

Table 1: Dev-set result of our method on subtask 1

$$\text{Weighted CE} = -\frac{1}{N}\sum_{i}\alpha_i \sum_{j\in\{0,1\}} y_{ij}\log p_{ij} \tag{2}$$

where $\alpha_i \in [0, 1]$ is set by assigning sample weights inversely proportionately to the class frequency.

4.2.2 Vector Scaling Loss

(Kini et al., 2021) proposed an extension of the VS-loss to handle imbalanced datasets, which is an improved version of cross-entropy loss but with the addition of three parameters that combine additive and multiplicative logit modifications. The VS-loss formula for multiclass datasets is as follows:

$$\ell_{\text{VS}}(y, f_w(x)) = -\omega_y \log\left(e^{\Delta_y f_y(x)+\iota_y} / \sum_{c\in[C]} e^{\Delta_c f_c(x)+\iota_c}\right) \tag{3}$$

weight parameters $\omega_\pm > 0$, additive logit parameters $\iota_\pm \in R$, and multiplicative logit parameters $\Delta_\pm > 0$:

4.2.3 Hybrid Loss Function

In data-imbalanced scenarios, using Focal loss, Dice loss, Tversky loss, and VS loss functions instead of standard weighted cross-entropy enhances model performance, as stated at (Mostafa et al., 2022). We tested various loss functions to see how well they performed in overcoming the imbalance problem in the provided dataset. The VS loss and Weighted cross-entropy(WCE) were the top performers, so we attempted to combine them. Because each loss function does not produce the same mistakes as the other, combining the two loss functions results in two predictions instead of simply one. Each of these predictions has its own loss. As a dynamic ensemble learning approach, gradients from all of these losses are propagated back through the model. The balancing weights α_{VS}, α_{WCE} are 0.7 and 0.3 respectively. The proposed hybrid loss function is defined as follows:

$$Hybrid.loss = \alpha_{VS}VS + \alpha_{WCE}WCE \tag{4}$$

4.3 Pre-Trained Model

Because the proposed dataset is a collection of tweets, we have to choose a pre-trained model that was trained on social media data (Twitter data) with dialect diversity, as the dataset contains 18 dialectics. According to (Abdul-Mageed et al., 2021a), fine-tuning phase performance increases if the model was pre-trained on the same dataset domain.

MARBERT-v2: Our model is based on the publicly available transformer model MARBERT-V2, which was trained on 1B multidialectal Arabic tweets (Abdul-Mageed et al., 2021a). It is based on the BERT-BASE architecture (Devlin et al., 2018) and has 163M parameters, including 12 encoder layers, 12 attention heads, and 768 hidden sizes, but without the next sentence prediction (NSP) component. MARBERT-V2 is an extension to MARBERT that has been trained on more data such as Books (Hindawi), El-Khair (El-Khair, 2016), Gigaword, OSCAR (Suárez et al., 2019), OSIAN (Zeroual et al., 2019), and AraNews dataset (Nagoudi et al., 2020), as well as a longer sequence length of 512 tokens totaling 29B. Figure 2 illustrates the proposed pipeline of our method.

5 Results

In the two main steps of the suggested technique, we tested with various settings. The best macro F1-score is obtained by eliminating the most common terms during the pre-processing step and then feeding the pre-processed data into MARBERT-V2 using the suggested hybrid loss function. The proposed methodology achieved an F1 score of 39%

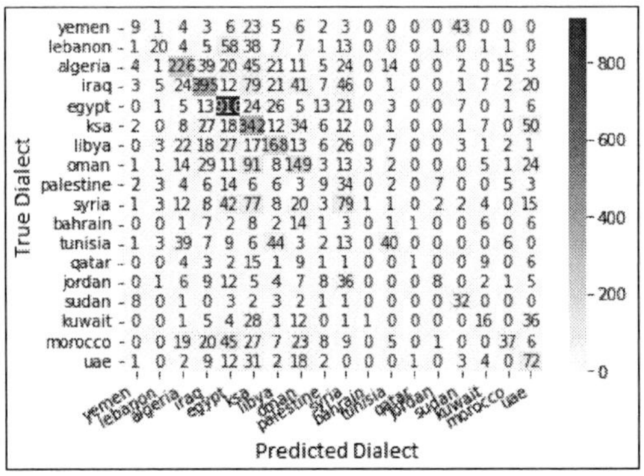

Figure 3: The confusion matrix of the proposed results

on the development set, 35.68% on test set A, and 17.1924% on test set B, and the average macro F1 score between the two test sets is 26.44%.

6 Discussion

As indicated in the Table 1, we tested the loss functions on the cleaned-only dataset first as a standalone loss and then as a hybrid loss between the two proposed loss functions in order to obtain the best results possible. As anticipated, VS loss outperformed Weighted Cross-Entropy Loss, scoring 34.207%, demonstrating that it is better able to address the issue of class imbalance. Additionally, we combined the two loss functions to create a hybrid loss, which performed better than the individual losses by achieving 34.274%. Utilizing multiple values for the removal threshold during the second phase of our method, which involves removing the most prevalent frequent terms, we found that the optimal value produced superior outcomes than utilizing the cleaned-data only, obtaining 34.461% with VS loss and 35.8% with the hybrid loss, which is the best results in our pipeline. Figure 3 illustrates the confusion matrix of the predicted results, demonstrating what we previously stated: the closer the countries are geographically, the more similar their dialects are. For instance, if we take the KSA dialect, it is most frequently confused with the UAE, Kuwaiti, and Omani dialects, and they are all GULF countries located on the same continent, thus closer to each other.

7 Conclusion

This paper outlines our method for solving Nuanced Arabic Dialect Identification (NADI) shared task 2022 subtask-1 (Country-level dialect identification). We eliminated the most frequent words from all tweets to reduce the likelihood that the model would become confused between the different dialects. Additionally, we used MARBERTv2 with a hybrid loss function approach during the modeling phase to effectively address the class imbalance issue in our dataset. The findings demonstrated that our method outperforms a standalone loss function and tweets without removing the most common terms, with an F1 score of 35.68% on test set A and 17.1924% on test set B, and the average macro F1 score between the two test sets is 26.44%. To further improve the model performance, we aim to develop better methods to handle the removal process of the standard terms. Also, collecting more data for the least common dialects may be significant in the performance.

Limitations

We employed the MARBERT-V2 pre-trained BERT-based model, which was trained on a large corpus with a reduced bias toward specific dialects. However, the proposed dataset sample size is insufficient to allow the model to generalize successfully to new data. The elimination of standard terms component is based just on frequency; introducing additional factors may improve performance.

Ethics Statement

The Arabic language is one of the world's most frequently spoken languages. Developing a system to recognize Arabic in its numerous dialects would benefit several applications in the Arabic language, such as offensive text identification on social media, because many internet users communicate using informal language (dialects).

Acknowledgements

This research is supported by the Vector Scholarship in Artificial Intelligence, provided through the Vector Institute. Also, We gratefully acknowledge support from Compute Canada.

References

Ahmed Abdelali, Hamdy Mubarak, Younes Samih, Sabit Hassan, and Kareem Darwish. 2021. Qadi: Arabic dialect identification in the wild. In *Proceedings of the Sixth Arabic Natural Language Processing Workshop*, pages 1–10.

Muhammad Abdul-Mageed, AbdelRahim Elmadany, and El Moatez Billah Nagoudi. 2021a. ARBERT &

MARBERT: Deep bidirectional transformers for Arabic. In *Proceedings of the 59th Annual Meeting of the Association for Computational Linguistics and the 11th International Joint Conference on Natural Language Processing (Volume 1: Long Papers)*, pages 7088–7105, Online. Association for Computational Linguistics.

Muhammad Abdul-Mageed, Chiyu Zhang, Houda Bouamor, and Nizar Habash. 2020. NADI 2020: The first nuanced Arabic dialect identification shared task. In *Proceedings of the Fifth Arabic Natural Language Processing Workshop*, pages 97–110, Barcelona, Spain (Online). Association for Computational Linguistics.

Muhammad Abdul-Mageed, Chiyu Zhang, AbdelRahim Elmadany, Houda Bouamor, and Nizar Habash. 2021b. NADI 2021: The second nuanced Arabic dialect identification shared task. In *Proceedings of the Sixth Arabic Natural Language Processing Workshop*, pages 244–259, Kyiv, Ukraine (Virtual). Association for Computational Linguistics.

Muhammad Abdul-Mageed, Chiyu Zhang, AbdelRahim Elmadany, Houda Bouamor, and Nizar Habash. 2022. NADI 2022: The Third Nuanced Arabic Dialect Identification Shared Task. In *Proceedings of the Seven Arabic Natural Language Processing Workshop (WANLP 2022)*.

Badr AlKhamissi, Mohamed Gabr, Muhammad El-Nokrashy, and Khaled Essam. 2021. Adapting marbert for improved arabic dialect identification: Submission to the nadi 2021 shared task. *arXiv preprint arXiv:2103.01065*.

Jacob Devlin, Ming-Wei Chang, Kenton Lee, and Kristina Toutanova. 2018. Bert: Pre-training of deep bidirectional transformers for language understanding. *arXiv preprint arXiv:1810.04805*.

Ibrahim Abu El-Khair. 2016. 1.5 billion words arabic corpus. *arXiv preprint arXiv:1611.04033*.

Abdellah El Mekki, Ahmed Alami, Hamza Alami, Ahmed Khoumsi, and Ismail Berrada. 2020. Weighted combination of bert and n-gram features for nuanced arabic dialect identification. In *Proceedings of the Fifth Arabic Natural Language Processing Workshop*, pages 268–274.

Abdellah El Mekki, Abdelkader El Mahdaouy, Kabil Essefar, Nabil El Mamoun, Ismail Berrada, and Ahmed Khoumsi. 2021. Bert-based multi-task model for country and province level msa and dialectal arabic identification. In *Proceedings of the Sixth Arabic Natural Language Processing Workshop*, pages 271–275.

Ganesh Ramachandra Kini, Orestis Paraskevas, Samet Oymak, and Christos Thrampoulidis. 2021. Label-imbalanced and group-sensitive classification under overparameterization. In *Advances in Neural Information Processing Systems*, volume 34, pages 18970–18983.

Ali Mostafa, Omar Mohamed, and Ali Ashraf. 2022. Gof at arabic hate speech 2022: Breaking the loss function convention for data-imbalanced arabic offensive text detection. In *Proceedinsg of the 5th Workshop on Open-Source Arabic Corpora and Processing Tools with Shared Tasks on Qur'an QA and Fine-Grained Hate Speech Detection*, pages 167–175, Marseille, France. European Language Resources Association.

El Moatez Billah Nagoudi, AbdelRahim Elmadany, Muhammad Abdul-Mageed, and Tariq Alhindi. 2020. Machine generation and detection of Arabic manipulated and fake news. In *Proceedings of the Fifth Arabic Natural Language Processing Workshop*, pages 69–84, Barcelona, Spain (Online). Association for Computational Linguistics.

Pedro Javier Ortiz Suárez, Benoît Sagot, and Laurent Romary. 2019. Asynchronous pipeline for processing huge corpora on medium to low resource infrastructures. In *7th Workshop on the Challenges in the Management of Large Corpora (CMLC-7)*. Leibniz-Institut für Deutsche Sprache.

Bashar Talafha, Mohammad Ali, Muhy Eddin Za'ter, Haitham Seelawi, Ibraheem Tuffaha, Mostafa Samir, Wael Farhan, and Hussein T Al-Natsheh. 2020. Multi-dialect arabic bert for country-level dialect identification. *arXiv preprint arXiv:2007.05612*.

Omar Zaidan and Chris Callison-Burch. 2011. The arabic online commentary dataset: an annotated dataset of informal arabic with high dialectal content. In *Proceedings of the 49th Annual Meeting of the Association for Computational Linguistics: Human Language Technologies*, pages 37–41.

Imad Zeroual, Dirk Goldhahn, Thomas Eckart, and Abdelhak Lakhouaja. 2019. OSIAN: Open source international Arabic news corpus - preparation and integration into the CLARIN-infrastructure. In *Proceedings of the Fourth Arabic Natural Language Processing Workshop*, pages 175–182, Florence, Italy. Association for Computational Linguistics.

Arabic dialect identification using machine learning and transformer-based models: Submission to the NADI 2022 Shared Task

Nouf AlShenaifi, Aqil Azmi
Department of Computer Science, King Saud University, Riyadh, Saudi Arabia
{noalshenaifi, aqil}@ksu.edu.sa

Abstract

Dialect is the language variation of a specific community. In this paper, we show the models we created to participate in the third Nuanced Arabic Dialect Identification (NADI) shared task (Subtask 1) that involves developing a system to classify a tweet into a country-level dialect. We utilized several machine learning techniques as well as deep learning transformer-based models. For the machine learning approach, we build an ensemble classifier of various machine learning models. In our deep learning approach, we consider bidirectional LSTM model and AraBERT pretrained model. The results demonstrate that the deep learning approach performs noticeably better than the other machine learning approaches with 68.7% accuracy on the development set.

1 Introduction

Dialect identification is the task of automatically identifying the dialect of a particular part of the text (Zaidan and Callison-Burch 2011). Arabic dialects differ by region, and there are no available dictionaries for their vocabulary or written rules for the words that are specific to those dialects. Developing an Arabic dialect identification system experimenting with different corpora and working at different levels of representation has attracted increasing attention in recent years (Elnagar et al. 2021). In this paper, we present our work to tackle the third Nuanced Arabic Dialect Identification (NADI) shared task that targets country-level dialects. We built multiple classifiers based on machine learning and deep learning techniques. We experimented with an approach of combining different Machine Learning models using a combination of n-grams and TF-IDF as features to enhance the performance. Another method applied in this study is a deep learning approach including Bidirectional Long-Short Term Memory (BiLSTM) model and pre-trained AraBert model. This paper is organized as follows: Section 2 details the used dataset. Section 3 presents the applied preprocessing steps and the proposed approach for Arabic Dialect Identification. In Section 4, we discuss the obtained results. Section 5 contains the conclusion.

2 Datasets

The dataset used in NADI 2022 shared task (Subtask 1) is the same as the prior NADI shared task (Abdul-Mageed et al. 2020) (Abdul-Mageed et al. 2021). It consists of 20k labeled tweets for training, 4,871 for development that covers 18 Arabic dialects. For testing, two test sets were provided TEST-A and TEST-B. TEST-A includes 18 country-level dialects. In the second test (TEST-B), K country-level dialects are covered where k is kept unknown. The training data which consists of 20K tweets is unbalanced as you can see in Figure 1. Figure 1 displays how tweets are distributed among Arab countries. Most of the tweets belong to Egypt (4283 tweets) and only 215 belong to Bahrain, Qatar, and Sudan. The provided data is normalized in which all URLs are replaced with the word 'URL' and mentions replaced with the word 'USER'. Around 10M unlabeled tweets were also provided to participating teams by the NADI shared task organizers.

Proceedings of the The Seventh Arabic Natural Language Processing Workshop (WANLP), pages 464 - 467
December 8, 2022 ©2022 Association for Computational Linguistics

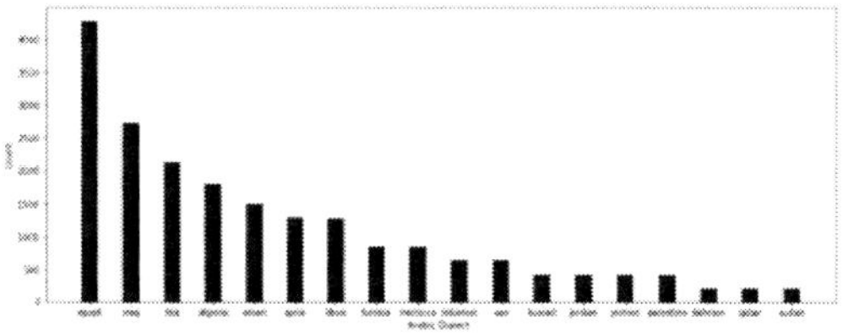

Figure 1: NADI 2022 shared task Training Dataset statistics.

3 Methodology

This section shows the models we used in our experiments starting with machine learning methods and moving on to deep learning and transformer-based approaches.

3.1 Data Preprocessing

Even though NADI training data set is normalized by replacing mentioned user with the token "user" and all links with the token "URL", further cleaning and preprocessing was required. Hence before training our proposed models, we used pre-processing steps including tokenizing, removal of punctuation marks, emojis, Arabic stop words and diacritics, and repeated chars such as "ههههههههههه". We also performed several experiments to test the effects of different preprocessing tasks such as stemming, and we found that stemming has a negative impact on the results. To deal with data imbalances, we applied Synthetic Minority Oversampling Technique (SMOTE) (Fernández et al. 2018) as an imbalance correction technique for oversampling imbalanced classification datasets.

3.2 Machine Learning-Based Models

3.2.1 Logistic Regression

Logistic regression is used to assess the statistical significance of each independent word with regard to probability (Shah et al. 2020). We have applied a logistic regression classifier on the concatenation of word n-grams (n=1 to 3) and char n-grams (n=1 to 4) TF-IDF features using one-vs-the-rest scheme for multi-class training.

3.2.2 Support Vector Machine

Support Vector Machine (SVM) which is based on structural risk minimization is recommended to use for handling large textual features (Fanny, Muliono, and Tanzil 2018). We build a Support Vector Machine (SVM) classifier for country-level dialect identification task based on CountVectorizer and TF-IDF word n-gram features. CountVectorizer to transform each tweet into a vector on the basis of the frequency of each word that appears in the whole dataset. For the extracted features, we used TF-IDF vectors with word n-grams where (n=1 to 3).

3.2.3 Ensemble Classifier

This classifier is a soft voting classifier of three individual machine learning models Stochastic Gradient Descent (SGD) Classifier, Multinomial Naive Bayes, and Bernoulli Naive Bayes as shown in Figure 2. Naive Bayes classifier is still used for text classification as a fast and easy to implement machine learning classifier (Kowsari et al. 2019). Stochastic Gradient Descent (SGD) is an efficient approach to fitting linear classifiers and regressors under convex loss functions such as Support Vector Machines and Logistic Regression. We used TF-IDF with character (2-5)-grams, and word (1-4) grams as a feature for training our ensemble classifier.

3.3 Deep Learning models

3.3.1 Embedding Layer with bidirectional LSTM model

Bidirectional Long-Short Term Memory (BiLSTM) network was used with pretrained word embeddings as an input. In word embedding, we obtain values for word vectors or embeddings by training a neural language model to capture semantic and syntactic relationships between words in the corpus (Soliman, Eissa, and El-Beltagy 2017) (Mikolov et al. 2017). In our model, we used Aravec (Soliman, Eissa, and El-Beltagy 2017)a pretrained word embeddings developed using Twitter data based on the continuous bag-of-words and another on the Skip-gram mode. We also built a word vectors model (word2vec model) using 300K tweets from the NADI unlabeled dataset (the 10M tweets) (Srinivasa-Desikan 2018). Fast text skigram model is trained on the corpus, to create an embedding matrix that contains embedding words each one represents a word in the corpus. Our BiLSTM model consists of an embedding layer, 128 hidden units, and a dense layer with 18 hidden units and softmax activation function to identify dialects. For the network configuration, we used 300 as input sequence length 0.1 for dropout rate, and 10 for epochs, because more than that the model overfits.

Moreover, Adam was the optimization technique we used, and Categorical cross-entropy was used as the loss function.

3.3.2 Fine-tuning Arabert Transformer

AraBERT is pretrained transformer model based on BERT transformer model (Devlin et al. 2018) specifically for the Arabic language (Antoun, Baly, and Hajj 2020). We used the pre-trained AraBERT model and fine-tuning hyperparameters for Arabic dialect identification tasks on NADI Dataset. We utilize the Hugging Face Trainer utility (McMillan-Major et al. 2021), which allows us to fine-tune AraBERT by changing parameter options. The final configuration of the model we used is Adam optimizer with 1e-8 for adam epsilon, Learning Rate of 1e-5, Maximum Sequence Length is 128, Batch Size is 40, and number of Epochs is 6.

4 Results & Discussion

In our experiments, we have reported the result of multiple models starting with machine learning approaches and moving on to transformer-based methods. The evaluation measures include F-score, Accuracy, Precision, and Recall. However, the Macro Averaged F-score is the official metric of evaluation. Table 1 shows the performance in terms of F1-score and accuracy of various Machine Learning and deep learning models evaluated on dev and test sets. According to the results shown in Table 1, the three best classifiers are Ensemble Classifier, Bidirectional LSTM, and Fine-tuning Arabert Transformer on both dev and test set for the first sub-task of NADI shared task. The best results on the development set are obtained by Embedding Layer with Bidirectional LSTM classifier with an F1-score of 50.5%. The obtained results show that deep learning approach significantly outperforms the other machine learning approaches.

Models	Dev		Test-A		Test-B	
	Acc	F1	Acc	F1	Acc	F1
Logistic Regression	36.9	19.1	7.8	5.5	17.6	7.9
SVM	40.9	19.4	36.9	16.1	21.3	7.4
Ensemble Classifier	46.2	24.4	39.1	18.8	24.4	9.1
Bidirectional LSTM	68.7	50.5	39.9	22.4	23.7	9.3
Fine-tuning Arabert Transformer	68.7	50.5	38.2	21.9	23.5	9.1

Table 1: The obtained results of the dev & test dataset.

5 Conclusion

In this paper, we present our submitted models to the third Nuanced Arabic Dialect Identification shared task. We conducted different experiments in which we tried different preprocessing procedures and several feature combinations for model training. We combined different machine learning approach such as (Logistic Regression, Support Vector Machine, and Multinomial Naive Bayes) to build a strong Arabic dialect identification System. We further developed a transformer-based model using Embedding Layer with a bidirectional LSTM model and Fine-tuning Arabert Transformer. The obtained results have shown that our transformer-based model outperforms all machine learning model on Macro-F1 evaluation measure.

References

Abdul-Mageed, Muhammad, Chiyu Zhang, Houda Bouamor, and Nizar Habash. 2020. "NADI 2020: The First Nuanced Arabic Dialect Identification Shared Task." *ArXiv Preprint ArXiv:2010.11334*.

Abdul-Mageed, Muhammad, Chiyu Zhang, AbdelRahim Elmadany, Houda Bouamor, and Nizar Habash. 2021. "Nadi 2021: The Second Nuanced Arabic Dialect Identification Shared Task." *ArXiv Preprint ArXiv:2103.08466*.

Antoun, Wissam, Fady Baly, and Hazem Hajj. 2020. "Arabert: Transformer-Based Model for Arabic Language Understanding." *ArXiv Preprint ArXiv:2003.00104*.

Devlin, Jacob, Ming-Wei Chang, Kenton Lee, and Kristina Toutanova. 2018. "Bert: Pre-Training of Deep Bidirectional Transformers for Language Understanding." *ArXiv Preprint ArXiv:1810.04805*.

Elnagar, Ashraf, Sane M Yagi, Ali Bou Nassif, Ismail Shahin, and Said A Salloum. 2021. "Systematic Literature Review of Dialectal Arabic: Identification and Detection." *IEEE Access* 9: 31010–42.

Fanny, Fanny, Yohan Muliono, and Fidelson Tanzil. 2018. "A Comparison of Text

Classification Methods K-NN, Naïve Bayes, and Support Vector Machine for News Classification." *Jurnal Informatika: Jurnal Pengembangan IT* 3 (2): 157–60.

Fernández, Alberto, Salvador Garcia, Francisco Herrera, and Nitesh v Chawla. 2018. "SMOTE for Learning from Imbalanced Data: Progress and Challenges, Marking the 15-Year Anniversary." *Journal of Artificial Intelligence Research* 61: 863–905.

Kowsari, Kamran, Kiana Jafari Meimandi, Mojtaba Heidarysafa, Sanjana Mendu, Laura Barnes, and Donald Brown. 2019. "Text Classification Algorithms: A Survey." *Information* 10 (4): 150.

McMillan-Major, Angelina, Salomey Osei, Juan Diego Rodriguez, Pawan Sasanka Ammanamanchi, Sebastian Gehrmann, and Yacine Jernite. 2021. "Reusable Templates and Guides for Documenting Datasets and Models for Natural Language Processing and Generation: A Case Study of the HuggingFace and GEM Data and Model Cards." *ArXiv Preprint ArXiv:2108.07374*.

Mikolov, Tomas, Edouard Grave, Piotr Bojanowski, Christian Puhrsch, and Armand Joulin. 2017. "Advances in Pre-Training Distributed Word Representations." *ArXiv Preprint ArXiv:1712.09405*.

Shah, Kanish, Henil Patel, Devanshi Sanghvi, and Manan Shah. 2020. "A Comparative Analysis of Logistic Regression, Random Forest and KNN Models for the Text Classification." *Augmented Human Research* 5 (1): 1–16.

Soliman, Abu Bakr, Kareem Eissa, and Samhaa R El-Beltagy. 2017. "Aravec: A Set of Arabic Word Embedding Models for Use in Arabic Nlp." *Procedia Computer Science* 117: 256–65.

Srinivasa-Desikan, Bhargav. 2018. *Natural Language Processing and Computational Linguistics: A Practical Guide to Text Analysis with Python, Gensim, SpaCy, and Keras*. Packt Publishing Ltd.

Zaidan, Omar, and Chris Callison-Burch. 2011. "The Arabic Online Commentary Dataset: An Annotated Dataset of Informal Arabic with High Dialectal Content." In *Proceedings of the 49th Annual Meeting of the Association for Computational Linguistics: Human Language Technologies*, 37–41.

NLP_DI at NADI Shared Task Subtask-1: Sub-word Level Convolutional Neural Models and Pre-trained Binary Classifiers for Dialect Identification

Vani Kanjirangat
IDSIA-USI/SUPSI, Switzerland
vanik@idsia.ch

Tanja Samardzic
URPP Language and Space, UZH
tanja.samardzic@uzh.ch

Ljiljana Dolamic
armasuisse S+T, Switzerland
Ljiljana.Dolamic@armasuisse.ch

Fabio Rinaldi
IDSIA-USI/SUPSI, Switzerland
fabio.rinaldi@idsia.ch

Abstract

In this paper, we describe our systems submitted to the NADI Subtask 1: country-wise dialect classifications. We designed two types of solutions. The first type is convolutional neural network CNN) classifiers trained on subword segments of optimized lengths. The second type is fine-tuned classifiers with BERT-based language specific pre-trained models. To deal with the missing dialects in one of the test sets, we experimented with binary classifiers, analyzing the predicted probability distribution patterns and comparing them with the development set patterns. The better performing approach on the development set was fine-tuning language specific pre-trained model (best F-score 26.59%). On the test set, on the other hand, we obtained the best performance with the CNN model trained on subword tokens obtained with a Unigram model (the best F-score 26.12%). Re-training models on samples of training data simulating missing dialects gave the maximum performance on the test set version with a number of dialects lesser than the training set (F-score 16.44%)

1 Introduction

Arabic Natural Language Processing (NLP) is traditionally faced with the problem of dialect identification. Although Arabic is spoken by a large community of about 400 million people, this community is distributed around different countries and extremely diverse in term of regional linguistic varieties, often called dialects. Modern Standard Arabic (MSA), which is the official language in many Arabic speaking countries is highly formal language used in books and official communication, but newspapers and online writing already show considerable diversification, which is greatly increased in the spoken language of everyday communication. MSA differs from regional varieties lexically, syntactically and phonetically (Zaidan and Callison-Burch, 2014).

In the long history of Arabic Dialect Identification (ADI), multiple datasets have been developed. Some of the most popular datasets include: The ADI VarDial dataset (Zampieri et al., 2017, 2018), which includes Arabic text that is both speech transcribed and transliterated (Malmasi et al., 2016; Ali et al., 2016). Arabic Online Commentary (AOC) is another dataset, which includes a large-scale repository of Arabic dialects obtained from reader commentary of online Arabic newspapers (Zaidan and Callison-Burch, 2011). Multi Arabic Dialect Applications and Resources (MADAR) corpus constitutes parallel sentences written in different Arabic city dialects from travel domain (Bouamor et al., 2019).

Classification methods tried out on these datasets range from feature-based machine learning approaches (Touileb, 2020; Younes et al., 2020; AlShenaifi and Azmi, 2020; Harrat et al., 2019), n-gram based language models (Çöltekin et al., 2018; Butnaru and Ionescu, 2018) and ensemble models El Mekki et al. (2020) to neural and pre-trained models (AlKhamissi et al., 2021; El Mekki et al., 2021; Elaraby and Abdul-Mageed, 2018; Ali, 2018).

In this paper, we describe the solutions submitted by our team to the Nuanced Arabic Dialect Identification (NADI) shared task 2022 (Abdul-Mageed et al., 2022), subtask-1, which targets a more fine-grained classification than in previous tasks. The NADI shared task focuses on the study and analysis of Arabic dialects at country-level, province-level and city-level. NADI 2020 (Abdul-Mageed et al., 2020) and 2021 (Abdul-Mageed et al., 2021) tasks focused on dialects across 21 Arab countries and 100 provinces.

This paper is organized as follows: The data

Proceedings of the The Seventh Arabic Natural Language Processing Workshop (WANLP), pages 468 - 473
December 8, 2022 ©2022 Association for Computational Linguistics

Models	Fscore(%)	Accuracy(%)
Unigram_CNN	17.06	32.45
BPE_CNN	17.17	33.97
AraBERT	21.38	37.54
Multi-dialect-Arabic-BERT	26.59	42.61

Table 1: Evaluation results on development set

	Average Positive Probabilities				
Dialect	**TEST-B**	**DEV1**	**DEV2**	**DEV3**	**DEV4**
Bahrain	0.8995	0.8907	0.8905	0.8965	0.8973
Jordan	0.8888	0.9053	0.9041	0.9146	0.9097
Lebanon	0.8557	0.8588	0.8622	0.8576	0.8605
Qatar	0.8984	0.8798	0.8788	0.8811	0.8837
UAE	0.9244	0.9009	0.9023	0.9019	0.9040
Oman	0.9203	0.9219	0.9219	0.9194	0.9228
Algeria	0.7978	0.8806	0.8588	0.8825	0.8836
Egypt	0.9432	0.9447	0.9456	0.9076	0.9496
Libya	0.8973	0.9185	0.9168	0.9215	0.9105
Palestine	0.8990	0.9086	0.9080	0.9227	0.9072
Tunisia	0.8589	0.9162	0.9141	0.9080	0.9185
Syria	0.8840	0.8969	0.8944	0.9020	0.8973
Morocco	0.8417	0.8735	0.8626	0.8767	0.8751
KSA	0.9408	0.916	0.9166	0.9205	0.9227
Yemen	0.8793	0.8899	0.8889	0.8991	0.8918
Kuwait	0.9459	0.9297	0.9296	0.9329	0.9299
Iraq	0.8652	0.8896	0.8857	0.8899	0.8623
Sudan	0.8276	0.8931	0.8990	0.9128	0.8975

Table 2: Comparing the average positive predicted probabilities for each binary classifier on simulated development set and TEST-B. The possible missing dialects identified by our approach are bolded.

statistics is described in Section 2, methods used are discussed in Section 3, experimental results are reported in Section 5, followed by conclusions in Section 6.

2 Data

The subtask 1 of NADI 2022 provides training and development sets with 18 country dialects. The training set constitutes 20,398 instances and development set 4871 instances. In the evaluation phase, two test sets were provided, TEST-A with 4871 instances and TEST-B with 1474 instances. TEST-A had all the 18 dialects as in the training set, while TEST-B had k missing dialects, where $k < 18$.

3 Models and Methods

We tried two kinds of solutions described in the following subsections.

3.1 Approach 1: Sub-word Level Convolution Neural Network

In our first solution, we train from scratch a Convolution Neural Network (CNN) on subword tokens produced with different algorithms. The CNN is an adapted version of the architecture proposed by Kim et al. (2016). This architecture is originally used for building a neural language model (NLM). To use this architecture for dialect classification, we take the CNN encoder part substitute the decoder part with dense and softmax layers. We used the CNN filter sizes as proposed by Kim et al. (2016). In general, the filter size can be seen as the length of n-grams and hence using different filters helps to capture text units of different spans.

To decide the optimal splits for input subword tokenization, we tune on the development set the vocabulary size (vocab_size) of two subword tokenization algorithms from the SentencePiece[1] library: the Unigram model and Byte Pair Encoding (BPE). We experimented with gradually increasing vocab_size, ranging from the character vocab_size to $0.4 * |V|$ following Mielke et al. (2019), where $|V|$ is the word-level vocabulary size, and kept the one which gave the best performance on the development set. The optimal vocabulary size turned out to be 20,045 for Unigram model and 7,045 for BPE.

3.2 Approach 2: Pre-trained Models

Our second solution makes use of pre-trained models, specifically BERT-based (Devlin et al., 2019) language-specific models. We used AraBERT (Antoun et al.)[2] and Multi-dialect-Arabic-BERT (Talafha et al., 2020)[3] models for our experiments. AraBERT is a BERT-based model, pre-trained additionally with Arabic articles from Wikipedia, OSCAR[4] and OSIAN corpus (Zeroual et al., 2019). Multi-dialect-Arabic-BERT model is initialized with the weights of Arabic-BERT model[5] and further trained on the 10M unlabelled tweets provided by NADI shared task. For loading and fine-tuning the pretrained models, we used the HuggingFace[6]

[1] https://github.com/google/sentencepiece
[2] https://huggingface.co/aubmindlab/bert-base-arabert
[3] https://huggingface.co/bashar-talafha/multi-dialect-bert-base-arabic
[4] https://oscar-corpus.com/
[5] https://huggingface.co/asafaya/bert-base-arabic
[6] https://huggingface.co/

transformer library and followed BERT single sentence classification pipeline.

For TEST-A, we used the fine-tuned AraBERT and Multi-dialect-Arabic-BERT models directly for the predictions. In TEST-B, we did additional adaptations, specifically to deal with the unknown or missing dialect(s) (described in Subsections 4.1 and 4.2).

4 Adaptation to Unknown Set of Dialects (TEST-B)

To deal with the missing dialects in TEST-B, we apply two additional techniques to the Multi-dialect-Arabic-BERT model as the baseline. These techniques are described in the remainder of this subsection.

4.1 Label Smoothing

Label smoothing helps to alleviate overfitting problem (Müller et al., 2019) and is used as an effective regularization technique in neural models. We used label smoothing (LS) with a specific α (hyperparameter) for fine-tuning the pre-trained model.

4.2 Binary Classifiers

In order to identify the possible missing dialects, we train binary classifiers, one for each dialect in the training set. Given an input sentence, we pass it through each of the 18 classifiers to identify whether the sentence belongs to the particular dialect class/not. For instance, if the classifier is for dialect *Egypt*, then it predicts whether the sentence dialect is Egypt/Not.

Uneven distribution of training data across dialects has a strong impact on models in such binary classification set-up causing strong preferences for some classes. To deal with this issue, we sample balanced datasets for each dialect class. For this, we label all the instances belonging to the particular dialect class as 1 and sample equal number of instances from the remaining classes in the training set without replacement and label it as 0. This helped in boosting the performance for some classes.

In an ideal situation, we expect that for a particular sentence input, only one of the 18 classifiers predicts 1, which means the sentence belongs to the respective dialect class. Further in the ideal scenario, for any sentence input, the missing dialects (in TEST-B) should not be predicted. But, since these country dialects are closely related and overlapping, misclassifications can occur quite often. To tackle this, we need to devise some approach to decide a threshold or some pattern that can help us in deciding the possible missing dialects.

To set the threshold for missing dialects, we simulate TEST-B conditions on the development set. We randomly removed some dialect classes from the development set and performed the evaluations. We performed multiple simulations and recorded the average correct prediction probabilities for each dialect class. We repeated the same for TEST-B. We then analyzed the probability distribution patterns and compared the average probabilities of each dialect from TEST-B with the simulated development sets. Further, we observed the change/ difference in probabilities and identified those dialects with an evident drop in average probabilities. The probabilities for four simulated development sets are tabulated in Table 2 with the missing dialects as: *DEV1: {'palestine', 'yemen', 'lebanon'}*, *DEV2: {'yemen', 'algeria', 'syria'}*, *DEV3: {'egypt', 'tunisia', 'morocco'}* and *DEV4: {'sudan', 'libya', 'iraq'}*. Based on these observations, we selected five dialects: {'Algeria', 'Tunisia', 'Morocco', 'Iraq' and 'Sudan'} as the missing dialects and retrained the Multi-dialect-Arabic-BERT model by removing these five dialects from the training set.

5 Experimental Settings and Results

The results obtained on the development set are reported in Table 1. The F-scores obtained with pretrained models (AraBERT 21.38% and Multi-dialect-Arabic-BERT 26.59%) is considerably higher than those obtained with the CNN models (Unigram_CNN 17.06% and BPE_CNN 17.17%).

Table 3 shows the official evaluation of our models on two test sets provided by the organizers. In TEST-A (with all the 18 dialects), we used the four models: *Unigram_CNN*, *BPE_CNN*, *AraBERT* and *Multi- dialect-Arabic-BERT*. In TEST-B (with missing dialects), we submitted five models: *Unigram_CNN*, *BPE_CNN*, *Multi- dialect-Arabic-BERT*, *Multi- dialect-Arabic-BERT_LS* (Multi- dialect-Arabic-BERT with Label Smoothing with α = 0.1) and *Binary classifiers + Multi- dialect-Arabic-BERT* (Binary classifiers with Multi- dialect-Arabic-BERT). In Binary classifiers + Multi- dialect-Arabic-BERT, we use the binary classifier approach as discussed in Section

Test Set	Models	Fscore (%)	Accuracy (%)
TEST-A	Unigram_CNN	16.18	31.39
	BPE_CNN	16.66	33.50
	AraBERT	19.99	36.65
	Multi-dialect-Arabic-BERT	26.12	42.07
TEST-B	Unigram_CNN	8.71	18.59
	BPE_CNN	7.58	19.34
	Multi-dialect-Arabic-BERT	13.47	27.88
	Multi-dialect-Arabic-BERT_LS	13.75	27.88
	Binary classifier + Multi-dialect-Arabic-BERT	16.44	27.68

Table 3: Official evaluation results on test set

4.2 for identifying the possible missing dialects and further retraining the model.

It can be observed that the best performance on TEST-A was achieved with Multi-dialect-Arabic-BERT model. On TEST-B, pretrained models work better with the best result achieved in the last setting (Binary classifiers + Multi- dialect-Arabic-BERT model).

Now, we discuss briefly the different outcomes on the two test sets. In both test sets, the best results are obtained by language specific pre-trained models. In TEST-B, all the scores are higher and the results with pretrained models are much better. We believe that this difference can be attributed to two factors. First, the smaller number of classes seems to make the task easier for all the models. Second, our adaptation techniques are better suited to the setting with pretrained models. Label smoothing helped in improving the performance slightly (Multi- dialect-Arabic-BERT_LS) and binary classifiers with model retraining brings additional improvement.

Overall, based on the official results, we achieved a F-score of 21.28%.

6 Conclusion

In this paper, we described and discussed two kinds of solutions for the NADI shared task, subtask 2: automatic country-wise identification of Arabic dialects. Among the solutions that we submitted, the language specific pre-traiend models gave the best performance in both TEST-A and TEST-B. Label smoothing and simulating the missing dialect scenario with binary classifiers were our techniques for TEST-B with unknown set of labels. These techniques improve the performance compared to the baseline setting. In TEST-B, adaptation techniques enable better performance on this set, but there is still a lot of room for improving the performance.

In future work, we aim to pursue the development of CNN architectures for fine-grained discrimination. We plan to investigate self-attention mechanisms with CNN and unsupervised deep embedding clustering.

References

Muhammad Abdul-Mageed, Chiyu Zhang, Houda Bouamor, and Nizar Habash. 2020. Nadi 2020: The first nuanced arabic dialect identification shared task. In *Proceedings of the Fifth Arabic Natural Language Processing Workshop*, pages 97–110.

Muhammad Abdul-Mageed, Chiyu Zhang, Abdel-Rahim Elmadany, Houda Bouamor, and Nizar Habash. 2021. Nadi 2021: The second nuanced arabic dialect identification shared task. In *Proceedings of the Sixth Arabic Natural Language Processing Workshop*, pages 244–259.

Muhammad Abdul-Mageed, Chiyu Zhang, Abdel-Rahim Elmadany, Houda Bouamor, and Nizar Habash. 2022. NADI 2022: The Third Nuanced Arabic Dialect Identification Shared Task. In *Proceedings of the Seven Arabic Natural Language Processing Workshop (WANLP 2022)*.

Ahmed Ali, Najim Dehak, Patrick Cardinal, Sameer Khurana, Sree Harsha Yella, James Glass, Peter Bell, and Steve Renals. 2016. Automatic dialect detection in arabic broadcast speech.

Mohamed Ali. 2018. Character level convolutional neural network for arabic dialect identification. In *Proceedings of the Fifth Workshop on NLP for Similar Languages, Varieties and Dialects (VarDial 2018)*, pages 122–127.

Badr AlKhamissi, Mohamed Gabr, Muhammad El-Nokrashy, and Khaled Essam. 2021. Adapting marbert for improved arabic dialect identification: Submission to the nadi 2021 shared task. In *Proceedings of the Sixth Arabic Natural Language Processing Workshop*, pages 260–264.

Nouf AlShenaifi and Aqil Azmi. 2020. Faheem at nadi shared task: Identifying the dialect of arabic tweet. In *Proceedings of the Fifth Arabic Natural Language Processing Workshop*, pages 282–287.

Wissam Antoun, Fady Baly, and Hazem Hajj. Arabert: Transformer-based model for arabic language understanding. In *LREC 2020 Workshop Language Resources and Evaluation Conference 11–16 May 2020*, page 9.

Houda Bouamor, Sabit Hassan, and Nizar Habash. 2019. The madar shared task on arabic fine-grained dialect identification. In *Proceedings of the Fourth Arabic Natural Language Processing Workshop*, pages 199–207.

Andrei Butnaru and Radu Tudor Ionescu. 2018. Unibuckernel reloaded: First place in arabic dialect identification for the second year in a row. In *Proceedings of the Fifth Workshop on NLP for Similar Languages, Varieties and Dialects (VarDial 2018)*, pages 77–87.

Çağrı Çöltekin, Taraka Rama, and Verena Blaschke. 2018. Tübingen-oslo team at the vardial 2018 evaluation campaign: An analysis of n-gram features in language variety identification. In *Proceedings of the Fifth Workshop on NLP for Similar Languages, Varieties and Dialects (VarDial 2018)*, pages 55–65.

Jacob Devlin, Ming-Wei Chang, Kenton Lee, and Kristina Toutanova. 2019. Bert: Pre-training of deep bidirectional transformers for language understanding. In *Proceedings of the 2019 Conference of the North American Chapter of the Association for Computational Linguistics: Human Language Technologies, Volume 1 (Long and Short Papers)*, pages 4171–4186.

Abdellah El Mekki, Ahmed Alami, Hamza Alami, Ahmed Khoumsi, and Ismail Berrada. 2020. Weighted combination of bert and n-gram features for nuanced arabic dialect identification. In *Proceedings of the Fifth Arabic Natural Language Processing Workshop*, pages 268–274.

Abdellah El Mekki, Abdelkader El Mahdaouy, Kabil Essefar, Nabil El Mamoun, Ismail Berrada, and Ahmed Khoumsi. 2021. Bert-based multi-task model for country and province level msa and dialectal arabic identification. In *Proceedings of the Sixth Arabic Natural Language Processing Workshop*, pages 271–275.

Mohamed Elaraby and Muhammad Abdul-Mageed. 2018. Deep models for arabic dialect identification on benchmarked data. In *Proceedings of the Fifth Workshop on NLP for Similar Languages, Varieties and Dialects (VarDial 2018)*, pages 263–274.

Salima Harrat, Karima Meftouh, Karima Abidi, and Kamel Smaïli. 2019. Automatic identification methods on a corpus of twenty five fine-grained arabic dialects. In *International Conference on Arabic Language Processing*, pages 79–92. Springer.

Yoon Kim, Yacine Jernite, David Sontag, and Alexander M Rush. 2016. Character-aware neural language models. In *Thirtieth AAAI conference on artificial intelligence*.

Shervin Malmasi, Marcos Zampieri, Nikola Ljubešić, Preslav Nakov, Ahmed Ali, and Jörg Tiedemann. 2016. Discriminating between similar languages and arabic dialect identification: A report on the third dsl shared task. In *Proceedings of the third workshop on NLP for similar languages, varieties and dialects (VarDial3)*, pages 1–14.

Sabrina J Mielke, Ryan Cotterell, Kyle Gorman, Brian Roark, and Jason Eisner. 2019. What kind of language is hard to language-model? *arXiv preprint arXiv:1906.04726*.

Rafael Müller, Simon Kornblith, and Geoffrey E Hinton. 2019. When does label smoothing help? *Advances in Neural Information Processing Systems*, 32:4694–4703.

Bashar Talafha, Mohammad Ali, Muhy Eddin Za'ter, Haitham Seelawi, Ibraheem Tuffaha, Mostafa Samir, Wael Farhan, and Hussein Al-Natsheh. 2020. Multi-dialect arabic bert for country-level dialect identification. In *Proceedings of the Fifth Arabic Natural Language Processing Workshop*, pages 111–118.

Samia Touileb. 2020. Ltg-st at nadi shared task 1: Arabic dialect identification using a stacking classifier. In *Proceedings of the Fifth Arabic Natural Language Processing Workshop*, pages 313–319.

Mutaz Younes, Nour Al-Khdour, and AL-Smadi Mohammad. 2020. Team alexa at nadi shared task. In *Proceedings of the Fifth Arabic Natural Language Processing Workshop*, pages 237–242.

Omar Zaidan and Chris Callison-Burch. 2011. The arabic online commentary dataset: an annotated dataset of informal arabic with high dialectal content. In *Proceedings of the 49th Annual Meeting of the Association for Computational Linguistics: Human Language Technologies*, pages 37–41.

Omar F Zaidan and Chris Callison-Burch. 2014. Arabic dialect identification. *Computational Linguistics*, 40(1):171–202.

Marcos Zampieri, Shervin Malmasi, Nikola Ljubešić, Preslav Nakov, Ahmed Ali, Jörg Tiedemann, Yves Scherrer, and Noëmi Aepli. 2017. Findings of the vardial evaluation campaign 2017. In *Proceedings of the fourth workshop on NLP for similar languages, varieties and dialects*.

Marcos Zampieri, Shervin Malmasi, Preslav Nakov, Ahmed Ali, Suwon Shon, James Glass, Yves Scherrer, Tanja Samardžić, Nikola Ljubešić, Jörg Tiedemann, et al. 2018. Language identification and morphosyntactic tagging. the second vardial evaluation campaign.

Imad Zeroual, Dirk Goldhahn, Thomas Eckart, and Abdelhak Lakhouaja. 2019. Osian: Open source international arabic news corpus-preparation and integration into the clarin-infrastructure. In *Proceedings of the fourth arabic natural language processing workshop*, pages 175–182.

Word Representation Models for Arabic Dialect Identification

Mahmoud S. Ali **Ahmed H. Ali** **Ahmed A. El-Sawy** **Hamada A. Nayel**
Department of Computer Science
Faculty of Computers and Artificial Intelligence
Benha University
{mahmoud.hassan,ahmed.ali,ahmed.el_sawy,hamada.ali}@fci.bu.edu.eg

Abstract

This paper describes the systems submitted by BFCAI team to Nuanced Arabic Dialect Identification (NADI) shared task 2022. Dialect identification task aims at detecting the source variant of a given text or speech segment automatically. There are two subtasks in NADI 2022, the first subtask for country-level identification and the second subtask for sentiment analysis. Our team participated in the first subtask. The proposed systems use Term Frequency Inverse/Document Frequency and word embeddings as vectorization models. Different machine learning algorithms have been used as classifiers. The proposed systems have been tested on two test sets: Test-A and Test-B. The proposed models achieved Macro-f1 score of 21.25% and 9.71% for Test-A and Test-B set respectively. On other hand, the best-performed submitted system achieved Macro-f1 score of 36.48% and 18.95% for Test-A and Test-B set respectively.

1 Introduction

Social media's widespread use has made it easy to collect user data in surpassing ways. These data can include behaviour and usage, content, and network (Abdul-Mageed et al., 2020). This work focuses on predicting social media user dialect based on language of his/her post. Dialect identification task comprises of some challenges such as finding the differences in writing style between men and women on social networks, ages of authors, or location (Abdul-Mageed et al., 2021b). The solutions to these questions are very important for new problems in the era of social networks such as fake news analysis, plagiarism detection, privacy and security issues.

The author profiling task aims at examining the written documents to extract pertinent demographic information from their authors (Aliwy et al., 2020). Lately, the research community concerning Arabic natural language processing started to pay attention to dialect identification. Nuanced Arabic Dialect Identification shared task (NADI 2021) aimed at predicting the dialect in Arabic Tweets (Abdul-Mageed et al., 2021b).

This work explores different vectorization techniques integrated with the various machine learning approaches. Term Frequency/Inverse Document Frequency (TF/IDF) and word embeddings have been used as vectorization models. Multinomial Naïve Bayes (MNB), Complement Naïve Bayes (CNB), Support Vector Machine (SVM), K-Nearest Neighbor (KNN), Decision Tree (DT), Random Forest (RF), and Multi-Layer Perceptron (MLP) have been used as classifiers due to their ability to deal with multi-class Classification problems.

The rest of the paper is organized as follows: section 2 presents the dataset; section 3 describes the system architecture. Experimental settings and results are given in section 4. Finally, conclusion and future work are presented in section 5.

2 Data

The NADI 2022 datasets that we used for building, developing, and evaluating the submitted systems were distributed by the task organizers (Abdul-Mageed et al., 2022).

The dataset targets nuanced Arabic dialect identification at the country level for Arabic tweets. It comprises training, development, and test sets. It covers 18 dialects (a total of approximately 20K tweets). The evaluation depends on two test sets, Test-A covers 18 country-level dialects, whereas the second test set (TEST-B) covers k country-level dialects. The value of k was kept unknown by the

Proceedings of the The Seventh Arabic Natural Language Processing Workshop (WANLP), pages 474 - 478
December 8, 2022 ©2022 Association for Computational Linguistics

task organizers

3 System Architecture

The general framework of our model is shown in Figure 1. The model consists of three main phases. The first phase is preprocessing where the raw data was prepared to further steps. The second phase is feature extraction and the third phase is training the model. After model construction, test set was fed to the model for model evaluation. The following are details of each phase.

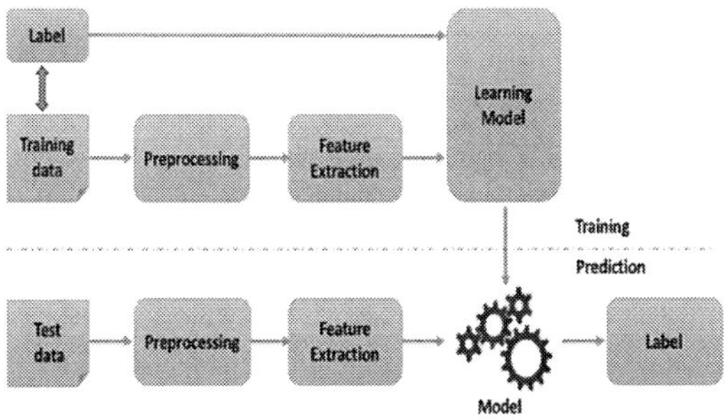

Figure 1: General architecture of the proposed models

3.1 Text Preprocessing

Text data sourced or generated by social media are unstructured and very noisy data. To overcome this issue some non-informative data or texts are removed such as emojis, Latin-characters, URLs, mentions, numbers, and non-Arabic characters. The preprocessing steps based on the work done by Nayel (2020); Ashraf et al. (2022a,b), have been applied to the tweets in detail:

- *Removing Non-Arabic letters* by deleting English letters, special symbols, numbers, Twitter markup, and Emoticons.
- *Text Normalization* by refining text to normalize different forms of some Arabic characters to unique form like, " ة " (an Arabic letter pronounced Haa) and " ه" to be " ه", removing redundant Arabic forms like, " يـة" (pronounced al and it is used as determiner).
- *Removing punctuation marks* such as $\{'+',' \#',' -',' \$', ...\}$ which increase the redundant features resulting a huge feature space dimension.
- *Decreasing the letter repetition*, cleaning the tokens from the redundant letters helps in reducing feature space. In our work, the letter is assumed to be redundant if it is repeated more than two times. For example, the word " عاااالم " (i.e., "global" will be reduced to " عالم ", also the word " راااائع " (i.e., "wonderful") will be reduced to " راائع "

3.2 Feature Extraction

In this work, TFI/DF and word embeddings (Word2Vec) vectorization algorithms were used with unigram features (words or tokens) to describe each tweet as a feature vector.

3.2.1 TF/IDF

In TF/IDF, the value of each component in this vector represents the weight of the corresponding feature (word) within a tweet. Assuming the vocabulary set V=v_1, v_2, ..., v_k that contains the unique tokens appeared in the corpus. Then, the tweet T_i can be represented as the following vector $T_i = < t_{i1}, t_{i2}, t_{i3}, \ldots, t_{ik} >$ and is calculated by the following formula:

$$t_{ij} = tf_{ij} * \log\left(\frac{N+1}{df_i + 1}\right)$$

Where, t_{ij} is the weight of a word j in tweet i, tf_{ij} is the count of word j in tweet i, N is the total number of tweets, and df_i is the count of word i in all tweets. We used unigram model in TF/IDF algorithm, in which each feature is a single word (token). For example, the sentence means which " جمعة مباركة تصبح على خير " "Happy Friday good night", has the following set of features (tokens) " جمعة ", " مباركة ", " تصبح ", " على ", " خير "

3.2.2 Word Embeddings

Another approach for word representation is word embeddings (Mikolov et al., 2013). One of the most effective embeddings model is Word2vec. Word2vec has a neural network structure, proposed by Google, to processes the text data. Word2Vec includes two learning models, Continuous Bag of Words (CBOW) and Skip-gram. CBOW predicts the word given its context, but Skip-gram predicts the context given a word. Word2Vec generates the word vectors through feeding the text corpus (which was available in this task) to one learning model.

First, Word2Vec builds a vocabulary from training corpus, which obtained from NADI 2022 subtask1, and learns the vector representations of each word. Also, Word2Vec calculates the cosine distance among each word. We implemented Word2Vec using gensim, which is a python library. First, we used the vocabulary from the entire training data. Then, to generate the word vectors, we employ the CBOW as it has higher computing speed than Skip-gram. After training step, each word is represented by a vector.

Then, a high dimension matrix has been constructed. Each row in matrix represents a training sample and columns represent the generated word vectors. Now, each word has multiple degrees of similarity, it can be computed via a linear calculation.

After we create the feature vector matrix of all training samples using the two algorithms, we go to the classification step, which will be described

3.3 Classification

In this work, the classification step was accomplished by applying seven classifiers. Then comparing the performance of each classifier and the best performed classifier was chosen to submit. Word2vec and TF/IDF have been used to represent the tweet tokens for each classifier. The following list is the classifiers have been used in this model:

- *The Complement Naive Bayes (CNB)* classifier was designed to correct the "severe assumptions" accomplished by the standard Multinomial Naïve Bayes (MNB) classifier. It is particularly suitable for imbalanced datasets, and this is proved in our results.

- *Support Vector Machine (SVM)* is a linear classifier which uses training examples or support vectors close to the boundaries of classes. SVM also can be used for classifying non-linear data using kernel functions such as, Linear, and RBF, which were used in this work.

- *K-NN* algorithm suppose that the similarity between the new example and available examples and put the new one into the category that is most similar to the available categories.

- *Decision Tree (DT)* classifier depends on the decision tree as a predictive model to go from observations about an item which represented in its branches to conclusions about the item's target value which represented in its leaves.

- *Random Forest (RF)* is a meta estimator that fits several decision tree classifiers on various sub-samples of the dataset and uses averaging to improve the predictive accuracy and control over-fitting.

- *Multi-Layer Perceptron (MLP)* is a fully connected class of feedforward Artificial Neural Network (ANN). An MLP consists of at least three layers of nodes: an input layer, a hidden layer and an output layer. Except for the input nodes, each node is a neuron that uses a nonlinear activation function

4 Experiments and Results

We proposed seven classifiers with TF/IDF, and five classifiers with Word2Vec. All algorithms were implemented on NADI 2022 shared task dataset for subtask1.

We calculated four evaluation metrics, Accuracy (Acc), Precision (P), Recall (R), and F1-score to measure the performance of our models. The macro-averaged f1-score is the official metric for subtask1.

Table 1 and Table 2 show the results for all runs of the development set classification using TF/IDF and Word2Vec representations respectively.

We implemented SVM with two different kernels, linear kernel and Radial Bases Function (RBF). Different numbers of hidden layers (h =10, 20, 30 and 40) have been implemented in MLP.

From Table 1 and Table 2, it is clear that MLP and CNB outperforms all other classifiers. We decided to submit the output of CNB, MLP (h = 20) and MLP (h = 30).

Table 3 and Table 4 shows the results of our submissions on Test-A and Test-B of subtask 1 respectively. For test-A set, MLP with 30 hidden layers and word embeddings (WE) outperforms all other classifiers. While accuracy of CNB with TF/IDF outperforms all other accuracies.

For test-B set, MLP with 30 hidden layers and word embeddings (WE) outperforms all other classifiers. While precision of CNB with TF/IDF outperforms all other precisions.

Algorithm	Accuracy	Precision	Recall	F1 (macro)
MNB	30.158	21.508	9.763	7.567
CNB	39.068	24.321	**19.893**	**20.475**
SVM (Linear)	**39.643**	**34.482**	14.893	13.407
SVM (RBF)	37.323	36.247	14.893	13.407
KNN	33.833	29.311	13.771	13.178
DT	25.662	12.740	12.005	11.920
RF	34.675	21.493	14.637	14.102
MLP (10 H)	31.102	16.984	16.181	16.222
MLP (20 H)	32.745	19.135	17.536	17.852
MLP (30 H)	32.622	18.276	17.328	17.457
MLP (40 H)	32.478	18.863	17.348	17.601

Table 1: Performance measure of the different classifiers on development set using TF/IDF for subtask 1.

Algorithm	Accuracy	Precision	Recall	F1 (macro)
SVM (Linear)	40.135	22.736	20.033	19.843
SVM (RBF)	**42.620**	**32.166**	14.647	12.804
KNN	35.024	25.217	14.647	12.804
DT	17.984	8.883	8.856	8.859
RF	37.056	18.579	13.937	11.162
MLP (10 H)	40.731	19.315	20.264	19.029
MLP (20 H)	38.883	21.710	**20.440**	**20.188**
MLP (30 H)	37.590	21.041	20.179	20.023
MLP (40 H)	36.769	20.414	19.740	19.620

Table 2: Performance measure of the different classifiers on development set using Word2vec model for subtask 1.

Algorithm	**Acc**	**P**	**R**	**Macro F1**
MLP(30)+WE	38.63%	**25.25%**	20.47%	**21.25%**
CNB+TF/IDF	**39.05%**	22.81%	**21.30%**	21.16%
MLP(20)+WE	38.97%	24.58	21.19 %	21.13%

Table 3: Results of our submissions on Test-A of Subtask 1.

Algorithm	**Acc**	**P**	**R**	**Macro F1**
MLP(30)+WE	**23.13%**	14.54%	**11.99%**	**9.71%**
MLP(20)+WE	22.73%	**16.88%**	11.80%	9.14%
CNB+TF/IDF	21.23%	11.41%	10.45%	7.78%

Table 4: Results of our submissions on Test-B of Subtask 1.

5 Conclusion and Future Work

In this paper, a simple framework for dialect identification has been introduced. Two main vectorization approaches (TF/IDF and Word Embeddings) have been compared. It is clear from results that word embeddings outperforms TF/ID. From this study, we can conclude that dialect identification of Arabic text is one of the most challenging tasks. The results of training using MLP (h=20 and h=30) with Word2Vec model achieved the best F1 macro-averaged score as the power of word embeddings in NLP. CNB with TF/IDF comes in the second as it can deal with unbalanced text data.

In future work, pre-trained models could be used to improve the performance of classification, such as BERT (Devlin et al., 2019), AraBERT (Antoun et al., 2020), MarBERT model (Abdul-Mageed et al., 2021a). Transfer learning can be applied that knowledge from one domain can be transferred to another domain.

References

Muhammad Abdul-Mageed, AbdelRahim Elmadany, and El Moatez Billah Nagoudi. 2021a. ARBERT & MARBERT: Deep bidirectional transformers for Arabic. In *Proceedings of the 59th Annual Meeting of the Association for Computational Linguistics and the 11th International Joint Conference on Natural Language Processing (Volume 1: Long Papers)*, pages 7088–7105, Online. Association for Computational Linguistics.

Muhammad Abdul-Mageed, Chiyu Zhang, Houda Bouamor, and Nizar Habash. 2020. NADI 2020: The first nuanced Arabic dialect identification shared task. In *Proceedings of the Fifth Arabic Natural Language Processing Workshop*, pages 97–110, Barcelona, Spain (Online). Association for Computational Linguistics.

Muhammad Abdul-Mageed, Chiyu Zhang, AbdelRahim Elmadany, Houda Bouamor, and Nizar Habash. 2021b. NADI 2021: The second nuanced Arabic dialect identification shared task. In *Proceedings of the Sixth Arabic Natural Language Processing Workshop*, pages 244–259, Kyiv, Ukraine (Virtual). Association for Computational Linguistics.

Muhammad Abdul-Mageed, Chiyu Zhang, AbdelRahim Elmadany, Houda Bouamor, and Nizar Habash. 2022. NADI 2022: The Third Nuanced Arabic Dialect Identification Shared Task. In *Proceedings of the Seven Arabic Natural Language Processing Workshop (WANLP 2022)*.

Ahmed Aliwy, Hawraa Taher, and Zena AboAltaheen. 2020. Arabic dialects identification for all Arabic countries. In *Proceedings of the Fifth Arabic Natural Language Processing Workshop*, pages 302–307, Barcelona, Spain (Online). Association for Computational Linguistics.

Wissam Antoun, Fady Baly, and Hazem Hajj. 2020. AraBERT: Transformer-based model for Arabic language understanding. In *Proceedings of the 4th Workshop on Open-Source Arabic Corpora and Processing Tools, with a Shared Task on Offensive Language Detection*, pages 9–15, Marseille, France. European Language Resource Association.

Nsrin Ashraf, Fathy Elkazzaz, Mohamed Taha, Hamada Nayel, and Tarek Elshishtawy. 2022a. BF-CAI at SemEval-2022 task 6: Multi-layer perceptron for sarcasm detection in Arabic texts. In *Proceedings of the 16th International Workshop on Semantic Evaluation (SemEval-2022)*, pages 881–884, Seattle, United States. Association for Computational Linguistics.

Nsrin Ashraf, Hamada Nayel, and Mohamed Taha. 2022b. A comparative study of machine learning approaches for rumors detection in covid-19 tweets. In *2022 2nd International Mobile, Intelligent, and Ubiquitous Computing Conference (MIUCC)*, pages 384–387.

Jacob Devlin, Ming-Wei Chang, Kenton Lee, and Kristina Toutanova. 2019. BERT: Pre-training of deep bidirectional transformers for language understanding. In *Proceedings of the 2019 Conference of the North American Chapter of the Association for Computational Linguistics: Human Language Technologies, Volume 1 (Long and Short Papers)*, pages 4171–4186, Minneapolis, Minnesota. Association for Computational Linguistics.

Tomás Mikolov, Kai Chen, Greg Corrado, and Jeffrey Dean. 2013. Efficient estimation of word representations in vector space. In *1st International Conference on Learning Representations, ICLR 2013, Scottsdale, Arizona, USA, May 2-4, 2013, Workshop Track Proceedings*.

Hamada Nayel. 2020. NAYEL at SemEval-2020 task 12: TF/IDF-based approach for automatic offensive language detection in Arabic tweets. In *Proceedings of the Fourteenth Workshop on Semantic Evaluation*, pages 2086–2089, Barcelona (online). International Committee for Computational Linguistics.

Building an Ensemble of Transformer Models for Arabic Dialect Classification and Sentiment Analysis

Abdullah Khered[1,2] , **Ingy Abdelhalim**[1] and **Riza Batista-Navarro**[1]
[1]The University of Manchester, UK
[2]King Abdulaziz University, Saudi Arabia
abdullah.khered@postgrad.manchester.ac.uk
ingy.abdelhalim@student.manchester.ac.uk
riza.batista@manchester.ac.uk

Abstract

In this paper, we describe the approaches we developed for the Nuanced Arabic Dialect Identification (NADI) 2022 shared task, which consists of two subtasks: the identification of country-level Arabic dialects and sentiment analysis. Our team, UniManc, developed approaches to the two subtasks which are underpinned by the same model: a pre-trained MARBERT language model. For Subtask 1, we applied undersampling to create versions of the training data with a balanced distribution across classes. For Subtask 2, we further trained the original MARBERT model for the masked language modelling objective using a NADI-provided dataset of unlabelled Arabic tweets. For each of the subtasks, a MARBERT model was fine-tuned for sequence classification, using different values for hyperparameters such as seed and learning rate. This resulted in multiple model variants, which formed the basis of an ensemble model for each subtask. Based on the official NADI evaluation, our ensemble model obtained a macro-F1-score of 26.863, ranking second overall in the first subtask. In the second subtask, our ensemble model also ranked second, obtaining a macro-F1-PN score (macro-averaged F1-score over the `Positive` and `Negative` classes) of 73.544.

1 Introduction

There are approximately 400 million Arabic speakers worldwide, spread geographically in 22 countries around the world (Boudjellal et al., 2021). With early manifestations of Arabic dating back to the 8th century BCE, the Arabic language has been redefined and refined over many decades across different continents. Many scholars struggled to define Arabic as a single language, with many considering Classical Arabic (CA)—the language of the Quran—as the ideal archetype. In modern times, Modern Standard Arabic (MSA) has been used in most official publications, broadcasts, political speeches, and written texts. However, most people use spoken varieties of Arabic in their daily lives. Some of these spoken varieties differ from each other significantly and are almost mutually unintelligible, whilst others bear strong similarities. These spoken variations of Arabic are commonly referred to as Dialectical Arabic (DA).

Thus far, the majority of the research in Arabic Natural Language Processing (NLP) has overlooked the variations across the different Arabic dialects (Oueslati et al., 2020), largely due to the lack of datasets that take the different DA types into consideration. The goal of the Nuanced Arabic Dialect Identification (NADI) shared task series is to diminish this research gap, by providing datasets where examples are organised according to dialects (Abdul-Mageed et al., 2020, 2021b, 2022). As part of the NADI 2022 shared task, organisers made available datasets that support two sub-tasks, namely, dialect identification (Subtask 1) and sentiment analysis of country-level dialectical Arabic (Subtask 2).

Recent advancements in NLP research have led to the development of transformer-based language models which learn contextual embedding representations of sequences, and which have been shown to obtain state-of-the-art performance on many NLP tasks (Vaswani et al., 2017; Liu et al., 2020; Nagoudi et al., 2022). MARBERT (Abdul-Mageed et al., 2021a) is a language model that was pre-trained specifically on DA, and formed the basis of our approach to the NADI 2022 shared tasks.

2 Datasets

NADI 2022 is the third in the NADI shared tasks series and consists of two subtasks. Similar to past editions of the shared task, the first subtask is a multi-class classification problem aimed at recognising the Arabic dialects used in tweets. Unlike in previous years, however, a new task focussing on sentiment analysis of dialectical Arabic tweets was

Proceedings of the The Seventh Arabic Natural Language Processing Workshop (WANLP), pages 479 - 484
December 8, 2022 ©2022 Association for Computational Linguistics

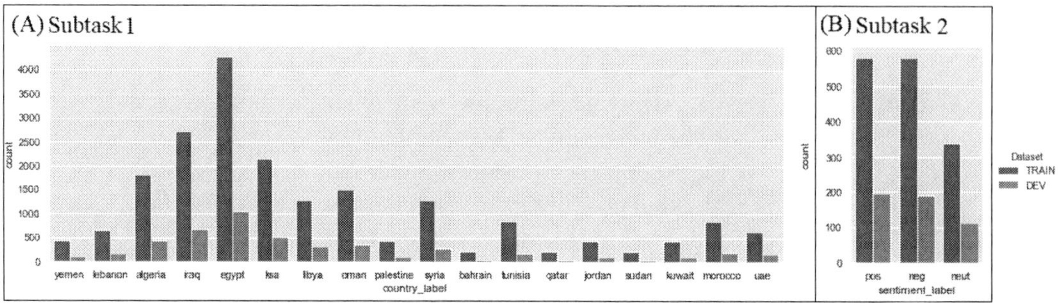

Figure 1: Label distribution of the training and the development sets for Dialect Arabic Identification (Subtask 1) and Sentiment Analysis (Subtask 2).

organised and put forward as the second subtask.

The organisers prepared a dataset of labelled tweets covering 18 Arab countries for the dialect identification subtask. It was split into training, development, and two test sets. Whilst the first test set (Test-A) covers 18 country-level dialects (as the training and development sets do), the second one (Test-B) includes an unknown number of dialects.

The distribution of examples across the different classes of interest for each of the subtasks is shown in Figure 1. As one can observe in Figure 1-A, the distribution across the 18 dialects is unbalanced, with `Eqypt` being the most frequently occurring label in the dataset for Subtask 1.

For the sentiment analysis subtask, the organisers provided a dataset of tweets labelled as any one of three classes: `Positive`, `Negative` and `Neutral`. It was divided into training, development and test sets. As shown in Figure 1-B, the `Positive` and `Negative` classes have an almost equal distribution between them, but the `Neutral` class has a slightly lower number of training samples.

The datasets for both subtasks were pre-processed whereby URLs were replaced with the token 'URL', and Twitter usernames were replaced with the token 'USER', in order to normalise them.

3 Methodology

Our approaches to the two subtasks are both underpinned by the first version of MARBERT, a language model that had been trained on a 128GB dataset containing both MSA and DA tweets (Abdul-Mageed et al., 2021a).

It is worth noting that we built our own version of the MARBERT model by continuing to train it for the masked language modelling (MLM) objective (Devlin et al., 2019); we describe this model in detail in Section 3.2 below. However, our experiments showed that using our own MARBERT model led to performance improvement only for sentiment analysis and not for dialect identification. Therefore this model formed the basis of our solution for Subtask 2 but not for Subtask 1.

3.1 Subtask 1: Dialect Identification

The original pre-trained MARBERT model was fine-tuned for dialect identification using the full training set for Subtask 1 that was provided by the NADI organisers. Considering the imbalance in the distribution of training samples across the different classes (as shown in Figure 1), it was unsurprising that when evaluated on the development set, the resulting sequence classification model is unable to predict the least represented classes (e.g., `Bahrain` and `Qatar`), but obtains satisfactory performance for the classes with sufficient examples.

Therefore, we investigated the use of undersampling, whereby the training samples belonging to the over-represented classes such as `Egypt` and `KSA` (Kingdom of Saudi Arabia), were reduced. Our undersampling technique is based on the removal of randomly selected samples (Chawla, 2010) from the over-represented classes; this led to the creation of a version of the dataset where the number of samples for each class was capped at 215 (i.e., the number of samples in the least represented dialects, namely, `Bahrain`, `Qatar` and `Sudan`). However, we also created other dataset versions where the number of samples per class was capped at 250 and 300. In this case, it was necessary to apply oversampling on the least represented classes (Chawla, 2010); to this end, randomly selected samples in those classes were duplicated. Our initial experiments showed that fine-tuning the original MARBERT model on these balanced versions of the dataset led to classification models that are able to predict the least represented dialects, although their performance on the sufficiently represented dialects was degraded compared with a model fine-tuned on the full training set.

Considering that fine-tuning on the full training set and fine-tuning on the balanced data, each has its own advantages, our solution for this subtask was based on combinations of models resulting from both.

3.2 Subtask 2: Sentiment Analysis

Taking the checkpoint for the original pre-trained MARBERT model[1], we continued to train it for masked language modelling using the dataset of 10 million unlabelled Arabic tweets, that was provided by the NADI organisers as part of the shared task. Out of these tweets, 90% were used for training, whilst the remaining 10% were used for validation. Both the number of epochs and batch size were arbitrarily set to 8 and the maximum sequence length was fixed at 512. The resulting model was then fine-tuned for sentiment analysis using the labelled tweets in the training set for Subtask 2. We also considered creating a version of the dataset where the dominant classes, i.e., `Positive` and `Negative`, are undesampled. However, models fine-tuned on this version obtained inferior classification performance. Thus, only models fine-tuned on the full training set comprise our solution for this subtask.

3.3 Hyperparameter Optimisation

For each of the subtasks, we trained a number of model variants using the full training sets for both Subtasks 1 and 2, and additionally, on the balanced versions of the training set for Subtask 1. These model variants are based on the exploration of a range of values for seed and learning rate. Specifically, seed values ranging between 20 and 300 (inclusive) were investigated; we found that setting the seed to 200 led to optimal performance in both subtasks, based on results on the respective development sets. Meanwhile, optimal performance was obtained by setting the learning rate to values ranging between $1.5e^{-5}$ and $2.5e^{-5}$ (inclusive).

The batch size was fixed at 32, while the number of epochs was arbitrarily set to 8. For every training run (on Nvidia A100 GPUs), the model trained in the epoch where the best macro-averaged F1-score was obtained, was considered as the best-performing model for that run.

3.4 Ensemble Models

After hyperparameter optimisation, the eight best-performing Subtask 1 models (according to F1-score), were selected: four based on training on the full training set, and the other four based on training on the balanced data. Meanwhile, for Subtask 2, we selected the five best-performing models (based on F1-score) trained on the full training set.

For each subtask, we aimed to identify an ensemble model (Rokach, 2019) that is based on the combination of the predictions of these best-performing models. In Subtask 1, for example, there are 255 possible combinations of the eight models (i.e., $2^8 - 1$ combinations). For each combination (ensemble), the average of the prediction probabilities output by the models for each class was taken as the basis for the overall prediction of the ensemble. A similar process was applied to the 31 possible combinations of the five models for Subtask 2 (i.e., $2^5 - 1$ combinations).

For each of the two subtasks, the three best-performing ensemble models were identified based on experiments on the corresponding development set and formed the basis of our official submission to NADI 2022.

4 Evaluation and Results

The performance of our ensemble models for the dialect identification subtask is summarised in Table 1. Our best-performing model (Ens 1.1) obtained a macro-averaged F1-score of 35.625 on the development set. Meanwhile, the macro-averaged F1-scores on the two test sets are: 34.778 on Test-A (the test set that covers 18 dialects) and 18.948 on Test-B (the test set with an unknown number of dialects). Nevertheless, it is worth noting that our best ensemble model ranks third when evaluated using Test-A, and ranks first when evaluated using Test-B, amongst the submissions from the 19 teams who participated in Subtask 1. If one takes the mean of the macro-averaged F1-scores on Test-A and Test-B as the overall performance for Subtask 1, our best ensemble model ranks second, with a mean score of 26.863.

With regard to the second subtask, we present the performance of our ensemble models for sentiment analysis in Table 3. Instead of the macro-

[1]`https://github.com/UBC-NLP/marbert#6-download-arbert-and-marbert-checkpoints`

Model	Eval. data	Macro-F1	Acc.
Ens 1.1	Dev	**35.625**	**53.890**
	Test-A	**34.778**	**52.333**
	Test-B	**18.948**	36.839
Ens 1.2	Dev	35.031	53.069
	Test-A	34.152	51.303
	Test-B	17.984	36364
Ens 1.3	Dev	34.937	52.782
	Test-A	34.248	51.366
	Test-B	18.435	**36.974**

Table 1: Results for Subtask 1 based on three different ensemble (Ens) models.

Model	Eval. data	Macro-F1-PN	Acc.
Ens 2.1	Dev	**77.262**	**72.400**
	Test	**73.544**	**67.700**
Ens 2.2	Dev	76.904	**72.400**
	Test	73.200	67.333
Ens 2.3	Dev	76.709	**72.400**
	Test	73.432	67.667

Table 2: Results for Subtask 2 based on three different ensemble (Ens) models.

averaged F1-score over all classes, a different metric (macro-F1-PN) based on the macro-averaged F1-score over the `Positive` and `Negative` classes only, was used in the evaluation of this subtask. Our best-performing ensemble model (Ens 2.1) obtained a macro-F1-PN score of 77.262 on the development set and 73.544 on the test set. This model ranks second amongst the submissions from 10 teams who participated in Subtask 2.

5 Discussion

To allow us to draw some insights on the class-level performance of our best-performing dialect identification model, we provide the confusion matrix based on the development set, in Figure 2.

As one can observe in the confusion matrix, the majority of the true samples from dialects such as `Egypt`, `KSA`, and `Iraq`, have been correctly predicted by our model. This can be explained by the fact that such classes are over-represented in the training data. However, the over-representation of such classes is likely to have also led to a detrimental effect, i.e., the model being biased towards such dominant dialects, as can be observed in the columns of the confusion matrix, where many samples tend to be wrongly predicted as `Egypt` or `KSA`, for instance. Meanwhile, as expected, the model

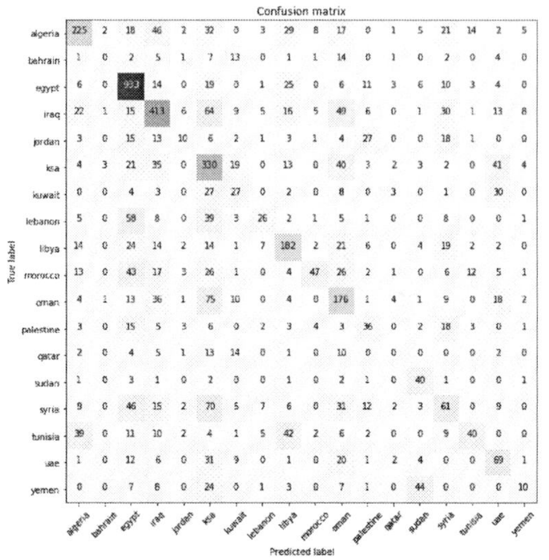

Figure 2: Confusion matrix for our best-performing dialect identification ensemble model, based on the development set.

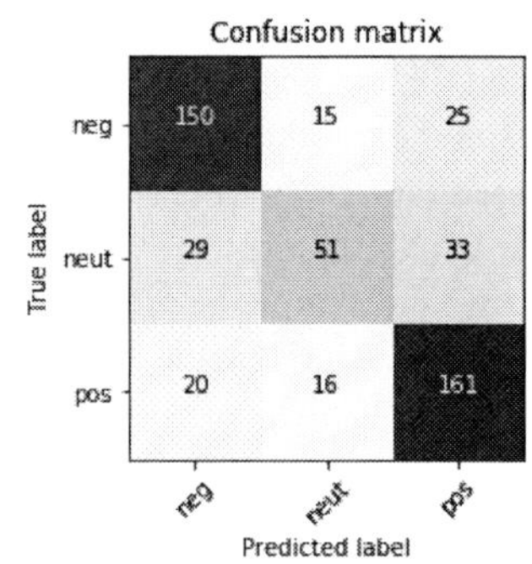

Figure 3: Confusion matrix for our best-performing sentiment analysis ensemble model, based on the development set.

obtained poor performance with respect to the least represented dialects such as `Bahrain` and `Qatar`. Also, our model tends to be confused by dialects which correspond to regions which are geographically close to each other and hence share certain dialects, e.g., `Oman` vs `KSA`, `Lebanon` vs `Egypt`.

As for our best-performing sentiment analysis model, the confusion matrix in Figure 3 shows that the model performs almost equally well on the `Positive` and `Negative` classes. Unsurprisingly, it does not perform as well for the `Neutral` class, which has a slightly lower number of training samples.

Hypothesising that limited context in any given tweet leads to wrong predictions, we investigated

	Tweet Text	English Translation	Gold	Pred.
1	الله يحفظوا و يحفظنا	May God protect him and protect us	Iraq	Oman
2	ربي يخليهم لك	May god keep them for you	Libya	Oman
3	لا دي مصرية	No, she is Egyptian	KSA	Egypt
4	بس حلو المسلسل	But the series is nice	Jordan	Iraq
5	اي لوف يو	I love you	KSA	Iraq
6	باك من قطر):	Back from Qatar :(	KSA	UAE
7	الله يحفظه ويطول بعمره	May Allah protect him and prolong his age	KSA	Oman
8	الله يسلمك ، امين	God bless you, amen	KSA	Oman

Table 3: Some of the incorrectly predicted samples, their English translation, their labels in the development set (Gold) and our model's predicted label (Pred).

whether the length of a tweet in terms of number of tokens, has a detrimental impact on model performance. There are 864 samples in the development set with at most four tokens; the macro-averaged F1-score obtained by our model on these samples is 25.180. In contrast, the same model obtained a substantially higher macro-averaged F1-score of 37.385 on the remaining 4007 samples which have four or more tokens. Moreover, as we increased the number of tokens being considered, the model's performance also improved: the macro-averaged F1-score on samples with no more than five tokens (1336 samples) and six tokens (1823 samples) is 26.126 and 28.323, respectively.

Based on the above observations and some samples (that we manually analysed), we argue that defining Arabic dialect identification task as a classification task with a large number of classes (e.g., 18), inevitably leads to overlap. In this scenario, a given tweet could easily qualify as belonging to more than one dialect, where even humans would disagree on the dialect used. This is because many countries may use the same phrase or wording; especially in cases where a tweet contains only a few tokens, it can be extremely hard to pinpoint its country or region of origin.

Table 3 shows some samples from the development set that were wrongly predicted by our model. These samples contain only a few tokens thus making it very challenging to identify their dialect. In fact, some of these samples cannot be identified as one dialect since they can be used in multiple countries. For example, the first four tweets (Samples 1, 2, 3 and 4) in Table 3 were labelled as being from a different dialect to what our model predicted them as; however, they can also be considered as the Egypt or KSA dialects since these phrases are commonly used in Egypt and Saudi Arabia. Moreover, we found samples that include English words, such as Sample 5 which was given KSA and Iraq as its label in the development set and by our model, respectively, when in reality it was not even written in Arabic. It is instead a transliteration of the English phrase *"I love you"*. Similarly, Sample 6 contains the word *"back"* transliterated into Arabic leaving only two Arabic words which translate to *"from Qatar"* from which it is impossible to detect a dialect even by a native Arabic speaker.

We also investigated some samples from neighbouring countries such as KSA, Oman and UAE (United Arab Emirates), which are all Gulf countries. As shown in Table 3, some samples (such as Samples 6, 7 and 8) are not easy to identify since there are some similarities between neighbouring countries' dialects. We thus believe that the task of identifying Arabic dialects could be more suitable as a multi-label classification task whereby each sample can be assigned more than one dialect.

6 Conclusion and Future Work

In this paper, we presented our ensemble-based approaches to the NADI 2022 subtasks: dialect identification and sentiment analysis. Our results demonstrate that an ensemble model consisting of a combination of MARBERT models fine-tuned in different ways, for each of the subtasks, obtains top-ranking performance. A potential future direction is the exploration of multi-task learning for jointly training a model on the two subtasks.

References

Muhammad Abdul-Mageed, AbdelRahim Elmadany, and El Moatez Billah Nagoudi. 2021a. ARBERT & MARBERT: Deep bidirectional transformers for Arabic. In *Proceedings of the 59th Annual Meeting of the Association for Computational Linguistics and the 11th International Joint Conference on Natural Language Processing (Volume 1: Long Papers)*, pages 7088–7105, Online. Association for Computational Linguistics.

Muhammad Abdul-Mageed, Chiyu Zhang, Houda Bouamor, and Nizar Habash. 2020. NADI 2020: The first nuanced Arabic dialect identification shared task. In *Proceedings of the Fifth Arabic Natural Language Processing Workshop*, pages 97–110, Barcelona, Spain (Online). Association for Computational Linguistics.

Muhammad Abdul-Mageed, Chiyu Zhang, AbdelRahim Elmadany, Houda Bouamor, and Nizar Habash. 2021b. NADI 2021: The second nuanced Arabic dialect identification shared task. In *Proceedings of the Sixth Arabic Natural Language Processing Workshop*, pages 244–259, Kyiv, Ukraine (Virtual). Association for Computational Linguistics.

Muhammad Abdul-Mageed, Chiyu Zhang, AbdelRahim Elmadany, Houda Bouamor, and Nizar Habash. 2022. NADI 2022: The Third Nuanced Arabic Dialect Identification Shared Task. In *Proceedings of the Seven Arabic Natural Language Processing Workshop (WANLP 2022)*.

Nada Boudjellal, Huaping Zhang, Asif Khan, Arshad Ahmad, Rashid Naseem, Jianyun Shang, and Lin Dai. 2021. ABioNER: a BERT-based model for Arabic biomedical named-entity recognition. *Complexity*, 2021:1–6.

Nitesh V. Chawla. 2010. *Data Mining for Imbalanced Datasets: An Overview*, pages 875–886. Springer US, Boston, MA.

Jacob Devlin, Ming-Wei Chang, Kenton Lee, and Kristina Toutanova. 2019. BERT: Pre-training of deep bidirectional transformers for language understanding. In *Proceedings of the 2019 Conference of the North American Chapter of the Association for Computational Linguistics: Human Language Technologies, Volume 1 (Long and Short Papers)*, pages 4171–4186, Minneapolis, Minnesota. Association for Computational Linguistics.

Qi Liu, Matt J Kusner, and Phil Blunsom. 2020. A survey on contextual embeddings. *arXiv preprint arXiv:2003.07278*.

El Moatez Billah Nagoudi, AbdelRahim Elmadany, and Muhammad Abdul-Mageed. 2022. AraT5: Text-to-text transformers for Arabic language generation. In *Proceedings of the 60th Annual Meeting of the Association for Computational Linguistics (Volume 1: Long Papers)*, pages 628–647, Dublin, Ireland. Association for Computational Linguistics.

Oumaima Oueslati, Erik Cambria, Moez Ben HajHmida, and Habib Ounelli. 2020. A review of sentiment analysis research in arabic language. *Future Generation Computer Systems*, 112:408–430.

L. Rokach. 2019. *Ensemble Learning: Pattern Classification Using Ensemble Methods*. Series in machine perception and artificial intelligence. World Scientific Publishing.

Ashish Vaswani, Noam Shazeer, Niki Parmar, Jakob Uszkoreit, Llion Jones, Aidan N Gomez, Łukasz Kaiser, and Illia Polosukhin. 2017. Attention is all you need. *Advances in Neural Information Processing Systems*, 30.

Arabic Dialect Identification and Sentiment Classification using Transformer-based Models

Joseph Attieh
Huawei Technologies Oy., Finland
joseph.attieh@huawei.com

Fadi Hassan
Huawei Technologies Oy., Finland
fadi.hassan@huawei.com

Abstract

In this paper, we present two deep learning approaches that are based on AraBERT, submitted to the Nuanced Arabic Dialect Identification (NADI) shared task of the Seventh Workshop for Arabic Natural Language Processing (WANLP 2022). NADI consists of two main sub-tasks, mainly country-level dialect and sentiment identification for dialectical Arabic. We present one system per sub-task. The first system is a multi-task learning model that consists of a shared AraBERT encoder with three task-specific classification layers. This model is trained to jointly learn the country-level dialect of the tweet as well as the region-level and area-level dialects. The second system is a distilled model of an ensemble of models trained using K-fold cross-validation. Each model in the ensemble consists of an AraBERT model and a classifier, fine-tuned on (K-1) folds of the training set. Our team Pythoneers achieved rank 6 on the first test set of the first sub-task, rank 9 on the second test set of the first sub-task, and rank 4 on the test set of the second sub-task.

1 Introduction

Arabic is the official language of 22 countries, recognized as the 4th most used language on the Internet (Guellil et al., 2021). Arabic can be classified into three types (Guellil et al., 2021), mainly Classical Arabic (CA), Modern Standard Arabic (MSA), and Arabic Dialects (AD). Unlike both CA and MSA, Arabic Dialects lack a standardized representation and data that cover their complex taxonomy. Several initiatives were made to advance the research in this field. One of the most prominent work has been carried out through the Nuanced Arabic Dialect Identification (NADI) shared tasks. The first two NADI shared tasks (Abdul-Mageed et al., 2020, 2021b) comprised country-level and province-level dialect identification.

Many participants presented their systems to the NADI shared tasks. Most of the systems submitted rely on the Bidirectional Encoder Representation from Transformers (BERT) (Devlin et al., 2019) models. For instance, Mansour et al. (2020) pretrained a multilingual BERT model on unlabeled Arabic tweets, then fine-tuned the model for the dialect classification task. Furthermore, Tahssin et al. (2020) fine-tuned the transformer-based Model for Arabic Language Understanding AraBERT (Antoun et al.) on an extended corpus constructed using a reverse translation of the given Arabic NADI dataset. Gaanoun and Benelallam (2020) employed Arabic-BERT (Safaya et al., 2020) alongside semi-supervised learning and ensembling methods in their system. El Mekki et al. (2020) introduced an ensemble that applies a weighted voting technique on two classifiers, the first based on TF-IDF with word and character n-grams and the second based on AraBERT. El Mekki et al. (2021) proposed a multi-task model that leverages MARBERT's contextualized word embedding (Abdul-Mageed et al., 2021a) with two task-specific attention layers, aggregated to predict both the province and the country of a given Arabic tweet.

The NADI 2022 shared task (Abdul-Mageed et al., 2022) provides two sub-tasks, mainly country-level dialect identification and sentiment analysis. Inspired by the previous submissions, we fine-tune AraBERT for each sub-task. The system for the first sub-task is a multi-task model that performs dialect identification by predicting the region, area, and country of the tweet. The system for the second sub-task is a distilled model from an ensemble of K models that were trained using K-fold cross-validation for sentiment classification.

This paper is structured as follows: Section 2 describes the data used. Section 3 gives an overview of fine tuning BERT models. Section 4 presents the systems submitted to Subtasks 1 and 2 respectively. We show the results on the NADI Subtasks 1 and 2 and discuss them in Sections 5 and 6. We conclude with Section 7.

Proceedings of the The Seventh Arabic Natural Language Processing Workshop (WANLP), pages 485 - 490
December 8, 2022 ©2022 Association for Computational Linguistics

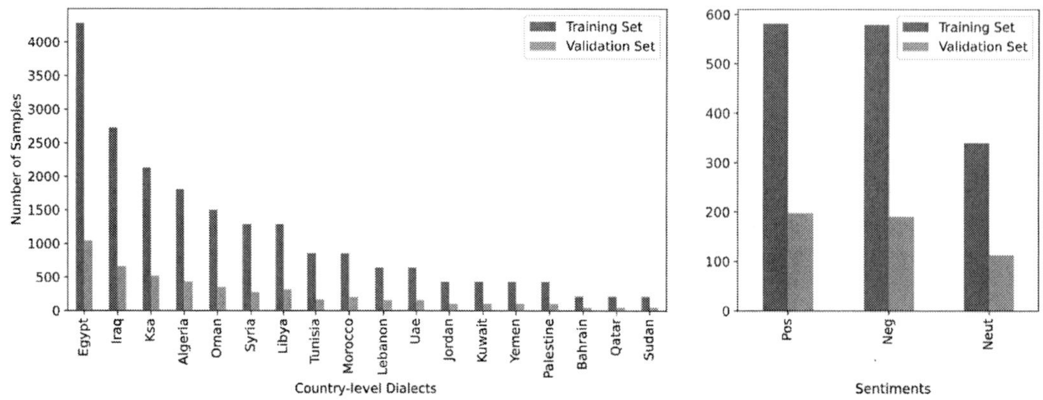

Figure 1: Label distribution in the training and validation sets of Subtask 1 and Subtask 2 respectively.

2 Data

2.1 Dataset Description

The systems were developed using the training and validation data provided by the task organizers. The training set for Subtask 1 consists of around 20,398 tweets with 18 different labels representing 18 country dialects, while the development set consists of 4,871 labeled tweets. The system submitted to this sub-task is evaluated on two test sets; the first test set (TEST-A) consists of 4,758 tweets covering 18 country-level dialects, whereas the second test set (TEST-B) consists of 1,474 tweets covering k country-level dialects.

The training set for Subtask 2 consists of 1,500 tweets labeled as either positive, negative, or neutral, while the development/validation set consists of 500 labeled tweets. The system submitted to this sub-task is evaluated on a test set of 3,000 unlabelled tweets.

Figure 1 shows that the distribution of the tweets for the country-level classification sub-task is highly unbalanced. This would raise some issues in correctly predicting the minority classes (i.e., the dialects that have a small sample of tweets in the training set). Moreover, Figure 1 shows that the number of samples in the training set provided for the second sub-task is quite small. This raises the need to have a language model that can perform the task given the small training set. This motivates the use of transfer learning and pre-trained language models for this sub-task.

2.2 Dataset Pre-processing

We apply the same pre-processing techniques for both Subtask 1 and 2. We first standardize the text by removing non-Arabic words, emojis, and URLs from the tweets. Then, we proceed by tokenizing the tweets using the AraBERT tokenizer.

2.3 Region and Area Inference

For the first sub-task, we infer two additional labels from the country-level label provided. We propose to classify the tweets into two regions (either Western or Eastern) and into four areas (Western, Egyptian, Levantine, or Peninsular gulf), as shown in Figure 2.

Western Dialect		Eastern Dialect			
Western Dialect		Egyptian	Levantine	Peninsular Gulf	
Morocco	Algeria	Egypt	Lebanon	Iraq	Bahrain
			Palestine	Kuwait	Yemen
Tunisia	Libya	Sudan	Syria	Oman	Qatar
			Jordan	KSA	UAE

Figure 2: Two additional labels were inferred from the country-level label for Subtask 1.

For instance, Morocco, Algeria, Tunisia, and Libya will belong to the Western region and to the Western area, while Egypt and Sudan will belong to the Eastern region and to the Egyptian area. We chose to add these additional labels to the task to encode some domain knowledge in the pre-trained language model.

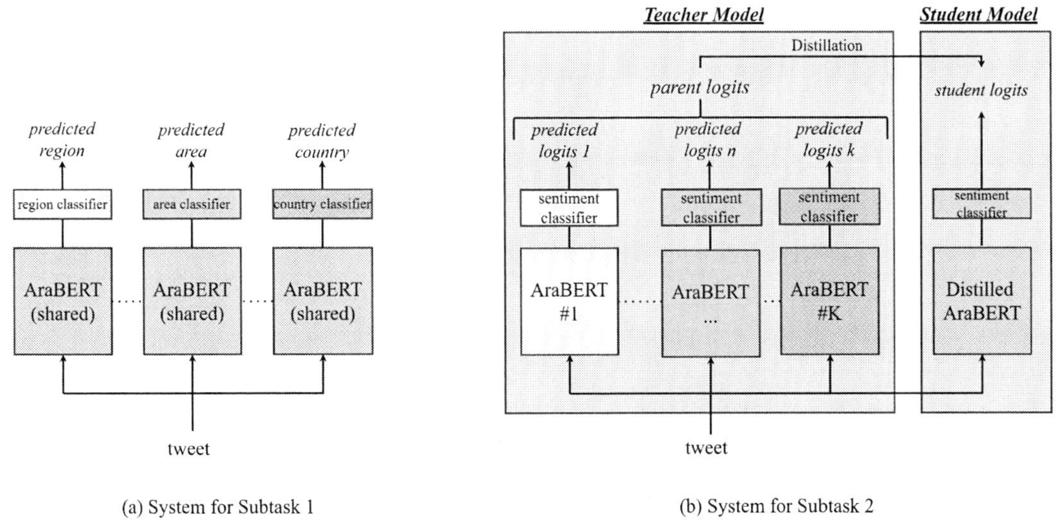

Figure 3: Systems used for the NADI subtasks.

3 Fine-tuning BERT

As mentioned in the previous sections, the two subtasks fall under the category of text classification. An intuitive solution would be to fine-tune a pre-trained language model on each sub-task by adding an output layer to the encoder and training the parameters of the network to predict the classes for the subtask.

Fine-tuning is a form of Transfer Learning, as it tailors the knowledge encoded in the model to the downstream task. Therefore, it is crucial to find an appropriate model to fine-tune. After investigating multiple BERT variants, we choose to use an Arabic pre-trained language model called AraBERT (Antoun et al.). AraBERT is trained on a huge corpus of Arabic text from a collection of publicly available large-scale raw Arabic text. The specific model employed in both subtasks is the *bert-large-arabertv02-twitter*. It is based on AraBERTv0.2-large, and it is pre-trained using the Masked Language Modeling task on 60M Multi-Dialect Tweets.

However, fine-tuning a BERT variant might not be sufficient to reach the desired performance on the sub tasks. Therefore, our contribution lies in employing multi-task learning for the first sub-task, and knowledge distillation from an ensemble of models for the second sub-task. All models have been trained on NVIDIA Tesla Volta V100.

4 Proposed Solutions

4.1 Subtask 1 - Multi-Task Learning

As mentioned in the previous section, a simple solution would be to fine-tune AraBERT to predict one dialect out of the 18 predefined dialects. We propose to encode more domain knowledge in AraBERT by training the model to predict the region and area of the tweet (as described in Figure 2). Learning these two labels jointly with the country-level dialect will help BERT acquire more knowledge for the country-level dialect identification task. To learn the region, area, and country-level dialect classes, we use multi-task learning. The Multi-Task model consists of a single shared AraBERT encoder. The pre-trained AraBERT model is fine-tuned using three task-specific classification heads (i.e., layers). Each classification head consists of a dropout layer of probability 0.1 followed by a linear layer that maps the CLS token embeddings of the AraBERT encoder to the number of predicted classes (2 classes for region, 4 for area, and 18 for country). We use the cross-entropy loss to compute the loss on the outcome of every classifier head. There are multiple strategies to combine the three losses. Since the losses assess different measures, we chose to fine-tune one loss at a time per batch. As seen in Figure 1, the dataset suffers from class imbalance. Therefore, we propose to randomly sample (with replacement) 500 sentences per country-level dialect. In other terms, the training set used for this model consists of 500

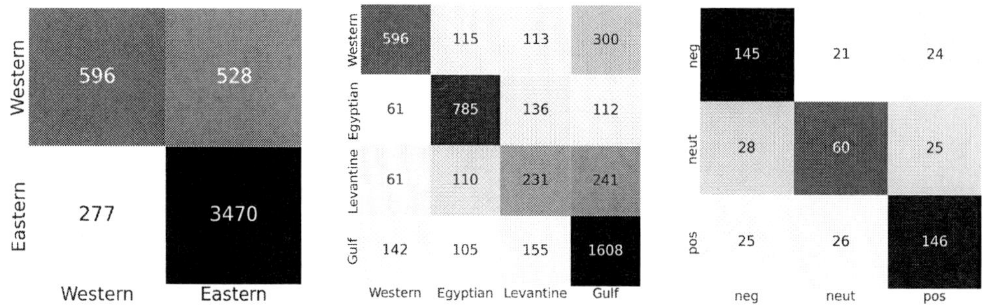

Figure 4: Confusion matrices for Region and Area of Subtask 1, and Sentiment of Subtask 2 on the dev set.

tweets for every label. This will guarantee that all classes participate in the training process equally. The model is trained using the Adam optimizer (Kingma and Ba, 2015), with a learning rate of 10^{-5}. After conducting multiple experiments, we chose to set the batch size to 64 and the number of epochs to 5. In this study, we report the results of the system that achieved the best score on the leaderboard.

4.2 Subtask 2 - Distilled Ensemble of K models

The proposed system relies on the same AraBERT model employed before. We propose to build an ensemble of K AraBERT models. To do so, we split the training set into K folds and we fine-tune an AraBERT model for each combination of (K-1) folds. Then, the output of this ensemble of K models (i.e., logits) is constructed by computing the average of the logits from all the K models. Using an ensemble is more robust and prevents overfitting since each model from that ensemble is exposed to a different subset of the training set. Furthermore, ensembles are known to usually achieve better performance compared to a single model. Afterward, we distill the knowledge from the ensemble teacher model to a single AraBERT student model by optimizing the following loss:

$$\begin{aligned} Loss &= (1-\alpha) \times CE(score, target) \\ &+\alpha \times MSE(student\_logits, teacher\_logits) \end{aligned}$$

CE stands for cross-entropy loss, while MSE stands for mean squared error loss. We set α to 0.95 and K to 10. The model is trained with a learning rate of 5×10^{-6} and a batch size of 32 for 6 epochs. It should be noted that the hyperparameters reported are the ones that resulted in the best performance on the validation set.

5 Results

We evaluate our systems on the validation set provided by the organizers. Table 1 presents the Macro-Averaged Precision, Recall, and F1 Score computed over the development sets and reported on the test set by the organizers for each sub-task. The first sub-task was evaluated on two test sets TEST-A and TEST-B: TEST-A covers 18 country-level dialects, while TEST-B covers k country-level dialects, where k was kept unknown. The second sub-task was evaluated by computing the metrics over the positive and negative labels only, on one test set of 3000 tweets. The official metric used is the Macro-Averaged F1-score. We report the confusion matrices of both systems on the development sets in Figures 4 and 5.

Table 1: Results of the systems on Subtasks 1 and 2.

Sub -task	Eval Set	Label	Macro Precision	Macro Recall	Macro F1 Score
1	DEV	Region	77.53	72.81	74.64
		Area	61.80	60.17	60.65
		Country	28.50	28.01	27.57
	TEST-A	Country	36.77	31.77	32.63
	TEST-B	Country	19.51	15.90	15.61
2	DEV	Sentiment (Pos, Neg)	68.06	67.84	67.93
	TEST	Sentiment (Pos, Neg)	66.08	65.87	73.40

6 Discussion

As we can notice, the simple task of predicting whether the dialect is Western or Eastern is challenging by itself. This clearly confirms that the task of dialect identification is not an easy task. Furthermore, we notice that the model has trouble distinguishing between the Levantine dialect and the Peninsular Gulf dialect. This is expected as these dialects are the most similar among all four families (area).

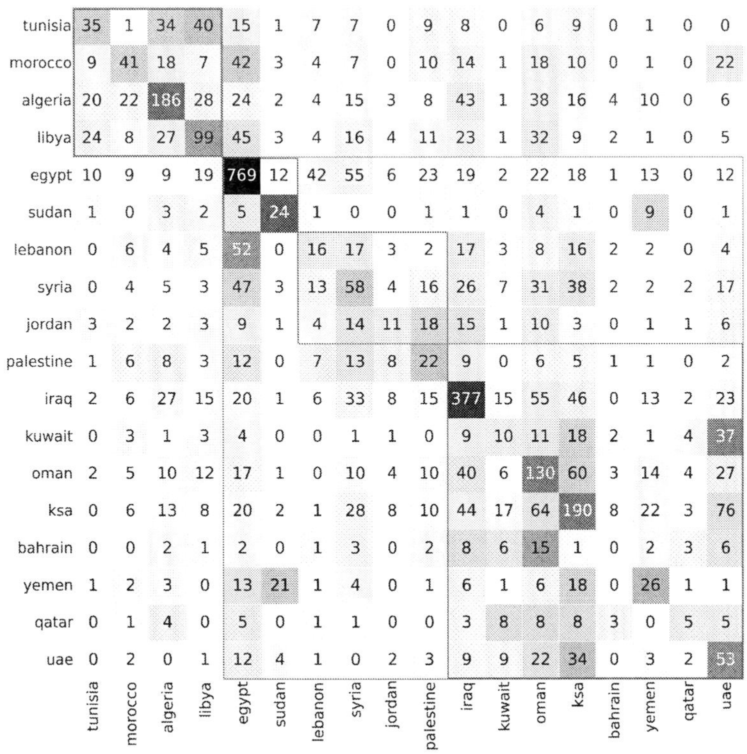

Figure 5: Confusion matrix for the country-level labels of Subtask 1.

Moreover, we notice that the confusion between dialects within the same area is higher compared to dialects from different areas (highlighted in Figure 5 by the clusters of values in red and green). This is expected as the training process injected knowledge that helps the model distinguish between the dialect classes (i.e., regions and areas). Therefore, a more fine-grained region-level and area-level classification should result in an improvement to the country-level dialect identification task.

We can also note the discrepancy in the performance of the model between TEST-A and TEST-B. In fact, TEST-A tests the model's performance on all the dialects, while TEST-B tests the performance on a subset of k dialects. TEST-B does not reflect the model's performance on all dialects, as the model might be tested on country-level dialects that are more difficult to predict.

As for Subtask 2, we can see that the Macro-Averaged F1 Score reported on the test set is higher than the score reported on the development set. This implies that distilling an ensemble of K models trained on different partitions of the training set helped the model generalize well on unseen data.

7 Conclusion

In this paper, we introduced two AraBERT-based systems to tackle dialect and sentiment classification. We conclude by confirming that dealing with Arabic dialect data is quite challenging. In future work, we propose to vary the training approach for every individual model in the ensemble, by changing the sequence length used, or even the training batch size per model. We also propose to build an ensemble of K multi-task models for Subtask 1.

References

Muhammad Abdul-Mageed, AbdelRahim Elmadany, and El Moatez Billah Nagoudi. 2021a. ARBERT & MARBERT: Deep bidirectional transformers for Arabic. In *Proceedings of the 59th Annual Meeting of the Association for Computational Linguistics and the 11th International Joint Conference on Natural Language Processing (Volume 1: Long Papers)*, pages 7088–7105, Online. Association for Computational Linguistics.

Muhammad Abdul-Mageed, Chiyu Zhang, Houda Bouamor, and Nizar Habash. 2020. NADI 2020: The First Nuanced Arabic Dialect Identification Shared Task. In *Proceedings of the Fifth Arabic Natu-*

ral Language Processing Workshop (WANLP 2020), Barcelona, Spain.

Muhammad Abdul-Mageed, Chiyu Zhang, AbdelRahim Elmadany, Houda Bouamor, and Nizar Habash. 2021b. NADI 2021: The Second Nuanced Arabic Dialect Identification Shared Task. In *Proceedings of the Sixth Arabic Natural Language Processing Workshop (WANLP 2021)*.

Muhammad Abdul-Mageed, Chiyu Zhang, AbdelRahim Elmadany, Houda Bouamor, and Nizar Habash. 2022. NADI 2022: The Third Nuanced Arabic Dialect Identification Shared Task. In *Proceedings of the Seven Arabic Natural Language Processing Workshop (WANLP 2022)*.

Wissam Antoun, Fady Baly, and Hazem Hajj. Arabert: Transformer-based model for arabic language understanding. In *LREC 2020 Workshop Language Resources and Evaluation Conference 11–16 May 2020*, page 9.

Jacob Devlin, Ming-Wei Chang, Kenton Lee, and Kristina Toutanova. 2019. BERT: Pre-training of deep bidirectional transformers for language understanding. In *Proceedings of the 2019 Conference of the North American Chapter of the Association for Computational Linguistics: Human Language Technologies, Volume 1 (Long and Short Papers)*, pages 4171–4186, Minneapolis, Minnesota. Association for Computational Linguistics.

Abdellah El Mekki, Ahmed Alami, Hamza Alami, Ahmed Khoumsi, and Ismail Berrada. 2020. Weighted combination of BERT and n-GRAM features for nuanced Arabic dialect identification. In *Proceedings of the Fifth Arabic Natural Language Processing Workshop*, pages 268–274, Barcelona, Spain (Online). Association for Computational Linguistics.

Abdellah El Mekki, Abdelkader El Mahdaouy, Kabil Essefar, Nabil El Mamoun, Ismail Berrada, and Ahmed Khoumsi. 2021. BERT-based multi-task model for country and province level MSA and dialectal Arabic identification. In *Proceedings of the Sixth Arabic Natural Language Processing Workshop*, pages 271–275, Kyiv, Ukraine (Virtual). Association for Computational Linguistics.

Kamel Gaanoun and Imade Benelallam. 2020. Arabic dialect identification: An Arabic-BERT model with data augmentation and ensembling strategy. In *Proceedings of the Fifth Arabic Natural Language Processing Workshop*, pages 275–281, Barcelona, Spain (Online). Association for Computational Linguistics.

Imane Guellil, Houda Saâdane, Faical Azouaou, Billel Gueni, and Damien Nouvel. 2021. Arabic natural language processing: An overview. *Journal of King Saud University - Computer and Information Sciences*, 33(5):497–507.

Diederik P. Kingma and Jimmy Ba. 2015. Adam: A method for stochastic optimization. In *3rd International Conference on Learning Representations, ICLR 2015, San Diego, CA, USA, May 7-9, 2015, Conference Track Proceedings*.

Moataz Mansour, Moustafa Tohamy, Zeyad Ezzat, and Marwan Torki. 2020. Arabic dialect identification using BERT fine-tuning. In *Proceedings of the Fifth Arabic Natural Language Processing Workshop*, pages 308–312, Barcelona, Spain (Online). Association for Computational Linguistics.

Ali Safaya, Moutasem Abdullatif, and Deniz Yuret. 2020. KUISAIL at SemEval-2020 task 12: BERT-CNN for offensive speech identification in social media. In *Proceedings of the Fourteenth Workshop on Semantic Evaluation*, pages 2054–2059, Barcelona (online). International Committee for Computational Linguistics.

Rawan Tahssin, Youssef Kishk, and Marwan Torki. 2020. Identifying nuanced dialect for Arabic tweets with deep learning and reverse translation corpus extension system. In *Proceedings of the Fifth Arabic Natural Language Processing Workshop*, pages 288–294, Barcelona, Spain (Online). Association for Computational Linguistics.

Generative Approach for Gender Rewriting Task with ArabicT5

Sultan Alrowili
Department of Computer Science
University of Delaware
Newark, Delaware, USA
alrowili@udel.edu

K.Vijay-Shanker
Department of Computer Science
University of Delaware
Newark, Delaware, USA
vijay@udel.edu

Abstract

Addressing the correct gender in generative tasks (e.g., Machine Translation) has been an overlooked issue in the Arabic NLP. However, the recent introduction of the Arabic Parallel Gender Corpus (APGC) dataset has established new baselines for the Arabic Gender Rewriting task. To address the Gender Rewriting task, we first pre-train our new Seq2Seq ArabicT5 model on a 17GB of Arabic Corpora. Then, we continue pre-training our ArabicT5 model on the APGC dataset using a newly proposed method. Our evaluation shows that our ArabicT5 model, when trained on the APGC dataset, achieved competitive results against existing state-of-the-art methods. In addition, our ArabicT5 model shows better results on the APGC dataset compared to other Arabic and multilingual T5 models.

1 Introduction

In many generative downstream tasks in Arabic NLP, such as Machine Translation and chatbot applications, addressing the correct gender is crucial to increase the quality of the generated text to reach human-level performance. This also leads to having a generated text that is less biased and discriminating against specific gender. Moreover, when used in Translation and chatbot applications, generative models such as T5 (Raffel et al., 2019), and BART (Lewis et al., 2020) may adopt a gender bias, which they learn from the pre-training corpora. Thus, the Gender Rewriting downstream task has recently received more attention in Arabic NLP. This attention can be seen with the introduction of the Arabic Parallel Gender Corpus (APGC) dataset (Alhafni et al., 2022a).

Current state-of-the-art methods to address the Gender Rewriting task uses a multi-stage model consisting of rule-based, morphological analyzer, and encoder-decoder GRU model (Alhafni et al., 2022b). However, one issue with using a multi-stage model is that it increases the complexity of the model. This motivates us to seek a more simple alternative approach. In this work, we hypothesize that generative models such as T5 and BART could address the gender rewriting problem when trained on the APGC dataset. Thus, in this work, we introduce a novel method to address the Gender-Rewriting task through our ArabicT5 model, a model that we pre-trained on a collection of Arabic corpora.

Thus, our contributions in this work can be summarized in the following points:

- We introduce ArabicT5: a new Arabic T5 model pre-trained on a 17GB of Arabic corpora, including Arabic Wikipedia and Arabic News articles. This model has many applications beyond the scope of this work, such as Question Answering, Text Classification, Question Generation, Machine Translation, and Text Summarization. We also released our ArabicT5 model and our codes to the public community. [1].

- We introduce a new approach in the Arabic NLP that uses Seq2Seq models to address the Gender-Rewriting task.

- We evaluate and compare our approach with our ArabicT5 against AraT5 (Nagoudi et al., 2022) , mT5 model: the multilingual variant of T5 (Xue et al., 2021), and the multi-step gender rewriting model by Alhafni et al. (2022b). We also show through our analysis how design factors such as the pre-training corpora affect the evaluation performance.

[1]Our ArabicT5 models can be accessed at https://huggingface.co/sultan/ArabicT5-Base, https://huggingface.co/sultan/ArabicT5-Large, https://huggingface.co/sultan/ArabicT5-xLarge and our GitHub page https://github.com/salrowili/ArabicT5.

Proceedings of the The Seventh Arabic Natural Language Processing Workshop (WANLP), pages 491 - 495
December 8, 2022 ©2022 Association for Computational Linguistics

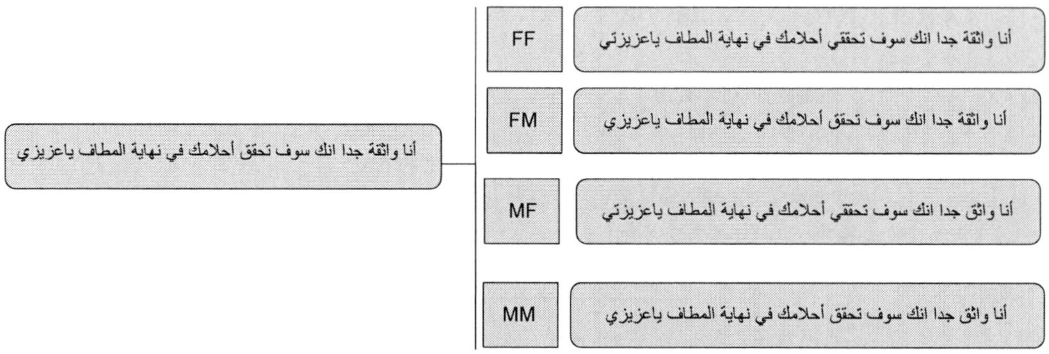

Figure 1: Example of the Gender-Rewriting task where we address different targeted genders. [FF: Female-to-Female, FM: Female-to-Male, MF: Male-to-Female, MM: Male-to-Male] .

2 Background

In this section, we will first explain the APGC dataset. Then, we will have an overview of the current state-of-the-art model; the multi-step gender rewriting model (Alhafni et al., 2022b). Then we will explain the T5, mT5 (Xue et al., 2021), and AraT5 models (Nagoudi et al., 2022).

2.1 Arabic Parallel Gender Corpus

Arabic Parallel Gender Corpus (APGC) (Alhafni et al., 2022a) is a new dataset introduced recently to address gender bias in natural language processing (NLP) applications. This dataset aims to address gender identification and rewriting sentence where the context involves one or two users (I and/or you). In Figure 1, we illustrate the structure of the APGC dataset.

2.2 The Multi-step Model Approach

The Multi-step Model (Alhafni et al., 2022b) represents the state-of-the-art model to address the Arabic Gender-Rewriting task. The Multi-step Model consists of multiple-stages including: (1) Gender Identification (GID), (2) Corpus-based Rewriter (CorpusR) (3) Morphological Rewriter (MorphR), and (4) NeuralR. The Gender Identification component aims to classify the word-level gender label for each word in the sentence using Arabic Transformer-Based models. The Corpus-based Rewriter (CorpusR) uses a bigram maximum likelihood estimator that uses the context to re-write desired word-level target gender. On the other hand, Morphological Rewriter (MorphR) component uses the morphological generator included in the CAMeL Tools. The last component in this Multi-step Model is the Neural Rewriter (NeuralR), a character-level attention-based encoder-decoder model. For both the encoder and decoder, it uses a GRU model (Chung et al., 2014).

2.3 T5

There are two common approaches where language models address downstream tasks. The first approach is the extractive approach, where we fine-tune the language model to extract specific spans (e.g., Question Answering) or predict a class in the Text Classification problem. Language Models that follow the extractive approach are models such as BERT (Devlin et al., 2019), ELECTRA (Clark et al., 2020), and ALBERT (Lan et al., 2019). On the other hand, generative models such as BART (Lewis et al., 2020), T5 (Raffel et al., 2019), and XLENT (Yang et al., 2019) are built to generate the target text to address the downstream task. For example, in T5, the Text-to-Text Transfer Transformer model, instead of extracting the spans that define the answer boundary, it generates the answer from the model parameters.

2.4 mT5

The mT5 model (Xue et al., 2021) is a multilingual variant of T5, which was pre-trained on the new Common Crawl-based dataset that consists of 6.3T tokens covering 101 languages. The mT5 model also uses a large vocabulary file that consists of 250K tokens.

2.5 AraT5

AraT5 (Nagoudi et al., 2022) is a newly introduced Arabic Language Model that pre-trains T5 on a collection of Arabic Corpora. AraT5 was pre-trained

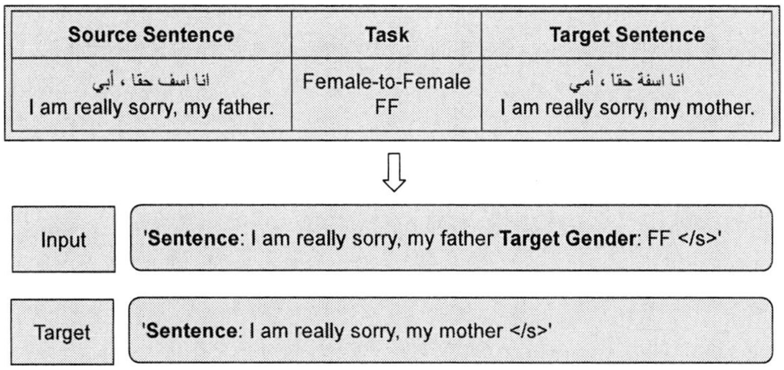

Figure 2: Example of our proposed method to address the Gender-Rewriting task. Both "Sentence" and "Target Gender" are used as tags and they are part of the input and target sentences.

for 80 days on the TPUv3-8 unit with a maximum sequence length of 128. AraT5 shows promising results on downstream tasks against Multi-lingual mT5 model. In our evaluation, we use three variants of AraT5, including:

- **AraT5-MSA$_{\mathbf{Base}}$**: pre-trained on Modern Standard Arabic (MSA) corpora (70GB) which include a collection of Arabic News articles and Arabic websites.
- **AraT5-Twitter$_{\mathbf{Base}}$**: pre-trained on Arabic Twitter Dataset (178GB).
- **AraT5$_{\mathbf{Base}}$**: pre-trained on 248GB of Arabic Corpora including Modern Standard Arabic (MSA) corpora (70GB) and dataset from Twitter (178GB).

3 Method

In this section, we will first explain how we build our new T5 model. Next, we will explain our method to address the Gender Rewriting task and the details of our environmental and evaluation setup.

3.1 Pre-training our ArabicT5 model

We build our ArabicT5 model by pre-training T5 model on a collection of Arabic Corpora including Arabic Wikipedia, News Articles (El-Khair, 2016), Hindawi Books [2] and Marefa encyclopedia [3]. We pre-train our ArabicT5 model using an efficient T5 implementation (Tay et al., 2021), which reduces pre-training and fine-tuning costs by studying T5 design factors (e.g., hidden size layers, attention heads, attention layers). We build our vocabulary using the SentencePiece model (Kudo and Richardson, 2018) and choose our vocabulary size as 32K tokens. In contrast to the AraT5 model, which only introduces the base model, we introduce based, large and xlarge models.

Our ArabicT5$_{\text{base}}$ model has 512 hidden size layers, eight attention heads, and 20 attention layers. We pre-train our ArabicT5$_{\text{base}}$ for 256K steps with a batch size of 256 (131,072 tokens) on TPUv3-32 unit. On the other hand, our ArabicT5$_{\text{large}}$ model uses 768 hidden size layers, 12 attention heads, and 16 attention layers. Moreover, we pre-train ArabicT5$_{\text{xlarge}}$ model which differ from ArabicT5$_{\text{large}}$ that it has more attention layers (36). We pre-train both our ArabicT5$_{\text{large}}$ and ArabicT5$_{\text{xlarge}}$ for 512K steps with a batch size of 512 (262,144 tokens) on TPUv3-128. For all models, we maintain all other settings set by (Tay et al., 2021) (e.g., learning rate, warm-up steps). We use the official TensorFlow implementation of T5 to pre-train our base and large models.

3.2 Preparing The Dataset

T5 models use a unified Text-to-Text framework that addresses all downstream tasks in Text-to-Text format as an input text and target text. For example, to address Text Classification problems such as Sentiment Analysis, we will add the sentence as the input text and the class (positive/negative) as the target text. To address the Gender Rewriting problem, we add the original sentence and targeted Gender (e.g., FF, FM, MF, MM) in the input text. Then we will add the output sentence which addresses the targeted gender in the target text. We will also add the flag </s> to mark the end of the sequence in both the input and target text. We illustrate our

[2] https://www.hindawi.org/books
[3] https://www.marefa.org/

Model	P	R	$F_{0.5}$	B
The Multi-Step Gender Rewriting Model (Alhafni et al., 2022b)	**88.8**	86.8	**88.3**	**98.1**
$mT5_{Base}$	71.6	82.0	73.4	97.5
$AraT5_{Base}$	72.8	83.6	74.7	97.7
$AraT5\text{-}MSA_{Base}$	72.6	83.8	74.6	97.7
$AraT5\text{-}Twitter_{Base}$	72.2	82.1	74.0	97.6
$ArabicT5_{Base}$ (ours)	72.1	85.5	74.4	97.7
$ArabicT5_{Large}$ (ours)	72.7	86.2	74.4	98.0
$ArabicT5_{XLarge}$ (ours)	73.0	**87.1**	75.4	98.0

Table 1: Evaluation Result of mT5, AraT5, ArabicT5 on the DEV set of APGC v2.1. [P: Precision, R: Recall, B: BLEU score] . We use reported results for the Multi-Step Gender Rewriting Model and generate the result for all other models.

method in Figure 2.

3.3 Experimental Setup

We fine-tune our ArabicT5, mT5, and AraT5 using the PyTorch XLA library `https://github.com/pytorch/xla`, which allows us to use Torch code on the TPUv3-8 unit. We fine-tune all models for 70 epochs with a learning rate of 1e-4. For evaluation, we follow a similar approach to (Alhafni et al., 2022b) by using the BLEU (Bilingual Evaluation Understudy) and MaxMatch (M2) scorer (Dahlmeier and Ng, 2012)[4]. We also adapt the same normalization script adapted by Gender Rewriting Shared Task [5].

4 Results and Discussion

In Table 1, we show the evaluation of both AraT5, mT5, and our ArabicT5 model with different scales (base, large, xlarge). In addition, we show the evaluation score of the current state-of-the-art model: The Multi-step Model by Alhafni et al. (2022b). We explain The Multi-step Model in detail in Section 2.2. This evaluation in Table 1 aims to compare the performance between single-stage seq2seq T5-based models against the current multi-stages state-of-the-art model.

We can observe from the results that there is a significant gap in performance between the Multi-Step Model and other Seq2Seq T5-based models. This gap is caused by the fact that these Seq2Seq models use a single-stage sentence-level approach. However, observe the close gap in blue score between all models in Table 1, which may caused by the fact that in the Arabic language, we only change a few letters in the sentence to address the right gender. In addition, we can attribute the significant gap in both Precision and $F_{0.5}$ scores between The Multi-Step Model and other Seq2Seq models to the multi-stage components used by Alhafni et al. (2022b). It also worth noting that our largest ArabicT5 models achieve the best recall score among all models showing the potential of seq2seq models.

On the other hand, the evaluation comparison between T5-based models, including mT5, AraT5, and our ArabicT5, shows how pre-training corpora significantly affect the performance in the Gender-Rewriting task. Our ArabicT5, pre-trained on modern classical Arabic corpora (Arabic Encyclopedias and Arabic news articles), shows superiority against other models that use Arabic website collection and Twitter Datasets.

We use our best-performing model $ArabicT5_{xLarge}$ to submit our prediction for the blind test dataset of Gender Rewriting task (Alhafni et al., 2022c) at the Seventh Arabic Natural Language Processing Workshop (WANLP 2022).

5 Conclusion

In this paper, we introduced a new Arabic T5 model pre-trained on 17GB of Arabic corpora. Also, we illustrate how our ArabicT5 model shows a competitive evaluation performance against the current state-of-the-art model and other Seq2Seq T5 models. For future work, we plan to add further stages to our ArabicT5 model to improve the evaluation performance on the Gender-Rewriting task.

[4]Alhafni et al. (2022b) states that "The M2 scorer computes the precision (P), recall (R), and F0.5 by maximally matching phrase-level edits made by a system to gold-standard edits"

[5]The normalization script can be accessed through this link `https://github.com/CAMeL-Lab/gender-rewriting-shared-task/blob/master/utils/normalize.py`

Acknowledgements

The authors would like to acknowledge the ultimate support from Google Research Cloud TRC for providing access to Tensor Processing Unit TPU. We use resources given from TRC to pre-train and fine-tune our ArabicT5 model. The author also would like to thank Patil Suraj who release a suite of codes and examples with T5 model to the public community which make our work easier.

References

Bashar Alhafni, Nizar Habash, and Houda Bouamor. 2022a. The Arabic parallel gender corpus 2.0: Extensions and analyses. In *Proceedings of the Thirteenth Language Resources and Evaluation Conference*, pages 1870–1884, Marseille, France. European Language Resources Association.

Bashar Alhafni, Nizar Habash, and Houda Bouamor. 2022b. User-centric gender rewriting. In *Proceedings of the 2022 Conference of the North American Chapter of the Association for Computational Linguistics: Human Language Technologies*, pages 618–631, Seattle, United States. Association for Computational Linguistics.

Bashar Alhafni, Nizar Habash, Houda Bouamor, Ossama Obeid, Sultan Alrowili, Daliyah Alzeer, Khawlah M. Ashnqiti, Ahmed ElBakry, Muhammad ElNokrashy, Mohamed Gabr, Abderrahmane Issam, Abdelrahim Qaddoumi, K. Vijay-Shanker, and Mahmoud Zyate. 2022c. The shared task on gender rewriting. In *Proceedings of the Seventh Arabic Natural Language Processing Workshop*, Abu Dhabi, UAE. Association for Computational Linguistics.

Junyoung Chung, Caglar Gulcehre, KyungHyun Cho, and Yoshua Bengio. 2014. Empirical evaluation of gated recurrent neural networks on sequence modeling.

Kevin Clark, Minh-Thang Luong, Quoc V. Le, and Christopher D. Manning. 2020. ELECTRA: Pre-training text encoders as discriminators rather than generators. In *ICLR*.

Daniel Dahlmeier and Hwee Tou Ng. 2012. Better evaluation for grammatical error correction. In *Proceedings of the 2012 Conference of the North American Chapter of the Association for Computational Linguistics: Human Language Technologies*, pages 568–572, Montréal, Canada. Association for Computational Linguistics.

Jacob Devlin, Ming-Wei Chang, Kenton Lee, and Kristina Toutanova. 2019. BERT: Pre-training of deep bidirectional transformers for language understanding. In *Proceedings of the 2019 Conference of the North American Chapter of the Association for Computational Linguistics: Human Language Technologies, Volume 1 (Long and Short Papers)*, pages 4171–4186, Minneapolis, Minnesota. Association for Computational Linguistics.

Ibrahim Abu El-Khair. 2016. 1.5 billion words arabic corpus. *arXiv preprint arXiv:1611.04033*.

Taku Kudo and John Richardson. 2018. SentencePiece: A simple and language independent subword tokenizer and detokenizer for neural text processing. In *Proceedings of the 2018 Conference on Empirical Methods in Natural Language Processing: System Demonstrations*, pages 66–71, Brussels, Belgium. Association for Computational Linguistics.

Zhenzhong Lan, Mingda Chen, Sebastian Goodman, Kevin Gimpel, Piyush Sharma, and Radu Soricut. 2019. Albert: A lite bert for self-supervised learning of language representations.

Mike Lewis, Yinhan Liu, Naman Goyal, Marjan Ghazvininejad, Abdelrahman Mohamed, Omer Levy, Veselin Stoyanov, and Luke Zettlemoyer. 2020. BART: Denoising sequence-to-sequence pre-training for natural language generation, translation, and comprehension. In *Proceedings of the 58th Annual Meeting of the Association for Computational Linguistics*, pages 7871–7880, Online. Association for Computational Linguistics.

El Moatez Billah Nagoudi, AbdelRahim Elmadany, and Muhammad Abdul-Mageed. 2022. AraT5: Text-to-text transformers for Arabic language generation. In *Proceedings of the 60th Annual Meeting of the Association for Computational Linguistics (Volume 1: Long Papers)*, pages 628–647, Dublin, Ireland. Association for Computational Linguistics.

Colin Raffel, Noam Shazeer, Adam Roberts, Katherine Lee, Sharan Narang, Michael Matena, Yanqi Zhou, Wei Li, and Peter J. Liu. 2019. Exploring the limits of transfer learning with a unified text-to-text transformer.

Yi Tay, Mostafa Dehghani, Jinfeng Rao, William Fedus, Samira Abnar, Hyung Won Chung, Sharan Narang, Dani Yogatama, Ashish Vaswani, and Donald Metzler. 2021. Scale efficiently: Insights from pre-training and fine-tuning transformers.

Linting Xue, Noah Constant, Adam Roberts, Mihir Kale, Rami Al-Rfou, Aditya Siddhant, Aditya Barua, and Colin Raffel. 2021. mT5: A massively multilingual pre-trained text-to-text transformer. In *Proceedings of the 2021 Conference of the North American Chapter of the Association for Computational Linguistics: Human Language Technologies*, pages 483–498, Online. Association for Computational Linguistics.

Zhilin Yang, Zihang Dai, Yiming Yang, Jaime Carbonell, Ruslan Salakhutdinov, and Quoc V. Le. 2019. Xlnet: Generalized autoregressive pretraining for language understanding.

AraProp at WANLP 2022 Shared Task: Leveraging Pre-Trained Language Models for Arabic Propaganda Detection

Gaurav Singh
Independent Research
gauravsingh141116@gmail.com

Abstract

This paper presents our approach taken for the shared task on Propaganda Detection in Arabic at the Seventh Arabic Natural Language Processing Workshop (WANLP 2022). We participated in Sub-task 1, where the text of a tweet is provided, and the goal is to identify the different propaganda techniques used in it. This problem belongs to multi-label classification. For our solution, we leveraged different transformer-based pre-trained language models with fine-tuning to solve this problem. In our analysis, we found that MARBERTv2 outperforms in terms of performance, where macro-F1 is 0.08175 and micro-F1 is 0.61116 compared to other language models that we considered. Our method achieved rank 4 in the testing phase of the challenge.

1 Introduction

Two thirds of EU citizens say they see false news at least once per week (Commission et al., 2018). Propaganda, misinformation, and fake news have the power to polarise public opinion, to encourage hate speech and violent extremism, and ultimately to weaken democracies. In general terms, the spread of propaganda can be harmful to a nation and can hurt the sentiments of its people in a negative way. Currently, propaganda (or persuasion) techniques have been commonly used on social media to manipulate or mislead social media users.

There are instances where propaganda is used to divert attention from important issues by passing on fake and irrelevant information. Propaganda introduces prejudice, by hiding the other side of things, proving them wrong by introducing an element of hypocrisy rather than by logically analyzing the facts. In a similar fashion, propaganda can also hamper the critical analysis of things and stop any meaningful discussion. Some of the techniques by which propaganda is spread are loaded language, name calling, repetition, exaggeration/minimization, flag waving and many others. A detailed analysis of the other forms in which propaganda is spread is given by (Da San Martino et al., 2019). Since there are many forms through which propaganda can be spread, its detection requires a deeper analysis of the context in which the statement is made, rather than by directly labelling the whole document as propagandistic. The goal of the shared task is to build models for identifying such techniques in the Arabic social media text (specifically Tweets).

In the the shared task of Propaganda Detection in Arabic at WANLP 2022 (Alam et al., 2022), it consists of two subtasks (optional):

Subtask 1: Given the text of a tweet, identify the propaganda techniques used in it (multi-label classification problem).

Subtask 2: Given the text of a tweet, identify the propaganda techniques used in it together with the span(s) of text in which each propaganda technique appears. This is a sequence tagging task.

We participated in Subtask 1 of the same. We fine-tuned the pre-trained language models to predict the propaganda techniques for the given sentences. This is multi-label classification where more than one class can be present for identifying the sentence. We considered two multilingual language models and six Arabic language specific transformer (Vaswani et al., 2017) based language models for our analysis. We found that MARBERTv2 outperforms all other models for the specific designed experiment settings.

2 Related Work

The identification of propaganda was mainly at the level of articles. Rashkin et al. (2017) created a corpus of news articles, which were divided into four categories: propaganda, trusted, hoax, or satire. Articles from eight sources were included, two of which are propagandistic. In another work by (Da San Martino et al., 2019), they introduced a

Proceedings of the The Seventh Arabic Natural Language Processing Workshop (WANLP), pages 496 - 500
December 8, 2022 ©2022 Association for Computational Linguistics

novel task by performing fine-grained analysis of texts by detecting all fragments that contain propaganda techniques as well as their type. There were eighteen propaganda techniques described from a novel corpus of news articles manually annotated at the fragment level. Dimitrov et al. (2021a) proposed a new multi-label multimodal task for detecting propaganda techniques used in memes from a carefully annotated new corpus of 950 memes with 22 propaganda techniques in text, image, or both. In addition, a shared task for detecting persuasive techniques in text and images was introduced at SemEval 2021. (Dimitrov et al., 2021b).

3 Data

The data of subtask 1 consists of ids, text, and propaganda techniques as labels. An example is provided in Figure 1. In our investigation, we found only 18 out of 21 classes annotated in the list of techniques provided by the organizer given in the training data. Most frequently occurring class is Loaded Language (32.8%), followed by Name Calling/Labeling, no techniques, Smears and Appeal to fear/prejudice and rest of the classes (20.3%), can be seen in the Figure 2. For training the system, we used the same training, development, and test data as provided by the organizer and the split of the data is given in Table 1.


```
{
  "id": "1389927866356412416",
  "text": "\"ده مش معتقل ده أحسن من اللوكاندة\"، جدل وسخرية من
    زيارات تنظمها وزارة الداخلية للسجون #مصر https://t.co
    /VkkCrRjOCF",
  "labels": [
    "Exaggeration/Minimisation",
    "Smears"
  ]
}
```


Figure 1: An sample data format from given data for subtask 1.

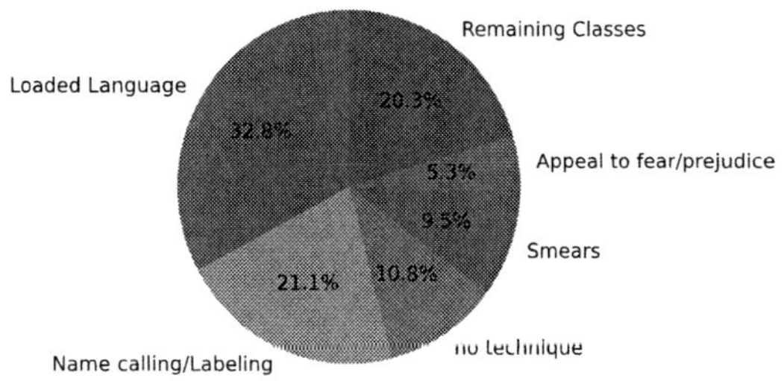

Figure 2: Class distribution in the training data including no technique.

Set	Number of Sample
Train	504
Development	52
Test	323

Table 1: Split of data provided by the organizer.

4 System Description

4.1 Model Description

In this work, we have used pre-trained transformer-based language models to identify the propaganda techniques in the sentences. Firstly, tokenized inputs were prepared based on the transformer-based language model's tokenizer for the given text, and then passed through the model, which produces contextualized word embeddings for all input tokens in our text. As we want a fixed-sized output representation, we need a pooling layer—several options like mean-pooling, max-pooling, min-pooling and many others. We simply average all contextualised word embeddings models by taking attention mask into account for correct averaging. Then, after a dropout layer was added, with a dropout rate of 0.3, we used stable dropout from the huggingface library because it is an optimised dropout model for stabilizing the training. A linear layer was added for projection into the prediction space based on the number of output classes, and a sigmoid activation function was added to each neuron output because we are dealing with multi-label classification problems.

We investigated multiple transformer-based language models, consisting of 2 multilingual models and 6 models specific to the Arabic language. A general overview showing the model architecture that we designed is depicted in Figure 3. We briefly describe the different transformer-based language models that we considered for Arabic propaganda detection.

bert-base-multilingual-cased: BERT (Devlin et al., 2018) is a transformer model pre-trained on a large corpus of multilingual data in a self-supervised fashion. A multilingual (mBERT) (Devlin et al., 2018) is a multilingual version of BERT. This model is case sensitive. It is pre-trained on the top 104 languages with the largest Wikipedia using a masked language modeling (MLM) objective.

xlm-roberta-base: RoBERTa (Liu et al., 2019) is a transformers model that was self-supervised pre-trained on a huge corpus. A multilingual version of RoBERTa is called XLM-RoBERTa (Conneau et al., 2019). 100 languages from 2.5TB of filtered Common Crawl data is used as its pre-training material.

bert-base-arabic: It is a pre-trained BERT base language model specifically designed for the Arabic language and was introduced by (Safaya et al., 2020). The pre-training procedure follows the training settings of BERT with some changes. It is trained for 3 million training steps with a batch size of 128, instead of 1 million with a batch size of 256. This model is pre-trained on ~8.2 billion words: Arabic version of OSCAR (Ortiz Suárez et al., 2020) - filtered from Common Crawl, Recent dump of Arabic Wikipedia and, other Arabic resources which sum up to ~95GB of text.

bert-base-arabert: AraBERT (Antoun et al.) is an Arabic pre-trained language model based on Google's BERT architecture (Devlin et al., 2018). It uses the same BERT-Base config. There is two versions of the model AraBERTv0.1 and AraBERTv1, with the difference being that AraBERTv1 uses pre-segmented text where prefixes and suffixes were split using the Farasa Segmenter (Darwish and Mubarak, 2016). We used AraBERTv1 for our task. The model is trained on 23GB of Arabic text consists of 70 million sentences with 3 billion words.

bert-base-arabertv2: This is similar to bert-base-arabert (Antoun et al.) but having few changes. The dataset consists of 77GB, equivalent to 200,095,961 lines or 8,655,948,860 words or 82,232,988,358 chars (before applying Farasa Segmentation). For the new dataset, authors added the unshuffled OSCAR corpus, after thoroughly filtering is done, to the previous dataset used in AraBERTv1 but with out the websites that authors previously crawled: OSCAR unshuffled and filtered (Ortiz Suárez et al., 2020), Arabic Wikipedia dump from 2020/09/01, the 1.5 billion words Arabic Corpus (El-Khair, 2016), the OSIAN Corpus (Zeroual et al., 2019) and, Assafir news articles. It used ~3.5 times more data, and trained for longer.

ARBERT: ARBERT (Abdul-Mageed et al., 2021) is a large-scale pre-trained masked language model focused on Modern Standard Arabic (MSA). For training, it used the same architecture as BERT-base: 12 attention layers, each has 12 attention heads and 768 hidden dimensions, a vocabulary of 100K Word Pieces, making ~163 million parameters. It is trained on a collection of Arabic datasets comprising 61 GB of text (6.2 billion tokens).

MARBERT: MARBERT (Abdul-Mageed et al., 2021) is a large-scale pre-trained masked language model focused on both Dialectal Arabic (DA) and MSA. Arabic has multiple varieties. To train it, randomly sampled 1 billion Arabic tweets from a large in-house dataset of about 6 billion tweets were obtained. Only considered those tweets with at least 3 Arabic words, based on character string matching, regardless of whether the tweet has a non-Arabic string or not. That is, authors did not remove non-Arabic so long as the tweet meets the 3 Arabic word criterion. The dataset makes up 128 GB of text (15.6 billion tokens). The same network architecture as ARBERT (BERT-base) is used, but without the next sentence prediction (NSP) objective since tweets are short.

MARBERTv2: From the results of ARBERT and MARBERT, they are not competitive on QA tasks. This can be because the two models are pre-trained with a sequence length of only 128, which does not allow them to sufficiently capture both a question and its likely answer within the same sequence window during the pre-training. To solve this problem, the authors further pre-train MARBERT on the same MSA data as ARBERT in addition to the AraNews dataset, but with a bigger sequence length of 512 tokens for 40 epochs. This pre-trained model called MARBERTv2 (Abdul-Mageed et al., 2021), to be noted it has 29 billion tokens.

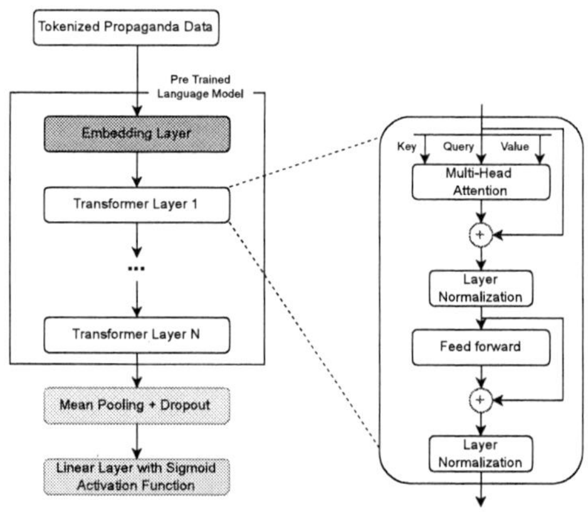

Figure 3: Fine-tuned model architecture with components built on the top of language model.

4.2 Experiment Settings

For our system, we fine-tuned the model architectures as discussed in Section 4.1. We used the AdamW (Loshchilov and Hutter, 2017) optimizer, and binary cross entropy has been used on the output layer. The system uses the same dataset as provided by the organizer. No other data has been used. There is no extra pre-training of language models that has been done. We did not apply any extra preprocessing to the text; we simply passed the full text to the tokenizer to create tokenized inputs for the model. We have provided metric scores as provided by the challenge's portal, i.e., macro-F1 and micro-F1. All the parameters, hyper-parameters and configurations are explained in Table 2. We used the Google Colab platform for training our system, which has 12.68 GB of RAM, a 14.75 GB NVIDIA Tesla T4 GPU, and Python language. Pytorch and the Huggingface library have been used for the implementation of the system.

Parameters	Values
Epoch	10
Learning Rate	5e-5
Weight Decay	1e-2
Batch Size	4
Max Length	64
Dropout Rate	0.3
Optimizer	AdamW
Activation Function	Sigmoid
Loss Function	Binary Cross Entropy

Table 2: Parameters used for training the system.

5 Results and Discussion

In Table 3, we scored the best macro-F1 score in the bert-base-arabic model, i.e., 0.16182, and the best micro-F1 score in the MARBERTv2 model, i.e., 0.61116. The performance analysis was done after the testing phase was completed. From a challenge perspective, micro-F1 is the official metric for scoring the submission. On that basis, the MARBERTv2 model outperforms all other models. The submitted result to the challenge portal during the testing phase is for the MARBERTv2 model, where we scored 0.600 as a micro-F1 score (see Table 4).

By carefully investigating Table 3, we can observe that the range of macro-F1 scores (minimum for bert-base-arabert and maximum for bert-base-arabic, with a range of 0.09527) is approximately three times the range of micro-F1 scores (minimum for mBERT-cased and maximum for MARBERTv2, with a range of 0.0389). Our hypothesis is that it is because of the highly unbalanced class distribution where about 5 classes constitute of 80% of all the labels and the rest of 20% labels are contributed by 13 classes.

Model	macro-F1	micro-F1
mBERT-cased	0.08468	0.57226
xlm-roberta-base	0.07632	0.59186
bert-base-arabic	**0.16182**	0.59735
bert-base-arabert	0.06655	0.59222
bert-base-arabertv2	0.09965	0.60140
ARBERT	0.13366	0.60448
MARBERT	0.06969	0.60343
MARBERTv2	0.08175	**0.61116**

Table 3: Performance scores of fine-tuned language models on testing data. Here, bert-base-multilingual-cased model referred as mBERT-cased.

Model	macro-F1	micro-F1
MARBERTv2	**0.105**	**0.600**

Table 4: Submitted model result from challenge portal in testing phase.

We understand that our approach is only applicable to more general aspects of Arabic propaganda detection. Further layers must be added to the setup to capture more specific knowledge about propaganda detection in the Arabic language specific to the given dataset.

6 Conclusion

In this work, our objective is to evaluate the performance of different transformer-based language models that are being built with simple fine-tuning. In the course of doing this, we achieved rank 4 on the challenge leaderboard without explicitly adding additional processing. We understand that propaganda detection is a challenging task. Our approach sets the baseline for the general aspects of Arabic propaganda detection. For future work, we can apply data augmentation, cross-validation, an ensemble of models, and further fine-tuning of model architecture specific to the task.

References

Muhammad Abdul-Mageed, AbdelRahim Elmadany, and El Moatez Billah Nagoudi. 2021. Arbert amp; marbert: Deep bidirectional transformers for arabic.

Firoj Alam, Hamdy Mubarak, Wajdi Zaghouani, Preslav Nakov, and Giovanni Da San Martino. 2022.

Overview of the WANLP 2022 shared task on propaganda detection in Arabic. In *Proceedings of the Seventh Arabic Natural Language Processing Workshop*, Abu Dhabi, UAE. Association for Computational Linguistics.

Wissam Antoun, Fady Baly, and Hazem Hajj. Arabert: Transformer-based model for arabic language understanding. In *LREC 2020 Workshop Language Resources and Evaluation Conference 11–16 May 2020*, page 9.

European Commission, Content Directorate-General for Communications Networks, and Technology. 2018. *Fake news and disinformation online*. Publications Office of the European Union.

Alexis Conneau, Kartikay Khandelwal, Naman Goyal, Vishrav Chaudhary, Guillaume Wenzek, Francisco Guzmán, Edouard Grave, Myle Ott, Luke Zettlemoyer, and Veselin Stoyanov. 2019. Unsupervised cross-lingual representation learning at scale. *CoRR*, abs/1911.02116.

Giovanni Da San Martino, Seunghak Yu, Alberto Barrón-Cedeño, Rostislav Petrov, and Preslav Nakov. 2019. Fine-grained analysis of propaganda in news article. In *Proceedings of the 2019 Conference on Empirical Methods in Natural Language Processing and the 9th International Joint Conference on Natural Language Processing (EMNLP-IJCNLP)*, pages 5636–5646, Hong Kong, China. Association for Computational Linguistics.

Kareem Darwish and Hamdy Mubarak. 2016. Farasa: A new fast and accurate Arabic word segmenter. In *Proceedings of the Tenth International Conference on Language Resources and Evaluation (LREC'16)*, pages 1070–1074, Portorož, Slovenia. European Language Resources Association (ELRA).

Jacob Devlin, Ming-Wei Chang, Kenton Lee, and Kristina Toutanova. 2018. BERT: pre-training of deep bidirectional transformers for language understanding. *CoRR*, abs/1810.04805.

Dimitar Dimitrov, Bishr Bin Ali, Shaden Shaar, Firoj Alam, Fabrizio Silvestri, Hamed Firooz, Preslav Nakov, and Giovanni Da San Martino. 2021a. Detecting propaganda techniques in memes. In *Proceedings of the 59th Annual Meeting of the Association for Computational Linguistics and the 11th International Joint Conference on Natural Language Processing (Volume 1: Long Papers)*, pages 6603–6617, Online. Association for Computational Linguistics.

Dimitar Dimitrov, Bishr Bin Ali, Shaden Shaar, Firoj Alam, Fabrizio Silvestri, Hamed Firooz, Preslav Nakov, and Giovanni Da San Martino. 2021b. SemEval-2021 task 6: Detection of persuasion techniques in texts and images. In *Proceedings of the 15th International Workshop on Semantic Evaluation (SemEval-2021)*, pages 70–98, Online. Association for Computational Linguistics.

Ibrahim Abu El-Khair. 2016. 1.5 billion words arabic corpus. *ArXiv*, abs/1611.04033.

Yinhan Liu, Myle Ott, Naman Goyal, Jingfei Du, Mandar Joshi, Danqi Chen, Omer Levy, Mike Lewis, Luke Zettlemoyer, and Veselin Stoyanov. 2019. Roberta: A robustly optimized bert pretraining approach.

Ilya Loshchilov and Frank Hutter. 2017. Decoupled weight decay regularization.

Pedro Javier Ortiz Suárez, Laurent Romary, and Benoît Sagot. 2020. A monolingual approach to contextualized word embeddings for mid-resource languages. In *Proceedings of the 58th Annual Meeting of the Association for Computational Linguistics*, pages 1703–1714, Online. Association for Computational Linguistics.

Hannah Rashkin, Eunsol Choi, Jin Yea Jang, Svitlana Volkova, and Yejin Choi. 2017. Truth of varying shades: Analyzing language in fake news and political fact-checking. In *Proceedings of the 2017 Conference on Empirical Methods in Natural Language Processing*, pages 2931–2937, Copenhagen, Denmark. Association for Computational Linguistics.

Ali Safaya, Moutasem Abdullatif, and Deniz Yuret. 2020. KUISAIL at SemEval-2020 task 12: BERT-CNN for offensive speech identification in social media. In *Proceedings of the Fourteenth Workshop on Semantic Evaluation*, pages 2054–2059, Barcelona (online). International Committee for Computational Linguistics.

Ashish Vaswani, Noam Shazeer, Niki Parmar, Jakob Uszkoreit, Llion Jones, Aidan N. Gomez, Lukasz Kaiser, and Illia Polosukhin. 2017. Attention is all you need.

Imad Zeroual, Dirk Goldhahn, Thomas Eckart, and Abdelhak Lakhouaja. 2019. OSIAN: Open source international Arabic news corpus - preparation and integration into the CLARIN-infrastructure. In *Proceedings of the Fourth Arabic Natural Language Processing Workshop*, pages 175–182, Florence, Italy. Association for Computational Linguistics.

TUB at WANLP 2022 Shared Task: Using Semantic Similarity for Propaganda Detection in Arabic

Salar Mohtaj[1,2] and Sebastian Möller[1,2]

[1]Quality and Usability Lab, Technische Universität Berlin, Berlin, Germany
[2]German Research Centre for Artificial Intelligence (DFKI), Labor Berlin, Germany
{salar.mohtaj|sebastian.moeller} @ tu-berlin.de

Abstract

Propaganda and the spreading of fake news through social media have become serious problems in recent years. In this paper, we present our approach for the shared task on propaganda detection in Arabic in which the goal is to identify propaganda techniques in the Arabic social media text. We propose a semantic similarity detection model to compare text in the test set with the sentences in the train set to find the most similar instances. The label of the target text is obtained from the most similar texts in the train set. The proposed model obtained a micro-F1 score of 0.494 on the test data set.

1 Introduction

Social media has played a crucial role in recent year, having a great impact on different areas such as communication, entertainment, and politics. Beside their positive applications, social networks became an easily accessible medium to spread disinformation and propaganda in recent years. Based on Hamilton (2021), propaganda differs from mis/disinformation in that it need not be false, but instead, it relies on rhetorical devices which aim to manipulate the audience into a particular belief or behavior (Hamilton, 2021).

In this paper we present our proposed approach for sub-task 1 of the propaganda detection in Arabic social media text shared task (*WANLP* 2022). *WANLP* 2022 shared task includes two sub-tasks; identifying the propaganda techniques in tweets as a multi-label text classification task, and identifying the propaganda techniques used in tweet together with the span(s) of text in which each propaganda technique appears as a sequence tagging task. We only submitted results for the first sub-task of the shared task. In this sub-task one or more propaganda techniques have been assigned to Arabic texts from social media (Alam et al., 2022). There are 21 propaganda techniques in the dataset that represent different approaches to manipulate the audience. More details about the different tasks can be found on the web-page of the shared task[1].

Although the first sub-task (identify the propaganda techniques) in a multi-label text classification problem, we used semantic textual similarity (STS) methods to identify related propaganda techniques to the instances in the test set. Based on the obtained results STS methods show competitive performance to the text classification models for the task.

The rest of the paper is organized as follow; Section 2 presents recent research on text based propaganda detection in social media. An overview of the data and the proposed approach are presented in Sections 3 and 4, respectively. We briefly review the obtained result and discuss it in Section 5. Finally, we conclude the paper and the system in Section 6.

2 Related Work

In this section we highlight some of the recent models for the task of propaganda detection using machine learning and Natural Language Processing (NLP) methods. The task of propaganda detection could be analyzed from two different perspectives; text analysis and network analysis perspectives (Martino et al., 2020). Here we focus on text analysis based models and review the recently developed models based on deep neural networks and pre-trained language models.

Vlad et al. (2019) proposed a model to detect propaganda in sentence level based on the BERT (Devlin et al., 2019) and an BiLSTM model. They formulated the task of propaganda detection as a binary classification task in which the model should distinguish propaganda and non-propaganda contents. The proposed model includes fine-tuning a pre-trained model on the task of emotion classification and feeding the output into a BiLSTM

[1]https://sites.google.com/view/propaganda-detection-in-arabic

Proceedings of the The Seventh Arabic Natural Language Processing Workshop (WANLP), pages 501 - 505
December 8, 2022 ©2022 Association for Computational Linguistics

architecture. The obtained results show that the model can significantly exceeds the baseline approach (Vlad et al., 2019).

In another study Vorakitphan et al. (2021) developed "protect" model for propaganda detection in text. As a propaganda detection pipeline, "protect" extract the text snippets from the input text, and then classify the technique of propaganda. The text snippets extractor module uses BERT pre-trained language model and feed the extracted text into the next step that is propaganda detection module. RoBERTa (Liu et al., 2019) pre-trained model is used for the classification task and propaganda detection.

As another research on propaganda detection as a text classification task, Barrón-Cedeño et al. (2019) proposed a binary text classifier based on different features includes readability level and writing style. They compared the performance of different supervised models such as logistic regression and SVMs for the task.

In addition to only text based models, some multimodal models have also been proposed in recent year to detect propaganda not only on text but also on images. As one of these efforts, a data set and a model are developed by Dimitrov et al. (2021) to propaganda identification in a multimodal setting. The compiled data set in this research contains 950 memes, each annotated with 22 propaganda techniques. It is collected from Facebook in includes different topics such as vaccines, COVID-19, and gender equality. They also proposed four different models, two unimodal and two multimodal models. For the unimodal setting, they used BERT and ResNet152 (He et al., 2016) for the text- and image-based models, respectively. The obtained results on the proposed data set show that the multimodal approach can outperform the unimodal training approaches.

In the proposed propaganda identification approach in this paper, we developed a model based on semantic similarity techniques unlike the highlighted researches in this section that formulated the task as a text classification problem.

3 Data

In this section we briefly describe the dataset for the first sub-task of *WANLP* 2022. The task organizers provided four data sets for sub-task 1 that includes train, development, dev_test and test sets. All the data sets are provided in *JSON* format that includes an id, the text of tweets and a list of labels for each instance.

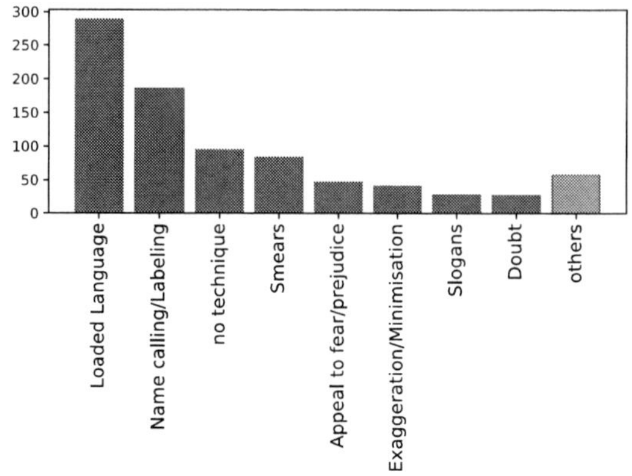

Figure 1: The distribution of top 8 most frequent propaganda techniques in the train set (504 data points). The "Others" represent the sum of the other techniques.

Table 1 highlights the main properties of the train and the test sets. As it is presented in the table, the instances in the test set tends to be shorter and also there are fewer number of words in the test set compared to the train data set.

There are a total number of 21 propaganda techniques in the data sets (Alam et al., 2022). Most of the techniques are presented and described in (Da San Martino et al., 2020). The distribution of ten most frequent techniques in the train set is depicted in Figure 1. As it is highlighted in the figure, "Loaded Language" is the most frequent propaganda techniques, followed by "Name calling/Labeling".

As the pre-processing step, we replaced twitter handles (i.e., the usernames) and URLs with constant texts ("username" and "weblink" respectively). These pre-processing steps have shown promising impact on the overal performance of related tasks like hate speech detection (Mohtaj et al., 2020). Although replacing URLs with the content of pages they refer to could be effective in related tasks like fake news detection (Mohtaj and Möller, 2022a), we decided to replace them with a constant text to prevent changing the length of input texts, drastically. The python regular expression package (re) has been used to replace the above mentioned texts in the data.

4 System

In this section we present the proposed model to detect the propaganda techniques in the social media

Attribute	Train set	Test set
Number of instance	504	323
Average length of instances (in words)	15.7	15.5
The length of longest instance (in words)	46	28
The length of shortest instance	5	6
Total number of words	7939	5273
Number of unique words	5069	3748

Table 1: The main properties of the train and the test sets.

text.

Although the first sub-task of the competition is a multi-label text classification task, we decided to use an STS based model to detect the most probable techniques for the instances in test set. From the provided definition for different propaganda techniques in (Da San Martino et al., 2020) and also from the provided data sets, lexicons play an important rule in a number of the techniques. For instance, "Loaded language" as the most frequent technique in the data set is defined as "using specific words and phrases with strong emotional implications to influence an audience" in (Da San Martino et al., 2020). Here, emotion lexicons are the main indicator of this propaganda technique.

Considering the role of lexicons and keywords on these techniques, using lists of related lexicons for each propaganda technique could show promising results on the task. However, due to lack of access to such resources in Arabic, we proposed an STS based approach to find the most similar instances in the train set to the unlabeled texts in the test set.

Word embedding models have shown promising performance on NLP tasks related to semantic textual similarity (e.g., plagiarism detection) (Asghari et al., 2019). However, it has been shown that the state-of-the-art contextual word embedding models (e.g., BERT) can outperform the traditional models in different NLP tasks like word similarity detection (Gupta and Jaggi, 2021) and hate speech and fake news detection (Mohtaj and Möller, 2022b). The overall proposed approach for *WANLP* 2022 to identify the most probable propaganda techniques for the instances in the test set is presented in Figure 2.

In the proposed model we used the Arabic BERT model (Safaya et al., 2020) to convert all the instances in the train and test sets into contextual vectors. We averaged word vectors to obtain the vector representation of sentences which resulted a vector with the length of 768 for each instance in the data sets. As the next step, we computed the cosine similarity between each instance in the test set (i.e., target sentence) with all of the instances in the train set. We took n most similar instance to the target sentence where the similarity is higher than a *threshold*. We named them as candidate sentences. Finally, top t frequent techniques in the candidate sentences have been chosen as the label of the target sentence. More details about the experiments are presented in Section 5.

5 Results and Discussion

In this section we briefly present our results based on the above mentioned model and discuss the main findings in the experiments.

As it is mentioned in the previous section, we tested three main hyper-parameters in our experiments; number of candidate sentences (n), minimum similarity threshold (*threshold*), and number of most frequent techniques to take from the candidate sentences (t). Table 2 summarizes the obtained results for different parameters on the validation set.

The Arabic BERT model has been used in all of the experiments to convert sentences to dense vectors. Although micro-F1 is the official evaluation metric that has been used by the shared task

Hyper-parameters			Macro F1	Micro F1
n	*threshold*	t		
20	0.4	3	**0.088**	0.475
10	0.4	3	0.072	0.459
5	0.4	3	0.065	**0.497**
5	0.5	3	0.058	0.435
5	0.5	1	0.036	0.298
10	0.5	1	0.037	0.310
5	0.6	3	0.009	0.050

Table 2: The obtained results by different hyper-parameters on the development set

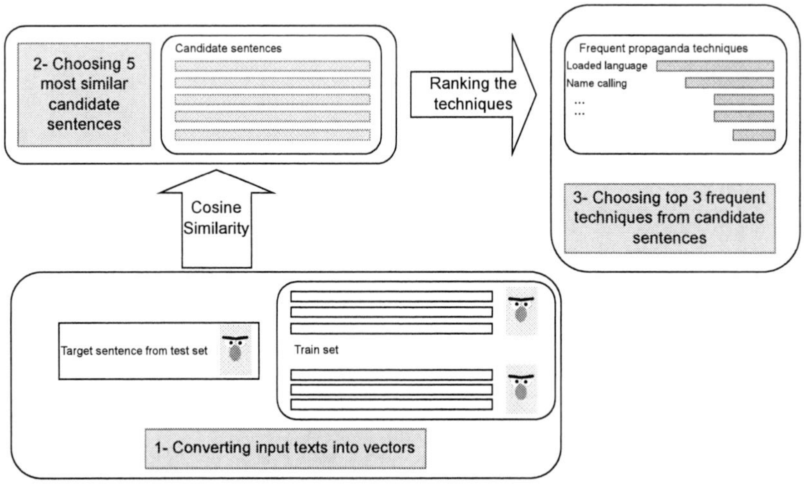

Figure 2: The overall process of choosing most probable propaganda techniques for a target sentence.

organizers to rank the models, the macro-F1 is also reported in the table. As it is highlighted in the table, the setting with 5 as the number of candidate sentences, 0.4 as the similarity threshold, and 3 as the number of top frequent propaganda techniques outperforms the other experiments. As a result, we submitted results on the test set based on this setting. The proposed model achieved the Micro F1 score of **0.494** and Macro F1 score of **0.076**.

One possibility to improve the overall performance of the proposed model would be using more than one hidden layer to convert the input text into vectors. In some studies on similar tasks like hate speech and fake news detection, it has been shown that using more than one layer for embedding could improve the performance of classification models (Mohtaj and Möller, 2022b).

6 Conclusion

In this paper we presented our model for the subtask 1 of the propaganda detection in Arabic social media text shared task (*WANLP* 2022). We proposed a model based on semantic textual similarity to compare instances in the test set with the labeled instances in the train set. The label of the test sentences obtained from the most similar sentences in the train set. Based on the results on the test set, the STS based model show a competitive performance compared to classification based models for the task.

For the future work, one can use different pretrained language models to convert raw input texts into vectors. Moreover, the hyper-parameters can be tuned in order to improve the overall performance of the model.

Acknowledgements

We would like to thank the organizers of *WANLP* 2022 shared task for organizing the competition and taking time on the inquiries.

References

Firoj Alam, Hamdy Mubarak, Wajdi Zaghouani, Preslav Nakov, and Giovanni Da San Martino. 2022. Overview of the WANLP 2022 shared task on propaganda detection in Arabic. In *Proceedings of the Seventh Arabic Natural Language Processing Workshop*, Abu Dhabi, UAE. Association for Computational Linguistics.

Habibollah Asghari, Omid Fatemi, Salar Mohtaj, Heshaam Faili, and Paolo Rosso. 2019. On the use of word embedding for cross language plagiarism detection. *Intell. Data Anal.*, 23(3):661–680.

Alberto Barrón-Cedeño, Israa Jaradat, Giovanni Da San Martino, and Preslav Nakov. 2019. Proppy: Organizing the news based on their propagandistic content. *Inf. Process. Manag.*, 56(5):1849–1864.

Giovanni Da San Martino, Alberto Barrón-Cedeño, Henning Wachsmuth, Rostislav Petrov, and Preslav Nakov. 2020. SemEval-2020 task 11: Detection of propaganda techniques in news articles. In *Proceedings of the Fourteenth Workshop on Semantic Evaluation*, pages 1377–1414, Barcelona (online). International Committee for Computational Linguistics.

Jacob Devlin, Ming-Wei Chang, Kenton Lee, and Kristina Toutanova. 2019. BERT: pre-training of deep bidirectional transformers for language understanding. In *Proceedings of the 2019 Conference of* the North American Chapter of the Association for Computational Linguistics: Human Language Technologies, NAACL-HLT 2019, Minneapolis, MN, USA, June 2-7, 2019, Volume 1 (Long and Short Papers), pages 4171–4186. Association for Computational Linguistics.

Dimitar Dimitrov, Bishr Bin Ali, Shaden Shaar, Firoj Alam, Fabrizio Silvestri, Hamed Firooz, Preslav Nakov, and Giovanni Da San Martino. 2021. Detecting propaganda techniques in memes. In *Proceedings of the 59th Annual Meeting of the Association for Computational Linguistics and the 11th International Joint Conference on Natural Language Processing (Volume 1: Long Papers)*, pages 6603–6617, Online. Association for Computational Linguistics.

Prakhar Gupta and Martin Jaggi. 2021. Obtaining better static word embeddings using contextual embedding models. In *Proceedings of the 59th Annual Meeting of the Association for Computational Linguistics and the 11th International Joint Conference on Natural Language Processing, ACL/IJCNLP 2021, (Volume 1: Long Papers), Virtual Event, August 1-6, 2021*, pages 5241–5253. Association for Computational Linguistics.

Kyle Hamilton. 2021. Towards an ontology for propaganda detection in news articles. In *The Semantic Web: ESWC 2021 Satellite Events*, pages 230–241, Cham. Springer International Publishing.

Kaiming He, Xiangyu Zhang, Shaoqing Ren, and Jian Sun. 2016. Deep residual learning for image recognition. In *2016 IEEE Conference on Computer Vision and Pattern Recognition, CVPR 2016, Las Vegas, NV, USA, June 27-30, 2016*, pages 770–778. IEEE Computer Society.

Yinhan Liu, Myle Ott, Naman Goyal, Jingfei Du, Mandar Joshi, Danqi Chen, Omer Levy, Mike Lewis, Luke Zettlemoyer, and Veselin Stoyanov. 2019. Roberta: A robustly optimized BERT pretraining approach. *CoRR*, abs/1907.11692.

Giovanni Da San Martino, Stefano Cresci, Alberto Barrón-Cedeño, Seunghak Yu, Roberto Di Pietro, and Preslav Nakov. 2020. A survey on computational propaganda detection. In *Proceedings of the Twenty-Ninth International Joint Conference on Artificial Intelligence, IJCAI 2020*, pages 4826–4832. ijcai.org.

Salar Mohtaj and Sebastian Möller. 2022a. The impact of pre-processing on the performance of automated fake news detection. In *Experimental IR Meets Multilinguality, Multimodality, and Interaction - 13th International Conference of the CLEF Association, CLEF 2022, Bologna, Italy, September 5-8, 2022, Proceedings*, volume 13390 of *Lecture Notes in Computer Science*, pages 93–102. Springer.

Salar Mohtaj and Sebastian Möller. 2022b. On the importance of word embedding in automated harmful information detection. In *Text, Speech, and Dialogue - 25th International Conference, TSD 2022, Brno, Czech Republic, September 6-9, 2022, Proceedings*, volume 13502 of *Lecture Notes in Computer Science*, pages 251–262. Springer.

Salar Mohtaj, Vinicius Woloszyn, and Sebastian Möller. 2020. TUB at HASOC 2020: Character based LSTM for hate speech detection in indo-european languages. In *Working Notes of FIRE 2020 - Forum for Information Retrieval Evaluation, Hyderabad, India, December 16-20, 2020*, volume 2826 of *CEUR Workshop Proceedings*, pages 298–303. CEUR-WS.org.

Ali Safaya, Moutasem Abdullatif, and Deniz Yuret. 2020. KUISAIL at SemEval-2020 task 12: BERT-CNN for offensive speech identification in social media. In *Proceedings of the Fourteenth Workshop on Semantic Evaluation*, pages 2054–2059, Barcelona (online). International Committee for Computational Linguistics.

George-Alexandru Vlad, Mircea-Adrian Tanase, Cristian Onose, and Dumitru-Clementin Cercel. 2019. Sentence-level propaganda detection in news articles with transfer learning and BERT-BiLSTM-capsule model. In *Proceedings of the Second Workshop on Natural Language Processing for Internet Freedom: Censorship, Disinformation, and Propaganda*, pages 148–154, Hong Kong, China. Association for Computational Linguistics.

Vorakit Vorakitphan, Elena Cabrio, and Serena Villata. 2021. PROTECT - A pipeline for propaganda detection and classification. In *Proceedings of the Eighth Italian Conference on Computational Linguistics, CLiC-it 2021, Milan, Italy, January 26-28, 2022*, volume 3033 of *CEUR Workshop Proceedings*. CEUR-WS.org.

SI2M & AIOX Labs at WANLP 2022 Shared Task: Propaganda Detection in Arabic, A Data Augmentation and Named Entity Recognition Approach

Kamel Gaanoun
SI2M Lab, INSEA
Rabat, Morocco
kgaanoun@insea.ac.ma

Imade Benelallam
SI2M Lab, INSEA
AIOX LABS
Rabat, Morocco
ibenelallam@aiox-labs.com

Abstract

This paper presents SI2M & AIOX Labs work among the propaganda detection in Arabic text shared task. The objective of this challenge is to identify the propaganda techniques used in specific propaganda fragments. We use a combination of data augmentation, Named Entity Recognition, rule-based repetition detection, and ARBERT prediction to develop our system. The model we provide scored 0.585 micro F1-Score and ranked 6th out of 14 teams.

1 Introduction

Even though the internet and social networks are tools for development and open doors to new opportunities, they also have a less attractive side. It is true that these tools are also used for bad purposes, such as the spread of propagandist messages when they are not identified as such by social media users. As part of cyber propaganda, or as part of the broader term "fake news" (Goswami, 2018), propaganda messages are used in social networks with the objective of convincing targeted populations in a biased way. Often, these messages aim to persuade their recipients to embrace ideas that are politically or ideologically motivated.

In light of the proliferation of such messages and the various upheavals the world is confronting today, researchers need to explore possible methods to detect cyber propaganda automatically. In contrast to English propaganda detection (Martino et al., 2020b), we note a flagrant lack of Arabic propaganda detection research, even if there are rare works dealing with this subject (Al-Ziyadi, 2019) or with close subjects like fake news (Nakov et al., 2022).

This work addresses this need, in order to build a system that can detect propaganda in tweets written in Arabic, as well as define the propaganda techniques employed. Indeed the dataset used in this paper contains 17 propaganda techniques, excluding "no technique", whose details are given by the organizers of the challenge (Alam et al., 2022) of which this work is part. Our system has the characteristic of combining a data augmentation method, Named Entity Recognition (NER), a rule-based approach, and the ARBERT model (Abdul-Mageed et al., 2020). The two main objectives are to answer the problem of the very limited amount of data available, and also to be able to detect as much as possible one of the most used propaganda techniques, namely "Name Calling/Labeling".

2 Related Work

Among the earliest definitions of propaganda is that of the Institute for Propaganda Analysis (Institute for Propaganda Analysis, 1938), which defined it in 1938 as "the expression of opinion or action by individuals or groups deliberately designed to influence opinions or actions of other individuals or groups with reference to predetermined end".

Apart from seeking the most comprehensive definition of the concept, several works have concentrated on categorizing propaganda techniques in order to better identify them. The first categorization was made by Clyde R. Miller (co-founder of the Institute for Propaganda Analysis) in 1937. Due to the proliferation of propaganda on social networks, these categorizations have become increasingly important over time due to the pressing need to detect propaganda automatically. The lack of annotated datasets dedicated to this problem, however, is one of the major obstacles. It was only in 2017 that the first datasets started to appear, namely the TSHP-17 (Rashkin et al., 2017), Qprop (Barrón-Cedeno et al., 2019) and PTC (Da San Martino et al., 2019b) in 2019.

In addition to detecting propaganda automatically, these datasets have also enabled us to detect the techniques in the texts in addition to specifying the relevant text fragments. Several works have emerged, mainly as system proposals within shared tasks. Like the Workshop on NLP4IF in

Proceedings of the The Seventh Arabic Natural Language Processing Workshop (WANLP), pages 506 - 510
December 8, 2022 ©2022 Association for Computational Linguistics

2019 (Da San Martino et al., 2019a) and SemEval-2020 Task 11 (Martino et al., 2020a), both based on the TPC corpus. In the two shared tasks, two objectives were targeted simultaneously, namely the detection of the propaganda texts and the specification of the article part in question. The most effective solutions proposed can be summarized in the use of BIO encoding (Morio et al., 2020), self-supervision with the RoBERTa Model (Jurkiewicz et al., 2020) and BERT word-level classification (Yoosuf and Yang, 2019).

3 Data

We received two datasets from the challenge organizers, one named Train for training the system, and the other named Dev for validating and selecting the best configuration. The datasets contain a list of sequences and the propaganda techniques contained within these sequences. Also, at the end of the challenge, we receive a third dataset to evaluate the system. Using this last dataset, named Test, the final scores of each team are calculated. There is also a second task for which the same data is provided along with the start and end of the techniques within each sequence.

Table 1: Datasets content

Dataset	Number of sequences
Train	504
Dev	52
Test	323

Table 1 shows the number of sequences included in each dataset. Moreover, we note that the Train dataset contains 17 propaganda techniques, while the Dev dataset contains 16. We present the distribution of these techniques in Table 2. There is an over-representation of "Loaded Language" and "Name Calling/Labeling", followed by "Exaggeration/Minimisation" and "Smears", whereas the other techniques are very scarce, such as "Thought-terminating cliché", "Flag-waving", "Causal Oversimplification", "Whataboutism", "Black-and-white Fallacy/Dictatorship", and "Presenting Irrelevant Data (Red Herring)", which only occurs six times at most.

Table 2: Propaganda techniques distribution

Propaganda technique	Train	Dev
Loaded Language	446	46
Name calling/Labeling	244	44
Smears	85	12
Appeal to fear/prejudice	48	7
Exaggeration/Minimisation	44	10
Slogans	44	1
Doubt	29	1
Glittering generalities (Virtue)	25	7
Appeal to authority	21	7
Obfuscation, Intentional vagueness, Confusion	9	3
Repetition	9	2
Thought-terminating cliché	6	1
Flag-waving	5	2
Causal Oversimplification	4	1
Whataboutism	3	1
Black-and-white Fallacy/Dictatorship	2	1
Presenting Irrelevant Data (Red Herring)	1	0

Additionally, we present the most frequent combinations of techniques within the Train dataset sequences in Figure 1.

4 System

In the following sections, we describe our four-step system.

4.1 Data augmentation

The first step is based on data augmentation. We use a strategy we call "MIX" adopted from (Gaanoun and Benelallam, 2020) work. The limited number of sequences available for training forces us to augment our data by generating synthetic sequences based on the mixture of subparts of the sequences we have. To do this, we take the following steps:

- Using Train and Dev sets including propaganda techniques tags (from second task data), we create a new dataset with one record per technique. The following is an example of retrieving two text chunks and their corresponding propaganda techniques:

  Sequence:

  [{'start': 1, 'end': 33, 'technique': 'Exaggeration/Minimisation', 'text': ده مش معتقل ده أحسن من اللوكاندة'},
  {'start': 37, 'end': 86, 'technique': 'Smears', 'text': «جدل وسخرية من زيارات تنظمها وزارة الداخلية للسجون»}]

Figure 1: Most frequent propaganda techniques combinations in Train set

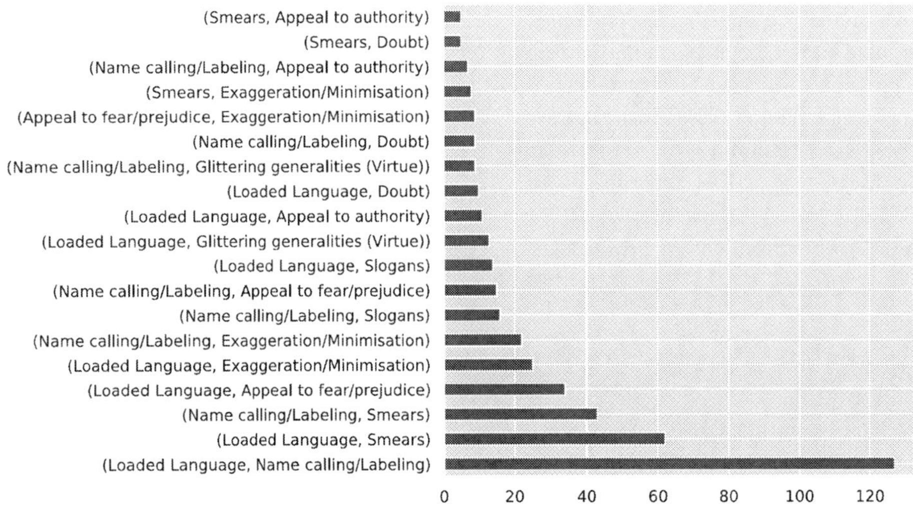

Produced records:

1. ده مش معتقل ده أحسن من اللوكاندة ، Exaggeration/Minimisation
2. جدل وسخرية من زيارات تنظمها وزارة الداخلية للسجون Smears

- Synthetic sequences composed of two techniques are created by randomly mixing the produced sequences. The final system is based on a mixed dataset of 2000 examples. To evaluate on the Dev set, the Mixed dataset is concatenated with the Train dataset. After the better system has been validated, we concatenate the Mixed Dataset with both Train and Dev to evaluate it on the Test Dataset.

4.2 ARBERT prediction

ARBERT is fine-tuned based on our training data in a multi-label configuration, resulting in a list of detected techniques and their associated probabilities. Using these predictions, we retain techniques with a probability higher than a threshold defined using the Dev set. We evaluate the results of a list of thresholds and select the one that yields the highest micro-F1 score for the Dev set. We select 0.3 as our threshold for assessing the Test set.

When no technique has a prediction probability greater than the selected threshold, we label it "No technique".

Table 3 presents ARBERT training configuration and used infrastructure.

Table 3: AEBERT and infrastructure configuration

GPU	NVIDIA Tesla T4
Hyperparameters	Epochs: 20, batch size:8, learning rate:5e-5, Embedding maximum length: 512
Training average time	14 minutes

4.3 Named Entity Recognition

Name calling and labeling are frequently used in propagandistic messages to target an organization or a person. The goal of this type of propaganda is to engender a predefined feeling towards the object of the propaganda, whether it is a personality, an organization, a group, etc. We have therefore made the link with the detection of organizations or persons in the texts and the use of the NER method in order to better detect this technique. In order to accomplish this, we use a model pre-trained on the NER task(Sahyoun, 2022) based on the AraBERT model (Antoun et al., 2020). When this model detects the entity "ORG" in the text, we consider it to include the technique of "Name calling/labeling". The entity "PER" for the detection of the quotation of persons was also tested but did not give better results, it was thus abandoned for our final system.

4.4 Repetition detection

The repetition of words is one propaganda technique used to convince the recipient that the message is true. To improve the detection of this technique we use a rule-based method while removing the Arabic stopwords available through the NLTK library. The repetition of one or two letter words is not considered in this step. Each time this method detects it and it is absent during ARBERT prediction, we add the "Repetition" technique.

Besides these 4 steps of the system, we also tried utilizing the PTC corpus (Da San Martino et al., 2020), which has the same purpose as the data used in this challenge, but is specific to English. Therefore, we proceeded to subtract the text chunks with their propaganda techniques. We then translated these chunks into Arabic using the Google Translate API[1]. Unfortunately, the use of this data did not improve the efficiency of the system, and was therefore not considered for further work.

5 Results

The results for the Dev and Test sets are presented in this section. To demonstrate the contribution of each of the steps considered in our system, we present the score obtained after applying each of these steps to the Dev set in Table 4. The final official results obtained on the Test set are presented in Table 5 .

Table 4: Dev set results for each step

Step	micro F1
Train set only	0.434
Mixed Data + Train set	0.455
Mixed Data + Train set + Repetition	0.459
Mixed Data + Train set + Repetition + NER (ORG)	0.56

Table 5: Official results on the Test set

micro F1	macro F1
0.585	0.137

We should point out that the official Test set result did not accounted for the label "No technique" in our predictions. This is because we used a capital N, whereas the organizers used a lowercase n for the final evaluation. The final result would have been 0.593 if this label had been considered.

[1]https://pypi.org/project/googletrans/

6 Discussion

The results show that the system's steps have a positive impact on the outcomes. Indeed, the score rises by 29% between the first step, which is solely based on the Train set, and the final step of the entire system. Furthermore, it appears that the use of NER has a significant effect on the final result, as the score knows the highest increase when using this method, recording a 22% increase. This finding is consistent with the fact that the name calling/labeling technique is the dataset's second most common technique. This result motivates future work to further investigate this idea by attempting to detect other majority techniques.

It is also worth noting that the data augmentation step contributed 5% to the improvement of the micro F1 score, whereas the detection of repetition contributed only 0.9%. The data augmentation step should be pushed in two directions: quantitatively by increasing the number of synthetic sequences generated, and structurally by prioritizing minority techniques or minority combinations in order to push the system to better predict these techniques.

7 Conclusion

This paper describes our contribution to the shared task of propaganda detection in WANLP 2022. We propose a system based on data augmentation, Named Entity Recognition (NER), repetition detection, and ARBERT prediction for subtask 1 dealing with multi-label classification techniques. Our analysis shows that NER and data augmentation have a significant impact on the final results, placing us sixth out of 14 competing teams.

References

Muhammad Abdul-Mageed, AbdelRahim Elmadany, and El Moatez Billah Nagoudi. 2020. Arbert & marbert: deep bidirectional transformers for arabic. *arXiv preprint arXiv:2101.01785*.

Wafa Saeed Murshid Al-Ziyadi. 2019. *Propaganda-based Classification of Arabic Newspapers*. Ph.D. thesis, Hamad Bin Khalifa University (Qatar).

Firoj Alam, Hamdy Mubarak, Wajdi Zaghouani, Preslav Nakov, and Giovanni Da San Martino. 2022. Overview of the WANLP 2022 shared task on propaganda detection in Arabic. In *Proceedings of the Seventh Arabic Natural Language Processing Workshop*, Abu Dhabi, UAE. Association for Computational Linguistics.

Wissam Antoun, Fady Baly, and Hazem Hajj. 2020. Arabert: Transformer-based model for arabic language understanding. *arXiv preprint arXiv:2003.00104*.

Alberto Barrón-Cedeno, Israa Jaradat, Giovanni Da San Martino, and Preslav Nakov. 2019. Proppy: Organizing the news based on their propagandistic content. *Information Processing & Management*, 56(5):1849–1864.

Giovanni Da San Martino, Alberto Barron-Cedeno, and Preslav Nakov. 2019a. Findings of the nlp4if-2019 shared task on fine-grained propaganda detection. In *Proceedings of the second workshop on natural language processing for internet freedom: censorship, disinformation, and propaganda*, pages 162–170.

Giovanni Da San Martino, Alberto Barrón-Cedeno, Henning Wachsmuth, Rostislav Petrov, and Preslav Nakov. 2020. SemEval-2020 task 11: Detection of propaganda techniques in news articles. In *Proceedings of the 14th Workshop on Semantic Evaluation*, SemEval '20, pages 1377–1414.

Giovanni Da San Martino, Seunghak Yu, Alberto Barrón-Cedeno, Rostislav Petrov, and Preslav Nakov. 2019b. Fine-grained analysis of propaganda in news article. In *Proceedings of the 2019 conference on empirical methods in natural language processing and the 9th international joint conference on natural language processing (EMNLP-IJCNLP)*, pages 5636–5646.

Kamel Gaanoun and Imade Benelallam. 2020. Arabic dialect identification: An arabic-bert model with data augmentation and ensembling strategy. In *Proceedings of the Fifth Arabic Natural Language Processing Workshop*, pages 275–281.

Manash Pratim Goswami. 2018. Fake news and cyber propaganda: A study of manipulation and abuses on social media. *Mediascape in 21st Century: Emerging Perspectives*, pages 535–544.

Institute for Propaganda Analysis. 1938. How to detect propaganda. *Bulletin of the American Association of University Professors (1915-1955)*, 24(1):49–55.

Dawid Jurkiewicz, ukasz Borchmann, Izabela Kosmala, and Filip Graliński. 2020. Applicaai at semeval-2020 task 11: On roberta-crf, span cls and whether self-training helps them. *arXiv preprint arXiv:2005.07934*.

G Martino, Alberto Barrón-Cedeno, Henning Wachsmuth, Rostislav Petrov, and Preslav Nakov. 2020a. Semeval-2020 task 11: Detection of propaganda techniques in news articles. *arXiv preprint arXiv:2009.02696*.

Giovanni Da San Martino, Stefano Cresci, Alberto Barrón-Cedeño, Seunghak Yu, Roberto Di Pietro, and Preslav Nakov. 2020b. A survey on computational propaganda detection. *arXiv preprint arXiv:2007.08024*.

Gaku Morio, Terufumi Morishita, Hiroaki Ozaki, and Toshinori Miyoshi. 2020. Hitachi at semeval-2020 task 11: An empirical study of pre-trained transformer family for propaganda detection. In *Proceedings of the Fourteenth Workshop on Semantic Evaluation*, pages 1739–1748.

Preslav Nakov, Alberto Barrón-Cedeño, Giovanni Da San Martino, Firoj Alam, Julia Maria Struß, Thomas Mandl, Rubén Míguez, Tommaso Caselli, Mucahid Kutlu, Wajdi Zaghouani, et al. 2022. The clef-2022 checkthat! lab on fighting the covid-19 infodemic and fake news detection. In *European Conference on Information Retrieval*, pages 416–428. Springer.

Hannah Rashkin, Eunsol Choi, Jin Yea Jang, Svitlana Volkova, and Yejin Choi. 2017. Truth of varying shades: Analyzing language in fake news and political fact-checking. In *Proceedings of the 2017 conference on empirical methods in natural language processing*, pages 2931–2937.

Abdulwahab Sahyoun. 2022. arabert-ner. `https://huggingface.co/abdusahmbzuai/arabert-ner`. [Online; accessed 05-September-2022].

Shehel Yoosuf and Yin Yang. 2019. Fine-grained propaganda detection with fine-tuned bert. In *Proceedings of the second workshop on natural language processing for internet freedom: censorship, disinformation, and propaganda*, pages 87–91.

iCompass at WANLP 2022 Shared Task: ARBERT and MARBERT for Multilabel Propaganda Classification of Arabic Tweets

Bilel Taboubi
bileltaboubi20@gmail.com

Bechir Brahem
bechir.brahem@outlook.com

Hatem Haddad
haddad.hatem@gmail.com

Abstract

Propaganda content has seen massive spread in the biggest social media networks. Major global events such as Covid-19, presidential elections, and wars have all been infested with various propaganda techniques. In participation in the WANLP 2022 Shared Task(Alam et al., 2022), this paper provides a detailed overview of our machine learning system for propaganda techniques classification and its achieved results. The task was carried out using pre-trained transformer based models: ARBERT and MARBERT. The models were fine-tuned for the downstream task in hand: multilabel classification of Arabic tweets. According to the results, MARBERT and ARBERT attained 0.562 and 0.567 micro F1-score on the development set of subtask 1. The submitted model was MARBERT which attained a 0.597 micro F1-score and got the fifth rank.

1 Introduction

Propaganda is one type of information that is shared deliberately for gaining political and religious influence. It is the systematic and deliberate way of shaping opinion and influencing the thoughts of a person for achieving the desired intention of a propagandist. In the age of "Post-truth" (Higgins, 2016), anti-scientific thinking and conspiracy theories the promotion of doctrines and ideologies that aim to manipulate and influence readers have rapidly spread through new communication mediums. In India, TV played a major role in the 2014 election, and some research has concluded that their results may have been swayed by propaganda techniques (Ward, 2014). Furthermore, social media platforms have known a widespread of propaganda, misinformation, and hate speech in their content. During the November 2012 Gaza conflict, Israel Defense Force and Hamas' Alqassam Brigades posted graphic images of death and suffering as well as explicit propaganda illustrations through their Twitter accounts(Seo, 2014). Social media platforms through their selective recommendation algorithms and their massive reach have fostered propaganda networks and "echo chambers" that amplify certain agendas and hide counter opinions and rebuttals. Propaganda actions may be now more effective than ever, representing a major global risk, possibly able to influence public opinion enough to alter election outcomes, decide wars, refuse Covid19 vaccines, and promote terrorism. For these reasons the need for modern automated and objective tools for uncovering propaganda is rising considerably.

2 Related Works

In the last few years research on detecting propaganda has seen a significant increase. The shared tasks found in workshops such as NLP4IF 2019(Yoosuf and Yang, 2019) and SemEval(Martino et al., 2020) (Semantic Evaluation) helped accelerate research on detecting propaganda and extracting the present propaganda techniques in a sentence or in a fragment of text. Also, apart from these workshops there exists work on binary classification of propaganda in the context of sentence-level and article-level(Oliinyk et al., 2020; Khanday et al., 2021).

On the other hand, Arabic propaganda detection research (Henia et al., 2021) is still lacking compared to its English counterpart (Taboubi et al., 2022). Our study presented in this paper attempts to classify propaganda techniques (multilabel classification) found in textual tweets using deep learning techniques and transformer architectures such as ARBERT and MARBERT.

3 Data

3.1 Data format and Characteristics

The data consists of a list of Arabic social media texts (tweets) and contained the list of propaganda techniques used in each tweet (table 1). The de-

Proceedings of the The Seventh Arabic Natural Language Processing Workshop (WANLP), pages 511 - 514
December 8, 2022 ©2022 Association for Computational Linguistics

tails of the dataset are reported in (Alam et al., 2022) and we used the dataset of task 1. The propaganda techniques used in the data are: Appeal to authority, Appeal to fear/prejudice, Black-and-white Fallacy/Dictatorship, Causal Oversimplification, Doubt, Exaggeration/Minimisation, Flag-waving, Glittering generalities (Virtue), Loaded Language, Misrepresentation of Someone's Position (Straw Man), Name calling/Labeling, Obfuscation, Intentional vagueness, Confusion, Presenting Irrelevant Data (Red Herring), Reductio ad hitlerum, Repetition, Slogans, Smears, Thought-terminating cliché, Whataboutism, Bandwagon, no technique. Our training dataset combined both files: "task1_dev.json" and "task1_train.json". This resulted in 556 data points. out of the 21 labels listed above, only 18 labels are present in the dataset. It is critical to note that the data is very unbalanced as some labels occur with orders of magnitude more than others. The propaganda technique "Loaded Language" was present in 346 tweets but "Presenting Irrelevant Data (Red Herring)" is present in only 2. This acute unbalance of the data is what pushed us to perform specific pre-processing methods on the data so that we give more chance to labels with lower frequency.

id	text	labels
7365	تحذيرات من حرب جديدة في حال فشل الانتخابات القادمة	Loaded Language Appeal to fear/prejudice
7375	"بوليساريو يروج زيفا لصور من ليبيا تدعي أنها لطائرة مغربية تم إسقاطها"	Smears Name calling/Labeling

Table 1: Two samples from our data. "text" is a string containing the Arabic tweet textual data. "labels" are the propaganda techniques used in the tweet

Figure 1 demonstrates the vast difference in the distribution of the labels' frequencies.

3.2 Data Preprocessing

Data preprocessing took the form of sequential steps listed here: remove emojis, normalization, remove links, remove special characters (i.e. ?,!,#), remove stop words.

4 System

To achieve the best results we have used language models (LMs) such as MARBERT and ARBERT (Abdul-Mageed et al., 2020). These models as their name suggest are based on the BERT (Bidirectional Encoder Representations from Transformers) (Devlin et al., 2018) language model which is a trained Transformer Encoder stack that uses bidirectional self-attention and was introduced by Google in 2018. While BERT focuses on the English language ARBERT and MARBERT were introduced to improve Arabic NLP tasks: ARBERT is pre-trained on standard Arabic language from sources such as Wikipedia and books. On the other hand, MARBERT focuses on dialectical Arabic. It is pre-trained on a large database of Arabic tweets On top of the BERT-based models, we have used global average pooling 1d and global max pooling 1d layers. Both of the pooling layers were concatenated and passed to a dropout layer and a final output layer.

We have tested both ARBERT and MARBERT with and without cross-validation. Cross-validation was done for 5 folds each with a percentage of 10% for the test. We also tested the models with and without the pooling layers. The training was done for 10 epochs using early stopping and we saved the best model on each epoch (according to the validation loss).

5 Results

We evaluated each model and each configuration at least 5 times and we calculated their mean and standard deviation. The results are plotted in (Fig 2)

F1 micro scores are presented in (table 2). From this table and its corresponding plot (Fig 2). From this table, we can see that the top 2 results are for ARBERT (without pooling and with cross-validation) mean: 0.567, std: 0.028 and MARBERT (with cross-validation and with pooling) mean: 0.562, std: 0.012. In the last two results, we have noted also their F1 macro scores: MARBERT mean:0.282, std: 0.023 and ARBERT mean: 0.243, std: 0.013

6 Conclusion

In this paper, we analyzed the performance of the pre-trained models ARBERT and MARBERT Despite the small-sized annotated data and huge unbalance presented in the provided data. To ob-

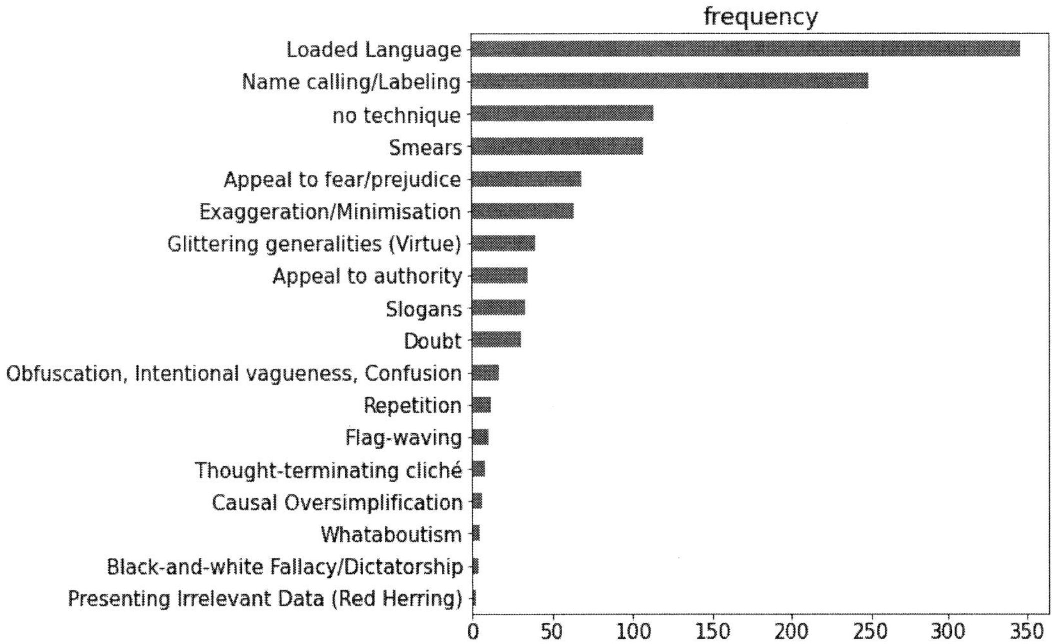

Figure 1: Horizontal bar plot that shows the distribution of the frequency of labels. It is clear from this plot that some labels are more present than others

with pooling		without pooling	
mean	std	mean	std
ARBERT with cross validation			
0.544	0.021	0.567	0.028
ARBERT without cross validation			
0.548	0.03	0.559	0.025
MARBERT with cross validation			
0.562	0.012	0.53	0.025
MARBERT without cross validation			
0.524	0.028	0.528	0.047

Table 2: Mean and standard deviation of the F1 micro score of the multiple runs for each model and training configuration

tain a good micro F1 measure for multilabel propaganda classification of Arabic tweets, different pre-processing techniques were applied to the data such as normalization, stopwords removal, etc. The submitted model MARBERT with pooling layers and trained with cross-validation splitting the data into 5 folds attained 0.597 for micro F1 and 0.191 macro F1 on the gold set reaching rank 5 on the leaderboard.

7 Limitations

Models attained unsatisfactory results for each of the micro and macro F1 measures and that is due to the low data distribution for many categories such as 'Whataboutism', and 'Black and white fallacy/Dictatorship'. Plus, the provided data was small in amount to train a model for multilabel classification with 18 categories. In the future, we will explore augmentation and resembling strategies to create a large balanced dataset for training and validating our proposed model and try to overcome our limitations.

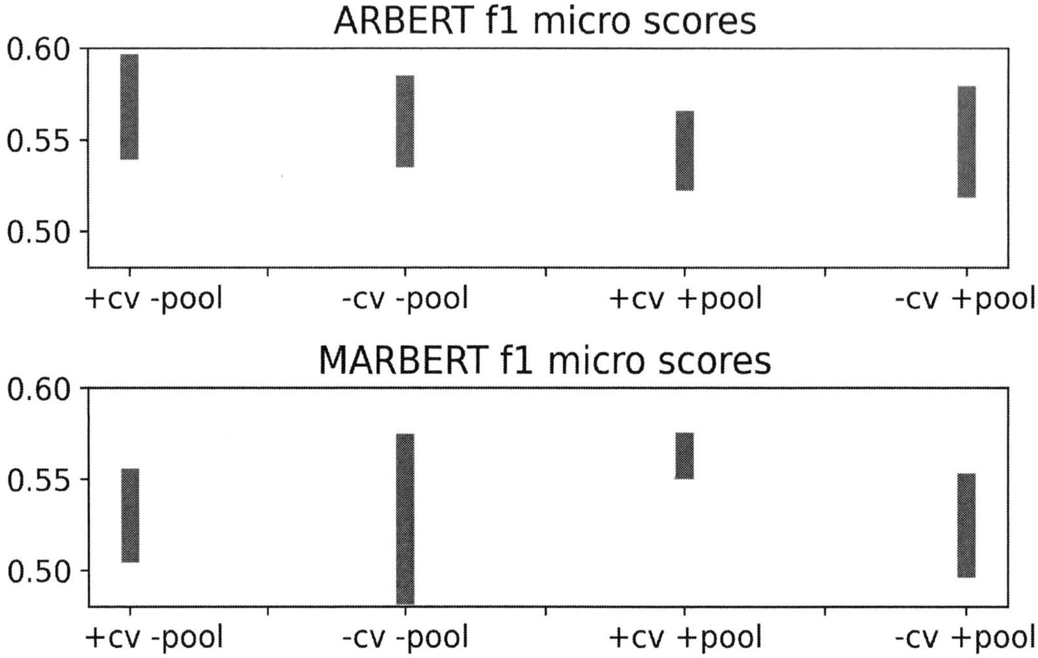

Figure 2: This figure plots the f1 micro scores and their errors for each training configuration. note that +cv (resp. -cv) means that the training was done with (resp. without) cross-validation. +pool (resp. -pool) means that the model used the two pooling layers (resp. did not use them)

References

Muhammad Abdul-Mageed, AbdelRahim Elmadany, and El Moatez Billah Nagoudi. 2020. Arbert & marbert: deep bidirectional transformers for arabic. *arXiv preprint arXiv:2101.01785*.

Firoj Alam, Hamdy Mubarak, Wajdi Zaghouani, Preslav Nakov, and Giovanni Da San Martino. 2022. Overview of the WANLP 2022 shared task on propaganda detection in Arabic. In *Proceedings of the Seventh Arabic Natural Language Processing Workshop*, Abu Dhabi, UAE. Association for Computational Linguistics.

Jacob Devlin, Ming-Wei Chang, Kenton Lee, and Kristina Toutanova. 2018. Bert: Pre-training of deep bidirectional transformers for language understanding. *arXiv preprint arXiv:1810.04805*.

Wassim Henia, Oumayma Rjab, Hatem Haddad, and Chayma Fourati. 2021. iCompass at NLP4IF-2021–fighting the COVID-19 infodemic. In *Proceedings of the second workshop on natural language processing for internet freedom: censorship, disinformation, and propaganda*, pages 115–118.

Kathleen Higgins. 2016. Post-truth: a guide for the perplexed. *Nature*, 540(7631):9–9.

Akib Mohi Ud Din Khanday, Qamar Rayees Khan, and Syed Tanzeel Rabani. 2021. Identifying propaganda from online social networks during covid-19 using machine learning techniques. *International Journal of Information Technology*, 13(1):115–122.

G Martino, Alberto Barrón-Cedeno, Henning Wachsmuth, Rostislav Petrov, and Preslav Nakov. 2020. Semeval-2020 task 11: Detection of propaganda techniques in news articles. *arXiv preprint arXiv:2009.02696*.

Vitaliia-Anna Oliinyk, Victoria Vysotska, Yevhen Burov, Khrystyna Mykich, and Vítor Basto Fernandes. 2020. Propaganda detection in text data based on nlp and machine learning. In *MoMLeT+ DS*, pages 132–144.

Hyunjin Seo. 2014. Visual propaganda in the age of social media: An empirical analysis of twitter images during the 2012 israeli–hamas conflict. *Visual Communication Quarterly*, 21(3):150–161.

B Taboubi, MAB Nessir, and H Haddad. 2022. icompass at checkthat! 2022: Combining deep language models for fake news detection. In *2022 Conference and Labs of the Evaluation Forum, CLEF 2022*, pages 694–701.

Patrick Ward. 2014. Modi and the tv media: propaganda or profits? *ElEctIon*, page 53.

Shehel Yoosuf and Yin Yang. 2019. Fine-grained propaganda detection with fine-tuned bert. In *Proceedings of the second workshop on natural language processing for internet freedom: censorship, disinformation, and propaganda*, pages 87–91.

ChavanKane at WANLP 2022 Shared Task: Large Language Models for Multi-label Propaganda Detection

Tanmay Chavan* and **Aditya Kane***
Pune Institute of Computer Technology, Pune
{chavantanmay1402, adityakane1}@gmail.com

Abstract

The spread of propaganda through the internet has increased drastically over the past years. Lately, propaganda detection has started gaining importance because of the negative impact it has on society. In this work, we describe our approach for the WANLP 2022 shared task which handles the task of propaganda detection in a multi-label setting. The task demands the model to label the given text as having one or more types of propaganda techniques. There are a total of 21 propaganda techniques to be detected. We show that an ensemble of five models performs the best on the task, scoring a micro-F1 score of 59.73%. We also conduct comprehensive ablations and propose various future directions for this work.

1 Introduction

The advent of social media has enabled people to view, create and share information easily on the internet. Such information can easily be accessed and viewed by a very large number of people in surprisingly short periods. Moreover, most social media websites have few restrictions over what the users choose to post and lack preemptive techniques to censor posts before they are uploaded. This has enabled the free flow of information from various strata of society which might have been restricted due to the lack of access to proper news sources. However, this has also led to a stark increase in the spread of propaganda through the internet. Information propagated through social media posts presents an individual's personal opinions, and hence is often biased and lacks rigorous fact-checking. Such problems are less frequently found in the original media sources of newspapers and TV news channels where their posts are subjected to a higher level of scrutiny.

The presence of propaganda online poses a serious threat to society as it can often polarize the majority opinion and lead to violent events. A wave of misinformation-based propaganda during the time of the COVID-19 pandemic(Cinelli et al., 2020) was observed. However, the problem of propaganda detection is much more complicated than it appears. The biggest challenge in propaganda detection is that the bulk of propaganda information is partially based on truths, but is presented in a manner that might be misleading or unnecessarily polarizing. It is also observed that propaganda posts are written professionally and are compelling which makes most of the readers believe the information to be authentic. All of these problems make it difficult to train a model to detect propaganda, and much more difficult to interpret the results of such models. The purpose of the shared task (Alam et al., 2022), a multi-label classification problem, is to come up with efficient methods for detecting propaganda on a dataset containing Arabic tweets.

Transformer-based models have achieved great success in text classification tasks. Additionally, ensemble-based models also outperform these individual models. Thus, we explore individual as well as ensemble of models for this task. Furthermore, we experimented with oversampling where we repeat the samples having minority labels. We also pretrained the DeHateBERT model on 1 million tweets to study the effect of domain-specific pretraining on downstream performance. We report the results of all these experiments and thereby propose an ensemble-based method for this task.

2 Related Work

Da San Martino et al. (2019) effectively addressed the problem of quantifying different types of propaganda into seventeen categories, which helps us distinguish between different types of propaganda. They also presented a corpus that contains information classified according to the seventeen classes. Previous shared tasks have generated successful results. The SemEval 2020 task 11 (Da San Mar-

*Equal contribution

Proceedings of the The Seventh Arabic Natural Language Processing Workshop (WANLP), pages 515 - 519
December 8, 2022 ©2022 Association for Computational Linguistics

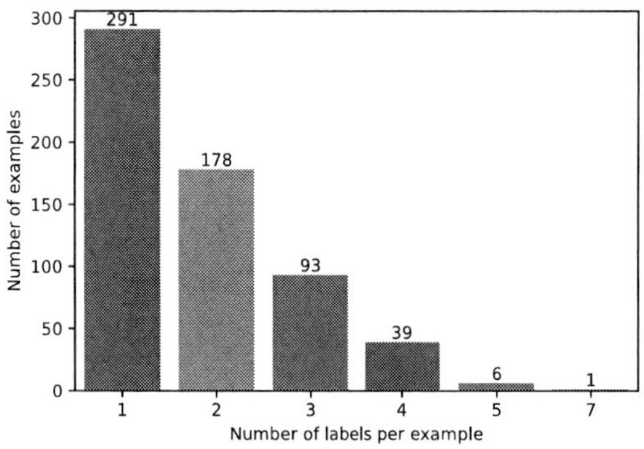

Figure 1: Distribution of label counts

tino et al., 2020) used the PTC corpus for building models to detect and classify propaganda. The SemEval task 6 (Dimitrov et al., 2021) helped develop novel approaches to detect propaganda in a multimodal environment. Yu et al. (2021) studied the topic of interpretability of propaganda detection and presented an interpretable model.

The use of BERT-based models which are pretrained on a large corpus has proven to yield better performance than most of the other deep learning-based approaches without pre-training(Min et al., 2021). There are several BERT models pre-trained on massive Arabic datasets available. We test some of these models for the task. AraBERT (Antoun et al., 2020), MARBERT, ARBERT (Abdul-Mageed et al., 2021) are some examples. However, most of these models are pretrained on structured data which significantly differs from tweets. Research has shown that domain-specific pretraining can yield better performance than general text pretraining(Brady, 2021). Hence, we used DeHateBERT (Aluru et al., 2020).

3 Data

The dataset consists of 504 training examples, 52 validation examples, and 52 testing examples. Our models were finally evaluated on a separate testing dataset, which consisted of 323 examples. Each example can have one or more of the 20 propagandist techniques[1]. Thus, it was a multi-label dataset. The number of label occurrences is illustrated in Figure 2. As shown in the figure, we see a skewed distribution. This shows that there is an imbalance. Given this problem of multi-label classification with a high class imbalance, we experimented with several architectures and found that DeHateBERT performed the best on the dataset. A full account of all of our successful experiments, as well as failed experiments, is given in Sections 5 and 6. We try multiple methods to mitigate this imbalance, as elaborated in Section 6. Since the dataset is a multi-label dataset, used one-hot encoding for each label to denote the ground truth labels.

Furthermore, we make some key observations about the number of labels per example in Figure 1. We observe that most examples have one label per example. We see that the number of examples having more than one label diminishes quickly, with only one example having 7 labels.

We use basic preprocessing to minimize the noise in the inputs. Firstly, we remove all links in the tweet. Then we remove the user mentions and hashtags (denoted by "@" and "#" followed by a string respectively). Finally, we replace underscores ("_") with space. This way, the separated words contribute to the semantics of the sentence. Note that we retain the emojis in the sentence since they also carry significant meaning and can aid the model to better detect sentiment.

4 System

Given this problem of multi-label classification with a high class imbalance, we experimented with several architectures and found that DeHateBERT performed the best on the dataset. A full account of all of our successful experiments, as well as failed experiments, is given in Sections 5 and 6.

We tried several models, namely AraBERT v1, v02 and v2, MARBERT, ARBERT, XLMRoBERTa (Conneau et al., 2020), AraELECTRA (Antoun et al., 2021). Note that the difference between AraBERTv2 and AraBERTv02 is that the former uses presegmented text whereas the latter uses the Farasa Segmenter (Darwish and Mubarak, 2016) to segment the text since Arabic is a language which requires its words to be segmented before being fed into the tokenizer. We used a specific variant of DeHateBERT, which is initialized from multilingual BERT and fine-tuned only on Arabic datasets. We found that this particular variant performed the amongst the best, in terms of micro-F1 on the test split of our dataset. Our model training is fairly straightforward. We train DeHateBERT on our multi-label dataset for 30 epochs and the best performing epoch is chosen based on validation micro-

[1] Complete list of propagandist techniques can be found at https://propaganda.qcri.org/annotations/definitions.html

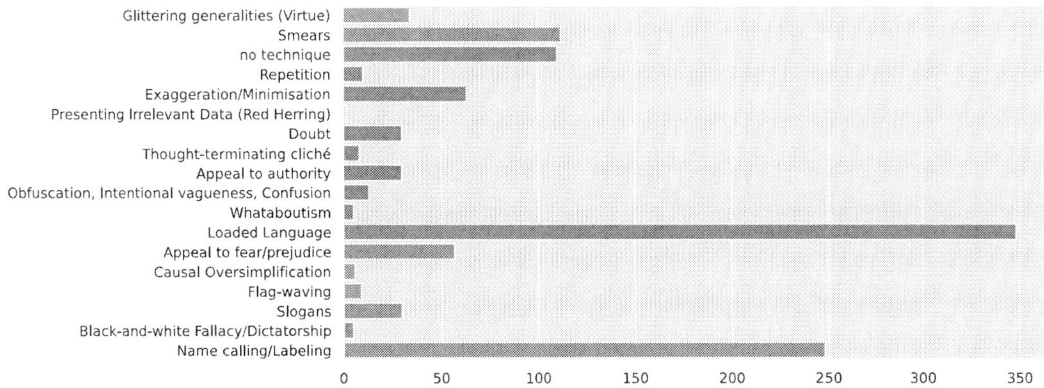

Figure 2: Data distribution

F1. We used a learning rate of $3e-6$. Note that we use binary cross-entropy loss, since we have multi-hot labels in our dataset.

We also create an ensemble of all the models. We use the five models namely DeHateBERT, ARBERT, AraBERTv02, AraBERTv01, and MARBERT. Our ensemble system is shown in Figure 3. We use the method of hard voting to obtain the final results. For each sample, we recorded the predicted labels of each of the five models. Then, for each of the 21 labels present, we check how many models predict that label. If majority of the models predict the label, we include that label for the sample in the ensemble output. We find that the ensemble of models had the best performance.

The dataset has a significant class imbalance. To overcome this, we tried to augment the dataset by oversampling. For oversampling, we duplicated the samples containing less frequent target classes. Thus we obtained a larger dataset containing duplicate samples but overall having lesser class imbalance. However, this did not yield better performance. We discuss this in detail in Section 6.

5 Results

The official scoring metric for the shared task is the F1 micro score. We present the results of the various models we tried in Table 1. We have used the official scorer module provided by the organizers. We can see that the ensemble has the highest score. MARBERT and DeHateBERT have roughly similar scores and perform better than other models. This can lead us to speculate that a model might perform better at classification tasks if it is pretrained on a corpus containing data from a similar source than a corpus with similar characteristics but having data from a different source. The oversampled DeHateBERT model has a lower performance compared to the model trained on the original dataset.

We can however see that ARBERT outperforms all other single models. Another key observation is that ARBERT outperforms MARBERT, which in turn outperforms all variants of AraBERT. An explanation for this is that AraBERT variants are trained on far less data than ARBERT and MARBERT. In the case of ARBERT and MARBERT, ARBERT is pretrained on a wide variety of sources as opposed to MARBERT and thus has better performance than MARBERT.

We can also speculate that the high performance of the ensemble is because the constituent models are pretrained on different datasets. This enables the ensemble to capture a wider array of semantic vocabulary and hence is better at predicting classes. The hard voting mechanism ensures that the ensemble will not predict too many classes for each sample and thus limits the number of false positives.

6 Discussion

We conducted several experiments apart from our best-performing model. Specifically, we tried pretraining on a large Arabic sentiment analysis tweet dataset as well as oversampling the classes having few samples.

We retrained the DeHateBERT model on 1 Million tweets from the Large Arabic Twitter Data for Sentiment Analysis dataset using the Masked Language Modeling technique. We found that pretraining on the sentiment analysis tweet dataset did not result in any gains to the model. We speculate

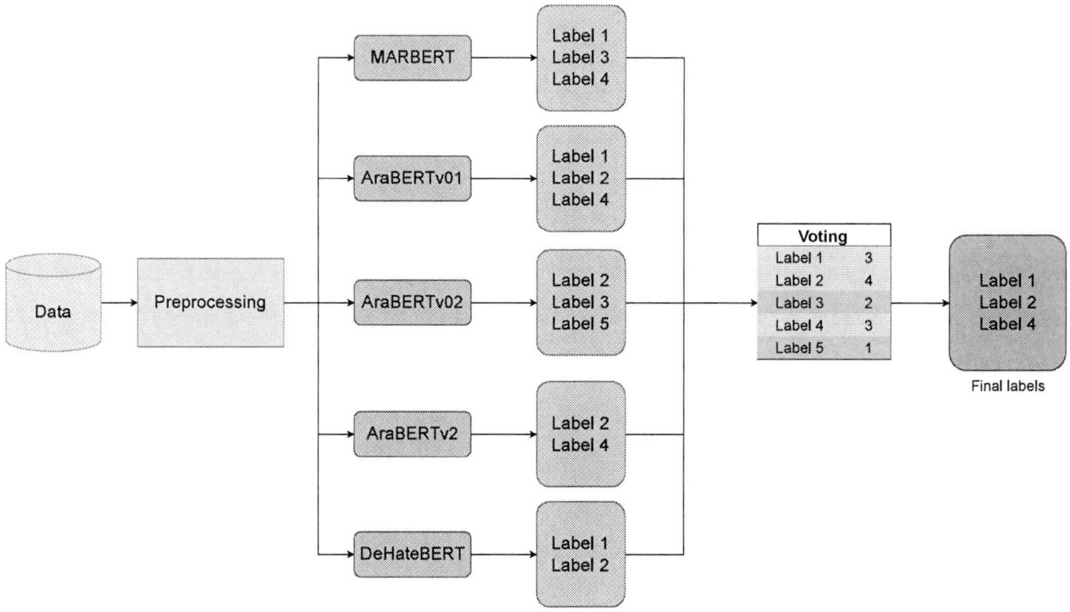

Figure 3: Ensemble system diagram. The ensemble works using a system of hard voting, wherein the prediction of each model is recorded and if the majority of models predict that label then it is declared to be one of the predicted labels. This figure illustrates this process in the multi-label setting.

Model	Micro-F1
AraBERTv01	54.195
AraBERTv2	50.841
AraBERTv02	53.996
AraBERTv02-twitter	54.135
DeHateBERT	56.484
Oversampling + DeHateBERT	52.529
MARBERT	**56.556**
ARBERT	**59.048**
Ensemble	**59.725**

Table 1: Results of our experiments on the WANLP-22 propaganda detection task dataset.

this is primarily because the number of tweets we pretrained the model on is less than the size the model was originally pretrained on.

In another attempt, we implement oversampling in the dataset, where we repeat samples of less frequent classes. We calculate the average number of examples for each class. Then, we get the oversampling factor, that is the number of times the examples must be repeated to reach the average number of samples. We further clip this factor to 10. Note that, since this is a multi-label scenario, we need to be careful not to use examples with the most frequently occurring classes, in which case the process will have no effect.

Currently, we use hard voting for choosing the final output of the ensemble. We believe better results can be obtained by having a more sophisticated method like using an SVM instead of hard voting.

7 Conclusion

This paper aims to articulate our approach for the WANLP 2022 Shared Task. We experimented with multiple transformer-based models, namely AraBERT, ARBERT, MARBERT and others. We also present ablations with monolingual pretraining, oversampling, and ensemble of the aforementioned transformer-based models. We show that the ensemble consisting of models pretrained on various sources of data has the best performance, with a Micro-F1 score of 59.73%. We foresee several possible future directions. One line of work can be to improve the ensemble mechanism as well as to better handle the class imbalance in multi-label setting. Another line of work can be to study the effects of domain-specific pretraining on downstream classification tasks like multi-label classification.

Acknowledgement

We thank Neeraja Kirtane for her reviews and inputs to this paper.

References

Muhammad Abdul-Mageed, AbdelRahim Elmadany, and El Moatez Billah Nagoudi. 2021. ARBERT & MARBERT: Deep bidirectional transformers for Arabic. In *Proceedings of the 59th Annual Meeting of the Association for Computational Linguistics and the 11th International Joint Conference on Natural Language Processing (Volume 1: Long Papers)*, pages 7088–7105, Online. Association for Computational Linguistics.

Firoj Alam, Hamdy Mubarak, Wajdi Zaghouani, Preslav Nakov, and Giovanni Da San Martino. 2022. Overview of the WANLP 2022 shared task on propaganda detection in Arabic. In *Proceedings of the Seventh Arabic Natural Language Processing Workshop*, Abu Dhabi, UAE. Association for Computational Linguistics.

Sai Saketh Aluru, Binny Mathew, Punyajoy Saha, and Animesh Mukherjee. 2020. Deep learning models for multilingual hate speech detection. *CoRR*, abs/2004.06465.

Wissam Antoun, Fady Baly, and Hazem Hajj. 2020. AraBERT: Transformer-based model for Arabic language understanding. In *Proceedings of the 4th Workshop on Open-Source Arabic Corpora and Processing Tools, with a Shared Task on Offensive Language Detection*, pages 9–15, Marseille, France. European Language Resource Association.

Wissam Antoun, Fady Baly, and Hazem Hajj. 2021. AraELECTRA: Pre-training text discriminators for Arabic language understanding. In *Proceedings of the Sixth Arabic Natural Language Processing Workshop*, pages 191–195, Kyiv, Ukraine (Virtual). Association for Computational Linguistics.

Oliver J. Brady. 2021. Aitbert : Domain specific pretraining on alternative social media to improve hate speech classification.

Matteo Cinelli, Walter Quattrociocchi, Alessandro Galeazzi, Carlo Michele Valensise, Emanuele Brugnoli, Ana Lucia Schmidt, Paola Zola, Fabiana Zollo, and Antonio Scala. 2020. The COVID-19 social media infodemic. *Scientific Reports*, 10(1).

Alexis Conneau, Kartikay Khandelwal, Naman Goyal, Vishrav Chaudhary, Guillaume Wenzek, Francisco Guzmán, Edouard Grave, Myle Ott, Luke Zettlemoyer, and Veselin Stoyanov. 2020. Unsupervised cross-lingual representation learning at scale. In *Proceedings of the 58th Annual Meeting of the Association for Computational Linguistics*, pages 8440–8451, Online. Association for Computational Linguistics.

Giovanni Da San Martino, Alberto Barrón-Cedeño, Henning Wachsmuth, Rostislav Petrov, and Preslav Nakov. 2020. SemEval-2020 task 11: Detection of propaganda techniques in news articles. In *Proceedings of the Fourteenth Workshop on Semantic Evaluation*, pages 1377–1414, Barcelona (online). International Committee for Computational Linguistics.

Giovanni Da San Martino, Seunghak Yu, Alberto Barrón-Cedeño, Rostislav Petrov, and Preslav Nakov. 2019. Fine-grained analysis of propaganda in news article. In *Proceedings of the 2019 Conference on Empirical Methods in Natural Language Processing and the 9th International Joint Conference on Natural Language Processing (EMNLP-IJCNLP)*, pages 5636–5646, Hong Kong, China. Association for Computational Linguistics.

Kareem Darwish and Hamdy Mubarak. 2016. Farasa: A new fast and accurate Arabic word segmenter. In *Proceedings of the Tenth International Conference on Language Resources and Evaluation (LREC'16)*, pages 1070–1074, Portorož, Slovenia. European Language Resources Association (ELRA).

Dimitar Dimitrov, Bishr Bin Ali, Shaden Shaar, Firoj Alam, Fabrizio Silvestri, Hamed Firooz, Preslav Nakov, and Giovanni Da San Martino. 2021. SemEval-2021 task 6: Detection of persuasion techniques in texts and images. In *Proceedings of the 15th International Workshop on Semantic Evaluation (SemEval-2021)*, pages 70–98, Online. Association for Computational Linguistics.

Bonan Min, Hayley Ross, Elior Sulem, Amir Pouran Ben Veyseh, Thien Huu Nguyen, Oscar Sainz, Eneko Agirre, Ilana Heinz, and Dan Roth. 2021. Recent advances in natural language processing via large pre-trained language models: A survey.

Seunghak Yu, Giovanni Da San Martino, Mitra Mohtarami, James Glass, and Preslav Nakov. 2021. Interpretable propaganda detection in news articles. In *Proceedings of the International Conference on Recent Advances in Natural Language Processing (RANLP 2021)*, pages 1597–1605, Held Online. INCOMA Ltd.

SIREN AI at WANLP 2022 Shared Task: AraBERT Model for Propaganda Detection

Mohamad Sharara, Wissam Mahmoud, Ralph Tawil, Ralph Chobok, Wolf Assi and Antonio Tannoury

Abstract

Nowadays, the rapid dissemination of data on digital platforms has resulted in the emergence of information pollution and data contamination, specifically mis-information, mal-information, dis-information, fake news, and various types of propaganda. These topics are now posing a serious threat to the online digital realm, posing numerous challenges to social media platforms and governments around the world. In this article, we propose a propaganda detection model based on the transformer-based model AraBERT, with the objective of using this framework to detect propagandistic content in the Arabic social media text scene, with purpose of making online Arabic news and media consumption healthier and safer. Given the dataset, our results are relatively encouraging, indicating a huge potential for this line of approaches in Arabic online news text NLP.

1 Introduction

People are moving away from traditional media and toward digital content in today's landscape, and with trust in traditional media at an all-time low of 32% (according to a Gallup Inc. poll), it's no surprise that people are turning to alternative sources for news. Furthermore, social media has recently evolved into a major source of news content, giving rise to the "fake news" phenomenon (S. Shaden et al., 2021), in which a large amount of false information circulates, often with malicious intent (P. Nakov et al., 2021). The associated propaganda, which is almost always present in fake news, is an important but often overlooked feature of such destructive content (S. Yu et al., 2021). The primary goal of propaganda is to influence the opinions of target individuals through language manipulation (D. Dimitrov et al., 2021). There are over 313 million people worldwide who speak Arabic, with roughly 90% of them getting their news from the internet and online content. Furthermore, the prevalence of "fake news" in online content, as well as its amplification by social platforms, poses a number of serious challenges to society (D. Marc et al., 2020). Propaganda techniques, for example, Obfuscation, Black or White Fallacy, Loaded language, Name calling, Straw man, Red Herring, Whataboutism, and others, can pose grave threats to society, economy, democracy, health, journalism, the environment, and a variety of other areas.

While there have been recent studies that developed machine learning models to detect fake news in a variety of languages (N. Preslav et al., 2021), the lack of research into Arabic is, to say the least, concerning. Propaganda Detection in Arabic is a collaborative effort (F. Alam et al., 2022) to combat fake news by developing models for identifying propaganda techniques in Arabic social media text. So far, recent efforts to detect propaganda in news items around the world (G. Da San Martino et al., 2019) have addressed this as a fine-grained problem of finding it within fragments, and as a result, transformer-based embeddings work reasonably well in such detection approaches.

As a result, in this article, we attempt to achieve the goal of our contributions by following the flow:

- Data processing (given a small balanced dataset)
- Design a transformer model prototype oriented to Arabic propaganda detection
- Optimize the algorithm using the ADAM optimizer
- Examine and evaluate F1 score performance

Proceedings of the The Seventh Arabic Natural Language Processing Workshop (WANLP), pages 520 - 523
December 8, 2022

2 Data

The dataset provided by the competition organizers (F. Alam et al., 2022) consisted of 504 Arabic tweets for training, each labeled by no more than five of several propaganda techniques. The no-technique label, which indicates that no propaganda technique was used in the tweet, was one of the labels. The majority of tweets were classified with one or two labels. In addition, a development set of 52 labeled tweets and a test set of 52 labeled tweets were provided. In terms of the total number of each label in the set and the number of labels per tweet, the latter two sets followed the same distribution as the training set. There was a total of 18 distinct labels, including the no-technique label. Labels included loaded language, Name calling, exaggeration, and so on.

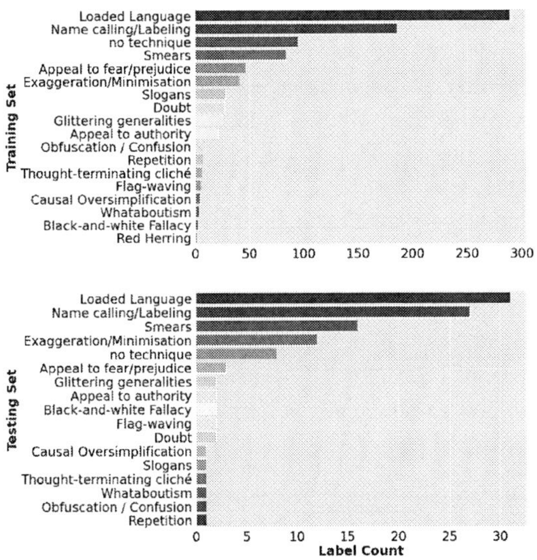

Figure 1: Label distribution across training and testing sets

The AraBERT model (W. Antoun et al., 2020) preprocessor was used to preprocess the training and testing sets. Preprocessing includes removing HTML markup, diacritics, tatweel, non-digit repetitions, and mapping Hindi numbers to Arabic, among so many other things. The highly skewed distribution of labels is a significant challenge in the competition. And, because the datasets are just so small, the model will be biased toward the most abundant label.

3 System

The model used for training is the AraBERT model's second version (W. Antoun et al., 2020). AraBERT is a powerful, cutting-edge transformer-based model for Arabic Language Understanding that has the same configuration as the base BERT model: twelve encoder blocks, twelve attention heads, seven hundred and sixty-eight hidden dimensions, five hundred and twelve maximum sequence lengths, and a total of approximately one hundred and ten parameters. The model included pre-trained embeddings that had been trained on approximately seventy million sentences from various sources.

The model was trained in the Google Collaboratory using a Tesla V100-SXM2-16GB GPU. The training set was divided into batches of sixteen each, with a gradient accumulation step of two, and an evaluation batch size of one hundred and twenty-eight. The optimization algorithm used is the ADAM optimizer, with an epsilon value of 10^{-8}, a learning rate of 0.00002, and iterates over twenty-five epochs. The overall training process took about five minutes, thanks to GPU parallelization. The model generates 18 probabilities, each of which corresponds to a propaganda technique, including no technique.

We used the following methodology to determine the output labels for each tweet based on those probabilities. We took the top five predictions from each tweet and discarded the rest. This is due to the fact that no tweet had more than 5 labels in the original data.

We had to optimize the threshold that will be used to filter out low probabilities from the top five. After some experimentation, we noticed that the most similar distribution was obtained with an optimal threshold of 0.35, assuming that the label distributions in the training, testing, and validation sets were the same.

We considered that if one of the remaining labels was 'no-technique', the corresponding tweet's labels would be all labels with a probability greater than that of the no-technique label. Otherwise, the tweet will be labeled as no-technique.

We merged the three labeled datasets before predicting the labels of the unlabeled datasets and submitting the samples after training, validating, and testing on the datasets and reaching the optimal configuration.

4 Results

Because the competition organizers set the Micro-F1 score as the primary metric to evaluate the performance of the models, we used it to examine our model performance. This is primarily due to the fact that our task is simply to maximize the number of correct predictions made by the classifier, and no class is more important than the other. In the table below, we show the experimental results of applying AraBERT to the multi-label classification problem for Arabic propaganda detection:

Metric	Training loss	Validation loss	Macro-F1 score	Micro-F1 score
Score	0.19	0.3	0.108	0.4108

Table 1: Performance of our developed model on the test dataset

It is worth noting that we were able to achieve a Micro-F1 of 0.61 while using data augmentation and attempting to optimize the classification layer weights. Due to other deadlines, this result was not submitted. A Micro-F1 score of 0.578 on the evaluation dataset was a very promising result that will be improved using the methods described in the following section.

5 Discussion

Given that the Micro-F1 score on the training set is around 0.88, it is clear that the training data is overfit. The used model is cutting-edge and does a good job of capturing the data's complexity. However, the true issue is that the dataset is not representative enough for the model to generalize outside of it.

To improve the model's performance outside of the training set, the first step would be to add a regularization to the model, such as L2 regularization, to reduce overfitting. However, given the small dataset size, this may not be so promising. The second optimization approach would be to augment the existing data by performing some transformation on the documents, such as random insertion, random deletion, and word swapping. The latter method will increase data diversity at a lower cost than collecting brand new labeled data. A third approach that could be used is to use class weights to compensate for class imbalances by penalizing misclassification by infrequent classes (flag-waving, for example) more than that of more abundant classes. Given enough time, the most time-consuming but effective thing that could be done is to collect or manually label more propaganda-related tweets so that we have more representative data for real-world tasks.

6 Conclusion

In this paper, we presented a transformer-based model that serves as a contribution framework to identify propaganda types in Arabic text social media content (tweets basically), by highlighting the propaganda strategies utilized (such as Obfuscation, Black or White Fallacy, Loaded language, Name calling, Straw man, Red Herring, Whataboutism, and others).

With a Micro-F1 score of 0.578 and given the relatively small dataset, the model appears promising, and we are confident that performance improvements can be expected with a more balanced and richer dataset.

We intend to improve the model in the future by focusing more on the labeled dataset and expanding it by either applying careful, well-structured augmentation to some data or by developing a platform to assist annotators in labeling data. This ensures that the model is constantly updated and improved. Furthermore, we intend to conduct extensive research on various aspects of propaganda in order to develop a general propaganda detection system, thereby broadening the scope of our work in relation to the existing platform, with the goal of making the online Arabic journey healthier and safer.

7 Acknowledgments

This work was supported by Siren Analytics. We thank our colleagues who provided insight and expertise that greatly assisted the research. We want to thank our senior AI engineers, Wissam Antoun and Fady Baly who provided insights and expertise that greatly assisted the research and implementation phase. We also want to thank Dr. Elie Badine, our AI Lead, for his advice and observations, which helped to improve this paper.

References

P. Nakov and G. Da San Martino, *"Fake News, Disinformation, Propaganda, and Media Bias," in Proceedings of the 30th ACM International Conference on Information & Knowledge Management, 2021, p. 4862–4865.*

S. Yu, G. Da San Martino, M. Mohtarami, J. Glass, and P. Nakov, *"Interpretable Propaganda Detection in News Articles," in Proceedings of the International Conference on Recent Advances in Natural Language Processing (RANLP 2021), 2021, p. 1597–1605.*

Alam Firoj, Mubarak Hamdy, Zaghouani Wajdi, Nakov Preslav and Da San Martino, Giovanni *"Overview of the WANLP 2022 Shared Task on Propaganda Detection in Arabic." Proceedings of the Seventh Arabic Natural Language Processing Workshop, Association for Computational Linguistics, 2022.*

G. Da San Martino, S. Yu, A. Barrón-Cedeno, R. Petrov, and P. Nakov, *"Fine-grained analysis of propaganda in news article," in Proceedings of the 2019 conference on empirical methods in natural language processing and the 9th international joint conference on natural language processing (EMNLP-IJCNLP), 2019, p. 5636–5646.*

Antoun Wissam, Fady Baly, and Hazem Hajj. *" AraBERT: Transformer-based model for arabic language understanding." arXiv preprint arXiv:2003.00104 (2020).*

Shaar Shaden, Firoj Alam, Giovanni Da San Martino, and Preslav Nakov. *"The role of context in detecting previously fact-checked claims." arXiv preprint arXiv:2104.07423 (2021).*

Nakov Preslav, David Corney, Maram Hasanain, Firoj Alam, and Tamer Elsayed. *"Automated Fact-Checking for Assisting Human Fact-Checkers." in IJCAI, 2021.*

Dimitar Dimitrov, Bishr Bin Ali, Shaden Shaar, Firoj Alam, Fabrizio Silvestri, Hamed Firooz, Preslav Nakov and Giovanni Da San Martino, *Detecting Propaganda Techniques in Memes, ACL, 2021.*

Djandji Marc, Antoun Wissam, Fady Baly, and Hazem Hajj. *" Multi-Task Learning using AraBert for Offensive Language Detection." in Proceedings of the 4th Workshop on Open-Source Arabic Corpora and Processing Tools, with a Shared Task on Offensive Language Detection, 2020, p.97-101.*

AraBEM at WANLP 2022 Shared Task: Propaganda Detection in Arabic Tweets

Eshrag A. Refaee
Faculty of Computer Sciences
Jazan University
erefaie@jazanu.edu.sa

Basem H. Ahmed
Dept. of computer science
Alaqsa University
basem@alaqsa.edu.ps

Motaz K. Saad
Faculty of Info Technology
The Islamic University of Gaza
msaad@iugaza.edu.ps

Abstract

Propaganda is information or ideas that an organised group or government spreads to influence peopleś opinions, especially by not giving all the facts or secretly emphasising only one way of looking at the points. The ability to automatically detect propaganda-related language is a challenging task that researchers in the NLP community have recently started to address. This paper presents the participation of our team AraBEM in the propaganda detection shared task on Arabic tweets. Our system utilised a pre-trained BERT model to perform multi-class binary classification. It attained the best score at 0.602 micro-f1, ranking third on subtask-1, which identifies the propaganda techniques as a multilabel classification problem with a baseline of 0.079.

1 Introduction

With the increasing popularity of social media (SM) in our modern society, social media platforms like Twitter have become essential means for influencing others. People on social media tend to convey their views and perspectives more freely. The ability of SM users to freely express their views has allowed interested parties to profile users based on how they express their opinions on social media. As such, the past few years have witnessed a great interest in targeting a broader spectrum of audiences via Twitter and other SM platforms. Parties like political and advertisement campaigns are competing to reach out to the broadest audience base possible and hence influence the general publicś view. It can be seen that the more ability a particular part has to influence peopleś opinions, the more powerful it becomes (Ferrara, 2017).

The term propaganda is defined in the Cambridge dictionary as information or ideas that an organised group or government spreads to influence people's opinions by not giving all the facts or secretly emphasising only one way of looking at the facts.[1] The spread of propaganda exploits the anonymity of the Internet, the micro-profiling ability of SM platforms, and the power of automatically creating and managing coordinated networks of accounts to reach a large number of SM users with persuasive messages (Martino et al., 2020). Spreading propaganda to promote a specific agenda has become a business (Chatfield et al., 2015).

In this context, the concept of automatic propaganda detection has risen recently (Alam et al., 2022). Researchers have focused on utilising state-of-the-art NLP techniques to develop systems for automatic propaganda detection. The main challenges in this regard include difficulty identifying and extracting the linguistic signs of propaganda use. This is particularly difficult due to the cunning and indirect ways propaganda can be expressed. As such, detecting propaganda-related techniques can be challenging even for a human expert. Regarding Arabic, propaganda detection can be a more challenging task due to several additional factors, including the limited availability of linguistic resources (e.g., corpus) and the morphologically-rich nature of the Arabic language (Refaee, 2017).

To bridge this research gap, a shared task about auto-detection of propaganda in Arabic social media has been launched.[2] subtasks in this shared task and a comprehensive description of the shared task are discussed in (Alam et al., 2022). In this work, our team participated in the first subtask-1, ranking our system in the third position.

2 Related Work

The literature on propaganda detection as an NLP task reveals an increasing interest in exploring this

[1] The Cambridge Dictionary. Available at:https://dictionary.cambridge.org/dictionary/english/propaganda Accessed on 03/10/2022

[2] EMNLP-2022, SHARED TASK ON PROPAGANDA DETECTION IN ARABIC. Available at https://sites.google.com/view/propaganda-detection-in-arabic/home?authuser=0 Accessed on 02/09/2022

Proceedings of the The Seventh Arabic Natural Language Processing Workshop (WANLP), pages 524 - 528
December 8, 2022 ©2022 Association for Computational Linguistics

research area (Martino et al., 2020). Previous work on propaganda detection indicates several common challenges associated with this task. Specifically, the limited availability of the annotated dataset, the ability to convey propaganda with means other than text (e.g., images) (Hashemi and Hall, 2019) and the difficulty of spotting direct and indirect propaganda techniques are among the most prominent challenges of the task of propaganda detection. A total of eighteen propaganda techniques have been identified in previous work. However, experts stated that propaganda techniques are not fixed and keep evolving (Martino et al., 2020).

Previous work on propaganda detection has mainly focused on English (Chaudhari and Pawar, 2022), as a well-resourced language. In addition, researchers highlighted that most propaganda-related languages tend to appear in biased news and SM platforms, unleashing different directions like promoting political agendas and radicalisation (Albadi et al., 2019). (Chaudhari and Pawar, 2022) summarised the features utilised in existing systems for detecting propaganda techniques. This includes user-based, time-based, metadata-based and context-based features, n-grams, and pre-trained models (e.g., BERT).

In (Heidarysafa et al., 2020), the authors performed text mining on some of the propaganda content published by ISIS to recruit women from around the world. The authors applied a lexical-based emotion analysis method to detect emotions most likely to be evoked in readers of these materials.

Regarding propaganda detection in Arabic, literature shows that few previous attempts have been made to address this issue (Hashemi and Hall, 2019; Abozinadah et al., 2015; Albadi et al., 2019). This need has provoked the lunching of a shared task of propaganda detection in Arabic and releasing a newly built dataset annotated specifically for propaganda techniques (Alam et al., 2022).

3 Data

In this work, we utilise the dataset released for the shared task described in this overview paper (Alam et al., 2022). Table 1 shows the characteristics of the corpus. Our team performed cleaning up and pre-processing using the steps utilised in previous NLP tasks on Arabic (Refaee, 2017, 2021):

- Normalising exchangeable Arabic letters: mapping letters with various forms (i.e., *alef and Hamza* and *yaa*) to their representative characters (Antoun et al., 2020).
- Text segmentation: was performed to separate the tokens based on spaces and punctuation marks using the tokeniser provided by the PyArabic package (Zerrouki, 2010).[3]
- Removing diacritics, any special characters, punctuation, non-alphabetic characters and repeated characters, e.g., *loooool.*
- Normalising URLs, usernames, and hashtags.

Data	Training	Dev.	Testing
Size	504	52	323
# of Tokens	7792	747	4994
Avg. # of Tokens	15.46	14.36	15.46
# of Chars	51602	6436	34027
Avg. # of Chars	1102.38	123.76	105.34

Table 1: Size of the dataset split.

Class	Dist.
Misrepresentation of Someone's Position (Straw Man)	0
Reductio ad hitlerum	0
Presenting Irrelevant Data (Red Herring)	1
Black-and-white Fallacy/Dictatorship	2
Whataboutism	3
Causal Oversimplification	4
Flag-waving	5
Thought-terminating cliché	6
Repetition	7
Obfuscation, Intentional vagueness, Confusion	9
Appeal to authority	21
Glittering generalities (Virtue)	25
Doubt	27
Slogans	28
Exaggeration/Minimisation	41
Appeal to fear/prejudice	47
Smears	84
Name-calling/Labeling	186
Loaded Language	289

Table 2: Class Distribution in The Training Corpus

[3]PyArabic is a publicly available Python library explicitly designed for the Arabic language. Available at `https://pypi.org/project/PyArabic/` accessed on 20/9/2022.

An initial observation reveals highly unbalanced classes in the obtained dataset, as shown in Table 2. Some classes have zero instances in the training set. Our team opted not to apply any technique to tackle class unbalancing. Instead, we decided to experiment with the original class distribution to explore how it would affect the overall system performance. It can also be seen that some propaganda techniques are more frequently occurring than others. For instance, the most commonly spotted propaganda techniques were *loaded language*, *name-calling*, and *labelling*. On the other hand, we noticed nearly a hundred tweets with no methods, which we decided to exclude from the dataset.

4 System

We explored approaches used in previous work on detecting propaganda or misleading language in social media. We noted that previous systems utilised different methods ranging from traditional machine learning (Habernal et al., 2017) to modern neural-based systems (Chetan et al., 2019).

Our team decided to use a pre-trained model, specifically BERT, which has performed well in previous work on propaganda detection in the news (Vlad et al., 2019; Badawy and Ferrara, 2018). The model has also been successfully used to detect auto-generated Arabic tweets, aiming to spot propaganda accounts (Harrag et al., 2021). We use BERT for multi-class binary label classification. The token size we use is 70 based on our calculation of the average tweet length. The output of running BERT on the shared-task dataset is several tensors, each associated with the possibility of the presence of propaganda techniques. To decide on the threshold, we ran several experiments and used the threshold 0.2, showing that any value above this threshold would be considered a presence of a propaganda technique. A possible future expansion of this work can include experimenting with a different threshold for each propaganda technique to test its impact on the overall system performance. We fine-tuned the pre-trained model using the training and development data.[4]

5 Results and discussion

We used the script the shared task organisers provided to evaluate our system. The best results submitted by our system were reported at a micro F-1 score of 0.602, ranking third place in the leaderboard of the shared task. The details of all results can be found in (Alam et al., 2022). Overall, the scores attained by the participating systems reflect the difficulty of the task of auto-detection of propaganda language in Arabic tweets. We believe a possible explanation is a small size and highly unbalanced annotated dataset provided with the shared task. Identifying and annotating propaganda techniques can be challenging even for a human expert, (Panda and Levitan, 2021) and as such, expanding the scale of the dataset by using methods like data augmentation might help improve the performance. Another issue is that some propaganda techniques, are more frequently used than others, like *loaded language*. As mentioned in section 3 and table 2, some classes have zero or very few train instances. In contrast, others are either less regularly used or can be conveyed cunningly, making them hard to detect and identify. Overall, the results of the shared task indicate that more research is still required to identify misinformation in Arabic more accurately.

Class	P	R	F1
Appeal to authority	0.00	0.00	0.00
Appeal to fear / prejudice	0.00	0.00	0.00
Black-and-white Fallacy / Dictatorship	0.00	0.00	0.00
Causal Oversimplification	0.00	0.00	0.00
Doubt	0.00	0.00	0.00
Exaggeration / Minimisation	0.00	0.00	0.00
Flag-waving	0.00	0.00	0.00
Glittering generalities (Virtue)	0.00	0.00	0.00
Loaded Language	0.72	0.97	0.83
Misrepresentation of Someone's Position (Straw Man)	0.00	0.00	0.00
Name calling / Labeling	0.59	0.80	0.68
Obfuscation, Intentional vagueness, Confusion	0.00	0.00	0.00
Presenting Irrelevant Data (Red Herring)	0.00	0.00	0.00
Reductio ad hitlerum	0.00	0.00	0.00
Repetition	0.00	0.00	0.00
Slogans	0.00	0.00	0.00
Smears	0.36	0.26	0.30
Thought-terminating cliché	0.00	0.00	0.00
Whataboutism	0.00	0.00	0.00

Table 3: Precision (P), Recall (R), and F1-Score for each class label

[4]Access to the source code of our system is available on `https://github.com/motazsaad/Arabic-Proagenda-Detection`

Figure 1: Receiver Operating Characteristic ROC curve for each class label

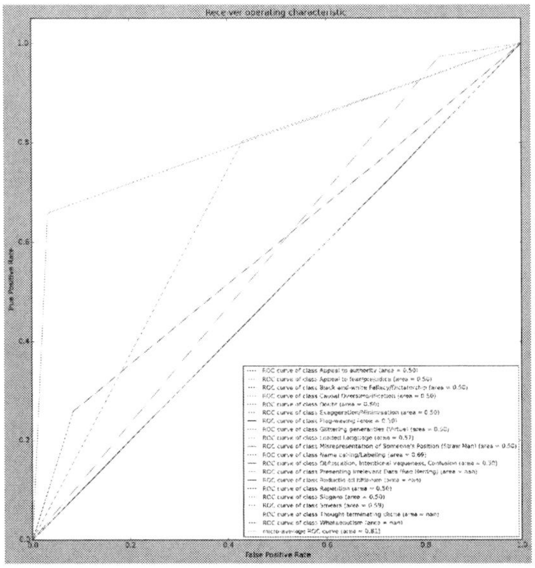

Tables 3 and 4 show the Precision (P), Recall (R), and F1-Score for each class label and the average scores. Figure 1 shows the Receiver Operating Characteristic ROC curve for each class label. It is clear from the tables and the ROC curves that classes with more training instances have better results than the ones with few or zero training instances. The nature of this shared task is very challenging, and the scarcity of the dataset adds more challenges to it.

Metric	P	R	F1
Micro avg	0.6	0.6	0.6
Macro avg	0.1	0.1	0.1
Weighted avg	0.5	0.6	0.6

Table 4: Average Precision (P), Recall (R), and F1-Score for all classes

6 Conclusion

The occurrence of propaganda and misleading information to promote a specific agenda has coincided with the growing popularity of SM platforms like Twitter. Before that, news outlets would generally be the primary source of information for people; hence, the broadcast news would usually come trustworthy with no need to question or cross-check their legitimacy. Contrarily, the broad spectrum of audiences on SM platforms and the ability to readily access and spread propaganda to promote specific agendas has attracted interesting parties (e.g., political, advertisement, radicalization). As such, the need for NLP researchers to come together to address propaganda and fake news detection, especially in social media, has emerged.

In this context, a shared task has been launched to detect propaganda techniques in Arabic tweets automatically, and an annotated dataset has been released as part of the shared task. Our team, AraBEM, has participated in subtask-1, which is about classifying propaganda techniques, and ranked in the third position attaining a micro F-1 score of 0.602 compared to a baseline of 0.079. We used a pre-trained BERT model and decided on 0.2 as the threshold for tensors to determine if a propaganda technique was spotted. Overall, the results indicate a good performance among the participating team. However, more investigations are still required to enhance the system's ability to identify propaganda techniques accurately. Future directions for expanding this research include experimenting with different pre-trained models and threshold settings. In addition, more investigations on data balancing methods like data augmentation would shed light on distinct possibilities for performance improvement. More experiments should be done to assess the systems' ability to detect the more cunning and indirect ways of creating and spreading propaganda.

References

Ehab A Abozinadah, Alex V Mbaziira, and J Jones. 2015. Detection of abusive accounts with arabic tweets. *Int. J. Knowl. Eng.-IACSIT*, 1(2):113–119.

Firoj Alam, Hamdy Mubarak, Wajdi Zaghouani, Preslav Nakov, and Giovanni Da San Martino. 2022. Overview of the WANLP 2022 shared task on propaganda detection in Arabic. In *Proceedings of the Seventh Arabic Natural Language Processing Workshop*, Abu Dhabi, UAE. Association for Computational Linguistics.

Nuha Albadi, Maram Kurdi, and Shivakant Mishra. 2019. Investigating the effect of combining gru neural networks with handcrafted features for religious hatred detection on arabic twitter space. *Social Network Analysis and Mining*, 9(1):1–19.

Wissam Antoun, Fady Baly, and Hazem Hajj. 2020. Arabert: Transformer-based model for Arabic language understanding. In *LREC 2020 Workshop Language Resources and Evaluation Conference 11–16 May 2020*, page 9.

Adam Badawy and Emilio Ferrara. 2018. The rise of jihadist propaganda on social networks. *Journal of Computational Social Science*, 1(2):453–470.

Akemi Takeoka Chatfield, Christopher G Reddick, and Uuf Brajawidagda. 2015. Tweeting propaganda, radicalization and recruitment: Islamic state supporters multi-sided twitter networks. In *Proceedings of the 16th annual international conference on digital government research*, pages 239–249.

Deptii D Chaudhari and Ambika V Pawar. 2022. A systematic comparison of machine learning and nlp techniques to unveil propaganda in social media. *Journal of Information Technology Research (JITR)*, 15(1):1–14.

Aditya Chetan, Brihi Joshi, Hridoy Sankar Dutta, and Tanmoy Chakraborty. 2019. Corerank: Ranking to detect users involved in blackmarket-based collusive retweeting activities. In *Proceedings of the Twelfth ACM International Conference on Web Search and Data Mining*, pages 330–338.

Emilio Ferrara. 2017. Contagion dynamics of extremist propaganda in social networks. *Information Sciences*, 418:1–12.

Ivan Habernal, Raffael Hannemann, Christian Pollak, Christopher Klamm, Patrick Pauli, and Iryna Gurevych. 2017. Argotario: Computational argumentation meets serious games. *arXiv preprint arXiv:1707.06002*.

Fouzi Harrag, Maria Debbah, Kareem Darwish, and Ahmed Abdelali. 2021. Bert transformer model for detecting arabic gpt2 auto-generated tweets. *arXiv preprint arXiv:2101.09345*.

Mahdi Hashemi and Margeret Hall. 2019. Detecting and classifying online dark visual propaganda. *Image and Vision Computing*, 89:95–105.

Mojtaba Heidarysafa, Kamran Kowsari, Tolu Odukoya, Philip Potter, Laura E Barnes, and Donald E Brown. 2020. Women in ISIS propaganda: a natural language processing analysis of topics and emotions in a comparison with a mainstream religious group. In *Science and Information Conference*, pages 610–624. Springer.

Giovanni Da San Martino, Stefano Cresci, Alberto Barrón-Cedeño, Seunghak Yu, Roberto Di Pietro, and Preslav Nakov. 2020. A survey on computational propaganda detection. *arXiv preprint arXiv:2007.08024*.

Subhadarshi Panda and Sarah Ita Levitan. 2021. Detecting multilingual covid-19 misinformation on social media via contextualized embeddings. In *Proceedings of the Fourth Workshop on NLP for Internet Freedom: Censorship, Disinformation, and Propaganda*, pages 125–129.

Eshrag Refaee. 2017. Sentiment analysis for micro-blogging platforms in Arabic. In *International conference on social computing and social media*, pages 275–294. Springer, Cham.

Eshrag A Refaee. 2021. A data-oriented approach for detecting offensive language in Arabic tweets. In *2021 International Conference on Software Engineering & Computer Systems and 4th International Conference on Computational Science and Information Management (ICSECS-ICOCSIM)*, pages 244–248. IEEE.

George-Alexandru Vlad, Mircea-Adrian Tanase, Cristian Onose, and Dumitru-Clementin Cercel. 2019. Sentence-level propaganda detection in news articles with transfer learning and bert-bilstm-capsule model. In *Proceedings of the second workshop on natural language processing for internet freedom: Censorship, Disinformation, and Propaganda*, pages 148–154.

Taha Zerrouki. 2010. PyArabic, an Arabic language library for python.

IITD at the WANLP 2022 Shared Task: Multilingual Multi-Granularity Network for Propaganda Detection

Shubham Mittal[1] **Preslav Nakov**[2]
[1] Indian Institute of Technology Delhi
[2] Mohammed Bin Zayed University of Artificial Intelligence
shubhamiitd18@gmail.com, preslav.nakov@mbzuai.ac.ae

Abstract

We present our system for the two subtasks of the shared task on propaganda detection in Arabic, part of WANLP'2022. Subtask 1 is a multi-label classification problem to find the propaganda techniques used in a given tweet. Our system for this task uses XLM-R to predict probabilities for the target tweet to use each of the techniques. In addition to finding the techniques, Subtask 2 further asks to identify the textual span for each instance of each technique that is present in the tweet; the task can be modeled as a sequence tagging problem. We use a multi-granularity network with mBERT encoder for Subtask 2. Overall, our system ranks second for both subtasks (out of 14 and 3 participants, respectively). Our empirical analysis show that it does not help to use a much larger English corpus annotated with propaganda techniques, regardless of whether used in English or after translation to Arabic.[1]

1 Introduction

Propaganda is information deliberately designed to promote a particular point of view and to influence the opinions or the actions of individuals or groups. With the rise of social media platforms, the circulation of propaganda is even more pronounced since it may be built upon a true fact, but exaggerated and biased to promote a particular viewpoint. Various propaganda detection systems have been developed in recent years (Da San Martino et al., 2019; Barrón-Cedeño et al., 2019; Barrón-Cedeño et al., 2019; Dimitrov et al., 2021a,b), but they all have been restricted to English due to the unavailability of labelled datasets (containing fine-grained annotations of textual spans) in other languages. To bridge this gap, the WANLP'2022 shared task on propaganda detection in Arabic (Alam et al., 2022) released a dataset of Arabic tweets (we will call it ARATWEET) that uses 20 propaganda techniques, thus enabling research beyond English.

There are two subtasks defined in this shared task for detecting the propaganda techniques used in a tweet: (1) identify the techniques present in the given Arabic tweet, and (2) identify the span(s) of use of each technique along with the technique. Subtask 1 can be viewed as a multi-label classification problem, where the tweet may contain any subset of the 20 propaganda techniques, even all or none of them. Subtask 2 can be seen as a multi-label sequence tagging problem, where the system needs to predict the labels for each of the tokens. Subtask 2 is more challenging than Subtask 1 due to the increased level of detail it asks for.

Our Subtask 1 system uses a multilingual pre-trained language model, XLM-R (Conneau et al., 2020) to estimate a Multinoulli distribution over the 20 propaganda techniques for a given Arabic tweet. For Subtask 2, we use the multi-granularity network (MGN) from Da San Martino et al. (2019), but we replace the BERT encoder with mBERT (Devlin et al., 2019). We call our resulting system mMGN. Our systems, which use only ARATWEET data, rank second for both subtasks.

We investigated cross-lingual propaganda detection by using the Propaganda Techniques Corpus (PTC) (Da San Martino et al., 2019), which consists of annotated English news articles. We trained mMGN on PTC and continued its training on ARATWEET. Surprisingly, we found that continued training hurts the model by 10.2 F1 points absolute. To alleviate the possibility of ineffective transfer from English in mBERT embeddings, we further translated the PTC to Arabic using Google Translate and we projected the span-labels using `awesome-align` (Dou and Neubig, 2021). Upon doing continued training with a subset of the translated data, having only sentences containing propaganda, we found that it does not help, but also does not hurt the model. We believe that the domain difference between the two dataset is quite large, and thus there are no benefits in cross-lingual transfer.

[1]The code is released at github.com/sm354/mMGN

Proceedings of the The Seventh Arabic Natural Language Processing Workshop (WANLP), pages 529 - 533
December 8, 2022 ©2022 Association for Computational Linguistics

Propaganda Technique	train		dev		test	
	count	length	count	length	count	length
Appeal to authority	21	93.4 ± 43.9	8	94.8 ± 37.3	1	142.0 ± 0.0
Appeal to fear/prejudice	48	49.2 ± 29.0	11	54.9 ± 38.0	25	44.8 ± 27.9
Black-and-white Fallacy/Dictatorship	2	60.5 ± 12.5	3	56.3 ± 20.4	7	49.6 ± 19.8
Causal oversimplification	4	80.0 ± 43.2	2	57.0 ± 18.0	4	57.3 ± 24.2
Doubt	29	52.4 ± 34.6	3	61.0 ± 53.7	19	39.5 ± 21.3
Exaggeration/Minimisation	44	23.7 ± 28.4	26	14.3 ± 6.8	26	29.1 ± 16.9
Flag-waving	5	57.6 ± 30.7	4	65.0 ± 19.6	9	60.1 ± 23.2
Glittering generalities (virtue)	25	81.4 ± 48.9	9	66.1 ± 17.2	1	104.0 ± 0.0
Loaded language	446	9.70 ± 7.10	88	12.7 ± 13.2	326	7.20 ± 4.70
Misrepresentation of someone's position	0	N/A	0	N/A	1	37.0 ± 0.0
Name calling/Labeling	244	13.8 ± 6.4	77	15.6 ± 8.4	163	14.1 ± 6.6
Obfuscation, intentional vagueness, confusion	9	48.8 ± 28.1	4	34.0 ± 22.1	6	43.3 ± 23.6
Presenting irrelevant data (red herring)	1	61.0 ± 0.0	0	N/A	0	N/A
Reductio ad hitlerum	0	N/A	0	N/A	0	N/A
Repetition	9	12.8 ± 11.0	3	11.3 ± 4.1	3	35.3 ± 17.3
Slogans	44	17.0 ± 6.6	2	26.5 ± 13.5	6	24.5 ± 11.7
Smears	85	73.8 ± 34.9	27	88.8 ± 53.3	50	55.8 ± 22.0
Thought-terminating cliché	6	28.2 ± 17.5	2	21.0 ± 7.0	0	N/A
Whataboutism	3	47.7 ± 15.3	2	64.5 ± 20.5	0	N/A
Bandwagon	0	N/A	0	N/A	0	N/A
no technique	95	N/A	15	N/A	44	N/A

Table 1: Instance count of propaganda techniques and their span length in characters (mean ± std-dev) in the ARATWEET partitions. N/A is for either *no technique* or for those propaganda techniques having zero instances to compute mean/std-dev (such as *Misrepresentation of Someone's Position*, *Reductio ad hitlerum*, and *Bandwagon*).

2 Data

The dataset released in this shared task, which we call ARATWEET, comprises Arabic tweets, most of which (but not all) contain some propaganda techniques.

Table 1 shows statistics about the propaganda technique in the partitions of ARATWEET. Techniques such as *Misrepresentation of Someone's Position (Straw Man)*, *Presenting Irrelevant Data (Red Herring)*, *Reductio ad hitlerum*, and *Bandwagon* are rarely present in the dataset. *Loaded Language* is the most frequently present technique, whereas *Appeal to Authority* has the longest span. There are also tweets present that do not contain propaganda (e.g., 95 tweets in the training set).

Table 2 shows aggregated statistics about all propaganda techniques in the different partitions[2] of the dataset.

	train	dev	test
#examples	504	103	323
#spans	1025	271	647
tweet len (t)	15.8±6.1	18.6±9.9	15.4±5.0
tweet len (c)	112.6±39.2	123.4±58	117.4±30.6

Table 2: Statistics about the ARATWEET. Tweet len is the average length in # tokens (t) and # characters (c).

[2]The *dev* partition in this work refers to the combination of dev and dev_test released in the shared task.

3 System Description

Subtask 1 is a multi-label classification problem, where the model needs to find which of the 20 propaganda techniques (if any) are present in the input tweet. Our system (shown in Figure 1) fine-tunes a multilingual pretrained language model, XLM-R, (Conneau et al., 2020) for this subtask.

Given an Arabic tweet, we first tokenize it into word pieces $[T_1, T_2, \ldots, T_n]$ using the XLM-R tokenizer. We the pass these pieces through XLM-R to obtain contextualised embeddings, from which we take the *CLS* token embedding and we pass it through a single fully-connected linear layer to obtain a 20-dimensional embedding. After passing it through a sigmoid non-linearity, we convert this embedding, representing logits, to probabilities $[p_1, p_2, ..., p_{20}]$, one for each propaganda technique. Using a threshold of 0.5, our system assigns label i if $p_i \geq 0.5$. When $p_i < 0.5 \; \forall \; i$, the model predicts *no technique* for the target tweet.

Subtask 2 is a multi-label sequence tagging problem, where we want to label the tokens of a given tweet with the propaganda techniques. Since the (training) data contains tweets that do not contain propaganda (as discussed in section 2), we use the multi-granularity network (MGN) (Da San Martino et al., 2019) to develop our Subtask 2 system.

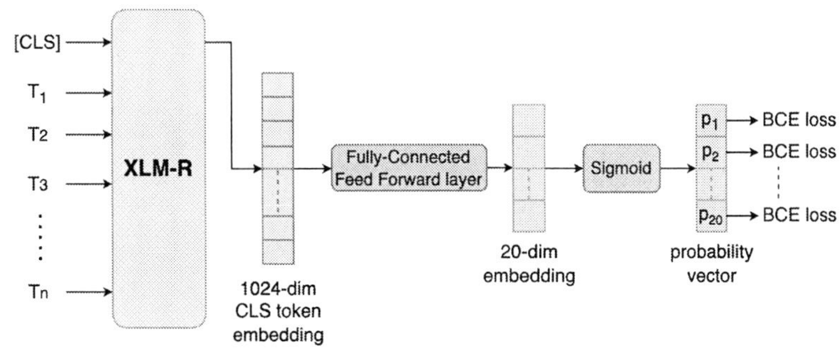

Figure 1: Our Subtask 1 system, which uses a pretrained XLM-R for multi-label classification. $T_1, T_2, T_3, \ldots, T_n$ are the tokens of the input tweet, and p_i is the probability of the tweet using i^{th} propaganda technique.

MGN uses BERT (Devlin et al., 2019) and models the task as a single-label sequence tagging problem, where either one of 20 techniques or none of them is assigned to each token. To improve the performance, it also adds a trainable *gate* to lower the probabilities for all tokens if the sentence does not contain propaganda.[3]

We replace BERT with mBERT in our MGN system, to obtain our multilingual multi-granularity network (mMGN) as our Subtask 2 system. mMGN can work for Arabic and for all other languages that are supported by mBERT.

4 Experiments

For evaluation, we use the official scorers that were released for the shared task. The official evaluation measure for Subtask 1 is micro-F1. However, the scorer also reports macro-F1. For Subtask 2, a modified micro-averaged F1 score is used, which gives credit to partial matches between the gold and the predicted spans.

We use the dev partition of ARATWEET to find the best model checkpoint and to report the scores on the finally released test set. Our models are trained on a single V100 (32GB) GPU.

Subtask 1 We empirically compare different pretrained language models (PLMs) as encoders for our Subtask 1 system and we report the scores in Table 3. With XLM-R encoder, our system achieves the best performance of 60.9 micro-F1. The hyperparameters of our Subtask 1 system include a maximum sequence length of 256, a batch size of 32, and 40 training epochs. We use two different learning rates: 1e-5 for PLM and 3e-4 for the remaining trainable parameters.

[3]We refer the readers to Da San Martino et al. (2019) for more detail.

	macro-F1	micro-F1
mBERT (Devlin et al., 2019)	8.1	54.3
AraBERT (Antoun et al., 2020)	**18.7**	59.4
XLM-R (Conneau et al., 2020)	18.3	**60.9**

Table 3: Performance(%) of our Subtask 1 system with different multilingual pre-trained LMs.

Subtask 2 We train the multilingual Multi-Granularity Network (mMGN) model on ARATWEET with a batch size of 16, a learning rate of 3e-5 for PLM and 3e-4 for other trainable parameters, and 30 epochs. This yields an F1 score of 35.5 on the test set, which is our best performance on this subtask.

Cross-lingual Propaganda Detection We ran several experiments using mMGN and the Propaganda Techniques Corpus (PTC), which is available in English (Da San Martino et al., 2019), to study cross-lingual transfer between English and Arabic in Subtask 2. In (1) ARATWEET, we train and test on ARATWEET, whereas in (2) PTC, we train on PTC data and we test in a zero-shot manner on ARATWEET. (3) TRANSPTC contains the translation of the PTC data from English to Arabic using Google Translate, followed by label projection using `awesome-align` (Dou and Neubig, 2021). Keeping only those translated sentences from TRANSPTC that contain propaganda gives (4) TRANSPTC+. (5) CTDTRANSPTC and (6) CTDTRANSPTC+ take the trained model from TRANSPTC and TRANSPTC+, respectively, and train it further on ARATWEET.

The performance across all settings is reported in Table 4. We can see that TRANSPTC is better than PTC by 0.6 F1 points, which suggests that the model learns better with the Arabic PTC.

	Precision	Recall	F1
ARATWEET	35.5	25.7	**29.8**
PTC	53.1	1.4	2.8
TRANSPTC	30	1.8	3.4
TRANSPTC+	34.2	10.6	16.1
CTDTRANSPTC	21	18.4	19.6
CTDTRANSPTC+	30.6	28.0	29.2

Table 4: Performance(%) of mMGN (on dev_test) using different training methodologies.

The 1.8 recall of TRANSPTC is quite low, which could be due to the high proportion of propaganda-free sentences in PTC, which makes the model reluctant to propose propaganda techniques. When training only on propaganda-containing translated sentences from PTC, TRANSPTC+ improves over TRANSPTC on recall and also on precision, resulting in a gain of 12.7 F1 points absolute. Continued training on ARATWEET, CTDTRANSPTC and CTDTRANSPTC+ yields sizable gains over the PTC-trained models TRANSPTC and TRANSPTC+. However, CTDTRANSPTC+ is worse than ARATWEET by 0.6 F1 points absolute, indicating that cross-lingual transfer is not helping, but also not significantly hurting the performance.

We posit that the large domain difference between the PTC and the ARATWEET datasets may be the reason for ineffective cross-lingual transfer. PTC contains news articles whereas ARATWEET contains tweets, which causes linguistic differences in the text such as the presence of URLs, emojis, or slang in the tweets. Tweets are also often shorter due to text length limit in Twitter, which may also confuse the model between the two datasets.

5 Conclusion

We described our systems for the two subtasks of the WANLP 2022 shared task on propaganda detection in Arabic. For Subtask 1, we used XLM-R to estimate a Multinoulli distribution over the 20 propaganda techniques for multi-label classification. For Subtask 2, we used a multi-granularity network with mBERT, addressing the subtask as a sequence tagging problem. The official evaluation results put our systems as second on both subtasks, out of 14 and of 3 participants, respectively. We further described a number of experiments, which suggest various research challenges for future work, such as how to effectively use data from different domains, and how to learn language-agnostic embeddings for propaganda detection.

References

Firoj Alam, Hamdy Mubarak, Wajdi Zaghouani, Giovanni Da San Martino, and Preslav Nakov. 2022. Overview of the WANLP 2022 shared task on propaganda detection in Arabic. In *Proceedings of the Seventh Arabic Natural Language Processing Workshop*, Abu Dhabi, UAE.

Wissam Antoun, Fady Baly, and Hazem Hajj. 2020. AraBERT: Transformer-based model for Arabic language understanding. In *Proceedings of the 4th Workshop on Open-Source Arabic Corpora and Processing Tools, with a Shared Task on Offensive Language Detection*, pages 9–15, Marseille, France.

Alberto Barrón-Cedeño, Giovanni Da San Martino, Israa Jaradat, and Preslav Nakov. 2019. Proppy: A system to unmask propaganda in online news. In *Proceedings of the AAAI Conference on Artificial Intelligence*, pages 9847–9848, Honolulu, HI, USA.

Alberto Barrón-Cedeño, Israa Jaradat, Giovanni Da San Martino, and Preslav Nakov. 2019. Proppy: Organizing the news based on their propagandistic content. *Inf. Process. Manag.*, 56(5):1849–1864.

Alexis Conneau, Kartikay Khandelwal, Naman Goyal, Vishrav Chaudhary, Guillaume Wenzek, Francisco Guzmán, Edouard Grave, Myle Ott, Luke Zettlemoyer, and Veselin Stoyanov. 2020. Unsupervised cross-lingual representation learning at scale. In *Proceedings of the Annual Meeting of the Association for Computational Linguistics*, pages 8440–8451.

Giovanni Da San Martino, Seunghak Yu, Alberto Barrón-Cedeño, Rostislav Petrov, and Preslav Nakov. 2019. Fine-grained analysis of propaganda in news article. In *Proceedings of the Conference on Empirical Methods in Natural Language Processing and the International Joint Conference on Natural Language Processing*, pages 5636–5646, Hong Kong, China.

Jacob Devlin, Ming-Wei Chang, Kenton Lee, and Kristina Toutanova. 2019. BERT: Pre-training of deep bidirectional transformers for language understanding. In *Proceedings of the Conference of the North American Chapter of the Association for Computational Linguistics: Human Language Technologies*, pages 4171–4186, Minneapolis, MN, USA.

Dimitar Dimitrov, Bishr Bin Ali, Shaden Shaar, Firoj Alam, Fabrizio Silvestri, Hamed Firooz, Preslav Nakov, and Giovanni Da San Martino. 2021a. Detecting propaganda techniques in memes. In *Proceedings of the 59th Annual Meeting of the Association for Computational Linguistics and the 11th International Joint Conference on Natural Language Processing*, pages 6603–6617.

Dimitar Dimitrov, Bishr Bin Ali, Shaden Shaar, Firoj Alam, Fabrizio Silvestri, Hamed Firooz, Preslav Nakov, and Giovanni Da San Martino. 2021b.

SemEval-2021 task 6: Detection of persuasion techniques in texts and images. In *Proceedings of the 15th International Workshop on Semantic Evaluation*, pages 70–98, Online. Association for Computational Linguistics.

Zi-Yi Dou and Graham Neubig. 2021. Word alignment by fine-tuning embeddings on parallel corpora. In *Proceedings of the 16th Conference of the European Chapter of the Association for Computational Linguistics*, pages 2112–2128.

Pythoneers at WANLP 2022 Shared Task: Monolingual AraBERT for Arabic Propaganda Detection and Span Extraction

Joseph Attieh
Huawei Technologies Oy., Finland
joseph.attieh@huawei.com

Fadi Hassan
Huawei Technologies Oy., Finland
fadi.hassan@huawei.com

Abstract

In this paper, we present two deep learning approaches that are based on AraBERT, submitted to the Propaganda Detection shared task of the Seventh Workshop for Arabic Natural Language Processing (WANLP 2022). Propaganda detection consists of two main sub-tasks, mainly propaganda identification and span extraction. We present one system per sub-task. The first system is a Multi-Task Learning model that consists of a shared AraBERT encoder with task-specific binary classification layers. This model is trained to jointly learn one binary classification task per propaganda method. The second system is an AraBERT model with a Conditional Random Fields (CRF) layer. We achieved rank 3 on the first sub-task and rank 1 on the second sub-task.

1 Introduction

Social media platforms have been one of the main mediums of communication and source of information for most internet users. These platforms, as useful as they might be, can also be used to deceive and manipulate individuals. This is mostly done through propaganda techniques. Propaganda can be defined as the expression of opinion that is crafted to deliberately manipulate people's beliefs, attitudes, or actions, achieving a set of specified goals (Smith, 2021). This is done by presenting certain arguments to divert the attention of the victims from everything but their own propaganda. Since fallacies and propaganda devices overlap, researchers have defined propaganda techniques in terms of argumentative fallacies (Miller, 1939; Weston, 2018).

Several initiatives were made to detect propaganda on social media. For instance, Da San Martino et al. (2019b) provided a fine-grained propaganda analysis and a corpus of news articles annotated with 18 propaganda techniques. This corpus was employed at SemEval-2020 for propaganda identification (Martino et al., 2020), then at NLP4IF-2020 for span detection respectively (Da San Martino et al., 2019a).

In this paper, we present our solution to the Propaganda 2022 shared task (Alam et al., 2022). The Propaganda 2022 shared task is one of the first shared tasks of its kind and is held with the 7th Arabic Natural Language Processing Workshop (WANLP 2022) co-located with the EMNLP 2022 Conference in Abu Dhabi (Dec 7, 2022). The goal of the task is to build models for identifying propaganda techniques in Arabic tweets. It provides two sub-tasks; the goal of the first sub-task is to detect the propaganda technique used in the tweet (if any), while the goal of the second sub-task is to identify the span of the text covered by each technique.

As mentioned by Da San Martino et al. (2019a), the best-performing systems in the propaganda shared tasks used Bidirectional Encoder Representations from Transformers (BERT) (Devlin et al., 2019) to generate contextual representations of the text. Therefore, we propose to fine-tune an Arabic variant of BERT called AraBERT for each sub-task. The system submitted to the first sub-task is a multi-task model that performs binary classification per propaganda technique. The system submitted for the second sub-task is an AraBERT model fine-tuned with a Conditional Random Fields (CRF) layer. Both systems achieved top rankings on the leaderboard; the first system ranked third with a micro-averaged F1-Score of 0.602, while the second system ranked first with a micro-averaged F1-Score of 0.396.

This paper is structured as follows: Section 2 describes the data used for each sub-task, as well as the data preprocessing techniques employed. Section 3 gives an overview of the fine-tuning process of BERT models. Section 4 presents the systems submitted to sub-tasks 1 and 2 respectively. In Section 5, we show the results and discuss them briefly. Finally, we present the related work section in Section 6 and conclude the paper with Section 7.

Proceedings of the The Seventh Arabic Natural Language Processing Workshop (WANLP), pages 534 - 540
December 8, 2022 ©2022 Association for Computational Linguistics

2 Data

2.1 Overall Description

The following propaganda task covers around 20 propaganda techniques, defined in terms of logical argumentative fallacies[1].

2.2 Dataset Split

Both systems presented in this paper are solely trained and validated on the data provided by the organizer. The training sets (i.e., train) for both sub-tasks consist of around 500 tweets each, while the development sets (i.e., dev and dev_test) consist of around 50 tweets each. The first sub-task provides the tweets labeled with the propaganda techniques present in these tweets. It should be noted that multiple propaganda techniques might be present in the same tweet. Tweets with no propaganda technique are labeled with "no technique". The second sub-task presents the tweets with the propaganda methods employed in each tweet with their span (i.e., start and end indexes of the text fragment containing the propaganda technique provided). It should be noted that both sub-tasks share the same tweets. The label distribution amongst the different sets is provided in the results sections in Table 2 for conciseness (the mismatch in the number of labels between the first sub-task and the second sub-task is because every propaganda technique can have multiple spans in the same text).

2.3 Dataset Preprocessing

2.3.1 Sub-task 1

The first sub-task is a multi-label classification task. We first standardize the text by removing non-Arabic words, emojis, and URLs from the tweets. Then, we proceed by tokenizing the tweets using the AraBERT tokenizer.

2.4 Sub-task 2

The second sub-task is a sequence tagging task. Therefore, we encode the input text based on the spans that represent the propaganda techniques. We experimented with different encoding schemes, displayed in Table 1. Preliminary experiments conducted with these encoding schemes showed that the *BIO data format* results in better performance for the task [2]. Therefore, we employ this format for the data.

[1] The propaganda techniques are defined in the following link: https://propaganda.qcri.org/annotations/definitions.html

[2] Results are not reported for conciseness.

Table 1: Encoding formats (**LL = Loaded Language** and **NC = Name calling/Labeling**)

Data Format		Notations	Encoding صدمة في تركيا بعد هذا القرار الروسي
BIO	B	first token in a span	B-LL O O O O B-NC I-NC
	I	token in a span	
	O	token outside of a span	
BIOUL	B	first token in a span	U-LL O O O O B-NC L-NC
	I	non-first and non-last token in a span	
	O	token outside of a span	
	U	unit-length span (span same size as token)	
	L	last token in a multi-token span	
IO	I	token in a span	I-LL O O O O I-NC I-NC
	O	token outside a span	

3 Fine-tuning BERT

As mentioned previously, the first sub-task is a multi-label text classification task, while the second sub-task is a sequence tagging task. We choose to fine-tune a pre-trained Bidirectional Encoder Representation from Transformer (BERT) model (Devlin et al., 2019) for each of these sub-tasks. This is usually done by adding an appropriate output layer to the BERT encoder and training the parameters of the network to predict correctly for the corresponding sub-task. It is a direct application of Transfer Learning, as the knowledge from the pre-trained model is transferred to the downstream task.

Therefore, finding an appropriate pre-trained model to fine-tune highly affects the performance of the model on the sub-task. Since we are dealing with Arabic tweets, we choose to build our systems using the Arabic pre-trained language model called AraBERT (Antoun et al., 2020). The specific model employed in both sub-tasks is the *bert-large-arabertv02-twitter*. It is based on *AraBERTv0.2-large*, first pre-trained on publicly available large-scale raw Arabic text, and then pre-trained again on 60M Multi-Dialect Tweets.

For the first sub-task, we propose to employ Multi-Task Learning to fine-tune AraBERT on the multi-label text classification task. As for the second sub-task, we propose to employ a CRF layer to fine-tune BERT for the sequence tagging task. All models have been trained on NVIDIA Tesla Volta V100.

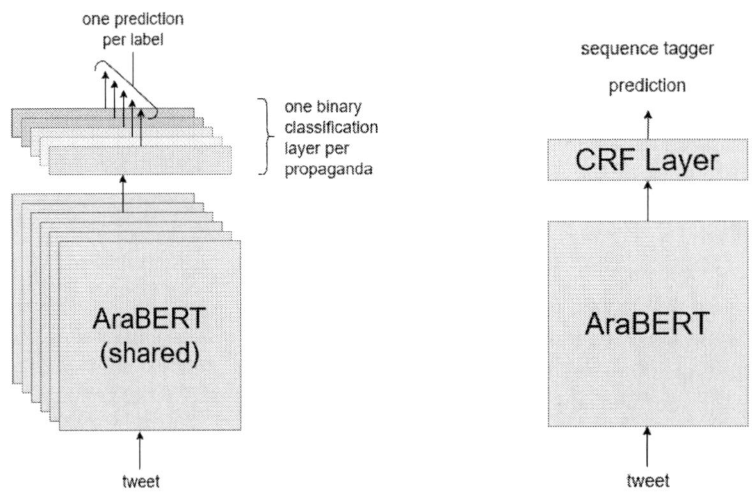

Figure 1: Diagrams for both systems 1 and 2 submitted for sub-task 1 and 2 respectively.

4 Systems

4.1 System 1 - Multi-Task Learning

For the first sub-task, we propose to use multi-task learning to perform multi-label text classification. We propose to encode more knowledge in AraBERT by training the model to predict different types of propaganda techniques, one technique at a time. In other words, AraBERT is fine-tuned to perform **n** binary classification, where n corresponds to the number of propaganda techniques. BERT will learn weights that will allow it to represent the text appropriately for the task, while at the same time fine-tuning the different binary classification layers to distinguish between the different techniques.

The Multi-Task model consists of a single shared AraBERT encoder. The pre-trained AraBERT model is fine-tuned using n task-specific classification heads (i.e., binary classification layers). Each classification head consists of a Dropout layer of probability 0.1 followed by a linear layer that maps the pooled embeddings of the AraBERT encoder to the number of predicted classes (2 classes at a time, since predicting each propaganda technique is a binary classification task). We use the cross-entropy loss to compute the loss on the outcome of every classifier head. Since the losses assess different measures, we chose to fine-tune one loss at a time per batch.

As mentioned earlier, the dataset used is a relatively small dataset, which makes the task more difficult to achieve. We train the model using the Adam optimizer (Kingma and Ba, 2015), with a learning rate of 10^5. After a couple of experiments, we set the batch size to 8 for the first 2 epochs, then to 1 for 2 epochs. This training scenario ensured that the model learns from the dataset without over-fitting (since the gradients would be computed differently throughout the different epochs).

As seen in Table 2, the dataset used suffers from class imbalance. Therefore, we propose to randomly sample (with replacement) 2000 sentences per propaganda label value from the training set (i.e., for the Smears classification head, we sample 2000 samples with a negative label and 2000 samples with a positive label). In other terms, the training set used for this model consists of 2000 tweets for every label. This will guarantee that all classes participate in the training process equally.

4.2 System 2 - CRF Layer

For the second subtask, we propose to fine-tune BERT using a Conditional Random Fields (Lafferty et al., 2001) layer. In general, CRFs are a generalization of Bayesian Networks and are used in applications in which the contextual information of the neighbors affects the current prediction (e.g., sequence labeling task). First, we encode the input text using the AraBERT model, and then we pass the output to the CRF layer to predict the label of the spans using the BIO data format. The model is trained to perform a multi-class classification, as the model will predict whether every token in the text is either the first token in the span (B-<type>), inside the span (I-<type>) or outside the span (O),

Table 2: Label distribution and F1 scores for both sub-tasks 1 and 2

Propaganda Techniques	Sub-task 1						Sub-task 2					
	TRAIN	DEV	DEV TEST	TEST	DEV TEST F1 Micro	TEST F1 Micro	TRAIN	DEV	DEV TEST	TEST	DEV TEST F1	TEST F1
Loaded Language	289	28	31	223	75.0	69.34	446	46	42	326	36.42	43.25
Name calling/Labeling	186	35	27	142	73.07	66.25	244	44	33	163	31.15	45.21
Smears	84	12	16	50	80.76	82.34	85	12	15	50	51.16	38.09
Appeal to fear/prejudice	47	7	3	25	88.46	90.71	48	7	4	25	18.18	42.23
Exaggeration/Minimisation	41	10	12	23	76.92	90.71	44	10	16	26	0	0
Slogans	28	1	1	7	98.07	97.73	44	1	1	6	0	5.40
Doubt	27	1	2	19	94.23	95.04	29	1	2	19	0	45.16
Glittering generalities (Virtue)	25	7	2	1	96.15	98.45	25	7	2	1	40	26.67
Appeal to authority	21	7	2	1	96.16	99.07	21	7	1	1	56.93	0
Obfuscation, Intentional vagueness, Confusion	9	3	1	6	98.07	97.83	9	3	1	6	0	0
Repetition	7	2	1	3	98.07	98.45	9	2	1	3	0	0
Thought-terminating cliché	6	1	1	0	100	100	6	1	1	0	0	100
Flag-waving	5	2	2	10	96.15	96.59	5	2	2	9	0	0
Causal Oversimplification	4	1	1	4	98.07	98.76	4	1	1	4	0	0
Whataboutism	3	1	1	0	98.07	100	3	1	1	0	0	100
Black-and-white Fallacy/Dictatorship	2	1	2	7	96.15	97.83	2	1	2	7	0	0
Presenting Irrelevant Data (Red Herring)	1	0	0	0	100	99.33	1	0	0	0	100	100
Misrepresentation of Someone's Position (Straw Man)	0	0	0	1	100	99.69	0	0	0	1	100	100
Reducto ad hitlerum	0	0	0	0	100	100	0	0	0	0	100	100
Bandwagon	0	0	0	0	100	100	0	0	0	0	100	100
No techniques	95	7	8	44	84.61	79.87	0	0	0	0	100	100
OVERALL	880	126	113	566	**59.07**	**60.2**	1025	146	125	647	**27.95**	**39.55**

where <type> represents the type of propaganda technique.

In the training process, we employ the negative log-likelihood loss, which is more suitable for this type of task than cross-entropy loss. We train the model using the Adam optimizer, with a batch size of 32 for 13 epochs.

5 Results and Discussion

Table 2 reports the size of the training set, development sets (dev and dev_test), and the testing set. Furthermore, it presents the Micro-averaged F1 Score on the dev_test and test sets for both tasks. We did not report the Macro-Averaged F1 Score as it is not the official metric of the task.

We conduct the analysis on the original training set. As mentioned previously, the training set is quite small (around 500 samples for training, covering 880 total labels). We notice that 51% of the tweets contain one propaganda technique, while 29% contain two propaganda techniques, and 20% of the tweets have more than three propaganda techniques. This makes the task quite challenging, as there might be instances with more than one propaganda technique present at the same time, while others with no propaganda technique at all. Therefore, treating the task as multiple binary classification techniques is suitable as we are able to independently predict the presence of different techniques, while at the same time learning their co-occurrence information through sharing the same base model.

For sub-task 1, the model's performance on the test set was on par with its performance on the dev_test set (similar F1-Scores achieved per label, and overall). For sub-task 2, the model generalized very well and scored a much higher F1-Score on the test set compared to the dev_test set.

We analyze these results with respect to the distribution of the samples among the different labels. We notice that 85% of the labels in the training set are covered by 9 propaganda techniques. Furthermore, the rest of the techniques have less than 10 samples in the training set. These samples might not be good representatives of their propaganda techniques that the multi-task model can generalize from. Perhaps training the multi-task model to achieve a higher performance on the 9 most common techniques would have resulted in a more accurate performance of the system. There is also a need to increase the number of instances of the propaganda techniques that rarely occur in the training set. This can be done using a data augmentation method guided using domain knowledge. On a last note, both systems were tested on the Straw Man propaganda technique that did not occur in any set.

6 Related Work

In this section, we present some of the previous work conducted for propaganda detection, also covering the Conference and Labs of the Evaluation Forum (CLEF) *CheckThat!* lab that employs fact-checking (where the propaganda sentences can be viewed as fake claims). Researchers provided multiple datasets to tackle the propaganda detection task. For instance, Rashkin et al. (2017) collected news articles from reliable and unreliable sources, and labeled them using distant supervision to four classes: propaganda, trusted, hoax, or satire. Habernal and Gurevych (2017) presented a corpus of 1.3k arguments annotated with five fallacies. Furthermore, Da San Martino et al. (2019c) presented a corpus of news articles annotated with 18 propaganda techniques. The annotations identify the minimal fragments related to the propaganda technique (i.e., the span), instead of flagging the whole sentence.

On another hand, CLEF provided the *CheckThat*! lab that supported the automatic identification and verification of claims in its multiple editions that are held every year (Atanasova et al., 2018; Barrón-Cedeño et al., 2018; Atanasova et al., 2019; Hasanain et al., 2019, 2020; Shaar et al., 2020; Nakov et al., 2021; Shaar et al., 2021b,a; Nakov et al., 2021, 2022a,b). The Lab provided multiple tasks around Fact-checking, with the following tasks: claim detection, claim matching, evidence retrieval, and claim verification. We briefly describe each task. The claim detection task estimates the check-worthiness of the claim by predicting which claims should be prioritized for fact-checking. The claim matching task determines whether a new claim is similar to a claim that has already been fact-checked; if a similar claim is found, there is no need to fact check the new claim again. The evidence retrieval task finds information that can verify a claim, by asking the participants to rank the set of evidence based on their usefulness for fact-checking a certain claim. Finally, the claim verification task is a Verdict Prediction task in which the claim is either deemed factually true, half-true or false based on the retrieved evidence.

7 Conclusion

In this paper, we introduced two AraBERT-based systems to tackle propaganda identification and span detection. We conclude that identifying propaganda techniques in Arabic tweets is a challenging task. The most challenging aspect of this task lies in the small dataset used (504 samples covering 880 labels) as well as the multi-propaganda aspect of the tweets. Even though the proposed systems did not employ any data augmentation technique, they achieved ranks 3 and 1 on sub-tasks 3 and 1. In future work, we propose to focus the training on the binary classification heads that handle propaganda issues that are more commonly faced by users on social media (such as Loaded Language and Name calling/Labeling). Focusing our attention on these classification heads would help build models that will protect the users from the most present propaganda attacks on the web.

References

Firoj Alam, Hamdy Mubarak, Wajdi Zaghouani, Preslav Nakov, and Giovanni Da San Martino. 2022. Overview of the WANLP 2022 shared task on propaganda detection in Arabic. In *Proceedings of the Seventh Arabic Natural Language Processing Workshop*, Abu Dhabi, UAE. Association for Computational Linguistics.

Wissam Antoun, Fady Baly, and Hazem Hajj. 2020. Arabert: Transformer-based model for arabic language understanding. In *LREC 2020 Workshop Language Resources and Evaluation Conference 11–16 May 2020*, page 9.

Pepa Atanasova, Lluís Màrquez i Villodre, Alberto Barrón-Cedeño, T. Elsayed, Reem Suwaileh, Wajdi Zaghouani, Spas Kyuchukov, Giovanni Da San Martino, and Preslav Nakov. 2018. Overview of the clef-2018 checkthat! lab on automatic identification and verification of political claims. task 1: Check-worthiness. *ArXiv*, abs/1808.05542.

Pepa Atanasova, Preslav Nakov, Georgi Karadzhov, Mitra Mohtarami, and Giovanni Da San Martino. 2019. Overview of the clef-2019 checkthat! lab: Automatic identification and verification of claims. task 1: Check-worthiness. In *CLEF*.

Alberto Barrón-Cedeño, T. Elsayed, Reem Suwaileh, Lluís Màrquez i Villodre, Pepa Atanasova, Wajdi Zaghouani, Spas Kyuchukov, Giovanni Da San Martino, and Preslav Nakov. 2018. Overview of the clef-2018 checkthat! lab on automatic identification and verification of political claims. task 2: Factuality. In *CLEF*.

Giovanni Da San Martino, Alberto Barron-Cedeno, and Preslav Nakov. 2019a. Findings of the nlp4if-2019 shared task on fine-grained propaganda detection. In *Proceedings of the second workshop on natural language processing for internet freedom: censorship, disinformation, and propaganda*, pages 162–170.

Giovanni Da San Martino, Seunghak Yu, Alberto Barrón-Cedeno, Rostislav Petrov, and Preslav Nakov. 2019b. Fine-grained analysis of propaganda in news article. In *Proceedings of the 2019 conference on empirical methods in natural language processing and the 9th international joint conference on natural language processing (EMNLP-IJCNLP)*, pages 5636–5646.

Giovanni Da San Martino, Seunghak Yu, Alberto Barrón-Cedeño, Rostislav Petrov, and Preslav Nakov. 2019c. Fine-grained analysis of propaganda in news article. In *Proceedings of the 2019 Conference on Empirical Methods in Natural Language Processing and the 9th International Joint Conference on Natural Language Processing (EMNLP-IJCNLP)*, pages 5636–5646, Hong Kong, China. Association for Computational Linguistics.

Jacob Devlin, Ming-Wei Chang, Kenton Lee, and Kristina Toutanova. 2019. BERT: Pre-training of deep bidirectional transformers for language understanding. In *Proceedings of the 2019 Conference of the North American Chapter of the Association for Computational Linguistics: Human Language Technologies, Volume 1 (Long and Short Papers)*, pages 4171–4186, Minneapolis, Minnesota. Association for Computational Linguistics.

Ivan Habernal and Iryna Gurevych. 2017. Argumentation Mining in User-Generated Web Discourse. *Computational Linguistics*, 43(1):125–179.

Maram Hasanain, Fatima Haouari, Reem Suwaileh, Zien Sheikh Ali, Bayan Hamdan, Tamer Elsayed, Alberto Barrón-Cedeño, Giovanni Da San Martino, and Preslav Nakov. 2020. Overview of checkthat! 2020i arabic: Automatic identification and verification of claims in social media. In *CLEF*.

Maram Hasanain, Reem Suwaileh, T. Elsayed, Alberto Barrón-Cedeño, and Preslav Nakov. 2019. Overview of the clef-2019 checkthat! lab: Automatic identification and verification of claims. task 2: Evidence and factuality. In *CLEF*.

Diederik P. Kingma and Jimmy Ba. 2015. Adam: A method for stochastic optimization. In *3rd International Conference on Learning Representations, ICLR 2015, San Diego, CA, USA, May 7-9, 2015, Conference Track Proceedings*.

John D. Lafferty, Andrew McCallum, and Fernando C. N. Pereira. 2001. Conditional random fields: Probabilistic models for segmenting and labeling sequence data. In *Proceedings of the Eighteenth International Conference on Machine Learning*, ICML '01, pages 282–289, San Francisco, CA, USA. Morgan Kaufmann Publishers Inc.

Giovanni Da San Martino, Stefano Cresci, Alberto Barrón-Cedeño, Seunghak Yu, Roberto Di Pietro, and Preslav Nakov. 2020. A survey on computational propaganda detection. *arXiv preprint arXiv:2007.08024*.

Clyde Raymond Miller. 1939. *How to detect and analyze propaganda*. Town Hall, Incorporated.

Preslav Nakov, Alberto Barrón-Cedeño, Giovanni Da San Martino, Firoj Alam, Rubén Míguez, Tommaso Caselli, Mucahid Kutlu, Wajdi Zaghouani, Chengkai Li, Shaden Shaar, Hamdy Mubarak, Alex Nikolov, and Yavuz Selim Kartal. 2022a. Overview of the clef-2022 checkthat! lab task 1 on identifying relevant claims in tweets. In *CLEF*.

Preslav Nakov, Giovanni Da San Martino, Firoj Alam, Shaden Shaar, Hamdy Mubarak, and Nikolay Babulkov. 2022b. Overview of the clef-2022 checkthat! lab task 2 on detecting previously fact-checked claims. In *CLEF*.

Preslav Nakov, Giovanni Da San Martino, Tamer Elsayed, Alberto Barrón-Cedeño, Rubén Míguez, Shaden Shaar, Firoj Alam, Fatima Haouari, Maram Hasanain, Watheq Mansour, Bayan Hamdan, Zien Sheikh Ali, Nikolay Babulkov, Alex Nikolov, Gautam Kishore Shahi, Julia Maria Struß, Thomas Mandl, Mucahid Kutlu, and Yavuz Selim Kartal. 2021. Overview of the clef-2021 checkthat! lab on detecting check-worthy claims, previously fact-checked claims, and fake news. In *CLEF*.

Hannah Rashkin, Eunsol Choi, Jin Yea Jang, Svitlana Volkova, and Yejin Choi. 2017. Truth of varying shades: Analyzing language in fake news and political fact-checking. In *Proceedings of the 2017 Conference on Empirical Methods in Natural Language Processing*, pages 2931–2937, Copenhagen, Denmark. Association for Computational Linguistics.

Shaden Shaar, Fatima Haouari, Watheq Mansour, Maram Hasanain, Nikolay Babulkov, Firoj Alam, Giovanni Da San Martino, Tamer Elsayed, and Preslav Nakov. 2021a. Overview of the clef-2021 checkthat! lab task 2 on detecting previously fact-checked claims in tweets and political debates. In *CLEF*.

Shaden Shaar, Maram Hasanain, Bayan Hamdan, Zien Sheikh Ali, Fatima Haouari, Alex Nikolov, Mucahid Kutlu, Yavuz Selim Kartal, Firoj Alam, Giovanni Da San Martino, Alberto Barrón-Cedeño, Rubén Míguez, Javier Beltrán, Tamer Elsayed, and Preslav Nakov. 2021b. Overview of the clef-2021 checkthat! lab task 1 on check-worthiness estimation in tweets and political debates. In *CLEF*.

Shaden Shaar, Alex Nikolov, Nikolay Babulkov, Firoj Alam, Alberto Barrón-Cedeño, Tamer Elsayed, Maram Hasanain, Reem Suwaileh, Fatima Haouari, Giovanni Da San Martino, and Preslav Nakov. 2020. Overview of checkthat! 2020 english: Automatic identification and verification of claims in social media. In *CLEF*.

Bruce Lannes Smith. 2021. Propaganda.

Anthony Weston. 2018. *A rulebook for arguments*. Hackett Publishing.

CNLP-NITS-PP at WANLP 2022 Shared Task: Propaganda Detection in Arabic using Data Augmentation and AraBERT Pre-trained Model

Sahinur Rahman Laskar[1], **Rahul Singh**[1], **Abdullah Faiz Ur Rahman Khilji**[1]
Riyanka Manna[2], **Partha Pakray**[1], **Sivaji Bandyopadhyay**[1]
[1]National Institute of Technology, Silchar, India
[2]Adamas University, Kolkata, India
{sahinurlaskar.nits, rahuljan, abdullahkhilji.nits}@gmail.com
{riyankamanna16,parthapakray,sivaji.cse.ju}@gmail.com

Abstract

In today's time, online users are regularly exposed to media posts that are propagandistic. Several strategies have been developed to promote safer media consumption in Arabic to combat this. However, there is a limited available multilabel annotated social media dataset. In this work, we have used a pre-trained AraBERT twitter-base model on an expanded train data via data augmentation. Our team CNLP-NITS-PP, has achieved the third rank in subtask 1 at WANLP-2022, for propaganda detection in Arabic (shared task) in terms of micro-F1 score of 0.602.

1 Introduction

Communities are significantly impacted by the propagation of rumors, false information, or incomplete information, particularly if the process is spearheaded by the media. In the minds of the target populations, who are consistently the targets of propaganda, the illusion becomes true. Propaganda is regarded as one of the most effective political tools in the modern period and consistently succeeds in drawing sizable populations. Social media is now utilized to distribute propaganda and bogus or misleading news to divert attention away from more pressing problems. Depending on the technology employed, a variety of materials and media are used to spread propaganda. The most modern methods (Vorakitphan et al., 2021) for detecting propaganda are based on language models, which mostly use transformer-based architectures. There are publicly available language models for Arabic, such as AraBERT (Antoun et al., 2020), AraGPT2 (Antoun et al., 2021b) and AraELECTRA (Antoun et al., 2021a). The challenging issue is the requirement of a sufficient amount of annotated multilabel dataset that must cover different varieties or types of propaganda in order to utilize advanced deep learning-based techniques. To encounter this issue, we have increased the train data by augmenting data to the original train set. We have noticed that people often use dictionary/root or stemmed words on social media platforms without adhering to proper grammar. Therefore, we have used Arabic Light Stemmer (Zerrouki, 2012) in the train data and prepared $1,008$ additional synthetic dataset that is directly augmented with the original train data. Moreover, AraBERT (Antoun et al., 2020) twitter-base model is utilized in this work and attains competitive results in terms of standard evaluation metrics (as reported in Section 5).

2 Related Work

In this section, we briefly present the related works of propaganda detection which have been studied recently. By identifying all text fragments that contain propaganda techniques and their type, the authors (Da San Martino et al., 2019) undertake fine-grained analysis of texts. They have contributed a corpus of news articles that are annotated using 18 propaganda techniques at the fragment level and designed a suitable evaluation measure. Also, a multi-granularity neural network is designed and attained better performance than the BERT-based baseline system. In (Dimitrov et al., 2021a), the authors introduce a multi-label multimodal task to detect the different types of propaganda techniques used in memes and release a corpus that includes 950 memes annotated with 22 propaganda techniques. (Dimitrov et al., 2021b) organizes SemEval-2021 task 6 which include subtasks of detecting the persuasion techniques in the text, the text spans where the persuasion techniques are used, and detection of particular technique present in the entire meme (text and image). They explored the benefits of text and image modalities for the detection techniques in the respective shared tasks. Moreover, (Yu et al., 2021) proposed to use of interpretable features with pre-trained language models for detecting deception techniques.

Proceedings of the The Seventh Arabic Natural Language Processing Workshop (WANLP), pages 541 - 544
December 8, 2022 ©2022 Association for Computational Linguistics

Train Set	Samples
Before Augmentation	504
After Augmentation	1512

Table 1: Data Statistics of train set (before and after augmentation) in subtask 1.

3 Dataset Description

The dataset[1] used has been provided by the organizers of WANLP 2022 for the shared task on Propaganda Detection in Arabic (Alam et al., 2022). The dataset consists of the text of Arabic tweets and the list of propaganda techniques used in them. There are a total of 21 propaganda techniques, namely, "Appeal to authority", "Appeal to fear/prejudice", "Black-and-white Fallacy/Dictatorship", "Causal Oversimplification", "Doubt", "Exaggeration/Minimisation", "Flag-waving", "Glittering generalities (Virtue)", "Loaded Language", "Misrepresentation of Someone's Position (Straw Man)", "Name calling/Labeling", "Obfuscation", "Intentional vagueness", "Confusion", "Presenting Irrelevant Data (Red Herring)", "Reductio ad hitlerum", "Repetition", "Slogans", "Smears", "Thought-terminating cliché", "Whataboutism", "Bandwagon", and a "no technique" label to indicate no propaganda techniques have been used. The train, validation, and final test set consist of 504, 104, and 440 number of tweets. For data augmentation, for each tweet in the training set, we have used an Arabic Light Stemmer[2] (Zerrouki, 2012) to get the root and stem and obtained synthetic data are added to the training set with the same labels. This brought up the number of training samples to 1512. Table 1 represents augmented train data that is used in this work and Figure 1 presents examples of synthetic data (stem and root).

4 System Description

The AraBERT (Antoun et al., 2020) twitter-base model is utilized for the task of multilabel propaganda classification and used example source code (Antoun et al., 2020)[3] for Text Classification. However, the example code (Antoun et al., 2020) is restricted for single-label classification. To prepare it for multi-label classification, we have changed the input labels to the model to be one hot encoded to indicate multiple labels and modify the macro-F1 scorer to give a score for multiple labels. We used data augmentation; in particular, generated synthetic training data using root and stem substitution from the original train samples and prepared additional synthetic examples. For preprocessing, the default ArabertPreprocessor[4] has been used. During training to get the predicted labels for one tweet, we selected the number of predicted labels corresponding to the number of true labels for that tweet. For training, we have used 0.1 drop-out, Adam optimizer with a default learning rate, and a batch size of 16. The model is trained on a single NVIDIA Quadro P2000 GPU for 5 epochs based on early stopping criteria, i.e, the model training is halted if it does not converge on the validation set for more than 5 epochs. The training process took less than 5 minutes. To make predictions with the model, the sentiment analysis pipeline is used from HuggingFace transformers[5], which returns scores corresponding to each of the labels for a given input. Then we selected all the labels that provide a score greater than or equal to 0.32 as the predicted labels. We observed multiple scores for predictions on the validation test set and found that most correct labels have a score greater than 0.30 and there was a large gap in the score for the labels that have scored less than 0.30.

5 Results

The WANLP 2022 shared task organizer (Alam et al., 2022) published the evaluation result[6] of the propaganda detection in Arabic. The shared task includes two subtasks, namely, Subtask 1: A multilabel classification problem (Given the text of a tweet, identify the propaganda techniques used in it). Subtask 2: A sequence tagging task (Given the text of a tweet, identify the propaganda techniques used in it together with the span(s) of text in which each propaganda technique appears). Herein, we have participated in Subtask 1 with a team named CNLP-NITS-PP and achieved the third ($3rd$) position where a total of fifteen (15) teams participated and four (4) teams participated in Subtask 2. The

[1] https://gitlab.com/arabic-nlp/propaganda-detection/

[2] https://github.com/linuxscout/tashaphyne

[3] https://github.com/aub-mind/arabert/tree/master/examples

[4] https://huggingface.co/aubmindlab/bert-base-arabertv02-twitter

[5] https://colab.research.google.com/drive/19zAYftPaXcNDZ6N6Pyj8K8BJXtkEgglx?usp=sharing

[6] https://sites.google.com/view/propaganda-detection-in-arabic/results?authuser=0

ID	Original Text	Stem	Root
1391667689656102914	RT @AJABreaking: | عاجل حركة حماس: ما يجري في المسجد الأقصى مجزرة حقيقية ستدفع سلطات الاحتلال الإسرائيلية ثمنها	RT @AJABreaking: | عاجل حركة حماس: ما يجري في المسجد الأقصى مجزرة حقيقية ستدفع سلطات الاحتلال الإسرائيلية ثمنها	RT @AJABreaking: | عجل حرك حمس: م جر ف لمسجد لءقصي مجزر حقق ستدفع سلطت لحتلل لءسرءل ثمنه
139257525971126 6821	رؤساء البرلمانات العربية يطالبون بتدخل دولي عاجل لوضع حد نهائي لممارسات إسرائيل "الإجرامية غير الإنسانية	رؤساء البرلمانات العربية يطالبون بتدخل دولي عاجل لوضع حد نهائي لممارسات إسرائيل "الإجرامية غير الإنسانية	رءسء لبرلمنت لعرب طلبن بتدخل دل عجل لضع حد نهء لممرست ءسرءل "لءجرم غر لءنسن
138621674411773 5425	▪ الهيئة القيادية العليا لأسرى حماس: تأجيل أو إلغاء الانتخابات سيكون له أثر خطير على شعبنا الفلسطيني وإيمانه بالاحتكام للعملية الديموقراطية.	الهيئة القيادية العليا لأسرى حماس: تأجيل أو إلغاء الانتخابات سيكون له أثر خطير على شعبنا الفلسطيني وإيمانه بالاحتكام للعملية الديموقراطية	لهء لقد لعل لءسري حمس: تءجل ء ءلغء لنتخبت سكن له ءثر خطر علي شعبن لفلسطن ءمنه بلحتكم للعمل لدمقرط

Figure 1: Examples of synthetic data (stem and root).

Team	Macro-F1	Micro-F1	Rank
mgamal88	0.185	0.649	1
Team_IITD	0.183	0.609	2
CNLP-NITS-PP	**0.068**	**0.602**	**3**
basem	0.068	0.602	3
josephattieh	0.177	0.602	3
gauravsingh	0.105	0.600	4
Team_iCompass	0.191	0.597	5
ArabicProcessors	0.137	0.585	6
mostafa-samir	0.186	0.580	7
SirenAI	0.153	0.578	8
earendil	0.111	0.565	9
mhmud.fwzi	0.087	0.552	10
Mohtaj	0.076	0.494	11
tesla	0.120	0.355	12
Baseline (Random)	0.043	0.079	13

Table 2: Our system's results (marked as bold) and other participants results on subtask 1 propaganda detection in Arabic.

automatic evaluation metric micro-F1 is mainly considered to evaluate the results of different submission teams. However, the task organizer also reports macro-F1. Table 2 presents the results of our system (marked as bold).

6 Discussion

In this work, we have presented preliminary experimental work in subtask 1 only at WANLP 2022 shared task. In future work, we need to explore and examine different deep-learning-based models such as AraGPT2, AraELECTRA, AraXLNet on the same benchmark data set released in this shared task and utilize another dataset, namely, PTC corpus[7] for both tasks, i.e., multilabel classification and sequence tagging tasks. Moreover, we will manually observe the benchmark dataset to identify the clue for the expansion of train data, the novelty in the multilabel annotation, preprocessing, and model training that could be increased accuracy in multilabel classification and sequence tagging tasks.

7 Conclusion

This paper demonstrates our work in subtask 1, propaganda detection in Arabic shared task at WANLP-2022. To handle the data scarcity problem in this shared task, we have proposed to use a data augmentation strategy and utilization of a domain-specific pre-trained language model (AraBERT twitter-base model) that shows remarkable results. This work motivates us to explore propaganda detection in Indian languages which will be beneficial for a multilingual country like India.

Acknowledgements

The authors would like to thank the Center for Natural Language Processing (CNLP), Artificial Intelligence (AI), and the Department of Computer Science and Engineering at the National Institute of Technology, Silchar for providing the requisite support and infrastructure to execute this work.

[7] https://propaganda.qcri.org/semeval2020-task11/

References

Firoj Alam, Hamdy Mubarak, Wajdi Zaghouani, Preslav Nakov, and Giovanni Da San Martino. 2022. Overview of the WANLP 2022 shared task on propaganda detection in Arabic. In *Proceedings of the Seventh Arabic Natural Language Processing Workshop*, Abu Dhabi, UAE. Association for Computational Linguistics.

Wissam Antoun, Fady Baly, and Hazem Hajj. 2020. Arabert: Transformer-based model for arabic language understanding. In *LREC 2020 Workshop Language Resources and Evaluation Conference 11–16 May 2020*, page 9.

Wissam Antoun, Fady Baly, and Hazem Hajj. 2021a. AraELECTRA: Pre-training text discriminators for Arabic language understanding. In *Proceedings of the Sixth Arabic Natural Language Processing Workshop*, pages 191–195, Kyiv, Ukraine (Virtual). Association for Computational Linguistics.

Wissam Antoun, Fady Baly, and Hazem Hajj. 2021b. AraGPT2: Pre-trained transformer for Arabic language generation. In *Proceedings of the Sixth Arabic Natural Language Processing Workshop*, pages 196–207, Kyiv, Ukraine (Virtual). Association for Computational Linguistics.

Giovanni Da San Martino, Seunghak Yu, Alberto Barrón-Cedeño, Rostislav Petrov, and Preslav Nakov. 2019. Fine-grained analysis of propaganda in news article. In *Proceedings of the 2019 Conference on Empirical Methods in Natural Language Processing and the 9th International Joint Conference on Natural Language Processing (EMNLP-IJCNLP)*, pages 5636–5646, Hong Kong, China. Association for Computational Linguistics.

Dimitar Dimitrov, Bishr Bin Ali, Shaden Shaar, Firoj Alam, Fabrizio Silvestri, Hamed Firooz, Preslav Nakov, and Giovanni Da San Martino. 2021a. Detecting propaganda techniques in memes. In *Proceedings of the 59th Annual Meeting of the Association for Computational Linguistics and the 11th International Joint Conference on Natural Language Processing (Volume 1: Long Papers)*, pages 6603–6617, Online. Association for Computational Linguistics.

Dimitar Dimitrov, Bishr Bin Ali, Shaden Shaar, Firoj Alam, Fabrizio Silvestri, Hamed Firooz, Preslav Nakov, and Giovanni Da San Martino. 2021b. SemEval-2021 task 6: Detection of persuasion techniques in texts and images. In *Proceedings of the 15th International Workshop on Semantic Evaluation (SemEval-2021)*, pages 70–98, Online. Association for Computational Linguistics.

Vorakit Vorakitphan, Elena Cabrio, and Serena Villata. 2021. PROTECT - A pipeline for propaganda detection and classification. In *Proceedings of the Eighth Italian Conference on Computational Linguistics, CLiC-it 2021, Milan, Italy, January 26-28, 2022*, volume 3033 of *CEUR Workshop Proceedings*. CEUR-WS.org.

Seunghak Yu, Giovanni Da San Martino, Mitra Mohtarami, James Glass, and Preslav Nakov. 2021. Interpretable propaganda detection in news articles. In *Proceedings of the International Conference on Recent Advances in Natural Language Processing (RANLP 2021)*, pages 1597–1605, Held Online. INCOMA Ltd.

Taha Zerrouki. 2012. Tashaphyne, arabic light stemmer.

NGU_CNLP at WANLP 2022 Shared Task: Propaganda Detection in Arabic

Ahmed Samir
Information Technology Institute
ahmedsamirio95@gmail.com

Abu Bakr Soliman
Nile University
ab.soliman@nu.edu.eg

Mohamed Ibrahim
New Giza University
mohamed.shafik@ngu.edu.eg

Laila Hesham
New Giza University
laila.afify@kaust.edu.sa

Samhaa R. El-Beltagy
New Giza University/Optomatica
samhaa@computer.org

Abstract

This paper presents the system developed by the NGU_CNLP team for addressing the shared task on Propaganda Detection in Arabic at WANLP 2022. The team participated in the shared tasks' two sub-tasks which are: 1) Propaganda technique identification in text and 2) Propaganda technique span identification. In the first sub-task the goal is to detect all employed propaganda techniques in some given piece of text out of a possible 17 different techniques, or to detect that no propaganda technique is being used in that piece of text. As such, this first sub task is a multi-label classification problem with a pool of 18 possible labels. Subtask 2 extends subtask 1, by requiring the identification of the exact text span in which a propaganda technique was employed, making it a sequence labeling problem. For task 1, a combination of a data augmentation strategy coupled with an enabled transformer-based model, comprised our classification model. This classification model ranked first amongst the 14 systems participating in this subtask. For subtask two, a transfer learning model was adopted. The system ranked third among the 3 different models that participated in this subtask.

1 Introduction

The term propaganda was coined in the seventeenth century as a means of disseminating noble ideas among groups of individuals. Over time, it has become known for referring to the use of infused ideas, news or partial arguments to groups of people with the intention of manipulating their beliefs and behaviors, typically, towards deceptive agendas. In today's world, we can find various forms of propaganda in almost every newspaper article, social media post or mass media broadcasting. It is rarely the case that individuals are simply informed without being pervasively biased. Moreover, propaganda propagation is no longer exclusively dominated by religious, political or demographic entities, but even by individuals where a variety of agendas are involved. With such huge proliferation and the expected undesired influences, it is of utmost importance to be able to detect faulty or misleading information for the purpose of efficiently and promptly handling the widespread of fallacies. However, detecting computational propaganda is a significantly involved task especially with the ever growing efforts to make it go inconspicuous. By leveraging tools from machine learning (ML), it is possible to automate the necessary NLP tasks required to detect such malicious agendas. Computational propaganda detection has gained immense attention [1, 2, 3, 4] in the NLP community. For example, Google and Facebook, are currently testing ML-powered fact-checking tools to investigate the authenticity of shared information for the purpose of fighting potential "infodemics" [5, 2] which are a form of propaganda. Typically, NLP tasks utilize several modeling approaches such as n-gram models and neural networks models. In n-gram modeling, n-words are being paired and processed. Neural networks are essential to the success of numerous NLP tasks.

NLP models have been revolutionized by the introduction of contextualized embeddings such as the the BERT transformer-based language model, first introduced by Google [6]. The idea of the BERT-model is that it can read a sentence simultaneously in both directions. Applying this to the task of propaganda detection is made possible through two subtasks. The first of which is the identification of the propaganda technique in the sentence together with the corresponding text span. The second subtask is concerned with the classification of the deployed propaganda technique out of the 18 well-known propaganda techniques [7].

In [8], a logistic regression-based model was proposed to detect a propagandist text, along with features acquired from Linguistic Inquiry and Word Count (LIWC) text analysis software, to solve a binary classification problem. Fine-tuning of the BERT transformer model was performed in [9] where, prior to using the BERT architecture, the authors initially concentrated on the pre-processing phases to offer additional details about the language

Proceedings of the The Seventh Arabic Natural Language Processing Workshop (WANLP), pages 545 - 550
December 8, 2022 ©2022 Association for Computational Linguistics

Dataset	Train	dev	dev_test
No. of Tweets	504	52	52

Table 1: Data Distribution for Subtask 1

model and current propaganda strategies. However, the author later utilised the BERT architecture to frame the work as a problem of sequence labelling. In [10], some linguistic characteristics and global noncontextual word embeddings were exploited.

This paper presents the system developed by the NGU_CNLP team for addressing the shared task on Propaganda Detection in Arabic at WANLP 2022 [11]. The team participated in the shared tasks' two sub-tasks which are: 1) Propaganda technique identification in text and 2) Propaganda technique span identification. In the first sub-task the goal is to detect all employed propaganda techniques in some given piece of text out of a possible 17 different techniques, or to detect that no propaganda technique is being used in that piece of text. As such, this first sub task is a multi-label classification problem with a pool of 18 possible labels. Subtask 2 extends subtask 1, by requiring the identification of the exact text span in which a propaganda technique was employed, making it a sequence labeling problem.

2 Subtask 1: Propaganda Classification

The first sub-task our team participated in, was a multi-label classification problem. In this subtask, the input is a single piece of text (a tweet), and the required output, is the set of the propaganda techniques used in it. The evaluation metric for this subtask was the micro-average F_1 score.

2.1 Initial Experimentation

Three labeled datasets were provided by the task organizers for training (train), validation (dev), and testing (dev_test) during the model development phase. The distribution of this data is shown in Table 1.

The total number of labels in this dataset was 18. Some of the tweets had as many as 5 labels, with the average number of labels/tweets being 1.75. Eight out of the 18 different labels/classes had less than 10 instances in the training dataset, i.e., they were very under-represented. Furthermore, careful analysis of the labels' distribution in the provided 3 datasets revealed that there is a discrepancy in the distribution of labels among them as shown in Figure 1.

To better understand the problem, gain insights into its challenges, as well as to establish a good baseline, we decided to apply traditional ML algorithms on the training data, and to test on the aggregated set of dev and dev_test data. Simple text pre-processing was carried out in this step which included normalization, diacritic removal, url removal and number removal. Text was then tokenized and represented as a bag of words. Classifiers that were used in this step included, Support Vector Machines ((with a multitude of k values), Naïve Bayes, Stochastic Gradient Descent, Logistic regression, Random Forests and simple K-nearest Neighbor. After experimenting with various configurations, the best result obtained was from the Linear Support Vector Machine with a micro average F_1 score of 0.44. However, looking at the F_1 scores of individual classes revealed that the majority of classes had zero as a score, highlighting the class imbalance problem seen in the training data.

2.2 Data Redistribution and Augmentation

To address the discrepancy in the distribution of labels in the provided datasets and to avoid the negative impact of this discrepancy on the quality of the prediction model, all three sets were merged and the re-split using multi-label stratification to ensure more uniform label distribution. The results of carrying out this step, are shown in Figure 2. Unfortunately, under-represented labels remained under represented even after the merge and re-split steps.

To overcome the fact that the training data size was quite small (only 504 instances) and in an attempt to provide more examples for under-represented labels thus addressing the class imbalance problem, means for expanding the training dataset were sought. The one that was adopted, was the translation of a similar dataset which is available in English to Arabic. The used dataset was taken from SemEval-2020 Task 11 [12] which targeted the detection of propaganda techniques in news articles. Data from the SemEval-2020 Task was translated to Arabic using the RapidAPI Translation tool [1].

Since the SemEval-2020 training data labels did not directly map to the labels used in the WANLP

[1] https://rapidapi.com/gofitech/api/nlp-translation/

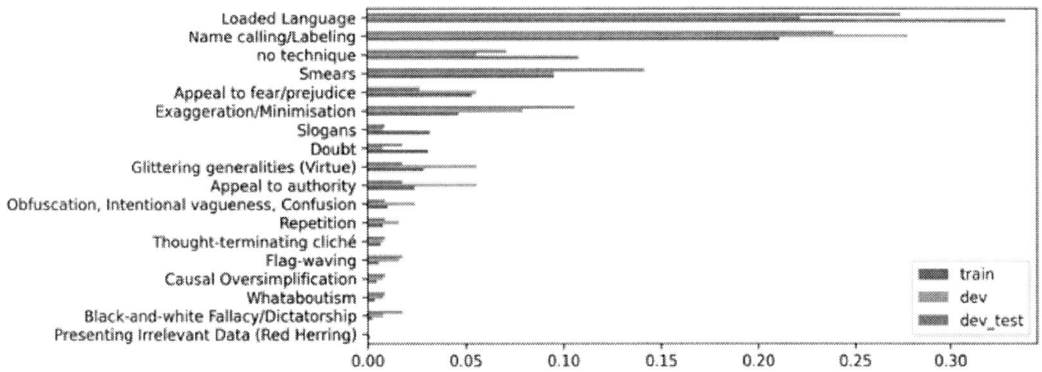

Figure 1: Label Distribution for Data of Subtask 1

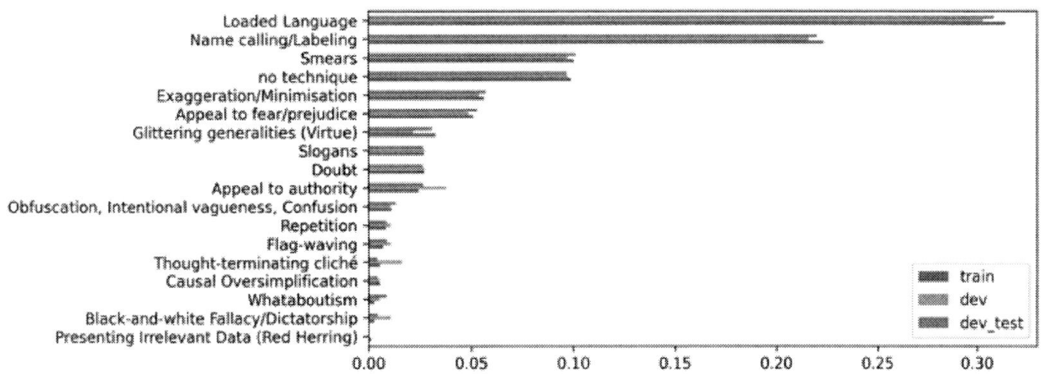

Figure 2: Data ReDistribution for Subtask 1

2022 shared task, a mapping function was created to convert the names of the SemEval labels to WANLP ones. In the end, 3,938 sentences were added to the original WANLP dataset bringing up the number of training instances from 504 to 4, 442.

2.3 Overview of the Adopted Model

Following the step described in the previous subsection, we decided to experiment with a more powerful prediction model. Since transformer based models have shown superior results in text classification tasks, the model we used was AraBERT [13]. Consequently, text preprocessing was done using the AraBERT preprocessor with the default configuration. Hyperparameters were tuned and optimized through the use of randomized grid search. The final used configuration was as follows:

- Proportion of extra data sampled to be in train dataset: 0.7
- Max. length of tokenization: 128
- Batch size: 8
- Number of epochs: 50 with early stopping
- Learning rate: 0.0001
- Learning rate scheduler: Linear
- Warm-up ratio: 0.1

The metric used for evaluation was the F_1 Micro score. The best configuration evaluation loss on the dev set can be seen in Figure 3.

This final configuration was used to train 5 models on 5-fold splits of the labeled data (train, dev and dev_test). The prediction probabilities of each model were averaged into the final prediction probabilities, and then the threshold for prediction was set (empirically) to be 0.4.

2.4 Final Results

For this shared task, the task organizers provided 440 unlabeled tweets. The model described in the previous section was used to predict various labels

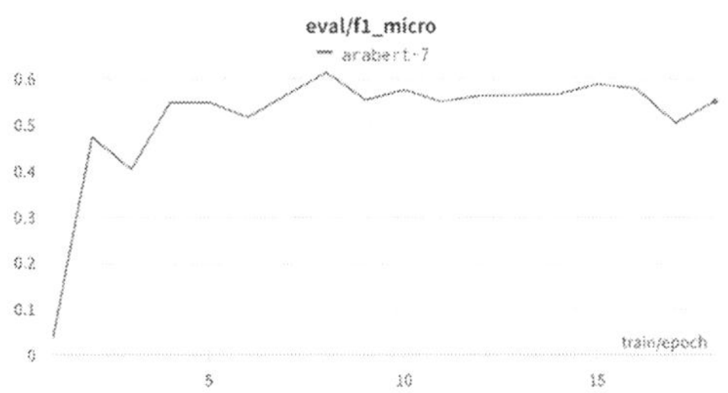

Figure 3: Model Performance for Subtask 1

for each tweet. The final results released by the task organizers have shown that the model that we have developed ranked at number one with an average micro F_1 score of 0.649. The next best performing system achieved a score of 0.609.

3 Subtask 2: Propaganda Span Detection

In the second task, the goal was not only to identify propaganda techniques used in a piece of text, but the exact text span that represents each technique. This can be thought of as a sequence tagging task or as a token classification [14].

3.1 Exploratory Data Analysis

The provided data distribution for this task was identical to subtask 1, except that here exact spans for each of the labels were provided. So similar to classes in subtask 1, some propaganda techniques (labels) such as Whataboutism and Causal Oversimplification were under represented while others such as Name calling/Labeling and Loaded Language were over represented. An example of a tweet taken from this dataset is shown in Figure 4. In this example, spans which are given in numbers representing their start and end positions, are mapped to their equivalent text fragments.

As can be seen in this example, it is possible to assign the same label more than once in the same tweet as well as to assign more than one label to the same span. So in the shown example, 'Loaded Language' appears twice, and the span (مقامر ومجنون) is labeled as both 'Loaded Language' as well as 'Name Calling/Labeling'. This pattern of multiple label assignment for the same span, appeared in 53 locations in the train dataset, 18 in the dev dataset and 16 in the dev_test dataset. The dataset used for training, was the augmented translated one described in Subtask 1.

ID	1399057217349881860		
Tweet	"مقامر ومجنون". الصحافة البريطانية تشن هجوماً حاداً على "غوارديولا" بعد ضياع دوري الأبطال		
Labels			
Span	مقامر ومجنون	مقامر ومجنون	هجوماً حاداً
Label	Name calling/Labeling	Loaded Language	Loaded Language

Figure 4: An Example of a Tweet taken from Subtask 2 Dataset

3.2 Preprocessing

One of the challenges of preprocessing the texts for this task, is that the final output must a span denoted in terms of the position of its first character and the positions of its last character in the text, which would then be compared with spans represented in a similar way in the test data provided. Preprocessing had to be handled carefully so that it does not change the order of the letters contained in the texts. This was done by applying only simple operations such as normalization. To get the data ready for the next step, we transformed the data into the widely used style of data representation BIO so that each span in the tweet is accompanied by a distinctive tag that indicates if it is outside the classification (O), the beginning of a classification (B), or within the classification span (I). When a single span was assigned to more than one technique, we neglected the technique that is most representative in the train dataset.

3.3 Overview of the Adopted Model

Using modern transformers and neural networks techniques, the proposed solution relied on employing a previously developed model that addresses a similar task in Arabic in order to transfer its experience for solving this particular problem. Specifically, we used the Marefa-NER model, which is one of the pre-trained templates available on the HuggingFace platform and which targets Named Entity Recognition (NER). The model was pretrained to identify 9 different types of entities within any news text or Wikipedia article.

After preparing the training data using the BIO format, a neural network was setup for a token classification problem, In other words, the network was responsible for assigning an appropriate class for each token in the text. Tokenizing the text was based on the originally followed strategy in Marefa-NER which was XLM-RoBERTa [15].

Hyperparameter tuning was performed through a series of experiments with the most important of these values being:

- Max. length of tokenization: 512
- Batch size: 8
- Number of epochs: 14 with early stopping
- Learning rate: 0.00001
- Learning rate scheduler: Linear
- Optimizer: Adam
- No. Hidden Layers: 24
- No. Attention heads: 16

Using the 'dev_test' dataset with the aim of optimizing the F_1-scores, Figure 5 shows the progress made with the F_1-scores during the training process while Figure 6 shows the training loss decreasing gradually.

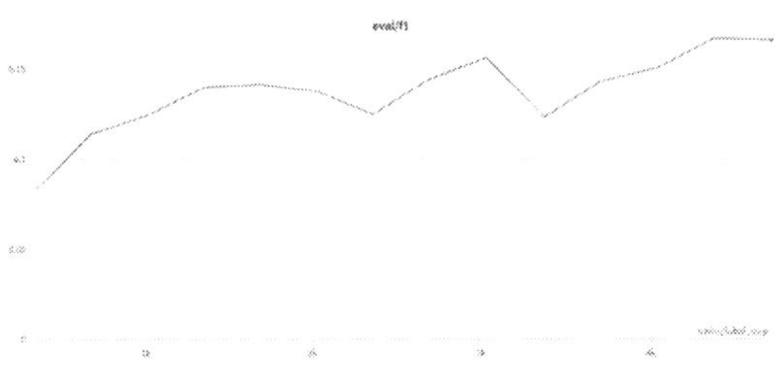

Figure 5: F_1-score of our Model during training for Subtask 2

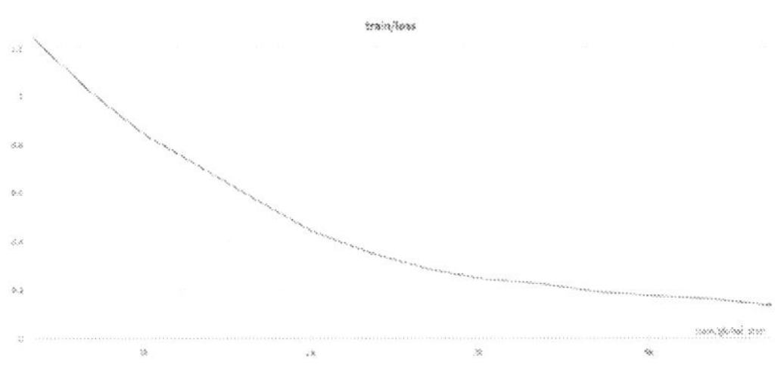

Figure 6: Training Loss of our Model for Subtask 2

After completing the whole training process, the model with the highest F_1-Score was retrieved and adopted. The best model results are shown in Table 2.

Training	Validation	F_1-score	Accuracy
0.1637	1.2753	0.1669	0.7815

Table 2: Model's validation results for subtask 2

4 Summary

The winning system for the propaganda classification task and the third-placed system for the propaganda span identification task has been described. Both of the developed solutions used transformer models. For subtask 1, the classification task was approached with the AraBert architecture and data augmentation. Final predictions were obtained based on an ensemble of 5 models. For subtask 2, the Marefa-NER model together with the XLM-RoBERTa as a tokenizer, were used to tackle the sequence tagging task with same translated data from subtask 1 to overcome the small and imbalanced dataset provided. An interesting future research direction would be to perform error analysis and conduct ablation studies to get more insights from the reported results and improve the models accordingly.

References

[1] Bolsover Gillian and Philip Howard. Computational propaganda and political big data: Moving toward a more critical research agenda. In *Big Data*, pages 273–376, April 2017.

[2] Akshay Jain and Amey Kasbe. Fake news detection. In *2018 IEEE International Students' Conference on Electrical, Electronics and Computer Science (SCEECS)*, pages 1–5, 2018.

[3] Hani Al-Omari, Malak Abdullah, Ola Altiti, and Samira Shaikh. Justdeep at nlp4if 2019 task 1: Propaganda detection using ensemble deep learning models. *Proceedings of the Second Workshop on Natural Language Processing for Internet Freedom: Censorship, Disinformation, and Propaganda*, 2019.

[4] Shaina Raza and Chen Ding. Fake news detection based on news content and social contexts: a transformer-based approach. *International Journal of Data Science and Analytics*, page 335–362, 2022.

[5] Zhijiang Guo, Michael Schlichtkrull, and Andreas Vlachos. A Survey on Automated Fact-Checking. *Transactions of the Association for Computational Linguistics*, 10:178–206, 02 2022.

[6] Jacob Devlin, Ming-Wei Chang, Kenton Lee, and Kristina Toutanova. BERT: pre-training of deep bidirectional transformers for language understanding. In Jill Burstein, Christy Doran, and Thamar Solorio, editors, *Proceedings of the 2019 Conference of the North American Chapter of the Association for Computational Linguistics: Human Language Technologies, NAACL-HLT 2019, Minneapolis, MN, USA, June 2-7, 2019, Volume 1 (Long and Short Papers)*, pages 4171–4186. Association for Computational Linguistics, 2019.

[7] Miller C. R. The techniques of propaganda. from "how to detect and analyze propaganda,". In Jill Burstein, Christy Doran, and Thamar Solorio, editors, *an address given at Town Hall*. The Center for learning, 1939.

[8] Jinfen Li, Zhihao Ye, and Lu Xiao. Detection of propaganda using logistic regression. In *Proceedings of the Second Workshop on Natural Language Processing for Internet Freedom: Censorship, Disinformation, and Propaganda*, pages 119–124, Hong Kong, China, November 2019. Association for Computational Linguistics.

[9] Shehel Yoosuf and Yin Yang. Fine-grained propaganda detection with fine-tuned BERT. In *Proceedings of the Second Workshop on Natural Language Processing for Internet Freedom: Censorship, Disinformation, and Propaganda*, pages 87–91, Hong Kong, China, November 2019. Association for Computational Linguistics.

[10] Tariq Alhindi, Jonas Pfeiffer, and Smaranda Muresan. Fine-tuned neural models for propaganda detection at the sentence and fragment levels. In *Proceedings of the Second Workshop on Natural Language Processing for Internet Freedom: Censorship, Disinformation, and Propaganda*, pages 98–102, Hong Kong, China, November 2019. Association for Computational Linguistics.

[11] Firoj Alam, Hamdy Mubarak, Wajdi Zaghouani, Preslav Nakov, and Giovanni Da San Martino. Overview of the WANLP 2022 shared task on propaganda detection in Arabic. In *Proceedings of the Seventh Arabic Natural Language Processing Workshop*, Abu Dhabi, UAE, December 2022. Association for Computational Linguistics.

[12] Giovanni Da San Martino, Alberto Barrón-Cedeño, Henning Wachsmuth, Rostislav Petrov, and Preslav Nakov. SemEval-2020 task 11: Detection of propaganda techniques in news articles. In *Proceedings of the Fourteenth Workshop on Semantic Evaluation*, pages 1377–1414, Barcelona (online), December 2020. International Committee for Computational Linguistics.

[13] Wissam Antoun, Fady Baly, and Hazem Hajj. AraBERT: Transformer-based model for Arabic language understanding. In *Proceedings of the 4th Workshop on Open-Source Arabic Corpora and Processing Tools, with a Shared Task on Offensive Language Detection*, pages 9–15, Marseille, France, May 2020. European Language Resource Association.

[14] Zhiyong He, Zanbo Wang, Wei Wei, Shanshan Feng, Xianling Mao, and Sheng Jiang. A survey on recent advances in sequence labeling from deep learning models, 2020.

[15] Alexis Conneau, Kartikay Khandelwal, Naman Goyal, Vishrav Chaudhary, Guillaume Wenzek, Francisco Guzmán, Edouard Grave, Myle Ott, Luke Zettlemoyer, and Veselin Stoyanov. Unsupervised cross-lingual representation learning at scale, 2019.

Author Index

Association for Computational Linguistics
209 N. Eighth Street
Stroudsburg, Pennsylvania 18360

ISBN 978-1-7138-9152-9

CURRAN ASSOCIATES INC.
proceedings.com